P9-DEM-334

READER'S DIGEST

Success with House Plants

READER'S DIGEST

Success with House Plants

The Reader's Digest Association, Inc.
Pleasantville, New York/Montreal

Edited and designed
by Dorling Kindersley Ltd

General editor	Anthony Huxley
Contributing editor	Richard Gilbert
Managing editor	Jackie Douglas
Art director	Roger Bristow
Art editor	Sheilagh Noble
Text editor	Donald Berwick
Editors	Lionel Bender
	Sybil del Strother
Designers	Debbie Lee
	Sue Rawkins
	Charlotte Westbrook
Assistant editor	Judith More
Special articles	Peter Black
	Lizzie Boyd
	Peter Chapman
	Gwen Goodship
	Margaret Martin
Photography	Michael Boys
Plant arrangements	John Vellam
Illustration style	Harry Titcombe

Reader's Digest Staff: Carroll C. Calkins, *Editor;* Richard J. Berenson, *Art Editor;* Thomas H. Everett, *Senior Horticulture Specialist N.Y. Botanical Garden.*

The credits and acknowledgments that appear on page 480
are hereby made a part of this copyright page.

Library of Congress Catalog Card Number 78-59802
ISBN 0-89577-052-0

Printed in the United States of America

Contents

How to use this book

Appreciating House Plants

The opening pages of *Success with House Plants* provide a largely pictorial introduction to the attractive and colorful world of the indoor gardener. Since the basic element in that world is the individual plant, the first section of this book, called *Appreciating House Plants,* offers a camera's-eye view of the shapes, textures, colors, and patterns to be found in the foliage and flowers of a single plant.

Using Plants Indoors

This section shows some of the many ways in which house plants can be made to relate to one another and to enhance their surroundings.

As will be obvious from a glance at these first two sections (pages 8–62), their contents are mainly suggestive. The rest of *Success with House Plants* is factual. The purpose of the book is to identify virtually all the indoor plants that any gardener is likely to acquire, and to explain how to keep those plants alive and healthy. The core of the volume is therefore an *A–Z Guide* (pages 64–398) that contains explicit advice about the cultivation needs of about 600 kinds of house plant.

The A–Z Guide to House Plants

Selection of plants House plants belong to many families and come from varied habitats. They succeed indoors under different growing conditions, but the most successful kinds are those that can be kept more or less permanently in average rooms. These plants often have decorative foliage rather than attractive flowers; in permanent house plants flowers are often a bonus. Many entries in the *A–Z Guide* are devoted to such plants.

Also included, however, are many temporary plants prized for their immediate display value—for instance, annuals, shrubs forced into flower in pots, and plants grown from

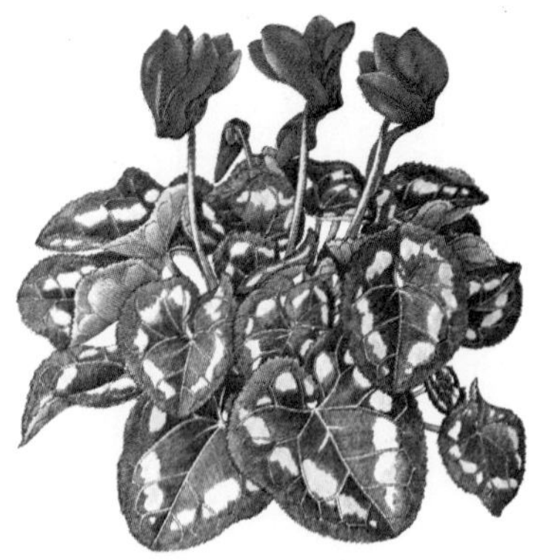

bulbs, corms, and tubers. This last group requires special treatment in the home, and certain commonly shared aspects of that treatment are discussed in the *A–Z Guide* under a general entry headed *Bulbs, Corms, and Tubers.* (There are also separate entries for individual genera.) Similarly, there are generalized entries for seven other groups that can be discussed *as* groups: *Bromeliads, Cacti,* other succulents (listed simply as *Succulents*), *Gesneriads, Ferns, Orchids,* and *Palms.*

Contents of entries Each entry in the *A–Z Guide* begins with a summary of the general characteristics of plants within a given genus, along with descriptions of selected species and forms recommended for their beauty, availability, or other qualities. There follows a series of basic instructions on proper care for the recommended plants. The instructions are grouped under the following headings: "Light," "Temperature," (which also includes a guide to maintenance of humidity where necessary), "Watering," "Feeding," "Potting and repotting," "Propagation," and, sometimes, "Special points" (which covers additional advice that seems important for the cultivation or display of a plant or group of plants).

In most cases the advice and accompanying illustrations in the *A–Z Guide* are enough to ensure successful cultivation of the plants under discussion. But all topics covered or even briefly mentioned here are reviewed in much greater detail in the several sections of *Success with House Plants* that follow the alphabetical guide. Within the *A–Z Guide* the reader is frequently referred, for further information, to specific pages elsewhere in the book. Even without cross-references, however, it is easy to find additional advice about any aspect of cultivation in one of the relevant sections by using the index.

Finder's guide This multi-reference chart (pages 399–408) is designed to help the indoor gardener choose the right plant for the right situation. At a glance the reader can find a plant with particular characteristics (a bushy one with variegated foliage, for instance, or a tall-growing specimen) or an appropriate plant for a given set of conditions (for example, a cool room with poor light).

Caring for House Plants

This section is composed of a number of self-contained articles (pages 410–461), each of which deals fully with a major aspect of proper care. There are discussions of light, temperature and humidity control, of watering and feeding, of potting and repotting techniques, and of propagation methods. In addition, there are

separate articles dealing with types of potting mixture, pruning, the training and support of certain kinds of plant, and such special cultivation aids as artificial light and hydroculture.

Plant health In this section the salient facts about identification and control of pests and diseases are outlined (pages 452–461). It includes a selective listing of modern fungicides and pesticides, with advice on when and how to apply them.

Families of house plants Here all the genera dealt with in the *A–Z Guide* are grouped under botanical family names (pages 462–463). Also indicated are the geographical range, types of habitat, and special characteristics, where significant, of each family.

Glossary

Technical terms have been kept to a minimum in *Success with House Plants*, but a few are unavoidable. Such terms, along with special horticultural uses of otherwise familiar words, are defined in the glossary.

Index

All Latin and common plant names used in the *A–Z Guide* are listed in the index along with usual entries.

The naming of plants

Growers throughout the world use Latin names for plants. This is a scientific necessity, since common names differ from place to place even when, as in America and Britain, the spoken language is the same. There is also an internationally recognized system of plant classification but the question of how plants are classified is too complex for discussion here. Relationships are based, broadly, on flower structure, and the subtleties of such structural distinctions are outside the scope of this volume. It must be emphasized, however, that closely related plants do not necessarily look alike; they may look very different.

Families and genera Plants are grouped, first of all, in families with names ending in -*aceae* or -*ae*—for example, *Bromeliaceae*, the bromeliad family, which includes pineapples and many botanically related but varied house plants. Within each family the main unit of classification is the genus (plural: genera). In referring to plants, the genus name—which is roughly equivalent to a surname—is always the first mentioned. (For examples of major groupings see *Families of house plants*, pages 462–463.)

Species and varieties Each genus can consist of a number of species, and the genus and species names form the first and second parts of the Latin name of a plant. Thus the pineapple is technically called *Ananas comosus*, and the popular house plant sometimes known as queen's-tears is technically called *Billbergia nutans*. Genus and species names are always printed in italics.

Within a species it is possible to have varieties that differ in minor ways but are distinct enough to warrant horticultural separation. The variety label, where there is one, forms a third part of a plant's full name. Varieties that occur in the wild always have Latin names. For instance, *Billbergia amoena* normally has green leaves, but it has a naturally occurring variety that has red, white- and yellow-spotted leaves which is called *B.a. rubra*.

Varieties that originate in cultivation (the majority of horticulturally interesting ones) are technically known as "cultivars." These may be given either Latin or vernacular names and are generally printed within single quotation marks. Thus, *Billbergia horrida* has a cultivar called *B.h.* 'Tigrina' in which the leaves are red.

Hybrids Although different species do not normally interbreed, interbreeding does occur, especially in cultivation (where it is often achieved artificially by plant breeders). The result of interbreeding of species within the same genus is an interspecific hybrid, or *cross*, which may be given an italicized Latin name or a single-quotes vernacular one. Technically, this should be preceded by an ×, as in *Billbergia* × *windii* (a hybrid between *B. nutans* and *B. decora*). In *Success with House Plants*, however, hybrids are clearly identified as such, and the × sign is not used. For instance you will find *B.* 'Fantasia,' not *B.* × 'Fantasia' (a cross between the plants *B. pyramidalis* and *B. saundersii*). Sometimes two or even more species from different genera are crossed. The result is a *bigeneric* hybrid (if only two genera are involved), a *trigeneric* hybrid (if three) and so on. For the sake of convenience, the term *intergeneric* can be used for any type of cross between genera. The name of the product of such a cross is often formed from a combination of parents' names. *Cryptbergia* is a hybrid, for example, between *Cryptanthus* and *Billbergia*. Again, although a hybrid genus is technically identified by an × (× *Cryptbergia*), this is not done in the following pages.

Name changes As a result of continuing research, the botanists who classify plants are frequently obliged to replace old names with new ones or to transfer a species to a new or different genus. Thus, *Billbergia amoena* used to be known as *B. pallescens*; and the plant formerly called *Billbergia marmorata* has been reassigned to the genus *Quesnelia*, so that its preferred name is now *Q. marmorata*. Such changes can obviously be confusing, and gardeners and nurserymen are often slow to accept them.

In this book the most up-to-date Latin name is normally used as the main reference for a plant, with any former name or names added parenthetically. But in a few cases where the change is too recent to have become generally known, the older and still commonly accepted name is used as the main reference, with parenthetical reference to the preferred new name.

Common names Plants that have common English-language names are also identified by these names in the *A–Z Guide*.

Summary Plants are listed in the *A–Z Guide* under the preferred genus name, with the family name beneath it. In descriptive matter, references may include any or all of the following kinds of identification:

GENUS *Billbergia*
FAMILY *Bromeliaceae*
SPECIES *Billbergia nutans*
COMMON NAME Queen's-tears
NATURAL VARIETY *B. amoena rubra*
CULTIVAR *B. horrida* 'Tigrina'
INTERSPECIFIC HYBRID *B.* 'Fantasia' *(B. pyramidalis × B. saundersii)*
INTERGENERIC HYBRID *Cryptbergia (Cryptanthus × Billbergia)*

Appreciating House Plants

It matters little whether an indoor garden is a few pots on a windowsill or a luxuriant garden room. Whatever the size of a collection of house plants, it adds a bright new dimension to the domestic scene. Even if you live in the country and have the green outdoors at the threshold, house plants bring a different view of the outdoor world into your home. Centuries of exploration, experimentation, and imagination have culminated in today's richness of choice for indoor gardeners. No matter what the outdoor climate, we can now enjoy the brilliant colors and fragrance of plants from tropical rain forests and arid deserts. And we can do so simply by staying home and tending our indoor gardens.

The range of plants suitable for growing indoors is so vast, and widens so swiftly as commercial growers produce more and more exotic varieties, that the choice can be bewildering. What plants should you acquire? Should you narrow down your collection and begin to specialize in cacti, or orchids, or bromeliads? Or should you broaden your horizons and search for splendid and startling new forms? In the end, of course, the answers to such questions must be dictated by personal tastes. Assuming that you can provide the right growing conditions for a plant, the ultimate decision as to whether it is right for *you* and *your* home is bound to depend on your instinctive reactions to one or more of the plant's attractive features.

When considering a plant in a florist's shop or at a nursery, however, do not forget that it is a living thing. Life means growth, and growth means change. You may find the current shape and size of the plant pleasing. Will they remain so? Only rarely do we buy mature plants, and a young specimen can shape up in surprising ways as it ages. A palm can take more than a decade to grow impressively tall and elegant. Some plants improve with age, but others deteriorate. The constant attraction of most permanent house plants lies in the foliage, but it sometimes lies in the flowers as well. Is the plant that you are contemplating buying going to flower attractively? When, and under what conditions? What will it look like during the annual rest period, if it has one? Questions like these are always worth asking. And there remains that basic question for the truly concerned gardener: How will this plant relate to the rest of the collection?

There is no reason why an outstanding collection of potted plants should not include a broad range of different species. Certain colors and textures clash with one another or with room furnishings, however. Moreover, attractive-looking combinations can work badly just because the various plants require different amounts of warmth and light. For these and other reasons, relationships among plants are more important than is realized by the person who casually acquires a plant just because he or she "likes the look of it." An informed interest in relationships often inspires the indoor gardener to begin to concentrate on a single type of plant.

Some people are cactus or orchid enthusiasts, others are bromeliad or fern connoisseurs, still others specialize in gesneriads, and so on. This type of specialization can be fun even on quite a small scale. In the genus *Peperomia,* for example, you can find infinite variety. Peperomias have leaves varying in shape from round to heart-shaped, in texture from smooth to hairy to quilted, in color from dark green to olive and gray, in pattern from variegations of silver and cream to pinks and purples. A *Ficus* collection would have even greater possibilities. The genus includes creeping and trailing plants, shrubs, and trees. And the foliage is as diverse as the natural habitats of the species, which come from such places as the rain forests of India, Malaysia, Africa, and South America, and the cool, high altitudes of the Himalayas and northern China.

Variety. Diversity. Change. These words and what they stand for are at the heart of the world of house plants. A potted plant is not a dainty *objet d'art*. It is a fascinating organism, which will respond dynamically to all the appreciative care you can give it.

FACING PAGE: *This* Cyperus alternifolius *bears unusual and curiously attractive flower heads; the fluffy starlike flowers emerge from green, arching, streamerlike bracts which are easily confused with leaves.*

The beauty of foliage

Variety in shape

The most dependably attractive feature of house plants is their foliage although different leaves obviously display a variety of attributes. Leaf shapes themselves are infinitely varied. Such descriptive terms as "strap-shaped," "egg-shaped" or round are commonly used. Leaf edges differ too. Some are gently waved, others are finely toothed or lobed. It is this immense variety of leaf forms and their arrangement that creates the fascinating combinations of outlines that we call foliage.

ABOVE: *Each grouping of leaves radiating symmetrically from a central point in* Heptapleurum arboricola *is a single, deeply divided leaf.*

TOP RIGHT: Asplenium nidus *has soft, gently waved leaves arranged in a circle like a crown of plumes. Note the dew on its moisture-loving green foliage.*

RIGHT: *The spoon-shaped leaves of* Aeonium arboreum *are arranged in a neat rosette, whose formality is emphasized by the prickly-looking tip of each upstanding leaf.*

FACING PAGE: *This erect palm, a* Chamaerops humilis, *has long leafstalks terminating in fan-shaped clusters of stiff, gray-green leaflets.*

Texture and form

One of the most distinctive qualities of any leaf is its texture. Where house plants are concerned it is true to say that there are as many subtle differences in leaf texture as in shape and size.

Compare the leaf, for instance, of a *Philodendron scandens* with that of a *Peperomia caperata*. They look somewhat alike because both are heart-shaped, but the resemblance ends there. The philodendron leaf is smooth and glossy, while the peperomia is deeply corrugated. And the severity of an aspidistra, with its medium green, lined leaves contrasts sharply with the hairy softness of a saxifrage or the waxy bloom of many bromeliads. Also, few leaves are really flat and without form. They can be as thick as they are broad; take a look at the lithops, for instance. Consider also how a leaf will curl over, either at the edges or over its length or width. Above all, leaves are seldom simply smooth surfaced. They are as diverse as the plants they grow on.

RIGHT: *Tough, leathery leaflets are strung like buttons along the hairy stems of* Pellaea rotundifolia, *a fern with highly unusual fronds.*

FACING PAGE: *The fresh, crisp appearance of the gracefully curling leaflets of a* Nephrolepis exaltata *frond is accentuated by the water droplets lying on its surface.*

ABOVE: *The quilted texture of these* Peperomia caperata *leaves is created by gentle undulations that pucker the surface between the veins.*

ABOVE: *The white mealy texture of the thick, wavy, strangely frilly-edged leaves of* Cotyledon undulata *adds to the bizarre appearance of this succulent plant.*

ABOVE: *As though polished to a bright glow, the leathery, sometimes dimpled leaves of the common rubber plant,* Ficus elastica, *are examples of perfect symmetry.*

The pattern on leaves

The decorative effect of foliage can be heightened and dramatized by endless variations of pattern. Although there is green in every normal living leaf (since chlorophyll is essential for growth), sometimes there are areas where chlorophyll is missing and these parts do not look green. The resultant color pattern is known as "variegation."

In most variegated leaves the basic green is marked with a recognizable pattern of white or gray, silver or cream, gold or yellow. The variegations can border leaf edges, follow veins, form a crosswise pattern, or they can be confined to one area, such as the central band of the leaf.

Whether these differences have come about naturally or by skilful propagation, variegated foliage often looks like the product of artistry.

ABOVE: *On the dark green background of a* Fittonia verschaffeltii argyroneura *leaf an intricate network of ivory white follows the length of the veins.*

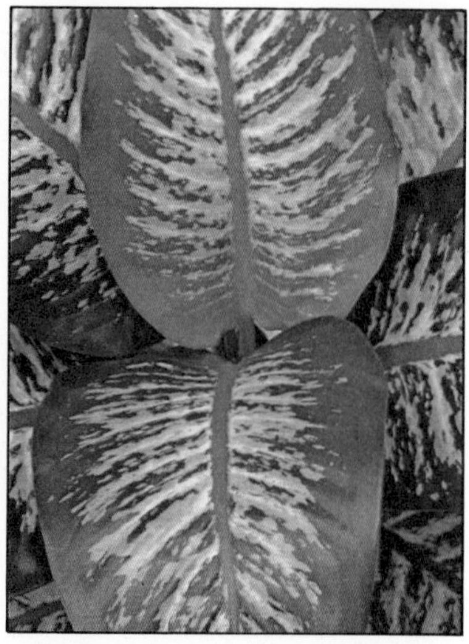

ABOVE: *Dieffenbachia variegations radiate from leaf midribs as if daubed carelessly on the veins instead of being delicately added like the markings on a fittonia.*

ABOVE: *Least symmetrical of these examples is this variegated pelargonium leaf, in which nothing is delineated; everything overlaps.*

LEFT: *There could hardly be a more rigid pattern than this one. The sculptured, angular appearance of white-bordered* Agave victoriae-reginae *leaves is almost menacing.*

FACING PAGE: *Contrast the shimmering, painted-fabric look of these* Calathea makoyana *leaves with the chiseled regularity of the agave (left).*

The drama of color

Although most variegated leaves have markings in shades of white, gray, and yellow, coloration is sometimes far more brilliant. A codiaeum, for instance, can regale the eye with a feast of yellows and oranges while a rhoeo or zebrina is usually colored purple.

Variegation is not confined to smooth leaves. The richness of colored patterns is often enhanced by leaf texture, which can either sharpen color contrasts or make them seem more mellow. On the wrinkled or corrugated surfaces of certain begonia leaves, for example, the colored markings stand out while those on a smooth tradescantia are more muted.

ABOVE: *Subtle and highly satisfying is the foliage of this* Rhoeo discolor, *its fleshy leaves softly streaked with violet-blue.*

LEFT: *This codiaeum presents a spectacle of radiating leaves with a pattern of bright colors following the leaf veins.*

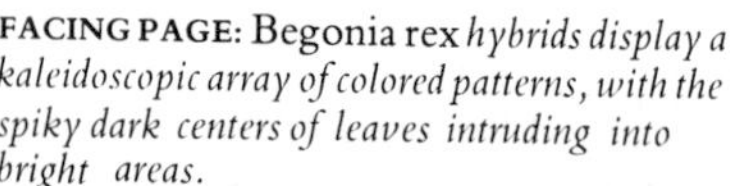

FACING PAGE: Begonia rex *hybrids display a kaleidoscopic array of colored patterns, with the spiky dark centers of leaves intruding into bright areas.*

ABOVE: *The violent contrast between the blood red central area of a neoregelia rosette and the rest of the plant is typical of this bromeliad at flowering time.*

The beauty of flowers

Simple and familiar forms

Not all house plants produce flowers, but those that do are often surprisingly generous with quantity, size, and color. And although some flowering forms are grown primarily for their foliage the annual or occasional bonus of the flowers can be well worth waiting for.

Yet there are many temporary plants so named because they are given house room only for the sake of their flowers. After a single flowering season they are either discarded or replanted outdoors. But those that grow healthily in the home for years, flowering almost continuously or for months at a time are probably the most satisfying. Familiar examples of this last group are the saintpaulias and the impatienses.

Whether permanent, temporary, or in between, flowering plants have an important part to play in every indoor garden. All-green foliage often forms the nucleus of house plant collections. Variegated leaves add splashes of lively color here and there. But no other feature can vie with an occasional flower in helping to create the atmosphere of a truly living garden.

ABOVE: *Giant clusters of radiant, trumpet-shaped, bright orange blooms rise above the strap-shaped leaves of clivias during the early spring.*

FACING PAGE: *A group of trumpet-shaped hippeastrum flowers majestically tipping their stiff stalk, is an annual, if short-lived, delight well worth waiting for.*

ABOVE: *The tiny flowers of this jasmine are pure white and sweetly fragrant. Clusters clothe the rambling stems all summer long.*

RIGHT: *Few flowers appear more ladylike than the delicate drooping blooms of fuchsias. And these plants will reward attention and care with a constant display of flowers throughout the summer.*

Unusual blooms

In some plants the true flowers are less notable than the bracts surrounding them. These highly flamboyant modified leaves are the main feature of such plants as poinsettias where nature, in fact, provided them to attract pollinating insects to flowers that wouldn't attract them otherwise. Sometimes, though, bracts and flowers have similar visual impact, but the bracts usually remain attractive long after the flowers have died. This is why such plants as aechmeas and aphelandras are useful indoors.

BELOW: *The flower head of* Aechmea fasciata *bears tiny blue flowers surrounded by spikily protective bracts that are attractive for months.*

ABOVE: *The common name for* Beloperone guttata *is, not surprisingly, shrimp plant. Tiny flowers peep from overlapping scalelike bracts.*

ABOVE: *This anthurium carries a large, glossy, white bract (called the spathe) and an erect flower spike (or spadix).*

The exotic world of orchids

For intriguing color combinations and durability there is nothing like an orchid flower. And although many orchids cannot be grown in normal rooms, those that can are no less exquisite. Indeed, few other flowers can compete with their beauty.

ABOVE: *Many cattleya flowers are notable for their frilly-edged lip, often in a contrasting color to sepals and petals. This is* C. *'Kaleidoscope.'*

RIGHT: *Miniature cymbidiums compensate for smallness with crowded flower sprays. This hybrid is* C. *'Showgirl Annie.'*

ABOVE: *Cymbidiums are among the easiest orchids to grow indoors.* C. *'Mary Princess Sunglow' has erect stems with glowing yellow blooms that last well in water.*

ABOVE: *Paphiopedilums are unmistakable, with their slipperlike lips. In* P. *'W. Churchill Personality Henry,' the top sepal is white spotted with purple.*

ABOVE: *The rosy-pink, 3-inch-wide flowers of* Cymbidium *'Invergarry Lewes' have strongly marked lips. The flowering season extends throughout winter and spring.*

When cacti burst into bloom

Contrary to popular belief, cacti bear flowers which are often beautiful and always stalkless, brilliantly colored, and long-lasting. The only drawback is that you may have to wait years before some types bloom.

RIGHT: *The magnificent bell-shaped blooms of an epiphyllum can measure 6 inches from top to bottom. They often appear in spring and fall.*

FACING PAGE: *The brilliant flowers of* Aporocactus flagelliformis *emerge from its spiny stems for two months every year.*

BELOW: *The odd flowers of a cleistocactus never open completely and only appear on very mature specimens.*

The fruits of flowers

When conditions are right, some indoor plants produce not only flowers but fruit. A few kinds, in fact, are lovely to look at and delightful to grow first for foliage, then for flowers, and finally, when the flowers have faded, for berries. One such plant is *Coffea arabica*, with glossy foliage and fragrant flowers that give way to shiny, red berries. Similarly attractive fruiting plants are citruses, capsicums and nerteras.

RIGHT: *The tiny green leaves of this* Nertera granadensis *are almost hidden beneath the hundreds of glowing berries produced by this unusual little plant.*

RIGHT: *The succulent orange to red berries of a* Solanum capsicastrum *are less tightly packed on the stems than those of nerteras but their larger size adds an extra dimension to their appearance.*

FAR RIGHT: *Orange trees bear "golden lamps in a green night," says the poet. The white flowers of* Citrus mitis *add stars to the image.*

Using Plants Indoors

There is an almost limitless choice of plants for indoor use. What the individual gardener selects must be partly governed, of course, by the conditions he or she can provide. But since most plants are surprisingly adaptable, there remains a large choice for almost any type of environment.

There are no rules for the kinds of plant that can be used to decorate a home. The selection is largely a matter of personal taste, but certain guidelines can prove useful. First of all, it is obviously sensible to select plants that suit normal home conditions rather than try to make either the plants or the home satisfy difficult requirements. To a certain degree, every house plant needs daily attention. If you spend too much time and effort on nursing frail specimens, routine care becomes a burden instead of the pleasure it can be. As a first step, then, assess your home environment, and choose plants to suit it. There is no need to turn every room into an indoor jungle. On the other hand, there are few rooms that will not benefit from the presence of a plant as long as it enhances or purposefully contrasts with the rest of the furnishings.

Scale and proportion also play an important role. Here, too, there can be no firm rules. For instance, although big plants are not generally recommended for small rooms, an attractive large plant can be used to round off a sharp angle or an awkward corner or to conceal ugly permanent fixtures. In general, though, large plants or massive displays on different levels belong in spacious areas, where a small specimen might look puny and lost. In a big, high-ceilinged room tall climbers and baskets of spreading, trailing plants help to tie the dimensions together. In a small room such vigorous plants can seem merely fussy and crowded.

The color scheme and type of furnishings should certainly be considered when you are choosing plants for a given position. A dark wall can make a poor background for richly colored or plain green foliage. But the darkness of the wall may well set off to dramatic effect the delicate tracery of pale green ferns or the sharply defined outline of a sansevieria. Light-colored walls—which, incidentally, benefit plants by reflecting light—are natural backdrops for almost any kind of plant, whether green, variegated, highly colored, or flowering. Concealed spotlights can add further emphasis at night to such sculptured plants as palms, cordylines, and large-leaved fig trees. Busily patterned and embossed wallpapers or chairs and sofas covered with richly designed fabric can be given a calming touch by a nearly plain-leaved plant, such as a *Schefflera actinophylla* or an *Asplenium nidus*.

One important consideration for some plants is the height and structure of the objects on which they are displayed. Table tops are ideal situations for small and medium-size group arrangements. Shelves and ledges provide perfect spots for single specimens placed at or below eye level. Above this height it is preferable to use plants that cascade over the edges of pots or baskets. Judiciously chosen ornamental containers can improve the decorative effect. If *too* ornamental, however, they are likely to weaken the impact of the plants themselves, especially in group displays.

The final selection must inevitably be a matter of personal judgment along with due consideration of plant needs. Move a plant or group of plants around until it appears to create a natural harmony or satisfying contrast with its surroundings. Try out the effects of plants in conjunction with mirrors and other hangings, with ornaments of metal, pottery, glass, and china, and with various lighting arrangements. Note changes in impact between day and evening hours. Often you will find the right plant for the right situation only after several experiments.

The following pages illustrate many ways in which plants can be used to enhance the beauty of your home.

FACING PAGE: *This display combines a tasteful blend of colors with gentle contrast of shape and texture. The dark green of the container ties together the varying greens of the three kinds of pilea; and the rough texture of the pottery, like that of the quilted leaves, is softened by the smooth wood of the old mirror shelf upon which the container stands.*

Plant shapes

The imaginative indoor gardener finds ways to take advantage of the wide difference in size and shape of house plants. It is exactly these differences that not only make for visually pleasing combinations, but also highlight individual outlines. A low, spreading plant, for instance, is given stature when planted beneath a stiff, upright species, and at the same time the low plant softens the shape of the taller. There are six basic growth patterns, and most indoor plants conform more or less to one of these. A plant can grow in a tight rosette; it can spread like a bush; it can be upright, extending vertically rather than horizontally; it can be grasslike; it can be treelike; or its stems are so weak that they must either climb up an external support or trail. Each of these growth patterns is shown here, and the pages that follow illustrate groups of plants with contrasting or harmonizing shapes.

Rosette

Saintpaulia hybrid

A rosette is a roughly circular cluster of leaves radiating from a central growing point. Many small plants—saintpaulias and some sinningias, for example—form flat rosettes that rise directly from the crown of the plant. Such low rosettes associate especially well with grasslike, bushy, or climbing foliage plants. The basically flat rosette is only one of several types, however. One variation of the pattern is found in many succulents where the leaves are arranged in symmetrical tiers to create a dense, solid rosette. Another variation is found among the bromeliads. In some bromeliads the leaves form a distinct flat rosette, but in others the long, nearly upright leaves are closely gathered around the base of the plant to form a watertight cup. These larger rosettes look best when associated with upright plant shapes or with trailing plants that contrast with the spreading appearance of the rosette.

Ananas comosus variegatus *Echeveria setosa*

Bushy

Coleus blumei

Bushy plants have several stems growing from potting-mixture level, giving the plants a spread almost equal to their height. For this reason, bushy plants are often used alone rather than in group displays. Some, such as the coleuses, branch freely only if the growing tips of all shoots are regularly pinched out. Others branch naturally to form increasingly thick plants. Among the most obvious examples are plants of the genera *Achimenes* and *Pilea*.

Upright bushy shapes make good backgrounds for small trailing plants. And some naturally climbing plants can be induced to become bushy by regular pinching out of growing points or drastic pruning.

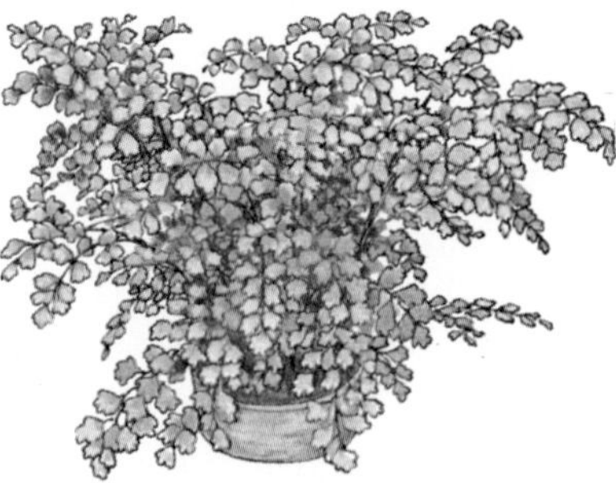

Adiantum capillus-veneris

Grassy

Acorus gramineus

The distinguishing characteristic of true grasses (members of the family *Gramineae*) are the slender but tough and wiry stems sheathed with narrow, pointed leaves. There are, however, other grasslike plants suitable for indoor cultivation which are highly regarded because they provide graceful contrasts in texture and outline to all other foliage plants. They can be upright, arching or even trailing in their habit. The grasslike acorus, for example, forms a clump of stiff, stemless leaves and, like the more drooping chlorophytum, adds an attractive element to plant groups.

One of the true grasses that has become popular as a house plant is *Stenotaphrum secundatum* which has stems that tumble over the pot edge. Like the grasslike *Scirpus cernuus*, it is best displayed in a hanging basket.

Stenotaphrum secundatum

Upright

Sansevieria trifasciata

Rosette-forming and bushy plants tend to grow outward instead of upright. By contrast, there are numerous species that extend their growth vertically rather than horizontally. These upright plants are often composed of non-woody stems that bear leaves all along their length. In some species there is a single stem, in others there are several. Not all upright plants have both stems and leaves. *Sansevieria trifasciata*, for example, is stemless, with sharp-pointed leaves rising straight upward. Columnar cacti, on the other hand, are leafless stems which can look particularly stark unless used in association with other plants. Irrespective of minor differences, upright plants are

Cereus jamacaru

Dieffenbachia exotica

perfect foils for low-growing, spreading rosettes and trailers. Conversely, single-stemmed plants such as dieffenbachias often drop their lower leaves with age and benefit from the complement of a smaller, bushy plant to conceal the otherwise ugly nakedness of the bare stem.

Treelike

Ficus benjamina

A typical tree has a single, upright trunk topped by a crown of branches and foliage. Many potted plants would become trees if permitted to grow unrestricted. *Ficus benjamina*, for example, grows to a 20-foot-tall tree in the wild. As a house plant it seldom exceeds 6 feet, but it is nevertheless treelike because its thin, upright, unbranched stem becomes like a woody trunk as it ages. Plants of such

Dizygotheca elegantissima

architectural proportions are effective when used as isolated focal points in spacious surroundings.

Although few house plants can reach treelike maturity when confined to a pot, several tree-shaped species are often found in indoor collections. *Dizygotheca elegantissima* is clearly treelike even when quite young, and its graceful leaf fronds look splendid standing above low rosettes and medium-size bushy plants. When mature, it deserves a place of its own.

Climbing and trailing

Cissus rhombifolia

A climbing plant normally grows in any direction that provides support to which it can cling. True climbers grow rapidly and are easy to cultivate indoors, but they must be given support in the form of trellises, stakes, moss poles, or even string. Many climbing plants, however, do equally well as trailers. Similarly, many plants that naturally creep or trail can be trained to climb. It is a characteristic of all these plants that their stems are too weak to grow unaided in any upright position. Such large vines as *Cissus antarctica* are equipped with thin, curling leaf tendrils by which they attach themselves to a support. They are ideal for framing archways and windows, or used as living screens for room dividers. Less vigorous climbers associate well with small and medium-size groups of rosettes and bushy plants.

Sedum morganianum *Asparagus sprengeri*

Natural trailers such as zebrinas and asparagus ferns display their handsome leaf colors and tumbling shapes best from a high position. The heavy, drooping stems of many succulents also show to best advantage in this way. Such succulents are among the trailers that cannot be trained to climb.

Grouping plants

Some foliage plants look more attractive when displayed as single specimens, but many not only look best but grow better in groups. A thriving plant community can be created by grouping a number of small pots on a window sill, in troughs, or, with larger plants, at floor level. Some of the most pleasing displays consist of growing plants together in a container.

The possibilities for attractive arrangements of compatible plants are endless. The only rule is that the grouped plants *must* be compatible—their needs must be similar. A satisfactory group can be composed of closely related plants, such as different kinds of cactus or bromeliad, or it can be based on harmonious or contrasting colors, shapes, and textures. Try using plain green leaves to accentuate the richness of colored leaves, or, conversely, put a green plant in the midst of brightly variegated foliage to provide a calming contrast. Similarly, a tall plant included in an otherwise low group offers a dramatic contrast. And a trailer cascading over the rim of the container will soften a severe design.

Even subtler groupings can be based on differing textures. Hairy and corrugated leaves are often effective in conjunction with smooth and glossy ones. Or a particular arrangement can emphasize the different shades of green in an all-green group.

It is generally wise, though, to avoid too many contrasts in a single display. Decide on a theme and build up a group based on color *or* shape *or* texture. And do not choose over-fancy containers whose design can detract from the natural beauty of the plants.

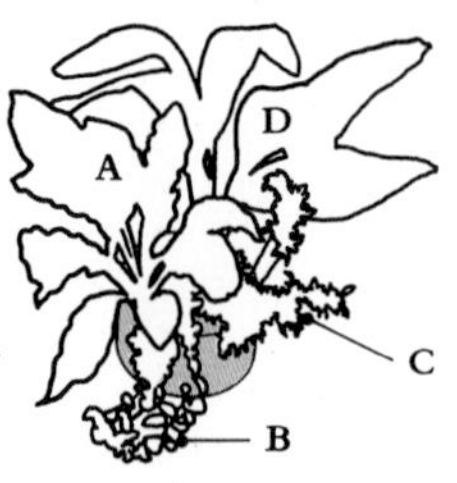

LEFT: *For subtle variety use differing shades of green. Use the dark green of an aspidistra* **(D)** *to complement a paler asplenium* **(A)**. *An arching pteris* **(C)** *and trailing ficus* **(B)** *add grace to the arrangement of glossy, light-reflecting leaves.*

LEFT: *Be sure that plants in a single container require similar growing conditions. This group of plain green nidulariums* **(D)** *along with the colorful dieffenbachia* **(C)**, *maranta* **(A)**, *and trailing scindapsus* **(B)** *must have a moderate amount of water and be kept out of direct sunlight.*

Planning groups

One popular way to build up a group of plants is to base it on shape. As shown here, a display can be roughly round or triangular, vertically or horizontally rectangular, etc. And whatever the shape, it can be further emphasized by a suitably shaped container. In choosing your plants, though, be sure that all of them relate to the planned shape and need similar growing conditions.

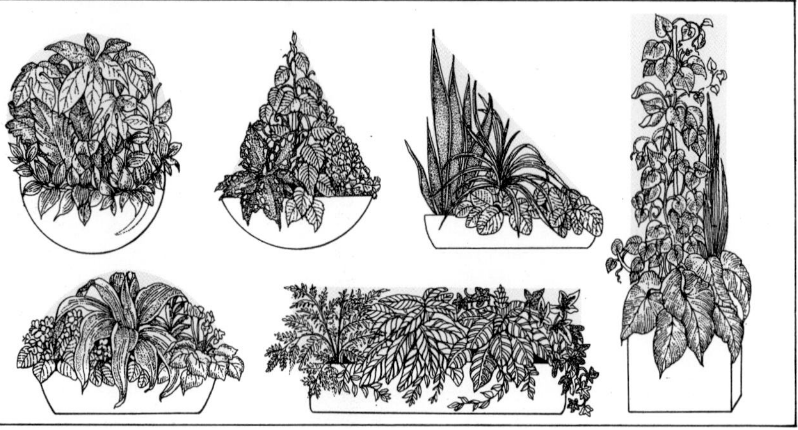

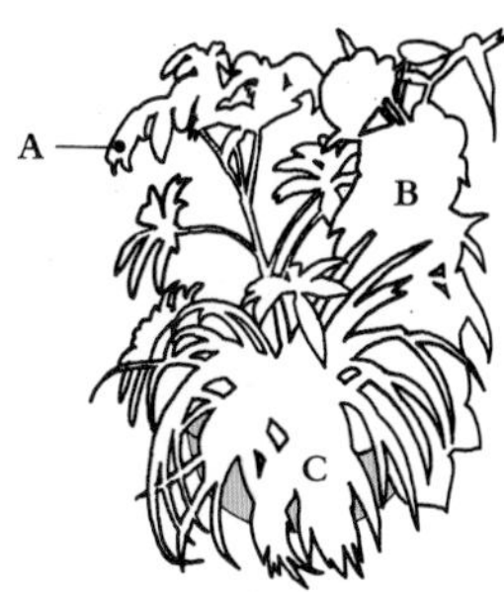

RIGHT: *In grouping tall and low plants, you can achieve balance by massing variegated leaves at the low level. Here the eye is drawn from high, green heptapleurum* (**A**) *and philodendron* (**B**) *to low, grassy, green and white chlorophytum* (**C**).

ABOVE: *Suit the container to the general contours of a display. This grevillea rises squarely above a fatshedera and ficus, creating a rectangular grouping for which the tall, square-cornered pot is highly appropriate.*

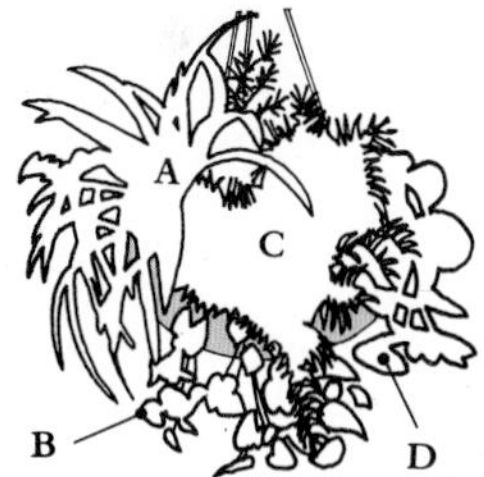

LEFT: *When filling a hanging basket with plants, do not let it seem to be weighed down by the load. Note here how the feathery asparagus* (**C**) *predominates over the broader-leaved chlorophytum* (**A**), *ficus* (**B**), *and scindapsus* (**D**).

Adding color to groups

The placement of bright-colored foliage within any group of house plants takes skill and care. Here are samples where colored foliage has been used to good effect.

RIGHT: *Soften the impact of flamboyant foliage by adding sober-colored leaves. Multicolored codiaeum* **(A)** *is less startling encircled by trailing ficus* **(B)** *spidery dizygotheca* **(C)** *and purple-blotched maranta* **(D)**

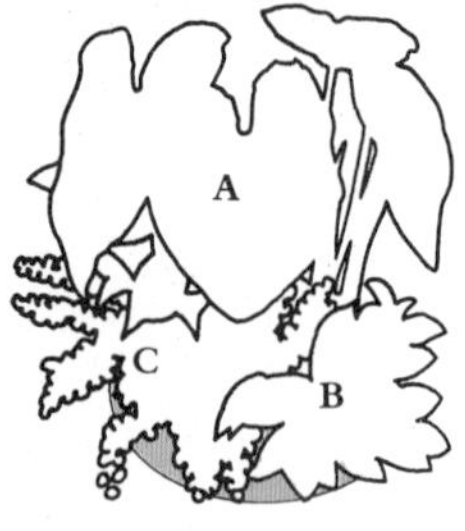

FACING PAGE: *Tissue-thin caladium leaves* **(A)** *need humid warmth to stay healthy. If you can maintain such conditions, mingle caladium with speckled dracaenas* **(B)** *on a bed of sprawling pellaea* **(C)** *for a truly incomparable display.*

ABOVE: *Use an extremely colorful grouping to enliven an otherwise dull area. But remember that this combination of purple gynura, pink-spotted hypoestes, silvery pilea, and bold-figured calathea would be over-dramatic for many positions.*

RIGHT: *Try to brighten a somber climbing cissus* **(A)** *by arranging plants with similar-shaped but richly colored leaves like begonias* **(B)** *around its base. The lamplight is not functional, merely decorative.*

Adding flowers to groups

A flowering plant, especially one that keeps its blooms for long periods, will often add a welcome extra dimension to a group of foliage plants. Flowers can be used either to complement or to contrast with leaf colors. In particular, a few floral shapes and colors are very useful for transforming small foliage arrangements into table centerpieces in place of cut flowers. Such temporary flowering plants as chrysanthemums and primulas can serve the same purpose, of course.

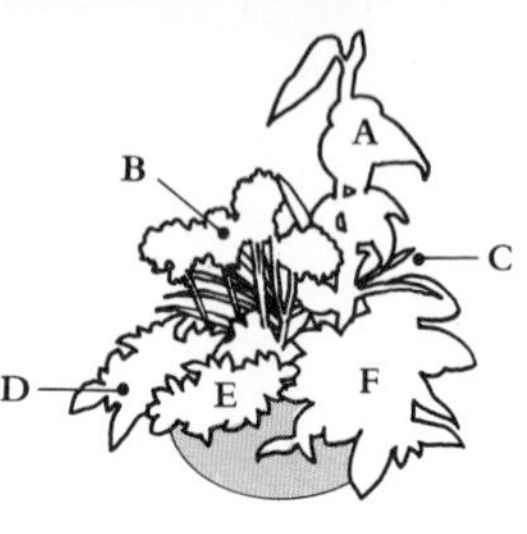

ABOVE: *Flowering kalanchoe* **(B)** *forms the brilliant red middle ground of this triangular group: low-growing variegated cleyera* **(F)**, *fittonia* **(E)**, *and peperomia* **(D)** *at the base, are flanked by thin-leaved codiaeum* **(C)**, *and philodendron* **(A)** *climbing a hidden stick.*

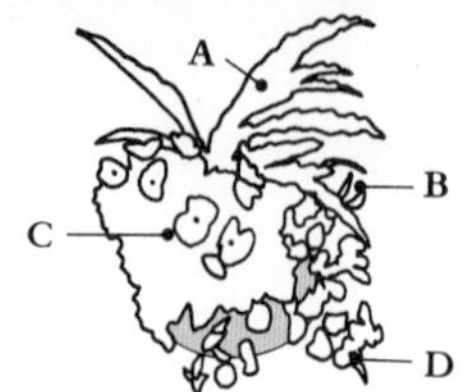

ABOVE: *To recreate this table display add splashes of pink begonia flowers* **(C)** *to a grouping of wavy calathea* **(A)**, *trailing plectranthus* **(D)**, *and* Peperomia caperata **(B)**, *with its protruding linear blooms.*

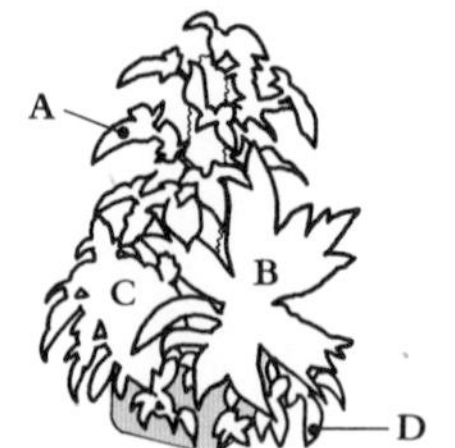

LEFT: *To make this attractive grouping use syngonium* **(A)** *trained up a moss pole, leathery-leaved aglaonema* **(B)**, *and brilliant pachystachys* **(C)**, *with silken-leaved tradescantia* **(D)**.

Contrasting shapes

The differing shapes of indoor plants are most successfully accentuated when one shape is placed in striking juxtaposition with an obvious opposite. Upright shapes associate with low rosettes, climbers with trailers.

RIGHT: *This is a well-considered, creative display, for not only do the low-lying pilea* **(C)** *and peperomia* **(B)** *contrast with tall sansevieria* **(A)**, *but the peperomia "flowers" reflect the shape of the tall, rigid leaves.*

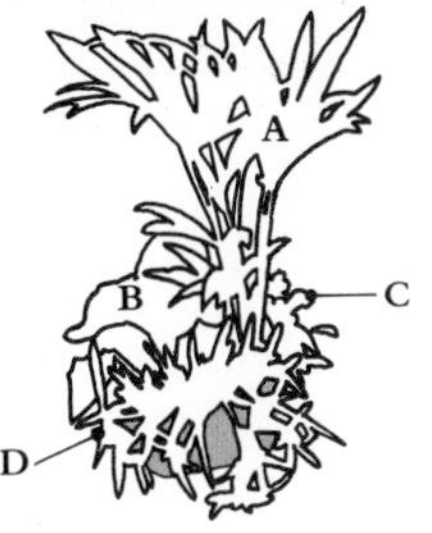

ABOVE: *Use a mirror to add depth to a studied arrangement like this one. The tall, graceful howea* **(A)** *looms over a mass of unruly, trailing stenotaphrum* **(D)** *backed by green-and-red fittonia* **(B)** *and golden-edged peperomia* **(C)**.

Plants in separate pots

A single container holding such varied plants as a climbing abutilon, trailing episcia, bushy aglaonema, clump-forming dieffenbachia and caladiums, and feathery dizygotheca makes a handsome display. But because they need different amounts of water, be sure to plant each kind in a separate pot. Note, too, that some must live in the shade of others and get less light. A creeping fittonia would be a good substitute for the episcia when its flowering period ends.

Brightening small areas

In every home there are small spaces in need of brightening up with some kind of ornament. Plants are not only ornamental but alive, and there are plants to suit almost any situation, no matter how restricted. Flowering pot plants in particular can add color and vitality to an otherwise "dead" spot.

A windowsill is an obvious choice for displaying single plants; even the narrowest sill can accommodate a couple of tiny cacti. But do not content yourself with the obvious for there are plenty of other possibilities. Use small plants, trailers, and climbers to decorate bookshelves, wall units, and kitchen cabinets and counters. Foliage plants add a welcome touch to small tables, narrow ledges and niches, desk tops, bathroom cabinets, and anywhere else that needs some living color to enliven a blank surface. Keep looking for new ideas—or invent positions to suit particular plants that especially appeal to you.

ABOVE: *Bring inanimate table-top ornaments to life by grouping them around a modest but attractive display of richly colored saintpaulias planted together.*

FACING PAGE: *Dramatize distinctions. This tall heptapleurum is strikingly placed to associate with a small fittonia and other low-lying objects for extra interest.*

ABOVE: *Try clothing naked window frames in cool azalea blooms. This springtime early morning sunlight will not harm the delicate white flowers.*

RIGHT: *Use a bright-hued plant—here a calceolaria—to enliven a deep wall niche. The light accentuates the glow but is too weak to help growth.*

Using medium-size areas

Almost every room has two or three areas too small for a functional piece of furniture and yet too large to be ignored. It is these gaps, whether they are wall, floor, window, or corner spaces, that plant life seems virtually born to fill. This is not to suggest that every available space should be occupied. A single, tastefully placed plant often lends just the right amount of warmth to a room. On the other hand, a group of plants carefully chosen and arranged can solve the same problem. In one corner of a high-ceilinged room, for instance, try placing an ornate china container holding several ferns or trailing cacti; it can surprise you by seeming to cast a glow over everything. Or a jutting wall angle may be just the place in which to display a foliage plant on a stool or low table. However, make sure that the positions chosen for plants not only suit the decor of a room, but also suit the requirements of the plant. It is no good trying to brighten a dingy corner with a plant that needs bright light. The plant will eventually suffer and will make the corner look even worse.

The best way to display medium-size plants is probably on a plant table or in a planter box. Such tables and boxes are available in a range of sizes

Lighting plants for effect

Take a tip from the museums; enhance the beauty of a valued specimen with "accent" lighting. Choose a lighting arrangement that suits the rest of your decor as well as the chosen plant and try to highlight the best feature of the plant—shape, color, form or texture. However, do not impair the health of the plant by expecting it to survive in this type of artificial light alone. Always remember that accent lighting is not a substitute for daylight (see "Artificial light," page 446).

Light a group of foliage plants from behind to achieve an unusual translucent stained-glass effect.

Use the light from an overhead skylight to silhouette the shape of a tall, dramatic plant like a dracaena.

A well-positioned spotlight accents not only the form of this dieffenbachia but also the pattern on its leaves.

and shapes, from round to square to rectangular, and are often large enough to contain several compatible plants. Ideally, they should be lined with waterproof material so that watering is not a problem, and fitted with casters so that they can be moved around as natural light intensity changes with the seasons. Casters also allow the display to be taken to the kitchen when a periodic overhaul becomes necessary. Some plant tables are built like portable carts, with two or more shelves.

ABOVE: *Use medium-size spaces even in such rooms as bedrooms for sizable plants. This citrus adds a bright touch with its colorful fruit.*

FACING PAGE: *The brassaia in the corner of this highly coordinated room, effectively breaks the monotony of the pattern.*

BELOW: *Exploit the beauty of an unused fireplace by framing such potted ferns as nephrolepis and pteris within it.*

ABOVE: *To create a stunning effect, mass pots of flowering plants such as cinerarias on a raised platform in a basket. Poinsettias and hydrangeas are larger but look just as effective.*

BELOW: *To increase the impact of a simple asplenium display, look for an interesting container, such as this ornate, wrought-iron one, in which to lodge the plants. The white container contrasts strongly with the leaves.*

Using large areas

Open-plan living rooms, studios, and offices are perfect settings for large plants and a floor-to-ceiling window can provide an almost open-air background for some such large, sculptured plant as a *Philodendron bipinnatifidum*, an orange tree, or a fatshedera. But beware of scorching sunlight. In more conventional settings graceful palms blend well with decorative or old-fashioned arrangements.

Never crowd a room with large plants. One or two well-positioned specimens will be far more effective than an overwhelming collection.

LEFT: *If you want to make this ascending garden for a stairwell, be sure there is enough light to maintain good health in such slow-growing, costly plants as howeas.*

FACING PAGE: *The dimensions of this modern, airy studio make a perfect setting for a single specimen plant, here an elegant, slim-stemmed, tall howea palm.*

BELOW: *Unusual plants often look best in unusual settings. Here, this* Euphorbia pseudocactus *adds a bizarre touch to an already exotic room.*

ABOVE: *It may take, as here, two medium-size fatsias in one large urn to fill a big empty space. Monsteras and large-leaved philodendrons can be used in the same way.*

ABOVE: *Use a huge, weeping ficus to soften the stark lines of tall, narrow spaces such as this one between French doors and a long window in a lofty room.*

Climbing and trailing plants

The common feature of trailing and climbing plants is their inability to grow upright without support. This characteristic makes them just right for decoration on the vertical plane. They can trail downward from wall pots, niches, ledges and shelves, or from freely suspended baskets. Or they can be trained to grow upward on some kind of support. Many plants can also be encouraged to grow both upward and downward around window frames and archways. *Philodendron scandens* and the ivies, for example, grow with equal success whether climbing or trailing. This ability to serve a dual purpose can result in some eye-catching arrangements. For instance, try grouping together a number of hedera varieties and permitting some of them to trail while training others up supports.

Small console tables fitted against walls are often used for holding trailing, arching, or climbing plants. Even if the light is not especially good, the ivies, many ferns, and trailing or climbing *Ficus pumila* are suitable for placement on some such table in a comparatively dim corner. A decorative container of rhipsalidopsises or schlumbergeras can also look attractive in such a position. But perhaps more appropriate for these plants is a high pedestal from which the succulent stems can cascade freely.

ABOVE: *If you want a splash of color,* Thunbergia alata, *a fast-growing, summer-flowering plant that winds around almost anything that gets in its way, can provide it.*

LEFT: *To relieve the cold lines of an open-plan landing, the foliage of a row of ficuses trails in front of colorful marantas standing on top of lower-floor cabinets.*

BELOW: *Even in this spacious and lofty room a 10-foot-high fatshedera-covered moss pole might look ungainly. But its height is offset by the neighboring bushy plant.*

BELOW: *The most effective — and least dangerous — way to display pendent, flowering, spiny aporocactus stems is in a hanging container kept above eye-level.*

FACING PAGE: *Pruning a fuchsia keeps it upright and tidy, but it can look even more stunning on a table in a garden room when, as here, the stems are allowed to droop and trail.*

ABOVE: *One way to control a long, trailing plant is to let it wander across netting. Note the curling tendrils of this passiflora which enable it to climb unaided.*

Decorative baskets

Of the many possible kinds of decorative container the hanging basket is probably the most useful (and most popular). There are endless variations, and you can even make your own. The all-important consideration in preparing an indoor container of any type, however, is that it must obviously be made waterproof.

Some hanging containers have chains and pulleys so they can be lowered for watering. Many indoor gardeners, however, prefer to use a separate pot within the container, so that plants can be removed for treatment whenever necessary.

ABOVE: *An unusual alternative to a hanging basket is a wicker stand. Straggling shoots of a trailing ivy look just as attractive displayed this way and should not be pruned.*

ABOVE: *This imaginatively-used wicker "pagoda" may seem a strange container, but cissus and ivy twining through its crevices and around its legs make an unusual focal point.*

Making a hanging basket

Many different plants are suitable for hanging baskets. Obviously your choice will be based on visual criteria, but there are other important points to consider before making the final selection: Have all the plants got the same cultivation needs? Is the display to be permanent or temporary? When these questions have been answered prepare the basket as follows:

For ease of working, rest the basket on the rim of a flat-bottomed bowl, and detach some chain ends.

Line the basket with two inches of damp sphagnum moss and a piece of plastic with holes for drainage.

When the plastic is weighted down with potting mixture, trim its edges so that they will not hang over the rim.

First arrange trailing plants around the basket rim. Support them with added mixture, firming it down.

After planting the trailers, put upright plants in the center of the basket, adding more mixture as necessary.

When the basket is filled, tuck in any plastic edges, and replace chain ends in their original positions.

ABOVE: *To beautify your kitchen with an easy-to-grow plant, hang a trailing plectranthus in a safe position, and spotlight it softly at night for added emphasis.*

FACING PAGE: *Macrame rope hangers for individual pots can be bought, but do-it-yourself fans enjoy making them. Note how these colors suit the ivy.*

Plant supports

Plants that climb by means of aerial roots, such as philodendrons and monsteras, grow best when they have a soft, moist medium over which they can scramble. Many florists sell ready-made moss poles for this purpose, but it is easy to make your own (see below). Soak the pole and let it drain before pushing it into potting mixture. Tie stems to the pole at intervals until the clinging aerial roots have taken firm hold. Keep the pole moist by spraying it, or trickle water down through the top of the pole.

A column or ball made on the same principle is a novel way to display small ferns. For instructions on how to build a fern column see page 207. A fern ball is simply a spherically shaped piece of chicken wire filled with moistened sphagnum moss into which the roots of small ferns are pushed through the mesh. A ball of this type suspended from a wall or ceiling hook is an attractive addition to any room. It need merely be taken down for watering at regular intervals. The best way to water it is by spraying or by immersing it in a pail of water.

Epiphytic plants, including the bromeliads and orchids, live on tree trunks and branches in the wild. Forest conditions can be simulated by growing such plants on what is known as either an "epiphyte branch" or "bromeliad log" (which may be merely a piece of driftwood or a slab of cork bark). In its simplest form such a support consists of several plants, with roots wrapped in damp sphagnum moss, wired onto a single piece of wood. More attractive and complex is a tree branch with several forks and hollows that provide homes for a wide variety of epiphytes. (See page 107 for instructions on making these.)

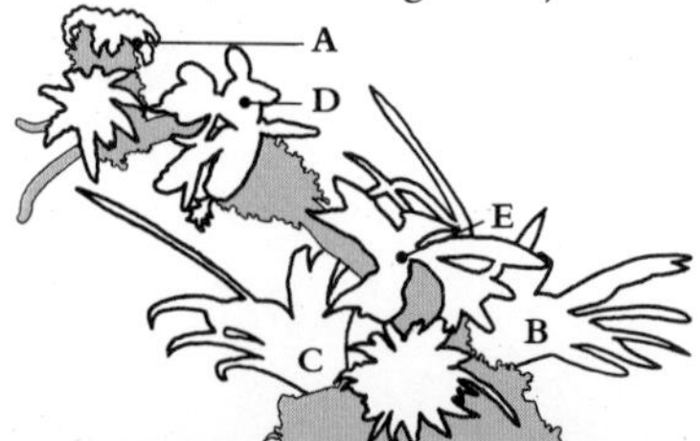

ABOVE: *If you insert a wire hoop in potting mixture, it can serve as a slender support around which to train the long stems of a graceful flowering stephanotis.*

BELOW: *This epiphyte branch holds three bromeliads—cryptanthus* **(A)**, *neoregelia* **(B)**, *vriesea* **(C)**; *a jungle cactus—rhipsalidopsis* **(D)**; *and a fern—platycerium* **(E)**. *All roots must be wrapped in moss which should be kept moist.*

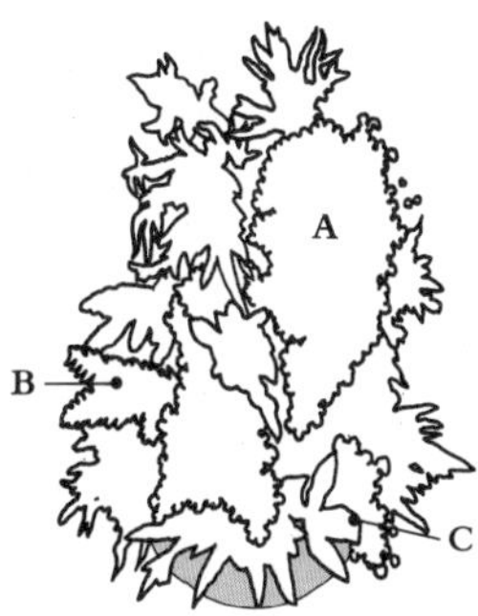

RIGHT: *You can grow a variety of ferns—here adiantum* **(A)**, *nephrolepis* **(B)**, *and pteris* **(C)** *on a wire column filled with moist sphagnum moss. Push roots through the mesh and into the moss at intervals so that the column is completely covered by the foliage.*

ABOVE: *To simulate its natural habitat, grow a climbing philodendron up a moss pole. Trickle water down the pole every day to keep the moss thoroughly moist.*

Making a moss pole

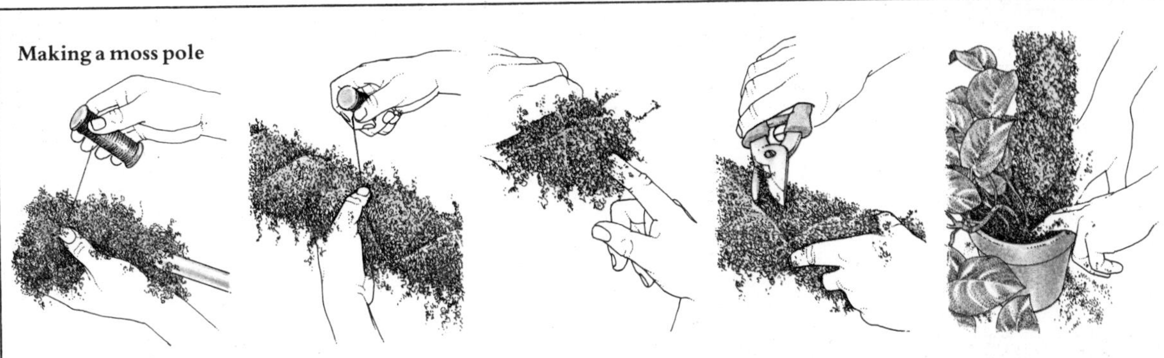

Wrap damp sphagnum moss thickly around a length of plastic tube or a wooden pole. Bind moss on tightly with soft wire.

Leave the bottom four inches bare (to be inserted in potting mixture). For security, criss-cross wire along the length.

If using tube, fill in the gap at the top by pushing sphagnum moss into the hole. Trim off straggling bits of moss.

Secure the pole base in the pot with plaster of Paris. Fill the pot with mixture, and finally, add the plant to be supported.

Room dividers

Potted-plant devices for separating one area of an open room from another can vary from a small group arrangement, terrarium, or bottle garden (see pages 54–57) set on a low table to a tall, living screen of rapid climbers, such as *Cissus antarctica*. A vital consideration is the shape and size of the room. In an average living room a floor-to-ceiling screen can merely serve to deny light to one small compartment. It is often much more effective to place single plants, or two or three, in strategic positions. Even in a spacious room a massive plant display should create a backdrop rather than a leafy wall.

Potted plants used as room dividers can be concealed in a deep, wide plant trough if this seems desirable. It is sometimes better, though, to place the plants alongside one another in decorative pots so that they can be turned toward the source of light as their individual needs dictate. Also consider the need for cleaning such plants. It is easier to sponge dust off large leaves than off small ones.

FACING PAGE: *Use mirrors to give a feeling of spaciousness to small rooms divided up by plants. This mirror image shows how a separate dining area has been created by fatshedera and asparagus on a bamboo trellis.*

BELOW: *A room divider need not look formal or meticulously designed. For a casual arrangement use several kinds of free-standing plant, and experiment with contrasts in height, shape, texture and so on.*

Creating a room divider

Pictured here are two types of divider. More like a true wall is the trellis, upon which syngonium stems are trained. To protect the floor, pots stand on a tray, while the trellis is supported by horizontal struts. Thus the divider is moveable—but with difficulty. A grouping of separate plants (here some dracaenas in matching pots) is obviously more flexible. And the feeling of a true room divider is heightened by using plants of varying sizes, whose foliage forms a more solid screen.

Using window areas

The light that comes into almost every home through windows is a necessity for the plants that grow in this artificial environment. But the intensity of the light varies greatly according to the time of year and the aspect. A south-facing window gets the greatest amount of light all year long. In fact, midday summer light through a south-facing window can be so intense that it must be filtered through a translucent curtain or blind in order to prevent scorching of leaves and loss of flower buds. True, cacti thrive at unshaded south-facing windows, and so do some (though not all) highly variegated foliage plants. But most plants do best in filtered southern light or—better still—at an east- or west-facing window.

Obviously, a window with a northern exposure admits the least amount of light, especially in winter. This does not mean, however, that the indoor gardener must forgo the pleasure of enlivening a north-facing window area with attractive plants. A number of green foliage plants—notably ferns, aspidistras, and sansevierias—grow satisfactorily in such a situation.

There can be other problems in window areas, though, regardless of the aspect. Radiators and air conditioners beneath windows cause hot or cold drafts and excessively dry air. That is why it becomes essential to create a humid micro-climate by standing certain plants on trays of moist pebbles and by mist-spraying their foliage at frequent intervals. Circulation of air is also important but ensure that plants are not in drafts.

FACING PAGE: *Try to suit plant shape to window shape. This round, north-facing window provides a graceful frame for a delicate maidenhair fern (adiantum).*

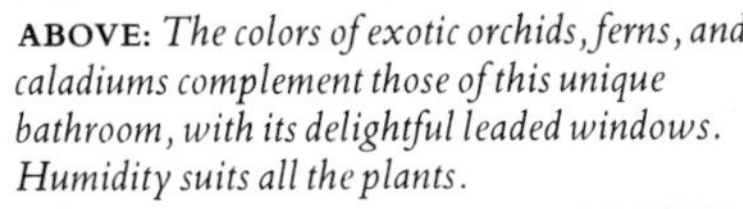
ABOVE: *The colors of exotic orchids, ferns, and caladiums complement those of this unique bathroom, with its delightful leaded windows. Humidity suits all the plants.*

BELOW: *You can create a three-dimensional still life with a nephrolepis fern, a few green apples, complementary wicker baskets, and bright light.*

ABOVE: *To decorate a sunny window ledge, build a small garden entirely of desert cacti, all of which need full sunlight. Note the varieties of shape, texture and color.*

RIGHT: *Light coming through this little window would be inadequate for many plants, but the sturdy, tolerant aspidistra continues to thrive. Do not be misled into thinking that an aspidistra needs poor conditions however.*

BELOW: *Groups need not be confined to window ledges. To soften the stark lines of a large window area consider hanging several containers at different levels; each will complement the other.*

Building window shelves

Disguise a dull view with an indoor window garden. The strong glass plant shelves at right are supported on an adjustable peg system while the wooden shelves shown far right are suspended on knotted rope "uprights." (Be sure to knot the rope at equal heights.) Choose plants whose light requirements suit the aspect of the window and if the window receives direct sunlight provide a translucent blind or curtain to shade plants from scorching midday sun.

ABOVE: *If you want to keep an azalea indoors and in bloom for as long as possible, place it in a cool position where it gets little, if any, direct sunlight. Note here how flower and room colors complement each other. After flowering has finished, put the plant outdoors to recover.*

BELOW: *A kitchen windowsill is ideal for a collection of small individual plants like these. Ivy hanging freely from a nearby shelf counterbalances the linear arrangement of other plants including ananas, saintpaulia, pelargonium, and sansevieria.*

ABOVE: *French doors leading onto a balcony seem to become part of the pleasant outdoor scene when framed with ivy. To protect the wooden molding round the doors, the fast-growing foliage must of course be trained up a separate support.*

RIGHT: *These floor-to-ceiling windows and vast skylight provide an exceptionally bright setting for indoor plants during the day, and an eyecatching framework for the artificially lit display at night.*

FACING PAGE: *It is unlikely that you will be able to find such a background for a plant display but notice how the green window areas reflect the color of leaves. The aged cycas is the focal point of this group and pelargoniums, hippeastrums, ficus, and lilies provide variety. Flowering plants are changed seasonally.*

ABOVE: *Try placing a scented pelargonium, which likes limited amounts of direct light at a window facing east or west. The delicate aroma will be released at the slightest touch.*

Creating a plant window

A special plant window is merely a double window with a large gap between the panes of glass. It serves as a container for plants that need humid warmth, and, if very elaborate, will have automatic mist-spraying, temperature control, lighting tubes, etc. Such sophistication is not vital, however. Note that among the typically suitable plants in the window illustrated here, only one plant not in a hanging basket is separately potted. This is because the potted plant, a medinilla, must be raised above ground level to keep its drooping flower heads from touching the damp mixture, which would rot them.

Plants in containers

Terrariums, plant cases, and bottle gardens have all developed from the so-called Wardian case invented by an English botanist, Nathaniel B. Ward, a century and a half ago. He found that some plants would grow indefinitely in sealed glass cases. The principle behind his discovery is this: Once humidity has been established in a sealed, transparent container, moisture from the soil and transpiration from the leaves of plants condenses, runs back into the soil, and thus creates a self-supporting environment.

Although many plants can live for years in sealed cases, condensation does cloud the glass. Some sort of ventilation is therefore necessary. In containers without automatic controls the lids or stoppers must be removed for a few days whenever the glass becomes badly clouded.

There are many possible types of glass or clear plastic container in which you can stand a potted plant. But some plants look better if planted in a layer of potting mixture (see "Bottle gardens," page 56, for instructions on how to prepare the mixture).

RIGHT: *The sedum in this candy jar is planted in mixture lying on drainage material. Pebbles around the sides and on the surface are for a purely decorative purpose.*

ABOVE: *Different containers—differing needs. Asparagus in a bell jar seldom requires water; an open-ended hanging bowl of pellaea needs constant care.*

RIGHT: *Terrariums of all shapes and sizes can be bought in specialty shops or made to order. Ficus, fittonia and microcoelum thrive in the moist air of this leaded-glass case, carefully designed to add elegance to any room.*

FACING PAGE: *You can often grow a humidity-loving maidenhair fern more easily in a covered container than under ordinary room conditions. This goblet makes a good table ornament with the spreading fronds suitably accommodated within the wide container.*

Finding interesting containers

Keep an eye out for unusual glass (or clear plastic) jars or bottles that can be used as containers for plants. Shapes pictured here are only a beginning. Be wary, though, of tinted glass; color blocks out light. Flaws or bubbles in old glass do no harm to plants and add charm to the display.

Bottle gardens

Narrow-necked, clear glass bottles of various sizes make handsome containers for a variety of moisture-loving plants. Any type of bottle is suitable as long as the neck is wide enough to let small plants pass through.

The narrow opening calls for special tools and a certain amount of dexterity. To avoid soiling the inside of the glass, all drainage material and potting mixture must be poured into the bottle through a funnel or cardboard tube. And thin, long-handled planting tools must either be acquired or constructed by wiring necessary implements to slender, sturdy, flexible sticks (see below for further details).

To prepare a bottle for plants, cover the base with a 1- to 2-inch-deep drainage layer consisting of charcoal chips mixed with small pebbles. Add a 2- to 4-inch layer of damp potting mixture. This should not be of a type that encourages fast growth. A combination of two parts of soil-based potting mixture, two parts of coarse sand, and one part of leaf mold or peat moss should suit most plants.

For obvious reasons, choose small, slow-growing plants and then plan the arrangement before placing plants in the bottle. In this way specimens can be moved around until they make the most satisfying display. Ensure that small plants are not hidden behind taller ones, that they are not positioned too close together, and that shapes and colors complement one another.

It is best to begin by inserting plants close to the edge of the bottle and then working toward the middle. Before lowering them into the bottle, remove as much soil as possible from the roots, and trim them back if necessary. The process of making holes in the mixture and easing the plants down into it is illustrated below. After planting has been completed, you can drop pebbles or small pieces of driftwood onto the surface of the mixture for additional visual effect.

Spray the bottled plants with a fine mist. Then, if necessary, clean the inside of the glass with a sponge attached to flexible wire. Put a stopper in the bottle and place it in good (but not too strong) light. Except for occasional ventilation and pruning, the display should need no further attention for many months.

ABOVE: *In general, avoid using colored bottles. This lightly tinted demijohn is suitable, though, for the microcoelum, peperomia, pteris fern, and acorus planted in it, since these plants do not require bright light.*

FACING PAGE: *To achieve a colorful effect, make a bottle garden including plants with variegated leaves. This display contains a dracaena, vriesea, fittonia, microcoelum, and cryptanthus of attractively contrasting heights.*

Making a bottle garden

To create a bottle garden you need the tools shown here. Near right are two sticks for use as tongs. You also need a spoon (top middle), wooden spool (top right), sponge (bottom middle) and sharp blade (bottom right), each tightly secured to a long stick or stiff wire. The spoon serves as a spade, the spool is used to firm the soil, the sponge is used for cleaning the glass, and the blade for pruning. Moisten the mix before putting it in the bottle and spray before corking plants up.

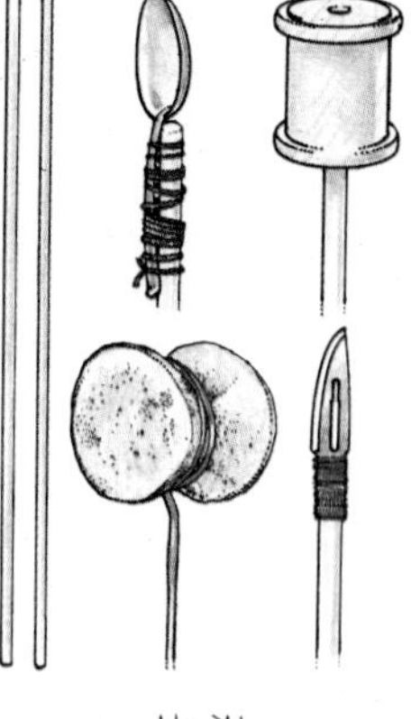

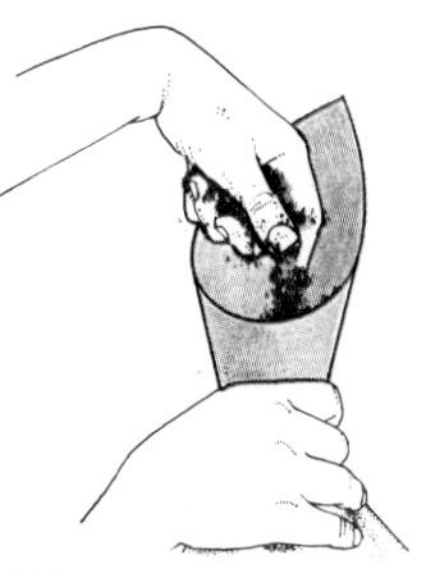

Trickle potting mixture down into the narrow-necked glass container through a paper funnel.

Use the spoon to smooth out the surface of the mixture, and then make a hole for the roots of the first plant.

Remove small plants from their current pots, and shake any excess potting mixture from their roots.

Holding a plant gently but firmly between two sticks, lower it into the scooped-out hole in the mixture.

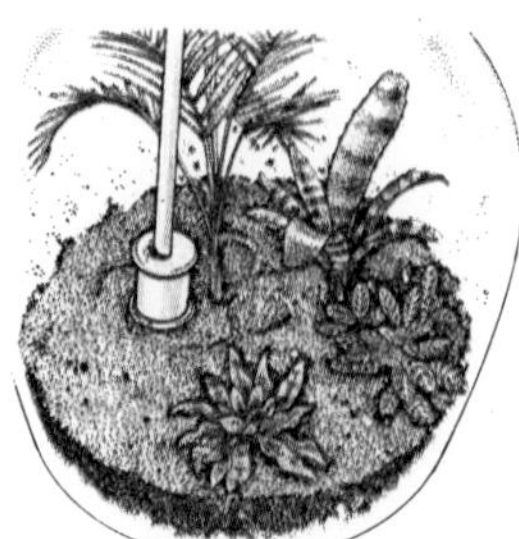

After repeating the process with more specimens, tamp down the mixture with the wooden spool.

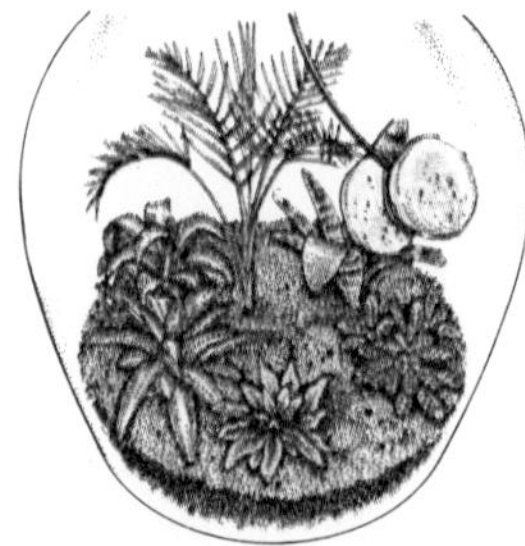

When the arrangement is complete use the moistened sponge to clean off the sides of the bottle.

Miniature gardens

Miniature gardens can be anything from a small replica of an outdoor garden to a little group of dwarf plants in a dish. Virtually any kind of dish or tray will make a satisfactory container as long as it is deep enough to hold a shallow layer of drainage material topped with a slightly deeper layer of potting mixture.

A miniature rock garden can form a charming centerpiece for a table. Built around stones carefully chosen to represent rocks and outcrops, such a garden can include small specimens of plain and variegated ivies, *Ficus pumila, Tolmiea menziesii,* etc. More elaborate and more colorful is a flower garden where imagination and patience can create a satisfying result.

Some of the most suitable plants for miniature gardens are cacti and other succulents, all of which have shallow root systems. Many of these plants will stay tiny and thrive for years in containers made to represent their natural habitats. In building this type of desert garden, try to choose plants that show the variety of shapes and textures.

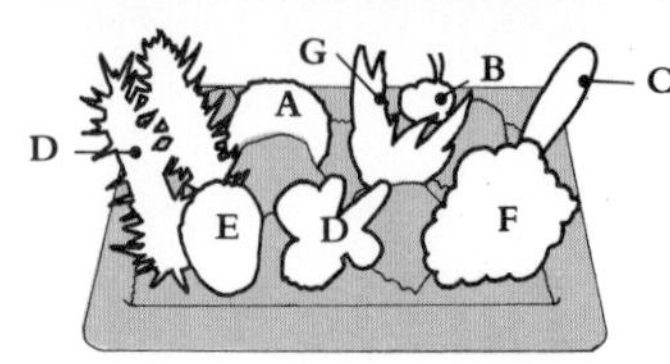

ABOVE: *To make a desert garden like this one, follow the step-by-step sequence outlined below. All these plants but one are cacti: a lobivia* **(A)**, *gymnocalycium* **(B)**, *cereus* **(C)**, *two opuntias* **(D)**, *espostoa* **(E)** *and a mammillaria* **(F)**. *The aloe* **(G)** *is a succulent.*

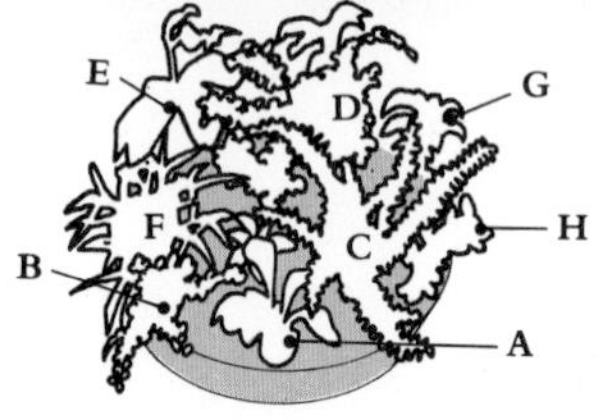

FACING PAGE: *Build this mossy glade for shade-loving plants. It will take months for asplenium* **(A)**, *pellaea* **(B)**, *nephrolepis* **(C)**, *adiantum* **(D)**, *dracaena* **(E)**, *codiaeum* **(F)**, *cleyera* **(G)**, *and fittonia* **(H)**, *to outgrow it.*

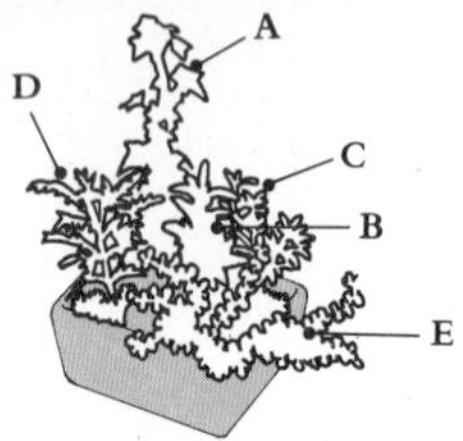

ABOVE: *Silver and gold predominate in this miniature garden where climbing ivy* **(A)**, *two types of euonymus* **(B and C)**, *graceful grevillea* **(D)**, *and trailing sedum* **(E)** *contrast pleasingly.*

Making a cactus garden

Put some gravel in a shallow container, and cover with suitable mixture.

With your finger mark out high and low areas and positions for shapely stones.

An aloe fits in well with cacti. To begin free its roots of the old potting mixture.

In adding other specimens, mix desert and jungle cacti. They do well together.

If plants are spiny or awkward to handle, use a stick to tamp down the mix.

You can make colorful paths by topping the mixture with small gravel chips.

Garden rooms

Grand conservatories are a thing of the past. Modern garden rooms, where they exist, are basically green, sunny, casually furnished extensions of the main part of the house. The ideal garden room is adjacent to the living room and is large enough to be full of plants without seeming to be too crowded to accommodate comfortable chairs. The chairs are made for lounging, with cushions covered in attractive fabric. In short, the room provides a relaxed environment for plants and people alike.

To facilitate gardening there is a water tap concealed in a corner. The floors (since this is an *ideal* room) are covered with tiles capable of standing up to dirt and water. The clear-glass roof slopes so as to shed rain, falling leaves, or snow. And there are windows on all sides, with easily drawn curtains or blinds.

By its nature a garden room admits more light than the average room, and so the possible range of plants is much extended. This is where such plants as bougainvilleas, grevilleas, hoyas, jacarandas, and many orchids are likely to thrive. If the roof is supported on stout joists, hanging baskets with trailing begonias, ferns, and flowering fuchsias can be suspended. Vines and other climbing plants can be encouraged to grow up the walls and creep along the ceiling. Greenhouse-type borders can be fitted at floor level.

Large garden rooms sometimes incorporate sunken pools and ornamental fountains. But such extras are luxuries. The garden-room attributes that really matter are light, comfort, color, fragrance, and the rich beauty of growing plant life.

ABOVE: *This colorful, airy garden room makes an attractive and unusual setting for an occasional meal on a cool summer evening. Candlelight adds to the calm atmosphere.*

FACING PAGE: *An old-style conservatory suggests repose. Vines clamber up the dome, the floor is covered with plants, and the chairs look cool and inviting.*

Gardens in the floor

To have a built-in garden in one part of a room you can box in a section of floor space. Provide a waterproof lining for the box, and either surround potted plants with peat moss or fill the space with potting mixture in which to plant specimens (as in the illustration, right). If you are building a new house, consider the possibility of providing a sunken area in the floor to be used as a permanent planter (far right).

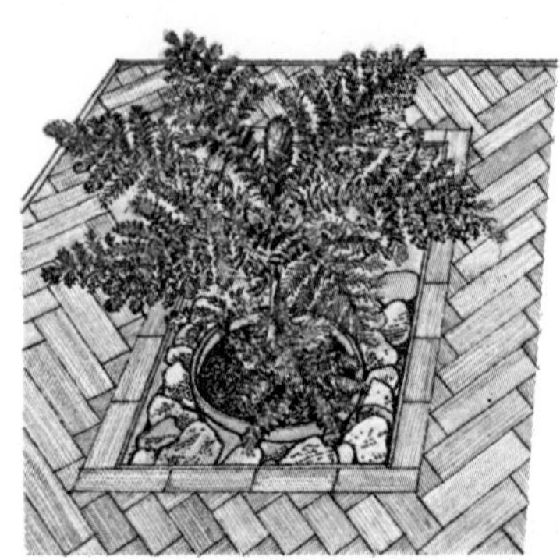

Patios and terraces

Patios, terraces and decks add another dimension to indoor gardening. In summer these extensions of the indoor living room are obviously made to order for the many house plants that benefit from a refreshing annual period in the open air. In particular, many cacti and other succulents tend to grow and flower better if given a few months of outdoor sunlight every year. And shrubby plants grown for their winter and spring flowers—azaleas and camellias for instance—can also be encouraged to flower indoors in succeeding seasons by being moved out to a deck or terrace (and, of course, being given proper care) at the end of each year's flowering period. In mild climates most foliage plants will do well if permitted to spend the summer in sheltered corners of a patio. Even in cooler areas such house plants as chlorophytums, asparagus ferns, fatsias, and hederas are hardy enough to stay healthy outdoors for some part of every year.

So if you have outdoor living space, no matter what you call it, make the most of it. In addition to benefiting many of your plants, it will give extra pleasure if it is decked with greenery.

RIGHT: *Rhododendrons, a bay tree, fatsia, and chamaedorea luxuriate in a sheltered corner of a terrace that gets a few hours a day of direct sunlight. This outdoor scene is linked to the room by a tall bougainvillea at the window.*

Natural surfaces

The natural elements of wood, stone, and brick are pleasing backgrounds for many plants. Near right: Green foliage in front of the arches of a brick wall in an old house softens harsh contours of the brick. Far right: The floor surface of a patio (whether cobblestones, patterned bricks, or concrete blocks, as suggested in this illustration) can be modified by the graceful leaves and flowers of plants that benefit from a period outdoors.

The A-Z Guide to House Plants

How to use the A–Z guide

Entries in the *A–Z Guide* are arranged alphabetically by genus name. If you do not know the genus of a plant but call it by a common name, consult the index, which lists common as well as Latin names. If you look up African violet, for example, you will be referred to *Saintpaulia*.

Pictured below is a reproduction of a small section of the guide: two consecutive pages containing the concluding portion of one entry (for plants of the genus *Platycerium*) and two complete entries (for *Plectranthus* and *Pleomele*). This representative sample contains most of the distinctive features of nearly all *A–Z Guide* articles. To help you make the most of what the guide has to offer, those features are pointed out and summarized in the accompanying notes.

Deviations from the dependable pattern illustrated here are rare. The exceptions exist only because of the special nature of certain genera. For instance, whereas *Plectranthus* and *Pleomele* are permanent (and therefore "typical") indoor plants, there are a few popular kinds that are only temporary (cinerarias and narcissi, for example). Proper treatment of temporary indoor plants seldom involves factors precisely parallel to those for permanent plants, and so the pattern must be broken. Occasionally, too, there are so many variations in form and growth habit within a single genus that the relevant facts cannot be presented without diverging from the established pattern. *Begonia* is an example. The several distinct types of begonia require

Procedures recommended in the text are often illustrated in step-by-step sequences nearby.

There is always a large illustration of a typical plant, which portrays shape, color, texture, and other major features. For genera with several recommended species the picture shows a specimen of one of the most common forms.

To show significant differences from the plant pictured in the main illustration, certain other recommended forms are often depicted. Sometimes, where the difference is in only one feature, such as leaf or flower shape, only that feature is illustrated.

Each article begins with a description of the general features of the genus, or—as in both Plectranthus *and* Pleomele*—not of the genus as a whole but of the forms that are in common use as house plants. This introductory section sometimes includes comments about growth habits and cultivation needs that seem worth emphasizing apart from recommendations in the* **PROPER CARE** *section.*

Recommended forms within the genus are listed in alphabetical order, with distinguishing features of each form clearly delineated. Species and varieties selected for recommendation are normally forms that are attractive, available, and not too difficult to grow. As shown in Pleomele, *some articles do not include specific recommendations, usually because little or no choice is possible for amateur growers.*

Vertical lines clearly mark the beginning and end of every article.

Tying a platycerium on bark

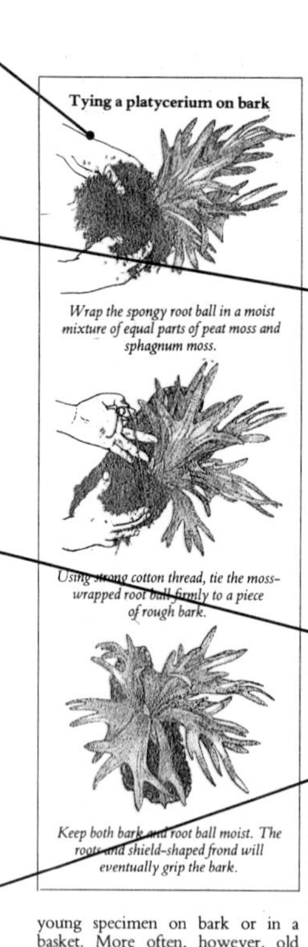

Wrap the spongy root ball in a moist mixture of equal parts of peat moss and sphagnum moss.

Using strong cotton thread, tie the moss-wrapped root ball firmly to a piece of rough bark.

Keep both bark and root ball moist. The roots and shield-shaped frond will eventually grip the bark.

young specimen on bark or in a basket. More often, however, old plants are broken up into several separate sections, but the breaking-up process may cause considerable damage to some sections.

Special points Platyceriums are not often troubled with pests, but scale insects (see page 455) sometimes infest the underside of the fronds. They can be treated by applying denatured alcohol on a fine-tipped brush direct to each of the insects.

Clean the fronds by leaving them in gentle rain in mild weather or by mist-spraying them; wiping them with a cloth or sponge will remove the attractive felty scurf. Do not allow water to remain on the fronds.

322

Plectranthus

LABIATAE

Candle plant
P. oertendahlii

ALTHOUGH the genus *Plectranthus* includes both short-shrubby and creeping plants, it is largely the creeping species that have become popular house plants. They are especially attractive in hanging baskets, from which they trail down as much as $1\frac{1}{2}$ to 2 feet. Most have soft, almost squared stems and soft, slightly furry leaves with shallowly scalloped edges; they emit a distinctive aromatic odor when touched. A plectranthus will root easily (at any point where a node touches the potting mixture), grow fast, and produce loose racemes of tiny, usually pale lavender flowers (similar to those of coleuses, to which these plants are closely related). The flowers are not particularly attractive and can be removed when they start to develop on the plant.

RECOMMENDED PLECTRANTHUSES

P. australis (Swedish ivy) has dark green, pointed-oval, $1\frac{1}{2}$-inch-long leaves. Unlike most other popular species, this is an erect, bushy plant, which can grow 3 feet tall.

P. coleoides is rarely available, but a variegated form, *P.c.* 'Marginatus,' is popular. It grows erect at first, but later trails. Its 2- to $2\frac{1}{2}$-inch-long, hairy, heart-shaped leaves have wide, creamy white margins.

P. nummularius, also a trailer, has plain green, fleshy, almost circular leaves up to $2\frac{1}{2}$ inches across.

P. oertendahlii (candle plant), the most popular plectranthus, has 1-inch, almost circular, bronze-green, softly felted leaves that are strongly veined with a silvery net and have purple margins. The undersides of mature leaves are also purple.

P. coleoides 'Marginatus'

P. australis (Swedish ivy)

PROPER CARE

Light These plants like three to four hours of direct sunlight every day. If they have inadequate light, leaf color becomes poor, and the gaps between leaves widen.

Temperature Plectranthuses grow well in warm rooms; they will thrive in temperatures of about 60°–70°F. In greater heat they need increased humidity. Stand pots on trays or saucers of damp pebbles. In winter it is advisable to give these plants a rest under cool conditions (55°–58°).

widely differing growing conditions, and the distinctions and comparisons essential for a meaningful discussion of the genus necessitate basic changes in the way the article is constructed. Even in such complex entries, though, the general approach is similar to that of a typical entry.

Note, finally, that eight of the articles in the *A–Z Guide* are not entries for single genera. Each of these articles deals with a group of plants belonging to different genera but having certain features in common. For example, under *Cacti* and *Orchids* you will find helpful discussions of those plants as groups, with emphasis on the cultivation needs peculiar to the group. Similar articles deal with bulbs, corms, and tubers; bromeliads; ferns; gesneriads; palms; and succulents other than cacti. In the individual entry for any genus belonging to one of those groups, you will be referred for further information to the general article. Following the introductory description of the general features of the genus *Blechnum*, for instance, the words "*See also FERNS*" appear.

For anyone in search of the right plant to buy rather than the right way to grow a plant, there is further guidance in the pages immediately following the *A–Z Guide*. Here you will find a multi-reference chart—the *Finder's Guide* (pages 399-408)—which suggests appropriate plants for virtually every indoor position or growth factor. Make a tentative choice with the help of the *Finder's Guide*. Then check your choice against all cultivation needs for that plant as they are described in the *A–Z Guide* entry. With these aids you will almost surely discover the right plant for the right situation with the minimum of effort.

The genus name in large type heads all entries except those dealing with groups of plants (see text block above).

The name of the family to which the genus belongs appears in smaller type under the genus name.

Cross-references direct the reader to pages where there is either more detailed information about the subject matter or explanatory material defining certain horticultural terms.

Where there is a generally accepted common name for the illustrated plant, the common name is printed before the technical one.

The illustrated plant is identified by its correct Latin name.

Here and there a single drawing dropped into the text illustrates an interesting point. The purpose of the picture is always clearly explained in a brief caption.

In nearly every case the six major aspects of **PROPER CARE** *are covered under six headings always in the same order. The seventh heading,* **Special points**, *appears where it is necessary.*

The **Special points** *category does not appear in all articles. It is reserved for matters not regularly covered under routine headings for* **PROPER CARE**. *Examples of such matters are pests, diseases, cleaning problems, and questions of pruning, handling, and display. Any of these can require special attention in specific cases, but they are not an important consideration with most house plants.*

ring Water actively growing plentifully enough to keep the g mixture thoroughly moist, ver allow pots to stand in water. ly growing trailers (those pro- g long stems) need very regular ing—as often as once a day— ularly if they are being displayed anging basket in a well-lit win- When plants are resting water gly, giving enough water to he potting mixture from drying ompletely. Lower leaves dry up ll if plants are allowed to dry out ore than a short time.
ng Apply standard liquid ferti- every two weeks to actively ing plants. A well-fed plect- us will produce large, lush foli- d strong stems.
ng and repotting Use a soil- potting mixture (see page 429). se plectranthuses are most at- ve when young, repotting is needed; old plants are best used opagation.
agation Tip cuttings 2–3 inches are easily rooted in the standard g mixture at almost any time. r them moderately and keep in bright filtered light. Once ng has occurred (as indicated by ppearance of new top growth), three or four cuttings together in ging basket and they will soon op into an attractive display of re plants. Alternatively, plant ngs singly in 3-inch pots of soil- l mixture.

this hanging basket P. oertendahlii is rained to grow up the cords as well as eing allowed to trail. The flowering episcia adds an extra touch of color.

cial points Remove the growing of all species of plectranthus re- ly in order to encourage frequent ching and the development of y growth.

Pleomele

AGAVACEAE

Song of India
P. reflexa variegata

PLEOMELES are decorative foliage shrubs that should technically be included in the genus *Dracaena*. They are so widely known as pleomeles, however, that the name is being retained here. The only species regularly grown indoors is *P. reflexa* (correctly, *D. reflexa*), which has erect, ½-inch-wide stems, each with a growing tip that leans at an angle of 45° from the vertical. The leaves, which grow in compact clusters, are lance-shaped, 5–9 inches long, and up to 1 inch wide. Those of the species are dark green, but in the popular variety *P.r. variegata* (song of India) they are medium green with lime green margins when young, turning light green with creamy yellow margins later on. As stems lengthen, lower leaves drop off; their weight causes the stems to topple unless tied to supporting sticks.

PROPER CARE

Light Give pleomeles bright light, but without direct sunlight.
Temperature Normally warm room temperatures are suitable. Minimum tolerable temperature: 55°F. Keep pots on trays of moist pebbles.

Watering Water moderately, enough to moisten the entire mixture, but letting the top half-inch dry out before watering again.
Feeding Apply standard liquid fertilizer every two weeks from early spring to fall.
Potting and repotting Use a soil-based potting mixture (see page 429) with the addition of a one-third portion of rough leaf mold or coarse peat moss. Move plants into pots one size larger in early spring. These plants grow best when lodged in pots that appear to be a size too small for them. After reaching maximum convenient size, topdress annually (see page 428).
Propagation Take a 4-inch-long tip cutting or basal shoot in early spring, remove its lower leaves, dip the cut end in hormone rooting powder, and plant it in a 3-inch pot of moistened equal-parts mixture of peat moss and coarse sand or perlite. Enclose the whole in a plastic bag or propagating case (see page 443), and keep it warm in bright filtered light. When roots are well developed, uncover the new plant, begin to water it sparingly, and apply liquid fertilizer every two weeks. About six months after beginning propagation, move the young plant into the recommended mixture, and treat it as a mature pleomele.

323

Abutilon

MALVACEAE

A. pictum
'Thompsonii'

ABUTILONS (flowering or parlor maples) are soft-woody shrubs with funnel- or bell-shaped flowers. Leaves vary considerably in size and shape, but most are hairy with three to five lobes. Leaf color is medium green, although most species grown as house plants have variegated foliage. Flowers are single-colored, in two colors, or in two shades of a single color. They appear from leaf axils throughout the summer and fall, either singly or in pairs, and they hang on thin, inch-long stalks. Some species form spreading shrubs up to 5 feet tall; others grow as trailing plants.

RECOMMENDED ABUTILONS

A. hybridum (flowering maple) is the name given to a group of hybrids of mixed parentage. There are many named varieties, which can grow to 5 feet tall with a 5-foot spread, and can begin to flower while very young. The pendent blooms are usually solitary, 2 inches long, bell-shaped, five-petaled, have prominent orange or yellow stamens, and are backed with a pale green, inch-long calyx (the papery, bractlike growth that protects the unopened flower bud). Some popular varieties are 'Boule de Neige,' which has white flowers with striking orange stamens; 'Golden Fleece,' with yellow flowers; and 'Master Hugh,' whose flowers are rose-pink.

A. megapotamicum, popularly called trailing abutilon, is a slender-stemmed, branching shrub often grown in hanging baskets or tied to sticks. Leaves are heart-shaped, pointed, toothed, and 2–4 inches long. The inch-long, bright red calyx of the pendent yellow flower half covers the $1\frac{1}{2}$-inch-long petals. In the center of each flower, and protruding $\frac{1}{2}$ inch beyond it, is a cluster of dark brown anthers. *A.m.* 'Variegata' has leaves splashed with yellow patches.

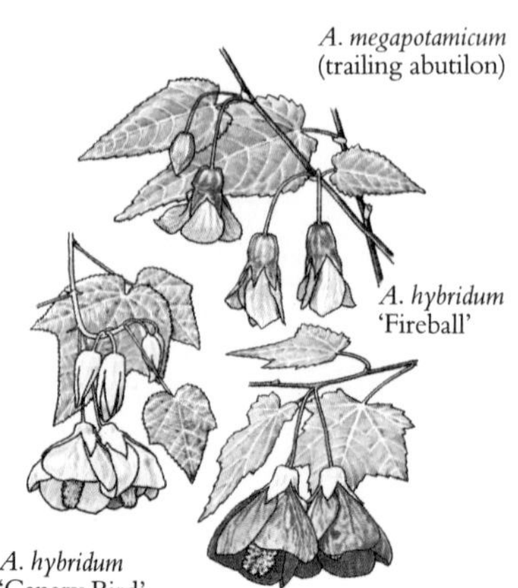

A. megapotamicum
(trailing abutilon)

A. hybridum
'Fireball'

A. hybridum
'Canary Bird'

A. pictum (formerly *A. striatum*) is chiefly grown in a form that has variegated leaves: *A.p.* 'Thompsonii' (sometimes called *A. thompsonii*). The rich mottling of yellow on dark green is caused by a harmless virus, which can be passed on to other abutilons only by means of grafting. The leaves are generally three- to five-lobed, 3–6 inches long, and nearly as wide; the flowers are salmon-colored with red veining, up to 2 inches long, and backed with a short, pale green calyx. Another form, *A.p.* 'Pleniflorum,' with many-petaled flowers, may have plain green or variegated leaves.

PROPER CARE

Light These plants need bright light with at least three to four hours of direct sunlight every day.

Temperature Abutilons grow well in normal room temperatures. Minimum temperature: 50°F.

Watering During the active growth period water moderately, enough to moisten the mixture throughout, but allowing the top half-inch to dry out between waterings. In the rest period water only enough to keep the mixture from drying out completely.

Feeding Apply standard liquid fertilizer every two weeks during the active growth period.

Potting and repotting Use a soil-based potting mixture (see page 429). Move plants into pots one size larger in spring. It is best to discard abutilons after two or three years.

Propagation The species may be grown from seed (see page 441), but variegated forms must be grown from cuttings. Take tip cuttings 3–4 inches long in spring or summer, dip cut ends into a hormone rooting powder, insert them in small pots in a mixture of equal parts of moistened peat moss and coarse sand or perlite, and cover each pot with a plastic bag. Place pots in filtered sunlight; cuttings will root in three to four weeks. Thereafter, move them into slightly larger pots of soil-based mixture, but keep the uncovered pots in filtered light for another two or three weeks and water just enough to keep the mixture barely moist. The plants can then be treated as mature abutilons.

Special points Abutilons may become spindly, and need cutting back in early spring. Remove any thin shoots that crowd the center, and reduce other stems by one-third.

Acalypha

EUPHORBIACEAE

Match-me-if-you-can
A. wilkesiana

THE genus *Acalypha* (copperleaf) includes one showy house plant notable for its flowers and several others that have tiny, insignificant flowers and are prized for their attractive foliage. All are fast growing and develop quickly into shrubs several feet high. To keep them within bounds many must be cut back annually and severely (taking out at least half the previous year's growth). Rather than do this, most indoor gardeners prefer to renew acalyphas from cuttings each year and to discard the overgrown plants.

RECOMMENDED ACALYPHAS

A. hispida (Philippine medusa, red-hot cattail, or chenille plant) is the species with conspicuous flowers. They are petalless, bright red, drooping, tassellike spikes (resembling strips of chenille), 12–18 inches long and about an inch wide; they grow from leaf axils in late summer and fall. The broadly oval leaves are 5–8 inches long, around 3 inches wide, slightly hairy and bright green, not copper-colored as are those of most acalyphas. The shrub itself can grow to more than 6 feet tall. There is a variety with white flowers, *A.h.* 'Alba.'

A. wilkesiana (Jacobs-coat, beefsteak plant, match-me-if-you-can, or fire dragon plant) can also grow to 6 feet tall. Its pointed-oval leaves, which are about 5 inches long and 2 inches wide, are a coppery green, mottled and streaked with copper, red, and purple. The following are among its most attractive varieties: *A.w.* 'Godseffiana' (sometimes called *A. godseffiana*), whose shiny green leaves have creamy white margins; *A.w.* 'Macrophylla,' which has leaves more nearly heart-shaped than oval, of russet-brown, with pale brown markings; *A.w.* 'Marginata,' which has heart-shaped, olive green leaves tinged with bronze and margined with a line of carmine-red; and *A.w.* 'Musaica' (giant red leaf), which has heart-shaped leaves that are bronze-green with orange and red markings.

A. hispida
(chenille plant)

PROPER CARE

Light These acalyphas need full sunlight, but it should be filtered through a translucent blind or curtain. In inadequate light they tend to become spindly; moreover, *A. hispida* will fail to produce its flowers, and the variegated-leaved forms will lose much of the leaf coloration that makes them so attractive.

Temperature Warmth is essential. Even during the winter rest period the temperature should not be permitted to fall below 60°F. Acalyphas will thrive in temperatures as high as 80°. But because they are particularly sensitive to dry air, the potted plants must be set on trays of moist pebbles or damp peat moss throughout the year. For increased humidity, mist-spray the foliage of *A. hispida* with water once a day from early spring until flowers begin to develop, after which further spraying becomes undesirable.

Watering During the active growth period water plentifully, as often as necessary to keep the potting mixture thoroughly moist, but never let the pot stand in water. During the winter rest period water only enough to keep the mixture from drying out.

Feeding Apply standard liquid fertilizer every two weeks during the active growth period only.

Potting and repotting Use a soil-based potting mixture (see page 429). Move small plants into pots one size larger whenever, on examination, roots are seen to fill their pots. This is best done in late spring but may be needed more than once a year. If plants are to be kept for more than one year, they should be repotted annually in late spring.

Propagation Acalyphas are most attractive when young. Plants are usually discarded in their second year after being used for propagation. The simplest way to increase a plant is to take tip cuttings 3–4 inches long in early spring. Alternatively, short sideshoots can be used. To encourage sideshoots, begin in early spring by cutting the old plant down to within a foot of the potting mixture. Keep the plant in bright filtered light. Mist-spray acalyphas daily, and water enough to keep the potting mixture moist. When new sideshoots are 3–4 inches long they should be removed—each with a heel attached (see page 437). After taking either tip or sideshoot cuttings, place

To propagate using a short sideshoot, remove the sideshoot with a sharp downward tug. Make sure that it comes away cleanly with a heel attached.

each in a 3-inch pot containing a moistened mixture of equal parts of peat moss and coarse sand or perlite. Enclose the pots in plastic bags, and place them in bright light filtered through a translucent blind or curtain at a temperature of at least 70°F. No further watering is required until new growth indicates that the cuttings have taken root. Then remove the plastic bags. Thereafter, water just enough to keep the potting mixture barely moist, and feed with half-strength liquid fertilizer every two weeks. When cuttings are a foot tall, move them into 4-inch pots containing the regular potting mixture. They can then be treated as mature plants.

Special points Acalyphas branch and become bushy naturally, and so it is never necessary to pinch out growing tips; in fact, the removal of growing points of *A. hispida* will usually cause a long delay in flowering.

Keep a careful watch for mealy bugs and red spider mites (see page 455), to which these plants are especially vulnerable. If unnoticed, such pests can do untold damage.

Achimenes

GESNERIACEAE

Achimenes hybrid

PLANTS of the genus *Achimenes* (Cupid's bower, magic flower, nut orchid) can produce a spectacular combination of foliage and flowers in spring and summer. All forms develop a root system which grows from a number of small rhizomes (about 1 inch long and $\frac{1}{4}$ inch thick), each of which sends up a single stem that carries opposite pairs of heart-shaped leaves on short stalks. An achimenes normally produces several such stems. The leaves are generally dark green, velvety, and tooth-edged. Flowers, which appear on short stalks from the leaf axils, consist of a narrow tube flaring out into five broad lobes. Each flower lasts for only a few days, but the flowering period is extensive.

Length of stems and size of leaves and flowers vary widely. Stems may be as short as 3 inches or as tall as 30 or more inches. The taller species tend to sprawl. Thus, some forms of achimenes are useful for planting in hanging baskets. After the flowering season the leaves begin to shrivel. When they have dried out, cut off the stems just above the surface of the potting mixture, and lay the dormant plant aside in its container till spring.

See also GESNERIADS.

RECOMMENDED ACHIMENESES

A. erecta (also known as *A. coccinea*) has trailing, hairy, green-to-reddish stems up to 18 inches long. The leaves, which are 1–2 inches long and $\frac{1}{2}$–1 inch wide, are dark green on the upper surface; the underside is pale green or red. Bright red flowers have $\frac{3}{4}$-inch-long tubes and are $\frac{3}{4}$ inch wide.

A. grandiflora has hairy, upright, green or red stems 12–18 inches tall. The leaves are hairy and rough, similar in color to those of *A. erecta,* and notably large—up to 6 inches long and 3 inches wide. Flowers are deep reddish purple, with a white throat, and they can be $1\frac{1}{2}$ inches long and $1\frac{1}{2}$ inches wide. *A. grandiflora* is one parent of the popular hybrid *A.* 'Purple King.'

A. longiflora has trailing stems about 24 inches long, and its markedly sawtooth-edged leaves are up to $3\frac{1}{2}$ inches long and $1\frac{1}{2}$ inches wide. The flowers are blue, with a white throat, and up to 2 inches long and 3 inches across the mouth. There is also a white-flowered form, *A.l. alba.* And *A.l. alba* is one of the parents of a hybrid, *A.* 'Ambroise Verschaffelt,' which has white flowers with purple lines running into the throat.

There are many hybrid forms of achimenes. Among several with reasonably short stems (6–12 inches high) and flowers that bloom close together, providing a mass of color: *A.* 'Tarantella,' with salmon pink flowers; *A.* 'Minuet,' with deep pink flowers; *A.* 'Fritz Michelssen' and *A.* 'Valse Bleu,' both with blue.

PROPER CARE

Light An actively growing achimenes does best in bright light but should never be subjected to the midday sun. During the long period of dormancy light is not a consideration.

Temperature During the active growth period, these plants thrive in temperatures ranging from about 60°

to 80°F. They tolerate temperatures as low as 55°, but they cannot stand temperatures above 80°. If high heat persists for more than a day or two, buds will turn brown and fail to open.

Dormant rhizomes may be stored in any cool spot, but they will not survive frost.

Watering Correct watering is especially important for the successful blooming of these plants. As soon as the rhizomes start into growth in early spring, begin to water plentifully, as much as necessary to keep the potting mixture thoroughly moist. If the mixture is allowed to dry out even for a short period, the plant is likely to return to dormancy. Increase frequency of waterings when plants are in flower, but limit the amounts; never let a flowering achimenes stand in water. After the flowering period, gradually reduce the quantity, and do not water at all during dormancy.

Feeding During the early weeks of the active growth period use a nitrogen-rich liquid fertilizer to encourage leafy growth. As buds form, change to a fertilizer that contains more phosphate and potash than nitrogen. Apply a one-eighth-strength dose of fertilizer at every watering until the flowering period has ended.

Potting and repotting Use an equal-parts mixture of peat moss, coarse sand or perlite, and vermiculite. To reduce acidity, add three or four tablespoonfuls of dolomite lime, lime chips, or crushed eggshells to four cups of mixture.

In early spring the clumps of newly sprouting rhizomes should be carefully shaken out of the previous year's potting mixture and, if desired, separated (they pull apart easily). Single rhizomes will soon form larger root systems if placed horizontally $\frac{1}{2}$ inch below the surface in shallow pots of fresh mixture. Plant three or four rhizomes in a 4-inch pot. For a hanging basket at least a dozen rhizomes are required. The potting mixture should not be packed down firmly. Over-firm packing causes waterlogging.

Propagation New plants are customarily grown from detached rhizomes, but an achimenes can also be propagated from a 3-inch tip cutting taken in early summer. A cutting will root easily in the recommended potting mixture if kept at normal room temperature in bright filtered light and watered plentifully.

Acorus

ARACEAE

Grassy-leaved sweet flag
A. gramineus 'Variegatus'

THERE are only two species in the genus *Acorus*, and only one of these, *A. gramineus* (grassy-leaved sweet flag), is often grown indoors. Its leaves, which grow in a dense clump or tuft rising from a slender rhizome that lies just below the surface of the potting mixture, are around $\frac{1}{4}$ inch wide and up to 18 inches long. There is a green flower spathe, but it is barely noticeable since it is so fine that it looks almost like another leaf. A variegated-leaved form, *A.g.* 'Variegatus,' has white stripes on its green leaves, as does the dwarf form *A.g.* 'Albovariegatus,' whose leaves rarely grow much longer than 6 inches. All forms provide a pleasant contrast with the more substantial foliage of other house plants. Although acoruses grow more or less continuously, active growth will slow down under reduced light.

A. gramineus *provides an elegant backdrop to a display containing contrasting plants of all kinds—bushy, trailing and upright.*

PROPER CARE

Light Medium light or direct sunlight filtered through a translucent blind or curtain will suit acoruses.

Temperature An indoor acorus will grow well in normally warm room temperatures but can also tolerate temperatures as low as 40°F. High humidity is essential; stand plants on trays or saucers of moist pebbles throughout the year, and mist-spray the leaves during warm periods.

Watering These plants must *never* be allowed to dry at the roots. Water plentifully as often as necessary to keep the potting mixture thoroughly moist. The pot may even be allowed to stand in a shallow saucer of water.

Because they are marsh plants, acoruses need more water than most other types. You can even stand the pots in water.

Feeding Apply standard liquid fertilizer every two weeks during spring and summer.

Potting and repotting Use a soil-based potting mixture (see page 429). In spring move small plants into pots or shallow pans one size larger if their tufts of leaves have completely filled the surface area of the mixture. Five-inch pots or half-pots are likely to be the largest size needed.

Propagation Propagate by separating overcrowded clumps in spring or summer. Carefully pull clumps apart with the fingers, making sure that a piece of the rhizome is attached to each section, and treat each divided clump as a mature plant.

Adiantum
POLYPODIACEAE

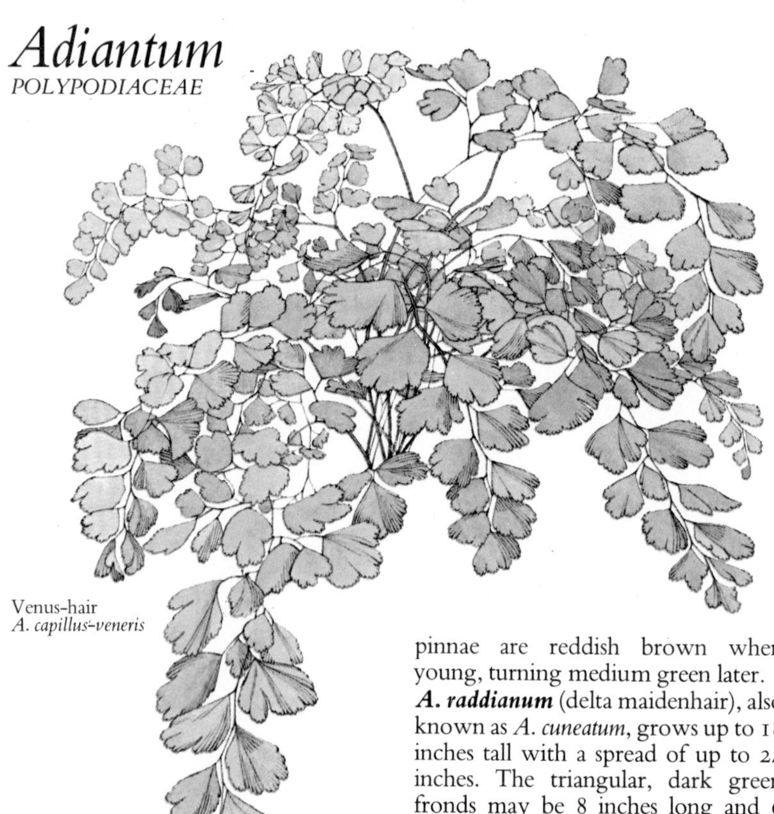
Venus-hair
A. capillus-veneris

ADIANTUMS, the most popular of all pot-grown ferns, are commonly called maidenhair ferns because their fine, shiny, often black leafstalks resemble human hair. They have fast-spreading rhizomes that grow horizontally just below the surface of the potting mixture. The fronds are 8–15 inches long and divided into many pinnae. Mature plants produce brown clusters of spore cases on the undersides of the pinnae.
See also FERNS.

RECOMMENDED ADIANTUMS

A. capillus-veneris, commonly called Venus-hair, rarely grows taller than 12 inches in a pot. It has roughly triangular light green fronds comprising many delicate-looking, fan-shaped pinnae. In particularly fine specimens the fronds may be up to 24 inches long and 10 inches wide, with individual pinnae an inch across.

A. hispidulum (Australian maidenhair) seldom grows more than 12 inches tall. Its fronds—usually 9–12 inches long and 6 inches wide—are roughly divided into several spreading sections much like the fingers of a hand. The almost oblong, leathery pinnae are reddish brown when young, turning medium green later.

A. raddianum (delta maidenhair), also known as *A. cuneatum*, grows up to 18 inches tall with a spread of up to 24 inches. The triangular, dark green fronds may be 8 inches long and 6 inches at their widest point and are divided into numerous delicate, wedge-shaped pinnae. There are many forms, all slightly different in scale, color, and general shape. The fronds of all forms, however, are semi-erect at first, drooping gracefully as they mature. One form, *A.r.* 'Fragrantissimum,' has denser foliage with a pronounced fragrance. Another, *A.r.* 'Fritz-Luthii,' is easy to grow and has longer fronds than the type plant.

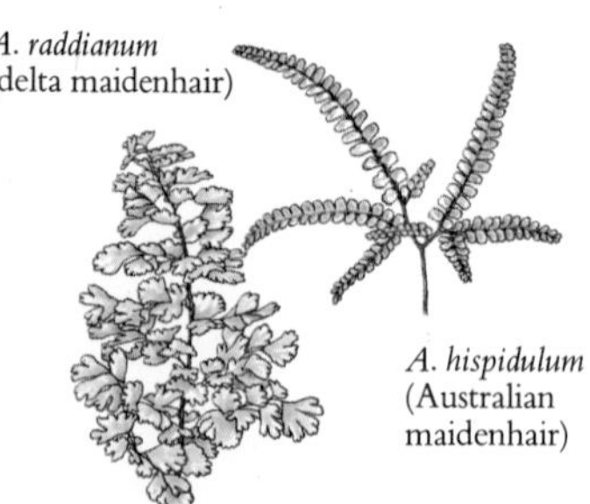
A. raddianum (delta maidenhair)
A. hispidulum (Australian maidenhair)

A. tenerum (brittle or fan maidenhair) grows up to 3 feet tall. Its triangular, pale green fronds are divided into many fan-shaped pinnae that may be deeply cut at the edges. There are several forms, some with rose-tinted fronds. *A.t.* 'Farleyense' (glory fern) has drooping fronds with deeply cut, frilly-edged pinnae; the fronds of *A.t.* 'Wrightii' are pink when young but turn fresh green, and their fan-shaped pinnae sometimes overlap each other.

PROPER CARE

Light Provide bright light, but do not subject these ferns to direct sunlight.

Temperature Adiantums will grow well in any normal room temperature and can tolerate temperatures down to 50°F. If the temperature rises above 75°, stand pots on trays of moist pebbles, and mist-spray daily to provide much-needed humidity.

Watering These ferns should be kept only slightly moist at the roots. The commonest cause of failure is to permit the root ball to dry out and then to soak the plant. Aim at a medium course by watering moderately—enough to make the mixture moist throughout but letting the top inch dry out between waterings.

Feeding Ferns, though not greedy, benefit from occasional feedings of standard liquid fertilizer during their active growth period. Recommended frequency of feedings depends on the type of potting mixture.

Potting and repotting The potting mixture for adiantums must be capable of holding water and yet of providing good drainage. A peat-based mixture is suitable, but only if the plant gets some fertilizer at least once every two weeks.

Feeding is much less important—fertilizer will do once a month—if equal parts of soil-based potting mixture (see page 429) and coarse leaf mold or coarse peat moss are used. Repot adiantums only when dark-colored roots appear on the surface of the mixture. The best time for repotting is early spring. Instead of being repotted, an older plant may have some outer roots carefully removed before being replaced in the same pot with the addition of fresh potting mixture.

Propagation New plants will grow from small sections of the rhizome with one or two fronds attached. Break off such sections whenever adiantums are being repotted. Alternatively, separate older plants into a number of clumps. Pot each growing section singly (or put several in a pan or hanging basket) in one of the recommended potting mixtures. Water new plants with extreme care, following watering instructions for mature plants; overwatering may well result in rotting.

Aechmea
BROMELIACEAE

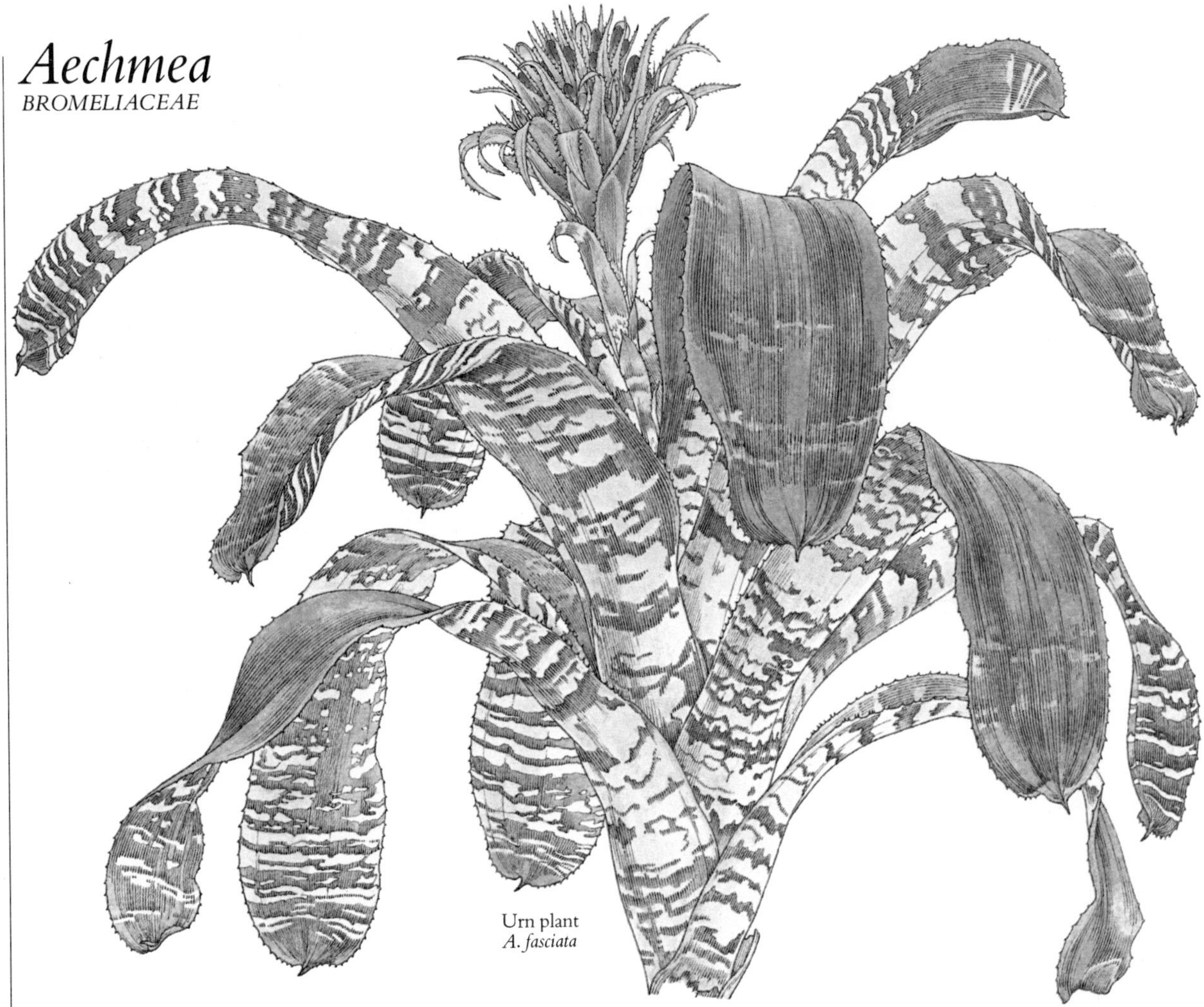

Urn plant
A. fasciata

IN the wild most aechmeas are epiphytic, and all species of this large genus come from humid tropical areas. The leaves have adapted to their environment, and are always arranged in a rosette, shaped to capture and hold water. Leaves of some kinds are clasped tightly together so as to form long tubes; in others the rosette is looser. But there is invariably a cuplike center in which water accumulates, and the flower stalk rises from this center, which should not be allowed to dry out. All aechmeas flower only when mature, and only once from each rosette, after which the rosette slowly dies. The foliage and colorful inflorescence remain decorative for several months after the small blooms have faded, however. During this period offsets appear around the base of the old rosette. Many indoor gardeners simulate natural conditions by growing these bromeliads on "epiphyte branches" (see page 107).
See also BROMELIADS.

RECOMMENDED AECHMEAS

A. chantinii has tough, arching leaves up to 18 inches long, which are gray-green, spiny-edged, and powdered with minute silvery white scales in crosswise bands. The inflorescence consists of a cluster of pointed, orange-red bracts, which droop as they open, to reveal a number of branched flower stems with upright yellow-and-red flowers. *A.c.* 'Pink Goddess' and *A.c.* 'Red Goddess' are varieties with pink and red bracts respectively.

A. fasciata (sometimes known as *A. rhodocyanea* or *Billbergia rhodocyanea*; commonly called urn plant) is the most popular aechmea. Its arching, gray-green, spiny leaves, which are cross-banded with sprinklings of white powder, can attain a length of 2 feet. When fully mature (usually after three or four years' growth), the plant sends up a strong flower stalk bearing a pink inflorescence up to 6 inches long. The large inflorescence consists mainly of bracts from between which emerge small, pale blue flowers that soon turn red. These disappear quickly, but the pink bracts remain decorative for up to six months. There are two variegated forms: *A.f.* 'Albo-marginata,' which has cream-colored

Along with other bromeliads, aechmeas look attractive on an epiphyte branch, anchored down by heavy stones.

bands bordering each leaf, and *A.f.* 'Variegata,' whose leaves have lengthwise cream stripes.

A. fulgens has broad leaves up to 16 inches long, which form a rather flat, open rosette. Only one variety, *A.f. discolor*, has become a common house plant. Its leaves are glossy olive green above, and deep wine purple dusted over with whitish powder on the underside. As the dark purple flowers die, attractive red berries appear, and these remain on the plant for several months at a time.

A. racinae (Christmas jewels) has soft, glossy, green leaves about 12 inches long and 1 inch wide arranged in a small, loose rosette. It normally flowers at Christmastime, when it produces a drooping flower stalk 12–18 inches long, bearing a cluster of about 12 oval, bright red, berrylike flowers with bright yellow-and-black petals projecting through the tip of the red oval. The flowers are followed by brilliant orange-red berries, which remain attractive for months.

Two of the most attractive small aechmeas—neither with leaves longer than 8 inches—are hybrids. *A.* 'Foster's Favorite' has shiny, deep wine red leaves forming a narrow tube but fanning out for about half their length. The flower spike, which tends to droop, carries deep purple flowers, which give way to dark red berries. The flowers are short-lived, but the berries last for two or three months. The leaves of *A.* 'Royal Wine' are olive green on top and wine-colored on the underside, and both surfaces look highly polished. Flowers are blue and berries orange. These two hybrids are extremely easy to grow indoors.

PROPER CARE

Light All potted aechmeas grow best in full sunlight. They will not flower successfully if kept at a distance from a sunny window.

Temperature These plants like temperatures of over 60°F, coupled with high humidity throughout the year. Pots should be stood on trays of moist pebbles. Aechmeas with thick, scaly leaves tolerate cool positions and dry air better than do those with soft, shiny foliage. Most of these plants, however, can survive short periods of cold without suffering unduly.

Watering Water moderately, enough to make the potting mixture thoroughly moist, but allow the top half-inch to dry out between waterings. In addition, make sure that the cup-like centers of plants have a constant supply of fresh water. Cups should be emptied and replenished periodically, to prevent water from becoming stale and smelly. In hard-water areas it is advisable to put aechmeas out in the soft rain from time to time (but only in mild periods); hard water disfigures the leaves by building up lime deposits.

Feeding Except in midwinter (when these plants may take a brief rest), provide half-strength standard liquid fertilizer once every two weeks. Apply the fertilizer not only at the roots, but over foliage and into the central cup.

Potting and repotting An equal-parts mixture of leaf mold, peat moss, and coarse sand or perlite is suitable. Most aechmeas produce rather little root, and therefore do best in small pots. Smaller plants will flower in 4-inch pots, and the 5-inch size suffices for most others. Repotting, if done at all, should take place just as new growth begins. To avoid top-heaviness, use clay pots rather than plastic ones.

Propagation When the offsets that appear around the base of a plant are about half the size of the parent plant, they can be cleanly detached—preferably in spring—and planted in 2- to 3-inch pots of the recommended potting mixture for adult aechmeas. If an offset has already produced roots of its own, they should be retained. For roughly the first four months, each little plant should be kept in bright but filtered light and should be watered very sparingly—just enough to keep the potting mixture barely moist. When it is well-established, the young aechmea can be moved into direct sunlight, and it can then be treated as a mature specimen.

Special points After a plant has flowered, some growers prefer not to remove offsets for propagation but to make room for the new rosettes to develop in the original pot. This is easily done by using a sharp kitchen knife to cut off the old rosette at the lowest possible point when it has become shabby and started to wither. Pots containing two or more rosettes can be exceptionally decorative, particularly when in flower.

Cutting off the old rosette close to the potting mixture allows new rosettes to develop in the original pot.

Propagating an aechmea

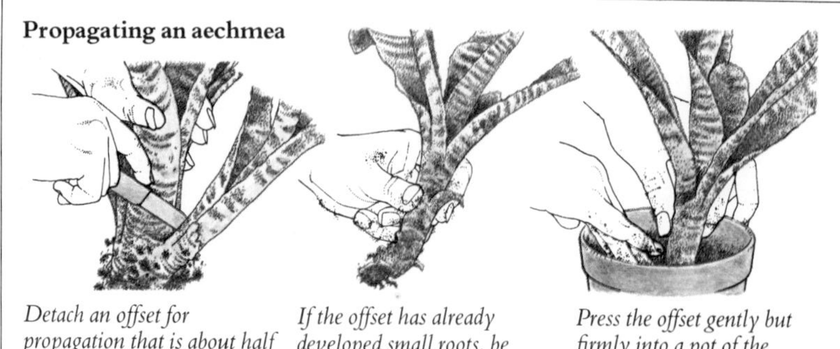

Detach an offset for propagation that is about half the size of the parent plant.

If the offset has already developed small roots, be careful not to damage them.

Press the offset gently but firmly into a pot of the mixture for adult aechmeas.

Aeonium

CRASSULACEAE

A. arboreum
'Atropurpureum'

AEONIUMS are a large group of succulents grown chiefly for their distinctive rosettes of fleshy, usually spoon-shaped leaves. For the most part, these rosettes are largely carried on woody stems, but some species have such short stems that they appear to be stemless. Some produce only a single rosette-topped stem; others have several. Leaves vary from thick and tough to soft and brittle. All rosettes constantly shed their lower leaves, and a characteristic of all the woody-stemmed aeoniums is that stems are scarred at whatever points leaves were attached.

Sprays of small, usually star-shaped flowers, mainly in cream and yellow-green shades, are produced from the rosette centers of mature plants. They may bloom at any season, but once a rosette has flowered—which may not occur before the plant is four or even five years old—it dies. Thus a plant with only one rosette dies after flowering. A plant that branches out and produces several rosettes usually flowers on most stems simultaneously, but one or two rosettes may fail to flower, and the plant will therefore remain alive until they do.

See also SUCCULENTS.

RECOMMENDED AEONIUMS

A. arboreum is treelike in that its woody stems branch out freely, but it is unlikely to exceed 3 feet in height. The 2- to 3-inch-long leaves of its rosettes are spoon-shaped and shiny green. One dark-colored form, *A.a.* 'Atropurpureum,' has slightly smaller deep purple leaves, but the coloring loses intensity if the plant is not grown in full sunlight. This is also true of *A.a.* 'Schwarzkopf,' a variety with almost black foliage.

A. canariense (giant velvet rose) produces a short, thick, trunklike stem, which rarely grows more than 1 foot high. The spoon-shaped leaves of the cupped rosettes are 4–12 inches long and 2–4 inches wide. Leaf color is pale green, and the leaves are edged with fine white hairs. In most specimens there is a single rosette, but some plants may produce one or two side rosettes. Pale yellow flowers are carried on a flower stalk 1–$1\frac{1}{2}$ feet tall.

A. domesticum See *Aichryson,* under which this species is now listed.

A. haworthii (pin-wheel) is usually small, seldom reaching 2 feet in height. Its tough, woody stems and many short branches are tipped with rosettes of thick, blue-gray leaves with reddish brown edges. Flowers are white or creamy yellow and sometimes tinged with pink.

A. haworthii
(pin-wheel)

A. tabuliforme

A. tabuliforme has such a short stem as to seem stemless. The light green and spoon-shaped leaves are tightly packed together, producing a distinctive platelike form. In the wild the plant grows on its side in crevices of rocks, so that water runs off the foliage. Thus the flat rosette should be

Plant A. tabuliforme *with the rosette at an angle, so that water can run off the foliage as it naturally does in the wild.*

planted with its tiny stem on a slant. The spike of bloom that sprouts from the mature rosette can grow to 18 inches in height. At its top appear many short branches, each tipped with several dull-yellow flowers.

A. undulatum (saucer plant) has a thick main stem that grows 2–3 feet tall, topped by slightly shiny, undulate, dark green leaves up to 6 inches long that form a 12-inch-wide rosette. The plant may also produce several rosette-crowned sideshoots, usually from the lower part of the main stem, and each rosette may carry a small cluster of long-stemmed, mustard yellow flowers.

PROPER CARE

Light To keep their form, aeoniums need full sunlight, even during rest periods when they are not actively growing. Too little light will result in elongated, prematurely falling leaves and gappy rosettes.

Temperature Aeoniums grow well in warm rooms (65°–75°F), but—like most other succulents—they are not tropical plants; if possible, they should be encouraged to rest during the winter months by being moved to a cool place (preferably around 50°).

Watering During the active growth period water moderately—enough to make the potting mixture moist throughout, but allowing the top half-inch of the mixture to dry out between waterings. During the rest period allow half of the potting mixture to dry out between waterings. Less than this will result in shriveled leaves. On the other hand, overwatering encourages soft, untypical growth, which is likely to droop.

Feeding Use standard liquid fertilizer every two weeks during the active growth period only.

Potting and repotting Use a porous potting mixture composed of one part coarse sand or perlite added to two parts of a standard soil-based mixture (see page 429). Because aeoniums can grow quickly, the taller kinds should be moved into pots one size larger every year, preferably just as new growth begins. Such smaller species as *A. haworthii* and *A. tabuliforme* will generally thrive for two or three years in 3-inch pots, after which they can be moved on. Newly potted plants should be especially firmly pressed into the potting mixture, and the taller types must be staked.

Propagation Because *A. tabuliforme* produces no sideshoots, new plants of this species can be raised only from seed—a procedure best left to commercial growers. The other, branching species are easy to propagate from tip cuttings. The best time to do this is early in the growth period. Cleanly detach a complete rosette together with 1–1½ inches of stem, dip the stem into hormone rooting powder to encourage quick rooting, and plant it in a moistened mixture of equal parts peat moss and coarse sand or perlite. Cuttings will root in two to three weeks in a warm room (65°–75°F) if given bright light and watered only enough to make the potting mixture barely moist. They can then be repotted in the mixture that is used for mature plants.

Aeschynanthus

GESNERIACEAE

Basket plant
A. speciosus

THERE are more than 100 species of the genus *Aeschynanthus* (basket plant), all of which are long-stemmed trailers with striking flowers. Most indoor specimens have fleshy, elliptic leaves pointed at both ends and growing in opposite pairs along the stem, which can grow to 2 feet long. In a few species the leaves are grouped in clusters. The decorative flowers appear either singly or in pairs from leaf axils, or in clusters at the tips of stems. In many forms there is a pronounced cuplike calyx from which the corolla extends. The slightly curved tube of the flower opens out into five lobes, with stamens usually visible at the mouth and the style eventually projecting beyond the mouth.

These plants normally have a summertime flowering season indoors, and individual flowers last for only two or three days. An aeschynanthus is displayed to best advantage in a hanging basket, where the broad surface area allows the trailing stems to root down at intervals and send out abundant sideshoots.

See also GESNERIADS.

RECOMMENDED AESCHYNANTHUSES

A. lobbianus has arching stems and dark green leaves that are 1½ inches long, ¾ inch wide, and have a slightly toothed, purplish edge. The bright red, 2-inch-long flowers, carried in pairs, project from blackish purple, 1-inch-long calyxes. Streaks of creamy white on the red lobes of the flower extend back into the throat, and the calyx and corolla are both hairy.

A. marmoratus is grown for its attractive foliage rather than the flowers. Its thick leaves, which can reach a length of 4 inches and a width of 1½ inches, are shiny green mottled with dark green on the upper surface and flushed with red on the underside. The green calyx is deeply cut into five narrow lobes, each about ¾ inch long, and it has a corolla about 1½ inches long that does not widen at the mouth. Flowers are greenish yellow splashed with dark brown in the throat. *A. marmoratus* is one of the parents of a hybrid, *A.* 'Black Pagoda,' that differs only in that its flowers are burnt orange in color and that it tends to produce them throughout the year.

A. pulcher is like *A. lobbianus* except that the calyx is green with a purple tinge and the corolla is 2½ inches long. Both calyx and corolla are less hairy.

A. speciosus is perhaps the most spectacular species. Its dark green leaves are carried along the stems in pairs or whorls of 3, but there are 4 to 8 leaves at the stem tip, where they surround a cluster of 6 to 20 flowers. The leaves are up to 4 inches long and 1½ inches wide, and their tips are more sharply pointed than their bases. The green calyx, about ¼ inch long, sheathes only a portion of the flower, which may be 4 inches long. Both calyx and corolla are slightly hairy. The flowers are orange, with the inside of the mouth orange-yellow and with a dark red bar across the lower lobes, which also have scarlet borders.

PROPER CARE

Light Provide bright light—but with no more than two or three hours of direct sunlight a day.

Temperature Normal room temperatures are suitable at all times as long as humidity is kept high. Place trays of moist pebbles below the trailing stems, and mist-spray plants daily during the flowering period.

Watering When an aeschynanthus is in flower, water it plentifully. At other times water moderately, enough to make the mixture moist throughout, but allow the top half-inch to dry out between waterings. If kept in humid warmth, these plants do not have a rest period, and so they require this much water all year long.

Feeding Use a liquid fertilizer containing an equal-parts mixture of nitrogen, phosphate, and potash. Apply a one-eighth-strength dose to these plants at every watering.

Potting and repotting Since these plants like an acid growing medium, coarse sphagnum peat moss may be used alone as the potting mixture. Equally suitable is an equal-parts mixture of peat moss, perlite, and vermiculite, which, if packed loosely, gives much-needed aeration around the roots. Shallow 5- or 6-inch pots or baskets are the best containers, with several young plants placed in each for good effect. Repotting may be done at any time of year. When roots fill the pot (see page 426), move plants into a pot one size larger. Or, preferably, shake the old mixture from the roots, cut them back by about one-third, and repot the plants in the same pot, but with fresh mixture.

Propagation Tip cuttings 4–6 inches long will root in three to four weeks at any season. Plant the cuttings in $2\frac{1}{2}$- or 3-inch pots of the recommended potting mixture thoroughly moistened, enclose them in plastic bags and keep them at normal room temperature in bright filtered light. When rooting has occurred, the bags should be removed and the new plants given just enough water to keep the potting mixture barely moist. About a week later pot several of the new plants together in a shallow 5- or 6-inch pot, and treat them as mature specimens. Make a particular effort to provide high humidity for these young plants.

Special points Keep a watch for aphids, which attack young leaves of an aeschynanthus (see page 455).

Agave

AGAVACEAE

A. victoriae-reginae

AGAVES are succulents with decorative sword-shaped leaves. They are often called century plants because of a mistaken notion that they flower only once a century. Actually, they can flower when they are about 10 years old (after which they usually die), but flowers are not normally produced on plants grown indoors. The thick, hard, fleshy leaves, at first tightly wrapped around each other to form a stiff and erect central core, gradually unfold and may eventually curl slightly over the edge of the pot. Many kinds of agave are fiercely spined, and the leaves of almost all are arranged in a rosette. The species vary considerably in size. Older basal leaves of all types dry up and can eventually be pulled off. This may result in scarred, woody stems.

See also SUCCULENTS.

RECOMMENDED AGAVES

A. americana (century plant), the commonest species, grows so big that it can be used indoors only when quite young. The leaves of a fully grown plant may exceed 6 feet in length. Without an obvious stem, it forms an open rosette of blue-green, spiny-edged leaves, each tipped with a dark brown needle-sharp point $\frac{1}{4}$ inch long. Among the variegated forms are: *A.a.* 'Marginata' with yellow leaf margins; and *A.a.* 'Medio-picta' with a central band of yellow bordered with green.

A. angustifolia is similar to *A. americana,* but more compact, with narrower, gray-green leaves up to $2\frac{1}{2}$ feet long that make a dense rosette. *A.a.* 'Marginata' has narrow white margins. Because of its eventual size, this species, too, is suitable for cultivation indoors only when young.

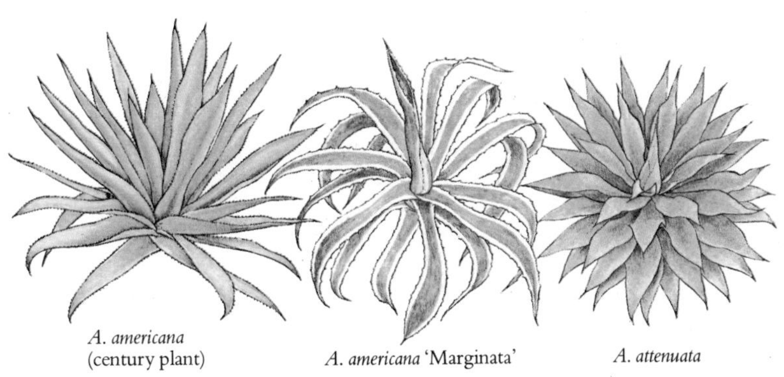

A. americana (century plant) — *A. americana* 'Marginata' — *A. attenuata*

A. attenuata also gets too big for indoor use after three or four years. It has soft, 1½-foot-long, broad but tapering leaves of an apple-green color, which have a firm point at the tip but no spines on the edges. Although the leaves are pliable, they can break if roughly handled.

A. fernandi-regis has a somewhat open rosette of tapering, 5-inch-long, dark green leaves, each one of which has narrow white margins and a ¼-inch-long spine at the end.

A. filifera is a slow-growing small agave—maximum height 10 inches—with a spherical rosette composed of stiff green leaves 10 inches long and 1 inch wide, which taper to a point and are edged in white. These white edges are actually threadlike fibers, which become partially detached and hang away from the leaves. There is a smaller form—no more than 6 inches tall—*A.f.* 'Compacta,' which has triangular green leaves with white stripes and a black tip, and short cobwebby threads. These plants can be grown indoors for many years.

A. parviflora is also small, slow-growing, and long-lived. Its stiff, narrow leaves, only 3–6 inches long, form a low rosette, and their edges split away into fine threads.

A. potatorum (also known as *A. verschaffeltii)* is a small, low-growing agave with 8-inch-long, blue-green leaves. Each leaf has a ¼-inch-long, slightly twisted, terminal spine and several prominent triangular, rust-brown marginal teeth.

A. victoriae-reginae makes a dense, tightly compressed rosette, which rarely grows taller than 9 inches but can attain a spread of about 18 inches. The dark green leaves are 6 inches long, roughly triangular, and beautifully marked with brilliant white, slightly raised patches, haphazardly arranged but especially concentrated along the margins. Their edges are unarmed, but every leaf has a blunt-looking although very hard and sharp point. Growth is so slow that only one or two new leaves a year can be expected, and mature plants are therefore rare and expensive. Certainly this is the most attractive of the many available agaves.

PROPER CARE

Light Provide the sunniest possible position for all species at all times. But if a plant has been subjected to some shade, it should be acclimatized to full sunlight gradually. Move such plants into bright light over the period of a week or two. A sudden change in light intensity can burn the foliage.

Temperature Agaves do best if kept at normal room temperatures during the active growth period and in a rather cooler environment (50°–55°F) throughout the rest period.

Watering During the active growth period water moderately—enough to make the potting mixture thoroughly moist—but allow the top two-thirds of the mixture to dry out between waterings. During the winter rest period water only enough to keep the potting mixture from completely drying out.

Feeding Apply standard liquid fertilizer every two weeks during the active growth period.

Potting and repotting Use a soil-based potting mixture with the addition of one-third coarse sand or perlite for drainage (see page 429). The smaller plants need repotting only every two or three years, but *A. americana* and its varieties and *A. attenuata* should be moved into pots one size larger every spring. Plants that have reached the maximum convenient pot size should be topdressed in spring (see page 428).

Propagation All species except *A. victoriae-reginae* produce offsets that can be detached—when 3–4 inches long for the larger kinds or 1–1½ inches long for the smaller kinds—and rooted in the standard potting mixture. Cultivation needs of offsets are those of mature plants—except that, until they are well rooted, offsets should be watered only enough to make the potting mixture barely moist. *A. victoriae-reginae* must be grown from seed (see page 441).

Special points A word of warning: Be sure to wear heavy gloves when you are working with thorny agaves. Keep the plants well out of the reach of children.

When pulling dead leaves off thorny agaves, be sure to wear protective gloves.

Aglaonema

ARACEAE

THE genus *Aglaonema* includes many decorative house plants notable for their subtly patterned gray, cream, and green leaves. Most of these upright plants are not as much as 3 feet tall. They have lance-shaped or oval leaf blades on leafstalks 1 foot long that arise from a central growing point. A plant may occasionally form a short, trunklike stem scarred with circular markings where leaves were once attached. A typically arum-shaped flower head comprising a white or yellow, 2-inch-long spathe with a central stalked spadix is produced in summer or early fall, and this is followed by red or orange berries. But aglaonemas are mainly grown for the effect created by their handsome foliage rather than for flowers.

RECOMMENDED AGLAONEMAS

A. commutatum, the most popular species, has given rise to many varieties with widely differing features. The plant has glossy, lance-shaped leaves, each about 8 inches long, 3–4 inches wide, and colored dark green with silvery gray markings. In older plants there is often a scarred, trunk-like stem. There are two interesting varieties: *A.c.* 'Pseudobracteatum' has foot-long leaves that are green with large patches of gray-green and creamy white, and its scarred stem is marked with white; and *A.c.* 'Treubii,' a notably compact plant, has 8-inch-long, 2-inch-wide, gray-green leaves blotched with yellowish green.

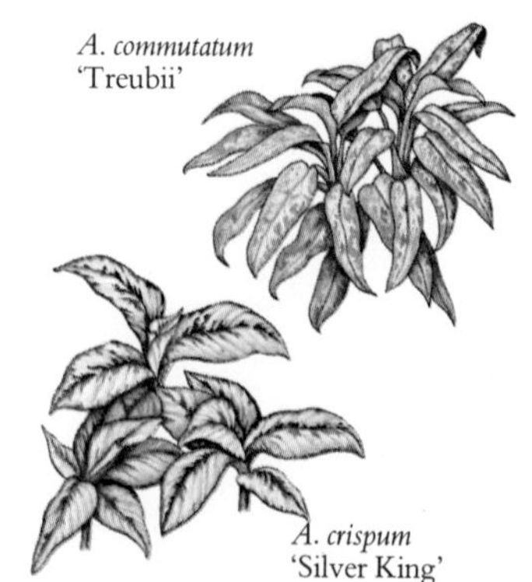

A. costatum (spotted evergreen) has 8-inch-long, 4-inch-wide leaves that are dark green with a white midrib. The leaf is irregularly spotted with small white dots. *A.c. immaculatum* is the name of a variety without spots.

Painted drop-tongue
A. crispum 'Silver Queen'

A. crispum (also called *A. roebelinii* and popularly known as painted drop-tongue) has thick, leathery leaves 1 foot long and 5 inches wide. They are gray-green except for the midrib and narrow borders, which are a muted olive green. The variety *A.c.* 'Silver Queen' has dark gray-green leaves heavily marked with silver. When several years old, *A. crispum* and its forms will have developed stout, scarred stems with 10 to 15 leaves clustered at the top.

A. modestum (Chinese evergreen) has waxy, undulate, medium green leaves 8 inches long and 4 inches wide. There is a variegated-leaved form, *A.m.* 'Variegatum,' with yellow patches on the green.

A. nitidum (often incorrectly called *A. oblongifolium*) has leaves up to 18 inches long and 6 inches wide. They are medium green, but in the form *A.n.* 'Curtisii' silvery markings run along the major veins.

A. pictum, which forms a stem that becomes gray with age, has slightly undulate leaves 5–6 inches long and 2 inches wide. They are a dark blue-green, with large, irregular patches of pale green and silvery gray and a prominent gray-green midrib. *A.p.* 'Tricolor' has yellowish green leaves spotted with lighter yellow.

PROPER CARE

Light Aglaonemas need medium light. Never subject them to direct sunlight, which can scorch the leaves.

Temperature Normally warm room temperatures are suitable. For extra humidity, stand the plants on trays of damp pebbles.

Watering During the active growth period water moderately— enough to make the entire mixture moist, but allowing the top inch of the mixture to dry out between waterings. During the rest period (which may be very short, or even nonexistent) water only enough to keep the mixture from drying out completely.

Feeding Use standard liquid fertilizer monthly except during the rest period.

Potting and repotting Use a soil-based potting mixture (see page 429). Move young plants into pots one size larger in the spring, but repot older plants only once every two or three years. These aglaonemas do not need large containers; they will thrive in 5- or 6-inch pots. When maximum convenient pot size has been reached, topdress annually (see page 428).

Propagation The best time to propagate is in the spring. Plant a basal shoot bearing three or four leaves, preferably with some roots already attached, in a pot containing a moistened mixture of equal parts of peat moss and coarse sand or perlite. Enclose the potted shoot in a plastic bag, and keep it in medium light. Rooting should occur in six to eight weeks, after which the new plant can be treated as mature.

If an old and unwanted plant is to be broken up, sections of the main stem can be used for propagation instead of basal shoots. Aglaonemas may also be air layered (see page 440).

Aichryson

CRASSULACEAE

A. laxum

AICHRYSON is a small genus of succulents closely related to aeoniums. They are freely branching shrublets that have rounded or somewhat spoon-shaped leaves covered with soft, fine hairs. Yellow daisylike flowers may be produced in small clusters at the ends of the branches in late spring or early summer. Some species sometimes—but by no means always—behave like annuals or biennials and die after flowering.

See also SUCCULENTS.

RECOMMENDED AICHRYSONS

A. domesticum (more often known as *Aeonium domesticum*) is a true perennial. Rarely over 10 inches tall, it has short stems topped by dark olive green, slightly furry, almost circular leaves packed into tight rosettes. The variety usually seen is *A.d.* 'Variegatum,' in which the leaves are so heavily marked with creamy white mottling that some look white. Flowers are rarely produced.

A. laxum (also known as *A. dichotomum*) tends to behave like an annual or biennial. Of dwarf-treelike appearance, it seldom grows over 1 foot high. Its many thin, forked branches bear 1- to 2-inch-long spoon-shaped (but nearly circular) leaves on short leafstalks. Clusters of many pale yellow flowers $\frac{1}{2}$ inch across are regularly produced. This plant is liable to die after flowering.

A. villosum, an untidy, straggling shrublet, may also behave like an annual. It grows to 8 inches tall and has $\frac{1}{2}$- to 1-inch spoon-shaped (but slightly rhomboidal) leaves on very short stalks. Clusters of $\frac{3}{4}$-inch golden yellow flowers appear in late spring, after which the plant may die.

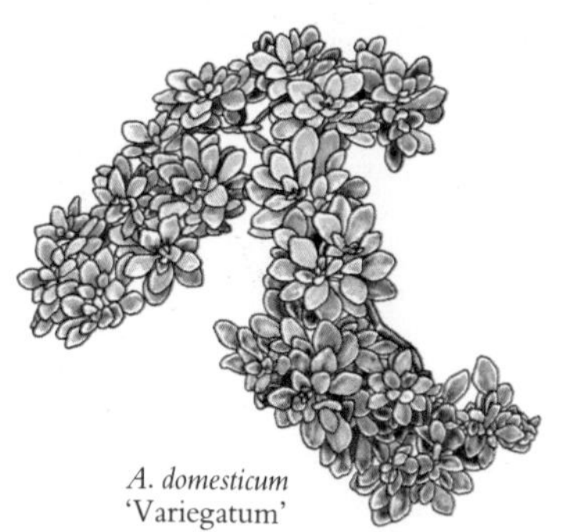

A. domesticum 'Variegatum'

PROPER CARE

Light Provide bright light with some direct sunlight. Aichrysons grow spindly and fail to bloom if they are grown in poor light.

Temperature These plants do well in a wide range of temperatures. Under normal room conditions, *A. domesticum* and other aichrysons that survive after flowering grow continuously. If they are kept in a place where the temperature falls below 55°F (and where light is poor), however, they will have a short winter rest period.

Watering During the active growth period water moderately—enough to make the potting mixture moist throughout, but allowing the top half of the mixture to dry out between waterings. During the rest period, if any, water only enough to keep the mixture from drying out completely.

Feeding In areas where light and temperature are low in winter (and plants have a rest period) apply standard liquid fertilizer every two weeks during the active growth period only. Elsewhere, these plants may be fed throughout the year.

Potting and repotting Use a soil-based potting mixture (see page 429). Because aichrysons have small root systems, they do not need large pots but should be able to mature and flower in 4- or 5-inch pots. If necessary, move small surviving plants into pots one size larger in spring.

Propagation Small tip cuttings root easily if taken in spring or summer. Take shoots 3 or 4 inches long, strip them of their lower leaves and plant them in a slightly moistened mixture of equal parts peat moss and coarse sand or perlite. Give the cuttings bright light and just enough water to prevent the mixture from drying out. Rooting should take place in three to four weeks. When rooted, plant the cuttings in 3-inch pots of soil-based mixture and treat them as adults.

Special points Aichrysons tend to lose their lower leaves. If too many leaves seem to be falling, the plants are probably getting too much hot, dry air or scorching sun. Move them to a more suitable position.

Allamanda

APOCYNACEAE

Golden-trumpet
A. cathartica

ALLAMANDA *cathartica* (golden-trumpet) is a climber with yellow flowers, and is best suited to plant windows (see page 53). Glossy, dark green leaves are 4–6 inches long and $1\frac{1}{2}$–$2\frac{1}{2}$ inches wide, and the flowers consist of a 1- to $1\frac{1}{2}$-inch-long tube flaring into five petals that span 5 inches. There is a compact variety, *A.c.* 'Grandiflora,' and another, *A.c.* 'Hendersonii,' whose buds are reddish brown before turning yellow.

PROPER CARE

Light Provide bright light, with three or four hours a day of full sun.

Temperature Warmth (at least 60°F) and high humidity are essential.

Watering During the active growth period water moderately. During the winter rest period water sparingly.

Feeding Apply standard liquid fertilizer to actively growing plants every two weeks.

Potting and repotting Use a soil-based mixture (see page 429). Move plants to larger pots in spring.

Propagation Plant 3- or 4-inch-long tip cuttings of early-spring growth in 3-inch pots of a moistened equal-parts mixture of peat moss and coarse sand or perlite. Place each cutting in a plastic bag or propagating case (see page 443), and stand it in bright filtered light at 70°F. When rooted, treat the young plants as mature allamandas. Move them into the standard mixture after two months.

Special points In late winter cut plants back by as much as two-thirds.

Aloe

LILIACEAE

Partridge-breasted aloe
A. variegata

THE genus *Aloe* includes hundreds of kinds of succulent with thick, tapering leaves that are generally arranged in rosette form. The leaves of some are free of protective spines, while others are fiercely armed with both spines and hooked teeth. Some aloes are stemless; some have stems permanently clothed with leaves; some have stems that become bare as they lose their leaves; and some of the forms with clothed stems topple over after they have grown a foot or more and continue to grow down the side of the pot. A number of them are suitable for the home only when young because they eventually grow too tall, but there are also many dwarf-growing kinds. Blooms, which appear from leaf axils at any time from late winter to early summer, normally consist of a spike of tubular orange or red flowers that are about $1\frac{1}{2}$ inches long. All aloes are easy to grow.
See also SUCCULENTS.

Do not worry when the stem of A. brevifolia *topples over the edge of its pot; this is its natural growth habit.*

RECOMMENDED ALOES

A. arborescens (candelabra aloe, candelabra plant, octopus plant, or torch plant) can grow to 15 feet tall; only young plants are suitable for use indoors. The narrow, tooth-edged leaves, which are 6–9 inches long and $\frac{3}{4}$ inch wide, form a loose rosette on the end of a bare woody stem. Offsets normally appear around the base when plants are two to three years old. Red flowers may be produced at the top of a long branched stem.

A. aristata (lace aloe) is stemless, with fleshy, dark gray-green leaves densely packed in a rosette. Each leaf is about 6 inches long and $\frac{3}{4}$ inch wide, spotted with tubercles, and has hard white edges. Orange flowers, which appear on a 12-inch stalk in early summer, last only a few days. Mature plants produce many offsets.

A. barbadensis (also called *A. vera*) is commonly known as medicine plant because its juices are excellent for healing burns. The plant forms a stemless clump of dagger-shaped leaves 1–2 feet long and 2–3 inches wide. Leaves are gray-green, faintly spotted with white, and edged with soft teeth in shades of pink or red. A stalk up to 3 feet long carries tubular, inch-long, yellow flowers. Offsets are produced from stolons just below the surface.

A. brevifolia (short-leaved aloe) has 3- to 4-inch-long and 1- to 2-inch-wide pale green leaves edged with prickly teeth arranged around a stem that eventually elongates and topples over. Flowers are pale pink on a stalk that can be up to 1 foot long. Offsets are produced from the lower leaf axils.

A. arborescens (candelabra aloe)

A. aristata (lace aloe)

A. brevifolia (short-leaved aloe)

A. ferox (Cape aloe) is of value as a house plant only when relatively young, while its bronze-green leaves are still of manageable size. The leaves are up to 3 feet long and 6 inches wide, broad, fleshy, and cupped. They have warty undersides and edges covered with brown spines, and they grow in two opposite ranks when young. Mature plants bear 3- to 4-foot-high racemes of red flowers. Offsets are not usually produced until the plant has grown too big for use indoors.

A. variegata (kanniedood aloe, partridge-breasted aloe, pheasant's-wings, or tiger aloe) is the most popular dwarf species. It has stems clothed with pointed triangular leaves 4–6 inches long and 1–$1\frac{1}{2}$ inches wide, which are at first arranged in three erect ranks then gradually spiral as the plant matures. They are dark gray-green in color, with pronounced markings or irregularly shaped transverse white bands. Plants rarely exceed 12 inches in height but often begin to flower when only 4–6 inches high. Coral pink flowers (seldom more than 10) appear on a foot-long stalk in late winter. These plants rarely shed leaves, and the stems eventually topple over with increasing weight. Some produce offsets at an early age, others not until they are mature.

PROPER CARE

Light Bright light suits all aloes. Those with spiny leaves usually do well in full sunlight, but the softer-leaved kinds such as *A. variegata* do best if sunlight reaches them indirectly—for instance, if it is filtered through a translucent blind or curtain. No aloe will thrive if permanently placed at a distance from a window.

Temperature Aloes grow well in normal room temperatures and are tolerant of dry air. To encourage flowering, however, give them a short winter rest at no more than 50°F.

Watering During the active growth period water plentifully as often as necessary to keep the potting mixture thoroughly moist. During the rest period water only enough to prevent the mixture from drying out. Do not permit water to collect in the tight rosette of such types as *A. variegata*.

Feeding Apply standard liquid fertilizer every two weeks during the active growth period.

Potting and repotting Use a soil-based potting mixture (see page 429). Most aloes should be moved into pots one size larger every spring. When maximum convenient pot size has been reached, plants should be top-dressed with fresh potting mixture once a year (see page 428). To prevent rot, make sure that plants with thick basal leaves are never buried deeper than they were before. A sprinkling of coarse sand or perlite over the surface of the mixture prevents rot at points where fleshy leaves of stemless aloes touch the soil.

Propagation Offsets can be taken from the base of a plant early in summer. These small new rosettes are often attached to the parent by a short underground stolon and may already have little roots, which should be retained for propagation. Because very tiny offsets are hard to root, they should not be removed for planting until their leaves have begun to open into the characteristic rosette shape. Plants that have a rosette of leaves on a long stem are likely to produce additional small rosettes low down on the stem, and these root more easily than those produced higher up. Offsets will root in two to three weeks in the standard potting mixture if some coarse sand or perlite is sprinkled at the base of the rosette to prevent rotting. Until offsets are well established, they should have bright light without direct sunlight and should be watered sparingly, only enough to moisten the potting mixture, allowing the top two-thirds of the mixture to dry out between waterings.

Special points Mealy bugs and root mealy bugs can be troublesome. The former hide deep in the crevices of rosette foliage, and the latter bury themselves in the roots, just below the surface of the potting mixture (see page 455).

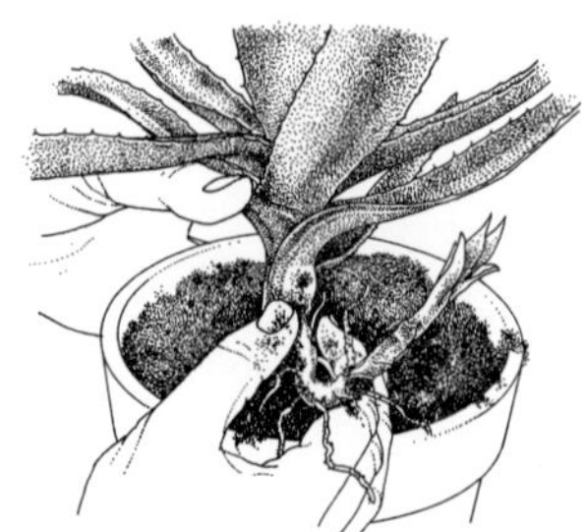

This offset has developed sufficiently to be detached from the parent plant for propagation.

Ananas
BROMELIACEAE

Variegated pineapple
A. comosus variegatus

THE genus *Ananas* includes the familiar edible pineapple as well as some plants grown indoors for their decorative foliage. The long, slender, usually sharp-toothed and spined leaves of these plants are arranged in a loose rosette; and in some species a stalk bearing pink bracts and blue flowers eventually rises from the center of the rosette. The part of the stalk that has borne the flowers may then thicken to form a fruit, which can take six or seven months to reach the typical pineapple shape. A cluster of short, tooth-edged leaves also develops at the top of the fruit. (When produced by indoor plants, such fruit is unlikely to be edible.)

All of these plants are slow-growing, and none has a regular annual rest period.

See also BROMELIADS.

RECOMMENDED ANANASES

A. bracteatus (red pineapple) grows large and makes a suitable house plant only while young. The most popular form is *A. b. striatus*, which has variegated leaves with 2-inch-wide lengthwise stripes colored green and cream, suffused throughout with pink. Two-year-old plants with leaves 9–12 inches long are of considerable decorative value, and the leaves are likely to remain reasonably short—under 4 feet—for 5 to 10 years. This species is unlikely to produce flowers and fruit indoors.

A. comosus (also called *A. sativus*), the familiar edible pineapple, grows much too big for use as a house plant. There is a decorative indoor form, however: *A.c. variegatus,* which has channeled and spiny leaves 1½ inches wide and up to 3 feet long; they are green with ivory-colored margins, but turn deep pink if given sufficient sunlight. Flowers, followed by a small (usually pink) fruit atop a 3-foot-tall stout stalk, may develop when the plant is about six years old, provided that it has been grown under ideal conditions, such as in a specially designed plant window (see page 53).

A. nanus is a dwarf plant that grows only 18 inches tall and 15 inches wide; thus it will reach maturity and bear flowers and fruit in a 4-inch pot. The dark green fruit, which is 1–2 inches long and bullet-hard (but pleasant-smelling), is held on an 18-inch-long stalk rising from the center of a rosette of dark green, very deeply arching leaves ¾ inch wide and 15 inches long. Unlike most plants of the genus, which grow in a single rosette form with only an occasional offset, this species may have many offsets clustered around the base.

PROPER CARE

Light All these plants like really bright light, including direct sunlight. The sunnier the position, the stronger the coloring of those species that have variegated leaves.

Temperature These plants require warm growing conditions. They do best when they also have high humidity, which can be provided by standing pots on trays or saucers of

damp pebbles or moist peat moss and also by occasional spraying of foliage.
Watering Water moderately, enough to make the potting mixture moist throughout, but allowing the top half-inch of the mixture to dry out before watering again.
Feeding Apply standard liquid fertilizer every two weeks throughout the year to these bromeliads.
Potting and repotting Use the potting mixture recommended for terrestrial bromeliads (see page 107).

A. nanus is usually sold in a 4-inch pot and can remain in that size indefinitely. Even large-growing species do not require very big pots, for they have relatively little root. While young, such species may need to be moved into pots one size larger every other spring. A 6- or 8-inch pot should be the largest size needed. It is best to use clay pots for these plants, since an ananas in a plastic pot may become top-heavy and topple over.
Propagation The most satisfactory way to propagate these plants is by means of offsets. Use a sharp knife for detaching an offset from the base of its parent when it is between 4 and 6 inches long (3–4 inches for *A. nanus*). Plant it in a 3-inch pot containing an equal-parts mixture of moistened peat moss and coarse sand or perlite, and enclose the whole in a plastic bag. Place it in a warm, slightly shaded position—for instance, at a bright window where the sunlight is filtered through a translucent blind or curtain. The offset should root in around eight weeks; it is unlikely to need any further water during that period.

When the offset is rooted, remove the pot from the bag, and water the plant sparingly—just enough to make the rooting mixture barely moist. When the plant begins to fill the pot with roots, slightly increase the amount of water. At this stage, begin to feed the rooted offset according to the recommendations given for a mature plant. About six months after it was first planted, move the offset into a 4-inch pot of regular potting mixture; thereafter, its cultivation needs are those of a mature ananas.

An alternative method of propagation is to cut off and root the crown of tooth-edged leaves at the top of the fruit. But because this procedure requires considerable skill and ideal rooting conditions, it is seldom successful.

Anthurium

ARACEAE

THE large genus *Anthurium* includes not only plants prized solely for their foliage, which are actually rather difficult to grow indoors, but also some more easily cultivated kinds that provide an additional bonus: striking and long-lasting flower spikes (technically known as inflorescences), each consisting of a large, flat spathe surrounding a thin, arched, or strongly twisted spadix. It is because of these distinctive inflorescences that some of the plants have acquired such popular names as flamingo flower and oilcloth flower (from the often brilliant color and shape of the spathe) or pigtail and tailflower (from the shape of the curly spadix). Although they usually flower in summer, plants grown in ideal conditions may produce flowers on and off almost all year round. Each inflorescence can last for eight weeks, or even longer.

In the wild, anthuriums grow either in the ground or epiphytically on trees. They have a small root system, with the leaves generally rising directly from a fleshy rootstock.

RECOMMENDED ANTHURIUMS

A. andraeanum (oilcloth flower, flamingo flower, or flamingo lily), the type species, is not often seen, since it has been superseded by a number of improved forms and many hybrids. Plants grown as varieties of *A. andraeanum* have deep green, leathery, arrowhead-shaped leaves 8–10 inches long and 5 inches wide, on leafstalks up to 10 inches long. The spathe, which may be white, pink, salmon, or red, is shield-shaped, 3–5 inches long, and shiny (as if lacquered); normally, too, it has a puckered surface. The offcenter fleshy spadix is cylindrical, 2–3 inches long, arched, and colored yellow shading into cream.
A. crystallinum, popularly called crystal anthurium or strap flower, is grown entirely for its highly decorative foliage. The leaves are heart-shaped, as much as 2 feet long and a foot wide. When young they are metallic purple, but they become a shimmering, deep emerald green as they age, with the prominent midrib and principal lateral veins etched in silver. Leafstalks are up to 15 inches long and hold the leaves up almost vertically. The inflorescence is insignificant compared with the foliage.
A. scherzeranum (flamingo flower, pigtail plant, or tailflower) has leathery, dark green, lance-shaped leaves up to 8 inches long and 3 inches wide on 6- to 8-inch-long stalks. The inflorescence has a 3- to 4-inch-long, waxy, bright scarlet spathe, which surrounds a curly orange-red spadix 2–3 inches long. In some forms the spathe is darker red spotted with white.

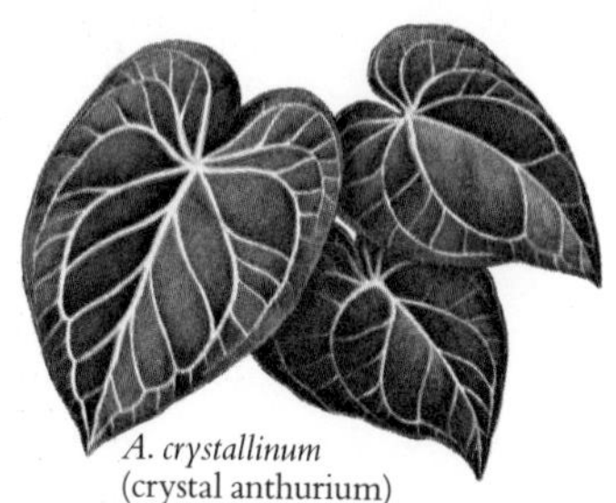
A. crystallinum
(crystal anthurium)

PROPER CARE

Light Anthuriums do not need bright light in order to bloom; in fact, they prefer medium light—as, for example, at a slightly shaded window—at all times. They should be kept close to the window, however. If grown too far from the source of light, their leaves elongate unattractively.
Temperature These plants do best at a fairly constant temperature of 65°–70°F, but they can tolerate temperatures down to 55° for short periods of time.
Watering While plants are actively growing, water them plentifully as often as necessary to keep the potting mixture thoroughly moist. During the rest period allow the top half-inch of the mixture to dry out between waterings. Some growers maintain that the water should be lime-free (soft), but this does not appear to be essential for most modern forms and hybrids.
Feeding Apply standard liquid fertilizer once every two weeks as long as plants are in active growth.
Potting and repotting The potting mixture should contain a high proportion of coarse peat moss or rough leaf mold or sphagnum moss. A peat-based mixture will do, providing it is kept well fed (see page 424), but the best potting mixture is one containing equal parts of coarse peat moss, soil-based mixture, and sand. Move small plants into pots one size larger every spring, making sure that they are inserted no deeper than before and

Flamingo flower
A. scherzeranum

that the pots have about 2 inches of clay-pot fragments in the bottom for drainage. Maximum size of pot needed for most indoor anthuriums is 5 or 6 inches.

Propagation Divide overcrowded clumps early in spring. Separate them carefully so that each section has some fleshy roots and a growing point. Plant each section in a small pot containing a peat-based potting mixture, place the pot in a position where it will receive medium light and a steady temperature of about 70°F, and water just enough to keep the mixture moist until roots have become active. It will help if some bottom heat can be provided by a simple electric propagator (see page 444).

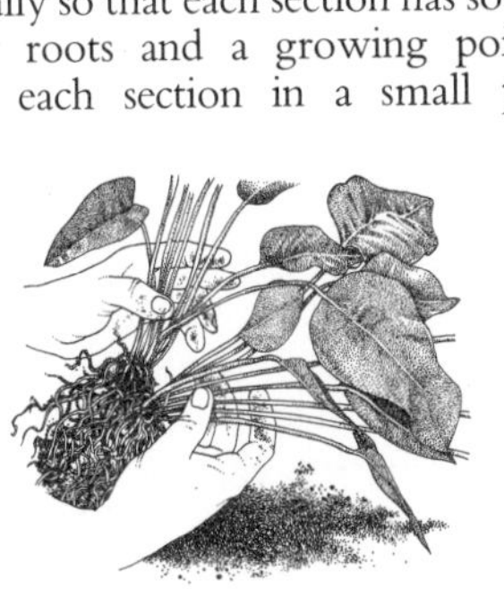

In pulling overcrowded clumps apart, make sure that each section bears both healthy leaves and roots.

Special points *A. crystallinum* (and other species grown mainly for their foliage) need extremely high humidity and are best grown in plant windows (see page 53). High humidity encourages flowering in both *A. andraeanum* and *A. scherzeranum*; create humidity by standing these plants on trays of wet pebbles or damp peat moss and moistening the leaves daily with a fine mist-spray. The inflorescences may need support; attach them to thin canes with soft twine or plastic-covered wire. The leathery leaves of these two species can be freed of dust by sponging, but regular spraying is the best way to clean the more delicate leaves of *A. crystallinum*.

If flower stalks begin to bend, push thin stakes into the soil around the sides of the pot and tie the stalks to them.

Aphelandra

ACANTHACEAE

Saffron spike
A. squarrosa 'Louisae'

THE genus *Aphelandra* includes about 80 species of tropical shrubs and herbaceous plants, but only two are commonly grown indoors. Both species grow 12–18 inches high on stout stems and have pointed-elliptic leaves of a dark glossy green with broad ivory white markings.

In spring these aphelandras produce flower spikes consisting of yellow or orange-yellow, flower-laden bracts 1–1½ inches long. The spikes appear at the top of the plant and sometimes there are additional spikes between the upper leaves. The small yellow flowers last for only a few days, but the cone-shaped spike of bracts remains attractive for several weeks. Unfortunately, aphelandras are not easy plants to bring into bloom. They are usually purchased when in flower and will flower again only under the right conditions. They are good plants for terrariums (see page 54).

RECOMMENDED APHELANDRAS

A. chamissoniana has close-set leaves 4–5 inches long, and narrow-pointed yellow flower bracts.

A. squarrosa (saffron spike or zebra plant) is normally seen in the compact form *A. s.* 'Louisae,' with leaves 8–12 inches long, and with broad, showy, yellow or orange-yellow flower bracts. Among the several other forms, *A. s.* 'Brockfeld' is notably compact, with dark green leaves; *A. s.* 'Dania,' with silvery leaf markings, is the most difficult to bring into bloom; *A. s.* 'Fritz Prinsler' has particularly sharp contrasts in its leaf coloring.

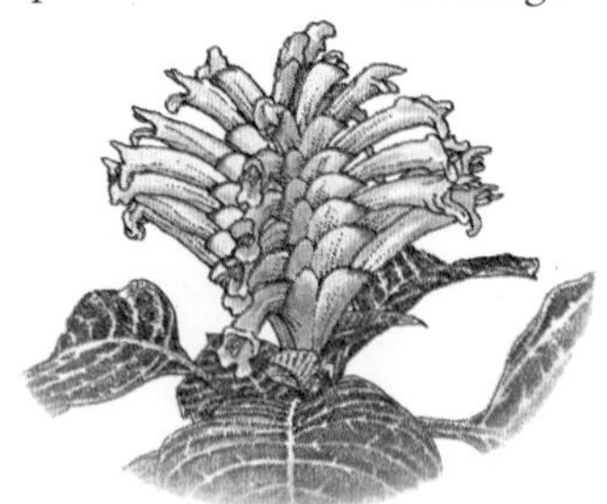

Long-lasting, showy yellow bracts encase short-lived flowers on a cone-shaped flower spike.

PROPER CARE

Light These plants need bright light but not direct sunlight.

Temperature During the active growth period give aphelandras high humidity along with temperatures of at least 65°F. Pots should be kept on trays of moistened pebbles. Immediately after flowering, give the plants a short winter rest in a relatively cool position, but not below 55°.

Watering During the active growth period water plentifully as often as necessary to keep the potting mixture thoroughly moist. During the short winter rest period make the entire mixture barely moist, allowing the top half to dry out between waterings; this should be just enough water to keep the leaves from drooping.

Feeding Aphelandras are greedy plants and must be given standard liquid fertilizer every week during the active growth period.

Potting and repotting Use a soil-based potting mixture incorporating peat moss or leaf mold (see page 429). Plants can be moved into pots one size larger as necessary. Most varieties will flower in 5- or 6-inch pots. A plant that has flowered should be cut back to a single pair of healthy leaves every spring before being repotted in fresh mixture. This will promote flowering. As much of the old mixture should be removed from the roots as can be done without harming them. This treatment often results in the production of two or three main shoots per plant instead of only one.

To prepare an aphelandra for repotting, use your fingers to loosen potting mixture gently from the tangled roots.

Propagation Propagate—preferably in late spring—by means of 2- to 3-inch-long tip cuttings. Plant them in the potting mixture recommended for mature aphelandras, moisten it well, enclose the whole in a plastic bag, and keep it in a warm, humid place in bright light filtered through a translucent blind or curtain. No further watering is necessary. Cuttings should root in six to eight weeks.

Special points Watch out for aphids, scale insects, and mealy bugs (see pages 454–455) as renewed growth begins, usually in early spring. The tender growing points of aphelandras are prone to attack by these pests.

Aporocactus

CACTACEAE

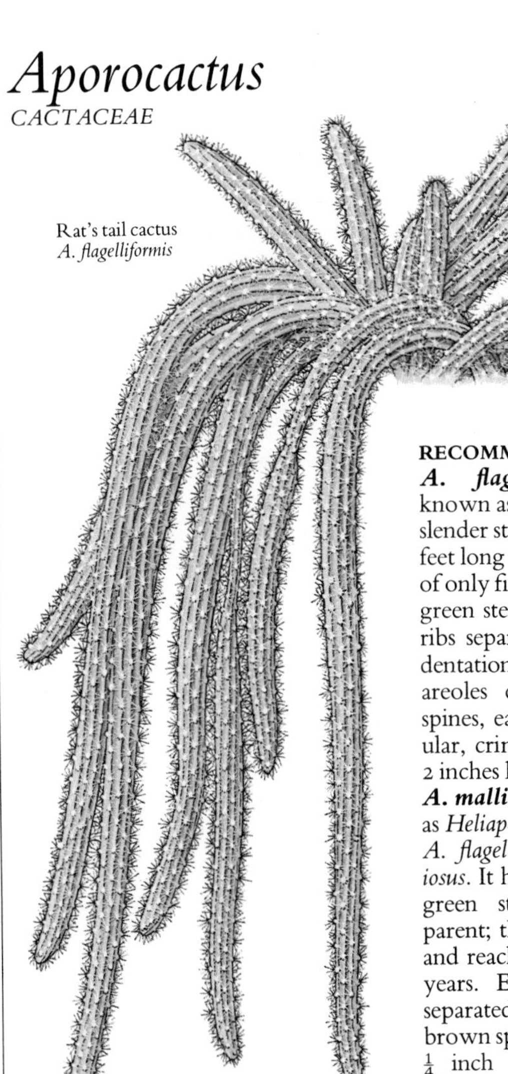

THERE are five species of aporocactus, but only one true species and a hybrid are popular house plants. These desert cacti have pendent stems that can grow several feet long, with areoles closely spaced along the ribs. Flowers are produced profusely in spring. The flowering season lasts for about two months, and individual blooms can last a week.

Their trailing stems make these cacti ideal plants for a hanging basket. Line the basket with sphagnum moss before filling it with potting mixture, and make sure it is hung where the prickly stems will not pose a threat to the unwary. If an aporocactus is grown in a pot, hang the pot up or attach it to a high shelf. If left free-standing, it can soon be overbalanced by the lengthening stems.

See also CACTI.

RECOMMENDED APOROCACTI

A. flagelliformis is commonly known as rat's tail cactus because of its slender stems, which can grow up to 6 feet long and ½ inch thick in the course of only five years. Each of these bright green stems has 8 to 12 narrow, low ribs separated by broad, shallow indentations. The small, slightly raised areoles carry clusters of brownish spines, each about ⅛ inch long. Tubular, crimson-pink flowers are about 2 inches long and 1 inch wide.

A. mallisonii (more correctly known as *Heliaporus smithii*) is a cross between *A. flagelliformis* and *Heliocereus speciosus*. It has stouter and shorter bright green stems than its aporocactus parent; they grow up to 1 inch thick and reach a length of 3–4 feet in five years. Each stem has 6 to 8 ribs separated by deep indentations, and the brown spines carried by the areoles are ¼ inch long. Cup-shaped flowers, which are more like those of the heliocereus parent, are 2 inches wide and bright red tinged with blue.

PROPER CARE

Light An aporocactus requires full sunlight. Hang the pot or basket in the sunniest window available. If possible, hang the plant outdoors in summer to give it fresh air and extra light.

Temperature During the active growth period normal room temperatures are suitable. In winter these plants should be rested at 45°–50°F, if possible, but they tolerate temperatures up to 60°.

Watering During the active growth period water plentifully, keeping the potting mixture thoroughly moist, but do not let plants stand in water. During the winter rest period keep the mixture from drying out.

Feeding Use tomato-type fertilizer every two weeks during the active growth period.

Potting and repotting An aporocactus likes a fairly rich potting mixture—ideally a combination of two-thirds soil-based mixture (see page 429) and one-third leaf mold. If leaf mold is not available, the plant can be grown successfully in ordinary soil- or peat-based mixture. Since the plant is fast-growing, it should be repotted annually—preferably when it has finished flowering, but not necessarily in a larger container. The main reason for repotting is to provide the plant with fresh potting mixture, for aporocacti use up nutriments swiftly. Use a container one size larger only when the current container is full of roots. Maximum convenient size is likely to be a 9-inch basket or 6-inch pot. If a plant has outgrown such a container, it should be discarded and restarted from a cutting.

Propagation To propagate, use either 6-inch tip cuttings or 6-inch segments of any part of the stem. Allow each cutting or segment to dry for three days; then insert it about an inch deep in a small pan or pot of the recommended potting mixture for mature plants; be sure that any stem segment is planted with the bottom end down. If this shallowly inserted cutting tends to fall over, it can be supported by being gently tied to a small wooden stick. Cultivation needs of the cutting are the same as those for mature aporocacti, and rooting will occur within a few weeks.

These plants can also be grown from seed (see *CACTI*, page 119).

In spring crimson-pink flowers adorn the trailing stems of A. flagelliformis *for up to two months.*

Araucaria

ARAUCARIACEAE

Norfolk Island pine
A. heterophylla

THE only araucaria grown indoors is *A. heterophylla* (formerly known as *A. excelsa*). This conifer is also called Norfolk Island pine, Christmas tree plant, Australian pine, or house pine. It can grow 200 feet tall in the wild, but it rarely exceeds 4–6 feet indoors, where it grows very slowly—no more than 6 inches a year. Its branches with $\frac{1}{2}$-inch needles clustered together in fan shapes are arranged in tiers. New growth—which is normally produced in the spring—is a bright fresh green, and this color is held until the fall, when it darkens. The branches are heavy but they need not be given any extra support, since the main stem turns woody in time.

Mature specimens develop dark green needles and woody stems in time, and their branches are grouped together in tiers.

PROPER CARE

Light These araucarias do best in medium light. They should not be placed too far from the window, however, or their needles will fall.

Temperature A wide range of temperatures (ideally 45°–75°F) can be tolerated. Above 80° these conifers must also have high humidity; mist-spray the foliage occasionally.

Watering During the active growth period water plentifully, as often as necessary to keep the potting mixture thoroughly moist, but never allow the pot to stand in water. During the rest period water moderately, enough to make the potting mixture thoroughly moist, but allow the top inch to dry out between waterings.

Feeding Apply standard liquid fertilizer every two weeks in the active growth period.

Potting and repotting Use a soil-based potting mixture (see page 429). Repotting should be needed only every two to three years, but plants can be moved in spring whenever roots appear on the surface of the mixture or through the bottom of the pot. Five-inch pots are normally the largest necessary, but large specimens may require 6- or even 8-inch pots.

Propagation Commercially, plants are grown from seed or cuttings, but neither method is practical for the indoor grower.

Ardisia

MYRSINACEAE

Coralberry
A. crenata

OF the large genus *Ardisia* only one species, *A. crenata* (commonly called coralberry or spiceberry because of its long-lasting bright red berries), is a popular house plant. The species is sometimes wrongly called *A. crispa*, the name of a very similar plant. When grown in a pot, this upright shrub reaches a maximum height of only about 3 feet, with a spread of no more than 12 to 15 inches. Its leaves are elliptically lance-shaped, up to 6 inches long and 2 inches wide, undulate, dark green, leathery, and shining. Thick clusters of star-shaped white or rose-pink $\frac{1}{4}$-inch flowers are produced from leaf axils, usually in early summer. These are followed by $\frac{1}{4}$-inch shiny berries held on nearly horizontal stalks. The berries gradually take on a bright red color and normally persist until flowering time the following year.

PROPER CARE

Light Provide bright light at all times, with several hours a day of direct sunlight.

Temperature Ardisias prefer to be grown cool, ideally at a maximum temperature of 60°F. In higher temperatures high humidity is essential to prevent the berries from falling prematurely; stand the plants on trays or saucers of moist pebbles, and mist-spray them daily.

Watering While plants are in active growth, water them plentifully as often as necessary to keep the potting mixture thoroughly moist. During the rest period allow the top half-inch of the mixture to dry out between waterings if plants are kept at normal room temperature; if the temperature can be held below 60°F, however, water even more sparingly, allowing at least half the potting mixture to dry out between waterings.

Feeding Apply standard liquid fertilizer every two weeks while plants are in active growth.

Potting and repotting Use a soil-based potting mixture (see page 429). Move young plants into pots one size larger each spring until they reach the 5-inch size where they will probably flower and fruit. Older plants tend to deteriorate and should be replaced when they have obviously begun to lose vigor.

Propagation Plants are normally raised from seed sown in spring (see page 441). Although this is possible in the home, it is easier to buy young plants, which are usually sold in 3-inch pots. An alternative method of propagation is to take heel cuttings from lateral shoots during late spring or early summer, pot them in an equal-parts mixture of peat moss and sand, and water them sparingly—just often enough to keep the mixture moist.

Ardisias can be propagated by means of sideshoot cuttings, which come away easily from the main stem with a small heel attached.

They should root in 6–8 weeks, especially if some form of bottom heat is provided from an electrically heated propagator (see page 444). If this is not feasible, enclose the potted cuttings in a plastic bag, and keep the bag in a place where it gets medium light and adequate warmth (not below 70°F) until roots have developed. Ardisias can also be air layered (see page 440).

Asparagus

LILIACEAE

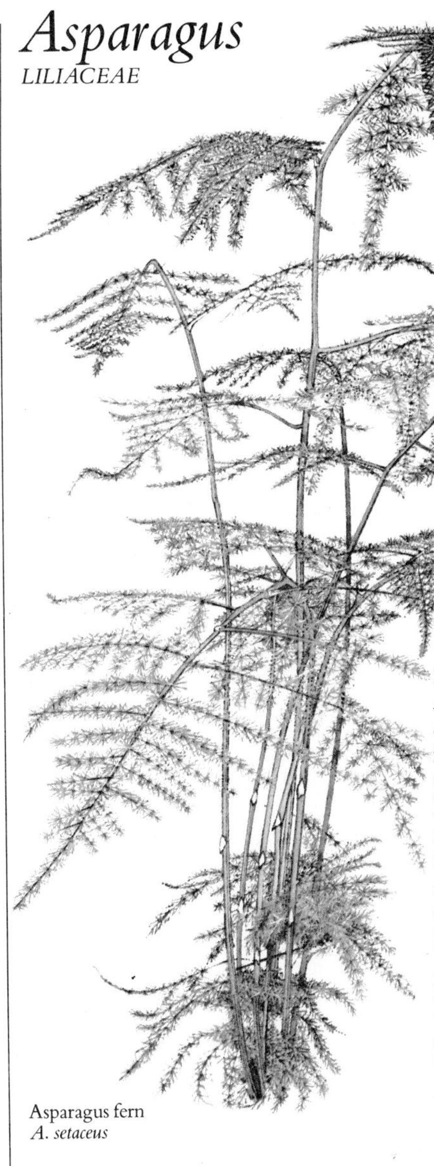

Asparagus fern
A. setaceus

THE genus *Asparagus*, which includes the edible vegetable *A. officinalis,* also includes a number of species and varieties grown indoors for their attractive feathery foliage consisting of finely divided and flattened modified branchlets resembling leaves. Most asparaguses have tuberous roots; some have thin intertwining stems; others produce plumelike fronds from a central crown. Flowers, which are small and insignificant though sometimes fragrant, are often followed by red, orange, or purple berries. Indoor asparagus plants are commonly called asparagus ferns because of their superficial resemblance to potted ferns. In fact, however, they are closely related to lilies, not to ferns.

RECOMMENDED ASPARAGUSES

A. asparagoides (also called *A. medeoloides*), commonly known as smilax, is a vigorous climbing plant with shiny, leathery, 2-inch-long branchlets; it winds its stems around the nearest available support. *A.a.* 'Myrtifolius' (formerly known as *Smilax myrtifolia*) is commonly called baby smilax, because it is smaller and much less vigorous than the original form.

A. densiflorus is not itself a familiar house plant, but is the species from which many familiar forms with plumed foliage have been evolved. Such plumed foliage may be either very full or quite sparse. *A.d.* 'Myers' (usually called *A. myersii*) is the well-known foxtail fern, an erect-growing form with foxtail-shaped fronds up to 15 inches long and $2\frac{1}{2}$ inches across. The most popular asparagus is *A.d.* 'Sprengeri' (emerald feather, emerald fern, or sprenger asparagus), which has pliable, drooping stems as much as 3 feet long. The stems are lightly covered with $\frac{1}{2}$- to $1\frac{1}{4}$-inch-long needle-like branchlets, which usually grow in groups of three at a node. *A.d.* 'Sprengeri' is ideal for use in hanging baskets or as a trailing plant in other types of container. *A.d.* 'Sprengeri Nanus' is a dwarf form; *A.d.* 'Sprengeri Robustus' is, as its name suggests, a very strong-growing one.

A. falcatus, commonly known as sicklethorn, is a climbing, woody-stemmed asparagus that bears narrow 2-inch-long branchlets.

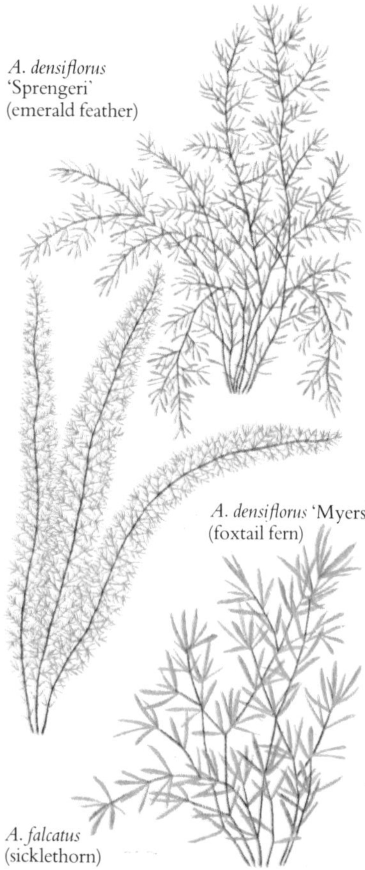

A. setaceus (more familiarly known as *A. plumosus*) has wiry stems and a flattened spray of bright green, ¼-inch-long branchlets. *A. setaceus* is widely known as asparagus fern (and sometimes called brides-bouquet fern, lacefern, or maidenhairfern). Branches of this plant are much used by florists as additional foliage with bouquets of cut flowers. *A.s.* 'Nanus' is a dwarf form, and *A.s.* 'Robustus' is an especially vigorous one. These plants do not climb when young, but as they mature they begin to send forth climbing stems which can be as much as 4 feet long. These stems are often bare at first, but they will eventually produce the characteristic tiny, bright green branchlets.

PROPER CARE

Light Bright light is essential for these plants. But never subject them to direct sunlight, which can badly scorch the leaves.

Temperature All asparagus plants do well in normally warm room temperatures, and they are also capable of tolerating temperatures which may be as low as 55°F.

Watering During the active growth period water plentifully as often as necessary to keep the potting mixture thoroughly moist, but never allow the pot to stand in water. During the rest period give these plants only enough water to keep the mixture from drying out. If the potting mixture dries out entirely at any time, loss of foliage is the inevitable result.

Feeding Apply standard liquid fertilizer every two weeks throughout the active growth period.

Potting and repotting Use a soil-based potting mixture (see page 429). Move plants every spring into pots one size larger until they are in the largest convenient size. Keep the level of the potting mixture well below the rim of the container, for thick asparagus roots tend to force the mixture upward. Forms of *A. densiflorus* grown in hanging baskets should be topdressed with fresh mixture in spring (see page 428), but should be taken out, divided, and replanted every third year.

Propagation Propagation in the home is usually done by dividing overcrowded clumps just as growth starts in spring. Remove any excess mixture from the tuberous roots and separate them with a sharp knife. Plant separate clumps in 3-inch pots of soil-based potting mixture and treat them as mature specimens. Although seed germinates well in a warm room, growth from seed is slow. On the whole it is better to buy new and vigorous small plants, which are frequently available, than to bother with home propagation.

Three asparagus species are displayed in this hanging basket—trailing A.d. *'Sprengeri,' dense* A.d. *'Myers' and upward-growing* A. setaceus.

Aspidistra

LILIACEAE

Cast-iron plant
A. elatior

THE only species of aspidistra cultivated indoors is *A. elatior* (sometimes wrongly named *A. lurida*), which can withstand poor conditions and will survive where few other house plants could; hence its name cast-iron plant, bestowed in Victorian days when the introduction of gas lighting produced fumes that killed most other plants. An indoor aspidistra will, however, respond well to good care. *A. elatior* has dark green, leathery leaves 15–20 inches long, which rise from a creeping rhizomatous rootstock lying half-buried in the potting mixture. Inconspicuous, dull-purple flowers are produced at soil level, but these are often hidden by the foliage. A less common form, *A.e.* 'Variegata,' has white or cream-colored stripes of varying widths running the length of the leaves.

PROPER CARE

Light Although aspidistras may be kept in dark corners and other poorly lit positions, they will produce little growth there, whereas they thrive in medium light—for instance, at a sunless window. The variegated form needs brighter light to maintain leaf color contrast, but keep it out of direct sunlight; strong sun can scorch its leaves.

Temperature The plant is so tolerant that it will flourish equally well in either hot or cold rooms.

Watering Water aspidistras moderately throughout the year, enough to make the potting mixture barely moist. The top two-thirds of the potting mixture must be allowed to dry out completely before watering again. A common sign of overwatering in aspidistras is the appearance of unsightly brown marks on the surface of the leaves.

Feeding Apply standard liquid fertilizer every two weeks during the active growth period.

Potting and repotting Use a soil-based potting mixture (see page 429). Aspidistras do best when left alone, and need repotting only at three- or four-year intervals. An overcrowded plant should be moved into a pot one size larger just as new growth begins in spring. Be sure there are plenty of clay-pot fragments in the pot for good drainage. Any plant that has reached maximum convenient pot size should be topdressed with fresh potting mixture every spring (see page 428).

Propagation Propagate by dividing overcrowded clumps in the spring. Each piece of rhizome should carry at least two leaves, and several pieces may be planted together in one 4-inch pot. Do not feed newly propagated plants; their roots should be encouraged to search for nutrients in the new potting mixture. Otherwise, cultivation needs of new plants are those of mature aspidistras. Regular feedings of standard liquid fertilizer can begin the following spring just at the start of the new active growth period.

This piece of aspidistra is particularly suitable for propagation since it carries both roots and leaves.

Asplenium

POLYPODIACEAE

Bird's nest fern
A. nidus

THE genus *Asplenium* (spleenwort) includes many species of fern, but only three of these ferns are popular as house plants. All three have decorative lance-shaped leaves and are easy plants to grow.
See also FERNS.

RECOMMENDED ASPLENIUMS

A. bulbiferum (hen-and-chicken fern, mother, or parsley fern) has foliage that closely resembles carrot leaves, but the medium green fronds are sturdier and more finely divided than those of carrot leaves. They are up to 2 feet long and 9 inches wide, and they grow on black stalks. Each frond is split into between 20 and 30 pinnae. Small brown bulbils from which arise replicas of the parent plant appear on the upper surface of several of the pinnae, eventually weighing the whole frond down slightly.

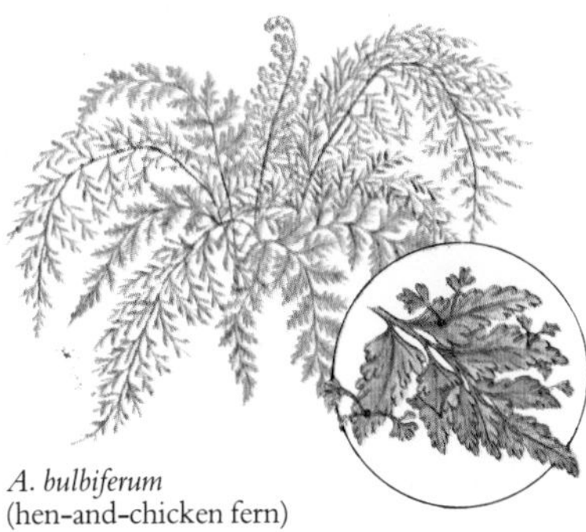

A. bulbiferum
(hen-and-chicken fern)

A. daucifolium, (better known as *A. viviparum*), is similar to *A. bulbiferum*, but has dark green, arching fronds divided into many lacy pinnae. Each frond can be up to 18 inches long and 6 inches wide supported on a green stalk. The pinnae are divided into needlelike segments about $\frac{1}{4}$ inch long. Small brown bulbils appear on the upper surface of some of the pinnae and are subsequently followed by miniature plants.

A. nidus gets its common name, bird's nest fern, from the fact that its shiny, undivided fronds are arranged in an upward-spreading, bowl-shaped rosette. These apple green, slightly undulate fronds may grow 4 feet long, but are more often about $1\frac{1}{2}$ feet long by 2–3 inches wide. Each one has a dark brown central rib that narrows and fades to merge with the color of the rest of the frond for the last third of its length. For the first few weeks, new fronds, which unroll from a central spongy, fibrous, dark brown core, are delicate and easily damaged. They should not have the dust wiped off them at this early stage. Harder, more mature fronds, on the other hand, will benefit from occasional wiping. Brown spore cases are arranged in herringbone fashion on the backs of some of the mature fronds. *A. nidus* does not produce offsets, but can live for years as a single-crowned rosette.

PROPER CARE

Light These aspleniums should be exposed neither to bright sunlight nor dense shade. Give them medium light all year long.

Temperature All these species do well in normal room temperatures. *A. nidus* cannot withstand temperatures below 60°F; *A. bulbiferum* and *A. daucifolium* can survive minimum temperatures of about 50°.

Watering During the active growth period water plentifully as often as necessary to make the potting mixture thoroughly moist. During the rest period water sparingly, enough to keep the mixture from drying out. It will not hurt these ferns to dry out for a while, but it is best to keep them evenly moist.

Feeding Give standard liquid fertilizer to well-established plants once a month during the active growth period only.

Potting and repotting For a suitable potting mixture see *FERNS*. Aspleniums have fine, dense, black roots, which form very solid root balls. Repotting is needed only when the root ball becomes so dense and crowded that the pot is full of roots (see page 426) and obviously the plant is not absorbing enough moisture when watered. When this occurs, move plants into pots one size larger in the spring. The roots will often adhere firmly to the sides of a pot, and it may be necessary to break the pot to remove the plant.

Propagation *A. bulbiferum* and *A. daucifolium* are easily propagated by means of the bulbils that grow on the mature fronds. When the bulbils are carrying three or four miniature fronds, they can be readily detached between the finger and thumb and then planted in small pots. Place the young ferns on the surface of the recommended potting mixture for ferns, and water them just enough to moisten the mixture. Enclose each potted plant in a plastic bag or propagating case, and keep it at normal room temperature in a slightly shaded position until further top growth begins to appear. Thereafter, gradually reduce the humidity by removing the plastic bag or uncovering the case for increasingly long periods over the next four weeks, and water the plant just enough to keep the mixture barely moist. Do not feed it. At the end of this time move the plant into a larger pot, and treat it as an adult. Propagation of *A. nidus* is possible only by spores and is impractical for most amateur growers.

Because asplenium roots tend to cling to the sides of the pot, it may be necessary to break it in order to remove the plant.

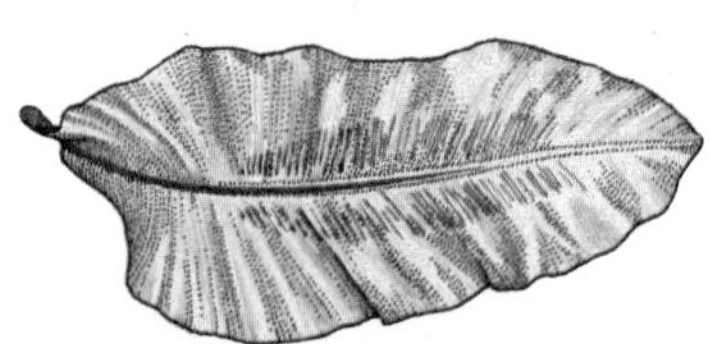

Propagation of A. nidus *is difficult, because each of the spore cases on this frond contains millions of spores that are nearly impossible to see, let alone handle.*

Propagating *A. bulbiferum*

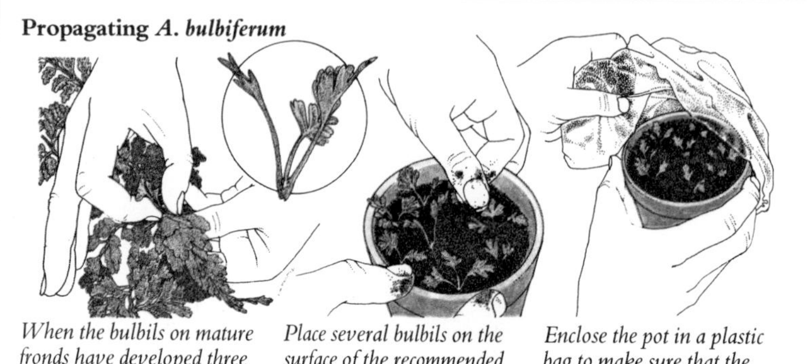

When the bulbils on mature fronds have developed three or four immature fronds, detach them from the parent.

Place several bulbils on the surface of the recommended potting mixture, and water them sparingly.

Enclose the pot in a plastic bag to make sure that the plants are kept in a humid atmosphere.

Astrophytum

CACTACEAE

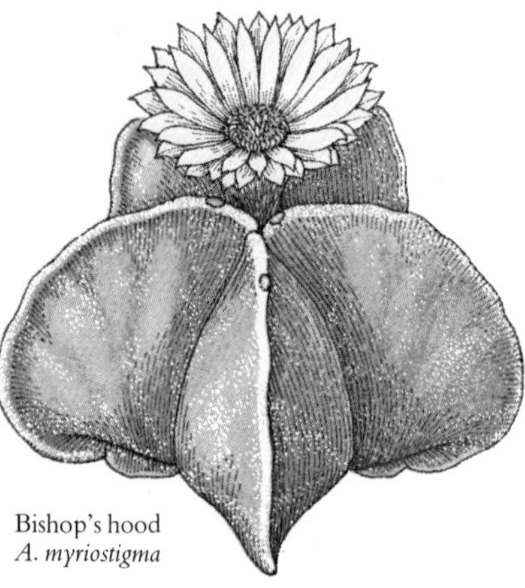

Bishop's hood
A. myriostigma

ASTROPHYTUMS are desert cacti, each with an unbranched stem that is roughly globular—often becoming elongated as the plant ages—and that is divided into wide segments, rather like those of an orange, by a small number of ribs. In mature plants the bottom of the stem tends to become woody. After a plant is at least three years old, cup-shaped flowers grow from areoles near the top of the stem; each flower lasts only a few days, but the plant continues to flower throughout the spring and summer. The two species described below are most suitable for cultivation in the home.

See also CACTI.

RECOMMENDED ASTROPHYTUMS

A. myriostigma (bishop's or monk's hood) loses its globular shape after about two years, when the stem begins to become cylindrical; it can eventually grow up to about 8 inches tall and 4 inches across. The basically green stem has no spines but is covered with tiny tufts of silvery hair (looking to the naked eye like scales or spots). These give the plant a grayish cast. There are from three to eight rather sharp-edged ribs. A form with four ribs, *A.m. quadricostatum*, is known as bishop's miter; another form, *A.m. nudum*, with five ribs, completely lacks the tufts of hair. The 2-inch-wide flowers of all forms are bright yellow with reddish throats.

A. ornatum (ornamental monk's hood or star cactus), which also elongates as it ages, can reach a height of over 1 foot and a diameter of around 6 inches. The dark green stem, obliquely banded by silvery scales, is sharply divided into segments by deep, narrow indentations between the eight ribs. Widely spaced areoles

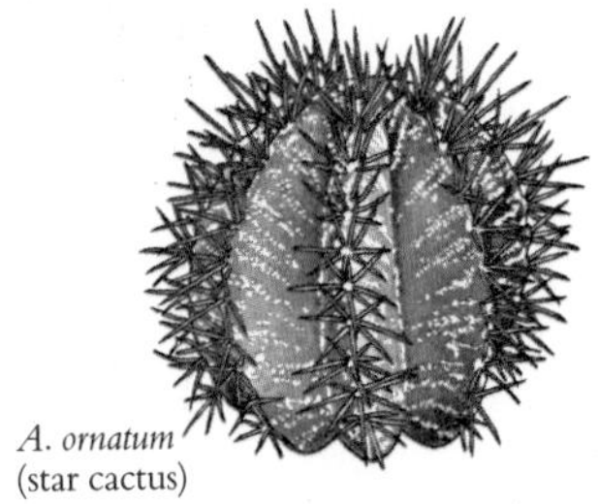
A. ornatum (star cactus)

on rib edges carry clusters of inch-long, stout, yellowish or brownish spines. Bright yellow flowers 3–4 inches wide appear when plants are about ten years old and 6 inches tall.

PROPER CARE

Light Astrophytums need plenty of full sunlight.

Temperature Normal room temperatures are suitable during the active growth period. From late fall to late winter give astrophytums a rest period at 45°–50°F.

Watering During the active growth period water moderately, but allow the top three-quarters of the mixture to dry out between waterings. During the rest period give only enough water to prevent the mixture from drying out completely.

Feeding In the active growth period only, apply a tomato-type fertilizer once a month to astrophytums growing in a soil-based potting mixture; once every two weeks to those in a peat-based mixture.

Potting and repotting Astrophytums do best in a mixture composed of one part coarse sand or perlite to two parts of either soil-based or peat-based mixture (see page 429). These cacti do not normally need to be moved into larger pots every year. Any plant up to 2 inches in diameter may be kept in a 3-inch pot. It is advisable, however, to remove plants from their pots in early spring; if the roots are tightly packed in the present pot, the plant should be repotted in a larger one. Otherwise, shake as much old mixture from the roots as possible, and replace the plant in its original pot with fresh mixture.

Propagation New plants can be raised only from seed sown in spring (see *CACTI*, page 119).

Aucuba

CORNACEAE

Japanese laurel
A. japonica 'Variegata'

THE genus *Aucuba* includes a few species, but only one, *A. japonica*, has become a popular house plant. Although an aucuba can reach a height of 15 feet outdoors, none of the several forms grown indoors is likely to grow more than 3 feet tall. Their oval leaves, which are arranged in pairs on ½-inch-long leafstalks, are 4–7 inches long, glossy, and coarsely toothed. All plants produce insignificant purple flowers in summer, and some produce small clusters of bright red berries in early winter.

All the many varieties of *A. japonica* have variegated leaves (those of the original species are mid-green). Probably the most popular is *A.j.* 'Variegata' (Japanese laurel or gold-dust tree); its leaves are heavily spotted with gold-colored markings. Two other attractive varieties are. *A.j.* 'Crotonifolia' (with at least half its mid-green leaf surface colored yellow or ivory) and 'Goldieana' (with a yellow center and green margins).

PROPER CARE

Light Indoor aucubas need bright light or filtered sunlight.

Temperature These plants are particularly good for use in cold, drafty positions; they can even withstand frost. But they cannot tolerate temperatures much above 75°F. In warm rooms be sure to provide a high degree of humidity.

Watering Throughout the year water aucubas plentifully as often as necessary to keep the potting mixture thoroughly moist, but never allow pots to stand in water.

Feeding Apply standard liquid fertilizer monthly throughout the year.

Potting and repotting Use a soil-based potting mixture (see page 429). These plants thrive in relatively small pots; a 5- to 8-inch pot gives adequate root room for quite a large plant. Small plants may be moved into pots one size larger in the spring when necessary. After maximum convenient pot size has been reached, an annual springtime topdressing (see page 428) is advisable.

Propagation Cuttings 4–6 inches long will root easily in spring if planted in small pots containing a moistened rooting mixture of peat moss and coarse sand or perlite. Place each pot in a plastic bag, and keep it at normal room temperature in filtered sunlight, giving no additional water until new growth indicates that rooting has occurred. Thereafter, remove the plastic bag, water the young plant sparingly and begin monthly feedings of liquid fertilizer. When the plant is 1 foot tall, move it into a 4-inch pot of standard mixture and treat it as a mature aucuba.

Special points If plants begin to get inconveniently large, cut them back in early spring.

Begonia

BEGONIACEAE

THE genus *Begonia* includes more than 2,000 species and hybrids, and they are as varied in appearance and habit as these numbers suggest. Some are valued mainly for flowers, some for decorative leaves, some for both leaves and flowers. Begonias range in size from tiny, ground-hugging creepers to stout-stemmed specimens 8–10 feet tall. Yet they all share a number of characteristics. Almost all forms have asymmetrical leaves; the leaves always grow alternately along the stems; and new leaves emerge from stipules (leaflike sheaths). And many begonias do not require continuous direct sunlight, a fact that makes them particularly suitable for indoor use.

Most kinds bear flowers in clusters on short stalks arising from or near leaf axils. There are separate male and female flowers on the same plant, however, each cluster normally composed of either all male or all female blooms. Male flowers tend to be the more eye-catching, partly because their petals are often of different shapes and sizes, whereas the petals of a female flower are more nearly alike. A distinctive feature of the female flower is the seed-bearing ovary, which looks like a three-lobed appendage immediately behind the petals. Female flowers, although they may slightly fade, usually last for weeks or even months, but the male flowers tend to drop off within two or three days of opening.

Because the genus is so large, it is generally divided into groups based on the differing storage organs or root structures of these plants. Some have fibrous roots (as most plants do). A second group consists of species in which roots grow down from a thick creeping rhizome. A third group includes tuberous species that have a fleshy, swollen storage organ at the base of the stem. In these pages fibrous-rooted and rhizomatous begonias are discussed together because their growth cycles and cultivation needs are similar—and are very different from those of the tuberous kinds.

B. 'Corallina de Lucerna'

Christmas-flowering begonia
B. cheimantha hybrid

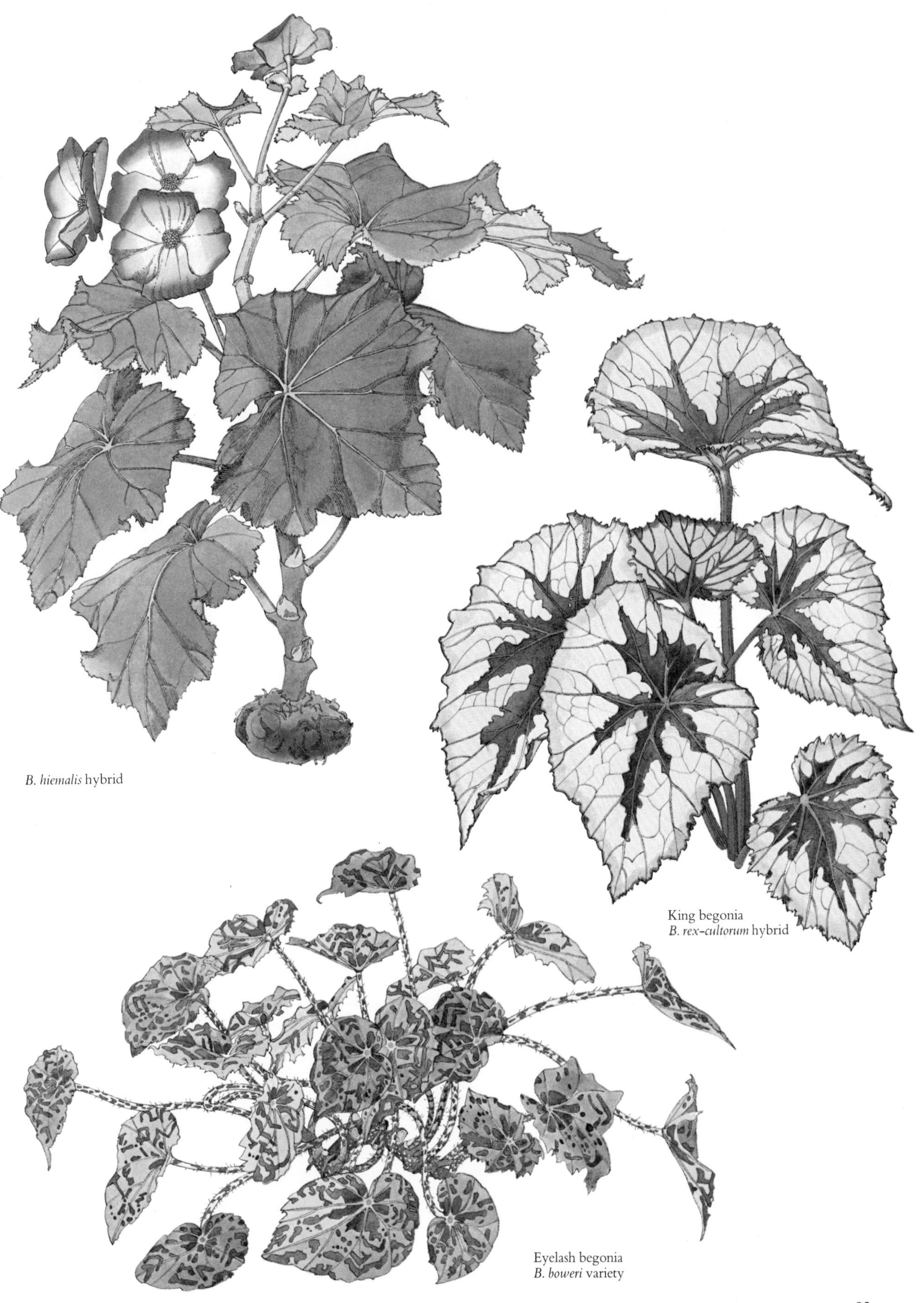

B. hiemalis hybrid

King begonia
B. rex-cultorum hybrid

Eyelash begonia
B. boweri variety

Begonia characteristics

This fibrous-rooted begonia has features in common with many begonias: stipules (**1**) *develop into asymmetrical leaves, which grow alternately; flowers grow in clusters, females with ovaries* (**2**), *males without* (**3**).

Fibrous-rooted and rhizomatous begonias

There are, roughly, three different kinds of fibrous-rooted begonia. Many species have smooth, rather woody stems marked here and there by swollen, knotted joints (nodes) a bit like the stems of bamboo. These plants usually have leaves like angel's wings—lobed near the top and acutely asymmetrical. A second kind of fibrous-rooted begonia has fleshy stems, and many parts of the plant—especially leaves and flowers—are covered with hairs. These plants (commonly known as hirsute begonias) are usually bushy, like those with bamboolike stems, although they will sometimes trail if left unsupported. So they are often grown in hanging baskets. Finally, there are the fleshy-stemmed wax begonias, whose crisp leaves are waxy, not hairy.

Most fibrous-rooted begonias flower profusely, and are grown both for their flowers and their decorative foliage. The flowers vary in size and color, but most have only a single layer of petals.

The rhizomatous begonias often have a thick, fleshy rhizome, which crawls over the surface of the potting mixture, sending down roots at intervals. The plants of most species grow less than 9 inches tall. The few that grow taller often need supporting with thin stakes. Many of these plants are without conventional, erect stems, but a few have much-branching, fleshy stems. Rhizomatous begonias are prized for their foliage. Leaves may be nearly circular, roughly star-shaped, or heart-shaped. Some plants have miniature leaves, some huge, some in between. Flowers are always small, each with only a single layer of petals.

RECOMMENDED BEGONIAS: FIBROUS-ROOTED

***B.* 'Alleryi,'** a hirsute begonia, grows 3–4 feet tall. Its pointed-oval, tooth-edged, hairy leaves are 6–9 inches long, 3–4 inches wide, and bronzy green with reddish purple veins on the underside. Rose-pink flowers ½ inch wide appear in summer and fall.

B. coccinea (angelwing begonia) has only a few bamboolike stems 3–4 feet tall. Leathery, obliquely oblong leaves are 4–6 inches long and 2–3 inches wide with slightly toothed, undulate edges. Leaf surfaces are grass green tinged at the edges with red above, and dull red below. The ½-inch-wide, waxy, coral red flowers appear in large, drooping clusters on red stalks from early summer to mid-fall.

B. compta has bamboolike stems. Some stems droop. Others grow erect up to 3–4 feet. Pointed-oval leaves, 3–6 inches long and 2–4 inches wide, are gray-green above marked with silvery white along the broad vein channels, and bright red below. The white, ½-inch-wide flowers are rarely produced indoors.

***B.* 'Corallina de Lucerna'** (sometimes called *B.* 'Lucerna') is a vigorous, bushy plant that grows to 6 feet tall. The bamboolike stems are green at first but turn woody and brown. Lance-shaped, glossy leaves 4–8 inches long and 2–4 inches wide are green with white spots above and deep red below. The deep pink to bright red, ½- to ¾-inch-wide flowers appear in pendent clusters of about 50 throughout most of the year.

B. luxurians (palm-leaf begonia) has fleshy, slightly hairy, red stems 2–3 feet tall and hairy, palmlike, light green leaves divided into as many as 17 lance-shaped leaflets 3–6 inches long and 1 inch wide. The creamy white, ½-inch-wide, hairy flowers seldom appear indoors.

B. maculata has much-branching bamboolike stems 2–3 feet tall, that are green when young but turn woody and brown. The lance-shaped, slightly tooth-edged leaves are up to 6 inches long and 4 inches wide, with rounded lobes at the top. Leaf color is dark green with silver markings above and crimson below. The ½-inch-wide, mostly pale pink flowers are carried on drooping, reddish flower stalks. Blooms may appear in all seasons, but are most abundant in summer. An attractive variety, *B.m.* 'Wightii,' has narrower, longer leaves with large silver spots and big white flowers.

B. metallica (metallic leaf begonia) is a hirsute begonia 3–4 feet tall. Its 6-inch-long and 4-inch-wide oval leaves are lobed, tooth-edged, and covered (as are the stems) with rough white hairs. Leaf color is olive green with a metallic gloss, and the deep-set veins are purple. The whitish, ½-inch-wide, summer-blooming flowers are covered with spiky pink hairs.

***B.* 'Preussen,'** has much-branching bamboolike stems that form a bush up to 18 inches tall. The pointed, heart-shaped leaves are 1½–2 inches long and wide, and bronze-green with some faint silver spotting. The continuously blooming pale pink flowers are about ½ inch across.

B. scharffii (often called *B. haageana*) is the most popular hairy-leaved begonia. Fleshy, upright stems 2–4 feet tall, and heart-shaped, acutely pointed leaves, are thickly felted with fine white hair. Each leaf is up to 10 inches long and 6 inches wide, olive green above and deep red below. Large clusters of white flowers 1–1½ inches wide bloom for most of the year. The petals are sprinkled with pink hairs.

B. schmidtiana is a creeping or trailing plant with fleshy, hairy stems up to 1 foot long. Heart-shaped, hairy leaves up to 3 inches long and wide are pale olive green with red vein areas above, and red underneath. Hairy, pale pink, ½-inch-wide flowers are produced continuously.

B. semperflorens-cultorum hybrids (often called *B. semperflorens* or wax begonias) are bushy plants with fleshy stems 6–15 inches tall, and waxy leaves. Leaves are roughly oval, 2–4 inches long, 1–3 inches wide, and any color from light green to bronzy red. The male flowers are ¾–1 inch across, with either a single layer, or several overlapping layers of petals. A mass of yellow stamens is usually visible in the center of flowers with only a few petals; in those with several layers the stamens are generally hidden behind the crowded petals. Female flowers are all single-layered, and the three-lobed ovary backing the petals looks extremely prominent. Flowers are produced continuously. They may be either white, pink or red. Popular *B. semperflorens-cultorum* hybrids include: *B.s.-c.* 'Dainty Maid' with shiny green leaves and many-petaled, white flowers with the outer petals tipped with pink; *B.s.-c.* 'Fiesta' with green leaves, and scarlet, single-layered flowers with prominent yellow stamens in the center of male blooms; *B.s.-c.* 'Gustav Lind' with shiny green leaves and many-petaled pink flowers; *B.s.-c.* 'Indian Maid' with bronze-colored leaves and single-layered, glowing, orange-pink flowers, with prominent yellow stamens in the male blooms; *B.s.-c.* 'Pink Camellia' with deep red-bronze leaves and many-petaled pink flowers.

B. semperflorens-cultorum (flowers)

***B.* 'Thurstonii'** has fleshy, red stems up to 2 feet tall, sparsely covered with white hairs. The almost round, hairless, glossy leaves up to 10 inches across are bronze-green on the upper surface and bright red underneath. The summer-blooming flowers are 1–1½ inches across, and pink with reddish hairs.

RECOMMENDED BEGONIAS: RHIZOMATOUS

B. boweri (eyelash begonia) is a bushy, stemless plant 6–9 inches tall. The small, heart-shaped leaves are deep emerald green, with black edging and with stiff hairs on leaf edges and leafstalks. Tiny, shell pink flowers are produced on 4- to 6-inch-long stalks in late winter and early spring.

B. deliciosa has fleshy, sturdy, erect, red stems up to 2 feet high. The deeply cut, much-lobed leaves are 6–10 inches long and up to 7 inches wide. They are red-tinged, olive green, heavily spotted with gray above, deep burgundy red below. The pink, 1-inch-wide, slightly fragrant flowers are produced in pairs from late summer through midwinter.

***B.* 'Erythrophylla'** (also called *B.* 'Feastii'; commonly known as pond-lily, kidney, or beefsteak begonia) is a hybrid up to 9 inches tall. This is an easy begonia to grow indoors. It has fleshy, shiny, almost round leaves 2–3 inches across that are olive green above, deep red below. Clusters of up to 30 light pink, ½-inch-wide flowers are produced in late winter and early spring. Two prized variants are: *B.* 'E. Bunchii' (lettuce-leaf begonia), with leaves crested and frilled at the margins; and *B.* 'E. Helix' (whirlpool begonia), with leaves in which overlapping basal lobes are spirally curled.

B. limmingheiana (often called *B. glaucophylla*) is a creeping, climbing, or trailing plant with light green, waxy, oval leaves up to 5 inches long and 3 inches wide. Brick red, winter-blooming flowers are 1 inch across.

***B.* 'Maphil'** (sometimes called *B.* 'Cleopatra') has many stems up to 6 inches tall, which carry star-shaped leaves 2 inches long and 1½ inches wide. Deeply divided into five pointed lobes and edged with bristly hairs, these leaves have red-spotted green leafstalks covered with white hairs. Leaf color is light chocolate brown, with major vein areas lined in greenish gold. Clusters of 10 or more pale pink flowers are produced on 12-inch-tall flower stalks in early spring.

B. masoniana (iron cross begonia) has heart-shaped leaves that are up to 6 inches long and wide, golden green, with a mahogany red, cross-shaped pattern in the center. Leaf surfaces are puckered, and covered with fine red hairs. Greenish, ¼-inch flowers with red hairs on petal undersides are comparatively rare indoors.

B. rex-cultorum hybrids (king, rex, or painted-leaf begonias) are grown for their extremely decorative foliage. The true *B. rex* species is probably no longer in cultivation. The leaves of most forms are obliquely heart-shaped and up to 12 inches long and 10 inches wide. They have 6- to 12-inch-long leafstalks arising directly from the rhizome. Some forms have sharply cut leaf edges, others have leaf lobes that are spirally curled. All have spectacular leaf coloring. Pale pink or white flowers ½ inch across sometimes appear in summer.

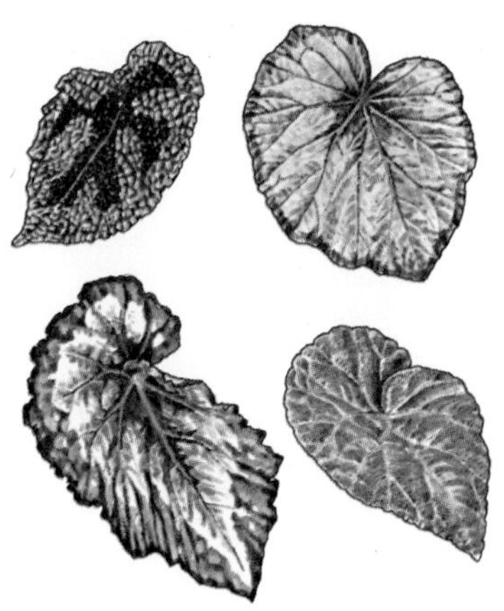

B. masoniana and *B. rex-cultorum* (leaves)

There are a number of dwarf or miniature forms of *B. rex-cultorum,* with a height of only a few inches and leaves as little as 3 inches long. The most suitable kinds of both full-size and dwarf plants for indoor use have crisp, thick, rough-textured leaves. Among the most satisfying forms are these: *B.r.-c.* 'King Edward IV,' which has large, reddish purple leaves with paler rose-pink spots; *B.r.-c.* 'Merry Christmas,' which has deep maroon-red leaves banded in pink, silver, and green; *B.r.-c.* 'President,' which has large, deep green leaves with extensive silver markings; and *B.r.-c.* 'Salamander,' which is a small, sturdy plant with almost totally silver leaves faintly threaded with deep green.

PROPER CARE: FIBROUS-ROOTED AND RHIZOMATOUS BEGONIAS

Light Fibrous-rooted and rhizomatous begonias grown primarily for their foliage need bright light without direct sunlight. Those grown principally for their flowers need three to four hours a day of direct sunlight.

Temperature Normal room temperatures are suitable for actively growing plants. Those that have a winter rest period should be kept at about 60°F—but not below 55°—during this period. All begonias suffer in dry air. For increased humidity stand pots on trays of moist pebbles, and suspend saucers of water under hanging baskets.

Watering Water actively growing plants moderately, allowing the top inch of the potting mixture to dry out before watering again. During any winter rest period water more sparingly, allowing the top half of the mixture to dry out between waterings.

Feeding Apply standard liquid fertilizer every two weeks to actively growing plants.

Potting and repotting Use either a peat-based potting mixture or a combination of equal parts of soil-based potting mixture (see page 429) and coarse leaf mold. Put an inch-deep layer of clay-pot fragments in the bottom of pots for extra drainage.

Move fibrous-rooted plants into pots one size larger every spring until maximum convenient pot size (probably 6–8 inches) has been reached. Thereafter, topdress annually with fresh potting mixture (see page 428). Rhizomatous begonias have shallow roots and are best planted in half-pots or pans. Move a small rhizomatous plant into the next size pot or pan only when the rhizome has grown across the entire surface of the potting mixture; do this preferably in spring. Discard aging rhizomatous begonias in favor of attractive new plants.

When potting or repotting a begonia, simply sprinkle some mixture around the roots, and tap the container briskly to settle the mixture. Do not firm it down with the fingers.

Propagation: fibrous-rooted kinds Take 3- to 4-inch-long cuttings of non-flowering shoots in spring or early summer. Trim each cutting immediately below a leaf, carefully remove the leaf, and dip the cut end of the stem in hormone rooting powder. Plant the cutting in a 3-inch pot of a moistened equal-parts mixture of peat moss and coarse sand or perlite, and enclose the whole in a plastic bag or propagating case (see page 443). Stand it in bright filtered light until renewed growth indicates that rooting has occurred (about three to six weeks). Uncover the rooted cutting, and begin to water it sparingly and to apply standard liquid fertilizer once every two weeks. Do not overwater, particularly not the hirsute begonias, which will rot if kept too wet. About six months after the start of propagation, move the young plant into a slightly larger pot of standard mixture, and treat it as a mature begonia.

Many of these begonias can also be propagated from seed. Seeds are very tiny and should not be buried when sown. Mix them with a little fine sand before sowing. (For raising plants from seed see page 441.)

Propagation: rhizomatous kinds Cut off 2- to 3-inch-long growing tips of rhizomes and treat them like stem cuttings of fibrous-rooted specimens (see above). Or, in spring, cut a rhizome into 2- to 3-inch-long sections, each with at least one growth point and treat cut ends of sections with sulfur dust. Plant each section half in and half out of slightly moistened rooting mixture in a 3-inch pot or pan. Use a rooting mix of equal-parts peat moss and coarse sand or perlite. Place the section either horizontally or vertically, depending on how the parent rhizome was growing in its container. Enclose each planted piece of rhizome in a plastic bag or propagating case (see page 443), and stand it in bright filtered light. Roots should form in four to six weeks. When two or three new leaves have appeared, uncover the little plant, repot it in an appropriate container of the recommended mixture for begonias, and treat it as a mature plant.

Most of the rhizomatous begonias named here can also be propagated every spring from leaf cuttings. (*B.* 'Erythrophylla' and *B. limmingheiana* are exceptions.) Take a healthy leaf with 1–2 inches of leafstalk attached, and plant the stalk at an angle of 45° in a small pot of the moistened rooting mixture recommended above (or insert several leaves in a small pan or seed tray). Enclose the whole in a plastic bag or propagating case, and stand it in bright filtered light. Rooting should occur in two to three weeks, and tiny plantlets should begin to appear from each leaf after a further two to three weeks. Several plantlets are generally clustered together. When each of them has produced at least two recognizable leaves, pot the plantlets up singly in 3-inch containers of the recommended potting mixture for mature begonias. Before treating the little plants as adults, however, dampen the mixture slightly and put the plants back in a plastic bag or propagating case for another four weeks. This will acclimatize them to normal room conditions.

Special points Some begonias—particularly *B.* 'Corallina de Lucerna,' *B. maculata,* and the tuberous *B. sutherlandii* (see opposite)—are susceptible to attack by powdery mildew, which shows up at first as small powder-coated spots on stems, leafstalks, and leaves (see page 456). As a preventive measure spray all begonias with a suitable fungicide at regular intervals (see page 459).

Tuberous begonias

Tuberous begonias are grown principally for their handsome flowers. Plants truly characteristic of the group have swollen underground stems (tubers) and are deciduous, with a period of total dormancy every year. Some kinds, however, do not lose their top growth in winter even though they are tuberous. They have a deep rest period. These plants are termed "semi-tuberous." There is a third group, composed entirely of winter-flowering plants (commonly called Christmas-flowering begonias), which are fibrous-rooted but have tuberous ancestors and the tuberous habit of dormancy after flowering. Plants of this type are usually grown as temporary indoor specimens, to be thrown away when flowering ceases.

See also BULBS, CORMS, and TUBERS.

RECOMMENDED BEGONIAS: TUBEROUS

B. cheimantha hybrids (Christmas-flowering or Lorraine begonias) are typical winter-flowering plants with fleshy, medium green stems up to 18 inches tall. Nearly round, glossy green leaves are 4–5 inches across. The pink flowers are often solitary, single-layered, and 2 inches across. Among the most popular are *B.c.* 'Gloire de Lorraine,' *B.c.* 'Lady Mac' (with white or pink flowers), and *B.c.* 'Melior.'

B. dregei (grapeleaf or mapleleaf begonia) is a semi-tuberous, bushy plant with erect, fleshy, red stems up to 3 feet tall. The maple-leaf-shaped, 3-inch-long and 4-inch-wide leaves are lightly toothed at the edges. Leaf color is light green with purple markings above, and reddish below. Small clusters of ½-inch-across, single-layered, white flowers are produced in spring and summer.

B. gracilis (hollyhock begonia) is a slender, erect-growing plant with a fleshy, rarely branching, green stem up to 2 feet tall. The fleshy, almost round, pale green leaves are scallop-edged and 2–3 inches across. Solitary, pink, single-layered flowers 1½ inches across appear on short stalks in summer. Mature plants require staking. All top growth dies down in early winter.

B. grandis (also called *B. evansiana;* commonly known as hardy begonia) has erect, fleshy stems, 2–3 feet tall. The much-branching stems are pale green, heavily marked at the nodes with red, and they carry glossy, heart-shaped leaves 3–4 inches long and 2–3 inches wide. Leaf color is medium green, with a ¼-inch red spot where the leaf joins the leafstalk, and with broad red markings around the veins on the underside. The pink, single-layered, fragrant flowers are up to 1 inch wide and appear in clusters of 10 or more on drooping flower stalks from late spring to fall. All top growth dies down in early winter.

B. hiemalis hybrids are typical winter-flowering plants, with red stems up to 18 inches tall. Among the most popular forms, known confusingly as *B.* 'Elatior' hybrids, are *B.h.* 'Fireglow' and *B.h.* 'Schwabenland.' Both have glossy, round, deep green leaves, 3 inches across. Their flowers are 2–2½ inches wide, single-layered, and bright red with a prominent yellow center.

B. sutherlandii has many delicate-looking, drooping, red stems, 15–18 inches long, that bear lance-shaped leaves 4–6 inches long and 2–4 inches wide. The leaves are bright green with fine red margins, and red leafstalks. Flowers are single-layered, coppery or salmon pink, and appear from early spring to late fall in clusters of 5 to 10. The top growth dies down completely when flowering stops.

B. tuberhybrida forms usually have fleshy, erect stems up to 1 inch thick and 15 inches tall, but a few hybrids have a trailing habit. The soft, easily damaged, pointed-oval leaves 6–9 inches long and 3–5 inches wide are dark green, but vein areas in some forms are a paler green. Flowers bloom in summer, normally in groups of three —one large male flower in between two smaller females—on 6-inch-long flower stalks arising from leaf axils. Male flowers are sometimes many-petaled and up to 6 inches across, whereas female flowers are single-layered and up to only 2 inches across. Flower color is white or any shade of pink, red, yellow, or orange. All *B. tuberhybrida* forms become totally dormant in winter.

***B.* 'Weltoniensis'** (the grapevine or summer lorraine begonia) is semi-tuberous with erect, much-branching, red stems up to 2½ feet tall. The roughly heart-shaped leaves grow 4 inches long and 3 inches across. They have a satiny gloss, are bright green with fine red veining and are held on 1½- to 3-inch-long leafstalks. Pink, ½-inch-wide, single-layered flowers are produced in small clusters from early spring to late fall.

PROPER CARE: TUBEROUS BEGONIAS

Light Give all tuberous begonias bright filtered light all year round. Light is not important during the dormant period for types that lose their top growth.

Temperature During the active growth period normal room temperatures are suitable. In temperatures above 65°F stand pots on trays of moist pebbles, or suspend saucers of water under hanging baskets. During the winter keep dormant forms at a temperature of about 55°. Semi-tuberous forms, which retain their foliage while resting, should ideally be kept at about 55° in bright filtered light during the winter. Winter-flowering begonias become totally dormant in summer, but they are best discarded after flowering.

Watering Water actively growing plants moderately, allowing the top inch of the mixture to dry out before watering again. As growth slows down, reduce amounts of water gradually. For the forms that lose their stems and foliage in winter, stop watering when the leaves begin to turn yellow. During the winter rest period of semi-tuberous types give just enough water to prevent the potting mixture from drying out.

Feeding Apply a high-potash liquid fertilizer to actively growing plants every two weeks.

Potting and repotting Use either a peat-based mixture or a combination of equal parts of soil-based mixture (see page 429) and coarse leaf mold. Put an inch-deep layer of clay-pot fragments in the bottom of pots for extra drainage. When potting or repotting, simply sprinkle some mixture around the tuber and roots, and tap the container briskly to settle the mixture. Start the tubers of *B. tuberhybrida* forms into growth in early spring by planting several in shallow trays of moistened peat moss, setting the tubers (with the concave side upward) half in and half out of the peat moss.

You may wonder which way up to plant a dormant tuber. Shoots emerge from the hollow, which should therefore face upward.

Stand each tray in bright filtered light for about three or four weeks, when 2 inches of top growth will have been made. Then move each specimen into a 3- or 4-inch pot of the recommended mixture for adult plants. The dormant tubers of other forms are smaller, and can be planted directly in 3- to 4-inch pots of the recommended mixture. Thereafter, treat all forms as mature tuberous begonias. The large-flowered hybrids may need to be moved into larger pots two or three times during the summer, but most other kinds can spend the entire season in the same container.

The semi-tuberous begonias should be moved into pots one size larger each spring. When repotting always keep the tuberous swelling at the same level in the mixture. After maximum convenient pot size (probably 6–8 inches) has been reached, topdress annually with fresh mixture (see page 428). Winter-flowering begonias are normally bought as young plants and do not need moving on into larger pots during their short stay in the home.

Propagation The best way to propagate *B. gracilis, B. grandis,* and *B. sutherlandii* is from the small tubers—usually known as bulbils—that appear in leaf axils in the fall. Detach these bulbils when top growth dies down. Store them in a container at about 55°F until the following spring. Then plant each bulbil in a 2- or 3-inch pot of the recommended potting mixture, just covering the bulbil with moistened mixture. Stand the pot in bright filtered light, and at first water only enough to make the mixture barely moist, but gradually increase the amount. Treat the rooted bulbil as a mature plant when it has made 3 inches of top growth. It will not reach full size or flower profusely until its second year.

B. sutherlandii *develops bulbils in some of its leaf axils during the fall. These can be detached and used for propagation.*

B. dregei and *B.* 'Weltoniensis,' the semi-tuberous forms, are normally propagated from 2- to 3-inch-long tip cuttings of new growth taken in late spring or summer. Trim each cutting immediately below a leaf, dip the cut end in hormone rooting powder, and plant it in a 2- or 3-inch pot containing a moistened equal-parts mixture of peat moss and coarse sand or perlite. Enclose the whole in a plastic bag or propagating case (see page 443), and stand it in bright filtered light. After rooting occurs (generally in three to four weeks), treat the rooted cutting as a mature begonia, but do not move it into the recommended potting mixture for mature plants until it has made at least 6 inches of top growth. (Winter-flowering begonias can also be propagated from tip cuttings, but this is a difficult process not recommended for amateur gardeners.)

To propagate *B. tuberhybrida* forms cut a large tuber into two or more sections in spring, making sure that each has a growing point. Treat the cut ends of sections with sulfur dust, and pot each one exactly as if it were a whole tuber (see "Potting and repotting," above).

Special points At the end of the growing season, the stems and leaves of deciduous begonias will gradually fall off. Do not pull away the stems since this could damage the tubers.

For susceptibility of these plants to mildew, see "Special points" for the fibrous-rooted and rhizomatous begonias, above.

Beloperone

ACANTHACEAE

Shrimp plant
B. guttata

ONE species of the genus *Beloperone, B. guttata* (also called *Drejerella guttata* or *Justicia brandegeana*), has become a common house plant. It is popularly known as shrimp plant because of its drooping, shrimp-like flower spikes. The most prominent parts of these spikes are terminal bracts, which are heart-shaped, reddish brown or pink, and up to 1 inch long. The bracts almost conceal white flowers that protrude from between them. The 4- to 5-inch-long flower spikes are produced continuously during the growing season, which lasts for as much as 10 months a year. The leaves, which have 1- to $1\frac{1}{2}$-inch-long leafstalks and are carried on upright woody stems, are 1–3 inches long, oval, fresh green, and slightly hairy.

Unless *B. guttata* is kept well trimmed, it tends to become a rather untidy shrub; also, if it is left alone, it usually grows over 2 feet tall. It therefore needs cutting back annually if it is to hold its shape and remain a manageable size at the same time (see "Special points").

There is also a rarer form with yellow bracts, *B.g.* 'Yellow Queen.' And a so-far-unnamed variety with dark red bracts is worth looking out for as well.

PROPER CARE

Light Bright light with some direct sunlight is essential for satisfactory production of the colorful bracts.

Temperature Normally warm room temperatures suit this plant, but too much heat makes for soft and spindly growth. The recommended winter temperature is 65°F.

Watering Water sparingly— enough to make the potting mixture barely moist, and allowing the top two-thirds of the mixture to dry out between waterings.

Feeding From late winter to early fall only, use standard liquid fertilizer once every two weeks.

Potting and repotting Use a soil-based potting mixture (see page 429) with the addition of a one-third portion of peat moss. Move these plants into pots one size larger every spring until maximum convenient size— probably 6 inches—has been reached. Thereafter, topdress annually (see page 428).

Propagation Tip cuttings 2–3 inches long will root easily in spring. Insert each cutting in a small pot containing a moistened mixture of equal parts of peat moss and coarse sand or perlite, enclose the pot in a plastic bag, and keep it in bright filtered light. Rooting should occur in six to eight weeks. To produce a bushy plant, pot three or four cuttings together in the recommended potting mixture for mature beloperones; water sparingly, and do not move the pot into direct sunlight for another month or two.

Special points Apart from periodical pinching out of growing points to encourage bushy growth, mature beloperones require cutting back annually. Cut away up to half the top growth (down to any leaf axil) just as the plant begins to make new growth in the spring.

The shape of a beloperone will benefit if as much as half of the top growth is cut back each year.

Bertolonia

MELASTOMATACEAE

B. marmorata aenea

THE small genus *Bertolonia* consists of creeping plants that have extremely decorative foliage with metallic coloring. The stems that crawl over the surface of the potting mixture turn upward toward the tips, but the plants never grow over 6 inches high. The oval to heart-shaped leaves are furry, often with a bristly upper surface, and always colored deep red or purple on the underside. Five-petaled pink or purple flowers are ½–1 inch in diameter and open singly on stiff stalks 3–4 inches long.

RECOMMENDED BERTOLONIAS

B. maculata has broadly oval leaves 2–3 inches long covered with coarse, bristly hair. The upper surface is velvety olive green with light moss green shading, thin reddish margins, and faint silvery green "feathering" that follows the veins in the center. Half-inch-wide, rose-colored flowers appear in batches several times a year.

B. marmorata has nearly pointed, heart-shaped leaves 5–8 inches long, which arch slightly toward the tips; they are vivid green, with a slightly satiny texture and—usually—five broad, silvery white lines running lengthwise along the veins on the upper surface. Purplish flowers, up to 1 inch across, appear at intervals throughout the year. A variety, *B.m. aenea*, has leaves of a coppery tinge and almost no silvery white markings.

PROPER CARE

Light Bertolonias need medium light. Avoid direct sunlight.

Temperature These plants like normal room temperatures and high humidity. Stand them on trays of damp pebbles but do not spray the foliage since water lodging on leaves can cause unsightly markings. Bertolonias are excellent for terrariums or plant windows (see page 53).

Watering During the active growth period water plentifully, keeping the mixture thoroughly moist. In the rest period water only enough to keep the mixture from drying out.

Feeding Apply standard liquid fertilizer every two weeks in the active growth period only.

Potting and repotting Use a potting mixture composed of equal parts of peat moss, leaf mold, and coarse sand or perlite. Bertolonias do best in small pots, half-pots, or shallow pans. Move small plants into larger containers only when leafy stems have covered the surface area and are trailing over the edges of the pots or pans.

Propagation Take tip cuttings in early spring. Plant each cutting in a small pot filled with slightly moistened potting mixture (as recommended above for mature plants), enclose the pots in plastic bags and stand them in medium light. Rooting should occur in six weeks. Thereafter, treat the bertolonias as mature.

Billbergia

BROMELIACEAE

BILLBERGIAS are the easiest and most adaptable bromeliads for indoor use. They usually have only five to eight narrow, stiff, sword-shaped leaves arranged in a tube-shaped rosette, of which the upper half flares outward. In some species the entire rosette is loose and looks thin, but in others it is tight enough to form a water-storing cup. The foliage and flower heads of the many kinds of billbergia vary considerably in size, shape, and coloring. But the flowers are generally tubular, have petals that arch outward, are backed with papery-looking bracts, and live for no more than a week or two. There is no regular flowering season for billbergias, which may bloom at any time of year. Nor do they have an annual rest period. Given adequate warmth, they will grow continuously.

See also BROMELIADS.

RECOMMENDED BILLBERGIAS

B. amoena rubra has leaves that are 2 feet long and 1½ inches wide arranged in a fairly tight rosette. Leaf color is rich red-bronze spotted with white and yellow. The leaves in the inner part of the rosette are blunt-ended, giving the impression of having been cut straight across. The pendent flowers are blue or blue-green, up to 3 inches long, and backed with very small, red bracts.

B. decora has 1½- to 2-foot-long and 2-inch-wide leaves arranged in a tight, tall rosette; they are gray-green dusted with mealy white cross-bands and edged with short brown spines. The drooping flower spike, also covered with white powder, carries small, greenish flowers, partly hidden by 3- to 5-inch-long, bright pink bracts.

B. distachia has leaves 18 inches long and 1½ inches wide; they are mid-green tinged with purple and covered with white scurf. The plant produces a number of rosettes, which cluster together. The pendent flowers are 2½ inches long, green tipped with blue, and backed with 3-inch-long, rose-pink bracts.

B. 'Fantasia' is a hybrid with leaves 15 inches long and 2–3 inches wide; they are splashed with cream and pink on coppery green. The blue flowers, carried on an upright spike, are 2–3 inches long, as are the red bracts.

Queen's-tears
Billbergia nutans

B. horrida gets its name from the menacing, $\frac{1}{4}$-inch-long, dark-colored spines that arm the leaf edges. The upright leaves, which do not arch or flare out as do those of most billbergias, are around 15 inches long and 2 inches wide; their color is mid-green with rather blurred, crosswise, gray stripes. The erect flower spike carries 2-inch-long, blue-tipped, pale green flowers and 2-inch-long, rose-red bracts. Unlike the flowers of most billbergias, these are fragrant, though only at night. There is a red-leaved form, *B.h.* 'Tigrina,' with bands of white scurf running along the underside of the leaves.

B. iridifolia has silvery gray leaves up to 12 inches long and $\frac{3}{4}$ inch wide, which curl at the ends. The 1-inch-long flowers, borne on drooping flower heads, have red sepals and yellow, blue-tipped petals, and the 3- to 4-inch-long bracts are rose-red.

B. nutans, known as friendship plant or queen's-tears, is the most popular of all bromeliads. Its arching leaves are 10–15 inches long and $\frac{1}{2}$ inch wide. Their olive green color may become reddish if the plant is grown in full sunlight. The 1-inch-long, pendent flowers have pink, blue-edged sepals and yellowish green, blue-edged petals, and they are backed with 2- to 3-inch-long pink bracts.

B. venezuelana, a robust, strikingly handsome plant, has 3-foot-long, 3-inch-wide leaves that are held in a rigid, upright rosette. They are deep green mottled with maroon and cross-banded with thin, silvery stripes. The flower spike, which may be 12 inches long, hangs on a long stalk that emerges through a gap between the leaves about halfway up the rosette, and the weight of the numerous flowers bears the spike down toward the base of the plant. Each flower is nearly 3 inches long and colored brilliant green with white sepals, and the 5- to 6-inch-long bracts are flared and bright pink.

B. venezuelana

B. vittata also has leaves 3 feet long and 3 inches wide arranged in an upright rosette. Leaf color is olive green to purplish brown, cross-banded with silvery white and lightly sprinkled with grayish scurf. The flowers, which are carried in a large, drooping head, are 2–3 inches long and have dark blue sepals and green, violet-tipped petals. The bright red bracts are 4 inches long.

B. zebrina is similar in shape and size to *B. venezuelana* and *B. vittata,* but its leaves are purple-bronze cross-banded with silvery scurf. The drooping flower stalk carries a large head of $1\frac{1}{2}$-inch-long flowers, which have green to yellowish green petals, backed with 2-inch-long pink bracts.

PROPER CARE

Light Bright light with at least three or four hours of direct sunlight every day is essential for good leaf color and regular flowering.

Temperature Billbergias grow well in normal room temperatures. *B. nutans* can also tolerate quite cold temperatures (down to 45°F).

Watering Throughout the year, water moderately, enough to make the mixture thoroughly moist, but allow the top half-inch of the mixture to dry out between waterings. In billbergias that form a water-holding cup in the center of the rosette, the cup should be kept topped up with fresh water. Central cups should be emptied (by turning plants upside down) and refilled with fresh water once a month. Rain or naturally soft water is most suitable for billbergias.

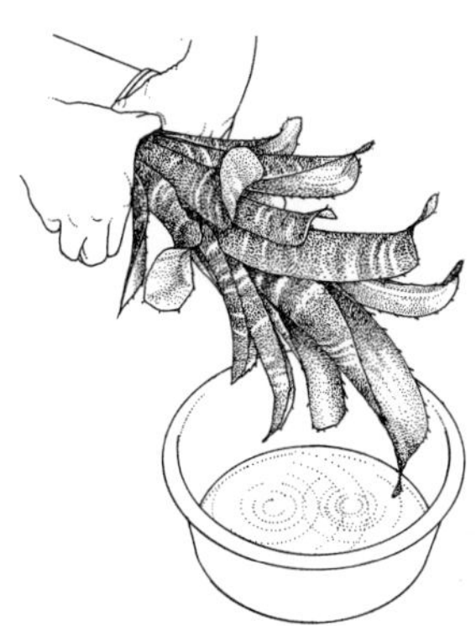

Empty the rosette centers of billbergias such as B. vittata *monthly in order to prevent unpleasant odor from stagnant water.*

Feeding Apply standard liquid fertilizer every two weeks. Let the liquid not only penetrate the potting mixture but splash over leaves and lodge in central cups.

Potting and repotting Billbergias are the least demanding of bromeliads where potting mixture is concerned; they grow well in either the standard bromeliad mixture (see page 107) or in an equal-parts combination of soil-based mixture (see page 429) and leaf mold. Because their roots are not extensive, they can be accommodated in relatively small pots. A 5-inch pot will allow several rosettes producing several flower heads to develop, but billbergias of a tall, tubular shape often look best when grown as single specimens. It is best to plant these latter types in heavy clay pots rather than plastic ones, to avoid the possibility of their being knocked over. Young plants of all kinds should be moved into pots one size larger in early spring when necessary.

Propagation Propagate in the spring by means of offsets, but do not remove them until they are 4–6 inches long and have begun to assume the characteristics of the parent plant. Very young offsets rarely root successfully. Plant offsets shallowly (retaining any roots that may already have developed) in small pots of bromeliad mixture, and place them in medium light. It may be necessary to insert a thin stake as support for an offset until it develops enough roots to anchor it down. Make the potting mixture barely moist, allowing the top inch or two of the mixture to dry out between waterings. Firm rooting is likely to occur in eight weeks. Thereafter, treat the plants in exactly the same way as mature billbergias.

Blechnum

POLYPODIACEAE

B. gibbum

THE genus *Blechnum* includes many very different kinds of fern, from small creepers to slow-growing upright plants that eventually develop a trunk and are not unlike true tree ferns. Those most commonly grown indoors tend to be of tropical or semitropical origin, since such ferns do well in fairly warm rooms and are more tolerant of a certain amount of dry air than are most others. Blechnums, like some other ferns, have both sterile and spore-bearing fronds. On mature plants the fronds are deeply divided into numerous pinnae.

See also FERNS.

RECOMMENDED BLECHNUMS

B. brasiliense (also known as *B. corcovadense*), the Brazil tree fern, begins life as a loose rosette of heavy lance-shaped fronds radiating from a brown central core. After some years it produces a dark brown scaly trunk up to 3 feet tall, topped by fronds up to 3 feet long and 1 foot wide. Each frond is divided into many paired leathery pinnae, which are coppery when young but turn mid-green with age. There is also a form *B.b.* 'Crispum,' with smaller, undulate fronds, which are usually red when they are young.

B. gibbum (formerly called *Lomaria gibbum*) is the most popular blechnum. It has a neat, symmetrical rosette of fronds up to 3 feet long and 1 foot wide, which eventually crowns a scaly, black trunk up to 3 feet tall. The many pinnae of each frond are shiny green and slightly drooping. There are several forms distinguished by having either narrower, wider, or more pointed pinnae. One smaller plant that is generally labeled *B. moorei*—with fronds only about 1 foot long—is regarded by some authorities as a form of *B. gibbum* rather than as a separate species.

B. occidentale (hammock fern) has creeping underground rhizomes and somewhat arching, rich green fronds up to 18 inches long and 5 inches wide. The fronds taper to a narrow point. The midrib of each frond is notably paler than the rest of it.

PROPER CARE

Light Bright light, but without any strong direct sunlight, is most suitable for blechnums.

Temperature These blechnums grow best in warm—not hot—rooms. Though tolerant of dry air, the plants should be given as much humidity as possible during the active growth period from mid-spring to late fall. Stand pots on trays of moist pebbles throughout the warmer months. With the resultant adequate humidity, they will tolerate temperatures slightly above 75°F. Lower temperatures are better in winter, though. Around 60° is ideal, but blechnums can even stand 50° if kept fairly dry.
Watering Water actively growing plants plentifully, as often as necessary to keep the mixture thoroughly moist, but never allow the pot to stand in water. If the temperature falls below 55°F water moderately, allowing the top half-inch of the mixture to dry out between waterings.
Feeding One or two applications of half-strength liquid fertilizer during the active growth period will suffice.
Potting and repotting Use equal parts of soil-based potting mixture and leaf mold (see page 429). Move plants into pots one size larger only when roots begin to appear on the surface of the mixture (about once every two years). Put a layer of clay-pot fragments in the bottom of pots for drainage, and add small chunks of charcoal to keep the mixture sweet.
Propagation Commercially, blechnums are grown from spores and sold as small plants, and this is often the only way to obtain specimens of *B. brasiliense* and *B. gibbum*. Occasionally, however, plants of these two species produce basal offsets, which can be detached from the parents, potted up, and treated as mature plants. With *B. occidentale,* the underground rhizome may be divided with hand forks, and each section repotted separately.

To propagate B. occidentale, *simply remove the plant from its pot and use hand forks to split the rhizome into sections. You can then repot the sections separately.*

Bougainvillea

NYCTAGINACEAE

Paper flower
B. glabra

BOUGAINVILLEAS (or paper flowers) are vigorous subtropical woody plants armed with spines. Though normally climbers—as seen outdoors in warm climates—they can be trained to keep bushy indoors, and there are some recently introduced dwarf-growing kinds that remain bushy without special attention. Their oval leaves are sparse and uninteresting, but they have decorative papery bracts surrounding small cream-colored flowers. Under good conditions these colorful bracts, which are mainly produced in spring and summer, persist for several weeks—and even longer for dwarf kinds. The bracts may be white, yellow, orange, pink, red or purple, and they usually appear in clusters of 10 to 20.

Bougainvilleas are not easy to grow indoors. Because they require better conditions than are normally available, they are grown most successfully in plant windows (see page 53). In naturally warmer areas they will do well in sunrooms or conservatories.

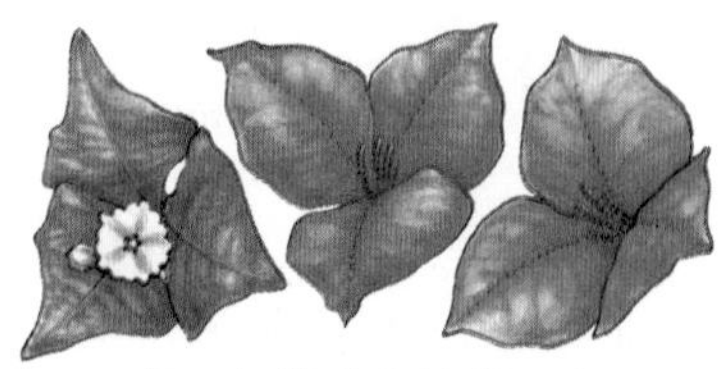

Bougainvillea hybrids (bracts)

RECOMMENDED BOUGAINVILLEAS

B. buttiana has given rise to a number of hybrid bougainvilleas, which are now the most popular forms. Because they are less vigorous than the species, they are more easily trained into shrub form and accommodated in the average-size room, where they can be kept for years in 6- to 8-inch pots. Best known are 'Mrs. Butt' (also called 'Crimson Lake'), with rose-crimson bracts; 'Brilliant,' with coppery orange bracts; and 'Temple Fire,' whose brick red bracts deepen in color as the flowering season progresses.
B. glabra is a vigorous climbing species, which flowers at an earlier age than most kinds. Purple or magenta bracts are produced in late summer and fall, and the varieties include other colors. Several variegated kinds are available. Two that are especially attractive: *B.g.* 'Harrisii,' with cream streaks along leaf-center and vein areas; *B.g.* 'Sanderana Variegata,' with leaves bordered in creamy white.

PROPER CARE

Light In order to bloom, bougainvilleas need at least four hours of direct sunlight every day during the active growth period, and they must have bright light at other times.

Temperature Normal room temperatures are suitable during the active growth period. In the winter rest period they should be kept cool—but not below 50°F.

Watering Water actively growing plants moderately, giving enough to moisten the mixture thoroughly; allow the top two-thirds to dry out between waterings. Amounts should be drastically reduced as the rest period approaches, and the mixture should just be kept from drying out during the winter rest.

Feeding Begin applications of standard liquid fertilizer as soon as growth starts in early spring, and continue once every two weeks throughout the flowering period.

Potting and repotting Use a soil-based potting mixture (see page 429), with a little extra peat moss well mixed in. Move young plants into pots one size larger in early spring. Older plants growing in the maximum convenient pot size— around 8 inches—should be topdressed (see page 428) with fresh potting mixture.

Propagation Home propagation should not be attempted unless the grower has a heated propagating case (see page 444). Cuttings of new growth 6 inches long may be taken in spring. After dipping the cut ends into hormone rooting powder, insert them in a moistened equal-parts mixture of soil-based potting mixture and coarse sand or perlite. The potted cuttings should then be placed in the propagating case and kept at 75°F in bright filtered light. Roots will form in eight weeks, after which plants can be repotted in standard mixture.

Special points Bougainvilleas in plant windows may make considerable growth—up to 6 feet—in one season, and at least a third of the season's growth should be cut away in early spring. At the same time, overlong shoots should be spur-pruned (cut back to leave just two or three growth buds on each shoot).

Bougainvilleas normally lose their leaves for a short period in winter. When conditions are not right for them indoors, leaf loss is likely to occur at any time.

Brassaia

ARALIACEAE

Queensland umbrella tree
B. actinophylla

THE house plant correctly called *Brassaia actinophylla* is more generally known by the earlier name *Schefflera actinophylla.* The plant is prized for its tough, shiny foliage, which radiates from a central point like the spokes of an umbrella. This explains its common names, Queensland umbrella tree, or starleaf. The five to seven leaflets of which each long-stalked leaf is composed are elongated ovals, each up to 12 inches long and shiny light olive green in color. A brassaia remains a manageable indoor shrub up to about 6 feet tall if given a good root run in a large container, or a smaller shrublet if kept in an 8-inch pot. Flowers are not normally produced indoors.

PROPER CARE

Light Provide bright light without direct sunlight.

Temperature The ideal temperature is 60°–65°F, but brassaias will do well in warmer rooms as long as the air is reasonably humid. In temperatures below 55° the leaflets may fall.

Watering During the active growth period water moderately, enough to make the potting mixture thoroughly moist, but allow the top two-thirds of the mixture to dry out between waterings. During the rest period water only enough to keep the mixture from drying out.

Feeding Apply standard liquid fertilizer every two weeks during the active growth period.

Potting and repotting Use a soil-based potting mixture (see page 429). Move plants into pots one size larger annually in early spring. After maximum convenient pot size has been reached, plants should be topdressed annually (see page 428).

Propagation Brassaias are usually propagated from seed, which must be fresh and needs bottom heat in order to germinate. This process, therefore, is best left to the professional. It is also possible to air layer these plants (see page 440).

Special points The large, shiny leaves of brassaias should be cleaned regularly with a damp sponge.

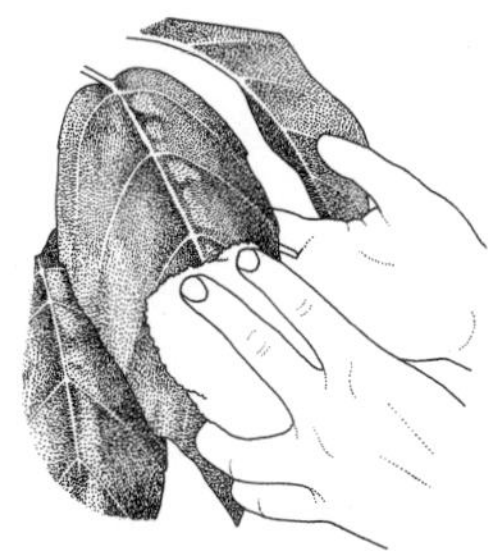

To keep the pores of brassaia leaves free of dust, make a point of sponging the leaves every two weeks.

Brassia
ORCHIDACEAE

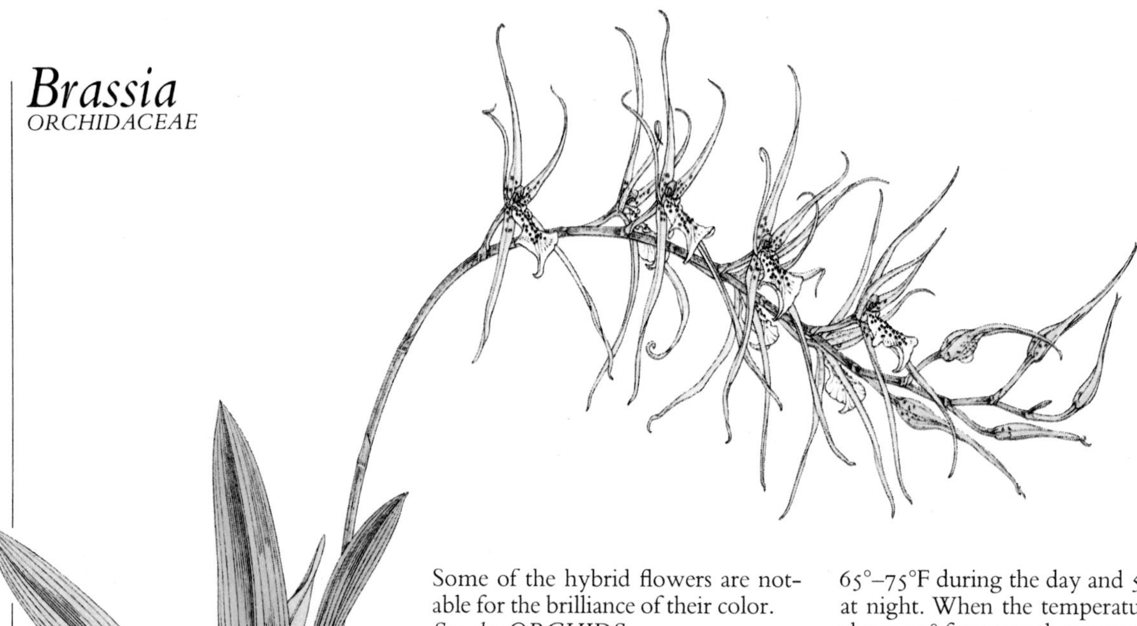

B. verrucosa

BRASSIAS are epiphytic orchids with unusually shaped flowers. Upright egg-shaped or cylindrical pseudobulbs are topped with two or three thick, leathery, narrowly elliptic, dark green leaves. Flower stems of all the species recommended here rise from the base of the pseudobulb. Each slightly arching stem carries a closely spaced row of flowers along its upper part. The distinguishing feature of brassia flowers is the extraordinary shape of the sepals and petals. They are so long and narrow, tapering to a point from such a narrow base, that each sepal or petal resembles a tail. The short lip often hangs down between the lower sepals, looking more like a tongue than a tail. Flowers are longer than they are broad. Because of the strange shape of their flowers brassias are sometimes called spider orchids.

There are a number of intergeneric hybrids with *Brassia* as one parent. Some of the hybrid flowers are notable for the brilliance of their color.
See also ORCHIDS.

RECOMMENDED BRASSIAS

B. caudata has cylindrical, usually yellowish green pseudobulbs, from 3–6 inches high and 1 inch wide, which carry two or three leaves 7–9 inches long and 2½ inches wide. Flower stems up to 18 inches tall can bear up to 12 fragrant flowers in late summer. Individual flowers are up to 5 inches long and 3 inches across. The sepals and petals are light greenish yellow spotted and barred with brown, especially near the base. The nearly triangular lip is light yellow with reddish brown spots.

B. verrucosa has flattened-egg-shaped, medium green pseudobulbs about 3 inches tall and 2½ inches wide. Each pseudobulb carries two leaves about 15 inches long and 2 inches wide. The flower stem, which can be 1–3 feet long, bears up to 16 fragrant blooms in spring and early summer. Each flower grows up to 5–6 inches long and 4 inches across. Some forms, with flowers 8–10 inches long and 4–5 inches across, are sometimes thought to be a separate species and are given the name *B. brachiata.* The sepals and petals are pale green spotted with dark green, red, or brownish purple, mainly near the base. The roughly diamond-shaped lip is white with dark green, wartlike spots.

PROPER CARE

Light Give brassias bright filtered light all year long. Never expose these orchids to direct sunlight.

Temperature Ideally, the year-long range of temperature should be 65°–75°F during the day and 50°–60° at night. When the temperature rises above 75° for more than two or three days at a time, stand containers on trays of moist pebbles, or suspend water-filled saucers below plants in hanging baskets or growing epiphytically on supports. In addition, mist-spray the foliage daily.

Watering Water actively growing brassias moderately, giving enough to thoroughly moisten the potting mixture at each watering, but let two-thirds of the mixture dry out before watering again. After flowering has ceased, encourage these plants to rest for a short time (about three weeks). During this rest period give only enough water to keep the mixture from completely drying out or the pseudobulbs from shriveling.

Feeding Give all actively growing plants a foliar feed at half strength with every third or fourth watering.

Potting and repotting Any of the potting mixtures recommended for orchids will be suitable (see page 289). Brassias can be grown in pots or baskets, or they can be grown epiphytically on a wooden support. Move plants into containers two sizes larger whenever more room for new pseudobulbs is required—about once in two or three years. The best time for repotting is spring.

Propagation Divide plants with sufficient pseudobulbs in the spring. Cut the rhizome into two or more segments, making sure that each section carries at least two pseudobulbs. Plant each segment in a 3- or 4-inch container or attach it to a support, and water very sparingly until new growth appears. Thereafter, treat the growing plant as a mature brassia.

BROMELIADS

Bromeliads are mainly tropical, rosette-forming plants that differ from most other flowering plants in that they absorb their food and moisture largely through leaves rather than roots. The main kinds of bromeliad are characterized below, along with general advice on proper care. A list of popular indoor genera follows this article. Consult separate articles for further details.

Bromeliads (airplants) are members of the family *Bromeliaceae*. These tropical or subtropical plants vary widely in shape and size. Even species of a single genus often differ drastically in appearance. Most bromeliads cultivated as house plants, however, are alike in being stemless, with strap-shaped, leathery, arching leaves arranged in a rosette, and with a central flower spike on a relatively long stalk.

The rosette may be just a loose open circle of leaves, or it may be more tubelike. In many bromeliads the leaves sheathe one another to form a cuplike, watertight vessel. In the wild, rainwater and dew collect in the cup, and the plants draw their water and food needs from this reservoir during dry periods. Bromeliads are unique among plants in that they need to have water around the growing point (situated at the center of the rosette). Water lodging permanently in the heart of any other non-aquatic plant would eventually kill it.

The majority of bromeliads grown as house plants are epiphytic, living on the trunks and branches of trees. Some attach themselves to rocks. The rest grow in the ground as most plants do. Within the same genus there are sometimes tree-dwelling, ground-dwelling, and rock-dwelling species. In fact, epiphytic and terrestrial bromeliads can often thrive equally well if forced to switch places and life styles. It is this ability, in particular, that allows some epiphytic kinds to be grown in pots like most other plants.

Practically all these plants have leaves capable of absorbing airborne plant food in addition to any that may be taken in through the roots. Even the minute scales that cover the leaves of some types are themselves able to take in food materials and moisture. In fact, many bromeliads have entirely ceased to rely on roots for their nourishment. Such plants now either produce no roots or use the few that they do produce as anchorage rather than for feeding.

The flowers of bromeliads, which can bloom at almost any time of year, are usually striking and brilliantly colored, and they are often partly encased in highly decorative, usually bright red or pink bracts. In some bromeliads the blooms rise barely above the average level of water stored in the cup of the rosette. Individual flowers are rarely bigger than ½ inch across, and they appear in succession on a broad, stalkless flower head. The leaves, or portions of leaves, at the rosette center often become bright-colored (usually red or purple) just before and during the flowering period. The brilliant coloring is nature's way of attracting pollinating insects and birds to the flowers.

Other bromeliads have a different type of floral arrangement consisting of a long, erect and sturdy flower spike that pushes up from the rosette center. The spike is topped by a bold, usually brightly colored flower head bearing flowers that are normally only ½ inch across but surrounded by brightly colored bracts. The leaves do not change their color during the flowering period.

Flowers of all bromeliads tend to be short-lived. The bracts of the long-stalked kinds and the striking leaf coloration of the others remain attractive for several weeks, however. Moreover, flowers of some kinds are followed by colorful berries. These normally remain attractive for several months before they shrivel and fall off.

As a rule, each rosette of leaves flowers only once and then slowly dies. The only exceptions among the bromeliads grown as house plants are the dyckias, the rosettes of which continue to grow. In all others the rosette remains attractive for several

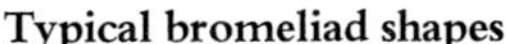

Typical bromeliad shapes

Although bromeliads are enormously varied, two types of rosette predominate: a loosely circular clump of leaves, as exemplified by tillandsias (top); and a tight-packed clump with a central cup, as seen in many cryptanthuses (bottom).

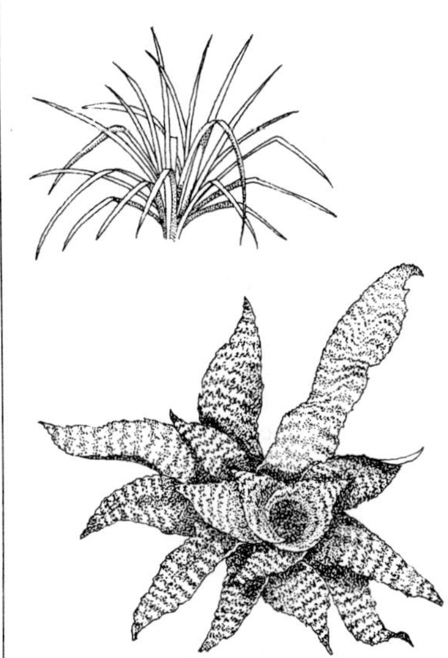

Flower arrangements

Flowers can half-hide in rosette cups, as in neoregelias (top), can emerge from upright, close-packed bracts, as in tillandsias (bottom left), or can be drooping, as in billbergias (right).

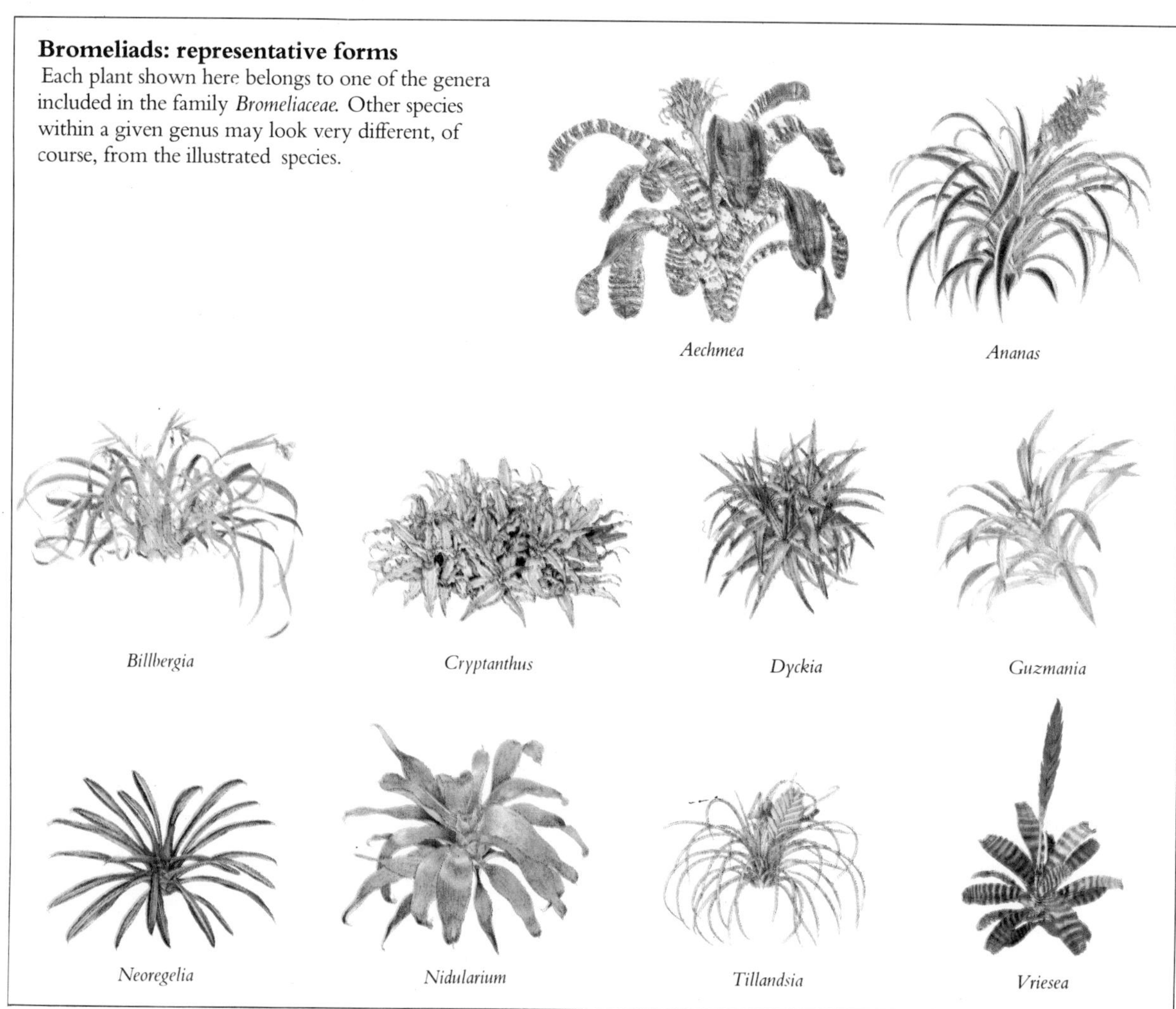

Bromeliads: representative forms

Each plant shown here belongs to one of the genera included in the family *Bromeliaceae.* Other species within a given genus may look very different, of course, from the illustrated species.

months before it finally yellows and dries up. Well before this time, however, offsets will have replaced the dying rosette.

Bromeliads flower only when they are mature. It may take as long as 20 years for some kinds to reach maturity. The most popular indoor bromeliads generally flower relatively early, when they are no more than two or three years old.

Epiphytic bromeliads

As each young epiphytic bromeliad grows it sends down wiry roots over the surface of the tree, clinging to the bark. The plant lives and grows not only by absorbing water and food from the atmosphere, but also by taking nourishment from any detritus (fallen leaves and other debris) that accumulates between the leaves. The roots of these bromeliads are used for support only.

Epiphytic bromeliads that grow on the lower parts of tree trunks in the wild tend to have soft and pliable leaves. Leaves of species that naturally grow closer to the tops of trees are likely to be harder and more leathery. The difference comes from the degrees of light and shade at different heights within the forest, and this helps to indicate the indoor lighting preferences of plants. Soft, thin-leaved bromeliads generally do best in bright filtered light, which suggests subdued or dappled light. Brighter light, including some direct sunlight, is better for plants with more leathery leaves.

Non-epiphytic bromeliads

The bromeliads that grow on the ground or in rock fissures normally live in open, warm, sunny places. Because they grow in exposed positions and are prey to grazing animals, many of them are armed with sharp spines and hooked teeth on the leaf edges. In this respect they resemble cacti and some succulents.

The rosettes are usually far more open and much less capable of storing water than are the rosettes of the epiphytes. Some (certain of the cryptanthuses, for example) have only five or six pointed leaves, which grow in a star shape against the ground. Some do not even have their leaves arranged in rosette shape. Most, though, are quite easily recognizable as bromeliads.

The best-known non-epiphytic bromeliad is the edible pineapple (*Ananas comosus*). It is also the only one grown as a commercial crop.

PROPER CARE

Light As was emphasized above, epiphytic bromeliads need either bright filtered light without direct sunlight or bright light with several hours a day of direct sunlight, depending on the texture of their leaves. For specific recommendations consult appropriate entries in the *A–Z Guide.* Terrestrial and rock-dwelling types generally require the brightest possible light to bring out the best leaf coloration and encourage flowering.

When light intensity is low or day length very short, bromeliads will usually stop growing and take a rest. However, they do not appear to grow as quickly during the long days of intense summer light as they do in spring and fall. There is no cause for concern about light, therefore, if a plant takes a brief summer rest.

Temperature Normally warm room temperatures are suitable for all bromeliads throughout the year. The thinner-leaved species in particular will die if exposed to temperatures below about 55°F. Even the few kinds (such as some billbergias) that can tolerate lower winter temperatures, will not react well to a prolonged period below 55°. Some leaf damage is inevitable after more than a few days of such temperatures.

Along with a fairly constant level of warmth, nearly all of these plants require high humidity when actively growing. Stand pots on trays of moist pebbles. In addition, whenever room temperatures remain above 65° for more than a day or two, mist-spray the foliage daily. During the warmer months it is advisable to put plants outdoors for an hour or so whenever there is a gentle rain. This permits them to take in moisture through their leaves. It is also beneficial in that the rain will wash away any accumulation of dust on the surfaces of the leaves.

Watering In those bromeliads with a central water-retaining cup, it is essential to keep the cup full of water at all times. To prevent the water in this reservoir from becoming stale, turn the plant upside down once a month, let the old water drain out, and refill the cup. Apart from this process, water the potting mixture for most types of bromeliad moderately, allowing the top half-inch of the mixture to dry out before watering again. During the brief rest period that some plants may take at some time in winter, give such bromeliads only enough water to keep the potting mixture from drying out completely.

In areas where the water is hard, use rainwater as much as possible. Hard water leaves unsightly lime deposits on the foliage. An alternative to rainwater is the meltwater that is produced by a defrosting refrigerator. Do not use this soft water while it is still ice-cold, though. Leave it out in a warm room for 24 hours before applying it to plants.

How to start a bromeliad log

For an unusual display of bromeliads and other epiphytes equip yourself with sphagnum moss, a reel of soft wire, lengths of plastic-covered wire, cork bark and shears.

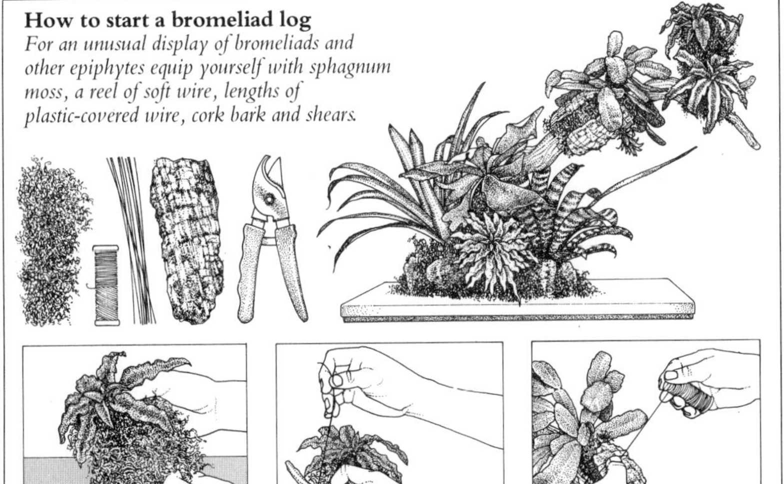

Wrap moistened sphagnum moss around the base of each rosette, making sure to cover the roots if there are any.

Fix the moss-covered base to the log with plastic-covered wire, twisting ends together. The wire is temporary.

Sandwich the moss between pieces of cork bark, and wrap them firmly into place on the log with reel wire.

Feeding Apply fertilizer to actively growing bromeliads according to the specific recommendations in appropriate *A–Z Guide* articles. Liquid fertilizer can be poured into either the potting mixture or the cuplike centers of rosettes, or it may be splashed over the leaves. Bromeliads grown in potting mixtures that contain a high proportion of peat moss need to be given some extra nourishment at regular intervals throughout the year. Bromeliads grown in a mixture that is largely soil-based should not be fed during any winter rest period that they may take. It is always better to give too little rather than too much of any type of fertilizer to bromeliads.

Potting and repotting Bromeliads need a potting mixture that is porous, spongy, and almost lime-free.

Satisfactory mixtures often consist of equal parts of coarse leaf mold and peat moss, or equal parts of a lime-free, soil-based mixture and peat moss. For specific recommendations, see the appropriate articles in the *A–Z Guide.*

Clay and plastic pots are equally satisfactory as containers unless plants are large, in which case a clay pot is more stable. As plastic pots retain moisture longer than clay ones, however, plants grown in them need watering less frequently than do those lodged in clay pots. It is usually advisable to provide extra drainage by putting some clay-pot fragments in the bottom of the pot.

Because bromeliads rarely have extensive roots, relatively small pots are big enough for most plants. The larger kinds can usually be brought to flowering size in 5- to 7-inch pots. Such low-growing plants as the cryptanthuses are unlikely to need pots (or half-pots) larger than 3 or 4 inches. Terrestrial plants do not have to be moved into larger pots until their roots completely fill the current ones. On the other hand, move young epiphytes into pots one size larger every spring until the maximum convenient pot size has been reached. Since bromeliads do not rely for all their food needs on the potting mixture, they do not require completely fresh mixture or even topdressing, as most other plants do.

Some epiphytic bromeliads—the small, gray-scaled tillandsias are an example—have virtually no roots if grown in potting mixture and do not thrive when they are planted in the conventional way. They prefer to grow *on* a suitable medium—for example, tree fern fiber, cork-oak bark, a fern slab, or piece of wood—rather than *in* one. To mount a plant on one of these materials, wrap the base of the plant (including roots, if any) in sphagnum moss, and tie the wrapped base to its support by winding plastic-covered wire around the moss and the supporting material. Fasten the ends of the wire firmly but in such a way that the wire can be easily untied. Hang the mounted specimen in a convenient place, and spray the moss at least once a day to keep it moist.

After supportive roots have grown over the sphagnum moss and turned around the mount, remove the temporary wire. To keep the plant alive and healthy, spray the plant, its roots, and the supporting material regularly throughout the year. The epiphytes can also be grown on so-called bromeliad logs (see page 107). These are detached tree branches that roughly simulate the plants' natural forest habitat. To work successfully, any such arrangement should be placed in a specially constructed plant window (see page 53), which can provide the high degree of humidity required. In a position where the plant gets ideal conditions, its roots function entirely as anchors, while the leaves absorb necessary water and plant food. Bind plants to epiphyte branches in the same way as they are attached to any other type of support, and give them the same subsequent treatment.

Alternatively, epiphytic bromeliads can be grown in such containers as slatted baskets and perforated clay pots that are traditionally used for other epiphytic plants such as orchids. When these containers are filled with a coarse-textured potting mixture, they allow excess water to drain away quickly, permitting air to penetrate through to the roots.

Some cryptanthuses and other terrestrial bromeliads can be induced to grow on pieces of very porous tufa stone or on shapely chunks of tree root or tree stump. If the stone or wood is kept permanently damp, a plant firmly bound to it will send its roots over the surface and into crevices in the stone or wood.

Propagation from seed

This shallow pan is just right for bromeliad seeds, which must be sown on the surface of rooting mixture.

Water newly sown seeds carefully. Note the fine-sprinkling head on this can. A free flow would bury seeds.

The pan is easily slipped into a plastic bag if you do not have a propagating case to assist germination.

Propagation The most convenient way to propagate bromeliads is by taking offsets from around the base of mature plants. Most bromeliads produce few offsets before flowering time. Then, practically all kinds begin to produce them directly from the base, or they send out offset-bearing stolons from the same point or from among the lower leaves. The offsets should not be cut away until they have begun to take on the characteristic rosette shape. If removed too early, while still little more than tightly rolled tubes of leaves, they will not root, or else they will take an inconveniently long time to do so. For the majority of species it is best to wait until the leaves are 3-4 inches long and arch over before taking an offset.

The best time for propagation is early spring. Try to cut or pull the offset away at a point as close as possible to the parent plant. During the period after the flowers of the parent plant have faded and while the old rosette is drying up and dying off, some bromeliads will produce as many as 10 offsets, all of which can be used for propagation. For further, more specific instructions consult individual articles in the *A–Z Guide*.

The vrieseas are a rather special case. Some forms do not produce offsets and must be grown from seed. Other forms produce only one new growth, which appears within the rosette of leaves, just off the center. Do not remove this single offset. Instead, allow it to grow on as the old rosette slowly dies off.

Bromeliads can also be raised from seed. In purchasing seeds make sure that they are freshly gathered, since they lose their viability quickly. Sow the seeds in spring, and use a shallow pan or half-pot filled with a mixture of two parts of peat moss to one part of coarse sand. Sprinkle the seeds thinly and evenly over the surface, pressing them down lightly without burying them. After thoroughly moistening the mixture, place the container in a plastic bag or (preferably) a heated propagating case (see page 444). At a temperature of 75°–80°F fresh seed will often germinate in a week or two.

Leave the seedlings, still enclosed in the bag or case, in a warm position that gets bright filtered light until they have made three or four leaves. Thereafter, gradually admit more air to the bag or case so as to accustom the seedlings to normal room conditions over a period of 7 to 10 days. After the seedlings are fully uncovered, begin to water them moderately, allowing the top half-inch of the seed-sowing mixture to dry out between waterings; and start once-a-month feedings of standard liquid fertilizer at half strength. When the seedlings have made at least six leaves, pot each young plant in a 2- or 3-inch pot of one of the recommended mixtures for adult bromeliads, and then treat it as a mature plant.

Young bromeliads barely 2–3 inches high that have been grown commercially from seed are available almost everywhere. They are usually sold for use in bottle gardens or terrariums (see page 54) and are inexpensive. This, of course, is the quick way to acquire a varied collection of these handsome plants. For specific kinds of bromeliad see:

Aechmea	*Guzmania*
*Ananas**	*Neoregelia**
Billbergia	*Nidularium*
*Cryptanthus**	*Tillandsia*
*Dyckia**	*Vriesea*

*Genera consisting entirely or largely of non-epiphytic species are marked with an asterisk.

Browallia
SOLANACEAE

Sapphire flower
B. speciosa 'Major'

BROWALLIAS (amethyst or bush violets) are prized for their vividly colored, usually sapphire blue flowers. When grown in pots, their slim, branching stems may need thin supports, but they also make attractive trailing plants if grown in baskets. Only two species are popular house plants; both flower in the fall and early winter, and most home growers treat them as temporary plants.

RECOMMENDED BROWALLIAS

B. speciosa itself is less popular than some of its forms. The kind most often grown is *B.s.* 'Major' (sapphire flower), which generally has erect stems 18–24 inches tall that carry slightly drooping, 2- to $2\frac{1}{2}$-inch-long, pointed-egg-shaped, bright green leaves on very short leafstalks. Violet-blue flowers 2 inches across, which are produced from leaf axils and borne on inch-long stalks, are tubular, but they flare out flat, dividing into five lobes. Most of the flowers have a white throat and some deep blue veining running along the lobes. Another popular form, *B.s.* 'Silver Bells,' is white-flowered.

B. viscosa, a more compact species, rarely grows taller than 12 inches. Its egg-shaped leaves are blunt-ended, 1–$1\frac{1}{2}$ inches long, hairy, mid-green and on short stalks. The bright blue flowers have white throats and are about an inch across. *B.v.* 'Sapphire' has flowers of a deeper blue; and those of *B.v.* 'Alba' are white.

PROPER CARE

Light Provide a position offering bright light with at least four hours of direct sunlight every day.

Temperature Browallias do best if they can be kept at a temperature of 55°–60°F; temperatures much over 65° will shorten the life of the flowers.

Watering Water moderately, enough to make the mixture thoroughly moist, but allow the top two-thirds to dry out between waterings.

Feeding Once new plants are established, begin applications of standard liquid fertilizer every two weeks, and continue throughout the whole of the flowering period.

Potting and repotting Purchased browallias will normally be in 5-inch pots of soil-based potting mixture and will not need repotting. They should be discarded after flowering.

Propagation Propagation is by seed. If it is sown in early spring, plants will begin to flower in early fall; later sowings will result in later flowering periods. Sow the seed thinly in small pots of moistened rooting mixture (see page 444). Place the pots in a plastic bag or small propagating case (see page 443) and keep them at a temperature of 60°–65°F in medium light. When seedlings are about $\frac{1}{2}$ inch tall, remove them from the plastic bag or propagator, water them enough to make the mixture barely moist, and leave them until they are about 2 inches tall. Then pot them individually in 3-inch pots of soil-based mixture (see page 429) and treat them as mature plants. They should be moved on into 5-inch pots after they have filled the smaller size with roots (see page 426). Alternatively, six or eight small plants can be placed in an 8-inch hanging basket.

Special points As browallias develop, nip out the growing tips of stems to encourage bushy growth.

Brunfelsia
SOLANACEAE

Yesterday-today-and-tomorrow
B. pauciflora calycina

POTTED brunfelsias are small shrubs—up to 2 feet high, with a 12-inch spread—that have 3- to 6-inch-long, lance-shaped, glossy, yet leathery leaves and showy, often fragrant, flowers. The one species grown indoors is *B. pauciflora calycina* (better known by its former name, *B. calycina*), which is commonly known as yesterday-today-and-tomorrow because of the way its flowers change color from one day to the next. Each bloom opens violet-purple, fades to pale lavender-blue, becomes almost white, and is dead by the fourth day. Flat, five-lobed flowers are up to 2 inches across, with a small, white, puckered "eye" (the entry point for insects to a short tube behind the floral surface). Flowers appear in clusters of up to 10 on the ends of long stems, but open singly. Under favorable conditions, all brunfelsias can bloom throughout the year. Two outstanding forms are *B.p.c.* 'Floribunda,' a profusely flowering miniature kind, and *B.p.c.* 'Macrantha,' with flowers measuring up to 3 inches across.

PROPER CARE

Light Bright light, including three or four hours of direct sunlight daily, is essential throughout the year for satisfactory flowering.

Temperature During the active growth period normal room temperature is suitable. Stand pots on trays of damp pebbles for increased humidity. Where warm, humid conditions are provided in winter, these plants will not have an appreciable rest period, but they will not suffer as a result. If such conditions are not provided, move brunfelsias to a really cool position—ideally, between 50° and 55°F—so that they can have a four- to six-week rest.

Watering In the active growth period water moderately, enough to make the mixture thoroughly moist, but allow the top half-inch of the mixture to dry out between waterings. If plants are given a rest, water them only enough during the rest period to keep the potting mixture from drying out completely.

Feeding Give actively growing plants standard liquid fertilizer every two weeks.

Potting and repotting Use a soil-based potting mixture (see page 429). Brunfelsias flower best when their roots are confined in small pots (5 or 6 inches at most). Repot in fresh mixture every spring, but do not increase pot size. Simply replace the old mixture with new.

Propagation Propagate in spring when tip cuttings of new growth are available. Dip a cutting 3–5 inches long in hormone rooting powder and plant it in a 3-inch pot containing a moistened equal-parts mixture of peat moss and coarse sand or perlite. Place the cutting in a plastic bag or propagating case (see page 443), and stand it in bright filtered light. When new growth is produced (in four to six weeks), uncover the young plant, begin moderate watering and apply standard liquid fertilizer every two weeks. About four months after the start of propagation, move the new brunfelsia into standard mixture and treat it as a mature plant.

Special points Prune old plants drastically in spring or just at the end of the rest period if they have one. Take out as much as half the previous year's growth. To encourage bushy growth, pinch out growing tips—this can be done at any time.

Bryophyllum

CRASSULACEAE

Devil's backbone
B. daigremontianum

ALTHOUGH the genus *Bryophyllum* should be included in the genus *Kalanchoe,* these plants are better known as bryophyllums; and so the old name is being retained here. Both species of indoor bryophyllum produce small plantlets on the edges or ends of their leaves, often when the parents themselves are only a few weeks old. The plantlets drop off and root wherever they fall, and there are usually several rooted plantlets growing at the base of older plants.
See also SUCCULENTS.

RECOMMENDED BRYOPHYLLUMS

B. daigremontianum (properly *Kalanchoe daigremontiana;* commonly known as devil's backbone) produces a single unbranched stem $1\frac{1}{2}$–3 feet tall, which carries opposite pairs of fleshy, shiny, lance-shaped leaves that are 4–10 inches long, grow at a 45° angle to the stem, and are bluish green with purple blotched undersides. The saw-toothed leaf edges curl slightly inward. The tiny plantlets that form in the gaps between the teeth often have $\frac{1}{4}$-inch-long aerial roots attached. One leaf can carry as many as 50 such plantlets in a single season. Pink flowers, which bloom only on a mature plant, are roughly tubular, 1 inch long, and pendent. They are carried in rather flat clusters atop foot-tall stalks in late fall and early winter.

B. tubiflorum (properly *Kalanchoe tubiflora;* popularly known as chandelier plant) has a main stem up to 3 feet tall and may also have shorter stems around the base. Leaves, which are arranged in threes around the stems,

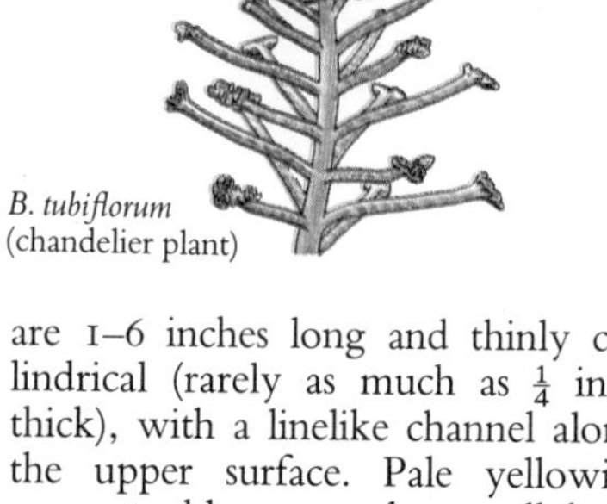

B. tubiflorum
(chandelier plant)

are 1–6 inches long and thinly cylindrical (rarely as much as $\frac{1}{4}$ inch thick), with a linelike channel along the upper surface. Pale yellowish green to blue-green leaves all have violet-brown spots; and every leaf bears four or more plantlets on its tip. In late winter orange-red, bell-shaped, inch-long flowers appear in a cluster of about 20 atop a foot-tall stalk.

PROPER CARE

Light These plants like bright light; do not subject them to direct sunlight.

Temperature Bryophyllums thrive in normal room temperatures.

Watering During the active growth period water moderately, but allow the top half-inch of the mixture to dry out between waterings. In the rest period water sparingly.

Feeding Apply standard liquid fertilizer once a month during the active growth period.

Potting and repotting Use a soil-based potting mixture (see page 429). Move small plants into pots one size larger every spring. A bryophyllum big enough to need a 6-inch pot is usually unshapely and best discarded.

Propagation Plantlets growing at the base of the plants may be dug up at any time, replanted in 2- to 3-inch pots of standard mixture, and treated as mature plants. Or plantlets may be picked from the leaves and shallowly planted in standard mixture.

BULBS, CORMS, and TUBERS

Plants that grow from bulbs, corms, or tubers have widely differing structures but are alike in possessing a fleshy organ from which roots are produced and in which food and water are stored. Because of this latter characteristic most have special cultivation needs. A list of plants commonly grown indoors follows this article. Consult separate articles for individual genera.

Because of their capacity for storing food and water, plants grown from bulbs, corms, or tubers can normally do without water for long periods even while in active growth. During the rest period, which is generally very pronounced, they frequently become completely dormant and need neither light nor water. Some kinds retain their foliage and roots throughout the year, however. These kinds can be considered permanent house plants.

Most people refer to all types as "bulbous." In fact, although bulbs, corms, and tubers all produce feeding roots below and leaves, flower stems, and flowers above, the three types of organ are different in many ways.

A bulb, for instance, is a modified leaf bud while tubers and corms are modified stems. Bulbs and corms produce roots from the base only; tubers can produce them from the top or sides as well. The top growth of bulbs and corms is stemless, with leaves and flower stalks sprouting directly from the neck; though many tubers also have stemless top growth, there are some that give rise to stems on which foliage and flowers are borne. Only one common house plant, the crocus, is grown from a corm, and crocuses can be treated exactly as if they were bulbous, although a corm's structure is distinct.

Like tubers, rhizomes are modified stems that generally grow underground. Since underground rhizomes are often swollen and act as food-storage organs, it is difficult to explain why they are not, nevertheless, tubers. Even so, it must be emphasized that rhizomes should not be confused with tubers. Rhizomatous plants are not discussed in this article.

Temporary indoor plants

Chiefly included in this category are hardy bulbs. A hardy bulb can not only withstand frost but is ordinarily unable to survive unless planted outdoors after flowering in the home. Such plants as hyacinths, narcissi, tulips, and certain scillas belong in this group, along with crocuses. These are single-season flowering plants.

The bulbs (or crocus corms) are bought dry and potted up in fall. There are many kinds that have been specially prepared for early flowering. By using these as well as unprepared bulbs and planting them at different times, indoor gardeners can prolong the flowering season. Individual bulbs flower for only two to three weeks.

It is best to pot up temporary bulbs as soon as they are acquired, otherwise they will start to sprout, and will probably fail to produce satisfactory flowers. Either soil-based or peat-based potting mixture can be used (see page 429), but some growers prefer packaged bulb fiber. Bulb fiber is composed, generally, of two parts of crushed oyster shell and one part of crushed charcoal added to six parts of peat moss. The resultant product is clean and easy to handle. Because it is exceptionally porous, it is recommended for use in watertight bowls. Do not use bulb fiber, however, for bulbs that are to be planted outdoors after flowering. For healthy outdoor growth later on, the best potting mixture for indoor use is soil-based. Since soil-based mixtures are not suitable for watertight containers, most growers do not try to preserve plants that have been grown in bowls.

Before potting bulbs, water the potting mixture or bulb fiber so that a clenched fistful feels moist without dripping. Position the bulbs close together, half-buried, with the necks well above ground. If possible, bury containers 6 inches deep outdoors, and cover them with peat. Otherwise, store them in a shaded outdoor spot under a heap of moist peat, keep them in a dark, unheated shed, or wrap them in black plastic bags and stand them on a window ledge in climates where they will not freeze.

Do not try to grow temporary bulbous plants if none of the above alternatives is possible. Top growth must be kept to a minimum while roots are developing, and the only way to do this is to deny the bulbs both light and warmth. Heat will stimulate top growth at the expense of roots, and the resultant weak root system will be unable to sustain leaf growth or flower production.

Containers under moist peat can be left untouched for 8 to 10 weeks. Any others should be inspected every two to three weeks to make sure they are not drying out and they should, if necessary, have a little water added. When the bulbs have produced leaves 1–2 inches tall, uncover the containers. Turn them two or three times a week to prevent lopsided growth. Water moderately, permitting the top half-inch of the potting mixture to dry out between waterings. Keep the temperature down to 45°–50°F until the leaves have made another 3–4 inches of growth. Once leaves are 4–5

Types of storage organ
Pictured here are a tulip bulb, a crocus corm, and a begonia tuber. They are alike in their ability to store food and water within the fleshy body, but each is different in structure from the others. The bulb is a modified leaf bud, the corm and tuber modified stems. Neither bulb nor corm produce stems. The tuber, on the other hand, is like a rhizome in that stems rise from it.

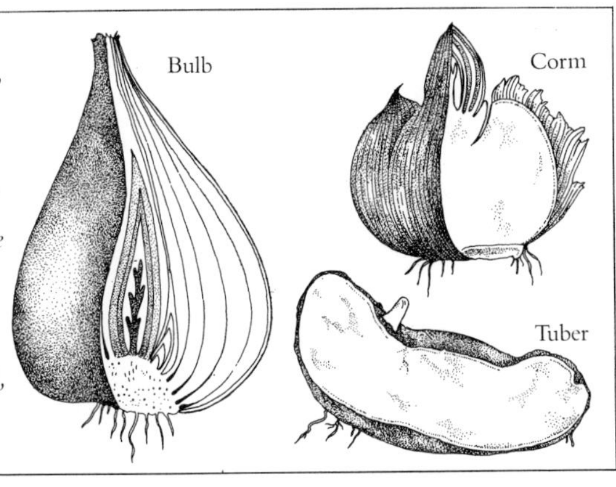

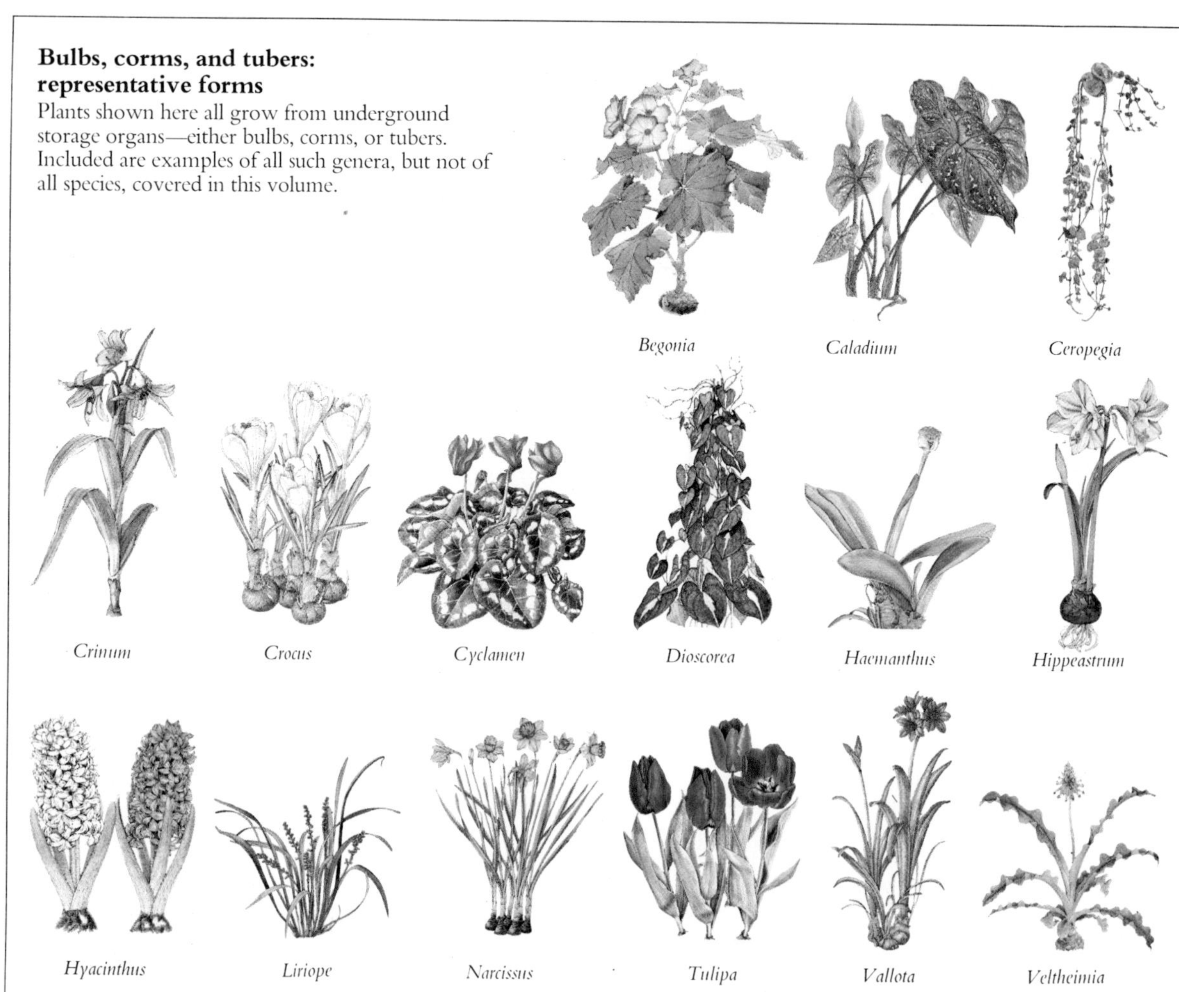

Bulbs, corms, and tubers: representative forms
Plants shown here all grow from underground storage organs—either bulbs, corms, or tubers. Included are examples of all such genera, but not of all species, covered in this volume.

inches high, all kinds except crocuses, which should remain as cool as possible until buds open, can be given warmer conditions—but not above 65°. Provide humidity by standing containers on trays of moist pebbles.

Some bulbs—narcissi and hyacinths, for example—can be grown in water alone. Instructions are given under appropriate entries in the *A–Z Guide.*

If the bulbs are to be replanted outdoors after flowering, cut off dead flower heads, leaving the green flower stem and the leaves, and either plant out the bulbs immediately or, if preferable, let them die down in their containers. In the latter case keep them in a bright, cool position and continue to water moderately until top growth has become entirely yellow, when it can be pulled off. Thereafter, allow the mixture to dry out completely; then shake the bulbs free of it, and store them in a dry place until they are planted in early fall.

Permanent indoor plants

This category includes most tuberous species. Their cultivation needs are very varied. Some have dormant periods without foliage, but others do not. Some can be kept in their pots during the rest period, but others should be stored in dry peat. Detailed instructions on how to care for specific plants appear under the appropriate entries in the *A–Z Guide.*

Permanent bulbs, on the other hand, all need generally similar treatment. They differ from the temporary kinds in that they must be kept indoors in cool weather. If conditions are right, they can live and bloom indefinitely. These plants do best if kept in potting mixture throughout the year without being permitted to dry out completely. This is because a few fleshy roots persist during the rest period, even when the normal feeding roots wither away, and these require moisture. If bought dry, pot up these bulbs without delay.

Plant bulbs singly, using pots about $1\frac{1}{2}$ times the diameter of the bulbs, which flower best when their roots are confined. Let one-third to one-half of each bulb project above the level of the potting mixture. The mixture should be soil-based, firmly packed, and evenly moist throughout. Water each potted bulb sparingly for the first two or three weeks, after which the amounts can be gradually brought up to levels recommended in specific *A–Z Guide* entries. Growth cycles vary, and instructions for proper care, particularly during the rest period, should be strictly observed.

All permanent bulbs can remain in the same pots for up to four years if they are regularly fed. After three or four years, though, the old potting mixture will need to be replaced. At this time repot as soon as the first signs of new growth appear, toward the end of the rest (or dormant) period. Begin by removing as much as possible of the old mixture. The best way to do this without damaging fleshy roots is to wash the mixture away under running water. Before replanting the bulb, pull off any young bulbs produced by the old one and pot them up separately (see "Propagation," below). The old bulb can usually go back into the original pot after the pot has been thoroughly cleaned. If necessary, use a slightly larger one. Fresh potting mixture can then be added.

When repotting a mature permanent bulb, pick away any young bulbs embedded in its long roots and use them for propagation.

In general, permanent bulbous plants need bright light, and often full direct sunlight, in order to prevent the leaves from becoming unattractively elongated. Sunlight after bulbs have finished flowering helps them in forming flowers the following year. Similarly, the permanent bulbous plants like normal room temperatures all year long, even during dormancy.

PROPER CARE

Feeding Temporary specimens do not require feeding. For those that are planted outdoors after flowering, a slow-acting fertilizer such as bone meal should be worked into the soil.

Begin feeding permanent bulbs two or three weeks after the first full watering at the start of the active growth period. (This will not be necessary for recently potted plants. Their fresh, soil-based potting mixture will provide enough nourishment until flowering time. After a plant has flowered, feeding becomes most important because it builds up the bulb for the following season.) Throughout the active growth period apply standard liquid fertilizer to all but recently repotted plants at regular intervals. Continue these feedings for all plants from the beginning of the flowering period until about two months before the rest (or dormant) period is expected. Then switch to a two-month-long routine of giving high-potash fertilizer, which assists in future flower formation.

Specific feeding instructions for tuberous plants are summarized in the relevant *A–Z Guide* entries.

Propagation Bulbs increase themselves by forming new bulbs, or offsets, which grow from the outside of the base. The offset begins life within the papery tunic of the parent bulb, then breaks through and develops its own tunic. It is usually easy to take an offset during the rest period. Sometimes, though, especially with bulbs that do not lose their leaves, it may be necessary to disentangle roots before the little bulb can be pried away.

Offsets can be potted and treated as adults but it normally takes them at least two years to reach flowering size. Propagation from seed takes even longer—an average of five years from sowing to flowering.

It is not possible to generalize about the propagation of tuberous plants. Most of them do not form offsets, but caladiums are an exception to this rule. Moreover, some tuberous plants—certain begonias, for instance—carry miniature tubers (often called bulbils) on the stems. And *Dioscorea discolor* produces miniature tubers at the ends of roots. All these can be used for propagation. But there are other ways of propagating tuberous plants.

One method is to cut the tuber into sections, each with a growth bud. If this is done, dust the cut surface with captan or sulfur dust (see page 459) to prevent decay. Then pot up each section and treat it as a full-size tuber.

The customary way to increase cyclamens is from seed. For other tuberous plants this is a difficult process.

Propagating pieces of tuber

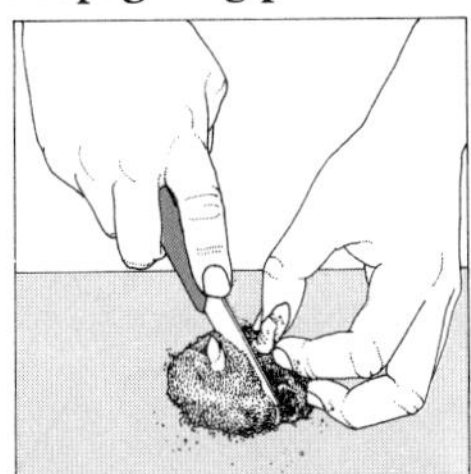

If a tuber has more than a single growth bud, make a clean cut that leaves a bud on each segment.

Cover each cut surface with a dusting of captan or sulfur dust to prevent planted segments from rotting.

If growth buds point straight upward when segments are potted, new top growth will be both straight and sturdy.

Special points Many flower stems, especially those of daffodils and tulips, sometimes need support. To provide this, push thin stakes into the potting mixture and loop twine or wool around them and the flower stalks (see page 432). The stems of some bulbs, notably hippeastrums, tend to lean toward the light as they develop. Turn such plants daily to avoid lopsided growth that would otherwise require support unnecessarily.

After the flowers of any plants growing from bulbs, corms, or tubers have faded, cut off the flower head but not the green stalk.

When cutting flowers from "bulbous" plants, do not destroy stalks. If left until they shrivel, stalks help build up further food material in storage organs.

For plants of the types discussed in this article see:

Bulbs	**Corms**
Crinum	*Crocus**
Haemanthus	**Tubers**
Hippeastrum	*Begonia*
*Hyacinthus**	*Caladium*
*Narcissus**	*Ceropegia*
*Tulipa**	*Cyclamen**
Vallota	*Dioscorea*
Veltheimia	*Liriope*

*Genera marked with an asterisk include temporary indoor forms.

CACTI

Cacti are succulent plants distinguished from all others by their areoles, which often carry spines and from which flowers are produced. The two distinct types of cactus—desert and jungle—are characterized below, along with general advice on providing proper care for both types. A list of cacti commonly grown indoors follows this article. Consult separate articles for individual genera.

The Latin name of the family to which the cacti belong is *Cactaceae,* and all the members of this family, with two exceptions, are succulent plants. (The exceptions, *Pereskia* and *Pereskiopsis,* need not concern us here because they are rarely grown as house plants.) Succulent plants are those that survive periods of drought by storing up water in their stems or leaves. There are succulents in a number of families, and some of them, such as many euphorbias, strongly resemble cacti. Like the cacti, these euphorbias have no leaves or only tiny ones, and they store water in their stems as cacti do. What chiefly distinguishes the cactus family from all others, including the succulent euphorbias, is what botanists call the "areole." If a plant has areoles, it must be a cactus; if a plant is a cactus, it must have areoles.

The flowers of a cactus always arise from its areoles, each of which can produce only one flower during the lifetime of the plant. As the cactus grows it forms new areoles, and so the plant continues to bloom. The areoles themselves are well-defined areas representing foreshortened branches. From the areoles sprout little tufts of spines, bristles, or hairs. These tufts are conspicuous in some species and hardly noticeable in others. They may be as tiny as $\frac{1}{16}$ inch across or as big as $\frac{1}{4}$ inch. They are always distributed over the stems, usually in rows. Although most cacti have spines, some are spineless. Even in spineless ones the areoles are present as minute hairy tufts. Conversely, the spiniest succulent that is not a cactus bears its spines directly on the stem surface, rather like thorns on a rose.

Cactus spines vary greatly in shape and size. Some are thick and sharp-pointed, others are merely bristly or hairlike. They may be straight or curved, long or short, hooked or, if hairlike, curly. In describing the spines of a cactus, it is convenient to make a distinction between the two types of growth, which are "radial" and "central." Radial spines project obliquely from the areoles, whereas the central spines, which are generally longer and fewer, jut more or less straight out.

Most cacti come originally from the Western Hemisphere. Those that now seem to be growing wild elsewhere have usually been introduced into their present environments from the Americas. Although the natural habitat of most of the genera used as house plants is the desert, there are others that come from tropical jungles. The two kinds—desert cacti and jungle cacti—are quite different, and so are many of their indoor requirements. In the following pages a general discussion of desert cacti as house plants precedes a similar discussion of the other kind. To avoid repetition where there are no notable differences in recommended treatment, the subject matter is fully explored in the desert-cacti section, with cross-references for the jungle type.

Desert cacti

Water is as essential to the cactus as it is to any other plant. The deserts of the American Southwest, Mexico, and South America where cacti grow wild have high summer temperatures, intense sunlight, and long periods of little or no rain, followed by short periods of heavy rainfall. During the drought the cacti draw upon the reserve of water in their stems. When it rains they replenish their stores.

Most plants lose a great deal of moisture through the stomata (pores) in their leaves. The absence or near-absence of leaves in cacti helps them to conserve water, and the green stems take over the food-making job that leaves normally perform. The stems of desert cacti are also shaped in a way that minimizes water loss. Most are globular, and several form tall, stout columns. Moreover, the surface of the stem is often divided into segments by wide or narrow ribs that run from the base to the top of the plant and enable the cactus to expand and contract with water intake or loss, like an accordion.

In ribbed cacti the areoles are always positioned along the ribs. There are, however, other arrangements of areoles. Some species have a number of tubercles—wartlike swellings—on the stem surface instead of ribs, and the areoles of these cacti appear in the tubercle centers. (See, for example, the genus *Mammillaria.*) In other plants, such as some forms of the genus *Opuntia,* the areoles are scattered over the surface, seemingly at random, though actually at regular intervals.

DESERT-CACTUS FLOWERS

Many people erroneously believe that cacti bloom only once every seven years. In fact, they are profusely flowering plants. Under the right conditions a mature desert cactus flowers annually, often throughout an extensive flowering season. It is true, however, that plants that grow very large in the wild are unlikely to flower on a windowsill. And some of the smaller cacti whose native environment is the slopes of the Andes cannot get enough light at lower altitudes to produce flowers. These are exceptions, however. Not only do most cacti eventually flower indoors, but many flower while still young, some even in 2-inch pots.

The flowers of desert cacti are generally either trumpet-shaped or bell-shaped with numerous straplike petals. The blooms arise directly from areoles, without stalks (and thus are unsuitable as cut flowers). In many species, the flowers are trumpet- or bell-shaped with petals that flare out from a long tubular base. Flower size varies greatly, from less than $\frac{1}{2}$ inch across, in some mammillarias, for instance, to 3 or 4 inches across in some kinds of echinopsis, where the flowers can exceed 9 inches in length. Color can be anything but blue.

Many desert cacti, such as the echinopsis and cereus, bloom at night, and their flowers are often sweetly

Cacti: representative forms

Each plant shown here belongs to one of the genera included in the family *Cactaceae.* Other species within a given genus may, of course, look very different from the illustrated species.

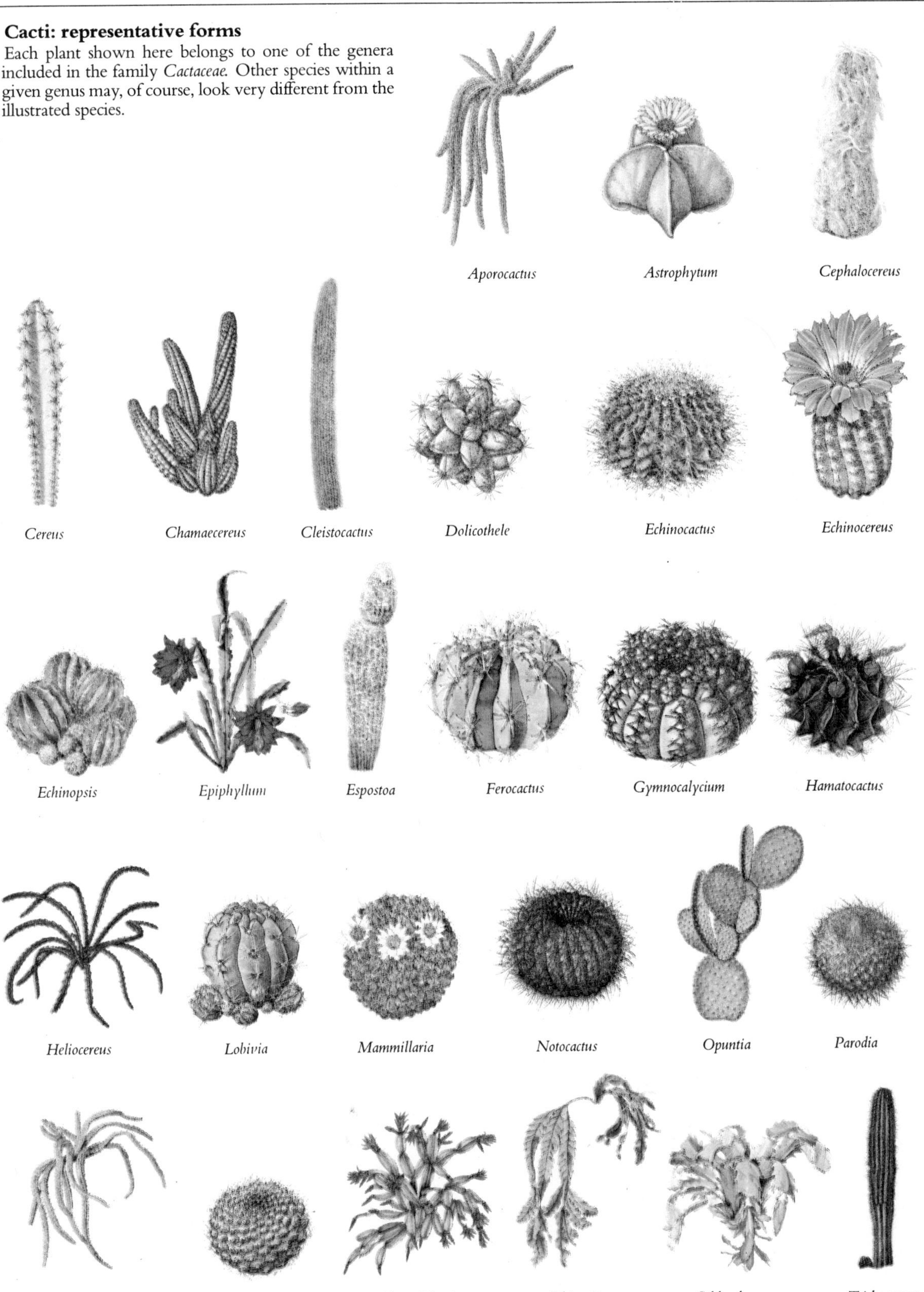

scented (an attraction for the moths that pollinate them in the wild). A few other types—gymnocalyciums, for instance—also emit a delicate perfume, but most cactus flowers, jungle as well as desert, are scentless. Apart from night-blooming species, desert cacti will usually open their flowers only in full sunlight. In prolonged spells of inadequate light, not only the flowers but even fully formed flower buds are likely to drop off the plant. Individual blooms are usually short-lived; in many cases they last only for a day. The flowering season can continue, however, for several months.

Normally, these plants begin to produce flowers in spring or early summer, but how well they flourish depends on growing conditions, particularly on the intensity and duration of light. It is nearly impossible to lay down hard and fast rules as to the precise way to treat desert cacti indoors. The individual entries for genera in this *A–Z Guide* include detailed suggestions for the best way to meet the requirements of specific plants. Information about the needs of desert cacti *in general* is given below.

Cacti are successfully grown as house plants in a broad range of indoor and outdoor environments. Indoor gardeners in the American Southwest or Mexico can keep their plants either at a brightly lit window or on an outdoor terrace, give them a watering now and then, and almost forget them; there will almost certainly be excellent growth throughout the year. Residents of colder, less sunny areas must pay more careful attention to the plants' special cultivation needs, and must work harder in order to supply those needs. No desert cactus discussed in this book, however, is really difficult to cultivate in any type of home or in any normal indoor climate. The basic requirements are the same for all species.

PROPER CARE

Light Since they come from regions where sunlight is intense, all desert cacti should be kept in the sunniest possible window. If denied full sunlight, the stems of these plants are likely to elongate and to lose their characteristic shape. Full sun is essential, too, for stimulating bud formation and hence flowering in the many kinds of cactus that, given the right conditions, will flower indoors.

Remember that the light through a window is one-sided. Turn plants regularly, preferably daily. Otherwise they are likely to become curved or in some other way distorted. If possible, place the plants in a sunny spot outdoors during the warmer months. No matter how bright the indoor position, conditions are better in summer sunshine and the fresh air of a garden, terrace, or even a south-facing balcony.

Temperature During the active growth period any normally warm room temperature is suitable for these plants. If kept in a small greenhouse in full summertime sunlight, desert cacti can sometimes become overheated. This is due mainly to insufficient ventilation, however, and overheating is unlikely in a living room. The difficult time for desert cacti is during the winter months, when they need to rest. Growers who keep them in greenhouses usually maintain a winter temperature of 40°–45°F for most kinds. It is only in areas with strong, steady winter sunlight that such plants may safely be encouraged to continue growing throughout the year. In a centrally heated room, where winter temperatures are likely to remain above 60° along with inadequate natural light, these cacti will produce "drawn," skinny growth.

Thus, if an unheated room is available, keep all desert cacti there during the winter rest period—provided, of course, that they continue to get full sunlight, and also that the room temperature never falls much below 40°. If it is not possible to move the plants to a cool position and they must remain in the usual place, pay particular attention to the following instructions for correct watering.

Desert cacti

Stem shapes

1 Cylindrical with leaves *(Opuntia subulata)* **2** Flattened, segmented *(Opuntia microdasys)* **3** Candelabra *(Cereus peruvianus)* **4** Columnar *(Cereus jamacaru)* **5** Pendent *(Aporocactus flagelliformis)* **6** Clustering *(Chamaecereus sylvestri)* **7** Star-shaped *(Astrophytum myriostigma)* **8** Globular with "chins" *(Gymnocalycium mihanovichii)* **9** Globular *(Notocactus ottonis)* **10** Pincushion *(Dolicothele longimamma)*

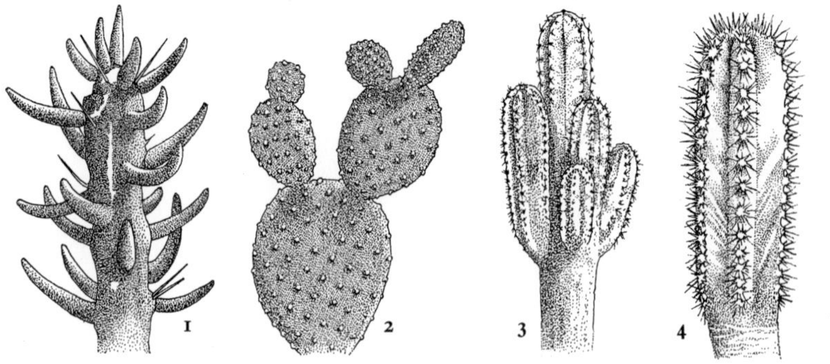

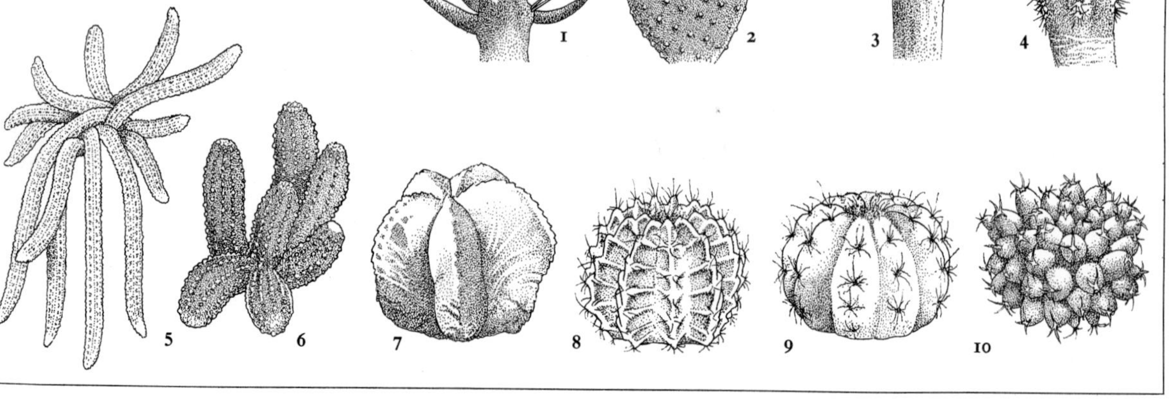

1 2 3 4 5 6 7 8 9 10

Watering The normal active growth period for desert cacti is the spring and summer months. Throughout this period give them plenty of water, soaking the potting mixture thoroughly at each watering but allowing the top half-inch of the mixture to dry out before watering again. The ideal way to water is to stand pots in bowls of water up to potting-mixture level until the mixture has become saturated, and then remove the pots and allow them to drain. Never let a pot stand in water longer than necessary to wet the mixture thoroughly. Because this is a rather time-consuming method for growers who have large collections of cacti, such people tend to cut corners by watering from above with a spouted can.

Many authorities strongly recommend watering early in the morning, but this too may not always be practicable. While plants are in active growth, early-morning watering is by no means essential. During the winter rest period, though, it *is* important to water well before noon; this allows time for any surplus moisture to dry up before the sun goes down. As explained above, it is best not to encourage desert cacti to grow during the short-day months, and they should have only enough water to prevent the mixture from becoming completely dry. If these plants are grown throughout the year in a greenhouse, they need no water at all in winter, but in a heated room the drier atmosphere makes some watering necessary. It is always better, though, to give a bit too little rather than too much water. Too much can cause rotting of cacti, particularly when they are resting.

Try not to splash water on the stems. If the water is hard, it can leave unsightly marks when it has dried. Use rainwater, in fact, if it is available.

Feeding Like most other house plants, desert cacti grown in a peat-based mixture need a dose of fertilizer once every two weeks or so during the active growth period. If the plants are grown in a soil-based mixture, which contains more natural food, less frequent applications are advisable. To encourage flowering, use a high-potassium, tomato type of fertilizer. Avoid the high-nitrogen type because it is likely to induce soft flabby growth at the expense of flowers. It is always better to give too little rather than too much fertilizer to a desert cactus. Above all, never feed a resting plant.

Potting and repotting In the wild most desert cacti have a widespread root system. The roots of a plant 6 inches across can extend, just below the soil surface, for a square yard. This enables them to collect a good supply of surface water in the form of dew. The roots of plants grown in pots are much more compact and the potting mixture must have especially good drainage in order to avoid the risk of rotting. Apart from the drainage requirement, desert cacti have no special potting-mixture needs. A suitable mixture consists of about one part of coarse sand or perlite to two parts of either soil-based or peat-based mixture (see page 429).

Desert cacti can be grown in either clay or plastic pots. The only important difference is that because plastic pots retain moisture longer than clay ones, there should also be longer intervals between waterings. If the potting mixture is sufficiently porous, as recommended, it will not be necessary to provide extra drainage by filling the bottom of the pot with clay-pot fragments. This would be a waste of valuable pot space. If a cactus is planted in a clay pot, however, place one fragment over the hole in the bottom in order to keep the potting mixture from falling through. This should not be necessary with plastic pots, which usually have a number of small drainage holes instead of a single big one.

The best time for repotting is early spring (although it can be done at any time except full winter). Every cactus should be removed from its pot at least once a year to see whether the roots form a tight mass that fills the pot. If

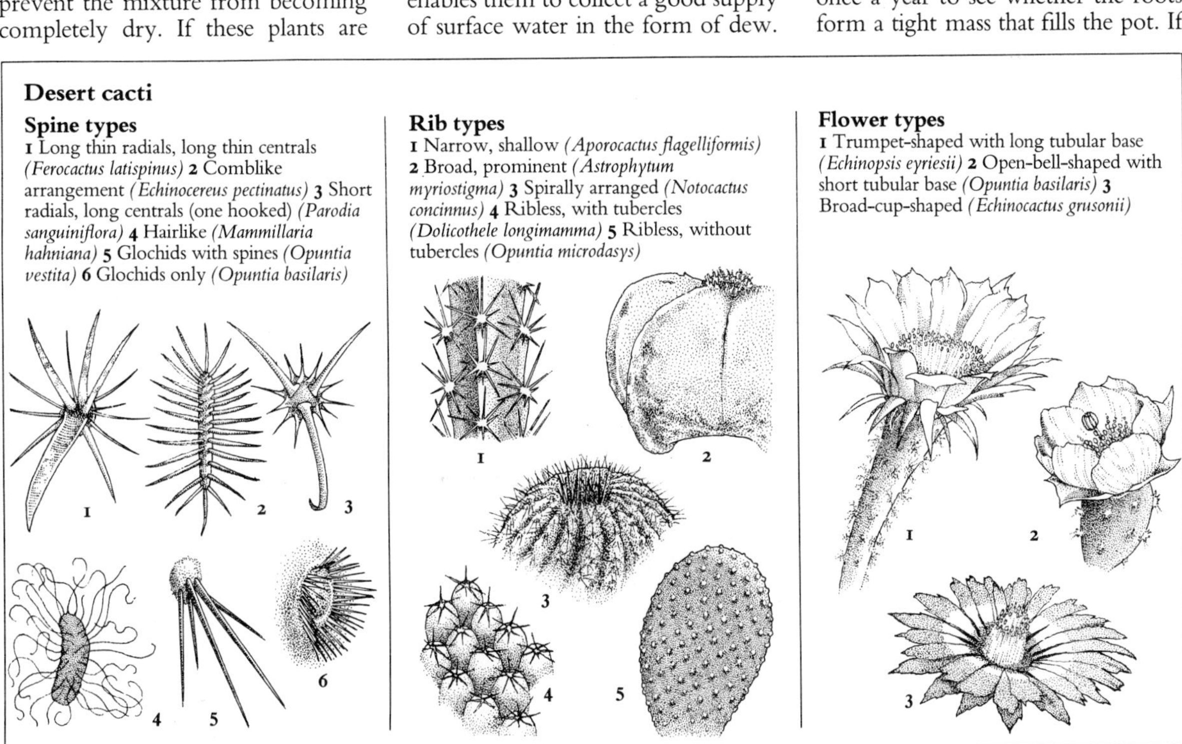

Desert cacti

Spine types
1 Long thin radials, long thin centrals *(Ferocactus latispinus)* **2** Comblike arrangement *(Echinocereus pectinatus)* **3** Short radials, long centrals (one hooked) *(Parodia sanguiniflora)* **4** Hairlike *(Mammillaria hahniana)* **5** Glochids with spines *(Opuntia vestita)* **6** Glochids only *(Opuntia basilaris)*

Rib types
1 Narrow, shallow *(Aporocactus flagelliformis)* **2** Broad, prominent *(Astrophytum myriostigma)* **3** Spirally arranged *(Notocactus concinnus)* **4** Ribless, with tubercles *(Dolicothele longimamma)* **5** Ribless, without tubercles *(Opuntia microdasys)*

Flower types
1 Trumpet-shaped with long tubular base *(Echinopsis eyriesii)* **2** Open-bell-shaped with short tubular base *(Opuntia basilaris)* **3** Broad-cup-shaped *(Echinocactus grusonii)*

they do, the plant must be moved to a pot one size larger. The handling of a spiny cactus involves risks to both handler and plant. Try wrapping a folded newspaper gently around the plant to protect the hands without crushing the spines. Alternatively, some experts use a small pair of tongs to grip the plant between the spines, usually at the base. To take the cactus out of its pot, begin by attempting to lift it carefully. If it does not budge, tap the pot, if it is clay, with moderate force; if plastic, squeeze it. A pencil pushed into drainage holes will also help to release the ball of potting mixture. Once the plant is free, shake as much mixture as possible from the roots, taking care not to damage them. If the roots have not grown enough to fill the present pot, replant the cactus in a clean pot of the same size, adding fresh mixture as required. Use a larger pot only if last year's size is obviously too small.

To replant the cactus, hold it at the right height in the pot by means of the folded newspaper or tongs. The "right" height is determined by the depth at which the cactus was originally potted; that depth should remain unchanged. While still holding the plant, let fresh potting mixture trickle down below and around the roots until they are well supported. A small trowel or a large tablespoon is ideal for use in the trickling-down process. Do not press the mixture firmly around the roots. A gentle knocking will suffice to tap an adequate amount into the pot.

Many desert cacti never exceed a height of 1–2 feet and a width of 4–6 inches indoors. The maximum necessary pot size for such plants is 6 or 7 inches. Others will require larger and larger pots. If a plant grows too big and if the owner prefers not to discard it, a possible alternative is to pull away some of the root mass so that the plant can be contained in a smaller pot. This is a risky operation, however, since it can cause rotting of the damaged roots. Anyone who nonetheless tries to save an outsize cactus by this method should be warned not to water the plant for several days after pulling the roots apart. The short rest will give the roots time to heal.

An assortment of cacti in bowls can be effective for a few years, until the plants (or some of them) become too large. Bowls without drainage holes are generally used. For adequate drainage there should be an inch-thick layer of gravel placed under the potting mixture in the watertight bowls, and the plants should be watered more sparingly than those in pots. If other succulents are also included in the display, choose plants whose active growth period coincides with that of the cacti. It is not generally advisable to mix desert cacti with jungle cacti in bowl arrangements (see "Jungle cacti," below).

The repotting process
Early spring is the best time to repot a desert cactus, which should be removed from its pot annually for inspection of its roots. Move the cactus to a larger pot only if its roots fill the current one. Otherwise, return the plant to its pot, which has been cleaned.

Wrap paper thickly around this spiny ferocactus before removing it from its pot.

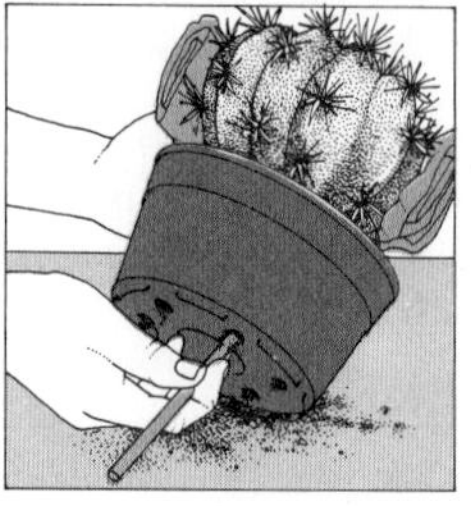
A pencil pushed through the hole in the bottom of the pot helps release the root ball.

Roots have not filled the pot. Before replacing the plant ease away some mixture.

Replace the cactus on a bed of fresh mixture in the bottom of its old pot.

Holding the plant at the correct depth, trickle fresh mixture around the sides.

For a miniature garden of cacti, choose an assortment of plants with different and contrasting characteristics and use them to offset one another.

Propagation A number of desert cacti produce offsets around the base of the plant, and these are often used for propagation. The best time to propagate is in the spring or summer. In some cacti—the echinopsis, for example—an offset can be pulled away easily with tongs. In others, such as many gymnocalyciums, the offset is more firmly attached and must be cut away with a sharp knife. If there is a cut surface, rotting can occur unless the offset is allowed to dry for a few days to let the cut harden. To propagate, insert the offsets in a single seed tray. There is no need to plant deeply. Simply push detached ends into the mixture far enough to hold them. Place pots or trays in a position where they get medium light, and give them just enough water to keep the potting mixture barely moist. After a few weeks the offsets will probably have rooted and can be treated as mature plants. Leave those in the seed tray until the following spring, when they will require repotting either singly or together in bowls.

To propagate any columnar cactus that branches cut off a branch and treat it in the same way as a detached offset. Branches are normally quite soft and can be cut easily with a sharp knife and the protective aid of some newspaper.

However, such a drastic operation may ruin the look of the parent plant. In order to propagate columnar cacti that do not normally branch—for instance, many of the cereuses—cut off a section of the stem, allow it to dry for a few days, and then pot it up as explained above. The stem-section method is advisable if the parent plant has become too tall for a house plant. A word of warning, though: Do not take sections less than 2 inches long from a stem that is an inch or more wide; it is difficult to root short pieces of this type.

The lower part of a cactus stem that has had its top cut off will send out shoots from around the cut surface, and these can be removed and treated as cuttings for propagation when they are 2 inches or more long. This is a good way of propagating non-branching and non-offset-producing plants that are columnar in shape. It is possible, but more difficult, to propagate a globular cactus in the same manner. If the stem is cut in two at the diameter, the lower half usually sends out shoots, which can be used as cuttings. The top half is harder to root, though, than is the stem section of a columnar plant. It will need drying out for at least a week before being planted and will require cultivation of a kind that inexperienced growers are well advised not to attempt.

Raising cacti from seed Almost all cacti, jungle as well as desert, are easy to raise from seed if the seed is reasonably fresh. Be sure to get seeds from a reputable source. They can be sown in either pots or seed pans, depending upon the quantity. Use pots at least 2 inches in diameter, because seeds need moisture, and very small pots tend to dry out too speedily. Several types of seed can be planted in the same large container, but be sure to mark out and label the placement of the different kinds so as not to become confused about them.

Put about ½ inch of some such drainage material as gravel or perlite on the floor of the container. Then fill it to within ½ inch of the top with a standard seed mixture (see page 444). Next soak the mixture in water and let it drain. When the excess water has drained away, scatter seeds thinly over the surface of the mixture; do not bury them. Plant large seeds, such as those of opuntias, individually and press them lightly into the surface. Finally,

Desert cacti: types of propagation

Offsets

Cacti that develop offsets around their base can be easily propagated. According to the type of cactus, the offsets can be pulled or cut away. The wound that you make in cutting will not heal if the offsets are planted immediately, and must therefore be allowed to dry.

In cutting away an offset from a spiny cactus such as a gymnocalycium, protect your hand with a thick glove.

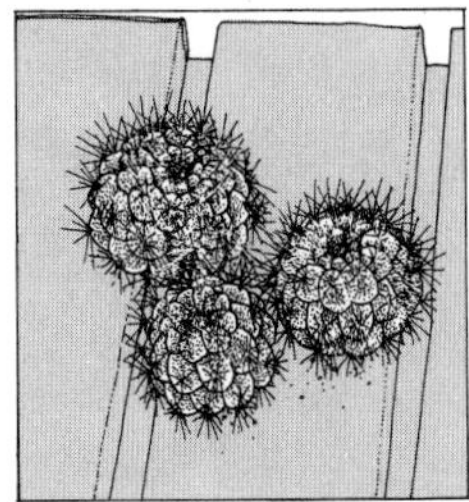

Leave the offset for a day or two to allow the cut surface to dry before planting it in standard mixture.

Use a pair of tongs to pull away an offset from a cactus such as this echinopsis.

If the offset has roots, ease it away carefully so as not to damage them.

Insert the offset into potting mixture. There is no need to plant it deeply.

Stem cuttings

Most branching cacti are propagated simply by cutting off a branch and replanting it. This will not spoil the look of the plant. A non-branching cactus can be propagated by means of a tip cutting, but this will leave a permanent scar: although in time new shoots will appear from around the edge of the scar. These in turn can be used for propagation.

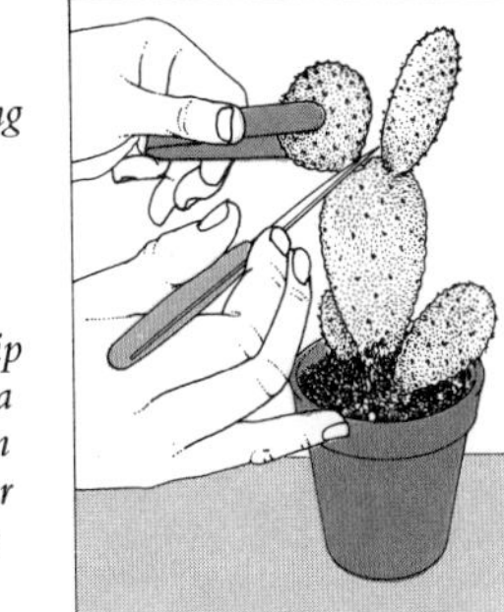

When cutting off a portion of stem from a segmented cactus such as an opuntia, hold the branch with tongs.

A piece at least 2 inches long can be cut off the top of a non-branching trichocereus and used for propagation.

Growing cacti from seed

Put a shallow layer of drainage material in a small pot, and fill the pot with standard seed mixture.

After watering the mixture plentifully, scatter small seeds over the surface without burying them.

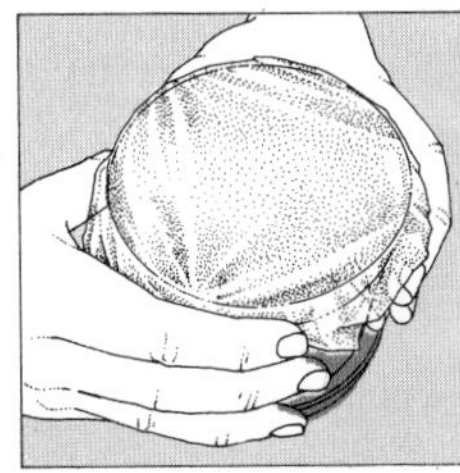

Cover the top of the pot with plastic and leave the pot in a warm place for the seeds to germinate.

lay a sheet of glass or plastic over the top of the container to conserve moisture, and place the whole in a warm position (78°-80°F is ideal). Light is not needed until seeds start to germinate. But because they will not all germinate at the same time, it is best to give the container medium light from the beginning. Never leave seedlings in full sunlight. Cactus seeds vary greatly in the time needed for germination, but most should be up within two to three weeks. When the first seedlings, which usually look like minute green balls, appear, raise the cover, and keep it in a slightly raised position to give the seedlings some much-needed air.

Desert-cacti seedlings benefit from being given a full year's uninterrupted growth before being potted up and treated as mature plants. The best time for sowing seeds, therefore, is spring. Seedlings will be ready for potting up the following spring, after a year in the seed container. During this first year, keep them at normally warm room temperatures, and water them often enough to keep the potting mixture slightly moist. When potting up young cacti, take care not to damage the roots, for root damage can kill a young plant. Before trying to move a plant, loosen the mixture around its roots. Then lift it gently, if necessary with a pair of blunt tongs. A 2-inch pot is big enough for a little cactus. If preferred, put several young plants about 1 inch apart in a pan, where they can remain until they almost, but not quite, touch each other.

Pests Neither desert nor jungle cacti suffer from many pests. The most troublesome are mealy bugs and root mealy bugs. When repotting cacti, always look for the whitish deposits on roots that indicate an infestation of below-ground mealy bugs. If humidity is very low, red spider mites can also be a nuisance. They can best be prevented by spraying plants regularly with plain water. Watch out, too, for tiny black flies hovering over the surface of the soil mixture. They are probably sciarid flies, whose grubs eat seedlings and roots. (For a full discussion of pests and how to combat them, see page 454.)

Potted cacti placed out of doors in summer are sometimes attacked by slugs. Slug pellets scattered over the surface of the potting mixture will usually deal with them.

Diseases Cacti are particularly susceptible to rot caused by fungi or bacteria. Watch out for soft brown or blackish marks on the stems, especially in places where there has been some local damage, and cut away such indications of rot as soon as they appear. Otherwise, the rot is bound to spread. Be sure to cut right back to healthy green tissue. Rotting at the base of a cactus is usually caused by compacted, over-wet potting mixture. If a sufficiently porous mixture is used, this should not occur. If it does occur, however, remove all infected tissue from roots as well as stems, and treat what remains of the plant as a cutting (see "Propagation," above).

A cactus may occasionally become marked with dry, brown, corky patches. If this happens at the base of a large columnar plant, it is merely an indication of ageing. Similar spots elsewhere or on the stems of other cacti may be due to damage from handling, poor ventilation, scorching sunlight through a windowpane, or sudden changes in temperature. Nothing can be done about such markings but they do not indicate rot and will not spread. Excess nitrogen in the potting mixture may also result in unsightly spots, notably on the stems of epiphyllums. This is one reason why high-nitrogen types of fertilizer are not recommended for cacti.

Soft brown or black patches on a cactus indicate rot. Cut back as far as healthy tissue to prevent the rot from spreading.

Cacti grown indoors tend to gather dust. Clean spineless plants by a gentle sponging with a weak detergent solution. The spiny cacti must be handled more gingerly but can usually be effectively washed down with a soft shaving brush rather than a sponge. (Do not try to wash plants that have hooked spines, however. They are too easily damaged.) When cleaning a cactus, protect the roots by laying a piece of plastic sheeting over the potting mixture to prevent undue wetting at the base of the plant.

Cleaning different kinds of cactus

To clean spiny stems use a shaving brush and a weak solution of detergent. Rinse with clean water.

To clean spineless stems sponge them down gently with a soft, damp cloth.

Jungle cacti

These plants, which are native to the tropical jungles of the New World, are mostly epiphytes. In the wild they usually grow in some such place as a pocket of leaf mold in the hollow of a tree branch. These soil pockets dry out quickly in spite of the humid jungle atmosphere, and thus the plants that grow in them need to be able to conserve water. Jungle cacti are succulent, therefore, but less so than desert cacti. The typical spherical or columnar shape of the desert plants does not exist in the jungle. Stems of these cacti usually consist of either flattened, joined segments or of long, trailing growths that are sometimes cylindrical, sometimes flattened and straplike.

The flattened stems—and, more particularly, the flat segments—look rather like leaves, and are often incorrectly called leaves, but all these cacti are leafless. Areoles are present, of course (otherwise the plants would not be cacti), but they are often very small. In some types they can be seen only through a magnifying glass. Jungle cacti do not have ribs, and the areoles are usually situated in notches along the edges of the stems. The long, stout spines of many desert cacti do not exist in jungle plants. Instead, all jungle-cactus areoles bear small bristles. On the whole, the stems are less interesting than those of desert cacti. These plants are prized mostly for their flowers and some for their berrylike fruits.

The flowers are notably varied in size. The largest of all cactus flowers, as well as some of the tiniest, are found in this group. An epiphyllum, for example, can produce blooms more than 6 inches across, while those of a rhipsalis rarely exceed ½ inch. Small flowers are usually produced in profusion, however, whereas the big ones are fewer in number. Flower shapes and colors are similar to those of the desert cacti, with the exception of the so-called Christmas cacti, which have oddly flattened blooms (see the genus *Schlumbergera*). The flowers are generally scentless unless they are nocturnal (white-flowered epiphyllums, for example, are heavily perfumed). For a fuller description of the flowers, see "Desert-cactus flowers," page 114.

Since jungle cacti grow under shady conditions in the wild, they do not need direct sunlight in order to flower. This means that they are really more suitable than their desert relations for indoor cultivation (at least where flowering is concerned). Individual flowers are no longer-lasting than those of the desert cacti. But the smaller-flowered plants will continue to bloom over a reasonably long period, and many of the others have two flowering periods a year.

Because their growth is less compact than that of desert cacti, jungle cacti frequently need to be supported on sticks. Often the best way to grow them is in hanging baskets, where they can trail down attractively. Details of the most suitable arrangements for specific types of jungle cacti are given in the appropriate entries in the *A–Z Guide*.

PROPER CARE

Light Jungle cacti must *never* be subjected to summer sunlight. Direct sunlight for even a few days during the summer months will surely kill them. Keep these plants in medium light throughout the year (although the winter sun will do no harm in regions where it is weak). If possible, place jungle cacti in the open air, ideally under a shady tree, during the warmer months. Although long stems are less likely to suffer from one-sided light than are the more rigid stems of desert types, regular turning of the plants when indoors will improve the look of the growth.

Temperature Normally warm room temperatures are suitable throughout the year since jungle cacti do not need a long winter rest in order to flower. They tend to grow almost continuously, even though most kinds do have a period of more active growth during the spring and summer. They cannot tolerate temperatures below about 50°F.

Since these plants come from humid jungles, the air in most rooms is too dry for them. To increase the humidity, spray them daily. If possible, use rainwater; hard water will spot the stems.

Watering During the spring and summer water these plants plentifully, often enough to keep the potting mixture thoroughly moist, but never allow the pots to stand in water. During the winter water more moderately. Make the potting mixture moist at each watering, but let the top half-inch of the mixture dry out before watering again. At the end of each flowering period give jungle cacti a two- to three-week-long rest. During those weeks water only enough to keep the potting mixture barely moist. Where water is hard try to use rainwater or distilled water.

Feeding Because flowering periods occur for various species at various times of year, the right time to fertilize is determined more by the growth of a plant than by the season. When flower buds begin to form, start to apply high-potassium, tomato-type fertilizer once every two weeks, and continue through the flowering period only. It is important to use a fertilizer free of excess nitrogen, which can cause brown spots on the stems.

Potting and repotting These cacti can be grown successfully in the potting mixture recommended for desert cacti—a standard soil- or peat-based mixture with the addition of a one-third portion of coarse sand or perlite (see above, page 117). Since leaf mold is the natural medium for jungle cacti, it may also be included in the mixture if available; add an amount equal to the portion of sand or perlite. The leaf mold is not essential, and neither is manure. But the addition of well-rotted or dried cow manure is bound to benefit the plants. Use a mixture of up to one-half manure to one-quarter each of soil-based mixture and coarse sand or perlite. Either clay or plastic pots will do.

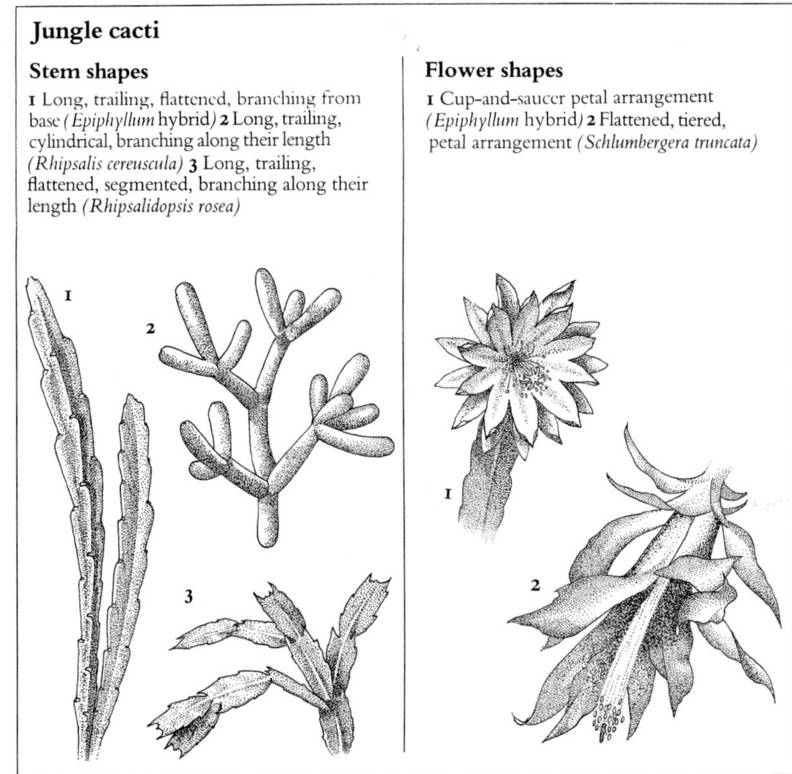

Jungle cacti

Stem shapes

1 Long, trailing, flattened, branching from base *(Epiphyllum* hybrid*)* **2** Long, trailing, cylindrical, branching along their length *(Rhipsalis cereuscula)* **3** Long, trailing, flattened, segmented, branching along their length *(Rhipsalidopsis rosea)*

Flower shapes

1 Cup-and-saucer petal arrangement *(Epiphyllum* hybrid*)* **2** Flattened, tiered, petal arrangement *(Schlumbergera truncata)*

Because jungle cacti do not have extensive root systems most can be grown in 4- to 5-inch pots. Once a year, at the end of a flowering period, examine the roots to see if they fill the pot. It usually takes only some gentle tapping to ease a plant out of its pot, and it will not harm the stems to hold them carefully while shaking the old potting mixture from the roots. If necessary, the plant can then be moved into a pot one size larger. Generally, however, a clean pot of the same size is suitable; it should be filled with fresh potting mixture. Do not use needlessly big containers. Most jungle cacti benefit from being slightly pot-bound.

Since many of these cacti have trailing stems, they are ideal plants for hanging baskets. The best sort of

The flowers at the ends of the trailing stems of schlumbergeras are shown off to good effect in a hanging basket.

basket is one with an open construction, usually made of wire. Line it with sphagnum moss, so that the potting mixture is contained within the moss lining, and then suspend it from a hook in the ceiling close to a suitable window, bearing in mind the need to avoid full sunlight.

Propagation To propagate jungle cacti that have many branches—the epiphyllum or the rhipsalis, for example—cut off a branch, using either a sharp knife or pruning shears (if the stem is tough), let the branch dry for a day, and then insert it about an inch deep into the normal potting mixture. Plant one such cutting in a 2-inch pot, several in a seed tray, or up to six around the inside rim of a 4-inch pot. The requirements of the cuttings are the same as those for adult plants.

Jungle cacti: stem propagation

Because jungle-cactus stems come in three different forms there are different ways to prepare them for propagation. No special rooting mixture need be used, and roots develop swiftly. Once cuttings are potted, they can, in general, be treated as adult specimens. Note the need for drying out cut ends in most forms.

Segmented stems

To take cuttings from plants such as schlumbergeras, cut off a stem with two or more segments at a joining point.

Insert the cut ends of several cuttings around the edge of a single pot of the standard potting mixture.

Branching stems

To propagate a cactus such as an epiphyllum, cut off several whole branches.

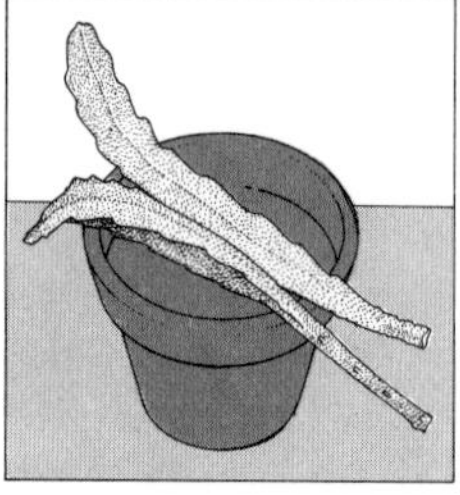

To heal the wounds, let cut surfaces dry out for 24 hours before planting them.

Insert branches an inch deep into potting mixture, planting several in a pot.

Columnar stems

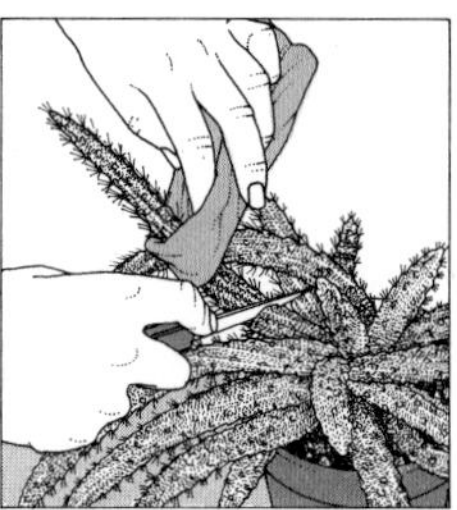

Cut several stems from cacti such as pfeifferas, wrapping a soft cloth around the stems.

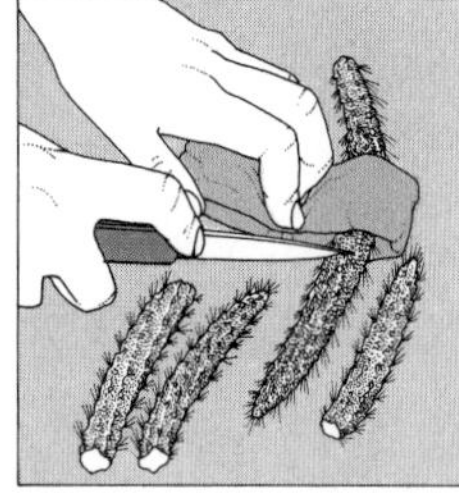

If necessary, cut stems into 4-inch pieces, and let them dry for 24 hours.

Plant stem portions the same way up as they were originally growing.

To propagate cacti with segmented stems, such as the schlumbergera, remove a portion consisting of two or more segments, and treat it just as if it were a cutting of a branching plant. With such jungle cacti as the pfeiffera, which have several unbranched stems, take a complete stem or a piece at least 4 inches long, and allow it to dry for 24 hours before potting up.

The best time for propagation from cuttings is spring or summer. For propagating jungle cacti from seed see "Raising cacti from seed," page 119.

Pests and diseases Jungle cacti are susceptible to the same pests and diseases as desert cacti.

For specific kinds of desert (D) and jungle (J) cacti see the individual articles in the *A–Z Guide:*

Aporocactus (D)
Astrophytum (D)
Cephalocereus (D)
Cereus (D)
Chamaecereus (D)
Cleistocactus (D)
Dolicothele (D)
Echinocactus (D)
Echinocereus (D)
Echinopsis (D)
Epiphyllum (J)
Espostoa (D)
Ferocactus (D)
Gymnocalycium (D)
Hamatocactus (D)
Heliocereus (J)
Lobivia (D)
Mammillaria (D)
Notocactus (D)
Opuntia (D)
Parodia (D)
Pfeiffera (J)
Rebutia (D)
Rhipsalidopsis (J)
Rhipsalis (J)
Schlumbergera (J)
Trichocereus (D)

Caladium

ARACEAE

Elephant's-ears
C. hortulanum hybrid

CALADIUMS (commonly called angel-wings, elephant's-ears, or heart of Jesus), are tuberous-rooted plants with heart-shaped or arrow-shaped leaves on long stalks rising directly from the tubers. The caladiums in cultivation are hybrids of mixed origin that are usually grouped under the name *C. hortulanum;* many are known by varietal names, of which there are dozens, but those normally available in florists' shops will probably be unnamed. All these plants need unusually constant high humidity to maintain healthy foliage; since this is difficult to achieve indoors, caladiums are often grown as temporary plants—very ornamental for the short period when they are in full leaf, but discarded when past their prime. It is not necessary to discard them, however. After the leaves have died down, dormant tubers can be kept in their pots and, given the right conditions, will produce new growth the following year.

The size of the paper-thin leaves varies considerably, but an average leaf is 12–15 inches long on a similar-length stalk. Color can be practically all white with just the faintest tinge of green along the veins; or the leaves can be spotted, veined, blotched, or marbled red, pink or white on green. Some kinds have much-smaller-than-average, predominantly green foliage, and these are far easier to grow than the others. Although all varieties have flowers, these plants are generally prized for their foliage only.
See also BULBS, CORMS, and TUBERS.

PROPER CARE

Light Caladiums require bright light but must not have direct sunlight.

The spectacular variations in coloring of caladium hybrid leaves are illustrated here.

Temperature A temperature of at least 65°–75°F, with a correspondingly high degree of humidity, is essential for plants in leaf; pots should be kept on trays of moist pebbles and foliage mist-sprayed daily. Caladiums must never be exposed to drafts, or the leaves will crumple up within an hour or two. Store dormant tubers in the dark at a temperature of about 60°.

Watering Caladiums are plants of tropical jungles. During the active growth period therefore, water them moderately, enough to make the entire mixture moist; but as leaves begin to dry out and die down, reduce the frequency of watering. The tubers require a rest period of at least five months, from early fall through early spring, and during those months they should be watered only sparingly (once a month, say).

Feeding Apply half-strength standard liquid fertilizer every two weeks in the active growth period only.

Potting and repotting Use a peat-based potting mixture and put plenty of clay-pot fragments in the bottom of the pot for drainage. Dormant tubers should be potted in fresh potting mixture in the spring. Three-inch pots are adequate for small tubers and for those with small leaves; 5-inch pots are best for larger plants. Tubers should be buried at about their own depth—for example, plant an inch-thick tuber an inch below the surface, etc. Maintain a temperature of at least 70°F to start tubers into growth.

This dormant tuber is being planted at about its own depth from the surface (as indicated by the dark shading in the cutaway picture above).

Propagation Detach small tubers from the parent at the time of restarting into growth. If it is potted up and cultivated as recommended above, each tuber will produce a new plant.

Calathea

MARANTACEAE

Cathedral-windows
C. makoyana

CALATHEA is a large genus of tropical plants all of which have decorative foliage. Although the leaves may seem to rise directly from the rootstock, they are normally connected to a short stem; in some species they appear in two ranks, the new leaves arising out of the sheathing of the stalks of older leaves. Leaf size and shape vary enormously—from 6 to 24 inches long, and from circular to strap-shaped. Flowers may be seen peeping through pale green bracts on mature plants, but they are insignificant and of little interest.

Note: Calatheas are closely related to marantas, and species from the two genera are often confused.

RECOMMENDED CALATHEAS

C. bachemiana has lance-shaped leaves held at a nearly 90° angle to upright leafstalks. Thus, although leaves can be 10 inches long and 2 inches wide on foot-long stalks, the plant tends to be comparatively low-growing. Leaf color is gray-green on the upper surface with broad, feathered, dark green markings fanning out alternately left and right of the central rib. The underside of the leaf is lightly shaded with purple across its entire surface.

C. lancifolia (often called either *C. insignis* or *Maranta insignis*) has uprightly held, lance-shaped, undulate leaves up to 18 inches long and 2 inches wide. Their pale green upper surface is marked with alternately large and small patches of darker green forking out from a dark green central vein; the underside is reddish purple. Leafstalks can be 10 inches long.

C. lindeniana has only a few leaves. They are elliptic, held upright, up to 15 inches long, and dark green, with olive green stripes running on both sides of the midrib and along the margins; the underside is maroon with darker markings. Leafstalks are up to 12 inches long.

C. makoyana (cathedral-windows, or peacock plant) has roughly oval leaves 10–12 inches long held upright on 10- to 12-inch-long stalks, and they turn slightly to display the underside as well as the upper surface. Both surfaces have very fine lines running from the central vein in a V-shape to the leaf edges, along with elliptic patches of different sizes following the thin lines. Patches on the green upper surface tend to be darker green; those on the pinkish maroon underside tend to be deep maroon. But leaf color in this species is variable, since it is greatly affected by growing conditions, especially the quality of light.

C. ornata has more or less erect leaves varying from oblong to lance-shaped and averaging 8 inches long. Their color is deep green above and deep purple-red beneath. The young leaves

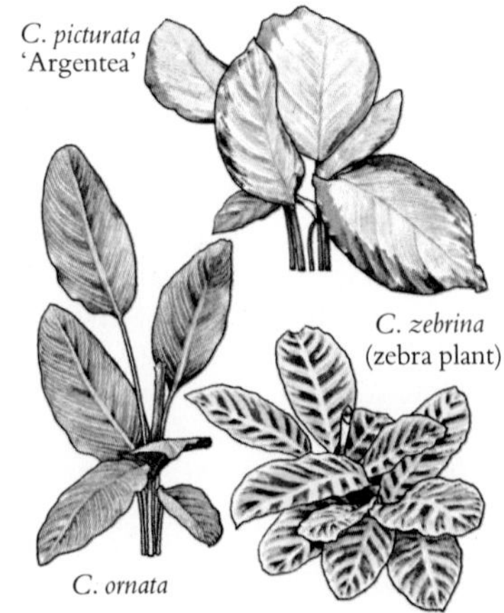

C. picturata 'Argentea'

C. zebrina (zebra plant)

C. ornata

are narrowly striped, usually with pairs of white lines (often tinged with pink) along the lateral veins. Two varieties—*C.o.* 'Roseolineata,' with pinker lines, and *C.o.* 'Sanderana,' with more strongly contrasted stripes and more uniformly erect leaves—are more frequently grown than the original species.

***C. picturata* 'Argentea'** has pear-shaped leaves that are more or less upright, 6 inches long, and 3 inches wide; the upper surface has a metallic silvery look except around the edges, which are emerald green, and the underside is maroon. Leafstalks are 3–4 inches long.

C. zebrina (zebra plant) has elliptic leaves up to 15 inches long, which have a velvety, emerald green upper surface with paler veins and midrib. The underside is purple. The leaves are held horizontally on erect stalks.

PROPER CARE

Light Calatheas prefer medium light—for example, at a tree-shaded window. Brighter light often spoils leaf coloring.

Temperature A temperature ranging between 60° and 70°F is ideal. In warmer rooms high humidity is essential, and the foliage should be mist-sprayed daily. Rainwater is excellent for this, since it leaves no unsightly white lime deposit.

Watering During the active growth period water plants plentifully—as often as necessary to keep the potting mixture thoroughly moist. In the rest period water moderately, enough to make the mixture moist, but allow the top half-inch of the mixture to dry out between waterings. Use lime-free water at room temperature.

Feeding Calatheas should be given generous amounts of standard liquid fertilizer every two weeks during the active growth period.

Potting and repotting Add up to one-third leaf mold or peat moss to a soil-based potting mixture (see page 429), or use a peat-based mixture. In the latter case, however, the mixture *must* be kept constantly supplied with standard liquid fertilizer when plants are in active growth. Healthy plants need to be moved into pots one size larger every year—preferably in late spring or early summer.

Propagation In late spring divide overcrowded clumps, making sure that some roots remain on each part. Plant the sections in 3-inch pots of moistened standard mixture, enclose them in plastic bags, and keep them in medium light. Remove the bags when new roots have formed.

Calceolaria

SCROPHULARIACEAE

Slipper flower
C. herbeohybrida

THERE are many species of this genus, but the only calceolarias generally grown indoors are the hybrids known as *C. herbeohybrida* (also called *C. crenatiflora* or *C. multiflora),* which are bushy plants with such common names as slipperwort and pocketbook, pouch or slipper flower. These have very decorative foliage and flowers but can be kept only for a single season. Commercial growers raise them from seed sown in early summer, overwinter the young plants cool at between 45° and 50°F, and sell them in early spring, when the flower buds are just beginning to open. They can then be enjoyed indoors for about a month of flowering time before being discarded.

Calceolaria leaves are large—up to 8 inches across—roughly heart-shaped, and grouped around the base of a single central stem. Above the leaves rise several branching stalks 1–2 feet tall, each carrying loose clusters of pouch- or slipper-shaped flowers, which vary in size (according to seed strain) from $\frac{1}{2}$ to 2 inches across, in any one of various shades of red, orange, yellow or reddish brown. Most of the flowers are spotted or blotched with a contrasting color.

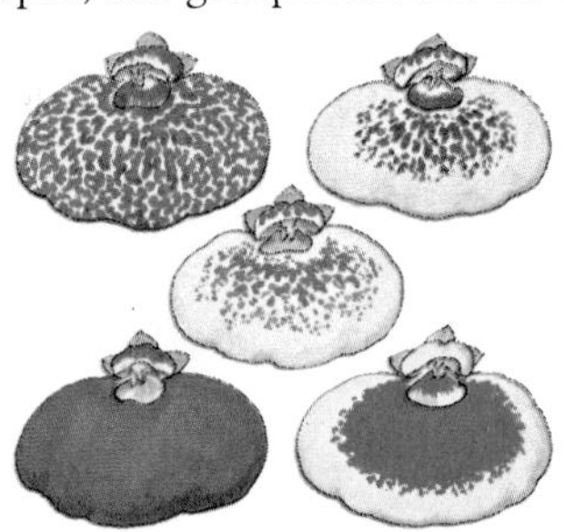

C. herbeohybrida (flowers)

To keep the plants flowering for as long as possible, these calceolarias should have bright light but not direct sunlight, be given the coolest possible position, and watered plentifully as often as necessary to keep the potting mixture thoroughly moist. Never allow the potting mixture to dry out; dry mixture can cause the plant to collapse. If this should happen through an oversight, immerse the pot in a pail of water, and allow the mixture to become thoroughly wet. When bubbles stop rising from the mixture, remove the pot and allow excess water to drain away. Standing the pot on a tray of damp pebbles or peat will also extend the life of a calceolaria by raising the humidity level.

A careful watch should be kept for aphids, (see page 454), which are these plants' greatest enemy. They can develop to epidemic proportions in a very few days.

Callisia
COMMELINACEAE

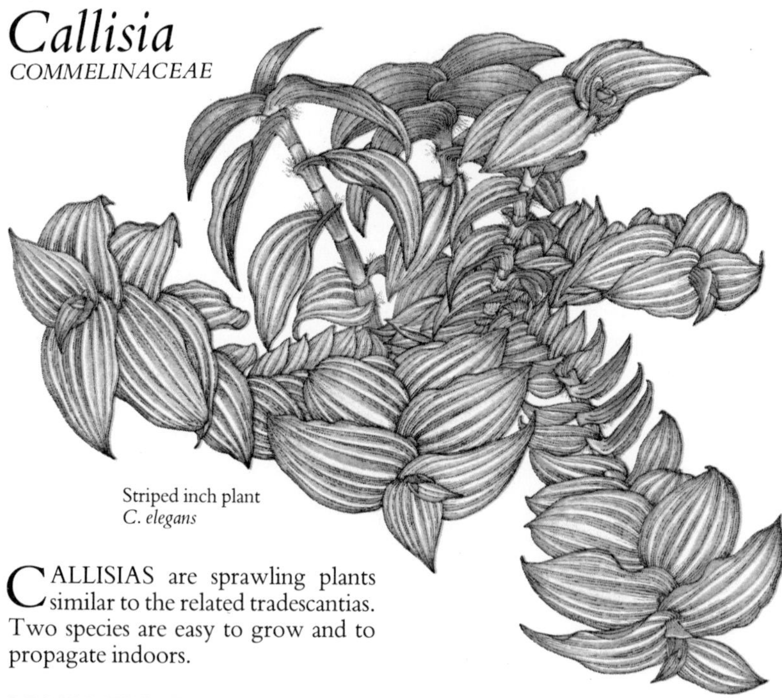
Striped inch plant
C. elegans

CALLISIAS are sprawling plants similar to the related tradescantias. Two species are easy to grow and to propagate indoors.

RECOMMENDED CALLISIAS

C. elegans (formerly called *Setcreasea striata;* popularly known as striped inch plant) has 2-foot-long stems that are erect when young but that hang down as they develop. The upper surface of the narrowly oval, 1- to $1\frac{1}{2}$-inch-long, pointed leaves is olive green liberally marked with lengthwise white lines; the underside is purple. The mature plant is unlikely to grow more than 3 inches tall, and it is best used as a hanging specimen, with the striped tops and richly colored undersides of the foliage in view. In bright light leaves almost overlap; in poorer light they grow about an inch apart. White, insignificant flowers are occasionally produced.

C. fragrans (also known as *Spironema fragrans* and *Tradescantia dracaenoides)* has elliptic, pointed leaves up to 10 inches long and $1\frac{1}{2}$ inches wide carried on fleshy stems up to 3 feet long. The fresh, glossy green leaves tend to become reddish purple in strong light. In young plants the short stems are arranged in a rosettelike shape, but they rapidly lengthen. The occasional flowers are fragrant. The upper leaf surfaces of a variety, *C.f.* 'Melnickoff,' have lengthwise white or cream-colored stripes of differing widths.

PROPER CARE

Light Give bright light with three or four hours a day of direct sunlight at all times.

Temperature Callisias thrive in warm rooms. It is advisable, however, to give them a short winter rest period at 50°–60°F, if possible.

Watering During the active growth period water plentifully, enough to keep the potting mixture thoroughly moist, but never allow pots to stand in water. In the rest period water sparingly, giving enough to make the mixture barely moist, and allow the top two-thirds to dry out between waterings.

Feeding Use standard liquid fertilizer once every two weeks in the active growth period only.

Potting and repotting Use either a soil-based or peat-based potting mixture (see page 429). Because *C. elegans* eventually loses compactness and richness of color, replace old plants with new. A 3-inch pot or half-pot is generally big enough for a plant's entire lifetime (about two years). *C. fragrans* grows fast and needs repotting every spring; large specimens may require 5- or 6-inch pots. If a plant begins to lose its lower leaves it too should be replaced.

Propagation Take 2-inch-long tip cuttings in spring or summer. Insert several cuttings of *C. elegans* or one cutting of *C. fragrans* in a 2- or 3-inch pot of standard potting mixture, and keep them in bright filtered light, watering sparingly. After two to three weeks, when roots have developed, treat the cuttings as mature callisias.

Callistemon
MYRTACEAE

Bottle-brush
C. citrinus

ONLY one species of the small genus *Callistemon, C. citrinus* (bottle-brush), is regularly grown indoors. The common name of this shrub is appropriate, for its flowers, which have no petals, are remarkable for their protruding, bright red stamens arranged in the shape of a bristly bottle-brush. The fine, silky hair which covers the stems and the branches of *C. citrinus* wears off with age. The leaves—usually bunched together tightly and held close to the branches—are stiff, gray-green, lance-shaped, and up to 3 inches long and $\frac{3}{4}$ inch wide. The cylindrical flower spikes that appear near the tips of branches in summer are 2–4 inches long. Each flower comprises hundreds of closely-packed hairlike stamens.

The best form of *C. citrinus* is *C.c. splendens,* whose brilliant crimson, $1\frac{1}{2}$-inch-long stamens form a "brush" 4 or more inches long. The graceful, open shrub can grow 4 feet tall in an

8-inch pot, but may be drastically pruned to keep it smaller (see "Special points," below).

PROPER CARE

Light These plants must have several hours of direct sunlight daily in order to bloom well.

Temperature Callistemons flourish in normal room temperatures during the growing season, but they should be given a cool resting period in winter (when they will require temperatures down to 45°–50°F).

Watering During the active growth period water plentifully as often as necessary to keep the potting mixture thoroughly moist, but never allow the pot to stand in water. During the rest period give only enough water to keep the mixture from drying out.

Feeding Actively growing plants should be given standard liquid fertilizer every two weeks.

Potting and repotting Use a soil-based potting mixture (see page 429). Move plants into pots one size larger each spring, just as they start into new growth. When a plant has reached maximum convenient pot size, topdress annually (see page 428), with fresh mixture.

Propagation In early summer take cuttings 3 or 4 inches long from non-flowering sideshoots of the current year's growth, preferably with a heel (a sliver of the old stem at the base of the cutting) attached. Plant each cutting in a 3-inch pot containing a moistened equal-parts mixture of peat moss and coarse sand or perlite, enclose it in a plastic bag or heated propagating case (see page 444), and stand it in bright filtered light. When rooting has occurred (generally after four to six weeks), uncover the pot and begin to water the new plant sparingly—just enough to make the mixture barely moist. When roots appear through the drainage hole of the pot, transfer the plant into a larger pot of standard potting mixture and treat it as a mature callistemon.

Special points If possible, stand callistemons outdoors in full sunlight from the end of the flowering period until the temperature drops to around 50°F. Then re-house them in the sunniest possible indoor position.

To keep plants shapely, cut them back immediately after flowering ceases. If necessary, cut out up to half the previous year's growth.

Camellia

THEACEAE

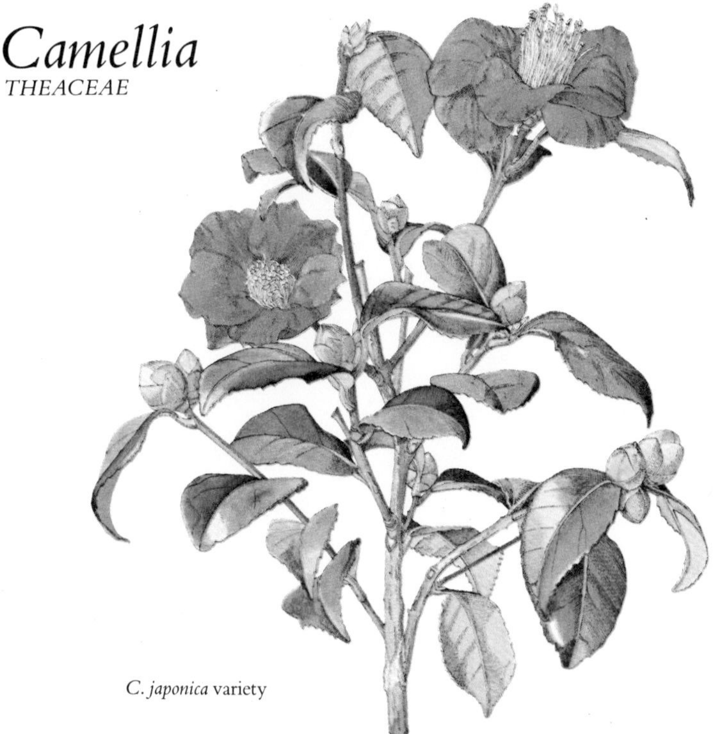

C. japonica variety

CAMELLIAS are flowering shrubs or small trees that produce striking flowers, mainly in late winter or early spring. Most indoor camellias are varieties of one species, *C. japonica*. The leathery, glossy leaves, which are about 4 inches long and 2 inches wide, are arranged alternately on woody stems. Flowers can be solitary or in clusters, and each bloom can be single (with only 5 petals encircling a mass of yellow stamens) or double (with more than 20 petals and no visible stamens) or semi-double (something in between). Flower size varies from 2 to 5 inches across, and color may be white, pink, red, or a combination of white and either red or pink.

RECOMMENDED CAMELLIAS

***C. japonica* 'Adolphe Audusson'** has double, blood red, 5-inch flowers that bloom in the spring.

***C.j.* 'Alba plena'** has double, white, 4-inch flowers that bloom in spring.

***C.j.* 'Alba simplex'** has single, white, 3-inch flowers that bloom in winter.

***C.j.* 'Pink Perfection'** has double, shell pink, 3-inch flowers that bloom in the spring.

***C.j.* 'Purity'** has double, white, long-lasting, 3-inch flowers that bloom in the spring.

***C.j.* 'William S. Hastie'** has double, crimson, 4-inch flowers that bloom in the spring.

PROPER CARE

Light Grow these plants in bright filtered light throughout the year.

Temperature In the dry warmth of the average home camellias will not flower, but they grow well in cool porches and conservatories. An ideal temperature during the bud-forming stage (fall and winter) is between 45° and 60°F. Camellias cannot survive for long in indoor temperatures above 65°. Stand pots on trays of moist pebbles, and mist-spray the plants at least once a day.

Watering During the active growth period water plentifully but never allow the pot to stand in water. During the rest period—about six weeks from the end of the flowering period until late spring or fall (depending on the variety)—water only enough to keep the mixture from drying out.

Feeding Apply standard liquid fertilizer every two weeks during the active growth period.

Potting and repotting Use equal parts of peat moss, coarse leaf mold, and a lime-free soil-based potting mixture (see page 429). Move plants into slightly larger pots in spring whenever necessary. After maximum convenient size has been reached, topdress (see page 428) at the end of each rest period.

Propagation Propagation is not a practicable procedure in the home.

Campanula

CAMPANULACEAE

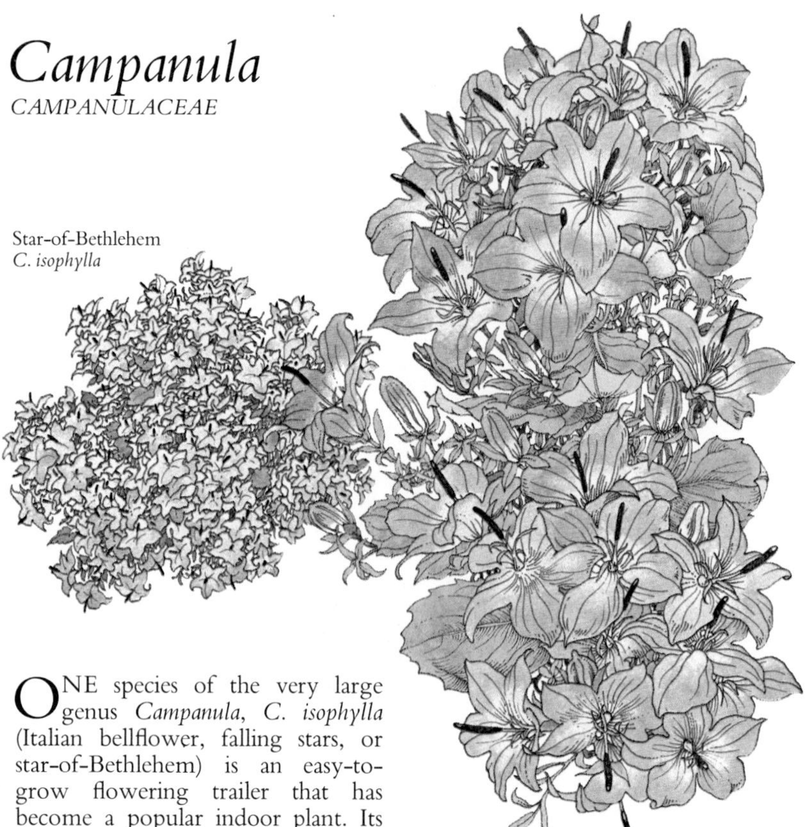

Star-of-Bethlehem
C. isophylla

ONE species of the very large genus *Campanula*, *C. isophylla* (Italian bellflower, falling stars, or star-of-Bethlehem) is an easy-to-grow flowering trailer that has become a popular indoor plant. Its small, heart-shaped, tooth-edged leaves are bright green and rather brittle. If stems or leafstalks are broken, they exude a milky white sap with a distinctive, but not unpleasant, odor. Star-shaped, cupped flowers, which are produced from leaf axils, are 1–1½ inches wide and pale blue. There is a white-flowered form, *C.i.* 'Alba,' and one form that has hairy, variegated foliage and slightly darker blue flowers, *C.i.* 'Mayi.'

C. isophylla is ideal for use in hanging baskets and raised pots. The many slender stems, each as much as 1 foot long, will trail down naturally, or else they can be trained upward on a small trellis. Flowers, which are normally produced between midsummer and fall, continue in succession for two or three months, usually becoming so numerous that they hide the foliage. Remove spent flowers (which can generally be pinched off with the fingertips) in order to prolong the flowering season. Cut back the long stems close to the potting mixture as soon as winter approaches.

PROPER CARE

Light Although these campanulas do not require full sunlight, they should have bright light, with or without some direct sunlight, at all times. This should ensure close growth and abundant flowers. Campanulas can bloom well in a sunless window but only if stood on the sill.

Temperature Since the flowers fade quickly in great heat, indoor campanulas should be given the coolest position possible in summer. In temperatures above 65°F provide high humidity by standing plants on trays of moist pebbles and mist-spraying them regularly; this will help prolong the flowering period. In winter these plants should rest in a really cool temperature—ideally around 40°, and certainly not above 50°; the rest may be started as soon as flowering finishes. Higher winter temperatures will curtail the next season's flowering.

Watering Campanulas like to have moist roots. During the active growth period and for the duration of the lengthy flowering period, they should be watered plentifully, as much as necessary to keep the potting mixture thoroughly moist—but never allow pots to stand in water (see "Special points," below). Even during the winter rest period these plants should be given some water—enough to moisten the potting mixture—at two-week intervals.

Feeding Apply standard liquid fertilizer once every two weeks, beginning when plants have filled their pots with roots (about six weeks after potting) and continuing until the flowering season ends.

Potting and repotting Use a soil-based potting mixture (see page 429). For best effect, plant three or four rooted cuttings in a single 3-inch pot in early spring; move them into slightly larger pots whenever roots appear on the surface of the potting mixture (normally, every two or three months). Maximum pot size required: probably 5 inches. To fill hanging baskets, take several plants from a few 3-inch pots at the time they need repotting. Since blue and white varieties bloom simultaneously, they can be effectively mixed together in one basket.

Propagation Take 2-inch-long tip cuttings (each with three or four pairs of leaves) from old plants just as new growth appears in early spring; handle them gently so as not to break the brittle stems and leafstalks. Dip cut ends in a hormone rooting powder to seal them and assist rooting. Gently insert each cutting about ½ inch into a moistened equal-parts mixture of peat moss and coarse sand or perlite, enclose the pot in a plastic bag, and keep it warm in medium light. The cutting will root in two to three weeks and can then be moved into the standard potting mixture for adult campanulas. After another three or four weeks of medium light and only moderate watering, the young plant can be subjected to brighter light and treated as a mature campanula.

Propagation can also be achieved by dividing established plants, but division is less satisfactory than the tip-cutting method because stems of divided plants are old and always appear rather woody. If plants *are* divided, the clump should be pulled apart into several sections and shaken free of most of the old mixture. Fresh potting mixture is important for the health of new plants.

Special points Although campanulas like plenty of moisture, fungus disease—especially gray mold (see page 456)—sometimes occurs if the soil retains too much water or if the plant is kept in excessively humid conditions. If this happens, a fungicide will kill the fungus, but the plant obviously needs drier soil and air.

Capsicum
SOLANACEAE

Christmas pepper
C. annuum

CAPSICUMS (ornamental peppers) are prized for their bright-colored, fleshy, podlike fruit. Most people buy the plants in fall or early winter with the fruit already formed, and discard them when the fruit has gone. The most popular forms are bushy and low-growing (12–15 inches tall and across). All capsicums bear fruit profusely. The stems are somewhat woody, with thin, dark green branches carrying usually lance-shaped, slightly hairy, green leaves $1\frac{1}{2}$–4 inches long and $\frac{1}{2}$–$1\frac{1}{2}$ inches wide on inch-long stalks. White flowers are produced from leaf axils in early summer, but are insignificant. The fruit that follows the flowers remains decorative for 8 to 12 weeks after which it wrinkles and drops off.

RECOMMENDED CAPSICUMS

C. annuum (Christmas pepper) is the most popular indoor species. The many forms are generally divided into five groups, of which only three—cherry, cone, and cluster peppers—are familiar potted plants.

Cherry peppers have berrylike, bright yellow or purplish white fruit 1 inch in diameter.

Cone peppers have cone-shaped or cylindrical fruit up to 2 inches long. Fruit color may be green, ivory white, yellow, orange, red, or purple, and the color may well change as the fruit ripens.

Cluster peppers have slender-pointed, 3-inch-long, red fruit, which grow in clusters of two or three.

PROPER CARE

Light These plants need bright light, with at least three or four hours a day of direct sunlight. In inadequate light the leaves will begin to wilt and drop off prematurely.

Temperature Capsicums do well enough in normal room temperatures, but the fruit remains decorative longer in a temperature of 55°–60°F. For increased humidity stand pots on trays of moist pebbles.

Watering Water plentifully, as often as necessary to keep the potting mixture thoroughly moist, but never let pots stand in water.

Feeding Apply standard liquid fertilizer every two weeks.

Potting and repotting Repotting is not required for these plants.

Propagation Capsicums are raised from seed. Since it takes professional care to bring them to the flowering and fruiting stage, however, this is not practicable in the home.

Carex
CYPERACEAE

Japanese sedge grass
C. morrowii 'Variegata'

ONLY one form of the large genus *Carex* is widely grown indoors: a variegated-leaved variety of *C. morrowii*, *C.m.* 'Variegata' (Japanese sedge grass). This stiff, grasslike sedge contrasts well with broad-leaved plants. Its clustered leaves, which grow from a rhizomatous rootstock running just below the surface of the potting mixture, are up to 1 foot long and $\frac{1}{4}$ inch wide. Leaves are yellowish green narrowly striped with white. Flowers are insignificant and rarely produced.

This plant grows more or less continuously, but active growth will slow down in the reduced light of winter.

PROPER CARE

Light Grow carexes in bright filtered light. Inadequate light will dull leaf-color contrast.

Temperature *C.m.* 'Variegata' can tolerate warmth (65°–70°F) only if humidity is kept high. In warm rooms it is advisable to stand plants on trays of moist pebbles and mist-spray them regularly. If possible, keep winter temperatures down to 50°–60°F.

Watering Although often found outdoors as waterside plants, indoor carexes should never be overwatered. Throughout the year water moderately, enough to make the mixture thoroughly moist, but allow the top inch of the mixture to dry out completely between waterings.

When using other specimens to contrast with grassy carexes in a display, choose plants needing similar growing conditions (here, scindapsuses and marantas).

Feeding Apply standard liquid fertilizer once a month during spring and summer only.

Potting and repotting Use a soil-based potting mixture (see page 429). A 5-inch pot is likely to be the biggest required. Move small plants into pots one size larger in spring whenever the tufts of leaves completely cover the surface area of the mixture.

Propagation Split mature plants into two or three clumps and plant each separately, preferably in spring. Do not divide a plant into more than three sections; very small clumps rarely grow well.

It would be possible to divide these two clumps further, but it would not be advisable. Clumps of carex that are too small will not develop healthily.

Caryota

PALMAE

Burmese-fishtail palm
C. mitis

CARYOTAS (fishtail palms) differ from other palms in that their fronds are bipinnate—i.e., each primary leaflet (pinna) is divided into secondary ones (pinnules). The gray-green leafstalks vary in length according to species, but the stalks of all species carry these bipinnate fronds, which are divided in herringbone fashion into sections that are again subdivided into many wedge-shaped leaflets; each secondary leaflet is folded into a V-shape with ragged edges, like a tattered fishtail. As caryotas age, the stem lengthens and the arching fronds grow several feet long and wide, but growth is slow—no more than a few inches a year for a stem that may reach an ultimate height indoors of 8 feet or more. Flowers and fruit are never produced on indoor caryotas.

See also PALMS.

RECOMMENDED CARYOTAS

C. mitis (Burmese-, crested-, or tufted-fishtail palm) can grow 8 feet tall—rarely more—in the home. The short stem of a 4-foot-tall specimen may carry six to eight deeply arching, bipinnate fronds on 1- to 2-foot-long leafstalks, and these form a sort of "crown" to the plant. Several smaller fronds are also generally clustered around the base of the main stem. The big fronds may be as much as 3 feet wide, with each light green secondary leaflet about 6 inches long and 5 inches wide; the leaflets grow close together in groups of 20 to 30.

C. urens (wine, jaggery, or sago palm) produces a stem up to 8 feet tall indoors. A 4-foot-tall specimen will usually have a crown of five or six drooping fronds, each up to 4 feet wide, borne on an 18-inch stalk, and divided into many sets of dark green, somewhat leathery, secondary leaflets about 5 inches long and 3 inches wide. These leaflets are more triangular in shape and have less jagged edges than those of *C. mitis*; and they are far less numerous, so that the fronds look looser and more open.

PROPER CARE

Light Caryotas grow best in full sunlight filtered through a translucent blind or curtain.

Temperature Caryotas like warmth and cannot tolerate temperatures below 55°F. In very warm rooms, however, increase humidity by standing the pot on a tray of moist pebbles or damp peat moss.

Watering These palms should be watered plentifully, as often as necessary to keep the potting mixture thoroughly moist, but never allow the pot to stand in water. Potted caryotas are not likely to have well-defined periods of growth and rest, but growth may slow down in fall and winter. In periods when plants appear to be growing more slowly than usual it is advisable to allow the top half-inch of the mixture to dry out completely between waterings.
Feeding Apply standard liquid fertilizer once a month from early spring to mid-fall only.
Potting and repotting Use a soil-based potting mixture (see page 429). Caryotas like to have their roots constricted and should therefore be grown in pots that seem too small for them. Move plants into pots one size larger only once every two or three years, at a time when they are just breaking into fresh growth. Put clay-pot fragments in the bottom of the pot for drainage, and pack the mixture firmly around the roots—taking care, however, not to break any of the thicker roots in the process. Once a plant is in a pot of maximum convenient size, give it an annual top-dressing (see page 428).
Propagation It is possible to propagate from seed sown in spring at a temperature of at least 75°F. *C. mitis* (not *C. urens*) can be propagated from suckers (basal growths) or offsets. Detach the growth when it is 9–12 inches tall, retaining some of the attached root, and plant it in a 3- to 4-inch pot of barely moistened soil-based potting mixture. Stand the pot (uncovered) in a warm place where it gets bright light filtered through a translucent blind or curtain, and water only enough to make the mixture barely moist, allowing the top half-inch of the mixture to dry out between waterings. New growth will indicate that rooting has occurred. Thereafter, the cultivation needs of the young plant are the same as those of a mature caryota.
Special points Brown leaflet tips on a caryota, as well as attacks by red spider mites (see page 455), usually indicate that the air is too dry. There is no need to worry, however, if an occasional frond turns entirely yellow and then brown before dropping off. It is entirely natural for one old frond to die off every year or so.

Catharanthus

APOCYNACEAE

Old-maid
C. roseus 'Ocellatus'

ONLY one species of the genus *Catharanthus* (sometimes confused with the genus *Vinca*) is grown indoors: *C. roseus* (Madagascar or rose-periwinkle, or old-maid), which is a small, upright shrub prized for its shiny green leaves and delicate-looking flowers. The glossy, oval leaves are 1–2 inches long, have a white center vein, and are borne in opposite pairs on slender stems. One or more flowers are produced at stem tips throughout a flowering period that generally lasts from mid-spring to early fall. Each flower has an inch-long tube flattened out into five lance-shaped petals at the mouth, which is up to $1\frac{1}{2}$ inches wide. Flower color is usually soft rose-pink or, occasionally, mauve. There is a white-flowered form, *C.r.* 'Albus,' and another, *C.r.* 'Ocellatus,' that has white flowers with a carmine-red center.

These plants are usually acquired in early spring and discarded when the flowering season has ended. They are not normally worth overwintering because only young plants tend to look healthy and flower profusely.

PROPER CARE

Light Bright light, including three or four hours of direct sunlight daily, is essential for good flowering.
Temperature Normal room temperatures are suitable at all times. A catharanthus cannot tolerate temperatures that fall below about 50°F.
Watering Water the potting mixture plentifully, but do not allow the pot to stand in water.
Feeding Once flowering has begun, apply standard liquid fertilizer every two weeks.
Potting and repotting Use a soil-based potting mixture (see page 429) when repotting these plants. Move them into pots one size larger every six to eight weeks. Probable maximum size needed: 4 or 5 inches.
Propagation Catharanthuses can be propagated from tip cuttings as well as from seed, but it is best to use seed, since plants grown by this method will flower more profusely. In late winter or early spring sow a few seeds in a shallow tray of moistened rooting mixture (see page 444), place the tray in a plastic bag or propagating case (see page 443), and stand it in a warm position where it will get bright filtered light. When the seeds have germinated—generally in two to three weeks—uncover the tray and begin watering the seedlings moderately (enough to make the mixture moist, but allowing the top half-inch to dry out between waterings) until they are about an inch high. Transfer each such seedling into a 3-inch pot of standard potting mixture, and treat it as a mature catharanthus.

Cattleya
ORCHIDACEAE

Cattleya hybrid

CATTLEYAS are epiphytic orchids with pseudobulbs up to 10 inches tall. Each pseudobulb is topped by one or two fleshy, strap-shaped, green leaves. New growth, which develops on a short rhizome from the base of the last pseudobulb, consists of an immature pseudobulb with a cluster of green leafy sheaths. The lower sheaths closely encase the growing pseudobulb. They gradually lose their green color, shrivel, and become white and papery. The upper one or two sheaths develop into the true leaves.

Flowers are produced either singly or in groups on a terminal flower stalk. Most flowers are waxy, fleshy, and have a tubular lip. There are many species and hybrids, all with incomparably beautiful flowers.
See also ORCHIDS.

RECOMMENDED CATTLEYAS

C. intermedia has cylindrical pseudobulbs 10–15 inches high and ½ inch in diameter, each topped by two 8-inch-long, 2-inch-wide, dark green leaves. A group of up to six rose-pink flowers each 4 inches across appear on a 4-inch-long stem in early summer and last for up to five weeks. The lip is dark purple. The variety *C.i.* 'Aquinii,' which has pink petals splashed with purple, has given rise to many splashed-petal varieties.

C. labiata has club-shaped pseudobulbs up to 10 inches high, 1 inch wide, and ¾ inch thick. One thick, leathery, medium green leaf up to 10 inches long and 3 inches wide tops each pseudobulb. A group of up to five fragrant flowers, each about 5 inches across, is produced in fall or early winter on a 3- to 4-inch-long stalk. Each bloom lasts for up to five weeks. Flower color is variable. The type plant has wavy-edged, rose-pink petals and sepals, and a dark crimson-magenta frilled lip streaked with bright yellow at the throat. There are many named varieties, which have larger flowers.

C. loddigesii has cylindrical pseudobulbs 8–12 inches high and ½ inch in diameter, each topped by two gray-green leaves 4–6 inches long and 1 inch wide. A group of up to six pale lilac flowers, each 4 inches across, is carried on a 6-inch-long stem in summer. Each flower lasts about four weeks. The deep purple lip can be splashed with yellow at the throat.

C. trianaei has club-shaped pseudobulbs 8–10 inches high, ¾ inch wide, and 1 inch thick, each with a single deep green leaf 6–10 inches long and 2–3 inches wide. A group of two to five flowers, each up to 7 inches across, is borne on a 4-inch-long stem in late winter. The flowers last about three weeks. Their color varies from light to deep lilac and the frilled lip is dark crimson-purple, marked with yellow at the throat.

PROPER CARE

Light Cattleyas need bright light without direct sunlight.

Temperature Warmth is essential. Minimum tolerable temperature for cattleyas: 55°–60°F. Protect these plants from sudden changes in temperature. For adequate humidity stand plants on trays of moist pebbles throughout the growing season, and mist-spray them daily whenever the temperature rises above 70°.

Watering During the active growth period water plentifully, but allow the potting mixture to dry out almost completely between waterings. During the six-week rest period that cattleyas take after flowering, water them just enough to prevent shriveling of the pseudobulbs.

Feeding Give a foliar feed with every third or fourth watering during the active growth period.

Potting and repotting Use any of the potting mixtures recommended for orchids (see page 289). Move plants into pots 2 inches larger whenever leading growth reaches the rim of the current pots. The best time to do this is at the end of the rest period. Place the old part of each plant against the rim of the new pot so that there is room for forward growth, and gently firm down the fresh mixture around the rhizome and roots. Water the mixture plentifully. Then move the repotted specimen into medium light for a week or two before exposing it to bright light. After maximum convenient pot size has been reached, divide the plant as suggested below.

Propagation To divide a cattleya, cut the rhizome into roughly equal halves. Disentangle the intertwined roots, cut away any rotting or broken ones, and repot each half of the plant in a suitable-size pot filled with thoroughly moistened, fresh mixture. Place pots in medium light until the rhizome pieces have made new roots (probably within four weeks). Then treat each plant as a mature cattleya.

Cephalocereus

CACTACEAE

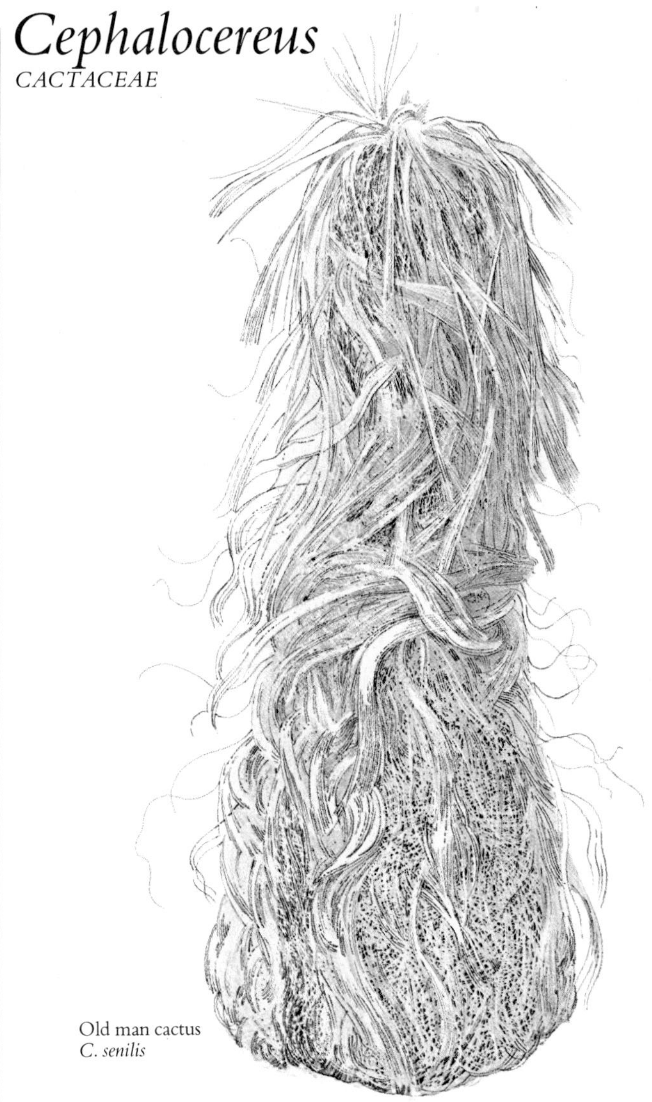

Old man cactus
C. senilis

THE only member of this genus of desert cacti commonly grown indoors is *C. senilis*, known as old man cactus because of the long, silvery white hairs that completely obscure the leafless, columnar stem. The stem is divided lengthwise into 20 to 30 shallow ribs, along the edges of which run rows of closely set areoles. Arising from the areoles are not only the hairs (which can grow up to 5 inches long) but from one to five yellow spines per areole. Avoid stroking the plant, since the hair conceals $1\frac{1}{2}$-inch-long spines. In the wild, *C. senilis* can grow up to 40 feet tall (when 200 years old), but as a slow-growing house plant it is unlikely to grow taller than 1 foot or to require a pot larger than 6 inches. Since the plant cannot reach maturity indoors, it will not flower.

See also CACTI.

PROPER CARE

Light In the wild these cacti are protected from intense sunlight by their hair; thus, the greater the intensity of light the longer and thicker are the hairs. If possible place plants at a window where they are likely to get constant sunlight.

Temperature In spring and summer, normal room temperatures are suitable for an actively growing cephalocereus. In winter, the plant should be encouraged to rest at a temperature below 65°F (though always above 45°). High winter temperatures coupled with the insufficient light of short winter days will cause unnaturally elongated stems.

Watering During the active growth period water moderately, enough to make the mixture moist throughout, but allowing the top half-inch to dry out between waterings. During the rest period water only enough to keep the mixture from drying out completely. Too much water during the short-day months encourages unnatural growth and can cause rotting of the base of the stem.

Feeding During the active growth period only, apply a tomato-type fertilizer once a month to plants grown in soil-based potting mixture, once in two weeks to those grown in peat-based mixture. Avoid splashing the hairs with fertilizer.

Potting and repotting Either soil-based or peat-based mixture can be used (see page 429) if made more porous by the addition of a one-third portion of coarse sand or perlite. These plants can usually be grown in 3-inch pots until they are 3–4 inches tall. Examine them each spring, however, to see if roots fill the pots (see page 426). When necessary, move plants into pots one size larger. If there is still room for roots to grow, replace plants in their original pots, which have been cleaned. Add fresh mixture as necessary.

Propagation *C. senilis* can be propagated only from seed (*see CACTI*, page 119).

Special points In time the white hairs of a cephalocereus tend to turn brownish. Some of this discoloration is due to dirt and can be removed by shampooing with a warm detergent solution and rinsing in clean water. Much of the darkening of hair, however, is due to age and must be accepted. (To avoid soaking the potting mixture with detergent, cover it up when washing the plant.)

The shaggy hair also provides a hiding place for such pests as mealy bugs (see page 455).

When shampooing a cephalocereus, be sure to cover the potting mixture to avoid soaking it with detergent.

Cereus

CACTACEAE

Peruvian apple cactus
C. peruvianus

CACTI of the genus *Cereus* form ribbed columns up to 30 feet tall when growing in the wild. Though less gigantic in pots, they are much admired for their almost sculptural, columnar shape, which contrasts impressively with that of most other plants in any collection of cacti. In an 8-inch pot one of these vigorous, fast-growing, desert plants can reach a height of 3 feet and a width of 6 inches in five or six years, after which it may produce funnel-shaped flowers in summer. These are up to 1 foot long, are often sweetly scented, and are nocturnal, opening at night and fading in early morning. Indoor gardeners with limited space need not be discouraged from growing one of these cacti because of size. If confined to a 4-inch pot, the plant will not grow any taller than about 2 feet. The only drawback is that it will be unlikely to flower at that size.

There are about 36 species of cereus, but only a few are in cultivation. Those described below are the most generally available.
See also CACTI.

RECOMMENDED CEREUSES

C. jamacaru is a bluish green single column that branches out toward the top in the wild, but that is unlikely to do so as a potted plant. It has six or more broad, prominent, notched ribs separated by deep, narrow indentations. Areoles in the notches are filled with white hairs, and each areole bears a cluster of 15 or more yellowish spines, which are unlikely to grow more than $\frac{1}{2}$ to 1 inch long indoors. Flowers, produced on large specimens only, are 8–12 inches long and have white petals tinged with green.

C. peruvianus (Peruvian apple cactus) is so similar to *C. jamacaru* that the two are often confused. Among the rather subtle differences: *C. peruvianus* has five to eight ribs; there are only about seven spines to each areole; the spines are more nearly brown than yellow; and petals of the 6-inch-long flowers are tinged with brownish green.

In any batch of *C. peruvianus* seedlings there may be at least one specimen of a naturally occurring variety known as *C.p.* 'Monstrosus'—a distorted form often sought after by collectors. Instead of having one center of growth at the top of the stem, this plant has numerous growing points and becomes covered with irregular, knoblike structures. It grows much more slowly than the type species and is harder to maintain in cultivation, for it apparently lacks the tolerance of adverse growing conditions characteristic of most types of cereus. If grown in badly drained soil, for example, *C.p.* 'Monstrosus' is likely to lose its roots and rot away.

C. peruvianus
'Monstrosus'

PROPER CARE

Light Grow these cacti in the fullest possible sunlight. Since the light coming from a window is one-sided, a columnar plant will tend to lean in that direction, and so it is important to turn such plants frequently. If possible, stand them outdoors during the summer months, for fresh air and extra sunlight will help improve their color and lengthen their spines.

Temperature Normally warm temperatures are suitable in spring, summer, and fall. For the winter these plants should be moved into a cool position (around 50°F, if possible), where they can rest. A cereus that tries to continue growing in the poor light of the short-day months will develop an abnormally thin, frail stem.

Watering During the active growth period water moderately, but allow the top half-inch of the mixture to dry out before watering again. During the winter rest period give just enough water to prevent the mixture from drying out.

Feeding During the active growth period only, use tomato-type fertilizer once every two weeks if the plants are in a peat-based potting mixture, once every four weeks if they are in a soil-based mixture.

Potting and repotting Either a peat-based or soil-based mixture will do (see page 429). For better drainage add one part coarse sand or perlite to two parts of the basic mixture. Plants up to 2 inches wide may be kept in 3-inch pots, but these cacti are fast-growing and may need to be moved into larger pots at least once a year. Remove every plant from its pot in early spring to see whether the roots are tightly packed. If they are, move the plant into a pot one size larger; otherwise, return it to its current pot, but topdress it (see page 428) with fresh potting mixture.

Propagation New plants are normally raised from seed. But, although these seeds germinate and grow up more quickly than those of most other cacti, seed propagation is still a slow process. A cereus can also be propagated by means of sections of stem rooted in the standard potting mixture (see *CACTI,* page 117), but this process is often impractical, since it involves the virtual destruction of the original plant. Amateur gardeners are well advised simply to buy small plants, which are easy to find.

Ceropegia
ASCLEPIADACEAE

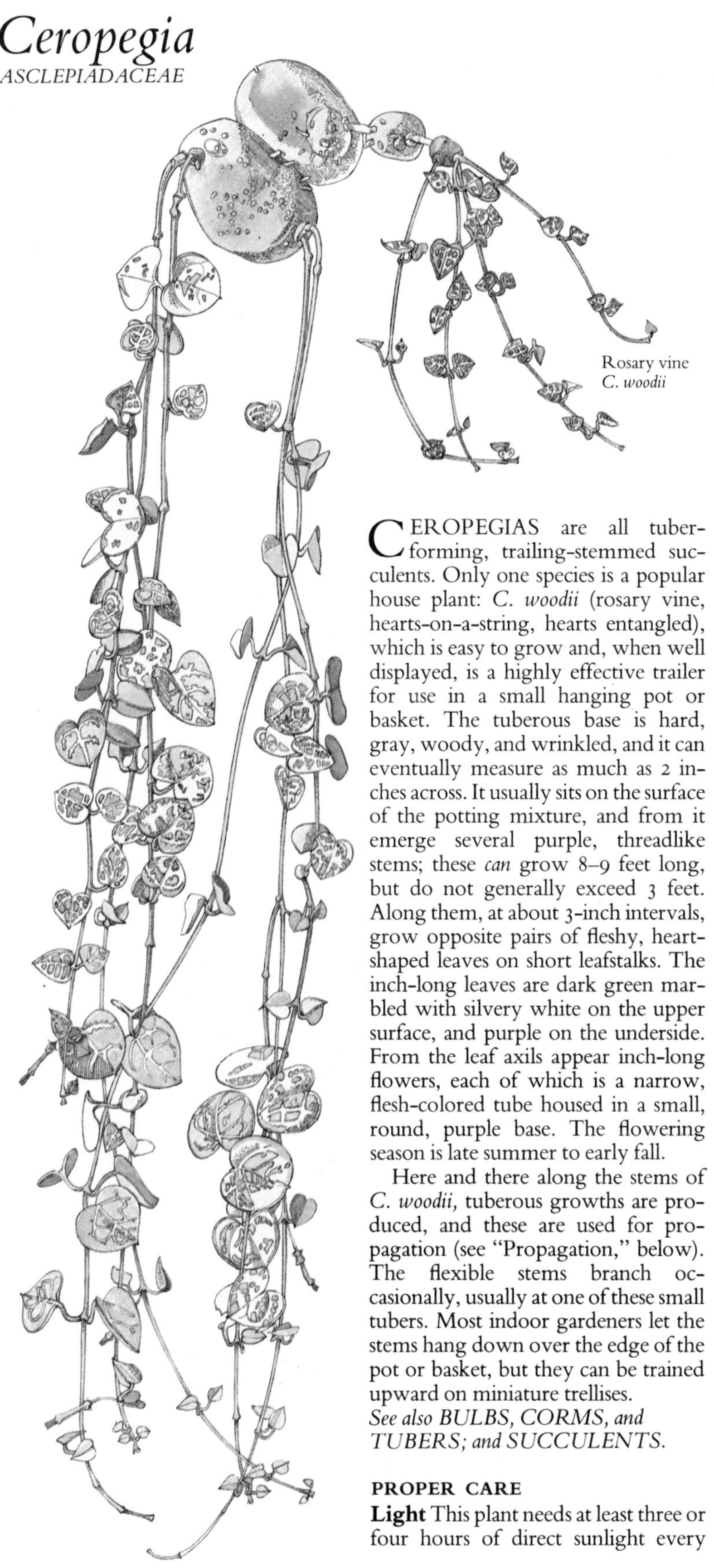

Rosary vine
C. woodii

CEROPEGIAS are all tuber-forming, trailing-stemmed succulents. Only one species is a popular house plant: *C. woodii* (rosary vine, hearts-on-a-string, hearts entangled), which is easy to grow and, when well displayed, is a highly effective trailer for use in a small hanging pot or basket. The tuberous base is hard, gray, woody, and wrinkled, and it can eventually measure as much as 2 inches across. It usually sits on the surface of the potting mixture, and from it emerge several purple, threadlike stems; these *can* grow 8–9 feet long, but do not generally exceed 3 feet. Along them, at about 3-inch intervals, grow opposite pairs of fleshy, heart-shaped leaves on short leafstalks. The inch-long leaves are dark green marbled with silvery white on the upper surface, and purple on the underside. From the leaf axils appear inch-long flowers, each of which is a narrow, flesh-colored tube housed in a small, round, purple base. The flowering season is late summer to early fall.

Here and there along the stems of *C. woodii,* tuberous growths are produced, and these are used for propagation (see "Propagation," below). The flexible stems branch occasionally, usually at one of these small tubers. Most indoor gardeners let the stems hang down over the edge of the pot or basket, but they can be trained upward on miniature trellises.

See also BULBS, CORMS, and TUBERS; and SUCCULENTS.

PROPER CARE

Light This plant needs at least three or four hours of direct sunlight every day. Too little light impairs leaf coloration and extends the gaps between the pairs of leaves.

Temperature Normal room temperatures are suitable for ceropegias throughout the year.

Watering In the active growth period water sparingly—just enough to make the potting mixture barely moist, allowing the top two-thirds of the mixture to dry out between waterings. During the winter rest period water very sparingly, giving just enough water to prevent the potting mixture from drying out completely.

Feeding During the active growth period give standard liquid fertilizer once a month—but only to fully mature, healthy plants.

Potting and repotting Use an equal-parts combination of soil-based potting mixture (see page 429) and coarse sand or perlite. Be sure to have about an inch of clay-pot fragments in the bottom of pots for quick drainage. Move small plants into pots one size larger in the spring; older plants will continue to thrive in 3- or 4-inch pots or half-pots for several years. When planting a few ceropegias in a single hanging basket, place the tubers about 1½–2 inches apart to get the most effective display.

Propagation At any time during the active growth period, propagate by means of the tuberous growths produced along the stems. After removing a stem tuber, set it in a small pot of the recommended potting mixture over which a half-inch layer of coarse sand or perlite has been sprinkled. Placing the tuber just on top of this will prevent rot. (Stem cuttings 2–3 inches long may be used instead; they should be planted in the same mixture, but some extra sand should be trickled down the hole made for the cutting as insurance against rotting.) The potted tuber (or cutting) should then be stood in medium light and watered very sparingly—allow two-thirds of the potting mixture to dry out between applications—until feeding roots are established. No new top growth will be apparent before these roots have been made; this may take around eight weeks, after which growth will be quite quick. When the young plant is established and growing well, move it gradually into a position where it will get direct sunlight. It can then be treated as a mature ceropegia.

Chamaecereus

CACTACEAE

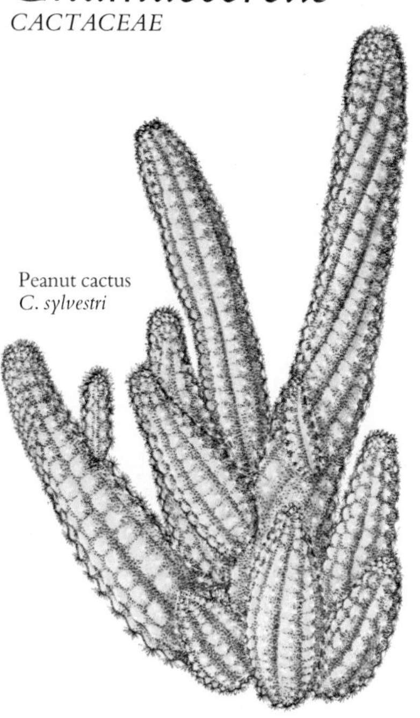

Peanut cactus
C. sylvestri

THERE is only one species of *Chamaecereus, C. sylvestri,* popularly known as peanut cactus because the young shoots somewhat resemble peanuts. With increasing age, however, the shoots of this desert cactus lengthen into cylindrical, fingerlike stems, which are pale green, very soft, and segmented lengthwise by 8 to 10 narrow, low ribs, with broad, shallow indentations in between. The main stems are about 6 inches long and ½ inch in diameter, and they tend to lie on the surface of the potting mixture, with many much smaller branches distributed among them. This cactus branches and spreads so rapidly that it will cover the surface of a 6-inch half-pot in two years. Each of the small areoles that are closely spaced along the ribs carries 10 to 15 short, whitish spines. Deep scarlet, cup-shaped flowers about

C. sylvestri hybrid (flower)

1 inch wide are produced from the areoles in early summer. Individual flowers last about a day, but the flowering period extends for two to three weeks, and *C. sylvestri* will produce numerous blooms during that period.

The species has been crossed with cacti of the genus *Lobivia* to produce attractive hybrids with flowers in a variety of colors—yellow, orange, red, and purple—and these are usually unnamed, sold as chamaecereuses by flower color. The stems tend to be thicker, more upright, and slower-growing than those of *C. sylvestri.*

Also in cultivation is a type of chamaecereus, *C.s.* 'Lutea,' with stems that are pale yellow instead of green. This plant is abnormal in that it does not possess chlorophyll (the green food-producing material characteristic of plant life). Thus it cannot be grown on its own roots and must be grafted onto another cactus, such as a cereus. In all other respects—including the production of scarlet flowers, which look particularly attractive against the yellow stems—the plant is indistinguishable from the normal chamaecereus. Though it cannot, obviously, be propagated from cuttings, amateur growers can buy young plants that are already grafted.

See also CACTI.

Because C.s. *'Lutea' has yellow stems that lack chlorophyll, it cannot survive on its own. Here it has been grafted onto a green cactus, which produces food for both.*

PROPER CARE

Light *C. sylvestri* needs direct sunlight; it forms thin, over-elongated shoots if grown in poor light. For a neat, attractive specimen that will flower well, keep the plant close to the sunniest window possible.

Temperature During the active growth period normal room temperatures are suitable. At other times this cactus will withstand temperatures down to freezing (although such an extreme is not advisable); ideally it should be given a winter rest in the coolest available position (no higher than about 45°F).

Watering During the active growth period water moderately, enough to make the mixture thoroughly moist, but let the top half-inch of the mixture dry out between waterings. During the rest period give limited amounts of water depending on the temperature. If a chamaecereus is kept very cool (below 40°F), it may be left completely dry for the winter; if kept in a warmer room, it will need just enough water to prevent the soil from becoming completely dry. In either case, the aim is to avoid stimulating the plant into growth during the short-day months of insufficient light.

Feeding In the active growth period only, use a tomato-type fertilizer once a month for plants grown in a soil-based potting mixture; once every two weeks for those grown in a peat-based mixture.

Potting and repotting Use either soil-based or peat-based potting mixture (see page 429), with the addition of a one-third portion of coarse sand or perlite for good drainage. Because this cactus has a shallow root system and spreads rapidly, it is best grown in a wide container about 3 inches deep; deep seed trays are ideal for large clumps. Move the plant into a container one size larger in the spring whenever the stems become crowded—or, alternatively, break it up and re-start it from cuttings.

Propagation *C. sylvestri* does not form seed; it is always propagated from cuttings—an extremely simple process. Remove a 2-inch-long branch from the main stem—it can be easily detached—and place it in a 2- or 3-inch pot of the kind of potting mixture in which the parent plant is growing; lay the cutting horizontally on the surface of the mixture. Or place several such cuttings in a large seed tray, spacing them 3 or 4 inches apart. If given the same conditions as the parent plant, new growth will soon be produced, and the young plants will probably be ready to flower by the following summer.

While the plant is being handled, small branches often break away from the main stem. These need not be wasted for they will root at almost any time. Unlike the cuttings taken from most cacti, these do not need to dry out for a few days before being potted up; the points of attachment of the branches are so narrow that there is little risk of rot at cut surfaces.

Chamaedorea

PALMAE

Parlor palm
C. elegans

THE few commonly cultivated species of this large genus have erect, woody stems and somewhat arching pinnate leaves (i.e. leaves divided into pairs of more or less twinned leaflets). Insignificant yellow flowers may be produced in small sprays on erect stalks that emerge from leaf axils when plants are three or more years old. In cultivation, most of these palms seldom grow more than 3 feet tall unless lodged in very big containers, and they are relatively easy to care for.

Chamaedoreas can tolerate dry air, but they do best when it is moist; leaf tips are likely to turn brown in dry conditions. It is advisable to stand potted palms on trays or saucers of damp pebbles during the active growth period, especially in hot rooms. *See also PALMS.*

RECOMMENDED CHAMAEDOREAS

C. elegans (parlor or good-luck palm) is one of the most popular indoor palms. (It was long known as *Neanthe bella*, and has also been called *Collinia elegans*.) When mature, this miniature palm, which takes several years to grow 3 feet high, has a short, green trunk and medium green, slightly arched leaves that vary in length from 18 to 24 inches. Each leaflet may be 6 inches long and 1 inch wide, and they are arranged almost in pairs along the yellowish leafstalk. The compact variety *C.e.* 'Bella' is the form most often seen in cultivation.

C. erumpens (bamboo palm) has a clump of stems that are smooth, green, slender, and sectional (knotted at intervals like bamboo). These tall-growing plants can reach a height of 8 feet. The 18- to 20-inch-long, slightly arching, deep green leaves are held on almost upright 6- to 10-inch-long leafstalks with as many as 10 pairs of leaflets, each 8–10 inches long and an inch wide (the terminal pair are somewhat wider than the rest). The leaves tend to cluster together on the stems, leaving whole sections bare.

C. seifrizii (sometimes sold as *C. graminifolia*) has delicate-looking, lacy leaves 2–3 feet long, with leaflets up to 15 inches long, at the top of slender, canelike stems that cluster together. Leaf color is a deep bluish green; maximum plant height, about 4 feet.

PROPER CARE

Light Chamaedoreas like bright filtered light. If kept at a distance from a window for extensive periods in winter, they begin to grow spindly.

Temperature Though chamaedoreas can tolerate a wide range, they do best in normally warm rooms (65°–75°F). Tolerable winter minimum: 55°. Stand the pots on trays of damp pebbles, and mist-spray the foliage regularly.

Even though chamaedoreas will tolerate dry air, it may cause their frond tips to turn brown. Increase humidity by standing the pots on trays of moist pebbles.

Watering Water plentifully as often as necessary to keep the potting mixture thoroughly moist during the active growth period, even permitting water to remain in the pot saucer. During the rest period water moderately, just enough to make the potting mixture barely moist, allowing the top two-thirds of the mixture to dry out between waterings.

Feeding Apply half-strength standard liquid fertilizer to these plants once a month during the active growth period only.

Potting and repotting Use a soil-based potting mixture (see page 429) with the addition of half as much extra peat moss or leaf mold. A 7-inch pot is likely to be the biggest needed. Repot a chamaedorea only when its roots have completely filled the pot (see page 426), and then move it into a pot just one size larger, working the mixture carefully around the brittle roots. It is essential to pack the mixture down firmly, but without damaging the plant. Root breakage will slow down development, and a plant with damaged roots may take several weeks to recover.

Propagation Propagation is not practicable in the home.

Special points If leaves become yellow and mottled, and especially if a thin webbing develops on their undersides, check for red spider mites (see page 455). Infestation is extremely unlikely, however, if adequate humidity is provided.

Chamaerops

PALMAE

European fan palm
C. humilis

THE genus *Chamaerops* has a single species, *C. humilis* (European fan palm or hair palm), which is the only palm native to Europe. It is a bushy shrub with 4-foot-high stems, and carries fan-shaped fronds with stiff, 15-inch-long, strongly toothed stalks. Each frond is about 2 feet across, dark gray-green, and cut almost to the stalk into many rigid, sword-shaped segments, which are usually split at the ends. Young fronds are often covered with fine gray hair, but this falls off as the frond opens. Flowers and fruit are never produced on plants indoors.

Of other popular forms, *C.h. arborescens* differs from the type species in having only a single stem up to 6 feet tall. The fronds of *C.h. argentea* are silvery gray instead of gray-green. *C.h. elegans* is less thickly bushy than the basic form. And both *C.h.* 'Canariensis' and *C.h.* 'Robusta' have fronds that are larger than those of any of the other forms.

See also PALMS.

PROPER CARE

Light Give these plants three to four hours of direct sunlight every day. A chamaerops will tolerate some shade, but its growth will be slower and the gaps between fronds greater if it has too little light.

Temperature Normal room temperatures are suitable for these plants. Minimum tolerable temperature: 50°F. If possible, give plants a winter rest period at 55°–60°.

Watering During the active growth period water plentifully as often as necessary to keep the potting mixture thoroughly moist, but never allow the pot to stand in water. During the winter rest period, if any, water these plants sparingly, allowing the top two-thirds of the mixture to dry out between waterings.

Feeding Apply standard liquid fertilizer to actively growing plants every two weeks.

Potting and repotting Use a soil-based potting mixture (see page 429). Once every two years, in the spring, move these palms into containers one size larger, until maximum convenient size—probably 8–12 inches—has been reached. Thereafter, topdress them with fresh mixture every spring (see page 428).

Propagation It is possible to propagate either from fresh seed sown in early spring at a temperature of at least 65°F, or from suckers (basal growths) whenever these appear. Take a sucker 8–10 inches long with some roots already attached, carefully pull it from the parent, plant it in a 5-inch pot of moistened soil-based potting mixture, and keep it at normal room temperature in bright filtered light. Water only sparingly, enough to make the mixture barely moist, until such time as new growth indicates development of active roots. Thereafter, treat the young plant as a mature chamaerops.

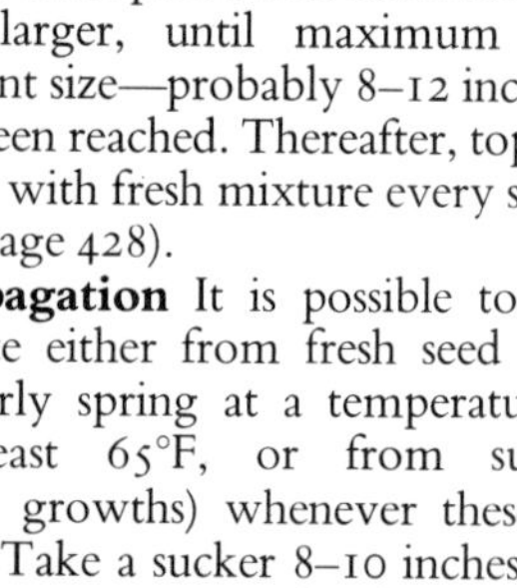

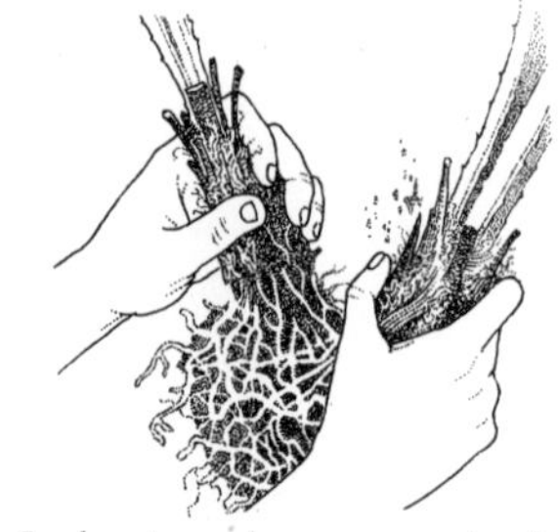

In choosing a chamaerops sucker for propagation, be sure to detach one with some roots already growing from it.

Chlorophytum

LILIACEAE

Ribbon plant
C. comosum
'Vittatum'

THERE are many chlorophytum species, but only *C. comosum* (ribbon plant or walking anthericum) is a popular indoor plant. However, a number of forms of this species exist. All produce clumps of soft, arching, lance-shaped leaves up to $\frac{3}{4}$ inch wide. During the active growth period, pale yellow stems up to 2 feet long arch upward between the leaves. They carry small six-petaled white flowers, which are succeeded by little plants appearing either singly or in groups. These plantlets weigh down the stems as they develop, rapidly producing roots (which, in nature, would grow into the soil around the parent). Some growers train the long stems upward over a hoop of pliable cane.

By training the long trailing stems of this plantlet-bearing plant over a hoop of pliable cane, you can both "frame" the specimen and save space.

Chlorophytums are very ornamental, especially when several plantlets are planted in a single hanging basket. When fully grown, they make an impressive display, particularly as seen against the bright light of a window.

RECOMMENDED CHLOROPHYTUMS

***C. comosum* 'Mandaianum'** has unusually short leaves—only 4–6 inches long—which are dark green with a yellow central stripe.

***C.c.* 'Picturatum'** has 12-inch-long medium green leaves with a yellow central stripe.

***C.c.* 'Variegatum'** has leaves up to 15 inches long of a fresh green color edged with white.

***C.c.* 'Vittatum,'** the familiar spider plant, has 6- to 12-inch-long leaves that are medium green with a central stripe, often quite wide, that is either white or pale cream.

PROPER CARE

Light For healthy growth and sharp contrast in the variegated foliage, these chlorophytums must have bright light, with some direct sunlight, especially during short winter days. Keep them out of hot midday sun, which may scorch the leaves.

Temperature Normally warm room temperatures are suitable. These chlorophytums do not thrive in temperatures below 45°F.

Watering During the active growth period, water plentifully as often as necessary to keep the potting mixture thoroughly moist. In the rest period water more moderately—enough to make the mixture moist throughout but allowing the top half-inch to dry out between waterings. Any further drying out may result in temporary bleaching of foliage (which will clear up when plants are watered) and permanent browning of leaf tips.

Feeding Every two weeks throughout the year, apply standard liquid fertilizer to established plants (those that have begun to produce plantlets).

Potting and repotting Use a soil-based mixture (see page 429). When potting or repotting, make sure to leave plenty of space for development of the mass of translucent water-storing tuberous roots that the plants produce; pots should allow the top of the root ball to lie an inch below the rim. Repotting becomes necessary when the fat roots have forced the mixture upward to rim level, so that it becomes difficult to add water. These chlorophytums may be moved into larger pots at any time.

When the strong chlorophytum roots have forced the mixture up to the pot rim, it is time to repot the plant. Be sure to leave an inch between root ball and rim.

Propagation Chlorophytums can be propagated easily by any one of three methods. Two of these methods involve cutting plantlets off the long stems when their leaves are 2–3 inches long, and stripping off the small lower leaves to prevent possible rot. If plantlet roots have already begun to grow, simply put them in a jar of water. Then transfer them into soil-based potting mixture when roots are at least an inch long. If a plantlet is still rootless, dip the lower part in hormone rooting powder, and insert it in a pot containing a moistened peat-based mixture or equal parts of peat moss and sand (see page 429). In a warm room (above 65°F) and medium light, rooting will quickly occur if the mixture is kept moist. Six to eight weeks after the start of propagation, move the plantlets into 3-inch pots of soil-based mixture, and treat them as mature plants.

The third method is a process similar to layering, (see page 439) which involves placing the lower parts of plantlets into small pots without detaching them from the parent, and fixing the plantlets down in close contact with the potting mixture. After six weeks or so, the young plants are well rooted and can be severed from the long stem and parent plants.

This is the method most likely to succeed; but it takes up a lot of space, since the pots for both parent and offspring must be kept together.

Two ways to propagate a chlorophytum

Detach single plantlets from stems and root them in water if they have developed rudimentary roots while on the parent.

Alternatively, place plantlets firmly in separate pots and leave them for six weeks before detaching them from the long stem of the parent plant.

Chrysalidocarpus

PALMAE

Yellow-palm
C. lutescens

ONLY one species of the genus *Chrysalidocarpus* is widely grown as a house plant: *C. lutescens* (yellow-, butterfly-, or golden-feather-palm). This plant—which used to be known as *Areca lutescens* and is still sometimes called areca palm—produces many reedlike stems in clusters, and these stems carry arching fronds on 2-foot-long, deeply furrowed, yellowish orange stalks. The fronds of a 5-foot-high chrysalidocarpus can be 3–4 feet long and are divided into many rather stiff, glossy, yellowish green segments up to 2 feet long and ½ inch wide. The segments are arranged in almost opposite pairs on a prominent midrib. Older stems are marked, like bamboo canes, with notches where fronds were formerly attached to them.

Development is relatively slow. An annual increase of 6–8 inches in height is average for a plant grown in good light at normal room temperature. Specimens in pots normally produce many small suckers at the base; these can be used for propagation.
See also PALMS.

PROPER CARE

Light These palms do best in direct sunlight filtered through a translucent blind or curtain.

Temperature Normally warm room temperatures are suitable. A minimum temperature of 55°F is essential for healthy growth.

Watering Water plentifully as often as necessary to keep the potting mixture thoroughly moist, but never allow the pot to stand in water. If the temperature falls as low as 55°F, give only enough water to keep the mixture from drying out completely.

Feeding Apply standard liquid fertilizer to actively growing plants every two weeks.
Potting and repotting Use a soil-based potting mixture (see page 429). Move plants into pots one size larger every second spring until maximum convenient pot size is reached; thereafter, topdress (see page 428) with fresh potting mixture annually. Make sure that the mixture is firmly packed around the roots, but be careful not to damage the thick taproots.
Propagation Propagation professionally is by fresh seed sown at a temperature of at least 65°F in late spring. If seed can be acquired, it is quite easy to germinate in the home (see page 441), but it will take several years to produce a plant with adult characteristics. These plants can be increased more simply by means of the basal suckers, which should be removed for propagation in spring. The ideal sucker is about 12 inches high and has some root growth (this can be ascertained when the plant is taken out of its pot for the operation).

To be suitable for propagation, a chrysalidocarpus basal sucker should be a foot tall with some dense root growth.

Plant each sucker in a 4- or 5-inch pot filled with a moistened mixture of two-thirds soil-based potting mixture (see page 429) and one-third coarse sand or perlite (the latter component to encourage active root growth). Enclose the whole in a plastic bag and keep it in a warm room in medium light for four to six weeks. Thereafter, remove the plastic bag and water the potted sucker sparingly, allowing the top inch of the mixture to dry out between waterings, until new growth indicates that roots are well established. Then treat the plant virtually as a mature specimen, but do not feed it for the first three or four months. It need not be moved into standard mixture until the following spring.

Chrysanthemum

COMPOSITAE

C. morifolium

CHRYSANTHEMUMS are temporary house plants and should not be kept indoors when their flowers have faded. The two species most commonly grown—*C. frutescens* (white marguerite, Paris daisy) and *C. morifolium* (sometimes called *C. hortorum*)—are bushy, soft-woody-stemmed plants with terminal clusters of daisylike flowers. In most other respects the species are quite different from each other. *C. frutescens* flowers only in summer, and the best time to buy an indoor specimen is late spring. *C. morifolium*, which naturally flowers in the short-day weeks of late fall or early winter, can be bought in full bloom at all times. Specialist growers restrict the amount of daylight throughout the year by "blacking out" plants of the latter species for several hours a day. This technique, along with the use of a dwarfing compound that limits plant height, has revolutionized commercial growing of all these chrysanthemums. Compact, flowering specimens are available from January through December.

RECOMMENDED CHRYSANTHEMUMS

C. frutescens can grow 3 feet tall. Potted plants, however, have usually had their growing shoots pinched out and are no more than 18 inches high. The leaves, carried alternately on short stalks, are pale green, 2–4 inches long, and up to 3 inches wide. Each leaf is deeply cut into lobed leaflets. The terminal clusters of flowers are often so numerous that they hide half the foliage. Each flower is 2–3 inches across, with a single, dense circle of white petals surrounding a yellow, raised disk. There is a variety with lemon yellow petals, *C.f.* 'Etoile d 'Or,' and one with rose-pink petals, *C.f.* 'Mary Wootten.' Flowers of the latter kind are 3–4 inches across.
C. morifolium is usually under 1 foot tall when sold in a pot. The leaves are like those of *C. frutescens*, but dark green rather than pale. Flowers may also be similar. Often, though, each flower has overlapping circles of petals so densely packed that they hide the central disk. The 1- to 3-inch-wide flowers may be white, cream, yellow, orange, pink, bronze, or purplish.

C. morifolium (flowers)

PROPER CARE

Light Unless *C. frutescens* has three or four hours a day of direct sunlight, some flower buds may fail to open. Place *C. morifolium* in a position where it will get bright light without, however, subjecting it to direct sunlight.

Temperature Keep these chrysanthemums cool. A temperature of 55°–65°F is suitable. Warmer conditions will shorten the flowering period greatly. For increased humidity stand pots on trays of moist pebbles, or place the potted plants in bowls of moist peat moss.

Watering Purchased chrysanthemums dry out quickly. Water them plentifully as often as necessary in order to keep the potting mixture thoroughly moist.

Feeding Fertilizing is not necessary for these temporary plants.

Potting and repotting No repotting is required. For decorative purposes, however, several specimens can be planted together in one bowl or basket. Simply knock plants out of their pots and group them together in a single large container. Fill in all empty spaces between root balls with moist peat moss.

Propagation Home propagation is impractical, and the indoor gardener is advised to purchase young plants.

Special points When buying potted chrysanthemums, make sure the flower buds are showing color. Tightly closed green buds often fail to open when brought indoors. Dwarfed specimens of *C. morifolium* can be planted outdoors after flowering in areas where winters are not severe. But although they thrive in the open air, they do not remain low-growing. In later years they can be expected to reach a height of 3–4 feet.

Although no chrysanthemum will show color in all its flower buds, avoid one with too many tightly closed, green buds. These often fail to open indoors.

Cineraria

COMPOSITAE

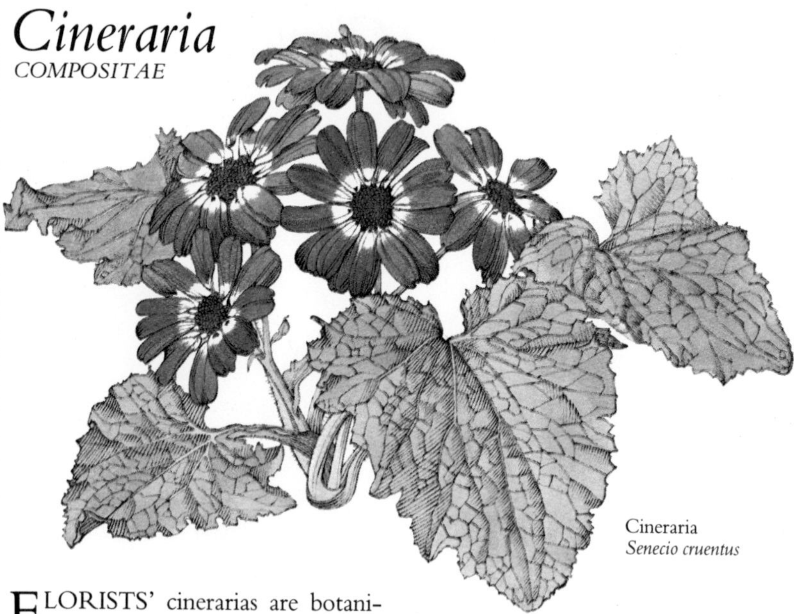

Cineraria
Senecio cruentus

FLORISTS' cinerarias are botanically included in the genus *Senecio* (as *S. hybridus* or *S. cruentus*), but they are so generally known under the popular name that they warrant separate treatment. (For other species, see *Senecio*.) Cinerarias, which are hybrids of complex origin, are late-winter and spring-flowering pot plants grown for their impressive heads of daisy-shaped flowers, each 1–3 inches wide. Commercial growers sow seed in late spring and early summer, overwinter young plants in greenhouses at a temperature of around 45°F, and sell them just as the first flower buds begin to open. Under the right conditions, plants continue to flower for several weeks, after which time they should be discarded.

Cinerarias vary in height (from 1 to 2 feet) and color. The most common floral pattern is a strong or pastel shade of red, blue, mauve, or purple surrounding a circle of white, which in turn surrounds a typical daisy center; but in some plants the flowers are a single color. They are normally carried in a flat or dome-topped cluster up to 9 inches across, virtually hiding the deep green, softly hairy leaves, which tend to be heart-shaped or nearly triangular with toothed edges. Leaf undersides in a number of forms are tinged with purple.

For their short stay in the house, give these plants bright light, but not direct sunlight, and keep them as cool as possible. To provide adequate humidity, which will help prolong the flowering period, stand them on trays of damp pebbles or moist peat moss, and water them plentifully as often as necessary to keep the potting mixture thoroughly moist. If the roots of a cineraria are allowed to dry out, it will collapse; and although it may appear to recover when watered, its life will have been appreciably shortened. There is no need to feed these plants during the short time that they are kept indoors.

Cineraria hybrids
(flowers)

In the event of the collapse of a plant soak the pot and potting mixture in a bowl or bucket of water for half an hour. When the potting mixture has been thoroughly moistened, allow the pot to drain and then return it to its normal position.

A watch should be kept for aphids which collect particularly around unopened flower buds (see page 454), and for whitefly (see page 456). Steps should be taken to eliminate these pests if they attack the plant.

Cissus

VITACEAE

Kangaroo vine
C. antarctica

THE several species of cissus popularly grown indoors are climbing foliage plants closely related to the grape vine. Cissuses can be used in many different ways; as climbers or trailers, or in bowls, pans, or hanging baskets. Most produce curly tendrils and attach themselves to any available support. Almost all are easy to grow because of their tolerance of widely differing conditions.

RECOMMENDED CISSUSES

C. antarctica (kangaroo vine or kangaroo ivy) is the best-known cissus. It can grow 6–10 feet tall indoors and is often trained on bamboo supports as a room divider, or as a backdrop to a collection of plants. Its pointed-oval leaves are shiny, medium green, and up to 4 inches long. They have lightly toothed edges and are produced singly on short, red leafstalks. Where overhead space is restricted, growing points can be picked out regularly to encourage the development of sideshoots. This will make the plants lower-growing and more bushy. If cissuses are permitted, they can produce at least 2 feet of new top growth in a single year. There is a very slow-growing dwarf form, *C.a.* 'Minima,' that produces spreading rather than upright branches. It is therefore ideal for hanging baskets.

C. discolor has many rather inappropriate common names (including rex-begonia vine), all of which try to describe its beautifully colored foliage. It has slender climbing stems and acutely pointed heart-shaped leaves 4–8 inches long, which are velvety green with silver and pale purple markings between the veins on the upper surface, and red below. This cissus is *not* easy to grow; it is suitable only for a large plant window (see page 53), where it can have warmth, high humidity, freedom from drafts, bright light without direct sunlight, and a precise watering program.

C. rhombifolia (grape ivy) was once known as *Vitis rhombifolia*, then as *Rhoicissus rhomboidea* (a name that many growers still use). Its tooth-edged leaves are actually composed of three leaflets, each of which is around 2 inches long and shaped somewhat like a rhomboid. They are carried on short stalks; the central stalk is longer than the two others. New growth often appears silvery because of the fine hairs that cover it; mature leaves are a glossy dark green with brown, finely hairy undersides. The tendrils have forked, curling ends. Growth can be rapid—2–3 feet a year—and plants can easily reach 10 feet or more if they are carefully trained up tall stakes. *C.r.* 'Ellen Danica' is a recently introduced variety that differs from the species in that its leaflets are larger and almost circular, with strongly lobed edges. *C.r.* 'Mandaiana' also has larger, more rounded leaflets; and the young plants have erect stems without tendrils, developing a climbing habit only after two to three years.

C. sicyoides (princess vine) is a rampant grower that requires plenty of space. Its leaves are heart-shaped, 4 inches long, light green (silvery gray when young), and slightly toothed.

C. striata (miniature grape ivy) is the smallest cissus in cultivation. It has thin, reddish shoots and leaves that are composed of five tiny leaflets radiating over a 3-inch spread on short

C. striata
(miniature grape ivy)

C. discolor
(rex-begonia vine)

C. rhombifolia (grape ivy)

leafstalks. Leaf color is bronze-green with pale vein markings above and pinkish undersides. *C. striata* is splendid for a small hanging basket, but it can also cling to supports.

PROPER CARE

Light Most cissuses will adapt to a wide range of light intensity. Ideally, they should be grown in bright light, but without direct sunlight throughout the year. Over-exposure to sun causes transparent leaf markings, which will eventually turn brown, especially on *C. antarctica*.

Temperature These plants like warmth, but do best if given a short winter rest period at around 55°F. *C. discolor* will lose most of its leaves if the temperature drops below 65° during the active growth period. It may well shed its leaves in winter.

Watering *C. discolor* must not be overwatered, since any excess will cause leaves to fall prematurely. Water plants of this species sparingly, giving just enough to make the entire potting mixture moist, and allow the top half of the mixture to dry out between waterings. Other species need more water. Water them moderately during the active growth period, enough to moisten the entire mixture at each watering, and allowing the top half-inch of the mixture to dry out before watering again. During the rest period water all these cissuses just enough to keep the mixture from drying out.

Feeding Apply standard liquid fertilizer every two weeks from early spring to early fall.

Potting and repotting Use a soil-based potting mixture (see page 429). Move plants into pots one size larger each spring. As long as they are adequately fed, quite large plants with a height or spread of 6 feet can be accommodated in 8- to 10-inch pots. After maximum convenient pot size has been reached, topdress these plants with fresh potting mixture instead of moving them on (see page 428).

Propagation Young tip cuttings 3–6 inches long will, if taken in spring, root in six to eight weeks under suitable conditions. Strip the lower leaves from the cuttings and dip the cut ends in a hormone rooting powder; plant four or five cuttings in a 3-inch pot containing an equal-parts mixture of moistened peat moss and coarse sand or perlite. Enclose the potted cuttings in a plastic bag, and stand in a warm place where bright light is filtered through a translucent blind or curtain. When new growth indicates that the cuttings are rooted, remove the bag and begin to water sparingly, enough to make the potting mixture barely moist but allowing the top inch of the mixture to dry out between waterings. When they are well established, repot the young plants in standard potting mixture. Their cultivation needs will then be those of mature cissuses.

If preferred, trailing shoots can be layered (see page 439) into a nearby pot of suitable rooting medium.

Special points Pinch out growing points periodically to promote branching. Any plants that lose a large number of lower leaves and become bare at the base should be cut back (if necessary, severely) in spring. Train vigorous stems into place, and, if necessary, tie them to their supports. It is advisable to shorten the main growth of large plants by a third in early spring. At the same time cut back lateral growths to a node within an inch or two of the main stems.

If the air in the room is especially dry, watch out for red spider mites, which may collect on the undersides of leaves (see page 455).

It is often best to keep the vigorous stems of cissuses neat by tying them to their supports with twine or raffia.

Trim sideshoots of a large cissus in spring, leaving them about an inch long, and cut back its main stems by a third (see inset).

Citrus

RUTACEAE

Calamondin orange
C. mitis

THE genus *Citrus* comprises about 15 species of small trees and shrubs, including those that bear lemons, limes, oranges, tangerines, and grapefruit. While still young and small, they make attractive house plants because of their lustrous dark green foliage, plentiful flowers, and bright-colored fruits. Citruses have glossy, roughly oval leaves on short leafstalks; and nearly all have spiny stems and branches and fragrant flowers. These are usually white and about an inch across, have five blunt-ended petals and prominent stamens, and may be carried either singly or in small clusters of up to five. The normal flowering season is late spring and summer, but occasional flowers may appear at any time of year. In good conditions some plants—especially the lemon—may flower almost continuously.

The fruit is green until fully developed, when it slowly ripens to yellow, yellowish green, or orange (according to species). The ripening process may take three months or more, and ripe fruit may remain on the branches for several months. Edible fruit can be expected from lemon and sweet-orange bushes. It is not uncommon for all these plants to bear flowers and fruit in various stages of development simultaneously.

RECOMMENDED CITRUSES

C. limon (lemon) is a tree that can grow 20 feet high in an orchard, but these are two forms that grow no taller than 4 feet when potted. *C.l.* 'Meyer' (Meyer's lemon) has leaves up to 4 inches long and rounded, thin-skinned, pale yellow fruit up to 3 inches in diameter. *C.l.* 'Ponderosa' (American wonder lemon) has similar leaves but a thick- and rough-skinned orange-yellow fruit up to 4½ inches in diameter.

C. limonia (formerly named *C. taitensis* or *C. otaitensis*; commonly known as Otaheite orange) is now considered to be a hybrid between the lemon and the mandarin orange, *C. reticulata*. This plant, which grows into a small, thornless bush, produces flowers with purple-tinged petals and rounded, deep yellow or orange fruits up to 2 inches in diameter.

C. mitis (calamondin orange), the most popular indoor citrus, is also a hybrid according to botanists, and should rightly be called *Citrofortunella mitis*. Whatever its name, the plant, which can grow 4 feet tall, is notable for its tendency to bear fruit when only a few inches high. It has many short branches with leaves 2–4 inches long, is thornless or nearly so, flowers intermittently, and bears fruit in profusion throughout the year. Fruits are bright orange, round, and 1¼ inches in diameter. They weigh down the ends of branches when three or more are clustered there.

Citrus varieties (fruits)

C. sinensis (sweet orange) is the only one of these plants that produces sweet-tasting fruit. The most common indoor form grows about 4 feet high in a 10- or 12-inch pot. Its stout stems have long, sharp spines and leaves up to 4 inches long. The smooth-skinned, bright orange fruit is usually about 2¾ inches in diameter and solitary.

PROPER CARE

Light Provide at least four hours a day of direct sunlight. Citruses do best if placed outdoors in bright light during the summer.

Temperature Normal room temperatures are suitable. For increased humidity stand citruses on trays of damp pebbles or moist peat moss, and mist-spray them occasionally. Maintain a winter temperature of at least 50°–55°F. They can tolerate readings as low as 40°, but stop growing actively below 50°.

Watering While plants are actively growing, water moderately, allowing the top inch of the mixture to dry out between waterings. In any resting period water only enough to keep the mixture from completely drying out.

Feeding Give actively growing citruses a high-potash, tomato-type fertilizer every two weeks. If light intensity is poor during the winter, do not feed plants till it improves.
Potting and repotting Use a soil-based potting mixture (see page 429). *C. mitis* will begin to flower and fruit well in a 5- or 6-inch pot, but most other kinds will not bloom until they are older and big enough to need 10-inch pots or larger tubs. Move plants into containers one size larger every spring until maximum convenient size is reached; thereafter, an annual topdressing (see page 428) of fresh potting mixture will suffice.
Propagation A citrus may be propagated by 3- to 6-inch-long stem cuttings. Dip each cutting in a hormone rooting powder, plant it in a small pot containing a moistened equal-parts mixture of peat moss and coarse sand or perlite, enclose the whole in a plastic bag, and keep it at a temperature of 65°–70°F in medium light. After rooting has taken place—in six to eight weeks—remove the plastic bag, and water the young plant just enough to keep the rooting mixture from drying out until new growth appears at the tip. Then begin monthly feedings of half-strength standard liquid fertilizer. When roots emerge from the drainage hole, move the plant into a larger pot of soil-based mixture, and begin to treat it as a mature citrus.

It is also easy to grow citruses from seeds. If planted in rooting mixture (see page 444) and kept moist and warm, most will germinate in four to six weeks, after which they should temporarily be given medium light, not direct sunlight. When seedlings are big enough to handle, pot them individually in small pots of soil-based potting mixture and treat them as adults. They will develop slowly into attractive foliage plants, but it may take as long as 7–10 years for them to flower indoors.
Special points If humidity is low, red spider mites are liable to appear on the undersides of citrus leaves (see page 455). Scale insects may also be found on leaf undersides, where they produce an excretion called honeydew that results in sooty mold (see page 457). Shorten overlong shoots of citruses by two-thirds in early spring. Nip out growing tips at practically any time to encourage bushy growth.

Cleistocactus

CACTACEAE

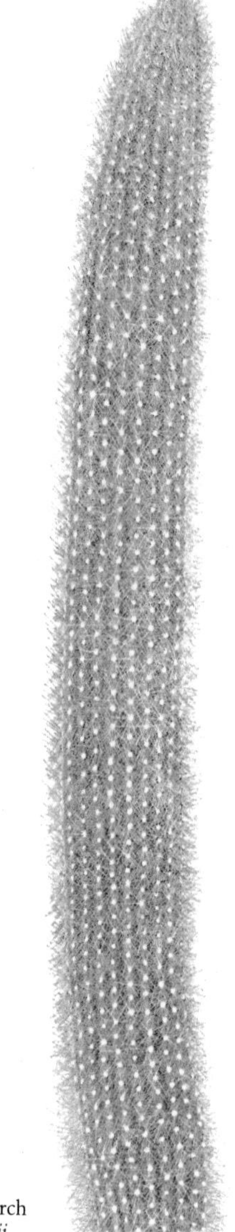

Silver torch
C. strausii

THERE are about 28 species of these tall, slender desert cacti, but only one, *Cleistocactus strausii*, is widely cultivated indoors. *C. strausii* (silver torch) has a green stem that looks silvery gray because of the short, whitish spines that completely cover it. The columnar stem has about 25 low, narrow ribs, and each of the small, white areoles spaced at $\frac{1}{2}$-inch intervals along the ribs carries at least 30 thin, $\frac{3}{4}$-inch-long, white spines, together with 4 somewhat stouter, pale yellow ones that are up to $1\frac{1}{2}$ inches long. The main stem often branches at the base, with upright-growing stems attached to the parent stem just above the surface of the potting mixture. In an 8-inch pot the plant will reach a height of 4 feet and will probably consist of several stems roughly equal in size.

Cleistocacti do not flower until they are 10 to 15 years old. When *C. strausii* has become 3 feet or more tall, it produces narrow, tubular flowers from areoles at the top of the main stem. The flowers are 3–4 inches long and carmine-red, and they appear in summer. They never open fully, and each one lasts only four or five days.
See also CACTI.

PROPER CARE

Light Like all desert cacti, *C. strausii* needs as much full sunlight as it can get. If possible, stand these plants in a sunny position outdoors during the summer months.
Temperature During the active growth period normal room temperatures are suitable. During the winter, however, give cleistocacti a rest period at 40°–50°F. If winter temperature is too high, plants will try to grow; and with the insufficient light of short winter days, growth is bound to be unnaturally thin.
Watering During the active growth period water moderately, enough to make the potting mixture moist, and allow the top half-inch of the mixture to dry out between waterings. In the winter rest period give only enough to keep the mixture from drying out.
Feeding Apply a standard tomato-type fertilizer during the active growth period only—monthly if the cleistocactus is growing in a soil-based potting mixture, once every two weeks if the mixture is peat-based.
Potting and repotting A porous potting mixture is essential. Add one part coarse sand or perlite to two parts of either soil-based or peat-based mixture (see page 429). *C. strausii* grows vigorously when young and needs to be moved into a pot one size larger every spring until an 8-inch pot has been reached. Thereafter, topdress plants (see page 428) with fresh potting mixture each spring.
Propagation It is possible to propagate by cutting a small branch from a cleistocactus and rooting it, but this inevitably leaves a disfiguring scar near the base of the main stem. It is therefore best to raise these plants from seed (see *CACTI*, page 114).

Clerodendrum

VERBENACEAE

Bleeding-heart vine
C. thomsoniae

THE only species of the genus *Clerodendrum* that has become a popular house plant is *Clerodendrum thomsoniae* (bleeding-heart vine), a vigorous twining shrub with striking flowers. It can grow inconveniently high—10 feet or more—but may be kept below 4 feet by having its stem tops pinched out regularly during the growing season; the stems themselves can also be trained around three or four thin stakes in the potting mixture. This species can make an attractive trailing plant when kept under control in a large hanging basket. Although not difficult to grow, it will not flower unless given adequately humid warmth during the active growth period. The leaves of *C. thomsoniae* are rather coarse, heart-shaped, up to 5 inches long and 2 inches wide, and colored deep green with slightly paler vein markings. Flowers, which are produced on wiry flower stalks at stem ends during the spring, summer, and early fall, grow in clusters of 10 to 30. Each flower consists of an inch-long, white (or else greenish white), bell-shaped calyx with a scarlet, star-shaped bloom peeping through a split in its tip. The contrast of scarlet and white is highly effective.

Although this is a naturally twining plant it will become straggly if not trained up stakes inserted into the potting mixture.

There is a variety, *C.t.* 'Delectum,' with rose-magenta flowers in very large clusters. Another variety, *C.t.* 'Variegatum,' has flowers like those of the type species, but its leaves are pale green at the margins and have light and dark green marbling in the central portion.

PROPER CARE

Light Grow clerodendrums in bright light filtered through a translucent blind or curtain. They will not flower without adequate light.

Temperature These plants will do well at normal room temperatures during the active growth period, but they should be given a winter rest in a cool position—ideally, if possible, about 50°–55°F. To ensure satisfactory flowering, provide extra humidity during the active growth period by mist-spraying the plants every day and by standing pots on trays or saucers of moist pebbles.

Watering During the active growth period water plentifully, as much as necessary to keep the potting mixture thoroughly moist, but never allow the pot to stand in water. During the rest period water only enough to keep the mixture from drying out.

Feeding Give actively growing plants standard liquid fertilizer every two weeks.

Potting and repotting Use a soil-based potting mixture (see page 429). Young plants should be moved into pots one size larger when their roots have filled the pot (see page 426), but mature plants will flower best if kept in pots that seem a little too small. Quite large specimens can be grown in 6- or 8-inch pots. Even when pot size is not changed, however, these clerodendrums should be repotted at the end of every rest period. Carefully remove most of the old potting mixture, and replace it with fresh mixture to which has been added a small amount of bone meal.

Propagation Propagate in spring from cuttings 4–6 inches long. Dip each cutting in a hormone rooting powder, and plant it in a 3-inch pot containing a moistened equal-parts mixture of peat moss and coarse sand or perlite. Enclose the pot in a plastic bag or heated propagating case (see page 444), and keep it at a temperature of at least 70°F in a position where it gets medium light. Rooting will take four to six weeks; when new growth indicates that it has occurred, uncover the pot, begin watering the young plant sparingly—just enough to make the potting mixture barely moist—and start applications of standard liquid fertilizer every two weeks. About four months after the beginning of the propagation process, move the plant into soil-based potting mixture. Thereafter, treat it as a mature clerodendrum.

Special points At the end of the rest period, as new growth becomes apparent, cut back at least half the previous year's growth in order to keep these plants within bounds.

Cleyera

THEACEAE

ONLY one species of cleyera is normally cultivated indoors: *C. japonica*, a branching shrub which, together with its more attractive variegated-leaved variety *C.j.* 'Tricolor' (otherwise known as *C. fortunei*), is quite easy to grow. The glossy, elliptic, blunt-tipped leaves, which are 3–4 inches long and around 2½ inches wide, are dark green in the species, marbled in pale and dark green and edged with yellow in the variegated form. Young leaves and those grown in very bright light may have a rosy tinge, particularly near the edges. The short-stalked leaves are arranged in two ranks on the branches, one on either side.

Plants that are cultivated in pots indoors seldom grow more than 2–2½ feet high. The plain green-leaved species sometimes produces small, white, scented flowers, but the variegated form rarely does so.

Note: *C. japonica* was once known as *C. ochnacea*, and is also often confused with *Eurya japonica*, a closely related and very similar plant.

PROPER CARE

Light Grow cleyeras in bright light; they benefit from some direct sunlight every day, but it is not essential.

Temperature These plants do well in normal room temperatures during the active growth period. During the winter rest period, however, they should ideally be kept quite cool (50°–55°F).

Watering Cleyeras have a dense root structure consisting of many finely branched roots that dry out rapidly. During the active growth period water moderately, as much as necessary to make the potting mixture thoroughly moist, and allow the top half-inch of the mixture to dry out between waterings. During the rest period let the top third of the mixture dry out between moderate waterings.

Feeding Apply standard liquid fertilizer every two weeks during the active growth period.

Potting and repotting Use a soil-based potting mixture (see page 429). Move plants into pots one size larger as soon as new growth begins each year. After they have reached maximum convenient pot size, an annual topdressing with fresh mixture at this time will suffice (see page 428).

Propagation Take tip cuttings 3–4 inches long in late winter or early spring. Strip away the lower leaves, dip the cut ends in hormone rooting powder, and plant them in a moistened mixture of equal parts peat moss and sand or perlite. Keep the cuttings in a warm place in bright light filtered through a translucent blind or curtain and water them moderately, enough to make the potting mixture moist. After roots have formed, probably in six to eight weeks, move the young plants into small pots of soil-based potting mixture and treat them as mature cleyeras.

Special points In hot rooms mist-spray cleyeras with water daily to discourage red spider mites (see page 455), which thrive in very warm, dry conditions. It will also help to stand the plants on trays of damp pebbles. If mites become really troublesome (as indicated by leaves' becoming yellowish with white webbing on the undersides), spray the plants with an appropriate insecticide.

Propagating a cleyera

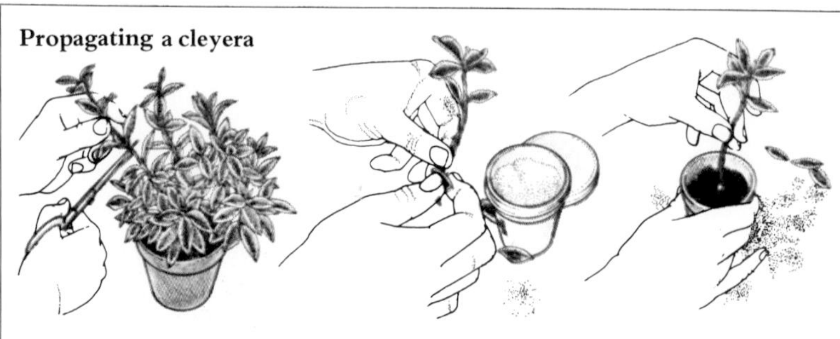

To propagate a cleyera, take a 3- to 4-inch tip cutting just below a pair of leaves.

Dip the cut end in hormone rooting powder after stripping off lower leaves.

With lower leaves removed, there is no risk of leaves rotting in damp mixture.

Clivia

AMARYLLIDACEAE

Kafir lily
C. miniata

THE genus *Clivia* comprises only three species, and only one, *C. miniata* (Kafir lily), is a familiar house plant. Clivias will develop into impressive plants, but only if they are given a cool winter rest. Their dark green, strap-shaped leaves, which vary in width from narrow to over 3 inches, fan out from a leeklike base consisting of thickly layered leaf bases. The spread of a single plant can exceed 3 feet. Roots are so thick and fleshy that they quickly fill pots, and some will appear on the surface of the potting mixture. In late winter thick flower stalks up to 18 inches long begin to push up between the leaves—always slightly off-center—and each stalk will carry up to 15 trumpet-shaped flowers, each 2–3 inches long, in the early spring. Flower color is usually a combination of yellow and bright orange or orange-red, but pure yellow and apricot-colored varieties are occasionally seen.

PROPER CARE

Light A window position that gets bright light with early-morning or late-afternoon sun is best. Midday sunlight can scorch the leaves. Too little light results in no flowers.

Temperature Though clivias thrive in warm rooms during the active growth period, they must be given a short early-winter rest period—six to eight weeks—ideally at a temperature slightly below 50°F. If this is not possible, they may be forced into premature bloom, with flower stalks failing to rise above the foliage. Too much warmth also shortens the life of the flowers.

Watering During spring and summer water plentifully, as much as necessary to keep the mixture thoroughly moist, but gradually reduce amounts in the fall, and keep clivias almost dry during the rest period. When flower stalks appear toward the end of the winter, begin a gradual increase in quantity and frequency of waterings.

Feeding Give clivias standard liquid fertilizer once every two weeks, beginning when flower stalks are half-developed and continuing until a month before watering is curtailed.

Potting and repotting Use a soil-based potting mixture (see page 429). Repot clivias only every three to four years; they flower best when pot-bound. Move a clivia into a bigger pot only when its roots fill the pot (see page 426). Topdress (see page 428) in years when plants are not moved into bigger pots. Be sure to pack the mixture firmly around the thick roots, and leave 2 inches between the surface of the mixture and the rim of the pot, for growing roots will force the mixture upward. Because the plants can become top-heavy, use clay, not plastic, pots. As a plant develops, it can be moved progressively into pots that are about 2 inches larger. When maximum convenient size—probably 10 inches—has been reached, topdressing every year is advisable. Carefully scrape away 2 inches of the old mixture, and replace it with fresh mixture enriched by a sprinkling of bone meal.

Clivias need repotting only when their roots appear on the surface of the potting mixture—about every three years.

Propagating a clivia

Examine the plant to find the point at which each offset is attached to the parent.

Use a sharp knife to cut off an offset with healthy roots and three long leaves.

In planting the offset, handle the roots gently. They are brittle and can snap off.

Both repotting and topdressing are best done in late winter, just as flower stalks begin to develop.

Propagation To propagate, use the offsets that emerge through the tangle of roots. Be sure to detach each offset carefully at the point where it meets the parent plant. Use a long, sharp knife. The best time to detach an offset is immediately after the last flowers of the season have dropped off, but not before the offset comprises at least three leaves 8–10 inches long. Plant it in a 3- to 5-inch pot containing an equal-parts mixture of peat moss and coarse sand or perlite, and keep it warm in medium light. Water it sparingly, enough to make the mixture moist, but allowing the top two-thirds of the mixture to dry out between waterings. When roots appear on the surface of the mixture, move the young plant into a soil-based mixture in a pot one size larger, and treat it as an adult. It will flower about a year after being detached from the parent plant. Propagation from seed takes seven or eight years.

Old plants can also be broken into separate crowns with the aid of a stout knife and potted up in 4- or 5-inch pots. In doing this be careful not to damage the fleshy roots.

Special points Flower trumpets fall as they fade, leaving behind embryo fruits. Remove these with a razor blade to prevent them from developing. If they are allowed to remain, they will grow large and absorb so much of the clivia's energy that the plant will be unlikely to flower the following spring. When the flower stalks begin to wither, pull them out from the cluster of leaves.

To enjoy a number of flower heads on a single clivia, never detach the offsets that these impressive plants normally produce.

Codiaeum

EUPHORBIACEAE

Croton
C. variegatum pictum

CODIAEUMS (crotons) are much-branching, bushy shrubs that seldom exceed 3 feet in height, with a spread of about 2 feet, indoors. There are only a few species of codiaeum, though there are many varieties with widely varying leaf shape, size, and color. Practically all the kinds of codiaeum now available are forms of just one variety of a single species, *C. variegatum pictum*. The smooth and leathery leaves generally have short stalks, but in almost all other respects codiaeum leaves differ enormously. They may be long and narrow, lance- or sword-shaped, broad and oval; they may have straight or undulate edges, or they may be twisted into a kind of spiral; their margins may be slightly indented in any one of a number of patterns, or they may be cut almost to the midrib. All available forms have variegated leaves, with colors appearing as spots, blotches, veining, etc., and the colors themselves are similarly variable. In some forms old and young leaves look alike; in others the colors change as they age. Mature plants produce fluffy, cream-colored flowers, but these are small and insignificant.

RECOMMENDED CODIAEUMS

C. variegatum pictum has a large number of forms, several of which are listed below. Leaf sizes are not indicated because they are too variable.

***C.v.p.* 'Aucubifolium'** has elliptic, glossy leaves, which are bright green with yellow spots.

***C.v.p.* 'Bruxellense'** has broad, lance-shaped leaves, which are bronzish at first but eventually turn red; veins are yellow.

***C.v.p.* 'Craigii'** has deep-cut, three-lobed, bright green leaves which have prominent yellow veins.

C. variegatum pictum forms (leaves)

***C.v.p.* 'Fascination'** has long, strap-shaped leaves colored in unpredictable patterns of green, red, and orange.

***C.v.p.* 'Gloriosum superbum'** has broad, slightly undulate leaves that narrow down to a pointed lobe near the tip; the color is green with yellow veins and margins, but the yellow deepens to golden orange as leaves age.

***C.v.p.* 'Imperialis'** (appleleaf) has elliptic leaves. The yellow leaf has roughly defined pink or red margins and a green midrib, both of which eventually turn deep metallic purple.

***C.v.p.* 'Punctatum aureum'** has long, narrow, glossy leaves, which are dark green spotted with yellow.

***C.v.p.* 'Reidii'** has oval-oblong leaves, which are basically green, but the green is strongly tinged with yellow, pink, and red, and the prominent veins are orange or red.

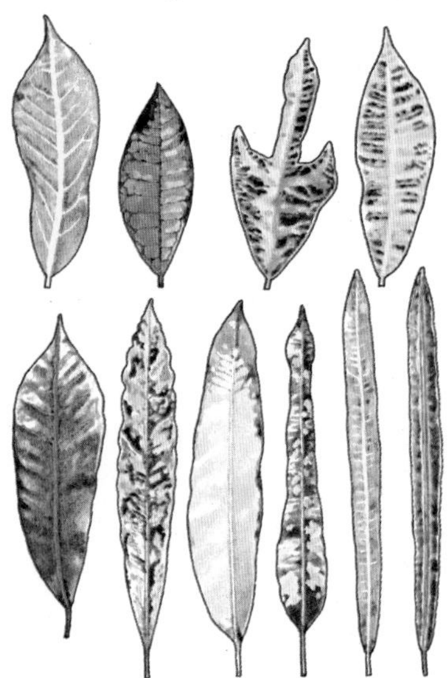

C. variegatum pictum varieties (leaves)

***C.v.p.* 'Spirale'** is descriptively named: Its narrow, multicolored leaves—green, red, and yellow in indefinable combinations—are twisted like corkscrews.

PROPER CARE

Light Bright light, with at least two or three hours of direct sunlight daily, is necessary for good coloration. The normal leaf loss of older codiaeums will be much increased in plants that get inadequate light.

Temperature Codiaeums grow well in normal room temperatures; do not let the temperature fall below 55°F. For adequate humidity stand pots on trays of damp pebbles.

Watering During the active growth period water plentifully—enough to keep the potting mixture thoroughly moist—but never allow pots to stand in water. In the rest period give only enough water to keep the mixture from drying out completely.

Feeding Apply standard liquid fertilizer every two weeks from the beginning of spring until late fall.

Potting and repotting Use a soil-based potting mixture (see page 429). Move plants into pots one size larger each spring until maximum convenient pot size (probably 8 inches) is reached; thereafter, annual topdressing (see page 428) with fresh potting mixture will suffice.

Propagation Propagate in early spring by means of 6-inch-long tip cuttings, preferably taken from side-shoots, which are likely to be smaller and less leafy than others. (Like most members of the *Euphorbiaceae* family, codiaeums are filled with a milky latex, which flows freely when stems are cut. Seal the cut ends by wetting them.) Plant each cutting in a 3-inch pot of a moistened equal-parts mixture of peat moss and coarse sand or perlite, enclose the whole in a plastic bag or heated propagating case (see page 444), and keep it in bright filtered light for four to six weeks. Thereafter, when fresh growth indicates that rooting has occurred, treat the new plant as a mature codiaeum. It will fill its pot with roots in five to six months, and should then be moved into a pot one size larger containing the recommended potting mixture for adult plants.

Codiaeums may also be propagated by air layering (see page 440), but this is a method taking a great deal of time and special care.

Special points Red spider mites can be troublesome; for preventive measures and treatment see page 455.

Since codiaeums normally branch out quite freely and become bushy without being cut back, pruning should not be necessary as long as a relatively large plant can be accommodated. If a plant becomes too big for the available position, however, cut it back as much as required. The best time to do this is in early spring, before new growth begins. Spray cut ends with water or dust them with powdered charcoal to stop the flow of latex. Stems that have been cut back will soon make new growth.

Coelogyne

ORCHIDACEAE

THE coelogynes grown as house plants are epiphytic, with short, upright pseudobulbs that are round, cylindrical, or cone-shaped. Each pseudobulb bears one to three leaves, and the terminal flower stem arising from its tip tends to droop. A mature plant will generally produce great numbers of fragrant flowers.

See also ORCHIDS.

RECOMMENDED COELOGYNES

C. cristata has a tightly packed cluster of shiny, light green, round or egg-shaped pseudobulbs. Each pseudobulb is 1–3 inches high and 1–1½ inches wide. Bulbs that have flowered gradually wrinkle and yellow. The pointed, strap-shaped, usually arching bright green leaves are 6–12 inches long and 2 inches wide. *C. cristata* is unusual in that its 12-inch-long flower stems rise from the base of the pseudobulbs. Each stem carries up to eight roughly bowl-shaped blooms, up to 4 inches across. The flower is entirely white, but five gold yellow lines run down the middle of the broad, three-lobed lip. Flowers generally appear in winter and early spring, and each bloom lasts several weeks.

C. flaccida has clusters of spindle-shaped, dark green pseudobulbs 2–4 inches tall and 1 inch wide. The pointed, strap-shaped, arching, dark green leaves are up to 9 inches long and 1½ inches wide. The 10-inch-long flower stem bears up to 12 star-shaped flowers, each 1½ inches across. The entire bloom is white or creamy white, but three red lines run down the middle of the small, narrow lip. Flowers generally appear in spring, and each lasts for several weeks.

C. pandurata (black orchid) has flattened-egg-shaped, medium green pseudobulbs 2–5 inches tall and 2½ inches wide that are set widely apart on the rhizome. The narrowly elliptic, shiny, slightly arching, bright green leaves are up to 18 inches long and 2½ inches wide. The 16-inch-long flower stem can carry up to 15 somewhat insectlike flowers, each 3–4 inches across. Sepals and petals are clear, pale green. The yellow-green, roughly fiddle-shaped lip is streaked and spotted with black. The flowering season is midsummer, and these flowers last a week or two.

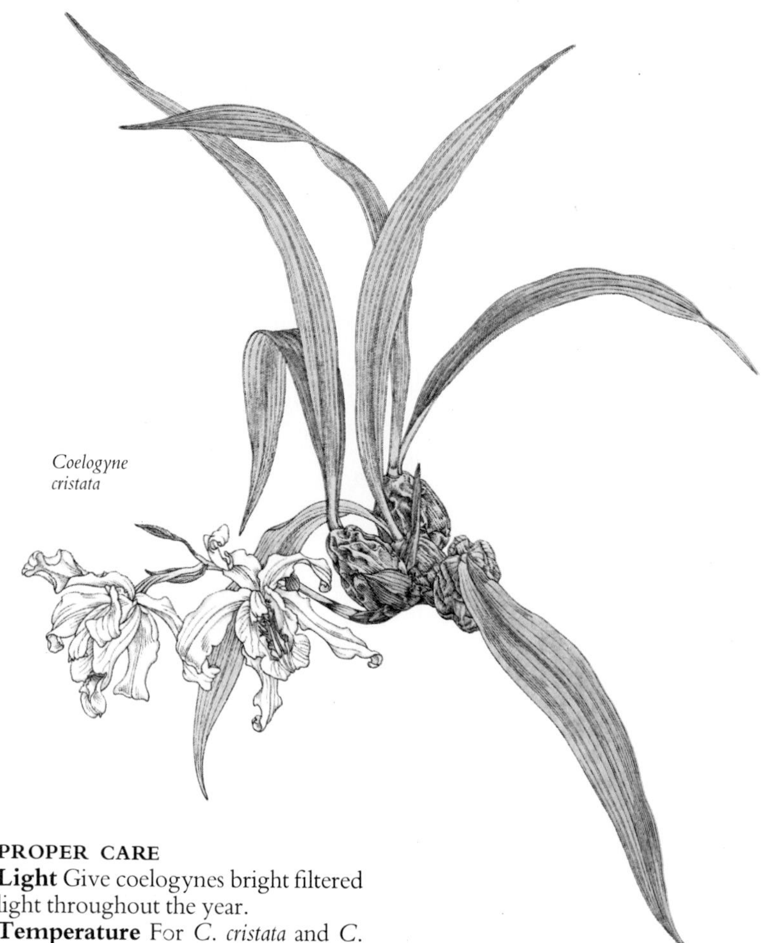

Coelogyne cristata

PROPER CARE

Light Give coelogynes bright filtered light throughout the year.

Temperature For *C. cristata* and *C. flaccida* temperatures should not exceed 75°F. Winter ranges of 55°–60° during the day and 45°–50° at night are best, but these orchids can tolerate up to 10° higher than the ideals. *C. pandurata* will do well in any normal room temperature at all seasons.

Watering *C. cristata* and *C. flaccida* normally need a winter rest period. During their active growth period water these plants plentifully, keeping the potting mixture thoroughly moist at all times. During the rest period give them only enough to keep the potting mixture from drying out. *C. pandurata* does not have a rest period so water plentifully at all times.

When watering coelogynes, do not let water rest on pseudobulbs around the new growth from which flower stems arise. To avoid this risk, stand containers in water below the level of new growths for 10 minutes at a time instead of watering from above.

Feeding Apply a foliar feed to actively growing coelogynes at every second or third watering.

Potting and repotting Use any of the recommended potting mixtures for orchids (see page 289). Grow these plants in pots or baskets, or attach them to a slab of tree fern. *C. pandurata*, however, looks best in a basket because of the wide spaces between the pseudobulbs. Coelogynes dislike being moved and they can usually be left undisturbed for at least four years. Repotting can be delayed by removing groups of the oldest pseudobulbs (the dying back-bulbs) from time to time. Use a sharp knife to cut through the rhizome, and fill the empty space with fresh potting mixture. In this way the removal of old growth makes room for the new. When repotting must be done, do it in spring. Disturb the roots as little as possible.

Propagation To propagate, cut off a piece of rhizome bearing at least one new pseudobulb and growing point as well as two or three older pseudobulbs. Do this just before the beginning of the flowering season. The larger the section of rhizome removed the better, since small pieces take several years to flower. Pot the rhizome section in recommended orchid mixture with its growing point toward the center of a small pot, and water it sparingly till new growth appears. Thereafter, treat it as a mature plant.

Coffea

RUBIACEAE

Coffee plant
C. arabica

THE only species of the genus *Coffea* grown as a house plant is *C. arabica*, a shrub that is actually the major source of the familiar coffee bean (really one of the two seeds held within a fleshy fruit). This shrub, which is single-stemmed when young but gradually becomes bushy, can grow 15 feet high in open ground but seldom exceeds 4 feet indoors. The glossy, dark green leaves, which are arranged on the stems in opposite pairs, are elliptic in shape, with pointed tips and undulating edges, and they grow up to 6 inches long and 2 inches wide. After a coffea is three or four years old, it can produce $\frac{1}{4}$-inch-wide, star-shaped, fragrant, white flowers from the leaf axils. Flowering generally occurs in midsummer or early fall, and the blooms are followed by $\frac{1}{2}$-inch-long fruits, which change color first from green to red and then to nearly black.

There is a dwarf form, *C.a.* 'Nana,' which may begin to bear flowers and fruit when only $1\frac{1}{2}$–2 feet tall.

PROPER CARE

Light Grow all of these plants in medium light—for instance, close to a slightly shaded window.

Temperature Normally warm room temperatures are suitable. These plants cannot tolerate low temperatures and will drop most of their lower leaves if the temperature falls below about 55°F for any length of time. The leaf tips will turn brown or black if the air is not sufficiently humid. In warm rooms, particularly during the active growth period, stand pots on trays of moist pebbles, and mist-spray the foliage at least twice a week.

Watering During the active growth period water plentifully as often as necessary to keep the potting mixture thoroughly moist, but never allow pots to stand in water. During the winter rest period make the potting mixture barely moist, giving only enough water to keep it from drying out completely.

Feeding Apply standard liquid fertilizer every two weeks from early spring to early fall.

Potting and repotting Use a soil-based potting mixture (see page 429), and put an inch-deep layer of clay-pot fragments in the bottom of the pot for drainage. Move plants into pots one size larger every spring, just as new growth begins.

Propagation Cuttings are difficult to root. The best way to propagate is from fresh seed sown in spring. (Note that freshness is essential.) Plant two or three seeds ½ inch deep in a 3-inch pot of moistened rooting mixture (see page 444), enclose the pot in a plastic bag or heated propagating case (see page 444), and stand it in medium light at a minimum temperature of 75°F. No additional water is needed until after germination, which should occur in three to four weeks. When the seedlings are about 1½ inches high, remove the covering, and pull up and discard all but the most promising-looking one. If necessary, gently firm the mixture around the base of this remaining seedling, and grow it on in the same pot. Begin to water very moderately and to apply the standard liquid fertilizer once a month. When the young plant has reached a height of 3–4 inches, move it into a 3-inch pot of soil-based potting mixture. Thereafter, its cultivation needs are the same as those of mature coffeas.

Special points Scale insects sometimes attack coffeas on the undersides of the leaves (for preventive measures and treatment see page 455).

Coleus

LABIATAE

Flame nettle
C. blumei

ALTHOUGH coleuses are perennials, many growers treat them as temporary foliage plants, to be enjoyed and then discarded when past their best. This is because they are sometimes difficult to overwinter, and also because they are very easy to grow from cuttings. Their soft, rather thin leaves vary considerably in shape, size, and color (which can be almost any shade of yellow, red, orange, green, or brown, or a mixture of three or more of these). Such flowers as they produce have little decorative value and are best nipped out when they are still developing; this helps keep the plants bushy.

C. blumei varieties (leaves)

Only one species, *C. blumei* (flame nettle or painted leaves), is commonly grown as a house plant. Some of its forms have heart-shaped leaves, and others have slender, sometimes contorted, pendulous leaves. Young seedlings only an inch or two high, but already showing their true color, can be bought in spring, and these may grow into plants 2 feet tall in one season. Named hybrids of this species are also frequently available. Some of the best of these are: *C.* 'Brilliancy,' which has crimson-red leaves that are marked with golden yellow at the edges; *C.* 'Candidus,' which has a white patch in the center of the undulate, pale green leaves; *C.* 'Golden Bedder,' which has lemon yellow leaves deepening to gold in bright light; *C.* 'Pink Rainbow,' which has undulate, coppery red leaves that are marked with green bands and bright carmine-red veining; and *C.* 'Sunset,' which has a pink patch in the center of its pale green leaves.

PROPER CARE

Light Provide bright light at all times—including several hours a day of direct sunlight, if possible. Insufficient light will result in spindly, elongated growth.

Temperature Coleuses do well in warm rooms. In temperatures above 65°F, though, the air should be humidified by standing plants on trays of damp pebbles or moist peat moss. If the temperature is allowed to fall much below about 55° leaves are in danger of wilting and dropping off.

Watering These plants should be watered plentifully as often as necessary to keep the potting mixture thoroughly moist. If the mixture is permitted to dry out for even a short period, the leaves will collapse; and although plants may appear to recover fully when they are watered once more, lower leaves will drop off.

Feeding Apply standard liquid fertilizer every two weeks throughout the active growth period.

Potting and repotting Use a soil-based potting mixture (see page 429). Young plants should be moved every two months into pots two sizes larger. Coleuses should not be underpotted; they need room for their active roots to develop.

Propagation Young, freshly rooted plants overwinter much better than older plants. Tip cuttings 2–3 inches long taken in early fall will root easily either in the standard potting mixture or water. If started in water, they should be moved into the potting mixture when roots are 2–3 inches long. Cuttings started in potting mixture will root in about two weeks if kept in a warm, brightly lit position, without direct sunlight. Water the cuttings enough to make the mixture moist, but allow the top half-inch of the mixture to dry out completely between waterings.

Special points In hot, dry rooms red spider mites can cause discoloration and leaf withering (see page 455). To prevent an infestation provide a humid atmosphere and spray plants with water occasionally. Wash off any heavy infestations of red spider mites under the water faucet.

All coleuses should have their growing tips nipped out regularly to help them remain bushy.

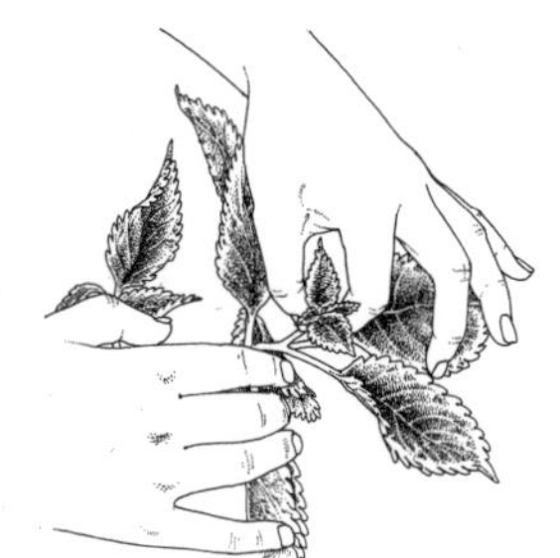

Pinching out all the growing points of coleuses several times a year helps them to stay bushy.

Columnea

GESNERIACEAE

THERE are basically two kinds of columnea: those with long, thin stems that are entirely trailing, and those with stems that are partially erect but deeply arching. Both kinds are prized for their abundant and spectacular flowers, which can bloom at almost any time of year. The short-stalked leaves are carried on the stems in opposite, often overlapping pairs. Paired leaves are frequently unequal in size and shape, and in some species the smaller leaf may be so tiny as to give the impression of alternating rather than paired leaves. Leaf shape is usually roughly elliptic, often more pointed at the base than at the tip.

Columnea flowers, produced from leaf axils either singly or in groups, always bear a five-lobed calyx and are brilliant in color and striking in shape. Each tubular corolla flares into five differently shaped lobes. The two upper lobes are joined together to form a down-curving hood above the others. As the flower opens, its stamens can be seen just under the outer end of the hood, and later the stigma also projects beyond the hood. It is the shape of the colorful open flower that has given columneas the common name of goldfish plant, for from some angles the flower resembles a head-on view of a fish. Up to 100 flowers may bloom simultaneously on one large plant, and each flower can last for four weeks. In some species the flower is followed by an attractive, often white berry cupped within the calyx.

See also GESNERIADS.

RECOMMENDED COLUMNEAS

***C.* 'Banksii,'** a long-established hybrid, has trailing stems to 4 feet long, with dark green, fleshy, nearly smooth leaves $1–1\frac{3}{4}$ inches long and $\frac{1}{2}–\frac{3}{4}$ inch wide. The flowers, each with a $\frac{1}{2}$-inch-long, green calyx, are about $2\frac{1}{2}$ inches long and scarlet in color, with yellow lines running into the mouth of the corolla. Flowering can continue throughout the year.

C. gloriosa has slender, trailing stems that grow to 3 feet long and branch only at the base. The dark green leaves, paired in generally unequal sizes, are $\frac{1}{2}–1\frac{1}{4}$ inches long, $\frac{1}{2}–\frac{5}{8}$ inch wide, and densely covered with purplish red hairs on the upper surface and reddish hairs on the lower. Leaf edges tend to turn under. The 3-inch-long flowers, carried singly on inch-long stalks, have a hairy green calyx about $\frac{1}{2}$ inch long. The scarlet corolla is covered with downy white hairs and has a bright yellow patch in the throat. Flowering is almost continuous, and each flower is followed by a particularly striking white berry that has a diameter of $1\frac{1}{4}$ inches when mature.

C. linearis is an erect species with branching stems up to $1\frac{1}{2}$ feet tall. Very short-stalked, equal-size pairs of narrow, glossy, dark green leaves are $3\frac{1}{2}$ inches long and $\frac{1}{2}$ inch wide. Deep pink, hairy flowers up to $1\frac{3}{4}$ inches long and with green, $\frac{3}{4}$-inch-long calyxes, are borne singly on $\frac{1}{2}$-inch-long stalks. Although this plant can bloom for most of the year, it flowers most freely in summer.

C. microphylla is a spectacular spring-flowering plant with thin, 6- to 8-foot-long, trailing and branching stems, which are densely covered with brownish red hairs. The stems carry nearly overlapping pairs of equal-size, almost round, dark green leaves up to $\frac{1}{2}$ inch in diameter; these too are densely covered with reddish hairs. Flowers, carried singly on $\frac{1}{4}$-inch-long stalks, bear $\frac{1}{4}$-inch-long, hairy calyxes, which are green tinged with red. Flower corollas are bright scarlet with a yellow throat, and are up to $3\frac{1}{2}$

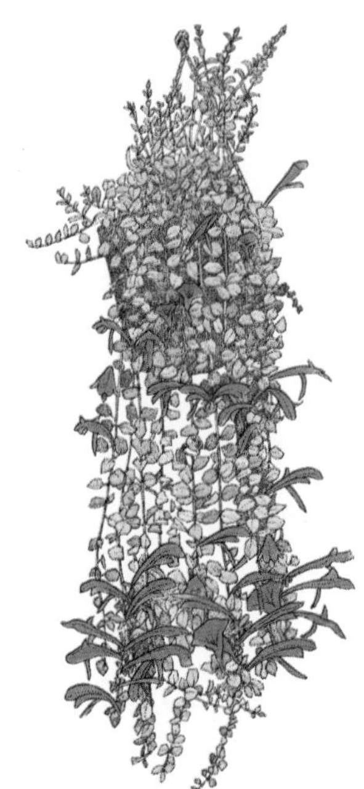

The long, trailing stems of C. microphylla *make it a particularly appropriate plant for display in a hanging basket.*

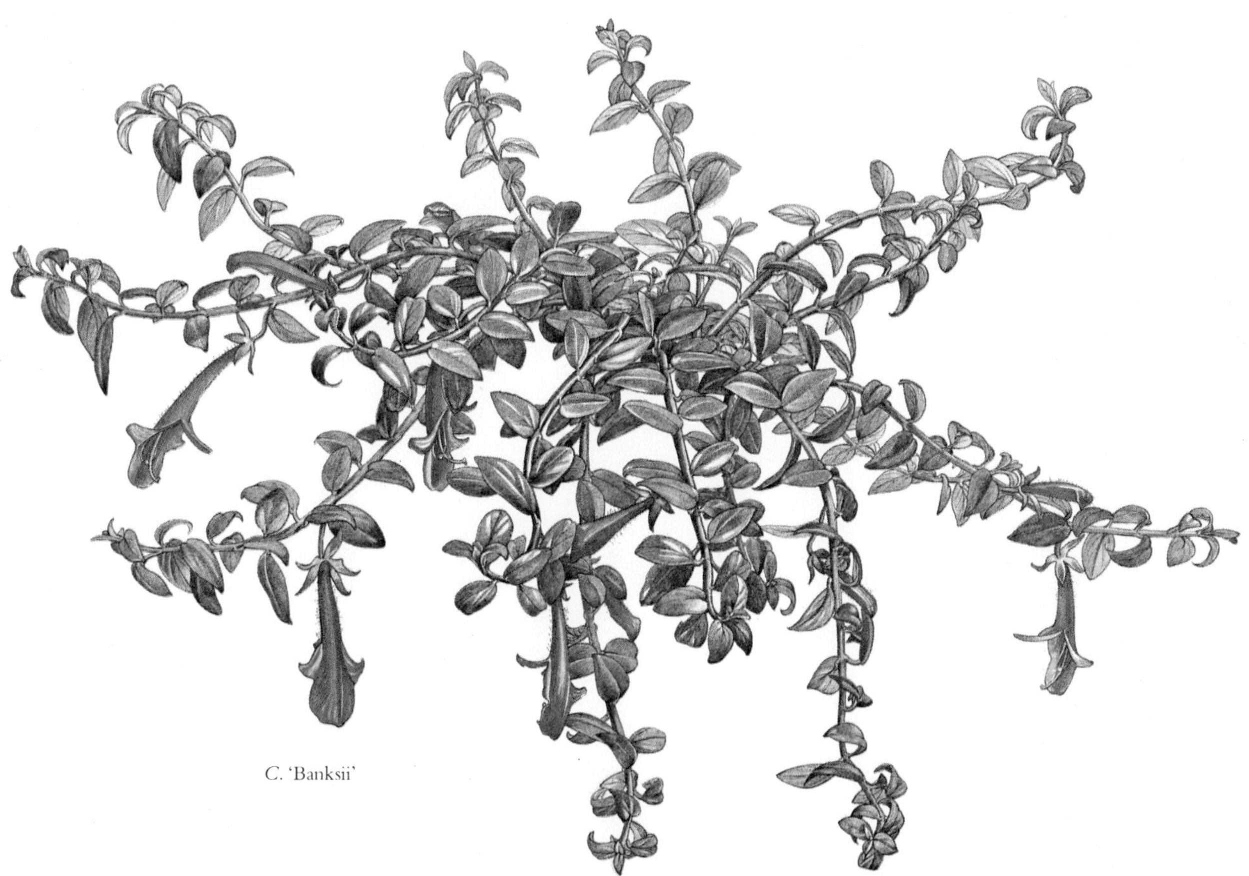
C. 'Banksii'

inches long. This plant looks best when it is allowed to trail in a hanging basket.

There are many recent columnea hybrids of varying parentage, most of them bred to give short-stemmed growth and long flowering periods. The following forms are particularly rewarding as well as conveniently compact for use in the home:

C. 'Alpha' has short, much-branching stems, with medium green leaves and numerous canary yellow flowers all year round. It will even flower on young rooted cuttings.

C. 'Chanticleer' is probably the easiest columnea to grow as a house plant. It is a short-stemmed, branching shrub with light green, velvety leaves and light orange flowers, which are produced during most of the year.

C. 'Christmas Carol' is a trailer with small, dark green leaves and large, deep red flowers, which bloom during most of the year.

C. 'Evlo,' a spring-flowering trailer, has dark coppery leaves and bright red flowers. Flower and leaf dimensions are similar to those of *C. gloriosa*, which is one parent of this hybrid.

C. 'Mary Ann' is a compact, branching trailer with narrow, dark green leaves and deep pink flowers, which are produced throughout the year.

PROPER CARE

Light Columneas like bright light without direct sunlight. The shorter-stemmed plants also do well in fluorescent light if placed about 15 inches below the tube. A few—including *C. microphylla* and C. 'Evlo,' among those recommended above—need the short day-length of winter in order to produce flowers. If such plants are being grown in artificial light, it should be adjusted accordingly (see page 446).

Temperature Normally warm room temperatures (65°–85°F) are just right for most of these plants throughout the year. *C. microphylla* and C. 'Evlo' need to be kept somewhat cooler (55°–65°) in winter, however, so as to flower in the spring. All columneas require high humidity at all times. Stand pots on trays of moist pebbles, and mist-spray plants in hanging baskets at least once a day. Water for spraying should be at room temperature. If cold water is sprayed, it can result in unattractive brown stains on the leaves.

Watering Although they need high humidity around the leaves, columneas cannot tolerate wet roots, which cause the stems to rot. During the active growth period (which is all year long, or nearly all year long, for most of these plants), water sparingly, enough to make the entire mixture barely moist, and let the top third of the mixture dry out between waterings. During the rest period, if any, water just enough to keep the mixture from completely drying out. Use water at room temperature to avoid brown spots on the leaves.

Feeding While a columnea is actively growing, give it a high-phosphate liquid fertilizer, one-quarter the recommended strength at every watering. Do not feed plants if they are having a rest period.

Potting and repotting Because columneas are epiphytic plants in the wild, they may be grown simply in coarse sphagnum moss. Or, if preferred, use a loosely packed equal-parts potting mixture of peat moss, perlite, and vermiculite. Shallow pots or pans about 4 inches in diameter or small, shallow baskets are best for growing columneas. When the roots of a plant fill its container (see page 426), move it into a container one size larger; or, alternatively, trim about one-third off the bottom of the root ball with a sharp knife, and repot the plant in the same size container, adding fresh potting mixture as required. Repot continuous-flowering columneas at any time, but this is best done just as the active growth period begins for other types.

Repotting without moving on

The roots of this plant have filled its current pot, which is of the largest convenient size.

By trimming away one-third of the root ball you can return the plant to the same pot with ample room for fresh potting mixture.

Propagation The best time to propagate is when repotting. Insert a tip cutting 3–4 inches long in a 3-inch pot of moistened vermiculite, and keep the pot at normal room temperature in bright filtered light, watering only often enough to keep the vermiculite barely moist. Rooting should occur in about four weeks, after which the new plant should be transferred to a 3-inch pot of the standard potting mixture for adult plants and treated as a mature columnea. For a really good display, plant three or four rooted cuttings in a single 10-inch hanging basket.

Columneas can also be grown from seed (see page 441).

Special points Inspect columneas regularly for pests. They are especially susceptible to attack by cyclamen mites and aphids. For preventive measures and treatment see page 454.

Cordyline

AGAVACEAE

Goodluck plant
C. terminalis

CORDYLINES are all single-stemmed, usually unbranched shrubs or small trees closely related to—and frequently confused with—dracaenas. Cordyline leaves are arranged in a loose rosette; as they age, the lower ones dry up and may be pulled off, leaving behind a stout but bare stem. Leaves of some forms are long, narrow, arching, without stalks, and of equal width for practically all their length; in others, they are shorter and broader—up to 4 inches wide, narrowing only at the tip and where they join leafstalks. Flowers, which are produced only on mature plants, are unlikely to appear in the home, where these plants rarely attain the size normally reached in the wild.

RECOMMENDED CORDYLINES

C. australis (often called *Dracaena indivisa* by florists; popularly known as giant or fountain dracaena, cabbage tree, or palm lily) has sword-shaped, arching, leathery, green leaves 2–3 feet long and 2 inches wide, each with a short, narrowed tip. In one form, *C.a.* 'Atropurpurea,' the midrib and base of the leaf are purple-marked; in another, *C.a.* 'Doucetii,' the entire leaf has lengthwise white stripes.

C. indivisa (blue dracaena) differs from *C. australis* in that its leaves are longer—3–4 feet—and wider—3 inches. Potted plants of this species obviously take up a great amount of space and are not often suitable for indoor use. In mild climates they are perhaps best grown out of doors—on a patio, for instance.

C. terminalis (formerly—and still inaccurately—called *Dracaena terminalis*; popularly known as goodluck plant, Polynesian ti plant, or tree of kings) has lance-shaped leaves up to 2 feet long and 4 inches wide, narrowing distinctly at the stalk as well as at the tip. Leaf color, which is rich crimson in young plants, gradually changes to coppery green with red shading. Among the many forms: *C.t.* 'Amabilis' has broad, shiny leaves colored bronze tinged with pink and edged with cream; *C.t.* 'Baptisii' has strongly arching leaves of deep green suffused with red and creamy yellow; those of *C.t.* 'Firebrand' (red dracaena) are shiny and purple-red with bronze shading; those of *C.t.* 'Rededge' are relatively small—up to 9 inches long and 2½ inches wide—slightly twisted, and bright green with red streaks; and *C.t.* 'Tricolor' is a broad-leaved form with red, pink, and cream coloring on a light green base.

PROPER CARE

Light *C. australis* and *C. indivisa* should be grown in full sunlight. *C. terminalis* and its varieties must not be subjected to direct rays of the sun, which would scorch their leaves; give them bright light filtered through a translucent blind or curtain.

Temperature *C. terminalis* requires normal room temperatures, but the other two species can tolerate temperatures as low as 50°F. Wherever possible, plants of the two hardier species should be kept outdoors during summer and fall.

Watering During the active growth period water plentifully as often as necessary to keep the potting mixture thoroughly moist, but never allow pots to stand in water. During the rest period water only enough to keep the potting mixture from drying out.

Feeding Apply standard liquid fertilizer every two weeks during the active growth period only.

Potting and repotting Use a soil-based potting mixture (see page 429). Move plants each spring into pots one or two sizes larger, until maximum convenient pot size (probably 8 to 10 inches) is reached. Thereafter, apply an annual topdressing (see page 428) of fresh potting mixture.

Propagation Cordylines may be grown from seed sown 1 inch deep in small pots of moistened rooting mixture (see page 444); this should be done in spring. Germination should occur in four to six weeks if pots are placed in a plastic bag or heated propagating case (see page 444) and stood in a warm position where they get bright filtered sunlight; no additional watering is necessary. When a seedling has made 2–3 inches of growth, it can be removed from the bag or case and treated as a mature plant.

Some species produce tip or basal shoots suitable for propagation. Take such cuttings when they are 4–8 inches long in spring or early summer, plant in a moistened equal-parts mixture of peat moss and coarse sand or perlite, enclose in a plastic bag or propagating case, and keep for four to six weeks in a warm room in bright filtered light. When top growth indicates that new roots are active, uncover the pots. Feed once a month with standard liquid fertilizer, and water just enough to make the mixture moist. After another four or five months, move the plants into 4- to 6-inch pots of the standard potting mixture for adult plants and treat them as mature cordylines.

Alternatively, 2-inch sections of old stem (with or without leaves) will normally root if each section includes at least one growth bud (a slight swelling under the bark). Plant the bottom end in the rooting mixture recommended above, and follow the same procedure that applies to tip or basal cuttings.

When C. terminalis *has become tall and leggy, the tip can be used for propagation and so can 2-inch segments of the tall, bare stem.*

Cotyledon

CRASSULACEAE

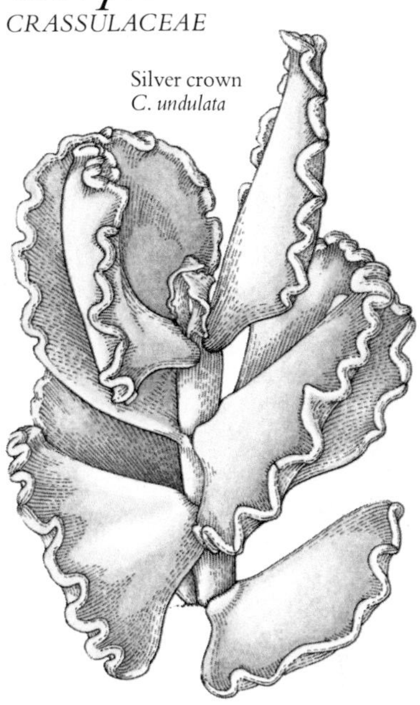

INDOOR cotyledons are shrubby succulents with fleshy, grayish leaves and bell-shaped flowers. Young plants have a single stem, which eventually branches. The stalkless leaves grow in opposite pairs and are usually covered with a fine white powder, or "bloom." These slow-growing plants take three or four years to reach a height of 20 inches. At about the same age they begin to produce bright-colored flowers in clusters of 10 to 20 on stalks up to 15 inches tall. The 1- to 1½-inch-long blooms have curled petal tips. Cotyledons bloom most commonly in summer, but may have some flowers in spring or fall. Each stalk retains a few flowers for up to four weeks.

See also SUCCULENTS.

RECOMMENDED COTYLEDONS

C. orbiculata grows 15–20 inches tall. The rigid, erect stems branch roughly every 6 inches. The leaves are shaped

like rounded triangles, with the apex at the point where they join the stems or branches. Individual leaves are 2–4 inches long and 1–2 inches wide, and gray-green thickly coated with white powder. Leaf edges are thinly marked with red. Flowers are either yellow or orange in color.

C. undulata (silver crown) also has rigid, branching stems. Wedge-shaped leaves about 2 inches long narrow to a point at the bottom where they join the stem, but widen to 3 inches at the scalloped top. Leaf color is grayish white, becoming pure white at the top leaf edge. The flowers are orange-colored.

PROPER CARE

Light Provide full sunlight all year long. Inadequate light causes spindly growth and poor leaf color.

Temperature Cotyledons do well in normal room temperatures.

Watering During the active growth period water moderately, enough to make the potting mixture moist throughout, and allowing the top inch of the mixture to dry out between waterings. Cotyledons profit from a short winter rest period. During the two or three months of least sunlight water them only enough to prevent the mixture from drying out.

Feeding Apply standard liquid fertilizer once every two weeks during the active growth period only.

Potting and repotting Good drainage is essential. Use a combination of two-thirds soil-based potting mixture (see page 429) and one-third coarse sand or perlite, and put a layer of clay-pot fragments ½ inch deep in the bottom of the pot. Move plants into pots one size larger every spring until maximum convenient size (probably 5–6 inches) has been reached. Thereafter, topdress each year in spring (see page 428).

Propagation Tip cuttings 3–4 inches long will root readily if taken in spring or early summer and left to dry for two or three days before being planted. Insert each cutting in a 3-inch pot of the recommended mixture. Cotyledon cuttings do not require a special rooting mixture. Simply stand the pot in a warm place where it gets bright filtered light and water sparingly until renewed growth indicates that rooting has occurred. Then move the plant into direct sunlight, and treat as a mature cotyledon.

Crassula

CRASSULACEAE

THE genus *Crassula* includes succulent plants of very different appearance and scale, often needing different treatment. Some are extremely simple, consisting of just a few leaves, whereas others are dense shrubs. All have leaves arranged in pairs on opposite sides of the stem. Most have unimpressive flowers, but those of a few—*C. falcata,* for instance—are very showy. There has been, and still is, confusion about the correct classification of some crassulas that superficially resemble one another. *See also SUCCULENTS.*

RECOMMENDED CRASSULAS

C. arborescens (Chinese or silver jade) forms a stout, trunklike stem up to 4 feet tall, which carries well-balanced branches bearing fleshy, almost round leaves that are gray-green with reddish edges and are 1–2 inches across. The balance of the branches is a distinctive feature of this plant, as of some of its close relatives; no training or pruning can improve their perfect treelike appearance. Flowers, which are rare in cultivation, appear in spring; they are tiny but numerous, star-shaped, and from white to deep pink in color. A variegated form, *C.a.* 'Variegata,' has yellowish leaf markings and is considerably slower-growing than the type plant.

C. argentea (also known as *C. portulacea,* and popularly as jade tree) also grows up to 4 feet tall, but its leaves are more spoon-shaped and are shiny jade green, often—but not always—with red edges. Tiny pink or white star-shaped flowers are regularly produced on mature plants during the winter, with many of them clustered together to form heads 2–3 inches across. Among variegated forms are *C.a.* 'Variegata,' which has greenish gray leaves with yellowish stripes, and *C.a.* 'Tricolor,' which is similar but has some pink coloring in the foliage.

There is considerable confusion about the naming of a form of crassula that has obliquely oval leaves of a silvery green, with darker markings. This plant is commonly known as *C. obliqua* but should probably be named *C.a.obliqua.*

C. falcata (airplane propeller plant, scarlet paintbrush, or sickle plant), which is still sometimes called by the long-discredited botanical name *Rochea falcata,* has sickle-shaped, gray-green leaves with a slightly roughened surface and a twist away from the stem; they can be up to 8 inches long. Although the plant is naturally bushy, with several growing points, it often develops only one stem up to 1 foot tall in cultivation. A dense cluster of little scarlet or orange-red flowers is produced in summer on a forked flower head 3–4 inches wide.

C. lactea (flowering crassula or tailor's patch) is perhaps the easiest crassula to grow indoors. It forms a 2-foot shrub with spreading branches that eventually droop down to soil level, but young plants are erect. The oval, pointed leaves are 1–2½ inches long and dark green with a line of white dots near the edge. Big, branching flower heads composed of quite large white flowers are produced in winter.

C. lycopodioides (toy cypress or moss, rat-tail or watch-chain crassula) is a small, much-branching plant suitable for use in a bowl or dish. Its slender, erect stems are almost hidden by minute, pointed, fleshy leaves that are packed tightly around each stem to form a four-sided column of scaly

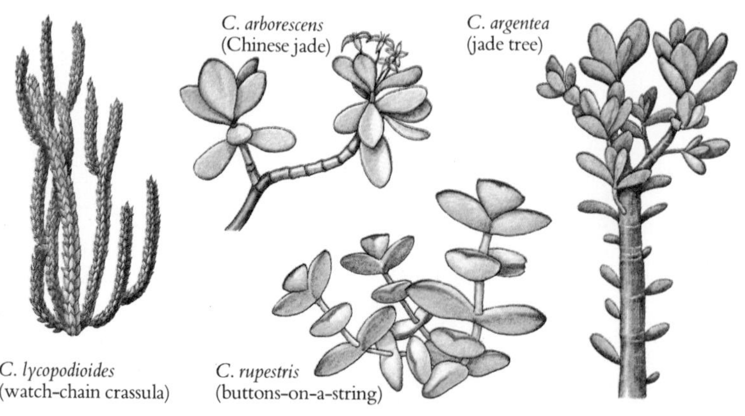

C. lycopodioides (watch-chain crassula)

C. arborescens (Chinese jade)

C. rupestris (buttons-on-a-string)

C. argentea (jade tree)

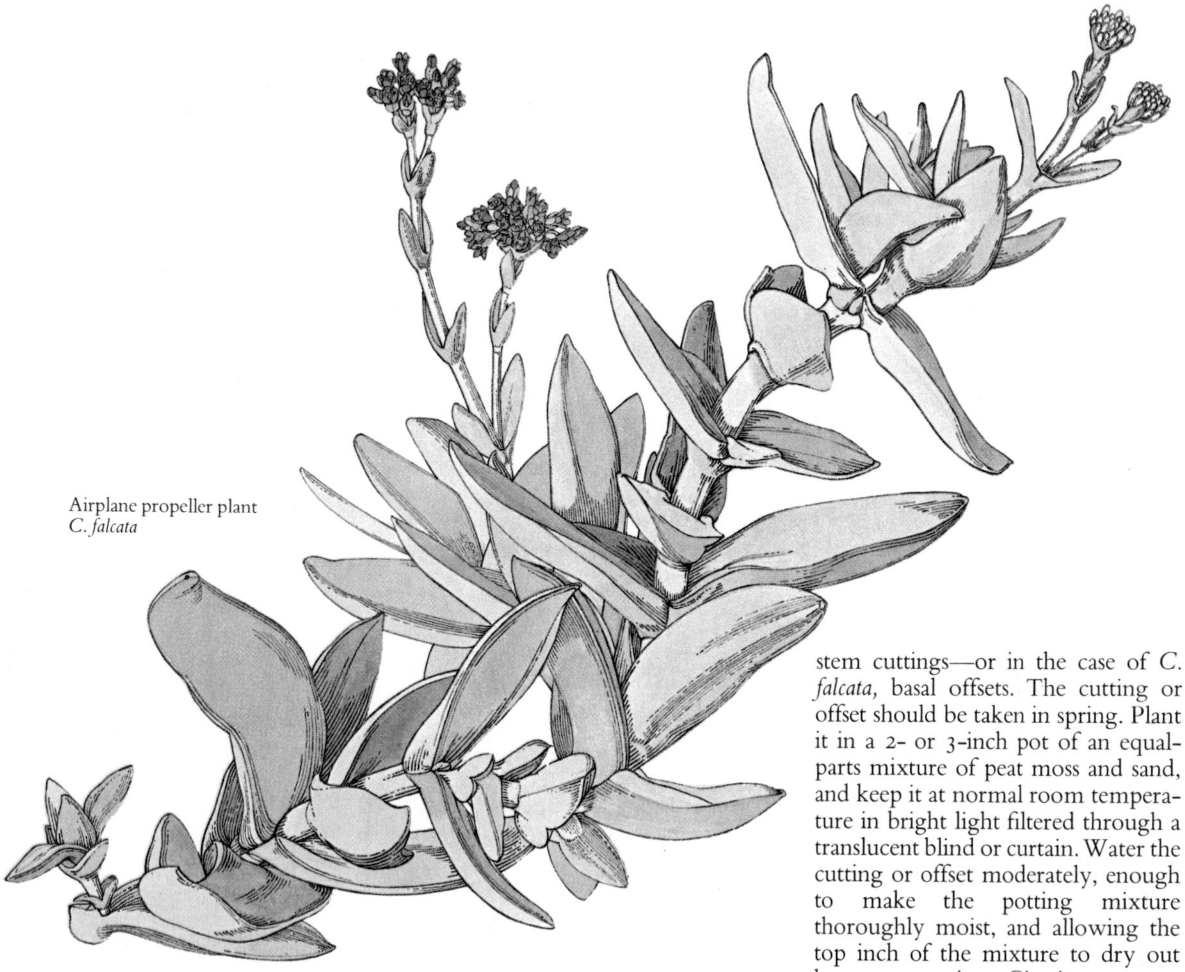

Airplane propeller plant
C. falcata

appearance. Greenish flowers are produced either singly or in pairs but are barely noticeable. These plants rarely grow taller than 9 inches.

C. rupestris has many popular names, including buttons-on-a-string, bead vine, rosary vine, and rosary plant. This crassula is a small spreading plant, with the stem appearing to pass through the ½- to 1-inch leaves like a string through beads. Leaves are fat, almost triangular, and blue-gray. The little pink flowers are produced in summer in clusters of 6 to 10 at the ends of the stems.

PROPER CARE

Light Crassulas need bright light, with some direct sunlight. No crassula will flower without sunshine, and inadequate light will cause all crassulas to develop spindly growth.

Temperature Most crassulas grow well in either warm or cool positions, but should not be subjected to temperatures above 55°F during the winter rest period, when they can tolerate temperatures down to 45°.

Watering During the active growth period water moderately, enough to make the mixture thoroughly moist at each watering, and always allow two-thirds to dry out between waterings. During the rest period water only enough to keep the potting mixture from drying out completely.

Feeding Apply standard liquid fertilizer every two weeks during the active growth period only.

Potting and repotting Use a mixture of three parts soil-based potting mixture (see page 429) to one part coarse sand or perlite. Most crassulas should be moved into pots one size larger only once every two years.

C. lycopodioides will continue to thrive in a 3-inch pot for several years, but the larger forms may be potted on up to 8- or 10-inch pots or small tubs.

Propagation Individual leaves of most crassulas will root readily in the recommended sandy potting mixture if kept in a warm room in a position where they get bright filtered light, but a more satisfactory way to propagate is by means of 2- to 3-inch-long stem cuttings—or in the case of *C. falcata,* basal offsets. The cutting or offset should be taken in spring. Plant it in a 2- or 3-inch pot of an equal-parts mixture of peat moss and sand, and keep it at normal room temperature in bright light filtered through a translucent blind or curtain. Water the cutting or offset moderately, enough to make the potting mixture thoroughly moist, and allowing the top inch of the mixture to dry out between waterings. Give it some standard liquid fertilizer once a month. When well rooted—in about three months—move the young plant into a one-size-larger pot of recommended mixture and treat it as mature.

Propagating a crassula

In taking a basal offset from C. falcata, *sever it close to the parent plant. Then plant the offset in a pot of rooting mixture.*

Crinum

AMARYLLIDACEAE

Spider lily
C. 'Powellii'

CRINUMS (spider lilies) are very large, bulbous, flowering plants with sword- or strap-shaped leaves. The bulbs may be 6 inches across, with "necks" up to 6 or even 12 inches long; clumps of bulbs form as the plants age. The species generally grown as house plants keep their leaves for at least one full year, after which the leaves slowly become shabby and untidy. When they finally drop off or are picked off, fresh new leaves appear. The plants therefore need considerable attention to keep the foliage presentable.

Clusters of five to eight impressive, trumpet-shaped flowers are produced in the fall on 2- to 3-foot-long flower stalks. Each of these long stalks may be an inch thick, and the flowers themselves are usually 3–5 inches long, with mouths up to 6 inches across. The handsome display of blooms lasts for about one month. Plants may take four years to reach flowering size.

See also BULBS, CORMS, and TUBERS.

RECOMMENDED CRINUMS

C. bulbispermum has a 3- to 4-inch-thick oval bulb from which rise about 10 spreading, sword-shaped leaves. Each slender-pointed leaf is 2–3 feet long and 2–3 inches wide. Flower color is white, deeply tinged with pink on the outer surfaces of the petals. One variety, *C.b.* 'Album,' has pure white blooms.

C. 'Powellii,' a hybrid of which *C. bulbispermum* is one parent, has a 4-inch-thick globular bulb and up to 20 sword-shaped leaves. Each leaf is 3–4 feet long and 3–4 inches wide near the base. The flowers are pinkish red, with green shading near the base of the petals. A variety, 'Ellen Bosanquet,' has shorter, broader leaves, and flower color is deep wine red.

PROPER CARE

Light Crinums need at least three hours a day of direct sunlight. Inadequate light will inhibit flowering and can also result in unnaturally elongated leaves.

Temperature Crinums grow well in normal room temperatures for most of the year, but need a three-month rest period at 50°F in midwinter.

Watering During the active growth period water plentifully, but never let the pot stand in water. During the winter rest period give just enough to prevent the mixture from drying out.

Feeding Apply standard liquid fertilizer once every three weeks during the active growth period only.

Potting and repotting Use a soil-based potting mixture (see page 429), in a pot that is only an inch or two wider than the bulb to be planted. If bulbs are small, plant two or three in a 10- or 12-inch pot or tub, standing each one half in and half out of the mixture. Leave plenty of space above the mixture, which will be forced upward as more roots are produced.

Once potted, crinums are most likely to flourish if left undisturbed. Do not attempt to separate bulb clumps or to move plants into bigger pots for at least three years. Instead, give the plants an annual spring top-dressing (see page 428).

Propagation To propagate, divide overcrowded clumps in spring by pulling them apart gently. Pot the bulbs up either singly or in groups of two or three. Then work the mixture around the fleshy roots, and press it down thoroughly. For six weeks after potting up, water sparingly. Thereafter, treat the plants as adults.

Special points When sections of leaves turn yellow or show signs of damage, cut away the unsightly portions. Entire leaves need not be cut away unless necessary.

Crocus

IRIDACEAE

Crocus hybrid

CROCUSES are all winter-flowering plants grown from small corms. Their slender, grooved leaves are dark green striped with white, and their cup-shaped flowers may be purple, mauve, white, bronze, yellow, or striped with two colors. The maximum height of these plants is about 4–5 inches. Outdoors they

Crocus hybrids (flowers)

produce roots and little or no top growth during the cold winter months and have a brief flowering period at the beginning of spring. After this, most of the leaves grow and die down within a couple of months. Crocuses to be used indoors should be encouraged to make root growth before top growth gets well under way, and they will do this only if kept cool. Ideally, planted-up bowls or pots should be buried outdoors beneath a thick covering of peat moss, and they should not be brought inside until the flower buds begin to show some color. Indoor plants can then be enjoyed while in bloom. When flowering has ended, they can be put outside again and can either be left to wither naturally in the pots—after which the corms should be dried for fall replanting in the open ground—or else they can be planted in the ground directly. They will not flower again indoors.

Dutch hybrids, which have flowers two or three times the size of the true species, make the most satisfactory house plants. Use only one flower color for each container, since different-colored hybrids may bloom at different times. Plant several corms

It is important when planting a number of corms together to keep them from touching one another.

together just below the surface of a soil-based potting mixture (see page 429) or prepared bulb fiber (see page 111). Containers may be shallow pots, half-pots, or bowls. Crocuses planted in bowls without drainage holes will need to be watered with extreme care, and it is always best to use bulb fiber for such plantings.

Plant crocuses early in the fall, water only enough to keep the potting mixture just moist, and place the plants in as cool and dark a position as possible if outdoor burial is not feasible. An ideal procedure for the apartment dweller is to cover the prepared pots or bowls with a black plastic bag and put them out on a ledge or balcony. Inspect them from time to time to make sure that no further watering is required. (It will not be necessary unless the potting mixture dries out completely.) Do *not* try to start the plants in a dark closet or cupboard, where temperatures are likely to be too high.

In mid-January the potted plants may be brought into gentle warmth (maximum 60°F). For their short stay in the home, keep them cool, out of direct sunshine but in bright light. Water them moderately.

See also BULBS, CORMS, and TUBERS.

Crossandra

ACANTHACEAE

Firecracker flower
C. infundibuliformis

THE only popular crossandra grown indoors is *C. infundibuliformis* (also called *C. undulifolia*; commonly known as firecracker flower). This shrubby plant can grow up to 2 feet tall. The glossy, lance-shaped, undulate, dark green leaves are 2–5 inches long and up to 2 inches wide, narrowing toward the ½- to 1-inch long leafstalk. In spring and summer, flowers appear in twos or threes on 6-inch-long spikes, which arise from terminal leaf axils and are partly hidden by small, triangular bracts. Each tube-shaped bloom flares out into a flattened, five-lobed disk 1½ inches across, and flower color varies from orange-red to salmon pink, but always with a yellow "eye." One form, *C.i.* 'Mona Walhed,' has dark leaves and salmon pink flowers, and rarely exceeds 12 inches in height.

PROPER CARE

Light Give crossandras medium light during the active growth period, but they need some direct sunlight during the short-day winter months.

Temperature These plants cannot tolerate temperatures below about 65°F. For high humidity stand them on trays of moist pebbles.

Watering During the active growth period water moderately, enough to make the mixture moist throughout and allowing the top half-inch to dry out between waterings. During the winter rest period give only enough to keep the mixture from completely drying out.

Feeding Apply standard liquid fertilizer once every two weeks during the active growth period only.

Potting and repotting Use a soil-based potting mixture (see page 429). Move small plants into pots one size larger each spring. Five- to 6-inch pots are likely to be the biggest needed. Thereafter, give an annual topdressing (see page 428) with fresh mixture.

Propagation In spring or in early summer, plant 2- to 3-inch-long tip cuttings in a moistened equal-parts mixture of peat moss and coarse sand or perlite. Place the cuttings either singly in 2-inch pots or several together in a seed tray. Enclose each container in a plastic bag or heated propagating case (see page 444), and keep the cuttings at a temperature of 70°F in bright filtered light. After rooting occurs (in four to six weeks) plant the rooted cuttings in 3-inch pots of the standard mixture and treat them as mature crossandras.

Special points In hot, dry rooms crossandras are susceptible to attack by red spider mites (see page 455).

Cryptanthus

BROMELIACEAE

Earth star
C. bivittatus

THE genus *Cryptanthus* (earth star) consists of low-growing terrestrial bromeliads that grow wild in rock fissures, on mossy tree roots and stumps, or in leafy jungle debris. The Latin name, "hidden flower," is appropriate since the unremarkable creamy or greenish white flowers that appear now and then tend to be partly hidden in leaf axils. These plants generally produce star-shaped rosettes of leaves that are tough, usually pointed but sometimes blunt-ended, and often have prickly margins. In most species the leaves grow flat on the potting mixture, and in some cases they are attractively wavy. Leaf coloring can be plain green, but is more often strongly patterned, with stripes or cross-bars in bright or muted shades. Leaves of a number of forms are covered with an attractive whitish scale, sometimes called "scurf" or "meal," which, unlike the bloom on leaves of many other plants, is not easily spoiled by touch. Cryptanthus roots are few; they serve mainly to anchor the plants rather than take in nutrients. These plants are excellent for use in bottle gardens and terrariums, and also for growing epiphytically on logs.

Because cryptanthus roots serve mainly to anchor, not to nourish, them, these plants are particularly suitable for display on epiphyte logs.

See also BROMELIADS.

RECOMMENDED CRYPTANTHUSES

C. acaulis (starfish plant) has slightly undulate mid-green leaves covered with light gray scurf. Among a number of varieties: *C.a.* 'Roseo-pictus,' *C.a.* 'Roseus,' and *C.a.* 'Ruber,' all with pink-tinged or reddish foliage. All are small—no more than 6 inches across—and easy to cultivate.

C. bivittatus has 3- to 4-inch undulate leaves colored greenish brown with two lengthwise red or pink stripes. *C.b.* 'Luddemanii' is similar but bigger, and *C.b.* 'Minor' is smaller.

C. bromelioides (sometimes known as *C. terminalis* var. *tricolor*) has the common name rainbow star. It is one of the most beautiful plants of this genus, but is also one of the most difficult to grow well because, for no apparent reason, it tends to rot at the base. Its undulate leaves, which are up to 1 inch wide and 7 inches long, are mid-green with ivory white edging and striping. If given enough bright light, the leaves—particularly those in the center of the plant—take on a pink hue. This is an unusual cryptanthus in that it grows upright rather than flat, and it also sends out stolons with plantlets on the end.

C. fosteranus is possibly the largest-growing species of the genus; mature plants can be as much as 20 inches across. The long, stiff, undulate leaves are both cross-barred and striped, and their overall color is a rather purplish copper-brown.

C. zonatus (zebra plant) has undulate leaves that are up to 9 inches long, brownish green cross-barred in green, white, and brown, and with a white scurf on the underside. The rosette grows to about 16 inches across. A few varieties of this species are available, the most attractive of which is *C.z.* 'Zebrinus' (peasant's leaf), with similar coloring but stronger contrast.

C. zonatus 'Zebrinus' (peasant's leaf)

PROPER CARE

Light Provide bright light at all times. A position at a sunny window will bring out the color of the leaves.

Temperature These plants grow well in warm rooms provided that the air is fairly humid. Keep pots on trays of moist pebbles.

Watering Water sparingly at all times—just enough to make the potting mixture barely moist, allowing the top two-thirds of the mixture to dry out between waterings.

Feeding Very little feeding is necessary. An occasional spray with a weak foliar fertilizer (see page 425) during the height of the growing season will help to improve leaf size and color.

Potting and repotting Use either a peat-based potting mixture or a mixture of equal parts of leaf mold and peat moss (see page 429). Plants should be grown in rather small pots, half-pots, or pans. Repotting is rarely necessary; a cryptanthus can be left in a 3-inch pot or half-pot, or in a 6-inch pan, until it has formed a clump of rosettes that need separating.

Propagation All these plants except *C. bromelioides* produce offsets between the leaves or at the base after flowering. In spring an offset can be potted in a 2½-inch pot containing a moistened equal-parts mixture of peat moss and sand. Enclose the whole in a plastic bag and keep it at normal room temperature in bright light filtered through a translucent blind or curtain. The offset will root in about three months. Transfer the rooted offset to a pot one size larger containing the recommended mixture for adult cryptanthuses and treat it as a mature plant. *C. bromelioides* plantlets can be used for propagation in exactly the same way.

Ctenanthe

MARANTACEAE

C. lubbersiana

PLANTS of the small genus *Ctenanthe* are closely related to marantas and calatheas, with which they are often confused. It may be helpful to remember that ctenanthes produce more compact clumps of leaves, and that the leaves are usually narrower, than those of the other two genera. All ctenanthes can grow up to 3 feet tall with a spread of 2 feet. They eventually produce sheathed stems that fork into two at a succession of nodes. The leathery, lance-shaped or nearly oblong leaves are produced on long stalks and are usually dull-surfaced rather than glossy. Bars of contrasting or muted coloring are likely to follow the main leaf veins in herringbone fashion. In addition to growing taller as they age, all kinds of ctenanthe produce basal offsets from slightly above or just below the soil level; thus they eventually become bushy clumps. Ctenanthe flowers are insignificant. The plants are grown for their attractively marked foliage.

RECOMMENDED CTENANTHES

C. lubbersiana is one of the most robust and fast-growing species. Its 9-inch-long, 2½- to 3-inch-wide leaves have rounded ends and short, pointed tips, with 4-inch-long leafstalks. Leaf color is light to medium green with yellowish patches on the upper surface, and pale green on the underside.

C. oppenheimiana, commonly called never-never plant, is popular chiefly in the variegated form *C.o.* 'Tricolor,' which has slender-pointed leaves 10–12 inches long and 3–4 inches wide with 6- to 8-inch-long stalks. Leaf color is dark green with irregular blotches of creamy yellow covering up to two-thirds of the upper surface.

C. oppenheimiana 'Tricolor' (never-never plant)

The deep red underside gives a reddish glow to the leaf, even from above. ***C. setosa*** has pointed-tipped leaves 18 inches long and 4 inches wide, with 6-inch-long, downy, purple stalks. Leaf color is pale green, with the main veins marked in dark green on the top surface only.

PROPER CARE

Light Ctenanthes do best throughout the year in bright light filtered through a translucent blind or curtain. Direct sunlight can cause the leaves of these plants to curl up.

Temperature Normal room temperatures are suitable for ctenanthes, which cannot tolerate temperatures below about 55°F. Stand pots on trays or saucers of damp pebbles for increased humidity.

Watering During the active growth period water moderately, enough to moisten the potting mixture throughout and allowing the top half-inch of the mixture to dry out before watering again. During the midwinter rest period water much more sparingly, giving only enough to keep the mixture from drying out completely.

Feeding Apply standard liquid fertilizer every two weeks during the active growth period only.

Potting and repotting Use an equal-parts combination of soil-based potting mixture (see page 429) and leaf mold. Move ctenanthes into pots one size bigger every spring until maximum convenient pot size (probably 6 to 8 inches) has been reached. Thereafter, topdress these plants annually with fresh potting mixture (see page 428).

Propagation In the spring take a stem cutting with three or four leaves on it, making the cut immediately below a node. Dip the cut end in hormone rooting powder, and plant it in a 3-inch pot of the mixture recommended for adult ctenanthes; water the mixture enough to make it just moist. Enclose the whole in a plastic bag or propagating case (see page 443), and keep it warm in medium light. Rooting will occur in four to six weeks; after that treat the new plants as mature ctenanthes.

Propagation is also possible from basal offsets. Carefully detach an offset from the parent plant and place the offset in a 3-inch pot of the recommended potting mixture. It can then be treated as a mature plant.

Cuphea

LYTHRACEAE

Cigar flower
C. ignea

THE genus *Cuphea* (firecracker plant) includes many species, but only a few of these small shrubs are used as house plants. They are prized for their bright-colored flowers, which bloom nearly continuously from early spring to late fall. Plants of the species named below can grow 2 feet high. They have leathery, lance-shaped leaves and many branches.

RECOMMENDED CUPHEAS

C. hyssopifolia (elfin herb, false heather) has dark green leaves $\frac{3}{4}$ inch long and $\frac{1}{4}$ inch wide crowded together on the stems. Bell-shaped, six-petaled flowers measure $\frac{1}{2}$ inch across and may be purple, pink, or white.

C. ignea (also known as *C. platycentra;* commonly called cigar flower) has medium green leaves 2 inches long and $\frac{1}{2}$ inch wide. Leaf edges turn red if plants get enough sunlight. The flower, which lacks petals, consists of a 1-inch-long, bright red calyx with a purple and white mouth. One form, *C.i.* 'Variegata,' has leaves flecked with yellow.

PROPER CARE

Light Give cupheas bright light, with three hours a day of full sunlight.

Temperature Normal room temperatures are suitable, but cupheas should have a winter rest at 50°–55°F.

Watering During the active growth period water moderately, allowing the top half-inch of the potting mixture to dry out between waterings. During the rest period give only enough to keep the mixture from drying out.

Feeding Apply standard liquid fertilizer every two weeks during the active growth period.

Potting and repotting Use a soil-based mixture (see page 429). Move plants into pots one size larger in spring, and again in midsummer. Maximum size needed is 6 inches since cupheas deteriorate and should be discarded when about two years old.

Propagation Take a 2- to $2\frac{1}{2}$-inch-long tip cutting in early fall, insert it in a 2-inch pot containing a moist equal-parts mixture of peat moss and coarse sand or perlite, enclose the whole in a plastic bag, and keep it in bright filtered light. After rooting occurs, repot the cutting in the standard potting mixture for cupheas, and treat it as a mature plant. But move it into full sunlight only gradually over a period of a couple of weeks.

Propagation is also possible from seed sown in early spring—though not for *C.i.* 'Variegata,' whose leaf markings can be passed along only by means of cuttings. (For propagation from seed see page 441.)

Cyanotis

COMMELINACEAE

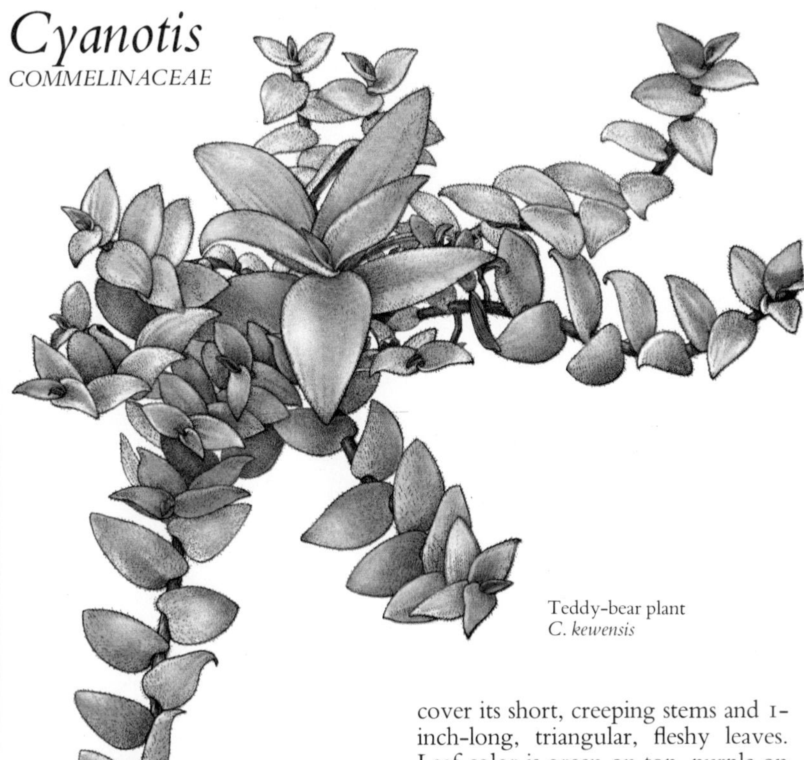

Teddy-bear plant
C. kewensis

ALL species of *Cyanotis* are small-leaved, low-growing plants that eventually begin to trail. Closely related to tradescantias, they have the same general appearance. But because they look best when growth is tight and compact and become weak and spindly unless they have very good light, they are a little more difficult to grow well than the tradescantias. They are particularly attractive when grown in hanging baskets.

These plants do not have a winter rest period. Active growth continues throughout the year.

C. somaliensis
(pussy ears)

RECOMMENDED CYANOTISES

C. kewensis is sometimes called teddy-bear plant or vine because of the fine gingery brown hairs that cover its short, creeping stems and 1-inch-long, triangular, fleshy leaves. Leaf color is green on top, purple on the underside. Three-petaled, violet-colored flowers are produced, but only rarely.

C. somaliensis (pussy ears) has 2-inch-long, shiny, green leaves edged with soft white hairs. The seldom-produced flowers are blue.

PROPER CARE

Light Bright light with some direct sunlight is essential throughout the year. It is a good idea to hang baskets in sunlit areas and to place pots on sunlit windowsills.

Temperature These plants will grow well throughout the year in normally warm room temperatures, but they need high humidity. Both species may develop brown leaf tips if the air is too dry. To increase humidity stand potted cyanotises on trays of moist pebbles and suspend saucers of water under hanging baskets.

Watering Water moderately all year long. Give enough to make the potting mixture moist throughout, allowing the top half-inch to dry out before watering again. Leaf color is improved if plants are occasionally allowed to dry out completely for very short periods (no more than a day or two). Avoid wetting the foliage when watering; the fine leaf hairs tend to trap water, which can cause unsightly marking.

Feeding Feeding is rarely necessary. Standard liquid fertilizer once every two months is enough.

Potting and repotting Though not technically succulents, plants of this genus are like the succulents in that they need a sandy potting mixture. Add a one-third portion of coarse sand, grit, or perlite to a soil-based mixture (see page 429). These plants have sparse roots and are slow-growing, and so they require little, if any, repotting. They usually look and grow best when planted in half-pots or shallow containers.

Propagation Propagate in the spring from tip cuttings that include about three pairs of leaves. Remove the bottom leaves before inserting cuttings in a moistened equal-parts mixture of peat moss and sand. Keep the cuttings in a warm position where they get bright light (preferably filtered through a translucent blind or curtain), and water just enough to keep the potting mixture from drying out, until fresh growth indicates that the cuttings are well rooted. Five or six can then be planted in a 3-inch pot of standard mixture for cyanotis plants. Thereafter, their cultivation needs are those of mature specimens. If cyanotis plants are well treated, they are likely to live for two or three years. After this time, old plants should be discarded and replaced by newly rooted cuttings.

Propagating from tip cuttings

Remove the lower leaves from suitable tip cuttings so that no leaves can rot as a result of touching the rooting mixture.

Insert several cuttings in a small pot of rooting mixture until new top growth indicates that rooting has occurred.

Cycas

CYCADACEAE

Sago palm
C. revoluta

THE plants included in the small genus *Cycas* are palmlike, but they are not palms. They belong to a group of plants called cycads, which are among the most primitive of flowering plants. *C. revoluta*, however, which is the only species that has become a fairly familiar house plant, is generally known as the sago palm. Potted plants of this species are so slow-growing that they often produce no more than one new leaf a year. Thus, although an individual specimen can eventually grow very big, most of those in pots are of manageable size because they are young (probably under 10 years old). The leaves, which are feathery-looking but quite stiff and hard, are arranged in a loose rosette. Each leaf is up to 3 feet long and is borne on a short-spined, four-angled stalk 3–4 inches long. The big leaf is itself divided into many 3- to 6-inch-long, needlelike leaflets, which are arranged in closely packed chevron-fashion on a $\frac{1}{4}$-inch-wide central rib. Some of the leaves stand almost vertical, but most of them arch outward. They rise from the dome of an oddly shaped, pineapplelike base with a rusty, felted covering. This base, which sits on top of the potting mixture, contains a reserve of water upon which the plant can draw in case of drought. Flowers do not develop on plants that are grown indoors.

PROPER CARE

Light In order to produce even one leaf a year, a cycas must be given bright light all year long, with or without direct sunlight (it will do equally well either way). Do not attempt to grow the plant in medium or poor light.

Temperature Normal room temperatures are suitable. These plants, however, are extremely tolerant of apparently adverse temperature and atmospheric conditions. They can tolerate relatively low humidity, and they are not harmed by temperatures falling as low as 55°F.

Watering During the active growth period (which is virtually all year) water moderately, enough to make the mixture moist throughout at each watering, and allowing the top half-inch of the mixture to dry out before watering again. During any rest period that may occur—possibly because of inadequate winter light—give cycases only enough water to prevent the mixture from drying out completely.

Feeding Apply standard liquid fertilizer once a month from early spring until early fall.

Potting and repotting Use a soil-based potting mixture (see page 429) with the addition of a one-third portion of coarse sand or perlite for extra drainage. Move these plants on to pots one size larger only when repotting is essential—roughly, when the pineapplelike base of a plant covers about two-thirds of the entire surface of the potting mixture. Repotting should not be necessary more often than about once in every two or three years.

Propagation Cycases are propagated commercially from seed. This type of propagation is a particularly slow process with these plants, however. Most indoor gardeners agree that it is not really feasible in the home.

Cyclamen

PRIMULACEAE

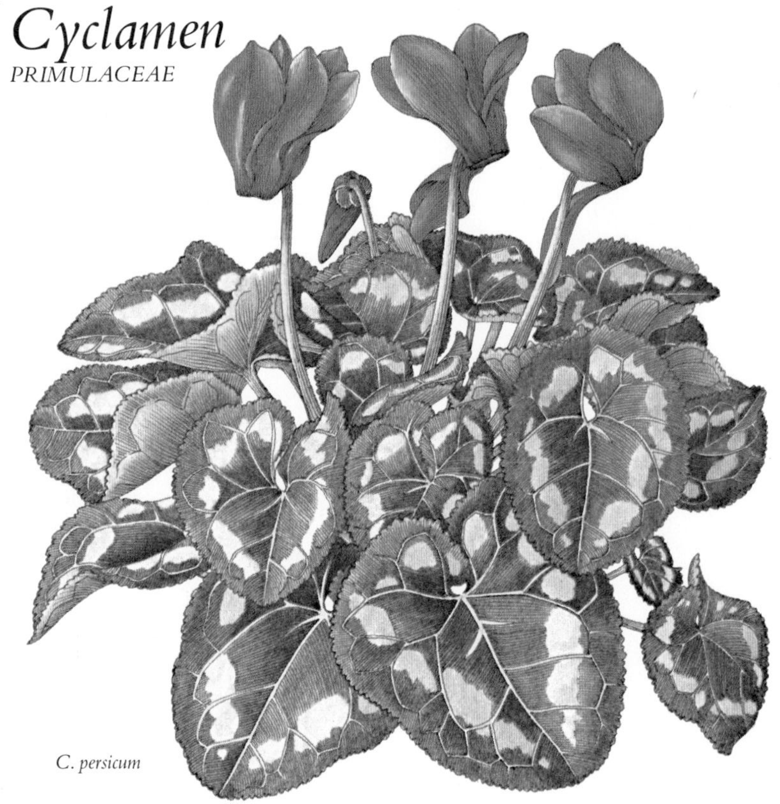

C. persicum

THE florist's cyclamen, *Cyclamen persicum,* is a tuberous-rooted flowering plant best treated as a temporary house plant, to be brought into the home just as the buds begin to open, enjoyed while flowering, and discarded (or passed on to a friend with a greenhouse) when flowering is over. Plants in bud normally appear on the market from the first weeks of September until around Christmas; those bought early are more likely to last well than later ones because they will not have suffered such a drastic change of conditions between the grower's greenhouse and the shop. Bought plants should remain decorative for two to three months.

Numerous flowers, produced on individual stalks 9 inches long or more, comprise several petals—of which there are usually five—standing almost erect. They may be pure white, deep red, or various shades of pink, salmon, mauve and purple.

C. persicum (flowers)

Some have white edging to the colored petals; some have ruffled petal edges; and some are more nearly like the wild species in that they are small, delicate, and pleasantly perfumed, whereas most cultivated forms are odorless and have flowers an inch or more long. The flower stalks rise up among leaves that are variably marked in silver, sometimes with a wide silver margin or irregular silver marbling. The leaves have 4-inch-long leafstalks that rise directly from the flattened, corky tuber.

Plants are usually bought either in 5-inch or 3-inch pots.

See also BULBS, CORMS, and TUBERS.

PROPER CARE

Light Cyclamens should be given bright light without direct sunlight.

Temperature Keep cyclamens cool at all times. A temperature of between 55° and 65°F is ideal, if possible. Warm conditions will greatly shorten the life of these plants, but plenty of humidity improves matters; this can be achieved by placing pots on trays of moist pebbles, or an individual pot can be kept in a bowl of moist peat moss.

Watering Cyclamen tubers are only half-buried in potting mixture, and water should never be poured onto the tubers, which are liable to rot. Instead, plants should be watered from below by placing the pots in a shallow water-filled bowl; this permits the potting mixture to take up as much water as it needs. After ten minutes the pots should be lifted out

This cyclamen is being removed to drain after standing in a water-filled saucer for ten minutes. Cyclamens should never be watered from above.

and allowed to drain. Some growers put pots of cyclamen on thin pieces of wet foam rubber (or fiberglass), which is kept moist by being placed in a shallow saucer or bowl of water; from this the plant automatically takes up its water needs. This is also an alternative way to achieve high humidity (see "Temperature," above).

Feeding Apply standard liquid fertilizer once every two weeks.

Special points Remove dead flowers as they fade, and it is important to remove the entire flower stalk along with the flower. This is easily done by twisting the stem and pulling sharply. Any damaged or yellowing leaves should also be cleanly pulled away.

As has been indicated, when plants have finished producing flowers, they can be discarded; but growers who want to try to bring them into flower another year (which is by no means easy to do) should begin by gradually reducing amounts of water until, in June, the leaves start to go yellow, after which no more should be given. Store the tubers in their pots dry and in a cool place until early fall, when signs of new growth will appear. Then remove the tuber from its pot, shake off the old soil, and repot into the same pot, using a soil-based potting mixture (see page 429).

Stand the pot in bright light, keep it cool, and water it sparingly, often enough to make the potting mixture barely moist until leaves are well developed. Thereafter, treat the plant as a mature cyclamen.

Cymbidium

ORCHIDACEAE

Cymbidium hybrid

THE genus *Cymbidium* includes about 40 species of terrestrial and epiphytic orchids. All cymbidiums suitable for use in the home are epiphytic. Most have short, erect pseudobulbs that arise from a woody rhizome and that carry leathery, ribbon-shaped leaves. Flowers are borne on either erect or drooping stems.

The best modern cymbidiums are miniature forms with pseudobulbs less than 2 inches tall and leaves that rarely grow longer than 12–15 inches. These plants can produce as many as 30 flowers, each up to 3 inches across, in a single season. Flowers can be scented, and any color from deep mahogany red to pink, yellow, green, or white. Individual blooms open along the flower stem during a period of several weeks in late spring and early summer. Each bloom lasts about six weeks. An established miniature cymbidium in a 6- to 10-inch pot can produce more than half a dozen flower stems in one season.

See also ORCHIDS.

RECOMMENDED CYMBIDIUMS

C. devonianum is a miniature species from which many hybrids are partly derived. Each 2-inch-tall pseudobulb carries three to five leathery, pale green leaves 7–14 inches long and 1½–3 inches wide. The flower stems are about 12 inches long, and every stem bears between 12 and 18 yellowish olive green flowers marked with deep purple. The lip is purplish red. Flowers are 1½ inches across.

***C.* 'Minuet'** is a hybrid with flower stems 10–16 inches tall. Each stem bears about 20 flowers 1–1½ inches across. Flower color is usually green, brown, or yellow, with the lip spotted in a darker shade.

***C.* 'Peter Pan'** is a hybrid with flower stems 10–14 inches tall. Each stem bears 10 to 15 flowers 1–1½ inches wide and greenish yellow. The lip is spotted with deep mahogany.

PROPER CARE

Light Grow cymbidiums in bright light without direct sunlight.

Temperature Throughout most of the year normal room temperatures are suitable if high humidity is maintained. Stand pots on trays of moist pebbles and mist-spray plants daily as long as the temperature remains at or above 65°F. Cymbidiums do best if given a brief winter rest at about 60°.

Watering Water moderately, giving enough to make the mixture moist throughout and allowing the top inch to dry out between waterings. Do not overwater or rotting will occur. During the short, ill-defined winter rest period, give only enough water to prevent the mixture from drying out.

Feeding Apply standard liquid fertilizer every two weeks to actively growing plants.

Potting and repotting Use a combination of one part of soil-based mixture (see page 429) and one part of sphagnum moss to two parts of osmunda fiber.Put an inch-deep layer of clay-pot fragments in the bottom of the pot. Immediately after the flowering period every second year, move plants into large pots. After maximum convenient size has been reached, divide plants as suggested below.

Propagation Divide an overcrowded plant immediately after it has finished flowering. Remove the plant from its pot, wash the old mixture away under running water, and cut through the rhizome with a knife. Each piece of rhizome must have at least two pseudobulbs and some roots attached. The backbulbs will not flower again, but the rhizome will eventually produce new pseudobulbs. Pot up each section in fresh mixture in a pot that allows space for forward growth. For the next four weeks water only enough to prevent the mixture from drying out. Mist-spray once a day. Thereafter, treat each plant as a mature cymbidium.

Cyperus
CYPERACEAE

Dwarf umbrella plant
C. alternifolius 'Gracilis'

MOST species of the genus *Cyperus* (umbrella sedge) thrive in boggy conditions, and the roots are adapted to exist in a constantly wet medium. All cyperuses have thin, rushlike, unjointed stems topped with narrow, usually radiating, leaflike bracts and brown or greenish white, grasslike flower heads. Most make dense clumps of many stems. Leaves may arise at the base of the stems, or are often reduced to barely visible sheaths around them.

RECOMMENDED CYPERUSES

C. albostriatus (often called *C. diffusus*) has stems 10–20 inches tall and some narrow basal leaves of similar length, together with purple sheaths. The heads have up to 24 narrow bracts 1–4 inches long; flowers are pale brown, and the overall color a bright pale green.

C. alternifolius (umbrella palm or plant) can grow up to 4 feet tall. The narrow stems are ribbed and almost triangular, and each head comprises about 12 thin, slightly drooping, pliable, leaflike bracts, much like the skeleton of an umbrella. Leaves are reduced to sheaths, and flowers are dull brown. *C.a.* 'Gracilis' (dwarf umbrella plant) is smaller in all respects, has rigid, rather dark green bracts, and rarely flowers. *C.a.* 'Variegatus' has soft, pliable bracts either striped with white or totally white, and there is also some white in the stems; often the variegation is short-lived, and the color reverts to green as the plant ages.

C. papyrus (Egyptian paper plant), the bulrush of the Bible, has been used for making paper since ancient times. This tall-growing plant needs a lot of space to grow to maturity. It has dark green, smooth, triangular stems up to an inch thick and 4–8 feet tall, each topped by a few bracts and a dense tuft of threadlike, pendulous growths 4–10 inches long; each "thread" is enclosed at the base by a short brown sheath and ends in a small flower.

Because of its need for humid warmth, *C. papyrus* is by far the most difficult species to grow. *C.p.* 'Nanus' (recently reclassified as *C. isocladus*), the miniature papyrus, grows 2 feet tall, but otherwise resembles its giant relation.

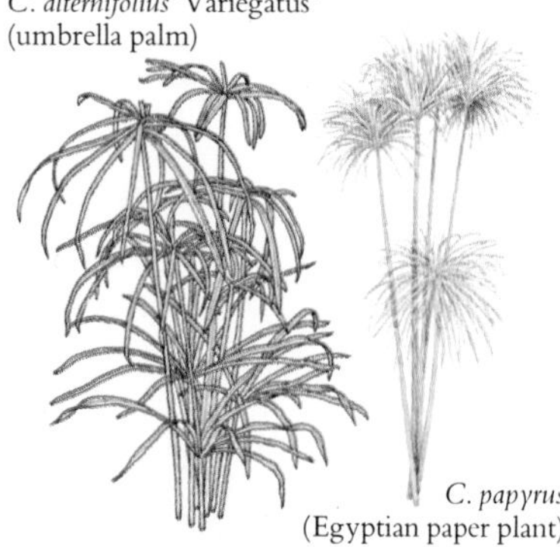

PROPER CARE

Light These plants can be grown in either full sunshine or slight shade. *C.a.* 'Variegatus' needs brighter light than the others. If a cyperus produces few new stems, this may indicate that it is getting too little light.

Temperature All plants of this genus do well in normal room temperatures, and all except *C. papyrus* can also tolerate temperatures down to about 50°F. *C. papyrus* needs a minimum temperature of 60°–65°.

Watering It is impossible to overwater *C. alternifolius* or *C. papyrus*. In both cases the root ball should be kept moist, and the best method is to stand the pot in a deep saucer of water and keep it filled up; the plant will then draw up its water needs—great quantities during active growth periods, less at times when the plant is resting. But pots must not be totally immersed, for stems may rot if they are below the waterline. It is also possible to grow these plants—notably *C. alternifolius*—in watertight containers

Because C. alternifolius *and* C. papyrus *roots thrive in wet conditions, these plants benefit from standing in water.*

filled with water and pebbles. *C. albostriatus*, however, needs to be watered only as much as necessary to keep the potting mixture moist, and the pot should never be allowed to stand in water.

If a cyperus is permitted to dry out for a short period, the bracts are likely to develop brown tips. This can also happen if the air is too dry, but adequate humidity is bound to result from standing the plants in water-filled saucers, as recommended above.

An unusual and attractive way to display C. alternifolius *is in a watertight container holding water and pebbles.*

Feeding Apply standard liquid fertilizer at monthly intervals during the active growth period.

Potting and repotting A soil-based potting mixture (see page 429) is best. Most of these plants are comparatively fast-growing and need moving on to bigger pots as soon as the clumps of stems begin to fill their present ones. Young cyperuses can be started in 3-inch pots, then moved to the 5-inch size. Most of the popular species look best, though, when growing in fairly small pots and appear out of scale in oversized containers.

C. papyrus is the exception, but even this tall-growing species will produce fine, long stems in an 8-inch pot. Repotting is best done when new growth starts in spring. Be sure to set the plant at the same level in the potting mixture, not buried deeper than before.

Propagation The best way to propagate is by dividing overcrowded clumps in spring. Remove the plant from its pot and, with a sharp knife, cut partly through the root ball from the top down—just deep enough to allow fingers and thumbs to be inserted between the roots to pry the tangled mass apart. This may take some force, since the roots can be densely packed. One plant may be divided into several clumps, each with three or four stems; the new clumps should be planted in 3-inch pots.

C. alternifolius can also be propagated from flower heads. Cut off a flower head, retaining half an inch of stem, and trim the bracts back by about half their length (to prevent excessive evaporation). Then either place the stem in water or set it in damp sand. Keep the cutting in bright light at 70°F, and, if it is in sand, keep the sand damp. When roots have developed on the flower head, the cutting can be transferred to a pot of the standard mixture for adult plants.

Propagating *C. alternifolius*

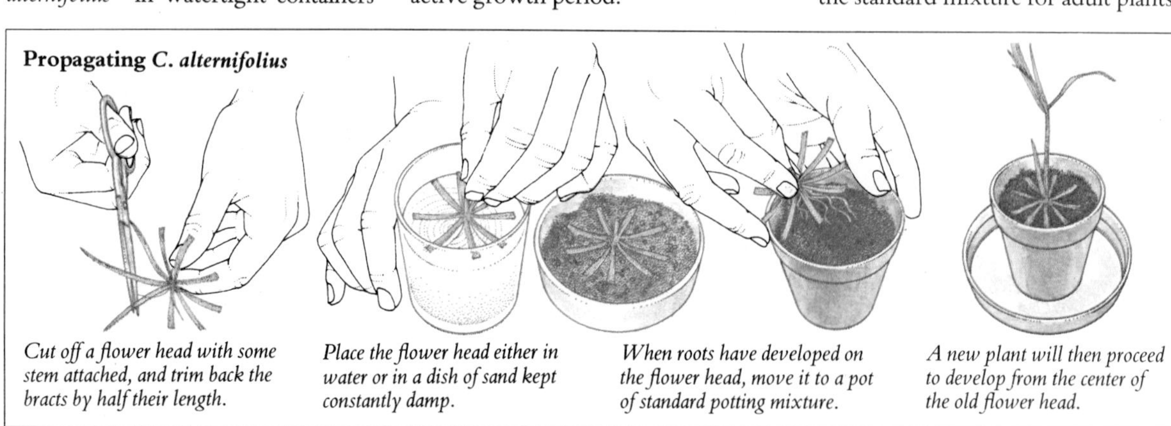

Cut off a flower head with some stem attached, and trim back the bracts by half their length.

Place the flower head either in water or in a dish of sand kept constantly damp.

When roots have developed on the flower head, move it to a pot of standard potting mixture.

A new plant will then proceed to develop from the center of the old flower head.

Cyrtomium

POLYPODIACEAE

Holly fern
C. falcatum

THE small genus *Cyrtomium* includes one species that has become a popular house plant: *C. falcatum* (holly fern), which is a very decorative, long-lasting fern with pinnae that look more like holly leaves than like the divisions of fronds. The base of the plant is a rhizome thickly covered with silvery, furry scurf, which also covers most of the 4- to 6-inch-long leafstalks that rise from the rhizome. Borne on these short stalks are leathery fronds up to 2 feet long, which are held stiffly erect, and each frond is divided into several pairs of 4-inch-long, oval, glossy, coarsely toothed, dark green pinnae. The spore cases that appear in small patches on the undersides of pinnae are green at first but gradually turn light brown. Among the many varieties, one of the most compact is *C.f.* 'Rochfordianum,' whose fronds are only about a foot long, but have large pinnae.
See also FERNS.

PROPER CARE

Light Provide bright filtered light. These ferns can tolerate quite poor light, but only for short periods. If not in a permanently bright position, they should be moved into better light for a few hours periodically—every other day, if possible.

Temperature Normal room temperatures are suitable, and these cyrtomiums can also tolerate temperatures down to 50°F. In warm rooms—above about 70°F—they should be given extra humidity by being stood on trays of damp pebbles.

Watering In a normally warm position these ferns do not have a winter rest period. Water them moderately enough to make the potting mixture moist throughout, and allowing the top half-inch of the mixture to dry out between waterings. If the indoor temperature ever falls below 55°F for more than a few days, water sparingly, allowing half of the mixture to dry out between waterings.

Feeding Apply standard liquid fertilizer at half strength every two weeks to actively growing plants.

Potting and repotting Use a potting mixture composed of half soil-based mixture (see page 429) and half leaf mold or coarse peat moss. In early spring, plants may be moved into pots one size larger, but only if roots have filled the pots (see page 426). These plants should never need larger pots than 6–7 inches. After this size has been reached, topdress annually (see page 428) with fresh mixture.

Propagation In early spring old plants can be pulled apart for propagation. A section of rhizome with three or four fronds attached will normally establish feeding roots quickly if it is planted just below the surface level of a 3-inch pot of the standard potting mixture well moistened. The rhizome section should have 2–3 inches of root already attached to it; if it does not, the potted section will need to be enclosed in a plastic bag or propagation case (see page 443) for two or three weeks. Otherwise, all that is necessary is to put the pot in bright filtered light, watering often enough to make the mixture barely moist, until new growth begins to appear. Cultivation needs thereafter are the same as those of mature plants.

The rhizome of this cyrtomium is hidden in the root ball, but it can easily be broken into sections. For propagation, each section needs at least three fronds.

Cytisus

LEGUMINOSAE

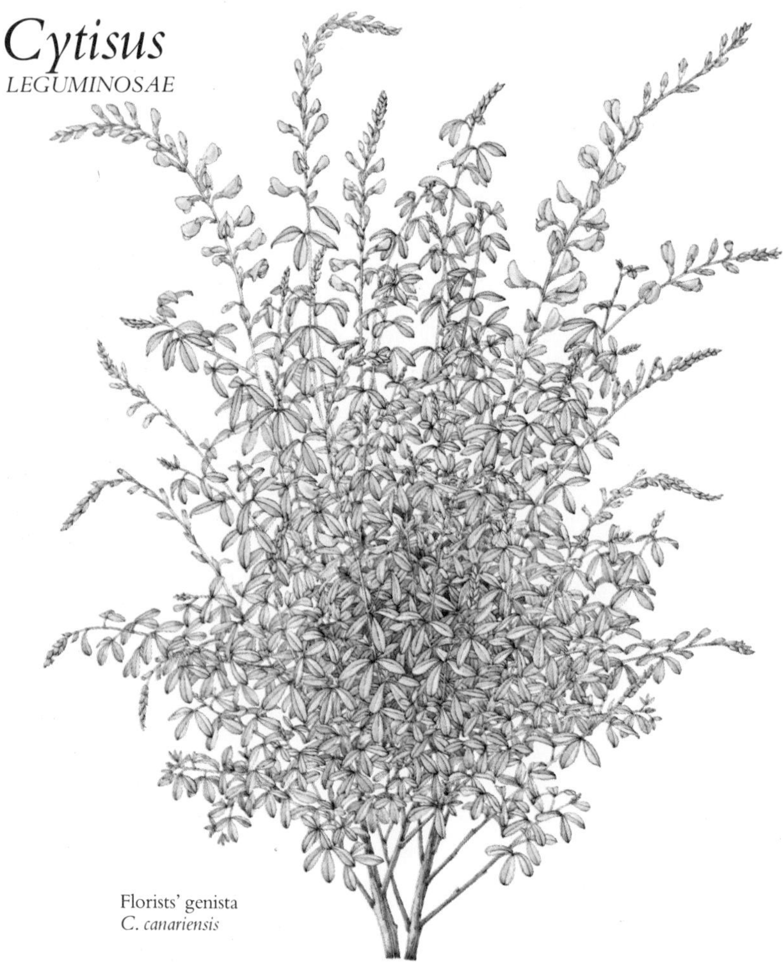

Florists' genista
C. canariensis

THE genus *Cytisus* (broom) includes many sorts of shrub and small tree, all notable for their clusters of sweet-pea-shaped, often scented flowers. The two species in general use as house plants are usually forced into bloom in early spring, brought indoors for two or three weeks, and then discarded. There are two reasons why they are rarely retained after flowering. First, they are not attractive during the 11 months or more that elapse before they bloom again. Secondly, they must overwinter in a cool place—preferably below 60°F—in order to flower the following year, and they do not flourish in normal room temperatures at any time.

RECOMMENDED CYTISUSES

C. canariensis (florists' genista) is a much-branching, bushy shrub that can grow up to 2 feet tall, with a spread of 18 inches. The medium green leaves consist of three oval leaflets, each $\frac{1}{2}$ inch long, $\frac{1}{4}$ inch wide, and covered with silky, white hair. The flowers are $\frac{3}{4}$ inch long borne in terminal clusters of 5 to 12. They are bright yellow and slightly fragrant, but short-lived. There is a variety, *C.c. ramosissimus*, which has smaller leaflets and fewer flowers per cluster, but more clusters per plant. The flowering period of *C.c. ramosissimus* is longer than that of the type species.

C. racemosus resembles *C. canariensis* in most respects. (In fact, some botanists believe it to be not a distinct species, but a hybrid, with *C. canariensis* as one parent.) Leaf color is dark green, and flower color is deep yellow. Flowers are longer-lasting than those of *C. canariensis*, and they are also set closer together in more numerous clusters.

PROPER CARE

Light In very early spring and during the flowering period give these plants bright light, with two or three hours a day of direct sunlight. During the rest of the year medium light is adequate for these cytisuses.

Temperature To make flowers last as long as possible, keep plants in a cool position—not above 60°F—throughout the flowering period. If they are to be retained for another year, stand them outdoors in the shade when flowering stops, and leave them there until late fall. Because they cannot withstand frost, bring them into a cool room (below 60°) before the first frost is expected.

Watering From early spring to early fall water plentifully as often as necessary to keep the potting mixture thoroughly moist, but never allow pots to stand in water. In fall and during the long winter rest period, keep the mixture from drying out.

Feeding Apply standard liquid fertilizer every two weeks in spring and summer only.

Potting and repotting Use a soil-based potting mixture (see page 429). Move plants into pots one size larger in early fall, taking care not to damage the roots. These plants react badly to root disturbance.

Propagation Commercial propagation of these plants is by seed, but it takes two or even three years for a flowering plant to be produced by this method. Propagation by stem cuttings is quicker and more satisfactory. Take cuttings 3–4 inches long in spring. Plant each cutting in a small pot containing a moistened equal-parts mixture of peat moss and coarse sand or perlite, and enclose the whole in a plastic bag or propagation case (see page 443). The cutting will usually root in four to six weeks if kept at 55°–60°F in bright filtered light. When new growth indicates that rooting has taken place, uncover the rooted cutting. Although it will not flower the first year, its cultivation needs are those of mature plants.

In early fall, move the young plant into a larger pot of the recommended soil-based potting mixture, and in midwinter begin monthly feedings of high-potash liquid fertilizer. Flowering should occur the following spring or summer, at which time the feeding requirements become those of a mature cytisus.

Special points Note that plants retained for a second year or propagated in the home will flower later than those forced into bloom by professional growers. The natural flowering season for a cytisus is between late spring and midsummer.

Davallia

POLYPODIACEAE

Deersfoot fern
D. canariensis

INDOOR ferns of the genus *Davallia* are distinguished by their furry rhizomes, which creep over the surface of the potting mixture and root down into it at regular intervals. The fur is composed of long, rusty brown or silvery gray hairs on $\frac{1}{2}$- to $\frac{3}{4}$-inch-thick rhizomes and is the reason why these plants have such common names as deersfoot and hare's foot fern. Arising from the rhizomes are 9-inch-long, gray-green stalks carrying fronds that are roughly triangular, usually around $1\frac{1}{2}$ feet long and 1 foot wide, and divided into three or four pinnae, each of which is again divided into many fine pinnules.

Davallias are excellent plants for hanging baskets or for shallow pans, where—because the rhizomes normally fork into two or more sections at the points where they root—the potting-mixture surface is quickly covered. Most forms are also remarkably tolerant of dry air and will thrive in rooms where many other ferns suffer from lack of humidity.
See also FERNS.

RECOMMENDED DAVALLIAS

D. canariensis (deersfoot fern) has triangular, medium green fronds and pale brown fur on the rhizomes. Each pinna is fine and triangular in shape.

D. fejeensis (rabbit's foot or hare's foot fern) has the largest fronds—sometimes 2 feet long—of the three species named here. They are also a paler green than the others. The fur is light brown.

D. fejeensis
(rabbit's foot fern)

D. trichomanoides (also known as *D. bullata* or *D. mariesii*; commonly called squirrel's foot or ball fern) has tan fur with some silvery gray hairs. The rhizome is slightly thinner than the others, and the dark green fronds are only about 9 inches long and 6 inches wide. The little pinnules have finely toothed edges.

PROPER CARE

Light These ferns will do best if they are grown in medium light.

Temperature Davallias grow well in normally warm room temperatures, but they can tolerate cooler conditons. Fronds may die off if the temperature falls below about 55°F, but new ones will grow as soon as warmer conditions prevail.

Watering Water moderately, enough to make the mixture moist throughout, but allow the top half-inch of the mixture to dry out before watering again. If the temperature is permitted to fall below 55°F for more than a day or two, give just enough water to keep the potting mixture from completely drying out until the temperature rises again.

Feeding Apply standard liquid fertilizer once every two weeks to actively growing mature plants.

Potting and repotting Use either a peat-based or a half soil-based, half leaf-mold potting mixture (see page 429). In spring move small davallias into pots that are one size larger. Take older plants out of their pots, trim away some of the outer roots, and detach some rhizomes before replanting them in the same pots (but using fresh potting mixture).

Propagation To propagate these plants, use 2- to 3-inch-long tip sections of rhizome, each with at least one to two fronds attached. In spring cut such sections from the parent plant with a sharp knife, and pin each section down with a loop of wire or hairpin so that it just sits on the surface of the rooting mixture in a 3-inch half-pot. Use a mixture of equal parts of peat moss and coarse sand or perlite, and moisten it slightly. Enclose the whole in a plastic bag or propagating case (see page 443), and keep it in bright filtered light at normal room temperature; no additional watering is required. When new fronds begin to appear—usually after three or four weeks—rooting will have taken place. Gradually reduce the humidity by uncovering the young plant for increasingly longer periods over the next two or three weeks, and give it just enough water to keep the rooting mixture from drying out. Do not feed the new plant. After a further three or four months move the plant into a slightly larger pot of the normal potting mixture, and treat it in the same way as a mature davallia.

Dendrobium

ORCHIDACEAE

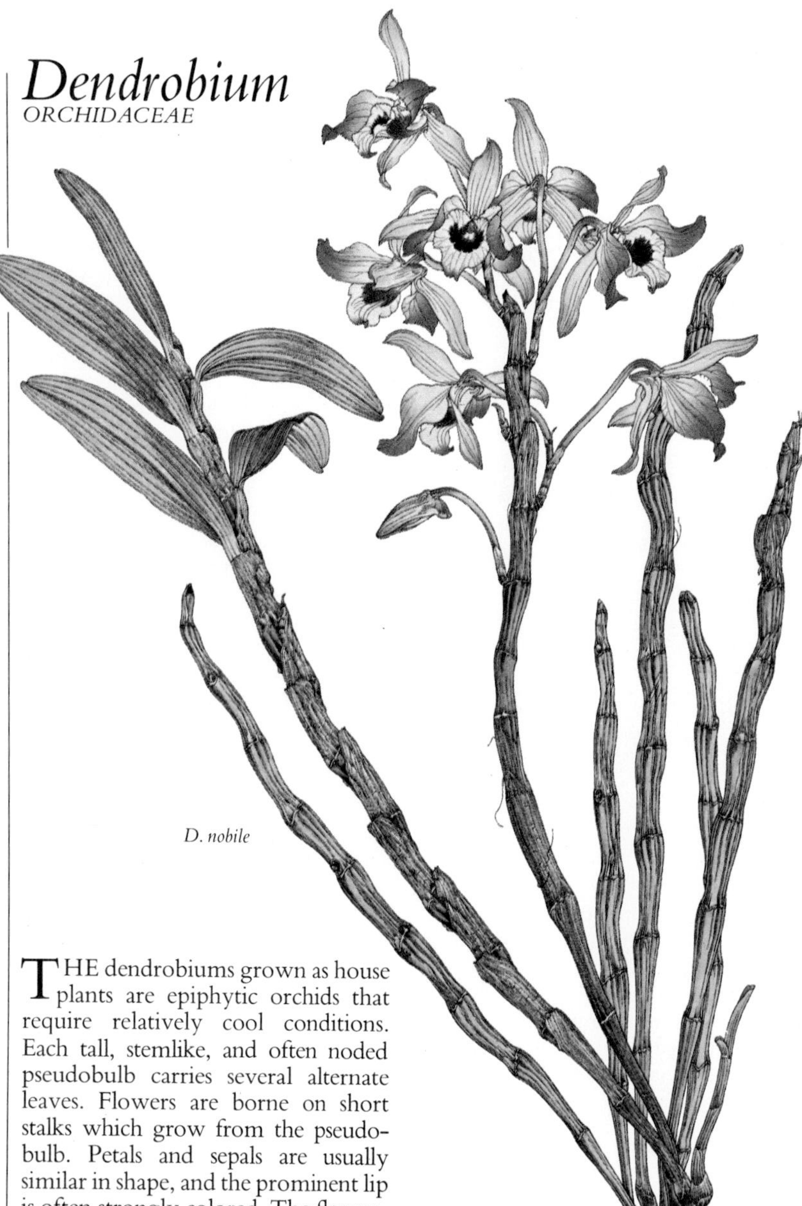

D. nobile

THE dendrobiums grown as house plants are epiphytic orchids that require relatively cool conditions. Each tall, stemlike, and often noded pseudobulb carries several alternate leaves. Flowers are borne on short stalks which grow from the pseudobulb. Petals and sepals are usually similar in shape, and the prominent lip is often strongly colored. The flowering season for the species below is late spring to early summer, and each flower lasts for four to six weeks.
See also ORCHIDS.

RECOMMENDED DENDROBIUMS

D. infundibulum has medium green pseudobulbs 10–20 inches tall, topped with several strap-shaped, dark green leaves about 3 inches long and ¾ inch wide. Flowers appear in groups of two to six. Each flower is about 4 inches across and white, with a deep yellow mark in the throat of the tubular lip. The petals are wavy-edged. Leaf sheaths that encase new pseudobulbs and flower buds are covered with short, black hairs, which become less noticeable as the new growth gets bigger and the buds open.

D. kingianum is a variable species with reddish green, tapering pseudobulbs 3–18 inches tall. Each pseudobulb is topped with three or four elliptic, grayish green leaves 3–6 inches long and about 1 inch wide. Fragrant, cup-shaped flowers ½ inch across are borne in terminal clusters of up to 12. Flower color varies from white to pink and deep mauve, with the lip edged in a contrasting color.

D. nobile has yellowish green pseudobulbs up to 4 feet tall, topped with several narrow leaves up to 4 inches long and 1 inch wide. The leaves are produced in early fall. In late spring, a pseudobulb that is about to flower loses its leaves and replaces them with branching flower stalks. Each stalk carries two to four flowers up to 3 inches across. The petals and sepals have wavy edges; the lip is large and rounded, with a tubular base. Color varies from lavender to deep purple, but the lip always has a deep maroon blotch in the center. There are many varieties, some with fragrant flowers.

PROPER CARE

Light Bright light is essential at all times, but filter strong direct sunlight through a translucent blind or curtain.

Temperature During the active growth period keep these plants within a temperature range of 60°–70°F and mist-spray them daily. During the winter rest period keep dendrobiums at 60°–65° during the day and 50°–55° at night.

Watering From the time flower buds start to appear and then throughout the active growth period, water plants moderately, but let the potting mixture dry out nearly completely before watering again. Do not let drops of water rest on new growths, which will rot if permitted to remain wet. During the winter rest period give only enough water to prevent the potting mixture from drying out.

Feeding During the active growth period only, apply a foliar feed with every third or fourth watering.

Potting and repotting Use any of the potting mixtures recommended for orchids (see page 289). These dendrobiums do best if grown in small conventional pots, with plenty of drainage material added. A plant with up to eight pseudobulbs can often thrive in only a 4-inch pot. Move plants to larger pots only when they are overcrowded. This is best done in spring, just as new growth begins.

Propagation To divide a large plant, cut the rhizome into segments each with at least four pseudobulbs, one of which should not have flowered. (Cut away and discard dead, brown pseudobulbs.) Plant each segment in a 3-inch pot of standard orchid mixture, and water it sparingly until new growth appears. Thereafter, treat the young plant as a mature dendrobium.

Some kinds of dendrobium produce new growths at the tops of old pseudobulbs. When such a growth has developed roots an inch or so long, it can be cut away, potted up in a 1½-inch pot, and treated as mature.

Special points *D. nobile* is prone to attack by red spider mites. For treatment see page 455.

Dichorisandra

COMMELINACEAE

Queen's spiderwort
D. reginae

THE genus *Dichorisandra* comprises a number of species, but only one of these large-leaved near-relatives of the common tradescantias, *D. reginae* (queen's spiderwort), is normally grown indoors. Its stems, which can grow more than 2 feet tall, are fleshy, reddish purple, flecked with green, and usually without branches; erect at first, they become sprawling under the weight of the leaves as they lengthen, and most of them have to be supported with thin stakes. The lance-shaped leaves are 5 inches long and 2 inches wide, are arranged in two opposite ranks on the stems, and have a shiny, deep emerald green surface with lengthwise silver stripes and silver flecking and a deep purple underside. Flowers are small, star-shaped, and blue-and-white; they appear in compact terminal clusters in late summer and early fall, but are of little interest compared with the foliage.

Only when the branches are supported by stakes are the dramatically colored but heavy leaves displayed to best advantage.

PROPER CARE

Light A dichorisandra needs medium light. It is adversely affected by bright light, but tends to develop awkwardly elongated stems and pale leaves if kept in poor light.

Temperature Normal room temperatures are suitable. If the temperature remains above 75°F, the plant will continue to grow throughout the year, with little or no rest period. But it reacts badly to dry air, which causes unsightly brown markings on the leaves. In hot, dry rooms stand it on a tray of damp pebbles, and mist-spray the foliage occasionally.

Watering Water moderately—enough to make the potting mixture moist throughout, and allowing the top half-inch to dry out between waterings. If there is no evidence of a rest period, continue moderate watering throughout the year. If active growth stops for a while, water more sparingly, allowing the top half of the mixture to dry out between waterings.

Feeding Apply standard liquid fertilizer every two weeks during the active growth period.

Potting and repotting Use a soil-based potting mixture (see page 429), with up to one-third extra peat moss for water retention along with good drainage. Move small plants into pots one size larger whenever their roots almost totally fill the pot (see page 426). Ordinarily, indoor dichorisandras are kept only for 18–24 months before being replaced, and so pots bigger than 5 inches are not required.

Propagation Take 3-inch-long tip cuttings, which are likely to have five leaves on them (two pairs and a terminal leaf), immediately below a node. Carefully remove the lower pair of leaves which would otherwise be buried, and insert a cutting with one or two others in a 3-inch pot containing equal parts of peat moss and coarse sand or perlite. Moisten the mixture, enclose the whole in a plastic bag, and keep it in a partially shaded position at normal room temperature for four to six weeks, during which time no more water need be given. If the potted cuttings are kept, instead, in a heated propagating case (see page 444), the rooting process and subsequent development of new plants will be greatly speeded up.

Remove rooted cuttings from the plastic bag or propagator, water them sparingly, and give half-strength liquid fertilizer every two weeks. Ten weeks after the start of propagation, move each new plant into a slightly larger pot of recommended mixture. Thereafter, treat each one as a mature dichorisandra.

Special points Discard old plants regularly in favor of young rooted cuttings. Keep a careful watch for aphids (see page 454), particularly at the growing tips.

Dieffenbachia

ARACEAE

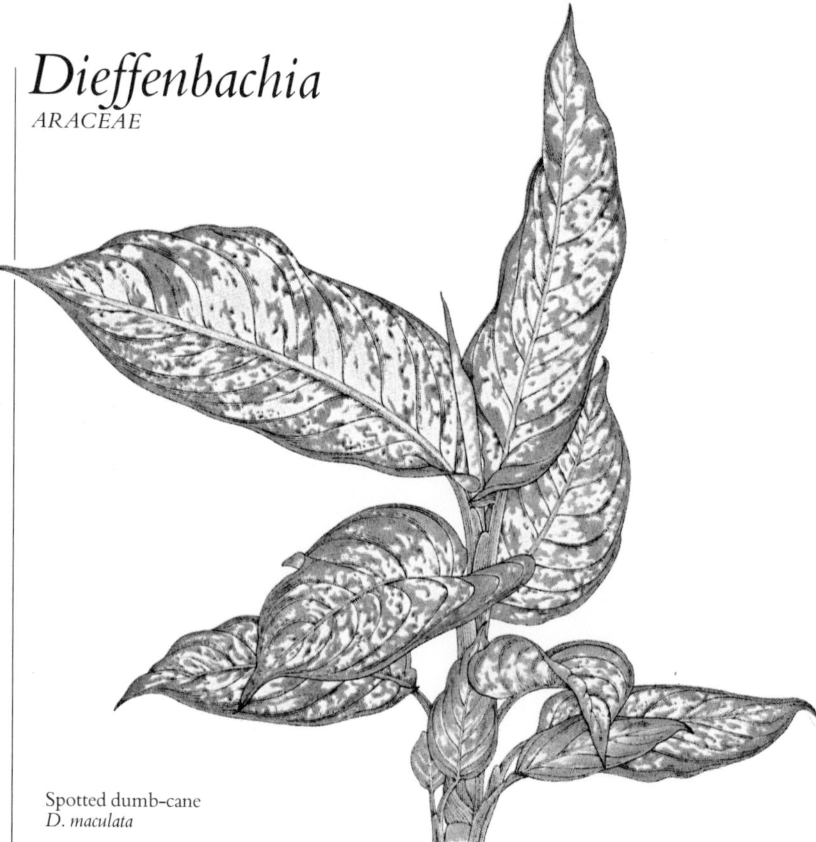

Spotted dumb-cane
D. maculata

DIEFFENBACHIAS (dumb-cane, dumb-plant, or tuftroot) are highly decorative foliage plants, some of which can grow over 5 feet tall indoors. Their thick, canelike, and unbranched stems carry rather soft and fleshy leaves on sturdy, sheathed stalks. The leaves generally spread outward and arch slightly downward. Although those of most species and varieties are basically green, some are so densely marked with yellow or white that the central area often seems to be one large patch of pale coloring. As dieffenbachias age, some of the lower leaves dry up and fall off or may be pulled off, leaving behind a scarred stem, which gradually lengthens. But the bare stem is likely to be at least partially hidden by the thick crown of downward-arching leaves. Mature plants may produce white or cream-colored typical arum flower heads, but these are of little interest.

RECOMMENDED DIEFFENBACHIAS

D. amoena, one of the most vigorous species, has elliptic-oblong leaves up to $1\frac{1}{2}$ feet long and 1 foot wide on 1-foot-long stalks. The dark green leaves are irregularly splashed with creamy white along the main veins.

D. bausei is a hybrid (between *D. maculata and D. weirii*) with lance-shaped leaves up to 1 foot long and 6 inches wide on 8-inch-long stalks. The yellowish green leaves have dark green margins and are marked with a few long, dark green patches and a number of small, white spots.

D. bowmannii has oval-elliptic leaves up to 2 feet long and $1\frac{1}{2}$ feet wide on 1-foot-long leafstalks. Leaf color is generally a mixture of light and dark green; and the margins and patches following the line of the main veins are dark green.

D. exotica has oval leaves 10 inches long and 4 inches wide on 4-inch-long stalks. Leaf color is dark green strongly marked with white and very pale green.

D. exotica

D. imperialis has leathery, oval leaves 2 feet long and 1 foot wide on 2-foot-long stalks. The leaves are dark green and irregularly spotted with yellow.

D. maculata (also called *D. picta*; commonly known as spotted dumb-cane) is the most popular species, and there are many varieties. Most forms have narrow, lance-shaped leaves with pointed tips; those of the type species are about 10 inches long and $2\frac{1}{2}$ inches wide, are borne on 5- to 6-inch-long stalks, and are deep green with irregular ivory white markings around the side veins. One attractive variety, *D.m.* 'Rudolph Roehrs' (yellow-leaf dumb-cane), has oval-elliptic leaves that are mostly creamy white when young but that develop yellowish green spots, a green midrib, and green margins.

D. oerstedii has leaves 10 inches long and 4–5 inches wide on 6- to 8-inch-long stalks. Leaf color varies from deep green to pale olive green. A variety, *D.o. variegata,* has an ivory white line on the leaf midrib.

PROPER CARE

Light Provide bright filtered light in spring, summer, and fall. During the short-day winter months the brightest possible light, including direct sunlight, is best.

Temperature Dieffenbachias need warmth and cannot tolerate temperatures below about 60°F. High humidity is also essential; plants should be stood on trays of damp pebbles.

Watering Water moderately, enough to make the entire mixture moist, but allowing the top inch of the mixture to dry out between waterings. In a suitably warm position these plants continue to grow throughout the year and will need the same type of watering at all times.

Feeding Give actively growing dieffenbachias standard liquid fertilizer every two weeks.

Potting and repotting Use a soil-based potting mixture (see page 429). Move small plants into pots one size larger every spring. An 8-inch pot is likely to be the biggest needed. If larger specimens are desired, move plants on every other year until a 10- or even 12-inch pot is reached.

Propagation A tip cutting 3–6 inches long will root at a temperature of at least 70°F if taken in spring or early summer. Take the cutting immediately below a node, strip off the lower leaves, dip the cut end in a hormone rooting powder, and plant it in a 4-inch pot containing a moistened equal-parts mixture of peat moss and coarse sand or perlite. Enclose the whole in a plastic bag or heated propagating case (see page 444), and keep it warm in bright indirect light. When the potted cutting has rooted (in four to six weeks) remove it from the bag or case, water it moderately, and apply standard liquid fertilizer at two-week intervals. Move the cutting into a 5-inch pot of standard mixture and treat it as a mature plant when it begins to fill the pot with roots.

It is also possible to propagate a dieffenbachia from a 3- or 4-inch-long section of the main stem. Take a section containing at least one growth bud, place it horizontally on the surface of a moistened equal-parts rooting mixture of peat moss and coarse sand or perlite, and treat it as a newly planted tip cutting. A dieffenbachia can also be air layered (see page 440).

Propagating a dieffenbachia

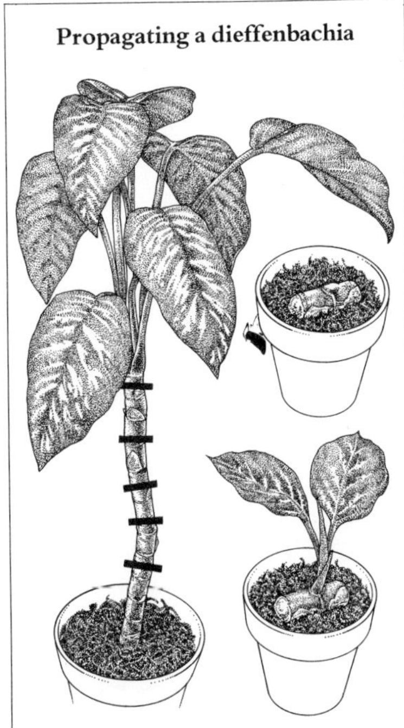

Lay a section of main stem containing at least one growth bud on the surface of a pot of damp rooting mixture. New growth will appear from the growth bud.

Special points Be sure to wash hands thoroughly after removing faded leaves or taking cuttings from dieffenbachias. The sap is poisonous. If it gets in the mouth, it causes swelling, pain, and temporary loss of speech—which explains one common name of the plant: "dumb-cane."

Dioscorea

DIOSCOREACEAE

Yam
D. discolor

PLANTS of the genus *Dioscorea* (yam) are tuberous-rooted vines. (Some have edible rootstocks, but these should not be confused with sweet potatoes, which are widely—but wrongly—called yams in the United States.) The only species of this genus commonly grown indoors, *D. discolor,* has a round rootstock that can eventually grow 2–3 inches across. In the spring it produces slender stems, which grow rapidly to a length of 10–15 feet in a single season. The wiry stems carry alternate heart-shaped leaves up to 8 inches long and 6 inches wide on 2½-inch-long leafstalks. Leaf upper surface is dark olive green, marked with patches of light green and silvery gray, and with prominent silver-and-pink veining. The underside of leaves is lusterless purple. Inconspicuous green flowers appear in late summer.

Growth of this plant stops in fall. Leaves turn yellow and drop off, and stems shrivel and die back.

See also BULBS, CORMS, and TUBERS.

PROPER CARE

Light During the active growth period provide bright light, with three or four hours a day of direct sunlight. During the dormant period light is not a consideration.

Temperature Normal room temperatures are suitable during the active growth period. Keep dormant dioscoreas cool, but do not subject them to temperatures below 55°F.

Watering At the start of the active growth period (in early spring), water sparingly, allowing the top two-thirds of the mixture to dry out between waterings. After the plant has made about 1 foot of growth, begin to water plentifully, enough to keep the mixture thoroughly moist, but never allow the pot to stand in water. When leaves begin to yellow in fall, gradually reduce amounts of water until leaves and stems have dried up. Then stop watering, and leave the tubers dry in their pots until spring.

Feeding Apply standard liquid fertilizer every two weeks from early spring until early fall.

Potting and repotting Use a soil-based potting mixture (see page 429). Repot mature tubers in clean pots every year. A 6-inch pot should be adequate for even the largest tuber. In early spring, before new growth starts, plant each tuber 1 inch deep in fresh, barely moistened mixture. If possible, keep the pot in a plastic bag or heated propagating case (see page 444) at about 70°F and in bright filtered light for 7–10 days. This environment will help tubers to grow.

Propagation Dioscoreas are propagated from small tubers that develop in fall on thickened white roots (which look very different from normal feeding roots). These tubers may be any size from that of a pea to that of a walnut. The tuber-bearing roots decompose during the winter, leaving the little tubers unattached. Start them into growth in spring by planting them in a tray filled with a moistened equal-parts mixture of peat moss and coarse sand, setting the tubers just below the surface. Stand the tray in bright light until the tubers have made shoots 1–2 inches tall. No further water is required if the tray is enclosed in a plastic bag or propagating case; otherwise, keep the rooting mixture from drying out completely. When shoots are 1–2 inches tall, transfer each tuber into a 3- to 5-inch pot of standard soil-based mixture, and treat it as a mature dioscorea.

Special points Provide support for the twining stems by inserting three or four thin stakes into the mixture around the rim of the pot.

Dipladenia

APOCYNACEAE

D. sanderi

THE only species of *Dipladenia* grown indoors, *D. sanderi*, now belongs to the genus *Mandevilla* and ought to be called *M. sanderi*. It is so widely known as dipladenia, however, that its former name has been retained here.

D. sanderi is a woody-stemmed plant that winds its stems around any available support. Showy flowers are borne in terminal clusters from late spring to early fall. The trumpet-shaped, five-petaled flowers, each of which may be 3 inches across, are rose-pink, with orange throats. The leathery, pointed-oval, glossy green leaves on ½-inch leafstalks grow in opposite pairs on the stems. Each leaf may be 2 inches long and 1 inch wide. These plants begin to flower at a relatively early age, when they are no more than 1 foot high and have not yet started to climb. They can be kept short and bushy by regular pruning. Alternatively, they can be encouraged to twine up thin supports pushed into the potting mixture.

PROPER CARE

Light Grow dipladenias in bright light filtered through a translucent blind or curtain; never subject them to direct sunlight. They will not flower if they are grown in insufficient light.

Temperature Normal room temperatures are suitable for actively growing plants. Lower the temperature to around 55°F during the winter rest period. For increased humidity stand pots on trays of moist pebbles.

Watering During the active growth period water moderately, giving enough at each watering to make the potting mixture moist, and allowing the top half-inch of the mixture to dry out between waterings. During the winter rest period give only enough to prevent the mixture from drying out.

Feeding Apply standard liquid fertilizer once every two weeks during the active growth period only.

Potting and repotting Use a soil-based potting mixture (see page 429). For improved drainage put a half-inch layer of clay-pot fragments in the bottom of the pot. Move plants into pots one size larger every spring until maximum convenient pot size (probably about 8 inches) is reached. Thereafter, topdress plants annually with fresh mixture (see page 428).

Propagation To propagate dipladenias, use 3-inch-long tip cuttings taken from the new growth produced in spring. Plant each cutting in a 3-inch pot containing a moistened equal-parts mixture of peat moss and coarse sand or perlite. Enclose the whole in a plastic bag or heated propagating case (see page 444), and place it in medium light. Dipladenia cuttings are unlikely to root successfully, or will be extremely slow to root, in a temperature below 75°–80°F. When new growth indicates that rooting has occurred, uncover the new plant. Still keeping it in a warm, shady spot, begin to water just enough to keep the mixture from drying out, and apply standard liquid fertilizer once a month until the roots nearly fill the pot (see page 426). When this happens, move the plant into a slightly larger pot of standard mixture, and treat it as a mature dipladenia.

Special points Dipladenias flower only on growth produced during the current year. In the fall, after the flowering period ends, prune away nearly all this growth. Disposing of much of the top growth will reduce the size of the plant that needs to be overwintered. It will also encourage the growth of flower-producing shoots in the following spring.

Dizygotheca

ARALIACEAE

DIZYGOTHECAS (false or finger aralias) are among the most delicate-looking of indoor foliage plants, with leaves that are divided into numerous leaflets arranged in roughly circular form at the tips of slender leafstalks. These tropical plants rarely exceed 6 feet in height, with a spread of about 20 inches, indoors.

Note: These plants used to be classified under *Aralia* (a very similar genus) and they may still be occasionally sold under that name.

RECOMMENDED DIZYGOTHECAS

D. elegantissima (often sold as *D. laciniata*) is a very slender plant. Its leaves comprise 7 to 10 narrow, leathery leaflets, each 3–4 inches long and ½ inch wide, with toothed, undulate edges. Leaf color is coppery red at first, but changes to a very deep green—in fact, almost black. The central stem and the leafstalks are all mottled with creamy white.

D. kerchoveana is similar to *D. elegantissima*, but its leaflets have a more prominent, whitish midrib.

D. veitchii has wider leaflets (up to 1 inch). The midribs are white and the undersides of the leaflets are a deep burgundy color.

D. veitchii

PROPER CARE

Light Dizygothecas like bright light but should not be placed in strong direct sunlight.

Temperature Warmth is essential (minimum temperature even during the rest period: 60°F), and so is humidity. Stand pots on trays or saucers of moist pebbles.

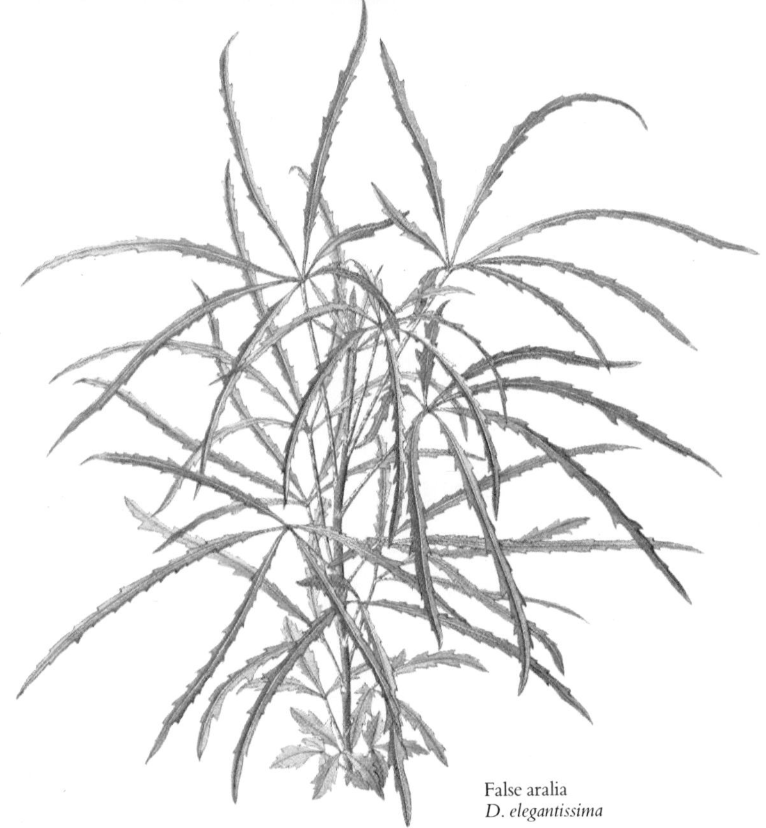

False aralia
D. elegantissima

Watering Water sparingly at all times, allowing the top two-thirds of the mixture to dry out before watering again.

Feeding Apply standard liquid fertilizer every two weeks during the active growth period.

Potting and repotting Use a soil-based potting mixture (see page 429). Dizygothecas are slow-growing and should be moved into pots one size larger only once in two years. This is best done in early spring. Do not use pots that are needlessly big. Once plants have reached maximum convenient pot size (probably 8–10 inches), topdress them (see page 428) with about an inch of fresh mixture every spring.

Propagation New plants are raised from seed—a method that may sometimes succeed in well-heated rooms (with fresh seed sown in spring). But young plants raised professionally are freely available, and this is the normal way to acquire a new dizygotheca.

Special points These plants do not normally branch but tend to grow straight up from the central growing point. For a bushy effect, plant two or three small specimens in one pot.

In this display the delicate foliage of dizygothecas contrasts with the bold leaves of begonias, codiaeums, aglaonemas and tradescantias.

Because dizygothecas grow upright and do not branch, the best way to achieve a full, bushy effect is to plant several in one pot.

Dolichothele

CACTACEAE

D. longimamma

THERE is only one species of the genus *Dolichothele*, *D.longimamma*. This desert cactus is so similar to the closely related mammillarias that it is often included in the genus *Mammillaria*. Like its near relatives, *D. longimamma* has a ribless stem that is covered with the conical, wartlike projections known as tubercles. These are arranged spirally, and each is about ½ inch across and carries an areole that bears around 10 whitish or pale yellow spines ½ inch long. When the plant is about five years old, its globular, green stem will probably have attained a girth of 6 inches. By then, too, a few offsets are likely to have formed around the base. In addition, branches are sometimes produced on the tips of tubercles. If a tubercle becomes very woolly and begins to grow noticeably thicker, this probably indicates that it is about to branch.

In summer this plant produces up to half a dozen bell-shaped yellow flowers, each about 2 inches across. Flower size is a distinguishing feature of *D. longimamma*; in general, mammillaria blooms tend to be smaller. Each flower lasts only a day or two, and there is normally only one flowering period per season (though a second one may occasionally occur). As in the mammillarias, the flowers are not produced from areoles at the tubercle centers, but from "secondary" areoles lying between tubercles at the top of the stem.

See also CACTI.

PROPER CARE

The cultivation needs of *D. longimamma* are exactly the same as those of mammillarias. For full details see *MAMMILLARIA*.

Dracaena
AGAVACEAE

DRACAENAS are highly regarded for their striking, usually variegated foliage. Most are naturally erect, single-stemmed shrubs; but some are low-growing, many-stemmed, and spreading; and some grow into tall trees. Flowers are rarely produced and generally unimportant. Many mature dracaenas have a palmlike appearance, with their narrow, lance-shaped, arching leaves, borne on top of tall, usually bare stems. They are often confused with cordylines.

Gold-dust dracaena
D. surculosa

Belgian evergreen
D. sanderana

D. fragrans 'Massangeana'

D. marginata 'Tricolor'

D. deremensis 'Warneckii'

RECOMMENDED DRACAENAS

D. deremensis, which has plain green leaves, is rarely seen, but two of its variegated forms are very popular. *D.d.* 'Bausei' grows 4 feet tall, with a spread of 15 inches. Its deep green leaves—18 inches long and 2 inches wide, narrowing to an inch-wide stalklike base near the stem—have a broad white stripe along the middle. *D.d.* 'Warneckii' differs only in that it has two stripes instead of a single one.

D. draco (dragon tree) can become huge in the wild but is rarely taller than 4 feet with a 2-foot spread indoors. The leathery leaves are blue-gray with thin red margins, acutely pointed, and up to 18 inches long and 2 inches wide. They are arranged in a low rosette in young plants but later appear at the top of a thick, woody trunk. The young leaves stand erect, but older ones arch downward.

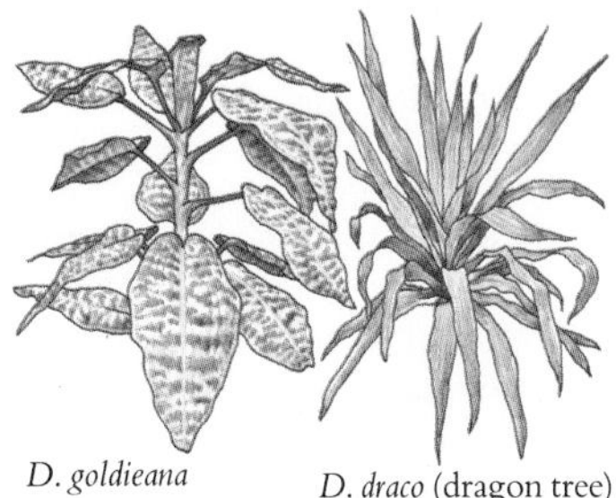

D. goldieana *D. draco* (dragon tree)

D. fragrans (so named because of its fragrant flowers, which are seldom produced in pots) grows 4–5 feet tall with a 2-foot spread. Its glossy green, loosely arching leaves are $1\frac{1}{2}$–3 feet long and 4 inches wide. The forms with variegated leaves are more popular than the basic type. The leaves of *D.f.* 'Lindenii' have broad, creamy white marginal stripes. Those of *D.f.* 'Massangeana' have a wide central stripe of yellow, which is sometimes bordered by one or two narrower yellow lines. Those of *D.f.* 'Victoria' (sometimes wrongly called *D. victoriae*) have broad margins that are bright yellow. All these plants begin shedding some of their lower leaves after a year or two and end up with an attractive leaf cluster on top of a stout but bare stem, sometimes with one or two leafy side branches.

D. goldieana is a most attractive low-growing plant, but a difficult one to grow well, since it needs very high humidity, complete freedom from drafts, and a constant temperature. It has a slender, unbranched, erect stem, usually no more than 1 foot high with a similar spread, which bears around 10 oval leaves 9–10 inches long and 5 inches wide on the ends of 2-inch-long leafstalks. The leaves are bright glossy green, with a yellowish midrib and irregular crosswise bands of silvery gray. The plant may produce an occasional tuft of tiny, scented, white flowers in the center of the leaf cluster.

D. hookerana has leathery, glossy green leaves with very fine, white, almost transparent margins. The leaves, which are sword-shaped, up to $2\frac{1}{2}$ feet long, and 2–3 inches wide, are stoutly ribbed on the underside. The stem is woody and trunklike, and it rarely branches; over the course of many years it can attain a height of 6 feet. There is a form, *D.h.* 'Latifolia,' which is very similar to the type species except that the leaves narrow a little at the point where they join the stem, and the middle of the leaf grows to a width of about $3\frac{1}{2}$ inches. Another form, *D.h.* 'Variegata,' differs from the plain green-leaved species in that it has some white striping in the leaves. This may be either a single white, lengthwise stripe 1–$1\frac{1}{2}$ inches wide or several fine lengthwise markings.

D. marginata—which is more tolerant of variable room conditions than are other dracaenas, and is therefore the easiest one to grow—can attain a height of 10 feet. It usually has a straight, bare stem topped with a cluster of about 30 arching leaves 2 feet long and $\frac{1}{2}$ inch wide, colored deep green with thin purple margins. As leaves age, they turn yellow, dry

Growth pattern of *D. marginata*

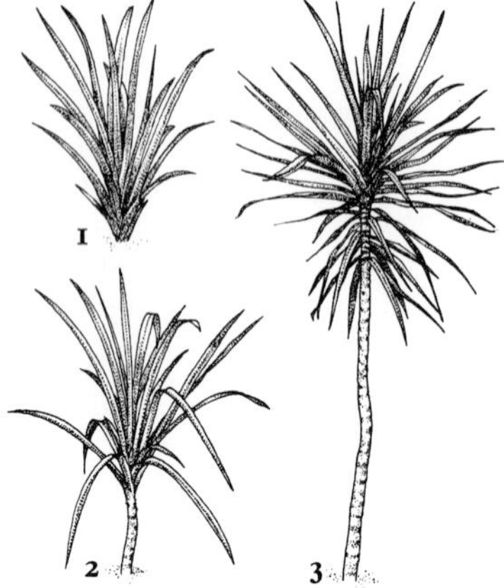

*When young (**1**),* D. marginata *has spiky leaves that grow up from its base. As the plant matures lower leaves droop and fall, leaving an elongated, bare stem (**2** and **3**).*

up, and fall off, leaving attractive triangular scars where they were attached to the woody stem. A splendid variegated form generally sold under the name *D.m.* 'Tricolor' has leaves striped with pink, cream, and green; it is one of the finest introductions of recent years, and is no harder to grow than the type plant.

D. sanderana (often wrongly called *D. sanderiana*; sometimes known as Belgian evergreen) is a slender, erect shrub with stiff leaves 9 inches long and 1 inch wide arranged openly around a stem that may branch, though only rarely. Leaf color is deep green with broad white margins. Branching, if it occurs, is from low down on the stem. Indoor height rarely exceeds 3 feet.

D. surculosa (better known by its former name *D. godseffiana*) is commonly called gold-dust or spotted leaf dracaena. Both of the popular forms—*D.s.* 'Florida Beauty' and *D.s.* 'Kelleri'—grow about 2 feet high with a spread of 15 inches, branch profusely, and bear whorls of two or three elliptic leaves 3 inches long and $1\frac{1}{2}$ inches wide on thin but wiry stems. The leaves are dark green spotted with cream. Those of *D.s.* 'Florida Beauty' are the more densely spotted—so densely, in fact, that many of the blotches merge to form a solid creamy white area—and those of *D.s.* 'Kelleri' are the thicker.

PROPER CARE

Light Dracaenas need bright light, but should not be placed in direct sunlight. The best possible position is one that gets two or three hours a day of sunlight filtered through a translucent blind or curtain.

Temperature *D. draco* will remain healthy in quite low temperatures (down to around 50°F), but all the others need warmth (65°–75° is ideal). If subjected to lower temperatures, their leaves droop and eventually fall off. Cooler conditions for only a week or two are not fatal, however; new leaves will appear within a few weeks of an early return to temperatures above 65°. Because high humidity is particularly necessary for dracaenas, keep the air moist by standing plants on trays or saucers of moist pebbles or damp peat moss and by occasionally mist-spraying the foliage.

Watering During the active growth period water plentifully, as often as necessary to keep the potting mixture thoroughly moist, but never allow the pot to stand in water. During the rest period water moderately, enough to make the potting mixture barely moist, but allow the top inch to dry out between waterings.

Feeding Apply standard liquid fertilizer every two weeks during the active growth period only.

Potting and repotting Use a soil-based potting mixture (see page 429). Because *D. goldieana, D. sanderana* and *D. surculosa* remain relatively small and do not need frequent repotting to sustain growth, they will thrive for years in quite small pots and will attain maturity in 5-inch pots. Dracaenas with larger leaves and a more robust habit should be moved into pots one size larger each spring until maximum convenient pot size (probably 8–10 inches) is reached.

Propagation Dracaenas can be propagated in spring or late summer from tip or stem cuttings or from basal shoots. Tip cuttings and basal shoots should be young, comparatively soft and 3–6 inches long. If older pieces of stem are used, they should be cut (by pruning shears, if necessary) into $1\frac{1}{2}$- to 2-inch-long pieces, each of which must carry at least one growth bud (a slight swelling noticeable under the soft bark of the stem). When planting these pieces, make sure they are placed the right end up—i.e., the way the stem originally grew.

Place each cutting or shoot in a 3-inch pot of slightly moistened rooting mixture consisting of equal parts of peat moss and coarse sand or perlite, enclose the whole in a plastic bag or heated propagating case (see page 444), and keep it in a warm, partially shaded position until rooted. No additional water will be required while the cutting is in the plastic bag or propagator (four to six weeks). After rooting has occurred, remove the pot from the bag or propagator and begin to water the new plant moderately, moistening the mixture at each watering and allowing the top half-inch of the mixture to dry out before watering again. In addition begin applying a half-strength standard liquid fertilizer at two-week intervals. When roots appear on the surface of the mixture, move the young plant into a pot one size larger containing the standard potting mixture for adult plants, and treat it as a mature dracaena.

Dyckia
BROMELIACEAE

D. brevifolia

DYCKIAS are spiny, stemless bromeliads resembling prickly succulents. Their rigid, heavily spined leaves usually grow in a tight rosette, and the leaves of most species have undersides that look striped because they are partially coated with silvery white scurf arranged in narrow lengthwise rows. In the spring bell-shaped flowers appear on long, slender flower stalks; these rise from one side—not the center—of the mature rosette, and because of this the rosette does not routinely die after flowering as do the rosettes of most other bromeliads. Dyckias form new rosettes rapidly, building up into relatively large clusters. The two species that have become popular choices as house plants are rather low-growing, with a spread of little more than 12 inches.
See also BROMELIADS.

RECOMMENDED DYCKIAS

D. brevifolia (often called *D. sulphurea)*, has sharply pointed, fleshy, green leaves 3–5 inches long and $\frac{3}{4}$ inch wide, edged with hooked spines only about $\frac{1}{8}$ inch long. The silvery white striping on the underside of the leaves is particularly well defined in this species. Bright orange flowers, each about $\frac{1}{2}$ inch long, appear at irregular but wide intervals along the last third of the length of the 2-foot-long flower stalk.

D. fosterana has shiny, stiffly arching, dull gray leaves up to 9 inches long and $\frac{3}{4}$ inch wide, viciously armed with $\frac{1}{4}$-inch-long hooked spines along the edges. In bright sunlight the leaf color changes to a rich metallic bronze. Orange-yellow flowers 1 inch long are borne on a 9- to 12-inch-long stalk.

PROPER CARE

Light Grow dyckias in direct sunlight for strongest leaf color and for short, sturdy growth.

Temperature Dyckias flourish in hot, dry conditions in the wild, so they are well able to withstand dry indoor heat. They have no definite resting period but grow steadily throughout periods of warmth. However, they can tolerate quite cool temperatures (as low as 50°F).

Watering Dyckias are well able to withstand long periods of drought (as well as short periods of general neglect). They do best, however, if watered moderately, enough to make the entire mixture moist at each watering, and allowing the top inch of the mixture to dry out before watering again. In areas where the quantity of sunlight is considerably reduced in winter, dyckias should be kept quite cool during the months of low light. At such times water them sparingly (no more than once a month), giving just enough each time to keep the potting mixture from drying out.

Feeding Apply standard liquid fertilizer to these plants once a month during spring, summer, and fall.

Potting and repotting Use a soil-based potting mixture (see page 429) with the addition of a one-third portion of coarse sand or perlite for good drainage. Pots should also have an inch-deep layer of clay-pot fragments in the bottom. Move dyckias into pots one size larger in the spring whenever their leaves have covered the entire surface of the potting mixture. The largest pot size needed will normally be 5 or 6 inches. Use stout gloves when repotting these plants (especially *D. fosterana)*, and handle the leaves with great care. Stiffly arching leaves are liable to break off suddenly under a rough touch.

Propagation Propagate in spring from offsets that appear in large numbers around the base of these plants. Remove the offsets with a sharp knife when they are $1\frac{1}{2}$–2 inches across. Place each little rosette in a small pot of very sandy potting mixture (one part soil-based mixture to one part coarse sand or perlite), and keep it in a position where it gets medium light, watering it just enough to keep the rooting mixture from drying out until renewed growth indicates that the offset has rooted. It can then be treated as a mature dyckia, and it should be moved into a larger pot of the recommended potting mixture for adult plants after the rosette leaves have completely covered the surface area of the rooting pot.

Special points Whenever possible, stand dyckias in a sunny position outdoors throughout the summer months. Do not expose them to outdoor brightness too suddenly, however. Instead, give them a little more sunlight each day over a period of 7 to 10 days. Bring the plants indoors again in early fall.

Echeveria

CRASSULACEAE

Baby echeveria
E. derenbergii

ECHEVERIAS, which range from very small, bushy shrubs to flat, stemless rosettes, vary widely in size, shape, leaf coloring, and texture. The fleshy leaves of these succulent plants are usually smooth and covered with a wax or bloom (which can be blemished if the leaves are handled). Some echeverias have hairy leaves, and the fine hairs are scattered over their stems as well. All leaves are easily broken and can snap off at the point where they join the main stem if carelessly knocked. As leaves age, they dry up and can be pulled away.

Bell-shaped flowers appear soon after the winter rest—or sometimes in early summer—from leaf axils toward the center of the rosette. The flowers are normally arranged on spikes (often curled at first but gradually straightening) carried on thin stems. Individual flowers open successively, starting from the base of the spike and finishing up at the tip.

The names of these plants are sometimes confusing. Many hybrids have been produced in recent years, including crosses between the genus *Echeveria* and other genera of the same family. These have been given names formed from a combination of the names of the parents—for instance, *Pachyveria,* from *Echeveria* crossed with *Pachyphytum*. Moreover, several species formerly included among the echeverias now belong to other genera (*Dudleya* and *Urbinia*), and so some familiar plants may now be listed under new, unfamiliar names. Among the echeverias themselves certain species and hybrids differ considerably in form from the type plant. For instance, they may have wavy leaf edging or may form a cristate rosette (that is to say one with a crested or cockscomb appearance).

See also SUCCULENTS.

RECOMMENDED ECHEVERIAS

E. affinis (sometimes sold as *E.* 'Nigra'), has thick, pointed, lance-shaped leaves, 2–3 inches long, which are arranged in a squat rosette with a spread of 4 inches. Leaves are waxy and very dark green; when the plant is grown in full sunlight and kept relatively dry, they go practically black. Late-winter flowers are red and arranged singly on a branched stem.

E. agavoides (sometimes known as *Urbinia agavoides)* has fleshy, triangular leaves $1\frac{1}{2}$–3 inches long, which are arranged in a tight rosette with a spread of 5–6 inches. The pale apple green leaves have pointed (not spined) brown tips and lack the usual coating of bloom or wax. If kept in full sunlight, the foliage may take on a reddish tinge, especially at leaf edges. Springtime flowers are red tipped with yellow. There is an attractive crested form, *E.a.* 'Cristata,' shaped like a large cockscomb.

E. derenbergii (baby echeveria or painted lady) has a short stem bearing one or more rosettes in a cushionlike clump, with new rosettes constantly appearing from leaf axils of the main plant. Spoon-shaped, blue-green leaves 1–$1\frac{1}{2}$ inches long have a waxy, silvery bloom and red tips. The multi-headed plants develop into fat cushions of fleshy leaves and produce numerous offsets. Curved flower stems up to 3 inches long carry orange-red flowers. Several such stems emerge from each rosette in spring and early summer. *E.* 'Doris Taylor' (woolly rose) is a hybrid with a short, trunklike, dark red stem supporting two (or, rarely, three) rosettes, each 7 inches across. The spoon-shaped leaves are pale green (tipped with red at certain seasons), up to 2 inches long, and covered with soft white hairs. In late winter orange-red flowers are produced on stems about 15 inches long.

E. elegans (Mexican gem or pearl echeveria) forms a tight stemless rosette 4 inches across. Mature plants produce offsets on long stolons that push out from below the lower leaves and form cushionlike clumps. All leaves are spoon-shaped, upturned,

E. setosa (firecracker plant)

E. harmsii

E. agavoides

E. gibbiflora 'Carunculata'

E. elegans (Mexican gem)

1–2 inches long, pale blue-green, thickly covered with a dusty white bloom, and almost transparent at the edges. In summer, pink-and-yellow flowers are produced on pink stalks up to 1 foot long.

E. gibbiflora, a robust plant, grows 2 feet tall, rarely branching into more than one stem. Leaves are spoon-shaped, 7–8 inches long, and gray-green with pink undertones. They form a tight rosette at the top of a stout stem. *E.g.* 'Carunculata' forms a looser rosette and has blisterlike lumps on its leaves; *E.g.* 'Crispata' has undulate leaf margins; and the leaves of *E.g.* 'Metallica' have a bronzy, metallic coloring. The pale red flowers of all these plants appear in winter on 9- to 12-inch-long stems that bear small leaves up their entire length.

E. harmsii (formerly known as *Oliveranthus elegans)* is much looser in form than most other echeverias. The main stem is topped by a rosette and also bears leaves from the axils of which rise secondary stems carrying smaller rosettes. The lance-shaped leaves are medium green, thinly edged with brown, and covered with short soft hair. Inch-long flowers, which appear on 6-inch-long stems in late spring and early summer, are often solitary rather than in spikes. Flower color is scarlet, with petal edges turned back to reveal a yellow lining.

E. leucotricha (white plush plant) is shrubby, with light green, lance-shaped, thick leaves 2–3 inches long, covered with fine, white, bristly hair. In bright light, especially just after the winter rest period, the leaf tips take on a bright reddish brown coloring. The plant branches profusely, grows slowly to about 9 inches tall, and in spring and summer produces red flowers on short stems, which appear from the edges of rosettes.

E. setosa (firecracker plant or Mexican firecracker) usually forms a flat rosette of thick, soft, densely packed 3-inch-long oval leaves. Fine silvery hairs thickly coat both the leaves and the short flower stems on which red-and-yellow flowers grow in summer.

E. shaviana is a flat plant with almost white, crinkled-edged, spoon-shaped leaves up to 3 inches long arranged in a rosette 4–5 inches across. In spring and summer, pink flowers grow on foot-long stems. Because offsets spoil the shape of the rosette, it is advisable to detach them when they appear.

PROPER CARE

Light Provide the brightest possible light—including direct sunlight—at all times. Inadequate light causes loose, uncharacteristic growth.

Temperature During the active growth period normal room temperatures are suitable. During the semi-dormant midwinter rest period, keep the temperature at about 55°–60°F, if possible.

Watering During the active growth period water sparingly, giving enough at each watering to make the entire mixture barely moist, but allowing a full half of the mixture to dry out before watering again. This short dry period promotes good leaf coloring and keeps plants true to character, whereas overwatering produces soft, "lush" growth, which is liable to rot. Avoid wetting foliage; drops of water remaining anywhere on the leaves can cause ugly scorch marks or rotting. Echeverias that grow flat and that completely cover the surface of the mixture can be watered only from below. Stand such plants in shallow saucers of water, and leave them for an hour or two—just long enough to moisten the mixture thoroughly.

During the rest period water only enough to keep the potting mixture from drying out. This will suffice to prevent foliage from shriveling.

Feeding Apply standard liquid fertilizer at slightly less than full strength every two weeks during the active growth period.

Potting and repotting Use a potting mixture composed of one-fifth coarse sand or perlite and four-fifths soil-based mixture (see page 429). Small, young plants should be moved into pots one size larger every spring, but more mature plants can be left for two years. Topdressing with fresh mixture will suffice in alternate years (see page 428). Pans or half-pots are suitable for the low-growing plants.

Put plenty of clay-pot fragments in the bottom of pots for good drainage. To avoid rot, do not replant the short, stemless kinds deeper than before. A sprinkling of coarse sand or perlite over the surface of the potting mixture will help surface drainage and keep low leaves away from the damp mixture. Some echeverias produce aerial roots. Such roots are not a sign that repotting is needed.

Propagation Echeverias may be propagated from seed (a slow process), leaf cuttings, branches carrying rosettes, or offsets. The last two methods are the quickest, for the rosettes or offsets are already recognizable plants before being detached from the parent. Remove the small rosettes and offsets—preferably no less than an inch across—from the plant with care, so as not to injure the parent. Strip away any lower leaves (to prevent leaf contact with the rooting medium); rosette stems should be cut down to a length of $\frac{3}{4}$ inch. Then place each rosette or offset into a pot of the recommended mixture. A sprinkling of coarse sand on top will encourage rooting by working in around the stem as the rosette or offset is gently pushed into the slightly moistened mixture. Rooting will usually occur in two weeks if the young plants are kept at normal room temperature in bright filtered light and watered just enough to keep the potting mixture from drying out completely.

Offsets are seldom produced by cristate forms, and the cristate plants

Propagating a rosette form

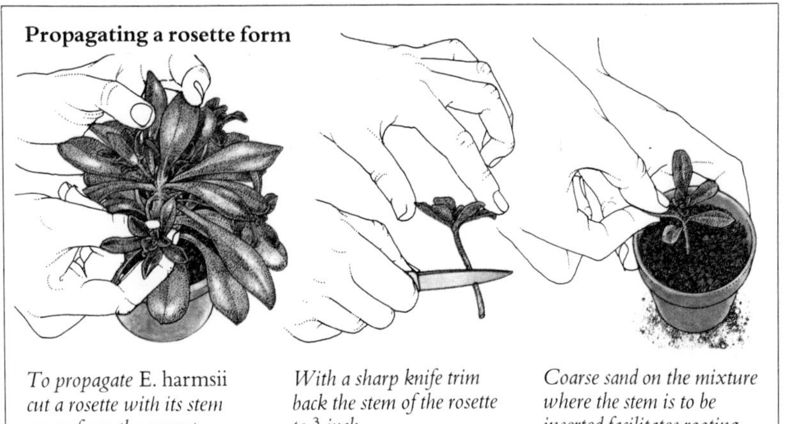

To propagate E. harmsii *cut a rosette with its stem away from the parent.*

With a sharp knife trim back the stem of the rosette to $\frac{3}{4}$ inch.

Coarse sand on the mixture where the stem is to be inserted facilitates rooting.

tend to lose their distinctive appearance if propagated by cuttings. The usual way to propagate these echeverias is to break them into small pieces and root each piece like any other section of plant.

To propagate types of echeveria that do not readily produce offsets, use single leaf cuttings. Choose a leaf that shows no signs of shriveling at the edges. It can come from any part of the plant, even from the flower spike of such tall-growing kinds as *E. gibbiflora,* which tends to produce few leaves in the main rosette. Carefully pull a leaf from the parent plant, and place it on a ¼-inch layer of coarse sand or perlite atop some slightly moist soil-based potting mixture (see page 429) in a shallow pan. Leave the uncovered cutting in a place where it gets bright light, but is shaded from direct sunlight, and water it just enough to keep the potting mixture from drying out completely. In two to three weeks, roots will sprout from the base of the leaf and penetrate the mixture. Soon after a plantlet will begin to grow from the point where root meets leaf. Once the roots have penetrated the potting mixture, water them sparingly, just enough to make the mixture barely moist. When the plantlet has grown to manageable size, pot it up and treat it as a mature plant. (Note, however, that leaf cuttings from some species—*E. leucotricha,* for example—will not produce plantlets.)

Special points The closely packed leaves of most echeverias provide perfect shelter for mealy bugs (see page 455), which may go unnoticed until they have done real damage. They can be eliminated with a fine-tipped brush dipped in denatured alcohol and applied directly to the insects.

Although dabbing each mealy bug with denatured alcohol individually is a lengthy procedure, it is the best way to rid close-packed leaves of these pests.

Echinocactus

CACTACEAE

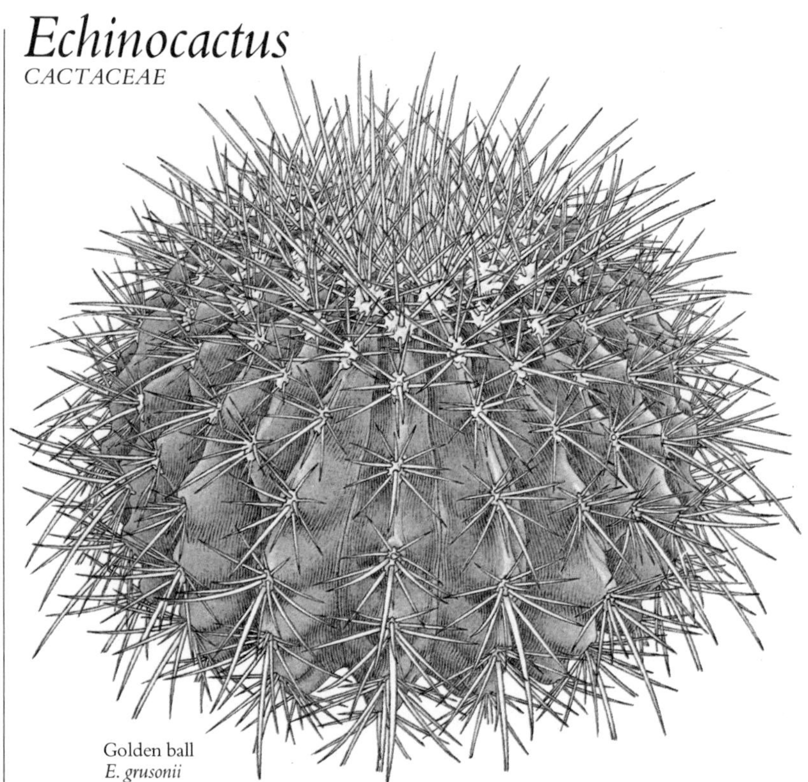

Golden ball
E. grusonii

ECHINOCACTI are all stout-spined, globular plants, some of which attain a diameter of several feet in the wild, but only after perhaps a hundred years of slow growth. Of the 16-odd species of this desert cactus only a few are in cultivation, and only one is likely to flower as a pot plant. *See also CACTI.*

RECOMMENDED ECHINOCACTI

E. grusonii (golden ball or barrel cactus) will probably have a diameter of 3–4 inches as a four-year-old seedling. The rate of growth slows down with age, however, and it will take 15 or 20 more years for the plant to add another 7 or 8 inches to its girth. Very young specimens are covered with tubercles (wartlike swellings) and look much like cacti of the genus *Mammillaria,* with which they are sometimes confused. As *E. grusonii* grows, the tubercles gradually become lined up in vertical rows and are less conspicuous. By the time a plant is 3 inches across, the tubercles will have merged, forming 20 to 27 narrow ribs separated by deep indentations. Areoles closely set along the ribs are filled with yellowish or whitish woolly hairs. The areoles at the top of the plant are so numerous that the crown of the "ball" appears covered in wool. The characteristic golden spines of the species also rise from the areoles. From 5 to 10 of the spines are ½ inch or more long, and another 3 to 5 of them may be twice as long.

Yellow, cup-shaped, 2-inch-wide flowers eventually appear from areoles on the crown of mature plants, but because *E. grusonii* does not bloom until fully mature, the flowers are never seen in room-size specimens. In areas with mild winter temperatures, however, this echinocactus can be grown outdoors and may ultimately become old and big enough to produce flowers in summer.

E. horizonthalonius, the one species that can be expected to flower indoors, is small and slow-growing. The rather flattened, grayish green stem ultimately reaches a height of only about 10 inches with a width of about 16 inches. The stem has 8 to 13 broad ribs, which are separated by deep, narrow indentations. The woolly areoles carry 6 to 9 thick, curved, grayish spines, which are up to 1½ inches long. Plants only 6 inches in diameter are already of flowering size. Their pink, bell-shaped flowers are about 2 inches wide at the mouth. They open during the summer months, and each flower lasts for several days.

PROPER CARE

Light Echinocacti need to be given direct sunlight throughout the year in order to produce long and well-colored spines.

Temperature During the active growth period normally warm room temperatures are suitable. Indoor echinocacti should be given a winter rest period, however—ideally, at about 50°F. Minimum tolerable temperature: 40°. At lower temperatures the surface of a plant may become discolored by the appearance of brown spots. On the other hand, if indoor winter temperatures rise much above 50°, the plant will be encouraged to continue growing; and with the often inadequate light of short winter days, the nearly spherical shape may elongate unattractively.

Watering During the active growth period water moderately, enough to make the potting mixture moist throughout, and allowing the top half-inch of the mixture to dry out before watering again. During the winter rest period water much more sparingly, giving only enough to keep the potting mixture from drying out completely. Too much moisture inevitably causes rotting to occur at the base of a resting echinocactus.

Feeding Use a standard tomato-type fertilizer during the active growth period. Apply the fertilizer once a month if the plant is growing in soil-based potting mixture, once every two weeks if the potting mixture is peat-based.

Potting and repotting Either soil-based or peat-based potting mixture is suitable (see page 429), but make it more porous by the addition of a one-third portion of coarse sand or perlite. Plants about 3 inches across can be accommodated for some years in 4-inch pots. Remove an echinocactus from its pot every spring to see whether it needs moving on. If it has grown so much that the roots fill the pot (see page 426), move the plant into a pot one size larger. Otherwise, gently shake the old potting mixture from the roots, and replace the plant in the original pot, which has been thoroughly cleaned. Add fresh mixture as necessary.

Propagation Potted echinocacti can be propagated only from seed (see *CACTI,* page 119). Seedlings can be raised easily, however, and in their first few years they grow rapidly.

Echinocereus

CACTACEAE

Hedgehog cactus
E. pectinatus

THERE are about 35 species of echinocereus (hedgehog cactus), and more than half of them have become common house plants, grown both for their colorful flowers and their attractive spines. The cylindrical stems of some of these desert cacti are more or less upright and rigid, whereas those of others are longer and softer and tend to sprawl. All echinocereuses are ribbed, with the ribs varying in size and shape according to species. Most of the plants produce branches, either from the base or farther up the stem. Some eventually form clumps. All begin to bloom when they are a few years old, producing short-lived, mostly cup-shaped flowers throughout the summer.

See also CACTI.

RECOMMENDED ECHINOCEREUSES

E. knippelianus is a small-growing plant. Its nearly globular stem attains a height of 3–4 inches and a breadth of 2–3 inches. Young plants remain solitary until about five years old and 3 inches high, when they begin to branch. The dark blue-green stem has five low, broad ribs, that bear small areoles. Each areole carries from one to three white, bristly spines about $\frac{1}{2}$ inch long. The pink flowers are up to $1\frac{1}{2}$ inches across.

E. pectinatus has a more nearly columnar, medium green stem, which can grow 10 inches tall and 3 inches wide in a 4-inch pot. It is slow-growing, however. A five-year-old specimen is unlikely to exceed a height of 3 inches; and this plant does not begin to branch until it is 4 or 5 inches high. Each of the many oval areoles on its 20 or so low, broad ribs carries up to 25 radial spines $\frac{1}{3}$ inch long and 2 to 6 shorter central spines. The species gets its name *pectinatus* (Latin for "comb-bearing") from the fact that the 25 radial spines are arranged in such a way as to look rather like the teeth of a comb. The white spines are so numerous that the whole plant appears white from a distance. The 3-inch flowers are violet-pink.

E. pentalophus (also known as *E. procumbens)* consists of profusely branching, light green stems that sprawl over the potting mixture and even droop over the sides of the pot. The stems are likely to be at least 6 inches long and 1 inch thick by the time the plant is five years old. There are either four or five broad, spirally arranged ribs with deep indentations in between. Small, wartlike tubercles on the ribs are tipped with whitish areoles, each of which bears from four to eight sharp-pointed, white radial spines about $\frac{1}{4}$ inch long and one brownish central spine up to $\frac{3}{4}$ inch long. The bright violet flowers are more nearly trumpet- than cup-shaped. Each one is 4 inches long and $3\frac{1}{2}$ inches across.

E. pentalophus

PROPER CARE

Light To stimulate flowering and help the plants retain their characteristic shape, give them the fullest possible sunlight. If at all feasible, stand them outdoors in the sun during the summer months.

Temperature During the spring and summer active growth period normal room temperatures are suitable, but these plants should have a winter rest period at a temperature below 50°F, if possible. They can withstand freezing conditions if kept completely dry in a cold frame or greenhouse.

Watering Water a fast-growing, sprawling echinocereus such as *E. pentalophus* plentifully during the active growth period; the potting mixture should be kept moist throughout as long as the pot is not allowed to stand in water. This much water can cause rot in slower-growing plants, however. Water such plants sparingly, barely moistening the mixture and letting the top two-thirds of the mixture dry out between waterings. During the winter rest period do not water plants that are kept at temperatures below 40°F. Give plants kept at 40° or higher just enough water to prevent the mixture from becoming completely dry.

Feeding During the active growth period only, apply a high-potassium, tomato-type fertilizer—monthly to plants in a soil-based potting mixture, once every two weeks to those in a peat-based mixture.

Potting and repotting Use a porous potting mixture: one part of coarse sand or perlite to two parts of soil-based or peat-based mixture (see page 429). For such slow-growing, upright plants as *E. knippelianus* and *E. pectinatus*, choose a pot that holds the root system comfortably, leaving a space of about ½ inch between the rim of the pot and the body of the plant. Provide a wider, shallower container for fast-growing, sprawling types.

Remove these plants from their pots every spring in order to see whether the roots of any of them completely fill the current pot. If they do, move the plant to a pot one size larger. Otherwise, shake away the old mixture and return the plant to its pot, adding fresh mixture as necessary.

Propagation To propagate a branching echinocereus, cut off a branch in spring or summer, using a sharp knife. Take care not to deface the parent plant if it is to be retained. Allow the branch to dry for three days, and then insert the cut end into a 3-inch pot of standard mixture. Treat the cutting as an adult, but shelter it from full sunlight for three or four weeks by placing it in the shade cast by other plants. Species that branch sparingly or not at all are best raised from seed (see *CACTI,* page 119).

Echinopsis

CACTACEAE

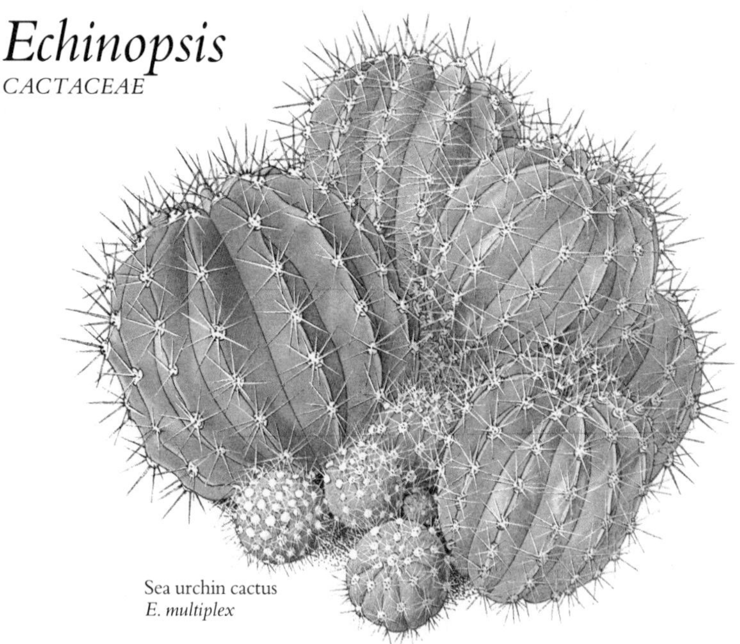

Sea urchin cactus
E. multiplex

PLANTS of the genus *Echinopsis* (sea urchin cactus or thistle globe) have notably beautiful flowers. The stems of these desert cacti are globular but tend to elongate into columns as they age. Flowering usually begins when plants are about three years old. Trumpet-shaped flowers appear from areoles toward the tops of stems, and the flowering period starts in early summer with a burst of up to 12 blooms at a time. Thereafter, flowers are produced spasmodically all summer long, usually two or three at once. In most species they open in the evening and are sweetly perfumed, but last only a day. Almost all specimens produce many basal offsets.
See also CACTI.

RECOMMENDED ECHINOPSISES

E. eyriesii has a dark green stem, with 11 to 18 narrow ribs bearing grayish areoles, each of which carries 14 dark brown spines less than ¼ inch long. Fragrant white flowers 8–10 inches long and 4–5 inches wide start to open at dusk, are fully open at night, and have wilted by the next afternoon.

E. multiplex has a pale green stem with 11 to 14 narrow ribs. Woolly areoles carry brownish, pointed spines, of which 5 to 9 are ¾-inch-long radial spines and 2 to 5 are 1½-inch-long central spines. The fragrant, night-blooming, pale pink flowers are 7–8 inches long and 5 inches wide.

In addition to the true species, there are many popular hybrids, most of which are crosses between *Echinopsis* and the genus *Lobivia*. The flowers of these plants (many of which are known as Paramount hybrids because they were developed in Paramount, California) are mostly day-blooming rather than nocturnal. Included among them are: 'Aurora' and 'Peach Monarch,' both with peach-pink flowers; 'Orange Glory' and 'Tangerine,' both with orange flowers; and 'Red Meteor' and 'Red Paramount,' both with red flowers. A night-blooming Paramount hybrid is 'Terracotta,' with pale peach-pink flowers striped in a darker shade of the same color. Outstanding non-Paramount, daytime-flowering hybrids are 'Golden Dream' and 'Green Gold,' both with scented, yellow blooms.

PROPER CARE

Light These plants need direct sunlight all year long. Do not subject night-blooming specimens to artificial lighting immediately following sunset. Buds open only after a period of full or partial darkness.

Temperature Normal room temperatures are suitable for actively growing plants, but a winter rest-period temperature below 50°F is essential for subsequent flowering.

Watering During the active growth period water plentifully, but never allow the pot to stand in water. During the rest period water only enough to prevent the potting mixture from becoming completely dry.

Feeding Apply a tomato-type liquid fertilizer every two weeks during the active growth period only.

Potting and repotting Use a mixture composed of one part of coarse sand or perlite to three of soil-based or peat-based mixture (see page 429). In potting, leave $\frac{1}{2}$ inch of space between the plant and the edge of the pot. Move plants to slightly larger pots every spring if roots are crowded. Otherwise, topdress them with fresh mixture at repotting time.

Propagation Normally a dead echinopsis flower leaves behind a fleshy berry. To prepare seeds for propagation, remove the berry, squeeze out the seeds, let them dry on a sheet of blotting paper, and store them in an envelope till sowing time (see *CACTI*, page 119). But be prepared for surprises. These cacti hybridize readily, and the eventual seedlings may not look like the parent.

To raise a plant that does resemble its parent, propagate from offsets in spring or summer. Offsets are easily detached. Plant them in appropriate-size pots of the recommended potting mixture by pressing them into the surface of the mixture, and treat them as adults. A word of warning, though: Some young echinopsises produce offsets too fast and become literally smothered by them, so that the main stem cannot reach flowering size unless many offsets are removed from the pot. It is best not to use such offsets for propagation since they are likely to prove as difficult to bring into flower as the parent plant.

Special points A night-flowering echinopsis normally blooms at about half an hour after dusk. If the plant is put in a dark cupboard for an hour or two before dusk, flowers will open before nightfall.

E. eyriesii

Elettaria

ZINGIBERACEAE

Cardamom
E. cardamomum

ELETTARIA *cardamomum* (cardamom) is the one species of the small genus *Elettaria* grown as a house plant. It is a plain green-leaved plant that can tolerate poor light and therefore can be used in positions where little else would survive. *E. cardamomum* has a stout rhizome that creeps just below the surface of the potting mixture, sending up stems that can grow $2\frac{1}{2}$ feet tall and $\frac{3}{4}$ inch thick. The leaves, which are carried on $\frac{3}{4}$-inch-long stalks, are a pointed-oval shape about 15 inches long and 3 inches wide. They grow in opposite pairs at $1\frac{1}{2}$- to 2-inch intervals all the way up the stems, and they are held semi-erect. So many stems are eventually produced that they crowd one another in the pot. Flowers appear only rarely and are insignificant.

PROPER CARE

Light This plant is one of the few that thrive in poor light. It will also flourish in medium or bright filtered light, but do not subject it to direct sunlight, because this would discolor the leaves.

Temperature Normal room temperatures are suitable for elettarias at all times. If the temperature falls below about 55°F, leaf edges are likely to turn brown.

Watering During the active growth period water moderately, enough to make the potting mixture moist throughout, but allow the top half-inch of the mixture to dry out between waterings. During the winter rest period give only enough to keep the mixture from drying out.

Feeding Apply standard liquid fertilizer every two weeks during the active growth period.

Potting and repotting Use a soil-based potting mixture (see page 429). Plant one rhizome in a 4- or 5-inch pot, and move plants into bigger pots when their stems have filled most of the surface area of the mixture. Repotting can be done in any season except winter. After maximum convenient pot size has been reached, topdressing with fresh potting mixture soon becomes difficult because of the crowded stems and leaves. When this happens, it is best to break up plants for propagation.

Propagation Divide overcrowded clumps in spring. Remove the plant from its pot, and carefully separate clumps of stems, making sure to retain as much as possible of the rhizome and fibrous roots. Treat each clump in the same way as a mature elettaria as soon as it has been potted up.

Epidendrum
ORCHIDACEAE

E. pentotis

MOST epidendrums used as house plants are epiphytes with pear-shaped pseudobulbs that bear up to six strap-shaped leaves at their tips. Flower stems develop between the leaves in late summer or fall, but the buds do not open until the following spring or summer. Individual blooms last about two to three weeks. Flowers of the species below usually have a starry appearance.
See also ORCHIDS.

RECOMMENDED EPIDENDRUMS
E. pentotis has light green, somewhat cylindrical pseudobulbs about 12 inches high and 1 inch thick, topped with two medium green leaves 4–5 inches long and 1 inch wide. Erect flower stems up to 4 inches long usually carry only two flowers each. The fragrant flowers, each about 3 inches across, bloom in late spring and summer. Sepal and petal color is yellowish or creamy white. The pointed-oval lip is white striped with purple.
E. vitellinum has bluish green pseudobulbs up to 3 inches high and $\frac{3}{4}$ inch thick, topped with two or three bluish green leaves 4 inches long and $\frac{1}{2}$ inch wide. Erect flower stems about 12 inches long carry up to 18 flowers each. The flowers are about $1\frac{1}{2}$ inches across and bloom in summer. The sepals and petals are bright orange-red, the tubular lip yellow.

PROPER CARE
Light Give epidendrums bright light all year long.
Temperature Maintain a daytime temperature of 70°F at all times. Minimum tolerable nighttime temperature: 55°. For adequate humidity stand pots on trays of moist pebbles, or place saucers of water under hanging baskets and epiphyte branches.
Watering Water actively growing plants moderately, but allow the potting mixture to dry out nearly completely between waterings. During the rest period (mid-fall to early spring), water them just enough to prevent the mixture from drying out.
Feeding Apply a foliar feed to actively growing epidendrums after every third or fourth watering.
Potting and repotting Use any of the recommended potting mixtures for orchids or grow plants on wooden supports. Repot in spring using larger containers only when the leading growth has reached the rim of the pot. After repotting, water plants sparingly and keep them in medium light for two weeks. Divide overlarge specimens for propagation.
Propagation Propagate in spring when the newest pseudobulb is about an inch tall. Cut the rhizome into segments each with at least three pseudobulbs, and make sure that one still carries leaves. Plant each segment in an appropriate-size container or on a small piece of supportive material. Moisten the potting mixture well, and then place the plant in medium light for four to five weeks. During this period water it sparingly. Thereafter, treat it as a mature epidendrum.

Epiphyllum
CACTACEAE

ALMOST all epiphyllums in general cultivation are hybrids between true epiphyllum species and other jungle cacti. These hybrids (popularly known as orchid cacti because of their big, bright-colored flowers) have flat, notched stems 2 feet or more long and up to 2 inches wide, which hang down unless staked. The stems branch profusely, usually from the base, forming clumps. Areoles in the notches often have tiny, bristlelike spines; only areoles on upper parts of stems normally carry any flowers. Flowering generally occurs in spring, but plants may bloom more than once in a year. The basically cup-shaped blooms can measure 6 inches or more across; some have cup-shaped inner petals and spreading outer ones. Flower color may be anything but blue. White flowers tend to be night-blooming and extremely fragrant. Up to 12 flowers may open at once, and each can last for several days.

The two hybrids named below are perhaps the most well-known of the indoor epiphyllums.
See also CACTI.

RECOMMENDED EPIPHYLLUMS
***E.* 'Ackermannii'** is remarkably prodigal with its flowers. It often produces cup-shaped, 4-inch-wide, bright red blooms in all four seasons.
***E.* 'Cooperi'** is a white-flowered, night-blooming type. Its open-funnel-shaped flowers are up to 4 inches wide and smell like lilies. The inner petals are snow white, the outer ones tinged with yellow and brown. Unlike most epiphyllum flowers, they arise from areoles positioned near the base of the stems.

E. 'Cooperi' (flower)

PROPER CARE
Light Give epiphyllums medium light. If possible, keep them in a shady spot outdoors in summer.

Orchid cactus
E. 'Ackermannii'

Temperature These plants require warmth with high humidity. Mist-spray them daily, and stand them on trays or saucers of moist pebbles.

Watering During spring and summer water plentifully, keeping the potting mixture thoroughly moist. Give plants a brief rest at the end of each flowering period by watering only enough during the next two to three weeks to prevent the mixture from drying out. At all other times water moderately, letting the top half-inch of the mixture dry out completely between waterings.

Feeding After flower buds start to form, apply a tomato-type fertilizer every two weeks. Stop feedings when most buds are open.

Potting and repotting Use a potting mixture composed of one part of coarse sand or perlite to three of peat-based mixture. Move plants into slightly larger pots every spring until they reach the 5- or 6-inch size. Thereafter, simply shake off the old potting mixture from the roots and replace plants in their pots, which have been cleaned. Add fresh mixture as necessary. Epiphyllums taller than 8 inches usually need to be staked unless permitted to trail in hanging baskets.

Propagation Propagate from cuttings taken in spring or summer. Remove a 5- or 6-inch-long branch, and allow it to dry for a day before inserting it an inch deep in a 4-inch pot of the mixture recommended for mature plants. Several such cuttings are usually planted around the rim of a single pot. Keep the potting mixture slightly moist until the cuttings root (in two to three weeks), after which they may be treated as mature plants.

True replicas of these hybrids can be obtained only from cuttings. Seed from hybrids is frequently offered for sale, but in general the results are unpredictable. Propagation from seed is only really useful when starting to build up a collection of epiphyllums (see *CACTI,* page 119).

Episcia

GESNERIACEAE

EPISCIAS are prized for both their foliage and their bright-hued, dainty flowers. A common name for the genus, carpet plant, derives from the tendency of these plants to form a spreading mat by means of creeping stolons, which grow from leaf axils on a short, thick central stem. At the tip of each stolon there is a cluster of leaves, which, on coming in contact with the potting mixture, will root into it, producing further central stems and stolons. The leaves of episcias are roughly oval and hairy, with an embossed or puckered surface and toothed edges. Flowers grow from leaf axils either singly or in small groups. Backed by a hairy calyx, each tubular corolla flares out into five rounded lobes that have finely toothed or fringed edges. The main flowering season generally begins in spring and lasts until fall.
See also GESNERIADS.

RECOMMENDED EPISCIAS

***E.* 'Acajou,'** a hybrid, has green stolons and silvery green leaves with a dark tan border. The leaves grow to 4 inches long and 2¾ inches wide. Bright red-orange flowers, which usually appear in groups, are up to 1 inch long and ¾ inch wide. This hybrid has such a long flowering period that it is almost everblooming.

***E.* 'Cleopatra,'** a hybrid, has reddish stolons carrying multicolored leaves up to 4 inches long and 2½ inches wide, with edges that curl under. An oak-leaf-shaped area of pale green around the midrib of the leaf is bordered in white, which in turn is bordered in pink. Red-orange flowers the same size as those of *E.* 'Acajou' and *E. cupreata,* are found singly or in pairs.

E. cupreata (creeping plant or flame violet) is a variable species with leaves 2–5 inches long and 1–3 inches wide. The leaves may be heavily embossed or nearly smooth, and their color ranges from deep coppery green to bright green, often with silvery or pale green markings around the main veins. Stolons are red or green. The red-and-yellow flowers, produced from leaf axils in threes or fours, are about 1 inch long and ¾ inch wide, with a throat that looks just like a white eye because of its soft lining of translucent hairs.

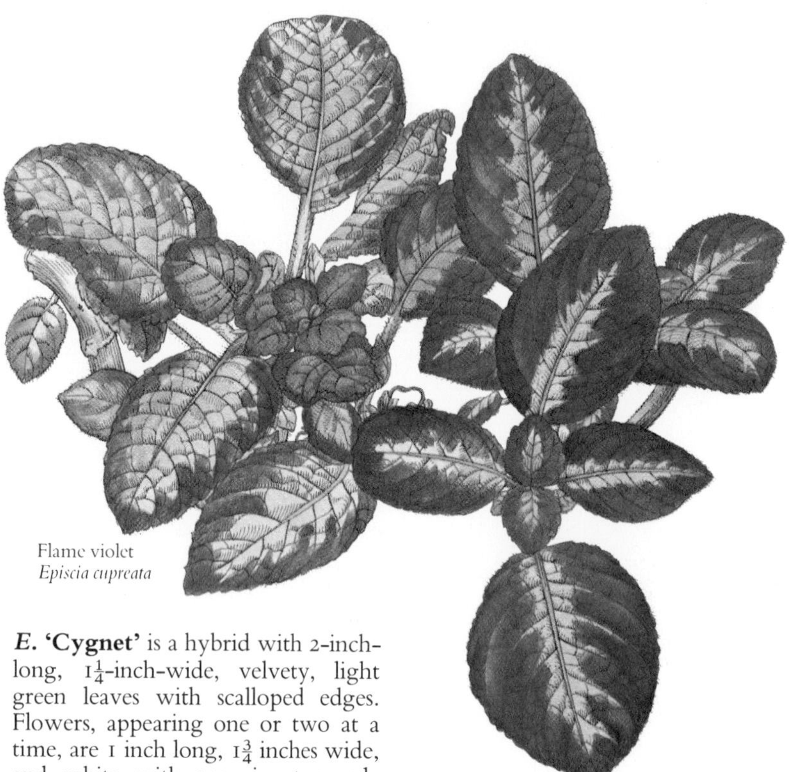

Flame violet
Episcia cupreata

***E.* 'Cygnet'** is a hybrid with 2-inch-long, 1¼-inch-wide, velvety, light green leaves with scalloped edges. Flowers, appearing one or two at a time, are 1 inch long, 1¾ inches wide, and white with prominent purple spots in the throat and deeply fringed mouth. This plant can be made to bloom all year long by constant removal of the greenish stolons. This encourages production of offsets from the base of the central stem, providing a continual supply of new leaf axils.

E. dianthiflora (lace flower vine) has green stolons bearing velvety, nearly round leaves with scalloped edges. The leaves, which can grow to 1½ inches across, have medium green upper surfaces, often with red veins, and pale green, green-veined lower surfaces. The 1¼-inch-long, white flowers, which grow from leaf axils singly, are speckled with pale purple in the throat, and the 1½-inch-wide mouth is deeply fringed. Blooms appear only for a short time in summer.

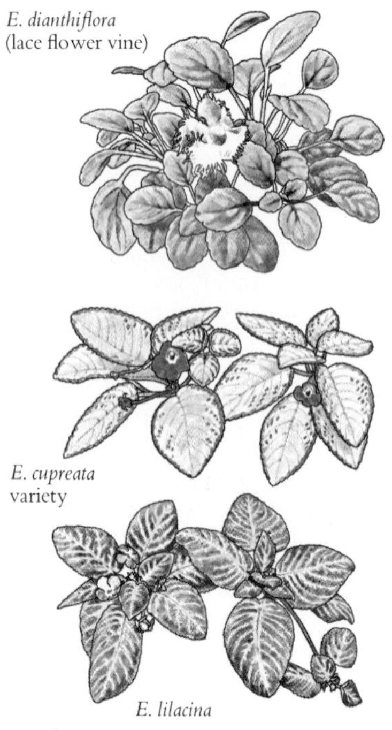

E. dianthiflora
(lace flower vine)

E. cupreata
variety

E. lilacina

E. lilacina has red or green stolons and leaves up to 4 inches long and 2½ inches wide. The heavily embossed leaves vary in color from dark bronzish green with a bright green central area to reddish. The flowers, in groups of two to four, are 1¼ inches long and 1½ inches wide. The corolla is white, and the pale lavender blue mouth has a pale yellow throat.

E. reptans (like *E. cupreata,* also called flame violet) has heavily embossed leaves up to 5 inches long and 2½ inches wide, carried on brownish stolons. Leaf color is dark or bronzish green, with silver markings along the veins. Slightly hairy flowers are produced in threes or fours, grow to 1½ inches long and 1 inch wide, and are rosy red with blood red throats lined with translucent hairs.

PROPER CARE

Light Episcias need bright light with several hours a day of direct sunlight. But keep them out of the midday sun. As a substitute for sunlight, place plants 4–6 inches below fluorescent tubes for 14 hours a day (see page 446). If an episcia seems to be losing leaf coloring, it may be getting too much direct sunlight; try reducing the amount for a few weeks. Reduce amounts, too, if humidity remains very high for any more than three days at a time.

Temperature Ideally, episcias should be grown in a daytime temperature of 70°–75°F, with a nighttime drop of 5°. They do best in temperatures above 60° and below 85°. They need high humidity; keep pots on trays of moist pebbles. Episcias thrive in terrariums (see page 54).

Watering Water plentifully as often as necessary to keep the potting mixture thoroughly moist, but do not let pots stand in water (except for *E.* 'Cygnet,' which does best if its roots are kept very wet). If the temperature falls below 60°F, give only enough water during the cool period to keep the mixture from drying out. Use water at room temperature in order to avoid damaging roots.

Feeding At every watering apply a liquid fertilizer containing equal amounts of nitrogen, phosphate, and potash, at one quarter of the recommended strength.

Potting and repotting Use an equal-parts combination of sphagnum peat moss, perlite, and vermiculite. The best containers are shallow pots, pans, or hanging baskets, since episcia roots spread just below the surface of the potting mixture. A wide surface area also allows stolons to root down. Repot when roots seem likely to fill the pot (see page 426). Move nearly pot-bound plants into slightly larger containers, or trim the root ball by about one-third and repot the plants into the same container, adding fresh mixture as required.

Propagation Because leaf clusters at the tips of stolons constantly put down roots, there is never a lack of new plants. Simply cut through a stolon with a sharp knife, pot the rooted plantlet, and treat it in exactly the same way as a mature episcia.

Special points Keep a careful watch for infestations of aphids on young leaves (see page 454).

Erica

ERICACEAE

French heather
E. hyemalis

THE genus *Erica* includes more than 500 species and many hybrids, all of which are popularly known as heaths or heathers. The few ericas grown indoors come from rather cool areas, and so require cool conditions. It is hard, therefore, to grow them satisfactorily, even on a short-term basis, in the home. For most growers they are best treated as temporary plants. Buy an erica just as its flowers begin to open, extend its life by keeping it cool, and discard it when it is no longer attractive.

All the plants named below are much-branched and woody-stemmed shrubs that do not grow more than 2 feet tall in pots. They have dense, needlelike leaves arranged in whorls on the stems and branches.

RECOMMENDED ERICAS

E. gracilis grows to $1\frac{1}{2}$ feet tall, with a spread of 1 foot. Its slender, erect stems bear tightly packed, hairless, pale green leaves $\frac{1}{8}$–$\frac{1}{4}$ inch long. The flower clusters consist of groups of four or more on each of several sideshoots. Flowers are globe-shaped, rose-pink, and about $\frac{1}{8}$ inch across, and they bloom in late fall and early winter. A form with white flowers is listed as either *E.g.* 'Alba' or *E. nivalis*.

E. gracilis

E. hyemalis (French heather) grows to 2 feet tall, with a spread of 15 inches. The erect branches bear tightly packed, threadlike, finely hairy, medium green leaves $\frac{3}{4}$ inch long. The pendent, tubular flowers, which bloom in winter, are white tinted with deep pink, up to $\frac{3}{4}$ inch long, and about $\frac{1}{4}$ inch across. They are produced from the main branches in tapering terminal flower heads. *E. hyemalis* is one parent of many hybrids with a variety of flower colors.

E. ventricosa is one of the few indoor species with a midsummer-to-fall flowering season. It grows to 2 feet tall, with a spread of 1 foot. The erect, rigid stems carry sharp-pointed, finely hairy, gray-green leaves $\frac{3}{4}$–1 inch long. The white or rosy flowers in the terminal clusters stand upright and are shiny, as if glazed. They are oval in shape, noticeably narrowing near the open end, and each flower is $\frac{1}{2}$–$\frac{3}{4}$ inch long and $\frac{1}{3}$ inch wide.

PROPER CARE

Light Grow ericas in bright light but out of direct sunlight, which would dry the leaves and cause them to fall.

Temperature The correct temperature range is 45°–50°F. If this cannot be maintained, keep the plants as cool as possible for the short time they will remain indoors. Increase humidity by standing pots on trays of moist pebbles, and mist-spray leaves daily.

The leaves of ericas become brittle and drop off if the air is too dry. For increased humidity mist-spray them daily, preferably with rainwater.

Watering Water ericas plentifully, often enough to keep the potting mixture thoroughly moist. Indoor ericas should never be permitted to dry out at the roots. Use either distilled water, rainwater, or water obtained from defrosting a refrigerator (which is simply atmospheric moisture that has become frozen). Water from the faucet often contains lime or other impurities to which ericas are extremely sensitive.

Feeding There is no need to feed these temporary plants.

Potting and repotting A purchased erica will be growing in a suitably lime-free potting mixture. Do not attempt to repot the plant.

Propagation Home propagation of ericas is not practicable. Healthy plants can usually be bought every year at the appropriate season.

Eriobotrya
ROSACEAE

Chinese loquat
E. japonica

ERIOBOTRYA *japonica* (Chinese loquat or Japanese plum), the only species of this small genus grown indoors, is a small tree with broad, olive green leaves that look embossed because the surface is raised above the lighter-colored veins. Young plants form a woody stem that eventually branches. The pointed-elliptic leaves, carried horizontally on short stalks, are 6–10 inches long and 3–6 inches wide. New leaves are sparsely covered with short, white hairs, which give them a silvery look, and their undersides may be slightly rust-colored. As leaves mature, the hairs and rusty color will disappear.

In warm climates, outdoor plants bear edible fruit, and potted eriobotryas are raised from the hard central seed (the stone) of the fruit. Although plants can grow 8–10 feet tall indoors, they are unlikely to produce flowers or fruit. Once eriobotryas become too big, they begin to lose their lower leaves and should be discarded.

PROPER CARE

Light Give these plants bright light, with at least two hours every day of direct sunlight.

Temperature Normal room temperatures are suitable, but eriobotryas do best if given a two- to three-month winter rest at 50°–55°F.

Watering During the active growth period water plentifully, as often as necessary to keep the potting mixture thoroughly moist, but never let the pot stand in water. During the rest period, if any, water only enough to keep the mixture from drying out.

Feeding Apply standard liquid fertilizer every two weeks to actively growing plants.

Potting and repotting Use a soil-based potting mixture (see page 429). Move plants into pots one or two sizes larger every spring until maximum convenient pot size (probably 8–10 inches) is reached. Thereafter, topdress annually with fresh potting mixture (see page 428).

Propagation Propagate in spring from eriobotrya stones (pits), which can be obtained occasionally from nurserymen. The fruits themselves (known as loquats) are also available in many food stores. In spring sow a single stone in a 3-inch pot of moistened rooting mixture (see page 444), and stand the pot in bright filtered light. Keep the rooting mixture just moist during the germination period of six to eight weeks. When the seedling has produced two or three leaves, transfer it to a 3-inch pot of standard mixture and treat it in the same way as a mature eriobotrya.

It may help to shorten the germination period of an eriobotrya pit by soaking it for 24 hours before planting it in moistened rooting mixture.

Espostoa
CACTACEAE

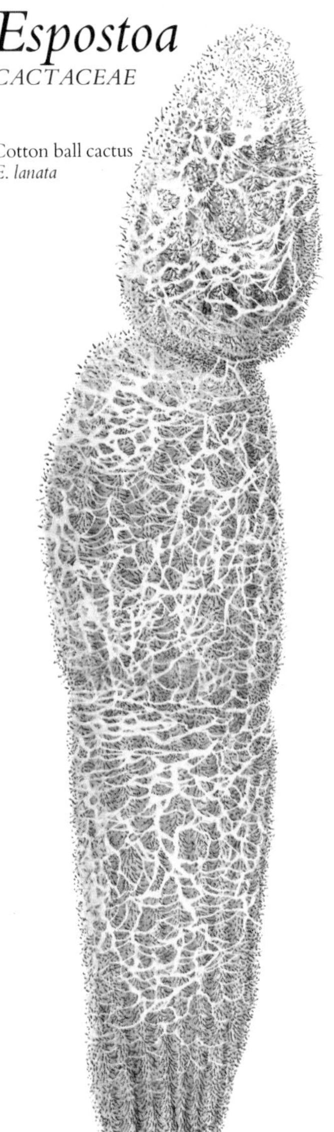
Cotton ball cactus
E. lanata

THERE are four species of *Espostoa*. The one most commonly grown indoors is *E. lanata* (cotton ball or new old man cactus). In a 6-inch pot this desert cactus will reach a maximum height of about 1 foot and a diameter of $1\frac{1}{2}$ inches after about ten years. The columnar green stem has some 20 low, broad ribs, with deep indentations in between. Each of the white areoles closely spaced along the ribs carries 12 yellowish white radial spines about $\frac{1}{2}$ inch long and 1 or 2 much longer, yellowish central spines. The areoles also produce silky, 1-inch-long, white hairs in such quantities that they hide most of the stem surface. *E. lanata* will not flower or branch as a house plant.

See also CACTI.

PROPER CARE

Light Always provide as much direct sunlight as possible for these espostoas.

Temperature During the active growth period (spring and summer) normal room temperatures are suitable. During the winter months *E. lanata* should be encouraged to rest. But since it comes from the warmer regions of Ecuador and Peru, this cactus should not be subjected to very low winter temperatures. If feasible, maintain a rest-period temperature of about 55°F.

Watering The roots of *E. lanata* rot if overwatered. Throughout the active growth period water sparingly, just enough to make the entire potting mixture barely moist at each watering, and allow the top two-thirds of the mixture to dry out before watering again. During the rest period give only enough to prevent the mixture from drying out completely.

Feeding If grown in a soil-based potting mixture, this slow-growing cactus does not need fertilizer. If grown in a peat-based mixture, apply a tomato-type liquid fertilizer every two weeks during the active growth period only.

Potting and repotting Provide a porous potting mixture by adding two parts of coarse sand or perlite to every three of either soil- or peat-based mixture (see page 429). A plant up to 3 inches tall may be grown in a 3-inch pot. Remove the plant from its pot and examine the roots every spring. If the root ball has become tightly packed, move the cactus into a pot one size larger. Otherwise, gently shake off the old mixture and replace the plant in its pot, which has been thoroughly cleaned. Add fresh mixture as necessary.

Propagation Nurserymen raise espostoas from seed, and young plants are generally sold when about two years old and 2–3 inches high. They are not difficult to grow from seed, however (see *CACTI*, page 119).

Special points Hairy cacti often pick up dust and look better if shampooed (see *CACTI*, page 120). The best time to shampoo an espostoa is just after repotting. Be sure to rinse the plant with clean water after using a detergent solution on it, and place it in an especially warm position to dry. If the lower hairs remain discolored after washing, this is probably due to age and cannot be prevented or repaired.

Eucalyptus

MYRTACEAE

Gum tree
E. gunnii

SPECIES of the genus *Eucalyptus* (gum tree, ironbark, or stringybark) are fast-growing trees and shrubs that make decorative foliage plants indoors, but only temporarily, since they grow very tall. Most have two distinct types of foliage: immature ("juvenile") leaves, and mature ones. Only the juvenile stage, when no flowers are produced, is normally reached in the home.

RECOMMENDED EUCALYPTUSES

E. globulus (Tasmanian blue gum) can be grown indoors only for a year or two, after which its rapid growth—3–4 feet a year—makes it too large. The juvenile leaves are almost stalkless, somewhat heart-shaped, 2–3 inches across, and gray-blue sparsely sprinkled with white powder.

E. gunnii is the most suitable indoor eucalyptus. Because ordinarily it cannot grow more than 12–18 inches a year in a pot, it remains a reasonable size for several years. Its juvenile leaves encircle the main stems, are more or less heart-shaped, 2–3 inches across, and of a dull gray-green color heavily sprinkled with white powder. The leaves of very young shoots are usually suffused with pink, particularly when the plant is grown in strong direct sunlight.

PROPER CARE

Light Eucalyptuses need full sunlight in order to maintain good leaf color.

Temperature These plants grow equally well in warm or cool rooms.

Watering While plants are actively growing, water moderately, moistening the potting mixture thoroughly at each watering, but let the top third of the mixture dry out before watering again. In winter, if plants are given a cool rest period (below 53°F), water only enough to keep the mixture from drying out completely.

Feeding Apply standard liquid fertilizer once every ten days, but only while plants are in active growth.

Potting and repotting Although some eucalyptuses cannot tolerate lime, these two species will grow well in almost any potting mixture. A rich soil-based mixture is best, however (see page 429). Move small plants into pots one or two sizes larger whenever necessary—certainly once every year, perhaps twice a year. Make sure that the potting mixture entirely covers the strange, swollen root structure.

Propagation Propagation is by seed. Sow seeds in spring in a moistened rooting mixture (see page 444) and place them in a heated propagating case (see page 444). While seeds are germinating, keep them in bright filtered light at a temperature of 70°–75°F. Seedlings (with two seed leaves) should appear within three weeks, and when each of them has developed two more leaves, pot the seedlings individually in 3-inch pots of standard potting mixture for mature plants. They can then be moderately watered—enough to make the mixture moist, but allowing the top inch of the mixture to dry out between waterings. When roots appear on the surface of the mixture, indicating that they have filled the pots, move the young plants into pots that are one size larger and treat them in exactly the same way as mature specimens.

Euonymus

CELASTRACEAE

E. japonica 'Microphylla Variegata'

THE genus *Euonymus* includes several species of bushy shrub with rigid, woody, much-branching stems. Only the variegated-leaved forms of one species, *E. japonica,* are generally grown indoors. They are difficult to grow in many homes since they need bright light without much warmth. Flowers are not produced indoors.

RECOMMENDED EUONYMUSES

***E. japonica* 'Albomarginata'** has medium green stems marked with yellow or cream-colored patches when young. As stems age they turn brown. Leathery, pointed-oval, slightly tooth-edged leaves are $1\frac{1}{2}$–$2\frac{1}{2}$ inches long, 1–2 inches wide, medium green with narrow white margins, and have $\frac{1}{2}$- to 1-inch-long stalks. The plant can grow 4 feet tall.

***E.j.* 'Aureo-variegata'** differs from *E.j.* 'Albomarginata' in that its leaves are blotched with yellow and lack the white margin.

***E.j.* 'Mediopicta'** differs in having a large, bright yellow patch in the middle of each leaf.

***E.j.* 'Microphylla Variegata'** is entirely different from the other three. Its stems are thin and dark green, and the plant grows only 18 inches tall. The leaves are very small, 1 inch long, $\frac{1}{8}$ inch wide, and dark green with narrow white margins. They have $\frac{1}{4}$-inch-long stalks.

PROPER CARE

Light During the active growth period provide bright filtered light. In winter, however, these plants must have three to four hours a day of direct sunlight (unaccompanied by any undue warmth).

Temperature During the active growth period these plants prefer cool conditions—between 55° and 60°F—but can tolerate indoor temperatures up to 65°. During the winter rest period they do best if kept at 50°–55°. In temperatures above 60° stand pots on trays of moist pebbles.

Watering During the active growth period water moderately, allowing the top half-inch of the potting mixture to dry out between waterings. In the winter rest period water sparingly—just enough to keep the mixture from drying out.

Feeding Apply standard liquid fertilizer every two weeks during the active growth period only.

Potting and repotting Use a soil-based potting mixture (see page 429). Move plants into pots one size larger every spring until they have reached maximum convenient size. Thereafter, topdress plants with fresh mixture annually (see page 428).

Propagation Take tip cuttings about 3 inches long in spring or in late summer. Trim each cutting to just below a pair of leaves, remove the lower leaves, and dip the cut end in hormone rooting powder. Plant the cuttings in a shallow tray containing a moistened equal-parts mixture of peat moss and coarse sand or perlite. Enclose the cuttings in a plastic bag or propagating case (see page 443), and stand them in bright filtered light. The cuttings may take up to six or eight weeks to root, but they should need no more water during this period. When rooting occurs, transfer the cuttings, two or three together, into 3- or 4-inch pots of soil-based mixture, and treat them as adults.

Special points Euonymuses are susceptible to a mildew disease that shows up as a white powder scattered over leaves and stems (see page 456). As a precaution, spray plants with a fungicide (see page 459) twice a year.

Euphorbia

EUPHORBIACEAE

THE genus *Euphorbia* (which includes the plants commonly called spurges) comprises more than 1,600 species of very variable form, habit of growth, and size. Some are prized for the colorful bracts that surround their insignificant flowers, some for their cactuslike form. Those grown as house plants may be soft-leaved shrubs, small trees, or heavily spined succulents. All have a milky juice (latex), which flows freely if a plant is cut or damaged, but which can be stopped by wetting the wound, for water causes the latex to coagulate. The juice can irritate sensitive skins; that of some species is poisonous and acrid, and it is therefore advisable to place euphorbias where they are unlikely to be knocked and out of the reach of young children.

Because their requirements are so varied, indoor euphorbias cannot all be treated as a single group. They are therefore separated here into three groups according to type and cultural requirements. The first group of house plant euphorbias all belong to the species *E. milii,* a spiny shrub. The second group includes all forms of *E. pulcherrima* (the poinsettia). In the third group are *E. pseudocactus* and *E. tirucalli,* two succulent types.

Euphorbia milii

The plant commonly called crown of thorns or Christ plant is one of the most popular euphorbias. It has been known by several Latin names (including, especially, *E. splendens),* but botanists now classify the species as *E. milii* with *E.m. splendens* as a variety of it. A dense shrub up to 3 feet tall, it has $\frac{1}{2}$-inch-thick dark brown stems armed on all sides and at frequent intervals with sharp spines of varying lengths (mostly around $\frac{3}{4}$ inch). Clusters of bright green, elliptic, 2- to-$2\frac{1}{2}$-inch leaves, which are produced near the growing tips of the stems, last for several months before dropping off, leaving the spiny stems permanently bare. Old leaves are not replaced and new ones will appear only on new terminal growth.

Flowers are tiny, but each is surrounded by a pair of $\frac{1}{2}$-inch kidney-shaped, bright red or yellow bracts, which look like petals. Clusters of

Crown of thorns
E. milii

from two to six of these paired, flowerlike bracts appear on 2-inch stalks at the ends of actively growing spiny stems; they are not produced on the old bare stems. A sticky substance on the flower stalks adheres to the fingers if touched. The main flowering season normally lasts from early spring through late summer, but flowering can be continuous if plants get exceptionally good light.

A number of forms are available, some of which have not yet been given varietal names. One, a shrub scaled down in all its parts, has almost circular leaves, smaller red bracts, and spines so soft that the stems can be handled without injury. Another form, *E.m. hislopii,* has 2- to 2½-inch-thick stems armed with inch-long spines; its lance-shaped leaves are an inch long, and its red or pink bracts are up to an inch across. *E.m. splendens* differs from the species in that it can grow 6 feet tall, its stems are ¾ inch thick, and its leaves are more oblong in shape than those of *E. milii*.

PROPER CARE

Light *E. milii* needs all the sun it can get. The brighter and more constant the sunlight, the longer its flowering season will be.

Temperature Warm rooms and dry air suit these plants, though they can, if necessary, tolerate temperatures as low as 55°F. If the air becomes any colder, leaves are likely to begin falling prematurely.

Watering Water plants grown in normal room temperatures moderately, enough to make the entire potting mixture moist, but allowing the top inch of the mixture to dry out between waterings. After the main flowering season ends, give a little less water; and if room temperature falls below 60°F for a long time, let the top half of the mixture dry out between waterings. Never let the roots dry out completely for dry roots cause premature leaf-fall.

Feeding Apply standard liquid fertilizer every two weeks from late spring to early fall. If plants are in such an ideal position that they continue to flower during the winter, feed them once a month.

Potting and repotting Use a combination of two-thirds of soil-based potting mixture (see page 429) and one-third of coarse sand or perlite for good drainage. Move plants into pots one size larger in early spring every second year. Older plants that have reached maximum convenient pot size should be topdressed (see page 428) with fresh potting mixture. It is essential to pack the mixture firmly around the roots of the plant when potting these euphorbias.

Propagation New plants can be raised from short tip cuttings taken in spring and early summer. Use a sharp knife or razor blade to cut off growing tips 3 or 4 inches long, and stop the latex flow immediately by spraying the old plant and dipping the cuttings in water. Allow cuttings to dry out for a day before setting them in small pots containing a slightly moist equal-parts mixture of peat moss and sand or perlite. It is important not to let the mixture become more than *slightly* moist; if too wet, the cuttings will rot before they can produce roots. Place the pots where they get bright light, but without direct sunlight, at normal room temperature, and make the mixture just barely moist, allowing the top two-thirds to dry out between waterings. When rooting occurs (in five to eight weeks), move the young plants into the standard soil-based potting mixture and treat them as mature specimens after they have made around 2 inches of top growth.

Because E. milii *is one of the spiniest of house plants, you must be particularly careful when taking cuttings.*

Poinsettia
E. pulcherrima

Euphorbia pulcherrima

The poinsettia (Christmas star, lobster plant, or Mexican flame leaf), which has become an essential element of the Christmas scene, is the descendant of a 6-foot-tall shrub that grows wild in Mexico. Growers in Scandinavia and California developed the strains that have been scaled down for use indoors. All poinsettias are winter-flowering shrubs notable for their colored bracts. Modern forms are often no taller than 12–15 inches with lobed or fiddle-shaped leaves that are 4–6 inches long, toothed and colored deep green etched with paler vein markings. The greenish yellow flowers are insignificant, but each cluster of tiny flowers is surrounded by 10 to 20 attractively colored bracts, which look like narrowly pointed (or roughly heart-shaped) broad leaves. In the most showy forms, these leaflike bracts are 8–10 inches long. There are many varieties, of which some of the most popular have been named by the California grower Paul Ecke for members of his family. Among them: 'Barbara Ecke Supreme,' a much-branching plant with very large cardinal red bracts closely surrounding the central flowers, and 'Mrs Paul Ecke,' with fewer stems and blood red bracts; also worth mention is 'Ecke's White,' which has long-lasting creamy white bracts.

Commercial growers subject their plants to a strict regimen that is almost impossible to follow in the average home. All poinsettias are short-day plants—i.e., flower-bud and bract formation can be initiated only by an eight-week period of no more than 10 hours of light and no less than 14 hours of total, uninterrupted darkness per day—and this can be achieved only through a high degree of control. In addition, the plants are treated with a dwarfing chemical that effectively reduces stem length. The resultant short-stemmed plants crowned by large and handsome bracts are normally sold when they are in full bloom in early winter, but they may also be timed for Easter.

PROPER CARE

Keep a potted poinsettia at normal room temperature in bright filtered light—for instance, full sunlight filtered through a translucent blind or curtain—and out of drafts. Water only when slightly drooping foliage indicates the need; the potting mixture should then be thoroughly saturated. No feeding is necessary. Under favorable conditions, the bracts will remain attractive for two months or even longer. Thereafter, most people discard the plant, but some amateur growers do try to keep poinsettias and bring them into flower again. This involves the following strict program (based on the assumption that the plant to be preserved has flowered around Christmas time):

After the bracts have faded and fallen, cut top growth down to 1 or 2 inches from the base, and allow the potting mixture to become almost—but never completely—dry. When growth stops, keep the dormant plant at normal room temperature, in bright filtered light until April; then flood it with water. The plant, still in its old pot, will soon begin to grow again. Two ways of proceeding are then possible. You can take 3-inch-long tip cuttings from the new sideshoots and root them to make new plants. Alternatively, you can allow the stump of the old plant to develop an entire new season's growth.

If you take tip cuttings, the cut ends should be treated with water to seal in the latex, and they should then be inserted in small pots containing a mixture of equal parts of peat moss and coarse sand or perlite. Keep the pots at normal room temperature in filtered sunlight and water only enough to make the mixture barely moist. Allow the top two-thirds to dry out between waterings. When rooting has occurred (normally in three or four weeks) and the cuttings are growing actively, move them into pots of fresh soil-based potting mixture (see page 429). If, instead of taking cuttings, you retain the old plant, shake off all the old potting mixture when the plant starts to grow again. Replant the newly growing poinsettia in fresh soil-based mixture. Warning: Do not use a larger pot than the original one for either a rooted cutting or a newly growing old plant. Bigger pots merely encourage the rapid growth of lush foliage at the expense of flowers and bracts; the result is likely to be a huge plant unrecognizable as a poinsettia.

Once repotted, treat the young plant or restarted old one as a purchased plant, except that it should be given monthly applications of a standard liquid fertilizer, until mid-September. Thereafter, it is vital to do precisely what commercial growers do: Give the plant no less than 14 hours of darkness per day—and it *must* be total darkness, unbroken even by the glow of a small light bulb. Obviously, this is a very difficult task in most homes. Moreover, even if such a regimen can be followed for the necessary eight weeks, the resultant plant will still be much taller than commercially produced poinsettias. The dwarfing chemical used by professional growers is rarely available for use by amateurs.

Succulent euphorbias

There are many succulent euphorbias, a number of which make excellent house plants, but only two will be discussed here: *E. pseudocactus,* because it is a good example of several similar cactuslike euphorbias; and *E. tirucalli,* because of its unusual, fascinating sticklike stems. Both types are grown for their decorative stems. Neither normally flowers indoors.
See also SUCCULENTS.

RECOMMENDED SUCCULENT EUPHORBIAS

E. pseudocactus is a thorny succulent shrub that can grow to 5 feet tall. As its name implies, it closely resembles a true cactus, with several upright leafless stems, which are four- or five-sided. These stems have yellowish fan-shaped markings on a bright green or grayish green background; they are $1\frac{1}{2}$–2 inches thick, but nipped in at 4-inch intervals all along their length, and have $\frac{1}{2}$-inch-long spines that lie in pairs along the prominent outer ridges. There is also a spineless form, *E.p. lyttoniana.*

E. pseudocactus

E. tirucalli (milkbush, finger tree, pencil tree, or rubber euphorbia) can grow 30 feet tall in the wild, but the house plant rarely exceeds 4 or 5 feet. When the plant is young, the many-branched stems carry minute leaves, but these soon disappear, leaving the stems smooth, cylindrical, glossy green, and pencil-thick. Most of them stand upright, producing branches by forking into two equal-size sections at frequent intervals.

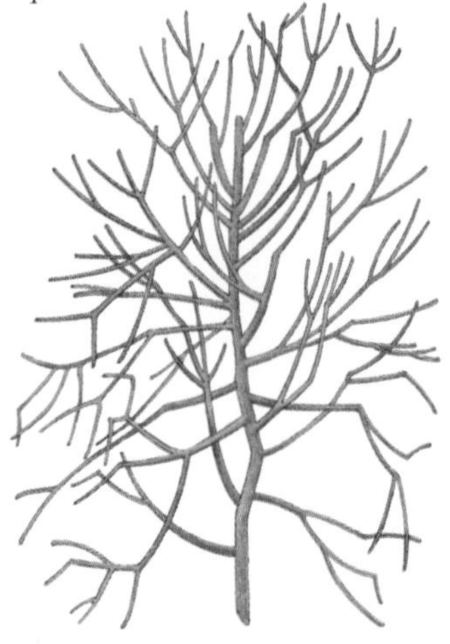

E. tirucalli (milkbush)

PROPER CARE

Light The succulent euphorbias need full sunlight all year long.

Temperature Normal room temperatures are suitable during the active growth period (spring, summer, and early fall), but these plants do best if given a winter rest period at 55°F, or even a few degrees lower.

Watering During the active growth period water sparingly, as much as necessary to make the entire potting mixture barely moist, but allow the top two-thirds to dry out between waterings. In mid-fall gradually reduce the amount of water given. During the winter rest period water only enough to keep the mixture from drying out.

Feeding Apply standard liquid fertilizer every two weeks during the active growth period.

Potting and repotting Use an equal-parts combination of soil-based potting mixture (see page 429) and coarse sand or perlite. Provide extra drainage by putting plenty of clay-pot fragments in the bottom of pots. Move plants into pots one size larger every spring; 6- to 8-inch pots should be the biggest needed.

Propagation Take stem cuttings in late spring or early summer. These succulent euphorbias produce a particularly large amount of milky sap, and it is essential to stop the flow of latex at the cut ends quickly by spraying the wound of the parent and dipping the cut end of the cutting in water. Allow each cutting to dry for several days before planting it in a moistened equal-parts mixture of peat moss and sand or perlite. After filling the pot with mixture, sprinkle coarse sand on the surface in the area where the stem is to be inserted. This will facilitate rooting and help prevent the possibility of stem rot. Leave the container uncovered at normal room temperature in a position where it gets sunlight filtered through a translucent blind or curtain, and water just enough to keep the mixture barely moist. Rooting should take place in six to eight weeks; once the young plants have begun to make new growth, thus indicating that rooting has occurred, pot them up in the normal mixture and treat them as mature plants.

Propagating a succulent euphorbia

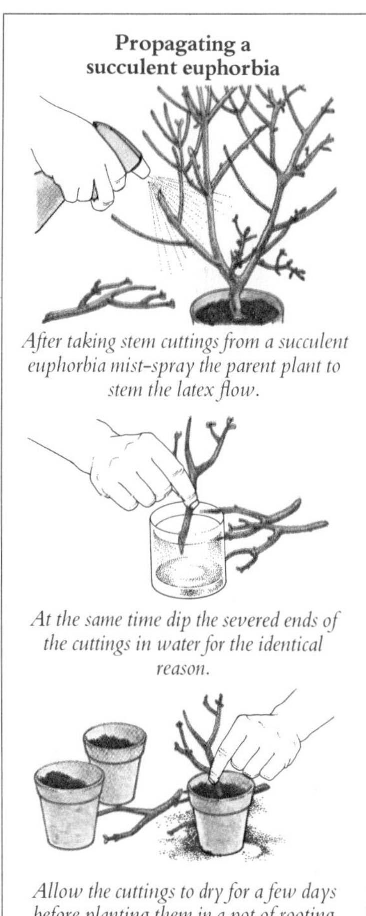

After taking stem cuttings from a succulent euphorbia mist-spray the parent plant to stem the latex flow.

At the same time dip the severed ends of the cuttings in water for the identical reason.

Allow the cuttings to dry for a few days before planting them in a pot of rooting mixture.

Exacum

GENTIANACEAE

German violet
E. affine

EXACUM *affine* (German or Arabian violet), the only species of this small genus generally grown indoors, is a profusely flowering perennial usually treated as an annual, to be enjoyed when in flower but discarded as winter approaches. Plants are raised commercially from seed either sown in early fall, over-wintered in a greenhouse, and finally potted up in early summer, or else sown early in spring; in the latter case the resultant plants are smaller and flower slightly later. The best time to buy an exacum is just as its first flowers begin to open, after which it should continue to bloom for several months.

On newly acquired exacums the stems are usually 3–4 inches long, but they lengthen to 9–12 inches in the course of the summer and fall. The leaves are 1 inch long, oval, shiny, and olive green, and they grow on ½-inch-long leafstalks clustered thickly on the stems. The flowers are pale lavender blue, have prominent golden yellow stamens, and are saucer-shaped, ½ inch across, and fragrant.

E.a. 'Atrocaeruleum' has darker lavender flowers; *E.a.* 'Blithe Spirit' has white flowers; *E.a.* 'Midget' is a dwarf-growing form with bright blue flowers.

PROPER CARE

Light Keep indoor exacums in bright light, but out of strong direct sunlight.

Temperature These plants will flourish in normally warm room temperatures, but they need high humidity. Keep pots on trays of moist pebbles, and spray plants regularly.

Watering Water plentifully as often as necessary to keep the potting mixture thoroughly moist.

Feeding Apply standard liquid fertilizer every two weeks as long as plants continue to flower.

Potting and repotting Use a soil-based potting mixture (see page 429). Spring-sown seedlings will live their four-month flowering life in a 3½- or 4-inch pot; older plants should be moved into 5-inch pots as necessary.

Special points Pick off flowers as they fade. This ensures a prolonged flowering period.

Pick off dead flowers to deprive an exacum of the chance to propagate itself. It will then continue to produce flowers in its effort to set seed.

Fatshedera

ARALIACEAE

THERE is only one fatshedera, *F. lizei* (commonly called aralia-ivy, botanical wonder, ivy-tree, or tree ivy). This is a bigeneric hybrid—a cross between species of two distinct genera, which are in this case *Fatsia japonica* 'Moseri' and *Hedera helix hibernica* (Irish ivy). In the hybrid the fatsia's wide spread has been replaced by smaller leaves on shorter stalks; the hedera's tough constitution has been retained without its tendency to sprawl; and the easy cultural needs of both remain. The plant has thin, erect stems that carry long-stalked leaves all along their lengths. Leaves are shiny, usually five-lobed, and up to 8 inches wide. A variegated form, *F.l.* 'Variegata,' has white markings, mainly on leaf edges.

Fatshederas normally grow 3–4 feet tall. They tend to flop over with increasing height and so need some support; thin stakes are ideal. Several young plants can be planted in one pot to produce a bushy effect.

PROPER CARE

Light Fatshederas adapt easily to most conditions but do best in medium light at or near a slightly shaded window. They should not be kept too far away from the window because too little light can result in thin, elongated main stems. *F.l.* 'Variegata,' which grows rather slowly, needs bright light but not strong sunlight.

Temperature While actively growing, this hybrid can tolerate a wide range of room temperatures. It prefers a cool position (below 50°F) during the rest period but will survive well enough in heated rooms provided the air is reasonably humid; stand the pot on a tray of moist pebbles. *F.l.* 'Variegata' likes more warmth at all times. Keep it above 60° even during the rest period.

Watering During the active growth period water moderately, allowing the top half-inch of the mixture to dry out between waterings. During the rest period, if any, reduce the amount, giving just enough to keep the mixture from drying out. Otherwise, continue to water as before to prevent the leaves from falling.

Feeding Apply standard liquid fertilizer every two weeks during the active growth period only.

Botanical wonder
F. lizei

Potting and repotting Use a soil-based potting mixture with the addition of one-third extra peat moss (see page 429). Well-established plants can be moved into pots one size larger every year; they should be planted very firmly, and new—possibly longer—stakes should be inserted to support the developing stems. After maximum convenient pot size is reached, annual topdressing with fresh mixture during the spring will usually suffice (see page 428).

Propagation Tip cuttings 3–4 inches long will root quickly if taken just as new growth begins, planted in a moistened peat-based mixture, enclosed in a plastic bag to maintain a moist atmosphere, and kept at a temperature of 60°–70°F in a position with medium light. When the cutting has rooted, uncover the plant and begin to water moderately, allowing a full inch of the mixture to dry out between waterings. Apply standard liquid fertilizer every two weeks. Ten weeks later, move the new plant into a slightly larger pot of the mixture for adult fatshederas and treat it as a mature specimen.

As fatshederas age, they lose their lower leaves; and plants that have become bare at the base are best used for cuttings. The old plants may be left in their pots, where they will sprout again. Alternatively, fatshederas can be air layered (see page 440).

Special points Keep a watch for aphids, particularly at the start of the active growth period. Scale insects and red spider mites are other possible pests. (See pages 454–455).

Fatsia

ARALIACEAE

FATSIA *japonica* (also known as *Aralia japonica* or *Fatsia sieboldii*), popularly called Japanese fatsia or aralia, is the only species of the genus. It has been used for over a century as both a garden plant and a decorative pot plant. A quick-growing shrub with woody stems that branch rather sparsely, especially on indoor plants, it often consists of a single stout stem bearing a large rosette of leaves at the apex. Plants can reach a height of 4–5 feet in two to three years. The leaves are shiny, 6–18 inches wide, and deeply incised into seven to nine lobes (looking like a huge many-fingered hand); and they are held on stalks up to 12 inches long.

Outdoors, the foliage is leathery and dark green, but indoors the plant produces softer and usually larger light green leaves. Young unfolding leaves are very tender and easily damaged; any blemish on them becomes magnified in maturity and never disappears again.

Outdoor plants annually produce large heads of white flowers in small individual clusters, but these seldom appear indoors except on old plants kept in very cool conditions.

A strain developed in France, known as *F.j.* 'Moseri,' is more compact, slower in growth, and with yellow coloring in the veins of the leaves. The leaves of a variegated form, *F.j.* 'Variegata,' have some white or cream coloring, especially on their edges; plants that are sometimes sold as *F.j.* 'Albo-marginata' appear to be identical with this form.

F. japonica
'Variegata'

PROPER CARE

Light Ideally, a fatsia should have bright light to keep its growth short and sturdy, but it can be grown in a sunless window provided that the light intensity is high. In poor light

Japanese fatsia
Fatsia japonica

the plant will become unattractively elongated, thin, and also very pale.

Temperature Fatsias grow best in cool conditions. In temperatures above 65°F the leaves become very soft and thin, and they are liable to flop, especially if humidity is low. For increased humidity in warm rooms stand plants on trays of moist pebbles. At temperatures slightly below about 60°, the leaves and stems acquire a desirable toughness and an ability to withstand temporary adverse conditions. Really cool conditions—around 45°—are advisable throughout the winter rest period.

Watering During the active growth period water plentifully as often as necessary to keep the potting mixture thoroughly moist. During the rest period water moderately, enough to make the entire mixture moist, but allow the top half-inch to dry out between waterings. If a fatsia is permitted to dry out completely, some of the lower leaves will drop off.

Feeding These strong-growing plants need feeding with standard liquid fertilizer every two weeks throughout the active growth period.

Potting and repotting Use a rich soil-based potting mixture (one with a higher than average amount of balanced fertilizer in it). Small plants should be moved into pots one size larger each spring until maximum convenient size has been reached. Fatsias require big pots (8–10 inches) in order to develop into large shrubs. Size may to some extent be restricted by the use of smaller pots, but this can result in distorted and unattractive growth. Clay pots are recommended. In plastic pots large plants such as these can easily become top-heavy.

Propagation The best way to propagate fatsias is by 2- to 3-inch stem cuttings, which can be taken at any time from new shoots that form at the base of plants. (Tip cuttings can also be used, but they usually carry large leaves, which make them hard to accommodate in a propagating case or plastic bag.) Strip the bottom leaves from cuttings, dip cut ends in hormone rooting powder, and plant the cuttings in 3-inch pots of a moistened mixture of equal parts peat moss and coarse sand or perlite. Enclose the potted cuttings in plastic bags or a heated propagating case (see page 444) and keep them at around 60°F in bright light filtered through a translucent blind or curtain. After four to six weeks new growth should begin to appear, indicating that cuttings have rooted. Remove the young potted plants from the bags or propagating case, begin watering just enough to keep the potting mixture barely moist. Once every two weeks apply standard liquid fertilizer. When plants are well established (probably between three and six months after the beginning of the propagation process), move them into slightly larger pots of the standard potting mixture for mature fatsias and treat them in exactly the same way as adult plants.

If fresh seed can be obtained, it is easy to raise these plants from seeds in a heated propagating case. Place seeds an inch deep in a moistened rooting mixture (see page 444) and keep them at a temperature of 60°–65°F in bright light filtered through a translucent blind or curtain. When seedlings are 1½–2 inches high, they can be planted in 2- to 3-inch pots of standard potting mixture and treated in the same way as mature fatsias.

Several new plants can be grown from one shoot as long as each piece contains at least one growing point (see inset).

Special points Fatsias can be kept from growing too big by drastic pruning. Half a plant's growth may be cut away in the spring. This also encourages branching.

Fatsia leaves drop off from time to time, and the loss of some of the lower, older ones should not automatically be taken as a signal that something is wrong.

In order to control the size of a fatsia, prune away up to half its growth in spring.

Faucaria

AIZOACEAE

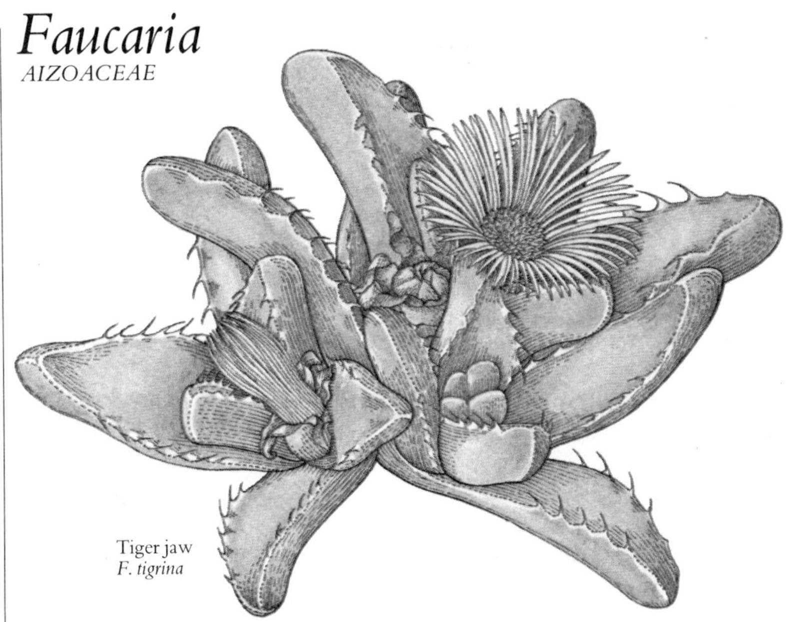

Tiger jaw
F. tigrina

FAUCARIAS are low-growing succulent plants, with four or five layers of leaves arranged in criss-cross opposite pairs, forming a thick, star-shaped rosette. Each pair of leaves is united at the base, and there are virtually no stems. The plants send out basal offsets that form crowded clumps. The roughly triangular leaves, which are usually edged with fiercely hooked teeth, have a flat upper surface, but the underside is convex (or "keeled"). Relatively large, daisylike flowers, which generally open in the afternoon, are produced from between the leaves in fall.
See also SUCCULENTS.

RECOMMENDED FAUCARIAS

F. tigrina (tiger jaw) has fleshy, pointed leaves $1\frac{1}{2}$–2 inches long and an inch broad at the base. Leaf color is grayish green marked with many small white dots. The teeth on the edges of young leaves interlock, but they later lengthen and separate to give a jawlike appearance. Flowers are golden yellow, stalkless, and can be up to 2 inches wide.

F. tuberculosa is like *F. tigrina* but has smaller leaves with raised, wartlike growths and many small white dots. Flowers are also a little smaller.

PROPER CARE

Light Faucarias must have at least three hours a day of direct sunlight all year long in order to flower.

Temperature During the active growth period normally warm room temperatures are suitable, but faucarias must have a cool winter rest period at a temperature around 50°F. Do not try to grow them if the combination of low temperature and winter sunlight cannot be achieved.

F. tuberculosa

Watering During the active growth period water faucarias plentifully as often as necessary to keep the potting mixture thoroughly moist, but never allow the pots to stand in water. During the winter rest period give only enough water to prevent the mixture from drying out.

Feeding During the active growth period only, apply standard liquid fertilizer at half-strength once a month. Too frequent feeding (or feeding at full strength) will result in soft, uncharacteristic growth.

Potting and repotting Use a mixture composed of two parts of soil-based mixture (see page 429) to one part of coarse sand or grit. Because faucarias have relatively little root, plant them in shallow pans or half-pots. When a clump has covered the surface of the mixture, move the plant into a container one size larger. Repotting should be necessary, however, only once in two or three years. The best time to pot is early spring.

Propagation Gently divide overcrowded clumps in late spring or early summer just after plants have restarted into growth. As individual plants are separated, some will come away with their roots attached. Insert each such rooted faucaria directly into a 2- or 3-inch container of the recommended potting mixture, and treat the new plant as a mature specimen. For the first week or two, however, keep the faucaria in medium light, well out of direct sunlight.

An individual plant without roots attached should be left unpotted for a few days to let the base of the plant dry up and harden. It may then be inserted in the recommended potting mixture. Be careful to surround the base with some additional coarse sand. This will help to prevent rotting and to encourage the development of roots. Keep the plant in medium light, and water only moderately until new growth indicates that rooting has occurred. Thereafter, treat the young plant as a mature faucaria.

Propagating rooted rosettes

In late spring remove the plant from its pot and divide the clump, making sure that each new plant will consist of at least one rooted rosette.

As soon as separated rosettes have been repotted, they can be treated as mature plants under temporarily reduced light.

FERNS

Ferns are foliage plants distinguished from almost all other plants in that they do not produce flowers and seeds but reproduce by means of spores. The main types of fern are characterized below, along with general advice on providing proper care. A list of ferns commonly grown indoors follows this article. Consult separate articles for discussions of individual genera.

There is no single family of ferns. These flowerless plants belong to several different families, and yet they have so many common characteristics that they can logically be discussed as a single group.

Wild ferns are distributed throughout the world. Those native to temperate areas, however, are of little interest to indoor gardeners, since they do not adapt well to the all-year-long warmth of the home. It is the ferns that grow naturally in warmer regions that are most generally suited to the growing conditions normally provided for house plants.

Many ferns are epiphytes. In other words, although their roots grow into the rotting vegetation that collects in the crevices of trees, they do not draw food from the trees upon which they are physically supported. But ferns can also be terrestrial. The terrestrial kinds thrive in the shady, humid atmosphere at the base of trees, or anywhere else at ground level where there is an adequate supply of leafmold-enriched soil for their roots. Both epiphytic and terrestrial ferns need high humidity to keep their fronds firm.

The fronds and feeding roots of most kinds of fern grow from rhizomes, which are fleshy stems that generally serve as storage organs. Rhizomes usually grow horizontally underground, but those of ferns of the genera *Phyllitis* and *Polystichum,* for instance, are stemlike, short, and branching. Rhizomatous stems of some blechnums look quite like thick tree trunks. Rhizomes of other ferns can creep or cling aboveground, as in the davallias and polypodiums, or they can extend horizontally underground, as in the adiantums. Fern rhizomes are always alike, though, in that they are coated, to a greater or lesser degree, in a furry, scaly covering that is black, brown, or silvery white.

The quantity of roots growing from the rhizome depends largely on the form of the rhizome itself. For instance, the underground rhizome of a terrestrial fern is certain to have a much denser root system than that of an epiphytic plant. In all types of fern though, the roots tend to be thin and wiry.

The fronds, which are a combination of stalk and leaflike blade, vary enormously in size and shape. Frond size can range in length from a few inches to several feet, and in width from an inch to as much as 3 feet. Frond stalks are virtually absent in plants of some genera (for instance, *Platycerium*), whereas in others, such as the polypodiums, they account for more than half the total length of the frond. The stalk, which may be green, brown, or black, extends into the frond blade, where it becomes the midrib. The color of the midrib, however, is normally the same as the color of the blade, not of the stalk.

In outline the blade of a fern frond may be simple and straplike, as in plants of the genus *Phyllitis*, or much divided and feathery, as in some aspleniums and blechnums. Among various shapes are the triangular fronds of adiantums and the startlingly antlerlike ones of the platyceriums. The separate segments of a compound (divided) fern blade are generally called pinnae (singular form: pinna). If a pinna is further divided, each segment of the pinna is correctly termed a pinnule. An extreme example of compound fronds is found among ferns of the genus *Davallia,* whose fronds can be quadripinnate—that is, with each pinna divided up completely into four separate sets of pinnules.

Since ferns are non-flowering plants, it follows that they do not produce seed for propagation. Instead, ferns reproduce themselves by means of spores, which are carried by the millions on some—not all—fronds. The spores are enclosed in spore cases called sori (singular form: sorus); and when these sori are ripe, they burst open to scatter the dust-fine spores. Clusters of sori are borne on the underside of a simple frond or on the underside of a pinna or pinnule in a compound frond. And the sori are arranged in a variety of special ways in

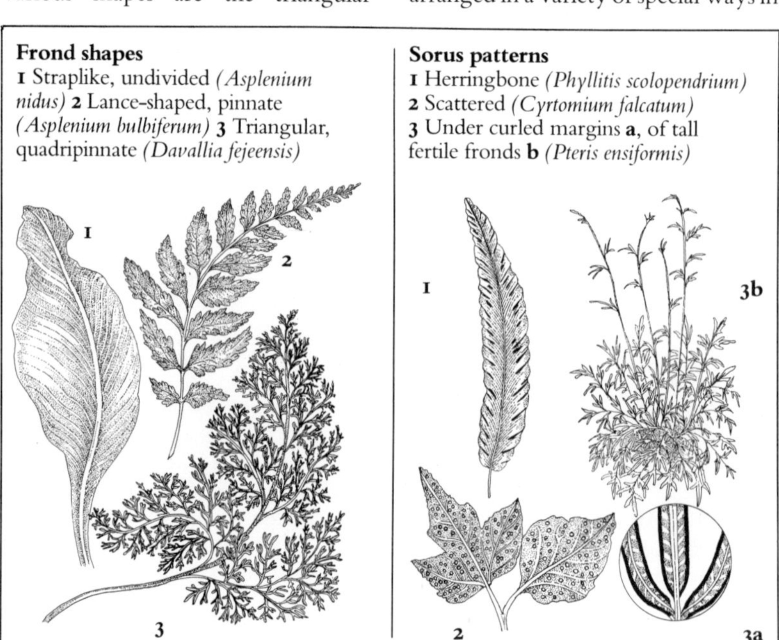

Frond shapes
1 Straplike, undivided *(Asplenium nidus)* **2** Lance-shaped, pinnate *(Asplenium bulbiferum)* **3** Triangular, quadripinnate *(Davallia fejeensis)*

Sorus patterns
1 Herringbone *(Phyllitis scolopendrium)*
2 Scattered *(Cyrtomium falcatum)*
3 Under curled margins **a**, of tall fertile fronds **b** *(Pteris ensiformis)*

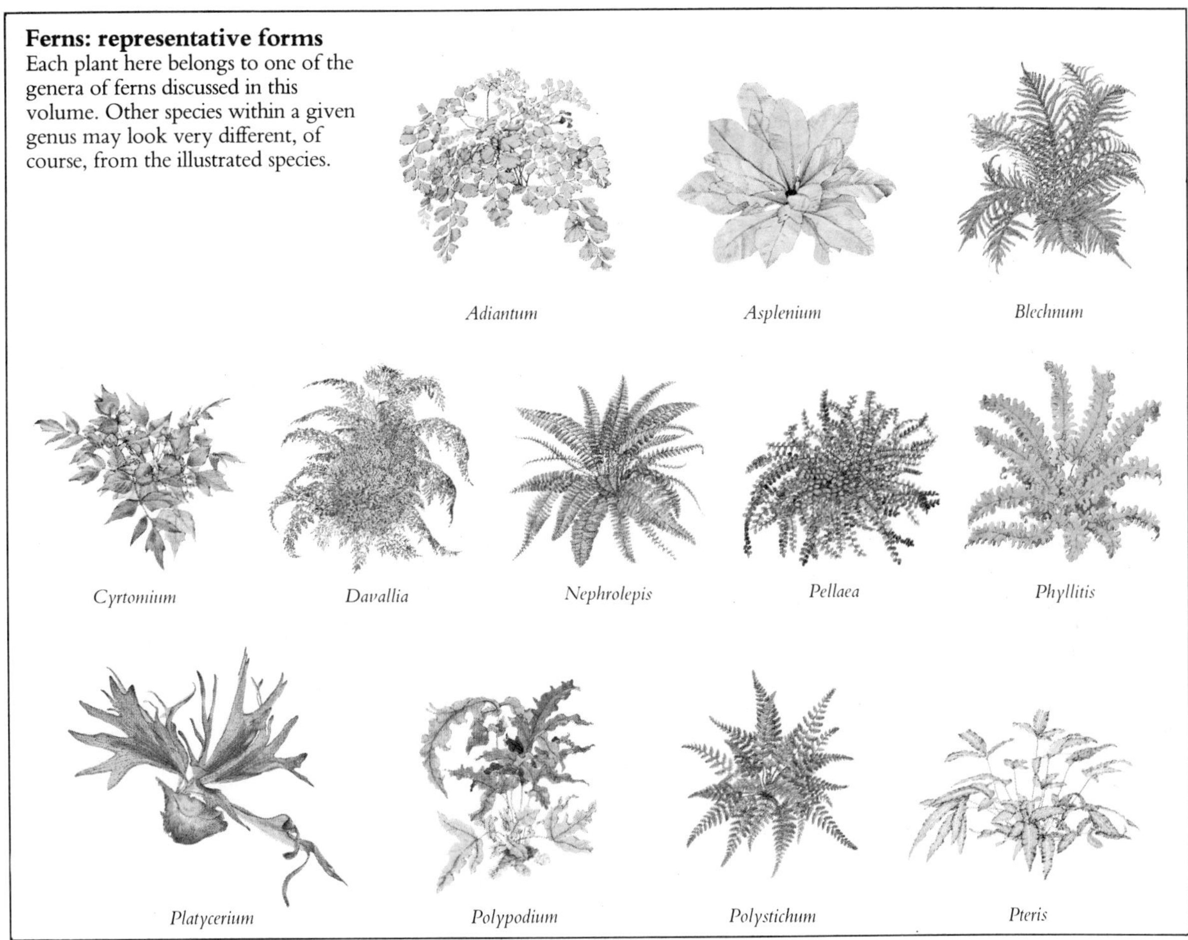

Ferns: representative forms
Each plant here belongs to one of the genera of ferns discussed in this volume. Other species within a given genus may look very different, of course, from the illustrated species.

Adiantum

Asplenium

Blechnum

Cyrtomium

Davallia

Nephrolepis

Pellaea

Phyllitis

Platycerium

Polypodium

Polystichum

Pteris

different kinds of plant. In fact, it is often possible to make an inspired guess as to the genus of a fern by the shape and position of its spore cases.

Certain ferns reproduce not only by means of spores but also by growing baby ferns on their fronds. The best example of this form of reproduction among the ferns that have become popular house plants is found in *Asplenium bulbiferum*. The little plantlets (generally known as bulbils, although they are not technically bulbs) can be easily detached and used for propagation (see below). At first each bulbil looks like nothing more than a small, round swelling. Gradually, as the swelling grows, minute fronds begin to unfurl and take on the shape of the parent fern.

Parts of a frond

Pinna
Pinnule
Midrib
Stalk
Rhizome

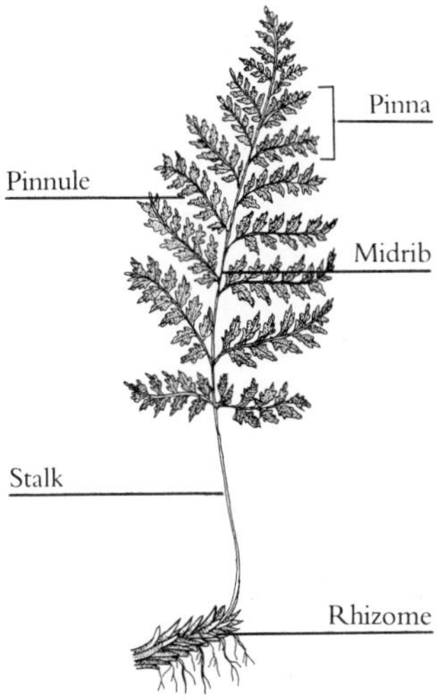

Often there can be as many as a dozen such plantlets growing on a single pinna. Under their weight the frond eventually droops down to ground level. If the base of a bulbil remains for a time on a suitable growing surface, the little plantlet will grow roots. In the wild the young fern then becomes independent of its parent, but natural rooting in this manner is unlikely to occur in the home.

Because ferns do not require direct sunlight or even particularly bright light, they are useful as decorative potted plants in many positions where other plants are often apt to languish. Most of them have the added advantage that if they are grown in conditions of warmth and fairly good light, they will continue in active growth and produce new fronds throughout the year. The only notable exceptions among common house plants are the adiantums, which benefit from a winter rest.

PROPER CARE

Light Although the native habitat of many indoor ferns is in tropical regions, they are invariably sheltered from direct sunlight by the foliage of the trees upon which or under which they grow. It is advisable, therefore, to give them either medium light or, at most, bright filtered light. Although direct sunlight will scorch the tender fronds of a plant at most times, however, early-morning winter sunlight will usually do no harm. In fact, this much sunshine will help to encourage continuous growth.

Many of these plants can tolerate the poor light of a dark corner for up to two or three weeks at a time, if necessary. They cannot continue to grow well, though, if the period of poor lighting lasts much longer.

To make sure that ferns grow evenly, turn each plant a quarter-turn around at two- or three-day intervals. This routine prevents the lopsidedness that occurs when fronds must all grow in the same direction in order to face the source of light.

Temperature Normal room temperatures ranging from 65° to 75°F are ideal for most kinds of fern. High humidity is essential along with warmth. Stand pots on trays of moist pebbles, and suspend saucers of water under hanging baskets at all times. Whenever the temperature remains above about 70° for more than a day or two, increase the humidity by mist-spraying the foliage at least once every day. Spraying should be done very carefully, however, since drops of water left on the fronds of certain kinds of fern (polypodiums, for instance) can mark and damage them. Spray with tepid, not with cold water, and hold the sprayer 2 feet away from the plant. At this distance the air around the plant becomes moist, while only a fine mist falls on the plant itself.

If, for any reason, indoor temperatures are permitted to fall below 65° in winter, there is no cause for concern. Virtually all ferns can tolerate temperatures down to about 50°. As the temperature falls, growth will slow down, and it will cease altogether at 50°, but without impairing the health of the plant. The fern will simply take a rest until the temperature rises again. During any such rest period watering should be drastically reduced (see below), but the plant still requires relatively high atmospheric humidity to prevent the fronds from wilting.

Watering The amount of moisture lost through the fronds of a fern is remarkable, even when the loss is reduced by the humidity of the surrounding atmosphere. Because of this, ferns generally need to be watered plentifully so that their roots are kept thoroughly moist (but never sodden) as long as temperatures remain at 60°F or above. The best way to water a fern is to stand the pot in a bowl and pour tepid water onto the potting-mixture surface, stopping as soon as the water begins to run out of the drainage holes into the bowl. During the next few minutes the water in the bowl will be drawn back into the potting mixture, and watering from above should again take place. Keep adding water in this manner until the excess remains in the bowl for about half an hour. Then remove the pot from the bowl, and

Stand the pot in a bowl, and water the mixture until water appears in the bowl. Allow this to be absorbed before watering again.

allow the mixture to drain for another half hour before replacing the fern.

Alternatively, ferns can be watered from below. This is simply a matter of pouring water into the bowl instead of onto the potting mixture, and continuing until water remains in the bowl for half an hour. Whichever method is used, some ferns do best if the potting mixture is allowed to dry out somewhat between waterings. Consult individual articles in the *A–Z Guide* for specific recommendations.

If indoor temperatures fall below 60° for more than two or three days, reduce the quantity of water given at each watering to only a moderate amount, and permit the top inch of the potting mixture to dry out before giving the plant just enough tepid water to moisten the mixture. If a fern fully enters a rest period (which is likely to happen only if the temperature drops down to 50°), make a further reduction. Until the temperature rises to 60° or above, water very sparingly, keeping the potting mixture just moist. All that the plant will need is enough to prevent the fronds from becoming limp. Too much water during a full rest period will almost certainly rot the roots of a fern.

If possible, use rainwater both for the roots and for mist-spraying the foliage of ferns. If there is no feasible alternative to the use of hard water from the faucet, make sure at least that the water is tepid or lukewarm. Some of the hardness can be boiled out of water, too (see page 423), but it is not necessary to do this. Ferns are generally as tolerant in this respect as in most others.

A fern growing in a basket can be a little more difficult to water than a potted plant. If the basket is small enough to be balanced in a bowl, it can be immersed for just long enough to moisten the potting mixture thoroughly. A larger basket may need to be watered in a sink or bathtub. However, the safest way to water ferns in baskets is to pour water gradually onto the surface of the mixture until it appears to be sufficiently moist. Though a rather tedious task, this method will ensure that the mixture does not become too wet.

Feeding Since all ferns are non-flowering foliage plants, lush growth is highly desirable. A fertilizer that encourages lushness is one in which there is a higher proportion of nitrogen than of phosphate and potash. It is also best to use a fertilizer that can be applied in liquid form. But all doses should normally be at only half-strength. Full-strength applications of nitrogen-rich fertilizer can cause root burn in many ferns.

Frequency of feeding depends on the type of mixture in which the plant is potted. An actively growing fern in soilless, peat-based potting mixture will do best if given fertilizer every two weeks. For a fern in soil-based mixture monthly feedings are sufficient because there are natural nutrients in the soil. During periods of slow growth, intervals between feedings should be longer, and fully resting plants should not be fed at all.

Occasional applications of a foliar feed are also advisable. These need not be at regular intervals. From time to time simply add some foliar feed to the water used in mist-spraying (see "Temperature," above).

Potting and repotting Ferns used as house plants grow in the wild in regions where there is always a plenteous supply of organic material in the soil. If the plant is epiphytic, it obviously has good drainage, and ground-level ferns in rain forests or jungles also live in comparatively porous earth. The potting mixture for an indoor specimen should therefore be rich in organic materials and must have good drainage.

The two potting mixtures generally recommended for ferns are suitable for either epiphytic or terrestrial plants. The epiphytes perhaps do best, however, in the first type of mixture: an equal-parts combination of peat moss, leaf mold, and coarse sand or perlite. The second type combines equal amounts of soil-based mixture and leaf mold, and it is particularly useful for large ferns because of its weightiness. A word of caution about using the soil-based mixture, though: Be sure that the soil has been sterilized (see "Potting mixtures," page 429). Add some charcoal granules to whichever of the two potting mixtures is used. Charcoal helps to prevent the mixture from turning sour.

Most ferns are not deep-rooted. The few that have deep roots (large blechnums, for example) need to be potted in standard containers, but shallow-rooted ferns do much better if lodged in shallow pans or half-pots, where their roots have plenty of room to spread out. In shallow containers, moreover, there is less chance for the potting mixture to become compacted and thus to block the necessary drainage. Several small, shallow-rooted ferns—phyllitises and some nephrolepises, for example—can also be grown together for display on a fern column. Keep such a column in medium light in a warm, humid position, and water the central column enough to keep the potting mixture and moss permanently moist.

Ferns with aboveground creeping rhizomes need a large surface area to spread over. Plant any such specimen in a container with a diameter two or three times its depth. If the specimen is extremely large, it will probably grow most successfully in a hanging basket because the rhizome can then creep over the whole basket surface. Large polypodiums, nephrolepises and davallias are in this category. They are good subjects for hanging baskets.

Repot a fern only when the roots have completely filled the pot (see page 426) or when a surface-creeping rhizome has covered the potting mixture and is beginning to spread beyond the rim. Under ideal conditions of light, warmth, watering, and feeding, ferns can require repotting every six or seven months. In less ideal conditions they can remain comfortably in the same container for up to two years. If repotting becomes necessary, try to do it in spring or early summer, and repot into a container only one size bigger. It is never a good idea to overpot a fern since if there is too much potting mixture in the container, the plant's watering needs will be more than met at each plentiful watering, and the mixture will remain too wet for the good of the roots.

After maximum convenient container size has been reached for any fern, the plant is perhaps best divided or used in some other way for propagation. It can be retained intact, however, if the root ball is trimmed by a third or a half. The fern can then be returned to its pot, which has been cleaned and filled with fresh mixture.

Propagation Depending on the type of fern, propagation is possible by one or more of several methods, all of which are best employed in early spring. The easiest method is division of the rhizome, but propagation by division is normally confined to plants (such as the adiantums or the polystichums) that have underground rhizomes. To divide a fern, begin by removing it from its container and carefully shaking the potting mixture away from the roots. Then, using a sharp knife, cut the rhizome into as many pieces as desired. Each piece can be quite small as long as there are a few fronds growing from it. Plant each piece of rhizome in a $2\frac{1}{2}$- to 3-inch pot containing either of the recommended potting mixtures. The mixture should be moist but not wet.

To aid recovery from the shock of division, the newly potted rhizome should be enclosed temporarily in a plastic bag or propagating case and placed in a warm, shady position. After a month or so, uncover the young fern gradually, watering very sparingly, over the course of the next three or four weeks. This will give it time to become accustomed to the less humid atmosphere of an open room. It can then be moved to its permanent position and treated as a mature plant.

For ferns with rhizomes that creep over the surface of the potting mixture the best method of propagation is to take tip cuttings of the rhizomes. The cutting should be made about two inches behind the growing tip of the rhizome, and there need not be a frond attached to the cutting. Place it on the surface of moistened potting mixture in a 3- or $3\frac{1}{2}$-inch half-pot, and secure the cutting lightly in position with a loop of wire. Enclose the

Making a fern column

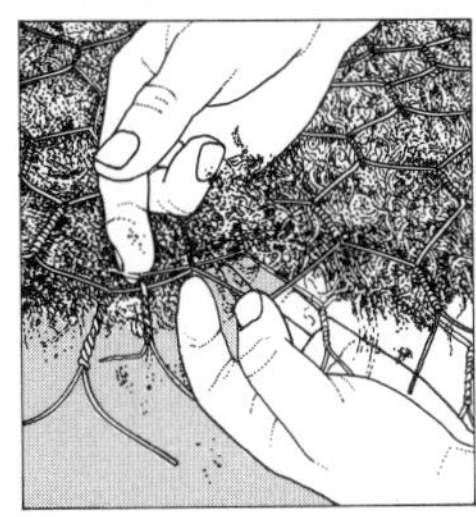

To create a display pole for a variety of ferns, begin by wrapping sphagnum moss loosely in chicken wire.

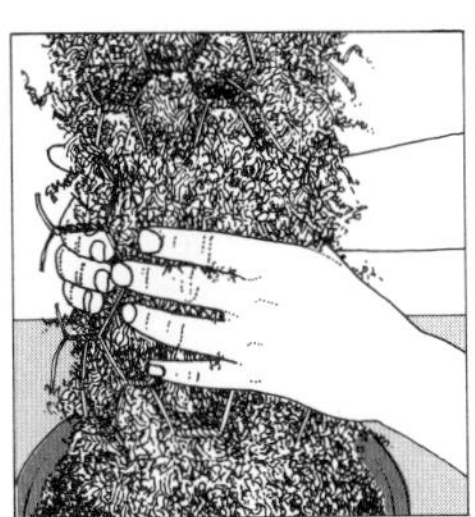

Shape the wire-enclosed cylinder of moss loosely around a pole embedded in a mixture-filled pot.

Pour standard mixture into all gaps between pole and moss. Plants will root into this mixture.

Tie off the top of the moss column with wire to hide the pole. The column now stands ready for its plants.

Start the display with a terrestrial fern such as a pteris. Make a hole for the root ball in the column.

Many sorts of fern can now be inserted in the same way. They will root into the mixture if it is kept moist.

whole in a plastic bag or propagating case, and place it in a warm, shady spot until the cutting has rooted, as evidenced by the growth of a tiny frond from the top. It can take four or five weeks for rooting to occur. Once the young frond has appeared, begin to uncover the rooted cutting, watering very sparingly and acclimatizing it to room atmosphere gradually over a period of two or three weeks. It can then be treated as a mature plant.

Tip cuttings of the runners that grow from the rhizomes of nephrolepises can be handled in similar fashion. Or if the runners are not cut away from the rhizome, they will root down into the potting mixture while still attached to the parent plant and can be cut off along with their roots. A rooted nephrolepis runner potted in a 3-inch container can be treated immediately as an adult fern.

For plants such as *Asplenium bulbiferum* the obvious way to propagate is by means of the baby ferns (bulbils) that grow on their fronds. Remove a bulbil with a piece of the pinna still attached to its base, and place it on the surface of moistened potting mixture in a $2\frac{1}{2}$-inch container. As in the propagation procedures for rhizome cuttings, enclose the bulbil in a plastic bag or propagating case until it has rooted, and uncover it gradually over about four weeks.

Growing ferns from spores Propagation from spores is not usually recommended for amateur growers since it takes much patience and special care. It is a highly gratifying procedure, however, for people who are willing to wait up to a year before anything looking like a young fern rewards their effort.

The first step of this method is to collect the spores. Choose a pinna with ripening sori. To test ripeness rub a finger tip against the sori; if the finger comes away looking slightly dusty, the spores are ready to be taken. Remove the pinna, place it underside down on a small sheet of smooth paper, and keep the paper in a warm position for a day or so. Meanwhile prepare the sowing medium, which may be either peat moss or leaf mold. Whichever it is, it must be sterilized and thoroughly moist. As a container, use either a $2\frac{1}{2}$-inch pot or small plastic box with a transparent lid. Fill the container with the moistened sowing medium to within $\frac{3}{4}$ inch of the top.

Propagating from a creeping rhizome

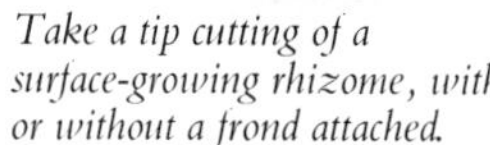

Take a tip cutting of a surface-growing rhizome, with or without a frond attached.

After placing the cutting on moist mixture in a pot, staple it loosely with wire.

Enclose the cutting in a plastic bag and keep it warm in medium light until it roots.

After about 24 hours innumerable spores should have been shed onto the paper. A gentle tap on the pinna will probably release many more. Distribute all the spores over the surface of the peat moss or leaf mold, and close the box lid or enclose the pot in a plastic bag. Then place the covered spores in a warm spot where they will get plenty of bright filtered light. Nothing is likely to happen for up to two to three months. The first sign of germination will be a slight greening of the sowing surface. From this point on begin to water the sowing medium, keeping it always moist but not sodden, so that humidity within the box or bag will be at a constantly high level. Gradually, then, a mosslike, green carpet will cover the surface. This carpet is composed of many small structures that represent the first stage in the life cycle of ferns but that are not at all shaped like young ferns.

When, after a further few months, tiny ferns are evidently starting to develop, prick out as many as desired into individual 1- to $1\frac{1}{2}$-inch pots (generally known as thumb pots) filled with the same sowing medium as that used for the spores. High humidity is still important for the delicate little ferns, which should therefore be kept well moistened in a plastic bag or propagating case placed in a warm spot where the young plants get bright filtered light. After the young ferns have attained a height of 1–2 inches, they will need to be fed. Give them a liquid nitrogen-rich fertilizer at one-eighth of the recommended strength once every two weeks. Move each plant to a pot one size larger when it has begun to fill its current pot with roots, and gradually increase fertilizer strength. By the time the young fern is ready to be moved into a 3-inch container, the plant is ready to survive and flourish in the recommended mixture for adult ferns.

Special points Ferns are susceptible to attack by several pests, and it is unfortunately true that certain insecticides are as apt to kill the fern as the pest. Never use an insecticide on a fern without a careful prior reading of the label. In many cases it will be found that pest control is possible without the use of exotic chemicals. For instance, aphids, which often attack young fronds, can be washed off with a weak detergent solution.

Denatured alcohol is an effective agent for control of two particularly troublesome pests, scale insects and mealy bugs. Scale insects are likely to occur along the veins on the undersurface of fronds. If a child's paint brush dipped in denatured alcohol is applied to the scales, they can be wiped off quite easily. Mealy bugs, sometimes found on new growth, can be treated in the same way. Try to use the alcohol sparingly on new growth, however, because too much of it can damage young fronds.

One other pest that must be mentioned is the eelworm, or nematode. This creature can enter a fern through the roots, and the first and only sign of infestation is distortion of the fronds. There is no known way to combat nematodes. Fortunately, they seldom infest ferns. One dependable form of insurance against infestation is the use of sterilized potting mixture.

For specific kinds of fern see:

Adiantum
Asplenium
Blechnum
Cyrtomium
Davallia
Nephrolepis
Pellaea
Phyllitis
Platycerium
Polypodium
Polystichum
Pteris

Ferocactus

CACTACEAE

Devil's tongue
F. latispinus

FEROCACTI (barrel or fishhook cacti) are a group of about 20 species of desert cactus noted for their stout spines, which are often hooked at the ends. (The prefix "fero-" comes from the Latin word for "fierce".) The roughly barrel-shaped stems of these plants do not normally produce either branches or offsets. In the wild most species can grow up to 5 feet tall and 3 feet wide. Potted specimens are unlikely to reach full maturity.

RECOMMENDED FEROCACTI

F. acanthodes can grow 3 feet tall and 1 foot across in cultivation, but as a house plant it is unlikely to need a pot larger than 6 inches. Specimens of suitable house-plant size are roughly spherical, with bright green stems that have about 20 broad, notched, wavy-edged ribs. The notches carry whitish areoles with sharp, red, curved, interlacing spines. The spines are sometimes attractively banded with yellow. The 10 radials are about 2 inches long and the 4 centrals (which are not hooked) are nearly twice this length. Spring blooming, yellow or orange flowers are unlikely to appear on indoor specimens.

F. fordii, a globular plant, attains an indoor diameter of about 6 inches. The grayish green stem has about 20 narrow, slightly notched ribs along which grayish areoles are spaced. Each areole has 15 needlelike, white, 1½-inch-long radial spines, and 4 brownish pink, stout, 2½-inch-long centrals. The lowest central spine is flattened, slightly hooked at the tip, and banded in a lighter color. Summer-blooming flowers are about 1½ inches across and pinkish white, striped with darker coloration. Flowers seldom appear before plants are many years old.

F. fordii

F. latispinus (devil's tongue) has a globular, grayish green stem that elongates as it ages. The stem has up to 12 broad, notched ribs. Whitish areoles in the notches carry 6 to 12 radial spines about 1 inch long and 4 central spines 1½ inches long. The radial spines are whitish, the central spines reddish; and the lowest spine of the red centrals is broader than the others and hooked (which explains the common name). The plant may eventually produce violet-colored flowers in summer, but only under ideal conditions. Although *F. latispinus* can reach an indoor height of 12 inches and a diameter of 8 inches in a 10-inch pot, the plant will take many years to achieve such dimensions. Most potted specimens are much smaller and retain their spherical shape.
See also CACTI.

PROPER CARE

Light In the wild, ferocacti are exposed to the full summer sun of desert regions. To make sure that they will have stout, highly colored spines, give the plants direct sunlight all year long. If possible, keep them in a sunny spot outdoors throughout the spring and summer months.

Temperature During the active growth period normally warm room temperatures are suitable. During the winter rest period keep these plants cool, but in temperatures well above freezing. A rest-period temperature of about 50°F is ideal.

Watering During the active growth period water moderately, enough to moisten the potting mixture at each watering, but allow the top half-inch of the mixture to dry out before watering again. During the winter rest period give only enough water to prevent the potting mixture from drying out completely.

Feeding Apply a high-potassium tomato-type fertilizer once a month during the active growth period.

Potting and repotting A porous potting mixture is essential. Add one part of coarse sand or perlite to three parts of either standard soil-based mixture or peat-based, soilless mixture (see page 429). A ferocactus needs a pot big enough not only to take its roots comfortably but to provide a space of about ½ inch between the plant and the rim of the pot. Remove the plant from the pot every spring at the beginning of the active growth period, and move it into a pot one size larger if the roots are found to be tightly packed in the current pot. If there is still room for growth, shake off as much of the old mixture as possible, and return the plant to its pot, which has been thoroughly cleaned. Add fresh mixture as necessary.

Propagation Because ferocacti do not usually have offsets or branches, young plants must be grown from seed. Seed is generally available, and these cacti are not difficult for amateur gardeners to raise (see *CACTI*, page 119). Commercial nurseries usually offer ferocacti for sale when the plants are about two years old and no more than 2 inches high.

Ficus

MORACEAE

THERE are over 800 species of the genus *Ficus* (Latin for "fig"), most of them natives of the warmer parts of the world. A number make excellent house plants—but not the edible fig, *Ficus carica*. The species now used indoors are prized for their evergreen foliage, and a suitable ficus can be found for any indoor situation. Included in the group are trees, shrubs, and climbers; some are suitable for narrow window sills, others must stand on the floor. Most of them adapt well to gradually changing conditions. Among them is one of the most common of all house plants, the rubber plant, *F. elastica*.

Mistletoe fig
F. deltoidea

Creeping fig
F. pumila

Fiddle leaf fig
F. lyrata

F. buxifolia
Rubber plant
F. elastica
Weeping fig
F. benjamina
Banyan tree
F. benghalensis
F. sagittata 'Variegata'

RECOMMENDED FICUSES

F. benghalensis (banyan tree) grows to a great height in its native habitat, where it also produces long aerial roots. Indoors it is chiefly valued for its much-branching habit and dark green oval leaves, which may be as much as a foot long. New leaves and stems are covered with fine russet hair. Because of this thin felted covering, the leaves

The leaves and stem of F. benghalensis *are covered in a fine hair, which makes them hard to wipe clean. Give them a fine mist-spray instead.*

are difficult to wipe clean; dust can, however, be washed off by gentle rain or a fine mist-spray.

F. benjamina (tropic laurel, Java or weeping fig) is a small, graceful tree that is useful when young for mixed plantings. It eventually grows to 6 feet tall, its weeping, treelike appearance becoming more and more pronounced. Leaves are 2–4 inches long, slightly undulate, and apple green when young but darker with age. The many short, twiglike branches and leafstalks have a stringy bark, which peels off and provides a home for scale insects, a troublesome pest with this plant. (Evidence of infestation is a sticky and/or sooty substance on the leaves. For treatment, see page 455.) Although the plant does not have a well-defined growing season or rest period, a number of leaves naturally turn yellow and fall off at the end of winter; but these are replaced in early spring by fresh growth. A form sold as *F.b. nuda* has slimmer, more tapering leaves and even more of a "weeping" habit than the species.

F. buxifolia is a comparative newcomer. Its name, meaning "boxlike," is appropriate, for its leaves, which are about an inch across and roughly triangular, are similar to those of plants of the genus *Buxus* (boxwood). This recently available species is a quick-growing shrub with thin, arching stems and copper-colored bark.

F. deltoidea (mistletoe fig) is the only popular indoor ficus that regularly produces fruit (inedible)—and at an early age. The small yellowish fruits grow on very short stalks from leaf axils. The plant gets its name from the greek capital letter Δ (Delta), which describes the shape of the leaves. An earlier name, *F. diversifolia,* meaning "with differing leaves," is frequently applied to this shrub, which has leaves that are 1–3 inches long, thick, dark green, and often very slightly spotted (almost pitted), and tapering toward the leafstalk. The plant rarely grows taller than 3 feet indoors, although it branches profusely and bears fruit throughout the year.

F. elastica (the familiar rubber plant) is the best-known indoor ficus. The original species is now rarely used as a house plant; improved forms are preferred. All of these have large, shiny, leathery leaves with prominent midribs, and the central stem tends to grow straight without branching or producing sideshoots. Branching can, however, be induced by cutting off the growing point. This will cause copious "bleeding" of latexlike sap, but the flow can be staunched by applying powdered charcoal or even cigarette ash to the wound. Among the many forms of *F. elastica: F.e.* 'Decora,' the most popular, has dark green oval-oblong leaves up to 15 inches long that stand at a 45° angle to the main stem, resisting the tendency to droop that characterizes the original species. New leaves emerge from a bright red protective sheath (which drops off), and the underside of the central vein is also red. *F.e.* 'Robusta' has larger, more rounded leaves than *F.e.* 'Decora'; its name is appropriate, for it is a notably sturdy plant. *F.e.* 'Black Prince' has leaves that are of a size and shape similar to those of *F.e.* 'Robusta,' but their color is an impressive greenish black.

There are also four popular variegated-leaved forms: *F.e.* 'Tricolor,' with pink and cream-colored

F. elastica 'Tricolor'

patches on a green ground; *F.e.* 'Schrijvereana,' with squarish patches of cream and pale green; *F.e.* 'Doescheri,' with gray and cream markings on the green leaves and a bright pink central midrib; and *F.e.* 'Variegata,' with leaves that are narrower and more drooping than those of the other forms. The leaves of *F.e.* 'Variegata' have a yellow border as well as yellow patches all over.

F. lyrata (sometimes called *F. pandurata*) is the fiddle leaf fig—so called because of its violin-shaped, puckered leaves. These can be as much as 15 inches long and 9 inches wide, are a

Staunching the flow of sap

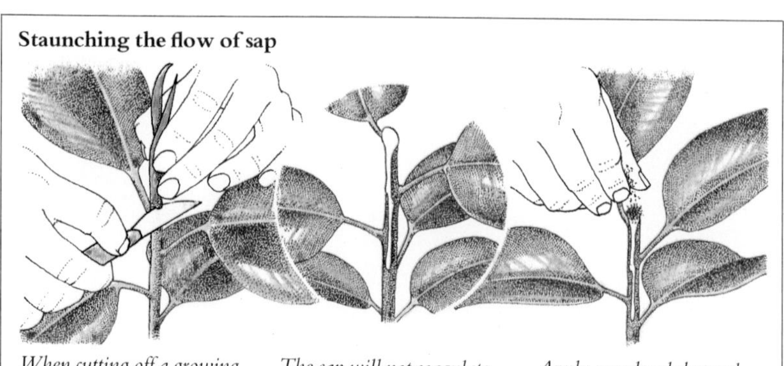

When cutting off a growing point of F. elastica, *be prepared for the flow of sap.*

The sap will not coagulate for some time unless measures are taken.

Apply powdered charcoal to the wound in order to staunch the flow.

medium green, and have undulate margins. The plant is fast-growing and, like *F. elastica,* tends to stay to a single stem. It can be induced to divide, however, by having its growing tip removed.

F. pumila (also known as *F. repens;* popularly called the creeping or climbing fig) is a small, much-branching, creeping plant with heart-shaped, thin, green leaves, which are less than an inch long and slightly puckered. It produces aerial roots if it has something moist and absorbent to cling to, and it looks very attractive when grown on a moss-covered pole. Most growers, however, use it as a trailing plant or as ground cover in plant troughs. There is a less familiar variegated form, *F.p.* 'Variegata,' with tiny white or cream-colored spots. This is a somewhat more demanding plant than the species: It needs slightly better light, warmer conditions, and more careful watering; moreover, some sections of it may revert to all green, and unless these green sections are removed they will take over.

F. religiosa is the Bo tree of India. Its thin, dark green leaves have distinctive long and slender tips, are carried on long leafstalks, are about 4 inches long and 2 inches wide, and have prominent light-colored veins. The plant grows fast and eventually becomes a large shrub.

F. retusa (sometimes known as *F. microcarpa* or by the common name Indian laurel) has deep green, elliptic, shiny, smooth, 3-inch-long leaves on short, erect, much-branching stems. It also bears small inedible fruit occasionally. Because this plant can withstand quite a lot of nipping out of shoots, it is often trained into specific shapes, such as standards and pyramids. If it is given its head, it will make a large shrub.

F. rubiginosa (also called *F. australis;* popularly known as the rusty fig) is a small, spreading tree with 3- to 6-inch-long, glossy, leathery, oval leaves that are dark green on top and rust-colored on the undersides. A form with variegated foliage, *F.r.* 'Variegata,' has deep green leaves that are marbled and margined with creamy yellow markings.

F. sagittata (also known as *F. radicans*) is a sturdy trailer with 2- to 3-inch-long, leathery, lance-shaped, green leaves and wiry stems. More popular because more attractive is the variegated form *F.s.* 'Variegata,' with grayish green leaves marked with ivory white.

PROPER CARE

Light Most of these plants do well either in medium light or in a position where they get some sun each day. *F. pumila,* however, likes more shade than the other types. The kinds with plain green foliage tolerate greater amounts of shade than do those with variegated foliage, which must have bright light with a few hours a day of direct sunlight. Otherwise the leaves are unlikely to retain their coloring and sharp contrasts.

Temperature Though most ficuses do best in normally warm room temperatures, they can be acclimatized gradually to a wide range of temperature. *F. pumila,* the one species that flourishes in cooler conditions, is almost capable of withstanding frost. In very hot rooms a careful watch should be kept for red spider mites (see page 455), which thrive in dry heat.

Watering *F. pumila* must never be allowed to become dry at the roots or its paper-thin leaves will shrivel and fall off. Water plants of this species moderately, giving enough to make the potting mixture thoroughly moist at each watering, and allowing only the top half-inch of the mixture to dry out before watering again. Most other species need much less water; let the top half of the mixture dry out before watering them. Overwatering will cause their lower leaves to fall.

Feeding Give standard liquid fertilizer every two weeks to actively growing plants only.

Potting and repotting Use a soil-based mixture (see page 429) for the larger-leaved types, but *F. pumila* and *F. sagittata* are best grown in a peat-based mixture. Do not overpot; these plants like slightly cramped root conditions. Use pots that look as if they are a size too small. Move plants into pots just one size larger when repotting becomes clearly necessary—as indicated by the emergence of a lot of root through the drainage hole, and possibly by the appearance of a network of fine roots on the surface. Repotting is best carried out in spring. When maximum convenient pot size has been reached, topdress plants annually with fresh potting mixture at the same time of year.

Propagation The two trailing types, *F. pumila* and *F. sagittata,* root easily from tip cuttings about 6 inches long, taken in spring and inserted in 3-inch pots of a moistened equal-parts mixture of peat moss and sand or perlite. Take the cuttings immediately below a node and carefully remove the lower pair of leaves before potting the cuttings in the rooting mixture. Enclose each potted cutting in a plastic bag, and keep it at normal room temperature in bright light filtered through a translucent blind or curtain. As soon as new growth appears, indicating that rooting has occurred, remove the bag and water the cuttings enough to keep the potting mixture just moist. When the new plant is well established—in about four months—move it into a pot one size larger containing the standard peat-based potting mixture. Thereafter treat it in the same way as a mature ficus.

Other types of ficus need somewhat greater skill. The large-leaved plants are usually slow to root from cuttings because water loss is very great. One possible method of propagation is air layering (see page 440)—a fascinating process, but one that takes a good deal of time and care, and thus requires much patience on the part of the amateur propagator.

Special points Every shiny-leaved ficus should have its leaves sponged regularly to free them of accumulated dust. Do this gently, especially when dealing with sensitive new leaves, which are easily damaged. Scars on young foliage remain unsightly for the rest of the plant's life. Ficuses with fuzzy (felted) leaves—such as *F. benghalensis*—should be sprayed clean, not wiped with a sponge.

When sponging a shiny-leaved ficus such as F. elastica, *use one hand to support each leaf so as not to put too much strain on its stalk.*

Fittonia

ACANTHACEAE

F. verschaffeltii

FITTONIAS are all small-leaved creeping plants indigenous to tropical rain forests. Most forms have 2- to 4-inch-long, somewhat pointed, oval leaves arranged in pairs with short stalks; but the distinctive feature of all fittonias is a fine network of colored veins that runs through the leaves. Plants of this genus also produce small yellow flowers in spikes, but these rarely develop indoors.

Fittonias are not easy to grow in the average home but are excellent for bottle gardens and terrariums (see page 54). They do best if given constant warmth, high humidity, and good light, but they must be sheltered from direct sunlight. Their roots need to be kept moist, but not wet. At regular intervals their growing points should be pinched out to encourage the production of sideshoots. And, since they lose their beauty as they age, fresh plants should be raised regularly from tip cuttings.

Low, creeping fittonias make an ideal foreground for taller plants in the humid atmosphere of a bottle garden.

RECOMMENDED FITTONIAS

F. gigantea is a bushy plant capable of growing 2 feet tall. Its dark green leaves have deep red veins and are 3–4 inches long.

F. verschaffeltii argyroneura 'Nana'

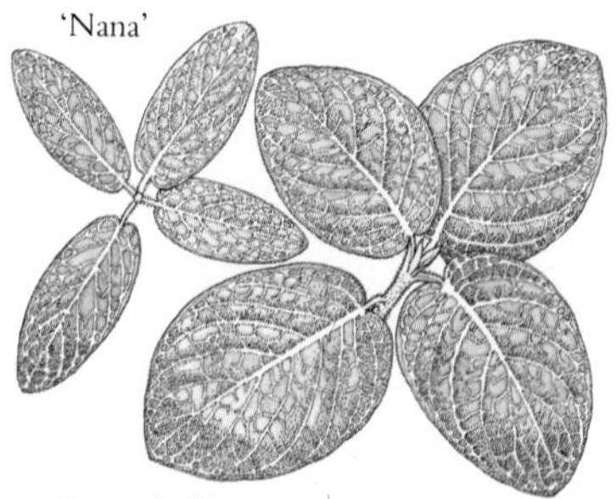

F. verschaffeltii argyroneura (mosaic plant)

F. verschaffeltii has 2-inch-long, olive green leaves netted with carmine-red veins; they are slightly more oval-shaped (i.e., less pointed) than those of *F. gigantea*. One of its varieties, *F.v. argyroneura* (mosaic or nerve plant), has similar leaves, but the veins are finer and silver-colored. There is now a delightful miniature form of this latter type, *F.v.a.* 'Nana,' which is reputed to be much easier to grow than the larger kind.

PROPER CARE

Light Keep actively growing fittonias in medium light, at a slightly shaded window. Direct sunlight damages their leaves. In winter, however, as the quality of light deteriorates, move these plants nearer to bright windows.

Temperature A perfect position would provide a steady temperature of 65°F. But fittonias will tolerate more or even less warmth—though no lower than 55°. For adequate humidity, stand pots on trays of damp pebbles, and give a fine mist-spray whenever possible.

Watering Careful watering is essential. If fittonias are allowed to become too dry, their leaves curl up and fall; if too wet, their stems rot. Water them regularly but sparingly. Keep the mixture just barely moist at all times.

Feeding Apply standard liquid fertilizer at half-strength to actively growing plants every two weeks.

Potting and repotting A peat-based potting mixture (see page 429) helps to provide the constant root moisture that these plants like. Repotting in larger containers is seldom necessary. Shallow pans or half-pots are best, for fittonias are naturally shallow-rooting. When initially potting up small plants or rooted cuttings, group several together for the best effect. Five or six cuttings in a 5-inch pan can remain there for a year or more.

Propagation Small tip cuttings comprising three or four pairs of leaves will root with comparative ease in standard potting mixture if they are given good indirect light and kept warm and moist. Another simple and sure way to propagate fittonias is by a process known as layering (see page 439). To do this, place the pot in which the plant is growing in a slightly larger bowl containing a peat-based potting mixture with a little coarse sand or perlite sprinkled over the surface. Train the growing tips of the plant over the edge of the container so that they come into contact with the mix in the outer bowl, and they will soon root. When this happens, detach the rooted tips from the parent plant; after two or three weeks they can be planted in groups in permanent containers. A 5-inch pan filled with fittonias will provide several batches of offspring in one season. If the parent plant is still handsome, it need not be discarded, for it will quickly replace tips that have been removed.

Fortunella

RUTACEAE

Nagami kumquat
F. margarita

FORTUNELLAS (kumquats) are miniature trees closely related to plants of the genus *Citrus*. They resemble orange trees in everything but size. Although all species can grow to 15 feet tall outdoors, potted plants are usually about 4 feet high. Some of these much-branching, bushy plants have spiny stems and branches; others are almost thornless. All have alternate, thick, leathery, slightly pitted leaves with short leafstalks. Leaf color is dark green on the upper surface, with a paler green underside. Heavily scented, five-petaled, white flowers $\frac{1}{2}$ inch across usually appear singly (rarely in small clusters) in spring and summer. They are produced on short stalks from leaf axils. The fruits that follow ripen slowly, eventually turning deep orange, and remain on the bush for a number of weeks before they drop off.

RECOMMENDED FORTUNELLAS

F. japonica has spiny stems bearing elliptic leaves 3 inches long and 2 inches wide. Each round, orange-yellow kumquat may be $1\frac{1}{4}$ inches in diameter. One form, *F. j.* 'Variegata,' has leaves flecked with white.

F. margarita (Nagami kumquat) has nearly thornless stems and lance-shaped leaves 4 inches long and $2\frac{1}{2}$ inches wide. The oval, darkish orange fruit can grow up to $1\frac{1}{2}$ inches long and $\frac{3}{4}$ inch across.

PROPER CARE

Light Give fortunellas as much direct sunlight as possible throughout the year.

Temperature During the active growth period normal room temperatures are suitable, but stand pots on trays of moist pebbles for increased humidity. Give plants a winter rest at a temperature of 55°–60°F, and let the pebbles dry out during this period. Lowest tolerable temperature: 50°.

Watering During the active growth period water plentifully as often as necessary to keep the potting mixture thoroughly moist, but never allow pots to stand in water. During the winter rest period water only enough to keep the mixture from drying out.

Feeding In the early weeks of the active growth period apply standard liquid fertilizer every two weeks. As soon as flower buds appear, change over to a high-potash, tomato-type fertilizer. Use this fertilizer for 8–10 weeks; then revert to the standard kind. Do not feed resting plants.

Potting and repotting Use a potting mixture composed of half soil-based mixture (see page 429) and half coarse leaf mold. If leaf mold is not available, substitute coarse-textured peat moss. Move plants into pots one size larger every spring until maximum convenient pot size (probably 10–12 inches) has been reached. Thereafter, topdress annually (see page 428) with soil-based mixture.

Propagation Fortunellas can easily be grown from seed, which should be sown very soon after being taken from the fruit. Sow each seed $\frac{3}{4}$ inch deep in a 2- to 3-inch pot of moistened rooting mixture, and enclose the whole in a plastic bag or heated propagating case (see page 444). Stand it in bright filtered light at a temperature of about 70°F until the seed has germinated. Uncover the seedling and begin to water it moderately, allowing the top half-inch of the mixture to dry out between waterings. In addition, begin to apply standard liquid fertilizer at two-weekly intervals. Repot the new plant when it has made two to three inches of top growth. Use the mixture recommended for adult fortunellas and treat it as a mature specimen.

Special points Fortunellas are susceptible to attack by scale insects and red spider mites. For treatment in these circumstances see page 455.

Remove any weak and twiggy growths or any overlong shoots that develop. The best time to do this is toward the end of the rest period.

Fuchsia

ONAGRACEAE

Lady's-eardrops
Fuchsia hybrid

FUCHSIAS (lady's-eardrops) are soft-wooded shrubs with colorful drooping blooms that are produced continuously over a long flowering period. There are literally hundreds of varieties; almost all fuchsias available today have been derived from several species after considerable hybridization. Some are trailers and look particularly attractive in hanging baskets; some grow tall and erect; a few are dwarf-size. Some produce few but very large flowers; others have many but smaller ones; a few are grown principally for their decorative variegated leaves. The lower-growing, small-flowered kinds make the most suitable house plants, since they are less affected than the others by the dry air and warm conditions that are likely to prevail indoors.

Fuchsia leaves vary in size and shape, but they are generally pointed oval, have slightly toothed edges, and are $1\frac{1}{2}$–$2\frac{1}{2}$ inches long and $\frac{3}{4}$–$1\frac{1}{2}$ inches wide. They grow on very short leafstalks (no more than 1 inch long) arranged in opposite pairs or groups of three to five on usually rigid—but sometimes pendent—stems. Although fuchsias may flower almost continuously outdoors in some areas, they are unlikely to bloom indoors for more than three or four months at a time. Flowers appear, often in pairs, from each leaf axil on thin, usually drooping 1- to 2-inch-long stalks. Each bloom usually comprises four (sometimes more) arching sepals, one or more bell-shaped or skirted corollas, long stamens, and an extremely long style. Flower color can be almost any combination of white, pink, red, magenta, and purple. Sepal color often, but not always, contrasts with that of the corolla.

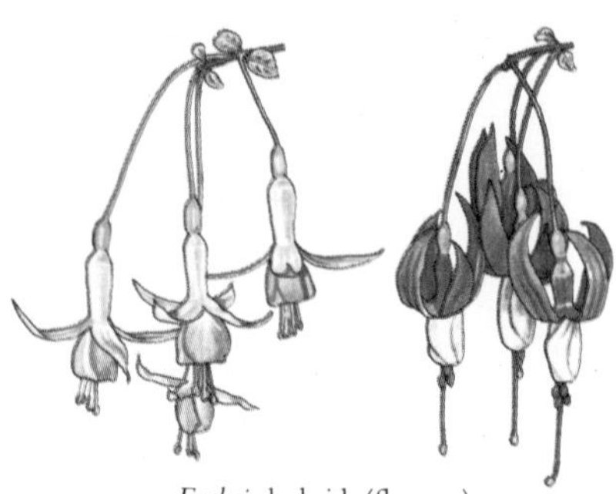

Fuchsia hybrids (flowers)

Mature fuchsias do not transfer easily from outdoors or from the humid atmosphere of the greenhouse into the relatively dry air of the home. They usually react by dropping many flowers and buds, and perhaps some leaves; and so they must be gradually acclimatized to indoor conditions. The best way to start growing fuchsias as house plants is to buy small plants (4–5 inches high) in spring. Such young potted plants may lose a few leaves when they are brought into the home, but they will not yet have buds or flowers, and they will have time to settle down in the home atmosphere before the flowering season begins. Everything possible should be done to make the air as humid as possible for these new arrivals. They should be stood on trays of damp pebbles and be mist-sprayed regularly, if possible more than once a day.

PROPER CARE

Light Fuchsias will not bloom unless they get really bright light, with at least three hours every day of strong direct sunlight.

Temperature Fairly cool conditions (around 60°F if possible) are best for these plants. In hot rooms the buds may fail to develop properly, and flowers (if any) will quickly fade. If plants are retained over the winter, they must have a cool resting period (see "Special points," below).

Watering During the active growth period water plentifully as often as necessary to keep the potting mixture thoroughly moist. In the fall gradually reduce amounts of water and extend the period between waterings to prepare the plants for their winter rest. During the rest period water only enough to keep the mixture from becoming completely dry.

Feeding Fuchsias are greedy and should be fed weekly with standard liquid fertilizer throughout the flowering period. Although resting plants should not be fed, it is advisable to begin giving standard liquid fertilizer to young plants once every two weeks during the spring months before flowering begins.

Blooms of a trailing fuchsia show to fine advantage in a hanging basket, along with leafy plants—for example, peperomias and star-shaped hederas.

Potting and repotting Use a soil-based potting mixture (see page 429). Fuchsias normally flower well in 5-inch pots; larger pots encourage the development of leaves at the expense of flowers. Young plants can be moved from 3-inch pots to the 5-inch size as soon as they have produced good top growth and begun to fill their pots with roots. In order to create attractive displays in hanging baskets, several small plants should be planted together; but it is best not to put different varieties in the same container, for vigor varies with variety, and one sort of fuchsia is likely to dominate the display to the detriment of the others.

Propagation Fuchsias are easy to propagate. This is possible either in fall, after which the new plants need to be overwintered, or in spring just after new growth begins on plants that have had a winter rest. Take tip cuttings 3–4 inches long, which have been cut immediately below a node, trim off the lower leaves, and plant the cuttings in 3-inch pots of a moistened equal-parts mixture of peat moss and sand or perlite. Enclose each potted cutting in a plastic bag or propagating case, and keep it in a warm position where it gets medium light. The cutting will root in three to four weeks. Spring-rooted cuttings can then be moved into 3-inch pots of standard potting mixture and treated as mature fuchsias. Fall-rooted cuttings should be uncovered and overwintered in a cool position (45°–50°F) in bright light without direct sunlight. They should be watered just enough to keep the leaves from drooping. In the following spring, such cuttings can be treated as mature plants, and they will normally flower earlier than spring-rooted plants. When either spring- or fall-rooted cuttings have made 2 or 3 inches of new growth, nip out the growing point. Four to six side branches will develop to form the flower-bearing branches of the new plant.

Special points When flowering stops in the fall, fuchsias are often discarded. They may be kept, however, if a suitable position for overwintering them, where they can be given an almost totally dormant resting period, is available. Cut away about half their growth, store the potted plants in a cool (45°–50°F), not necessarily well-lit position and water them sparingly (see "Watering," above). During the rest period all leaves will fall off, and the stems will become quite woody. In early spring trim them to about one-third their original height, then bring them into bright light at normal room temperature and water them enough to make the potting mixture moist, but allowing the top two-thirds of the mixture to dry out between waterings. Some varieties naturally branch and form bushy plants, but others do so only if the growing tip is nipped out at an early stage. As soon as new growth begins, repot plants. Shake off the old mixture, and move them into a fresh mixture in the same-size pots as before—or in smaller ones if roots can be fitted in. Feed growing plants sparingly at first (see "Feeding," above). Otherwise, treat them in the same way as mature specimens.

If you want to keep a fuchsia for another year, cut off half its growth after flowering, and give it a winter rest.

Fuchsias are particularly susceptible to attack from aphids and whitefly (see pages 455 and 457). Spray plants with a suitable insecticide whenever evidence of these pests appears.

Gardenia

RUBIACEAE

GARDENIAS are low-growing, bushy shrubs mainly prized for their fragrant flowers. They are not difficult plants to grow, but they require particular attention in order to flower. The only indoor species is *G. jasminoides* (frequently known as *G. grandiflora* and *G. florida*), which is popularly called common gardenia or Cape jasmine (though not related to true jasmines). As a potted plant, it rarely exceeds 18 inches in height or spread, even though it is capable of growing 6 feet tall in climates where it can be grown outside.

The 4-inch-long leaves of *G. jasminoides* are shiny, dark green, leathery, lance-shaped, and usually arranged in opposite pairs, but sometimes in whorls of three or more. The flowers, which may be fully double (with many petals) or semi-double (with only two layers of slightly arching petals), are 2–4 inches across and appear, usually singly, from leaf axils near the ends of the shoots. Several forms of the species are cultivated. Among them are *G.j.* 'Belmont' (the variety often sold as cut flowers by florists), which is a densely bushy plant and bears large, many-petaled, white flowers that turn cream-colored as they age; *G.j.* 'Fortuniana' (also known as *G.j.* 'Florida'), a less bushy plant with medium-size, rather waxy, pure white, many-petaled flowers that turn yellowish with age; and *G.j.* 'Veitchii,' with dense growth and medium-size, many-petaled flowers that remain pure white.

Most gardenias bloom naturally during the summer months, but they

To bring a gardenia into flower in early winter, pick off all flower buds that develop in the summer and early fall.

Common gardenia
Gardenia jasminoides

can be brought into flower in early winter by disbudding (having their flower buds picked off at an early stage) throughout summer and early fall. This process is more usual with *G.j.* 'Veitchii' than with other forms.

PROPER CARE

Light Gardenias do best in bright light. Always keep them out of direct sunlight, however.

Temperature The key to success in bringing gardenias into flower is to maintain a steady temperature of 62°–63°F during the period when flower buds are forming; a sudden change in either direction is practically certain to cause the buds to drop off. When plants are not forming flower buds, the range can be that of a fairly normal room: 60°–75°F. A high degree of humidity is also essential when flower buds are forming. To achieve this, stand the pots on trays of moist pebbles or peat moss, and spray plants at least once a day with a fine mist-spray (using water at room temperature). But try not to wet the flowers if plants are in bloom, for water on the petals causes discoloration.

Watering Gardenias do not have a well-defined rest period. They grow less actively, though, during the winter in areas where the winter months bring on a considerable reduction of light. In such places water these plants moderately during summer, giving enough at each watering to make the potting mixture moist throughout and allowing the top half-inch of the mixture to dry out before watering again. During the winter months (roughly October through February) allow the top 1–2 inches of the potting mixture to dry out completely before watering again.

Such reduced winter watering is desirable even with plants that are forced into winter flowering. In areas with less winter reduction of light, watering can remain unchanged throughout the year. Always use slightly warm, preferably lime-free water for these plants.

Feeding Apply "acid" fertilizer every two weeks, but only from March through September, to these lime-hating gardenias.

Potting and repotting Most growers use a lime-free potting mixture even though gardenias can tolerate a little alkalinity. A mixture of equal parts leaf mold and peat moss is excellent. If a proprietary peat-based potting mixture is used (see page 429), make sure it is suitable for lime-hating plants, since some are not. Because there is relatively little nutritional value in leaf mold and none in peat moss, it is especially important to give the regular feedings recommended above if this mixture is used. It is also possible to use a soil-based potting mixture (see page 429), as long as it is non-alkaline. The feeding regime is less essential with soil-based mixtures than with soilless ones.

Repot gardenias only when their roots have nearly filled the pot (as indicated by their appearance at the surface or outside the bottom drainage hole). These plants flower best when in pots that are just a little too small for vigorous stem growth. Any repotting should be done when plants begin to grow in the spring, and the root ball should be disturbed as little as possible.

Propagation Gardenias can be propagated from 3-inch-long tip cuttings taken in early spring. Dip these in hormone rooting powder, and plant them in small pots of moistened peat-based potting mixture suitable for lime-hating plants. Place the potted cuttings in a heated propagating case (see page 444) or alternatively, enclose them in plastic bags and keep them at a temperature of 60°–65°F in bright light filtered through a translucent blind or curtain. Rooting should occur in four to six weeks. In late summer move the rooted cuttings into pots a size larger containing the potting mixture recommended for mature plants. Water them moderately, and feed them at least once a month until they are well developed. Then treat them as mature plants.

Special points Some early-spring pruning is usually necessary to keep the shrubs low and bushy. Nip out growing points of any long new shoots on young plants, and cut out half or even two-thirds of the old wood of mature plants. Be careful, however, not to nip out flower buds. Stems can always be cut back later after the flowers have died. The cuts should be made immediately above points where growth-producing buds point outward rather than toward the center of the plant.

In pruning gardenias, make cuts just above outward-pointing growth buds, so that new growth will not overcrowd the center of the bush.

Gasteria
LILIACEAE

Wart gasteria
G. verrucosa

THE genus *Gasteria* (Dutch wings, lawyer's tongue, or ox-tongue) includes about 50 species of small, often stemless, succulent plants, which produce basal, clustering offsets. The leaves of most species are arranged in two flattened rows, but a few species form rosettes. These plants are highly regarded for both the general effect of the foliage and the small but attractive flowers produced along the lengths of long flower stalks in late spring and summer. Each stem carries 15–20 of these flowers, which are no more than an inch long and tubular, but curved and swollen at the base. The rather slight resemblance of the swollen base of individual flowers to a miniature belly has given rise to the generic name *(gaster* is the Latin word for belly). Flower color is orange or red, sometimes tipped with green. Gasterias make ideal house plants because they thrive in the warm, dry air of a living room. They also flourish in shade rather than bright light. In the wild, they tend to grow within the shade of larger plants, and it is for this reason that they are more shade-tolerant than most other succulents. They are essentially summer plants, for they must have a cool winter rest and they grow very slowly in spring and fall. The species that are described below are representative of the two types of leaf formation.
See also SUCCULENTS.

RECOMMENDED GASTERIAS

G. liliputana, one of the smallest gasterias, has pointed lance-shaped leaves $1\frac{1}{4}$–$2\frac{1}{2}$ inches long and about $\frac{1}{2}$ inch wide, which are arranged in the form of a spiral rosette. The leaves are dark green flecked with white. Leaf undersides are keeled.

G. liliputana

G. maculata, a larger plant than *G. liliputana,* is one of the most popular gasterias. Its blunt-tipped, tongue-shaped, glossy leaves are about 6 inches long and generally close to 2 inches wide. Leaf color is dark green abundantly marked with white spots or bands. While the plant is young, the leaves are arranged in two flattened rows. This arrangement persists in some specimens. In others the plant tends to form a spiral rosette as it ages.

G. pseudonigricans has pointed-tipped, tongue-shaped, glossy leaves arranged in two rows. Each leaf is 5–6 inches long, about $1\frac{1}{2}$ inches wide, and dark green covered with white spots. The leaves are usually almost horizontal at the base but tend to arch upward at the tip.

G. verrucosa (rice or wart gasteria) has leaves that taper gradually to a point. Each leaf is 4–6 inches long and about $\frac{5}{8}$ inch wide, somewhat concave above and rounded on the underside, and dark green covered with small, white warts. Leaves are always arranged in pairs, forming two distinct rows.

PROPER CARE

Light Give gasterias medium light—near a north-facing window, for example. Although they can tolerate somewhat brighter light, they should never be exposed to direct sunlight, particularly in summer. The summer sun will turn the leaves brownish.

Temperature During the active growth period normal room temperatures are suitable. During the winter rest period keep these plants in a cool position. They should rest at about 50°F, if possible.

Watering During the active growth period water moderately. Give enough at each watering to make the potting mixture moist throughout, but allow the top half-inch of the mixture to dry out before watering again. During the winter rest period water sparingly. Moisten the mixture at each watering and allow the top two-thirds of the mixture to dry out completely before watering again.

Feeding It is not advisable to feed gasterias. There is enough nourishment in the potting mixture, and any additional fertilizer causes them to make unnaturally lush growth.

Potting and repotting To make sure that the potting mixture is sufficiently porous, add one part of coarse sand or perlite to three parts of standard soil-based mixture (see page 429). Because gasterias normally produce a number of offsets, grow each plant in a broad container or pan rather than in an ordinary pot. Repot every year at the beginning of the summer growth period. Move the plant into a slightly larger container only if the current one allows no room for further production of offsets. A space of about $1\frac{1}{2}$ inches between the edges of the container and the plant should suffice for a year's new growth. A pot size of 6–8 inches should be the biggest required. If the current container is large enough and can continue to hold the roots without crowding, simply clean it and replant the specimen in fresh potting mixture. Some gasterias produce offsets so profusely that they become unsuitably large after a few years unless the offsets are regularly removed.

Propagation The best and simplest way to propagate gasterias is by means of offsets, which are easy to separate from the parent plant by a gentle tug. If an offset has roots already formed, plant it in the recommended potting mixture and treat it as a mature gasteria. If the offset is rootless, leave it in the air to dry for two or three days before pressing it lightly down into the surface of the potting mixture. If given the same care as adult plants, it should develop roots and begin to grow actively within a few weeks. The best time to propagate is during the summer months.

Gasterias can also be raised from seed. Because they hybridize readily, however, this is not a dependable method by which to reproduce a particular kind of plant.

Propagating a gasteria

Remove offsets from the parent plant at any time during the summer. They should come away with no difficulty, and will probably have roots of their own.

Press a rooted offset into the recommended potting mixture for adult plants and treat it at once as a mature gasteria.

Geogenanthus

COMMELINACEAE

Seersucker plant
G. undatus

ONLY one species of the very small genus *Geogenanthus* is grown as a house plant: *G. undatus* (often called *Dichorisandra musaica undata;* commonly known as seersucker plant). This low-growing plant produces two or three unbranching, usually erect, fleshy stems, each up to 10 inches long. The stems carry oval leaves 3–5 inches long and 2–4 inches wide with $\frac{1}{2}$-inch-long leafstalks. These fleshy, somewhat leathery leaves have a curiously puckered surface. Leaf color is deep green with lengthwise silvery green stripes on the upper surface, and wine red below. The lightly quilted, seersuckerlike texture of the leaves justifies the plant's common name. Although grown principally for its decorative foliage, *G. undatus* also produces attractive $\frac{1}{2}$-inch-wide, pale violet flowers with fringed petals. Small clusters of these flowers are produced in summer on short flower stalks arising from leaf axils at the ends of the stems. Each bloom opens in the morning and fades in early afternoon.

PROPER CARE

Light Give *G. undatus* bright filtered light throughout the year.

Temperature These plants need warmth. A minimum temperature of 65°F is essential at all times. Because they are sensitive to dry air, provide extra humidity by standing pots on trays of moist pebbles.

Watering Water moderately at all times. Give enough at each watering to moisten the mixture throughout, allowing the top half-inch to dry out before watering again.

Feeding Although *G. undatus* does not have a regular annual rest period, it grows most vigorously during the months from early spring to late fall. Apply standard liquid fertilizer every two weeks during those months only.

Potting and repotting Use a potting mixture composed of equal parts of leaf mold, peat moss, and coarse sand or perlite. Move a plant into a pot one size larger whenever roots fill the pot (see page 426). Since young plants are more attractive than older ones, it is usually best to propagate often rather than move plants into pots bigger than 6 inches.

Propagation Propagate in spring from tip cuttings 2–3 inches long. Trim the stem of each cutting just below the bottom leaf, remove that leaf, and plant the cutting in a 2- or 3-inch pot containing a moistened equal-parts mixture of peat moss and coarse sand or perlite. Enclose the whole in a plastic bag or propagating case (see page 443), and stand it in a warm place where it gets bright filtered light. After rooting occurs (usually in three to five weeks), uncover the new plant gradually, acclimatizing it over a period of two or three weeks to normal room humidity. Do not move it into the recommended potting mixture for adult plants, however, until roots have begun to appear on the surface of the rooting mixture.

Gesneria
GESNERIACEAE

G. cuneifolia

THE gesnerias grown as house plants, which are slow-growing, short-stemmed, and generally rosette-forming, will flower throughout the year if given the right conditions. The virtually stalkless, alternate, prominently veined, green leaves are somewhat elliptic in shape. Flowers grow continuously from the leaf axils on long stalks, either singly or in groups of up to four. Tubular in shape, the corolla widens only slightly at the mouth; each tube is backed by a five-lobed green calyx. Stolonlike runners spread out underground from the parent plant, and new rosette-shaped plants arise wherever the tips of the runners break the surface of the potting mixture. Because gesnerias need high humidity, they grow best in terrariums (see page 54).
See also GESNERIADS.

RECOMMENDED GESNERIAS

G. cuneifolia, the only widely grown species, has a stem that grows thicker and taller so slowly that it attains a height of 6 inches and width of $\frac{1}{3}$ inch only when several years old. As the green, sometimes red-tinged, hairy stem ages, it branches, producing further rosettes of leaves on the new stems, all of which become slowly covered with white hairs. The leaves, which grow to 6 inches long and $1\frac{1}{4}$ inches wide at the widest point, have a dark green upper surface and a pale green underside. Long white hairs cover the prominent veins of the underside only. One-inch-long flowers, with minutely fringed, $\frac{1}{2}$-inch-wide mouths, are carried on erect, hairy, 2-inch-long, green stalks. The flowers are bright red tinged with orange in the throat, and they are covered with short, white hairs. Flowers will continue to be produced from a leaf axil even after the leaf has dropped off. An easy-to-grow variety, *G. c.* 'Quebradillas', has yellow-and-orange flowers. And G. 'Lemon Drop' is a hybrid very similar to G. *cuneifolia,* which is one of its parents, but its flowers are pure yellow.

A gesneria will benefit from the high humidity and constant warmth of a bottle garden, and so will probably flower throughout the year.

PROPER CARE

Light Gesnerias need bright light throughout the year. Give them three or four hours a day of direct sunlight, but keep them out of the midday sun. As a good alternative use fluorescent light (see page 446) for about 12 hours a day, with the plants placed about 15 inches below the tubes.

Temperature These plants need a minimum of 65°F at all times. For high humidity place pots on saucers of moist pebbles. *G. cuneifolia* is unlikely to grow well outside the ideal environment of a terrarium unless it is mist-sprayed several times a day.

Watering Water these plants plentifully, as often as necessary to keep the potting mixture thoroughly moist, but never allow pots to stand in water. If the mixture is allowed to become even slightly dry, flowering will be severely curtailed.

Feeding At every watering apply a weak dose—one-eighth the recommended strength—of liquid fertilizer with a high-phosphate content.

Potting and repotting In the wild, gesnerias grow on limestone cliffs. The best potting mixture, therefore, is composed of equal parts of sphagnum peat moss, perlite and vermiculite, with the addition of a tablespoonful of dolomite lime or lime chips to every cup of the basic mixture. Use shallow, 6-inch pots to encourage the production of runners. There is no need to move these plants into larger containers. Simply trim back the roots of each plant by a third about once a year and set the plant lower in its old pot, which has been cleaned. Add fresh mixture as necessary.

Propagation To produce more gesnerias, use the young plants that grow from the underground runners. Separate as many as required by cutting through the runners with a sharp knife. Pot up the plants individually, and treat them as mature gesnerias.

GESNERIADS

The Latin name of the gesneriad family is *Gesneriaceae*. There are more than 120 genera with over 2,000 species in the family. Most gesneriads have brightly colored flowers, which differ from most other flowers in that the petals are joined at their base to form a tubular corolla. A list of genera commonly grown indoors follows this article. Consult separate articles for individual species.

Within the family of gesneriads there are three different root systems. Some types have fibrous roots like those of most other plants, some have scaly rhizomes with feeding roots, and some are tuberous. Fibrous roots are the most common. They are found in such terrestrial gesneriads as the episcias, saintpaulias, and streptocarpuses and in such epiphytes as the aeschynanthuses and columneas. Given ideal growing conditions, all the fibrous-rooted gesneriads can grow actively throughout the year.

Rhizomes are modified stems, and the scales of scaly rhizomes are modified leaves. The rhizomes of gesneriads generally grow horizontally underground, spreading out in all directions from the base of the visible stem. These plants tend to have an annual dormant period during which their stems and leaves die back to the ground. Dormancy can last for only a few weeks as in some kohlerias, or for several months, as in the smithianthas. At the end of the dormant period when favorable conditions of light, warmth, and moisture return, the tip of each scaly rhizome grows upward and produces new top growth. If a scaly rhizome is broken into pieces, each piece can send up a stem to make a new plant.

The most widely grown tuberous gesneriads are the sinningias including the popular kinds commonly known as gloxinias. The tuber is a woody, fleshy swelling at the base of the stem. Its function is as a food store for new top growth produced after the annual dormancy period, which these plants also tend to take. A gesneriad tuber is shaped like a flattened ball, with the upper surface slightly hollowed, and it is from the hollowed-out area that the stems arise. Hairlike roots grow out thickly from the upper and side surfaces of the tuber, but *not* from the bottom. This is a point to remember when potting up a dormant tuber. The growing points from which the stems rise on a tuber are known as its "eyes," and any piece of tuber with an eye can be used for propagation.

Apart from their variety of root systems gesneriads also produce many different kinds of top growth. Some have long, trailing stems bearing pairs of lance-shaped or elliptic, fleshy leaves. Most aeschynanthuses and columneas are in this category, and such plants are ideal for display in hanging baskets. Other kinds of gesneriad—the smithianthas, for example—have erect stems with pairs of leaves that are often hairy, oval or heart-shaped, and tooth-edged. A third group, which includes many saintpaulias, miniature sinningias, and streptocarpuses, have extremely short stems (or no stems at all) and rosettes or whorls of often oval or round leaves. Even the flowers, similar as they are, can be borne in many different ways: singly, in clusters, on stalks arising from leaf axils, at the tops of stems, even from near the base of the midrib of leaves (as in stemless streptocarpuses).

PROPER CARE

Light Since the gesneriads grown as house plants come from bright tropical regions, almost all of them need bright light for good growth. But they cannot tolerate direct midday sunlight, which scorches delicate and fleshy leaves and can cause stunted growth in some genera. The best position for most of these plants is at an

Flower types

Blooms are usually five-petaled and tubular. The tube can be short, as in saintpaulias (left), or long as in aeschynanthuses (right). Note the paired saintpaulia stamens and the joined ones of the aeschynanthus.

Root systems

Most gesneriads have fibrous roots (top right), such as saintpaulias. A few—notably sinningias—have roots emerging from a tuber (left). Some, such as smithianthas, root from rhizomes (bottom).

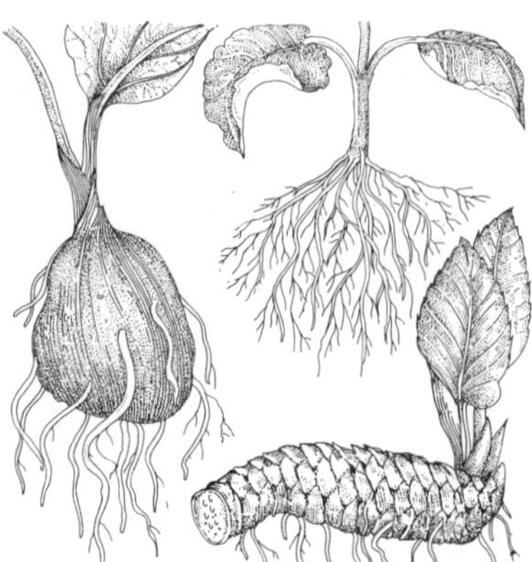

Growth habits

Terrestrial gesneriads tend to grow bushily or in tufts, as the streptocarpus (left) does. There are also epiphytic gesneriads, however. Columneas such as the one at the right grow high on trees in their native jungle.

Gesneriads: representative forms

Gesneriads belong to a plant family notable for tubular flowers, attractive foliage (which is often as brightly colored as the flowers), and variety of growth habits. One representative from each genus discussed in this volume is illustrated here. In most cases, of course, there are many different species within each of the illustrated genera, and plants of species other than those pictured here may look very different.

Achimenes

Aeschynanthus

Columnea

Episcia

Gesneria

Gloxinia

Kohleria

Saintpaulia

Sinningia

Sinningia (florist gloxinia)

Smithiantha

Streptocarpus

east- or west-facing window, where they will get a few hours a day of morning or afternoon sunlight. A gesneriad at a south window should have the light filtered through a translucent blind or curtain. On the other hand, inadequate light will result in weak, spindly stems and virtually no flowers at all.

A constant intensity of light is important for members of this family. The easiest way to provide a dependable degree of light intensity throughout the year is to place fluorescent light tubes (see page 446) above the gesneriads. If given the right kind of artificial light for ten to fourteen hours a day every day, plants that do not require a period of dormancy will be likely to continue in active growth throughout the year. The best possible placement of plants under fluorescent tubes can be ascertained only by experimentation. The correct distance between light tube and gesneriad foliage can be anything from 6 inches to 14 inches. For dormant plants, of course, light is not a consideration.

Temperature In the wild the gesneriads discussed in this article are accustomed to warm temperatures with little fluctuation. Basically, they require a daytime temperature of about 65°–75°F in order to grow well. An average nighttime drop of 5° from the daytime level does no harm. Most genera can tolerate temperatures down to about 55° in winter, but growth at temperatures below 65° slows down; at 55° it can stop altogether. (For precise recommendations consult specific articles in the *A–Z Guide*.) Plants that go into dormancy, such as those of the genus *Achimenes* and some sinningias, can survive temperatures down to 45° during the dormant period as long as they are kept dry throughout. Temperatures above about 80°F are also likely to cause slowing of active growth in some genera (saintpaulias, for example) and damage in others, such as the smithianthas. It is advisable, therefore, to keep the air circulating gently during any period of high temperature. Moreover, increased humidity is essential at such times. During warm periods always stand pots on trays of constantly moist pebbles, or suspend saucers of water under hanging baskets. In addition, mist-spray the area around each plant from time to time, but always with tepid water. Be careful not to let a heavy mist fall on a gesneriad because large drops of water can mark delicate foliage. Holding the sprayer about two feet away from the plant should guarantee a harmlessly fine mist.

Watering Water needs of gesneriads differ considerably. Follow the advice given in specific entries of the *A–Z*

Guide. A common requirement, however, is good drainage. Although roots may be kept constantly moist, they should never be allowed to become sodden in waterlogged mixture.

It is a good idea to water some kinds of plant by standing the pot in a larger vessel and pouring water into the vessel until the surface of the potting mixture has become thoroughly moist. If this method of watering is used, be sure to let any excess water drain away before returning the plant to its normal position. In addition, water the plant from the top about once in every four to six weeks. This will wash out the salts that might otherwise collect in the top layer of the potting mixture, with consequent damage to the roots. When watering from the top for this purpose, do not stand the plant in a saucer, but let the excess water run out and away.

Another safe way to water gesneriads is to prepare apparatus for drawing water up from a small reservoir by capillary action. This involves the insertion of a wick into the potting mixture (see page 423).

To keep a plant watered in your absence, stand the pot over a "reservoir" of water. Insert one end of a wick into the potting mixture, while allowing the other end to trail in the water.

Obviously, plants that are resting or dormant should be given little or no water. Be sure to follow recommendations as set forth in appropriate *A–Z Guide* entries.

Feeding As with other flowering house plants, and especially because they are grown in a peat-based mixture, gesneriads need regular applications of fertilizer to keep them growing and flowering. Give actively growing plants a liquid fertilizer that has equal amounts of nitrogen, phosphate, and potash or else one with less nitrogen (depending on the recommendations for specific plants in the *A–Z Guide*). It is sometimes advisable to use the former type of fertilizer for a young plant and to change to the second as the plant matures. Gesneriads with continuous growth should be fed throughout the year, of course. And a weak foliar feed may be added to the mist spray (see "Temperature," above) occasionally. Take extra pains to avoid marking the foliage, however, when the water has fertilizer in it.

The hairlike roots of all these plants are easily damaged by excess amounts of fertilizer. For this reason it is wise to use liquid fertilizer in a weaker solution than that recommended on the label. To compensate for the weakness apply fertilizer more frequently. "Little and often" is a good rule when feeding gesneriads.

If a specimen is watered by a capillary-action, wick-watering system, it is a simple matter to add fertilizer to the water reservoir so that the plant is being constantly fed. In this case, though, never use a stronger than one-eighth-strength solution.

Potting and repotting Gesneriads need a potting mixture that is basically composed of organic material. It must have good drainage qualities and yet be able to retain water well enough to stay moist. And it must be open and airy so that the fine roots can spread through it. The best potting mixture, therefore, includes equal amounts of sphagnum peat moss, perlite, and vermiculite. Most gesneriads do best in a mixture that is just on the acid side of neutral (see page 430). Add about a tablespoonful of dolomite lime or lime chips to each cup of mixture in order to achieve this effect. But follow the *A–Z Guide* directions; some plants—certain aeschynanthuses, for example — prefer a more acid mixture, and so no lime should be added.

Commercial mixtures formulated specifically for gesneriads are also widely available.

All gesneriads are shallow-rooted and should be grown in shallow pots. Plastic pots are better than clay pots because they are more moisture-retentive. Hanging baskets are appropriate for such trailing plants as the columneas or for stolon-producing plants such as the episcias. Pot size must depend upon the size of plant, but remember that gesneriads that grow continuously will usually flower most profusely if they are nearly pot-bound. They should be moved into pots one size larger only when their roots fill the pot. If the grower prefers not to move a specimen to a bigger pot, it is often possible simply to trim the root ball by one-third and replace the plant in its old pot with the addition of some fresh potting mixture.

The best time to repot varies according to species. Gesneriads with a distinct rest period, however, are normally repotted in early spring, immediately before active growth begins. This is also the right time to repot plants that have been completely dormant.

Propagation Many gesneriads can be propagated by stem, tip, or (in the case of the episcias) stolon cuttings. In taking a cutting always use a very sharp knife. Whether it is a stem, tip, or stolon cutting, and regardless of the species, simply insert the cut end in a pot of moistened potting mixture, enclose the pot in a plastic bag or propagating case (see page 443), and keep the covered cutting warm, generally in bright filtered light until it roots. Always acclimatize the young plant to the lower humidity of a room by uncovering it just a little further every day during a period of several days. For more detailed advice about watering, feeding, etc., consult appropriate entries in the *A–Z Guide.*

Gesneriads with scaly rhizomes often produce so many rhizomes in a single growing season that no other form of propagation is necessary. The gardener need merely separate the rhizomes as desired or break a single rhizome into pieces and pot up each piece. If the potting mixture is kept slightly moist in bright filtered light, the rhizome segment will soon send up a stem to make a new plant.

Large tubers can be cut up for propagation in a similar way. The best time to do this is in the spring as new growth begins after dormancy. Be sure that each planted piece of tuber has an eye. To guard against disease, dust all the cut edges with a fungicide before potting. And keep the mixture only just moist until growth is well advanced. Otherwise, there is a risk of rot invading the tuber.

Still another way to propagate some gesneriads (including the saintpaulias) is by growing new plants from leaves. Any leaf can be used for propagation as long as it is fully grown but not old. The stalk should be trimmed with a sharp knife, inserted in moistened potting mixture, enclosed in a plastic bag or propagating case, and placed in a light warm position (see *Propagation,* page 439). The leaf should root in about a month, and plantlets will appear after another month. When the plantlets are large enough to handle, they can be gently pulled away from the mother leaf and potted individually.

It is also possible to grow plantlets by cutting the vein of a leaf and laying the leaf flat on the surface of potting mixture. This is a method often used with sinningias. Interestingly enough, if a sinningia leafstalk is inserted in mixture, it will produce a tuber, from which top growth will eventually arise, whereas the cut-vein method produces plantlets that are perfect replicas of the parent plant.

Propagation from seed is comparatively easy for all gesneriads. The seeds are tiny and should be sown thinly on the surface of the rooting mixture. Because they must have light in order to germinate, the seed tray must not be covered by opaque material. The best sort of tray is a transparent plastic box with a close-fitting transparent lid. Use the recommended potting mixture for mature gesneriads, rubbing it well between the hands to break up lumps in the peat moss, and put only enough in the box to half-fill it. After sowing the seeds on the thoroughly moistened mixture, place the covered box in a warm position where it gets bright filtered light. Germination should occur within a month, but it will take longer if the seeds are not fresh.

Once seeds have germinated, be careful not to let the minute roots dry out. Visible condensation under the box lid does not necessarily indicate that the rooting mixture is adequately moist: On the contrary, it indicates that water has emerged from the mixture, which might therefore be drying out. Tip the seedbox gently sideways whenever it seems advisable to return the condensation to the mixture. The seedlings should be large enough to handle in about two months. Thin them out only if they are too crowded in the box. About once a week give them a one-eighth-strength dose of liquid fertilizer high in nitrogen. And before transplanting them acclimatize them gradually to room conditions by raising the lid of the box a little more each day. Thereafter, each seedling can be treated as a mature specimen.

Pests The most likely pests are aphids, which feed on young shoots of gesneriads. Look for them in particular between baby leaves. Search, too, for early signs of mealy bugs around stem bases in leaf axils and on leaf undersides. Thrips can be an intruder from outdoors and will attack and distort flower buds. But the most dangerous of all pests is the cyclamen mite, which can completely destroy a plant by feeding on its growing center. Once these pests attack they are virtually uncontrollable, and the best thing to do is to burn the plant. (For detailed information about pest control see pages 454–456.)

There are two pests that can be brought indoors in unsterilized potting mixtures. Root mealy bugs can be dealt with by pesticides. But there is no way to control nematodes, and a plant that has been infested should be destroyed. The best way to fight both these pests is to keep them out. Never use unsterilized potting mixture for planting gesneriads.

Diseases An occasional problem that affects gesneriads is mildew, which humidity encourages. This is why a gentle circulation of air around these plants is essential. If mildew does appear, a fungicide should control it effectively. Watch out, too, for crown and root rot, which can swiftly spread through a gesneriad that is kept too wet and either too hot or too cold. (For further information about plant diseases see pages 456–458.)

One disorder that can worry gesneriad growers is ring spot, which appears as white or cream-colored rings on leaves. This is not a disease. It is probably caused by watering with cold water in warm weather. The circular marks are permanent and can be unsightly. The obvious way to avoid ring spot is to use tepid water at all times.

To keep plants free of both pests and diseases, obey a simple rule: Do not put newly acquired plants into a collection of gesneriads until their overall health has been established. The new specimens should remain in quarantine for at least four weeks before being placed with the other plants in the collection.

For specific kinds of gesneriad see:

Achimenes	*Gloxinia*
Aeschynanthus	*Saintpaulia*
Columnea	*Sinningia*
Episcia	*Smithiantha*
Kohleria	*Streptocarpus*
Gesneria	

Two ways to propagate gesneriads

Leaf-vein cuttings

Many gesneriads can be propagated from leaf cuttings, with the result that plantlets grow either from leafstalks or cut veins. The vein-cutting method often gets quickest results. This is especially true of sinningias, since only a tuber will grow from a sinningia leafstalk, whereas careful cutting of the veins can produce several plantlets from a single leaf.

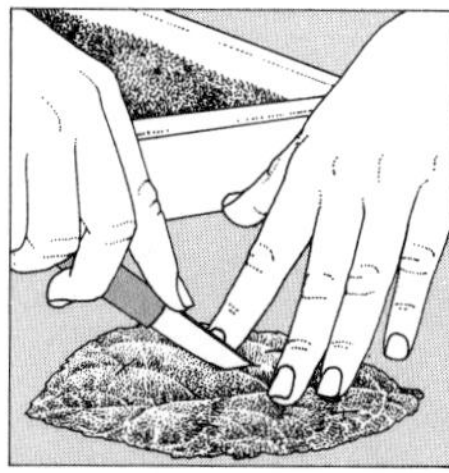

Cut through the underside of main veins at various points. Lay the leaf so that the cut veins touch the mixture.

Keep the cutting in bright light, after placing it under glass. Plantlets will soon develop at cut places.

Rhizome segments

One of the easiest ways to propagate rhizomatous gesneriads—such as smithianthas—is to divide the numerous tiny rhizomes produced by a plant in the course of a single season. It is even possible to break a rhizome into a number of pieces, and pot each piece up separately.

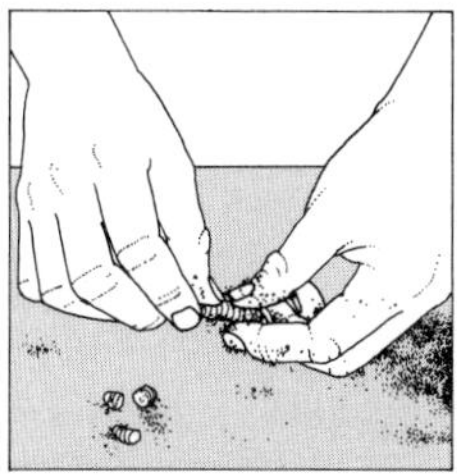

You do not need a knife to separate rhizomes. Just divide them in spring.

Plant each segment in a small pot, an inch below the surface of the mixture.

Gloxinia

GESNERIACEAE

G. perennis

THE true genus *Gloxinia* is a small group of plants with underground scaly rhizomes. Plants of this genus should not be confused with the so-called gloxinias of horticulture (florist gloxinias), which are tuberous-rooted members of the genus *Sinningia.*

Only two species of *Gloxinia* are commonly grown as house plants. One of them, the tree gloxinia, sometimes called *G. lindeniana,* is often classified as *Kohleria lindeniana* and is listed and described in this volume under the genus *Kohleria. G. perennis,* the other—and more popular—species, produces many rhizomes, each $\frac{1}{4}$ inch thick and several inches long, every year. A single upright stem can rise from the tip of each rhizome. The stems are green, often spotted with red, and grow up to 30 inches tall. They tend to sprawl with increased height unless staked. Oval, scallop-edged, slightly hairy, short-stalked leaves 3–7 inches long and $2\frac{1}{2}$–6 inches wide grow from the stems in opposite pairs. They have a glossy, deep green upper surface, with a paler green underside that may be flecked with red. Hairy, somewhat bell-shaped, $1\frac{1}{2}$-inch-long, lavender flowers grow singly from leaf axils on the upper half of the stem. A dark violet spot at the base of the throat is visible in the mouth of each flower.

G. perennis flowers in midsummer before the plant reaches maximum height. Its stems and leaves die back gradually in early fall, and the plant is dormant throughout the winter.

See also GESNERIADS.

PROPER CARE

Light During the active growth period *G. perennis* requires three or four hours a day of direct sunlight. Keep it out of the strong midday sun, however. When the plant is dormant, light is not a consideration.

Temperature All actively growing gloxinias will thrive at temperatures between 65° and 85°F. Temperatures outside these limits are harmful. Dormant rhizomes can withstand temperatures down to 45° if kept dry. During the active growth period place pots on trays of moist pebbles.

Watering When new shoots emerging from rhizomes indicate the start of active growth, begin to water moderately, giving enough to make the mixture moist throughout at each watering, but let the top half-inch of the mixture dry out between waterings. As dormancy approaches, reduce quantity and frequency over a period of three weeks until the stems have died back. Leave the mixture dry until repotting time the following spring.

Feeding Apply a high-phosphate liquid fertilizer at every watering during the active growth period. The dose should be one-quarter the recommended strength.

Potting and repotting Use a potting mixture composed of three parts sphagnum peat moss, two parts vermiculite, and one part perlite, adding a tablespoonful of lime chips or crushed egg-shells to each cup of mixture. Leave the dormant plant in its pot until early spring. Then remove the rhizomes, carefully shake off the previous year's mixture, and pull the rhizomes apart. Plant them singly about an inch deep in 5- or 6-inch pots of fresh, moist potting mixture, and place the pots in bright filtered light. Keep the mixture just moist, and do not feed until stem growth begins. Thereafter, treat the young plants as mature specimens.

Propagation The multiplying rhizomes normally provide plenty of new plants. It is possible to propagate *G. perennis* from seed, but this method requires care and attention.

Special points To encourage the plant to branch, pinch out the tips of all stems when they are 6 inches tall.

Graptopetalum

CRASSULACEAE

G. pachyphyllum

PLANTS of the genus *Graptopetalum* resemble some forms of the related genus *Echeveria.* Graptopetalums are small, compact, succulent plants grown for their interesting shapes and delicate flowers. The smooth, thick, lance-shaped leaves of all types are arranged in rosettes on short, profusely branching stems. If grown in good light, these leaves assume various soft shades of white, gray, or blue. Clusters of small, bell-shaped flowers are borne on 6-inch-long stalks that arise from leaf axils in spring. Individual flowers last for only a day or two, but the flowering period lasts for several weeks. Mature plants produce basal offsets freely.

See also SUCCULENTS.

RECOMMENDED GRAPTOPETALUMS

G. pachyphyllum is an attractive dwarf plant with thick, 1-inch-long stems carrying rosettes of bluish leaves. Each rosette is about 1 inch in diameter, and the individual leaves are $\frac{1}{2}$ inch long, $\frac{3}{16}$ inch wide, and $\frac{3}{16}$ inch thick. Red flowers are about $\frac{3}{4}$ inch long and $\frac{1}{4}$ inch across.

G. paraguayense (ghost or mother of pearl plant) has $2\frac{1}{2}$-inch-long stems that are normally upright but sometimes become prostrate. Rosettes 5 inches across are borne on the ends of stems and branches. Each rosette consists of whitish gray leaves 2–3 inches long, 1 inch wide, and $\frac{3}{4}$ inch thick. Leaf upper surfaces are flat, the undersides keeled. White flowers are up to $\frac{1}{2}$ inch long and $\frac{3}{16}$ inch across.

PROPER CARE

Light These plants need as much direct sunlight as possible to maintain characteristic growth and coloring.

Temperature During the active growth period (spring through fall) normal room temperatures are suitable. During the winter rest period keep these plants cool—at around 50°F, if possible.

Watering During the active growth period water moderately, giving enough at each watering to make the potting mixture moist throughout but allowing the top half-inch of the mixture to dry out before watering again. During the rest period water only enough to prevent the mixture from drying out. Avoid wetting the foliage. Drops of moisture on the rosettes can cause unsightly spotting.

Feeding It is not necessary to feed graptopetalums at any time.

Potting and repotting Use a potting mixture composed of one part of coarse sand or perlite to three parts of standard soil-based mixture (see page 429). Graptopetalums grow and spread rapidly, and they are best planted in pans or half-pots. Move each plant to a container one size larger every spring until the plant begins to lose its attractive shape because of loss of leaves. Pull off shriveled leaves when plants are being repotted. By the time a graptopetalum outgrows a 5-inch pan or half-pot, it has probably lost too many leaves to be worth retaining. Discard any such specimen after restarting from offsets.

Propagation Propagate from basal offsets taken in spring or summer. Remove an offset rosette by cutting its stem at the base with a sharp knife, and strip off the lower leaves to expose about $\frac{1}{2}$ inch of stem. Allow the cutting to dry for two days before pushing the stem gently into a 2-inch pot of the potting mixture recommended for adult plants. Place the pot in bright filtered light, and water moderately until rooting has occurred. Thereafter, treat the rooted offset as a mature graptopetalum.

Graptopetalums are not normally propagated from seed.

Special points Like the related echeverias, graptopetalums are prone to attack by mealy bugs. Examine plants carefully for this pest from time to time, and take appropriate measures to combat them. (See page 455. See also *Echeveria,* "Special points.")

Grevillea

PROTEACEAE

Silk-oak
G. robusta

GREVILLEA *robusta* (silk-oak) is the only species of grevillea grown as a house plant. This fast-growing evergreen tree—often seen in gardens in warmer parts of the U.S.—has finely bipinnate leaves 6–15 inches long that look like fern fronds; and young specimens are often included by nurserymen in mixed boxes of ferns offered for sale. In two to three years a grevillea grown indoors can become 6 feet tall, with a spread of around 18 inches. The dark green foliage, which is tinged brown when young, is slightly downy, with a silky underside. Flowers are not produced on plants grown indoors.

PROPER CARE

Light Grevilleas like direct sunlight but will grow well in medium light—for instance, at a sunless window—during the summer. In winter, these plants should be moved to the brightest possible position.

Temperature Tolerant of a wide range of temperatures, indoor grevilleas will grow quickly in warm rooms if the air is sufficiently humid, and more slowly in cool rooms. In temperatures above 65°F, stand pots on trays of moist pebbles or peat moss. Tolerable winter minimum is 45°.

Watering While grevilleas are growing rapidly, water them moderately, enough to make the mixture moist throughout at each watering but allowing the top half-inch of the mixture to dry out before watering again. At other times water more sparingly, allowing fully half the mixture to dry out before giving more water.

Feeding Apply standard liquid fertilizer every two weeks only while plants are growing rapidly.

Potting and repotting Although these plants will grow well enough in a standard soil-based mixture, they prefer a neutral or slightly acid potting mixture. If possible, use a lime-free soil-based mixture (see page 429). Move grevilleas into pots two sizes larger every spring. If the growth of a plant is exceptionally vigorous, it may be necessary to move it twice in a single year. Do not do this, however, at any time between mid-fall and the early spring.

Propagation Commercially, propagation is carried out from seeds, and is perhaps best left to the grower with a greenhouse. Small seedlings are generally available for purchase in spring from nurserymen. If seed is obtained, it can be germinated in a heated propagating case (see page 444), or on a well-lighted, but not sunny, windowsill at 55°–60°F. Use a lime-free seed mix, and keep it permanently moist (see page 444). When the seedlings are $1\frac{1}{2}$–2 inches high, pot them individually in 3-inch pots, and treat them as mature grevilleas.

The 2-foot grevillea and the hedera are the tall plants here. They back the lower-growing stromanthe, cyclamen, kalanchoe, peperomia and maranta.

Guzmania

BROMELIACEAE

G. lingulata minor

GUZMANIAS form a rosette of soft leaves, which are usually glossy and either plain green or else marked with fine brown or red lengthwise—or, rarely, crosswise—lines. Some forms have decorative foliage; others are prized chiefly for their flower heads, which may be either on tall stalks or on stumpy ones in the center of the rosette. The short-lived flowers are normally white or yellow, but the long-lasting bracts as well as the rest of the flower head may be a brilliant red or orange. The flowering season is usually late winter. *See also BROMELIADS.*

RECOMMENDED GUZMANIAS

G. lingulata is quite a variable species; individual specimens differ considerably in some respects. Characteristic of the species are smooth green leaves $1\frac{1}{2}$ feet long and an inch wide, with a flower stalk up to 1 foot long bearing small yellow flowers in the center of a cup-shaped or funnel-shaped flower head of 2-inch-long crimson bracts. Among a number of forms are *G. l. cardinalis,* which is a little larger than the species plant and has bracts of an even stronger red; and *G. l. minor,* which grows less than 12 inches tall, with leaves only about 4 inches long and a cup-shaped flower head on a short, stumpy stem carrying variably colored bracts.

G. monostachia (formerly called *G. tricolor*) has bright green leaves up to 15 inches long and a long-stalked, poker-shaped flower head comprising 1-inch-long white flowers and greenish white bracts striped with purplish lines and tipped with orange or red. The leaves of a variegated form, *G. m. variegata,* are striped with white.

G. monostachia

G. musaica has somewhat tougher leaves, which grow up to 2 feet long and are bright green, cross-banded with dense, wavy-edged patches of fine brown lines above and purple lines beneath. The flower stalk, which is up to 15 inches long, is capped with 20 or more flesh-colored, waxy, $1\frac{1}{2}$-inch-long, oval flowers within yellow, pink-striped bracts.

G. zahnii has slender, almost transparent leaves each up to 18 inches long, which are conspicuously striped lengthwise with fine red lines on both upper and lower surfaces. The center of the rosette is a strong coppery red. The yellow or white flowers are surrounded by red bracts and appear on a foot-long stalk that also has small red bracts along its length.

Note: New and increasingly spectacular *Guzmania* hybrids—for instance *G.* 'Orangeade' and *G.* 'Omer Morobe'—are constantly being produced by breeders, and are gradually becoming available.

PROPER CARE

Light Guzmanias like bright filtered light. They will not flower too far from a window.

Temperature Give these plants temperatures above 65°F, with high humidity. Stand pots on trays of damp pebbles, and mist-spray foliage every day.

Watering Keep the potting mixture moist by watering plentifully. The rosette will hold some water, but not much. Keep it topped up with plain water except when in bloom.

In their native rain-forests guzmania rosettes are seldom dry. Keep them topped up, preferably with rainwater.

Feeding Apply standard liquid fertilizer every two weeks not only to the potting mixture but over the foliage and into the central cup.

Potting and repotting Use the potting mixture recommended for bromeliads (see page 107). Since these plants have little root, 3- or 4-inch pots should be large enough. If a plant needs more room, move it into a pot one size larger in the spring.

Propagation In spring cut offsets from the parent, but not before the offsets are 3 inches long. Insert each offset in a 2- to $2\frac{1}{2}$-inch pot of bromeliad mixture, keep it in bright filtered light, and water it moderately. When the offset is well rooted (in about six months) move it into a pot one size larger and treat it as mature.

Gymnocalycium

CACTACEAE

Rose-plaid cactus
G. quehlianum

THE genus *Gymnocalycium* (chin or rose-plaid cactus) comprises about 40 species of desert cactus, together with many varieties. Certain plants that botanists consider varieties are often noted as "species," and it is therefore possible to buy the same plant under more than one name. All gymnocalyciums have attractive flowers, but the varied spine formation makes these cacti extremely attractive even when not in bloom. The green stems are mostly globular in shape, ribbed, and often with clefts beneath the spine-bearing areoles, giving a "chin" effect. Characteristic of the genus are the completely hairless flower buds ("gymnocalycium" means "naked bud").

Even when mature, these cacti are comparatively small, and so a good collection can be housed in a fairly limited space. Some species form offsets when quite young, others remain solitary, and a few form clumps of smaller stems. Gymnocalyciums generally begin to flower when about 2 inches in diameter, but some bloom when only half this size. The flowers, which are flat or slightly vase-shaped and are carried on a flower tube, are white, pink, red, or yellowish. They measure 1–3 inches across and appear toward the tops of plants throughout the warmer months.

See also CACTI.

RECOMMENDED GYMNOCALYCIUMS

G. baldianum (sometimes called by its former name of *G. venturianum*) reaches a diameter of about 3 inches and has broad, prominent ribs and pronounced "chins." Flowers are up to 2 inches in diameter; their color is most commonly brilliant red, but may be pink in some specimens. The whitish or yellowish spines are all radials, and each spine is $\frac{1}{4}$ inch long.

G. bruchii (sometimes called *G. lafaldense*) is a small, clump-forming plant, with individual globular stems up to an inch across and the whole clump reaching a spread of about 4 inches. Each stem has 12 flattish ribs. The flowers, also about an inch in diameter, are delicate pink, and the thin, white, $\frac{1}{4}$-inch-long spines are in starlike clusters. The spines are generally radials, but there is an occasional brownish central spine. *G. bruchii* is a profusely flowering, compact plant.

G. denudatum (spider cactus) forms a flattened sphere up to 4 inches high and 6 inches across. It has broad, prominent ribs; thick, curved, $\frac{1}{2}$-inch-long, radial spines, which are grayish tipped with brown; and white flowers up to 3 inches across.

G. mihanovichii is a variable species with many varieties. It can reach a diameter of about 3 inches but flowers freely when much smaller. The prominent ribs are sharply angled, and the whole plant often has reddish banded markings. The yellowish spines, all of which are radials, are fairly thin, curved, and about $\frac{1}{2}$ inch long. The flowers are 1–2 inches in diameter and greenish yellow or pink. This plant has given rise to varieties with bright red stems, known as 'Ruby Ball' or 'Hibotan' cacti. These lack chlorophyll and must therefore always be grown by being grafted on to the top of a green cactus base.

G. platense reaches a diameter of about 4 inches. It has pronounced tuberclelike "chins" and spreading, whitish spines, all radials, which are red at the base and about $\frac{1}{2}$ inch long. The flowers are about 3 inches across and white, but tinged with green and red at the base.

G. quehlianum is flattened rather than globular. It attains a diameter of about 6 inches and a height of no more than about 2 inches. The stem, which is of a dull bluish green color, has 8 to 12 broad, prominent ribs, with pronounced "chins" below the rounded, woolly areoles. Each areole bears five or six rather thin radial spines $\frac{1}{4}$–$\frac{1}{2}$ inch long, and these tend to curve inward toward the stem. They are yellowish, darkening to brownish red toward the base. There are no central spines. The abundantly produced flowers are 2 to 3 inches across, basically white but tinged with red at the center. A variety of this species, *G. q. zantnerianum* (sometimes sold as *G. zantnerianum*) differs markedly in only one respect: Its flowers are pinkish rather than white and have a darker red center.

G. saglione, one of the largest gymnocalyciums, has deeply grooved "chins." It seldom flowers before it is 7–8 inches across, but it is most attractive while still small. Its stout, curved spines are reddish brown but become paler with age. Each areole bears up to 12 radial spines 1–1$\frac{1}{2}$ inches long and 2 or 3 slightly shorter centrals. Flowers

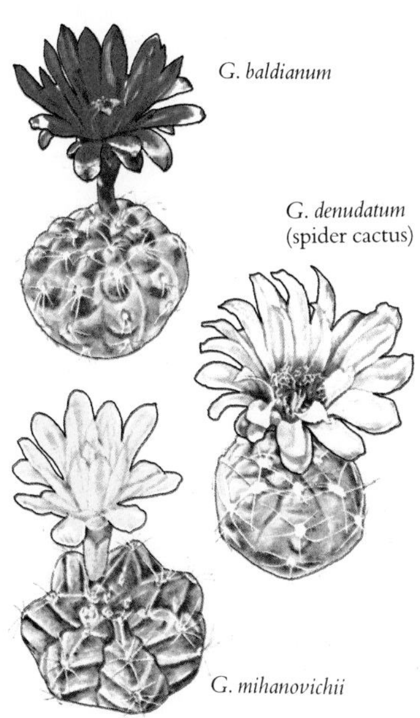

G. baldianum

G. denudatum (spider cactus)

G. mihanovichii

are funnel-shaped, greenish to pink, and about $1\frac{1}{2}$ inches across. The spines of a variety, *G. s. tilcarense,* are less noticeably curved.

PROPER CARE

Light Grow the plants in bright light. Otherwise, they lose their globular shape, become elongated, and are unlikely to flower well.

Temperature These desert cacti can tolerate a winter temperature of about 40°F, and thus are never likely to suffer from cold indoors. In fact, too much winter warmth may discourage flowering the following year. In winter, therefore, they should have the coolest available position consistent with the best light. During the summer gymnocalyciums can stand almost any amount of heat.

Watering In spring and summer water gymnocalyciums plentifully—enough to keep the potting mixture thoroughly moist, though never soggy. Reduce the quantity as winter approaches, and give only enough throughout the winter months to prevent shriveling.

Feeding Actively growing plants may be fed once every two weeks. Use the high-potassium type of fertilizer normally given to tomatoes.

Potting and repotting Add a one-third extra portion of coarse sand or perlite to any good soil-based potting mixture or soilless mixture (see page 429). Plants should be moved into pots one size larger in spring if roots appear to be filling the pots. Most species can be grown successfully in a maximum pot size of 4 inches. Either clay or plastic pots will do, but be sure to put a few clay-pot fragments in the bottom for drainage.

Propagation When offsets appear, detach them with a sharp knife, allow them to dry for a few days to harden the cut surface, and then push them lightly into rooting mixture (see page 444). They may be placed either singly in 3-inch pots or several together at inch-wide intervals in a 6-inch half-pot. The best time to do this is spring or early summer. Place the potted offsets in a warm, shady position, and water them only enough to keep the mixture just moist. When roots emerge from the drainage holes of pots, transfer the rooted offsets into pots one size larger containing the potting mixture for adult plants, and thereafter treat them as mature.

Gynura

COMPOSITAE

Purple passion vine
G. sarmentosa

GYNURAS are chiefly prized for their softly hairy, velvety purple leaves. The two kinds usually grown as house plants have purple hair on both upper and lower surfaces of leaves, stems, and flower heads. In spring or summer they produce rather unpleasantly scented, orange-colored flowers, which are best picked off before they open. When the leaves of

G. sarmentosa
(flower)

most gynuras are new and developing, they have an even stronger purple coloring than they have when mature.

There is considerable confusion about the naming of species within this genus. The confusion results partly from the fact that two distinct types of growth can appear on certain plants at different times. In addition, the two kinds of gynura that are generally grown as house plants have a number of popular (and often overlapping) names, and this probably adds to the confusion.

RECOMMENDED GYNURAS

G. aurantiaca (purple velvet, or royal velvet plant) has stems that are erect at first, though they later sprawl about. In the wild the stems can grow to be 8–9 feet long. Leaves are roughly oval,

G. aurantiaca
(purple velvet)

rather coarsely toothed, and up to 8 inches long and 4 inches wide. Commercial growers often prune the plant considerably to keep it compact, and this may well make it lose its initially upright look.

G. sarmentosa shares many of the common names given to *G. aurantiaca,* and it is also called purple passion vine. It is almost certainly not a true species but is a variety of *G. aurantiaca.* The word "vine" in the common name is appropriate for the plant, which is a twining or trailing form incapable of supporting itself. The leaves are 3–4 inches long and of about the same width. This plant is especially effective when it is used in hanging baskets or is otherwise permitted to trail so as to exhibit to the full extent the color of its foliage.

PROPER CARE

Light Some direct sunlight every day is essential for close growth and strikingly colored foliage. Too little light will cause shoots to elongate and develop pale green growing tips.

Temperature Gynuras grow well in normal room temperatures as long as humidity is high enough, and they can survive in temperatures down to 55°F. Stand pots on trays or saucers of moist pebbles.

Watering Avoid wetting the foliage. The fine hairs on the leaves are liable to trap beads of moisture which can cause unsightly spots. Water moderately in warm conditions, allowing the top inch of the mixture to dry out between waterings. In relatively cool temperatures—below about 60°F—give only enough to keep the potting mixture from drying out.

Feeding Apply standard liquid fertilizer throughout the year, but no more than once a month. Overfeeding produces coarse, soft growth.

Potting and repotting Use a soil-based mixture (see page 429). Both types of gynura grow rapidly and need to be moved into larger pots in spring, but two years is the maximum time that these plants remain attractive. After that, new plants should be started from cuttings.

Propagation Gynuras are very easy to propagate by tip cuttings taken in early spring. Insert three or four cuttings 3–4 inches long in a 3-inch pot containing an equal-parts mixture of peat moss and sand, and keep them warm in bright filtered light, watering just enough to keep the mixture barely moist. Rooting will normally take place in two to three weeks. After a further four to five weeks, begin applications of standard liquid fertilizer once every two weeks. When plants have made about 6 inches of new growth, move them into a 4- or 5-inch pot of standard mixture, and treat them as mature gynuras. For the fullest effect several young plants should be kept in a single container.

Special points *G. sarmentosa* should be nipped out regularly to encourage bushy growth; otherwise the plant will become thin and lanky.

Aphids are apt to attack young growth. They are easy to spot against the purple foliage, and single aphids can be picked off by hand. If they become too well established, use a suitable pesticide (see page 460).

Haemanthus

AMARYLLIDACEAE

African blood lily
H. albiflos

THE genus *Haemanthus* (African blood lily) consists of bulbous plants with showy flowers. Some species are deciduous and must be rested almost dry for two or three months; others have brief rest periods but retain their leaves. The bulbs of some species produce offsets. Flowers of all species are short-lived; flower size and coloring differ considerably.
See also BULBS, CORMS, and TUBERS.

RECOMMENDED HAEMANTHUSES

H. albiflos is not deciduous. It has fleshy, rounded-oblong leaves 9–12 inches long and 4 inches wide, which are dull-surfaced, dark green, and bordered with fine, white hairs. Each bulb usually has four stalkless leaves arranged in arching pairs. Every spring a new pair is produced from the "crease" between the upper pair of leaves. Soon afterward the lower pair dry up, when they can be pulled away. A single, cup-shaped head composed of many flowers appears in late summer or early fall on a 9-inch-long, ¾-inch-thick, green stalk. The 2-inch-wide flower head consists of 8 to 10 petallike, inch-long bracts enclosing dozens of inch-long stamens. The bracts are white marked with fine green lines, and the stamens are white tipped with yellow. When the plant is several years old, it produces offsets.

H. coccineus (blood lily) has stalkless, fleshy, strap-shaped, dark green leaves up to 2 feet long and 6 inches wide. There are usually two per bulb, and they develop fully after the bulb has flowered. They remain through winter and spring, dying down in early summer. After a short rest period a green, red-spotted flower stalk begins to rise from the leafless bulb. By early fall the 10- to 12-inch-long, inch-thick stalk carries a 2½-inch-wide, cup-shaped flower head composed of six or eight bracts 1½–2 inches long surrounding 1½-inch-long stamens. Bracts are blood red, stamens orange-red tipped with yellow. Offsets are not produced.

H. katharinae produces stems up to 2 feet tall, which carry 9- to 12-inch-long, 4- to 6-inch-wide, lance-shaped leaves with inch-long stalks. The leaves, usually kept throughout the year, are undulate and medium green with pale green veins. In summer a green flower stalk (often spotted with red at the base) rises from the bulb. The stalk carries a globe-shaped, salmon red flower head 6 to 9 inches across, which consists of tubular flowers, each up to 2 inches long. Inch-long stamens jut out from the tips of the tubes. Offsets are not produced.

H. multiflorus has three or four pointed-oval leaves about 10 inches long and 4–5 inches wide. These are arranged on inch-long stalks around a 6- to 9-inch-long stem. The stem and leaves appear in early spring and are shed in fall. The flower head on its foot-long stalk is generally bright red, appears in late spring, and is less than 6 inches in diameter. Offsets are not produced by these bulbs.

PROPER CARE

Light Provide bright light, with some direct sunlight every day. Light is not important during dormancy.

Temperature Room temperature is suitable. Avoid temperatures below 55°F, even in dormancy.

Watering Water moderately, allowing the top half-inch of the potting mixture to dry out between waterings. When the leaves of a deciduous haemanthus begin to yellow, gradually reduce the amount, and give dormant bulbs only enough to keep the mixture from becoming completely dry. During the winter water species that retain their leaves only enough to keep the mixture from drying out.

Feeding Apply a high-potash liquid fertilizer to actively growing plants every two weeks.

Potting and repotting Use a soil-based potting mixture (see page 429). When planting bulbs, choose pots that allow an inch of space between the bulb and the rim. Move a haemanthus into a larger pot only when its roots appear on the surface of the mixture or the bulb edges approach the edge of the pot. Otherwise, topdress it (see page 428) in early spring.

Propagation When *H. albiflos* has produced a group of bulbs, the group may be divided in early spring just as the parent plant starts into new growth. Plant bulbs separately, half-burying them in the potting mixture. Water each newly potted bulb sparingly for four or five weeks, and do not feed it until the plant is well established. Otherwise, treat the bulb as a mature plant. Haemanthuses that do not produce offsets can be propagated only from seed.

Hamatocactus

CACTACEAE

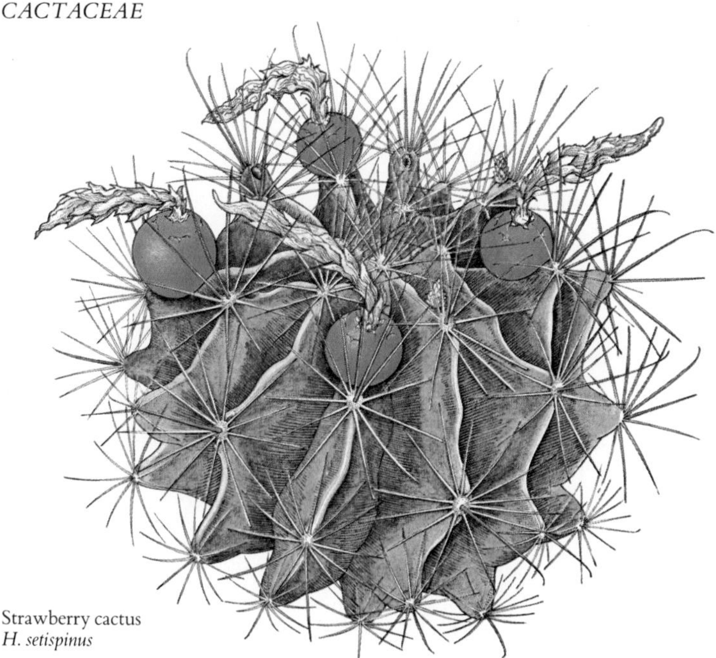

Strawberry cactus
H. setispinus

THESE desert cacti have a single stem and do not normally produce offsets. Yellow flowers arising from areoles near the top are cup-shaped and 3–4 inches across. Three or four flowers will appear simultaneously throughout summer and early fall. They last for several days.

See also CACTI.

RECOMMENDED HAMATOCACTI

H. hamatacanthus (sometimes called *Ferocactus hamatacanthus*; popularly known as Turk's head) has a dark green, globular stem that gradually elongates. A 10-year-old specimen in a 6-inch pot will be up to 9 inches tall and 5 inches across. The 13 to 17 prominent, narrow ribs have notched edges that carry whitish areoles, each of which bears 8 to 12 thin, 1-inch-long radial spines and 4 stouter, 2-inch-long, hooked centrals. When young, all spines are red, but they fade to whitish. Flowering begins when the plant is 4–5 inches tall.

H. setispinus (strawberry cactus) has a dark green stem that reaches a height of 6 inches and a width of 4 inches in a 5-inch pot. It has about 12 narrow, notched ribs, which carry gray areoles. Each areole bears 12 to 15 thin, inch-long, brownish radial spines and 1 to 3 longer, stouter centrals, which are hooked. The flowers are followed by berrylike fruits.

PROPER CARE

Light Always give these cacti direct sunlight in order to encourage flowering.

Temperature Normal room temperatures are suitable during the active growth period, but hamatocacti need a winter rest at about 50°F. Minimum tolerable temperature: 40°.

Watering During the active growth period water moderately, but let the top half-inch of the mixture dry out between waterings. In winter give only enough to prevent the mixture from drying out.

Feeding Apply tomato-type, high-potassium fertilizer every two weeks during spring and summer.

Potting and repotting Use a mixture of one part coarse sand or perlite to three parts of standard soil- or peat-based mixture (see page 429). Remove each plant from its pot every spring, and move it to a pot one size larger if roots have filled the old pot. Otherwise, shake off as much mixture as possible and replace the plant in its pot, which has been cleaned. Add fresh mixture as necessary.

Propagation These plants are raised from seed (see *CACTI*, page 119).

Special points The areoles of *H. setispinus* tend to excrete a substance that encourages the growth of a black mold. If stickiness appears, rinse it off with warm water, and keep the plant in a warm place until dry.

Haworthia

LILIACEAE

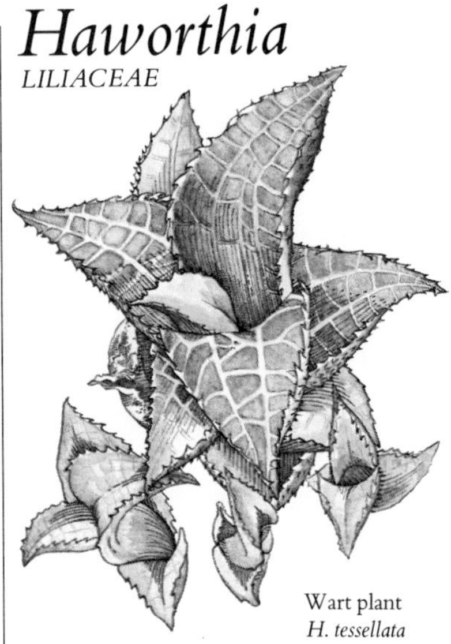

Wart plant
H. tessellata

AMONG the more than 160 species of haworthia (wart plant), which are small succulents, several are prized as house plants because of their interestingly shaped and colored leaves. These thick, stalkless leaves are arranged in a rosette around an often hardly visible stem. Some haworthias are low and compact while others grow quite tall, with several rows of overlapping leaves. A number of plants have relatively hard, tough leaves; others have soft, fleshy leaves. There are sometimes small translucent areas on the upper surface of the soft leaves. In the wild, these haworthias live nearly buried in sand, and they get much of their light through these "windows" during dry seasons.

Flowers of all species are whitish, narrowly tubular, less than 1 inch long and $\frac{1}{4}$ inch across, and carried in clusters on long, thin, wirelike stems. Since the blooms are uninteresting, many growers cut the flower stems off as soon as they appear. Plants can flower at almost any time.

Haworthias are easy-to-grow and unlike most succulents, they thrive in partial shade. And those recommended below produce many offsets, which can be used for propagation.
See also SUCCULENTS.

RECOMMENDED HAWORTHIAS

H. cuspidata forms clusters of low-growing, 3-inch-wide rosettes. Each tightly packed rosette consists of stiffly pointed, soft, pale green leaves that arch strongly outward and hide the short stem. Individual leaves are triangular, about 1 inch long, $\frac{1}{2}$ inch broad at the base, and up to $\frac{1}{2}$ inch thick. Leaf surfaces are flat and slightly translucent toward the tips above, and rounded and keeled toward the tips on the undersides.

H. margaritifera (pearl plant) has lance-shaped, rather tough, dark green leaves thickly spotted with pearly white warts. Stems are very short, and the many-leaved rosettes, which can attain a diameter of 6 inches and a height of 3–4 inches, appear to be stemless. A cluster of rosettes forms quickly (within about a year). The lower, older leaves of each rosette stand erect, but the younger ones toward the rosette center curve inward. The $\frac{1}{4}$-inch-thick leaves are about $3\frac{1}{2}$ inches long and $1\frac{1}{4}$ inches wide at the base. Leaf upper surfaces are flat, while the undersides are keeled toward the tips.

H. reinwardtii has stems about 6 inches long densely packed with triangular, tough, dark green leaves, each of which curves inward. Individual leaves are about $1\frac{1}{2}$ inches long, $\frac{1}{2}$ inch thick, and $\frac{1}{2}$ inch wide at the base, and they are covered with tiny, pearly warts. Leaf upper surfaces are flat, the lower surfaces rounded and keeled toward the tops. Overlapping leaves are so numerous that they hide the stems. Offsets look rather like fir cones at first, and a cluster of them forms within a year or two. The species is extremely variable, with a number of widely differing forms.

H. reinwardtii

H. margaritifera (pearl plant)

H. tessellata forms clusters of almost stemless rosettes about 2 inches high and 3 inches across. The green or brownish leaves are tooth-edged, broadly triangular, about $1\frac{1}{2}$ inches long, 1 inch wide, and $\frac{1}{4}$ inch thick at the base. Each leaf narrows down to a fine point at the tip. Leaf upper surfaces are slightly rounded, translucent, and marked with a network of whitish lines. The undersides of the leaves are completely covered with whitish warts.

PROPER CARE

Light Never place haworthias in direct sunlight. If exposed to summer sun, foliage will shrivel. Medium light suits all types at all times.

Temperature Normal room temperatures are satisfactory at all times, but haworthias do best if winter temperatures are kept below about 60°F. They have a rest period from midwinter to late spring and can survive temperatures down to 40°. They do prefer more warmth even while resting in winter and spring, however.

Watering During the active growth period water moderately, enough to make the potting mixture moist throughout but allowing the top half-inch to dry out between waterings. During the rest period water only enough to prevent the potting mixture from drying out completely. Never let the mixture become completely dry, however. Although haworthias are succulent plants, they cannot survive total drought.

Feeding It is neither necessary nor advisable to feed haworthias.

Potting and repotting Use a porous potting mixture composed of one part of coarse sand or perlite to two parts of standard soil-based mixture (see page 429). Since haworthias are shallow-rooted, half-pots are best suited to the clustering habit of the plants. In potting a specimen, always leave a $1\frac{1}{2}$- to 2-inch space between the edges of the cluster and the rim of the pot to allow for new growth. Repot in spring at the start of the growth period. After pulling or cutting off any dead or shriveled leaves, move each plant into a larger pot only if the rosette cluster covers the entire surface of the mixture. The largest pot size needed will be 5–6 inches. A plant that has grown beyond that size should be split up.

Propagation Remove offsets in summer; they pull away easily. Pot up immediately any offset with roots already attached and treat it as a mature plant. Allow an offset without roots to dry for three days, however. Then press it into the potting mixture, and treat it as an adult.

Haworthias grow readily from seed (see *SUCCULENTS,* page 379). These plants hybridize so easily, however, that the results are likely to turn out unpredictable.

Hedera
ARALIACEAE

THE small genus *Hedera* (ivy) includes only a few species, but many varieties, of woody-stemmed, climbing plant. A few of these grow 20 feet or more and have large leaves, but most are prized for their dense, low growth and small leaves. The leaves of all types are leathery, and they are often lobed. Most hederas produce short aerial roots from the nodes of stems. When the roots come in contact with a suitable damp surface, they attach themselves to it.

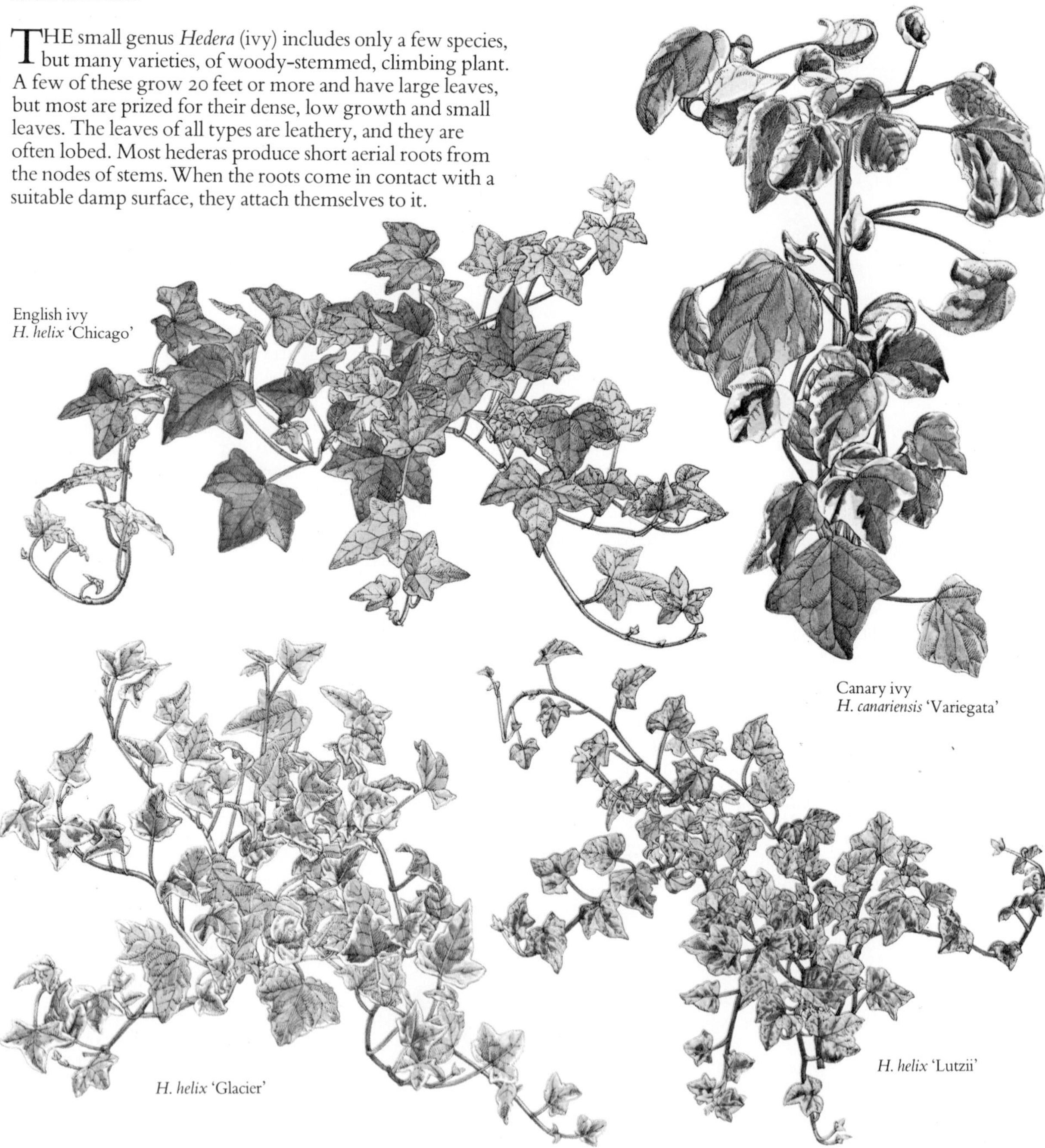

English ivy
H. helix 'Chicago'

Canary ivy
H. canariensis 'Variegata'

H. helix 'Glacier'

H. helix 'Lutzii'

RECOMMENDED HEDERAS

H. canariensis (Canary or Algerian ivy) is a tall-growing species with triangular, slightly lobed leaves that are 5 inches long and 6 inches wide. The leaves are dark green with fine, pale green veins, but the stems and leafstalks are deep red. The leaves of a smaller, variegated-leaved form, *H.c.* 'Variegata' (sometimes called *H.c.* 'Gloire de Marengo' or, popularly, Hagenburger's ivy), are 3–4 inches long and 2 to 3 inches wide, with patches of gray-green and bold creamy yellow margins.

H. colchica (colchic, fragrant, or Persian ivy) also grows tall. It has heart-shaped, deep green leaves 10 inches long and 8 inches wide. A variety, *H.c.* 'Ravenholst,' has red leafstalks.

H. helix (English ivy) has typically "ivy-shaped" leaves with three to five lobes, of which the one at the apex is the longest and most pointed. The original species has been superseded by its many varieties. Most of the following plants are "self-branching" (each stem tends to branch naturally at frequent intervals), and this makes the plants attractively dense and bushy. As

Hedera leaf shapes and markings

indicated in the list, however, some varieties of this species will become bushy only if their growing tips are pinched out frequently.

***H.h.* 'Chicago'** has 1- to 1½-inch-long and 1½-inch-wide, medium green leaves. The leaves of one of its forms, *H.h.* 'Chicago Variegata,' are creamy-edged. Those of another, *H.h.* 'Golden Chicago,' are marked with golden yellow patches.

***H.h.* 'Cristata'** (parsley ivy) has 1½- to 2-inch-long and 2-inch-wide medium green leaves that are so notably undulate as to seem curly-edged.

***H.h.* 'Emerald Gem'** and *H.h.* 'Emerald Jewel' both have 1-inch-long and 1½-inch-wide, sharply pointed, emerald green leaves.

***H.h.* 'Glacier'** has 1½-inch-long and 1-inch-wide leaves that are medium green with gray-green blotches, white marginal patches and pink edges. For dense growth this plant needs pinching out two or three times a year.

***H.h.* 'Jubilee'** has 1-inch-long and ¾- to 1-inch-wide dark green leaves variegated with gray and white. This variety is notably dense.

***H.h.* 'Little Diamond'** has roughly diamond-shaped, 1-inch-long and ¾-inch-wide, medium green leaves thinly bordered with white. It needs pinching out to become bushy.

***H.h.* 'Lutzii'** has 1½-inch-long and 1-inch-wide, dark green leaves covered with pale green and yellow spots. Not self-branching, it needs pinching out two or three times a year.

***H.h.* 'Sagittifolia'** has arrow-head-shaped, 2-inch-long and 1½-inch-wide, dark green leaves. A variegated form, *H.h.* 'Sagittifolia Variegata,' has light green and pale yellow markings. These plants make excellent trailers, but growing points must be pinched out if bushy growth is desired.

PROPER CARE

Light Hederas need bright light. Variegated forms should have two or three hours of sunlight a day in order to retain their color contrast, but the other types do best if kept out of direct sunlight. In inadequate light, gaps between leaves lengthen, and plants become increasingly spindly.

Temperature Ivies can tolerate a broad range of room temperatures, but they do not thrive in situations where the temperature is permitted to fluctuate widely. In temperatures above 65°F provide extra humidity. During the winter months encourage them to take a short rest by keeping them cool. A temperature of 50° is ideal.

Subtle variations in shape and color among species of hedera grown together create an attractive display.

Watering During the active growth period water moderately, allowing the top half-inch of mixture to dry out between waterings. In the rest period water sparingly, allowing half the mixture to dry out between waterings.

Feeding Apply standard liquid fertilizer to actively growing plants every two weeks.

Potting and repotting Use a soil-based potting mixture (see page 429). Move small plants into pots one size larger whenever pale roots emerge through drainage holes. Maximum pot size needed should be 5 or 6 inches. Topdress annually those plants that are not being moved on (see page 428). For the best effect put four to six small plants in a single hanging basket.

Propagation Hederas are easy to propagate. Three- to 4-inch-long cuttings will root quickly in a glass of water kept at normally warm room temperature in bright indirect light. When the roots are 1 to 1½ inches long, plant two or three cuttings together in a 3-inch pot of the standard potting mix recommended for adult plants.

Alternatively, insert three or four tip cuttings in a 3-inch pot containing a moistened equal-parts mixture of peat moss and coarse sand or perlite, and enclose the whole in a plastic bag or heated propagating case (see page 444). Given adequate warmth and bright indirect light, the cuttings will root in two to three weeks, after which they should be uncovered, watered moderately, and fed monthly with standard liquid fertilizer. When their roots have filled the pot and have begun to grow through the drainage hole, transfer the cuttings into a larger pot of standard mixture and treat them as mature plants. Hederas can also be propagated by layering (see page 439).

Special points Ivy kept in a warm room is susceptible to attack by red spider mites (see page 455). Spray the leaves with water once or twice a week, and put foliage under running water at least once a month to discourage and dislodge the mites.

If plants do not rest, weak growth may be produced during the winter months because of insufficient light. Cut weak shoots out with a knife or a pair of scissors in early spring. Over-long shoots may be shortened back at any convenient time.

Rooting a tip cutting

To propagate a hedera begin by taking a tip cutting from just above a growth bud.

When placed in water, the cutting will quickly develop roots long enough for it to be potted on.

Heliocereus

CACTACEAE

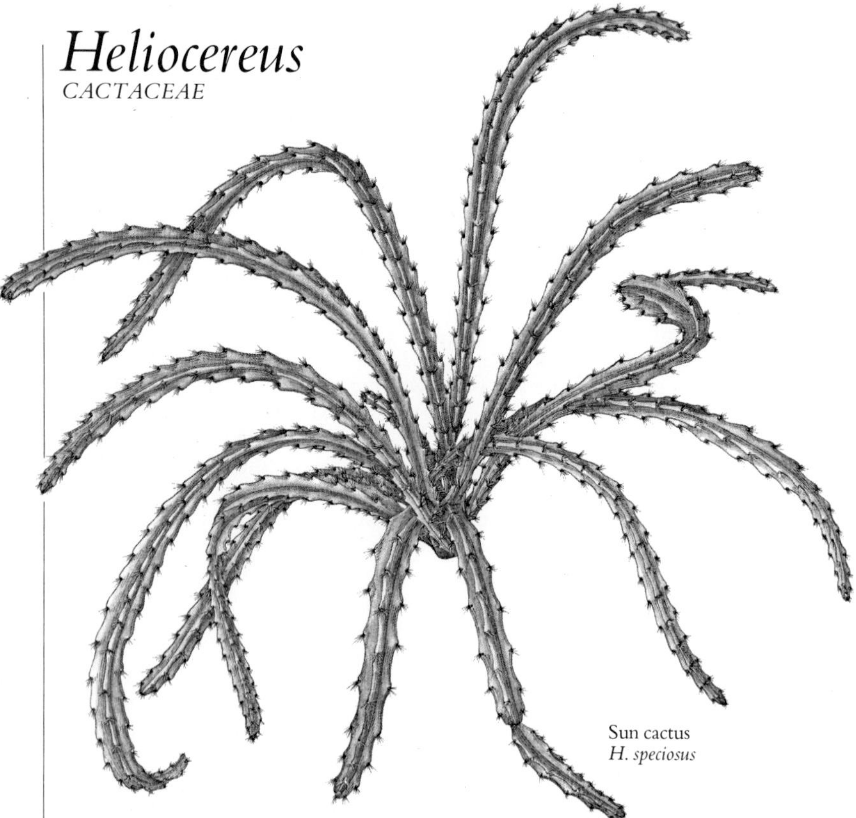

Sun cactus
H. speciosus

ONLY one of the five species of the genus *Heliocereus* is normally grown indoors: *H. speciosus* (sun cactus). This jungle cactus, notable for its beautiful flowers, has slender, trailing, bright green stems that branch from the base. Each stem, which can grow 3 feet long and 2 inches wide, has three to five narrow ribs separated by broad, shallow indentations. The undulate edges of the ribs carry woolly areoles, spaced about 1 inch apart, and every areole carries five to eight thin spines $\frac{1}{2}$ inch long. The spines vary in color from whitish to brown.

The funnel-shaped flowers, which appear from areoles in almost any part of the long stems, are slightly scented, about 6 inches long and 4 inches across, and bright scarlet with a bluish sheen in the throat. This cactus is one ancestor of a great number of *Epiphyllum* hybrids, many of which have flowers with the characteristic coloration of *H. speciosus.* Heliocereus flowers are produced in spring and summer, usually only one at a time, and remain open for several days. There is a variety, *H.s. albiflorus* (also known as *H.s. amecamensis* or, sometimes, *H. amecamensis*), with pure white flowers.

H. speciosus albiflorus
(flower)

See also CACTI.

PROPER CARE

Light These jungle cacti benefit from limited amounts of direct sunlight so give them bright light. Never leave them in midday sun.

Temperature Normal room temperatures are suitable for heliocereuses throughout the year.

Watering Although heliocereuses do not have well-marked periods of active growth and rest, they tend to grow most actively in spring and summer. During those seasons water plentifully enough to keep the mixture thoroughly moist, but never allow the plants to stand in water. Water more moderately during the rest of the year, allowing the top half-inch of the potting mixture to dry out between waterings. Never permit the potting mixture to dry out completely.

Feeding Give heliocereuses a high potassium, tomato-type of fertilizer when flower buds start to form. Apply the fertilizer every two weeks until flowering has finished.

Potting and repotting Use a rich equal-parts potting mixture composed of standard soil-based mixture (see page 429), coarse sand or perlite, and leaf mold. An alternative mixture in places where leaf mold is unobtainable is one part of coarse sand or perlite with three parts of either soil- or peat-based mixture. The best time to repot is just after the plant has finished flowering. Take it out of its pot (holding the stems gently in a folded newspaper), and examine the roots. If they are tightly packed, move the plant into a pot one size larger. If the roots have plenty of space to grow in, moving on is not necessary. Simply remove as much of the old mixture as you can without damaging the root system, and replace the plant in its old pot, which has been cleaned. Add fresh mixture as necessary.

Sprawling growth makes these cacti particularly suitable for planting in hanging baskets. Those grown in pots need support to keep upright. Provide this by tying stems to sticks pushed into the potting mixture. A 6-inch pot is likely to be the largest, even for a plant with 3-foot-long stems.

Propagation A heliocereus is best propagated by means of stem cuttings taken in spring or summer. Cut off a branch 4–6 inches long close to the potting-mixture level, and allow the cutting to dry for one or two days. Then insert it about an inch deep into a 3-inch pot of the recommended mixture for heliocereuses. Keep the cutting at normal room temperature in medium light, watering often enough to keep the mixture barely moist, until new growth indicates that rooting has occurred. Thereafter, treat the new plant as a mature specimen.

Propagation is also possible by taking a 1- to 2-foot-long stem and cutting it crosswise into three or more sections. These can be handled in the same way as the single short cutting, but be sure to plant each section the right way up. A stem section will not produce a normal plant if the end that was closer to the roots of the parent plant is pointed upward instead of being inserted in the potting mixture.

Hemigraphis
ACANTHACEAE

Red ivy
H. alternata

ONLY one true species of the genus *Hemigraphis, H. alternata,* (formerly *H. colorata*), and one hybrid, *H.* 'Exotica,' are widely grown indoors. Both kinds are popularly known as red ivy or red-flame ivy. Alike in most respects, they have fleshy, wine red stems up to 1 foot long that tend to creep or trail, making the plants ideal for growing in hanging baskets. Oval to heart-shaped leaves up to 3 inches long and 2 inches wide are arranged along the stems in opposite pairs on ½- to 1-inch-long, wine red leafstalks. Leaf edges are toothed, and leaf color is metallic, purplish gray on the upper surface and deep wine red on the underside. Inconspicuous, short-lived, white flowers ½–¾ inch long appear in terminal spikes at the end of summer. The stems root down wherever nodes touch the potting mixture.

RECOMMENDED HEMIGRAPHISES

H. alternata has more nearly heart-shaped leaves than *H.* 'Exotica.' The vein areas of the leaves are notably sunken and conspicuous.

***H.* 'Exotica'** differs in that its leaves have a deeper purple hue, and leaf surfaces are more puckered than those of *H. alternata.*

PROPER CARE

Light Give these plants bright light without direct sunlight. Do not keep them more than 4 feet away from a window, however, or they will become spindly.

Temperature Keep the temperature at 65°–75°F throughout the year, with correspondingly high humidity. Stand pots on trays of moist pebbles, and suspend saucers of water under hanging baskets. Mist-spray the foliage daily whenever the temperature rises above 70°.

Watering During the active growth period water plentifully, but never allow pots to stand in water. During the short winter rest period (no longer than about two months) give only enough water to keep the potting mixture from drying out completely.

Feeding Apply standard liquid fertilizer every two weeks throughout the active growth period.

Potting and repotting Use a potting mixture composed of equal parts of peat moss and coarse leaf mold. Move potted plants into pots one size larger every six or eight weeks throughout the active growth period. When maximum convenient pot size (probably about 6 inches) has been reached, replace the plants with newly rooted cuttings. Replant hanging baskets every year.

Propagation It is easy to propagate hemigraphises from tip cuttings 2–3 inches long at any time of year. Stand the cuttings in water in opaque glass jars and keep them in bright filtered light. They will develop roots in two to three weeks. As soon as the roots are about an inch long, plant three or four cuttings together in a 3-inch pot of the recommended potting mixture (or put five or six in a hanging basket), and treat them as mature plants. Alternatively, root cuttings directly in the mixture. Take each cutting just below a node, strip off the lower leaves, and dip the cut end in hormone rooting powder. Then insert three or four cuttings together in a 3-inch pot of moistened mixture, enclose the whole in a plastic bag, and stand it in bright filtered light for three weeks. The cuttings will have rooted by then so uncover them and treat them as adults.

Heptapleurum
ARALIACEAE

HEPTAPLEURUMS are closely related to plants of the genus *Brassaia* (formerly *Schefflera*). They are often sold under these names. Like brassaias, they do not flower indoors. Only one species, *H. arboricola,* has been identified, but there are two varieties. Although both can rapidly become 6 feet tall with an unbranched stem, they can be encouraged to become bushy by having their growing tips pinched out. Even with several stems, they have an open look because each leaf has a semi-erect leafstalk 9–12 inches long. The leaf is divided into 7 or more leaflets, each on its own inch-long stalk. The short stalks radiate in an almost complete circle from the tips of the long stalks.

These plants grow continuously, although usually at a slower pace during the winter.

RECOMMENDED HEPTAPLEURUMS

***H.a.* 'Geisha Girl'** has slender, green stems, with shiny, dark green leaves borne alternately at 2- or 3-inch intervals. The leaflets are oval with rounded tips, 2–5 inches long, and about 1 inch wide.

***H.a.* 'Hayata'** differs from *H.a.* 'Geisha Girl' in that its leaves are gray-green and much less shiny. The leaflets are acutely pointed at the tips.

PROPER CARE

Light Heptapleurums must have two or three hours a day of direct sunlight. In inadequate light leafstalks grow abnormally long.

Temperature A minimum temperature of 60°F is essential all year long. Maintain high humidity by standing plants on trays of moist pebbles.

Watering Water moderately, but allow the top half-inch of the potting mixture to dry out between waterings. Never permit the mixture to become drier than this, but, conversely, never give so much water at a single watering that the mixture becomes thoroughly wet.

Feeding Apply standard liquid fertilizer every two weeks from early spring to late fall.

Potting and repotting Use a soil-based potting mixture (see page 429). Move heptapleurums into pots one size larger in spring until maximum

Heptapleurum arboricola
'Hayata'

convenient pot size has been reached. Thereafter, topdress them annually (see page 428).

Propagation Propagate in spring from tip or stem cuttings 3–4 inches long. Take each cutting immediately below a leaf node, strip off any lower leaves, and dip the cut end of the cutting in a hormone rooting powder. Plant the cutting in a 3-inch pot containing a moistened equal-parts mixture of peat moss and coarse sand or perlite, and enclose the whole in a plastic bag or heated propagating case (see page 444). Maintain a temperature of 65°–75°F; at lower temperatures these cuttings are likely to rot before they can root. In bright filtered light and steady warmth a cutting should root in three to four weeks. When renewed growth indicates that rooting has occurred, acclimatize the new plant to room conditions over a period of two weeks by opening the bag or case a little more every day, and water the plant only enough to keep the rooting mixture barely moist.

When the plant is uncovered, place it in bright light, water moderately, and apply standard liquid fertilizer monthly until a fine network of roots has appeared on the surface of the rooting mixture. This will have occurred by the time two or three new leaves have been produced. Thereafter, move the plant into a slightly larger pot of soil-based mixture, and treat it as a mature heptapleurum.

Special points Provide thin stakes for stems where necessary. The main stem will need to be tied to a stake at intervals as it grows taller, although this will be less necessary if growing tips are pinched out regularly.

Hibiscus

MALVACEAE

Rose of China
H. rosa-sinensis variety

TWO species of the large genus *Hibiscus* are grown indoors. Both are much-branching shrubs that can grow 6 feet or more unless kept within bounds by drastic pruning. Leaves on leafstalks 1–2 inches long tend to be roughly pointed-oval, 2–3 inches long and $1\text{–}1\frac{1}{2}$ inches wide, dark green, and tooth-edged. Funnel-shaped, short-lived flowers appear singly from leaf axils at tips of stems and branches throughout late spring and summer, with occasional blooms at other times.

RECOMMENDED HIBISCUSES

H. rosa-sinensis (rose of China, blacking plant) has 5-inch-wide, deep crimson flowers consisting of a single

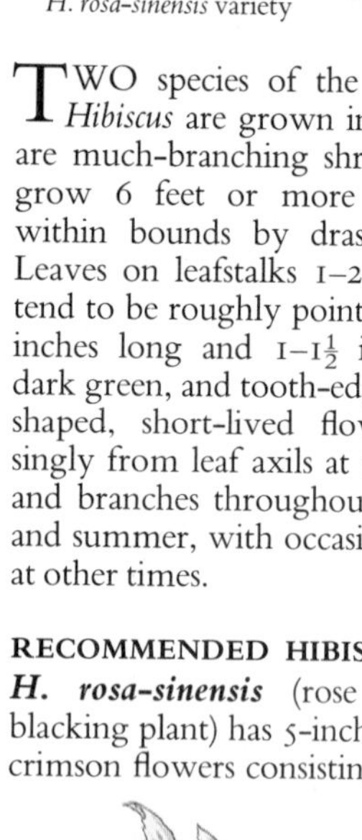

H. rosa-sinensis variety

H. schizopetalus (Japanese hibiscus)

layer of five petals. There are several varieties, some with five petals, some with more; and flowers may be white, yellow, pink, orange, or red. Stamens in five-petaled forms are united in a tubular column up to 2 inches long, whereas stamens in many-petaled forms tend to grow in a loose cluster. One five-petaled, scarlet-flowered form, *H.r-s.* 'Cooperi,' has leaves that are marked with olive green, pink, and white.

H. schizopetalus (Japanese hibiscus) has slender stems that usually need supporting. Orange-red, 2-inch-wide, pendent flowers with 2-inch-long stalks have fringed, backward curving petals, with a 3-inch-long staminal column projecting beyond them.

PROPER CARE

Light Give these plants bright light, with some direct sunlight, every day.

Temperature During the active growth period normal room temperatures are suitable. But keep the temperature at about 55°F during the two- to three-month winter rest.

Watering During the active growth period water moderately, allowing the top half-inch of the mixture to dry out between waterings. During the rest period water only enough to keep the mixture from drying out.

Feeding Apply high-potash liquid fertilizer every two weeks during the active growth period.

Potting and repotting Use a soil-based potting mixture (see page 429). Move plants into pots one size larger every spring until maximum convenient pot size has been reached. Thereafter, topdress them annually (see page 428).

Propagation Propagate in spring or summer by 3- or 4-inch-long tip or heel cuttings. Plant each cutting in a 3-inch pot containing a moistened equal-parts mixture of peat moss and coarse sand or perlite. Enclose the whole in a plastic bag or propagating case (see page 443), and stand it in bright filtered light. After rooting occurs, uncover the cutting and begin feeding as well as moderate watering. About three months after the start of propagation move the new plant into a 4-inch pot of soil-based mixture, and treat it as a mature hibiscus.

Special points In early spring cut away unwanted growths, and shorten stems and branches to within 6 inches of the base.

Hippeastrum

AMARYLLIDACEAE

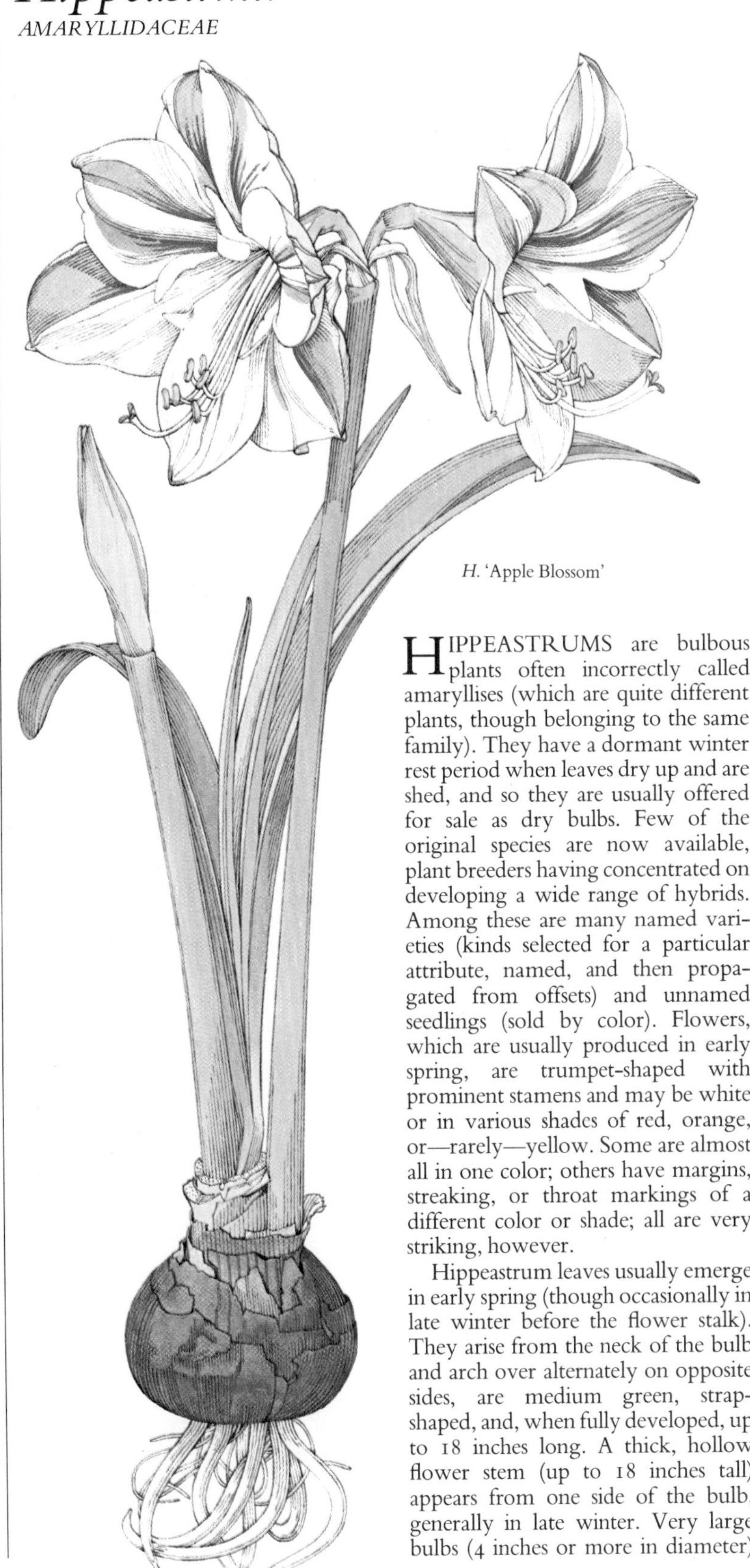

H. 'Apple Blossom'

HIPPEASTRUMS are bulbous plants often incorrectly called amaryllises (which are quite different plants, though belonging to the same family). They have a dormant winter rest period when leaves dry up and are shed, and so they are usually offered for sale as dry bulbs. Few of the original species are now available, plant breeders having concentrated on developing a wide range of hybrids. Among these are many named varieties (kinds selected for a particular attribute, named, and then propagated from offsets) and unnamed seedlings (sold by color). Flowers, which are usually produced in early spring, are trumpet-shaped with prominent stamens and may be white or in various shades of red, orange, or—rarely—yellow. Some are almost all in one color; others have margins, streaking, or throat markings of a different color or shade; all are very striking, however.

Hippeastrum leaves usually emerge in early spring (though occasionally in late winter before the flower stalk). They arise from the neck of the bulb and arch over alternately on opposite sides, are medium green, strap-shaped, and, when fully developed, up to 18 inches long. A thick, hollow flower stem (up to 18 inches tall) appears from one side of the bulb, generally in late winter. Very large bulbs (4 inches or more in diameter) may produce two flower stems, one following the other. Every stem carries two, three, or four blooms, and in particularly fine types every bloom can be as much as 6–7 inches across. Each lasts for two to three weeks. Some bulbs have been especially treated to flower earlier than normal—usually in time for Christmas and the New Year. They are cared for, however, in exactly the same way as the other bulbs are.

The newly purchased hippeastrum bulb has a perfect embryo flower already formed. All that need be done the first year is to pot the bulb up and care for it until it flowers. Thereafter, some skill is required to make sure that it blooms in subsequent years.

See also BULBS, CORMS, and TUBERS.

Hippeastrum hybrids (flowers)

PROPER CARE

Light Hippeastrums need bright light, with some direct sunlight, throughout the active growth period; during the dormant period light is unimportant. Too little light when a plant is in active growth results in elongated leaves and in no flowers the following year. A continuous position in bright sunlight from the time flowers fade until mid-fall will contribute more than any other factor to subsequent flowering.

Temperature Normally warm room temperatures encourage fast growth and bring hippeastrums into early bloom, but too much heat will considerably shorten the life of the flowers. A temperature no higher than about 65°F is advisable for hippeastrums at flowering time.

Watering Newly potted bulbs should be watered sparingly—just enough to keep the potting mixture barely moist—until roots develop (as indicated by the appearance of healthy new growth). Thereafter, water more moderately, but let the top half of the mixture dry out between waterings. When plants are in full growth, water enough to keep the potting mixture constantly moist. After the active growth period has ended, some growers continue watering (on a reduced scale) for quite a while, but it is probably best to stop in mid-fall, so that bulbs begin to get an enforced rest. After watering stops, the foliage will become yellow and wither away. If watering is continued too long, the past year's foliage will remain green and may become unwieldy and unattractive. Keep the potting mixture completely dry throughout the rest period, which lasts until new growth (usually the tip of the flower bud) begins to appear.

Feeding Apply standard liquid fertilizer once every two weeks from the time the flowers have finished blooming until midsummer. Then switch to a high-potash fertilizer, such as is usually recommended for tomatoes; this will help to mature the bulb and ensure a flowering stalk the next year. Discontinue feedings entirely after mid-fall.

Potting and repotting Use a rich soil-based potting mixture (see page 429) and put plenty of clay-pot fragments in the bottom of the pot to aid drainage. New bulbs should be set singly in 5- or 7- inch pots; half-bury the bulb, leaving its neck and shoulders clear of the potting mixture. Some growers believe that soaking the bases of dry bulbs for 24 hours in shallow saucers of water assists initial growth. The mixture should be settled firmly around the bulb and any existing roots.

Hippeastrums, like all amaryllids, dislike root disturbance and flower best when left alone. For three or four years after the initial potting, simply take the bulb out of its pot with the tangled root ball intact, remove a little loose mixture from above and between the roots, replace the bulb in the same pot, and work some fresh mixture into the spaces made. Do this when the first signs of new growth appear, just at the beginning of the active growth period. Repot completely at three- or four-year intervals. Shake the bulb free of the old mixture and replant it in completely fresh potting mixture.

Hippeastrum: the annual cycle

A dry bulb may have some shriveled roots, which can be fleshed out by being soaked in water before potting. The flower bud should emerge first, followed by leaves that last until the plant becomes dormant.

Propagation Small bulbs are produced around the base of the parent bulb and can be detached when about $1–1\frac{1}{2}$ inches across, keeping as much root as possible attached to them. This is best done at the time of repotting. Plant young bulbs initially in 3-inch pots, but otherwise treat them just the same as you would mature bulbs—but move them into slightly larger pots each year until they have grown to flowering size ($3–3\frac{1}{2}$ inches across).

Hippeastrums may also be raised from seed—a process involving a three- to five-year wait for flowers. (Seedlings are not given a rest period but are kept growing through to flowering size without a break.) Obviously, the use of offsets is an easier way to increase plants, but seedlings can produce interesting surprises in color and markings.

Special points Prepare bulbs for the dormant period by removing all the dried foliage. Leave them in their pots of mixture, and store the pots in a thoroughly dry place at a temperature of about 50°F. Bulbs that have been treated to bloom early must be particularly well tended to ensure flowering. If a hippeastrum produces lots of leaves at the beginning of the growing season, it is unlikely that the bulb will flower; the first thing to emerge from the bulb is usually the flower bud.

Howea
PALMAE

Curly palm
H. belmoreana

THE genus *Howea* (sentry palm) includes only two species, both of which have become popular house plants. These slender palms used to be classified as belonging to the genus *Kentia,* and they are still sold in some places as kentia palms. The two species are alike in that they are single-stemmed and have dark green, arching fronds cut almost to the midrib into many 1- to 1½-inch-wide and 1½- to 2-foot-long leaflets (or pinnae). Another common characteristic is their ability to thrive under what might seem to be difficult indoor conditions. Flowers and fruit are not produced in the home.

See also PALMS.

RECOMMENDED HOWEAS

H. belmoreana (curly palm) can eventually grow to 8 feet tall, with a 6-foot spread. As it ages, the stem forms a short trunk, which thickens at the base. On top of the stem are rather short leafstalks—only 10–18 inches long—which are nearly erect. An extension of each leafstalk becomes the midrib of the frond, whose leaflets grow close together and are also held somewhat upright. By forming a kind of trough, the leaflets give the frond an erect but gracefully arching appearance. Frond size varies considerably with the age of the palm, but tends to reach an indoor maximum of 18 inches long and 18 inches wide.

H. forsterana (flat- or thatch-leaf palm), eventually grows up to 8 feet tall with a possible spread of up to 10 feet. Its leafstalks, which may grow to 3 feet long, support flat-topped fronds with leaflets drooping from the extended midrib. The leaflets are spaced about an inch apart on the extension of the leafstalk that forms the rib of the frond, and they are held horizontally rather than nearly vertically (as in *H. belmoreana*). This is the main difference between the two species. The way in which the leaflets are carried affects the shape of the whole palm. Because of the lower, more spreading nature of the fronds of *H. forsterana,* it occupies much more space than the other species. There are two less obvious differences: The stem of *H. forsterana* is not thickened at the base, and the undersides of its leaflets sometimes have spots or scaly patches on them.

PROPER CARE

Light Howea palms do well in either bright or medium light, and so they may be placed at either a fairly sunny or entirely sunless window. If they get too little light, however (as in a position at some distance from a window), they will slowly deteriorate. An ideal position is one that provides filtered sunlight. If a plant is intended for a dark corner, it can be kept healthy by being put into filtered sunlight for a few hours every other day.

Temperature These plants grow well in normal room temperatures and are able to tolerate reasonably dry air. Do not expose howeas to temperatures below about 55°F.

Watering During the active growth period water plentifully, as often as necessary to keep the potting mixture thoroughly moist, but never allow the pot to stand in water. During the rest period give only enough water to keep the mixture from drying out.

Feeding Apply standard liquid fertilizer to actively growing plants every two weeks.

Potting and repotting Use a soil-based potting mixture (see page 429). Move plants into pots one size larger in late spring every second year until maximum convenient pot size has been reached (usually 10–12 inches). Thereafter, an annual topdressing can replace repotting (see page 428). It is essential to press mixture down firmly around the roots of howeas.

Propagation These palms can be propagated only by sowing fresh seed and permitting it to germinate at a temperature of 80°F. A heated propagating case is, therefore, essential (see *PALMS,* page 293). Seedlings grow very slowly. It may take six years to produce a typical howea.

Special points To wash off accumulated dust, stand howeas outdoors in gentle, warm rain or under a tepid indoor shower. Do not use commercial leaf-cleaning products, which are liable to damage the foliage.

Hoya

ASCLEPIADACEAE

Honey plant
H. carnosa

HOYAS are climbing or trailing plants with thick, fleshy leaves and clusters of waxy, star-shaped flowers. Some species are also sweet-scented. The climbing kinds, which can grow many feet tall, are usually grown on small indoor trellises or are trained around wires or stakes. The smaller trailers look attractive when grouped together in a hanging basket. The leaves grow in opposite pairs and have short leafstalks. Clusters of long-lasting flowers are produced every year (normally throughout the summer) on 1½- to 2-inch-long stalks. Each cluster is composed of up to 30 ½-inch blooms and is carried on a 1-inch-long woody spur that arises from a leaf axil.

RECOMMENDED HOYAS

H. australis is a fast-growing climber with waxy, pointed-oval leaves 2–3 inches long and 1½ inches wide. Leaf color is dark green, occasionally spotted with silver. The flowers, which grow in clusters of about 15, are white with a red center.

H. bella (miniature wax plant) is a small, branching plant that grows upright until it becomes about a foot tall, then begins to trail. Its non-glossy, roughly heart-shaped leaves are about an inch long and ½ inch wide and are gray-green with a narrow, brown band running down the center. The flowers grow in clusters of 8 to 10 and are white with a purple center.

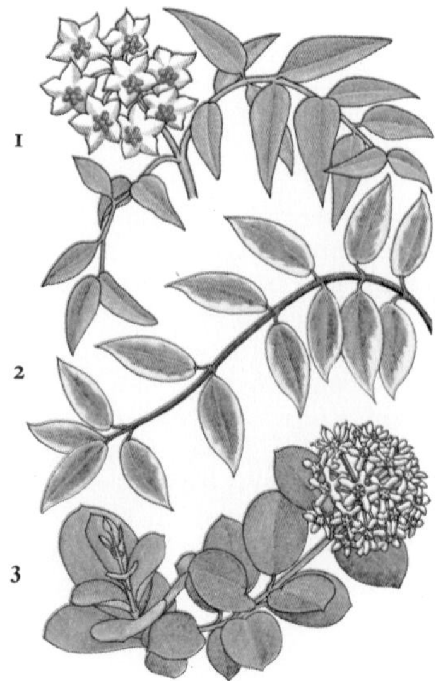

1 *H. bella* (miniature wax plant) **2** *H. carnosa* 'Variegata' (golden wax plant) **3** *H. australis*

H. carnosa (honey or wax plant) is a fast-growing climber with glossy, elliptical, dark green leaves 3 inches long and an inch wide. Flowers, in clusters of 10 to 30, are white to very pale pink, always with a red center. There are two variegated-leaved forms: *H.c.* 'Exotica,' with a broad yellow stripe down the center of each leaf; and *H.c.* 'Variegata' (golden wax plant), with leaves broadly bordered in creamy white, which may even be pink-tinged.

PROPER CARE

Light Three to four hours a day of direct sunlight are essential for healthy growth and flowering.

Temperature Normal room temperatures are suitable for these hoyas.

Watering During the active growth period water moderately, allowing the top half-inch of the mixture to dry out between waterings. During the rest period water only enough to keep the mixture from drying out.

Feeding Give hoyas a high-potash liquid fertilizer once every two weeks during the active growth period only.

Potting and repotting Use a soil-based potting mixture (see page 429). Move climbing hoyas into pots one size bigger each spring until maximum convenient pot size is reached. Move trailing plants on only once in two years. After reaching maximum pot size, topdress these plants (see page 428) instead of moving on.

Propagation Propagate in spring by means of stem cuttings 3 or 4 inches long. Take each cutting immediately below a pair of leaves, dip cut ends in a hormone rooting powder, and plant two or three together in a 2- or 3-inch pot containing a moistened equal-parts mixture of peat moss and coarse sand or perlite. Enclose the whole in a plastic bag or propagating case and stand it in medium light until rooting occurs (normally, in six to eight weeks). Uncover the new plants, and begin to water sparingly. After further top growth appears, start regular feedings. About three months after the start of propagation move the new plants into soil-based mixture, and treat them as mature hoyas.

Special points When removing spent blooms, be careful to pick off only the flowers and flower stalks. Hoya spurs produce flowers year after year. Destruction of spurs means reduction of future quantities of flowers.

Hyacinthus

LILIACEAE

Dutch hyacinth
Hyacinthus hybrid

THE hybrid hyacinths now available are heavily scented, spring-flowering bulbous plants, that can be enjoyed for a few weeks while developing, and then for two or three weeks when in bloom. There are three main types. The most popular is the Dutch hyacinth, which produces a single flower spike 4–6 inches long on a stalk 2–3 inches long. The spike is crowded with bell-shaped flowers 1–2 inches long. They have arching petals, which may be white, red, pink, yellow, or blue. The early-flowering Roman hyacinth produces two to three thinner flower stalks only 6 inches high, with fewer, more widely spaced white, pink, or blue blooms. The multiflora, or cynthella, hyacinths produce several 6-inch stalks per bulb, with loosely carried blooms in the basic color range. The leaves of all three types are basal and variable in length and width, and they surround the central flower spike or spikes.

Dutch hyacinth bulbs are normally sold by size, in centimeters. Those of 19-centimeter circumference (about 8 inches) are said to be of "exhibition" size and produce the broadest and tallest flower spikes. The average size is 17–18 centimeters, and the smallest offered are 16–17 centimeters. For most indoor displays, a large group of smaller-sized bulbs is probably just as effective as fewer exhibition-sized ones, especially since the very big spikes produced by the latter are hard to support if grown in bowls. Roman and multiflora hyacinths never need support. The bulbs are surrounded by paper-thin tunics, that may be silvery-white or purple-blue, depending on variety. And some hyacinth bulbs have been "prepared" so that they will bloom earlier than normal.

Bulbs are generally sold in early fall and should be planted before the beginning of winter. By planting different kinds of bulb over a several-week period, it is possible to have flowers throughout two or three months. Plant them either in soil- or peat-based potting mixture (see page 429) or in bulb fiber (a mixture of peat moss, charcoal pieces, and—often—crushed oyster shell). It is best not to put hyacinths of different flower colors in the same container, since these rarely flower at the same time. For the best effect, plant several similar bulbs close together, but not touching, in a single container. Single bulbs are frequently planted in bulb glasses. The bulb is placed in the neck of the glass, that has been filled with water to a point just below the base of the bulb (*not* touching the bulb), which will send roots down into it.

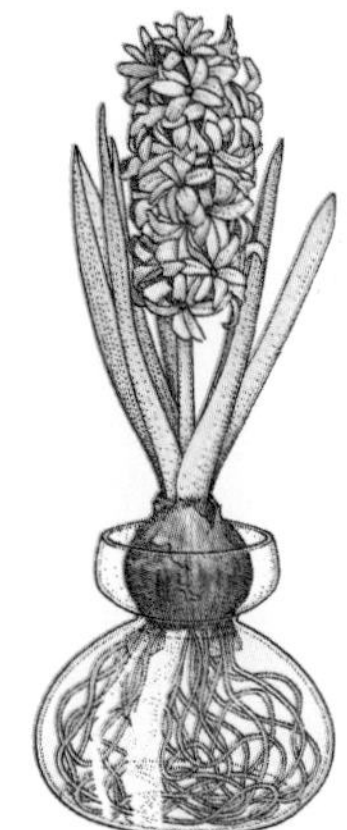

The narrow neck of a bulb glass supports the bulb, so that it remains dry while sending roots down into the water.

Bulbs planted in a potting mixture should be only half-buried. Pots, bowls, or pans may be used, and they need not have drainage holes—though it is probably better to use a bulb fiber in a container without a hole. The mixture should be moist, but not very wet, when bulbs are inserted. It may be lightly watered when planting is complete, to settle the mixture around the bulbs. Thereafter, keep them cool (below 50°F) and dark for eight to ten weeks (or about six weeks for "prepared" bulbs); this ensures early production of a good root system. Commercial growers plant hyacinths in fall and bury them under peat moss until they are rooted. Instead, wrap the container in a black plastic bag and store it in a cool place.

After plants have served their time in the dark, acclimatize them gradually to the light, watering enough to make the potting mixture moist, allowing the top half-inch to dry out between waterings. Keep them cool until the flower bud has emerged from the neck of the bulb. Provide bright light with some direct sunlight throughout both the leaf- and bud-producing stages. Some thin sticks may need to be inserted into the mixture and the heavy flower heads tied to them with raffia or thin twine. When flowering has finished, plant the bulbs outdoors. They cannot be used again as house plants.

See also BULBS, CORMS, and TUBERS.

Hydrangea

SAXIFRAGACEAE

H. macrophylla 'Hortensia'

ONLY one species of the genus *Hydrangea, H. macrophylla,* is a common house plant. Even this one is difficult to carry over from one year to another indoors because it requires constantly cool, airy conditions in order to bloom. Thus, potted hydrangeas are usually bought when budding in early spring, kept for a few weeks while flowering, and then either discarded or planted outdoors. There are a number of varieties of *H. macrophylla,* but the ones normally grown in pots are all forms of *H.m.* 'Hortensia.' They are all low-growing shrubs, usually with a height and spread of no more than 1 or 2 feet. Each plant has a short, woody stem and from four to eight branches, which carry opposite pairs of shiny, pointed-oval leaves 3–6 inches long and 2–4 inches wide. The leaves have 1-inch-long stalks. The main stem and branches may each terminate in a rounded flower head 5–8 inches wide which is composed of many four-petaled flowers up to 1–1½ inches wide. Occasionally there are small specimens available that have only an unbranched main stem with a single flower head at its top.

Flowers of *H.m.* 'Hortensia' have greenish buds that open white, pink, red, purple, or blue. Flower color of all hydrangeas is affected by the degree of acidity or alkalinity of the soil in which they grow (see page 430). Pink- or red-flowered kinds develop blue or purple flowers when grown in acid or neutral potting mixtures, and the normally blue-flowered kinds turn pink or purple-red in alkaline potting mixtures.

PROPER CARE

Light Grow hydrangeas in bright light but not in direct sunlight.

Temperature Flowers of a potted hydrangea will last for up to eight weeks if kept in a cool position (below 60°F). In normal room temperatures the blooms are likely to fade within three or four weeks.

Watering Water plentifully as often as necessary to keep the potting mixture thoroughly moist. Never allow the mixture to dry out, or the plant will collapse. If this happens, immerse the pot in a bucket of water until the root ball is thoroughly soaked. Even if this treatment succeeds, however, the current flowering period of the plant will have been shortened.

Feeding Apply standard liquid fertilizer every two weeks as long as the plant remains indoors.

Potting and repotting Repotting is not necessary for these temporary plants. Most specimens will recover and thrive if planted in a sheltered position outdoors.

Propagation Propagation is not practical in the home. Although stem cuttings of hydrangeas will root quite easily, the resultant plants are unlikely to produce flowers indoors.

Hypoestes

ACANTHACEAE

PLANTS of the genus *Hypoestes* are shrublike—sometimes with a soft woody base—and have attractively spotted leaves. Only one species, *H. phyllostachya* (better known as *H. sanguinolenta*), is grown as a house plant. Among its common names are baby's tears, flamingo plant, freckle face, polka-dot plant. Although this plant can grow quite big, its maximum suitable height and spread are about 15 inches, for it tends to become straggly with age and should be replaced by a younger specimen. The pointed-oval leaves are 2½ inches long and 1½ inches wide, dark olive green heavily spotted with light (but conspicuous) pink markings, and arranged in opposite pairs on 1½-inch-long leafstalks. Short side growths develop from every leaf axil, making the plant dense and bushy. In early spring small lilac-colored flowers are produced, but they are insignificant and can simply be removed.

In one of the available varieties, *H.p.* 'Splash,' the pink markings are brighter and larger than those of the type plant, and the spots sometimes merge to form ½-inch patches of pink.

PROPER CARE

Light These plants do best in full sunlight filtered through a translucent blind or curtain. If they are given the wrong kind of light, their characteristic leaf markings will become duller and less numerous.

Temperature Normal room temperatures are suitable; these plants cannot survive in temperatures below about 58°F.

Watering During the active growth period water moderately, enough to make the entire potting mixture moist, but allow the top half-inch of the mixture to dry out between waterings. During the brief winter rest period water sparingly, giving just enough to make the mixture barely moist and allowing the top half to dry out between waterings.

Feeding Apply standard liquid fertilizer every two weeks during the active growth period.

Potting and repotting Use a soil-based potting mixture (see page 429). Move young plants into pots one size larger whenever their roots have filled the pot (see page 426). These plants do

Baby's tears
H. phyllostachya

not require large pots; 5-inch pots will usually suffice for mature specimens.

Propagation Plants may be raised either from seed sown in a rooting mixture in early spring (see page 445) or from tip cuttings taken at any time of year. Take a cutting 3–4 inches long and either root it in water or place it in a 3-inch pot containing a moistened equal-parts mixture of peat moss and sand. Enclose the cutting to be rooted in the mixture in a plastic bag and keep it at a temperature of 65°–70°F in bright light filtered through a translucent blind or curtain; no further watering is necessary. Once the new plant is well developed (in six to eight weeks), remove the plastic bag and begin to water the plant sparingly, just often enough to keep the potting mixture barely moist. (Transfer a cutting rooted in water to a pot containing rooting mixture when its roots are about 2 inches long.)

Let the young plant make appreciable top growth and fill the 3-inch pot with roots (see page 426) before transferring it to a 4-inch pot of standard potting mixture, after which its cultivation needs are the same as those of mature plants.

Propagating a hypoestes

After taking a tip cutting for propagation, be sure to remove the lower leaves before placing it in water to root.

Impatiens

BALSAMINACEAE

PLANTS of the genus *Impatiens* (busy Lizzy, patient Lucy, patience plant) are bushy, succulent-stemmed, and almost perpetual-flowering. They were given their botanical name because of the apparent impatience with which they discharge their seeds when ripe, and their common names because of the persistence with which they flower. Most plants that are grown today are hybrids, notable for their compact low-growing habit, for their relatively large flowers with a long spur, for their wide color range, and for their profuse flowering. A few of the true species are also sometimes available, however.

Under the right conditions this colorful display of impatiens hybrids will bloom attractively throughout the year.

RECOMMENDED IMPATIENSES

I. petersiana grows 2–3 feet tall, branches freely, and has shiny, bronze-red, elliptic leaves up to 3 inches long. Throughout most of the year flat, carmine-red flowers up to 2 inches across are produced at the tips of stems that are light bronze, often flecked with red, and slightly translucent. This plant fails to bloom if it is in much too large a pot, where new roots find space to grow at the expense of flower production.

I. repens is a creeper, which roots at the nodes when they touch any suitable material. The stems are red, the leaves heart- or kidney-shaped, $\frac{1}{2}$ inch across, and waxy. Each solitary bright yellow flower is up to $1\frac{1}{2}$ inches long, bonnet-shaped with a long spur; they appear on short stalks in leaf axils.

Busy Lizzy
Impatiens petersiana

I. wallerana (formerly *I. holstii* or *I. sultanii*) is the tall, lanky ancestor of a vast number of hybrids that have all the good habits and none of the drawbacks of the species. Only one direct form of the species is grown indoors: *I.w.* 'Variegata,' which has carmine flowers 1–2 inches across and 2- to 3-inch-long, acutely pointed leaves of pale green margined with white. It can become spindly, however. There are a number of better variegated-leaved kinds.

Among the many hybrid strains of *I. wallerana* are plants with flowers of all shades of white, pink, red, and orange, as well as bicolored (for instance, red or pink striped with white), and some kinds have more than a single layer of petals. Foliage may be elliptic or heart-shaped, and colored any shade of green with or without a bronze sheen and red or brown speckles on the undersides. Some forms have names, but most are unnamed and sold by color alone. Seedlings begin to flower when they are only an inch or two tall, and they rarely stop. None of the new compact strains is likely to grow more than 12–15 inches tall.

Startling new hybrids, most with flowers much larger than those of *I. wallerana,* have recently been developed as a result of a plant-collecting expedition to New Guinea. Some of the most colorful have strongly variegated foliage, and the largest flower size is reputed to be over 3 inches. Among them:

'Aflame,' is an especially compact form, with leaves 3 inches long and 1½ inches wide, which are marbled green and yellow with some red markings. Its 1½-inch flowers are pale pink.

'Arabesque,' a vigorous grower, has leaves up to 6 inches long and 3 inches wide, which are green with yellow centers and red veining. The 3-inch flowers are bright pink.

'Cheers' is a small plant with crinkly-surfaced, 3-inch-long leaves that are yellow thinly striped with green. It sometimes produces 1-inch coral flowers with paler spurs, but is grown primarily for the foliage.

'Red Magic' has bronze-red leaves 3 inches long and 1½ inches wide. It grows 2 feet tall and has 2-inch scarlet flowers with a prominent spur.

None of the above-named plants has been fully tested indoors. Their long-term behavior will have to be established before they can be recommended unreservedly to home growers. So far, however, they appear to be no more difficult than other hybrids.

PROPER CARE

Light These plants should not be subjected to hot direct sunlight, but they do need bright light. In particular, *I. repens* must have bright light in order to flower.

Temperature Normal room temperatures are suitable, but at temperatures above about 75°F these plants like high humidity. Place plants on saucers of moist pebbles, and mist-spray the foliage daily. This is essential for *I. petersiana, I. repens,* and the New Guinea hybrids. No impatiens can tolerate temperatures below 55°.

Watering Water moderately, allowing the top half-inch of the mixture to dry out between waterings. Never permit pots to stand in water. If the amount of light reaching plants is reduced, they will enter a rest period, when they should be watered more sparingly, allowing the top third of the mixture to dry out between waterings. Never let the mixture dry out completely, however.

Feeding Apply standard liquid fertilizer every two weeks throughout the active growth period.

Potting and repotting Use a soil-based potting mixture (see page 429). Move permanent plants into pots that are one size larger when the pots become full of roots (see page 426). A 5-inch pot should normally be the largest size required.

Propagation Modern hybrids are usually treated as annuals and discarded toward late fall, when they begin to go out of bloom in average room conditions. If kept, they tend to become unsightly. During the summer, however, tip cuttings 2–3 inches long can be rooted in water and transferred to soil-based mixture when ½-inch-long roots have formed. Or cuttings may be planted directly in an equal-parts mixture of peat moss and sand or perlite for later transferral to soil-based mixture. Treat well-rooted cuttings as mature plants.

Impatienses can be grown from seed sown in shallow trays of rooting mixture (see page 445) early in spring. Seeds are usually sold in mixed or separate colors; the selection is given a name describing the attributes of the strain. Enclose trays in a plastic bag and keep them in bright filtered light at a temperature of 65°–70°F. When plantlets are about 1½ inches high, carefully transplant them into small individual pots filled with soil-based mixture. Plants will begin to flower after about six weeks.

Special points Hot, dry air and exposure to full sunlight may encourage red spider mites. Watch out, too, for aphids and whitefly (see pages 454–6).

Iresine

AMARANTHACEAE

Beefsteak plant
I. herbstii

IRESINE *herbstii* (beefsteak plant or bloodleaf), the most popular indoor species of this genus, is prized for the unusual color of its foliage. In pots, *I. herbstii* forms small, shrubby plants up to 2 feet high with a similar spread. The soft, succulent stems, and the leaves that they carry, are red. The heart-shaped leaves have 1- to 2-inch-long leafstalks, and are up to 3 inches long and 2 inches wide. The veining of the leaves is a paler red than the rest of the surface. Flowers are insignificant and they are rarely produced indoors. There is a variety, *I.h.* 'Aureoreticulata,' that differs from the type species in that the red leaves have a greenish tinge, and the leaf veins are broadly traced in yellow.

PROPER CARE

Light Bright light, with at least two or three hours of direct sunlight every day, is essential for the production of healthy, colorful leaves.

Temperature Normal room temperatures are suitable all year long, even during the rest period. Iresines react badly to dry air, however. For increased humidity stand the pots on trays of moist pebbles.

Watering During the active growth period water iresines plentifully as often as necessary to keep the potting mixture thoroughly moist, but never allow the pot to stand in water. During the winter rest period give these plants only enough water to keep the mixture from drying out.

Feeding Apply standard liquid fertilizer once every two weeks during the active growth period only.

Potting and repotting Use a soil-based potting mixture (see page 429). Move each plant into a pot one size larger whenever its roots begin to appear on the surface of the potting mixture; this is likely to be necessary twice in a single growing season. A 6-inch pot should be the biggest required. A plant that has grown too large for a 6-inch pot should be used for propagation because iresines become less decorative as they age.

Propagation Propagate in the spring by means of tip cuttings 2–3 inches long. Put a cutting in plain water in an opaque glass jar or other container and keep it in bright filtered light. When the roots are ½–1 inch long, plant two or three cuttings together in a 3-inch pot of soil-based mixture. Iresines make the best display if grouped in a single pot in this fashion. Treat water-rooted plants as mature iresines as soon as they have been potted, except that they should be watered only moderately, allowing the top half-inch of the mixture to dry out between waterings, during their first three or four weeks in the pot.

Some growers prefer to root iresine cuttings in a conventional rooting mixture rather than in water. For this procedure trim each tip cutting immediately below a node, and dip the cut end in hormone rooting powder before planting. Insert two or three cuttings in a 3-inch pot containing a moistened equal-parts mixture of peat moss and coarse sand or perlite. Enclose the whole in a plastic bag or propagating case (see page 443), and stand it in bright filtered light. When rooting has occurred (in two to three weeks), uncover the rooted cuttings, water them moderately, and apply standard liquid fertilizer every two weeks. Six or eight weeks after the start of propagation move the young plants (still together) to a slightly larger pot of soil-based mixture and treat them as mature iresines.

Special points To encourage bushy growth, regularly nip out the growing tips of these plants at two- or three-month intervals.

Ixora

RUBIACEAE

Flame of the woods
I. coccinea

AMONG plants of the genus *Ixora* are low-growing tropical shrubs notable for their brightly colored flowers, which are composed of many small blossoms massed together into dense, flat-topped flower heads. These plants cannot tolerate much variation from ideal growing conditions, and so they are generally grown in greenhouses. However, an ixora that thrives will repay careful treatment. Of the few species that make good house plants the most likely to succeed is *I. coccinea* (flame of the woods, jungle geranium), along with several kinds developed from it.

It takes up to five years for *I. coccinea* to grow to its maximum height of 4 feet. It is a much-branching shrub, with leathery, shiny, pointed-oblong leaves up to 4 inches long and 2 inches wide arranged in pairs or whorls of three or more on ½- to 1-inch-long stalks. Leaf color is dark green (often bronzish when the leaves are new). Tubular flowers, which are up to 2 inches long and fiery red, open at the mouth into four petals arranged in the form of a ½-inch-wide cross. The entire flower head has a diameter of 3–5 inches. Normal flowering period is summer, but occasional flowers also appear in the fall. Various kinds of ixora which have *I. coccinea* as a parent produce differently colored blooms, chiefly in shades of orange, yellow, and pink, as well as red. One of the most popular is *I.c.* 'Fraseri,' which has salmon pink flowers.

PROPER CARE

Light Ixoras must have at least four hours a day of direct sunlight.

Temperature Warmth is essential. These plants cannot tolerate temperatures below 60°F. For extra humidity stand pots on trays of moist pebbles during the active growth period, but do not continue this treatment during the winter rest period.

Watering Water moderately during the active growth period, allowing the top half-inch of the mixture to dry out between waterings. During the winter rest period give only enough to keep the mixture from drying out.

Feeding Apply standard liquid fertilizer every two weeks during the active growth period only.

Potting and repotting Use an equal-parts potting mixture of peat moss, leaf mold, and coarse sand or perlite. Move plants into pots one size larger each spring until maximum convenient pot size (probably 6–8 inches) has been reached. Thereafter, topdress ixoras each spring with fresh mixture (see page 428).

Propagation Propagate from stem cuttings 2–3 inches long taken in spring. Trim each cutting immediately below a leaf, remove that leaf, and dip the cut end in hormone rooting powder. Plant the cutting in a 2- or 3-inch pot containing a moistened equal-parts mixture of peat moss and coarse sand or perlite. Enclose the whole in a plastic bag or propagating case (see page 443), and stand it in bright filtered light at a temperature of 70°–80°F. When the cutting has rooted—probably in four to six weeks—uncover it gradually over a two- or three-week period in order to acclimatize the new plant to the less humid atmosphere of the room. When the cutting is fully uncovered, begin to water moderately (allowing a full inch of the mixture to dry out between waterings) and to apply standard liquid fertilizer once every two weeks. About three months after the start of propagation move the new plant into a slightly bigger pot of the recommended potting mixture for adult plants, and treat it as a mature ixora.

Jacaranda

BIGNONIACEAE

J. acutifolia

JACARANDAS are shrubs or small trees that can grow 30 feet tall in the wild. The only species grown indoors, *J. acutifolia* (sometimes called *J. mimosifolia* or *J. ovalifolia*), is single-stemmed at first but begins to branch into several stems when it reaches a height of about 2 feet, and it becomes a graceful shrub with fernlike foliage. The bipinnate, bright green leaves up to 15 inches long and 4 inches wide are divided into 20 or more opposite pairs of pinnae; each pinna is further divided into many pairs of tiny oval pinnules or leaflets. Jacarandas grown as house plants do not produce flowers. As they age, they lose some of their lower leaves and much of their beauty. When this happens, replace them with young seedlings (see "Propagation," below).

PROPER CARE

Light Give bright light, and at least three hours a day of direct sunlight.

Temperature Jacarandas do well in normal room temperatures for most of the year. They should have a winter rest period at about 60°F, however, and can, if necessary, tolerate temperatures down to 45°.

Watering During the active growth period water moderately, giving enough to moisten the potting mixture thoroughly, but allow the top half-inch of the mixture to dry out before watering again. During the rest period water only enough to keep the mixture from drying out.

Feeding Apply standard liquid fertilizer every two weeks during the active growth period.

Potting and repotting Use a soil-based potting mixture (see page 429). Move a jacaranda into a pot two sizes larger every spring until maximum convenient pot size (probably 8–10 inches) has been reached. Thereafter, topdress the plant (see page 428) annually. If a jacaranda becomes too big it can be pruned in spring.

Propagation Jacarandas are best raised from seed. Soak the hard-coated seeds in water for 24 hours to soften the outer covering. Then plant each seed in a 2½- to 3-inch pot of moistened rooting mixture (see page 444), and stand the pot in bright filtered light, watering only enough to make the mixture barely moist. Germination should occur within two to three weeks. When the seedling is 6–8 inches high, move it into a 4- or 5-inch pot of the standard potting mixture for adult jacarandas, and treat it as a mature plant.

Jacobinia
ACANTHACEAE

J. pauciflora

THERE are about 300 species in the genus *Jacobinia* (more correctly known as *Justicia)*, but only two of them are grown as house plants. These small shrubs, which have many soft-wooded stems and branches (usually more erect than spreading) and rather coarse-textured leaves, are chiefly prized for their tubular, two-lipped flowers. Because jacobinias grow vigorously and become straggly and unattractive unless drastically pruned, they are usually kept for only a year or two and discarded after propagation.

RECOMMENDED JACOBINIAS

J. carnea (Brazilian plume, king's crown, or pink acanthus) grows to 4 feet tall, with a spread of 2 feet. Acutely pointed, dark green leaves held in opposite pairs on 2-inch-long leafstalks are 6 inches long, $2\frac{1}{2}$ inches wide, and are deeply veined. Cone-shaped flower heads 4–6 inches long appear at stem ends in late summer and early fall. Each flower head consists of many rosy pink flowers 1–2 inches long supported by closely packed green bracts.

J. pauciflora grows 18–24 inches tall, with a 15-inch spread. Medium green leaves held in opposite pairs have tiny stalks and are up to $\frac{3}{4}$ inch long and $\frac{1}{2}$ inch wide. Small clusters of drooping, 1-inch-long scarlet flowers with yellow tips begin to appear from leaf axils during late fall. Flowering may continue throughout the winter and into early spring.

J. carnea (Brazilian plume)

PROPER CARE

Light Jacobinias need bright light, with three to four hours a day of direct sunlight, throughout the year.

Temperature All jacobinias do well in normal room temperatures from early spring to late fall. *J. carnea* should be given a long winter rest period, ideally at about 55°F; *J. pauciflora* needs to rest from the time flowering stops (often not until the end of the winter) until new growth starts in spring or early summer. Both species need high humidity for active growth. While temperatures remain above 55°, stand plants on trays or saucers of moist pebbles and mist-spray regularly.

Watering Water actively growing plants plentifully as often as necessary to keep the mixture thoroughly moist, but never allow the pot to stand in water. During the rest period keep the mixture from drying out.

Feeding Apply standard liquid fertilizer every two weeks to actively growing plants.

Potting and repotting Use a soil-based potting mixture (see page 429). Move jacobinias into slightly larger pots whenever roots begin to appear through drainage holes or on the surface of the mixture. This may be necessary several times during the active growth period. After a specimen has reached maximum convenient pot size (probably 6–8 inches for *J. carnea*, 5–6 inches for *J. pauciflora*), use the plant for propagation rather than attempting to retain it (see "Special points," below).

Propagation Jacobinias root easily in the spring from 2- to 4-inch-long stem or tip cuttings. Trim each cutting to just below a node, and remove any leaves that might otherwise come into contact with the rooting medium. Dip the cut end in hormone rooting powder, and plant the cutting in a 3-inch pot containing a moistened equal-parts mixture of peat moss and coarse sand or perlite. Enclose the whole in a plastic bag or propagating case (see page 443), and place it in bright filtered light. The cutting will normally root in two or three weeks, after which it should be uncovered. Water the rooted cutting moderately, allowing the top half-inch of the rooting mixture to dry out between waterings, and apply standard liquid fertilizer once every two weeks. About six to eight weeks after the start of propagation, when the young plant seems well established, move it into a 4-inch pot of standard soil-based mixture, and treat it as a mature plant.

Special points To encourage bushy growth, pinch out all growing tips during the early stages of growth. Do not attempt to keep a jacobinia for more than a second year. Old specimens that have been cut back are far less satisfactory as house plants than cuttings started in the spring.

Jasminum

OLEACEAE

Common white jasmine
J. officinale

THERE are many species of jasmine (or jessamine), of which three are grown indoors—all for their flowers. Two are strong climbers, which will cling to any available support, and their blooms are heavily scented; the other is a rapid-growing, rambling, scentless shrub. In all three species, the flower consists of a stem-like basal tube flaring out into four to nine rounded petals, and the leaves are arranged along the stems in opposite pairs, each leaf comprising three or more leaflets up to 3 inches long.

J. mesnyi
(primrose jasmine)

RECOMMENDED JASMINUMS

J. mesnyi (also known as *J. primulinum,* commonly called yellow or primrose jasmine) has four-angled, rambling stems, with leaves divided into three leaflets. In spring it produces solitary, short-tubed, bright yellow flowers with darker centers. These blooms often have more petals than those of the other indoor jasmines, but they are not scented. The plant must be tied to thin sticks for support.

J. officinale (common white jasmine) is a climber with slender, squarish stems and leaves that consist of five or seven leaflets and are almost always stalkless. Clusters of strongly perfumed, long-tubed flowers appear from midsummer to mid-fall at the ends of the stems. The flowers are most often white, but they are pale pink in some forms.

J. polyanthum, also a climber, has a single long stem at first but eventually branches profusely. Its leaves are made up of five to seven leaflets. The long-tubed fragrant flowers, produced in large clusters from leaf axils near the stem ends, are rosy pink on the outside and pure white inside, and appear from midwinter until mid-spring. Young plants of this species are particularly prized by many indoor gardeners because they flower well when only six months old—much sooner than other species do.

PROPER CARE

Light Jasmines need bright light and some direct sunlight to flower.

Temperature These plants like relatively cool conditions. But they will do quite well at about 60°F.

Watering During the active growth period water plentifully—enough to keep the potting mixture thoroughly moist. At other times give just enough to make the mixture moist, allowing the top half-inch of the mixture to dry out between waterings.

Feeding Apply standard liquid fertilizer once every two weeks during the active growth period only.

Potting and repotting Use a soil-based potting mixture (see page 429). Move young plants of *J. mesnyi* and *J. polyanthum* into pots one or two sizes larger in the summer, *J. officinale* in early spring. After they reach the 8- to 10-inch pot size, annual topdressing (see page 428) with fresh potting mixture will suffice.

Propagation In midsummer or early fall plant short tip cuttings (taken just below a node) or heel cuttings (taken from sideshoots with a small section of main-stem wood attached) in 3-inch pots of moistened equal-parts mixture of peat moss and sand. Enclose the pots in plastic bags, and place them in bright filtered light. When the young plants are well developed (generally after about four weeks), move them into 4-inch pots of the recommended potting mixture for adult plants and treat them as mature jasmines.

Special points Encourage newly rooted cuttings to develop several growing points by taking out the main growing point when the stem is about 1 foot long. Jasmines grow rapidly and need thinning out and possibly severe pruning; cut back stems that have flowered as far as required. Plants in 5- to 8-inch pots should be kept to about 3 feet in height; one way to keep them within reasonable limits is to train new growth around an inverted hoop of rattan cane or wire.

Kalanchoe

CRASSULACEAE

K. blossfeldiana variety

KALANCHOES are all succulent plants of varying size and form. Some are grown primarily for their decorative foliage, others for their clusters of long-lasting flowers. All have fleshy leaves and can therefore tolerate dry air as well as short periods of drought. The foliage types can be kept for years. But *K. blossfeldiana,* the most popular flowering species, is usually discarded after flowering, because it produces unattractive growth and does not readily flower again indoors.

Some botanists consider that the genus *Kalanchoe* should include all plants originally included in the genus *Bryophyllum,* but in this book they are treated separately. Kalanchoes normally carry their flowers erect, but those of bryophyllums are pendent. *See also SUCCULENTS.*

RECOMMENDED KALANCHOES

K. beharensis (felt-bush, or velvet-leaf) is one of the most striking foliage species. It can grow several feet tall in the wild but is unlikely to exceed 18–24 inches indoors. The leaves are up to 12 inches long, triangular or spade-shaped, with undulate edges and a shallow channel down the center; each is covered with dense, fine hair, which is rusty brown on the upper surface and paler beneath. As the plant develops, it loses its lower leaves, usually retaining 8 or 10 pairs toward the top of a stout, woody stem. It rarely branches and eventually becomes top-heavy and in need of support from a small stake. Pink flowers are produced in the wild, but seldom indoors.

K. blossfeldiana is rarely seen in its original form, having been superseded by a number of improved forms. These have become popular flowering plants, to be bought in full bloom, especially around Christmas time, and discarded when the flowering season has passed. Most are 12–15 inches tall and bushy, the leaves are thick, fleshy, dark green (often edged with red), more or less circular, and 1–1½ inches long. The small flowers are arranged in dense clusters of between 20 and 50, each cluster spreading at least 1½ inches. Miniature forms never more than 6 inches high include *K.b.* 'Tom Thumb,' *K.b.* 'Vulcan,' and *K.b.* 'Compacta Lilliput,' all with red flowers. Less frequently seen are some yellow and orange-flowered kinds, larger in all their parts, such as *K.b.* 'Orange Triumph' and *K.b.* 'Goldrand.' All will continue to bloom for two or three months.

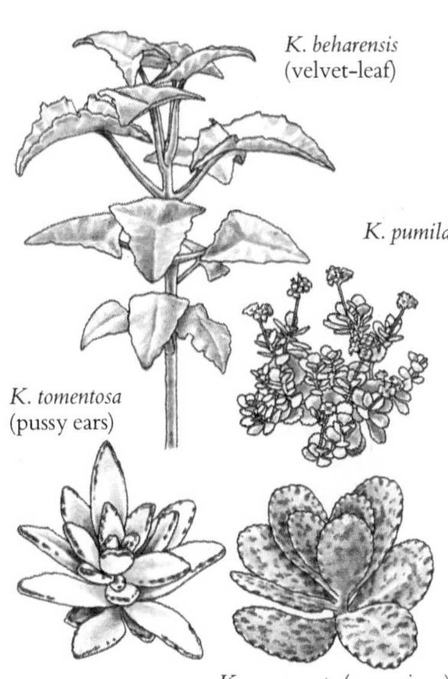

K. beharensis (velvet-leaf)

K. pumila

K. tomentosa (pussy ears)

K. marmorata (pen wiper)

K. marmorata (also known as *K. somaliensis* and commonly called pen wiper), a bushy plant up to 1 foot tall, has shiny, fleshy, oval leaves up to 4 inches long; they are blue-gray with brown markings and have indented edges. The white flowers are seldom produced on indoor plants.

K. pumila, which grows up to 1 foot tall, has attractive foliage and pretty flowers. The 1- to 1½-inch oval leaves are coarsely toothed and thickly coated with a brilliant white powder. Weak stems, which are also powdered white, bend with the weight of the fleshy leaves. Pinkish violet flowers up to ½ inch across are clustered in terminal groups of six or more and are produced in late winter. This plant is especially effective when it is displayed in a small hanging basket.

K. tomentosa (pussy ears or panda plant) is a very handsome foliage species. It has loose rosettes of oval leaves borne on woody stems up to 18 inches high. The 1½- to 3-inch-long leaves are covered with fine, bristly hairs, which are silver-colored except in patches at the edges, where they change to rusty orange on young leaves or chocolate brown on older ones. Flowers are not often produced.

PROPER CARE

Light Kalanchoes should be grown in a sunny window.

Temperature All species grow well in normal room temperatures; but those grown primarily for foliage—as well as *K. pumila*—should be given a winter rest period, if possible, at 50°–55°F (never below 45°)

Watering During the active growth period water sparingly—just enough to keep the potting mixture moist, allowing the top half of the mixture to dry out between waterings. During the rest period give only enough water to keep the mixture from drying out. Kalanchoes—particularly the

large foliage types—become abnormally gross and flabby if overwatered.
Feeding Apply standard liquid fertilizer every three or four weeks from early spring to the end of summer. Feed *K. blossfeldiana* every two or three weeks while in flower.
Potting and repotting Use a soil-based potting mixture (see page 429) with the addition of a small amount of coarse sand or perlite. Plants that are not to be discarded should be moved each spring into pots one size larger. Good drainage is important; have a half-inch layer of clay-pot fragments at the bottom of the pot. Maximum pot size needed: 5 inches, except for *K. beharensis,* which may eventually require an 8-inch pot.
Propagation To propagate all kinds take tip cuttings in spring and root them in 3-inch pots filled with a mixture of peat moss and sand. Put pots in a warm position in bright filtered light. Water the mixture whenever the top half-inch dries out. When roots have formed and new growth appears, move each young plant into a pot of standard mixture. Make sure that the pot is large enough to hold the roots. Thereafter, treat the plant as a mature kalanchoe.

The sheer size of the top of a growing shoot of *K. beharensis,* with leaves up to 12 inches long, makes it difficult to treat as a cutting. It is easier, if slower, to produce new plants of this species from leaves. Detach a mature, still sound leaf and cut away some of the outer edge with a razor blade to expose the internal flesh. Peg this with wire, or weight it down with small stones, onto a bed of damp sand. Small plantlets are usually produced at the cut edges. To produce plantlets while the leaf is still attached to the parent plant, slice off its edge as described above and, in addition, make three or four cuts at intervals along the leaf from the edge to the central channel area. Plantlets will then sprout on the cut edges. When plantlets produced by either method are an inch or more long, gently detach them from the original leaf and press them lightly into a moistened mixture of peat moss and sand to form adequate roots, after which pot them on and treat them as mature plants.

K. blossfeldiana is hardly worth propagating since it is hard to bring into bloom in the home and can be bought cheaply full of buds.

Kleinia

COMPOSITAE

Hotdog plant
K. articulata

ALL plants formerly called kleinias now belong to the genus *Senecio,* and the genus *Kleinia* no longer technically exists. The plants listed below, however, are still widely sold under the old name, and so it is retained here. Kleinias are small shrubs, usually with fleshy, succulent stems and leaves. Flowers are not dependably produced indoors, but they are attractive when they appear. They grow in tightly packed heads on stalks up to 10 inches long. Each flower is 1 inch wide and can be white, yellow, or red. The active growth season for these plants is winter—which is partly what makes them particularly suitable for indoor cultivation—but they tend to flower, if at all, in summer.
See also SUCCULENTS.

RECOMMENDED KLEINIAS

K. articulata (more properly called *Senecio articulatus*; commonly known as the hotdog plant) can attain a height of 1–2 feet. The fleshy stems branch profusely from the base. Each stem consists of jointed segments 6 inches long and ¾ inch thick. The stems are covered with a pale gray, waxy coating, which is easily rubbed off by careless handling. During the winter growing period a large number of flattened, non-succulent, and roughly arrow-shaped leaves appear at the tip of each stem on leafstalks 1–2 inches long. Each dark green leaf has three to five lobes, is about 1 inch long and ½ inch wide, and lasts only through the growing period. In spring all leaves shrivel and fall off. Yellowish white flowers are sometimes produced during the fall.
K. tomentosa (properly called *Senecio haworthii*) has branching, non-segmented stems 8–10 inches long. The medium green of not only the stems but also the leaves is hidden by a dense covering of short white hairs. Cylindrical, fleshy, stalkless leaves, each about 1½ inches long and ½ inch thick, are closely packed all along the length of the stems. Under ideal conditions leaves remain on the plant throughout the year, including the rest period. This species is extremely sensitive to less than ideal conditions, though, and may shed its leaves if disturbed by sudden movements or drafts. Once a specimen begins to lose leaves, the best course is to propagate from stem cuttings and to discard the damaged plant.

PROPER CARE

Light Give kleinias direct sunlight at all times, especially during the winter period of active growth.
Temperature Normal room temperatures are suitable throughout the year. An ideal temperature during the winter growth period is 65°–70°F. All

kleinias can survive temperatures down to 40°, if necessary, but only at the expense of healthy growth.

Watering Although these plants rest from early spring to early fall, they require moderate watering all year long. Give them enough at each watering to make the potting mixture moist throughout, but allow the top half-inch of the mixture to dry out before watering again. If kleinias are given too much water, rotting can occur. Be especially careful not to overwater plants during their winter growth period; because of the limited amount of sunlight in winter, water evaporates slowly. If the temperature is permitted to drop to 50° or less, give no water at all unless the sun is shining brightly enough throughout the day to dry out any surplus moisture around the base of plants.

Feeding It is neither necessary nor advisable to feed kleinias.

Potting and repotting Use a porous potting mixture consisting of one part of coarse sand or perlite to two parts of standard soil-based mixture (see page 429). Repotting is best done in late fall, but it is not necessary to move kleinias into larger pots every year. A 3-inch pot is normally big enough for a plant until it has grown over 6 inches tall. When its roots have filled the current pot (see page 426), gently shake off the old potting mixture and repot the plant in a pot one size bigger. After the maximum convenient pot size (probably 4–5 inches) has been reached, propagate the plant from cuttings and discard the parent. When handling a kleinia, hold it far down on the stems to avoid damaging the waxy or hairy coating.

Propagation Propagate *K. tomentosa* from 3-inch-long stem cuttings taken in late summer or early fall. Remove lower leaves, if any, from each cutting, leaving at least an inch of bare stem at the bottom. Allow the cut surface to dry for three days, and gently press the cutting down into a 3-inch pot of the recommended mixture for adult kleinias. Use a single stem segment, regardless of its length, for propagation of *K. articulata*. Segments can ordinarily be pulled apart easily and need not be given the three-day drying-out period before being planted in the recommended mixture. Treat potted-up cuttings of all kleinias as mature specimens. They will root and produce top growth swiftly.

Kohleria

GESNERIACEAE

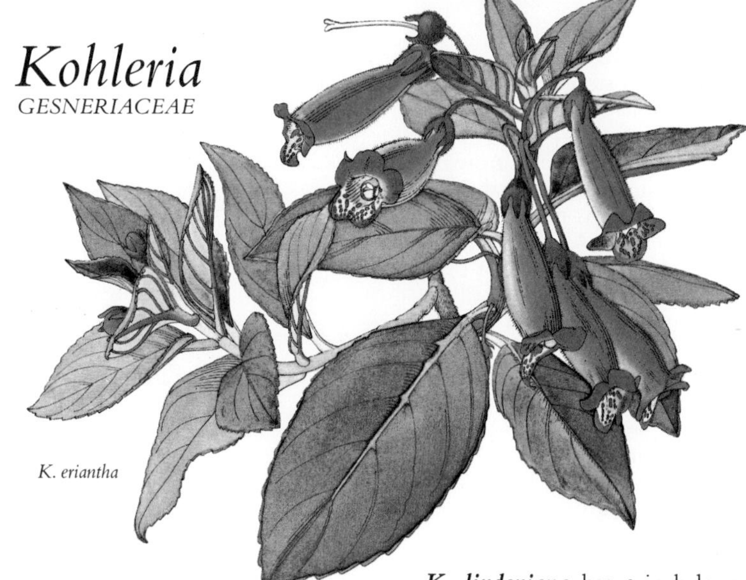

K. eriantha

KOHLERIAS are all attractive flowering plants that produce many underground, ¼-inch-thick, scaly rhizomes in a single year. Some kinds can grow and flower throughout the year indoors. A densely hairy stem rising from the tip of each rhizome bears tooth- or scallop-edged leaves either in opposite pairs or in whorls of three or four. Hairy, bell-shaped flowers, carried on drooping stalks, are produced either singly or in small clusters from upper leaf axils. Each flower has a hairy, green calyx, whose lobes sometimes curve outward and upward. Flower color ranges from red to pink, lavender, and white, and the five-lobed mouth is often speckled.

See also GESNERIADS.

RECOMMENDED KOHLERIAS

K. eriantha has rhizomes up to 6 inches long, each producing a stem that can grow 4 feet tall. If confined to 4- or 5-inch pots, however, the stems will not exceed the more suitable indoor height of about 18 inches. Stem hair may be either red or white. The hairy, elliptic leaves grow up to 5 inches long and 2½ inches wide and each has a 1-inch-long stalk. Leaf color is medium green, but there is a distinct border of fine red hairs. Flowers, usually in clusters of three or four, grow on 4-inch-long, reddish stalks. Each flower is about 2 inches long, with a mouth ¾ inch wide. Flower color is orange-red, speckled with yellow at the mouth. Normal flowering time is late spring; but this species can flower all year long.

K. lindeniana has 3-inch-long rhizomes and slender, reddish, 12-inch-tall stems covered with white hair. The heart-shaped leaves with 1½-inch-long stalks grow 1¼–3 inches long and ¾–2 inches wide. Upper surfaces of leaves are velvety and deep green, with silvery, pale green veins; lower surfaces are hairy and pale green flushed with red. Flowers, which grow either singly or in pairs, are borne on 2½-inch-long stalks. Each bloom is ½ inch long and about 1¼ inches wide at the flared end. Flower color is white, with a yellow throat marked by a patch of dark lavender. Normal flowering time is late summer through early fall.

***K.* 'Rongo'** is probably the best kohleria hybrid for indoor use. The rhizomes are 2 inches long, and the white-haired stems are up to 12 inches tall. Hairy, medium green leaves are about 4 inches long and 2 inches wide, and are carried on 2-inch-long stalks. Flowers, usually produced singly on 2½-inch-long stalks, are 2 inches long and an inch wide at the mouth. Flower color is bright magenta, with white veining on the mouth. This plant can flower throughout the year.

PROPER CARE

Light Actively growing kohlerias need bright light with some direct sunlight, but keep them out of the midday sun. In the dormant period, if any, light is unimportant.

Temperature Normal room temperatures up to about 80°F, with a 5°–10° drop overnight, are ideal for active growth. If the temperature drops below 50°, kohleria stems and leaves die down, and the dormant rhizomes are best stored barely moist in pots at 45°. Stand actively growing plants on trays of moist pebbles.

Watering Water actively growing plants moderately, allowing the top half-inch of the mixture to dry out between waterings. After a plant has flowered, reduce water gradually over a period of about two weeks until the mixture remains barely moist. Thereafter, if the plant is to be kept active throughout the year, resume moderate watering. Give dormant rhizomes just enough water to prevent the mixture from drying out completely.

Feeding Apply standard liquid fertilizer to actively growing kohlerias (one-quarter of the recommended strength at every watering).

Potting and repotting Use a mixture of three parts of sphagnum peat moss, two parts of vermiculite, and one part of perlite, with a tablespoonful of dolomite lime added to every two cups of mixture. Pull rhizome clusters apart once a year—dormant clusters in spring, active ones immediately after cutting back the stems at any time of year (see "Special points," below). Repot the rhizomes individually in 4- or 5-inch pots of fresh potting mixture. Plant each rhizome about ½ inch below the surface. If a rhizome has been dormant, when new growth appears work up to normal watering and feeding gradually over the course of two or three weeks. As soon as active rhizomes are repotted, treat them as mature kohlerias.

Propagation Separation of rhizomes generally provides plenty of new plants. If more are desired, take 3-inch-long tip cuttings in spring and root them in small pots of the recommended potting mixture for mature plants. Cover each potted cutting with a plastic bag after moistening the mixture, and place the pot in bright filtered light. When new growth becomes evident, open the bag gradually over a two-week period and water only enough to make the mixture barely moist. Move the plant into a larger pot and treat it as a mature kohleria about six or eight weeks after the start of propagation.

Special points Cut *K. eriantha* and *K.* 'Rongo' stems back to just above the potting-mixture surface after they finish flowering. Stems of these two species should begin to produce new growth within a few weeks if kept in a warm, bright position.

Laelia

ORCHIDACEAE

L. purpurata

LAELIAS are epiphytic orchids with pseudobulbs that bear one, or sometimes two, fleshy leaves, slightly channeled into a V shape, with a distinct midrib. A single flower stem arising from the top of the pseudobulb can carry from one to several blooms, each lasting for up to six weeks. The flowers have a somewhat starry shape, with a lip that is usually tubular or trumpet-shaped. These orchids have a winter rest period, which sometimes coincides with the flowering period.

See also ORCHIDS.

RECOMMENDED LAELIAS

L. anceps has 3- to 5-inch-tall, four-angled pseudobulbs that are medium green, often flushed with purple. Each pseudobulb bears one or two leaves 10 inches long and 1½ inches wide. The arching flower stem 18–24 inches long carries four to eight winter-blooming flowers, each about 4 inches across. Sepals and petals are pinkish purple, and the tubular, crimson-purple lip is sometimes marked with yellow at the base of the throat. There are many popular varieties.

L. cinnabarina has 6- to 12-inch tall, cylindrical, reddish green pseudobulbs, each of which bears one or two leaves 12 inches long and ½–1 inch wide. The upright flower stem is about 10 inches long and carries 5 to 15 winter-blooming flowers, each up to 2½ inches across. The narrow sepals and petals are bright orange-red. The small, tubular lip is darker orange.

L. purpurata has 18-inch-tall, narrowly club-shaped, medium green pseudobulbs, each of which bears a single leaf 20–30 inches long and 2–3 inches wide. The thick, upright, flower stem 10–12 inches long carries up to seven summer-blooming flowers, each of which is 8 inches across. The wavy-edged sepals and petals are pale pink to white. The tubular lip has a flared mouth and is dark purple to crimson. An especially attractive variety of this species is *L.p.* 'Werkhauseri,' which has a white flower, with the lip color tending toward a bluish violet.

PROPER CARE

Light Give laelias bright light, but avoid strong midday sunlight, which can burn the leaves.

Temperature Give laelias a daytime temperature as close as possible to 60°F, with a nighttime temperature 10° cooler (though not below 48°), all year long. During the warmer months place pots on trays or saucers of moist pebbles, and mist-spray all plants daily.

Watering During the active growth period water moderately, but let the top two-thirds of the potting mixture dry out between waterings. During the winter rest period give only enough water to keep the pseudobulbs from shriveling.

Feeding Give a high-nitrogen foliar feed to these orchids with every third or fourth watering during the active growth period only.

Potting and repotting Laelias can be grown in any of the recommended potting mixtures for epiphytic orchids (see page 289). The smaller-growing species can also be grown epiphytically on supports. Move plants into pots two or three sizes larger at the start of the active growth period whenever the tip of the rhizome has reached the edge of the pot. Water newly repotted plants sparingly, and keep them in a cool position where they get only medium light for the first three or four weeks. Mist-spray the foliage once a day during these weeks. Thereafter, the repotted plants can be treated normally.

Propagation After a laelia rhizome has produced eight or more pseudobulbs, it can be divided at the beginning of any active growth period. Cut through the rhizome in such a way that at least four pseudobulbs are attached to the front portion. Then leave the plant in its pot, still undivided, until the back segment produces a new pseudobulb. When this new growth is 3–4 inches high, remove the whole plant from the pot, and finish the division, cutting through roots and potting mixture with a sharp knife. Before potting up the back half of the plant, use a sterilized knife to cut off any backbulbs that have lost their leaves and turned brown. Both halves of the old plant can then be potted separately in suitable containers and treated as repotted specimens (see "Potting and repotting," above).

Laeliocattleya

ORCHIDACEAE

Laeliocattleya hybrid

LAELIOCATTLEYAS are hybrid orchids resulting from crossing plants of the two genera *Laelia* and *Cattleya*. As a result of further crossings within this hybrid group, there is a wide range of plant sizes, characters, and flower colors. The hybrid forms named below tend to produce fragrant flowers during the cooler months.
See also ORCHIDS.

RECOMMENDED LAELIOCATTLEYAS

***L.* 'Anna Ingham'** has flower stems that carry up to five flowers, each 6–7 inches across. Flower color varies from dark reddish purple to deep mauve. The dark magenta or purple lip has a throat veined with gold.

***L.* 'Derna'** has flower stems that carry only one or two flowers, each 5 inches across. Flowers are yellow, the purple lip streaked with gold.

***L.* 'Dorset Gold'** has flower stems with up to six 5-inch-wide flowers. The yellow petals are edged with red, and the ruffled lip is red-purple streaked with gold in the throat.

PROPER CARE

Light Grow laeliocattleyas in bright filtered light except during the short-day months, when they need some direct sunlight every day.

Temperature Normal room temperatures are ideal at all times. Minimum tolerable temperature: 55°F. Stand pots on trays of moist pebbles, and mist-spray daily above 70°.

Watering Water plants moderately, but allow the potting mixture to dry out almost completely before watering again. During the six-week rest period immediately after flowering water only enough to make the mixture barely moist.

Feeding Apply a foliar feed to actively growing plants with every third or fourth watering.

Potting and repotting Use any of the potting mixtures recommended for orchids (see page 289). Move plants into pots about 2 inches larger whenever the pseudobulbs have covered the surface of the mixture. The best time to repot is at the end of a rest period. When a plant has been repotted, water thoroughly, soaking the mixture. For the next four to six weeks, however, just mist-spray the plant daily and keep it in medium light. Thereafter, treat it as a mature specimen. After maximum convenient pot size has been reached, divide plants for propagation.

Propagation Carefully remove an over-large plant from its pot, and divide the rhizome into two roughly equal parts. Disentangle as many of the intertwined roots as possible, and cut away any rotting or damaged roots. Plant each separate half in a small, clean pot of fresh mixture. For four to six weeks place the pots in medium light, and give only enough water to make the mixture barely moist. Thereafter, treat each young plant as a mature laeliocattleya.

Lantana
VERBENACEAE

Yellow sage
L. camara

LANTANAS are all low-growing shrubs prized for their clusters of small, fragrant flowers. The genus *Lantana* includes many species, but only one, *L. camara* (yellow sage), flourishes indoors. In the wild this flowering shrub grows 4 feet tall, but a potted lantana can be kept to 10–15 inches high by pruning (see "Special points," below). The plants are generally sold in late winter or early spring when in bud, and they are often thought of as temporary plants, to be discarded after flowering. This is a false impression, however. They can be kept for years if properly pruned.

The elliptic, medium green leaves are up to 3 inches long and $1\frac{1}{2}$ inches wide, rough-surfaced, and coarse-textured. Leaves have slightly toothed edges, have $\frac{1}{2}$-inch-long stalks and appear in opposite pairs or whorls of three. The flowering season lasts from late spring to mid-fall. Round, 2-inch-wide flower heads are produced from leaf axils on 2-inch stalks. Each head consists of densely packed, tubular flowers. Individual flowers open successively, in rows starting from the outside of the circle. Whatever their color, it changes (usually darkening) as they age. Thus, a single flower head can contain blooms of two or three related colors—for instance, yellow, orange, and reddish. There are a number of named forms, with primarily white, yellow, orange, pink, or red flowers.

PROPER CARE

Light Grow lantanas in bright light, with at least three hours a day of direct sunlight, all year long. If they have too little sunlight, these plants will not be able to flower.

Temperature Normal room temperatures are suitable from early spring to the end of the flowering period. But move plants to a cooler position for a short winter rest at about 50°F, if possible. While lantanas are in normal room temperatures, increase the humidity by standing pots on trays of moist pebbles.

Watering During the active growth period water plentifully as often as necessary to keep the potting mixture thoroughly moist, but never allow pots to stand in water. During the rest period water only enough to keep the mixture from completely drying out.

Feeding Apply standard liquid fertilizer every two weeks during the active growth period.

Potting and repotting Use a soil-based potting mixture (see page 429). Move small plants into pots one size larger whenever roots appear through drainage holes and on the surface of the mixture. Repotting may be necessary two or three times a year, but do not use needlessly large pots. Lantanas flower best in pots that seem slightly too small for them. A 6- to 8-inch size is the largest likely to be required for a small, bushy plant. When the maximum convenient size has been reached, simply topdress plants (see page 428) with fresh potting mixture every spring.

Propagation Propagate in midsummer from stem cuttings. Take 3-inch cuttings of non-flowering shoots immediately below a leaf, strip off lower leaves that might come in contact with the rooting medium and dip the cut ends in a hormone rooting powder. Plant the cuttings in a moistened equal-parts mixture of peat moss and coarse sand or perlite—either several together in a shallow seed tray or singly in a 3-inch pot. Enclose each container of cuttings in a plastic bag or propagating case (see page 443), and stand it in bright filtered light. After rooting occurs (probably in two to three weeks), uncover the new plants, water them sparingly, and apply standard liquid fertilizer every two weeks. When the plants have made 2–3 inches of new growth, move them into direct sunlight. At this stage pinch out all the growing points to encourage bushy growth. Early the following spring move cuttings rooted in 3-inch pots into bigger pots of soil-based mixture and treat them as mature lantanas. Pot up cuttings rooted in trays separately in 3-inch pots of soil-based mixture in early fall, and treat them as mature lantanas. It is easy to propagate from seed sown early in spring, but the seedlings that result will be of mixed coloring and quality.

Special points Young lantanas rooted from cuttings are likely to flower more profusely than older plants. The young ones can be kept down to a suitable size for indoor use by having all their growing points nipped out when small (as suggested above in "Propagation"). As plants age, they will retain their shape and much of their ability to flower freely if cut back to within 4–6 inches of the base in late winter or early spring.

These plants are particularly susceptible to attack by whiteflies, which tend to congregate on the leaves (see page 456). Use a suitable insecticide to combat these pests.

Liriope

LILIACEAE

Big blue lily-turf
L. muscari

THE genus *Liriope* includes several species of stemless plant, but the only one popularly grown as a house plant is *L. muscari* (big blue lily-turf). It is valued both for its graceful, grassy leaves and its flowers, which grow on a flower spike in a shape somewhat resembling that of the grape hyacinth. The leathery, arching, deep green leaves of a liriope rise in tufted clumps from a mass of fleshy roots carrying tuberlike swellings. Each grasslike leaf may be up to 18 inches long and ¾ of an inch wide. The plant has an annual winter rest period, but its leaves are retained throughout the year. Lilac-colored flower spikes 9–12 inches long rise from leaf axils in late summer and early fall. Each of these spikes is tipped by a 2- to 3-inch-long cluster of closely packed dark violet flowers. Individual flowers are bell-shaped, about ¼ inch long, and ¼ inch wide at the mouth.

There are a number of named varieties of *L. muscari*. One variegated-leaved form, *L. m.* 'Variegata,' is identical with the species except that new leaves have lengthwise yellow stripes until they become 6–12 months old, after which they turn completely green. Other varieties differ only in flower color. The flowers of *L. m.* 'Grandiflora,' for instance, are light lavender, and those of *L. m.* 'Munroe White' are white.

PROPER CARE

Light Grow these liriopes in bright light without direct sunlight. If given inadequate light, they will never produce flowers.

Temperature Liriopes will tolerate a wide range of temperature and will withstand any summer heat. But they should be kept cool in winter, preferably not above 50°–55°F. This makes them excellent for cool rooms.

Watering During the active growth period water moderately, enough to make the potting mixture moist at each watering but allowing the top half-inch of the mixture to dry out before watering again. During the winter rest period water only enough to keep the mixture from drying out.

Feeding Apply standard liquid fertilizer every two weeks during the active growth period.

Potting and repotting Use a soil-based potting mixture (see page 426). Move plants into pots one size larger in spring, but only when the tufts of leaves have covered the entire surface of the mixture. After a plant has filled a 6-inch pot, do not move it on. Instead, break it up for propagation.

Propagation To propagate a liriope, break or cut the thickened base into pieces, each with 8 to 10 leaves attached. Plant individual pieces in 3-inch pots of standard potting mixture, and treat them as mature liriopes.

Lithops

AIZOACEAE

Living stones
L. fulleri
L. lesliei

PLANTS of the genus *Lithops* are known as living stones, mimicry plants, or stonefaces because of their resemblance to the stones among which they grow in their desertlike habitat. Each plant has a short underground stem that rises from a relatively long taproot. This buried stem carries a pair of thick and fleshy semicircular leaves (which are sometimes unequal in size) that are fused together for most of their length. At the top of the line of fusion there is a slit, or fissure, from which a single, daisylike flower is produced in late summer or early fall. The fused leaves rarely exceed a total of 2 inches in diameter, but flowers can be larger. The upper surface of the leaves may be flat or domed, plain or attractively patterned. Leaf color can be virtually any shade or combination of shades that blend with the arid, rocky background. After a lithops has flowered, the old leaves gradually wither and dry up as a new pair emerges to replace them.

Although many lithopses remain solitary, some, such as both of those named below, form clumps. It may take years, however, for certain species to produce two or three pairs of low-lying leaves.

See also SUCCULENTS.

RECOMMENDED LITHOPSES

L. fulleri has domed leaves ¾ inch to 1¼ inches thick, with a ¼-inch-deep fissure. The sides of the leaves are colored a deep dove gray, and the top surfaces are dove gray marked with rust-colored lines and rows of dark brown spots. The white, 1-inch flowers bloom in fall.

L. lesliei has flat-topped leaves up to 1½ inches thick with a ¼-inch-deep fissure. Leaf color is variable, running from pinkish gray to olive green (depending on the quality of light), with rust-colored spots on the upper surface. It has 1¼-inch-wide flowers which bloom in late summer, and are golden yellow, with pink shading on the underside of the petals.

PROPER CARE

Light Give these plants at least three or four hours a day of direct sunlight all year long.

Temperature Normal room temperatures are suitable. A lithops can tolerate temperatures down to freezing but should not generally be subjected to temperatures below 50°F.

Watering Water sparingly from late spring until the flower dies in the fall, giving just enough to make the potting mixture barely moist, and letting the top two-thirds of the mixture dry out between waterings. From fall to spring these plants have a rest period, during which new leaves replace the old ones. During this period the water in the old leaves supplies the needs of the new; give plants no further water until the following season.

Feeding It is not necessary to feed these plants at any time.

Potting and repotting Use an equal-parts mixture of soil-based potting mixture (see page 429) and coarse sand or perlite. For good drainage put an inch-deep layer of clay-pot fragments in the bottom of the pot. Use a standard-depth pot. A shallow pan may appear to be more suitable for the low top growth, but it will not be deep enough for the searching taproot. Even though the two species of lithops recommended above are clump-forming, the clumps form so slowly that the potting mixture provides nourishment for a long time. Plants need to be moved on only when they begin to crowd each other in the pot—usually about once every three or four years.

Propagation Divide overcrowded clumps in early summer. Keep a newly divided lithops in bright filtered light, and water it sparingly. Withhold water during the rest period. Move the plant into full sunlight in late spring, when it should be ready to flower. Plants can also be grown from seed, but seedlings take several years to reach flowering size.

Livistona

PALMAE

Chinese fan palm
L. chinensis

ONLY a few of the many species in the genus *Livistona* are suitable for use as house plants, and only two species are widely grown. In the wild these fan-leaf palms can develop into tall trees, but those grown in pots do not usually become big enough to produce substantial single stems, and so they remain small, stemless shrubs. Their fan-shaped leaves have toothed stalks, are up to 2 feet long and 2 feet wide and are deeply cut along much of their length into many 1- to 1½-inch-wide, pointed segments. The tips of these segments droop for the last 2 or 3 inches of their length. The uncut lower portion appears pleated.
See also PALMS.

RECOMMENDED LIVISTONAS

L. australis (sometimes also called *Corypha australis;* popularly known as Australian fan-palm) has dark green leaves with slender stalks up to 18 inches long.

L. chinensis (often called *Latania borbonica;* popularly known as Chinese fan or fountain palm) has shiny, bright green leaves that are more rounded than those of *L. australis*. The leafstalks are 12–15 inches long.

PROPER CARE

Light Grow livistonas in bright filtered light without any direct sunlight.

Temperature Normal room temperatures are suitable, but livistonas can also tolerate temperatures that fall to 45°F.

Watering Water moderately, just enough to make the potting mixture moist, but allow the top half-inch of the mixture to dry out before watering again. If winter room temperature remains above 60°F, these palms do not have a rest period. If the temperature is permitted to fall much below 55°, however, active growth will be temporarily interrupted. During any such period give only enough water to keep the mixture from drying out.

Feeding Give standard liquid fertilizer to actively growing plants once every two weeks.

Potting and repotting Use a soil-based potting mixture (see page 429). Move plants into pots or tubs one or two sizes larger every other spring until maximum convenient container size (probably 10 or 12 inches) has been reached. Thereafter, an annual topdressing with fresh potting mixture will suffice (see page 428). In working with these palms be careful not to damage the main roots.

Propagation Livistonas are propagated from fresh seed. Since this is an extremely slow process, indoor gardeners usually buy small plants raised by commercial growers.

Lobivia
CACTACEAE

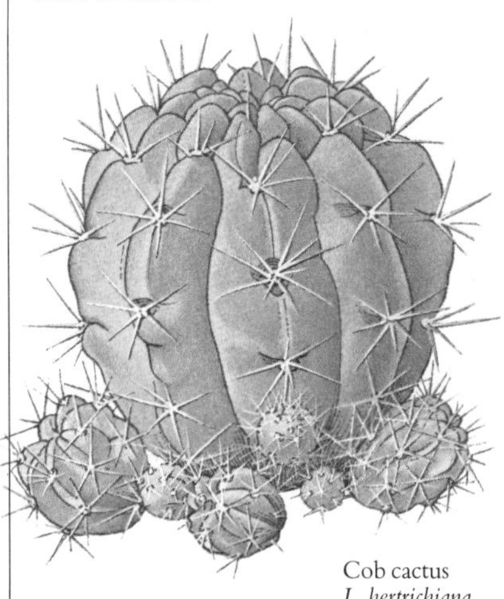
Cob cactus
L. hertrichiana

THE word "lobivia" is an anagram of Bolivia, the country where most of these desert cacti (commonly known as cob cacti) grow in the wild. Although botanists disagree about the number of species in the genus *Lobivia,* there are probably about 70. All kinds are cylindrical or globular and clump-forming. All, too, have attractive, scentless, usually highly colored flowers, each of which opens in the morning and fades by evening.
See also CACTI.

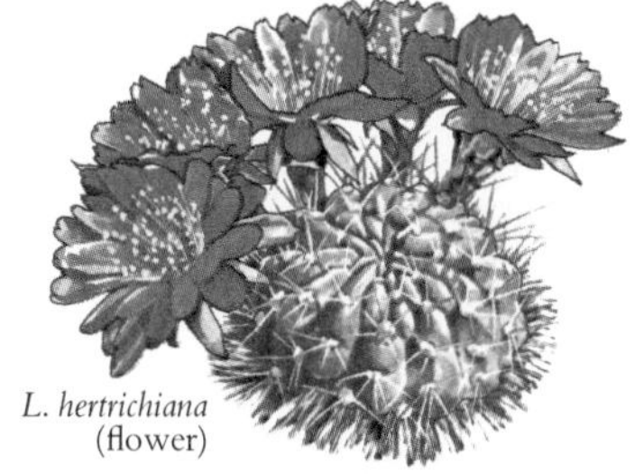
L. hertrichiana (flower)

RECOMMENDED LOBIVIAS

L. hertrichiana is one of the more familiar species. Although virtually any lobivia is worth growing, this species has been singled out because it is representative of the rest in both its physical features and its cultivation needs. Its globular, glossy, dark green stems attain a diameter of about 4 inches by the time the plant is five or six years old. At that age it will already have produced many offsets from the base. Each stem has 11 prominent, deeply notched ribs separated by deep, broad indentations. Round, white-wooly areoles arise from the notches along the edges of the ½-inch-wide ribs. Each areole carries six to eight brownish radial spines ½ inch long, together with a single yellowish central spine up to 1 inch long. Cup-shaped scarlet flowers about 3 inches long and 2 inches across begin to appear in early summer. They open several at a time. And although each flower is short-lived, the flowering period can last for several weeks.

There are many splendid hybrids of this genus crossed with plants of the genera *Chamaecereus* and *Echinopsis.*

PROPER CARE

Light To make sure that lobivias develop strong spines and flower profusely, give them the maximum amount of full sunlight all year long. If possible, keep them in a sunny spot outdoors during spring and summer.

Temperature Most lobivias are high-altitude plants and come from regions with cold, dry winters. Give them a rest during the winter months by keeping them in a cool position, preferably in a place where the temperature remains slightly below 50°F. During the active growth period normal room temperatures are suitable.

Watering During the active growth period water moderately, enough to moisten the entire mixture, but allowing the top half-inch of the mixture to dry out before watering again. During the rest period water only enough to prevent the mixture from drying out. The lower the temperature, the less the need for water.

Feeding Apply a high-potassium, tomato-type fertilizer every two weeks during the active growth period.

Potting and repotting These plants grow well in either a soil- or peat-based mixture (see page 429) made more porous by the addition of one part of coarse sand or perlite to every three of the standard mixture. Because lobivias are usually shallow-rooted, spreading plants, they are best potted in wide, shallow containers, such as half-pots or deep pans. A specimen will not need a container larger than 5 inches until its offsets begin to grow and multiply. An 8- or 9-inch pot or pan may then be needed.

Every spring remove the plant from its pot, trying not to damage or lose any of the offsets. Hold the entire plant body in folds of newspaper while turning the pot upside down. A gentle tapping of the pot should release the cactus. If any offsets appear to be pressing against the sides of the pot, either move the plant into a larger pot or remove some of the offsets. If roots have filled the original pot, repot the plant in a container one size larger. Otherwise, gently shake the old potting mixture from the roots, and repot the cactus in the original container. Add fresh mixture as necessary. Whether returning the plant to the same pot or transferring it, bury the roots at about the same level as before.

Propagation Propagation is by means of offsets. These will often have their own well-developed root systems. Whether they are rooted or not, it is easy to pull them gently away from the parent plant. There will be little or no "wound," and it will not be necessary to let the small plants dry out before potting them. Simply press them into the surface of the standard potting mixture for lobivias, after making a small depression in the mixture for the roots, if there are any. Place each offset in a 2- or 3-inch pot and treat it as a mature specimen. This form of propagation can be carried out at any time of year except during the rest period, but it is best to propagate in spring or summer.

Lobivias can also be raised easily from seed (for full instructions see *CACTI,* page 119).

Propagating a lobivia

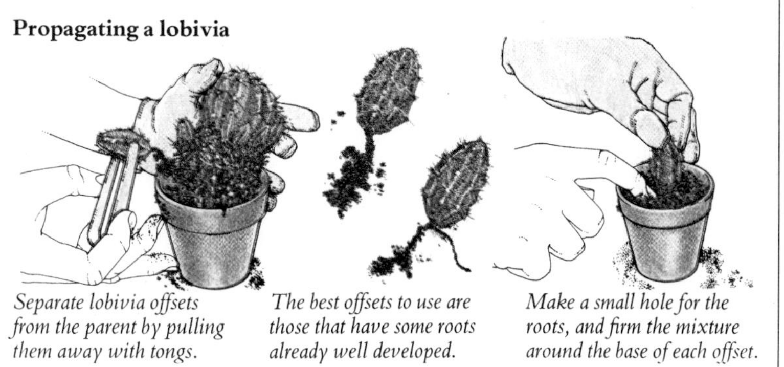
Separate lobivia offsets from the parent by pulling them away with tongs. *The best offsets to use are those that have some roots already well developed.* *Make a small hole for the roots, and firm the mixture around the base of each offset.*

Lycaste

ORCHIDACEAE

L. aromatica

THE genus *Lycaste* includes some of the easiest orchids to grow indoors. All the species used as house plants are epiphytic, with egg-shaped pseudobulbs that become furrowed and wrinkled with age. Each pseudobulb carries one to three dark green leaves at its tip. The leaves are narrow at the base, widening to four times the basal width and then narrowing down to a point. Upright flower stems rise from the bases of the newer pseudobulbs, and each stem bears a single waxy, fragrant, long-lasting flower. Flower shape may be rather flat with outspread or bowl-shaped sepals. The sepals are always much larger than the petals, and the lip is relatively small. Lycastes require a fairly long winter rest period. Some of these plants, however, can bloom in winter.

In addition to the species named below there are many attractive hybrids, which in several cases have exceptionally large flowers.

See also ORCHIDS.

RECOMMENDED LYCASTES

L. aromatica has pseudobulbs 2–3½ inches tall and 1–2 inches wide. There are usually three leaves 7–10 inches long and 3 inches across at their widest. Each pseudobulb produces several 3- to 6-inch-long flower stems, each carrying a nearly flat 3-inch-wide flower. Sepals are reddish yellow, petals golden yellow, and the lip orange-yellow spotted with red. The flowering season can last through spring and early summer.

L. cruenta has pseudobulbs about 4 inches tall and 2 inches wide. There are usually three leaves up to 15 inches long and 6 inches wide. Each pseudobulb produces several 7-inch-long flower stems, each carrying a bowl-shaped flower up to 3 inches wide. The sepals are yellow to yellowish green, the petals orange-yellow spotted with red at the base, and the lip orange-yellow blotched with blood red at the base. Flowers generally open in the spring.

L. deppei has somewhat flattened pseudobulbs about 4 inches tall and 2 inches wide, with usually three leaves 9–12 inches long and 4 inches wide. Each pseudobulb produces several 6-inch-long flower stems, each carrying a flower 3–4 inches wide. The outspread, pale green, carmine-spotted sepals surround the small, white petals and white, red-streaked lip. Flowers usually open in the spring and early summer months.

PROPER CARE

Light Give lycastes medium light throughout the year.

Temperature Ideally, daytime temperatures should be as close as possible to 65°F, and there should be a 10° drop in temperature during the night. These orchids will readily survive more heat in summer, however, and will not suffer if the daytime temperature drops to about 60° for short periods. Provide adequate humidity for these orchids at all times.

Watering During the active growth period water moderately, but allow the potting mixture to dry out almost completely between waterings. At the start of the rest period, usually in mid-fall, withhold water entirely for two full weeks. Thereafter, give just enough to keep the mixture from drying out and to prevent the newest pseudobulbs from shriveling.

Feeding Give lycastes a foliar feed with every third or fourth watering during the active growth period only.

Potting and repotting Use any of the recommended potting mixtures for epiphytic orchids (see page 289), and add a handful of broken-up pieces of charcoal to each 4- to 5-inch potful of mixture. Pots should be half-filled with clay-pot fragments for extra drainage. The best time to repot is spring. These orchids can be kept in pots up to about 9 inches, or they can be grown epiphytically.

Propagation Plants can be easily divided in spring at repotting time. Cut rhizomes at the point of branching, so that each piece of rhizome has a growing point and at least two pseudobulbs. Place each rhizome segment on the surface of standard potting mixture in a 4- or 5-inch pot, with the cut end near the edge of the pot (or attach the segment to a support, where it will grow epiphytically). Water the plant sparingly, for six weeks. Thereafter, treat it as a mature lycaste.

Mammillaria
CACTACEAE

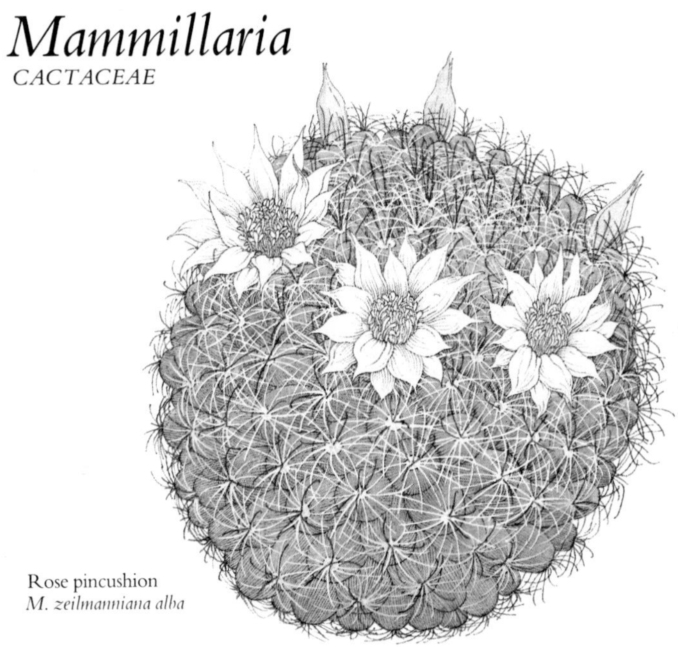

Rose pincushion
M. zeilmanniana alba

MAMMILLARIA, which includes more than 300 species of desert cactus, is the largest genus in the cactus family. Some are so difficult to grow that they present a challenge to even the most experienced grower, but others are fast-growing plants ideal for any indoor collection. They are either globular or columnar and vary in size from a 2-inch-wide plant to giant clusters more than a yard across. Yet there are no species that are too large to be successfully cultivated to flowering size indoors.

Mammillarias are low-growing plants that are often clump-forming, producing many offsets or branches from the base. One of the notable features of the genus is the absence of ribs. These have been replaced by prominent spirally arranged tubercles, which carry spine-bearing areoles on their tips. Spines are variable. Some species have bristly or hairy ones; others have stouter, sometimes hooked ones; but the thick, awllike spines characteristic of many desert cacti do not exist among the mammillarias. Another notable feature of these plants is that flowers arise from secondary areoles on the stem surface between the tubercles, not from the spine-bearing ones on the tubercle tips. The flowers form a ring around the top of the plant and are produced on the part of the stem that has grown during the previous year. Thus, if a plant has grown poorly one year, it is unlikely to bloom well the next.

The small, bell-shaped flowers are usually produced in spring or early summer. Although individual flowers last for only a few days, the flowering period can extend through two or more weeks. Flower color tends to be creamy white or red. In general, plants with creamy flowers bloom at a younger age and smaller size than the red-flowered kinds. An exception is *M. zeilmanniana* (see below). Sometimes a ring of red berries appears on mammillaria stems in spring, following the previous year's flowers. The berries remain on the plant until fall, forming a circle below the present year's blooms.

The plants described below are all relatively easy to grow.
See also CACTI.

RECOMMENDED MAMMILLARIAS

M. bocasana (powder-puff or snowball cactus) is a clustering plant, which eventually forms a "cushion" consisting of many individual heads. Each of these in a five-year-old specimen is likely to be almost globular, with a diameter of about 2 inches. The whole clump can have a spread of 8 inches or more at that age. The blue-green stems are thickly covered with ½-inch-high tubercles. Each of the areoles on the tips of the tubercles carries 25 to 30 spreading, silky, hairlike, white spines about an inch long. These interlacing spines cover the plant like a silvery veil. In addition, each of the spine-bearing areoles carries two to four yellowish central spines 1¼ inches long. These are stouter than the white spines, and at least one is hooked. Yellow flowers about ¾ inch long and ⅓ inch across appear every spring while the plant is still young.

M. celsiana consists of a single stem until it is about five years old. Thereafter, it usually begins to branch from the base, and it can eventually form a cluster of 2-inch-thick stems about 4 inches high. Although each stem is bluish green, the numerous spines give the stem a pale-honey tinge. The tubercles are about ⅓ inch high and are tipped by areoles, each bearing both radial and central spines. The 20 or more radials are slender, white, and about ⅓ inch long; the 4 to 6 centrals are quite tough, deep yellow, and ¾ inch long. It is the mixture of white and yellow spines that gives this plant its characteristic color. In spring *M. celsiana* produces carmine flowers, each ½ inch long and about ¼ inch across. In common with most of the red-flowered kinds, this mammillaria is unlikely to flower until it is at least four or five years old.

M. elegans is a cylindrical plant. At about five years of age, when the main stem is about 4 inches tall and 3 inches thick, it begins to form a cluster from the base. The pale green stems are completely masked by dense white spines that arise from areoles on the tips of ¼-inch-high tubercles. Each areole carries 25 to 30 stiff radial spines about ¼ inch long, together with 1 to 3 centrals 1 inch long, and all the spines are white. The deep carmine flowers, which open in early spring, are about ½ inch long and ⅓ inch across. Flowering normally begins when plants are four or five years old.

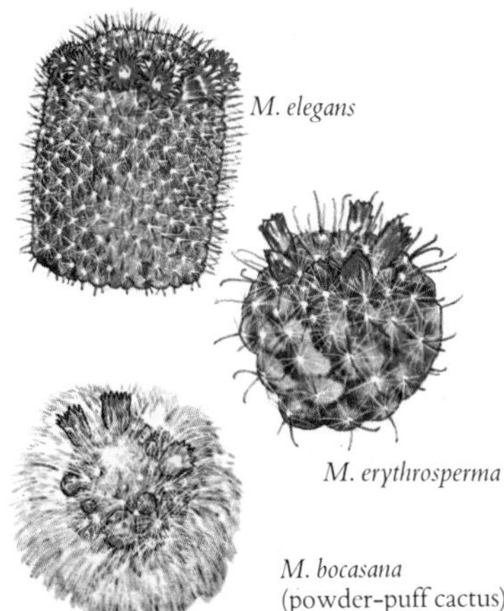

M. elegans

M. erythrosperma

M. bocasana (powder-puff cactus)

M. erythrosperma forms cushionlike clumps that can measure up to 2 feet across in the wild. As a house plant it will probably fill a 6-inch-wide container by the time it is five years old. Each globular stem is about 2 inches tall and dark green, covered with $\frac{1}{2}$-inch-high tubercles. From 15 to 20 slender, white spines radiate from each spine-bearing areole in a starlike pattern. These $\frac{1}{2}$-inch-long spines give the plant a slightly frosted appearance, in spite of the fact that there are also 1 to 3 $\frac{1}{2}$-inch-long brownish central spines to each areole. One of the central spines is always hooked. The flowers are about $\frac{3}{4}$ inch long and wide. Their color is deep reddish, with a satinlike sheen. Flowering time is spring, beginning when plants are about three years old.

M. gracilis has bright green cylindrical stems about 4 inches long and $1\frac{1}{2}$ inches thick. They are erect columns at first, but soon start to sprawl. Profusely produced offsets are globular or slightly elongated, and they are so loosely attached to the parent stems that they fall away at the slightest touch; areoles at the tips of tubercles $\frac{1}{3}$ inch high carry 12 to 14 white radial spines in a starlike arrangement, along with 3 to 5 brown central spines. The radials are $\frac{1}{2}$ inch long, the centrals three times this length. Whitish flowers, produced in spring, are about $\frac{3}{4}$ inch long and $\frac{1}{2}$ inch across. The plant can be expected to bloom when about two years old. The very easily detached offsets make *M. gracilis* a particularly easy cactus to propagate (see "Propagation," below).

M. hahniana (old lady cactus) is a globular cactus that can grow 4 inches tall. Solitary at first, it begins to produce offsets when four or five years old. The most notable feature of this species is its white hair, which hides the grayish green stems. What looks like white hair consists of a vast number of 2-inch-long, curly, hairlike bristles, which are carried by the secondary areoles. The primary areoles at the tips of the $\frac{1}{2}$-inch-high tubercles are themselves woolly, and each bears about 30 white radial spines $\frac{1}{4}$ inch long and two white centrals $\frac{1}{2}$ inch long. Crimson flowers $\frac{3}{4}$ inch long and $\frac{1}{2}$ inch across open in late spring to early summer. This mammillaria will not flower until the main stem is 2 inches in diameter and four years old.

M. microhelia is clump-forming, with bright green columnar stems that can grow 6 inches tall and 2 inches thick. The tubercles are about $\frac{1}{4}$ inch high, and the areoles on their tips carry about 50 golden yellow radial and 1 to 4 reddish brown central spines. The radials, arranged in starlike fashion, are $\frac{1}{3}$ inch long; the centrals are $\frac{1}{2}$ inch long. Cream-colored flowers $\frac{1}{2}$ inch long and wide appear in late spring to early summer. Flowering begins after the plant is about three years old.

M. prolifera (silver cluster cactus) has cylindrical stems that form clusters at a remarkable rate. Even stems smaller than 1 inch across produce offsets, and the clump of plants eventually grows very big. A specimen four years old can easily cover the surface of a 6-inch container. Individual stems are dark green, up to $2\frac{1}{2}$ inches tall and $1\frac{1}{2}$ inches thick, and are covered with extremely soft tubercles $\frac{1}{4}$ inch high. The areoles bear up to 40 thin, white radial spines about $\frac{1}{2}$ inch long, together with 4 to 9 yellowish centrals $\frac{1}{3}$ inch long. Long, white bristles in grooves between the tubercles give the plant a somewhat woolly appearance. Creamy white flowers $\frac{1}{2}$ inch long and nearly the same width appear in late spring and early summer. Flowering begins when plants are about two to three years old.

M. zeilmanniana (rose pincushion), one of the most beautiful mammillarias, is an exception to the general rule that red-flowered plants of this genus do not bloom until they are several years old: It produces a profusion of deep cerise flowers while still quite young and small. The young plant is solitary but slowly forms a cluster of individual, nearly globular stems, which are glossy green, about $2\frac{1}{2}$ inches high and 2 inches across. A four-year-old specimen is likely to fill a 4-inch container. The tubercles are $\frac{1}{4}$ inch high, and each areole has 15 to 18 radial white and 2 to 4 central brown spines, all about $\frac{1}{2}$ inch long. One of the centrals is hooked. *M. zeilmanniana* flowers in summer; each of the many blooms is $\frac{1}{2}$ inch long and $\frac{3}{4}$ inch across. A white-flowered form, *M. z. alba,* is identical except for the pure white color of its flowers.

PROPER CARE

Light For attractively colored spines and good flowering, give mammillarias direct sunlight all year long.

Temperature During the spring and summer active growth period, normal room temperatures are satisfactory for these plants, but they do best if kept in a sunny position outdoors during these months. Give mammillarias a winter rest at about 50°F, if possible. If necessary, they can survive a minimum temperature of 40°. But do not keep them growing in well-heated rooms during the short-day months. If encouraged to continue growing when there is insufficient light for proper growth, they will lose their shape and ability to flower.

Watering In spring and summer water moderately, enough to make the potting mixture moist at each watering, but allowing the top half-inch of the mixture to dry out before watering again. As plants begin to form clusters, be careful not to let excess water remain on the surface of the mixture between the stems. Puddles of this sort can easily cause rotting. For this reason some indoor gardeners prefer to water mammillarias from below. To do this, stand each pot in a pan containing 2 inches of water, and leave the pot there until the surface of the potting mixture has become moist to the touch. Leave the pot in water for two or three minutes once a week. During the winter rest period give only enough water to prevent the mixture from drying out.

Feeding During the active growth period apply a high potassium, tomato-type fertilizer once a month to plants growing in soil-based potting mixture, once every two weeks to those in peat-based mixture.

Potting and repotting Use a potting mixture consisting of one part of coarse sand or perlite to three parts of either soil- or peat-based mixture (see page 429). Plants that form large clusters do better in a broad pan than in a pot. A cluster 3 inches across needs a 4-inch pan. Solitary specimens or those with only a few branches or offsets may be grown in an ordinary pot; a 3-inch pot will suit a plant 2 inches across. Repot mammillarias in early spring. Carefully remove each plant (or plant cluster) from its container, lifting the plant by holding it near the base with tongs or forceps. Grasp plants that have hooked spines with special caution, because the hook is difficult to remove, if it catches in anything (such as clothing), without tearing away the areole.

If roots have filled the present container, move the plant into a slightly larger one. Otherwise, gently shake away as much as possible of the old potting mixture and replace the mammillaria in the original container, which has been thoroughly cleaned. Add fresh mixture as necessary.

Propagation Mammillarias are raised commercially from seed. Some indoor gardeners prefer to propagate from the seed of their own plants. Remove the berries produced following the flowering season in the fall. Squeeze the pulp containing the seeds onto a piece of blotting paper, and put the paper in a dry place for several days. Then pick off the seeds, and store them in labeled envelopes until sowing time the following spring. (See *CACTI*, page 119.)

Saving seed for propagation

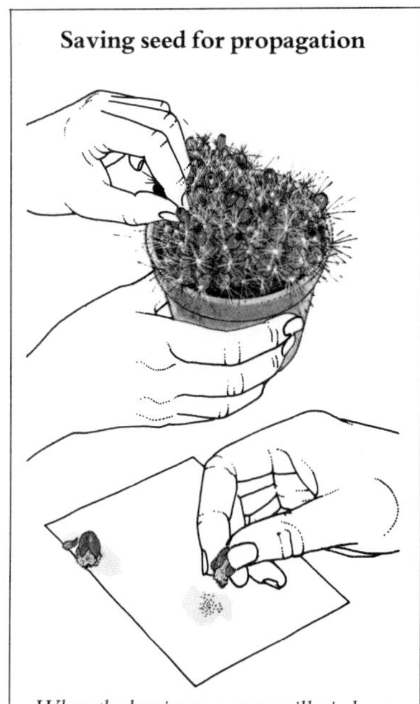

When the berries on a mammillaria have ripened, remove several and squeeze out the pulp onto blotting paper. After the pulp has dried, you can pick out the seeds.

Clustering plants can also be propagated from branches or offsets in spring and summer. This is the quickest way to produce a flowering-size plant. Cut or pull away a branch and allow it to dry for several days. Then push the cut end into the surface of a 2- or 3-inch pot of standard potting mixture. The easily detached offsets of some species do not even need to be dried, but can be potted up without delay. Treat newly potted branches and offsets as mature mammillarias; they will root within a few weeks.

Manettia

RUBIACEAE

Firecracker vine
M. inflata

MANETTIA *inflata* (sometimes called *M. bicolor*; popularly known as firecracker vine) is the only species of the genus grown as a house plant. It is a climber with striking flowers, which bloom from early spring to late fall. The thin, twining stems are usually trained up slender sticks pushed into the potting mixture. But the stems can also be allowed to trail. Pointed-oval leaves about 2 inches long and 1 inch wide have inch-long leafstalks. The leaves hide most of the stem. Tubular, $\frac{3}{4}$-inch-long, hairy flowers are red tipped with yellow. They are backed by a green calyx divided into five arching sections, and are carried on 1- to $1\frac{1}{2}$-inch-long stalks arising from leaf axils.

PROPER CARE

Light Manettias need bright light without direct sunlight all year long.

Temperature During the active growth period normal room temperatures are suitable. An ideal temperature during the winter rest period is 55°–60°F.

Watering During the active growth period water plentifully as often as necessary to keep the potting mixture thoroughly moist, but never allow the pot to stand in water. During the rest period give just enough to keep the mixture from drying out completely.

Feeding Apply standard liquid fertilizer every two weeks during the active growth period only.

Potting and repotting Use a soil-based potting mixture (see page 429). Move plants into pots one size larger whenever roots begin to appear on the surface of the mixture (perhaps as often as twice a year) until maximum convenient pot size (probably 8–10 inches) is reached. Thereafter, topdress (see page 428) with fresh potting mixture every spring.

Propagation Take tip cuttings 2–3 inches long from non-flowering shoots in spring or summer. Cut just below a pair of leaves, remove the lower leaves, and dip the cut ends in hormone rooting powder. Plant two or three cuttings near the rim of a 3-inch pot containing a moistened equal-parts mixture of peat moss and coarse sand or perlite. Enclose the whole in a plastic bag or propagating case (see page 443), and stand it in bright filtered light. After rooting occurs (normally in three or four weeks) uncover the cuttings. Water them moderately, moistening the mixture at each watering but allowing the top inch to dry out before watering again, and apply standard liquid fertilizer every two weeks. Move the young plants together into a 4- or 5-inch pot of soil-based mixture when roots appear through the drainage hole or on the surface. Thereafter, treat the young plants in the same way as mature manettias.

Special points Cut back manettias by as much as half in spring whenever it seems desirable, in order to improve the shape of the plants.

Maranta
MARANTACEAE

Prayer plant
M. leuconeura erythroneura

THE low-growing marantas used as house plants are popularly called prayer plants because they tend to fold their leaves together at night. Some members of the genus are sometimes confused with members of three other genera—*Calathea, Ctenanthe,* and *Stromanthe*—to which *Maranta* is related. As a rule, though, maranta leaves are smaller. Only one species, *M. leuconeura,* is commonly grown indoors, but it has several forms, with varying leaf size and pattern. The species itself has a spreading habit and oval leaves up to 5 inches long and 3 inches wide. Upper leaf surface is pale green with a satiny luster, liberally sprinkled with dark green or light brown feathery markings; the underside is gray-green occasionally shot with reddish purple. New leaves appear from the short, sheathed leafstalks. Flowers are insignificant.

The most familiar variety, *M. l. leuconeura* (often known as *M. l.* 'Massangeana' or *M.* 'Massangeana'), has leaves with paler margins and midribs, almost black markings about the midribs, and deep purple undersides. The leaves of *M. l. erythroneura* are nearly oblong and are deep olive green, with light green markings along the central rib, many bright red lateral veins leading away from it, and purplish red undersides. All the leaves of *M. l. kerchoviana* (rabbit's foot or rabbit tracks) have light green upper surfaces, with squarish, deep green or deep brown markings on each side of the midrib; the undersides are pale blue-gray. This last plant is particularly prone to closing its leaves at nightfall.

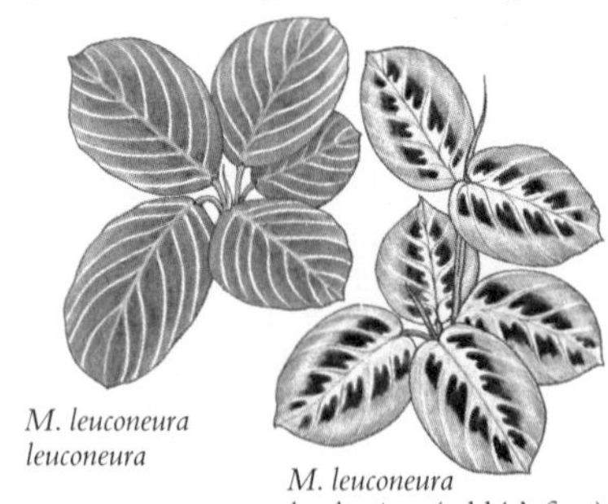

M. leuconeura leuconeura

M. leuconeura kerchoviana (rabbit's foot)

PROPER CARE

Light Marantas should be grown in medium light. Strong sunshine makes the leaves fade and develop dry, brown edges.

Temperature An ideal year-long temperature is 65°–70°F. Whenever the temperature climbs much above 65°, increase the level of humidity by standing the plants on trays of moist pebbles and mist-spray them. Try to use soft rainwater, which does not make unsightly lime-deposit marks on the leaves. Marantas will not thrive in temperatures below 55°.

Watering Water plentifully, as much as necessary to keep the potting mixture thoroughly moist, in the active growth period. During the winter rest period water sparingly, allowing the top half of the mixture to dry out between waterings.

Feeding Apply standard liquid fertilizer once every two weeks during the active growth period.

Potting and repotting Use a soil-based potting mixture (see page 429). Move marantas into containers one size larger in spring. They do not have a deep root system and grow well in shallow pans or half-pots.

Propagation Propagate either by dividing large clumps in spring or by cuttings taken during the warmer months. Take cuttings 3–4 inches long, with three or four leaves, and trim off any leafstalk sheaths that would be below the potting-mixture surface when planted. Plant each cutting in a 2- to 3-inch pot containing a moistened equal-parts mixture of peat moss and sand, enclose it in a plastic bag, and keep it in a fairly shady place. Rooting should occur in four to six weeks; thereafter move the new plant into a shallow pan or half-pot of standard soil-based potting mixture and treat it in exactly the same way as a mature maranta.

Propagating from cuttings

When propagating a maranta, use a sharp blade to slice off a cutting with at least three leaves.

Trim off any leafstalk sheaths that would otherwise be buried in rooting mixture when the cutting is potted.

Maxillaria

ORCHIDACEAE

M. praestans

MAXILLARIAS suitable for indoor cultivation are epiphytic, with pseudobulbs that carry leathery, dark green leaves. The leaves normally arise from the tip of the egg-shaped pseudobulbs. Flowers are borne singly on stalks that grow upright from the base of the newest pseudobulbs, and each pseudobulb can produce several flower stalks at a time. Sepals and petals are usually rather long, narrow, and pointed. As a result, the flowers tend to have a starry, insectlike appearance.
See also ORCHIDS.

RECOMMENDED MAXILLARIAS

M. picta has pseudobulbs about 3 inches long, which become furrowed with age. Each pseudobulb bears one, or rarely two, narrowly strap-shaped leaves 9–15 inches long and ½ inch wide. Each flower stalk is about 8 inches tall, and the flowers are likely to be about 2 inches across, with inward-arching sepals and small petals. Sepals and petals are creamy yellow with maroon markings. The cream-colored lip is striped with maroon. Most flowers open in winter and early spring, during the rest period.

M. praestans has 1-inch-long pseudobulbs that each bear one strap-shaped leaf 6–7 inches long and 1–1½ inches wide. The 4- to 5-inch-long flower stalks grow almost upright. Each stalk carries a flower 1–1½ inches across, with small, upward-pointing petals and lip surrounded by much larger, outspread sepals. The sepals and petals are reddish brown, but marked lengthwise with fine, yellow lines. The lip is dark red and encloses the bright yellow column. Flowering season varies, but is likely to be in the early summer.

M. tenuifolia has a rhizome that grows vertically rather than horizontally. The pseudobulbs that are spaced at intervals along this climbing rhizome are only about 1 inch long. Each carries one narrow, channeled, strap-shaped leaf 12–15 inches long. The newer pseudobulbs produce many 2-inch-long flower stalks, each with a single flower 1½–2 inches across. The narrow, pointed sepals and petals are dark red with yellow spots and blotches. The nearly oblong lip is blood red, with a yellow, purple-spotted lower end. Flowering normally occurs in summer and fall.

PROPER CARE

Light Give maxillarias bright filtered light throughout the year. Do not expose these plants to direct sunlight, which scorches the leaves.

Temperature During the active growth period keep daytime temperature around 70°F, with a nighttime level 10° lower. During the winter rest period it is advisable not to exceed 60° during the day, again with a lower level at night. Provide adequate humidity at all times by placing potted plants on trays of moist pebbles. For maxillarias growing on supports epiphytically a daily mist-spray should suffice.

Watering During the active growth period water these plants moderately, allowing the top half-inch of the mixture to dry out before watering again. During the winter rest period water sparingly, giving only enough to prevent the mixture from drying out completely. This applies even to *M. picta*, which flowers during the rest period. At the end of the flowering season give almost no water at all for a three-week period.

Feeding Apply a foliar feed with every third or fourth watering during the active growth period only.

Potting and repotting Use any of the recommended potting mixtures for epiphytic orchids (see page 289). Move plants in spring into slightly larger pots only when they have outgrown their current ones. After repotting, water sparingly for a few weeks, until the roots have taken hold. Small plants grow well in 3- to 5-inch pots or on supports such as blocks of osmunda fiber. Larger plants do better in shallow pans or in slatted baskets. If *M. tenuifolia*, with its vertically growing rhizome, is lodged in a pot, put an upright, 2-inch-wide, 1-foot-long slab of tree fern in the pot to give the plant support.

Propagation Maxillarias can be divided in spring. Cut through the rhizome with a sharp knife, making sure that each segment has a growing point and at least two unwithered pseudobulbs. Plant the segments individually in pots of standard mixture, allowing about an inch of space for further growth (or attach the segments to separate supports, where they can grow epiphytically). Water only sparingly for the first six weeks. Thereafter, treat the new specimens as mature maxillarias.

Medinilla

MELASTOMATACEAE

M. magnifica

PLANTS of the genus *Medinilla* can be epiphytes growing in the forks of tree branches, but more often they are shrubs. The only species of this tropical plant that is grown indoors, *M. magnifica,* is well named, for it produces magnificent drooping floral clusters. It is extremely difficult to grow, however, even in the controlled conditions of a warm and humid greenhouse. As a house plant it is likely to flourish only if grown under the best possible conditions. Another problem with this handsome shrub is that it eventually becomes bulky and takes up a good deal of space. Most amateur indoor gardeners who successfully grow medinillas have found it best to keep them in specially constructed plant windows (see page 53).

M. magnifica can grow 8 feet tall in the wild, but indoor plants are unlikely to exceed 4 feet in height, with a similar spread, in 10- or 12-inch pots. The woody, four-angled stems and numerous branches carry coarse-textured, strongly undulate, leathery leaves arranged in opposite pairs. The medium green leaves which are stalkless, are pointed-oval in shape, up to 12 inches long and 5 inches wide. Drooping flower stalks up to 18 inches long are produced at the tips of branches in late spring. Every flower stalk carries a number of pinkish, papery bracts, each 2–4 inches long and 2 inches wide. The bracts are arranged in two or three tiers along the flower stalk, and between each tier hangs a cluster of about 20 cherry red flowers. At the tip of the stalk, however, is a very large cluster of up to 40 blooms. Each bell-shaped flower is up to ½ inch long and wide and is borne on a short stalk of its own.

PROPER CARE

Light Medinillas must have bright light filtered through a translucent blind or curtain.

Temperature Give these plants temperatures of 65°–80°F throughout the year. Temperatures may be slightly lower during the winter rest period, but medinillas should never be exposed to below 55°. They need high humidity, too, in order to flower. Stand pots on trays of moist pebbles, and spray the foliage daily whenever the temperature is above 65°. During the rest period allow the trays of pebbles to dry out, but do not discontinue the spraying unless temperatures drop below 65° for more than two or three days at a time.

Watering During the active growth period water moderately, giving enough at each watering to make the potting mixture moist throughout but allowing the top half-inch of the mixture to dry out before watering again. During the rest period give only enough to keep the potting mixture from drying out completely, and do not begin to water moderately again until new flower stalks become visible in early to mid-spring.

Feeding Begin to apply standard liquid fertilizer once every two weeks as soon as flower buds start to open. Stop feedings in early fall even though the active growth period has not yet come to an end.

Potting and repotting Use a combination of one-third soil-based potting mixture (see page 429), one-third coarse leaf mold, one-sixth peat moss, and one-sixth coarse sand or perlite. In early spring move each plant into a pot one size larger, taking great care to damage the roots as little as possible. After the maximum convenient pot size (probably 10–12 inches) has been reached, topdress the plants every spring with fresh potting mixture (see page 428).

Propagation Although medinillas can be propagated from tip cuttings, home propagation is not normally feasible. Leaves at the top of growing shoots are awkwardly large, and very humid conditions and high, constantly even temperatures are required for successful rooting. Most indoor gardeners who grow these plants acquire them as young specimens from professional growers.

Special points Medinillas are extremely susceptible to attack by red spider mites (see page 455). The regular spraying recommended above (see "Temperature") should help to prevent a heavy infestation. When spraying, pay particular attention to the undersides of leaves; this is where the mites tend to collect.

Prune plants immediately after the last flowers have faded, probably in early summer. Cut back unwanted, spindly branches almost to the base, and shorten by half all long branches, whether or not they have flowered.

Microcoelum

PALMAE

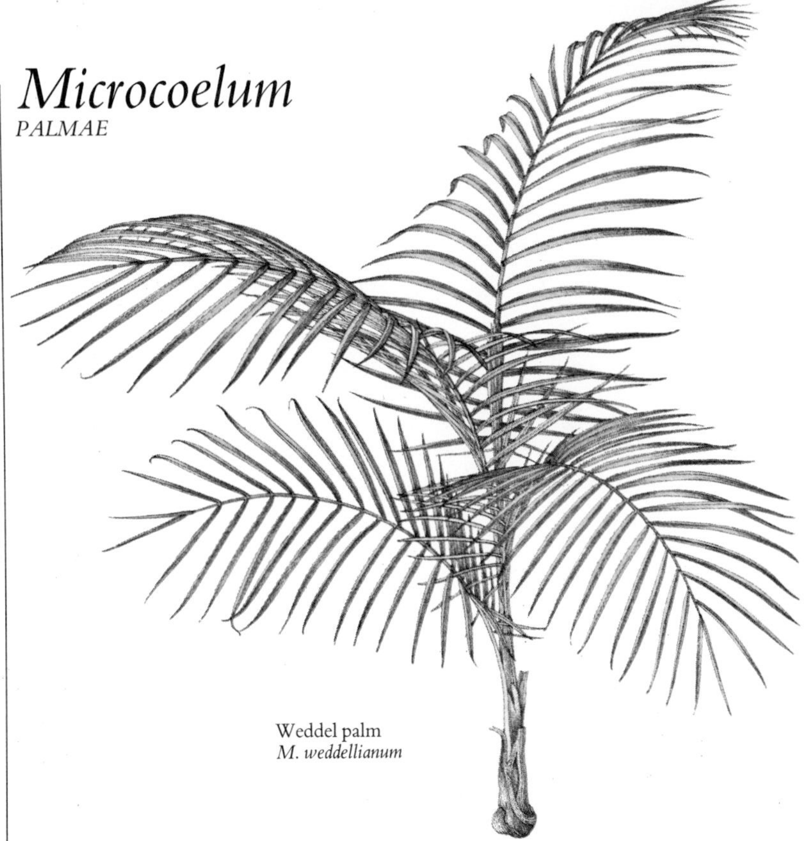

Weddel palm
M. weddellianum

THE genus *Microcoelum* includes just two species, and only one, *M. weddellianum* (weddel palm), is used as a house plant. This compact palm is still sold in many places as either *Cocos weddelliana* or *Syagrus weddelliana,* two names now considered invalid.

M. weddellianum rarely grows taller indoors than 4 feet, with a 2-foot spread. Young plants are generally bought when they are only 9–12 inches high, with three or four 8- to 10-inch-long fronds. As the plants age, the fronds lengthen and broaden; they can eventually become about 3 feet long and 9 inches wide. A potted microcoelum rarely produces a trunk of any length. The shiny, dark green fronds, which are divided into many pinnae (or leaflets), spread out from a very short, thickened base. Each frond, carried on a stalk 3–6 inches long, has a central rib covered with black scales. There are 20 to 30 slender pinnae on each side of the rib, and these are evenly arranged—though not quite opposite one another—in herringbone fashion. Flowers are not produced on plants grown indoors.
See also PALMS.

PROPER CARE

Light Give these palms bright light, but without any direct sunlight.

Temperature Microcoelums do well in temperatures between 60° and 80°F. They should not be exposed for long periods to temperatures below or above that range. They are extremely sensitive to dry air, which will cause the fronds to turn brown and shrivel. Stand the potted plants on trays of moist pebbles throughout the year.

Watering Water moderately at all times, giving enough to make the mixture moist, allowing the top half-inch to dry out before watering again. Should temperatures fall below 60°F, allow the top inch of mixture to dry out between waterings.

Feeding Apply standard liquid fertilizer once a month throughout the active growth period.

Potting and repotting Use a soil-based potting mixture (see page 429). It is vitally important not to give these palms larger pots than they actually require. Repotting becomes necessary only when the thickened base of a microcoelum begins to force its way up out of the pot. This will not happen more often than once every two or three years. Repot in a slightly larger container, when required, in spring.

Propagation Microcoelums are propagated from seed. This is an extremely slow process, and is therefore best left to commercial growers.

Miltonia

ORCHIDACEAE

THOUGH the genus *Miltonia* is fairly small, there are many varieties and innumerable hybrids. These epiphytic orchids are unmistakable because of their large, almost flat flowers which resemble pansies. Miltonias, in fact, are commonly called pansy orchids. In general they have flattened-egg-shaped pseudobulbs about 2–4 inches high and $1\frac{1}{2}$ inches wide, but only $\frac{1}{2}$ inch thick. Each pseudobulb, which is usually smooth, shiny, and grayish green, normally carries from one to three pale green, almost translucent leaves at its tip. The leaves tend to be long, narrow, and gracefully arching.

Upright flower stems 6–18 inches tall rising from the base of pseudobulbs carry from one to as many as ten short-stalked flowers. Flower texture, especially of the hybrids, is velvety. The petals and sepals, which are almost oblong in shape, give the impression of overlapping. Flowers vary in size from about 2 to 4 inches across, depending on species or variety. They are richly colored, and there is almost always a contrasting blotch on the upper part of the big, broad, two-lobed lip. The flowers of many forms are sweetly scented. The main flowering season is late spring through summer, but flowering sometimes occurs again in the fall. Each bloom lasts four to five weeks.

Miltonias do not have a distinct rest period but tend to grow throughout the year under the right indoor conditions. Because they are sensitive to temperature changes, it is advisable to keep them in a terrarium (see page 54). It is virtually impossible to single out specific miltonia hybrids (which are usually grown in preference to the species), as particularly suitable or attractive for indoor use; there are too many. However, instead, a number of species and varieties that are relatively easy to grow indoors have been selected below as being representative of the genus. Indoor gardeners are advised to acquire specimens when they are in flower.
See also ORCHIDS.

RECOMMENDED MILTONIAS

M. spectabilis has pseudobulbs 3–4 inches tall each bearing two strap-shaped leaves up to 6 inches long.

Pansy orchid
Miltonia hybrid

Flower stalks 6–8 inches tall are each topped by a single flower up to 4 inches across. Flower color is variable but sepals and petals are usually white or cream, and the lip is wine purple marked with a central blotch and several veins of darker hue. The lip margins are wavy, and edged with white or pale rose. Blooms usually appear in late summer or early fall. There is a more popularly grown form, *M.s.* 'Moreliana,' with maroon to purple sepals and petals, and with the wine purple lip more heavily veined than in the type plant.

M. vexillaria has pseudobulbs up to $2\frac{1}{2}$ inches tall, each bearing at least three strap-shaped leaves 8–12 inches long. Flower stalks grow to 20 inches tall; several may be produced at one time from each pseudobulb. The stalks are each topped by three or more notably flattened, fragrant flowers each 3 inches across. Flower color is pale lilac to rosy red, with the large lip (up to $2\frac{1}{2}$ inches across) darker in color than the rest of the flower, and with a prominent yellow crest. Flowering season is spring to early summer. A highly floriferous form, *M.v.* 'Volunteer,' has lavender pink flowers veined with deep purple, and with a white and yellow blotch on the lip.

M. warscewiczii has dark green pseudobulbs up to 4 inches high each carrying a solitary strap-shaped leaf up to 7 inches long. The flower stalks grow to 12 inches long and each bears several flowers about $1\frac{1}{2}$ inches across. The petals and sepals of the flowers are cinnamon brown tipped with yellow; they have undulating edges. The lip is almost circular, and rosy purple with white at the tip and with a roughly central brown blotch. Flowers appear between midwinter and early spring. There is a white-flowered form, *M.w. alba,* in which the lip is blotched with lilac, and another, *M.w. xanthina,* with flowers that are yellow except for a white border on the petals and sepals.

PROPER CARE

Light Miltonias do best in medium light for most of the year. Too much bright light will turn the thin foliage yellow. During the short-day winter months, however, give plants bright light, with two or three hours a day of direct morning or late-afternoon sun.

Temperature Keep the daytime temperature at about 70°F and the nighttime temperature at about 65°. Do not permit the temperature to rise above 75° or to fall below 62° at any time. High humidity is essential. Stand plants on trays of moist pebbles, and mist-spray them every morning.

Watering Water moderately, allowing the top half-inch of the mixture to dry out before watering again. It is best to water early in the day so that the foliage is dry by nightfall.

Feeding Give a high-nitrogen foliar feed with every third or fourth watering during the warmer months, and with every sixth or eighth watering at all other times.

Potting and repotting Use any recommended potting mixture for epiphytic orchids (see page 289). Grow each miltonia in the smallest pot that will allow for the further growth of two or three pseudobulbs. Repot only when necessary. The best time for repotting is in summer, immediately after flowering has ceased.

Propagation When a plant becomes inconveniently large, divide it in summer by cutting through the rhizome, making sure that each segment retains at least two pseudobulbs. Plant segments in the smallest suitable pots of moist potting mixture. Keep pots in medium light, and do not water apart from a daily light mist-spray during the first four weeks. Thereafter, treat each young plant as a mature miltonia.

Special points Remove dying flowers and leaves without delay. If they come into contact with healthy leaves, these may be blemished.

Black spots on leaves indicate that the temperature has fallen too low. Either raise the temperature or decrease the humidity.

Mimosa

LEGUMINOSAE

Touch-me-not
M. pudica

MIMOSA *pudica* (humbleplant, sensitive plant, or touch-me-not) is the only species of the genus *Mimosa* grown as a house plant. Although it is related to the popular florists' mimosa, which is so highly regarded for its sweetly scented yellow flowers, *M. pudica* is a very different kind of plant. The florists' mimosa, in fact, belongs to an entirely different genus, *Acacia,* and *M. pudica* resembles its familiar relative only in the general shape of the leaves and blossoms. As an indoor plant it is valued not only for its feathery leaves and fluffy, ball-shaped flowers, but also for the fascinating way in which the leaves behave when they are touched. If a leaf is handled, no matter how gently, it almost immediately folds in on itself, and the leafstalk reacts by drooping downward, taking the folded blade with it. This sometimes sets off a chain reaction, with several leaves falling onto one another, causing the apparent collapse of a whole small section of the foliage. The collapse is merely temporary, though. After a short time—normally, about half an hour—the plant will have fully recovered. Some authorities suggest that it may be unwise to touch-test *M. pudica* too often, however. It is evident that some specimens have been thought to react less quickly and to recover less efficiently when they have been purposely "played with" a bit too frequently.

This shrublike plant grows to 20 inches tall, and its much-branching stems carry light green leaves with leafstalks up to 4 inches long. The stems are spiny and are sparsely coated with fine, white hairs. The leaves are bipinnate—that is, they are divided into several sections (pinnae), each of which is further subdivided into many little leaflets (pinnules). The narrow, 1- to 2-inch-long pinnae are composed of elliptic, $\frac{1}{4}$-inch-long pinnules arranged in rows of opposite pairs. From mid-spring to early fall, clusters of five to eight mauve-pink flowers appear on short stalks from the leaf axils. Every flower consists of hundreds of fine filaments and looks like a fluffy pompon $\frac{1}{4}$–$\frac{1}{2}$ inch across. The leaf axils, too, are usually tufted with bristly, white hairs $\frac{1}{8}$ inch long.

M. pudica is a perennial and may be kept alive indefinitely under the right conditions. Because it tends to become unsightly as it ages, however, most experienced indoor gardeners prefer to discard each specimen when it has finished flowering at the end of a single season. Plants are generally acquired in early spring and retained until mid-fall.

PROPER CARE

Light Grow this mimosa in bright light. In order to bloom successfully throughout the summer months, it must have at least three or four hours a day of direct sunlight.

Temperature Normally warm room temperatures are suitable for mimosas throughout the year. Because *M. pudica* needs high humidity, stand pots on trays of moist pebbles.

Watering Water moderately, giving enough at each watering to make the potting mixture moist but allowing the top inch of the mixture to dry out before watering again.

Feeding Apply a high-potash liquid fertilizer once every two weeks.

Potting and repotting Although best treated as a temporary plant to be retained for one season only, *M. pudica* requires repotting several times during that period. Use a soil-based potting mixture (see page 429), and move each plant to a slightly larger pot whenever the roots have totally filled the current pot. Root ends appearing through the drainage hole at the bottom of the pot will indicate that repotting is necessary. The plant flowers best and its foliage is at its most characteristic, however, when the roots are confined in a relatively small space. A 5-inch pot should be the largest required. The sensitive leaves of a newly repotted mimosa may seem to be alarmingly droopy, but they should recover swiftly.

The leaflets of M. pudica *will fold up when touched. This cannot be avoided during repotting, but should not be done otherwise.*

Propagation Propagation is from seed sown in early spring in 3-inch pots of rooting mixture (see page 444). Plant two or three seeds in one pot, place the pots in bright filtered light, and give only enough water to make the mixture barely moist. After the seeds have germinated (probably in no more than two or three weeks), discard those seedlings that look least strong and healthy. When the remaining seedlings have grown about $1\frac{1}{2}$ inches high, repot them singly in 3-inch pots of the standard soil-based potting mixture, and treat the young specimens as mature mimosas.

Monstera

ARACEAE

Swiss cheese plant
M. deliciosa

WHEN growing in the wild, plants of the genus *Monstera* climb up the trunks and along the branches of trees, clinging to the bark by means of thick aerial roots, which not only anchor the plant to the tree but also take up water and nutrients. Only one species, *M. deliciosa,* is a popular house plant; others occasionally used indoors are less decorative. The shiny leaves of a mature *M. deliciosa* grow up to 18 inches across, have 12-inch-long stalks, and are basically heart-shaped, but deeply incised from the edges almost to the central vein, and perforated in the remaining sections. This breaking up of the leaf area helps the wild plants withstand high tropical winds—and perhaps explain the origin of one of their common names, hurricane plant. Other common names are splitleaf, Swiss cheese, and window plant.

Mature monsteras with active aerial roots have the most attractive leaves, with the most pronounced incisions and holes. Young plants have leaves that may be entirely unbroken. Immature monsteras are sometimes sold as *Philodendron pertusum* (not a valid name). As they develop, they acquire the characteristic perforations and split edges. The inflorescence, which is rarely produced indoors, is a half-oval, creamy white spathe with a thick 10-inch-long spadix in the middle. The spadix develops into a white, edible fruit that tastes something like pineapple. It can occur at any time of year once the plant reaches maturity.

Indoor monsteras make dramatic plants whether they are young specimens with only three or four leaves or tall, mature ones that need to be supported on stout canes or poles. If treated well, they can grow very big—10–15 feet tall and 6–8 feet across—and thrive indoors for years. Moss-covered poles that simulate the bark of trees the plants climb on in the wild add considerably to the health of monsteras grown indoors. There is a form, *M. d.* 'Variegata,' with leaves splashed with white or cream-colored patches of irregular shapes and sizes.

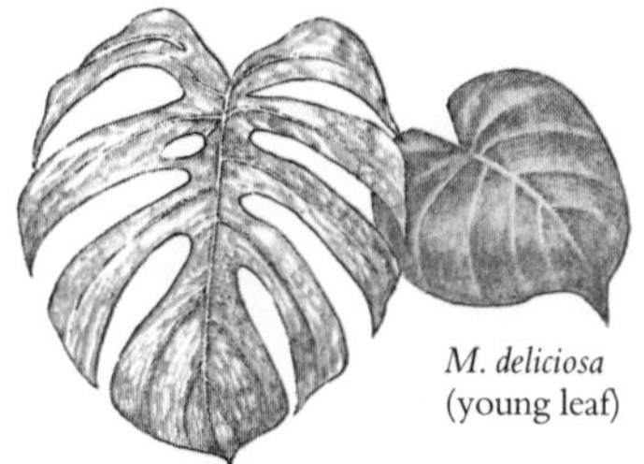

M. deliciosa (young leaf)

M. deliciosa 'Variegata' (leaf)

PROPER CARE

Light Actively growing monsteras do best in bright filtered light, but plants may be placed in direct sunlight in winter. In an inadequately lit position the long leafstalks will become extended and the leaves smaller and somewhat less divided.

Temperature Normal room temperatures are suitable. In temperatures above 70°F place pots on trays of damp pebbles for increased humidity.

Watering Water sparingly, making the potting mixture barely moist and allowing the top third to dry out before watering again.

Feeding Apply standard liquid fertilizer once every two weeks during the active growth period only.

Potting and repotting Use a soil-based potting mixture (see page 429) with the addition of a one-third portion of coarse leaf mold. Move plants into pots one size larger each spring until maximum convenient pot size is reached. Thereafter, topdress plants (see page 428) with fresh potting mixture annually.

Propagation Home propagation is difficult because of the awkwardly large expanse of leaf and consequent high loss of moisture through transpiration. A tip cutting, including at least two leaves, will root in spring, however, if it is planted in a 4-inch pot containing a moistened equal-parts mixture of peat moss and sand. Enclose the cutting in a plastic bag, and keep it warm in bright filtered light. When new growth indicates that the cutting has rooted, repot it in the mixture recommended for adult plants, and treat it as mature.

If it proves impracticable to root cuttings, plants can be air layered (see page 440)—a reliable but slow method. Seed, too, will germinate easily in a warm room, but plants from seed lack attractive incised leaves for at least two years.

Special points Keep the leaves clean by frequent sponging. Train aerial roots to moss-covered poles if these are used; if not, train them into the potting mixture.

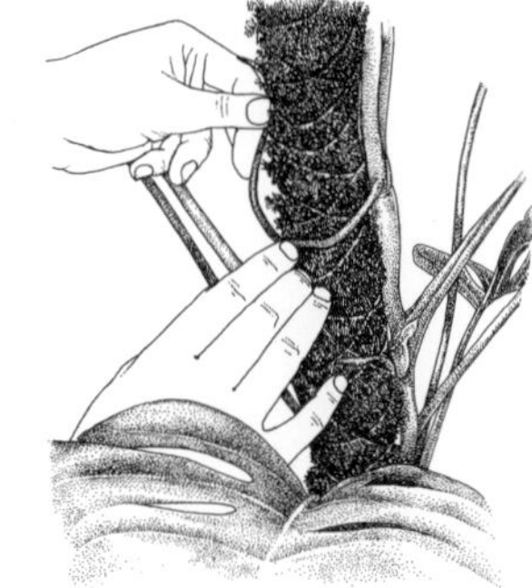

In addition to tying M. deliciosa *to a moss-covered pole, assist its aerial roots to penetrate the support as if in the wild.*

Myrtus

MYRTACEAE

Dwarf myrtle
M. communis 'Microphylla'

THE genus *Myrtus* (myrtle) consists of about sixteen species of shrub or small tree with aromatic foliage and white or pink flowers. Those most commonly grown as house plants are small forms of the Mediterranean myrtle, *M. communis,* which is capable of growing 15 feet tall in its native habitat but usually only 2–3 feet high indoors. The species is a much branching shrub with densely crowded, pointed-oval leaves, which are dark green, shiny, and fragrant when crushed. The scented flowers have a diameter of $\frac{3}{4}$ inch and are composed of a mass of yellow stamens concealing five small, white or pale pink petals. Flowers are produced singly on short flower stalks in late summer.

RECOMMENDED MYRTUSES

M. communis boetica has $1\frac{1}{2}$-inch-long leaves with a pronounced fragrance.

***M.c.* 'Microphylla'** (dwarf myrtle), the most common variety, grows no taller than about 2 feet and bears leaves less than an inch long. *M.c.* 'Microphylla' can be pruned and trained into practically any shape (see "Special points," below).

M.c. tarentina is compact, and its inch-long leaves are unusually tough. The stems and leafstalks are covered with a dense, white down.

***M.c.* 'Variegata'** has sharply pointed leaves up to 2 inches long. Each green leaf is bordered with creamy white.

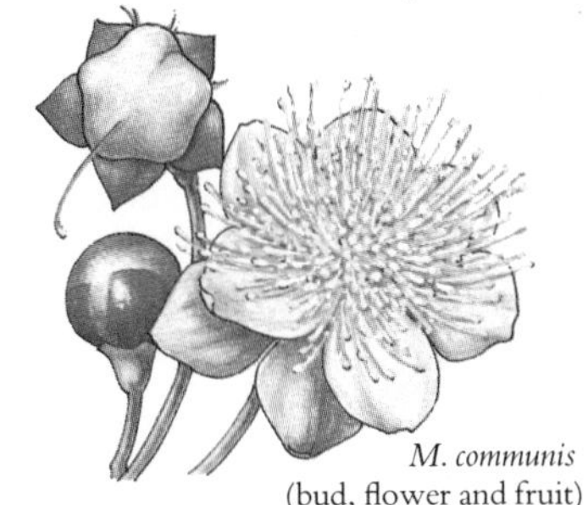

M. communis
(bud, flower and fruit)

PROPER CARE

Light Provide the brightest possible light at all times. If these plants are placed more than a foot or two away from a fully sunlit window, they are likely to become spindly. Turn them regularly to avoid lopsided growth.

Temperature Although *M. communis* prefers relatively cool conditions, all its forms grow well in normal room temperatures. If possible, however, give them all a winter rest period at about 45°F. Otherwise, the relatively warm, dry air will make the leaves fall. Fresh air during the active growth period will toughen up growth, and so these plants may be stood in a sunny position outdoors throughout the summer months.

Watering During the active growth period water plentifully. During the rest period water only moderately, giving enough to make the potting mixture moist throughout at each watering but letting the top inch of the mixture dry out before watering again. If at all possible, use rainwater or some other calcium-free water.

Feeding Do not feed these plants until they have been lodged in the same pot for more than three months. Thereafter, apply standard liquid fertilizer every two weeks during the active growth period only.

Potting and repotting Use a soil-based potting mixture (see page 429) with the addition of a one-third portion of leaf mold or peat moss. The basic mixture should be lime-free, because myrtuses do best in a neutral or slightly acid medium (see page 430). As plants get bigger, move them into increasingly larger pots, one size at a time. This is best done just as new growth is starting in the spring. It is important to pack the mixture firmly around the roots and to set these plants at the same level in successive pots—never deeper than before. Once a myrtus is lodged in a pot of maximum convenient size (probably 7 or 8 inches), simply topdress (see page 428) each spring with fresh mixture.

Propagation Cuttings with a short heel (that is, with a little of the old bark attached) are normally used for propagating these plants. The process requires patience, since rooting may take six to eight weeks. Insert several cuttings together around the rim of a 3-inch pot containing a moistened rooting mixture (see page 444), and enclose the whole in a plastic bag or propagating case. Keep it in medium light—at a slightly shaded window, for instance—at a temperature of about 60°F. When new top growth appears, move the rooted cuttings individually into 3-inch pots of the recommended potting mixture for adult plants. Thereafter, treat the new specimens as mature myrtuses.

Special points These small shrubs can be kept in shape by judicious pruning, which should be done only when strong growing shoots that might spoil a plant's symmetry become apparent. Too much pruning will reduce the likelihood of flowers, but a certain amount of regular pinching out of growing tips is essential for building up dense growth.

Narcissus

AMARYLLIDACEAE

Daffodil
N. 'Carlton'

NARCISSI are bulbous plants grown for their fresh-colored, graceful flowers, some of which are scented. Outdoors these plants bloom in late winter or early spring. Indoors, however, the bulbs can be "forced" to flower earlier. Potted narcissi can be enjoyed while coming into flower and during the brief flowering period, but they must be discarded when the flowers have faded. Bulbs will not flower twice indoors.

Most kinds of narcissus fall into one or another of several distinct groups. Of these the bunch-flowered (polyanthus) types, which are mostly forms of *N. tazetta,* are most successful indoors. A number of large-flowered kinds are also suitable, among them some of the trumpet-shaped narcissi generally known as daffodils. (Plants usually *called* narcissi are forms with large or small cups rather than trumpets.) Many of the plants—the *N. tazetta* forms in particular—grow well on a bed of moist pebbles. The large-flowered kinds do best in pots of soil-based mixture, which gives them much-needed stability when in flower. *See also BULBS, CORMS, and TUBERS.*

RECOMMENDED NARCISSI

The large-flowered daffodils recommended for use indoors include: *N.* 'Mount Hood' (with ivory white petals and a creamy white trumpet); *N.* 'King Alfred' (with golden yellow petals and trumpet); *N.* 'Celebrity' (with white petals and a pale yellow trumpet); *N.* 'Carlton' (whose soft-yellow flowers have a relatively short, broad, frilled trumpet); *N.* 'Jack Snipe' (with white, arching petals and a short, frilled, primrose yellow trumpet); and *N.* 'Valiant Spark' (with bright buttercup yellow petals and a short, bright tangerine-orange trumpet).

N.t. 'Cheerfulness' *N.* 'Mount Hood'

N.t. 'Geranium'

N. tazetta types suitable for use indoors include: *N.t.* 'Cheerfulness' (a pale, creamy yellow, many-petaled form with orange petals in the center); *N.t.* 'Cragford' (white-petaled, with a very short, brilliant orange-scarlet cup); *N.t.* 'Geranium' (white-petaled, with an orange-red cup); *N.t.* 'Paperwhite' (white-petaled with a short white cup); and *N.t.* 'Soleil d'Or' (yellow, with an orange cup). All bear three or four blooms per stalk.

PROPER CARE

It is possible to buy narcissus bulbs (usually of the *N. tazetta* forms) that have been subjected to a special cooling treatment that makes them flower earlier than untreated bulbs. These "prepared" bulbs (always clearly labeled as such) may be started into growth either in the light, or in the dark. The main disadvantage of untreated bulbs is that they *must* be started in the dark. The best time for planting is early fall, and a cool temperature for the first few weeks is essential.

Planting on pebbles Use a waterproof container at least 4–5 inches deep, and cover the bottom with pebbles. Place 5 or 6 "double-nosed" bulbs (those partially divided into two flowering-size sections, but remaining attached to each other) or 8 to 10 fair-sized single bulbs on top of the pebbles. Stand the bulbs together, almost (but not quite) touching, and put more pebbles around them as a support. Add only enough water to reach a point just below the bases of the bulbs. As roots are produced, they will work their way down to the water. This method is a form of hydroculture (see page 448). Store the container in a cool place (not above 48°F), and top it up with water from time to time.

The bulbs should remain at this low temperature (and, if untreated, in the dark) until they have made about 3 inches of growth, and flower buds have appeared through the necks of the bulbs. This will take 8–10 weeks for untreated bulbs, less for prepared ones. Thereafter, move the container

These specimens of N.t. *'Geranium' have been brought into flower on wet pebbles in a watertight container. The result is an eye-catching display.*

gradually (over a period of about a week) into a brightly lit position. Once acclimatized the plants need as much direct sunlight as they can get.

Planting in mixture For growing narcissi in potting mixture or bulb fiber (see page 111), use either waterproof containers (such as decorative bowls) or pots or pans with drainage holes. Plant several bulbs together, each bulb half in and half above the fiber or mixture, which may be either soil- or peat-based (see page 429). Make sure that the fiber or mixture is moist, not sodden, before planting. Store the container in the coolest possible position, and in the dark (preferable even for prepared bulbs). Commercial growers "plunge" narcissi potted in fiber or mixture in the ground under a thick layer of peat moss. If it is impossible to provide such outdoor treatment, enclose the potted bulbs in black plastic bags and place the bags in a cool position.

Examine the container once or twice during the next few weeks. If the potting mixture appears to be drying out, add just enough water to keep it evenly moist. When the bulbs have made 3 inches of top growth and flower buds have cleared the necks, treat these narcissi in the same way as those planted on pebbles.

Special points Do not subject budding narcissi to room temperatures above about 60°F. Heat will cause flower buds to shrivel. It will also shorten the life of any that do develop.

Neoregelia

BROMELIACEAE

Blushing bromeliad
N. carolinae 'Tricolor'

NEOREGELIAS are bromeliads with brilliantly colored foliage usually arranged in a flattish rosette shape. During the flowering period, which can occur at any time of year, there are striking changes of color in the leaves of most species. In some, for example, the leaf tips turn bright red, in others the inner leaves of the rosette redden. Whatever the change, the remarkable color remains attractive for several months. Insignificant flowers—usually white or blue—grow from a compound head situated deep in the cuplike center of the rosette. Neoregelias have no clearly-defined rest period; they grow slowly and more or less continuously throughout the year.

See also BROMELIADS.

RECOMMENDED NEOREGELIAS

N. carolinae (blushing bromeliad) and its varying forms are rarely more than 9 inches tall, with shiny, medium green leaves about a foot long and $1\frac{1}{2}$-2 inches wide. Flowers are violet-colored or lavender. *N. c.* 'Marechalii,' the most compact variety, has slightly shorter, broader leaves, and the center of the rosette turns carmine-red when the plant is about to flower. *N. c.* 'Meyendorffii' has copper-tinged olive green leaves, that become dark maroon in the rosette center at flowering time. The most popular variety is *N. c.* 'Tricolor,' with leaves that are striped in white and rose-pink, as well as green. As *N. c.* 'Tricolor' matures, the whole leaf area becomes suffused with pink, and with the approach of flowering time the central leaves turn brilliant red.

N. concentrica has stiff, broad leaves a foot long and 4 inches wide edged with short, black spines; the leaves are pale green lightly flecked with purple on the upper surface, and pale green striped with silvery gray on the underside. Prior to flowering, the rosette center turns a rich purple. The flowers are bright blue.

N. marmorata has leaves up to 15 inches long and $2\frac{1}{2}$ inches wide, that are light green heavily marbled on both sides with reddish brown. Flowers are pale lavender-blue. (Most of the plants sold under this name are, in fact, hybrids between *N. marmorata* and *N. spectabilis.*)

N. sarmentosa is one of several creeping species, which often form a number of rosettes on stolons 6–12 inches long. There are never more than about ten leaves to a rosette; each leaf is up to 10 inches long and an inch wide, deep green but sometimes shaded with purple in the leaf axils, and sprinkled with white scales on the underside. Flowers are white. This species of neoregelia does not change color at flowering time.

N. spectabilis (painted fingernail or fingernail plant) has 15-inch-long, 2-inch-wide, olive green leaves, gray-striped on the underside and tipped at flowering time with inch-long red "fingernails." Flowers are blue.

PROPER CARE

Light For compact, brilliantly colored foliage and dependable flowering these plants need bright light with some direct sunlight.

Temperature All neoregelias will thrive in normal room temperatures. They cannot tolerate temperatures below 50°F. Provide a humid atmosphere by standing pots on trays of moist pebbles, and mist-spray plants daily when they are being grown in warm, dry conditions.

Watering Water plants moderately, enough to make the potting mixture moist throughout, but allow one-third of the mixture to dry out between waterings. The cuplike centers of rosettes should also be filled and kept topped up; keep this water fresh by upturning the plant once a month, draining old water, and replacing it.

Feeding Give all neoregelias half-strength liquid fertilizer every two weeks, applying it not only to the potting mixture but over the foliage and into the center of the rosette.

Potting and repotting Use a potting mixture consisting of equal parts of leaf mold, peat moss, and sand. Small plants should be moved to pots one size larger in spring. Neoregelias, however, are unlikely to require pots bigger than the 5-inch size.

Propagation Spring is the best time to propagate. Use young rosettes produced near the base of plants or on the ends of stolons. Basal rosettes may already have rooted down into the potting mixture; when carefully detaching them, keep as much root attached as possible. Place each basal rosette in a 3-inch pot of a moistened equal-parts mixture of peat moss and sand, enclose it in a plastic bag, and keep it in a warm place where it will get medium light. After the rosette is well rooted (in about six to eight weeks), transfer it to a 3-inch pot of the recommended potting mixture for mature neoregelias. Thereafter, treat it in the same way as a mature plant.

Small stolon rosettes should be rooted while still attached to the parent plant. The process is similar to layering (see page 439).

Nephrolepis

POLYPODIACEAE

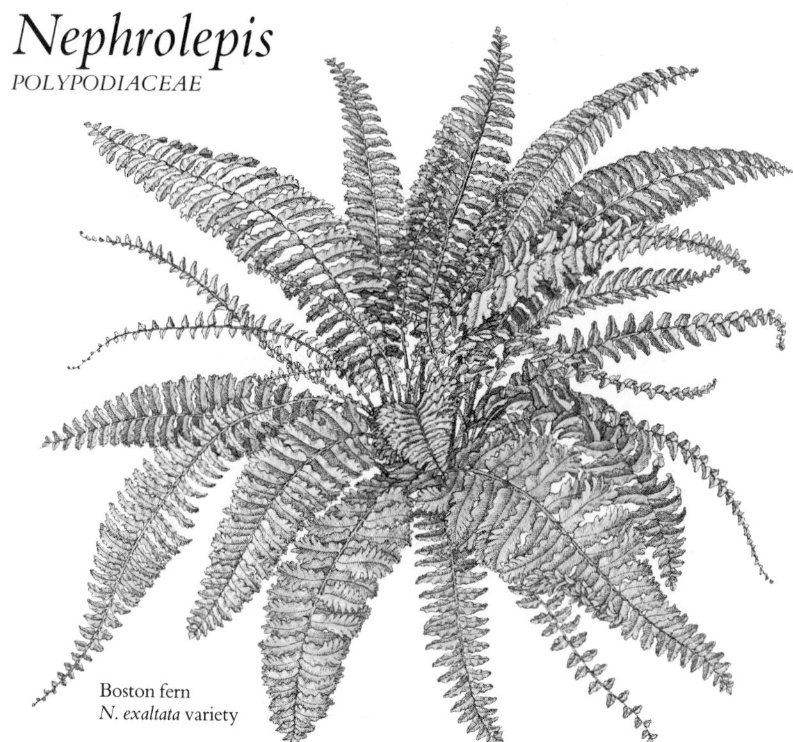

Boston fern
N. exaltata variety

TWO species of the genus *Nephrolepis* are popular indoor ferns. There are a number of widely differing forms of both species, and so the indoor gardener has a broad choice of plant size and shape. In all forms the fronds rise from an upright under ground rhizome, the top of which is visible as a short, thick stem. Each long, arching frond is divided into many narrow pinnae, which grow alternately on either side of the midrib. On the underside of each pinna there are two rows of kidney-shaped, brown spore cases, one on each side of the central vein. These plants look particularly attractive when they are grown on pedestals. Given the right conditions, they grow actively all year long.

Numerous slender, furry runners grow out from the rhizome and creep along the surface of the potting mixture, putting down roots and producing new plants at their tips.

See also FERNS.

RECOMMENDED NEPHROLEPISES

N. cordifolia (erect swordfern) has light green fronds that grow up to 2 feet long. The fronds are 4 inches wide at the base, narrowing down to $\frac{1}{4}$ inch at the tip, and the straight-edged pinnae are about $\frac{1}{2}$ inch wide. In one popular variety, *N.c.* 'Plumosa,' the color of the fronds is darker green, and the extreme tip of each of the pinnae is cut, giving a fringed, slightly feathery look to the entire plant.

N. cordifolia (erect swordfern)

N. exaltata is similar to *N. cordifolia*, but the fronds can grow 4–6 feet long. More important than the species are the varieties, among which are the plants familiarly known as Boston ferns. In the most popular varieties each pinna is itself cut into a number of segments, so that plants have an exceptionally feathery appearance. The fronds are much shorter than those of the species. *N.e.* 'Whitmanii' and *N.e.* 'Rooseveltii,' for example, have finely divided feathery fronds only 3 feet long.

PROPER CARE

Light Provide bright light, without direct sunlight. If necessary, these ferns can tolerate medium light for periods up to four or five weeks.

Temperature Normal room temperatures are suitable throughout the year. Minimum tolerable temperature: 50°F. For a nephrolepis grown at temperatures above 70° increase the humidity by standing the pot on a tray of damp pebbles, and mist-spraying the foliage daily.

Watering Never allow these ferns to become dry at the roots. As long as room temperature remains above 55°F, water plants plentifully as often as necessary to keep the potting mixture thoroughly moist. If the temperature falls below 55° for more than a day or two, allow the top third of the potting mixture to dry out completely between waterings.

Feeding Apply standard liquid fertilizer every two weeks to plants actively growing in peat-based potting mixture. Feed actively growing plants that are in a soil-based mixture once every four weeks.

Potting and repotting Use either a standard peat-based potting mixture or a combination of half soil-based mixture and half leaf mold (see page 429). When the roots of a nephrolepis have filled its current pot (see page 426), repot in the spring, moving the plant into a pot only one size larger. After maximum convenient pot size has been reached, remove the plant from its pot every spring, carefully trim away some of the outer roots, and replace the plant in the same pot, which has been thoroughly cleaned. Add fresh mixture as required.

Propagation Propagate whenever desirable by potting up a plantlet taken from any point where the tip of a runner has rooted down. Use a sharp knife to cut through the runner about 2 inches from the tip, thus releasing the rooted plantlet. Plant it in a 3-inch pot of the preferred potting mixture for adult plants, and treat it in the same way as a mature specimen.

Plants of the type species can also be propagated by spores, but this is a slow process (see *FERNS*, page 208). Spore propagation of the interesting varieties of these ferns is not possible because the spores are not viable.

Special points In some of the extremely feathery forms of *N. exaltata* one of the fronds of a plant occasionally reverts to the type species. Cut out any long, insufficiently segmented fronds as soon as they appear. If permitted to survive, they will take over the plant.

Nerium

APOCYNACEAE

Common oleander
N. oleander

ONLY two or three species of nerium exist, and only one of these is widely cultivated: *N. oleander* (sometimes called *N. indicum* or *N. odorum*; popularly known as common oleander or rose bay). This shrub—prized for its terminal clusters of flowers—can grow 20 feet tall outdoors, but its height rarely exceeds 6 feet in a pot. Stems are woody and generally erect, branching every $1\frac{1}{2}$–2 feet into two or more stems. The leathery leaves are narrowly lance-shaped, up to 10 inches long and 1 inch wide, with a prominent central rib and a lusterless, deep green color. They appear on short stalks in groups of three, equally spaced around the stems; some tend to droop, some are horizontal, but most grow upward at a 45° angle. Flowers, which are 1–2 inches across, are borne in groups of six or eight on the branched ends of stems. In warm climates neriums are rarely out of bloom, but a potted indoor specimen is likely to bloom only in midsummer.

Typical flower color is rose-pink, but there are varieties with red, purple, yellow, orange and white flowers. All of these may exist in both single- and double-flowered forms; the former have five petallike lobes spreading out flat from a tubular base, whereas the double-flowered sorts have many petals and resemble roses in shape. Some flowers are scented, others are not. Of the scented forms, a red double-flowered kind (which is often sold as *N. odorum*) is the most popular. Also popular is a variegated-leaved, pink-flowered form, *N.o.* 'Variegata,' which has wide, deep yellow striping on its leaves.

N. oleander 'Variegata'

PROPER CARE

Light These plants require bright light, including direct sunlight, all year round. Flowers are produced only on woody stems that have been well ripened by the sun.

Temperature Indoor neriums will do well in normal room temperatures. However, give them an annual rest period at a temperature below 60°F, if possible. They can withstand temperatures as low as 45°.

Watering During the active growth period water moderately, enough to make the potting mixture thoroughly moist, but allow the top half-inch of the mixture to dry out between waterings. During the rest period water just enough to make the potting mixture barely moist. Never let it get completely dry, however.

Although neriums can withstand periods of drought when planted in the open, many of the flower buds fail to develop if the roots of a potted plant are permitted to dry out.

Feeding Apply standard liquid fertilizer every two weeks during the active growth period.

Potting and repotting Use a soil-based mixture (see page 429). In the spring move plants into pots one size larger if roots have completely filled their pots (see page 426). After maximum convenient pot size has been reached, move plants into small tubs or topdress annually with fresh mixture (see page 428). Pack the potting mixture firmly around the roots.

Propagation Tip cuttings 3–6 inches long will root easily in early summer. Cut them cleanly just below a node, strip off the three bottom leaves that would otherwise be buried in the rooting mixture, and insert the cuttings 1½–2 inches deep in a moistened equal-parts mixture of peat moss and sand. Place the cuttings at normal room temperature in bright filtered light, and water just enough to keep the rooting mixture barely moist. Replant them in potting mixture and treat them as mature plants when roots appear through drainage holes.

Cuttings can also be rooted in water. Transfer them into potting mixture when roots are an inch long.

Special points Keep a careful watch for scale insects (see page 455), which are particularly likely to attack neriums. These pests appear on the undersides of leaves, often close to the central rib. Use a fine brush dipped in denatured alcohol to kill them and spray the plants with an insecticide.

Stickiness and sooty mold on nerium leaves are signs of scale insects. Kill these pests with denatured alcohol.

Prune by half their length all the shoots that have flowered as soon as the last bloom has faded. Also cut back any long side shoots.

Warning: Neriums should never be placed within reach of young children. Every part of this attractive plant is poisonous if eaten.

Nertera

RUBIACEAE

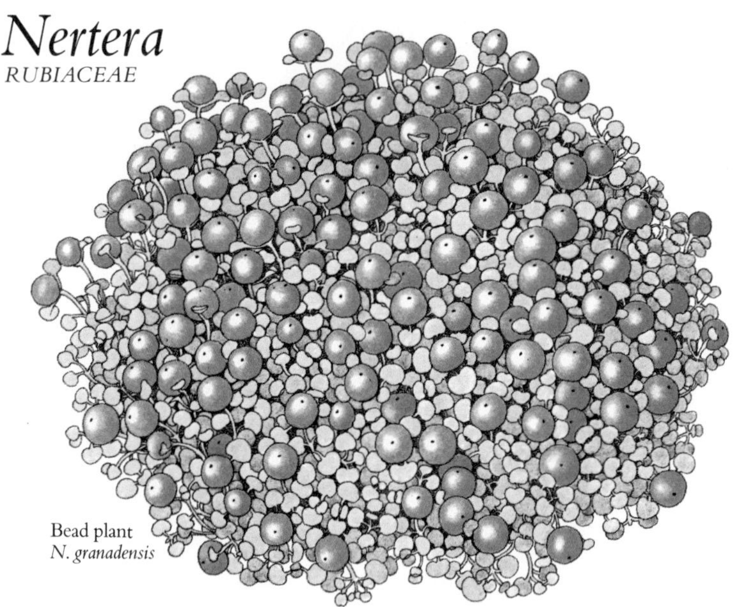

Bead plant
N. granadensis

NERTERAS are very decorative creeping plants with pea-size, orange-colored berries. The only species commonly grown indoors is *N. granadensis* (also known as *N. depressa*; popularly called bead plant, coral moss, and English or hardy baby tears). The thin, closely matted stems of this plant run along the surface of the potting mixture, rooting into the mixture at the nodes. The stems, which can grow up to 10 inches long, carry medium green, broadly oval, fleshy, stalkless leaves ¼ inch across. A fully mature plant is likely to form a low mound 2–3 inches high. Insignificant, stalkless flowers, which are produced in early summer, appear from leaf axils. The flowers are tiny and greenish yellow, and they give way to shiny, orange-red berries ¼ inch in diameter. These berries are fully developed by late summer, and they remain on the plant for several months. They are often so numerous that they almost hide the foliage.

Many home growers treat nerteras as disposable plants, replacing older specimens with new ones every year. It is not necessary to do this, however. Under the right conditions nerteras can be kept for a number of years.

PROPER CARE

Light Grow nerteras in bright light, making sure that they get at least three hours of direct sunlight every day.

Temperature Nerteras will flower and set fruit best if kept in an airy position at a temperature of 50°–60°F. Ideally, these plants should be kept outdoors throughout the months from late spring until the berries have formed. In placing them outdoors be sure to choose a position where they get some direct sunlight and are sheltered from summer storms. Indoors they can tolerate warmer conditions than the recommended temperature range. But they grow very fast in warm rooms (over 65°), and thus tend to produce too much foliage. To bear flowers and berries successfully, nerteras require high humidity. While they are kept indoors, stand the containers on trays or saucers of moist pebbles. And spray plants lightly with water once a day from the time that flowers begin to appear until all berries have fully developed.

Watering Water moderately, giving enough at each watering to make the potting mixture thoroughly moist, but allowing the top half-inch of the mixture to dry out before watering again. These plants should never be allowed to dry out completely, not even during the rather short winter rest period. While plants are resting, continue moderate watering, but allow the top inch of the mixture to dry out between waterings.

Feeding Excessive feeding stimulates the growth of foliage at the expense of flowers and berries. Apply standard liquid fertilizer to these plants only during the few summer months between the end of the flowering period and the time when berries are fully matured. Even then, be sure not to apply fertilizer to the plants more often than once a month.

Potting and repotting Use a combination of two-thirds of soil-based potting mixture (see page 429) and one-third of an equal-parts mixture of peat moss and coarse sand or perlite. Nerteras are normally grown in 3-inch pots. Because they have relatively shallow roots, however, they are more suitably lodged in 3- or 4-inch pans, and they need never be moved on into larger containers.
Propagation Commercially, these plants are grown from seed, but this is a slow and not very dependable process. Instead, divide old plants in the spring, setting five or six small clumps of stems around the edge of a 4-inch pan containing the standard mixture.

Propagating a nertera

Divide a nertera that has lost its berries into small clumps and place these around the edge of a pan of standard mixture.

Space the clumps evenly so that they will gradually cover the surface of the mixture. Eventually they will look like one plant.

Alternatively, plant several short tip cuttings (1–2 inches long) together in a 2-inch pot containing an equal-parts mixture of moistened peat moss and sand. Enclose the cuttings in either a plastic bag or propagating case (see page 443) and place them in bright filtered light at a temperature of about 60°F. When renewed top growth indicates that roots are well established, move each group of cuttings directly into a 3-inch pot of the recommended mixture for adult specimens, after which the needs of the young plants are those of mature nerteras.

Nicodemia

LOGANIACEAE

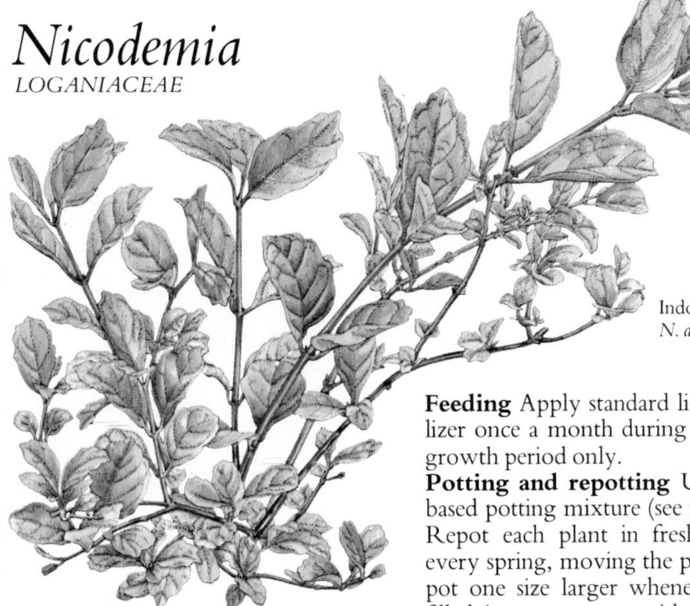

Indoor oak
N. diversifolia

BOTANISTS have recently agreed that nicodemias should really be included in the genus *Buddleia*. The only species of nicodemia commonly grown as a house plant, however, is still being sold as *N. diversifolia*, and so, although it should be called *Buddleia indica*, its former name is retained here. *N. diversifolia* (indoor oak) is a bushy shrub that can grow about 18 inches tall in an 8-inch pot. The woody, brown stems bear leaves 1–2 inches long and $\frac{3}{4}$–1 inch wide with $\frac{1}{2}$-inch-long leafstalks. Flowers are not produced indoors. The leaves of *N. diversifolia*, which closely resemble oak leaves, are roughly oval, but lobed and scalloped, and they have a quilted surface. Leaf color is green, but young leaves are often tinged with red, and take on a metallic blue sheen as they age. Leafstalks are bronzish.

PROPER CARE

Light Grow these plants in bright light, with three to four hours a day of direct sunlight. If grown in inadequate light, they become spindly.
Temperature Normal room temperatures are suitable throughout the year. Nicodemias can also tolerate temperatures as low as 50°F.
Watering During the active growth period water moderately, giving enough at each watering to make the potting mixture moist throughout but allowing the top half-inch of the mixture to dry out before watering again. During the rest period give only enough water to keep the mixture from drying out completely.
Feeding Apply standard liquid fertilizer once a month during the active growth period only.
Potting and repotting Use a soil-based potting mixture (see page 429). Repot each plant in fresh mixture every spring, moving the plant into a pot one size larger whenever it has filled its current pot with roots (see page 426). After the maximum convenient pot size (probably 6–8 inches) has been reached, an annual spring topdressing (see page 428) will suffice.
Propagation Take tip cuttings 3–4 inches long in early spring. Cut immediately below a node, remove the bottom leaf or leaves, and dip the cut end of each cutting in hormone rooting powder. Plant the cutting in a 3-inch pot containing a moistened equal-parts mixture of peat moss and coarse sand or perlite, and enclose the whole in a plastic bag or propagating case (see page 443). Stand it in bright filtered light. When renewed growth indicates that the cutting has rooted, uncover it, and begin to water it moderately and to feed it monthly. In late summer transfer the young plant into the standard soil-based potting mixture, using a slightly larger pot only if roots are obviously becoming crowded in the 3-inch size. The plant can then be treated in exactly the same way as a mature nicodemia.
Special points These plants are particularly subject to attack by red spider mites (see page 455), especially in warm rooms (above about 65°F). Symptoms of heavy infestation are yellowing leaves and fine webbing in leaf axils. Wash off as many of the mites as possible under running water, and use an appropriate insecticide (see page 460). Mist-spray the foliage of plants grown in warm rooms with tepid water twice a week.

Nicodemias are naturally bushy shrubs, but it is advisable to pinch out some of the growing tips every spring.

Nidularium
BROMELIACEAE

N. innocentii

PLANTS of the genus *Nidularium* have soft, glossy, strap-shaped, sometimes spiny-edged leaves that are arranged in a rosette. The central portion of the basically green rosette becomes bright-colored (usually red) when the plant is about to flower. This color is often limited to a tuft of modified leaves only 2–3 inches long, but it can also affect the bases of the longer leaves that form the rosette. Small, tubular flowers appear from a flower head within the central tuft. The flowers are short-lived, but the bright leaf coloring lasts for several months. Nidulariums flower only when they are mature (rarely before they are three or four years old), and they flower only once from the one rosette, which slowly dies after flowering. At flowering time and for some months thereafter, however, the plant produces offsets from the axils of the lower leaves. Thus, when the parent rosette has died and must finally be discarded, younger plants are ready to take its place.

The flowering season for nidulariums is not clearly defined. Flowering can occur at any time of year, and plants in bloom or about to bloom can be purchased at almost any season.
See also BROMELIADS.

RECOMMENDED NIDULARIUMS

N. fulgens (blushing bromeliad) has a rosette with a spread of up to 18 inches. The leaves, which are pale green spotted with slightly darker green, are about 12 inches long and 2 inches wide, with prominent, spiny edges. At flowering time the rosette center flushes bright cerise. At the same time dark blue, white-edged flowers appear within it.

N. fulgens
(blushing bromeliad)

N. innocentii is similar in size and shape to *N. fulgens*. The color of the leaves, though, is metallic and deep green, and the undersides of the leaves are notably glossy. The rosette center turns brownish red at flowering time (usually in fall). Flowers are white. One variety, *N. i. nana,* which has shorter, somewhat broader, olive green leaves with glossy purple undersides, rarely attains a spread of more than 9 inches. Another, *N. i. lineatum,* is the same size and shape as the species, but its leaves are pale green striped lengthwise with broad bands of white. And *N. i. striatum* is like *N. i. lineatum,* but with fewer, narrower, white or cream-colored markings.

N. purpureum forms a looser, more upright rosette than most other nidulariums. Its leaves are 12–15 inches long and 2–2½ inches wide, deep green with a purplish tinge, and shiny maroon-red on the undersides. At flowering time the center becomes brownish red, and the flowers are normally rose-colored.

PROPER CARE

Light Grow these plants in bright filtered light.

Temperature Normal room temperatures, to a minimum of 55°F, are suitable. Because nidulariums need high humidity, stand the pots on trays of moist pebbles.

Watering Water moderately at all times, giving enough to moisten the potting mixture thoroughly, but allowing the top half-inch of the mixture to dry out before watering again. Fill the central "cup" with water as needed. But turn plants upside down to empty the cup every month or so, and refill it with fresh water.

Feeding Give actively growing nidulariums standard liquid fertilizer at half strength once every two weeks.

Potting and repotting Use a potting mixture recommended for bromeliads (see page 107). Nidulariums will grow well in relatively small pots. A 3- to 4-inch pot should be the largest required. Move a plant into a slightly bigger pot only when its roots completely fill the current one (see page 426). The best time to do this is in spring.

Propagation Most nidulariums produce offsets on short, woody stolons that grow from the lower leaf axils. When an offset has three or four leaves that have begun to open into the characteristic rosette-shape, it is ready for springtime propagation. With a sharp knife cut away the offset with a short length of the stolon attached, and plant it in a 2- or 3-inch pot containing a moistened equal-parts mixture of peat moss and coarse sand or perlite. Enclose the whole in a plastic bag or propagating case (see page 443), and keep it warm in bright filtered light. After new roots have become established—in four to eight weeks—uncover the young plant and begin to water it sparingly, allowing the top inch of the rooting mixture to dry out between waterings. About three months after the start of propagation, begin monthly applications of liquid fertilizer at half strength. Wait for a further three months before transferring the plant into standard bromeliad potting mixture. Thereafter, treat it as a mature nidularium.

Notocactus

CACTACEAE

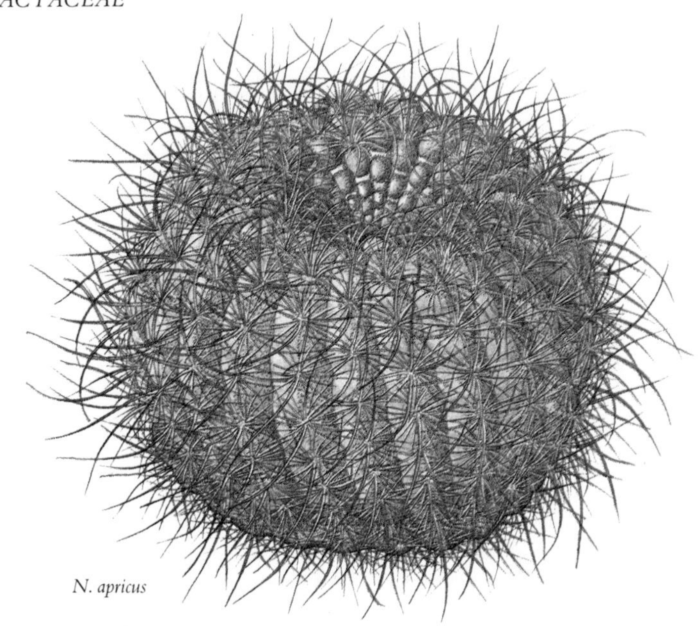

N. apricus

THE genus *Notocactus* comprises about 25 species of leafless desert cacti, grown for both their attractive spine formations and beautiful flowers which are produced profusely in most kinds. The non-branching, usually bright green stems of notocacti are globular although some species become cylindrical as they age. They are always ribbed lengthwise, with areoles closely set along the ribs. The areoles bear clusters of spines that radiate outward. Three or four spines in the center of the cluster are generally of a different color and length from the others. Some species produce offsets, but many remain solitary. Funnel- or cup-shaped flowers, often three or four at a time, appear at the tops of notocacti throughout the summer. Each flower lasts about a week, and (as in all flowering cacti) there is only one flower per areole in the course of a single season.

See also CACTI.

RECOMMENDED NOTOCACTI

N. apricus has a stem that remains globular and reaches a diameter of 3–4 inches. The areoles along the 15 to 20 blunt ribs carry tufts of 18 to 20 bristly, yellowish radial spines, as well as 4 stiffer central spines. Each of the radial spines is about ½ inch long, and each of the centrals is up to 1 inch long and reddish at the base. Three-inch-long and 2-inch-wide, funnel-shaped flowers, which begin to appear only after the stem has achieved a diameter of about 2 inches, are a bright, shining yellow, with reddish edges. Specimens three years old or more sometimes produce offsets around the base.

N. concinnus, with a globular or slightly flattened stem up to 3 inches across, has around 15 prominent, narrow ribs. These are notched all along their length, and white-woolly areoles are spaced ¼ inch apart between the notches. Every areole bears 10 to 12 bristly, pale yellow spines ¼-inch-long, together with 4 brownish central ones, each up to ¾-inch-long, which are very thin and somewhat twisted. The funnel-shaped flowers are about 2 inches long and 2½ inches wide at the mouth. Their outer petals are reddish, the inner ones bright satiny yellow. This species does not produce offsets.

N. leninghausii (golden ball cactus), one of the biggest notocacti, differs from the other kinds in that it flowers less freely and is grown mainly for its shape and spine clusters. When about three years old, the globular plant starts to elongate into a column. Eventually, after 20 years or more, the column can reach a height of well over 2 feet and a width of 3–4 inches. Its stem is almost completely hidden by clusters of up to 19 spines. Up to 15 of the spines are radial, ¼ inch long, and yellowish. They surround 3 or 4 inch-long golden spines carried on closely set areoles along the 30-odd broad, low ribs. When *N. leninghausii* is about 6 inches tall, it normally begins to produce a few funnel-shaped bright yellow flowers about 2 inches long and 2 inches wide at the mouth. Offsets may also appear at the base. However, not all specimens bloom or produce offsets.

N. ottonis also remains spherical. Its stem has a dozen or so broad, rounded ribs carrying areoles with clusters of 10 to 12 bristly, brown, ½-inch-long spines and 3 or 4 tiny, darker-colored central ones. When the stem is about 2 inches across, at about three years of age, offsets are produced at the base; and the whole plant ultimately forms a 6-inch-wide clump of stems, each of which is only 2–3 inches across. When the plant is about three years old, funnel-shaped, bright yellow flowers up to 2½ inches long and 3 inches wide begin to appear, generally only one or two at a time. There are a number of varieties of *N. ottonis* that differ from the species in minor ways, mostly in color and length of spines.

N. scopa tends to become cylindrical as it ages; when about 10 years old, it is likely to be about 7 inches tall and 3–4 inches wide. At this age and size it can produce offsets, although most plants of the species remain single-stemmed. The stem, which is a much paler green than those of most other species, has 30 to 40 low, rounded ribs, with white areoles carrying clusters of 40-odd bristly spines. The outer spines in each cluster are white and about ¼ inch long, and the inner ones are brown and up to ½ inch long. Flowers are funnel-shaped, lemon yellow, 2 inches long, and 2 inches wide at the mouth. Among the many varieties of *N. scopa,* the one that is most commonly available is *N.s. ruberrima,* which can be distinguished from all the other forms by the attractive crimson-red spines (central as well as outer) that it carries.

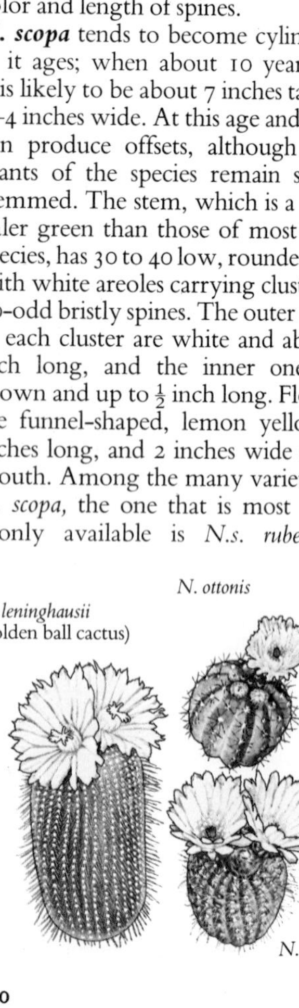

N. ottonis

N. leninghausii (golden ball cactus)

N. scopa

PROPER CARE

Light To maintain the shape and encourage flowering, give notocacti as much full sunlight as possible throughout the year.

Temperature Normal room temperatures are suitable during the spring and summer active growth period. During the winter rest period keep these plants cool—ideally at a temperature of about 50°F.

Watering During the active growth period water moderately, giving enough to moisten the entire potting mixture at each watering, but allow the top half-inch of the mixture to dry out before watering again. During the winter rest period water notocacti only enough to keep the mixture from drying out completely.

Feeding Use a full-strength, high-potassium, tomato-type liquid fertilizer every two weeks during the spring and summer active growth period only.

Potting and repotting Use a porous potting mixture composed of one part coarse sand or perlite to three parts of a soil-based or peat-based mixture (see page 429). Keep plants up to 2 inches in diameter in 3-inch pots. Always remove any larger notocactus from its pot at least once a year, preferably in early spring, in order to examine the roots; if they are tightly packed in the pot, move the plant into a pot one size larger. Otherwise, shake off as much of the old potting mixture as possible, and replace the plant in the original pot, adding fresh potting mixture as required.

Propagation Offsets, if any, can be used for propagation at any time in spring or summer. Cut them away cleanly, let them dry out for three days to harden the cut surfaces, and then press them gently into the recommended potting mixture for mature notocacti—either individual offsets in 2-inch pots or several in a large seed tray. If the mixture is kept just moist at normal room temperature in medium light, the offsets should be rooted in two to three months.

Notocacti can also be raised from seed. *N. ottonis* is a particularly easy species to propagate by this method. (See *CACTI,* page 119.)

Odontoglossum

ORCHIDACEAE

PLANTS of the genus *Odontoglossum* are mainly epiphytic orchids which have flattened, egg-shaped pseudobulbs that generally rise from the rhizome in small groups. A pair of leaves or occasionally three, grow from the top of each pseudobulb. Each usually strap-shaped, light green leaf is folded lengthwise into a V-shape from the midrib. The often arching flower stem that grows from the base of each pseudobulb carries as many as 30 fleshy, long-lasting, sometimes fragrant flowers. Each flower is normally borne on a short stalk, and the flowers are arranged alternately along the upper two-thirds of the stem. Flowers have a flat appearance with the petals and sepals either widely spaced or partially overlapping. Flowering can be almost continuous under the right conditions. There are a great number of hybrids, both natural and cultivated.

See also ORCHIDS.

RECOMMENDED ODONTOGLOSSUMS

O. bictoniense has pseudobulbs 3–7 inches tall that carry two or three lance-shaped leaves up to 12 inches long. The erect flower stem grows 2½ feet high and bears about 12 flowers, each 1½ inches across. The flowering season normally extends from fall through early spring. The petals and sepals are yellow-green heavily spotted with chestnut brown. The heart-shaped lip can be a soft pink or almost white with yellow markings.

O. crispum has 4-inch-tall pseudobulbs, each carrying two strap-shaped leaves 9-12 inches long. The arching flower stem up to 2½ feet long bears as many as 30 flowers up to 5 inches across. Flowering is generally in late winter and early spring. Flower color is variable, but is most commonly white with the lip covered with red spots and yellow markings.

O. grande (tiger orchid) has 3- to 4-inch-tall pseudobulbs each carrying two leaves up to 9 inches long. Unusually for orchids, the leaves have short stalks. The 12-inch-tall flower stem bears up to seven flowers, each about 7 inches across. Flowers normally bloom in late summer through to late fall. The petals and sepals are all bright yellow with crosswise

Tiger orchid
O. grande

cinnamon brown stripes. The short, rounded lip can be cream-colored or pale yellow.

O. pulchellum (lily-of-the-valley orchid) has pseudobulbs 2–3 inches tall, each carrying two narrow, 8- to 12-inch-long leaves. The erect, 10-inch-high stem bears 5 to 10 fragrant flowers, each one about 1 inch across. Flowering season is usually spring. The flowers are white, and the lip has a yellow crest. The flowers appear to be upside down, with the lip on top.

PROPER CARE

Light Give actively growing odontoglossums bright filtered light. During the short winter days they will benefit from some direct sunlight.

Temperature These plants need a temperature of around 60°F at all times. Even at this relatively cool temperature they need a high degree of humidity. Stand them on trays of moist pebbles. Whenever indoor temperatures rise above 60°F, mist-spray plants twice a day.

Watering Water actively growing plants moderately but allow a full half of the potting mixture to dry out before watering again. During the short rest period, give only enough to keep the mixture from drying out.

Feeding Apply a foliar feed to actively growing plants with every third or fourth watering.

Potting and repotting Use a mixture of two parts of finely chopped osmunda fiber to one part of sphagnum moss, with a little coarse sand added. Fill pots with clay-pot fragments for a third of their depth. Every year, either just before roots become active in spring, or in early fall, move plants into larger pots. After maximum pot size has been reached, divide plants as suggested below.

Propagation To propagate, divide overcrowded clumps at repotting time. When cutting a rhizome into pieces, choose sections that contain a group of about four pseudobulbs. At least one of these must have new growth or a growth bud. Pot each section of rhizome in a small pot filled with fresh, barely moist mixture. Place the pot in medium light and water sparingly for four to six weeks. Thereafter treat the young plant as a mature odontoglossum.

Oncidium

ORCHIDACEAE

THE genus *Oncidium* (dancing-lady orchid) includes more than 400 species of epiphytic orchids. The species commonly grown as house plants generally have egg-shaped pseudobulbs with two large, medium green leaves growing from the apex. The flower stem that rises from the base of the pseudobulb can be either erect or arching, up to several feet long. The flowers are usually small and numerous, and are often borne on short branches of the main flower stem. Flower color varies from brown, red, pink, green, or white. A characteristic of many oncidium flowers is a ridge at the base of the lip, often with raised spots on it.
See also ORCHIDS.

RECOMMENDED ONCIDIUMS

O. crispum has slightly flattened, 4- to 5-inch-tall pseudobulbs generally topped with a pair of nearly oblong leaves 6–8 inches long and 2 inches wide. The arching flower stem is 2–4 feet long and carries up to 40 flowers, each 2–4 inches across. Flowers are chestnut or copper brown marked with yellow, and with yellow margins. The petals and sepals have deeply undulate edges. The normal flowering season is during the fall.

O. ornithorhynchum has pseudobulbs 1–2 inches tall, each topped with a pair of strap-shaped leaves 7–10 inches long and ½ inch wide. The arching flower stem is about 3 feet long and carries up to 50 blooms, each only ¾ inch across. The fragrant flowers are rose-colored apart from a yellow crest on the fiddle-shaped lip. Flowering season is fall through winter.

O. wentworthianum has slightly flattened, 3-inch-tall pseudobulbs, each topped with a pair of strap-shaped leaves about 10 inches long and ½ inch wide. The 4-foot-long flower stem has many small branches, each branch bearing numerous 1-inch-wide flowers. There can be up to 50 blooms on a single main stem. The flowers are yellow blotched with red-brown. The lip is lobed at the base. This species flowers in summer.

PROPER CARE

Light Give these orchids direct sunlight, except at midday. Oncidiums will benefit from some supplementary

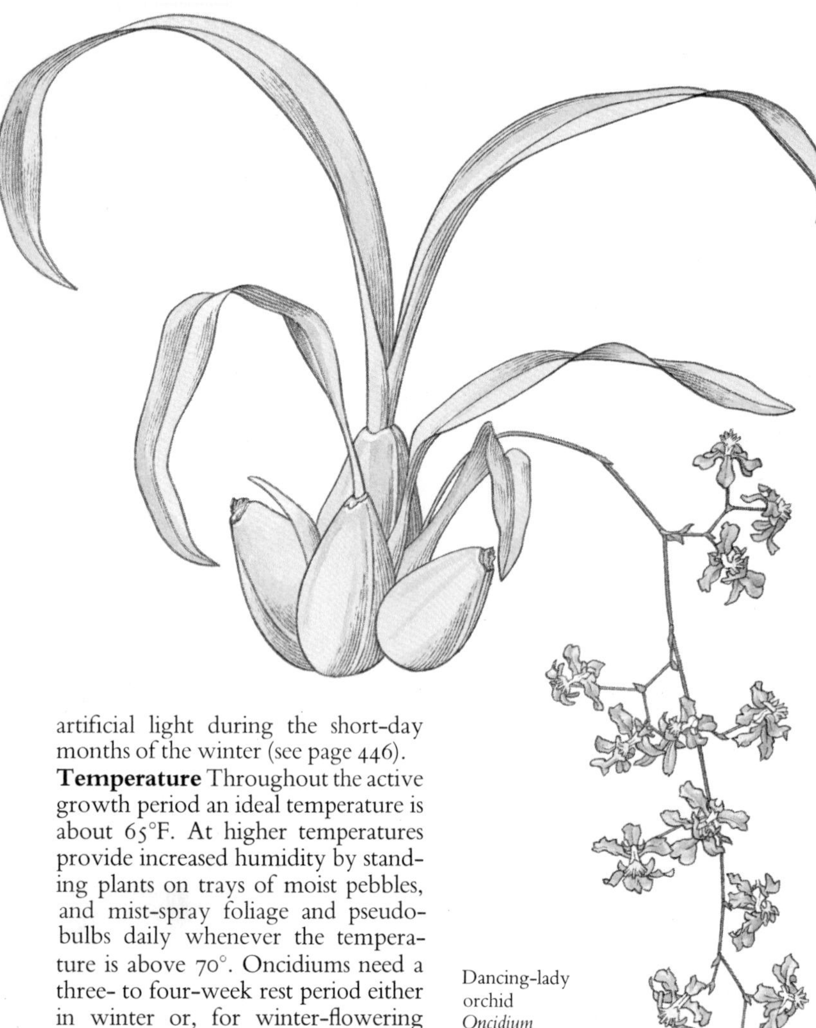

Dancing-lady orchid
Oncidium ornithorhynchum

artificial light during the short-day months of the winter (see page 446).

Temperature Throughout the active growth period an ideal temperature is about 65°F. At higher temperatures provide increased humidity by standing plants on trays of moist pebbles, and mist-spray foliage and pseudobulbs daily whenever the temperature is above 70°. Oncidiums need a three- to four-week rest period either in winter or, for winter-flowering plants, immediately after flowering ceases. During the rest period reduce the temperature to around 55°, and decrease the humidity by allowing the pebbles to dry out.

Watering Water actively growing plants sparingly, giving enough at each watering to make the potting mixture moist throughout but allowing the top half of the mixture to dry out between waterings. During the rest period give only enough to keep the pseudobulbs from shriveling.

Feeding Apply foliar feed to actively growing plants with every third or fourth watering.

Potting and repotting Use a porous potting mixture composed of one part of sphagnum moss to two parts of osmunda fiber, and add a little coarse sand. Fill at least a third of the pot with clay-pot fragments for drainage. Move plants into pots one size larger every spring until maximum convenient pot size has been reached. Thereafter, divide plants for propagation. If a large display of plants in a single pot is desired, repot every second or third spring. To do this, clear the spent mixture from the roots, and cut the rhizome into sections, each with at least two pseudobulbs. Cut away any rotting or damaged roots, and then arrange the pieces of rhizome around the inside rim of the old pot, which has been cleaned and filled with fresh mixture. Point the new growth toward the center of the pot, and it will grow over the unoccupied surface of the mixture.

Propagation Divide inconveniently large plants in spring as suggested above (see "Potting and repotting"). To create two or more new plants repot the small groups of pseudobulbs individually in appropriate-size pots. For the first four to six weeks water new plants only enough to make the mixture barely moist, and give them bright filtered light. Thereafter, treat them as mature oncidiums.

Ophiopogon

LILIACEAE

White lily turf
O. jaburan 'Variegatus'

ONLY one species of the small genus *Ophiopogon* is grown as a pot plant: *O. jaburan* (white lily turf), which is a clump-forming, grasslike plant. The tufted, leathery, dark green leaves rise directly from the rootstock and are up to 2 feet long but only about ½ inch wide. Loose clusters of 6 to 20 pendent flowers appear in summer (and sometimes early fall) at the ends of flattened stalks 9–15 inches long. Each flower stalk arises from the center of a tuft of leaves. Individual flowers are tubular, ½ inch long, and either white or white tinged with lilac. The flowers may be followed by deep blue, pea-size berries, which appear in late fall. *O. jaburan* resembles, and is often confused with, its close relation *Liriope muscari*, but a close comparison of their flowers will reveal that the flowers of ophiopogons are slightly larger and droop rather more loosely on the flower stalk.

There are a number of variegated-leaved forms, in all of which the leaves have narrow lengthwise stripes of white, cream, or yellow. Among such varieties are *O.j.* 'Argenteo-vittatus,' *O.j.* 'Aureo-variegatus,' and *O.j.* 'Variegatus.' One non-variegated form, *O.j.* 'Caeruleus,' has plain dark green leaves and violet-blue flowers.

PROPER CARE

Light Grow these plants in bright light, but without direct sunlight. They will not flower if given inadequate light.

Temperature Although ophiopogons can tolerate a fairly wide range of temperatures, they do best in relatively cool positions (55°–65°F) throughout the year. Do not subject them to temperatures below about 50°, however.

Watering During the active growth period water ophiopogons moderately, giving enough at each watering to make the potting mixture moist throughout but allowing the top half-inch of the mixture to dry out before watering again. During the winter rest period water these plants much more sparingly, giving only enough to keep the potting mixture from drying out completely.

Feeding Apply standard liquid fertilizer every two weeks during the active growth period only.

Potting and repotting Use a combination of one-third of coarse sand to two-thirds of soil-based potting mixture (see page 429). Move plants into pots one size larger in the spring whenever it becomes necessary (that is, if and when the tufts of leaves entirely cover the surface of the potting mixture). When maximum convenient pot size (probably 5–7 inches) has been reached, break plants up into smaller pieces, which can then be used for propagation.

Propagation Propagate an ophiopogon in the spring by dividing overcrowded clumps. In breaking off sections of the rootstock, be sure that each section bears at least 8 to 10 leaves and retains as many of the cordlike roots as possible. (If the roots are very tangled, wash away the potting mixture under running water. It should then be easier to disentangle them.) Plant sections separately in 3-inch pots of the potting mixture that is recommended for adult plants, and treat each section in exactly the same way as a mature ophiopogon. However, do not feed the new plants for the first three or four months.

Oplismenus

GRAMINEAE

Ribbon grass
O. hirtellus 'Variegatus'

OPLISMENUS *hirtellus* 'Variegatus' (often called *Panicum variegatum*; popularly known as basket or ribbon grass) is a highly decorative, variegated-leaved grass that is the only representative of the small genus *Oplismenus* commonly grown as a house plant. It has profusely branching stems that grow upright when young, but later trail to a length of 15 inches. Stalkless leaves, which grow on alternate sides of the stems, are thin, flat, lance-shaped, acutely pointed, and up to 2 inches long (but only ½ inch wide). Leaf color is medium green, with white lengthwise stripes. When grown in sufficiently bright light, however, much of the white changes to pink, and some of the older leaves become tinged with purple. Little green flowers on wispy, erect stalks are produced on mature plants in summer, but they are uninteresting and hardly noticeable.

These plants can be grown in pots, but are most attractive in small hanging baskets. After a year or so they tend to lose leaves and look shabby, and so they should be discarded and replaced annually.

PROPER CARE

Light Grow oplismenuses in bright light, including two or three hours a day of direct sunlight, throughout the year. Stems grow unattractively long and leaves lose their distinctive coloration if plants get inadequate light.

Temperature Normal room temperatures are suitable, but an oplismenus will tolerate temperatures down to 55°F.

Watering During the active growth period water plentifully to keep the potting mixture thoroughly moist. During the winter rest period water only enough to prevent the mixture from drying out completely.

Feeding Apply standard liquid fertilizer once every month to actively growing plants.

Potting and repotting Use a soil-based potting mixture (see page 429). For a hanging basket, put 15 to 20 rooted cuttings in a single 6- or 8-inch basket. Fewer than about 15 will create a thin, spindly display. Plants grown in pots do not need to be moved into bigger pots. Simply replace a year-old potful with a fresh supply of rooted cuttings, using new potting mixture, at any time during the spring or summer.

Propagation Tip cuttings 2–3 inches long will root with extreme ease in spring or summer. Insert six to eight cuttings around the rim of a 3- or 4-inch pot containing moistened soil-based potting mixture, and enclose the whole in a plastic bag or propagating case. Keep the covered cuttings warm in bright filtered light, and they will root in about two weeks. Thereafter, treat them as mature plants, keeping them in the pot or replanting them in a hanging basket.

Opuntia

CACTACEAE

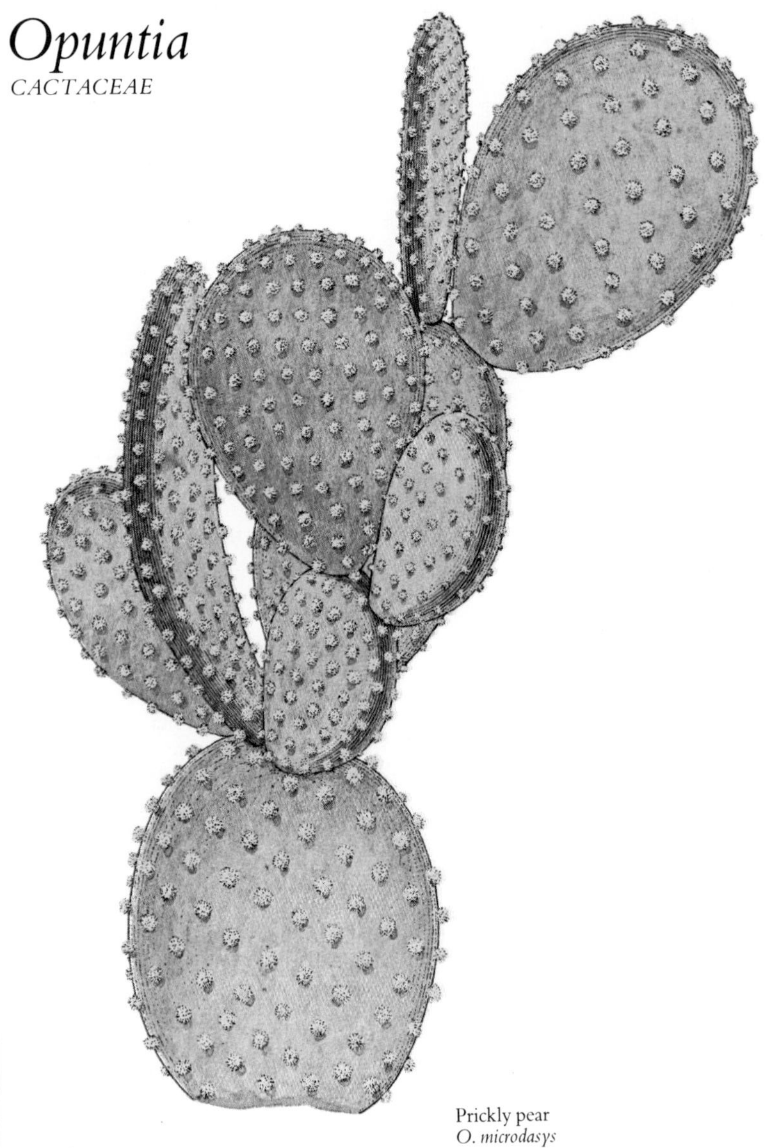

Prickly pear
O. microdasys

THE opuntias are one of the largest and most widely distributed groups of cactus. They are highly variable in shape and size. Among them are straight, usually unbranched, columnar forms; dwarf plants with small, more or less cylindrical, jointed segments, which grow in dense clumps; and specimens with stems that consist of many flattened, joined segments, which are often fiercely spined. It is opuntias of this last type that are popularly called prickly pears because of their spiny, pear-shaped fruits (which are rarely produced in potted specimens). Unlike the stems of many other desert cacti, those of opuntias are not ribbed. Cylindrical types usually have low, flattened, wartlike tubercles on which the spine-bearing areoles appear. Species with flattened stem segments have areoles spaced over the surface at regular intervals.

Spine formation of different kinds of opuntia varies as greatly as the shape of their stems. Some have no spines at all, some have a few bristles, and some have spines as formidable as any in the whole family of cacti. Although the spines of a number of species are distinctly differentiated as radial and central, the spines of most opuntias point directly outward from the areoles. In all species, however, there are minute barbed bristles known as "glochids." These occur in bunches on the areoles, regardless of the type of spine. Though barely visible to the naked eye, the glochids readily penetrate the human skin and are extremely difficult to remove. So handle these cacti with great care.

These soft, leaflike growths on a newly produced segment of an opuntia will eventually be replaced by spines.

Opuntias do not have leaves in the usual sense, but small, soft-textured cylindrical "leaves" sometimes appear on new growth. These soon shrivel and fall off. Most species do not flower in the home, either. Many grow very big in the wild and then produce magnificent blooms, but they are cultivated as house plants mainly for their attractive shape and spines. In order to flower they need to grow far too large for the average domestic situation. Even the dwarf forms, which are generally rare in cultivation, cannot easily be brought to flower, since their natural habitat is on mountain summits. At lower levels the light intensity is inadequate for flowering.
See also CACTI.

RECOMMENDED OPUNTIAS

O. basilaris becomes a spreading bush about 3 feet high in the wild. In cultivation it is a slow grower and unlikely to need a pot larger than 4 or 5 inches. It takes about five years for potted plants of this species to reach a height of 8–12 inches. There is a single flattened stem at first, but this usually branches profusely from the base. Each branch consists of two or three flattened segments, oval in shape, about 4 inches long, 3 inches broad, and about ⅜ inch thick. Stem color is purplish blue. The areoles, which are spaced about ⅜ inch apart over stem surfaces, have tufts of reddish glochids and usually no spines. This is one of the few opuntias that will flower fairly easily indoors, though not before it is four or five years old. The flowers appear in spring or summer on the ends of the topmost stem and branch segments. Each carmine-red bloom is open-bell-shaped, 2–3 inches long and wide. Individual flowers last for only about two days, but, unless all buds develop at the same rate, other flowers will follow over a period of a week or so. They are without fragrance.

O. *cylindrica* has a columnar, bright green stem that can attain a height of several feet and a diameter of up to 2 inches in a 6-inch pot. The plant does not branch naturally. If the top of the stem is cut off, however, the bottom part will send out four or more branches from near the cut surface, eventually producing a candelabrum effect. Although the end result is not true to type, many growers find it a most attractive addition to their cactus collections. The entire stem is covered with flat, diamond-shaped tubercles, each with an areole in the center. The areoles carry several ¼-inch-long, whitish spines in addition to the whitish glochids. Cylindrical leaves appearing along with new growth on stem ends are ¼–½ inch long, but soon drop off. Like most opuntias *O. cylindrica* will not produce flowers when it is grown as a pot plant.

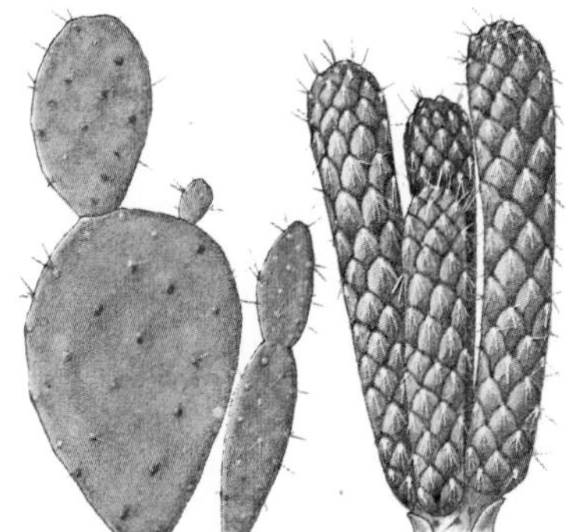

O. robusta *O. cylindrica*

O. *imbricata* has many cylindrical, much-branching segments, each of which will grow up to about 3 inches long and 1 inch thick in a potted specimen. The plant itself is variable in size, since it grows like a tree in the wild. Normally, a plant in a 4-inch pot grows 8–12 inches high, with a similar spread. Large specimens tend to sprawl and shed segments, which drop off under their own weight. The segments are covered with rounded tubercles, and new growth has small, temporary, cylindrical leaves. Large, yellowish areoles, each centered in a tubercle, carry a few whitish glochids and up to 20 stout, white-to-yellow spines 1–1½ inches long. Any indoor flowering is highly unlikely.

O. *microdasys*, a very popular plant, is a profusely branching species, with many flattened, oval segments, each up to about 3 inches long, 2 inches wide, and ¼ inch thick. The segments are yellowish green and spineless, but the areoles, which are spaced close together over the surface of every segment, are packed with beautiful (but extremely prickly) golden yellow glochids. A healthy specimen of *O. microdasys* can grow 12 inches tall, with a 12-inch spread, in a 6-inch pot. But it will reach such a size only after five or six years. Occasionally, potted plants of the species will produce pale yellow flowers about 1½ inches long and of similar width, but these cannot be counted on.

O. *robusta* is a large, vigorous plant. It branches profusely and attains treelike dimensions in the wild. The flattened segments, which are grayish green with a powdery bluish coating, are almost circular. They vary in size from 2 or 3 inches to more than a foot across, with a width of ¼–½ inch. As a house plant *O. robusta* can be kept small if planted in pots no bigger than 6 inches. If it grows too large—over about 12 inches high—it can be restarted by propagation from stem segments. Areoles with brownish glochids are spaced about ½ inch apart over the surface of every segment. Each areole has a few very short, yellowish spines, but spines in abundance—in addition to yellow flowers—are found only in non-potted plants of this species.

O. *rufida* (cinnamon cactus or red bunny ears) is sometimes classified as a variety of *O. microdasys,* which it resembles. It is a somewhat smaller plant than the other, and its segments are shorter and thicker—1–2 inches long, under 2 inches wide, and about ⅜ inch thick. Segment color is dark grayish green, and the closely set areoles carry tufts of reddish brown glochids. There are no spines. Indoors the plant is unlikely to reach a height and spread of more than 8–10 inches in a 4-inch pot. *O. rufida,* however, does sometimes produce bell-shaped, yellow or orange flowers about 1 inch long and wide. Flowering season is spring or summer.

O. *salmiana* has many profusely-branching, cylindrical segments, each of which grows up to about 6 inches long and ⅜ inch diameter. Segment color is a deep green, sometimes suffused with pink. The plant can reach a height of about 12 inches and a spread of 6–8 inches in a 4-inch pot. Small areoles sparsely spaced over the smooth stems and branches each have a bunch of whitish glochids and three to five ¼-inch-long, yellow spines. This is the easiest of all opuntias to bring into flower indoors. Even plants about 5 inches high will readily produce numerous, whitish, open-bell-shaped flowers, each about 1½ inches long and wide. The slender stems of this opuntia will need supporting. Tie them to sticks that have been inserted into the potting mixture.

O. *subulata* closely resembles *O. cylindrica.* Like the latter it does not normally branch as a pot plant unless the columnar, medium green stem is cut across, in which case side branches will form near the cut surface, producing a candelabrum effect. Of the two species *O. subulata* is the more robust and sturdier. It is a particularly vigorous grower and in only four or five years can attain a height of more than 6 feet and a diameter of 2–3 inches in a 6- to 8-inch pot. The best way to keep it from growing too tall is to induce branching by cutting off the top of the stem. Areoles in the center of the broad, flat tubercles that cover the stem surface carry a few yellowish glochids, along with one or two stiff, pale yellow spines 1–2 inches long. Toward late spring every year the cylindrical stem (and branches, if any) will begin a period of active growth, accompanied by the appearance of cylindrical leaves at the top. The leaves will be 2–3 inches long and about ¼ inch across, and they will persist throughout the summer, shriveling and dropping off as winter approaches. *O. subulata* blooms indoors very rarely; its flowers are red.

O. *vestita* (cottonpole cactus or old man opuntia) is one of the columnar opuntias that branch naturally. The pale green stem, which grows about 18 inches tall and 1 inch wide, usually branches toward the top. The surface is warty, and the round, yellowish areoles at the center of the warts bear four to eight sharp, stiff spines ½–¾ inch long, as well as many white glochids and a quantity of long white hairs. The hairs almost cover the stem, giving the plant an attractively shaggy appearance. The cylindrical leaves produced on new growth at the ends of the main stem and branches are about ½ inch long and last for several weeks before dropping off. *O. vestita* is one of the smaller columnar species and should not require a pot larger than 4 inches. It is unlikely to flower as a house plant.

PROPER CARE

Light Opuntias need as much direct sunlight as they can get throughout the year. If kept in an inadequately lit position, their stems will be uncharacteristically elongated. The stems of flat-segmented species will become thin, straggly, and almost cylindrical in shape. There is no real alternative to unobstructed sunlight. If possible, place all opuntias in a sunny spot outdoors during the spring and summer growing period.

Temperature For most opuntia species normal room temperatures are suitable at all times, though a winter temperature of 45°F is preferable if feasible. A higher winter temperature, however, is not only preferable but essential for two species, *O. microdasys* and the very similar *O. rufida*. If these two opuntias are wintered at temperatures below 50°, brown markings will probably disfigure their stems.

Watering During the spring and summer active growth period water moderately, giving enough to moisten the potting mixture throughout, but allowing the top half-inch of the mixture to dry out before watering again. These plants can tolerate rather more water than can most desert cacti. Some of the taller flat-segmented types are even liable to wilt in summer if allowed to become too dry—an unusual reaction for a desert cactus. They will recover quickly, however, when watered. During the winter rest period give the plants only enough to prevent the potting mixture from becoming completely dry. Be careful not to splash water on the segmented kinds; drops of water can spot the stems permanently. This is particularly important with *O. robusta*, whose bluish "bloom" is very easily disfigured.

Feeding Give these plants a high-potassium, tomato-type fertilizer once every two weeks throughout the active growth period.

Potting and repotting For a good porous potting mixture add one part of coarse sand or perlite to every four of a standard soil- or peat-based mixture (see page 429). Most opuntias need to be repotted annually. To determine whether a given plant needs repotting, remove it from its pot and examine the roots in spring. The prickliness of many of these plants makes this a hazardous operation. Wrap a thick fold of newspaper around the plant to protect the hands. Grip the stem or stems gently as near to the base as possible in order to avoid damaging the spines or glochids. If examination indicates that the plant's roots have not yet filled the current pot, simply clean the pot and replace the plant in fresh potting mixture, after having gently removed as much of the old mixture from the roots as possible. If, as is more likely, the current pot is full of roots, move the plant on to a pot one size larger.

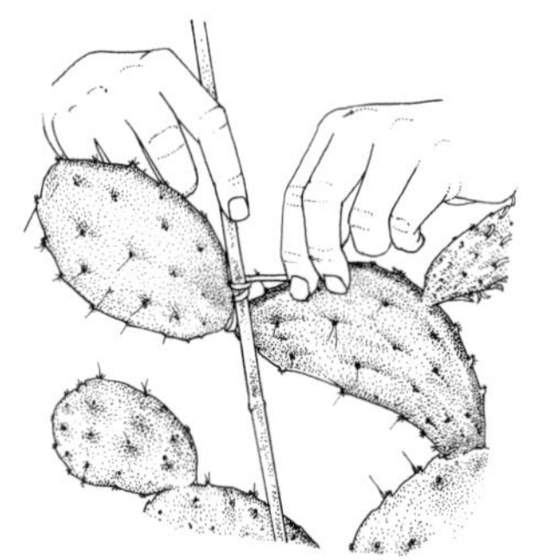

Keep segmented opuntia stems from sagging by tying them at joining points to a stake inserted into the mixture.

Many of the opuntias grown as house plants would become sprawling bushes or clumps in the wild. Because of this tendency to sprawl, potted specimens sometimes need some extra support. If a plant starts to sag over the side of the pot, insert a stake in the potting mixture, and attach the plant to it in such a way as to counterbalance the tilt effectively.

Propagation The segmented types of opuntia are exceedingly simple to propagate. At any time in spring or summer remove a stem segment, either by pulling it off or by cutting it cleanly with a knife. Allow the detached segment to dry for about three days. Then insert the cut end in a 2- or 3-inch pot of the recommended potting mixture for opuntias. Let the exact size of the pot be determined by the size of the segment. Once it is potted up, treat it as a mature plant. Rooting should occur in a few weeks.

It is equally easy to propagate a columnar opuntia, but propagation from a cutting of a single-stemmed, unbranching plant will necessitate changing the plant's appearance. As already explained above (see *O. cylindrica* and *O. subulata*), this is because cutting away a portion of the stem induces uncharacteristic branching. Whether the plant is naturally branching or single-stemmed, take a cutting at least 2–3 inches long, allow it to dry for four to five days, and then treat it precisely in the same way as prescribed above for stem segments.

Opuntias can also be raised from seed, which is readily available, at least for the more common species. The seeds are large—up to ¼ inch across—and are planted individually. They normally germinate within a week, and the resultant seedlings are remarkable in that they do not look like small cacti. Each seedling consists of two thick seed-leaves that spread outward. At first there are no signs of spines or glochids. These come later, when a small, spiny growth appears between the leaves. This enlarges and becomes the main stem. Later, the seed-leaves wither away. (For further information about raising cacti from seed, see *CACTI*, page 119.)

Propagating O. *subulata*

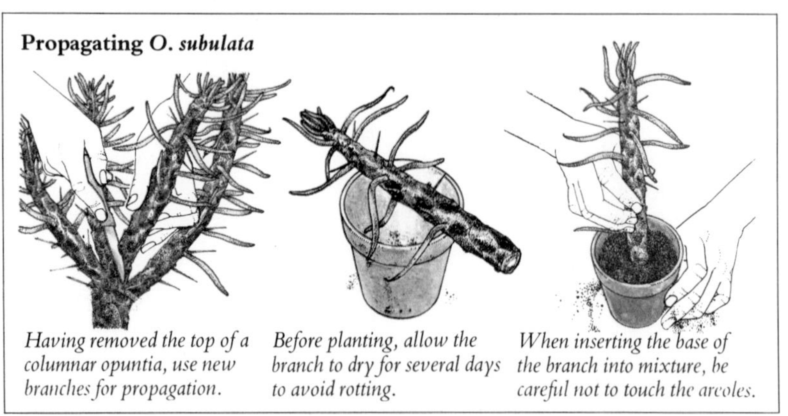

Having removed the top of a columnar opuntia, use new branches for propagation.

Before planting, allow the branch to dry for several days to avoid rotting.

When inserting the base of the branch into mixture, be careful not to touch the areoles.

ORCHIDS

Orchids form probably the largest flowering-plant family. They vary enormously in most respects, but are alike in producing fascinating flowers. As an indoor group, they have different needs from those of most others, and for successful cultivation those needs must be met. A list of suitable indoor orchids follows this article. Consult separate articles for discussions of individual genera.

It is widely believed that orchids are very difficult to grow and require conditions that only greenhouses can provide. This is not true. Although orchids need special treatment, more than a dozen kinds can be grown quite readily in an ordinary home environment. It *is* true that successful flowering depends on the indoor gardener's ability to maintain rigorous standards for proper care. That is why some growers prefer to keep their orchids in terrariums or plant windows (see pages 53-54), where full control of light, temperature, and humidity is possible. With suitable attention, however, these plants can be kept blooming for many years.

The family *Orchidaceae* includes about 750 genera, more than 20,000 species, and many thousands of man-made hybrids. About half the species are terrestrial (growing on the ground), and half are epiphytic (clinging to trees, shrubs, or rocky surfaces). Most kinds of orchid in cultivation are epiphytes; in fact, only one genus of terrestrial plant—*Paphiopedilum*—is a relatively common house plant.

Most terrestrial orchids have thick and fleshy roots with fine, fibrous roots attached to them, as do most terrestrial plants. These roots take up the orchids' nutrient needs. The epiphytic species usually have aerial roots in addition to a root system at the base. In the wild these aerial roots enable the plants to climb or creep along their various supports. Normally, such roots are thick and cylindrical, and they cling to any suitably moist surface such as damp bark.

Stems, leaves, and flowers of epiphytic orchids tend to grow in one of two ways. Some plants—those of the genus *Vanda*, for example—have a single main stem rising from a tuft of roots at the base. The stem, which normally grows upright, is clothed with leaves along its length, and it can attain a height of several feet in potted specimens. Occasionally there may be sideshoots, but these are smaller and much less vigorous than the main stem. Flower stalks appear from between leaf axils near the top, and aerial roots tend to protrude from lower leaf axils. These roots may or may not cling to any available moist surface. Such plants are technically known as *monopodial* orchids (meaning, roughly, that they are "single-footed").

The second pattern of growth is more common than the monopodial. Epiphytic orchids known as *sympodial* usually have many stems, all of which rise from a horizontal rhizome. In the wild the rhizome runs over the surface of the support; and in pots it sits on the surface of the potting mixture, sending feeding roots down into the mixture. Thick stems, which are called *pseudobulbs*, rise from the rhizome at intervals. These pseudobulbs are so named because, like bulbs, they are storage organs for food and water and can carry plants through short periods of drought. The pseudobulbs are usually light green in color, but they vary widely in shape and size. They are either rounded, spindle-shaped, bamboolike, cylindrical, or egg-shaped. They can look like ordinary stems or elongated bulbs, or they can be more or less flattened out.

Pseudobulbs range in size from under an inch to several feet high. In most indoor orchids, however, they grow no taller than about 8 inches. Each pseudobulb has one or more leaves at its tip, possibly with a few more along the side or base. Eventually a flower stem appears from either the top or base of the pseudobulb, but this may take a few years. Each pseudobulb usually flowers only once, and then slowly dies.

A new pseudobulb is produced annually at the end of a new short length of rhizome. Meanwhile, pseudobulbs that have flowered are gradually withering and drying up, but it may take a pseudobulb and its leaves up to five years to die completely. In some species, however, all the leaves of a pseudobulb that has flowered die off together naturally during an annual rest period. Old pseudobulbs are generally called backbulbs because of their location on the rhizome (always to the rear of the continuously forward-growing tip).

It is not possible to generalize about orchid leaves. They may be almost any shape or size, thin or thick, leathery, fleshy, or papery. Most are a single shade of green, but some are spotted or marbled with other colors.

In terms of flower pattern, however, virtually all orchids are alike. An orchid flower always has six symmetrically-arranged petallike segments (though there may appear to be fewer, because twin segments are sometimes joined together, often with a clearly visible seam). The uppermost segment and the lower, twin segments, which are all generally called sepals, are usually alike in size, shape

Types of growth

Monopodial orchids such as vandas (top), have a single stem. Sympodial orchids, for example, the odontoglossums (bottom), have several stems arising from a rhizome. These are thickened and are called pseudobulbs.

Orchids: representative forms

Each plant shown here belongs to one of the genera included in the family *Orchidaceae*. Other species within a given genus may, of course, look very different from the illustrated species.

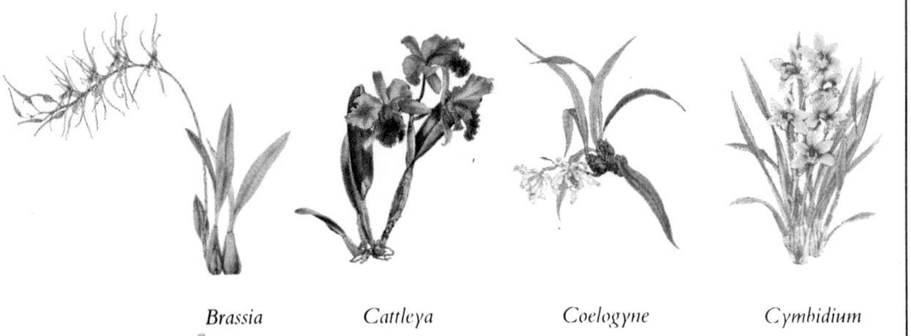

Brassia *Cattleya* *Coelogyne* *Cymbidium*

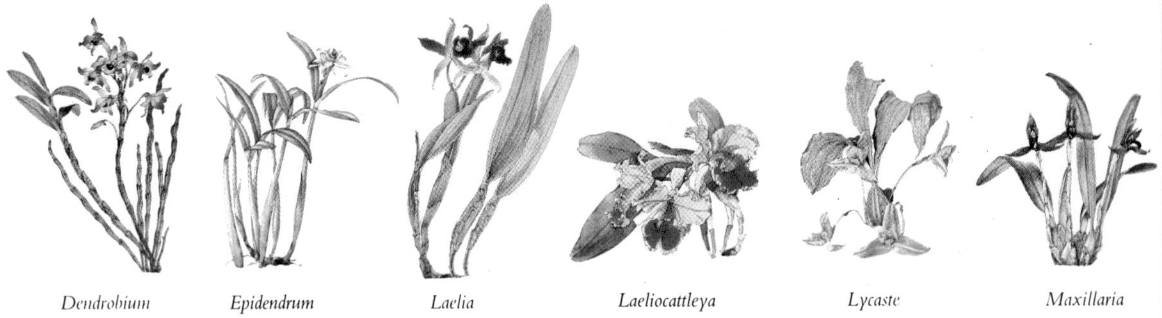

Dendrobium *Epidendrum* *Laelia* *Laeliocattleya* *Lycaste* *Maxillaria*

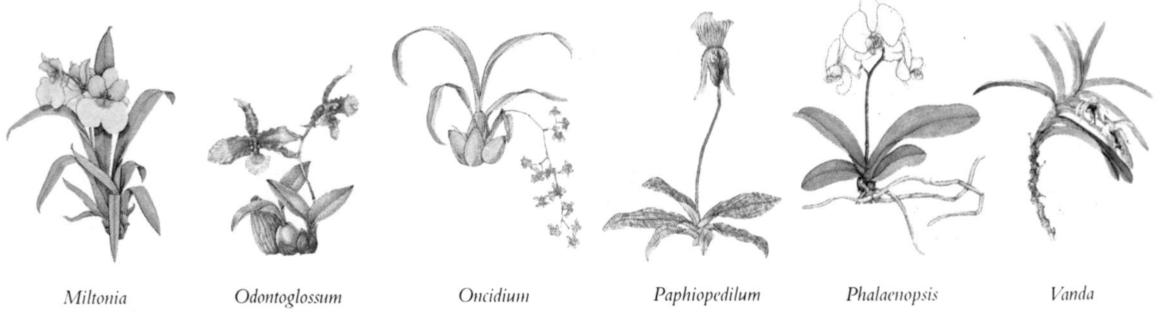

Miltonia *Odontoglossum* *Oncidium* *Paphiopedilum* *Phalaenopsis* *Vanda*

Orchid flower structure
An orchid flower always has three petals alternately arranged with three petallike sepals. The lowest segment, an unusual petal, is known as the lip and the central structure carrying the reproductive organs is the column.

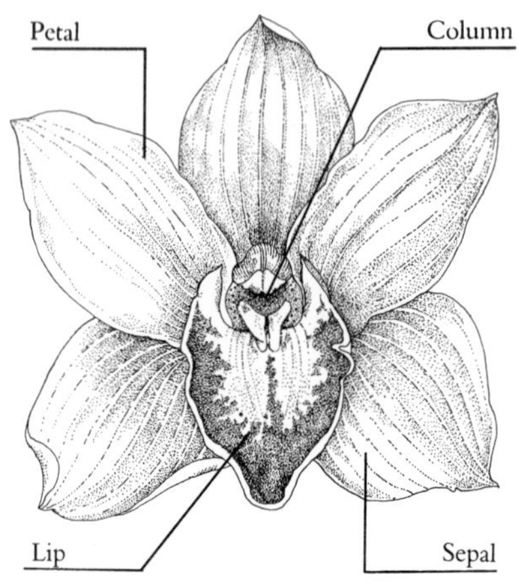

and color. The twin petals flanking the upper sepal tend to be larger than these, which they otherwise resemble. The third petal, which is the lowest of all the segments, is called the lip and is always different in shape and color from the others. In the center of the flower is an erect structure, called the column, that bears the reproductive organs of the orchid.

Although the general pattern of these flowers is unmistakable, they come in a vast variety of shapes, sizes, and colors. They may be produced on the flower stem singly or in clusters. Flower stalks can be erect or drooping, and the flowers can be scentless or delicately scented. Most have a fleshy, waxy texture, and each bloom is long-lasting (usually 3-6 weeks, but sometimes up to 12 weeks). It is advisable to cut flowers as soon as they begin to fade. Unlike most flowers, if orchids are cut early, they usually last as long standing in water as they do on the plant.

PROPER CARE

Light In the wild most orchids grow in direct or dappled sunlight, with some shade provided by surrounding foliage. It is therefore best, in general, to give indoor specimens bright filtered light or to grow them at a window where they get a few hours of morning or afternoon sunlight. The only exceptions among the orchids discussed in this book are the lycastes, miltonias and paphiopedilums, which do best in medium light and should never be exposed to direct sunlight.

During the short-day winter months move epiphytic plants to a position where they get the maximum amount of direct sunlight. If possible, give the epiphytes some supplementary artificial light in winter for six to eight hours a day (see page 446), so that they have a minimum of ten hours of light altogether.

Temperature These plants normally require a steady level of warmth throughout the year, even during the brief rest period that some of them take. Future flowering can be prevented by failure to keep within stated temperature ranges. In warm climates it can be helpful to stand most epiphytic orchids in a slightly shaded spot outdoors during the summer.

High humidity is essential for all types. Except during the short rest period, if any, stand plants on trays of damp pebbles or moist peat, and mist-spray the foliage once or twice a day in temperatures above about 70°F. Similarly, suspend a saucer of moist pebbles under hanging baskets, and give at least one mist-spray a day to plants grown in baskets or on some such support as a piece of tree bark.

Watering The commonest cause of failure with orchids is overwatering. Most actively growing potted orchids should be watered moderately at every watering, but it is often advisable to let the potting mixture dry out almost completely between waterings. With a free-draining mixture of the kind recommended below, waterings are unlikely to be necessary more often than once a week. Orchids growing on pieces of osmunda fiber or similar fibrous supports may need more frequent soakings, but plants should never be watered before the base begins to feel dry. The easiest way to water an epiphytic orchid grown in a hanging basket or on a wooden support is to soak the container (or the supportive material, together with the base of the plant that rests on it) in a bucket for a few minutes. Water plants in pots in the usual way.

A number of orchids have a distinct rest period, when growth all but stops and when the leaves of some of the species drop off. This is most likely to occur in the fall and winter, and may last for no more than a few weeks. Give resting orchids only enough water to keep the potting mixture from drying out completely.

Feeding Although orchids grown under the right conditions do not normally require extra nourishment, a little feeding is often beneficial. Bear in mind, however, that overfed orchids produce soft, lush growth at the expense of flowers. It is enough, as a general rule, to give actively growing plants a foliar feed after every third or fourth watering.

Potting mixtures All mixtures used for orchids must be free draining. This is provided for potted terrestrial orchids by growing them in a mixture of equal parts of fibrous loam, leaf mold or peat moss, chopped sphagnum moss, and coarse sand or perlite.

Traditional potting-mixture formulas for epiphytic orchids almost always include osmunda fiber, which is simply the dried root of the osmunda fern chopped across the grain into pieces up to 2 inches long. This extremely porous material can be procured in several grades, from fairly fine to very coarse, and the right grade mixed with other recommended ingredients will provide the right degree of drainage. Osmunda fiber, however, is both expensive and hard to find in some places. A satisfactory popular substitute is shredded tree bark (usually fir). Both tree bark and osmunda fiber can be purchased in the form of slabs or blocks on which orchids can also be grown.

A good general-purpose potting mixture for epiphytic orchids consists of two parts of osmunda fiber or shredded bark to one part of sphagnum moss. Some growers add a light sprinkling of coarse bonemeal to the mixture for its long-term nutritive value. A number of prepackaged mixtures are also available.

Potting and repotting Terrestrial orchids are normally grown in standard pots. The epiphytic kinds can also be planted in conventional containers, but they tend to do better in special, perforated clay pots, in slatted wooden or wire baskets, or attached to sections of tree branch or tree-fern stem or to slabs of bark or osmunda fiber. For added drainage, pots should be half full of clay-pot fragments; and baskets should be lined with a thin layer of sphagnum moss to prevent the potting mixture from dribbling through gaps in the slats or wire mesh.

It is unnecessary to repot most orchids more often than once every two years. Repot just as new root growth begins (normally in spring). When potting or repotting, cut away any dead or damaged roots with a sharp knife, and carefully remove the residue of the old potting mixture from among the remaining roots of the plant. If the plant has a single stem, position it in the middle of the new container. If the plant is rhizomatous, place the rhizome on the surface of the mixture in such a way that the back of the rhizome, or oldest pseudobulb, nearly touches the edge of the pot, with the growing point toward the middle. This will permit growth toward the other side as the rhizome sends down roots and, in epiphytic plants, produces new pseudobulbs. Do not use larger containers than are required for two years' growth.

Pack the potting mixture firmly around the thick feeding roots, pushing it down among them with a pencil-shaped piece of wood, but taking care not to damage them. Allow enough space above the level of the mixture for moderate waterings. But never water newly potted orchids moderately until their roots have become established in the fresh medium. For the first three or four weeks it is usually sufficient to mist-spray the foliage once a day.

Plants lodged on such supports as blocks of wood, tree fern, or blocks of osmunda fiber are not rooted in potting mixture. Instead, the base of any such plant should be soaked in water and allowed to drain for half an hour before being secured to its support. Place a handful of sphagnum moss

Propagating sympodial orchids

Divide pseudobulbs by slicing the rhizome. Each division should have several pseudobulbs and leaves.

After two months, remove a division from its container, and carefully disentangle roots from old mixture.

Plant the division in a 3- or 4-inch pot, packing fresh mixture firmly around the roots with your fingers.

under the moist base of the orchid, spread its roots gently over the supportive surface, and tie them down with copper wire or nylon string.

Propagation The easiest way to propagate all sympodial orchids is by division of the rhizome. As a first step in dividing such a plant, cut through the rhizome a month or two before actually dividing the top growth. This gives the cut ends time to heal before removal and repotting. Ideally, each section should carry two or three pseudobulbs or clumps of leaves. After removing the plant from its container or support, disentangle the roots and replant each section singly in an appropriately sized container or on a separate support. It is also sometimes possible to plant several pieces of detached rhizome together in a large hanging basket. Water newly separated orchids sparingly—a daily overall mist-spray may be sufficient—until new growth indicates that additional rooting has occurred. Thereafter, treat each section as a mature plant.

Monopodial orchids can be propagated from sideshoots or from tip cuttings. In taking a cutting, be sure it includes at least two aerial roots. Plant it in a 3-inch pot, tucking the aerial roots into the potting mixture, and keep it warm in bright filtered light. For the first four to six weeks water sparingly. Thereafter, the young plant can be treated as an adult. Do not throw the old plant away after removing its growing tip. If mist-sprayed daily, it will produce a new growth or two somewhere along the stem. When such growths have produced aerial roots, they can be used for further propagation.

Special points A weekly sponging of leaves is advisable for all indoor orchids. Scale insects and mealy bugs sometimes attack these plants, lurking in particular under the dried-up leaves on pseudobulbs and at the base of old flower stalks after these have been cut back. For pest control see pages 460-461.

For specific kinds of orchid see:

Brassia	*Lycaste*
Cattleya	*Maxillaria*
Coelogyne	*Miltonia*
Cymbidium	*Odontoglossum*
Dendrobium	*Oncidium*
Epidendrum	*Paphiopedilum*
Laelia	*Phalaenopsis*
Laeliocattleya	*Vanda*

Osmanthus

OLEACEAE

False holly
O. heterophyllus
'Variegatus'

PLANTS of the genus *Osmanthus* are slow-growing shrubs and trees with hard, prickly leaves that resemble holly leaves. Only one species is generally grown as a house plant: *O. heterophyllus* (frequently called *O. aquifolium* or *O. ilicifolius*; popularly known as false holly or the holly osmanthus). This dense, woody-stemmed shrub can attain a height of 3 feet and a spread of 2 feet when planted in an 8- to 10-inch pot. The prickly, glossy, medium green leaves, which are about 2½ inches long and 1½ inches wide, have ½-inch-long leaf-stalks and are arranged in opposite pairs. The shape of leaves—even of those on the same plant—will vary. Some may be elliptic, with a few large, spiny teeth along the edges and with one exceptionally long spine at the tip. Others may be more nearly egg-shaped and smooth-edged, with only the one spine at the tip. An indoor osmanthus does not normally produce flowers.

The most popular indoor form is *O.h.* 'Variegatus,' a variegated-leaved kind with creamy white markings, sometimes tinged with pink, at the leaf margins. Another form, *O.h.* 'Purpureus,' has purplish black leaves that turn to green flushed with purple as they age. A miniature variety, *O.h.* 'Rotundifolius,' rarely grows taller than 18 inches. Its dark green leaves can be as much as 1½ inches long and 1 inch wide.

PROPER CARE

Light Give osmanthuses bright light, with three or four hours a day of direct sunlight, throughout the year.

Temperature An osmanthus does best in a relatively cool and well-ventilated position, such as an unheated porch. This is one of the few house plants that can even tolerate drafts. Keep the temperatures below 55°F at all times, if possible.

Watering During the active growth period water moderately, giving enough at each watering to make the potting mixture moist throughout but allowing the top half-inch of the mixture to dry out before watering again. During the winter rest period give only enough to prevent the mixture from drying out completely.

Feeding Apply standard liquid fertilizer once every two weeks during the active growth period only.

Potting and repotting Use a soil-based potting mixture (see page 429). Repot each osmanthus in fresh mixture every spring, but do not move it into a larger pot until it has filled the current pot with roots (see page 426). After maximum pot size (probably 8–10 inches) has been reached, top-dress each spring (see page 428).

Propagation Propagate from tip cuttings 3–4 inches long taken in spring. Cut immediately below a node, remove the lower leaves from each cutting, and dip the cut end in hormone rooting powder. Plant the cutting in a 3-inch pot containing a moistened equal-parts mixture of peat moss and coarse sand or perlite. Enclose the whole in a plastic bag or heated propagating case (see page 444), and stand it in bright filtered light at a temperature of 65°F. After rooting has occurred (probably in six to eight weeks), uncover the cutting and move it to a position where it gets some direct sunlight. Begin to water moderately every two weeks, but do not feed the rooted cutting. About four months after the start of the propagation process, transfer the young plant into soil-based mixture, and treat it as a mature osmanthus.

Special points Cut back unwanted growths in spring. To induce bushy growth nip out growing tips every three or four months.

Pachyphytum

CRASSULACEAE

Moonstones
P. oviferum

PLANTS of the genus *Pachyphytum* (blue haze) bear a close resemblance to the related echeverias. Pachyphytums are small shrubs with short, branching stems that carry fleshy, often strikingly colored leaves normally arranged alternately along the length of the stems. Flower stalks 2–6 inches tall arise from leaf axils in spring and summer. Each stalk is tipped with a cluster of bell-shaped, five-petaled flowers about $\frac{3}{4}$ inch long and $\frac{1}{2}$ inch across at the flared end. These plants, however, are prized mainly for the beauty of their leaves.

See also SUCCULENTS.

RECOMMENDED PACHYPHYTUMS

P. amethystinum (also known as *Graptopetalum amethystinum*) has stems about 4 inches high and $\frac{1}{3}$ inch thick. The stems are erect at first but tend to flop over as they mature. The plump, pointed-oval leaves are about $1\frac{1}{2}$ inches long, $\frac{2}{3}$ inch broad, and $\frac{1}{4}$ inch thick. Although they are spaced out alternately along the branching stems, they look from above like a thick rosette of leaves. Leaf color is basically blue-gray, but attractively tinged with amethyst. The pink or whitish flowers open in summer.

P. amethystinum

P. bracteosum has stems up to about 6 inches high and $\frac{1}{2}$ inch thick. They carry rosettelike clusters of plump, bluntly pointed, spoon-shaped leaves. Each leaf is about 3 inches long and 1 inch wide toward the tip, tapering at the base to $\frac{1}{2}$ inch wide and $\frac{1}{4}$ inch thick. Leaf color is grayish, and the leaves are coated with a dusty white bloom, which is easily blemished.

P. oviferum (moonstones) is the most popular pachyphytum. The stems, which grow up to 6 inches long and $\frac{1}{2}$ inch thick, carry rosettelike clusters of egg-shaped leaves, each approximately 1 inch long and $\frac{3}{4}$ inch broad and thick. An entire leaf cluster has a spread of about 4 inches. Leaf color is grayish tinged with pink, and the leaves are coated with a dusty white bloom which is easily rubbed off. Flowers are bright red.

***P.* 'Pachyphytoides'** is an intergeneric hybrid between a species of pachyphytum and a variety of echeveria. The latter parent has given this plant a size not found among true pachyphytums. The stems can grow 16 inches tall and 1 inch thick, and they bear leaves 3–4 inches long, 1 inch broad, and $\frac{1}{2}$ inch thick. Each long, plump, bluntly rounded leaf is greenish white tinged with purple. Pale pink flowers, which can appear at almost any time of year, are borne on stout stalks up to 20 inches long.

PROPER CARE

Light To preserve the bright color of leaves and to prevent the plants from becoming unnaturally elongated, give pachyphytums as much direct sunlight as possible.

Temperature Normal room temperatures are suitable during most of the year. Pachyphytums should be encouraged to have a winter rest, however (see "Watering," below). An ideal temperature to help slow down growth during the winter is 50°–60°F.

Watering Water actively growing plants moderately, giving enough at each watering to make the potting mixture moist throughout but allowing the top half-inch of the mixture to dry out before watering again. Like many members of the *Crassulaceae* family, pachyphytums do not have a definite rest period. They do best, however, if active growth is permitted to slow down considerably during the winter, since continuous growth during the short-day months is likely to result in distortion. Give less water in winter, therefore, along with cooler temperatures. Moisten the potting mixture throughout at each watering, but allow a full $1\frac{1}{2}$ inches to dry out before watering again.

Feeding Do not feed these plants. It is not advisable to use fertilizers for pachyphytums at any time.

Potting and repotting Use a potting mixture composed of one part of coarse sand or perlite to every two parts of standard soil-based mixture (see page 429). These plants grow quickly so move them into pots one size larger every spring. Maximum pot size required is likely to be 5–6 inches. Thereafter, either topdress plants annually (see page 428) or, probably preferably, cut them up for propagation. To avoid damaging leaves, particularly of *P. bracteosum* and *P. oviferum*, hold plants by the base of the stems whenever possible during the repotting process. If a specimen has begun to look straggly, discard it and replace it with a rooted cutting.

Propagation It is extremely easy to propagate pachyphytums from stem cuttings in the spring. Using a sharp knife or pruning shears, cut off a 3- to 4-inch-long side branch of any one of these plants. Allow the branch to dry for two or three days, and then push the cut end into a 3-inch pot of the potting mixture recommended for mature plants. The potted cutting can be treated immediately as an adult specimen. It should root and produce new top growth within four weeks.

Pachystachys

ACANTHACEAE

P. lutea

THE only species of the small genus *Pachystachys* that is grown indoors is *P. lutea,* a low-growing shrub with tubular flowers that protrude from decorative bracts. *P. lutea,* which was introduced into cultivation only recently, will grow 18 inches high in a 7-inch pot. (It *can* grow taller in a bigger pot, but at the risk of losing its lower leaves.) The erect stems, which become woody with age, carry shiny, lance-shaped, dark green leaves arranged in opposite pairs. The leaves are about 6 inches long and have a puckered surface, strongly marked veining, and slightly undulant margins. Each stem becomes tipped with an erect flower head 4–6 inches long consisting chiefly of upright, heart-shaped, golden yellow bracts with green tips. The 2-inch-long, white flowers that seem to push their way through the bracts are produced successively from the base of the flower spike upward. Although each bloom lasts only a few days, the plant flowers continuously throughout the summer, and the bracts retain their color for 8 to 12 weeks.

PROPER CARE

Light Grow these plants in bright filtered light at all times. Though they cannot tolerate full sunlight, they will not flower if given inadequate light.

Temperature Normal room temperatures, with a minimum of 60°F, are suitable at all times.

Watering Water moderately, just enough to moisten the mixture, but let the top half-inch of the mixture dry out before watering again. A pachystachys does not generally have a noticeable rest period.

Feeding Apply standard liquid fertilizer every two weeks. If a plant still fails to bloom when it has reached a height of 12–15 inches, change to a high-potash fertilizer to encourage flowering. At the end of the first successful flowering season, change back to the normal feeding program.

Potting and repotting Use a soil-based potting mixture (see page 429). Move plants into pots one size larger every spring until they reach the 7- or, at most, 8-inch size. Thereafter, annual topdressing (see page 428) with fresh potting mixture will suffice.

Propagation Propagate in spring by means of tip cuttings 3–4 inches long taken from the lower branches. Take each cutting immediately below a pair of leaves, remove that bottom pair, dip the cut end of the cutting in hormone rooting powder, and insert it in a 2- or 3-inch pot (or plant several cuttings around the rim of a 4-inch pot) filled with a moistened equal-parts mixture of peat moss and coarse sand or perlite. Enclose the whole in a plastic bag or heated propagating case (see page 444), and stand it in bright filtered sunlight at a temperature of 70°F. When new growth indicates that rooting has occurred, remove the covering and begin moderate waterings (see "Watering," above). About 8 to 10 weeks after the start of propagation move each cutting into a 4-inch pot of the standard potting mixture and treat it in the same way as a mature pachystachys.

Propagating a pachystachys

In spring take a tip cutting below a pair of leaves. Before placing the cutting in mixture, remove these bottom leaves and dip the cut end in hormone rooting powder.

PALMS

Palms are mainly tropical plants distinguished in the wild for their usually tall, unbranched trunks topped by a crown of fan-shaped or feathery fronds. The kinds commonly grown as house plants are characterized below, along with general advice on providing proper care. A list of popular indoor palms follows this article. See separate articles for discussions of individual genera.

The palm family, *Palmae,* consists of more than 200 genera and almost 3,000 species. A number of these are naturally quite low-growing, clustering shrubs, but most palms eventually mature into tall, long-trunked, unbranching trees. When grown as house plants, the latter type rarely grow big enough to have long trunks. Under average indoor conditions a typical palm will produce only one, two, or at most three new fronds a year. It takes so long for seedlings of some kinds to become salable that commercial growers have found it uneconomic to grow many species. Thus only a few species have remained popular house plants.

Many potted palms acquired at a juvenile stage remain immature for the duration of their long lives indoors, and they differ considerably from the full-grown shrubs or trees that they would become under outdoor conditions. This is true not only of the size of stems (if any) and leaves but of overall appearance and characteristic growth habit.

Some types (such as microcoelums) have a solitary, unbranched stem that develops into a short trunk or stumpy base even on potted specimens. Others (such as howeas) are stemless or nearly so. These plants form a cluster of leafstalks that appear aboveground before the plants are old enough to produce a true stem. Still other types (such as chrysalidocarpuses) form a clump of thin true stems.

It is characteristic of every palm that each of its stems has only one growing point from which all the leaves develop. This growing point (called the terminal bud) is situated in the middle of the group of leaves. In most palms the terminal bud is partly hidden within a tight package of the erect leaves. If the terminal bud is damaged or destroyed, it is not replaced and the plant will eventually die. Although individual leaves may be removed, these plants cannot be cut back in any other way.

Palm leaves, which are usually called fronds, are of two distinct kinds: feathery (as in chamaedoreas and phoenix palms) or fan-shape (as in chamaeropses and washingtonias). Plants with feathery fronds are generally known as pinnate palms, those with fan-shape fronds are termed fan-leaf palms. Both kinds of leaf are likely to have stalks with a broad, thickened base. The leafstalk itself can be smooth and shiny or hairy, spiny, or tooth-edged. The stalk of a fan-shape frond terminates at the start of the broad blade. In pinnate palms, however, the extended leafstalk becomes the midrib of the blade, and the blade is divided into a number of segments arranged along the midrib. These segments are known as leaflets, or sometimes pinnae.

In fan-leaf palms the frond blade spreads out in fanlike fashion from an axis (or common point) at the tip of the leafstalk. The blade may be divided into segments for only a short distance from the edge of the "fan," or it may be deeply divided into dagger-shaped segments that run all or most of the way to the axis. These segments are usually referred to as such rather than as leaflets. More often than not, the leafstalks of these fronds are spined or tooth-edged.

In all mature palms sprays of small, ball-shaped, greenish or yellow flowers are produced in spring or summer on short stalks arising from the center of the cluster of leafstalks. The only indoor specimens that are likely to reach flowering size are the smaller chamaedoreas, which can bloom when only four or five years old. Fruit is seldom produced indoors.

Because palms are so often seen in poorly lit rooms and hotel foyers, it appears that these plants actually thrive on neglect. Certainly, most

Pinnate frond types

Feathery, or pinnate fronds, have an extended leafstalk from which two ranks of leaflets grow. Leaflets can be spiky, as in phoenixes (top), or soft, as in chrysalidocarpuses (middle). Caryota leaflets (bottom) are themselves divided.

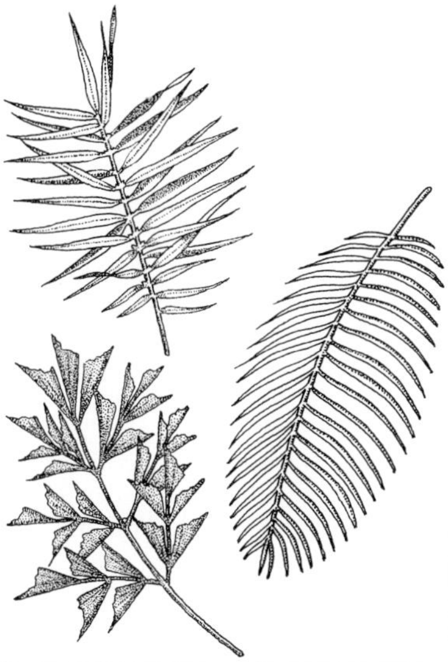

Palmate frond types

Palmate fronds have leaflets arranged in a fanlike group. Segments are partially separated, as in washingtonias (top), or completely, as in rhapises (middle) and trachycarpuses (bottom).

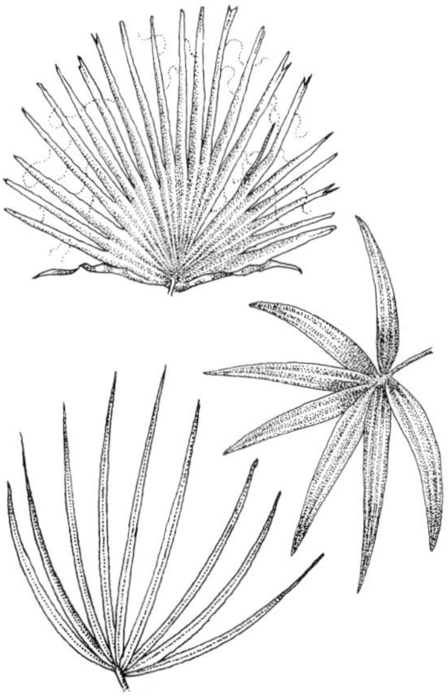

Palms: representative forms

Each plant here belongs to one of the genera included in the family *Palmae.* Other species within a given genus may, of course, look very different from the illustrated species.

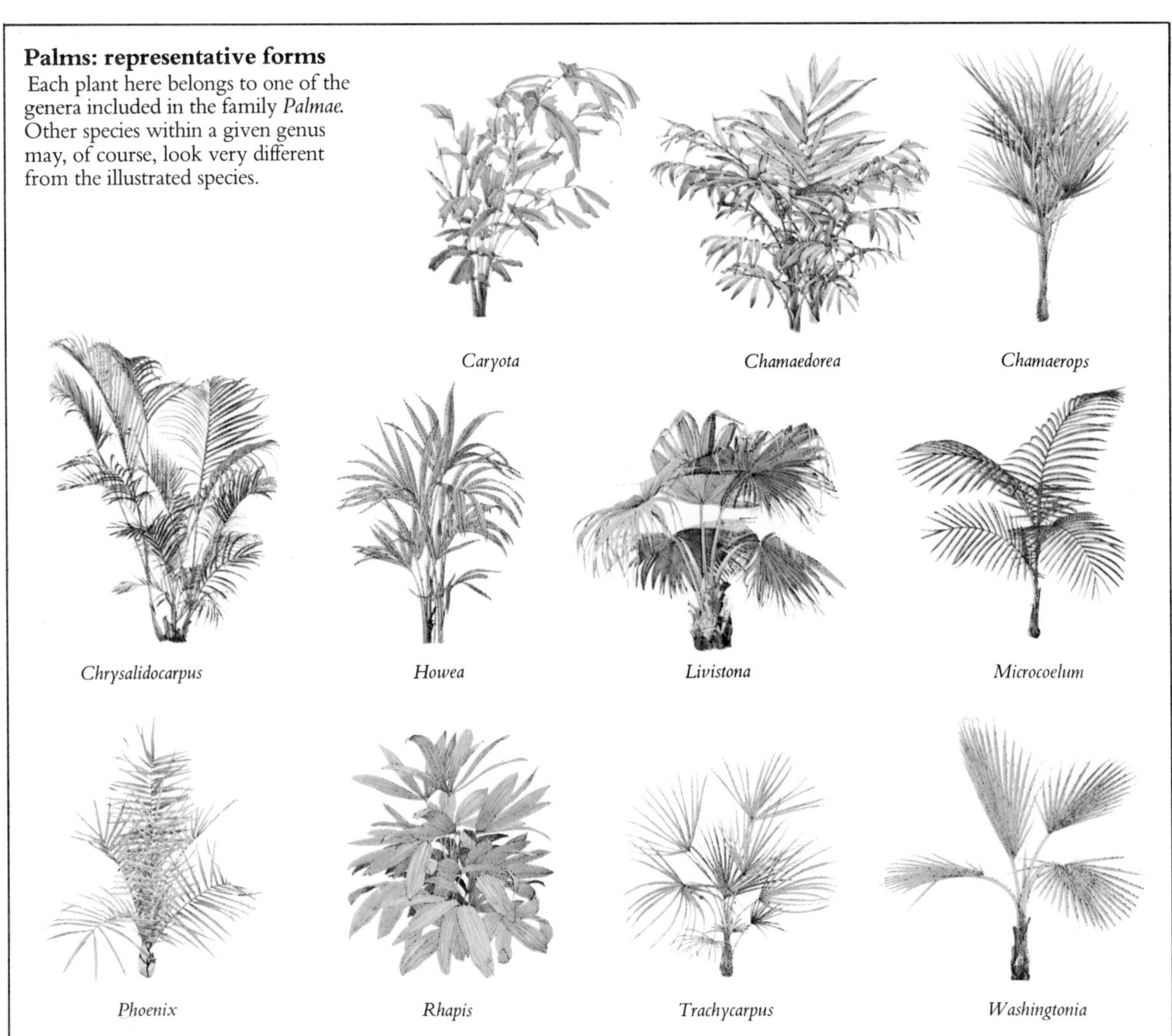

palms can tolerate a wide range of light intensity, with hot and dry air, and with a faulty watering program. But all kinds will develop into much finer plants if given reasonable and intelligent treatment.

During the poorly lit days of winter, indoor palms will normally have a two- to three-month rest period. Active, though slow, growth will usually begin in mid-spring and continue until late fall. Most types will benefit from being stood in a sheltered but sunny position outdoors during the warmer months. This is not essential for their well-being, however. All the palms recommended in this book are relatively easy to grow in the conditions provided by an average room.

PROPER CARE

Light Most palms come from regions where sunlight is intense. Since potted specimens are still in a juvenile form, however, they would be shaded from strong sunlight by other vegetation at a similar stage in the wild. Most of these plants, therefore, will grow best in bright light, with only two or three hours a day of direct sunlight, throughout the year. Some (as specified in the *A–Z Guide*) prefer bright filtered light. Although palms can tolerate poor light for periods of several months duration, with totally inadequate light these plants will make very little growth and will slowly deteriorate. To keep a poorly lit palm healthy, simply move it into a more brightly lit position for two or three hours every other day.

Temperature Throughout the active growth period any normally warm room temperature will suit all these palms. During the winter rest period hardier kinds—*Chamaerops, Livistona,* Phoenix, Rhapis, Trachycarpus, and *Washingtonia*—can all tolerate temperatures down to about 45°F, but the other kinds should never be subjected to temperatures below 55°. Palms do not suffer from slightly dry air, but very dry air will cause frond tips to turn brown. In any case a somewhat humid atmosphere adds considerably to the attractiveness of the foliage, and so it is advisable to stand all palms on trays of damp pebbles during the active growth period.

Watering Water requirements vary. See specific entries in the *A–Z Guide* for precise recommendations. In general, actively growing palms should be watered plentifully, enough at each watering so that some excess water runs out of the drainage holes in the bottom of the pot or tub. Some of these plants may even be allowed to stand in water for a while, but not for more than half an hour at any time. Amounts of water to be given during the rest period depend largely on the winter temperature in which plants are grown. The cooler the room, the smaller the quantity of water required. Even in warm conditions, however, these plants must be encouraged to have a winter rest, and one way to do this is to keep the mixture barely moist for two to three months.

Feeding Feed actively growing palms as recommended in appropriate A-Z entries. Do not continue feedings during the winter rest period.

Potting and repotting Most palms will thrive in a soil-based mixture, sometimes with the addition of some extra peat moss or leaf mold. Because good drainage is essential, all pots should have an inch-deep layer of coarse gravel (preferably pea-size pebbles or rough stones) in the bottom.

Some palms produce thick, fleshy, white roots, which wind around the outer edges of the potting mixture and tend to push their way through the drainage holes in the container. Finer feeding roots, like coarse hair, can also spread over the surface of the mixture. The fine roots are not a cause for concern, but care should be taken at all times not to damage the thick roots. A little root damage will not kill a plant, but growth can be stopped or badly slowed down for several weeks.

Repotting is normally necessary only when palms have filled their pots with roots (see page 426), and this should happen no more often than every two or three years. In repotting a palm, be sure to press the potting mixture firmly round the plant, taking care not to break the thicker roots. Clay and plastic pots are equally suitable for small palms. For large specimens, however, clay pots or wooden tubs are preferable as they will prevent topheaviness. Leave a gap of 1-2 inches between the surface of the mixture and the rim of the pot. This not only allows adequate watering space but provides room for the expansion of the fleshy roots, which tend to push up the mixture as they fill the pot. In years when palms are not being repotted or after maximum container size has been reached, topdress plants in the spring (see page 428), replacing the top inch or two of potting mixture with fresh mixture. It is advisable to add a little slow-release fertilizer to this topdressing material.

The repotting process

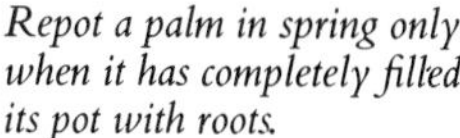

Repot a palm in spring only when it has completely filled its pot with roots.

Place an inch-deep layer of coarse gravel in the bottom of a clean pot for drainage.

Press fresh mixture round the root ball but leave space for water and root expansion.

Propagation Commercially, palms are raised from seed. But some seeds take up to two years to germinate, and it takes several years for seedlings to assume palmlike characteristics. Most indoor gardeners therefore prefer to buy young potted palms rather than to attempt propagation from seed.

There are a few kinds of palm that produce suckers or offsets that can be detached and potted up, preferably in spring. When an offset has at least three well-developed fronds, cut it away from the parent plant with a sharp knife, and then insert it in an appropriate-size pot filled with a moistened equal-parts mixture of peat moss and coarse sand or perlite. Enclose the whole in a plastic bag or propagating case (see page 443), and stand it in bright filtered light at a temperature of 70°-75°F. Firm rooting can take up to 12 weeks, during which time water the offset enough to prevent the potting mixture from drying out completely. When the offset appears to have developed new roots, as indicated by renewed top growth, uncover the young plant, water it sparingly, and begin to apply standard liquid fertilizer once a month. Do not move newly rooted offsets into the recommended mixture until the following spring. Thereafter, treat the plant as a mature palm.

Special points Most palms like airy conditions but they cannot tolerate drafts, extreme heat, or sudden changes in intensity of light. If moving a plant outdoors, acclimatize it gradually to breezes and brighter light. And be sure to bring plants inside before the onset of cool weather. In mild weather at any season, half an hour outdoors in gentle rain will rid the fronds of the dust that settles on them. Otherwise, wash plants under the bathroom shower, or mist-spray the foliage, or sponge off each frond.

Scale insects and red spider mites sometimes infest palm fronds. If infestation is suspected, use an appropriate pesticide (see page 461).

For specific kinds of palm see:

Pinnate	**Fan-leaf**
Caryota	*Chamaerops*
Chamaedorea	*Livistona*
Chrysalidocarpus	*Rhapis*
Howea	*Trachycarpus*
Microcoelum	*Washingtonia*
Phoenix	

Propagating palms with offsets

In spring, cut an offset bearing leaves and roots away from the parent plant.

Place the offset in a small pot and fill the pot with moistened potting mixture.

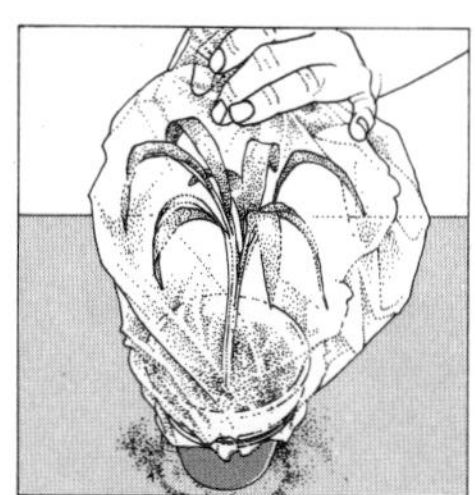

To encourage rooting, enclose the potted offset in a plastic bag for a few weeks.

Pandanus

PANDANACEAE

Veitch screw pine
P. veitchii

THE genus *Pandanus* (screw pine) includes many species of large shrub and tree. The spiral arrangement of the leathery, shiny leaves gives the genus its popular name. Mature plants develop a woody stem that can reach 9 inches tall. At its top is a rosette-shaped tuft of stalkless, sword-shaped, gracefully arching leaves, each several feet long. When two or three years old, the plant begins to send down stiltlike, ½-inch-thick, fleshy roots from below the lower leaves. These aerial roots pierce the potting mixture and prop up the plant. In mature plants small suckers develop at the base of the stem. These root easily and grow fast if they are detached and used for propagation.

P. veitchii (Veitch screw pine), the best-known indoor species, has dark green leaves striped lengthwise, frequently near leaf edges, in white, cream, or dull yellow. The 3-inch-wide leaves grow up to 3 feet long, so that a six- to eight-year-old plant can be 4 feet tall, with a spread of 3 feet. Beware of the finely toothed leaf edges, which can cut the hands. The more compact form, *P.v.* 'Compacta,' has leaves only 15–24 inches long and 1½–2 inches wide. Leaf color differs in that the margins are edged with white and the striping is more pronounced. The plant grows nearly as tall as the type species, but because the leaves are shorter the spread is barely more than 2 feet.

PROPER CARE

Light These plants must have at least three hours a day of direct sunlight.

Temperature Normal room temperatures are suitable. Minimum tolerable temperature: 55°F. If the air is too dry, leaf edges and tips will turn brown. Stand the plants on trays or saucers of moist pebbles.

Watering During the active growth period water plentifully often enough to keep the potting mixture thoroughly moist, but never allow the pot to stand in water. During the winter rest period give only enough to keep the mixture from drying out.

Feeding Apply standard liquid fertilizer every two weeks during the active growth period only.

Potting and repotting Use a soil-based potting mixture (see page 429). Move plants into containers one size larger every spring until maximum convenient size is reached. Thereafter, topdress annually (see page 428) with fresh mixture. The aerial roots of a mature pandanus tend to push the plant upward so that its base rises, as if on stilts, out of the pot. When repotting or topdressing a plant, leave extra space between the potting-mixture surface and the rim of the pot. In early fall add fresh mixture to cover any roots that have been exposed during the active growth period.

Propagation Propagate in early spring by cutting off suckers and planting each one in a 3- or 4-inch pot filled with a moistened equal-parts mixture of peat moss and coarse sand or perlite. Enclose the potted sucker in a plastic bag or propagating case (see page 443), and stand it in bright filtered light. When rooting has occurred (in four to six weeks), uncover the sucker gradually, acclimatizing it to less humid room conditions over a period of about two weeks. For the next month or so, water moderately, allowing the top inch of the rooting mixture to dry out between waterings. After the young plant appears to be well established in its pot, treat it as a mature plant, but do not expose it to direct sunlight. Move it into a 5-inch pot of soil-based mixture about four months after the start of propagation, and treat it as a mature pandanus.

Paphiopedilum

ORCHIDACEAE

Slipper orchid
P. callosum

PAPHIOPEDILUMS are commonly called slipper orchids because the pouch-shaped lip of their flowers looks very much like a slipper or moccasin. These plants are terrestrial and stemless. Strap-shaped, pointed leaves arising in separate clumps directly from a short rhizome are thick and fleshy, with a prominent midrib. The flowers, which vary tremendously in size, shape and color, are borne on a stalk that appears from the center of a group of leaves. The flowers are fleshy in texture; most of them have a polished, waxy, almost artificial look. The top (dorsal) sepal is usually in a contrasting color to the petals and lip. The pouchlike lip hides the lower sepals, which are joined together. The flowering season is generally fall to spring, and each flower lasts 8–12 weeks.

There are thousands of hybrids between the species of paphiopedilum. *See also* ORCHIDS.

RECOMMENDED PAPHIOPEDILUMS

P. callosum has leaves up to 12 inches long and 2 inches wide. Leaf color is dark green mottled with bright green. The 18-inch-long flower stem carries one or two 3- to 4-inch-wide flowers. The dorsal sepal and petals are white with purple and green stripes. The petals curl downward and have hairy, black, raised spots along the top edge. The lip is reddish purple. The main flowering season is mid-spring.

P. fairieanum has pale green leaves up to 8 inches long and 1 inch wide. The 12-inch-long flower stem carries one or two $1\frac{1}{2}$- to 2-inch-wide flowers. The dorsal sepal and petals are white veined with thin, purple lines. The petals arch downward, turning upward at the ends (somewhat like an old-fashioned moustache), and they have tiny black hairs along the top edge. The lip is green flushed with red, and with purple veining. The flowers appear in fall.

P. hirsutissimum has leaves up to 10 inches long and 1 inch wide. Leaf color is dark green slightly mottled with light green. The flower stem, which is up to 10 inches long and covered with tiny black hairs, carries a single 5-inch-wide flower. The wavy-edged dorsal sepal is a pale green densely marked toward the bottom center with purple-brown spots. The wavy-edged petals are green with pale pink tips and are spotted with reddish brown. The lip is green tinted with brown and covered with brown spots and blotches. The normal flowering season is spring.

P. insigne has medium green leaves up to 10 inches long and 1 inch wide. The flower stem is up to 10 inches long and carries one or two 4-inch-wide flowers. The dorsal sepal is white tinted green in the center and heavily spotted with brown and purple. The petals and lip are yellowish brown lightly spotted with purple-red. The flowering season for *P. insigne* is late winter. There are many different forms of this species.

P. spiceranum has 6-inch-long, 1-inch-wide, bright green leaves with purple undersides. The 8-inch-long flower stem carries one or two $2\frac{1}{2}$-inch-wide flowers. The dorsal sepal is white with a lengthwise purple stripe in the center. The petals are yellowish green with a crosswise crimson line in the center. The lip is crimson. Flowers appear in fall.

P. venustum has leaves 6 inches long and 1 inch wide. Leaf color is bluish green mottled with dark green. The flower stem is up to 12 inches long and bears only one 2-inch-wide flower. The dorsal sepal is white with several lengthwise green stripes. The petals are pale green tinged with pink at the ends, and they have hairy, black, raised spots along the edges. The lip is beige streaked with brown. Flowering season is late fall to early spring.

PROPER CARE

Light Grow paphiopedilums in medium light, and never expose them to any direct sunlight. Supplementary fluorescent light from late fall into early spring will promote good flowering (see page 446).

Temperature Normal room temperatures are suitable. For adequate humidity stand plants on trays of damp pebbles throughout the year, and mist-spray the foliage daily when temperatures rise above 70°F.

Watering Water moderately during periods of active growth, but allow the top one to two inches of the mixture to dry out before watering again. During the six weeks after flowering, when all paphiopedilums make little new growth, water them sparingly, allowing the potting mixture to dry out almost completely between waterings.

Feeding Apply a foliar feed to paphiopedilums with every third or fourth watering, except during the six-week period of slow growth.

Potting and repotting Use any of the recommended potting mixtures for orchids (see page 289). For all species but *P. callosum* add three or four $\frac{1}{2}$-inch-square pieces of limestone to the drainage material in the bottom of the pot. Move plants into pots one size larger at the end of the flowering period whenever clumps of leaves completely cover the surface of the potting mixture. Be sure to keep leaf bases level with the top of the mixture; burying them deeper will cause rotting. After maximum convenient pot size has been reached, propagate paphiopedilums by division.

Propagation Divide any plant that has made six or more clumps of leaves. At the end of the flowering season shake away the old potting mixture from the roots, remove any dead roots, and carefully cut or pull the rhizome into pieces, making sure that each piece has at least two clumps of leaves attached. Gently disentangle as many of the roots as possible rather than cutting them apart. Plant each piece in a 3-inch pot, place it in medium light and mist-spray daily for three weeks. Thereafter, treat it as a mature plant.

Special points Paphiopedilum roots are easily damaged and are susceptible to rot if overwatered.

Flower buds sometimes tend to hang downward. To remedy this fault insert a thin stick in the potting mixture, and tie the flower stem to it. If the last tie is made just below the bud, flowers open in an upright position.

Parodia

CACTACEAE

P. chrysacanthion

PARODIAS are desert cacti with stems that are globular at first but tend to become broadly cylindrical with age. Most species have spirally arranged tubercles about $\frac{1}{8}$ inch high, but in some kinds the tubercles merge to form spiral ribs. All tubercles carry areoles at their tips. As many as a dozen cup-shaped flowers appear at once from areoles at the tops of stems in late spring followed by occasional blooms throughout the summer. Individual flowers last up to four days. Some parodias form offsets readily, others produce none or only a few. *See also CACTI.*

RECOMMENDED PARODIAS

P. aureispina (golden Tom Thumb) forms a column up to 8 inches high and 5 inches across when only seven years old. Each areole carries roughly 40 thin, white radial spines and 6 thicker, golden yellow central spines, all about $\frac{1}{2}$–$\frac{3}{4}$ inch long. One of the central spines is hooked. The bright green stem is almost hidden by the mass of spines. Flowers are buttercup yellow and $1\frac{1}{2}$ inches across.

P. chrysacanthion remains almost globular even after seven years, when it reaches a diameter of 4–5 inches. Stem color is pale green, which the spines do not entirely hide. Each areole bears 30 to 40 slender, pale yellow radial spines about $\frac{1}{2}$ inch long, and 3 to 5 golden yellow centrals up to 1 inch long. Golden yellow flowers are 1 inch across.

P. sanguiniflora has a dark green stem that is likely to become cylindrical—about 5 inches high and 4 inches wide—after seven years. The tubercles tend to merge into ribs as some plants get older. Each of the areoles carries about 15 white, $\frac{1}{3}$-inch-long radial spines and 4 brown, 1-inch-long centrals. One of the centrals is hooked at the tip. Flowers are blood red and 2 inches across.

PROPER CARE

Light Grow parodias in direct sunlight all year long.

Temperature Normal room temperatures are suitable during the active growth period. During the winter rest period give parodias temperatures of about 50°F, if possible.

Watering During the active growth period water moderately, allowing the top half-inch of the potting mixture to dry out between waterings. During the winter rest period give only enough to prevent the mixture from drying out completely.

Feeding Apply a high-potassium, tomato-type fertilizer once a month during the active growth period only.

Potting and repotting Use an equal-parts combination of coarse sand or perlite and soil-based or peat-based mixture (see page 429). Shallow-rooted parodias should be grown in half-pots. In early spring move plants to pots one size larger if current containers are packed with roots or if stems have begun to press against container sides. The biggest pot likely to be needed is the 6-inch size. If a current pot is still large enough, clean it thoroughly and replace the plant after shaking away as much as possible of the old mixture. Add fresh mixture as required.

Propagation In early summer, cut away offsets of clump-forming kinds from parent plants with a sharp knife. Let each offset dry for three days, then press it into a 2-inch pot of the recommended mixture, and treat it as a mature parodia. It may be three months before growth starts.

Parodias that do not produce offsets can be raised from seed. (See *CACTI,* page 119.)

Special points The roots of parodias sometimes rot away. If a specimen has lost its roots, cut off any dark, rotted tissue at repotting time and treat the plant in the same way as if it were an offset (see the "Propagation" section above). If rootlessness is discovered during the winter rest period, remove the cactus from its pot, store it in a dry place where it gets full sunlight, and repot it in spring.

Passiflora

PASSIFLORACEAE

Passion flower
P. caerulea

THE genus *Passiflora* includes about 400 species of vigorous climbing plants. Their long, thin stems attach themselves to any available support by means of spiraled tendrils, and most species are capable of growing 20 feet or more. Only one species, *P. caerulea* (passion flower), is commonly grown as a house plant. It is relatively easy to grow; and, unlike most other passifloras, it will flower when still young, even in a small pot.

P. caerulea has wiry, dark green, angular stems bearing leaves that are basically fan-shaped, but deeply lobed into between five and nine almost separated sections. The leaves, each of which has a spread of about 4 inches, are shiny and deep green, with 1- to $1\frac{1}{2}$-inch-long leafstalks. Short-stalked, saucer-shaped flowers open up from fat, pale green, oval buds that appear singly along the stems throughout the summer and early fall. Each 3-inch-wide flower consists of five white petals and five white sepals of equal lengths encircling a wheel-shaped collection of fine, colorful filaments, with five prominent golden anthers and three brown stigmas in the center. The filaments are purple at the base, white in the middle, and blue at the tip. In the wild and in the garden the flowers are followed by 2-inch-long, yellow-to-orange, fleshy fruits, but these are not produced indoors. The plants require supports to cling to, and they benefit from drastic pruning (see "Special points," below).

PROPER CARE

Light Grow this plant in bright light throughout the year. It should have between three and four hours a day of direct sunlight.

Temperature During the active growth period a passiflora will thrive in a warm room, but it needs a winter rest period in a cool position, ideally at a temperature of about 50°F.

Watering During the active growth period water plentifully as often as necessary to keep the potting mixture thoroughly moist, but never allow the pot to stand in water. During the rest period give only enough to keep the potting mixture from drying out.

Feeding Apply standard liquid fertilizer every two weeks during the active growth period only.

Potting and repotting Use a soil-based potting mixture (see page 429). Although a young plant will flower in a 4-inch pot, it must be moved into the 6-inch size the following spring. Thereafter, move it into a pot one size larger in the spring whenever necessary. Because large pots encourage stem and leaf growth at the expense of flowers, use pots no larger than 8 inches, and topdress with fresh mixture (see page 428) annually.

Propagation Propagate in summer by 3- to 4-inch-long stem cuttings. Take each cutting just below a leaf, remove the lower leaf, dip the cut end in a hormone rooting powder, and plant the cutting in a 3-inch pot filled with a moistened equal-parts mixture of peat moss and coarse sand. Enclose the whole in a plastic bag or propagating case (see page 443), and stand it in bright filtered light. Rooting should occur in three to four weeks. When new growth begins to appear, uncover the plant, move it into bright light, and begin to apply standard liquid fertilizer every two weeks. Water only sparingly, however, and stop feeding the new plant at the beginning of winter. Leave it in its pot, and give it the winter rest recommended for mature plants. In early spring move the young plant into a 4-inch pot of standard mixture, and treat it as a mature passiflora.

Special points In early spring cut young plants (but not recently rooted cuttings) down to within 6 inches of the potting-mixture surface. Prune older plants as much as necessary, and cut back every side branch to 2 or 3 inches. Drastic pruning of older plants will not affect them adversely.

Provide all plants with thin supports to which tendrils can cling. Guide young growth by twining it gently around the supports until the stems produce tendrils. Passifloras are particularly attractive when trained over two hoops of stout wire. Place the hoops opposite each other in the potting mixture.

Pedilanthus

EUPHORBIACEAE

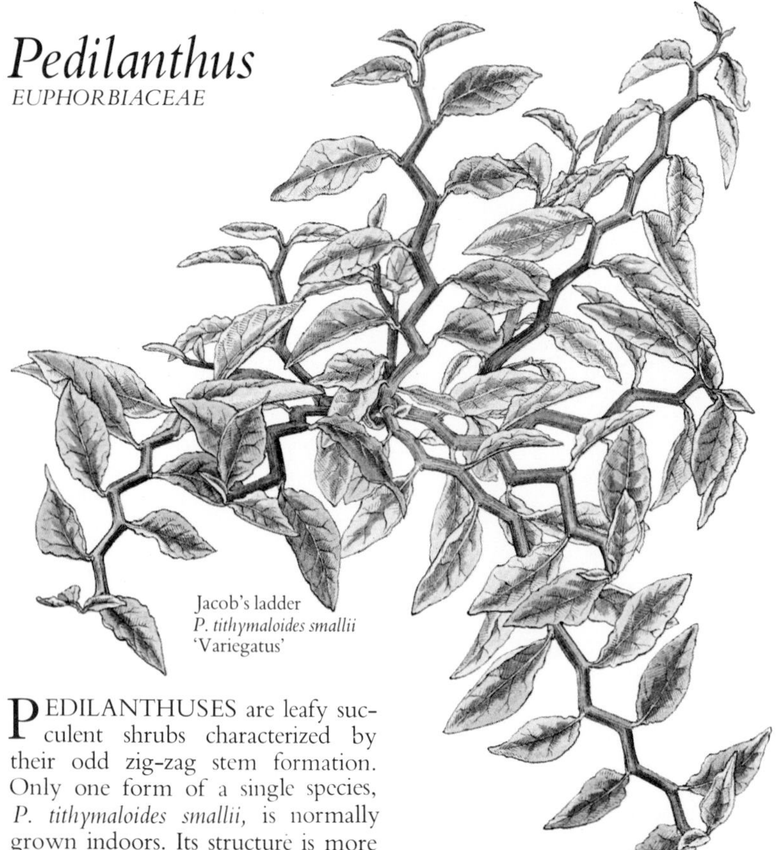

Jacob's ladder
P. tithymaloides smallii
'Variegatus'

PEDILANTHUSES are leafy succulent shrubs characterized by their odd zig-zag stem formation. Only one form of a single species, *P. tithymaloides smallii,* is normally grown indoors. Its structure is more compact than that of the species plant, *P. tithymaloides.* Because its stems zig-zag even more than those of other pedilanthuses, it is commonly called devil's-backbone or Jacob's ladder. The stems, which are green and usually grow about 2 feet long, change direction every inch or so, first to the left and then to the right, forming an open-centered but bushy shrub. The pointed-oval leaves are dull apple green in color, up to 3 inches long and 2 inches wide, and have a heavy crease—like the keel of a boat—on the underside. They grow on alternate sides of the zig-zagging stem, one leaf emerging at each point where the direction changes.

There is also a variegated-leaved form, *P. t. s.* 'Variegatus.' Its leaves have broad but rather indistinct creamy white leaf margins, which are lightly tinged with pink.

Although mature plants growing in the wild produce dense clusters of red (or occasionally pink or purple) flowers, they rarely occur indoors.
See also SUCCULENTS.

PROPER CARE

Light Provide bright light, with about two or three hours of direct sunlight every day.

Temperature Pedilanthuses do best if kept in warm rooms (65°–80°F) and in dry air. These plants can tolerate brief periods of lower temperatures, but they should never be subjected to temperatures much below 55°.

Watering Beware of overwatering. Throughout the year water sparingly, giving only enough at each watering to make the entire potting mixture barely moist, and allowing the top half of the mixture to dry out before watering again. If room temperature falls below 60°F, be even more sparing. Too much water can result in mildew or—worse—in rotting of the main stem at soil level.

Feeding Apply standard liquid fertilizer once a month while plants are actively growing.

Potting and repotting Use a soil-based potting mixture, with the addition of up to one-third extra coarse sand or perlite for drainage (see page 429), and plant very firmly. These pedilanthuses do best in rather small pots, where their roots are somewhat constricted. They should be moved into pots one size larger only when the roots have become extremely crowded (about once every two years). The best time for repotting is at the beginning of the growth period. After maximum convenient pot size (likely to be 5 or 6 inches) has been reached, topdress with fresh potting mixture every second spring (see page 428).

Propagation Cuttings of pieces or tips of stem 2–6 inches long are used in propagation. Like all other members of the family *Euphorbiaceae,* these plants produce a milky white latex, which flows profusely when a cutting is taken. Stop the flow by immersing cut ends in water. Allow them to dry for 24 hours before inserting them in a slightly moist, very sandy rooting mixture (two-thirds sand, one-third peat moss). If bottom heat can be provided by a small electric propagator, it will assist rooting considerably (see page 444). Do not cover the cuttings with plastic bags, for a moist atmosphere encourages mildew. Water only enough to keep the potting mixture barely moist until the cuttings are well rooted. Then pot each cutting, using the soil-based mixture recommended above.

Special points The latex produced by these plants is acrid. Take care to avoid getting it into the eyes or into cuts in the skin.

Propagating a pedilanthus

When propagating a pedilanthus from tip cuttings, be prepared for the flow of milky latex that will ooze from the wound.

Stem the flow of latex by dipping the severed end of the cutting in water. Do not touch cut ends; latex can harm skin and eyes.

Pelargonium

GERANIACEAE

PELARGONIUM is the correct generic name for the small shrubs commonly called geraniums. (It is a confusing fact that there is also a genus *Geranium*; but the familiar plants we call geraniums do not belong to it.) The pelargoniums popular as house plants are prized for either their striking flowers or their attractive, sometimes scented leaves, and most of them are hybrids.

P. domesticum variety

P. peltatum variety

P. hortorum variety

Oakleaved geranium
P. quercifolium

Each of the many kinds of indoor pelargonium can be considered as belonging to one of four main groups: *P. domesticum* hybrids (regal or Lady Washington geraniums); *P. hortorum* hybrids (zonal or bedding geraniums); *P. peltatum* hybrids (ivy-leaved geraniums); and the scented-leaved pelargoniums—a small number of species and hybrids grown for their leaves rather than their flowers. There are also miniature and dwarf forms that reach only 6–10 inches in pots.

Indoor pelargoniums are mainly bushy shrubs with soft-wooded, much-branching, brittle stems. The leaves, which may be of many shapes and sizes, have leafstalks that are more or less equal in length to the leaf blades themselves. The most common leaf shape is circular with slightly lobed edges, and all leaves have a distinctive scent when fingered. Clusters of flowers on short individual stalks are often grouped in rounded heads at the ends of long flower stalks. Each of the flowers can be small and unimpressive or big and brilliant, but all have one or more layers of five spoon-shaped petals, two pointing upward and three downward. Flower color can be white or virtually any shade of pink or red. Most pelargoniums have a long flowering season.

Pelargonium hybrids (flowers)

RECOMMENDED PELARGONIUMS

***P. domesticum* hybrids,** which normally grow 15–24 inches tall, have rough-textured, plain green, oval leaves 2–4 inches long and up to 3 inches wide. Leaf texture is a little rough, and leaf edges are slightly scalloped as well as undulate. The funnel-shaped flowers, which normally consist of a single layer of petals, are 2–2½ inches wide. They are produced in groups of up to ten at or near the tips of stems and younger branches. A darker coloring near the bottom of each petal usually creates the effect of an "eye" in the center of the flower funnel. There may also be fine, hairlike, dark-colored lines spreading out from the eye.

The flowering season of *P. domesticum* (early spring to midsummer) is a shorter one than that of most pelargoniums, but the flowers are impressive. They are sometimes abundant enough to hide the foliage at the top of a plant.

The following hybrids of *P. domesticum* are both attractive and generally available as well:

***P.d.* 'Chorus Girl'** has ruffled petals of an attractive lavender color almost covered with bright salmon blotches.

***P.d.* 'Conspicuous'** has showy flowers whose petals have deep red veins and are blotched with black.

***P.d.* 'Dawn'** has flowers of an apricot color that is unusual for pelargoniums.

***P.d.* 'Easter Greetings'** is a profusely flowering variety that has petals of cherry-rose covered with orange-brown markings.

***P.d.* 'Grand Slam'** has flowers of a rich rose-red color.

***P.d.* 'Pink Bonanza'** has strawberry pink flowers.

***P.d.* 'Snowbank'** has white ruffled petals some of which are marked with a pink central blotch.

***P. hortorum* hybrids** can grow more than 4 feet tall. The round, scalloped-edged, 3- to 5-inch-wide leaves with 1½- to 3-inch-long stalks are usually medium green with a contrasting color (generally dark maroon) ringing a "zonal" area in the middle. The marking around the zone may be pronounced or just faintly defined. Some forms have multicolored leaves, with bands of cream, red, or orange following the pattern of the zonal marking. Leaves are borne on leafstalks 1½–3 inches long. Flowers are produced in large, round-headed clusters on 9-inch stalks from leaf axils. Each flower is about 1½ inches wide—much smaller than the flowers of the regal *P. domesticum*—but the flowering season is much longer. Some specimens flower continuously, except during the brief rest period.

The following named hybrids of *P. hortorum* are highly recommended:

***P.h.* 'Apple Blossom'** has large white flowers, which are tinged with pink at the centers.

***P.h.* 'Blaze'** is a compact, free-flowering variety, which has bright red petals.

***P.h.* 'Mrs. Cox'** has medium green leaves heavily marked with red, yellow and brown bands. Single-layered flowers are pale salmon pink but this variety is grown principally for its impressive leaves.

***P.h.* 'Happy Thought'** has leaves of soft green with a yellow center and single-layered flowers of crimson. This variety lacks the usual zonal markings.

***P.h.* 'Irene'** has medium green leaves with maroon zonal markings and bears double crimson flowers.

***P.h.* 'Mamie'** has flowers of a particularly brilliant red.

***P.h.* 'Snowball,'** just as the name implies, has large, round white flowers.

The 'Carefree' strain of pelargonium is rapidly gaining in popularity and includes a wide range of colors bearing that name.

***P. peltatum* hybrids** are low-growing plants that are especially suitable for hanging baskets because their stems, which can grow 3 feet long, can be permitted to trail. The stems are brittle, however, and will break if roughly handled. The often shiny leaves, held on 1½- to 2-inch-long leafstalks, are 2–3 inches long and wide, and they are sometimes shaped like ivy leaves. Flowers 1–1½ inches wide are carried in small clusters on 6- to 9-inch-long stalks. Flowering is profuse in spring, although flowers also appear from time to time throughout summer and fall.

The following hybrids of *P. peltatum* are among the most desirable:

***P.p.* 'Apricot Queen'** has salmon pink flowers that turn pale pink (almost white) before they die.

***P.p.* 'Barbary Coast'** has large lavender flowers.

***P.p.* 'Charles Turner'** has long, trailing stems, which carry deeply cut leaves of medium green and large rose-pink flowers.

***P.p.* 'Mexican Beauty'** has long trailing stems and blood red flowers.

Scented-leaved forms Although all pelargonium leaves have an easily recognizable scent when fingered, there are several species and a few hybrids that have an especially pleasant scent.

Some of them grow exceedingly tall, and do not make suitable house plants. A few, however, are relatively small and have attractive foliage (but comparatively insignificant flowers). They are excellent plants for positions where people are apt to brush gently against them in passing. The following kinds are recommended for both appearance and odor.

***P.* 'Cinnamon'** has attractive deep green leaves which smell rather like cinnamon, hence its name.

***P. tomentosum* 'Peppermint'** is a trailing form with velvety green leaves and the scent of mint.

***P.* 'Mabel Grey,'** a hybrid, can grow 2 feet tall and has roundish, rough-surfaced, deeply indented leaves 3 inches across. Leafstalks are 3 inches long. The leaves have a strong lemon-grapefruit fragrance.

P. quercifolium (oakleaved geranium) can grow as much as 3 feet tall. The 2-inch-long and $1\frac{1}{2}$-inch-wide, medium green leaves are quilted and deeply lobed. Leafstalks are 2–3 inches long. The scent of this species is pungent and distinctive.

Rejuvenating old pelargoniums

Old plants should be repotted every spring. Begin by shaking off spent mixture.

Cut away at least half of the top growth to encourage the development of new shoots.

To keep plants in a relatively small pot, trim long, thick roots and repot plants in fresh mixture.

PROPER CARE

Light Pelargoniums need at least four hours a day of direct sunlight in order to flourish and flower well.

Temperature Normal room temperatures are tolerable at most times. If possible, give plants a winter rest at a temperature of about 50°F.

Watering Water actively growing plants moderately. Give enough to make the potting mixture moist throughout at each watering, allowing the top half-inch of the potting mixture to dry out between waterings. *P. domesticum* hybrids differ from other pelargoniums in that they need to be rested for six to eight summer weeks immediately following the flowering period. During this warm-weather rest period give them only enough water to keep the mixture from becoming completely dry. In early fall gradually increase amounts given until *P. domesticum* specimens are being watered normally again (see "Potting and repotting," below). During the winter rest period water all pelargoniums only enough to keep the potting mixture from completely drying out.

Feeding Apply a high-potash liquid fertilizer every two weeks to actively growing plants only.

Potting and repotting Use a soil-based potting mixture (see page 429), and provide good drainage by placing a half-inch layer of clay-pot fragments at the bottom of the pot. Pelargoniums will flower more profusely and have better leaf coloring if they are grown in relatively small pots. Move young plants into larger pots in spring or when too many roots are coming through drainage holes, but it should rarely be necessary to use pots bigger than 5 inches. Replant older pelargoniums in fresh mixture once a year. Except for varieties of *P. domesticum* remove plants from their pots every spring. Shake away spent potting mixture, cut back by half the top growth and any long, thick roots, and plant each specimen in a clean pot of fresh mixture.

Treat *P. domesticum* hybrids in the same way, but remove them from their pots after their late-summer rest rather than in spring. When they have been cut back and potted in fresh mixture, start them into growth by watering them—sparingly at first, but gradually increasing the amount as new top growth is produced.

Do not use pots bigger than 4 inches for dwarf and miniature forms. They grow uncharacteristically tall in larger pots.

Propagation Use 3- to 4-inch-long tip cuttings ($1\frac{1}{2}$–2 inches for dwarf and miniature kinds) taken in summer. Cut a strong-growing shoot immediately below a node, remove any flowers or buds as well as the lowest leaf, and dip the cut end of the shoot in a hormone rooting powder. Plant the cutting in a 2- to 3-inch pot (or plant several around the inside rim of a 4-inch pot) filled with a moistened equal-parts mixture of peat moss and coarse sand or perlite. Stand the pot in bright light filtered through a translucent blind or curtain. Water sparingly, making the potting mixture barely moist, until renewed growth indicates that roots have formed. Rooting should occur in two to three weeks, after which the amount of water given may be gradually increased. After a further three or four weeks move the pot into direct sunlight, and treat the plant as a mature pelargonium. When the pot is completely filled with roots (see page 426), move the young plant into a slightly larger pot of standard soil-based potting mixture (or, if several cuttings were rooted in a single pot, plant them individually in 3-inch pots).

Special points Pinch out the growing tips of young pelargoniums to encourage the development of new sideshoots. And do not neglect to prune older plants every year (see "Potting and repotting," above). Because old woody growth will always send out new shoots, pruning can be as drastic as desired.

Pelargoniums are susceptible to a disease known variously as "blackleg," "black rot," or "black stem rot," which turns stems black where they touch the surface of the potting mixture (see page 453). The rot spreads quickly and can result in the collapse of the entire plant. This disease is often caused by too much moisture in the potting mixture or in the air. Remember that pelargoniums, unlike most plants, do best in fairly dry air. Take good care not to bruise cuttings when preparing them for propagation; they are particularly prone to attack by blackleg. Other diseases, especially mildew, are often spread by yellowing, dried, or dead foliage and by spent flowers. Remove such foliage and flowers regularly.

Pellaea

POLYPODIACEAE

Button fern
P. rotundifolia

THE large genus *Pellaea* (cliffbrake fern) includes two species commonly grown as house plants. The fronds of the two species are very different, but all indoor pellaeas are alike in three respects: They have furry, wiry frond midribs and stalks; the stalks rise directly from a much-branching rhizome; and some of the fronds are composed of pinnae with edges that curl down, concealing spore cases produced all around the underside. Pinnae on fronds that do not carry spore cases have edges that are slightly toothed and do not curl.

Under ideal conditions, these ferns do not have a distinct rest period. They grow actively throughout the year, though growth does slow down perceptibly during the short-day winter months.
See also FERNS.

RECOMMENDED PELLAEAS

P. rotundifolia (button fern) does not conform to the popular image of a fern. Its fronds, which can grow 12 inches long and about $1\frac{1}{2}$ inches wide, arch downward and spread out almost like the stems of a trailing plant. Each frond consists of a short stalk bearing 12 to 20 pairs of leathery, dark green pinnae growing alternately along the midrib, with a single pinna at the tip. The midrib and stalk are almost black. The paired pinnae are nearly round, with a diameter of about $\frac{1}{2}$ inch. The terminal pinna is more nearly oval and is roughly $\frac{3}{4}$ inch long and $\frac{1}{2}$ inch wide.

P. viridis (green cliffbrake), with upright, bright green fronds, has a bushy look. The fronds can grow to a length of 30 inches. Each frond consists of a stalk up to 6 inches long bearing a 2-foot-long, triangular blade that is divided into about 15 pairs of alternate, lance-shaped pinnae. The largest pinnae are about 4 inches long and 1 inch wide. The midrib and stalk are green at first but they become glossy black as the frond matures.

P. viridis (green cliffbrake)

There are two popular varieties of this species, *P.v.* 'Macrophylla' and *P.v.* 'Viridis.' In both varieties the overall shape, size, and color of the fronds are similar to those of the species. The pinnae of *P.v.* 'Macrophylla,' however, are larger than those of the species, there are fewer pairs (about 10), and the pinnae may become lobed at the base as they mature. *P.v.* 'Viridis' has a more delicate look than *P.v.* 'Macrophylla' because, although its fronds are the same size, they are divided into about 20 pairs of pinnae.

PROPER CARE

Light Pellaeas grow best in medium light. Never try and grow them in direct sunlight.

Temperature Normal room temperatures are suitable throughout the year. Winter temperatures down to 50°F will not harm pellaeas, however. When temperatures rise above 70° for more than three or four days, mist-spray these ferns with tepid water once a day.

Watering Water plentifully, enough to keep the potting mixture thoroughly moist, but do not let pots stand in water. If room temperatures fall below 55°F for more than a day or two, water sparingly during this period, allowing the top third of the mixture to dry out completely between waterings.

Feeding Apply standard liquid fertilizer to pellaeas once every two weeks if they are planted in peat-based potting mixture; once every four weeks if in a soil-based mixture.

Potting and repotting Use either a peat-based potting mixture or a combination of half leaf mold, half soil-based mixture (see page 429).

P. rotundifolia is not deep-rooted and should be potted in a shallow pan or half-pot, but *P. viridis* and its varieties need full-size pots. Move plants into pots one size larger only when their roots fill the current pot (see page 426). When maximum convenient pot size (probably 6–8 inches) has been reached, either divide the fern for propagation or trim away some of the outside roots and replace the plant in its pot, which has been cleaned and filled with fresh mixture. In repotting, place the rhizome horizontally just below the surface of the mixture. The best time for repotting is spring.

Propagation Propagate any oversize plants in spring. Cut the rhizome into segments, each with fronds and roots attached, and plant each segment in a 3-inch pot of either of the recommended potting mixtures.

New plants can also be grown from spores (see *FERNS,* page 208).

Pellionia

URTICACEAE

P. daveauana

INDOOR pellionias, which are all creepers with attractively patterned, multicolored leaves, are particularly useful for covering the surface of the potting mixture in which taller plants are growing and for hiding the edges of troughs and similar containers. Their trailing stems also show to good advantage in hanging baskets. As the

A creeping pellionia does not necessarily need other plants to offset it; in this hanging basket, the green foliage and purple stems create their own contrast.

stems grow, they root down wherever a node meets the potting mixture. The leaves of the two species commonly grown as house plants are variable in shape, but are always arranged in two ranks, one leaf beyond the other on either side of the stem. Pinhead-size, dull-green flowers are grouped together in dense clusters on short flower stalks near the base of these creeping plants.

RECOMMENDED PELLIONIAS

P. daveauana has pinkish stems capable of growing more than 2 feet long, which carry 1½- to 2½-inch-long leaves with very short leafstalks. Apart from having slightly jagged edges, leaves can vary a great deal in shape and color. They vary from roughly oblong to oval; and whereas some are almost entirely pale apple green, others are finely veined with darker green, still others have wide bronzy olive green borders, and some are almost black.

P. pulchra (rainbow vine or satin pellionia) has pale purple stems up to 18 inches long, and 1½-inch-long leaves more nearly uniform than those of *P. daveauana*. Leaf shape is generally oval, and color is deep emerald green, with broad, almost black vein areas and light purple undersides. The very short leafstalks are often hidden by small, pointed bracts that are only ¼ inch long and wide.

PROPER CARE

Light These plants like bright light. They should never be exposed to direct sunlight, but sunlight filtered through a translucent blind or curtain is beneficial.

Temperature Indoor pellionias like normal room temperatures. They cannot withstand temperatures below about 55°F.

Watering During the active growth period water plentifully as often as necessary to keep the potting mixture thoroughly moist, but never let the pot stand in water. During the rest period give only enough to keep the potting mixture from drying out.

Feeding Apply standard liquid fertilizer to these plants once every two weeks during the active growth period only.

Potting and repotting Use a soil-based potting mixture (see page 429), with the addition of up to one-third rough leaf mold or coarse peat moss. These plants will grow well in small pots or half-pots; in spring, however, if they have filled their pots with roots (see page 426), move them into pots one size larger. When planting pellionias in hanging baskets, use at least six plants for an 8-inch basket, and plant them close to the edges.

Propagation Tip cuttings 2–3 inches long will root if taken in spring or early summer, planted in a moistened mixture of equal parts peat moss and sand, sealed in a plastic bag, and kept for three to five weeks in a warm place where they get bright filtered light. When rooted, transfer the cuttings to pots containing the potting mixture recommended for mature plants; place one cutting in a 3-inch pot, or three cuttings around the edges of a 4- to 5-inch pot or half-pot.

Pellionias can also be propagated by a process similar to layering (see page 439)—a sure method and a relatively simple one.

Pentas

RUBIACEAE

Egyptian star cluster
P. lanceolata

THE only species of the small genus *Pentas* grown as a house plant is *P. lanceolata* (sometimes known as *P. carnea;* commonly called Egyptian star cluster). This soft-wooded, bushy shrub, which generally grows only 12–18 inches high when potted, is mainly winter-flowering, and the clusters of small, star-shaped flowers are extremely attractive. The much-branching, nearly upright stems carry lance-shaped, bright green, hairy leaves 3–4 inches long and up to 1 inch wide. The leaves, which have short leafstalks, are arranged in opposite pairs or whorls of three or more. Each little flower consists of a tubelike base about 1 inch long flaring out into a five-petaled "star" that measures no more than $\frac{1}{2}$ inch across. Groups of 20 or more such blooms, each borne on a short flower stalk, cluster together at the ends of stems and branches. The resultant nearly flat-topped flower head can be up to 4 inches across. Flower color is white, pink, lavender, or magenta. Of the few named varieties, perhaps the most familiar is *P.l.* 'Orchid Star,' which has lavender flowers. Although the normal flowering season is early fall to midwinter, some blooms can appear at other times as well.

PROPER CARE

Light Bright light, with at least four hours a day of direct sunlight, is essential throughout the year.

Temperature Pentases grow best in temperatures of 65°F or more, but they also do well in somewhat cooler conditions. Absolute minimum: 50°.

Watering Water actively growing plants moderately, enough each time to make the entire mixture moist, but allowing the top half-inch of the mixture to dry out before watering again. Pentases should be encouraged to have a six- to eight-week rest when the main flowering period is over. During this rest period give only enough water to prevent the potting mixture from completely drying out.

Feeding Apply standard liquid fertilizer every two weeks except during the late-winter rest period.

Potting and repotting Use a soil-based potting mixture (see page 429). Move plants into pots one size larger in the spring until they are three years old. Because plants tend to become straggly, replace them by newly rooted cuttings every two or three years.

Propagation Tip cuttings of non-flowering shoots will root at any time in spring or summer. Take a 2- to 3-inch-long cutting just below a leaf, strip away the lower leaves, dip the cut end in a hormone rooting powder, and plant the cutting in a 3-inch pot filled with a moistened equal-parts mixture of peat moss and coarse sand or perlite. Enclose the potted cutting in a plastic bag or propagating case (see page 443), and stand it in bright filtered light. When rooting occurs—normally in three to four weeks—uncover the new plant and begin to water and feed it as if it were fully grown, but do not expose it to direct sunlight. After a further four weeks move the plant into a 4-inch pot of standard mixture and treat as mature.

Peperomia

PIPERACEAE

MORE than a dozen species and varieties of peperomia are in common use as house plants. The usually low-growing foliage of these plants is diverse in size, shape, color, and texture. The odd-shaped flowers, however, are generally immediately recognizable (though times and frequency of flowering vary). Most types produce a long, thin, white or cream-colored flower spike.

Here, the random markings on leaves of P. obtusifolia *'Variegata' offset the regular banding of* P. argyreia *and the corrugated texture of* P. caperata.

RECOMMENDED PEPEROMIAS

P. argyreia (formerly known as *P. sandersii*; commonly called watermelon peperomia) has thick, smooth, leaves up to 4 inches long and 3 inches across. They are nearly round, but taper to a point at the end. Prominent alternate bands of silver and darker green, which radiate outward from the off-center point at which each green leaf joins its stalk, give the leaf a heart-shaped look. The dark banding follows the principal leaf veins. Leafstalks are red, and the 3- or 4-inch flower spikes are white. Overall height (including the flower spike): no more than 1 foot.

P. caperata has heart-shaped, dark green leaves up to $1\frac{1}{2}$ inches long with a corrugated surface; the green looks almost black in the base of the corrugations. Leafstalks are red or pink; white flower spikes of varying lengths may be produced throughout summer and fall. The plant does not normally grow above 10 inches high. Of the several varieties, the most

P. caperata

common are *P.c.* 'Emerald Ripple,' a shorter plant, with smaller, waxy leaves in a denser cluster; *P.c.* 'Little Fantasy,' a dwarf form; and *P.c.* 'Variegata' (also known as *P.c.* 'Tricolor'), which has smaller leaves that have broad white borders.

P. fraseri (also known as *P. resediflora*) has untypical fluffy, scented flowers on flower spikes as much as 2 feet tall. Small (1 inch across), heart-shaped leaves with red undersides are arranged in widely spread whorls of up to six along slender stems.

P. glabella has fleshy, medium green, almost oval leaves 1½ inches long on slender pink stems. The plant may either sprawl or grow upright but its height rarely exceeds 6 inches. Its thin, greenish flower spikes are 3–6 inches tall. There is a branching variegated form, *P.g.* 'Variegata,' with white-margined leaves.

P. griseoargentea (also known as *P. hederifolia*; commonly called ivy or silverleaf peperomia) has metallic-looking, slightly quilted, shield-shaped leaves 2½ inches across. They are gray-green with a silvery shimmer, darker veins and pink stalks. The plant grows to a height of 6 inches. Greenish white flower spikes on reddish stems are 8–10 inches tall. *P.g.* 'Nigra' differs in that its vein channels are of a much darker green.

P. magnoliifolia (formerly called *P. tithymaloides*) is a robust plant with glossy, 6-inch-long, dark green, oval leaves. Flower spikes are seldom produced. After growing 12 inches tall, the stems may flop over and crawl across the surface of the potting mixture. A variegated form, *P.m.* 'Variegata,' has red-spotted stems, and half the leaf area is yellow-green.

P. obtusifolia (baby rubber plant) has long stems and fleshy, glossy, rounded but blunt-ended leaves 3–4 inches long. Leaf color is a deep purplish green, and the stems are slightly purple. Maximum height is about 1 foot. White flower spikes only 2–3 inches long appear between late spring and early fall. Among the several variegated forms: *P.o.* 'Alba,' with pale lemon yellow new leaves, deepening in color as they age; *P.o.* 'Albo-marginata,' with silvery white borders on a gray-green leaf; *P.o.* 'Variegata' and *P.o.* 'Greengold,' both with patches of cream or yellow on a green-gray ground. There are also dwarf forms, such as the compact *P.o.* 'Minima,' with leaves 1½ inches long.

P. orba itself is rarely seen, but it has given rise to several attractive dwarf varieties. The most popular is *P.o.* 'Astrid' (also known as *P.o.* 'Princess Astrid'), a bushy, branching plant with red-spotted stems and spoon-shaped, light green leaves. The leaves are covered with very fine hairs, are 1½

1 *P. argyreia* (watermelon peperomia) 2 *P. griseoargentea* (ivy peperomia) 3 *P. scandens* 'Variegata' 4 *P. verticillata* 5 *P. magnoliifolia* 'Variegata' 6 *P. obtusifolia* (baby rubber plant)

to 2 inches long, and have 1-inch-long stalks. Creamy white flower spikes appear occasionally.

P. scandens (also known as *P. serpens*) is never commercially available, but a variegated form, *P.s.* 'Variegata,' has become popular. This climbing or trailing plant, which can grow several feet long, has pointed, heart-shaped leaves about 2 inches long; most of the leaf surface is shiny and pale yellow when young, but gradually becomes green-centered with creamy margins. Leafstalks are 1 inch long and light pink. In cultivation, flowers do not normally appear.

P. verticillata can grow over a foot tall. It has 2-inch-long, sharply-pointed, slightly shiny leaves in whorls of three to five, with up to 3-inch gaps between the whorls. Extremely slender and cream-colored flower spikes 6 inches long appear at the ends of long stems.

PROPER CARE

Light Green-leaved peperomias need to be shaded from the hot sun during the sunniest months, but those with variegated foliage like a few hours of sunshine every day. Therefore these plants should be positioned so that they are quite close to a bright window, especially in winter.

Temperature Peperomias thrive in normal room temperatures. Even when not actively growing, they must have a temperature of at least 55°F. But although they look succulent, they are not desert plants; to develop to best advantage, they need high humidity during the growing season. In very warm rooms the plants will lose many of their leaves unless stood on trays of moist pebbles or in larger pots of damp peat moss.

Watering The easiest way to kill peperomias is to overwater them. Too much water, even for a short period, will result in considerable leaf loss and may even bring on complete collapse of the plants. Water only when clearly needed—and then very sparingly. Allow the potting mixture to dry out almost completely between waterings. The thick, fleshy leaves of most of these plants enable them to withstand short periods of drought. If at any time the leaves look unusually transparent, this probably indicates that the plant is in need of water.

Feeding From mid-spring to fall only, apply standard liquid fertilizer once a month at half strength. Too much feeding will result in soft, untypical growth, and eventually the plant is likely to collapse.

Potting and repotting Peperomias are best grown in a peat-based potting mixture. Because they have little root, they do well in small pots, half-pots, shallow pans, bowls, and hanging baskets. Young plants may need to be moved into pots one size larger in the spring. Mature plants in 4- or 5-inch pots are unlikely to need repotting. All pots should have a $\frac{3}{4}$-inch layer of clay-pot fragments in the bottom for adequate drainage.

Propagation All types can be propagated from 2- to 3-inch-long tip cuttings. Take cuttings in spring or early summer, and insert several together in 2- to 3-inch pots containing a barely moist equal-parts mixture of peat moss and coarse sand or perlite. Keep the potted cuttings at a temperature of about 65°F in bright light but out of direct sunlight, and water them very sparingly.

Leaf as well as tip cuttings can be used for propagating *P. argyreia, P. caperata* and its forms, and *P. griseoargentea*. Young but fully developed leaves should be used. Even parts of a leaf of *P. argyreia* can be rooted (it can be cut into quarters and the cut edges placed in contact with a rooting medium). However, the whole leaf blade with a 1-inch-long stalk attached is much more likely to root successfully. Insert the stalk in a 2-inch pot of slightly moist rooting mixture and push it down just to the point where leaf blade joins stalk. Water the potted leaf sparingly until it is rooted, just moistening the mixture when it has almost dried out.

Tip cuttings are likely to root in four to six weeks. Leaf cuttings may take a little longer. Move rooted tip and leaf cuttings into larger pots only when they have completely filled their pots with roots and clearly need more space. It is normally most effective to put several rooted cuttings in a single pot or hanging basket.

Using leaves for propagation

When the stalks of certain peperomia leaves are inserted in rooting mixture, tiny replicas of the parent plant will appear and can be detached for propagation.

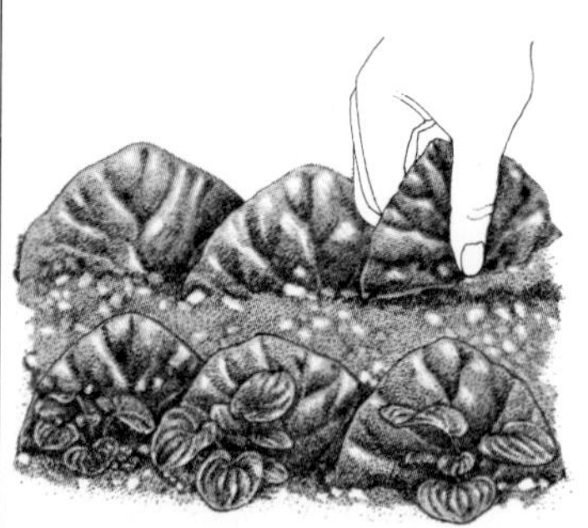

P. argyreia *can also be propagated from cut sections of the leaf blade that have been implanted vertically in rooting mixture.*

Special points Occasional pinching out of growing points during spring and summer will induce plants to produce more sideshoots and become bushier; trailing kinds can be cut back in spring when necessary. However, too much nipping out of growing points reduces the likelihood of many flowers being produced.

Pfeiffera
CACTACEAE

P. ianothele

THE only species of pfeiffera commonly grown as a house plant is *P. ianothele,* a jungle cactus with slender, pendent, pale green stems, that branch profusely from the base. The stems can grow to about 18 inches long and $\frac{3}{4}$ inch wide. Each stem has four prominent, narrow ribs, with deep, broad indentations in between. Reddish areoles on the ribs carry six or seven thin, brownish spines about $\frac{1}{4}$ inch long. During the summer pinkish white, cup-shaped flowers about 1 inch across are produced along the length of the stems. Each bloom lasts for several days and is followed by a plump red berry about $\frac{1}{2}$ inch in diameter. Since areoles that have flowered once can never do so again, a stem that flowers well one year is unlikely to produce many flowers for another year or two, until it has lengthened enough to bear a number of new areoles. If such stems are used as cuttings for propagation, however, they will quickly elongate and flower profusely.

See also CACTI.

P. ianothele (flowers)

PROPER CARE

Light These jungle cacti need bright light, but without strong sunlight. An ideal position is one that gets early morning sun but is protected from full sunlight during the rest of the day. *P. ianothele* will do best if kept outdoors in spring and summer. Place it in a partially shaded position.

Temperature Normal room temperatures are suitable throughout the year. In winter pfeifferas tend to rest, or at least to grow only slowly, but they do not require low temperatures during the rest period.

Watering During the active growth period water plentifully, enough to keep the potting mixture thoroughly moist; as soon as the surface of the mixture looks dry, give more water. During the winter rest period allow the top inch of the mixture to dry out between waterings.

Feeding Apply a high-potash, tomato-type fertilizer every two weeks to actively growing plants.

Potting and repotting Plant pfeifferas in either soil- or peat-based potting mixture (see page 429), but it should be made more porous by the addition of one part of coarse sand or perlite to every three of the standard mixture. Use pots or baskets large enough to provide a half-inch space between the root mass and the sides of the container. Examine the roots every spring and if they are crowded, move the plant into a container one size larger. A 4- or 5-inch pot should be the biggest needed. If the roots are not crowded, gently remove as much of the old potting mixture as possible, and replace the plant in its old container, which has been thoroughly cleaned and filled with fresh mixture.

Pfeifferas look particularly attractive when planted in a hanging basket. If grown as an upright specimen, the plant must be supported by sticks inserted into the potting mixture.

Propagation The berries that follow the flowers on a pfeiffera contain seeds in a juicy pulp. In late summer or early fall, when the berries are ripe, they split and can then be pulled off the plant for propagation purposes. To harvest the seeds, squeeze them onto a sheet of blotting paper, where the pulp will dry out in a few days. Rub the seeds clean, and store them in an envelope for sowing the following spring. Young plants will develop very quickly from seed. (For raising cacti from seed see page 119.)

In order to have a plant that will reach flowering size more quickly, take 4-inch-long stem cuttings in spring or summer, and allow each to dry for a day before inserting it $\frac{1}{2}$ inch deep in a 2-inch pot of the mixture recommended for adult plants. Give cuttings only enough water to make the mixture barely moist, and do not feed them. Otherwise, treat them as mature pfeifferas. Begin the normal watering and feeding program as soon as fresh growth appears (probably in about three weeks).

When cutting up a long stem, remember to mark the top or bottom of each piece. If cuttings are inadvertently planted the wrong way up, they will root, but the resultant plants are unlikely to develop normally.

Special points Containers of plants kept outdoors in spring and summer are best suspended from branches of trees. Beware of slugs if the containers are placed on the ground.

Phalaenopsis

ORCHIDACEAE

Moth orchid
Phalaenopsis hybrid

PLANTS of the genus *Phalaenopsis* (moth orchids) are mainly single-stemmed epiphytes. The thick, upright stem up to 3 inches high carries wide, fleshy, alternate leaves that are limp. Some aerial roots are produced on the stem among the lower leaves. Similar roots cover the mixture.

Arching flower stalks that rise from the leaf axils can be 3 feet long, with branches 10 inches long. Stalks bear up to 30 pansylike flowers in an inflorescence resembling a flight of moths. Flowering occurs at any time and each flower lasts up to 3 weeks.

In addition to the species named below there are many hybrids with superior flowers.

See also ORCHIDS.

RECOMMENDED PHALAENOPSISES

P. amabilis has leaves up to 12 inches long and 4 inches wide, which are dark green with reddish undersides. The flower stalks carry 20 to 30 flowers, each 4 inches across. Flowers are white, but the lip is spotted red, with a yellow flush in the throat.

P. schillerana has leaves about 18 inches long and 3 inches wide, which are dark green mottled with silver-gray and reddish purple underneath. Flower stalks carry up to 30 blooms, each $2\frac{1}{2}$ inches across. Sepals and petals are pale pink with reddish brown spots on the two lower sepals. The throat of the pink lip is yellow with reddish brown markings.

P. stuartiana has gray-green silver-mottled leaves up to 15 inches long and 3 inches wide. Flower stalks carry up to 20 flowers, each about 2 inches across. Sepals and petals are white, but this is heavily speckled with reddish purple on the bottom half of the lower sepals. The lip is yellow with purplish red spots, and the throat is pink.

PROPER CARE

Light Give these plants bright filtered light throughout the year. During the short-day winter months some supplementary artificial light (see page 446) will encourage flowering.

Temperature A minimum temperature of 68°F throughout the year is essential, along with high humidity. Stand plants on trays of moist pebbles, and mist-spray daily.

Watering Water plants moderately, allowing the top half-inch of the mixture to dry out between waterings. It is best to water in the morning (see "Special points," below).

Feeding Apply standard liquid fertilizer every two weeks or a foliar feed with every third or fourth watering.

Potting and repotting Use osmunda, bark (see page 289), or peat-based mixture. For good drainage put a $1\frac{1}{2}$-inch-deep layer of clay-pot fragments in the bottom of pots. These orchids do well in wooden or wire baskets lined with sphagnum moss. Every two years move plants into slightly larger containers.

After removing a plant from its container, clear the old mixture from the roots and cut away any dead roots before repotting. Plants in maximum-size pots should be replanted in fresh mixture once every two years. Immediately after repotting, move plants into a shaded position for three or four weeks. Repot at any time that plants are not in flower.

Propagation Phalaenopsises can produce shoots at the base, or in the joints of branches of flower stems after the season's flowers have died. Leave growths on the plant until their roots are at least 1 inch long. They can then be carefully cut away and planted individually in 3-inch pots of the recommended potting mixture. Keep each potted cutting in a warm room in bright filtered light, and water sparingly for the first six weeks. Thereafter, treat it as a mature plant.

Special points To extend the flowering period, cut back flower stems after flowers fade to just below the point where the earliest flowers appeared. New blooms will appear on side-shoots growing from this point.

Never permit beads of moisture to rest on phalaenopsis leaves. These orchids are susceptible to rot and fungus infection, and black spots will appear on the foliage if moisture remains on them throughout a single night.

Philodendron

ARACEAE

PHILODENDRONS (tree lovers) belong to a large genus of mostly climbing plants prized for their striking, leathery leaves. Flowers are rarely produced in potted specimens and are relatively insignificant when they do appear. In the wild the stems of most species grow up the trunks and branches of trees by sending out aerial roots at each leaf node; the roots attach themselves to the surface of the bark. These aerial roots can take up nutrients, but the main source of food for philodendrons is the soil and is taken up by the roots that penetrate it. Indoors, climbing species can reach a height of 6–8 feet when they are trained up stakes or moss-covered poles (see "Special points," below). Some of the smaller-leaved kinds, however, are often grown as trailers. The few species that do not climb form an upright stem that rarely grows more than 6 inches tall. This short, usually stout stem carries a loosely arranged rosette of leaves.

The leaves of different species of philodendron vary considerably. They may be heart-, lance-, arrow-, or spatula-shaped. They may be smooth-edged, slightly indented, or so deeply lobed that they appear to be divided into leaflets. Many look entirely different in shape and size when the plant is mature from the way they looked when the plant was young. This last characteristic should be borne in mind when the amateur gardener is buying a philodendron. Young plants sold as distinct species can disappoint by growing into familiar ones. Leaf color is normally glossy green, sometimes with some red coloring on the underside, occasionally with a reddish tinge across the whole leaf surface. The leafstalks are between 2 inches and 2 feet long.

RECOMMENDED PHILODENDRONS

P. angustisectum (also known as *P. elegans*) has climbing stems that can grow 4–6 feet tall indoors when supported on a stake. The leaves are broadly oval, 15 inches long and 12 inches wide, and deeply cut into many narrow, dark green, fingerlike segments, often little more than 1 inch wide. The leafstalks are about 12 inches long.

P. bipennifolium, commonly called panda plant, fiddle-leaf, or horsehead philodendron, is a climbing plant that can rapidly grow to 6 feet tall. Leaves on young plants are somewhat heart-shaped. As a plant ages, however, its leaves become roughly fiddle-shaped (narrowed in the middle, like a violin), but with a pointed tip and two pronounced lobes at the stalk end. These leathery, pale olive green leaves are up to 15 inches long and 8 inches wide on 12-inch-long stalks. Plants of this species need to be supported by stout stakes.

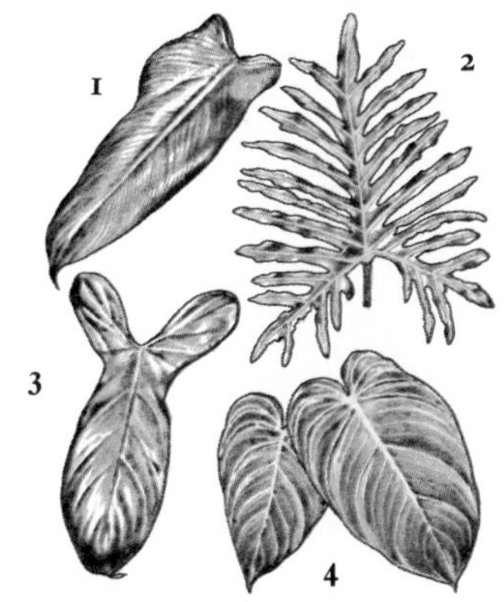

1 *P. wendlandii* **2** *P. bipinnatifidum*
3 *P. bipennifolium* (panda plant)
4 *P. melanochrysum* (black-gold philodendron)

P. bipinnatifidum is a large non-climbing species that can attain a height of 4 feet in a pot. The roughly arrow-shaped, dark green leaves are 15 inches long and 15 inches wide with 12- to 15-inch-long leafstalks arranged in a loose rosette radiating from the central crown. The leaves are so deeply incised that they appear to be cut into separate leaflets, but they are not; the cut goes almost—but not all the way—to the midrib. The plant eventually produces a short, thick, trunklike stem. Leaves of young plants are more nearly heart- than arrow-shaped, and their edges are only slightly indented, giving no indication of the deep marginal serration typical of the leaves in mature plants.

P. 'Burgundy' is a hybrid of mixed parentage. It climbs much more slowly than most—no more than 3–6 inches a year—and seldom requires the support of anything bigger than a short stake. Its spread exceeds its height because the closely spaced leaves are held upright on 12-inch-long, horizontal leafstalks. The stalks, as well as the stout stems that bear them, are red. The lance-shaped, 12-inch-long, 4-inch-wide leaves are olive green on the upper surface and deep burgundy red on the underside. For their first few weeks, however, new leaves are bright red.

P. erubescens (redleaf or blushing philodendron) is a strong climber that grows over 6 feet tall when well staked. The leaves are arrow-shaped, 10 inches long, and 7 inches wide, with shiny, dark green upper surfaces and coppery undersides. The 10-inch-long leafstalks as well as the central stems are reddish purple.

P. imbe can attain a height of 8 feet in only a few years if supported by strong stakes. The thin but firm-textured leaves are heart-shaped, 10 inches long, 5 inches wide, and mid-green. They are borne on 12-inch-long leafstalks, which extend horizontally from the stems, so that the plant has a layered appearance. In some forms of this species the leafstalks and undersides of leaves are faintly tinged with red.

P. melanochrysum (often called *P. andreanum*; popularly known as black-gold philodendron) is a slow-growing climber that can attain a height of 6 feet. Its leaves are heart-shaped when the plant is young, but they lose their curves and become elongated as the plant ages. The upper surface of the leaves, which can grow 2 feet long and 9 inches wide, is a velvety, blackish green, with prominent pale green vein areas. The leaves hang down from 18-inch-long leafstalks that are held in a semi-upright position. This species needs to be attached to a moist, moss-covered stake in order to show to best advantage.

P. pedatum (sometimes called *P. laciniatum)* climbs so slowly that a 4-foot stake will normally support it until it is several years old. Its shiny, mid-green leaves are about 10 inches long and 7 inches wide and are carried on 10-inch-long leafstalks. Each leaf is basically divided into five lobes. The lobe at the leaf tip is spear-shaped, and the four other lobes may themselves be double-lobed.

P. scandens (heartleaf philodendron) is the most popular small-leaved climbing philodendron, and one of the easiest of all house plants to grow. Its slender stems carry heart-shaped leaves 4 inches long and 3 inches wide with 2- to 3-inch-long leafstalks. The leaves, which have acutely pointed

Philodendron
continued

P. 'Burgundy'

Heartleaf philodendron
P. scandens

P. selloum

tips, look slightly bronzish and almost transparent when they are new, but they quickly become deep green as they grow to maturity. This plant can be grown as a climbing or trailing specimen, depending on whether its long stems are trained up supports or are allowed to trail over the rims of pots or hanging baskets. Experienced growers recommend regular pinching out of the growing tips in order to make *P. scandens* bushy. Otherwise, the stems tend to grow too long, giving the plant a skimpy look.

P. selloum does not climb. It forms a rosette of leaves that eventually rise from a short, thick, trunklike stem. The 12- to 18-inch-long, 12-inch-wide leaves have arching, 18- to 24-inch-long stalks. This species is very similar in appearance to *P. bipinnatifidum*, except that the leaves are smaller and less incised.

P. wendlandii is a non-climbing species with a rosette of 12- to 18-inch-long, lance-shaped leaves with 6- to 9-inch-long leafstalks. Each glossy, dark green leaf has a prominent midrib, which widens from a thin, raised line at the tip of the leaf to a 1-inch-wide bar at the base.

PROPER CARE

Light Grow philodendrons in bright filtered light, but out of direct sunlight. Although they will survive in poor light, the stems will elongate unnaturally, and the plants will lack their characteristic close growth and striking leaf color.

Temperature Normal room temperatures are suitable. Philodendrons cannot tolerate temperatures below about 55°F.

Watering During the active growth period water moderately, giving enough at each watering to moisten the potting mixture throughout, and allowing the top half-inch of the potting mixture to dry out between waterings. During the short midwinter rest period water only enough to keep the entire mixture from drying out completely.

Feeding Throughout the months while philodendrons are actively growing apply standard liquid fertilizer once every two weeks.

Potting and repotting Use a combination of half soil-based potting mixture (see page 429) and half leaf mold or coarse peat moss. Move philodendrons into containers one size larger only when their roots have completely filled the current ones (see page 426). Do this at any time of year except during the short rest period. After the maximum convenient pot size (probably 10 or 12 inches) has been reached, an annual spring topdressing with fresh potting mixture (see page 428) will help keep these plants healthy.

The best type of container for big specimens of the three large-leaved, non-climbing philodendrons—*P. bipinnatifidum*, *P. selloum*, and *P. wendlandii*—is a small tub 12–15 inches across. Such tubs have a broader, firmer base and less height than the standard pots. Plants that are grown in them are far less likely to become dangerously top-heavy than those philodendrons that are grown in the standard containers.

Propagation To propagate climbing philodendrons, use 3- to 4-inch-long tip cuttings taken in late spring or early summer. Take each cutting immediately below a node, remove the lower leaf or leaves, and plant the cutting in an equal-parts mixture of moistened peat moss and coarse sand or perlite. Plant three or four small-leaved cuttings together in a 3-inch pot, larger-leaved cuttings singly in 4- to 6-inch pots. Enclose the potted cutting (or group of cuttings) in a plastic bag or propagating case (see page 443), and stand it in bright filtered light at normal room temperature. Rooting should occur in three to four weeks. When renewed growth indicates that the new roots are well developed, remove the pot from the bag or case and begin to water sparingly (just enough to make the potting mixture barely moist), and to apply monthly doses of standard liquid fertilizer. About three months after the start of the propagation process, move each singly potted cutting into a slightly larger pot of the recommended potting mixture for adult plants, and treat it as a mature philodendron. Move the several cuttings of small-leaved plants to a larger pot whenever necessary, but keep them together. This helps to produce a bushy plant.

Propagation by tip cuttings is easy for *P. scandens*, with its small-size leaves. It is more difficult for some of the larger-leaved climbers. In propagating the climbing species other than *P. scandens* be particularly careful to protect cuttings from rough handling during the root-developing period. Damage to roots at this stage can be fatal to the plants.

Non-climbing species of philodendron are best raised from fresh seed. Sow seeds $\frac{1}{2}$ inch deep in an appropriate rooting mixture in the spring, and keep the containers at a temperature of 80°–85°F. When the seedlings are 2 inches high, pot them up individually in 2- or 3-inch pots of the recommended potting mixture, and treat them in exactly the same way as mature plants. (For raising plants from seed, see page 441.)

Special points As indicated above, most climbing species of philodendron are usually tied to a stake or to several thin sticks inserted into the potting mixture for support. These plants are more attractive, however, if instead of being tied to the supportive structure they can be made to cling to it with their aerial roots. For this to happen they must be given a moist surface to cling to, since aerial roots will not grip dry wood. One way to achieve the desired effect is to tie sphagnum moss to a stake, building the moss up around the stake until it forms a 2- to 3-inch-thick covering over the full length of the stake above potting-mixture level. Alternatively, nail a piece of rough-textured cork-bark to the stake. The moss or the bark must then be sprayed with water at least once a day. Some initial tying-in may be necessary until the aerial roots get a firm hold on the support. Be sure to use moss- or bark-covered stakes that are tall enough to accommodate the eventual total growth of the plants. It is difficult to add height to supports as plants continue to grow.

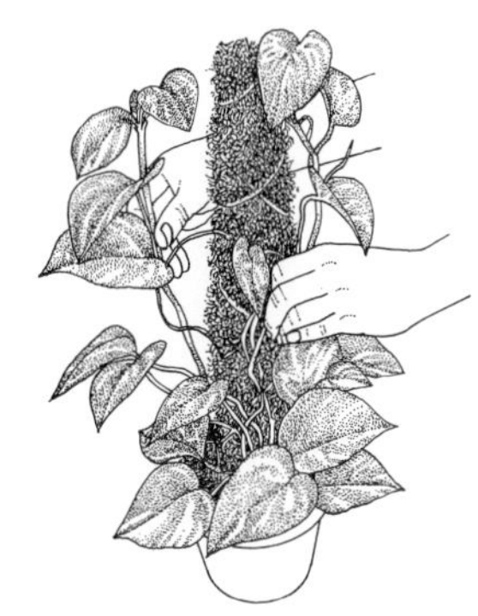

In the wild this plant would climb naturally with the help of its aerial roots, but house plants need some added assistance.

Phoenix

PALMAE

Canary date palm
P. canariensis

THE three species of the genus *Phoenix* commonly grown indoors are extremely decorative and comparatively slow-growing. Although they may eventually grow too big, this is unlikely to happen for many years. All species have durable pinnate fronds (fronds divided into many leaflets, or pinnae) arching outward and downward from a central rib. Most of these phoenixes have a stumpy, almost bulbous base. A brown thread connects the pinnae of each frond, but the thread drops away as the frond opens up. The pinnae are always partly folded or pinched together at the point where they join the leafstalk. Because flowers and fruit (dates) are not produced until a phoenix palm is quite old, indoor plants are unlikely to bloom.

Phoenix palms are variable plants, partly because of natural variations and partly because they hybridize freely. Many forms may be hybrids.

See also PALMS.

RECOMMENDED PHOENIXES

P. canariensis (Canary date palm) is the hardiest and most popular species. It has a husklike stem consisting of wide, emerald green leaf bases partly covered with brown, fibrous hair. The dark green fronds are finely divided, and their stalks are a paler green. The pinnae are quite stiff but not easily damaged. The many pinnae of each frond are all arranged in roughly herringbone fashion, some in opposite pairs, some not. The pinnae vary to a considerable degree in length, shorter ones near the base and tip of the frond and longer ones in the middle. This palm will grow 6 feet tall, with fronds up to 3 feet long, in a small tub. **P. dactylifera** (date palm) has blue-green fronds with long pinnae that are prickly but not spined, arching from a slender green stem. This plant grows quite a lot bigger and more swiftly than *P. canariensis,* but it is a less attractive plant.

P. dactylifera (date palm)

P. roebelenii (miniature date palm)

P. roebelenii (sometimes confused with *P. loureirii*) is popularly known as the miniature date palm. It has a thick crown of narrow, arching, dark green fronds, which are much finer than those of the other types and have a thin layer of white scales upon them. The short, slender stem eventually becomes roughened as old leaf bases accumulate along its length. Although the plant normally has only a single stem, it sometimes produces several. To maintain single-crowned plants which look better as pot specimens, remove surplus stems while they are still young. *P. roebelenii* rarely grows taller than 3 feet, but it can achieve a spread of as much as 4 feet, with 3-foot-long fronds.

PROPER CARE

Light *P. canariensis* and *P. dactylifera* like direct sunlight. *P. roebelenii* does best when kept in filtered light, but it will also thrive in full sunlight.

Temperature All these palms grow well in normally warm room temperatures, but they do best if they are encouraged to have a winter rest period at about 50°–55°F.

Watering Water sparingly, making the mixture barely moist during the rest period. When active growth begins, increase amounts of water gradually, and water plentifully during the active growth period, giving as much as necessary to keep the mixture thoroughly moist. Never allow pots to stand in water, however. As winter approaches, begin to reduce amounts gradually once more.

Feeding Apply standard liquid fertilizer to established plants once every two weeks during the active growth period only.

Potting and repotting Use a soil-based potting mixture (see page 429). Repot these palms in pots 2 inches larger every two or three years just as new growth starts in spring. One sign that a plant needs a bigger pot is the appearance of many fine roots on the surface of the potting mixture. In repotting, it is essential to pack the mixture down firmly, but be careful not to damage the thicker roots. Ten-inch and 12-inch pots are big enough for 4-foot-tall specimens; small tubs should be used for larger ones. Leave enough space between the mixture surface and the rim of the pot to take plenty of water. Once maximum convenient container size has been reached, an annual topdressing (see page 428) with an inch or two of fresh mixture will suffice.

Propagation Commercially, phoenix palms are raised from seed. This is a slow process, however, and is not recommended for amateur growers. Some indoor gardeners plant date stones. The stones germinate easily in spring if they are placed in a very warm position and kept moist, but the first leaf is a single undivided section, and it may take two or three years for leaves with divisions to appear. Set the stones individually in 3-inch pots or start them in seed boxes (see page 441). In the latter case, pot in 3-inch pots after they have germinated and have made about 2–3 inches of growth. Thereafter their cultivation needs will be those of mature phoenix palms.

If sucker shoots at the base of *P. roebelenii* are carefully detached, they should have some roots already formed, and such shoots can be used for propagation. Pot each shoot in a 3-inch pot of the standard potting mixture, place it in bright filtered light, and water it sparingly—just enough to keep the mixture barely moist. After new top growth indicates that the shoot is well rooted, treat the young plant in the same way as a mature phoenix palm.

Phyllitis

POLYPODIACEAE

ONLY one species of the genus *Phyllitis, P. scolopendrium* (hart's tongue fern), is commonly grown as a house plant. Tufts of fronds unfurl from an upright, branching rhizome that lies partly above, partly below the surface of the potting mixture. The rhizome, which is covered with light brown, furry scales, is usually hidden by the frond stalks. Depending on their age and growing conditions, the stalks are from 1 to 10 inches long, and their color is black at the base shading to green at the point where they become the midrib of the blade. Frond blades are straplike, pointed at the tip, lobed at the base, and medium green in color. In the wild each blade can grow 20 inches long and 5 inches wide, but in potted plants they are seldom more than half that size. The fronds grow erect at first, but arch over as they lengthen. Spore cases grow in a herringbone pattern on the back of most of them. The edges of blades can be undulate and sometimes frilled, and the tip of each blade can be either pointed or crested like a cockscomb. These differently shaped blades can all be present at one time on the same plant. In fact, it is this characteristic of *P. scolopendrium* that chiefly appeals to many indoor gardeners. In decorative groupings the shape of these ferns, along with their fresh coloring, makes an interesting contrast with flowering plants.

There are a number of varieties of *P. scolopendrium* with frond blade margins or tips that are non-variable in shape. *P.s.* 'Capitatum' has frond blades with undulating edges and heavily crested tips. The blades of *P.s.* 'Crispum' have deeply indented and greatly undulating or frilled edges (like an Elizabethan ruff) with a simple pointed tip. *P.s.* 'Crispum cristatum' has frond blades with crested tips as well as very frilled edges.

Phyllitises grow actively throughout the year under ideal conditions. Growth slows down, however, during the short-day winter months.

See also FERNS.

PROPER CARE

Light Medium light is best for these ferns throughout the year. They should never be subjected to direct sunlight, which will scorch the fronds.

Phyllitis scolopendrium 'Crispum'

Temperature Phyllitises grow well in normal room temperatures and can also tolerate temperatures down to 50°F. They need high humidity in warm positions. When the temperature rises above about 65°F, stand these ferns on trays of damp pebbles.

Watering Water moderately, giving enough at each watering to make the potting mixture moist throughout but allowing the top half-inch of the mixture to dry out before watering again. If room temperature is allowed to fall below 55°F for more than two or three days at a time, water more sparingly during this cool period, allowing a full half of the mixture to dry out between waterings.

Feeding Use half-strength standard liquid fertilizer. Frequency of feeding depends on the type of potting mixture. For plants that are potted in soil-based mixture monthly feedings are adequate. For those grown in peat-based mixtures apply fertilizer once every two weeks.

Potting and repotting Use either a peat-based mixture or one composed of half soil-based mixture (see page 429), half leaf mold. If a peat-based mixture is used, add a tablespoon of lime chips to each cupful of mixture in order to neutralize the acidity of the peat (see page 430). Repotting is necessary only when roots fill the pot (see page 426). When this happens, move plants into pots one size larger in spring. After maximum convenient pot size (probably 6–8 inches) has been reached, use the plants for propagation, or carefully cut away about one-third of the root ball and replace plants in the same size pots, adding fresh potting mixture at the same time. When repotting, always plant rhizomes vertically, with half of each rhizome below and half above the surface of the potting mixture.

Propagation Propagate old plants in spring by cutting off small branches of the main rhizome. Make sure that each cutting bears a tuft of fronds. Plant cuttings individually in 3-inch pots of one of the recommended potting mixtures, only half-burying each cutting. Place the potted cuttings in medium light at normal room temperature, and make the mixture barely moist throughout until new growth develops. Thereafter, treat the new plants as mature phyllitises.

These ferns may also be propagated from spores at any time of year (see *FERNS*, page 208).

Pilea

URTICACEAE

PILEAS are attractive foliage plants, some of which are creeping, others upright-growing. They tend to deteriorate as they age, either by becoming straggly or bare at the base, or by the inability of stems to support the growth. The creeping kinds look particularly effective when grown in shallow pans, where they can spread into large, fat cushion shapes. Those with textured and colored leaves contrast well with the foliage of other plants, with which they may be freely grouped together.

P. spruceana *'Norfolk' is a creeping plant that spreads rapidly over the surface of the mixture. For this reason it is well-suited to being grown in a shallow pan.*

RECOMMENDED PILEAS

P. cadierei (aluminum plant or watermelon pilea), the most popular species, is an extremely easy-to-grow, upright plant. After about a year, however, when it has reached a height of 10–12 inches, it may drop its lower leaves, leaving bare basal stems. Leaves are thin, up to 3 inches long, oblong-oval, and arranged in opposite pairs. Their edges are slightly incised, and the surface has four rows of raised silvery patches between the green vein areas. Tiny flowers may appear at any season but are scarcely noticeable. A dwarf variety, *P. c.* 'Minima,' is very similar but it has leaves about half as big as those of the type species, and it seldom grows to become any more than 6 inches in height.

P. involucrata (Pan-American friendship plant) has fleshy, deeply quilted leaves clustered in tight rosettes at the ends of 3- to 6-inch-long stems. Leaves are almost circular but pointed, of variable sizes ranging from 1–3 inches, and have scalloped edges; the dark green upper surfaces take on a coppery sheen in brightly lit positions, and the undersides are deep purple. Clusters of tiny pink flowers are produced in summer.

Watermelon plant
P. cadierei

The best form of *P. involucrata* is a plant usually sold as *P. mollis* (or, more popularly, *P.* 'Moon Valley'), which differs in that its leaves are puckered and have upper surfaces of a remarkably fresh green, with bronze coloring in the vein crevices. This is one of the most beautiful of all pileas.

P. microphylla (also called *P. muscosa*) is known as the artillery plant because of the explosive way in which, when the flowers are mature, it expels a cloud of pollen over an area of 3 feet or more. The fine medium green foliage is arranged in flattened sprays similar to the feathery fronds of ferns; individual leaf sections are $\frac{1}{4}$ inch long. Plants rarely exceed 10 inches in height. Inconspicuous greenish yellow flowers bloom throughout the summer. One form, *P. m.* 'Variegata,' has pink and white markings all over its tiny green leaves.

P. nummulariifolia (creeping charley) is a swift-growing, tiny-leaved creeping plant suitable for use in hanging baskets. Branches are thin and reddish. Leaves are pale green, quilted, almost circular, and $\frac{3}{4}$ inch across. Small, insignificant flowers are produced throughout the whole summer.

P. spruceana (which some authorities believe is the same species as *P. involucrata*) has several varieties, two of which are extremely popular. *P. s.* 'Norfolk' is a creeper with almost circular leaves ranging in size from $1\frac{1}{2}$ to 3 inches across, arranged in crosswise pairs that form tight rosettes. Each leaf is striped with silver and bronze; it takes on a deep copper hue in bright light or a bluish silver hue in shaded conditions. The plant branches often and, creeping quickly over the potting mixture, regularly roots down into it at the leaf nodes.

P. involucrata (Pan-American friendship plant)

P. spruceana 'Norfolk'

P. spruceana 'Silver Tree'

P. s. 'Silver Tree' is a short, upright-growing plant, with 3-inch-long, triangular, quilted leaves that have depressed vein areas; they are bronzish green, with a broad silver band running through the center. Plants sometimes sold as *P. s.* 'Bronze' or *P. s.* 'New Silver' seem to be identical with 'Silver Tree,' and so those names probably should not be used.

PROPER CARE

Light Pileas do well in semi-shade and can be grown at a short distance from a window in summer. Avoid very bright light—especially direct sunlight—at all times.

Temperature These tropical plants like a combination of heat and humidity. Pots should be stood on trays of moist pebbles. Pileas cannot tolerate temperatures below 55°F.

Watering Water sparingly, making the entire potting mixture barely moist but never letting the mixture get too wet. Let the top two-thirds of it dry out between waterings.

Feeding Apply standard liquid fertilizer once every two weeks, from mid-spring through summer only.

Potting and repotting Use either an equal-parts mixture of peat moss and soil-based potting mixture (see page 429) or a peat-based mixture. In the latter case, however, regular feeding during the spring and summer is not merely advisable but essential. Pileas do not have a large root system and will thrive in 3- to 4-inch pots or shallow pans. Because they deteriorate, they should not be moved on; it is better to restart from cuttings.

Propagation Propagate pileas in late spring. Take young tip cuttings up to 3 inches long, dip their cut ends in hormone rooting powder and insert each in a 2- to 3-inch pot of gritty rooting mixture (one part of coarse sand or perlite to two of peat moss). Each cutting will root in three to four weeks if placed in a warm, shady position and watered just enough to keep the mixture barely moist. When the cutting is well rooted, move it into the recommended potting mixture for pileas and treat it as a mature plant.

Special points The main shoots of these plants naturally divide into side branches, and dense growth is usually automatic. But it may be advisable to nip out over-long shoots sometimes, thus balancing growth and encouraging further division.

Piper

PIPERACEAE

P. crocatum

THE genus *Piper* (pepper) includes more than 1,000 species, among them *P. nigrum,* from which comes the familiar condiment. The pepper plant most commonly grown indoors is *P. crocatum*, a climbing or trailing vine that is prized for its colorful leaves. It is often grown upright and trained around three or four thin stakes, but it also makes an attractive display when permitted to trail down from a hanging basket.

Attaching P. crocatum *to three or four sticks inserted into the mixture will turn the plant from a trailer into a climber.*

P. crocatum has slender stems bearing pointed, heart-shaped leaves up to 5 inches long and 4 inches wide. The leaves have reddish, 1-inch-long leafstalks, which are attached not at the end of the leaf, but slightly toward the middle. Leaf surfaces are puckered. The upper surface is olive green heavily spotted with pinkish silver markings. The pink tinge is most pronounced wherever a marking occurs near main veins. Leaf undersides are unmarked deep maroon. The plant does not produce flowers when it is grown indoors.

PROPER CARE

Light Grow these plants in direct sunlight filtered through a translucent blind or curtain.

Temperature Pipers must have warmth (a minimum of 60°F), or they will shed most of their leaves. They do not flourish if subjected to fluctuating temperatures and dry air. Keep the temperature as constant as possible, and increase the humidity by standing pots on trays of moist pebbles. Mist-spray the foliage once a week. This plant is particularly suitable for growing in a large terrarium or special plant window (see page 53).

Watering Throughout the year water moderately, enough to make the potting mixture moist throughout, but allowing the top inch of the potting mixture to dry out before watering again.

Feeding Except in midwinter, feed plants every two weeks with standard liquid fertilizer. Pipers do not have a distinct rest period, but they grow less actively in winter.

Potting and repotting Use a soil-based potting mixture (see page 429). Pipers have small root systems and should not be planted in needlessly big pots. A 5- or 6-inch pot should be the biggest needed for a potted specimen. Move a plant into a pot one size larger only when it has made so much top growth that there is an obvious imbalance between top growth and pot size—a relatively dependable indication of the need for more root space. Repotting may be done at any time, as long as plants are actively growing. For the best effect in a hanging basket, plant two or three young pipers in an 8-inch basket, and replace them with fresh specimens every second year.

Propagation Propagate in late spring or early summer by stem cuttings 3–4 inches long. Trim each cutting just below a leaf, remove the bottom leaf, dip the cut end of the stem in hormone rooting powder, and plant it in a 2- or 3-inch pot of a moistened equal-parts mixture of peat moss and coarse sand. (Do not substitute perlite for the sand. Perlite retains too much moisture for these plants.) Place the cutting in a plastic bag or heated propagating case (see page 444), and stand it in bright filtered light at a temperature of about 75°F. When renewed growth shows that rooting has occurred—normally in four to six weeks—uncover the rooted cutting gradually over the course of about two weeks. The objective is to acclimatize the new plant to the less humid air outside the bag or propagating case. Water very sparingly until the plant has made some further top growth. It is probably best to wait for 10 or 12 weeks after the start of propagation before beginning to feed the plant. When roots have filled the pot, as indicated by two or three inches of top growth, move the young plant to a slightly larger pot of soil-based potting mixture, and begin to treat it as a mature piper. At this point, instead of repotting the plant singly, it can of course be planted along with others in a hanging basket.

Pisonia

NYCTAGINACEAE

Birdcatcher tree
P. umbellifera variegata

THE only pisonia that has become a familiar house plant is a variegated-leaved variety of *P. umbellifera* (which has also been called *Heimerliodendron brunonianum*) known as *P.u. variegata*. This much-branching shrub rarely exceeds a height of 3–4 feet when grown in a pot. The smooth, roughly oblong leaves are up to 15 inches long and 5 inches wide on leafstalks up to 2 inches long. Leaf color is deep green heavily marked with irregular patches of creamy yellow. Because of a sticky gum that coats the midribs of the leaves, pisonias are sometimes called birdcatcher trees. Flowers are not produced on plants grown indoors.

PROPER CARE

Light Provide bright light, with three to four hours a day of direct sunlight. Pisonia leaves lose their brilliant color if light is inadequate.

Temperature Normal room temperatures are suitable all year long. Pisonias cannot tolerate temperatures below 50°F.

Watering During the active growth period water moderately, enough to moisten the potting mixture at each watering, but allowing the top inch of the mixture to dry out before watering again. During the winter rest period give only enough to keep the mixture from drying out completely.

Feeding Apply standard liquid fertilizer every two weeks during the active growth period only.

Potting and repotting Use a soil-based potting mixture (see page 429). Move young plants into pots one size larger every spring until maximum convenient pot size (probably 8 to 10 inches) has been reached. Thereafter, topdress plants annually with fresh mixture (see page 428).

Propagation Propagate from tip cuttings 3–4 inches long taken in spring. Trim each cutting immediately below a node, dip the cut end in a hormone rooting powder, and plant it in a 3-inch pot containing a moistened equal-parts mixture of peat moss and coarse sand or perlite. Cover the whole with a plastic bag, or put it in a propagating case (see page 443), and stand it in bright filtered light. When new growth indicates that rooting has occurred (usually after four to six weeks), uncover the new plant, begin to water moderately, and start once-a-month applications of liquid fertilizer. After another five or six months, transfer the young pisonia to a 4-inch pot of standard potting mixture, and treat it as a mature plant.

Pittosporum

PITTOSPORACEAE

Australian laurel
P. tobira

PITTOSPORUMS are shrubs or small trees prized for their leathery, shiny leaves and sweetly scented summer flowers. The most decorative indoor species is *P. tobira* (Australian laurel or houseblooming mock orange), which rarely grows taller than 4–5 feet in a large pot or tub. It is a much-branching shrub with elliptic leaves arranged in whorls or loose rosettes on woody stems. Leaves are rounded at the tip but pointed at the end adjoining the leafstalk. They are up to 4 inches long and 1 inch across, and their edges roll back slightly toward the underside. Leafstalks are only $\frac{1}{4}$–$\frac{1}{2}$ inch long. The fragrant flowers are tubular, up to $\frac{1}{2}$ inch long, and white or pale yellow. They grow in flat-headed clusters up to 2 inches wide. There is also a variegated-leaved form, *P.t.* 'Variegata,' with white- or cream-colored markings along the leaf edges. Pittosporums make excellent plants for cool rooms and unheated porches.

PROPER CARE

Light Give pittosporums bright light, with at least three hours every day of direct sunlight.

Temperature Normal room temperatures are suitable except during midwinter, when plants should be rested at around 50°F, if possible.

Watering During the active growth period water plentifully as often as necessary to keep the potting mixture thoroughly moist, but never allow pots to stand in water. During the rest period give only enough water to keep the mixture from drying out.

Feeding Apply standard liquid fertilizer every two weeks during the active growth period only.

Potting and repotting Use a soil-based potting mixture (see page 429). Move plants into containers one size larger every spring until maximum convenient pot or tub size (probably 10 or 12 inches) is reached. Thereafter, topdress each spring (see page 428) with fresh mixture.

Propagation Propagate in late spring from tip cuttings 2–3 inches long taken from new growth. Trim each cutting immediately below a node, remove any lower leaves that might come into contact with the rooting mixture, and dip the cut end in a hormone rooting powder. Plant the prepared cutting in a 2- or 3-inch pot containing a moistened mixture of equal parts of peat moss and coarse sand or perlite. Enclose the whole in a plastic bag or propagating case (see page 443), and keep it in medium light. Cuttings will root in about six weeks. When new growth indicates that rooting has occurred, uncover the young plant, and begin to water sparingly, allowing the top two-thirds of the mixture to dry out between waterings. Acclimatize the plant to brighter light over a period of a week or two. When it has made 2–3 inches of new growth, start to feed the plant. And when its roots appear on the surface of the potting mixture, move it into a larger pot of standard mixture. Thereafter, treat it in the same way as a mature specimen.

Pittosporums can also be propagated from seed (see page 441).

Special points Occasional pruning is advisable. This is best done in spring. Cut away any overlong, unwanted shoots or thin, twiggy growths, making each cut immediately above a whorl or rosette of leaves.

Platycerium

POLYPODIACEAE

PLATYCERIUMS (often known as staghorn ferns) are epiphytic rainforest ferns that adapt well if gradually acclimatized to indoor conditions. They all have two kinds of frond. One, at the base of the plant, is shield-shaped and clasps the plant's support; the other is spreading or drooping, and forked like a stag's antlers, which gives the genus its common name.

The single flat frond is sterile (incapable of producing spores), and its main function in nature—apart from holding the plant to its support—is to trap debris that can be broken down into nutrients as it falls from the branches of the host tree. In time this frond becomes brown and papery, and a new green one forms in its place. More decorative are the fertile antler-shaped fronds, which are normally several in number, fleshy, and deep green overlaid with fine, white, felty scurf. When mature, they have brown spores arranged in dense clusters on their undersides, mainly concentrated at the tips of the fronds. The overlay of white scurf gives the fronds a silvery green appearance. All these plants do best when they are grown on pieces of rough bark or tree fern.

See also FERNS.

RECOMMENDED PLATYCERIUMS

P. bifurcatum (also known as *P. alcicorne*; commonly called antelope ears or elk's horn-fern) is much the easiest species to grow indoors. The single sterile frond is constantly being replaced, each new one appearing as a small silver spot on top of its predecessors and gradually spreading over the dry, brown, papery surface of the earlier ones. When young, the new "shield" is a soft peppermint green, which gradually turns brown. At first it clings tightly to the brown patch below it, but it unfurls for the last inch or two of its growth, and it is this upward-turning section that catches falling leaves and any other tree debris in the wild.

The fertile fronds develop from the center of the sterile one; they can extend up to 3 feet, with each of the terminal "antlers" as much as 9 inches long. These long fronds are often semi-erect, with the divided parts drooping a little. There are a number of different forms, with fronds of either a darker or lighter green and with longer or shorter end segments.

P. grande is bigger than *P. bifurcatum*, and the sterile fronds are of a paler green than those of *P. bifurcatum*. The fronds also tend to turn upward for a greater part of their length, to be undulate, and to divide at the ends. The fertile fronds may be up to 4 feet long, and they droop considerably. The overlay of felty scurf is less thick than that of *P. bifurcatum*.

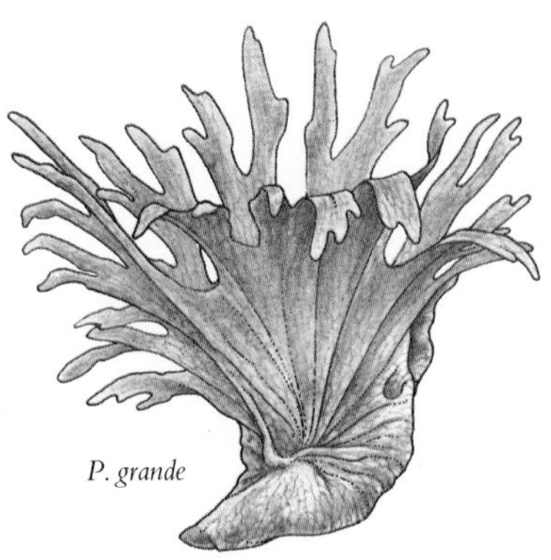
P. grande

PROPER CARE

Light In nature, platyceriums usually grow high up in the branches of trees; thus, they thrive in bright light. Strong direct sunlight, however, will rob the fronds of much of their color and may cause unsightly marking.

Temperature Platyceriums like temperatures up to 75°F as long as humidity is kept high. Plants should be mist-sprayed once a day when they are grown in warm rooms. An ideal summer temperature is about 70°, the winter minimum about 55°. Airy, well-ventilated situations suit these plants best. For this reason it is advisable to grow them suspended on pieces of bark or in hanging baskets.

Watering During the spring and summer give platyceriums enough water at every watering to make the potting mixture thoroughly moist, but allow the mixture to dry out almost completely before watering again. During the rest period water all these plants much more sparingly, giving only enough to make the mixture barely moist throughout. Because the "shield" frond often covers the surface of potting mixture, it may be virtually impossible to water some potted platyceriums from above. The way to solve this problem (and probably the best way to water all these plants, whether they are growing in

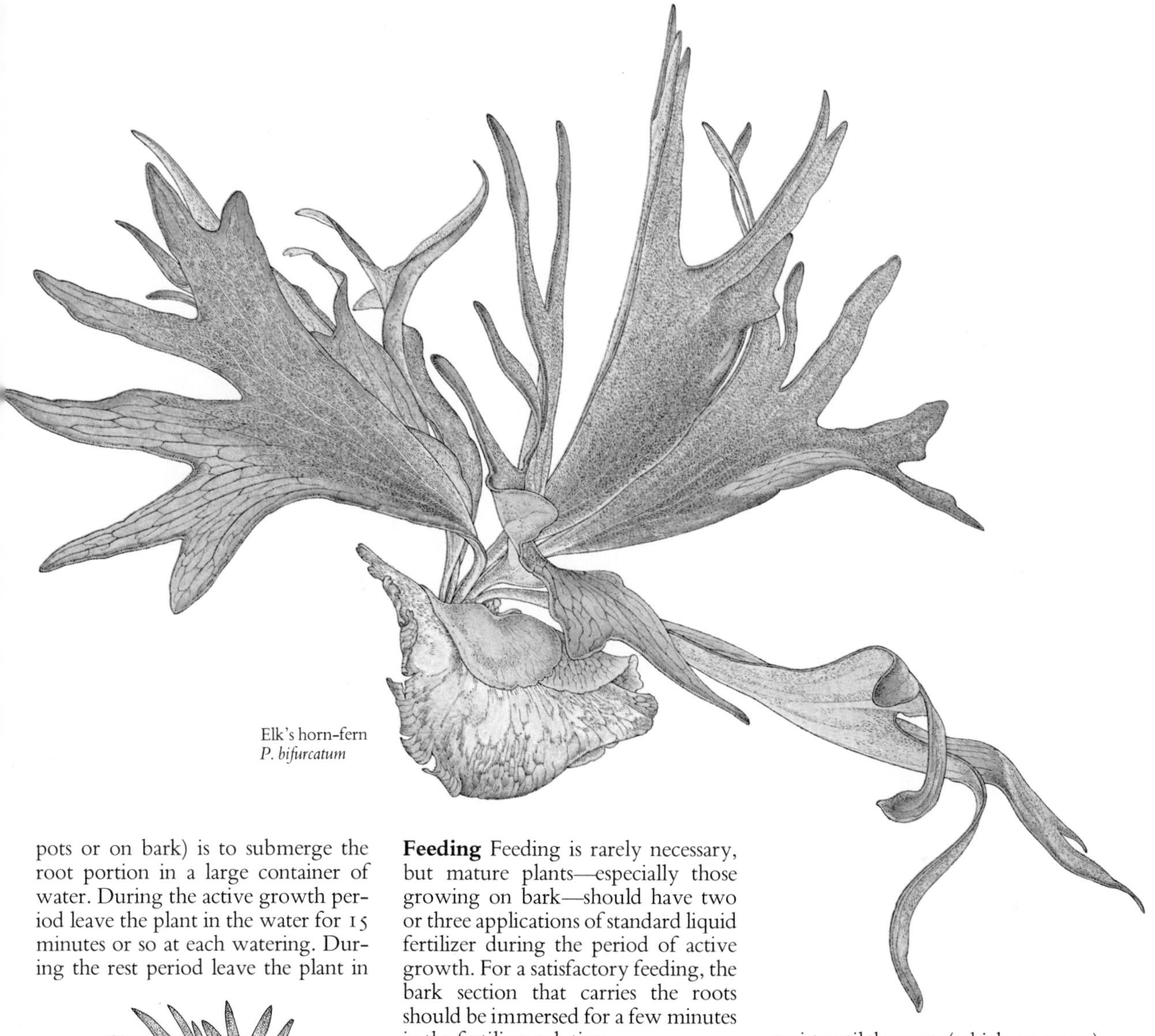

Elk's horn-fern
P. bifurcatum

pots or on bark) is to submerge the root portion in a large container of water. During the active growth period leave the plant in the water for 15 minutes or so at each watering. During the rest period leave the plant in

Because potted platyceriums can be difficult to water from above, it is best to submerge pots for a few minutes at a time whenever watering becomes necessary.

the water for no more than one or two minutes at a time. Whether the plant is growing actively or resting, do not soak it again until it is obviously in need of water, as indicated by abnormally droopy fronds or by an evident loss of weight of the plant.

Feeding Feeding is rarely necessary, but mature plants—especially those growing on bark—should have two or three applications of standard liquid fertilizer during the period of active growth. For a satisfactory feeding, the bark section that carries the roots should be immersed for a few minutes in the fertilizer solution.

Potting and repotting There are three ways to grow platyceriums. The most natural is to let them attach themselves to the rough and moist surface of a piece of bark or similar material; another way is to plant them in wooden hanging baskets; the least satisfactory way is to pot them. Plants are often sold growing on pieces of tree fern or bark. When sterile fronds of such plants have almost covered their backing, fasten the plant onto a larger piece of material, either tying or carefully nailing the two together.

To fasten a plant initially to bark wrap the small, spongy root mass in an equal-parts mixture of very coarse peat moss and sphagnum moss, and tie this bundle securely to the backing with strong cotton—*not* nylon—thread. Keep both bark and root mass moist until the roots (which are sparse) and the sterile frond have adhered to the support. Or plant the fern in a small, wooden, slatted hanging basket (like those used for orchids) filled with a similar mixture of peat and sphagnum moss. When established, the plant will grasp the slats firmly.

Platyceriums can be grown in pots only when small, since as they grow they wrap their supportive fronds around the pot, which must be broken to sever their hold. It becomes extremely difficult to move them into larger containers.

Propagation Propagation is usually from spores and is not practical in the home. Large plants occasionally develop more than one growing point, and a small side growth can be detached without harming the rest of the plant; this can be treated as a new

Tying a platycerium on bark

Wrap the spongy root ball in a moist mixture of equal parts of peat moss and sphagnum moss.

Using strong cotton thread, tie the moss-wrapped root ball firmly to a piece of rough bark.

Keep both bark and root ball moist. The roots and shield-shaped frond will eventually grip the bark.

young specimen on bark or in a basket. More often, however, old plants are broken up into several separate sections, but the breaking-up process may cause considerable damage to some sections.

Special points Platyceriums are not often troubled with pests, but scale insects (see page 455) sometimes infest the underside of the fronds. They can be treated by applying denatured alcohol on a fine-tipped brush direct to each of the insects.

Clean the fronds by leaving them in gentle rain in mild weather or by mist-spraying them; wiping them with a cloth or sponge will remove the attractive felty scurf. Do not allow water to remain on the fronds.

Plectranthus

LABIATAE

Candle plant
P. oertendahlii

ALTHOUGH the genus *Plectranthus* includes both short-shrubby and creeping plants, it is largely the creeping species that have become popular house plants. They are especially attractive in hanging baskets, from which they trail down as much as 1½ to 2 feet. Most have soft, almost squared stems and soft, slightly furry leaves with shallowly scalloped edges; they emit a distinctive aromatic odor when touched. A plectranthus will root easily (at any point where a node touches the potting mixture), grow fast, and produce loose racemes of tiny, usually pale lavender flowers (similar to those of coleuses, to which these plants are closely related). The flowers are not particularly attractive and can be removed when they start to develop on the plant.

RECOMMENDED PLECTRANTHUSES

P. australis (Swedish ivy) has dark green, pointed-oval, 1½-inch-long leaves. Unlike most other popular species, this is an erect, bushy plant, which can grow 3 feet tall.

P. coleoides is rarely available, but a variegated form, *P.c.* 'Marginatus,' is popular. It grows erect at first, but later trails. Its 2- to 2½-inch-long, hairy, heart-shaped leaves have wide, creamy white margins.

P. nummularius, also a trailer, has plain green, fleshy, almost circular leaves up to 2½ inches across.

P. oertendahlii (candle plant), the most popular plectranthus, has 1-inch, almost circular, bronze-green, softly felted leaves that are strongly veined with a silvery net and have purple margins. The undersides of mature leaves are also purple.

P. coleoides 'Marginatus' — *P. australis* (Swedish ivy)

PROPER CARE

Light These plants like three to four hours of direct sunlight every day. If they have inadequate light, leaf color becomes poor, and the gaps between leaves widen.

Temperature Plectranthuses grow well in warm rooms; they will thrive in temperatures of about 60°–70°F. In greater heat they need increased humidity. Stand pots on trays or saucers of damp pebbles. In winter it is advisable to give these plants a rest under cool conditions (55°–58°).

Watering Water actively growing plants plentifully enough to keep the potting mixture thoroughly moist, but never allow pots to stand in water. Actively growing trailers (those producing long stems) need very regular watering—as often as once a day—particularly if they are being displayed in a hanging basket in a well-lit window. When plants are resting water sparingly, giving enough water to keep the potting mixture from drying out completely. Lower leaves dry up and fall if plants are allowed to dry out for more than a short time.

Feeding Apply standard liquid fertilizer every two weeks to actively growing plants. A well-fed plectranthus will produce large, lush foliage and strong stems.

Potting and repotting Use a soil-based potting mixture (see page 429). Because plectranthuses are most attractive when young, repotting is rarely needed; old plants are best used for propagation.

Propagation Tip cuttings 2–3 inches long are easily rooted in the standard potting mixture at almost any time. Water them moderately and keep them in bright filtered light. Once rooting has occurred (as indicated by the appearance of new top growth), place three or four cuttings together in a hanging basket and they will soon develop into an attractive display of mature plants. Alternatively, plant cuttings singly in 3-inch pots of soil-based mixture.

In this hanging basket P. oertendahlii *is trained to grow up the cords as well as being allowed to trail. The flowering episcia adds an extra touch of color.*

Special points Remove the growing tips of all species of plectranthus regularly in order to encourage frequent branching and the development of bushy growth.

Pleomele

AGAVACEAE

Song of India
P. reflexa variegata

PLEOMELES are decorative foliage shrubs that should technically be included in the genus *Dracaena*. They are so widely known as pleomeles, however, that the name is being retained here. The only species regularly grown indoors is *P. reflexa* (correctly, *D. reflexa*), which has erect, $\frac{1}{4}$-inch-wide stems, each with a growing tip that leans at an angle of 45° from the vertical. The leaves, which grow in compact clusters, are lance-shaped, 5–9 inches long, and up to 1 inch wide. Those of the species are dark green, but in the popular variety *P.r. variegata* (song of India) they are medium green with lime green margins when young, turning light green with creamy yellow margins later on. As stems lengthen, lower leaves drop off; their weight causes the stems to topple unless tied to supporting sticks.

PROPER CARE

Light Give pleomeles bright light, but without direct sunlight.

Temperature Normally warm room temperatures are suitable. Minimum tolerable temperature: 55°F. Keep pots on trays of moist pebbles.

Watering Water moderately, enough to moisten the entire mixture, but letting the top half-inch dry out before watering again.

Feeding Apply standard liquid fertilizer every two weeks from early spring to fall.

Potting and repotting Use a soil-based potting mixture (see page 429) with the addition of a one-third portion of rough leaf mold or coarse peat moss. Move plants into pots one size larger in early spring. These plants grow best when lodged in pots that appear to be a size too small for them. After reaching maximum convenient size, topdress annually (see page 428).

Propagation Take a 4-inch-long tip cutting or basal shoot in early spring, remove its lower leaves, dip the cut end in hormone rooting powder, and plant it in a 3-inch pot of moistened equal-parts mixture of peat moss and coarse sand or perlite. Enclose the whole in a plastic bag or propagating case (see page 443), and keep it warm in bright filtered light. When roots are well developed, uncover the new plant, begin to water it sparingly, and apply liquid fertilizer every two weeks. About six months after beginning propagation, move the young plant into the recommended mixture, and treat it as a mature pleomele.

Plumbago

PLUMBAGINACEAE

Cape leadwort
P. auriculata

THE only species of the genus *Plumbago* grown indoors is *P. auriculata* (formerly *P. capensis;* commonly called Cape leadwort). The thin straggly stems of this shrubby plant can grow 4 feet long and need to be tied to supports. The short-stalked, elliptic, medium green leaves are up to 2 inches long and tend to curl downward. Terminal clusters of up to 20 flowers are produced from spring to fall. Each flower has a thin, $1\frac{1}{2}$-inch-long tube flaring into five pale blue petals, which form a 1-inch-wide disk. A thin, dark blue line runs down the center of each petal. There is a white-flowered variety, *P.a.* 'Alba.'

PROPER CARE

Light Give plumbagos full sunlight.

Temperature During the active growth period normal room temperatures are suitable. In winter keep plants at 45°–50°F, if possible.

Watering During the active growth period water plentifully, but never allow the pot to stand in water. During the rest period give only enough water to prevent the mixture from drying out completely.

Feeding Apply a high-potash liquid fertilizer every two weeks during the active growth period only.

Potting and repotting Use a soil-based potting mixture (see page 429). Move plants into pots one size larger in early spring. An 8-inch pot should be the largest size needed. Topdress annually once it has been reached.

Propagation Take 3- to 4-inch-long cuttings in spring or summer (use shoots that are neither soft and fleshy nor hard and woody). Insert each cutting in a 3-inch pot of moistened equal-parts mixture of peat moss and coarse sand or perlite, enclose the whole in a plastic bag or propagating case, and stand it in bright filtered light. When rooting has occurred, remove the covering, begin to water moderately (allowing the top half-inch of the mixture to dry out between waterings), and apply standard liquid fertilizer once a month. When the young plant is a foot high, nip out the growing tip to encourage branching, transfer the plant to a slightly larger pot of standard mixture, and treat it as a mature plumbago.

Special points Because flowers are produced only on current growth, prune plants every spring. Cut out weak growths and trim off two-thirds the length of the main stems. Shoots sprouting from old woody stems will produce the next crop of flowers.

Podocarpus

PODOCARPACEAE

PODOCARPUS *macrophyllus* (also called Buddhist pine or Japanese Yew) is the only species of this genus that is commonly grown as an indoor plant. It is a conifer that grows very big in the wild, but remains a shrub or small tree when grown in a pot or tub. The much-branching stems are upright, but the branches tend to droop a little as they lengthen. They carry flat leaves (which are really needles) $2\frac{1}{2}$–4 inches long and about $\frac{1}{4}$ inch wide, each with a well defined midrib. The leaves, which cluster together so closely that they half hide the stems, are pale green when plants are young, but darken to deep green. They are hard and not easily damaged. Some of them undulate slightly or curl under at the tips. Catkinlike flowers are not produced indoors.

PROPER CARE

Light This conifer does best in bright light filtered through a translucent blind or curtain, but it grows quite well if given some direct sunlight and some shade every day.

Temperature In normally warm room temperatures a podocarpus will grow almost continuously throughout the year. If winter indoor temperatures fall below about 55°F, the plant will take a short rest. Minimum tolerable temperature: 50°.

Watering Water actively growing plants moderately, enough at each watering to moisten the potting mixture throughout, but allowing the top half-inch of the potting mixture to dry out before watering again. During the rest period, if any, give only enough to keep the potting mixture from completely drying out.

Feeding Apply standard liquid fertilizer every two weeks while the plants are in active growth.

Potting and repotting Use a soil-based potting mixture (see page 429). Move plants into containers one size larger every spring until maximum convenient size (probably 10–12 inches) is reached. Podocarpuses should never be placed in over-large containers. They are sensitive to the airless, waterlogged conditions that often result. Repotting is only really necessary when plants have completely filled their pots with roots. Thereafter topdress (see page 428) annually with

Buddhist pine
P. macrophyllus

fresh mixture. A podocarpus can attain a height of 6 feet—rarely more—in a 10- or 12-inch pot or tub.

Propagation *P. macrophyllus* is propagated by means of tip cuttings. This is best done in spring. Take 3- to 4-inch-long tip cuttings in spring, trim them immediately below a node, strip off all lower leaves that might come in contact with the rooting mixture, and dip the cut ends in a hormone rooting powder. Plant two or three cuttings in a single 3-inch pot containing a moistened mixture of equal parts peat moss and coarse sand or perlite. Enclose the whole in a plastic bag or propagating case (see page 443), and stand it in medium light. Because podocarpus stems are hard and woody, rooting may take up to eight weeks, but no additional watering should be necessary during this period. When new growth indicates that the cuttings have rooted, treat them as adults. Move them singly into 3-inch pots of the standard potting mixture when their roots have filled the first pot.

Special points Some form of light staking is advisable for the main stems of a potted podocarpus. The side branches usually look best when they are unsupported, however.

If a plant with a bushier appearance is required, cut back all side branches by half. New growth will readily develop. Although such pruning can be done at any time of year, it is best done in spring or summer.

Propagating a podocarpus

Be sure to take young, green tip cuttings from a podocarpus. Older growth is too woody to root easily.

You must remove several of the tightly packed leaves before dipping cuttings in hormone rooting powder.

Because cuttings take so long to root, the bag must be sealed tightly enough to retain moisture over this period.

Polypodium

POLYPODIACEAE

THE species of the genus *Polypodium* most commonly grown indoors is *P. aureum* (also called *Phlebodium aureum*; popularly known as hare's foot fern). The fronds of this fern rise from a creeping, branching rhizome that lies partly above, partly below the surface of the potting mixture. The rhizome, which is likely to grow in a shape that follows the contours of the container, has a diameter of about 1 inch and is covered with furry, orange-brown or white scales. The fronds have stalks up to 2 feet long that are green at first but turn brown with age. The extension of each stalk that serves as the midrib of the frond blade adds a further two feet to the length. The blade itself surrounding the midrib is triangular in shape, and up to $1\frac{1}{2}$ feet across at the base. It is composed of up to 10 pairs of opposite, light green pinnae, with a single terminal pinna. The paired pinnae are up to 9 inches long, the terminal pinnae about 3 inches shorter. All pinnae are 2 inches wide. Clusters of golden brown spore cases are arranged in a line on either side of the central vein on the underside of most pinnae. As each frond ages, dies, and drops away, it leaves a scar not unlike a small footprint on the rhizome at the point where the stalk was attached. Given the right conditions, these polypodiums will grow actively throughout the whole year, although growth slows down slightly during the short-day months of winter.

This is the underside of a mature polypodium frond, showing how spore cases are arranged on both sides of the main veins.

There is an extremely attractive variety, *P.a.* 'Mandaianum,' with silvery blue-green fronds. Each shimmering pinna of this form has wavy, ruffled edges.

Hare's foot fern
Polypodium aureum

PROPER CARE

Light Medium light is best for these ferns. They cannot tolerate direct sun.

Temperature Normal room temperatures are suitable at all times. If necessary, though, polypodiums can tolerate temperatures down to 50°F provided they are kept drier than normal during periods when the temperature remains below 55° for more than a few days. In temperatures above 70° increase the humidity by standing containers on trays of moist pebbles, and mist-spray the foliage daily. Use a fine mist since large drops of water can discolor the fronds.

Watering Water plants plentifully, as often as necessary to keep the potting mixture thoroughly moist. If room temperature drops below 55°F for more than two or three days, water more moderately, allowing the top half-inch of the mixture to dry out between waterings.

Feeding Apply standard liquid fertilizer at half strength once a week.

Potting and repotting Use a potting mixture composed of half leaf mold, half soil-based mixture (see page 429). To allow the rhizome plenty of room to branch and spread, plant each polypodium in a wide, shallow container rather than an ordinary pot. Move plants into larger containers whenever rhizomes have completely overgrown the surface of the mixture. Repotting is best done in spring. After maximum convenient container size (probably 8–10 inches) has been reached, use the plant for propagation.

Propagation In spring cut off 2- to 3-inch-long tip sections of the branching rhizomes and place each section in a $3\frac{1}{2}$-inch half-pot of the potting mixture recommended for adult plants. Moisten the mixture well. To assist rooting, peg down each section horizontally on the surface of the mixture with a loop of wire or a hairpin. Enclose the whole in a plastic bag or heated propagating case (see page 444), and keep it in medium light at 65°–70°F until rooting has occurred (probably in four to five weeks). After new growth has developed, gradually acclimatize the young plant to normal room humidity by uncovering it for progressively longer periods over the course of about one month. During this time make sure that the potting mixture remains just moist. Thereafter, treat the plant in the same way as a mature polypodium.

These plants can also be propagated from spores (see *FERNS,* page 208). This method needs patience.

Polyscias

ARALIACEAE

P. balfouriana
'Marginata'

PLANTS of the genus *Polyscias* are shrubs or trees with decorative, usually variegated leaves. In the wild, with a free root run, they grow very tall, but indoors, within the confines of a pot, they become compact shrubs rarely more than 3 feet high. There are about 80 species in the genus. Only a few types are in general use as house plants, however.

RECOMMENDED POLYSCIASES

P. balfouriana (Balfour aralia) has much-branching stems that are green speckled with gray. They retain this coloration instead of turning brown and woody with age, as do the stems of most other species. The shiny, dark green leaves change their structure as the plant ages. A young plant generally has single, round, semi-erect, 2-inch-wide leaves held on 3-inch-long leafstalks. In older plants, however, the characteristic leaf is composed of three round leaflets, each of which is held on a short stalk at the end of the main leafstalk. The leaflets, which are 2–4 inches in diameter, have a slightly puckered surface, and their shallowly scalloped margins are sometimes, but not always, split a little at the edges.

Leaf color in the species is dark green, but there are two variegated-leaved varieties more popular than the type plant. The leaflets of one, *P.b.* 'Marginata,' are bordered in creamy white. The leaflets of the other, *P.b.* 'Pennockii,' have pale yellow-green markings all along the main vein areas. *P.b.* 'Pennockii' leaflets also tend to be about an inch larger than those of the other kinds.

P. guilfoylei (geranium leaf aralia) is more nearly a small tree than a shrub, and is normally too big for indoor use. But one of its varieties, *P.g.* 'Victoriae,' which grows no more than 3 feet tall, is an excellent house plant. It is much less bushy than *P. balfouriana,*

P. guilfoylei
(geranium leaf aralia)

and its leaves are notably larger and more divided. Each leaf has a 3- to 6-inch-long leafstalk, and is divided into three to seven leaflets, each one 2–3 inches across with a short stalk of its own. The full spread of the leaflets is 12–15 inches. Their shape is indeterminate, and most of them are themselves divided or randomly split, some with lobes, some with toothed edges. Leaf color is gray-green, and most—but not all—of the leaflets have narrow white margins.

PROPER CARE

Light Grow these plants in bright light, but without direct sunlight.

Temperature Warmth is essential. Do not subject a polyscias to temperatures below 65°F. Increase the humidity by standing plants on trays of moist pebbles.

Watering Water moderately throughout the year, moistening the potting mixture well at each watering but allowing the top half-inch of the mixture to dry out before watering again.

Feeding Apply standard liquid fertilizer every two weeks from early spring to late fall. Although these plants do not have a well-defined rest period, they grow more slowly during the winter months.

Potting and repotting Use a soil-based potting mixture (see page 429). Move plants into pots one size larger in early spring, and again in late summer if necessary (as indicated by the appearance of many roots through the drainage hole). After maximum convenient pot size (probably 8 or 10 inches) has been reached, topdress plants with fresh potting mixture every spring (see page 428).

Propagation Propagate from tip cuttings 3–4 inches long taken in early spring. Trim each cutting to just below a leaf, remove the lower leaf, and dip the cut end in a hormone rooting powder. Plant the cutting in a 3-inch pot containing a moistened equal-parts rooting mixture of peat moss and coarse sand or perlite, and enclose the whole in a plastic bag or heated propagating case (see page 444). Stand it in bright filtered light at a temperature of not less than 70°F, and rooting—as indicated by the appearance of new top growth—will occur in two to three weeks. Give the newly rooted cutting more air gradually by opening the plastic bag or lifting the propagator lid a little at a time over the course of a week or so. After the young plant has been acclimatized to normal room conditions in this way, treat it as a mature polyscias. In early summer transfer it into a 4-inch pot of soil-based potting mixture.

Propagating a polyscias

After taking a tip cutting for propagation, be sure to remove the lower leaves before planting it in rooting mixture.

Polystichum

POLYPODIACEAE

THE only species of the genus *Polystichum* that is much used as a house plant is *P. tsus-simense.* The fronds of this fern rise from a rhizome that grows partly under, partly above the surface of the potting mixture. As it ages, the rhizome, which is covered with almost black scales, branches. Thus, clumps of fronds arise from a number of growing points. Before unfurling, all the tightly coiled clumps of fronds are densely covered with silvery white scales. Mature frond blades are somewhat triangular in shape, up to 12 inches long, and up to 5 inches wide at the base. The frond stalks, which are covered with dark brown scales, are about 5 inches long. Each frond blade consists of many pairs of lance-shaped, deep green pinnae up to $2\frac{1}{2}$ inches long and 1 inch wide. The pinnae grow alternately on either side of the midrib, and every pinna is divided into many pairs of $\frac{1}{2}$-inch-long, $\frac{1}{4}$-inch-wide pinnules. These pinnules are deeply toothed along the edges, and they are also tipped with sharp points not unlike those that tip holly leaves. On the

A typical polystichum frond is bipinnate, and each tiny pinnule carries many minute spore cases on its underside.

backs of pinnules of mature fronds are tiny, round, dark brown spore cases. These spore cases are evenly spaced between the central vein and the margins of the pinnule.

P. tsus-simense will grow actively throughout the year if it is given truly ideal conditions. The rate of growth slows down somewhat, however, during the course of the short-day winter months.

See also FERNS.

PROPER CARE

Light Provide medium to bright light, all year long. *P. tsus-simense*

Polystichum tsus-simense

should not be subjected to any direct sunlight, which will scorch the fronds.
Temperature This polystichum can tolerate any room temperature down to 55°F. When the temperature rises above 65°, extra humidity will greatly benefit the plant. Stand pots on trays of damp pebbles, and mist-spray plants daily with tepid water.
Watering Never allow the potting mixture to dry out. Water polystichums plentifully as often as necessary to keep the potting mixture thoroughly moist. But if temperatures fall much below 60°F and remain low for more than two or three days, water more moderately during this period, allowing the top inch of the potting mixture to dry out completely between waterings.
Feeding Give plants half-strength applications of standard liquid fertilizer once every two weeks if they are potted in a peat-based mixture. Polystichums that are grown in a soil-based mixture need feeding less frequently—once a month is enough.
Potting and repotting Use either a peat-based mixture or one composed of half soil-based mixture (see page 429) and half leaf mold. Move plants into pots one size larger whenever their roots fill the pot (see page 426). The best time for repotting is early spring. After maximum convenient pot size (probably 8–10 inches) has been reached, divide up polystichums for propagation.
Propagation It is best to propagate in early spring by dividing an over-large polystichum. Using a sharp knife, cut a rhizome into as many sections as desired, making sure that each section has some roots and bears a clump of fronds. Plant the sections individually in 3-inch pots of moistened soil- or peat-based potting mixture, and then treat the newly potted ferns as mature plants. In potting rhizome sections, plant them horizontally half in, half out of the mixture.

Polystichums can also be propagated from spores at any time of year (see *FERNS*, page 208).

Primula
PRIMULACEAE

ALTHOUGH some of the perennial primulas make excellent house plants, most are treated as annuals, to be enjoyed while in bloom and then disposed of. Those that are to be carried over to another season require cool, light, and airy conditions. All tender primulas (those that cannot withstand frost) bloom principally in late winter and early spring, but some flower at other seasons. All have circular flowers that are borne in sprays or whorls of 6 to 10 on erect stems arising from basal clusters of radiating leaves.

RECOMMENDED PRIMULAS
P. kewensis grows about 15 inches tall and is the only yellow-flowered indoor primula. The fragrant flowers are $\frac{3}{4}$ inch across and produced in whorls, one above another, on 10- to 12-inch-long stalks from midwinter to spring. The leaves are an elongated oval shape with toothed, wavy edges. The whole plant, apart from the blooms, is covered with a fine white powder. Non-powdery strains are available, but they are less appealing.

P. obconica

P. sinensis

P. kewensis

Fairy primrose
P. malacoides

P. malacoides (fairy or baby primrose) is a small mauve-flowered wild species. There are some excellent indoor forms up to 18 inches tall with bright pink, red, or white flowers. From midwinter to spring the best of these forms carry between 20 and 30 $\frac{1}{2}$-inch blooms in tiers, on slender stems above hairy, pale green, scallop-edged leaves.

P. obconica has its numerous 1-inch flowers arranged in an upright umbel at the top of a 1-foot-tall flower stalk. Flowers can be pink, red, salmon, mauve, or white, each with a large apple green central "eye." Flowers are very long-lasting; plants bloom from midwinter through early summer. The almost circular leaves are coarse and hairy, slightly indented, with wrinkled edges. Modern hybrids have few hairs on upper leaf surfaces, but more on the undersides and leafstalks. Warning: Some people are allergic to the fine hairs and develop a skin rash after handling *P. obconica*.

P. sinensis has hairy, lobed leaves and produces a flower spike on a short stalk, which elongates as the flowers open and eventually reaches a length of 1 foot. Each spike comprises two or three tiers of 1- to $1\frac{1}{2}$-inch flowers, mostly in shades of pink or purple with a yellow central "eye." Most of the modern cultivated forms have delicately fringed and undulate petals.

PROPER CARE

Light Provide bright light, including some sunshine, at all times.

Temperature Primulas purchased already in flower are best kept between 50°–55°F. Room temperatures over 60° will shorten the life of the flowers. If plants are brought into warmer rooms temporarily, give them added humidity by standing them on a tray of moist pebbles, and mist-spray the plants frequently.

Watering Water plentifully, enough to keep the entire potting mixture thoroughly moist, but never let the pot stand in water.

Feeding Apply standard liquid fertilizer every two weeks during the entire flowering period, beginning when flower stalks appear.

Potting and repotting Use a soil-based potting mixture (see page 429). Small plants, which can usually be bought in early fall, should be quickly moved into 4- or 5-inch pots to give them room for development.

Propagation Commercially, primulas are grown from seed, but it is not practicable to do this in the home.

Special points Of the four kinds recommended here, *P. obconica* and *P. sinensis* can be grown on for a second year; the others are best discarded after flowering. The flowering period can in all cases be prolonged by picking off dead flowers as soon as they fade. In the second year *P. obconica* will bloom spasmodically through late summer and fall before the main winter-spring flush of flowers.

To prolong the flowering period of primulas pick off fading flowers. The plants will continue to flower in their effort to produce seed.

To keep these plants through a second season, give them maximum ventilation and keep them cool and in light shade during the summer, with just enough water to prevent the mixture from drying out. An outdoor position on a shaded balcony or in a cold frame in the garden might be the right place for them. Then, in early fall, gently pull out dead and yellowed leaves, topdress plants (see page 428) with fresh potting mixture, and restart them into growth by gradually increasing the amounts of water given.

Any yellowing of young primula leaves may indicate a magnesium deficiency. To overcome this apply Epsom salts (magnesium sulfate) at the rate of $\frac{1}{4}$ ounce in 2 pints of water.

Inspect a primula kept for a second season in early fall. After pulling away dead leaves, topdress the plant with fresh mixture.

Pseuderanthemum

ACANTHACEAE

Purple false eranthemum
P. atropurpureum

PSEUDERANTHEMUMS (previously listed as belonging to the genus *Eranthemum*, and still often sold under that name) are low-growing plants and small shrubs with highly decorative, usually variegated leaves. The species that is most commonly grown as a house plant, *P. atropurpureum* (purple false eranthemum), is a shrub capable of growing 3 feet tall. It becomes straggling as it ages, however, and usually only remains attractive while small. However, if plants are discarded while they are still small, they are unlikely to reach flowering size. The rigid stems carry opposite pairs of elliptic leaves 4–6 inches long and up to 2 inches wide, which are held on 1-inch-long leafstalks. The glossy leaves are basically purple and green in color, with pink, white, and cream blotches. None of these colors is well defined; they merge into one another. In the summer mature plants produce 6-inch-long flower spikes at the tips of stems. Each of these spikes consists of many slender, tube-shaped flowers about an inch long. Flower color is white spotted with pink.

PROPER CARE

Light Give these pseuderanthemums bright filtered light all year long.

Temperature These plants need warmth and cannot tolerate temperatures below 60°F. Because they also require high humidity, stand pots on trays of moistened pebbles.

To keep pseuderanthemum leaves in good condition, provide humidity by standing pots on saucers of moist pebbles throughout the year.

Watering Throughout the year water moderately, making the potting mixture moist throughout at each watering but allowing the top half-inch of the mixture to dry out before watering again.

Feeding Apply standard liquid fertilizer every two weeks from early spring to late fall.

Potting and repotting Use a soil-based potting mixture (see page 429). Move each small plant into a pot one size larger whenever roots begin to appear through drainage holes and on the surface of the mixture. After maximum convenient pot size (probably about 6 inches) has been reached, use the plant for propagation, and then discard it.

Propagation To propagate, take a tip cutting 2–3 inches long, preferably in spring. Trim the cutting immediately below a pair of leaves, strip off the lowest leaves, and dip the cut end in hormone rooting powder. Plant the cutting in a 3-inch pot filled with a moistened equal-parts mixture of peat moss and coarse sand or perlite, and enclose the whole in a plastic bag or heated propagating case (see page 444). Stand it in bright filtered light at a temperature of 70°–75°F until renewed growth indicates that rooting has occurred. Uncover the rooted cutting, and begin to water and feed it as if it were a mature plant. About 10 weeks after the start of propagation move the young plant into a 4-inch pot of soil-based mixture.

Pteris

POLYPODIACEAE

PTERIS (table fern) is a large genus, with several species that have become familiar house plants. Indoor pterises produce clumps of fronds from short underground rhizomes. As the upright fronds grow tall, they tend to arch over at the tip. Plants of some species have two kinds of frond: short, sterile ones and longer ones with spore cases on the underside margins. Plants of other species have only a single type of frond, which is either sterile or fertile. In all forms the spore cases are protected by pinna (or sometimes pinnule) margins, which curl over the cases. As a result, fertile pinnae always appear to be straight-edged even though they are toothed, whereas the toothed edges of sterile pinnae are invariably visible.

Given ideal conditions, these plants will grow actively all year long.
See also FERNS.

RECOMMENDED PTERISES

P. cretica (Cretan brake) has only one kind of frond, which is about 12 inches long, 8 inches wide, and light to medium green. The frond stalk is about 6 inches long and is black. Each frond blade has up to four pairs of pinnae and a single terminal pinna. Each strap-shaped pinna is up to 4 inches long and about $\frac{3}{4}$ inches wide, and it tapers to a point. In fertile specimens the spore cases can be borne on all pinnae. A variety, *P.c.* 'Albo-lineata,' has a narrow band of creamy white on either side of the midrib of each separate pinna.

P. ensiformis (sword brake) has two types of frond. The fertile fronds have medium green, narrowly triangular blades, up to 14 inches long and 8 inches wide, with stalks about 6 inches long. Each blade has up to eight pairs of pinnae, each up to 4 inches long and $\frac{1}{4}$ inch wide. The sterile fronds also have triangular blades, but they reach only 8-9 inches long and 6 inches wide, with stalks up to 4 inches long. The sterile frond blades have six pairs of pinnae, each up to 3 inches long and $\frac{1}{2}$ inch wide. The pinnae of both kinds of blade are sometimes divided into small pinnules. An especially decorative variety is *P.e.* 'Victoriae,' with pinnae (and occasionally pinnules) colored silvery white along their midribs.

Cretan brake
P. cretica 'Albolineata'

P. tremula (Australian brake or poor man's cibotium) is a much larger and faster-growing species than the other two. It bears only one type of frond, with a yellow-green, triangular blade up to 2 feet long and 1 foot wide. The medium green stalk is up to 15 inches long. Each blade has about four pairs of lance-shaped pinnae, each up to 6 inches long and 2 inches wide. All the pinnae are themselves divided into small pinnules, and so the fronds have a feathery, carrot-top appearance. In a mature plant the apparently straight-edged pinnules have noticeably dark margins because of the many brown spore cases on the underside.

PROPER CARE

Light Give these ferns bright light throughout the year, but never expose them to direct sunlight.

Temperature Normal room temperatures are suitable for pterises throughout the year. Whenever temperatures remain above 65°F for more than two or three days stand pots on trays of moist pebbles, and mist-spray plants daily. Minimum tolerable temperature: 55°.

Watering These plants cannot tolerate dryness at the roots. Water plentifully at all times, giving enough to keep the potting mixture thoroughly moist. If indoor temperatures ever drop below 60° for more than a day or two, water moderately during this period, allowing the top half-inch of the potting mixture to dry out between waterings.

Feeding Apply a half-strength standard liquid fertilizer once every two or four weeks, depending upon the type of potting mixture. The more frequent feedings are required for plants in a peat-based mixture.

Potting and repotting Use either a peat-based mixture or an equal-parts combination of soil-based mixture and leaf mold (see page 429). Move plants into pots one size larger in the spring, but only when roots fill the pot (see page 426). In repotting, bury the rhizome just below the surface of the potting mixture. After maximum convenient pot size (probably 8–10 inches) has been reached, use plants for propagation.

Propagation Propagate in spring by dividing large pterises. Using a sharp knife, cut the rhizome into sections, making sure that each section carries a clump of fronds and feeding roots. Plant each section in a $3\frac{1}{2}$-inch pot of fresh, moist mixture, and treat the newly potted fern as a mature pteris.

Production of spores is so heavy that young pterises are often found growing in the pots of neighboring plants. These tiny ferns can be rescued, potted up in 2-inch pots, and grown on as adult specimens. Otherwise, spores can simply be used for propagation in the normal way (see *FERNS,* page 208).

Special points Cut away the older, outer fronds of pterises if they become shabby-looking. There are generally new fronds ready to unfurl from the many growing points on the rhizome.

Punica

PUNICACEAE

Dwarf
pomegranate
P. granatum 'Nana'

THE genus *Punica* contains two species, only one of which, *P. granatum,* can be grown indoors—and then only in a miniature form, *P.g.* 'Nana' (dwarf pomegranate). The plant grows slowly to a height of 3–4 feet, forming a compact, bushy shrub. The leathery, glossy, lance-shaped leaves grow on short, twiggy branches. Leaves are medium green, about 1 inch long and $\frac{1}{2}$ inch wide, and have short leafstalks. They appear in opposite pairs or whorls of three or four. Inch-long, orange-red, bell-shaped flowers with crinkled petals are backed by purplish red calyxes. They grow at the tips of side branches either singly or in groups of two or more.

The flowering period, which extends from late spring through summer, is followed by fruiting. Each rounded, yellow or yellow-orange fruit is up to 2 inches across, and the tufted calyx is still attached at the apex. The abundant fruits usually weigh down the thin branches. Although edible when fully ripe, the fruit is not very palatable. *P.g.* 'Nana' loses most of its leaves after the fruiting period.

PROPER CARE

Light During the active growth period give punicas bright light, with three or four hours a day of direct sunlight. During the rest period medium light is adequate.

Temperature During the active growth period normal room temperatures are suitable. Move plants to a cooler position—preferably about 55°F—in late fall after they have dropped most of their leaves.

Watering During the active growth period water plentifully as often as necessary to keep the potting mixture thoroughly moist, but never allow pots to stand in water. During the rest period give only enough to keep the mixture from drying out completely.

Feeding Apply standard liquid fertilizer every two weeks during the active growth period.

Potting and repotting Use a soil-based potting mixture (see page 429). Move plants into pots one size larger only once in two years, since punicas flower best when their roots are slightly restricted. Repot in spring just as plants start into growth. After maximum convenient pot size (probably 6–8 inches) has been reached, topdress plants with fresh mixture every spring (see page 428).

Propagation Propagate in midsummer by means of sideshoots 2–3 inches long. Take each cutting with a heel attached. Dip the heel end in hormone rooting powder, and plant it in a 3-inch pot containing a moistened equal-parts mixture of peat moss and coarse sand. Enclose the whole in a plastic bag or propagating case (see page 443), and stand it in bright filtered light. Take care not to disturb the cutting during the next six to eight weeks, after which renewed growth should indicate that roots have formed. Uncover the rooted cutting, and begin to water moderately, allowing the top inch of the rooting mixture to dry out between waterings. Keep the cutting in medium light at a temperature of about 55°F throughout the winter. In the spring move it into bright filtered light until it has made 2–3 inches of new growth. Then move the plant into a 4-inch pot of soil-based mixture and treat it as a mature punica.

Special points Pruning is not normally necessary. If any stems seem weak and crowded, however, cut them out in early winter.

Rebutia

CACTACEAE

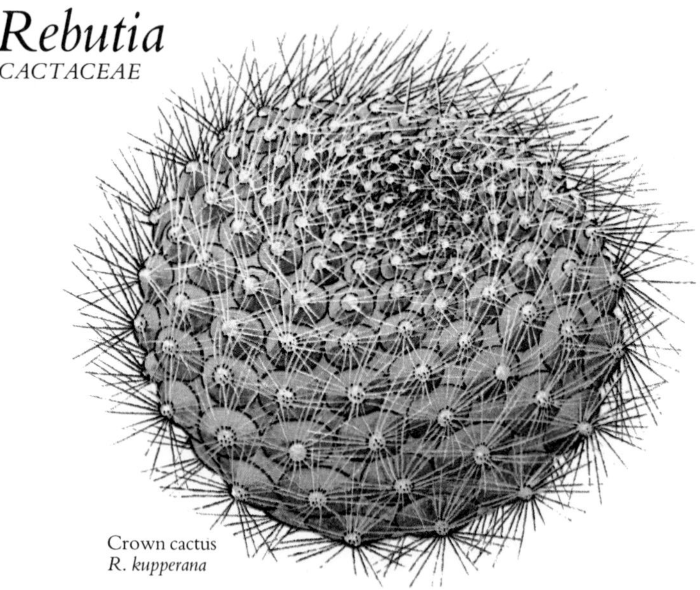

Crown cactus
R. kupperana

REBUTIAS (crown cacti) are a group of about twenty species of small desert cacti that form many offsets, mostly at the base of the main stem. The stems are either spherical or cylindrical and bear spirally arranged rows of tubercles, each with an areole at its tip. Because rebutias are so small, they are ideal for the indoor gardener who has limited space for plants. Their special attraction is that they are not only small but showy, with highly colored, funnel-shaped flowers produced profusely in late spring and early summer. The flowers, appearing from around the lower part of the clustering stems, often form complete circles of blooms around separate stems. Flowers open in the morning and close in late afternoon, each one lasting for two or three days. Because the buds do not usually open simultaneously, the flowering period can extend through several weeks. In a general collection of cacti the rebutias are normally the first to flower every year. They begin to flower while they are still young (some when only 1 inch across), but are short-lived in comparison with most other desert cacti. It is not unusual for a plant about five years old to flower itself literally to death: It may become covered with blooms, and then turn brown and die. *See also CACTI.*

For an impressive display of brightly colored flowers, do not separate clumps of rebutias. Flowers appear only from lower areoles.

RECOMMENDED REBUTIAS

R. callianta has bright green stems that can grow up to 6 inches tall and $2\frac{1}{2}$ inches wide. The cluster of stems can fill a 6-inch container when the plant is less than five years old. There are up to 27 rows of tubercles, and each tubercle is tipped with an areole carrying from 12 to 22 slender whitish, interlacing, $\frac{1}{4}$-inch-long spines. The blood red flowers, each about $1\frac{1}{2}$ inches long and wide, open in the early part of summer.

R. kupperana has dark green stems up to 4 inches tall and 2 inches wide. It forms its clusters relatively slowly and may take six or more years to fill a 6-inch container. The stems have about 15 rows of $\frac{1}{8}$-inch-high tubercles, and the areoles carry 13 to 15 brownish radial spines about $\frac{1}{4}$ inch long, together with 1 to 3 dark brown centrals that are more than twice the length of the radials. Deep red flowers, each an inch or more long and wide, open in early summer. *R. kupperana* flowers tend to appear somewhat higher up the stem than is usual among cacti of this genus, and they rarely form a complete ring around the plant.

R. minuscula (red crown) has nearly spherical, pale green stems, each up to 2 inches across. The plant grows so fast that its many offsets will fill a 6-inch container in three or four years. The tubercles are about $\frac{1}{10}$ inch high and are arranged in 20 rows. Each areole carries 20 to 25 thin, whitish spines only $\frac{1}{8}$ inch long. The pale red flowers about $1\frac{1}{2}$ inches long and $\frac{3}{4}$ inch wide start to open in the late spring.

R. minuscula has a number of forms. Two of the most attractive are *R.m. grandiflora,* with red flowers $2\frac{1}{2}$ inches long and 2 inches wide, and *R.m. violaciflora,* with violet flowers $1\frac{1}{2}$ inches long and 1 inch wide. The flowers of *R.m. violaciflora,* which often have downward-curving petals, bloom somewhat earlier than do those of most rebutias. (These two varieties are sometimes sold as *R. grandiflora* and *R. violaciflora* because they used to be considered as separate species.)

R. senilis (fire crown) has pale green, spherical stems that grow up to 3 inches across. They sometimes form a cluster about 6 inches across in less than four years. The tubercles are $\frac{1}{10}$ inch high. The areoles carry 35 to 40 white, hairlike spines about $1\frac{1}{4}$ inches long that give the stems a silvery appearance. Pale red flowers $1\frac{1}{2}$ inches long and 1 inch wide open in late spring. Two of the many varieties of this plant are *R.s. kesselringiana,* with golden yellow flowers, and *R.s. lilacino-rosea,* with lilac-pink flowers.

R. xanthocarpa has pale green stems up to 3 inches tall and 2 inches wide. The cluster can attain a spread of 6 inches in four years. The $\frac{1}{10}$-inch-high tubercles are tipped with areoles that carry 15 to 20 white radial spines about $\frac{1}{4}$ inch long. This is one of the smallest-flowered rebutias, with pale pink flowers that are only $\frac{3}{4}$ inch long and $\frac{1}{2}$ inch wide. They appear in late spring. The most attractive variety is *R.x. salmonicolor,* which has salmon pink flowers.

PROPER CARE

Light Although classed as desert cacti, rebutias do not come from the more extreme desert regions. Their natural habitat is the semi-desert grassland, where surrounding vegetation gives them some protection from the sun. Do not subject them to long periods of intense summer sunlight. During the rest of the year, however, give them as much direct sunlight as possible. They will not thrive if they are grown in shade.

Temperature During the active growth period normal room temperatures are suitable for these plants. In order to produce an abundance of flowers they must have an annual winter rest period, preferably at a temperature somewhat below 50°F. They can tolerate winter temperatures as low as 35°–40°.

Watering During the active growth period water moderately, enough to make the potting mixture moist throughout at each watering, but allow the top half-inch of the mixture to dry out before watering again. During the winter rest period give these plants only enough water to prevent the potting mixture from drying out completely.

Feeding For rebutias grown in soil-based potting mixture, use a high potassium, tomato-type fertilizer once every four weeks during the active growth period only. For plants grown in peat-based mixture use the same fertilizer, but apply it more often—ideally, once every two weeks during the active growth period.

Potting and repotting Use a porous potting mixture consisting of one part of coarse sand or perlite to three parts of either soil-based or peat-based mixture (see page 429). Because rebutias are shallow-rooted as well as spreading plants, they do better in broad pans or half-pots than in ordinary pots. A single-stemmed plant 2 inches wide requires a container with a 3-inch diameter, but most rebutias of this size will already have several offsets and will need a correspondingly larger pan or half-pot.

At the beginning of the growing period remove each rebutia cluster from its container. If the container is found to be full of roots, or if the offset stems have begun to press against the sides, move the plant into a container one size larger. If there is still room for growth, however, remove as much of the old potting mixture as possible without damaging the roots, and replace the plant in the original container, which has been thoroughly cleaned. Add as much fresh potting mixture as required to bring the level of mixture up to the original level on the stem. Rebutias are not fiercely spined and are quite easy to handle in comparison with most other cacti. While working with the plant, fold newspaper around it, more to protect the plant than the fingers.

Propagation The easiest way to propagate is from offsets, which come away cleanly when gently pulled. Press the offset down into a small container of either soil-based or peat-based potting mixture, and treat it immediately as a mature specimen. It will soon root and begin producing offsets of its own. Do not take too many offsets from a single plant, or the naturally clustered shape of the cactus may be spoiled.

Propagation from offsets ensures the continuing existence of plants that are true to type. It is also easy to raise rebutias from seed, and many indoor gardeners enjoy doing so, especially because even one-year-old seedlings will sometimes flower; flowering can certainly be expected the second year. Not only is commercial seed readily available, but rebutias are often self-fertilizing, and seed pods usually form after flowering. Because the plants hybridize readily, however, the indoor gardener can never be sure that seedlings will turn out as anticipated, particularly if different species are in flower at the same time. Gardeners who do not mind uncertainty can harvest their own seed when the pods split. Rebutia pods are dry, not mucilaginous, and so the seeds can simply be shaken out and stored for sowing the following spring. (For seed raising see *CACTI,* page 119.)

Rhapis

PALMAE

Little lady palm
R. excelsa

THE two species of *Rhapis* (lady palm) that can be grown indoors are slow-growing palms with fan-shaped, dark green leaves cut lengthwise into a number of almost entirely separate, thin segments. The leaves are borne on 9- to 12-inch-long stalks along unbranched, rigid stems that are produced in clumps. Each stem is covered with a rough, dark brown fiber. Some of these palms can grow several feet tall if planted in 10- to 12-inch pots. Eventually the lower leaves dry up and fall off (or should be pulled off as they become unsightly). When they drop, they take some of the brown fiber with them, revealing the smooth, deep green, naked stems underneath. These retain scars at 2- to 4-inch intervals, where the leafstalks were attached.
See also PALMS.

RECOMMENDED RHAPISES

R. excelsa (sometimes called *R. flabelliformis*, commonly known either as bamboo palm or little lady palm), the smaller of the two species, has clustered stems up to 1 inch thick. Each leaf is composed of five to eight blunt-tipped, tooth-edged segments 9 inches long and up to 2 inches wide. *R. excelsa* is unlikely to grow more than 5 feet tall indoors. A variegated-leaved form, *R.e.* 'Zuikonishiki,' has yellow markings on each of the segments and is rarely any taller than 2 feet.

R. excelsa
'Zuikonishiki'

R. humilis (slender lady palm or reed rhapis) can grow 8 feet tall but has stems only ½ inch thick; they are so thin as to be reedlike in appearance. The leaves, which are more broadly rounded than those of *R. excelsa*, are divided into 10 to 20 pointed-tipped segments up to 12 inches long and of varying widths (from ¼ to 1½ inches).

PROPER CARE

Light Grow these plants in bright filtered light. During the winter months, however, give them three to four hours of direct sunlight each day.

Temperature Rhapis palms do well not only in normal room temperatures but also in cool conditions down to about 45°F. Under the cooler conditions they simply take a winter rest or grow more slowly.

Watering Water actively growing plants moderately, giving enough at each watering to make the potting mixture moist throughout, but allowing the top half-inch of the mixture to dry out before watering again. During the rest period, if any, water more sparingly, allowing the top 2 inches to dry out between waterings.

Feeding Apply standard liquid fertilizer about once a month to actively growing rhapis palms.

Potting and repotting Use a soil-based potting mixture (see page 429). Do not move these plants into larger pots more often than once in two years; grow them in pots that look a little too small for them. After reaching maximum convenient pot size (probably 12 inches), give the plants a topdressing with fresh potting mixture (see page 428) every spring.

Propagation Rhapis palms produce suckers from the base of the plant, and these can be used for propagation in spring. Cut off a basal sucker, preferably one with some roots already attached to it, and plant it in a 3- to 5-inch pot of the recommended potting mixture for these plants. Place the pot in a warm position in medium light, and water the sucker sparingly. Give it just enough at each watering to make the entire mixture barely moist, and allow the top inch of the mixture to dry out before watering again. As soon as new growth becomes apparent, the young palm can be treated as a mature specimen.

These palms can also be propagated from seed (see *PALMS*, page 295), but it takes a great deal of time and patience. The other method is both quicker and surer.

Rhipsalidopsis

CACTACEAE

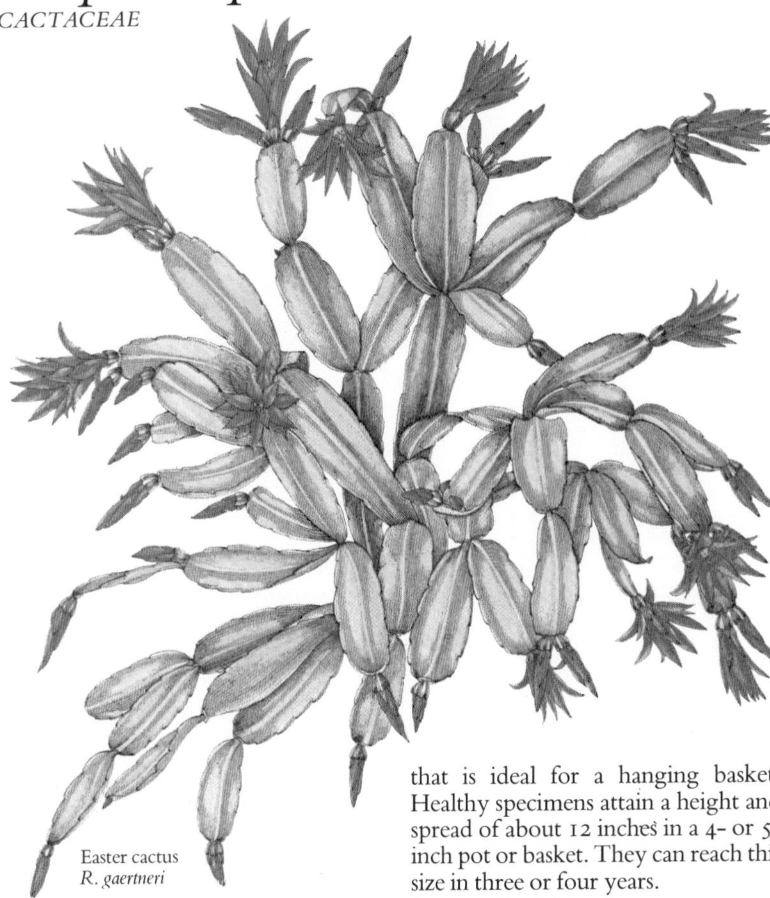

Easter cactus
R. gaertneri

INDOOR gardeners prize the two species of this jungle cactus, together with a number of hybrids from crosses between them, for their beautiful flowers, which are produced in profusion in early spring. Although individual flowers last for only two or three days, the flowering period extends over several weeks, and even very small plants will bloom. The stems consist of numerous small, flat (or sometimes angled), bright green segments with notched edges. Each segment carries minute areoles in the notches. The stems branch freely, and there is an elongated areole on the end segment of each branch. It is from the elongated areoles on new branches that the flowers arise, either singly or in pairs. All the areoles bear yellowish or brownish bristles. Since these bristles are not hard or sharply pointed, the plants are quite safe to handle, and no protection is necessary for the fingers. The stems are erect at first. As more segments are formed, however, they begin to droop, forming a plant that is ideal for a hanging basket. Healthy specimens attain a height and spread of about 12 inches in a 4- or 5-inch pot or basket. They can reach this size in three or four years.

See also CACTI.

RECOMMENDED RHIPSALIDOPSISES

R. gaertneri (formerly called *Schlumbergera gaertneri;* popularly known as the Easter cactus) has thin, flat stem segments up to 1½ inches long and ¾ inch wide. The open-bell-shaped, scarlet flowers measure 1–1½ inches across at the mouth.

R. rosea has stem segments that may be either flat or three- or four-angled. Each segment is no more—often less—than ¾ inch long and ½ inch wide. The 1-inch-across, rose-pink flowers are more flattened and starlike than those of *R. gaertneri*.

R. gaertneri and *R. rosea* have been crossed to produce a number of attractive hybrids, which have been given such names as *R.* 'Paleface,' *R.* 'Salmon Queen,' *R.* 'Spring Dazzler,' and *R.* 'Spring Princess.' The plants themselves tend to resemble *R. gaertneri* rather than *R. rosea* in stem-segment shape and form. The hybrid flowers are mainly open-bell-shaped, but they often have pointed, starlike petals. Flower color varies, and can range from pink to crimson.

PROPER CARE

Light These jungle cacti should not be exposed to any direct sunlight. Medium light suits them best. They will benefit from being placed outdoors in summer only if they are kept in a shady spot.

Temperature Normal room temperatures are suitable throughout the year. These cacti do not need a cool winter rest period. They cannot tolerate temperatures below 50°F.

Watering From very early spring to the end of the flowering period water plentifully as often as necessary to keep the potting mixture thoroughly moist, but do not allow containers to stand in water. When flowering has ended, give the plants a brief late-spring rest by watering only enough to prevent the mixture from drying out during a period of two to three weeks. Thereafter, water moderately, allowing the top half-inch of the mixture to dry out between waterings, until the following spring. If, for any reason, the indoor temperature falls much below about 60°F for more than a few days, give these plants only enough water during that period to keep the potting mixture from drying out completely. In a normally warm room a rhipsalidopsis will flourish in moist conditions. It will benefit from a daily mist-spraying with clean water. Use room-temperature rainwater, if possible, for all watering.

Feeding When flower buds begin to form in very early spring, start to apply a high-potassium, tomato-type fertilizer every two weeks. For a plant potted in soil-based mixture no further feeding is necessary after the last buds have opened. For a plant in peat-based mixture, discontinue feedings during the two or three weeks immediately following the flowering season (see "Watering," above). Then resume feedings—but only at four-weekly intervals—throughout the rest of the year.

Potting and repotting Use either a soil-based or peat-based potting mixture (see page 429). The latter is preferable. In either case add one part of coarse sand or perlite to three parts of the mixture; good drainage is essential. The best time for repotting is just after the brief rest period in late spring or early summer. Remove each plant from its container at that time, and shake as much potting mixture from the roots as possible. If the roots have completely filled the old container, move the plant into a slightly larger one. Otherwise, clean the old container and replace the plant. Add fresh mixture as necessary. These cacti do not have extensive roots, and a 4- to 5-inch container should be the biggest needed. If a specimen is planted in a hanging basket, line the basket with sphagnum moss in order to retain the potting mixture.

Displaying rhipsalidopsises

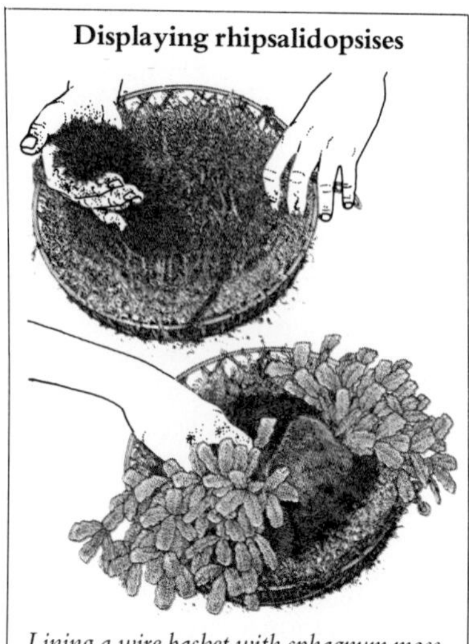

Lining a wire basket with sphagnum moss before planting rhipsalidopsises not only holds potting mixture in but also improves the look of the display.

Propagation Few cacti are easier to propagate than these. At any time in the spring or summer remove one (or, preferably, two) of the stem segments. They can usually be detached from the rest of the stem with a gentle tug. The two detached segments should not be separated from each other, of course. Press the segment (or the bottom one of the two if two are taken) deep enough into the standard potting mixture to permit the cutting to stand upright. Use a 2-inch pot, or plant several such cuttings in a larger pot or pan. Treat potted segments immediately as mature plants.

A rhipsalidopsis will not produce seed unless it is deliberately cross-pollinated. Seed, which is generally labeled "rhipsalidopsis hybrid," is available in many places however, and propagation from seed is not difficult (see *CACTI,* page 119).

Rhipsalis

CACTACEAE

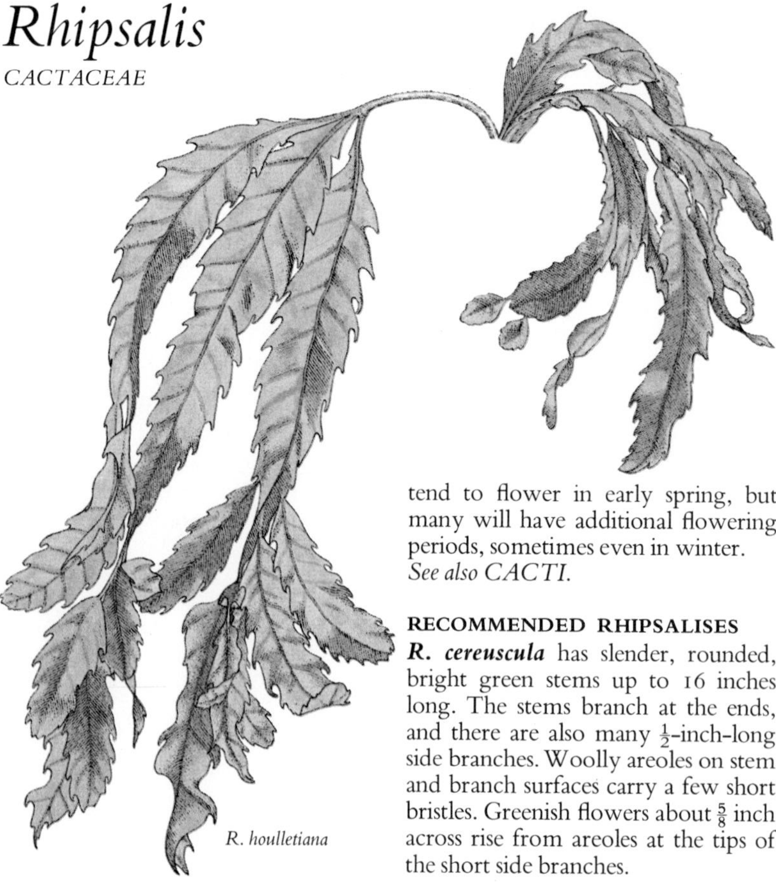

R. houlletiana

PLANTS of the genus *Rhipsalis* are jungle cacti with trailing, branching stems that do not conform to most people's idea of what a cactus looks like. Stems of the few species in general cultivation differ greatly. Some are rounded, thin, and interlacing, and it is their appearance that has given the genus its name (*Rhipsalis* derives from a Greek word meaning "wickerwork"). In other species the stems consist of many rounded, jointed segments, and in still others the stems are flat and straplike. Rounded stems generally have tiny areoles scattered over the surface, while areoles on flattened stems are usually situated in notches along the edges. The areoles are sometimes woolly, and they often bear bristles or hairs rather than spines. The pendent stems of all species commonly used indoors make these plants ideal for hanging baskets.

Rhipsalis flowers are small but attractive, numerous, and sometimes fragrant. The generally star-shaped blooms last for a few days, and they may be followed by small, often white, berrylike fruits. These remain on the plant for several weeks. Plants tend to flower in early spring, but many will have additional flowering periods, sometimes even in winter. *See also CACTI.*

RECOMMENDED RHIPSALISES

R. cereuscula has slender, rounded, bright green stems up to 16 inches long. The stems branch at the ends, and there are also many $\frac{1}{2}$-inch-long side branches. Woolly areoles on stem and branch surfaces carry a few short bristles. Greenish flowers about $\frac{5}{8}$ inch across rise from areoles at the tips of the short side branches.

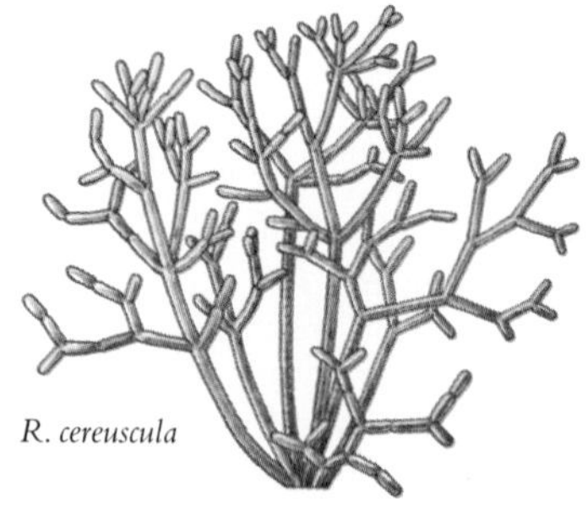

R. cereuscula

R. crispata has 2-foot-long, pale green stems composed of flattened, jointed segments, each up to 4 inches long and 2 inches broad. Stem edges are notched, and yellowish flowers about $\frac{1}{2}$ inch across appear from almost invisible areoles in the notches. The stems do not trail as readily as those of most other kinds, but they eventually become pendent.

R. houlletiana has rounded, pale green stems 6–8 inches long and $\frac{1}{4}$ inch thick. Each stem may bear two types of branch: very slender, rounded ones up to 12 inches long, and flattened, leaflike ones up to 10 inches long and 1 inch broad. The flat branches, which are tough and leathery, have sharply notched edges, and there are tiny areoles with scarcely visible bristles in the notches. Yellowish white flowers $\frac{1}{2}$ inch wide are produced in profusion, but only on the flat branches. Flower-bearing branches trail; other stems and branches are more upright.

R. pilocarpa has rounded, interlacing, dark green stems about 16 inches long and up to $\frac{1}{4}$ inch thick, with riblike furrows running along the length. Sweetly scented white or cream-colored flowers, produced mainly on areoles at the ends of stems, are up to $\frac{3}{4}$ inch across.

PROPER CARE

Light Like other jungle cacti, these plants need shade; with too much sunlight the stems tend to turn reddish and shrivel. Give them medium light, and put them in a shady spot outdoors, if possible, during late spring and throughout the summer.

Temperature Normally warm room temperatures are suitable for all rhipsalises throughout the year as long as the air is sufficiently moist. For extra humidity stand pots on trays of moist pebbles, and suspend saucers of water beneath hanging baskets. In addition, mist-spray these plants daily—with soft water, if at all possible (see "Watering," below).

Watering These jungle cacti should never be allowed to dry out completely. When they are most actively growing, during spring and summer, water plentifully, enough to keep the potting mixture thoroughly moist but do not allow the container to stand in water. In the winter, under normal living-room conditions, water plants moderately, moistening the mixture throughout at each watering but allowing the top half-inch to dry out before watering again. Because rhipsalises dislike calcium, try to use soft water at all times. Rainwater is ideal for watering these plants.

Feeding Use a tomato-type fertilizer once a month throughout the year, and step up the frequency to once every two weeks during flowering periods. Begin the more frequent feedings as soon as flower buds appear, and continue them until the last buds have opened.

Potting and repotting A peat-based, soilless potting mixture is ideal for these cacti. But be sure to provide extra drainage by adding one part of coarse sand or perlite to three parts of the basic mixture. For plants kept in hanging baskets, line the baskets with sphagnum moss to retain the potting mixture. Because rhipsalises have small root systems, they do not need large containers. Thus, a plant with stems long enough to hang down a foot or more can be lodged in a 3- or 4-inch pot or basket. Repot every rhipsalis once a year, however, even though it may not need moving on to a larger container. Simply remove the old potting mixture, clean the pot thoroughly, and repot the plant in fresh mixture. Do this at any time except midwinter. In general, these plants are not hard to handle. In repotting a specimen with stems composed of jointed segments, however, remember that the segments are easily broken apart and must therefore be treated with care.

Propagation It is easy to propagate from cuttings taken in spring or summer. Simply detach a segment of a segmented type or cut a branch from any of the others, and press the cut end of a 2- or 3-inch piece into the usual potting mixture. Such cuttings need no special care in order to root and can be treated immediately as mature plants. Three or four cuttings may be started into growth in a single 2- or 3-inch pot. When they begin to develop, pot them up separately, or else plant a few of the same sort together in a hanging basket.

With *R. houlletiana,* which has two distinct types of branch, a cutting of one kind can produce a typical plant. Sometimes, however, a specimen with only a single kind of branch will result. The only way to avoid this possibility is to propagate from seed (see *CACTI,* page 119). Unfortunately, the kinds of seed available in garden centers are rather limited.

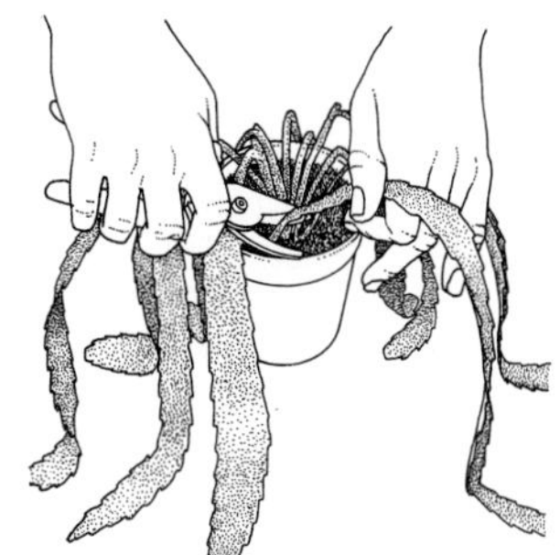

You must cut off a whole branch when propagating a rhipsalis, even if you then cut the branch into several smaller pieces.

Rhododendron

ERICACEAE

THE very large genus *Rhododendron* contains two species that provide forms commonly grown as house plants: *R. obtusum* (kurume azalea) and *R. simsii* (sometimes incorrectly known as *Azalea indica* or *R. indicum*). The kinds seen indoors, which are almost invariably hybrids of mixed parentage, are all small shrubs rarely more than 18 inches in height and spread, and they have 1-inch-long, leathery, generally egg-shaped leaves. Funnel-shaped flowers are borne at the ends of the stems.

These hybrid forms are usually grown indoors for a single season as temporary winter- and early-spring-flowering plants, but it is possible to keep them alive and attractive for several years under the right conditions (see "Potting and repotting," below). In their natural state both species flower in mid-spring, but commercial growers start batches of plants into growth at different times, to produce a succession of well-budded plants that will bloom at various periods from early winter well into spring.

RECOMMENDED RHODODENDRONS

R. obtusum hybrids have glossy leaves, and the young stems are usually covered with a soft, flat layer of brown hair. The 1-inch-wide flowers may be solitary, in pairs, or in groups of three, and colored white, magenta, or any shade of pink or red.

R. obtusum hybrid (flower)

R. simsii hybrids are the large-flowered "azaleas" of florists' shops. The leaves are sometimes glossy, but practically all varieties have some bristly hairs on leaf margins. Flowers are carried in small clusters of two to five; each flower is $1\frac{1}{2}$–2 inches across and may be single or double, sometimes

Rhododendron simsii hybrid

with ruffled petals. Color range is the same as that of *R. obtusum,* except that the flowers of *R. simsii* are sometimes attractively bicolored.

PROPER CARE

Light Potted rhododendrons in bud or bloom should be placed in bright light but out of direct sunlight. When not flowering, they do best if given only medium light, as at a sunless window, although a brightly lit position in a cool room is also suitable.

Temperature Keep these plants in as cool a position as possible (preferably 45°–60°F). If rhododendrons are brought into warm rooms (above 70°), the roots will dry out quickly, flowers will flop, and leaves will fall. Move plants gradually from cool into warmer positions if absolutely necessary, but flowers will last much longer if they are kept cool.

Watering To make sure that indoor rhododendrons are permanently moist at the roots (they are almost always potted in pure peat moss), water them plentifully, giving enough at each watering to keep the potting mixture thoroughly moist. They dislike lime, so use soft, lime-free water. If water containing lime has to be used, plants may become chlorotic, with the result that their leaves will turn yellow (see page 458). To counteract this, water with a sequestrene compound. Stand pots on trays or saucers of damp pebbles for extra humidity.

Feeding Apply a lime-free liquid fertilizer once every two weeks from late spring to early fall.

Potting and repotting Use a lime-free combination of one part of soil-based potting mixture (see page 429), two parts of peat moss, and one part of coarse sand or perlite. Although it is not possible to retain these plants for any longer than one season entirely indoors, they *can* be kept indefinitely in the right circumstances. When flowers have faded, place the plants in the coolest possible position, water them moderately—enough to make the potting mixture moist throughout but allowing the top half-inch of the mixture to dry out before watering again—and put them outdoors on mild days. After all danger of frost has passed, stand them in the shade outside, preferably with the pots sunk into the ground (only if the soil is low in lime). Keep each such plant moist, spray with clear water on hot evenings, and feed with lime-free fertilizer. Then bring it indoors for another flowering season just as winter begins (but before the first frost).

One way to provide extra humidity for a potted rhododendron is to stand it in a larger pot of peat moss kept constantly moist.

Once more, keep the potted plant cool while buds develop; hot, dry air will cause buds and, possibly, leaves to drop off. A cool conservatory or greenhouse at 45°–55°F is ideal at this stage. From the beginning of the flowering period until the flowers fade, brighter light and more warmth (though not above 70°) become tolerable to the plant.

Plants should be transferred to pots one size larger every two or three years, after flowering but before being moved outdoors. *R. obtusum* hybrids are hardy plants and can be planted permanently in the garden after flowering if it should happen that they are no longer desired as house plants.

Propagation Rhododendrons can be propagated by means of tip cuttings of new growth taken in spring. Plant a 2- to 3-inch-long cutting in a 3-inch pot of moistened rooting mixture consisting of two parts of coarse sand or perlite and one part of peat moss, enclose the potted cutting in a plastic bag or propagating case (see page 443), and keep it in a shady position. When the cutting is well rooted (in about 8-12 weeks), transfer it to a 3-inch pot of the mixture recommended for mature plants. Thereafter, it may be treated as an adult rhododendron.

Special points The larger the plant, the more easily it is carried over into another year. Most young specimens have been removed prematurely from nursery beds, have had their roots pruned, and have been packed into small pots. Thus, often they cannot tolerate the treatment that is necessary for them to continue growing and flowering in subsequent years.

Rhoeo

COMMELINACEAE

Boat lily
R. spathacea 'Variegata'

THE only species of this genus is *R. spathacea* (also known as *R. discolor,* commonly called boat lily, Moses in the cradle, or three-men-in-a-boat). *R. spathacea* forms a loose rosette of mostly upright leaves of 9–12 inches long, 2½ inches wide, and dark green with purplish red undersides. As plants age, a short, fleshy stem is formed. Small, white flowers cupped by striking purple-green, boatlike bracts grow low down among the leaf bases. Flowers are short-lived but profuse, and bracts stay decorative for months.

There is a handsome variegated-leaved form, *R.s.* 'Variegata' (or *R.s.* 'Vittata'), whose leaves have bright yellow, lengthwise stripes; the yellow may be tinged with pink if the plant is grown in bright light. A more compact form, with tighter rosettes of 5- to 6-inch-long leaves, has recently been introduced. Rhoeos are particularly attractive in hanging baskets.

PROPER CARE

Light Provide bright light, but keep plants out of direct sunlight.

Temperature Rhoeos need a minimum temperature of 60°F. Because they cannot tolerate dry air, stand these plants on trays of moist pebbles.

Watering During the active growth period water plants plentifully. At other times give just enough to keep the entire mixture barely moist, allowing the top two-thirds to dry out between waterings.

Feeding Apply standard liquid fertilizer once every two weeks during the active growth period only.

Potting and repotting Use either a peat-based or soil-based potting mixture (see page 429). Repot annually in spring until maximum convenient pot size is reached. Thereafter, topdress plants with fresh mixture (see page 428) every spring. Rhoeos are not deep-rooted and may be grown in shallow pots or pans.

Propagation The offsets produced around the base of plants, usually after flowering, can be removed when 3–4 inches long. Plant them singly in 3- or 4-inch pots containing an equal-parts mixture of peat moss and sand, and treat them as mature rhoeos.

Seed can also be used for springtime propagation. Sow fresh seeds ½ inch deep in 3-inch pots of moistened rooting mixture (see page 444), enclose the pots in plastic bags or a propagating case (see page 443), and keep them warm in medium light. When the seeds have germinated (in four to six weeks), uncover the pots, use standard liquid fertilizer once a month, and water moderately, giving enough to make the mixture moist throughout but allowing the top half-inch to dry out between waterings. When plantlets are about 4 inches high, move them singly into 4-inch pots of standard mixture, and treat them as mature rhoeos.

Be sure to choose a basal offset that has developed some roots of its own when propagating a rhoeo.

Rhoicissus

VITACEAE

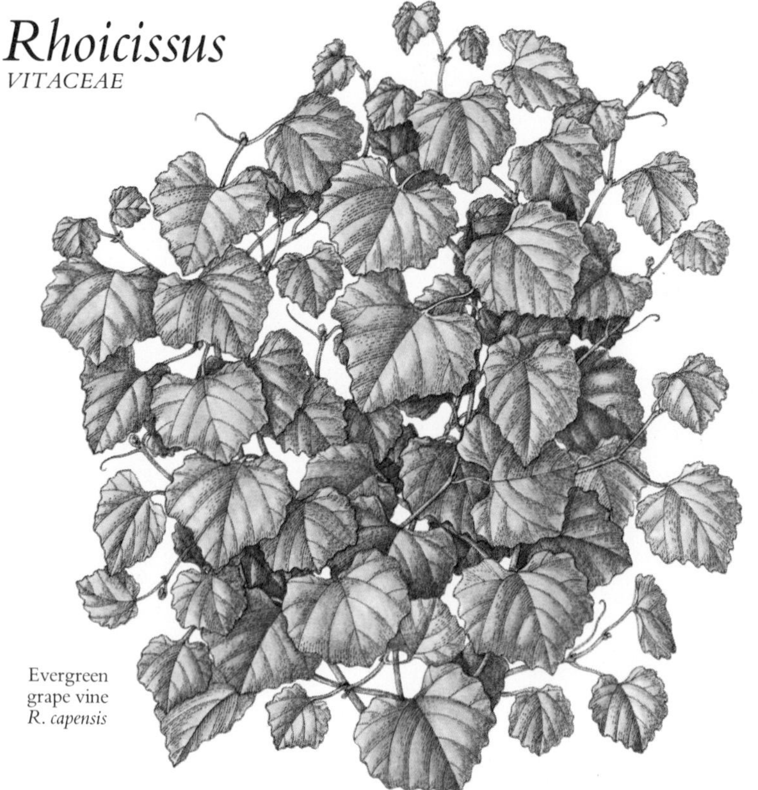

Evergreen grape vine
R. capensis

THE only species of rhoicissus commonly grown indoors, *R. capensis* (evergreen grape vine), has sturdy climbing stems bearing glossy leaves up to 8 inches across. Leaf shape varies from roughly circular with deep indentations to roughly heart-shaped with shallow indentations. All leaves have toothed, slightly undulate edges and are colored bright emerald green, with paler veins above, and rusty brown beneath. The plant, which clings to any available support by wiry tendrils, is easy to grow and can rapidly become 4–6 feet tall.

Note: For *Rhoicissus rhomboidea* see *Cissus rhombifolia*.

PROPER CARE

Light Provide bright light, but without direct sunlight.

Temperature Either warm or cool conditions suit this adaptable plant. If possible, give it a winter rest period at 50°–55°F.

Watering During the active growth period water plentifully, as often as necessary to keep the potting mixture thoroughly moist. During the rest period water sparingly, giving only enough water to make the potting mixture barely moist, allowing the top two-thirds of the mixture to dry out between waterings.

Feeding Apply standard liquid fertilizer once every two weeks during the active growth period only.

Potting and repotting Use a soil-based potting mixture (see page 429). Move plants into pots one size larger each spring, as long as this is practical. After maximum convenient pot size has been reached, an annual topdressing (see page 428) with fresh potting mixture will suffice.

Propagation Propagate from tip cuttings 3–4 inches long taken just as new growth begins in spring. Dip cut ends in hormone rooting powder, and set three or four cuttings in a 3-inch pot containing a moistened equal-parts mixture of peat moss and sand. Enclose the whole in a plastic bag, and keep it in a warm place where it gets bright light filtered through a translucent blind or curtain. After cuttings have rooted—in four to six weeks—pot them individually in the standard mixture and treat them in exactly the same way as mature plants.

Special points Pinch out growing tips regularly to promote bushy growth, and tie in any stray shoots to supporting sticks in the position required. Cut back plants that have grown undesirably big as drastically as required. Older stems will normally send forth new growth.

Rochea

CRASSULACEAE

R. coccinea

ROCHEAS are small shrubs grown primarily for their clusters of flowers. These succulent plants rarely grow more than about 1½ feet tall, with a spread of about 8 inches. Their much-branching stems are 1–2 feet long, with a diameter of ⅓ inch. The leathery, medium green leaves arranged alternately along each stem are roughly elliptic with pointed tips; each leaf grows about 1 inch long, ½ inch wide, and ⅛ inch thick. Flower clusters at the tips of stems and branches are 2–3 inches across. Individual blooms are narrowly tubular (up to 1 inch long), flaring into five tiny petals at the end. Flower color is usually red or white. The flowering period is spring and summer.

See also SUCCULENTS.

RECOMMENDED ROCHEAS

R. coccinea, the best-known species, has bright red flowers. More popular than the species, however, are two of its varieties: *R.c.* 'Flore-albo,' with pure white flowers, and *R.c.* 'Bicolor,' with red-and-white flowers. All the forms have a pleasant hyacinthlike odor when in bloom.

R. versicolor has somewhat narrower, more nearly lance-shaped leaves than those of *R. coccinea.* Flower color varies widely. It may be white, pale yellow, or pink, and the outer surface is often speckled with red.

PROPER CARE

Light Give rocheas direct sunlight at all times. In inadequate light they will not remain compact and bushy.

Temperature Normal room temperatures are suitable for these rocheas throughout most of the year. However, they should be encouraged to enter a rest period during the short-day winter months by being kept in a cool position throughout this time. A winter temperature of 50°–60°F is a good level to aim for.
Watering Water actively growing rocheas moderately, giving enough at each watering to make the potting mixture moist throughout, but allowing the top half-inch of the mixture to dry out before watering again. During the winter months, when the plants should be growing much less actively, water them only sparingly, allowing the top two-thirds of the mixture to dry out between waterings. Overwatering in winter encourages rocheas to continue active growth at a time of year when there is inadequate light for normal growth (see "Light," above).
Feeding As soon as flower buds appear, begin to apply a high-potassium, tomato-type liquid fertilizer to all rocheas once every two weeks. Continue these regular feedings only until the moment when the last flowers have faded and died.
Potting and repotting Grow rocheas in a porous potting mixture consisting of one part of coarse sand or perlite to two parts of standard soil-based mixture (see page 429). Move each plant into a pot one size larger every spring. But if a specimen has lost many lower leaves during the winter and looks untidy, it is probably best to discard the plant and replace it from a cutting. Maximum pot size likely to be required before plants begin to deteriorate is 5–6 inches.
Propagation Rocheas are easy to propagate from stem cuttings taken in spring or summer. Using a sharp knife or pruning shears, remove a 3- to 4-inch-long branch. Allow it to dry for two or three days, and then insert the cut end in a 3-inch pot of the mixture recommended for mature rocheas. Treat the cutting as an adult plant immediately. It should root and begin producing new top growth in three to four weeks.

Propagation from seed is also possible (see *SUCCULENTS*, page 379), but this is a slow method, and, since the results are often unsatisfactory, it is not always recommended for the amateur indoor gardener.

Rohdea

LILIACEAE

Lily of China
R. japonica

THE small genus *Rohdea* includes only one species that is a popular house plant: *R. japonica* (lily of China). This hard-leaved, durable plant has a short, thick, underground rhizome. From this rise many thick, arching, leathery leaves, which grow in tufts arranged, roughly, in two ranks. Each leaf is strap-shaped, up to 1 foot long and 3 inches wide, and slightly undulate. Leaf color is non-glossy green. In early spring a foot-long flower stalk rises from the middle of the plant. The stalk is tipped with a 2-inch-long spike of closely packed blooms, each no more than $\frac{1}{8}$ inch long. Flower color is usually either white or pale yellow. In late summer or early fall the flowers are followed by small red berries.

Two fine examples of the many variegated-leaved forms are *R. j.* 'Marginata,' which has very dark green (almost black) leaves edged in white; and *R.j.* 'Variegata,' which has green leaves striped lengthwise with white or yellow.

PROPER CARE

Light Grow rohdeas in medium light. They cannot tolerate direct sun. Although they can be grown in quite dark corners, they are unlikely to flower if kept far from a window.
Temperature Rohdeas do best in relatively cool conditions (55°–65°F). If possible, keep them at about 50° during the winter rest period. In normally warm room temperatures (above 65°) stand pots on trays or saucers of moist pebbles.
Watering During the active growth period water plentifully. During the rest period water only enough to keep the mixture from drying out.
Feeding Apply standard liquid fertilizer every two weeks during the active growth period only.
Potting and repotting Use a combination of equal parts of soil-based potting mixture (see page 429) and peat moss or leaf mold. In planting a rhizome or portion of rhizome bury it horizontally just below the surface of the mixture. Repot at the end of the flowering season, moving each plant into a pot one size larger until maximum convenient pot size has been reached. Thereafter, topdress the plant annually at the beginning of the flowering period (see page 428).
Propagation Divide overcrowded tufts of leaves in the spring. If an older plant grows too big, take it out of its pot, scrape away most of the old potting mixture from around the rhizome and roots, and separate the tufted growths. Be sure to retain at least two inches of rhizome with every group of leaves. Plant each piece of rhizome in a 3-inch pot of the potting mixture recommended for adult plants, and treat it as a mature rohdea.

Rosa
ROSACEAE

China rose
R. chinensis variety

THE only roses that can be grown indoors are miniature forms, most of which are derived from the dwarf-growing China rose, *R. chinensis*. There has been much hybridization, of course, and the varieties now available are of mixed parentage. There are bushy forms of these small shrubs, climbing forms (which are usually grown on miniature trellises), and forms suitable for training as "standards" (shrubs with a single main stem topped by a shaped head of branches). On average, indoor roses grow 9–12 inches tall. The stems are soft-wooded, much-branching, but rarely thorned. The medium green leaves are composed of five or seven oval, tooth-edged leaflets. Flowers can have only a single circle of petals or many; they can be from $\frac{1}{4}$ to $1\frac{1}{2}$ inches across, fragrant or without fragrance, and of many different colors.

R. chinensis varieties (flowers)

Miniature roses are sometimes classified by flower type, such as hybrid tea types, whose tight, slender flower buds, usually produced singly on long flower stalks, open out to display a full center; Floribunda types, whose flowers of varying forms are carried in clusters; and the Moss Rose types whose stems and flower buds, usually produced in groups of three or four, are covered with a fine, soft mossy growth. The amateur grower can choose from dozens of named varieties, and new types become available every year.

As house plants, roses are often treated as temporary acquisitions, to be retained only for six or eight weeks—from the time their first flower buds begin to open until the last flowers have faded. There is no need to discard them, however, if they can be given an annual rest period in a cold position.

PROPER CARE

Light Actively growing plants need plenty of bright light. They will not flower well without 14–16 hours of bright light every day. Supplementary artificial lighting (see page 446) is necessary in most areas if some growth is to occur during the short-day months. Place fluorescent lamps no more than 3–4 inches above the tops of the plants. During the winter rest period, potted roses lose all their leaves. Once leafless, the quality of light they receive is unimportant.

Temperature During the active growth period normal room temperatures are suitable, but plants that are to be retained must have a two-month rest period in the cold (preferably below 45°F). If they are kept cold—perhaps on an outside window ledge, porch, or balcony—through November and December, they can begin active growth again in January and can be in flower before the end of winter. Whenever possible, plants should be gradually acclimatized to the temperature changes between periods of active growth and rest. One way to do this is by moving them by degrees from a position in sunny warmth to a shaded position in a cooler room, and vice versa.

Watering During the active growth period water moderately, enough to make the potting mixture moist throughout, but allowing the top half-inch to dry out between waterings. During the rest period give only enough to keep the mixture from drying out completely.

Feeding Apply standard liquid fertilizer once every two weeks in the active growth period only.

Potting and repotting Use a soil-based potting mixture (see page 429). These miniature roses flower best when their roots are restricted and when top growth is regularly cut back (see "Special points," below). They should be grown in 4- or 5-inch pots and replanted in fresh potting mixture every year, just as new growth starts after the winter rest.

Propagation The best time to propagate is early spring. Indoor miniature roses are generally grown from stem cuttings or seed. Take tip cuttings 2–3 inches long, dip the cut ends in hormone rooting powder, and plant each cutting in a 3-inch pot of a moistened equal-parts mixture of peat moss and sand. Enclose the whole in a plastic bag, and place it in a warm room in bright filtered light. When rooting has occurred—in six to eight weeks—uncover the cutting, water it just enough to keep the entire potting mixture barely moist, and begin to apply standard liquid fertilizer at two-week intervals. After a further three or four months transfer the young plant to a pot of soil-based mixture and treat it as a mature miniature rose.

Only two kinds of seed, *R. chinensis* 'Minima' and *R. polyantha* 'Nana,' are generally available. Most of the named forms cannot be grown true to type from seed. If seed is used, set a single seed in a 2- or 2½-inch pot of moistened rooting mixture (see page 444), or space out a number of seeds in a small seed tray. Plant seeds ½ inch deep, enclose them in a plastic bag, and keep cool—if possible, at around 50°F—for three or four weeks before bringing them into normal room temperature. As soon as shoots appear, remove the plastic bag. Thereafter, give them bright light filtered through a translucent blind or curtain, and water them just enough to keep the entire rooting mixture barely moist. When seedlings are 1–2 inches high, begin to use standard liquid fertilizer every two weeks. They should be ready for moving into 3-inch pots of standard potting mixture and bright light when they are 3–4 inches tall. Water the young plants more generously, but always allow the top inch of the mixture to dry out between waterings. Supplementary fluorescent light can help to hasten growth at this point (see page 446). When the plants are 5–6 inches tall, move them into 4-inch pots and treat them as mature roses.

Special points Prune these roses at the end of the rest period, using sharp scissors to remove up to half the previous year's growth. Make cuts directly above growth buds (preferably those that point away from the center of the plant, so as to produce an open-centered bush). Throughout the growth period use scissors to remove faded flowers, cutting away 2 inches of stem with each flower. This is a kind of growth-period pruning.

High humidity during the active growth period is essential and will help to discourage red spider mites (see page 455), which often attack indoor roses. Stand plants on trays of damp pebbles or moist peat moss, and mist-spray the foliage daily. A free circulation of air helps to keep the plants healthy. Place them near an open window whenever possible.

Ruellia

ACANTHACEAE

Trailing velvet plant
R. makoyana

THE only species of the genus *Ruellia* commonly grown as a house plant, *R. makoyana* (monkey or trailing velvet plant), is prized for its winter-blooming flowers and satiny leaves. Because of its trailing, much-branching stems which grow 2 feet long, *R. makoyana* is an ideal plant for a hanging basket. The stems carry opposite pairs of oval, 3-inch-long and 1- to 1½-inch-wide leaves on 1-inch-long stalks. Leaf color is violet-tinged olive green with prominent silvery veins on the upper surface, and deep purple on the underside. Rose-red, trumpet-shaped flowers are 2 inches long and 2½ inches wide at the flared end. They are produced singly in leaf axils near growing tips.

PROPER CARE

Light Give ruellias bright light without direct sunlight. Inadequate light during the winter months will shorten the flowering period.

Temperature Keep plants in a warm, moist atmosphere. Stand pots on trays of moist pebbles, and suspend saucers of water under hanging baskets. In temperatures above 70°F mist-spray foliage daily. Minimum tolerable temperature: 55°.

Watering Water plants moderately, but allow the top half-inch of the potting mixture to dry out between waterings. At the end of the annual flowering period give plants a six- to eight-week rest by watering them only enough to keep the mixture from drying out completely.

Feeding Apply standard liquid fertilizer every two weeks except during the short rest period.

Potting and repotting Use a mixture of half peat moss or leaf mold and half soil-based mixture (see page 429). Half-pots, pans, or hanging baskets are the most suitable containers for these shallow-rooted plants. When a specimen begins to fill its container with roots, move it into a slightly bigger one in the spring.

Propagation In summer take 3- to 4-inch-long tip cuttings, each with three or four pairs of leaves, cutting just below a node. Strip off the bottom leaves, and dip the cut end of each cutting in hormone rooting powder. Insert the cuttings singly in 2- to 3-inch pots containing a moistened equal-parts mixture of peat moss and coarse sand or perlite. Place each cutting in a plastic bag or propagating case (see page 443), and stand it in bright filtered light. When rooting has occurred, uncover the cutting and water it sparingly. After 2–3 inches of new growth have been produced, begin to apply standard liquid fertilizer every two weeks. Some 10 to 12 weeks after the start of propagation move the new plant into a 4-inch pot of the recommended mixture for adult plants (or put three or four rooted cuttings together in a hanging basket). Thereafter, treat the plants as mature ruellias.

Special points Aphids often attack the tender growing tips of ruellias. For treatment see page 454.

Saintpaulia

GESNERIACEAE

SAINTPAULIAS (African violets), which are prized for their abundant and colorful flowers, are perhaps the most popular of all house plants. There are more than twenty species in the genus, but only a few are of interest to the average indoor gardener, who is likely to prefer striking modern varieties and hybrids to plants of the type species. The kinds recommended below include outstanding modern forms as well as the five species from which most new kinds have been bred.

All saintpaulias have shallow root systems and either a short stem topped by a rosette of leaves or a creeping, branching, trailing stem bearing alternate leaves. The leaves of the species are generally round or oval, somewhat hairy, medium green on the upper surface, and pale green on the underside. Leafstalks are fleshy and pale green.

S. 'Ballet Eva'

S. 'Rhapsodie Venus'

S. 'Winter's Dream'

S. 'Rhapsodie Gigi'
S. 'Coral Caper'
S. 'Blue Nimbus'

In mature plants flower stalks grow from all leaf axils. Each stalk branches near the tip, and a small, pale green calyx bearing a corolla with five lobes grows from each branch. The corolla is tubular but no more than $\frac{1}{8}$ inch long, and the lobes spread so widely that they look like five separate petals. Flowers of the species are single—they have only one layer of these petals—but a number of the varieties and hybrids are many-petaled, or double. In most forms the two upper lobes of the flower are much smaller than the other three, but some kinds have star-shaped blooms with equal-size lobes. Flower color ranges from white through numerous shades of blue, purple, pink, and red. Tiny, golden yellow pollen sacs are highly noticeable in the center of the flower.

Modern growers have a choice of thousands of varieties of saintpaulia. There should be no cause for concern, therefore, if some of the forms named below are unavailable in a given area. African violets to everyone's taste can be acquired in almost any nursery at almost any time. And if these plants are grown under the right conditions, they will continue to grow and produce flowers throughout the year. Flower and leaf sizes cannot always be predicted, however, since the size of varieties and hybrids frequently depends on growing conditions.

RECOMMENDED SAINTPAULIAS

***S.* 'Ballet'** hybrids have medium to dark green oval or pointed-oval leaves with scalloped edges. Flowers are five-lobed or many-lobed. Lobe edges are ruffled. Flower color is white, pink, purple, blue, or blue with white edges. Leaf and flower size vary, but the rosette-shaped plant will grow about 12 inches across. These hybrids are especially easy to grow

***S.* 'Bicentennial Trail'** is a large trailer with lance-shaped, medium green leaves and deep pink, many-lobed flowers. Like all the larger trailing saintpaulias, this plant is attractive in a hanging basket. The stems of this plant root down in the potting mixture from leaf nodes.

S. confusa is a rosette-forming species with nearly round, slightly scallop-edged, hairy leaves $1\frac{1}{2}$ inches long and $1\frac{1}{4}$ inches wide on 3-inch-long stalks. Each flower stalk grows up to 4 inches long and carries up to four blue-violet flowers $1-1\frac{1}{4}$ inches across.

S. 'Eternal Snow' has medium green leaves and large, many-lobed, white flowers. This rosette-forming plant grows to 15 inches across.

S. grandifolia has much thinner, larger leaves than those of the other recommended rosette-forming species. The leaves are oval with scalloped edges and grow to 4 inches long and $3\frac{1}{2}$ inches wide on 4-inch-long stalks. Flower stalks are about $2\frac{3}{4}$ inches long and carry up to twenty $\frac{3}{4}$-inch-wide, deep violet flowers.

S. grotei is an ancestor of many trailing saintpaulia forms. Its creeping, branching stems will grow to 8 inches long. Nearly round leaves up to 3 inches across have slightly sawtoothed edges and are covered with short, velvety hairs. Leafstalks are up to 10 inches long. Flower stalks about 7 inches long carry two to four 1-inch-wide flowers that vary from blue-violet at the edges to deep violet in the center.

S. ionantha is a rosette-forming species with oval, slightly scalloped, hairy leaves that grow up to 3 inches long and $1\frac{1}{2}$ inches wide on $2\frac{1}{2}$-inch-long stalks. Leaf undersides sometimes have a reddish tinge. Flower stalks up to 5 inches long carry two to eight violet-colored flowers $1-1\frac{1}{4}$ inches across.

S. 'Little Delight' is a miniature rosette-forming hybrid, with a diameter rarely exceeding 6 inches. The medium green leaves are roughly lance-shaped. The flowers are many-lobed and white with purple edges.

S. 'Midget Bon Bon' has variegated, light green and white leaves. The flowers are five-lobed and pale pink. The mature plant measures no more than 6 inches across.

S. 'Mini-Ha-Ha' is also under 6 inches in diameter. It has dark green, lance-shaped leaves and many-lobed mauve flowers with purple shading.

S. 'Optimara' hybrids are recent introductions and each is named after a State. They have rosettes of medium green, roundish leaves with slightly scalloped edges. Flowers are five-lobed, often with ruffled edges, and colors include white, red, and blue.

S. 'Pink N Ink' is a rosette-forming hybrid up to 10 inches across, with medium green, roundish leaves. The many-lobed, star-shaped flowers are pink splashed with purple.

S. 'Pixie Trail' is a miniature trailer. It has medium green heart-shaped leaves and five-lobed pink flowers. Unlike the large trailers, which are generally lodged in hanging baskets, this little plant is best grown in a shallow pot.

S. 'Rhapsodie' hybrids, (many of which are now known as S. 'Melodie' hybrids), have dark green, roundish leaves with slightly scalloped edges. Flowers are five-lobed or many-lobed, and flower color is pink, red, or blue. Plants of this type grow about 12 inches across and, like S. 'Ballet' hybrids, are very easy to grow.

S. schumensis, a rosette-forming plant, is an ancestor of many of the non-trailing miniature saintpaulias. It is small-growing, with $1\frac{1}{4}$-inch, round, scallop-edged, hairy leaves on 2-inch-long stalks. The flower stalks are also about 2 inches long, and they carry up to five 1-inch-wide, pale mauve flowers, which are spotted with violet on the upper lobes.

S. 'Tommie Lou' hybrids are extremely popular variegated-leaved plants. The oval, slightly scalloped leaves have dark green centers, with feathery white or cream markings and solid white or cream borders. Flowers are five-lobed or many-lobed, and any color within the range for saintpaulias. The whole rosette can grow to about 16 inches in diameter.

S. 'Violet Trail,' a large trailing plant, has heart-shaped leaves that are dark green on the upper surface and red on the underside. The glistening, mauve-violet, five-lobed flowers of this hybrid are fairly unusual in that they are star-shaped, with all lobes equal in size.

PROPER CARE

Light Provide bright light without direct sunlight throughout the year. Two or three hours a day of filtered sunlight will benefit saintpaulias, but they should never be subjected to midday sunlight, not even if filtered, for it can scorch both leaves and flowers. Saintpaulias grow well in artificial light. If fluorescent lighting is available, place plants 12 inches below the tubes for about 12 hours a day (see page 446). Given adequate light along with other satisfactory conditions, flowering should be continuous.

Temperature These plants flourish in 65°–75°F warmth. Even a 5° fluctuation from this range will eventually cause growth to stop. High humidity is essential; stand pots on trays of moist pebbles, and suspend dishes of water under hanging baskets.

Watering Water plants moderately, enough to make the potting mixture moist at each watering but allowing the top half-inch of the mixture to dry out before watering again. If indoor temperature falls below 60°F for more than a day or two, reduce the frequency of watering, permitting a full inch of the mixture to dry out between waterings. Too much water at any time can cause the roots of saintpaulias to rot.

Feeding At every watering give all saintpaulias a one-quarter-strength dose of liquid fertilizer containing equal amounts of nitrogen, phosphate, and potash.

Potting and repotting Use a mixture of equal parts of sphagnum peat moss, perlite, and vermiculite, and add three or four tablespoonfuls of dolomite lime to every four cups of the mixture. Plant rosette-forming saintpaulias in shallow pots or pans. To determine the right size of container, measure the diameter of the rosette, and choose a pot or pan with a diameter only about one-third that of the plant. A 5- or 6-inch container should be the largest needed. Miniature and young trailing types can also be grown in pots or pans, but large mature trailers are best grown in hanging baskets, where their stems have plenty of room to root down.

Rosette-forming saintpaulias are best grown in pots with a span one-third that of the plant (see scale above).

Saintpaulias do best when somewhat potbound. Repot these plants in slightly larger containers only about two months after roots have filled the current containers (see page 426). This can be done in any season as long as indoor temperature is above 60°F. When repotting, it is advisable to remove the outer ring of leaves if the leafstalks have been damaged by being pressed against the container rim. Remove each leafstalk by a sharp tug sideways; do not cut stalks away. It is important to break off the entire leafstalk because any stub that remains can rot and infect the main stem.

Holding leafstalk between forefinger and thumb, carefully pull away the whole of a damaged leaf and its stalk when repotting a saintpaulia.

Propagation The easiest way to propagate saintpaulias is by rooting individual leaves, which will then produce plantlets. Remove a leaf (with its stalk) from the second or third row from the outside of the rosette (or take one from near the end of the stem in a trailing plant). With a sharp knife trim the leafstalk down to a length of 1–1½ inches, and insert it ½–¾ inch deep in a 2- to 2½-inch pot of moistened potting mixture. Enclose the whole in a plastic bag or propagating case (see page 443), and keep it in bright filtered light at 65°–75°F. Little or no further watering should be necessary for 7–10 weeks, or as long as it takes for a clump of plantlets rising from the base of the leafstalk to emerge from the surface of the mixture. During the course of the next four weeks uncover the plantlets by degrees until they are fully out of the protected atmosphere. Meanwhile, give just enough water to prevent the potting mixture from drying out, and apply standard liquid fertilizer at one-eighth strength once every week. When plantlets have grown 1½–2 inches tall, carefully pull them away from the mother leaf and move them into individual 2- to 2½-inch pots. Thereafter, treat them as adults.

Saintpaulia leaves can also be rooted in water (see page 439).

Special points Saintpaulias are extremely susceptible to attack by aphids, cyclamen mites, mealy bugs, and root mealy bugs (see pages 454–455). To forestall infestation of a whole collection, always isolate each newly acquired plant for at least a month. During this time any pests that infest the new plant can be dealt with.

Sanchezia

ACANTHACEAE

S. speciosa

THE only species of the genus *Sanchezia* widely grown as a house plant is *S. speciosa* (often, but incorrectly, called *S. nobilis glaucophylla* or *S. glaucophylla*). This erect-growing shrub, which attains an indoor height of no more than 3 feet, has woody, branching stems that carry opposite pairs of stalkless leaves. Each lance-shaped leaf has a pointed tip, a narrowed base, and bluntly toothed edges. Individual leaves are 9–12 inches long and 3–4 inches wide, and leaf color is dark green with some pale yellow or white markings around the midrib and main vein areas. In early summer clusters of tubular, yellow flowers, each up to 2 inches long, are produced at the tip of short flower stalks. Each cluster consists of 8–10 flowers, and the entire cluster is surrounded by a pair of oval, bright red bracts 1–1½ inches long.

There are a number of varieties of *S. speciosa* all characterized by broad or strongly marked coloration along the midrib and veins. One of the most attractive forms is *S.s. variegata,* which has very strong white, cream, and yellow markings.

PROPER CARE

Light Grow sanchezias in bright light filtered through a translucent blind or curtain throughout the year.

Temperature Normal room temperatures are suitable throughout the year. Never subject these plants to temperatures below 55°F. During the active growth period they need high humidity so stand plants on trays of damp pebbles. Let the pebbles dry out, however, for the whole of the winter rest period.

Watering During the active growth period water moderately, giving just enough at each watering to make the potting mixture moist throughout and allowing the top half-inch of the mixture to dry out before watering again. During the winter rest period give only enough to keep the mixture from drying out completely.

Feeding During the active growth period apply standard liquid fertilizer every two weeks.

Potting and repotting Use a soil-based potting mixture (see page 429). Sanchezias grow rapidly and need to be moved into slightly larger pots twice or even three times in one growing season. Move plants on whenever they begin to fill their pots with roots (see page 426). When a plant has grown to a height of 2½–3 feet and is becoming too big for a 7- or 8-inch pot, discard it rather than moving it on to a larger pot (see "Special points," below).

Propagation Propagate in midsummer from cuttings of the sideshoots that develop below flower stalks. Each cutting should be 3–4 inches long, taken immediately below a node, and stripped of the bottom pair of leaves. Dip cut ends in hormone rooting powder, and plant three or four cuttings around the edge of a 4-inch pot containing a moistened equal-parts mixture of peat moss and coarse sand or perlite. Enclose the whole in a plastic bag or propagating case, and stand it in bright filtered light. When renewed top growth indicates that rooting has occurred (normally, in four to six weeks), uncover the rooted cuttings and begin to water very sparingly and to apply standard liquid fertilizer every two weeks. In early fall remove the cuttings from the rooting mixture, and plant each cutting separately in a 3-inch pot of soil-based mixture. Thereafter, treat the young sanchezias in the same way as mature specimens.

Special points Because young plants are much more attractive than older ones, it is generally advisable to replace mature plants with rooted cuttings every other year.

Sansevieria

AGAVACEAE

Mother-in-law-tongue
S.trifasciata 'Laurentii'

COMMONLY called by such names as mother-in-law tongue, good luck plant, lucky plant, devil's tongue, and bowstring hemp, sansevierias are popular and easy to grow. Growth is comparatively slow, and plants last for many years. There are numerous species of two main types: tall-growing plants with stiff, erect, lance-shaped leaves; and dwarf-growing rosette forms. The tall-growing kinds are decorative in groupings, where they can be used to provide compact vertical contrast with different kinds of lower-growing bushy or rosette plants.

Most sansevierias have an attractive marbled pattern on the foliage. The leaves rise directly from a thick rhizome that runs just below the surface of the potting mixture. Every leaf is tipped with a narrow awl-shaped point, and care should be taken not to damage it; a leaf with a broken tip stops growing. Flowers—which appear only erratically—are whitish or yellowish, narrow-petaled, in clusters on an erect spike, and often fragrant.

RECOMMENDED SANSEVIERIAS

S. cylindrica is a rarely-seen tall-growing species with cylindrical leaves about 1 inch thick and up to 3 feet long fanning out from the narrow base. Plants are rigid, ribbed lengthwise, and dark green cross-banded with gray-green when young.

S. liberica has thick, stiff leaves up to 3 feet long, striped lengthwise with wide bands of almost pure white.

S. trifasciata (mother-in-law tongue), with 12- to 18-inch-tall, dark green, marbled, and slightly spiraled foliage, is not in itself a popular indoor plant,

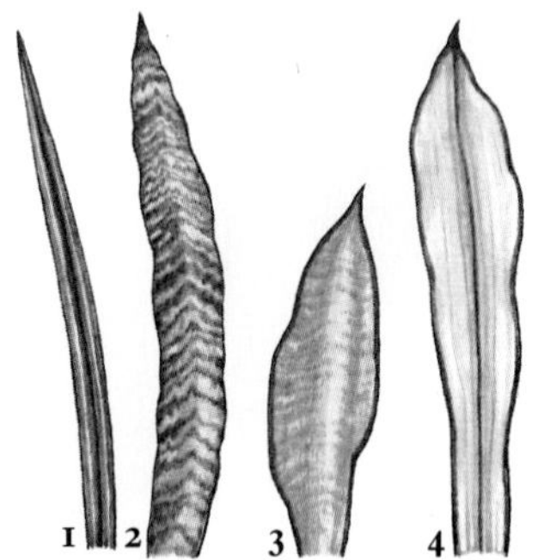

1 *S. cylindrica* **2** *S.trifasciata*
3 *S.trifasciata* 'Moonshine' **4** *S. liberica*

but among its various forms are the most familiar of all sansevierias. One form, *S.t.* 'Bantel's Sensation,' has some portions of its tall leaves striped lengthwise in cream color, while other portions retain the marbling of the species. Another form, *S.t.* 'Craigii,' has very broad, creamy yellow bands running along the leaf margins. Most popular of all is *S.t.* 'Laurentii,' whose leaves are edged in golden yellow. The sword-shaped leaves of all these closely-related plants can grow up to 4 feet tall.

S.t. 'Moonshine' is a recently introduced variety. Its leaves are 9–12 inches long, 3–4 inches wide, and very pale green bordered by a fine dark green line.

One form of *S. trifasciata,* 'Hahnii,' is unlike the others in that it grows as a squat rosette of leaves no more than 6 inches tall. It is found in a variety of colors and patterns. *S.t.* 'Golden Hahnii,' for instance, has bold golden yellow margins and stripes on the

S.trifasciata
'Golden Hahnii'

green leaves; *S.t.* 'Silver Hahnii' has silver green leaves lightly flecked with dark green markings.

S. zeylanica has gray-green leaves with dark green cross-bands. They are 24–30 inches long, channeled with a V section, and arranged in a rather loose, spreading rosette.

PROPER CARE

Light Sansevierias like bright light and can stand plenty of direct sunlight. They will tolerate a certain amount of shade—for example, at a slightly shaded window—without detriment to their growth, but will virtually stop growing if they are forced to live in poor light for any length of time. Plants that have been living in the shade should not be moved to a sunny position without gradual acclimatization; sudden prolonged exposure to sunlight can result in leaf burn.

Temperature As natives of the tropics, these plants thrive in the warmth; from 65°–80°F suits them ideally. Take care never to subject them to temperatures below 55°.

Watering During the active growth period water moderately, giving enough to make the potting mixture moist throughout at each watering, but allowing the top inch of the mixture to dry out before watering again. During the rest period allow at least half of the potting mixture to dry out between waterings. Overwatering leads to rot and causes the large leaves of tall-growing types to topple over at the point where they join the rootstock. To prevent rot in rosette types, do not let water settle in the center of plants.

Feeding Do not overfeed these sansevierias. Apply standard liquid fertilizer once a month to all plants during the active growth period, but only at half strength.

Potting and repotting For open, quick drainage add one-third coarse sand or perlite to a soil-based potting mixture (see page 429), and put plenty of clay-pot fragments into the bottom of the pot.

Sansevierias do not mind cramped root conditions and so can be left undisturbed for several years. Fleshy, usually cream-colored roots will often appear on the surface of the potting mixture, but these plants do not need repotting until they crack their pots. Ideally, however, they should be moved on shortly before reaching that stage. In upright-growing plants repotting is advisable when the leaves occupy most of the pot surface. With the rosette-forming *S.t.* 'Hahnii' and its varieties, the only way to check is by examining the roots; if they are packing the pot so that little soil is visible, repot them immediately. This procedure is best done in early spring. Use clay pots for the tall plants, which tend to be top-heavy. In years when plants are not repotted, topdress them (see page 428) with fresh potting mixture, first scraping away some of the loose old mixture carefully so as not to do any inadvertent damage to any near-surface roots.

Propagation It is possible to propagate sansevierias by leaf cuttings or—much more satisfactorily—by dividing up overcrowded clumps of leaves. In order to propagate by means of this second method, detach clusters of leaves from the rootstock with a sharp knife when the leaves are 6 inches long for taller types, 2 inches for rosettes. Most clusters will have some roots attached and can be planted directly in the normal mixture; those without roots will root quickly in a mixture of peat moss and sand.

For leaf cuttings, slice leaves crosswise into 2-inch-long pieces, remembering which is top and which is bottom, because cuttings must, of course, be planted right end up. Push three or four leaf sections about $\frac{1}{2}$ inch into a moistened mixture of peat moss and sand in a 3-inch pot, place them in bright light in normally warm room temperatures and water sparingly, just enough to make the potting mixture barely moist. Eventually, rhizomes will be produced, but it is a slow process. Moreover, the yellow-bordered varieties of *S. trifasciata* do not pass on any of their characteristic leaf coloration when they are propagated by this means.

Note: When new rhizomes are sufficiently developed for potting up in the normal mixture, it is best to cut away the old leaf sections.

Special points Keep a careful watch for vine weevils which often eat pieces from the edges of leaves, causing irreparable damage. For treatment of these pests see page 456.

Topdressing a sansevieria

Because these plants like cramped roots, do not repot each year. Instead remove the top inch of the old potting mixture.

Replace this with fresh mixture and firm it down, taking care to cover any exposed roots.

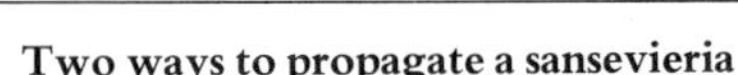

Two ways to propagate a sansevieria

The easiest way is to detach offsets from the rhizomatous rootstock and pot them up.

A slower method involves taking leaf cuttings. Use a sharp knife to remove a whole leaf.

Chop the leaf into 2-inch-long pieces, remembering which way up they are to be planted.

Plant several of these pieces together in a small pot. In time young shoots will appear.

Saxifraga
SAXIFRAGACEAE

Mother-of-thousands
S.stolonifera

ONLY one species of this very large genus is suitable for use as a house plant: *S. stolonifera* (formerly known as *S. sarmentosa*), which has been aptly termed mother-of-thousands because of its many offspring. It is also known by a number of such inappropriate and misleading common names as beefsteak geranium, strawberry geranium, and strawberry begonia. It is a stemless plant that grows no more than about 9 inches tall, with loose rosettes of almost circular leaves up to 4 inches across, graceful flower spikes, and attractive trailing shoots that carry miniature plantlets. The leaves are deep olive green, roundly toothed, netted above with fine silver veining, and colored reddish purple beneath. They are borne on leafstalks up to about 4 inches long, and the stalks as well as the leaves are covered with short, soft hairs, which are reddish when young but gradually turn green. The red, threadlike stolons that bear the little plantlets closely resemble strawberry runners. They are of varying lengths (sometimes as much as 3 feet long); they emerge from the center of the plant and they occasionally divide into several threads. Some of the plantlets at the ends of stolons remain small while attached to the parent plant. Others grow larger, often attaining proportions almost as great as those of the parent plant, and can more readily be used for propagation (see below).

The flower spikes, which are up to 18 inches long, are produced in late summer. They carry loose clusters of star-shaped flowers that are white with a yellow center. Each flower is about 1 inch across, with two of its petals appreciably longer than the rest. One of the forms, *S.s.* 'Tricolor' (magic carpet), is smaller than the others, and its leaves, which have cream-colored edges, turn rose-pink if the plant is grown in good light. *S.s.* 'Tricolor' is less vigorous than the type plant in terms of both rate of growth and of plantlet production, however.

These plants are not dense enough to fill hanging baskets by themselves, but they look most attractive in small hanging pots, where their trailing shoots and decorative, colorful leaves are displayed to full advantage.

The long, threadlike stolons that bear the little plantlets of S.s. *'Tricolor' look decorative in hanging pots, but are delicate and easily damaged.*

PROPER CARE

Light A little direct sunlight every day (an hour or two of early-morning sun, if possible) helps saxifrages to keep their leaf coloring, but do not place them in hot, prolonged sunshine. The variegated-leaved form *S.s.* 'Tricolor,' however, must have at least three hours a day of direct sunlight or the leafstalks will become long and spindly, and much of the leaf contrast will be lost.

Temperature *S. stolonifera* grows best in fairly cool conditions—ideally, 50°–60°F. It can, however, tolerate somewhat higher daytime temperatures during the active growth period (from spring to late fall). *S.s.* 'Tricolor' will thrive if it is kept in normally warm room temperatures throughout the year. If indoor temperatures rise above 65°, all saxifrages require high humidity. Stand potted plants on trays of pebbles kept permanently moist, and suspend dishes of water under hanging baskets. Keep plants in a well-ventilated position, but out of drafts. Minimum tolerable temperature: 40°F.

Watering During the active growth period water plentifully, as much as necessary to make the potting mixture thoroughly moist, but never allow the pot to stand in water. After plants have flowered, gradually reduce the amount of water given over a period of about two weeks. During the rest period give only enough water to keep the potting mixture from completely drying out.
Feeding Give standard liquid fertilizer once a month during the active growth period only.
Potting and repotting Use a soil-based potting mixture (see page 429). For extra drainage put an inch-deep layer of clay-pot fragments in the bottom of containers. In the spring move young plants into pots one size larger as needed. Old plants become straggly, and so these saxifrages are not normally retained for more than two or three years, especially since young plants not only look better than old ones but begin producing plantlet-bearing stolons early in life (see "Propagation," below).
Propagation Propagation is extremely easy by means of the stolon-borne plantlets. Detach these from the parent and plant them individually in 2- to 3-inch pots containing an equal-parts mixture of peat moss and sand. If placed at a slightly shaded window in a warm room and watered just enough to make the rooting mixture barely moist, they will root in a few weeks and can then be moved into pots of the standard mixture and treated as mature plants. Alternatively, leave young plantlets attached to the parent and anchor them down with pegs in contact with rooting mixture in nearby pots. Cut them away from the parent when they have sent roots into the mixture. This process is similar to layering (see page 439).

A saxifrage is easily propagated. Simply cut off the little plantlets and pot them up separately.

Schizocentron
MELASTOMATACEAE

Spanish shawl
S.elegans

BOTANISTS have recently decided that *Schizocentron elegans* (Spanish shawl) should be included in the genus *Heterocentron;* its correct name is *H. elegans*. It is still better known by its earlier name, however, so that name has been retained here.

S. elegans is a creeping or trailing plant with slender, slightly hairy, reddish stems. These stems are noded at intervals and root into the potting mixture wherever the nodes come in contact with it. Thus, the plant eventually forms a dense mat. In hanging baskets the stems trail down for 1–2 feet, producing short, reddish branches at frequent intervals. The dark green leaves, which are arranged in opposite pairs on stems and branches, are pointed-oval, $\frac{1}{4}$–$\frac{3}{4}$ inch long, and up to $\frac{1}{2}$ inch wide, with $\frac{1}{4}$-inch-long leafstalks. *S. elegans* flowers in summer. Each deep purple bloom appears at the tip of one of the branches on a $\frac{3}{4}$-inch-long stalk. The flower, which measures 1 inch across, consists of four evenly spaced, rounded petals, with a cluster of prominent purple stamens in the center.

PROPER CARE

Light Give these plants bright filtered light. Unless they have adequate light all year long, they will produce few, if any, flowers.
Temperature Schizocentrons do well in normal room temperatures if the air is sufficiently humid. For increased humidity stand pots on trays or saucers of moist pebbles, and suspend saucers of water under hanging baskets. Do not expose these plants to temperatures below 55°F.
Watering Water moderately all year long, allowing the top half-inch of the mixture to dry out before watering the plant again.
Feeding Apply standard liquid fertilizer once a month all year long.
Potting and repotting Use an equal-parts combination of soil-based potting mixture (see page 429) and coarse leaf mold or peat moss. Move plants to pots one size larger only when they have filled their current containers with roots (see page 426). The maximum pot size needed is likely to be 5–6 inches. Discard plants in hanging baskets every two or three years, and replace them with cuttings.
Propagation A 3-inch-long tip cutting that includes three or four pairs of leaves will root at almost any time. Take each cutting just below a node, and remove the bottom pair of leaves. Plant three or four cuttings together in a 3-inch pot containing a moistened equal-parts mixture of peat moss and coarse sand or perlite. Enclose the whole in a plastic bag or propagating case, and stand it in bright filtered light. After rooting has occurred (probably in three to four weeks), uncover the pot and begin to water sparingly, allowing the top two-thirds of the rooting mixture to dry out between waterings. In addition, start monthly applications of standard liquid fertilizer. About three or four months from the beginning of propagation, transfer the three or four rooted cuttings into a 4-inch pot of the recommended mixture for adults, and treat the combined planting as a mature schizocentron. For a hanging basket plant 9 to 12 cuttings together.

Schlumbergera
CACTACEAE

Claw cactus
S. truncata

THERE are only three recognized species of schlumbergera, and specimens grown as house plants are more likely to be hybrids than representatives of the true species. In the wild these jungle cacti inhabit moist tropical forests, where they grow in pockets of leaf debris in the clefts of tree branches, and they do best if indoor conditions approximate those of their natural habitat. A good average specimen is likely to have a height and spread of about 12 inches. The densely branching, mainly pendent stems consist of many thin, flat, medium green segments. Each of these joined segments is $1-1\frac{1}{2}$ inches long and $\frac{3}{4}-1$ inch wide and has a prominent midrib. The precise shapes and other features of the segments vary considerably among the species and hybrids. Minuscule areoles, some of which bear tiny bristles, are situated in notches along the edges of the segments. There is a bigger, elongated areole at the tip of the end segment of each stem, and flowers arise in abundance from these terminal areoles. Each areole can produce a single bloom or a pair, and there is a relatively long flowering period sometime in early or late winter.

The appearance of flowers during the Christmas season in some of the hybrids has given rise to the name Christmas cactus, loosely applied to several forms. The flowers are unusual for cacti, since they are not symmetrical in shape but have different right and left halves (as do snapdragons or pea flowers). Each bloom is about 1 inch across and $1\frac{1}{2}-3$ inches long, and the longer flowers may seem to consist of separate tiers of petals. Individual blooms last for a few days, and a specimen with many buds may flower for several weeks.

See also CACTI.

RECOMMENDED SCHLUMBERGERAS

S. 'Bridgesii' (also called *S.* 'Buckleyi'; popularly known as Christmas cactus) is a hybrid between *S. truncata* and the rarely seen species *S. russelliana*. The stem segments have rounded notches and rounded ends.

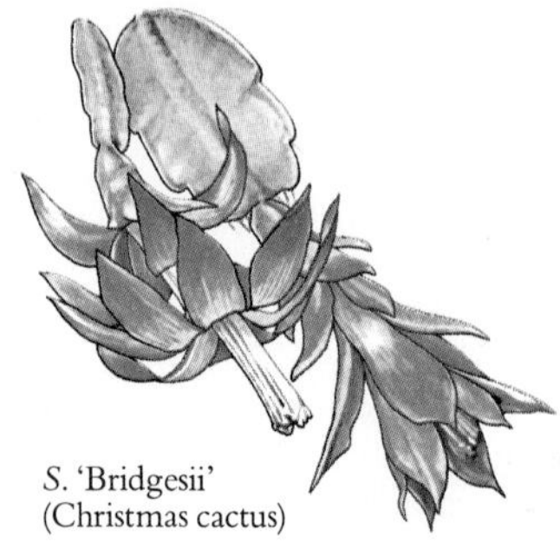

S. 'Bridgesii'
(Christmas cactus)

The flowers are magenta and appear around Christmas or somewhat later.

S. truncata (also called *Zygocactus truncatus;* commonly known as claw, crab, or Thanksgiving cactus) has stem segments with deeply incised notches along the edges and pronglike projections, not unlike a crab's claws, at the ends. The pink to deep red flowers have attractively turned-back petals and usually begin to appear a few weeks before Christmas. *S. truncata* is a parent of most of the schlumbergera hybrids. There are many of these, and they are sold under a variety of names that are apt to differ in different places at different times. Some have rounded stem segments, others have the more pointed type (and these latter are often informally called crab cacti). The flowers also differ considerably in shape, and flower color may be white or almost any shade of pink or red.

In addition to hybridizing these plants, professional growers have produced a novelty form of the Christmas cactus which can occasionally be obtained. A schlumbergera is grafted onto the top of a tall, single-stemmed cactus, and as the schlumbergera grows, its many stems arch over to form a "weeping" plant. In a large specimen the graft is completely hidden and when the plant is in full flower, the effect is impressive.

PROPER CARE

Light Like other jungle cacti, schlumbergeras should never be exposed to full summer sunlight. Medium light at a partly shaded window is best throughout spring, summer, and fall. The less powerful winter sun is not so likely to harm these plants. Flower buds start to form in early fall, and full flowering is initiated by the restricted light of shortening days. Once these cacti have begun to bud, do not keep them in a living room where artificial lights may be burning virtually all evening every day. To encourage the abundant flowering characteristic of healthy schlumbergeras, either move plants to rooms generally left unlighted after dark or cover budding plants with black plastic sheets when lights are switched on. If a specimen that should flower in late December does not usually flower till well after Christmas, try helping it by giving it an extensive period of artificial short days: Beginning in early fall, put the plant in a dark place every day at twilight, and keep it there till morning. This must be done very carefully (see "Special points," below).

Temperature Normal room temperatures are suitable throughout the year. All schlumbergeras will benefit from being placed in a shady spot outdoors during late spring and summer, but move them back indoors before the start of cold weather.

Watering Although these are generally winter-flowering plants, their stems grow most actively during the months from early spring to early fall. During the entire year except for a brief period following the end of the flowering period, water plentifully as often as necessary to keep the potting mixture thoroughly moist, but do not allow pots to stand in water. When flowering ceases (probably in late winter), reduce amounts, and water only moderately—enough to moisten the mixture at each watering but allowing the top half-inch of the mixture to dry out before watering again. Resume plentiful waterings as soon as new stem growth starts in spring. For increased humidity mist-spray the plants daily, especially in spring and summer. Because schlumbergeras dislike hard water (water with a high calcium content), use rainwater, if possible, for all watering purposes. Never permit the potting mixture to dry out completely.

Feeding Except during the brief period of moderate watering immediately following the end of the flowering period, apply a high-potassium, tomato-type fertilizer once every two weeks throughout the year.

Potting and repotting Although actively growing schlumbergeras require plentiful watering, they must not be permitted to get waterlogged. To avoid this possibility, use a peat-based potting mixture made more porous by the addition of one part of coarse sand or perlite to every three parts of the standard mixture. Grow plants in ordinary pots or hanging baskets. The latter are particularly suitable for larger specimens; to retain the potting mixture in the baskets, line them with sphagnum moss.

Repot every year when plants have finished flowering. Move each plant into a container one size larger only if roots have filled the current one. Otherwise, shake off the spent potting mixture, replace the plant in its container, which has been cleaned, and add fresh mixture as necessary. Schlumbergeras do not have large root systems, and a specimen a foot across can be grown in a 4- or 5-inch pot or basket.

Propagation Schlumbergeras are easy to propagate from cuttings at any time in the spring or summer. Remove a section of stem consisting of two or three joined segments, allow it to dry for a few hours, and push the bottom segment gently into a 3-inch pot of the potting mixture recommended above. Insert the segment just deep enough to support the whole cutting. Several such cuttings may be inserted around the edge of a larger container, if desired. Treat the cuttings as mature plants. They should start into growth within four weeks.

Seed is sometimes available, usually of "mixed hybrids." Raising these cacti from seed presents no problems (see *CACTI*, page 119), but it will be three or four years before the resultant plants can be evaluated.

Special points Although it is common to see schlumbergeras covered with buds or in full bloom in florists' shops at Christmastime, do not be disappointed if plants grown in the home fail to flower by the calendar. They will usually bloom later. Professional nurserymen have perfected the art of forcing these plants for the Christmas market.

Some growers find that flower buds drop off after they have formed. This can result from such obvious causes as drafts, sudden changes of temperature, or either dried-out or waterlogged roots. There is another possibility, however: If these plants are turned around when buds are small, the buds themselves are likely to try to turn to face the light, and the effort will weaken them. So when moving a budding schlumbergera (as recommended above, under "Light"), be careful not to change the plant's position relative to the source of light.

Scilla

LILIACEAE

SCILLAS (wood-hyacinths) are small, bulbous-rooted plants notable for the brightly colored flowers of some kinds, the speckled or striped leaves of others, and both foliage and flowers of still others.

Indoor scillas include two distinct kinds, the hardy and the tender. Hardy types, which can withstand extreme cold, will not bloom if kept indoors for more than a single season. They are treated as temporary house plants, to be enjoyed while in flower but to be discarded (or planted out of doors) when flowering stops. The tender kinds, which cannot tolerate extreme cold, are generally kept indoors for several years. Although they have a winter rest period, their leaves remain decorative throughout the year, whereas the bulbs of the hardy species lose all their top growth after the end of the flowering season. Flowers of hardy scillas are generally more brightly colored than those of the tender forms.

The bulbs of both kinds are about $\frac{1}{2}$ inch in diameter, usually green or cream-colored, and covered with a thin, papery skin (known as the "tunic"). This tunic can be shiny and almost transparent, permitting the basic green or cream color to show through, or it is opaquely deep purple or brown tinged with purple. Hardy species are bought as single bulbs and remain single. The tender species produce offsets profusely, so that a tightly packed cluster of small bulbs can cover the surface of a pan of potting mixture within a few years. The leaves of all scillas are stalkless, broadly lance-shaped, from 2 to 9 inches long, and $\frac{3}{4}$–1 inch wide. Leaf color is rich, shiny green in the hardy species, and variously patterned in the tender kinds. Up to three or four flower stalks rising among the leaves from the center of each bulb bear several pendent, bell-shaped flowers.

See also BULBS, CORMS, and TUBERS.

RECOMMENDED SCILLAS

S. adlamii, a tender species, has fleshy, 8- to 9-inch-long leaves that are olive green striped lengthwise with fine, brown lines. Very small, deep purple flowers, produced in the spring, are massed close together at the end of

Wood-hyacinth
Scilla violacea

each slender, 3- to 4-inch-long stalk. The bulb is dull green, and it has a transparent tunic.

S. ovalifolia is a tender species with fewer leaves than most other scillas. Sometimes there are only two or three 2½- to 3-inch-long leaves to each bulb. Each leaf has undulate edges and is pale green, spotted with darker green on the upper surface. Tiny, greenish flowers appear in spring. They are arranged in a loose, 2- to 3-inch-long spike at the end of a flower stalk 4–6 inches long. The pale green bulb has a transparent tunic.

S. siberica (Siberian squill), a hardy species, has narrow, channeled, bright green leaves 6 inches long. Deep blue flowers, produced in early spring, are ¾ inch across and are generally arranged in threes at the top of each 3- to 5-inch-long flower stalk. The bulb is white, with a deep violet-purple tunic. There is a white-flowered form, *S.s.* 'Alba'; and another, *S.s.* 'Atrocoerulea' (spring beauty), with deeper blue, earlier-blooming flowers.

S. tubergeniana is a hardy plant with apple green leaves up to 4 inches long. Flowers ¾ inch wide appear in early spring and are pale blue, with a threadlike, deeper blue line running down the center of each petal. The flowers are arranged in threes at the top of 3- to 5-inch-long stalks; some are pendent, some are held erect and some extend horizontally. The bulb is yellowish, with a transparent tunic.

S. violacea (now officially *Ledebouria socialis*), the most familiar of the tender scillas, has fleshy, pointed leaves 2–4 inches long. Leaf upper surfaces are silvery gray blotched and banded with olive green, and the undersides are deep violet. Dense clusters of tiny, green flowers edged with white are produced in spring on flower stalks 3–6 inches long. The bulb is purplish, with a transparent tunic.

PROPER CARE

Light The tender scillas require bright light with three to four hours a day of direct sunlight. Bulbs of the hardy species (which are best planted in fall) should be kept in the dark for the first 10 to 12 weeks, while roots and top growth are forming. In late winter as soon as the flower buds begin to appear, introduce the plants gradually (over a period of about 10 days) to bright filtered light. Do not subject them to direct sunlight at any time.

Temperature During the active growth period of the tender scillas normal room temperatures are suitable. During the rest period keep them at 50°–60°F, if possible. Potted bulbs of the hardy species need temperatures no higher than about 50° throughout most of the winter. Once flower buds are showing, temperatures up to 60° become tolerable. Although hardy scillas will flower at temperatures above 60°, warmth will shorten the life of the flowers.

Watering During the active growth period water tender species moderately, allowing the top half-inch of the mixture to dry out before watering again. During the rest period water these scillas only enough to prevent the mixture from drying out.

During the long period while hardy bulbs are forming roots in the dark, test the potting mixture every two weeks to make sure that it remains moist. If necessary, add just enough water to keep the mixture from drying out. From the moment that flower heads emerge from the necks of the bulbs until all flowering stops, water plentifully.

Feeding It is not necessary to feed the hardy species during their short life indoors. Apply standard liquid fertilizer to the tender kinds once a month during the active growth period.

Potting and repotting Use a soil-based potting mixture (see page 429), and plant all scilla bulbs in pans or half-pots. Plant bulbs of the hardy species in early fall, burying several bulbs just below the surface of the potting mixture in a single container. Set the bulbs so that they almost, but not quite, touch one another, water enough to moisten the mixture without making it sodden, and place the container in a cool, dark position. If necessary, enclose the potted bulbs in a plastic bag and put it on a shady window ledge or balcony. Darkness and cold are essential if the bulbs are to make roots before making top growth. (For further instructions on care see "Light," "Temperature," and "Watering," above.)

Pot up the bulbs of tender scillas in the spring. Put no more than three bulbs in a single 4- or 6-inch pan or half-pot. Space the bulbs evenly over the surface, and bury only the bottom half of each bulb in the potting mixture. During the first four to six weeks do not feed the plants, and water sparingly, allowing the top half of the mixture to dry out between waterings. When the new roots should be well established, treat the plants in the normal way. Break up overcrowded clumps every two or three years.

Propagation Hardy scillas are not propagated indoors. To propagate the tender kinds break bulbs away from clumps after the flowers have faded (normally, in late spring), and pot them up as recommended above (see "Potting and repotting").

Scindapsus

ARACEAE

Golden hunter's robe
S.aureus

PLANTS of the genus *Scindapsus* (devil's ivy) are climbers that are closely related to philodendrons. The familiar indoor species *S. aureus* has recently been classified as belonging to another genus *(Epipremnum),* but the plant is still so widely known as a scindapsus that the earlier name is being retained here.

In the wild these plants climb high up the trunks and along the limbs of trees by attaching fleshy aerial roots to the rough bark. Indoors, they grow 4–6 feet tall. Their leathery, usually shiny-surfaced, heart-shaped leaves are arranged alternately on 2- to 3-inch-long leafstalks. Flowers are not produced indoors. All forms of scindapsus can be trained to grow upright on stakes, wires, or strings. They can also be encouraged to use their aerial roots to support themselves on slabs of rough tree bark as long as the bark is kept constantly moist. Or they can trail down from either pots or hanging baskets. (For plant supports see page 432.)

RECOMMENDED SCINDAPSUSES

S. aureus (now correctly called *Epipremnum aureum;* commonly known as golden hunter's robe, pothos vine, or Solomon Island's ivy) has angular, yellowish green stems and bright green leaves irregularly marked with yellow. On young plants leaves are 4–6 inches long and wide, but they can be twice as big on older plants growing in large pots. One form, *S.a.* 'Golden Queen,' has stems and leaves almost completely golden yellow. Another, *S.a.* 'Marble Queen,' has stems and leafstalks that are white marked with green, and leaves that are white to cream-colored flecked with green and gray-green markings. A third form, *S.a.* 'Wilcoxii,' has green and yellow leaves in which colored areas are sharply defined.

***S. pictus* 'Argyraeus'** (formerly *Pothos argyraeus*) is the only form of this species grown in the home. Its rounded stems are olive green. The 2- to 3-inch-long, lusterless leaves are dark olive green with gray-green spots on the upper surface. Leaf undersides are pale green without markings.

S.pictus 'Argyraeus'

PROPER CARE

Light Bright filtered light throughout the year is best for these plants. At low light levels the leaves lose much of their color contrast.

Temperature Normal room temperatures are suitable during the active growth period. Give scindapsuses a winter rest around 60°F, if possible. They can tolerate a minimum of 50°. For increased humidity in warm rooms stand pots on trays of damp pebbles, and suspend saucers of water under hanging baskets.

Watering During the active growth period water moderately, allowing the top half-inch of the potting mixture to dry out before watering again. During the winter rest period give just enough to prevent the potting mixture from drying out completely.

Feeding Apply standard liquid fertilizer every two weeks during the active growth period.

Potting and repotting Use a soil-based potting mixture (see page 429). Move plants into pots one size larger every spring until maximum convenient size (probably 8 inches) has been reached. Thereafter, topdress every spring (see page 428). If planting in a hanging basket, place five or six rooted cuttings around the rim of the basket. These will have enough space for only two or three years. After that replace them with newly rooted cuttings in fresh mixture.

Propagation Propagate in spring from tip cuttings 3–4 inches long. Take each cutting immediately below a node, remove the bottom leaf, and dip the cut end in hormone rooting powder. Plant three or four cuttings together around the rim of a 3-inch pot containing a moistened equal-parts mixture of peat moss and coarse sand or perlite. Enclose the whole in a plastic bag or propagating case (see page 443), and stand it in bright filtered light. After rooting occurs (in four to six weeks), uncover the cuttings, water them moderately, and apply standard liquid fertilizer once a month. About three months after the start of propagation move each plant singly into a 3- or 4-inch pot (or several into a hanging basket) of soil-based mixture and treat them as mature specimens.

Special points Prevent a scindapsus from growing too big by cutting back stems of larger plants every spring to a point just in front of a healthy leaf.

Scirpus

CYPERACEAE

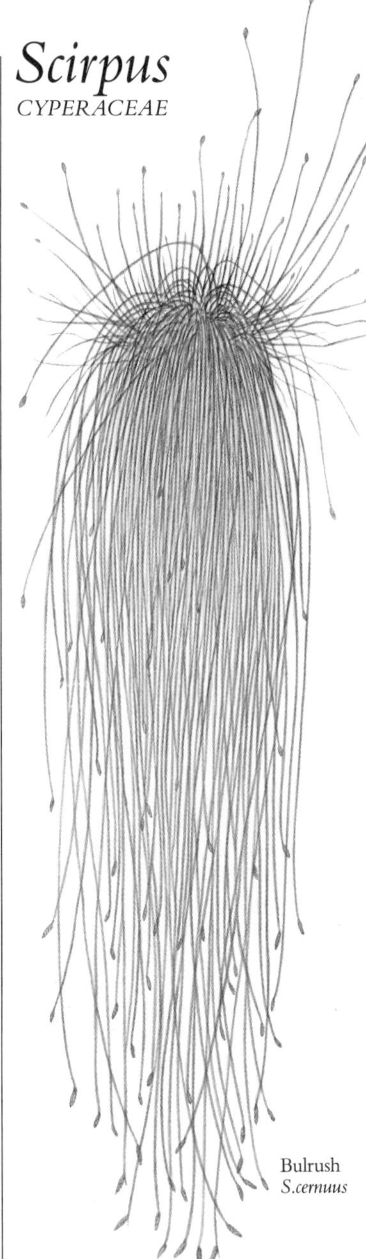

Bulrush
S.cernuus

THE genus *Scirpus* (bulrush) includes over 300 species of stemless plant that thrive on marshy land and in shallow water. The only species generally grown indoors, *S. cernuus,* is a graceful, grasslike plant that produces dense tufts of threadlike, fresh green leaves arising directly from a creeping underground rootstock. The cylindrical leaves, which resemble stems, grow about 10 inches long, and each carries at its tip a white to cream-colored flower no bigger than a pinhead. Flowers can appear at any time. Although not particularly interesting in themselves, they provide an attractive contrast to the slim, green line of the leaves. New leaves stand erect at first, but they begin to arch downward as they age. For this reason scirpuses usually show to best advantage when they have been planted in hanging baskets.

PROPER CARE

Light Give scirpuses medium light. Unlike most house plants, they thrive in a position at a north-facing window or even at a window that is obscured by a nearby obstruction.

Temperature Normal room temperatures are suitable. These plants, however, grow actively all year long in temperatures above 55°F. They can tolerate lower winter temperatures (down to about 45°) but should be given a rest (see "Watering," below) if indoor temperatures are likely to remain unusually low for more than two or three days.

Watering During the active growth period (which may be continuous) water plentifully as often as necessary so as to keep the potting mixture thoroughly and constantly moist. Pots may even be permitted to stand in water. Hanging baskets filled with scirpuses will dry out very quickly; they may need a daily soaking in a bucket of water during this period. If temperatures fall below 55°F at any time, encourage these plants to take a rest period by watering very sparingly, giving only enough to keep the potting mixture from drying out completely.

Feeding Apply standard liquid fertilizer to actively growing plants once every four weeks.

Potting and repotting Use a soil-based potting mixture (see page 429). Move scirpuses into slightly larger pots or hanging baskets whenever the tufted growths completely cover the surface of the mixture. Pots bigger than 5 inches should not be necessary, since young plants are more attractive than old ones. Split up any clump that has reached the 5-inch size, and use the pieces for propagation.

Propagation Propagate scirpuses by dividing overcrowded clumps, preferably in the spring. Pull the clumps apart gently, making sure that each section retains at least 20 leaves. Plant the sections either singly in 3-inch pots or group three or four together in a single hanging basket, and treat them immediately in exactly the same way as mature plants.

Sedum

CRASSULACEAE

THERE are several hundred species of sedum (stone crop or gold moss); some are fairly large shrubs, others are low-growing creepers or trailers. There is enormous variety within the genus, but most forms are alike in having fleshy, and much-branching stems thickly clothed with fleshy, stalkless leaves. The species commonly grown as house plants are valued mainly for their decorative foliage. Flowers are not always produced in indoor specimens. When they do appear, they are normally grouped at stem tips in attractive flower heads 2–3 inches across, with each starlike bloom only $\frac{1}{4}$–$\frac{1}{2}$ inch wide. Flower color is usually white, but can be various shades of pink or yellow. The flowering season is generally spring or summer, although a few types are winter-flowering.

See also SUCCULENTS.

RECOMMENDED SEDUMS

S. adolphi (golden sedum) attains a height and spread of only 6 inches. The upright stems bear elliptic, bluntly pointed leaves 1 inch long, $\frac{5}{8}$ inch broad, and $\frac{1}{4}$ inch thick. Leaf color is yellowish green edged in red. White flowers may appear in spring.

S.rubrotinctum (Christmas cheer) *S.adolphi* (golden sedum)

S.sieboldii 'Medio-variegatum'

S. allantoides is a bushy plant that grows 12 inches high, with a similar spread. The thick leaves, arranged alternately on drooping stems, are

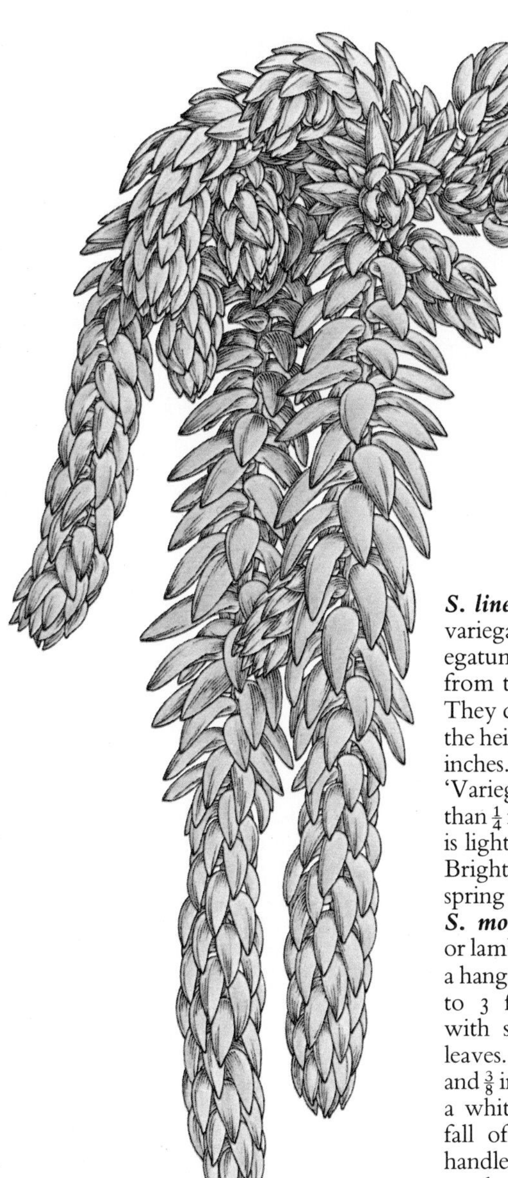

Donkey's tail
S.morganianum

roughly club-shaped, about 1 inch long, and ¾ inch across. Leaf color is green, but covered with dusty grayish white bloom. Greenish white flowers are produced in summer.

S. bellum, which grows about 6 inches high with a spread of up to 12 inches, has stems that branch only from the base. The rounded leaves closely spaced along the stems are spoon-shaped, about 1 inch long, ½ inch wide, and ¼ inch thick. They are covered with so much powdery white bloom that their bright green color is hardly visible. During its first year *S. bellum* produces a flower stem, but the white flowers do not appear until late winter of the second year.

S. lineare is chiefly seen indoors in a variegated-leaved form, *S.l.* 'Variegatum.' The stems of this plant arch from the base and become prostrate. They can grow to 10 inches long, but the height of the plant never exceeds 3 inches. The lance-shaped leaves of *S.l.* 'Variegatum' are 1 inch long and less than ¼ inch broad and thick. Leaf color is light green edged in creamy white. Bright yellow flowers appear in late spring or summer.

S. morganianum (donkey's, horse's, or lamb's tail), an appropriate plant for a hanging basket, has trailing stems up to 3 feet long completely covered with small, overlapping, cylindrical leaves. Each leaf is about ¾ inch long and ⅜ inch thick, and is pale green with a whitish bloom. Because the leaves fall off easily, this plant should be handled with extreme care. It may produce rose-pink flowers in early spring, but it does not flower readily.

S. pachyphyllum has erect, branching stems up to 12 inches high closely covered with cylindrical, gray-green leaves 1½ inches long and ½ inch in diameter. The blunted tips of the leaves are often tinged reddish. Bright yellow flowers appear in early spring.

S. praealtum (more technically called *S. dendroideum praealtum)* has upright, much-branching stems up to 2 feet tall. Broadly lance-shaped, shiny, medium green leaves 2–3 inches long, ¾ inch wide, and ¼ inch thick are clustered at the ends of the stems and branches. Bright yellow flowers may appear in early spring.

S. rubrotinctum (Christmas cheer) forms a plant 4–6 inches high. Thin stems branching from the base bear clusters of very fleshy, roughly egg-shaped leaves at the tips of branches. The leaves, which grow about ¾ inch long and ¼ inch thick, are bright green if the plant is kept cool and wet, but they turn red under hot, dry conditions. As the stems elongate, they tend to root down at points of contact with the potting mixture. Yellow flowers are produced in the winter, but rarely indoors.

S. sieboldii which grows only about 4 inches high, has trailing stems up to 9 inches long. Nearly circular, slightly tooth-edged, gray-green leaves about ¾ inch across and ¼ inch thick are arranged in groups of three along the stems. Pink flowers appear in fall. The most popular form of this species is *S.s.* 'Medio-variegatum,' which has pink-tinged green leaves blotched with white or creamy white in the center. This plant is ideal for hanging baskets. Although the stems tend to die back after flowering, they resume active growth swiftly in the spring.

PROPER CARE

Light Give sedums full sunlight at all times. Inadequate light weakens their attractive coloring and causes stems to become straggly.

Temperature During the active growth period normal room temperatures are suitable for sedums. During the rest period (which takes place in winter, even for plants that are likely to flower in late winter) keep the plants reasonably cool—around 50°F, if possible. Minimum tolerable temperature: 40°.

Watering During the active growth period water moderately, giving enough at each watering to make the potting mixture thoroughly moist but allowing the top half-inch of the mixture to dry out before watering again. During the rest period water sedums sparingly, allowing a full two-thirds of the potting mixture to dry out between waterings.

Feeding It is not necessary to feed sedums at any time.

Potting and repotting Use a combination of one part of coarse sand or perlite to two parts of standard soil-based mixture (see page 429). Sedums do best in broad, shallow pans, half-pots, or hanging baskets, where they have room to spread. Move plants into slightly larger containers every spring; to accommodate the new season's growth, allow a space of about $1\frac{1}{2}$ inches between the plant and the edges of the container. Since young sedums are normally more attractive than older specimens, it is usually best to discard plants when they have grown too big for 6- to 8-inch containers and to restart the plants from cuttings.

Propagation To propagate these plants take stem cuttings 2–3 inches long at any time in spring or summer. Remove the lower leaves of each cutting as far as an inch above the cut, and allow the cutting to dry for one or two days before inserting the cut end in a 2- to 3-inch pot of the mixture recommended for mature sedums. Thereafter, treat the newly-potted cutting as an adult specimen, and transfer it to a larger, shallow container when necessary.

Propagating a sedum

Use a knife to take a 2- to 3-inch-long stem cutting from a mature sedum, taking care not to destroy the look of the plant in the process.

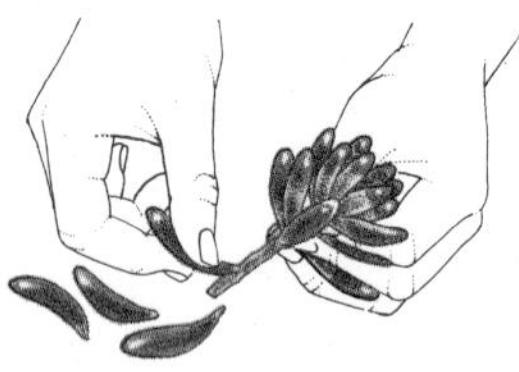

In order to prevent rotting, remove the tightly packed leaves from the lower part of the stem. Leave the cutting to dry for a day or two.

Insert the cutting in a small pot of standard mixture so that none of the remaining leaves touches the surface. Begin treating the plant as mature.

Selaginella

SELAGINELLACEAE

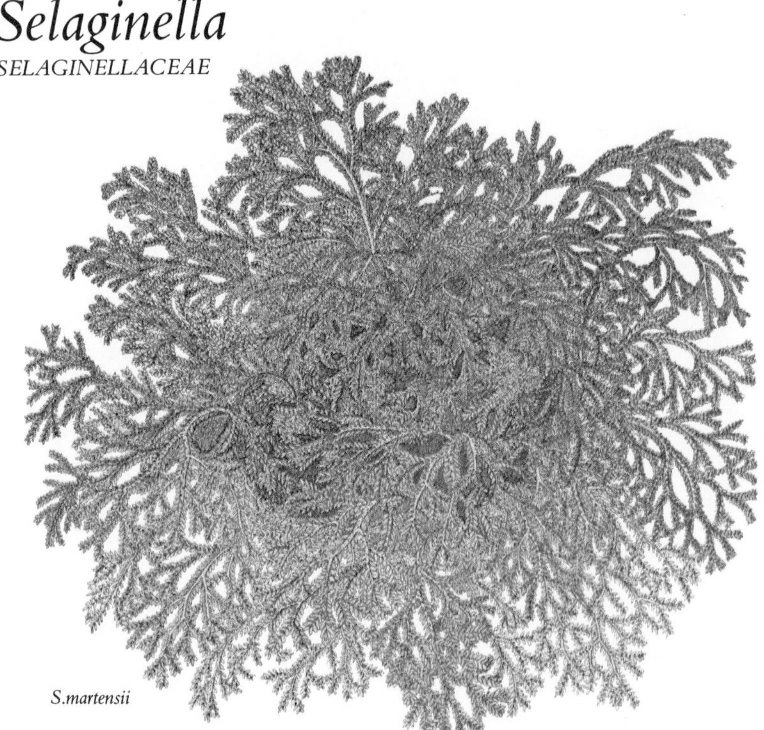

S.martensii

THE large genus *Selaginella* includes several species that are grown indoors for their decorative foliage. These plants do especially well in terrariums (see page 54), which give them the constantly moist conditions that they need. They can be low, mosslike hummocks; otherwise they are profusely branching plants that have either upright or else creeping stems. Their tiny leaves usually grow in ranks of four around each stem; the ranks extend from the base of the stem to about $\frac{1}{2}$ inch below the tip. The tip itself carries spores; although selaginellas are not ferns, they resemble ferns in that they produce spores instead of seeds.

RECOMMENDED SELAGINELLAS

S. apoda has creeping stems up to 4 inches long that bear pale green leaves. This species forms a dense, mosslike mat of foliage.

S. emmeliana (also called *S. pallescens*; popularly known as mossfern or sweat plant) has nearly erect stems that branch from the base upward and grow to 12 inches tall. Because the branching causes the stems to fan out, the whole plant looks somewhat like a large ball of fernlike foliage. The minute leaves are pale green with a white edge. There is also a variety, *S.e.* 'Aurea,' with golden green leaves.

S. kraussiana (spreading clubmoss or trailing selaginella) is an exceptionally quick-growing, creeping species. The 12-inch-long stems root down as they branch, forming a mat that takes its color from the masses of bright green leaves. The plant is often used as attractive ground cover in terrariums. The variety, *S.k.* 'Aurea,' has golden green leaves.

S. martensii is different from the other common indoor species. Its stems, which grow up to 12 inches long, branch less profusely. For about half their length they are erect, but the rest of the stem tends to arch over. Supporting the stems are strong, stiff,

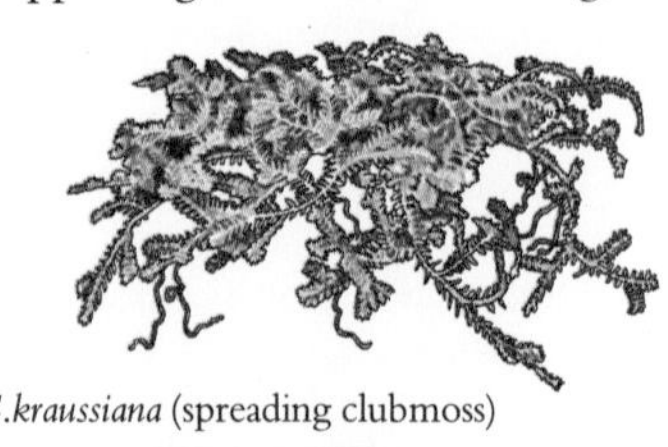

S.kraussiana (spreading clubmoss)

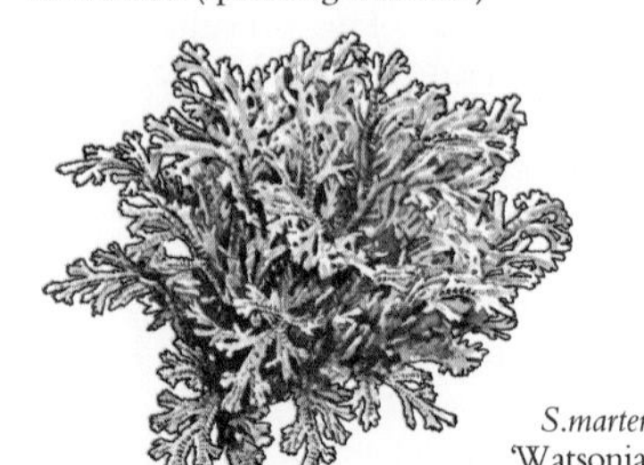

S.martensii 'Watsoniana'

stiltlike roots, which grow downward into the potting mixture from leaf joints on the lower part of the stems. The fleshy, glistening, medium green leaves are about ½ inch long—larger than those of the other species described here. *S.m. variegata* is a variety with silvery-white-tipped leaves. *S.m.* 'Watsoniana' has pale leaves tipped with silver.

PROPER CARE

Light Selaginellas do best in shade. Keep them in medium light throughout the year.

Temperature Normally warm room temperatures are suitable at all times. These plants will grow continuously if they are kept in a warm, humid atmosphere. In low humidity the tiny leaves will dry out, curl, and turn brown. So mist-spray the plants with tepid water at least once a day unless they are in the controlled atmosphere of a terrarium. Never use cold water for the spray; cold water will damage the foliage irreparably.

Watering Throughout the year water plentifully as often as necessary to keep the potting mixture thoroughly moist, but never allow the pot to stand in water.

Feeding Selaginellas do not require heavy feeding. Apply standard liquid fertilizer at one-quarter strength every two weeks.

Potting and repotting Use a peat-based potting mixture to which a one-third portion of coarse sand has been added for good drainage. Shallow pans are the best containers for selaginellas. Move each plant into a larger container every spring until maximum convenient size (probably 6–8 inches) has been reached. Thereafter, repot the plant every spring in a container of the same size, which has been cleaned and filled with fresh potting mixture. The quick-spreading growth may be a problem, but it can be controlled by judicious trimming. Cut the plant back by as much as half, if necessary.

Propagation When trimming plants in spring, take cuttings 2–3 inches long, and insert each cutting ½ inch deep in a pan of well-moistened potting mixture. Keep the cutting warm in medium light, and water it only moderately until rooting has occurred (probably in two weeks). Thereafter, treat the new plant as a mature selaginella.

Senecio

COMPOSITAE

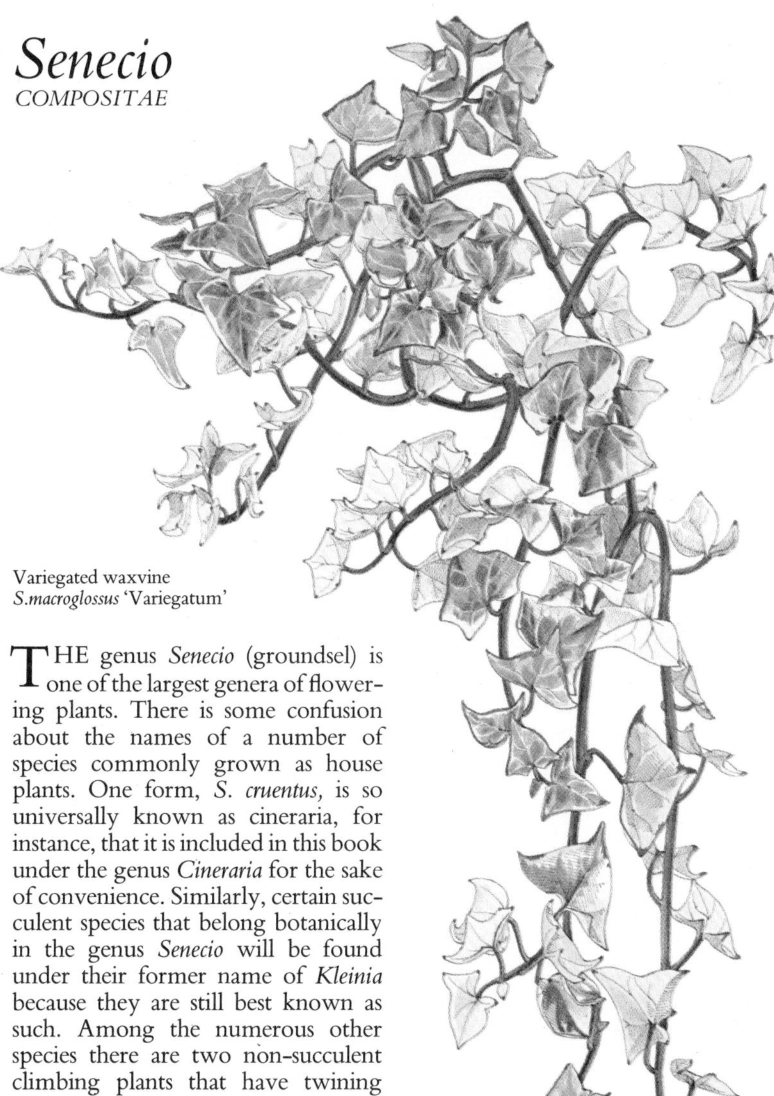

Variegated waxvine
S.macroglossus 'Variegatum'

THE genus *Senecio* (groundsel) is one of the largest genera of flowering plants. There is some confusion about the names of a number of species commonly grown as house plants. One form, *S. cruentus,* is so universally known as cineraria, for instance, that it is included in this book under the genus *Cineraria* for the sake of convenience. Similarly, certain succulent species that belong botanically in the genus *Senecio* will be found under their former name of *Kleinia* because they are still best known as such. Among the numerous other species there are two non-succulent climbing plants that have twining stems that can be trained up thin stakes or allowed to trail in hanging baskets.

The leaves of these two senecios are smooth, soft, and fleshy, and they are shaped like ivy leaves (shallowly cut into blunt or slightly pointed lobes). Leaf shape, even on the same plant, is variable, however. Leaves are carried alternately on the stems and have leafstalks at least as long as the blade. Flowers are yellow and daisylike. These plants rarely flower indoors; but when they do, the flowering period coincides with the rest period.

RECOMMENDED SENECIOS

S. macroglossus (waxvine) has roughly spear-shaped, three- to five-lobed, deep green leaves 2½ inches long and 2 inches wide. The more popular variegated-leaved form, *S.m.* 'Variegatum' (variegated waxvine), has slender, purple stems that carry purple-stalked, medium green leaves haphazardly marked with pale cream-colored streaks and patches. The leaves of some shoots are cream-colored all over. (These chlorophyll-free shoots cannot be used for propagation because they are unable to survive when detached from the parent.) If flowers are produced, they appear singly or in small clusters at the ends of shoots and are up to 2 inches across.

S. mikanioides (German, water, or parlor ivy) has medium green stems carrying dark green leaves 2–4 inches long and wide on medium green leafstalks. Each leaf has five to seven pointed lobes, with sunken veins radiating from the leafstalk to the tips of the lobes. Clusters of fragrant flowers about ¼ inch across are occasionally produced at the ends of shoots.

PROPER CARE

Light These senecios must have bright light, including two to three hours each day of direct sunlight, throughout the year.

Temperature Normal room temperatures are suitable during the active growth period. During the winter rest period cooler conditions (ideally, 50°–55°F) are advisable. Minimum tolerable temperature: 45°.

Watering During the active growth period water moderately, allowing the top half-inch of the mixture to dry out before watering again. During the winter rest period give only enough to keep the potting mixture from drying out completely.

Feeding Apply standard liquid fertilizer every two weeks during the active growth period.

Potting and repotting Use a mixture of one part of coarse sand or perlite to three parts of soil-based mixture (see page 429). In the spring move overcrowded plants into pots one size larger, but do not retain these senecios longer than about 18 months because young plants are more attractive than older ones. A 6- to 7-inch pot or hanging basket should be the largest needed.

Propagation Take tip cuttings at any time from early spring through summer. Trim each 2- or 3-inch-long cutting just below a node, remove the lowest leaf, and stand two or three cuttings in an opaque glass jar of water. Keep them warm in bright filtered light until roots an inch long have formed. Then transfer the cuttings together into a 3- or 4-inch pot of the mixture recommended for adult plants, and treat the potful as a mature senecio.

Alternatively, insert two or three prepared cuttings in a 3-inch pot containing a moistened equal-parts mixture of peat moss and coarse sand or perlite. Stand the pot in bright filtered light, watering just enough to keep the rooting mixture from drying out completely, for about seven weeks. Then repot the group of rooted cuttings in a 4-inch pot of the recommended potting mixture, and treat the potful as a mature plant. If planting in a hanging basket, group together at least six or eight of the rooted cuttings.

Special points Watch out for aphids, which tend to collect on the growing tips of these senecios (see page 454).

Setcreasea

COMMELINACEAE

Purple heart
S.purpurea

THE genus *Setcreasea* has recently been redefined, and some plants previously included are now assigned to *Callisia*. *S. purpurea* (purple heart), the only species grown indoors, is a trailer with lance-shaped leaves 4–6 inches long and 1 inch wide. Leaves and stems are all a rich violet-purple. Small, three-petaled, bright magenta-pink flowers are produced in leaf axils in summer. Blind flowering stems (those that do not grow beyond the leaf axil that produced the flowers) should be cut off every year when flowering ceases. Setcreaseas are attractive growing either singly in a 3- or 4-inch pot or grouped together in a larger pot or hanging basket.

If a setcreasea is planted with a tradescantia in one pot, keep them in direct sunlight to maintain intense leaf color.

PROPER CARE

Light For best leaf color, plants should have three or four hours of direct sunlight every day.

Temperature Setcreaseas grow especially well in warm rooms (above 65°F), but they can tolerate temperatures down to about 45°.

Watering Throughout the year, water plants moderately, giving enough to moisten the potting mixture thoroughly but allowing the top half-inch of the potting mixture to dry out between waterings.

Feeding Apply standard liquid fertilizer monthly to all well-established plants (those that have been potted for over two months) while they are actively growing.

Potting and repotting Use a soil-based potting mixture (see page 429). Setcreaseas are fast-growing and may need to be moved into larger pots every six months or so. But because these plants lose their beauty with age, it is best to discard them after 18–24 months.

Propagation Propagate from 3-inch-long tip cuttings taken in spring or summer. Remove the lower leaves to prevent burial in the mixture. Insert the cuttings in the standard mixture, place them in bright filtered light for two to three weeks and water them just enough to make the entire mixture barely moist. Treat rooted cuttings as mature plants.

Special points Handle setcreaseas as little as possible, because the leaves become slightly glossy and much less attractive if the thin, delicate bloom is rubbed off.

Siderasis

COMMELINACEAE

S. fuscata

THE genus *Siderasis* consists of a single species, *S. fuscata,* which is a low-growing, rosette-shaped tropical plant prized for its beautiful flowers as well as its large, richly colored leaves. Unfortunately, this is an extremely difficult plant to grow successfully. It is best grown in a terrarium (see page 54) or plant window (see page 53). Under the right conditions active growth will continue all year long.

The elliptic leaves of *S. fuscata* rise directly from a short underground stem, are up to 8 inches long and 3 inches wide, and are arranged in a spreading rosette that is rarely more than 3 inches high. The upper surface of each leaf is pale olive green, with a ¼-inch-wide, white stripe running lengthwise down the middle; the underside is entirely purplish red. Short, very fine, rust-colored hairs densely cover the plant. In late summer hairy flower stalks appear from near the center of the rosette. Each stalk bears a 1-inch-wide, three-petaled flower. Flower color varies from violet to rosy purple. Mature plants produce offsets from the base.

PROPER CARE

Light Medium light is essential. Keep these plants out of bright light, and never subject them to direct sunlight.

Temperature *S. fuscata* should have steady 70°–75°F warmth, with fluctuations of no more than four or five degrees. Because these plants are extremely sensitive to dry air, provide humidity by standing them on saucers or trays of moist pebbles at all times.

Watering Water moderately all year long, while allowing the top half-inch of the mixture to dry out between waterings. Be careful not to overwater. These plants are particularly likely to rot at the point where the leaves join the underground stem.

Feeding Apply standard liquid fertilizer once a month. Do not increase the frequency of feedings. Overfeeding encourages soft, sappy growth.

Potting and repotting Use an equal-parts combination of soil-based potting mixture (see page 429), coarse leaf mold or peat moss, and coarse sand (not perlite, which retains too much water). Put a half-inch layer of drainage material in the bottom of the pot. Siderasises do not need large pots, and mature plants can be grown in the 5-inch size. Move small plants into slightly bigger pots in the spring until such a size has been reached. Then divide clumps for propagation.

Propagation Divide overcrowded clumps of rosettes at any time. In separating individual rosettes from the base of the plant be careful not to damage rooted stems. Plant each offset rosette in a 3-inch pot of the recommended potting mixture, make the mixture moist, and enclose the whole in a plastic bag or heated propagating case (see page 444). Stand it in medium light at about 75°F for 10 days. Then uncover the young plant and treat it as a mature siderasis.

Sinningia

GESNERIACEAE

THE most familiar plants of the genus *Sinningia* are commonly known as florist gloxinias (not to be confused with plants of the genus *Gloxinia*). The gloxinias are mostly varieties of one species, *S. speciosa.* But the genus *Sinningia* includes several types of plant that are different in many respects from one another. They can be separated into three categories. First, there are those that were classified until recently in the genus *Rechsteineria;* botanists now agree that these plants are sinningias. The second category includes not only the familiar gloxinias but also the velvet slipper sinningias. Finally, there is a group of miniature species and hybrids with special characteristics. All three groups have only two obvious features in common: They produce brightly colored flowers, and their stems rise from fibrous-rooted tubers. Roots grow from the upper surface of the tubers instead of from the underside. And in most specimens several stems rise from a single tuber.

See also GESNERIADS.

The rechsteineria group

The hairy, erect stems of these plants carry hairy and short-stalked leaves. Flowers grow in clusters from upper leaf axils. Each flower is backed by a five-lobed calyx and consists of a narrow, tubular corolla with a five-lobed mouth. The end of the flowering season is followed by a dormant period during which top growth dies down. The dormant period is short, though, because new stems can sprout before earlier ones die down.

RECOMMENDED KINDS

S. cardinalis (cardinal or helmet flower) has medium green stems that grow up to 10 inches tall and are thinly coated with white hairs. The broadly oval, pointed-tipped, hairy leaves are 3–6 inches long and 2–4½ inches wide and have scalloped edges. Leaf upper surface is medium green marked with darker green around the veins, and the underside is pale green. Blood red flowers open over a period of about three months in fall. Each bloom has a hairy, ¼-inch-long, and medium green calyx clasping the base of a hairy, 2-inch-long corolla. The top two corolla lobes are joined and

Cardinal flower
S.cardinalis

Florist gloxinia
S.speciosa hybrid

jut forward above the lower lobes, rather like the open visor of a helmet.

S. leucotricha (Brazilian edelweiss) has stems and leaves thickly covered with white hair. The stems, which grow to 10 inches tall, bear leaves in whorls of four. The rounded-oval leaves are 6 inches long and 4 inches wide and have turned-down edges. Veins on the leaf undersides are very strongly marked, partly because hairs on the undersides are especially short. The soft green color of stems and leaves just shows through the coating of hair. Pink flowers open over a period of two months in summer and fall. Each flower has a hairy, ⅛-inch-long, pale green calyx backing the inch-long corolla. The flower is nearly cylindrical in shape.

Velvet slipper gloxinias

Plants of this group have velvety leaves and short stems. Flowers are trumpet-shaped, with a spreading, five-lobed calyx and a five-lobed mouth. Flower color ranges from white to red to purple. These plants have a five- to six-month period of complete dormancy.

RECOMMENDED KINDS

S. regina (Cinderella slippers) has hairy, purplish stems up to 8 inches tall. Closely spaced, oval, velvety, tooth-edged leaves have 1- to 2½-inch-long, purplish leafstalks. The leaves are 4–8 inches long and 3–6 inches wide, dark green with white veins on the upper surface, and purplish on the underside. Four to six 2- to 4-inch-long flower stalks grow from each leaf axil, and each stalk carries a pendent flower. The corolla is backed by a ½-inch-long, green calyx, whose pointed lobes extend outward like a star. The 1½-inch-long corolla widens to 1¼ inches across the flared end, where the bottom lobe juts forward, giving the bloom its slipperlike appearance. The violet flowers, which appear in late summer, have throats spotted with purple.

S. speciosa (Brazilian or florist gloxinia) is a parent of innumerable forms. The species has hairy, purplish stems up to 12 inches tall. Opposite pairs of oval, velvety, scallop-edged leaves on 1½-inch stalks grow 8 inches long and 6 inches wide. Leaf color is medium green with pale green veins on the upper surface, and pale green flushed with red on the underside. One to three 4-inch-long flower stalks, each bearing a pendent flower, rise from each upper leaf axil. The 1½-inch-long corolla projects from a ¾-inch-long, starlike calyx. The top two corolla lobes curve slightly backward, while the other three jut forward. Flowers can be white, red, or violet, sometimes banded with yellow or white, and the throat is sometimes red-spotted. The flowering season lasts for two months in the summer.

The most popular descendants of *S. speciosa* tend to be virtually stemless, with larger leaves and bigger, more brilliantly colored flowers than the species. The blooms are symmetrically trumpet-shaped and evenly lobed, and they are often held erect so that the throat is visible. The corollas of some hybrids have many more than the normal five lobes, and the lobes have ruffled margins, so that the flowers appear to consist of several layers of petals. New varieties of these forms come and go too swiftly to warrant permanent recording.

Miniature sinningias

The miniature species and hybrids are the most profusely flowering sinningias. These little plants are often stemless rosettes, but some kinds produce stems up to 3 inches tall. Under ideal conditions they grow actively and flower all year long. They are good subjects for a terrarium (see page 54). The species most generally grown indoors is *S. pusilla,* which is also one parent of most of the popular hybrids. *S. pusilla* has stems less than ½ inch tall and nearly round leaves ½ inch across on ⅛-inch-long stalks. The scallop-edged leaves are covered with tiny, erect hairs, and leaf color is medium green with darker veining on the upper surfaces, pale green with reddish veins below. Trumpet-shaped flowers produced singly from leaf axils on 1-inch-long stalks are backed by ⅛-inch-long, green calyxes. The corolla grows up to ¾ inch long and ½ inch wide at the flared end, and its two upper lobes are smaller than the forward-jutting lower three. Flower color is violet or lavender, sometimes with dark lines running into a white throat. There is also an attractive white-flowered form, called *S.* 'White Sprite.'

S. pusilla and its varieties are ever-blooming. As one flower-bearing stem begins to die back, new stems rise from the top of the pea-size tuber. The plant constantly sheds seeds that grow into new plants. Among the many miniature hybrids that have *S. pusilla* as one parent are: *S.* 'Bright Eyes,' which has light purple flowers with darker lobes; *S.* 'Dollbaby,' with lilac to bluish flowers suffused with white; *S.* 'Little Imp,' which has lavender flowers with dark magenta lobes; *S.* 'Pink Petite,' with pink flowers; and *S.* 'Wood Nymph,' a tiny plant that has reddish purple flowers with white-spotted throats.

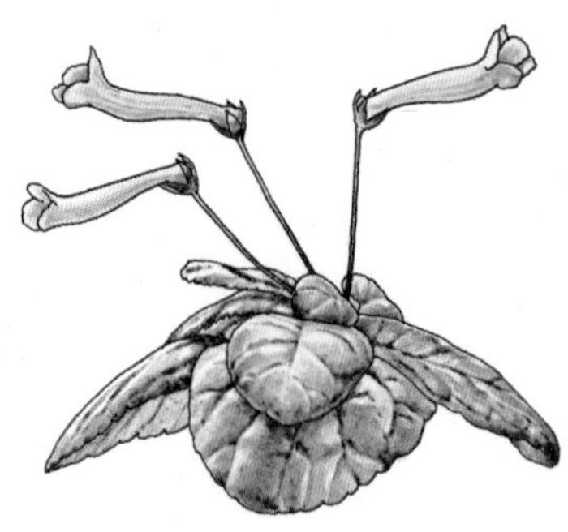

S. 'Pink Petite'

PROPER CARE

Light Give actively growing sinningias bright filtered light. Light is not a consideration during any period of dormancy. Miniature forms do especially well if grown under fluorescent lights (see page 446). Give them 12 hours a day of the artificial light, and position them about 10 inches below the tubes.

Temperature All actively growing sinningias do well in temperatures between 65° and 75°F, but they need adequate humidity. Stand pots on trays of moist pebbles. If the temperature rises above 75°, mist-spray the air above the foliage. Do not spray the foliage directly; drops of water will mark leaves and flowers. During the dormant period keep tubers at a temperature of 45°–60°.

Watering Water actively growing plants plentifully, but never let pots stand in water. If the temperature drops below 65°F, reduce amounts until the temperature rises again. During the cool period water velvet slipper gloxinias and miniature plants moderately, allowing the top inch of the mixture to dry out between waterings; but give plants of the rechsteineria group only enough to keep the mixture from drying out, thus avoiding the risk of rotting tubers. As dormancy approaches and leaf color fades, gradually reduce amounts of water until stems die down. Keep dormant tubers dry.

Feeding For sinningias that have a dormant period apply a high-phosphate liquid fertilizer at half strength every two weeks starting when flowering stops and ending when top growth has died down. Do not feed these plants at any other time. Give a one-eighth-strength dose to ever-blooming miniature forms once in two weeks throughout the year.

Potting and repotting Use a potting mixture composed of equal parts of sphagnum peat moss, perlite, and vermiculite, adding half a tablespoonful of dolomite lime or lime chips to each cup of mixture. The larger sinningias are likely to need 4½- or 5-inch pots, but the 2- to 2½-inch size should suffice for miniature forms. Pot up dormant tubers in early spring, making sure that the upper surface of each tuber is level with the surface of the barely moist mixture. Water sparingly at first, increasing amounts gradually as top growth progresses. Remove tubers of the velvet slipper gloxinias from their pots when dormancy begins again, but do not disturb tubers of rechsteineria sinningias during dormancy. The latter plants are best left in the same pots for three or four years. Thereafter, repot them in pots one size larger, or replace them. Repot miniatures in fresh potting mixture about once a year (at any time).

Propagation To propagate all but the miniature kinds, use 1- to 4-inch-long cuttings of young stems. Take each cutting in early summer, and insert it in a 1½- to 2½-inch pot of moistened potting mixture. Enclose the whole in a plastic bag or propagating case, and stand it in bright filtered light for about four to six weeks, when renewed growth should indicate that a tuber and roots have formed. Uncover the young plant only slightly at first, and remove it from the protected atmosphere gradually over a four-week period, keeping the potting mixture moist (but not sodden). Thereafter, treat the rooted cutting as a mature plant.

All sinningias can also be grown from seed or from leaf cuttings (see *GESNERIADS,* page 225). Many of the miniature types shed seeds that become new plants. These can be potted up separately at any time.

Smithiantha

GESNERIACEAE

Temple bells
S.zebrina

SMITHIANTHA (temple bells) is a small genus of four or five species. They are plants for only temporary display, however, because the flowering season is followed by a several-month-long period of total dormancy (see "Special points," below). All species have a root system growing from several scaly rhizomes, each of which can grow 2 inches long and ½ inch in diameter, and from which rise simple or branched stems bearing opposite pairs of hairy, heart-shaped leaves with sharp-toothed edges. The tubular, pendent flowers are about 2 inches long, with a five-lobed mouth, and are borne on short stalks placed alternately along the stem above the leaves, thus forming a terminal flower spike. Flowers normally appear in midwinter, opening in quick succession from bottom to top of the spike, and they remain attractive for at least one month.

See also GESNERIADS.

RECOMMENDED SMITHIANTHAS

S. cinnabarina (often incorrectly called *Naegelia cinnabarina*) has stems 18–24 inches tall and dark green leaves up to 6 inches long and 5 inches wide; a dense covering of red hairs gives the leaves a velvet sheen. The brick red flowers have pale yellow or white bands on the lower side and in the throat, which is spotted with pale red. The inner surfaces of the five lobes are spotted too, and have pale lines running back toward the throat.

S. fulgida differs from *S. cinnabarina* in that it has plain green leaves and scarlet flowers with red-spotted yellow throat and lobes.

***S. zebrina*,** which can grow 30 inches tall, has leaves up to 7 inches long and equally wide; they are dark green with brown or purple coloring around the veins. The outside of the flowers is red banded with yellow; the throat is yellow spotted with red; and the two upper lobes are orange-yellow and smaller than the three other lobes, which are yellow.

Note: Many hybrids are more useful as indoor plants than the true species, for they grow only 8–12 inches tall. Flowers are usually some shade of red, orange, or yellow, with differing patterns of spots and lines. Two popular examples: S. 'Golden King' has gold flowers spotted with red, and S. 'Little One' has red-and-yellow flowers.

PROPER CARE

Light Smithianthas grow best in medium light, which can be provided either by shaded daylight or fluorescent tubes (see page 446). Bright light can cause ugly, stunted growth.

Temperature Warm, humid conditions are essential. The temperature should not be permitted to fall below 65°F, but care should be taken to avoid excessive dry heat. Smithianthas are good subjects for plant windows (see page 53).

Watering Water moderately, but allow the top half-inch of the mixture to dry out before watering again. Overwatering, like dry heat, can cause leaves to turn brown.

Feeding Smithianthas need regular feedings of standard liquid fertilizer. Quarter-strength fertilizer at every watering is a good general rule.

Potting and repotting Use a soilless mixture such as three parts sphagnum peat moss, two parts vermiculite, and one part perlite, with the addition of a small amount of dolomite lime, lime chips, or crushed eggshells to reduce the acidity of the peat moss (see page 430). Pot single scaly rhizomes in large half-pots when they are starting to sprout. Large pots are necessary because the shallow root system of smithianthas can be extensive.

Propagation The easiest way to propagate is by dividing the rhizomes into two or three sections before growth starts. Pot up each section and treat it as a single scaly rhizome (see "Potting and repotting," above). Another method is to grow new plants from seed sown very thinly on the surface of the recommended soilless potting mixture in early spring. If the mixture is kept evenly moist (*not* soaked) and placed in a slightly shaded position where a temperature between about 60° and 70°F can be maintained, germination should occur in a month. When seedlings have two to four leaves, separate them, move them on to other pans, and grow them as mature plants. As growth continues, move them on from 2-inch to 4- or 5-inch half-pots. They can be expected to flower nine or ten months after sowing.

Special points After flowering, let smithianthas die down and the rhizomes dry off. When thoroughly dry, shake them out of the pot, pack them in peat moss or vermiculite, and store until ready for potting.

Solanum

SOLANACEAE

False Jerusalem cherry
S.capsicastrum

THE genus *Solanum* (nightshade) includes about 1,700 species of shrub and climbing plant, only two of which are popular house plants. These two species are both bushy shrubs that grow up to 18 inches tall, with a spread of about 18 inches. Their twiggy branches carry small, dark green leaves and insignificant star-shaped flowers, which bloom in summer. The flowers are followed by highly decorative, long-lasting, non-edible berries. Solanums are usually acquired in late fall or early winter, at a time when the berries have started to change color—from green through yellow and orange to orange-red—and are generally discarded when, after a few months, the berries have shriveled and fallen off. This is a waste, however. These plants will bloom and fruit again the following year under the right conditions, provided they can be kept outdoors during the summer months.

RECOMMENDED SOLANUMS

S. capsicastrum (false Jerusalem cherry) has slightly hairy, lance-shaped leaves with ¼-inch-long stalks. Each leaf is up to 3 inches long and 1½ inches wide and has undulate edges. The leaves are densely arranged along the many short branches that develop from the woody stems. Flowers appear from leaf axils, usually in twos or threes, on 1-inch-long flower stalks. Each flower is about ½ inch across and white, with a central core of orange-yellow stamens. The oval berries that follow in late fall to early winter are ½-¾ inch in diameter and are green, backed by green bracts. The bracts remain green, but the shiny berries gradually turn orange-red as they ripen, and they remain attractive for most of the winter months. There is a variegated-leaved form, *S.c.* 'Variegatum,' that has leaves splashed with creamy yellow or, in some cases, edged with creamy white.

S. pseudocapsicum (Jerusalem cherry) is similar in most respects to *S. capsicastrum,* but is more robust and therefore easier to grow. The berries, too, are slightly larger, rounder, and more nearly scarlet in color. They also last somewhat longer than do those of *S. capsicastrum*. There are two dwarf forms, *S.p.* 'Nanum' and *S.p.* 'Tom Thumb,' which rarely grow taller than 10–12 inches but which carry berries just as big and long-lasting as those of the species.

PROPER CARE

Light Stand solanums in direct sunlight indoors throughout the fruiting period (beginning in early fall and ending in early spring). Plants to be retained for a second year must be kept outdoors, but sheltered from the midday sun, throughout late spring and for the whole summer.

Temperature During the fall and winter months keep these plants at a temperature no higher than about 60°F, if possible, and give them high humidity. Warm rooms and dry air will considerably shorten the life of the berries. Stand the plants on trays or saucers of moist pebbles, and mist-spray them once a day. During late spring and summer, while they are outdoors, normal summer temperatures are suitable. In dry weather mist-spray specimens being kept outdoors daily. Be sure to bring the plants indoors before there is a risk of frost. Minimum tolerable temperature: 50°.

Watering Water plentifully as often as necessary to keep the potting mixture thoroughly moist, but never let the pots stand in water. If a plant is to be retained for a second season, give it a short rest period for four or five weeks just before putting it outdoors. During this period water only enough to keep the potting mixture from drying out completely.

Feeding Apply standard liquid fertilizer every two weeks, except during the brief rest period.

Potting and repotting Plants acquired in late fall or early winter will not need repotting until mid-spring. To keep them for a second fruiting season, move them into pots one size larger (probably the 5-inch size) before placing them outdoors. Use a soil-based potting mixture (see page 429). A young solanum raised from seed should be moved into a bigger pot whenever root crowding is indicated by the appearance of roots on the surface of the potting mixture or through drainage holes. Solanums are not normally retained for a third fruiting season.

Propagation Seed sown in the early spring will flower and fruit the same year. Sow the seed in a small pot or shallow pan of moistened rooting mixture (see page 444), spacing the seeds half an inch apart just below the surface of the mixture. Place the container in a plastic bag or propagating case (see page 443), and keep it in bright light filtered through a translucent blind or curtain until germination occurs (probably in two to three weeks). Uncover the container, and grow the seedlings on in a position where they get bright light, with at least two hours a day of direct sunlight. Water enough to keep the rooting mixture just moist throughout, and begin to feed the seedlings when they are 2–3 inches high. About eight weeks after the start of propagation transplant the young plants singly into 3-inch pots of soil-based potting mixture, and treat them as mature solanums. If possible, place them outdoors and keep them there until berries begin to form in the fall.

Special points In late spring, just before putting a mature plant outdoors, prune it drastically, cutting out two-thirds of the previous year's growth. For bushy growth thereafter, pinch out the growing tips of new growth in spring. Mist-spray solanums daily throughout the entire flowering period in order to encourage the fruit to set.

Sonerila
MELASTOMATACEAE

S.margaritacea

SONERILA *margaritacea,* a low-growing, bushy plant with beautifully marked leaves, is the only species of this genus commonly grown indoors. Red, creeping stems, which grow 10 inches long, carry opposite pairs of lance-shaped leaves 4 inches long and 2 inches wide. The leaves are dark green spotted with silvery white above, and plain deep purple below. The 2-inch-long leafstalks are red. In summer and fall small clusters of three-petaled, ½-inch-wide, and rosy purple flowers are produced on 2- to 3-inch-long stalks. The flower stalks rise from near the growing points of stems and branches. These tropical plants grow actively all year long.

There are several varieties of *S. margaritacea* with leaves marked with silver to a widely varying degree.

PROPER CARE

Light Give sonerilas bright filtered light all year long.

Temperature Sonerilas need a minimum temperature of 65°F along with high humidity at all times. They are ideal for growing in the controlled atmosphere of terrariums (see page 54) and bottle gardens (see page 56).

Watering Water moderately at all times, allowing the top half-inch of the potting mixture to dry out between waterings.

Feeding Apply standard liquid fertilizer every two weeks.

Potting and repotting Use an equal-parts mixture of peat moss and leaf mold. Because sonerilas have shallow roots, plant them in half-pots, pans, or bowls. Move plants into pots one size larger every spring until the 5- or 6-inch size has been reached. Larger specimens are best replaced with younger plants, since they tend to lose their bottom leaves as they age.

Propagation Propagate at any time from mid-spring to early fall by 2- to 3-inch-long stem cuttings taken from near the base of the plant. Trim each cutting to just below a pair of leaves, remove the bottom leaves, and dip the base of the cutting in hormone rooting powder. Plant two or three cuttings together in a 3-inch pot containing a moistened equal-parts mixture of peat moss and coarse sand or perlite. Enclose the whole in a plastic bag or propagating case, and stand it in a warm place in bright filtered light. After rooting occurs (in three to four weeks), acclimatize the rooted cuttings to normal room conditions over a period of 7–10 days by uncovering them gradually. Water cuttings sparingly until roots are well established, when moderate watering and feeding may begin. About three months from the start of the propagation process, transfer young plants together into 4-inch pots of the mixture recommended for adult plants, and treat them as mature sonerilas.

Sparmannia
TILIACEAE

SPARMANNIAS (indoor linden) are shrubs which can grow 6–10 feet tall indoors. Only *S. africana* and its varieties, the double-flowered *S.a.* 'Flore Pleno' and the dwarf *S.a.* 'Nana,' are commonly grown as house plants. *S. africana* (zimmer linden or African hemp) has 9-inch-long, roughly heart-shaped, pale green, slightly hairy leaves carried on leafstalks 6–9 inches long. When young, the main trunk and branches are also pale green as well as hairy, but they turn brown as they grow older.

Use a clay pot with soil-based potting mixture to counterbalance the weight of a mature sparmannia.

Long-stalked clusters of white, four-petaled flowers appear most often in late winter to early spring. A plant blooming in a cool room can continue to produce flowers for most of the year. Flower buds are pendent but straighten up as they open, displaying prominent yellow, often purple-tipped stamens. Individual flowers fade after a few days, but remain for some weeks and should be removed once unsightly.

Some specimens of the basic species rarely flower, and the double-flowered form does not bloom readily, either. If flowers are desired, therefore, the dwarf form is the best one to acquire.

Sparmannias are at their most attractive when about two years old. It is advisable to take cuttings every other year and to discard parent plants when the cuttings have rooted.

Zimmer linden
S. africana

PROPER CARE

Light Sparmannias grow best in bright filtered light. Without good light every day, the plants will not flower and may develop over-lengthy leafstalks. They should not be exposed to direct sunlight, however; it can scorch the thin leaves.

Temperature Sparmannias do best in a temperature of about 60°F. In warmer rooms increase the humidity by placing plants on trays or saucers of moist pebbles.

Watering Water actively growing plants moderately, enough to make the potting mixture moist throughout, but allowing the top half-inch of the mixture to dry out between waterings. If, however, a sparmannia has filled the pot with roots, the mixture should be kept constantly moist during the active growth period. During the rest period water more sparingly, giving all these plants only enough to keep the potting mixture from drying out completely.

Feeding Apply standard liquid fertilizer once every two weeks from spring (or earlier, if flower buds appear before that) to fall.

Potting and repotting Use a soil-based potting mixture (see page 429). Move plants into progressively larger pots as they fill their pots with roots. This may be necessary more often than once a year, but repotting is not advisable for sparmannias in late fall or winter. A 10-inch pot will accommodate a 6-foot specimen.

Propagation In the spring tip cuttings about 6 inches long will root easily either in water or in a moistened equal-parts rooting mixture of peat moss and sand. Keep the cutting in a warm place where it gets medium light, and move it into a 3-inch pot of standard mixture when it is well rooted; thereafter, treat it as a mature plant. Cuttings rooted in spring will often produce flowers by late winter.

Special points Encourage young rooted cuttings to branch by pinching out the main shoot in spring. Old, oversize plants can be cut down drastically (taking away half the growth), but this process usually leaves unsightly stumps. It is far better to start anew. No staking is necessary for tall plants, because their stems are rigid enough to support them.

Spathiphyllum

ARACEAE

SPATHIPHYLLUMS are stemless plants grown for their glossy leaves and arum-shaped flower heads. Many kinds have become popular house plants, but most of these are hybrids. All spathiphyllums have short underground rhizomes that send up clusters of lance-shaped or elliptic, dark green leaves on sheathed leafstalks. Flower heads arising from centers of leaf clusters are produced mainly in spring or summer (occasionally in early fall) on long stalks that tower above the foliage. Each flower head consists of a large, white spathe surrounding an erect, 2- to 3-inch-long spadix colored white, cream, or green. The usually fragrant flower head keeps its original color for only about a week. The spathe gradually changes from white to light green and remains attractive for a further five or six weeks. It then begins to become unsightly, and is best removed.

RECOMMENDED SPATHIPHYLLUMS

***S.* 'Mauna Loa,'** a hybrid, can grow 2 feet tall. Its leaves, on stalks 10–12 inches long, are up to 9 inches long and 5 inches wide. This plant flowers mainly in spring, although it sometimes blooms intermittently throughout the year. The flower stalk can be 15–20 inches long, and the pointed-oval spathe backing the cream-colored spadix is 4–6 inches long and up to 4 inches wide.

S. wallisii, the only true species commonly grown indoors, rarely grows more than 12 inches high. Its leaves, on 6-inch-long stalks, are 6 inches long and 3 inches wide. The flowers, which appear in spring and often again in late summer, are borne on stalks 8–10 inches long. The cream-colored spadix rises from the base of a pointed-oval spathe 3–4 inches long and 2–3 inches wide.

PROPER CARE

Light Grow all spathiphyllums in medium light. Direct sunlight will burn the leaves.

Temperature Normal room temperatures are suitable for these plants. Minimum tolerable temperature: 55°F. Spathiphyllums are particularly sensitive to dry air and should be kept on trays of moist pebbles throughout

Spathiphyllum 'Mauna Loa'

the year. In temperatures of 65° and above there is unlikely to be a noticeable rest period. Growth may slow down during the winter, however.

Watering Water moderately, enough at each watering to make the potting mixture moist throughout but allowing the top half-inch of the mixture to dry out before watering again. If the temperature falls below 60°F for more than a day or two, reduce the quantity of water, making the potting mixture barely moist. Never let the mixture dry out completely.

Feeding Apply standard liquid fertilizer every two weeks from early spring to late fall (when spathiphyllums grow most actively). Continue feedings throughout the year for plants that are actively growing in peat-based mixture.

Potting and repotting Use either a peat-based potting mixture or an equal-parts combination of soil-based mixture (see page 429), leaf mold, and coarse sand or perlite. Move plants into pots one size larger every spring until the maximum convenient pot size (probably 6–8 inches) has been reached. Thereafter, topdress plants annually with fresh potting mixture (see page 428).

Propagation Propagate in spring by dividing overcrowded clusters of leaves. Pull rhizomes apart gently, making sure that each piece has at least two or three leaves attached. Plant individual pieces in 3-inch pots of either of the recommended mixtures, burying each piece at the same depth as the entire rhizome was planted. Do not feed the newly potted rhizome sections for three months. Otherwise, treat them as mature spathiphyllums.

Special points Red spider mites will attack spathiphyllums, if humidity is low (see page 455). Mist-spray foliage at least once a week, concentrating on leaf-undersides, which is where these mites collect.

Stapelia

ASCLEPIADACEAE

STAPELIAS (carrion flowers) are succulent plants with thick, four-angled stems that usually branch from the base and grow up to about 8 inches long. They appear to be leafless, but the edges of the stems carry closely set, soft "teeth," which are in reality vestigial leaves. The great fascination of these plants is their remarkable flower formation. The five-petaled flowers, which grow singly on short stalks arising from the bases of stems, are star-shaped and may measure from under 2 inches across in some species to more than 12 inches in others. Flower color is brownish, yellowish, or purple, often with the basic color mottled or striped with another. The flowers of some species are coated with short hairs. The odor that these flowers emit—often not unlike the stench of decaying animal flesh—seems highly unpleasant to most people. For this reason, and also because they are not easy to grow successfully, stapelias have never been popular house plants. The flowers are nevertheless both interesting and beautiful. Flowering occurs at any time from late spring to early fall, and each bloom lasts for several days. When the flower fades, it is followed by a horn-shaped pod neatly packed with silky, tufted seeds.

See also SUCCULENTS.

RECOMMENDED STAPELIAS

S. gigantea (giant stapelia, giant toad plant, or Zulu giant) has one of the biggest flowers of any known plant: 12 inches across (sometimes a little more). The petals, which are yellow with crosswise red lines, are thickly covered with pale purple hairs. The flowers grow from the lower part of smooth, upright, pale green stems 6–8

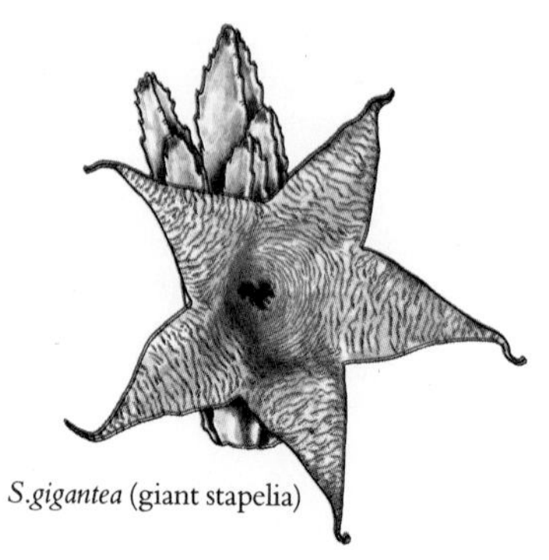

S.gigantea (giant stapelia)

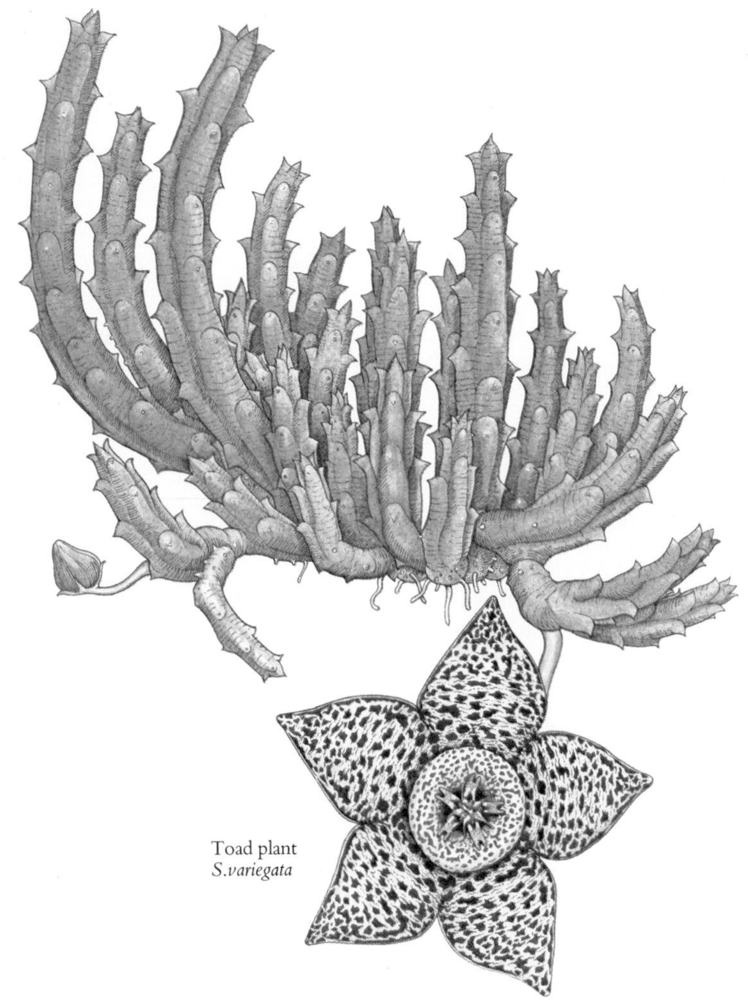
Toad plant
S.variegata

well before the surface of the potting mixture has time to become even slightly moist.

Feeding Apply a liquid high-potassium, tomato-type fertilizer once a month during the active growth period only. Add the fertilizer to the water in which the pots are placed for watering.

Potting and repotting Use a porous potting mixture consisting of equal parts of coarse sand or perlite and standard soil-based mixture (see page 429), but use only the sand or perlite for the top inch of the mixture. Stapelias grow rapidly. Start them in 3-inch pots, but move each plant into a pot one size larger when its stems appear to be crowding against the edges of the pot. This should be done in spring, so that the new season's growth will be unhindered, but it may be necessary to repot again in later summer or fall. Try to disturb roots as little as possible during the repotting process. The maximum pot size required for most stapelias is 6 inches because these plants do not have very extensive root systems.

Propagation Stapelias can be raised very easily from seed. Seeds will germinate in less than a week at 70°F, and young seedlings grow fast. Such smaller-growing plants as *S. variegata* will probably flower within three years of sowing the seed. Larger ones may take a year or two longer. (See *SUCCULENTS,* page 379.)

Cuttings taken in summer can also be used for propagation. It is often possible to pull away a single stem complete with roots. Let the stem stand for a day; then plant it in a 3-inch pot of the mixture recommended for adult stapelias. Alternatively, cut a stem from the plant with a sharp knife, allow it to dry for four or five days, and gently press the cut end into a 3-inch pot of mixture. In either case treat the cutting immediately in the same way as a mature specimen.

Special points Stem rotting is a constant danger with stapelias. After taking a stem cutting for propagation, do not permit the cut surface of the parent plant to become moist. If water touches the wound during the first three or four weeks, rot can set in and destroy the entire plant.

Keep an eye out for fungus attack, especially in winter. If black marks become visible (usually at stem tips), use a fungicide (see page 456).

inches long and about 1 inch across. *S. gigantea* flowers in mid- to late summer, but it flowers neither dependably nor profusely. When they do appear, the spectacular blooms have only a faintly unpleasant odor.

S. variegata (starfish plant, starflower, or toad plant), the most commonly grown species, is one of the smaller stapelias. It has stems up to 6 inches long and $\frac{1}{2}$ inch across, and the flowers are 2–3 inches across. The stems are shiny and bright green, with brownish markings. They grow upright at first but tend to sprawl as the plant ages. The hairless flowers, abundantly produced in summer, are yellow spotted with dark purplish brown. They smell rather like an overflowing garbage can.

PROPER CARE

Light To encourage flowering, grow stapelias in direct sunlight throughout the year.

Temperature Warm, dry air is right for these plants. Never let the temperature fall much below 60°F. Although some species can tolerate lower temperatures, stapelias are likely to develop black spot and other fungus diseases in cool conditions.

Watering Water with great caution at all times. If the potting mixture is too wet, these plants tend to rot at the base. If the mixture is allowed to become too dry, the stems shrivel and die back from the tips. The best way to water is from below. During the active growth period stand pots in about three inches of water until the potting mixture is thoroughly moist. Remove pots from the container of water as soon as the sandy surface of the mixture is damp to the touch. Do not water again until the top two inches of the mixture have dried out. During the winter rest period stand pots in water for only five minutes every two weeks, removing the pots

Stenocarpus

PROTEACEAE

Firewheel tree
S.sinuatus

STENOCARPUS *sinuatus* (fire-wheel tree or wheel of fire) is the only species of the genus *Stenocarpus* grown as a house plant. Within the confines of a pot or tub it grows no more than about 6 feet high. The plant rarely branches naturally, so it is advisable to encourage it by nipping out the growing point of the main stem. The popular names for this plant derive from its wheel-shaped, bright red flowers, but these are not produced on potted plants.

Indoor stenocarpuses are valued for their deeply lobed leaves, which grow alternately along the stem and branches. These leaves are up to 18 inches long and 9 inches wide, and they are lobed into several segments roughly paired on either side of a prominent midrib, with a single segment at the tip end. Some forms of *S. sinuatus* have smaller, lance-shaped leaves that are either undivided or only slightly lobed, but these forms are less attractive than the larger-leaved plants and are rarely used as house plants.

All *S. sinuatus* leaves are glossy-surfaced and pale green, which is tinged with red on the underside. Leaf midribs are a paler shade of green. Leafstalks are 1–3 inches long and the same color as the leaf midribs. Leaves are bronzish in color during the first week or two after they open.

PROPER CARE

Light Grow stenocarpuses in bright light, with at least three hours a day of direct sunlight.

Temperature This plant grows well either in normally warm room temperatures or under cooler conditions. It cannot tolerate temperatures below 50°F, however. When grown at temperatures below 65°, the leaves are hard and leathery; in warmer positions they will be bigger and softer.

Watering During the active growth period water plentifully as often as necessary to keep the potting mixture thoroughly moist, but never allow the pot to stand in water. During the winter rest period water sparingly, giving only enough to keep the mixture from drying out completely.

Feeding Apply standard liquid fertilizer every two weeks during the active growth period only.

Potting and repotting Use a soil-based potting mixture (see page 429). Move plants into pots one or two sizes larger every spring until maximum convenient pot size (probably 10 or 12 inches) has been reached. Thereafter, annual topdressing with fresh mixture will suffice (see page 428).

Propagation Indoor stenocarpuses can be raised from seed sown in a shallow seed tray in early spring. Bury the seeds $\frac{1}{4}$ inch deep in moistened rooting mixture (see page 444), and place the tray in a plastic bag or propagating case (see page 443). Keep it in bright filtered light at a temperature of at least 65°F until germination occurs. Uncover the seedlings, and begin to water them sparingly, permitting the top one-third of the rooting mixture to dry out between waterings, until the seedlings are 2 inches high and have two true leaves. Transfer each such seedling into a 2- or 3-inch pot of soil-based mixture, and treat it as a mature stenocarpus.

Stenotaphrum

GRAMINEAE

Buffalo grass
S.secundatum 'Variegatum'

STENOTAPHRUMS, which all belong to the large grass family, have bright-hued, attractive, and bladelike leaves. Only one form of one species of stenotaphrum is a popular house plant: *S. secundatum* 'Variegatum' (buffalo grass). This plant can add an air of lightness to a mixed planting of darker green-leaved plants or it can be very attractive on its own in a hanging basket. It has creeping, flattened stems that will take root at whatever point the swollen joints (nodes) touch the potting mixture. From these nodes rise small clusters—usually four—of pale cream-colored leaves, many of which are marked with fine green lines, and may or may not be bordered in green as well. They vary in length from 3 to 12 inches but they are of equal width—about $\frac{1}{2}$ inch—for the whole of their length, and they all have bluntly rounded ends.

Some of the leaves eventually lose their color and die. They can easily be pulled off without harming the rest of the plant in any way. The flowers, however, inconspicuous at best, are rarely produced indoors.

PROPER CARE

Light Provide bright light with at least three or four hours of direct sunlight daily. Inadequate light causes leaves to lose much of their brilliance and become more green. If grown in very bright light, some clumps of leaves will become tinged with pale mauve, particularly at the bottom, near the nodes.

Temperature Potted stenotaphrums thrive and grow very quickly in any normal room temperature. They cannot tolerate temperatures lower than about 55°F. Because high humidity will prevent the premature yellowing of leaves, stand pots on trays or saucers of damp pebbles; spray plants in hanging baskets daily.

Watering During the active growth period water plentifully, enough to keep the potting mixture thoroughly moist—but never allow the pot to stand in water. In the rest period water only enough to keep the potting mixture from drying out completely.

Feeding Apply standard liquid fertilizer once a month during the active growth period only. Do not over-feed plants, or the leaves will become unattractively large and limp.

Potting and repotting Use a soil-based potting mixture (see page 429) and shallow pots, half-pots, or pans. Since these stenotaphrums grow on the surface of the mixture, they do not need deep pots. Move plants into larger containers when the creeping stems have covered the surface and are beginning to hang over the edge; repot several times a year if necessary. Young plants are much more desirable than old ones, and the maximum lifetime of an indoor stenotaphrum should be no more than two years.

Propagation In spring or early summer, cut off clumps of leaves attached to nodes with an extra half-inch of stem attached. Plant three or four such clumps around the edge of a shallow 3-inch container filled with an equal-parts mixture of peat moss and coarse sand or perlite. Keep the container of cuttings at 65°–75°F in bright filtered light, and water it often enough to make the potting mixture barely moist throughout. When new growth covers the entire surface of the mixture—in around three months—move the group of young plants into a larger pot of the standard potting mixture and treat in exactly the same way as mature stenotaphrums.

Stephanotis

ASCLEPIADACEAE

Wax flower
S. floribunda

ONLY one species of the genus *Stephanotis, S. floribunda,* is a familiar house plant. Popularly known as floradora, Madagascar jasmine, or wax flower, it is a climbing shrub grown principally for its waxy, white, very fragrant flowers. The leaves are dark green, leathery, shiny, oblong-egg-shaped, and up to 4 inches long and 2 inches wide. They appear in opposite pairs on ½-inch leafstalks, and each leaf has a prominent central rib of a lighter green color. The 1½-inch-long flowers, which usually appear in spring and may continue into the summer, are narrowly tubular, flaring out into five pointed lobes, and are produced from the leaf axils in loose clusters of ten or more. Growth may be vigorous; if a stephanotis is trained up a trellis in a large plant window, it can grow more than 12 feet tall. Where space is limited, it can be trained around a hoop of wire or cane inserted in the sides of the pot.

PROPER CARE

Light Provide bright light, but keep these plants out of direct sunlight, which will damage the foliage.

Temperature An ideal temperature for indoor stephanotises is 65°–70°F, but they also do well in warmer rooms, given high humidity. It is important to keep the temperature as constant as possible, because they react badly to fluctuations. In fact, if stephanotises are to be regarded as permanent house plants, they are best kept in the controlled conditions of a large plant window or conservatory (see page 53).

Watering During the active growth period water plentifully as often as necessary to keep the potting mixture thoroughly moist. In the rest period water sparingly only when the top half of the mixture has dried out—but never allow the mixture to dry out completely. Spray plants with a fine mist-spray daily whenever the temperature rises above 70°F.

Feeding Apply standard liquid fertilizer every two weeks in the active growth period.

Potting and repotting Use a soil-based potting mixture (see page 429). Move plants into pots one size larger in early spring. Flowering-size stephanotises can generally be accommodated in 5- or 6-inch pots, but move healthy plants that continue to grow into 8-inch pots. Thereafter they should merely be given an annual springtime topdressing of fresh potting mixture (see page 428).

Propagation When propagating a stephanotis take 3- to 4-inch-long tip cuttings from non-flowering lateral shoots in spring or early summer. Dip the cut ends in hormone rooting powder, and plant each cutting in a 3-inch pot containing equal parts of peat moss and coarse sand or perlite. Enclose the potted plant in a plastic bag or heated propagating case (see page 444) and keep it at a temperature of around 65°F in bright light without direct sunlight. Given just enough water to keep the potting mixture moist, rooting should occur in eight to ten weeks. When roots are well developed, move the cuttings into the normal soil-based mixture.

Special points Scale insects are likely to attack these plants. They are found on the undersides of leaves (usually against the midrib) and are easily recognized as small, brown, rounded bodies that exude a sticky substance. Remove larger insects manually, and spray with an appropriate insecticide (see page 455).

Strelitzia

STRELITZIACEAE

Bird of paradise flower
S.reginae

STRELITZIAS are clump-forming plants with big, dark green leaves on long leafstalks in a fanlike arrangement, and strangely shaped, strikingly colorful flowers. Some species are treelike and have trunks up to 25 feet tall in the wild, but only one species is widely grown indoors: *S. reginae* (bird of paradise flower, crane flower, or crane lily). *S. reginae* is a large plant in the wild, but its growth is considerably restricted in a pot or small tub, where it will grow no taller than 3–4 feet. This restriction encourages early flowering. The leathery leaves, which are oblong to spear-shaped, 12–15 inches long, and 3–6 inches wide, have sturdy, cylindrical leafstalks 12–30 inches long. The stalks rise from sheaths in the base of the plant. These strelitzias flower when they are about six years old. Thereafter, they produce crested flower heads every year on 3- to 4-foot-long stalks that rise from the axils of the lower leaves in spring and early summer. The remarkable flower head consists of an 8-inch-long, boat-shaped bract held in a nearly horizontal position, from which a succession of three-petaled flowers emerge during the course of several weeks. These erect blooms, each up to 6 inches long, give the flower head its crested appearance. Jutting out from the center of each flower is a tonguelike projection 6–8 inches long and 1 inch wide. The boatlike bract is green, sometimes flushed with purple or red; the flowers are bright orange; the tonguelike projections are dark blue or purple. Apart from its need for sunlight along with a cool winter rest period, this exotic plant is not particularly difficult for the amateur indoor gardener to grow.

PROPER CARE

Light Give these strelitzias bright light, with at least three or four hours a day of direct sunlight. They will not flower if grown in inadequate light.

Temperature During the active growth period strelitzias will do well in normal room temperatures. They need a long, cool rest period during the fall and winter months, however, when the temperature should be kept at around 55°F.

Watering During the active growth period water moderately, giving enough at each watering to make the potting mixture moist throughout but allowing the top inch of the mixture to dry out before watering again. During the rest period give just enough to prevent the mixture from drying out completely.

Feeding Apply standard liquid fertilizer every two weeks during the active growth period only.

Potting and repotting Use a soil-based potting mixture (see page 429). Move young plants into containers one or two sizes larger each spring until maximum convenient pot or tub size (probably 8–12 inches) has been reached. Thereafter, topdress with fresh mixture in the spring (see page 428). Apart from the annual topdressing, do not disturb mature, flowering plants. They are likely to stop flowering for a year or two if subjected to any sort of displacement.

Propagation Propagate strelitzias in spring by dividing old, overcrowded clumps or by gently separating a section with two or three leaves with some roots attached from any mature plant. Pot the small section in a 5- or 6-inch pot of soil-based mixture, and place it in a warm spot in bright filtered light (but no direct sunlight) for six weeks. During this period do not feed the small plant, and water it sparingly, allowing a full half of the mixture to dry out between waterings. By the end of the sixth week the roots will have become active in the new pot, so treat the plant as a mature specimen. It will normally flower in two to three years.

S. reginae can also be grown from seed. This is an extremely slow process, though. It involves a wait of possibly as long as 10 years before flowers are produced.

Special points Scale insects sometimes attack strelitzias. Look for them from time to time near the midrib on the undersides of leaves, which is where they are usually found. For treatment see page 455.

Streptocarpus

GESNERIACEAE

S. 'John Innes' hybrid

PLANTS of the genus *Streptocarpus* (cape primrose) are of two types: stemless and stemmed. The stemless kinds are more common as house plants, because they have given rise to many attractive, profusely flowering hybrids. Some of the stemless kinds are unique in that they form only one big leaf, and die after flowering. Because the leaf can grow inconveniently large, single-leaf streptocarpuses are rarely grown indoors. Other stemless types are longer-lasting. Some have smaller leaves growing from the base of a large leaf. Others have several leaves of the same size arranged in rosette form. The popular hybrids belong to this last group. In all the stemless types the leaves are stalkless. Flower stalks rising from near the bottom of the midrib of each leaf carry small clusters of flowers. In the stemmed streptocarpuses the much-branching stems bear leaves in opposite or alternate pairs or in whorls of three or four, and the flower stalks rise from leaf axils. Some species have several flowers on each stalk, and others have only one per stalk.

The flowers of all streptocarpuses have a tiny, five-lobed calyx backing a tubular corolla that flares out into a five-lobed mouth. Flowers are followed by spirally twisted, frequently attractive seed pods. To promote flowering of the hybrids, however, pods should be removed as they form. *See also* GESNERIADS.

RECOMMENDED STREPTOCARPUSES

***S.* 'Constant Nymph,'** the most popular hybrid, is a rosette-forming plant with medium to dark green, strap-shaped leaves up to 12 inches long and $2\frac{1}{2}$ inches wide. Several 6-inch-long flower stalks grow from each midrib base, and each stalk bears two to six flowers up to $1\frac{1}{2}$ inches long and 2 inches across. Flower color is blue with dark blue lines running from the lower lobes of the corolla into the pale yellow throat. Flowers bloom from spring to fall.

***S.* 'John Innes' hybrids** have leaves and flowers like those of *S.* 'Constant Nymph.' Flower stalks are up to 8 inches tall, and flower color ranges from pale pink to deep purple to blue. Corolla lobes of some forms have markings extending into the throat. These hybrids will flower all year long under the right conditions.

S. polyanthus is mainly a single-leaved type, but some forms grow secondary leaves. The big, downy, slightly scallop-edged, medium green leaf can grow 12 inches long and 6 inches wide. The secondary leaves are similar but only 2 inches long and ½ inch wide. Up to a dozen 12-inch-tall flower stalks bear from 7 to 30 flowers each. The flowers are 1½ inches long and across, yellow, with blue, tooth-edged lobes. The main flowering season is from spring to fall.

S. rexii is a rosette-forming plant with oval, hairy, ruffled, slightly scallop-edged, medium green leaves up to 10 inches long and 4 inches wide. About four 6- to 8-inch-tall flower stalks, each with up to three flowers, are produced from each mature leaf. The 2-inch-long, 1-inch-wide flowers are bluish mauve with violet lines running from the lower lobes into the throat of the corolla. Under the right conditions flowering is continuous.

S. saxorum has branching stems up to 12 inches long, which tend to lean over sideways. Oval, velvety, gray-green leaves are arranged in opposite pairs or whorls of three at stem and branch tips. The 1-inch-long and ¾-inch-wide leaves have turned-under margins and prominently veined, pale green undersides. Flower stalks 3 inches long carry solitary flowers 1 inch long and 1½ inches across. The hairy, white corolla has a pale lilac mouth. Flowering time is spring and summer.

***S.* 'Wiesmoor' hybrids** are rosette-forming plants with strap-shaped, medium green leaves up to 12 inches long and 3 inches wide. At least five stalks 6–15 inches long carry three or four flowers each. The 2-inch-long, 3-inch-wide flowers are markedly funnel-shaped, and the flared ends are fringed or ruffled. Flower color ranges from white through blue to dark red, often with dark markings on the lower lobes. The flowering season lasts from spring to fall.

PROPER CARE

Light Give actively growing plants bright light without direct sunlight. In the rest period, if any, medium light is adequate. *S. saxorum* can tolerate medium light at all times.

Temperature All streptocarpuses will grow actively throughout the year in normally warm room temperatures. At temperatures above 75°F provide extra humidity by standing pots on trays of moist pebbles, and keep the roots cool by covering the surface of the potting mixture with a constantly moist layer of sphagnum moss. If indoor temperatures fall below about 55° for more than a day or two, all streptocarpuses (with the probable exception of *S. saxorum)* will have a rest period.

Watering Water moderately, allowing the top half-inch of the potting mixture to dry out between waterings. During any rest period, allow a full inch of the potting mixture to dry out between waterings.

Feeding Apply a high-phosphate liquid fertilizer at half strength every two weeks to actively growing plants.

Potting and repotting Use a potting mixture composed of equal parts of sphagnum peat moss, perlite, and vermiculite. For a well-aerated mixture the peat moss should be rough-textured and lumpy, and the perlite should be fairly coarse-grained. Add half a tablespoonful of lime chips to every cup of mixture. Use shallow pots or pans for these shallow-rooted plants, and move the plants into slightly larger containers only when roots fill the pot (see page 426). Repotting is best done just after a heavy bout of flowering. Six-inch containers should be the largest required.

Propagation Except for *S. saxorum*, propagate in spring from leaf cuttings. Remove a leaf, and cut it across its width into two or three sections. Insert the base of each section ½ inch deep in a 2½-inch pot of the mixture recommended for adult plants. Place the pots in medium light, and keep the mixture barely moist. Plantlets should appear at the bottom of the sections in four to six weeks. When a plantlet is 2–3 inches tall, pull it away from the parent section, plant it in a 2½-inch pot, and treat it in the same way as a mature specimen.

Propagate *S. saxorum* from 2- to 3-inch-long tip cuttings taken in spring. Insert each cutting ½ inch deep in a 2-inch pot of moistened potting mixture, and place it in medium light. Water sparingly, enough to make the mixture barely moist throughout until new growth indicates that rooting has occurred. Thereafter, treat the rooted cutting as a mature plant.

Special points Mildew is a possibility (see page 456) if streptocarpuses are given high humidity without adequate air circulation. (Do not, however, subject the plants to cold drafts.) Watch out, too, for mealy bugs (see page 455) on leaf undersides.

Strobilanthes

ACANTHACEAE

Persian shield
S. dyeranus

THE genus *Strobilanthes* (Mexican petunia), a large and variable group, includes only one species commonly grown as a house plant, *S. dyeranus* (Persian shield). This is an erect-growing and much-branching shrub, which is an attractive foliage plant when young but becomes faded and straggly as it ages. Plants are best discarded when more than 15–18 inches high. The soft-woody, hairy stems of strobilantheses carry pointed-oval leaves up to 6 inches long and 2 inches wide on 1-inch-long leafstalks. The finely tooth-edged leaves have a dark green upper surface with a pronounced bluish, metallic sheen that does not quite extend to the green margins; the underside is deep purple. Pale blue flowers (which are seldom produced on young plants indoors) are funnel-shaped and 1½ inches long. They rise in small spikes from leaf axils in late summer.

PROPER CARE

Light Give these strobilantheses bright, filtered light all year long.

Temperature Normal room temperatures are suitable. A strobilanthes cannot tolerate temperatures below about 55°F.
Watering Water actively growing plants moderately, giving enough at each watering to make the potting mixture moist throughout and allowing the top half-inch of the mixture to dry out before watering again. Encourage plants to have a short winter rest by giving only enough water to prevent the mixture from completely drying out during a two- or three-month rest period.
Feeding Apply standard liquid fertilizer to actively growing plants every two weeks.
Potting and repotting Use an equal-parts combination of soil-based potting mixture (see page 429) and leaf mold. Move plants into pots one size larger whenever roots appear on the surface of the mixture (an indication that the roots have begun to fill the pot). When a plant has reached the 6-inch pot size, it is probably past its prime, or nearly so, and should be replaced by a young specimen. As they age, these plants lose much of their leaf coloring and become leafless at the bottom of stems.
Propagation Propagate in spring by 2- to 3-inch-long stem cuttings that have been trimmed to just below a leaf. Remove the lower leaf to prevent possibly harmful contact between a leaf and the potting mixture, and dip the bottom of the cutting in hormone rooting powder. Plant each cutting in a 2- or 3-inch pot containing a moistened equal-parts mixture of peat moss and coarse sand or perlite, and enclose the whole in a plastic bag or heated propagating case (see page 444). Stand it in bright filtered light at a temperature of 65°–70°F until renewed growth indicates that rooting has occurred (probably in three to five weeks). Uncover the rooted cutting, and begin to water (giving only enough to make the mixture barely moist) until 2–3 inches of new top growth has developed. Thereafter, begin to water normally, and start regular feedings as recommended above. About two months after the beginning of the propagation process move the plant into a slightly larger pot of the potting mixture recommended for adult plants, and treat the young strobilanthes in exactly the same way as a mature specimen.

Stromanthe

MARANTACEAE

S. amabilis

THE genus *Stromanthe* contains only two species grown indoors. Their oval-oblong leaves are blunt-ended, but with a small pointed "tail." Each leaf is herringboned with darker markings from the central prominent vein. Both species have a creeping rhizome and produce fanlike sprays of leaves. New leaves are tightly rolled at first; they emerge from the stalks of older leaves.
Note: Stromanthes are closely allied to marantas and calatheas and may be sold under those names.

RECOMMENDED STROMANTHES

S. amabilis is of notably compact habit. Its leaves are 6–9 inches long and 2 inches wide, with gray-green bands on their green upper surfaces; the undersides are gray-green.
S. sanguinea has glossy leaves up to 20 inches long and 6 inches wide. Their pale green upper surfaces have dark emerald green markings spreading out from a wide, central, indented vein; the undersides are wine-purple.

PROPER CARE

Light Stromanthes like medium light. To avoid scorched foliage, keep them out of direct sunlight, especially during the summer months.
Temperature These plants need high humidity along with normal room temperatures. They are suitable plants for a terrarium (see page 54).
Watering Water moderately at all times, allowing the top inch of the mixture to dry out between waterings.
Feeding Use half-strength standard liquid fertilizer once every two weeks from early spring to late fall.
Potting and repotting A peat-based potting mixture is best (see page 429). Repot stromanthes only when top growth begins to extend beyond the edge of the containers; it is best done in late spring or summer. Shallow pots or pans are ideal for these plants.
Propagation Divide overcrowded clumps of leaves just as plants begin to make new growth. Carefully detach a section of rhizome bearing two or three leaves from the main rootstock and place it in a 2- or 3-inch pot of moistened peat-based potting mixture (with a little sand added). Enclose the whole in a plastic bag, and keep it in a warm place in medium light until roots have developed. Then remove the new plant from the bag and treat it as a mature stromanthe.
Special points Keep stromanthes out of drafts. *S. amabilis* is suitable for bottle gardens (see page 56).

SUCCULENTS

Succulent plants, which are alike in having an unparalleled ability to store water in their tissues, do not all belong to a single family; a number of families have succulent members. A list of genera that include succulents commonly grown indoors follows this article. Consult separate articles for discussions of individual succulent species other than the cacti listed on page 122.

In temperate climates most plants living in the wild get enough water for their needs throughout the year. In parts of the world with scarce or intensely seasonal rainfall, however, perennial plants need to be able to store up water during rainy periods in order to stay alive during periods of drought. These plants, which have evolved abundant water storage tissue, are known as succulents. The water-storage tissue is generally concentrated in plump, fleshy leaves (leaf succulents) or in thick, juicy stems (stem succulents). The stem succulents are often leafless or nearly so, since the stems of such plants have taken over the food-making process along with water storage. Among house plants the most familiar stem succulents are the cacti, which all belong to a single family (see *CACTI*, pages 114-122).

Other succulents are distributed among several plant families. Unfortunately, not even the strict definition of a succulent plant as one that stores water in its tissues applies to every plant that is generally considered to belong to the group. For example, certain drought-resistant species such as the agaves and some of the aloes contain little water-storage tissue. Yet they are always included among the succulents, and their cultivation needs are basically similar.

Practically all of the succulent indoor plants other than the cacti belong to one of these seven plant families: *Agavaceae*, *Aizoaceae*, *Asclepiadaceae*, *Compositae*, *Crassulaceae*, *Euphorbiaceae*, and *Liliaceae*. Most, though not all, are natives of arid grasslands and other semi-desert regions, but they are enormously diverse, not only in shape and form but also in their degree of succulence. Some, such as *Euphorbia pseudocactus*, are, as the name of the species suggests, like a typical cactus, with extremely succulent, columnar, and spine-covered stems. Others, such as the agaves, with their thin, strap-shaped leaves, seem to be virtually non-succulent. Many leaf succulents—echeverias, for instance—form rosettes of more or less fleshy, tightly packed leaves. Such plants appear to have little in common with, for example, stapelias, which are fleshy, stemmed plants with vestigial leaves.

It is impossible, therefore, to make meaningful generalizations about the appearance of the foliage of succulent plants. And it is equally difficult to describe a "typical" flower. Whereas cacti all have a basically similar flower (the characteristic bloom of the family *Cactaceae*), other succulents have flowers typical of the particular family to which they belong. All these plants produce flowers in the wild, but many of them cannot be expected to do so under the artificial conditions of indoor cultivation. Those that do not bear any flowers or that have small, uninteresting flowers are grown as house plants for their interesting, often bizarre shapes or for the attractive coloration of stems or leaves.

Among this wide variety of plants are many that are easy to grow in the home, but there are some that come from such specialized habitats that they are a challenge to the most experienced grower. On the whole, however, succulents make especially satisfactory house plants because they can tolerate more neglect than most other indoor plants.

PROPER CARE

Light The main problem with almost all succulents grown as house plants is light. With the exception of some of the members of the family *Liliaceae*, notably the haworthias and gasterias, which do best if given some shade, most of these plants need as much direct sunlight as possible. This means that the only really suitable spot for a succulent plant is at or near the sunniest window in the house.

Since all the light streaming in through a sunlit window is one-sided, succulent plants should be given a quarter turn regularly to forestall distorted growth. Turn each specimen once every day during the brightest seasons. If a plant seems to be looking "drawn" (with top growth abnormally long and thin), it is probably getting insufficient light. This can be particularly noticeable in the case of such compact, rosette-forming plants as echeverias. A healthy echeveria has a flattened rosette. With inadequate light the rosette elongates and looks unattractively flabby.

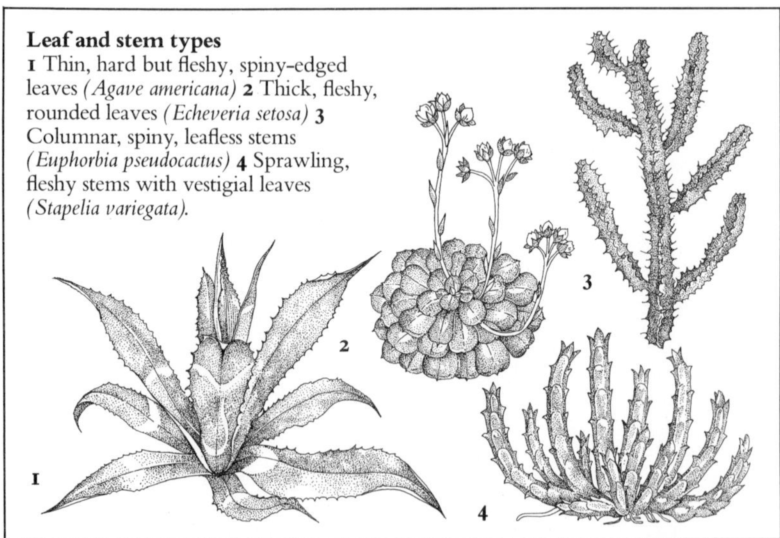

Leaf and stem types
1 Thin, hard but fleshy, spiny-edged leaves (*Agave americana*) 2 Thick, fleshy, rounded leaves (*Echeveria setosa*) 3 Columnar, spiny, leafless stems (*Euphorbia pseudocactus*) 4 Sprawling, fleshy stems with vestigial leaves (*Stapelia variegata*).

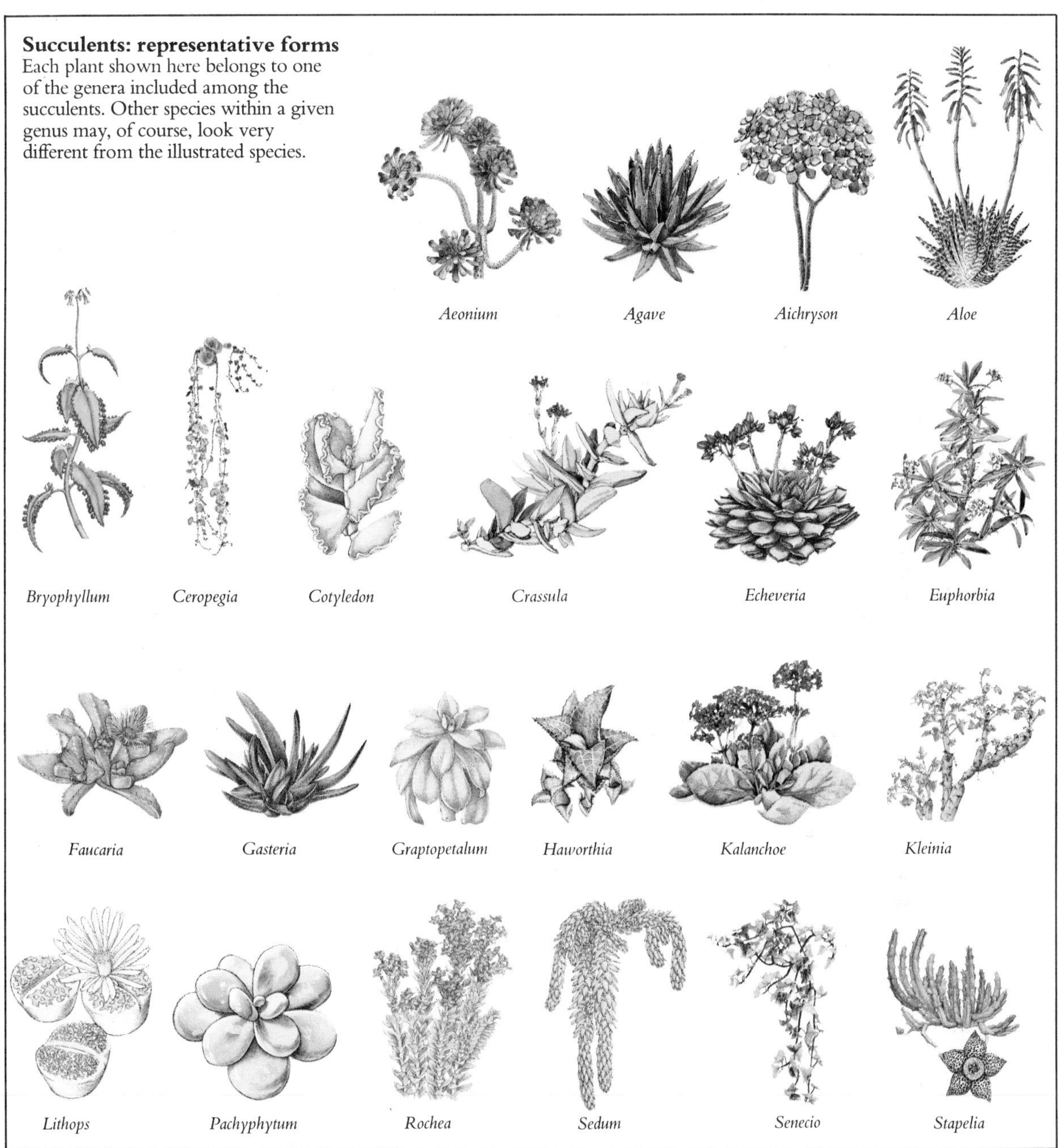

Succulents: representative forms
Each plant shown here belongs to one of the genera included among the succulents. Other species within a given genus may, of course, look very different from the illustrated species.

Temperature The warmth and the comparatively low humidity of a modern living room are singularly suitable for most succulent plants throughout the year. Winter warmth does not normally affect the flowering adversely. Some succulent species will not thrive, however, unless they are encouraged to have a cool winter rest period. Consult appropriate articles in the *A–Z Guide* for the precise recommendations for specific plants.

Like most house plants, succulents benefit from being placed outdoors in their pots during the bright, warm days of spring and summer. When doing this, though, exercise a certain amount of caution. In general, succulent plants with small, delicate leaves or with leaves that are coated with white powder or bloom should not be left out in the rain. Some echeverias and pachyphytums come in this category. If placing them outdoors, put them under a glass or transparent plastic cover to protect the leaves from possible heavy-rain damage. Tougher plants such as agaves can safely be left in a sunny outdoor position all through the warmer months. Such succulent members of the family *Liliaceae* as the aloes, gasterias, and haworthias will also flourish in the open air, but not in full sunlight. Obviously, all succulent plants must be brought back to indoor warmth well before the onset of cold weather.

Watering Because of their natural defenses against drought, succulents do not wilt as swiftly as other plants when deprived of water. This tolerance must not be abused, however.

It is a popular misconception that because these plants often grow in sandy, rainless deserts or near-deserts, they require little or no water. In fact, it is just as possible to kill a succulent plant by neglecting watering instructions as it is to kill a begonia; it merely takes longer. Some growers, aware of this truth, overreact to it. So as not to neglect their succulents, they water these plants as freely as non-succulents—a generosity that can do as much harm as stinginess, since it can cause rotting, particularly during the annual rest period.

In the wild, succulent plants tend to grow during the wetter season of the year (which may be summer or winter, depending upon where a plant comes from) and to rest during the dry season. This provides the most important clue to the successful cultivation of virtually every succulent. Water it reasonably freely during the period of active growth, and give it only enough during the rest period to prevent it from drying out completely. For precise watering instructions consult appropriate entries in the *A–Z Guide*.

Many succulent plants have delicate stems or leaves, which careless splashes of water can easily deface with permanent markings. The best way to water any of these plants is to stand the pot in a vessel containing about 2 inches of water and let capillary action suck up the water until the surface of the potting mixture has become moist. Then remove the pot, and allow it to drain. Never let pots stand in water for longer than it takes to moisten the mixture right through to the top. If it is inconvenient, for any reason, to water each succulent separately in this fashion, use a narrow-spouted can, and take special care to avoid splashing the leaves or stems. It is usually not advisable to water again, even during the active growth period, before the top half-inch of the potting mixture has dried out completely. Rainwater is best if it is available, but these plants will also tolerate ordinary drinking water.

Feeding During the active growth period the more rapidly growing succulents will benefit from applications of liquid fertilizer about once every two weeks. For some plants a standard fertilizer will do, but others need a high-potassium fertilizer of the kind ordinarily used on tomatoes. There are only a few such succulents, but feeding instructions for them in the *A–Z Guide* should be followed carefully. If they get too much nitrogen, their top growth is likely to become soft and weak, and flowering can be inhibited. Slow-growing succulent plants do not normally benefit from feeding of any sort.

Potting and repotting Beware of excess water around the roots of a succulent plant even if it is being watered according to the strictest instructions. The best way to avoid the risk of rotting roots is to provide exceptionally good drainage. If using a soil-based potting mixture, always add a quantity of coarse sand or perlite, mixing it thoroughly into the basic mixture. The usual proportions are about one part of the sandy substance to two of the standard mixture, but some succulents require an even greater degree of drainage. Correct proportions are always indicated in *A–Z Guide* entries.

Either clay or plastic pots can be used. The main difference between the two kinds is that plants in plastic pots need less frequent waterings than those in clay. Plants that produce many branches from the base and eventually form clumps or that spread in other ways are more conveniently grown in pans or half-pots than in conventional pots. And trailing succulents, like any other trailing plants, are generally displayed to best advantage in hanging baskets. Remember, though, that whatever the type of container, no matter how decorative, it will not function well unless it has adequate drainage holes. To improve the drainage even further, put a layer of clay-pot fragments at the bottom before filling the container with the recommended potting mixture.

Most succulents need to be repotted in slightly larger pots once a year, but a slow-growing plant will not be damaged if repotted only every second or third year. The best time to remove a plant from its pot is at the beginning of the active growth period. To ease a specimen out of a clay pot, push a stick or pencil gently into the drainage hole, meanwhile holding the base of the upside-down succulent and tugging lightly. A plant in a plastic pot should emerge easily with a slight squeeze of the pot. If, on removing the plant, its roots are found to have filled the pot, a larger container is clearly in order. Moving on will also be necessary if the plant has formed clumps or offsets that are crowding against the sides of the current pot. Otherwise, simply clean the current pot thoroughly, shake as much spent mixture as possible away from the roots, and return the plant to the pot. Add fresh mixture as needed, but build the mixture up only to the same level on the plant as before.

Most succulent plants other than cacti are easy to hold in the hands during the repotting process. The danger is not to the hands in most cases, since these plants seldom have fierce spines. The dusty bloom on the leaves of some succulents, however, is easily smudged and some of these plants are brittle. The best way to handle such plants is to hold them by the base of the stem as close as possible to the surface of the potting mixture. Wrap a folded newspaper lightly but securely around spiny euphorbias or agaves with sharply pointed leaves.

The biggest pot size required will depend upon the particular plant. Succulents, however, rarely need containers larger than 6–8 inches. Any larger plant is best discarded after being restarted from cuttings.

Propagation Most succulents are among the easiest of house plants to propagate. Non-branching specimens frequently produce offsets, usually from around the base. These can often be gently pulled away, planted in small pots, and treated immediately as mature plants. If the offset must be cut away instead of being detached with a light pull, give the cut surface a chance to heal by letting the offset dry out for two or three days before planting it. It does not matter whether or not the offset already has roots of its own. A rootless offset will soon develop roots if placed on the surface of moist potting mixture and given an appropriate amount of light and warmth.

Some succulents—notably members of the family *Crassulaceae*—can be propagated from leaf cuttings. These should be removed as carefully as possible and allowed to dry out for two or three days. The dry leaf can then be laid on the surface of the potting mixture, or, if it is a long, strap-shaped leaf, its base can be just pushed into the mixture. Where propagation from leaf cuttings is feasible, this method is recommended in the *A–Z Guide* entry. For a full discussion of the technique see page 439.

The two other major types of succulent are the branching plants and the clump-producing members of the family *Aizoaceae* (like faucarias and lithopses). The clumps of the latter type can easily be pulled apart and potted up immediately. And a branch of any succulent that branches naturally can be cut away, allowed to dry for three days, and treated as if it were an offset. The only difference is that such a branch may need to be tied to a short stick for support if it cannot stand upright on its own.

The best time to undertake any of the methods of propagation summarized above is during the active growth period of the particular plant (usually some time in spring or summer). See specific entries in the *A–Z Guide* for more detailed information.

Raising succulents from seed In spite of the varied families of succulents, the method of growing these plants from seed is much the same for all. If only one type of seed is to be sown, use a single 2-inch pot, which can be either clay or plastic. If several different kinds of seed are being sown, either use a separate pot for each kind or divide an ordinary seed pan into carefully labeled sections. Put about ½ inch of gravel or perlite in the bottom of the pot or pan, and fill it up to within ½ inch of the rim with a standard rooting mixture. Because the seeds of most succulents cannot tolerate excess water, it is a good idea to mix one part of medium-coarse sand into three parts of standard mixture. This will improve the drainage.

Give the rooting mixture just enough water to moisten it evenly throughout. Next sprinkle a little fine sand over the top, covering the mixture thinly but entirely. This provides a fine, level surface for the seeds. Then scatter seeds thinly over the surface. Do not bury them. The seeds of various succulent plants are of different sizes. None are extremely large, and so the bigger ones present no problems. Some types of seed (especially of the family *Aizoaceae*) are so small, however, that they are dustlike. Take care not to let them blow away.

Cover the container with a piece of glass or clear plastic to conserve the moisture, and keep the seeds at a temperature of at least 70°F—a level most easily reached in late spring or summer which is also the best time to sow seeds. Light is not needed at first.

Two ways to propagate succulents

Propagation by leaf cuttings

Use a sharp knife to cut a leaf from a succulent such as a crassula.

Allow the cut end to dry. If the leaf is short lay it on the surface of the mixture to root.

To root a long leaf such as one from Crassula falcata*, insert its base in the mixture.*

Propagation from seed

Prepare a seed pan by covering a layer of gravel with damp rooting medium.

Cover the mixture with sand to provide an even surface for seeds.

Sprinkle seeds thinly, sowing each kind in a separate section of the pan.

If the container is placed near a window, put a sheet of thin paper over it to protect the seeds from direct sunlight. As soon as some of the seeds germinate, this diffused light or any sort of bright filtered light becomes essential. In addition, when germination begins, ventilate the seedlings by keeping the glass or plastic cover slightly open. Most succulent seeds should germinate within two to three weeks, but some take longer. Seeds of stapelias and ceropegias, on the other hand, germinate with startling rapidity, and their seedlings often appear in a few days. Therefore it is best to use individual pots rather than to sow several types in one container.

The worst enemy of seedlings is a fungus that causes damping-off disease. To overcome this problem there are commercial preparations with which rooting mixture can be treated before seeds are sown. The best preventive measures, however, are clean containers and good ventilation once seeds have germinated. Keep the mixture slightly moist at all times, and do not expose seedlings to direct sunlight during their first year. Bright filtered light is best. Many kinds of seedling can remain in the original container for a year. Move rapidly-growing kinds into individual 2-inch pots of standard mixture if they seem to be getting overcrowded. At this stage the young plants are ready to be treated as mature specimens.

Pests and diseases The mealy bug and root mealy bug find an ideal hiding place among the tightly packed leaves or roots of many succulents. And plants put outdoors in spring and summer are subject to attack by slugs and snails. (For a discussion of pests and diseases see pages 452-459.) The following genera are either entirely composed of succulent plants or include one or more succulent species. For cactus species see page 122.

Aeonium	*Gasteria*
Agave	*Graptopetalum*
Aichryson	*Haworthia*
Aloe	*Kalanchoe*
Bryophyllum	*Kleinia*
Ceropegia	*Lithops*
Cotyledon	*Pachyphytum*
Crassula	*Rochea*
Echeveria	*Sedum*
Euphorbia	*Senecio*
Faucaria	*Stapelia*

Syngonium

ARACEAE

Arrowhead plant
S. podophyllum

THE genus *Syngonium* (formerly called *Nephthytis)* includes about 20 species of tropical vine that closely resemble certain climbing philodendrons. Like the climbing philodendrons, syngoniums are peculiar in that the leaves produced by mature plants are different in shape from those produced by young specimens. As a syngonium ages, it carries both types of leaf, and it also gradually develops a climbing or trailing stem. Stems of indoor syngoniums, therefore, can either be trained up thin stakes pushed into the potting mixture or be permitted to grow in hanging baskets.

Leaves of most syngoniums are leathery and glossy, with sheathed stalks that tend to be equal in length to the leaves. In young plants each leaf is usually undivided, though deeply lobed (there are generally either three or five lobes). Mature plants normally have leaves divided into distinct segments (or leaflets), and a single leaf may consist of as many as nine of these. The middle segment (like the middle lobe of the leaf in younger plants) is invariably the largest. Stems of young plants are fleshy and slender and have prominent nodes. Stems of older plants harden and thicken to a diameter of up to $\frac{3}{4}$ inch, and an indoor length of 6 feet. Flowers are calla lily-shaped, but are rarely produced indoors.

RECOMMENDED SYNGONIUMS

***S. angustatum* 'Albolineatum'** (called arrowhead vine) is a variety whose leaves change in both shape and color from the juvenile stage of the plant to its maturity. Juvenile leaves are about 3 inches long, 2 inches wide and triple-lobed, with the large middle lobe shaped like an arrowhead. Leaf color is green with widespread white or silvery markings along the midrib and main veins. As they age, plants produce leaves up to 9 inches long and wide. Each leaf is divided into three or five distinct segments, and leaf color is plain green except for the white midrib of each segment.

S. auritum (five fingers) has fleshy, dark green leaves that are 6 inches long, 3 inches wide, and triple-lobed when the plant is young. The mature leaves are up to 15 inches long and 12 inches wide, and each leaf is composed of five separate segments. A long, elliptic central segment is flanked by a pair of medium-size segments held at right angles to the middle one, and there are a pair of very small opposite leaflets at the base.

S. podophyllum (arrowhead plant or vine) usually produces medium green, rounded leaves 6 inches long and 4 inches wide with three deep-cut lobes when the plant is young. Mature plants produce leaves up to 12 inches long and wide divided into five or seven segments. There are a number of interesting varieties of *S. podophyllum*. One of the best-known forms is *S.p.* 'Emerald Gem,' a compact variety with shorter leafstalks than those of most syngoniums. Its crinkled leaves grow up to 8 inches long and 6 inches wide in both juvenile and mature plants. Leaf color is a dark green, with lighter green zones along the length of the veins.

PROPER CARE

Light Give syngoniums bright filtered light throughout the year. Never subject them to direct sunlight.

Temperature Normal room temperatures are ideal. Syngoniums cannot tolerate temperatures below 55°F. Whenever indoor temperatures are above 65°, increase the humidity for actively growing plants by standing pots on trays of moist pebbles.

Watering Water actively growing plants moderately, allowing the top half-inch of the mixture to dry out before watering again. Syngoniums normally have a short winter rest period, during which they should be given only enough water to keep the mixture from drying out completely.

Feeding Apply standard liquid fertilizer every two weeks to actively growing plants.

Potting and repotting Use an equal-parts combination of soil-based potting mixture (see page 429) and coarse leaf mold or peat moss. Repot each syngonium every spring, moving the plants into pots one size larger when roots have filled the current pots (see page 426). These plants do not require large containers. A 5- or 6-inch pot or a 6- to 8-inch hanging basket should be the maximum required. After such a size has been reached, topdress plants every spring with fresh mixture (see page 428).

Propagation Propagate in late spring or early summer from tip cuttings 3–4 inches long. Take each cutting just below a node, strip off the bottom leaf, and dip the cut end in hormone rooting powder. Plant two or three prepared cuttings together in a 3- or 4-inch pot of a moistened equal-parts mixture of peat moss and coarse sand or perlite. Enclose the whole in a plastic bag or propagating case, and stand it in bright filtered light. After rooting has occurred (normally, in four to six weeks), uncover the pot and begin to give the rooted cuttings just enough water to make the rooting mixture barely moist. After another month begin to apply monthly doses of standard liquid fertilizer. Four or five months after the start of propagation transfer the young plants, in groups, into the potting mixture recommended for mature specimens and treat them as adult syngoniums. In transferring the plants keep them together. For hanging baskets plant two or three groups in each basket.

Tetrastigma

VITACEAE

Chestnut vine
T. voinieranum

THE vigorous large-leaved vines of the genus *Tetrastigma* are represented indoors by only one species, *T. voinieranum* (formerly known as *Cissus voinieranum*). This plant is commonly called either chestnut vine (because its leaves resemble those of horse chestnuts) or lizard plant (because it sometimes drops whole sections of its growth, as a lizard loses its tail when alarmed). Under the right conditions the plant grows extremely fast, and some growers regard it as coarse. Its stems, which can be $\frac{1}{2}$–$\frac{3}{4}$ inch thick, are produced in jointed segments a few inches long, each segment growing at a slight angle to the previous one. The leaves, carried on 4- to 12-inch-long stalks, are composed of several (usually five) glossy green, widely separated leaflets, each of which is 4–8 inches long, slightly toothed at the edges, and carried on a 2-inch stalk of its own. Stems and leaflet undersides are heavily felted with fine russet-colored hairs.

The spiraled tendrils of this vine cling firmly, holding the heavy stem and leaf sections to any available support. When a section of growth falls off, no permanent harm results; the plant often produces a similar-size stem section from the same joint. A well-cared-for tetrastigma will cover 6 feet of trellis or wall in a single year. For this reason, the plant is really suitable only for very large indoor areas. It does not produce flowers and fruit when it is grown indoors.

PROPER CARE

Light Provide bright light at all times, but keep these plants out of direct sunlight.

Temperature Indoor tetrastigmas grow well in any normal room temperature and will tolerate a certain amount of dry air. The temperature should never be permitted to fall below 55°F; and it should be kept as constant as possible, because violent fluctuations in temperature seem to be a major cause of the shedding of sections of growth.

Watering During the active growth period water tetrastigmas moderately, giving enough to make the potting mixture thoroughly moist, but allowing the top half-inch of the mixture to dry out between waterings. During the rest period water only when half of the mixture has dried out.

Feeding Apply standard liquid fertilizer every two weeks during the active growth period only.

Potting and repotting Use a soil-based potting mixture (see page 429) for tetrastigmas. It is advisable to move these plants into pots two sizes larger every spring. After maximum convenient pot size (probably between 10–12 inches) has been reached, annual topdressing with fresh potting mixture will suffice (see page 428).

Propagation Propagate whenever convenient by means of a 9-inch-long tip cutting with at least one leaf attached. Dust the cut end with hormone rooting powder, plant it in a 3-inch pot containing a well-moistened mixture of peat moss and sand, and cover the whole with a plastic bag or place it in a heated propagating case (see page 444). Keep the cutting at 60°–75°F and in bright light filtered through a translucent blind or curtain, but do not water it.

The cutting should root in six to eight weeks. Thereafter, uncover the young plant and begin to water it just enough to make the potting mixture barely moist, but allowing the top half of the mixture to dry out between waterings; and it should be fed standard liquid fertilizer once a month for four or five months. When the plant appears to be well established, move it into a 5-inch pot of soil-based potting mixture, after which its cultivation needs are exactly the same as those of a mature tetrastigma.

Special points It is essential to provide substantial support for these large-leaved climbers. Push a stick into the potting mixture close to the base of the plant and tie the stem at regular intervals to this support.

Thunbergia

ACANTHACEAE

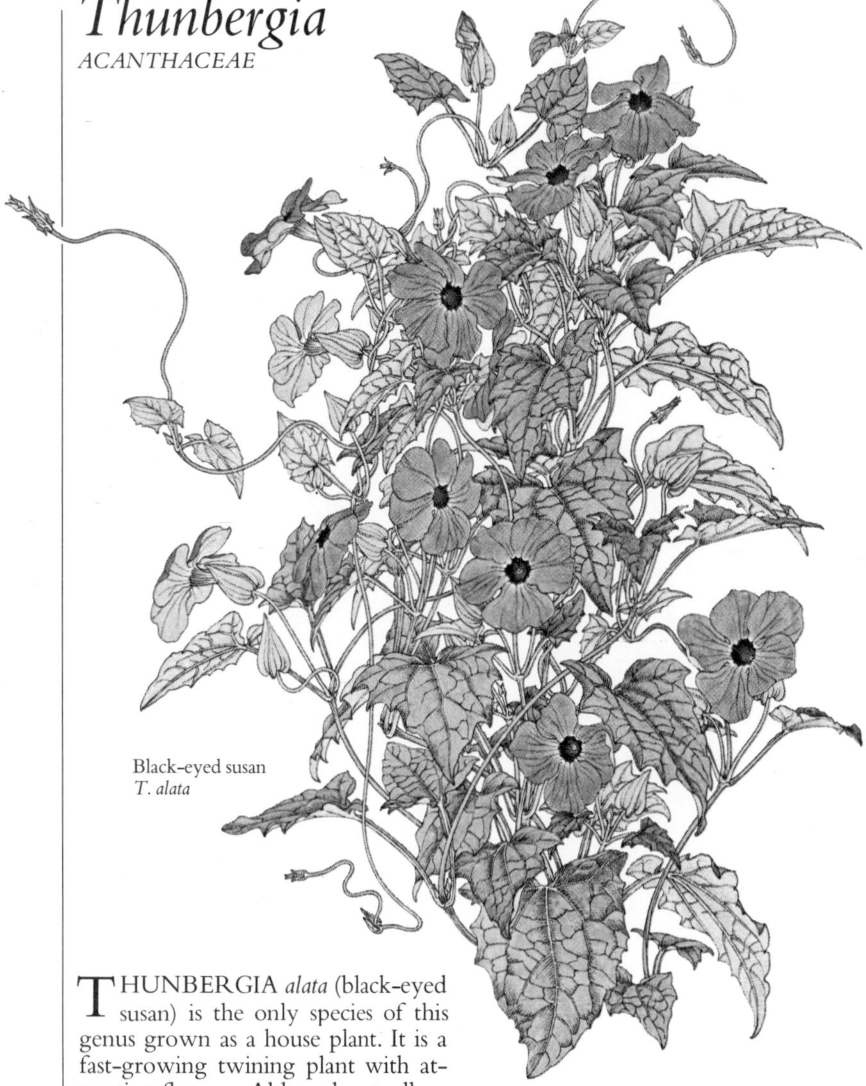

Black-eyed susan
T. alata

THUNBERGIA *alata* (black-eyed susan) is the only species of this genus grown as a house plant. It is a fast-growing twining plant with attractive flowers. Although actually a perennial, it is usually treated as a temporary house plant, to be enjoyed during the flowering period—which normally lasts from late spring to late fall—and then discarded. Its leaves are tooth-edged, triangular to arrow-shaped, up to 3 inches long and wide, borne on slender stalks along the twining stems. Two-inch-wide flowers, which are produced on short stalks from the leaf axils, consist of an inch-long tube flaring out into five petallike lobes. Petal-lobe color varies, but in all forms there is a central deep chocolate brown "eye" (the entry point to the tube for insects); the tube itself is dark purple, and each flower is backed with a pair of $\frac{3}{4}$-inch-long, pale green bracts. In the most common form of *T. alata, T.a.* 'Aurantiaca,' the lobes are orange-yellow; in *T.a.* 'Alba,' white; in *T.a.* 'Lutea,' bright yellow.

Buy young thunbergia plants only a few weeks old in the spring. They usually twine around three or four thin sticks pushed into the edge of the pot but they will also climb up a string fixed to the side of a window. In either case, they should be cut down and discarded when flowering stops.

PROPER CARE

Light Thunbergias must have bright light with two to three hours a day of direct sunlight to flower properly.

Temperature These thunbergias will do well in any normal room temperature during their stay in the home. Nevertheless, they can tolerate much cooler conditions—down to 50°F.

Watering Water young plants moderately, enough to make the potting mixture moist at each watering, but allowing the top half-inch of the mixture to dry out before watering again. As these swift-growing plants get bigger and begin to flower, they need more water. Throughout the flowering period water them plentifully, as often as necessary to keep the mixture thoroughly moist.

Feeding Give standard liquid fertilizer to flowering plants every two weeks throughout the year.

Potting and repotting Use a soil-based potting mixture (see page 429). Young thunbergias should be moved on when they grow too big for their original pots. As soon as a number of roots begin to appear through the drainage hole in the bottom of a pot, move the plant into a pot two sizes larger. Probable maximum pot size needed: 6 inches.

Propagation Seed can be grown indoors without much difficulty if sown in early spring. Three seeds should be planted in a single 3-inch pot containing a moistened soil-based potting mixture. They will usually germinate in three to five weeks if kept in a warm room in a position where they get bright filtered light, and are watered enough to make the mixture moist, but with the top half-inch of the mixture allowed to dry out between waterings. The new plants will grow quickly and may be transferred to individual 3-inch pots and treated as mature thunbergias when they are 6 inches high.

Special points Be sure to remove faded flowers by nipping them out with the fingertips. If this is not done regularly, the flowering season will be needlessly brief.

It is vital to remove dead flowers: As well as curtailing the flowering season they spoil the look of the plant.

Tibouchina

MELASTOMATACEAE

Glory-bush
T. urvilleana

THE only species of *Tibouchina* commonly grown as a house plant is *T. urvilleana* (also called *T. semidecandra;* popularly known as glory-bush, princess-flower, or purple glory tree). This plant is a shrub that grows up to 4 feet tall indoors. Its four-angled stems and branches are soft, green, and covered with fine, reddish hairs when young. Later the stems turn woody and brown. The velvety, pointed-oval, paired leaves are medium to deep green, with prominent, pale green, lengthwise veins and finely toothed edges. Each leaf is 2–4 inches long and 1–1½ inches wide. The striking saucer-shaped, five-petaled flowers are a rosy purple to violet color, with a cluster of protruding purple stamens in the center. Each flower is about 3 inches across. They are produced in clusters at branch tips from midsummer to early winter.

PROPER CARE

Light Give tibouchinas bright filtered light from early spring to mid-fall. During the short-day months keep plants in a position where they get four hours a day of direct sunlight.

Temperature During the active growth period normal room temperatures are suitable. During the midwinter rest period temperatures of about 50°F are best. Stand actively growing tibouchinas on trays or saucers of damp pebbles.

Watering During the active growth period water plentifully as often as necessary to keep the potting mixture thoroughly moist, but never allow pots to stand in water. During the rest period give only enough to make the mixture barely moist throughout.

Feeding Apply standard liquid fertilizer every two weeks during the active growth period.

Potting and repotting Use a soil-based mixture (see page 429). Move plants into larger pots every spring until maximum convenient size is reached. Thereafter, topdress annually with fresh mixture (see page 428).

Propagation Take stem or tip cuttings 3–4 inches long in spring. Trim each cutting to just below a pair of leaves, remove the bottom leaves, and dip the cut end of the cutting in hormone rooting powder. Plant the cutting in a 3-inch pot containing a moistened equal-parts mixture of peat moss and coarse sand or perlite. Enclose the whole in a plastic bag or propagating case (see page 443), and stand it in a warm room in bright filtered light. When new growth appears, uncover it and begin to water it moderately. After a further eight weeks, move the young plant into a 4-inch pot of standard mixture and treat it as a mature specimen.

Special points Shorten main shoots by half their length, and cut sideshoots back to two pairs of leaves each spring.

Tillandsia

BROMELIACEAE

THE genus *Tillandsia* includes many widely varying forms of bromeliad. Tillandsias range in size from tiny, lichenlike plants to immense rosettes of leaves, and their native habitats range from humid rain forests to arid deserts. Those in common use as house plants have little or no root and absorb most or all of the water and food they need through their leaves. This makes them suitable for epiphyte branches (see page 107). *See also BROMELIADS.*

RECOMMENDED TILLANDSIAS

T. cyanea has many 1- to 1½-foot-long and ½- to 1-inch-wide leaves. These narrow, pointed-tipped leaves are arranged in a loose rosette. Their color is gray-green, with reddish brown, lengthwise stripes on the undersides. A 2- to 3-inch-long flower stalk appearing from the center of the mature rosette carries a fan-shaped flower head 4–6 inches long and 2 inches wide. This hard flower head, which lasts for up to 10 weeks, is composed of a number of smooth, overlapping, rose-colored bracts. The actual flowers, which appear singly from the notches formed on the edge of the flower head by the overlapping of the bracts, are tubular flaring out into three broad petals. Flower color is bright violet-blue, and each bloom measures 2 inches across at the mouth.

As with most bromeliad rosettes, the rosette flowers only once and then gradually dies. Offsets are produced from leaf axils, and these may be either used for the purpose of propagation or

Here two dissimilar tillandsias, T. cyanea *and* T. usneoides, *are being displayed together on an epiphyte log.*

Tillandsia cyanea

else left in the pot after the withered old rosette has finally been detached.

T. lindenii is similar to *T. cyanea* in almost all respects. It differs mainly in that the flower stalk can be as much as 12 inches long, and flower color is deep royal blue with a white throat.

T. usneoides (Spanish moss or graybeard) consists of threadlike stems covered with silvery gray scales that are, in reality, minute, scaly leaves. In the wild this virtually rootless plant hangs from trees and rocks in long, tangled festoons. *T. usneoides*, therefore, is not used as a potted plant. Instead, many indoor gardeners attach a few sections of the tangled mass to a 2-inch-square piece of cork or bark, tying the fine stems on loosely with plastic-coated or copper wire and hanging the cork on a hook. The stems trail as they lengthen. The tiny, pale green flowers that appear in the leaf axils of wild Spanish moss rarely bloom indoors.

PROPER CARE

Light Tillandsias used as house plants do best in bright filtered light.

Temperature These plants will grow actively throughout the year if the temperature is kept above 60°F; they cannot tolerate temperatures below 55°. For increased humidity, stand the potted species of tillandsia on trays of moist pebbles, and mist-spray them two or three times a week. Mist-spray *T. usneoides* daily.

Watering The negligible roots of *T. cyanea* and *T. lindenii* need little water. If the foliage is mist-sprayed regularly as advised above (see "Temperature"), enough water will seep down into the potting mixture. In addition, submerge *T. usneoides,* along with its base, in water for 10 minutes a week.

Feeding Give a half-strength dose of standard liquid fertilizer to most potted tillandsias once a month. *T. usneoides* needs nothing.

Potting and repotting For *T. cyanea* and *T. lindenii* use one of the potting mixtures recommended for bromeliads (see page 107). These plants will flower and form offsets in 4-inch pots and do not need to be moved to bigger ones. For *T. usneoides* see "Recommended tillandsias," above.

Propagation Remove offsets of *T. cyanea* and *T. lindenii* from the parent plant at any time after their leaves have attained a length of 3 inches. Plant each offset in a 2- or 3-inch pot containing an equal-parts mixture of peat moss and coarse sand or perlite, and enclose the whole in a plastic bag or propagating case (see page 443). When roots have developed, treat the young plant as a mature specimen. Transfer it into a 4-inch pot of standard bromeliad mixture about six months after the start of propagation.

To propagate *T. usneoides,* detach a few stems, and wire them to a piece of cork or bark, as suggested in "Recommended tillandsias," above.

Tolmiea

SAXIFRAGACEAE

TOLMIEA *menziesii* (mother of thousands, piggy-back plant, or youth on age) is the only species of this genus. Its 4-inch-long leafstalks, rising from a main stem so short as to be barely noticeable, carry heart-shaped, lobed, tooth-edged leaf blades 2–3 inches across. The plant grows to a height of about 12 inches and a spread of 15 inches. Its common names derive from the fascinating habit of producing plantlets on a number of the older leaves. Each plantlet grows on the upper surface of a leaf at the junction of the leaf and its stalk. This extra weight bears down the slender leafstalks, so that many of them seem to be trailing. Thus, tolmieas look especially attractive in hanging baskets. Both the fresh green leaves and their leafstalks are covered with soft hair. The greenish white flowers are insignificant and rarely produced on plants grown indoors.

PROPER CARE

Light Tolmieas thrive in either bright or medium light. The leaves of those kept in relatively low light are a paler green, and the stalks of such plants tend to elongate.

Temperature Normal room temperatures are suitable.These plants are tolerant of a wide range of temperatures, however. They will do well in any temperature down to 50°F.

Watering Throughout the warmer months, during the active growth period, water these plants moderately. Give enough to moisten the potting mixture throughout, but allow the top half-inch of the mixture to dry out before watering again. During the short winter rest period water tolmieas only enough to keep the potting mixture from drying out completely.

Feeding Apply standard liquid fertilizer every two weeks during the active growth period.

Potting and repotting Use a soil-based potting mixture (see page 429). Plant three small tolmieas together in a 3-inch pot. Alternatively group four to six plants in a hanging basket. Move the plants on to larger containers only when they have filled the present ones with roots (see page 426). Repotting can be done at any time of the year. Because newly rooted plants grow best and look healthiest, it is

Mother of thousands
T. menziesii

advisable to replace older tolmieas rather than to repot them more than once or twice.

Propagation Propagate tolmieas in spring or summer. Cut off a leaf that has a well-developed plantlet on it leaving about 1 inch of its stalk attached, and plant it in a 2- or 3-inch pot containing a moistened rooting mixture of equal parts of peat moss and coarse sand or perlite. Make sure that the stalk is buried and the plantlet-bearing part sits on the surface of the rooting mixture. Keep the pot in bright light, watering only enough to make the rooting mixture barely moist, until new growth indicates that rooting has occurred (normally, in two to three weeks). Thereafter, treat the plantlet as a mature tolmiea. In another five or six weeks transfer it from the rooting mixture into the standard soil-based potting mixture. The "mother" leaf may remain green for several months, but it will eventually dry up and can then be carefully removed from the new plant.

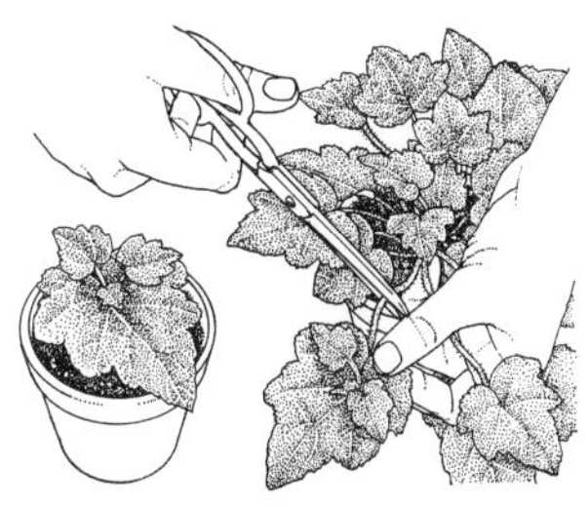

Cut off any tolmiea leaf carrying a small plantlet. Make sure that the joint between leafstalk and blade is in close contact with the mixture.

Alternatively, the plantlet-bearing leaf can be propagated while still attached to the parent plant by a process similar to layering (see page 439). Fill a 3-inch pot with the rooting mixture recommended above, and place the pot close to the parent plant. Use a short piece of wire (a hair-pin, for example) or a small stone to fasten the leaf down onto the mixture in the prepared pot. Keep both pots in a warm room in bright light, and water the leaf sparingly, just enough to keep the rooting mixture from drying out completely. Roots will develop at the point where the leaf touches the mixture. After rooting has occurred (probably in two or three weeks), sever the large leaf from the parent plant and treat the newly rooted plantlet as a mature tolmiea.

Tolmieas grow extremely quickly and the indoor gardener will be in possession of an attractive house plant only 5 or 6 months after the start of the propagation process.

Trachycarpus

PALMAE

THE single species of the genus *Trachycarpus* grown as a house plant, *T. fortunei* (windmill palm), has a slender stem that bears fan-shaped leaves with finely toothed stalks several feet long. In the wild, *T. fortunei* grows to about 40 feet tall, but growth indoors is slow and plants are unlikely to reach a height of more than 8 feet in the home. When young, the leaves are pleated and they are covered with fine, short, gray or light brown hair. As the leaves age, this woolly covering disappears, and the pleats divide almost to the base into many stout but pliant segments, each up to 12 inches long and 1–1½ inches wide. Individual segments are sometimes pleated into two or three folds. The mature leaves are up to 2 feet wide and dark green above, bluish green below, and the main stem, which does not normally branch, becomes covered with a coarse brown fiber. Eventually the leaves turn from green to yellow to brown, but they do not fall off. They should be gently pulled away or cut off when they become unsightly. The tips of leaf segments, in particular, become discolored with age and are liable to split along an inch or more of their length. This is natural and is not necessarily a sign of ill-health. An affected tip can be cut off without detriment to the rest of the leaf. The flowers and fruit produced by mature trachycarpuses are not found on indoor specimens.

The young pleated leaf emerging from the middle of mature leafstalks will gradually grow taller, and its pleats will divide into separate segments.

See also PALMS.

Windmill palm
Trachycarpus fortunei

PROPER CARE

Light Throughout the year, trachycarpuses need bright light with three or four hours a day of direct sunlight. New growth will be limited if plants receive insufficient light.

Temperature These plants not only grow well in normally warm room temperatures but are also completely unharmed by temperatures down to 45°F. If possible, stand trachycarpuses outdoors in a sheltered but sunny position from late spring to mid-fall. This will promote new growth and encourage the development of stiff, healthy leaves.

Watering Water actively growing plants moderately, giving enough water to make the potting mixture thoroughly moist, but allowing the top half-inch of the mixture to dry out before watering again. In a normally warm room a trachycarpus will not have a regular rest period, but its growth will slow down or even stop whenever the temperature drops below 55°F. At such times, water only once a month, and sparingly—just enough to make the potting mixture barely moist throughout.

Feeding Apply standard liquid fertilizer to actively growing plants once every two weeks.

Potting and repotting Use a soil-based potting mixture (see page 429). Move small trachycarpuses into pots one or, at the most, two sizes larger every second or third spring until the maximum convenient container size (likely to be 10–12 inches), is reached. Thereafter, topdress plants annually (see page 428) with fresh potting mixture.

Propagation Trachycarpuses are propagated by fresh seed sown in early spring. Seed takes up to a year to germinate, however, and the seedlings are also slow-growing—they may take several years to assume palmlike characteristics. The best way to acquire trachycarpuses, therefore, is to purchase young plants from nurseries or garden centers.

Special points Stand any plants not kept outdoors in the milder months in gentle rain, or wash them carefully under a cool shower if this is not possible, in order to free them of the accumulation of dirt and dust that collects on the leaves.

Tradescantia

COMMELINACEAE

TRADESCANTIAS are easy-to-grow, small-leaved, trailing plants with many popular names including inch plant and wandering Jew. The trailing stems, which grow more than a foot long, have prominent nodes and change direction slightly at each node. Leaves are generally pointed-elliptic in shape and stalkless. In the spring and summer, clusters of small, three-petaled, white, white-and-pink, or pink flowers, appear at the ends of the trailing stems. Individual blooms last just one day. All tradescantias tend to lose their lower leaves with age and should be propagated regularly.

RECOMMENDED TRADESCANTIAS

T. albiflora, a white-flowered, plain green, shiny-leaved tradescantia, is a familiar house plant only in several variegated forms. Among them are *T.a.* 'Albovittata' (giant white inch plant), with white stripes on its green leaves; *T.a.* 'Aurea,' whose leaves are almost entirely yellow; and *T.a.* 'Tricolor,' with leaves striped in both white and light purple. Leaves of all these are 2–2$\frac{1}{2}$ inches long, and the plants bloom infrequently.

T. fluminensis 'Variegata'

T. sillamontana (white velvet)

T. blossfeldiana 'Variegata' (flowering inch plant)

Wandering Jew
T. fluminensis 'Quicksilver'

T. blossfeldiana (flowering inch plant) has fleshy leaves up to 4 inches long; they are dark olive green with deep purple undersides. The ½-inch flowers that appear in spring are pink in the upper half, white in the lower. Fine whitish hair covers the flowers, stems, and leaves. One form, *T.b.* 'Variegata,' has leaves that may be green, wholly cream-colored, or striped half green and half cream—all on a single plant. When grown in bright light, the cream sections of this form take on a strong pink hue.

In propagating the variegated form it is essential to use shoots carrying leaves with at least a third of green coloring in them. The stems bearing all-cream leaves will not root.

T. fluminensis (wandering Jew) is similar to *T. albiflora,* but its leaves, which are up to 2 inches long and have deep purple undersides, are more pointed. White-striped and cream-striped forms are available; the most popular of these is *T.f.* 'Variegata.' *T.f.* 'Quicksilver' is an extremely fast-growing, robust variety, which does not lose its lower leaves as easily as some of the other tradescantias do; it has evenly striped green-and-white, 3-inch-long leaves (without purple undersides), and the starlike white flowers are carried in larger clusters than in the other forms.

T. navicularis (chain plant) is a low- and slow-growing creeper, which has closely packed, 1-inch-long, fleshy, coppery green, triangular leaves. Each leaf has a crease along the central vein, short hairs along the edges, and purple dots on the underside. The flowers are a bright pink.

T. sillamontana (white velvet) has flattened ranks of extended-oval leaves that are 2½ inches long and colored peppermint green. The leaves and stems are all heavily felted with long, white, woolly hair; and the magenta-pink flowers also contrast strongly with the leaf coloring.

PROPER CARE

Light Tradescantias need bright light, with some direct sunlight every day. Given insufficient light they will lose much of their decorative leaf coloring. *T. sillamontana* in particular must have direct strong light, or its stems will elongate unnaturally.

Temperature Do not subject these plants to temperatures below 50°F; they grow best in humid warmth. An ideal temperature range throughout the year is 70°–75°.

Watering Water actively growing tradescantias plentifully, as much as necessary to keep the potting mixture thoroughly moist. At other times make the potting mixture barely moist throughout, allowing the top two-thirds of the mixture to dry out before watering again. But water *T. navicularis* and *T. sillamontana* only sparingly at all times.

Feeding Apply standard liquid fertilizer once every two weeks from early spring to late fall.

Potting and repotting A soil-based potting mixture (see page 429) is best for most tradescantias, but *T. navicularis* and *T. sillamontana* should have up to a one-third portion of coarse sand or perlite added to the mixture for better drainage. A 4- to 6-inch pot is the largest size needed for any of the stronger-growing plants and a 3-inch half-pot or pan will suffice for the slow-growing *T. navicularis* for several years. Move young plants into larger pots whenever it becomes necessary, but discard aging plants in favor of newly-rooted cuttings.

Propagation Take tip cuttings at virtually any time. Insert four to six 3-inch-long cuttings in a 3-inch pot containing an equal-parts mixture of peat moss and sand. Keep the pot in a warm place in bright filtered light, watering just enough to keep the rooting mixture barely moist. Roots will develop in about two weeks. Groups of rooted cuttings can then be planted together in larger pots of the recommended mixture for mature plants and treated in the same way as adult tradescantias. In propagating *T. navicularis* and *T. sillamontana* there is a possibility that the cuttings may rot. To forestall rotting, sprinkle some coarse sand or perlite into the holes made for the cuttings.

Alternatively, cuttings 2–3 inches long root easily in small—preferably opaque—glasses of water that are kept in bright light filtered through a translucent blind or curtain. When the roots have grown 1–2 inches long, pot up the cuttings and treat them as mature tradescantias.

Special points Nip out the growing tips of most tradescantias regularly to encourage bushy growth. Remove any drying leaves from the base of the trailing stems.

Trichocereus
CACTACEAE

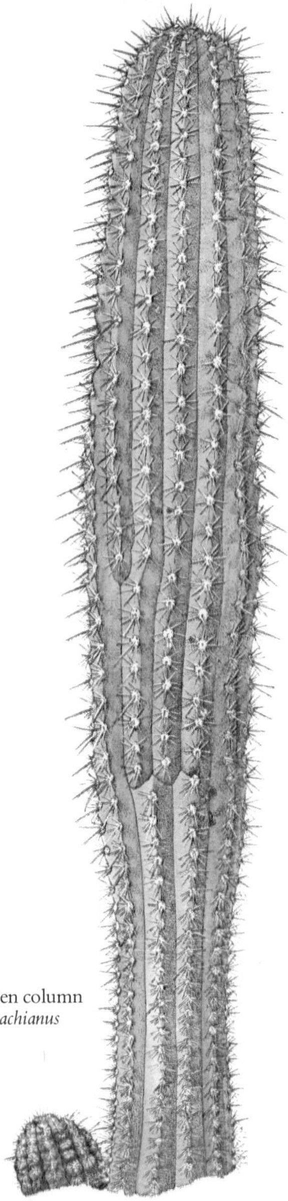

Golden column
T. spachianus

THE only species of this desert cactus commonly grown as a house plant is *T. spachianus* (golden column or white torch cactus), which forms an erect column, usually branching from the base. The bright green stem can reach a height of 5 feet, but it is relatively slow-growing. A five-year-old plant is unlikely to be more than about 8 inches high and 1–1½ inches across. The stem has 10 to 15 broad ribs, with deep indentations in between. The areoles spaced about ⅜ inch apart along the ribs are yellowish at first but they gradually turn grayish. Each areole bears around eight brownish yellow, radial spines and one or two central spines of the same color. The radials are bristlelike and up to ½ inch long; the centrals are slightly thicker and longer.

T. spachianus does not flower until it is at least 12 inches tall, at which time the plant will be 8 to 10 years old and will have several branches. Because the plant takes so long to bloom, it is generally grown for its impressive columnar form and colorful spines rather than for its flowers. When the flowers do appear, they are produced profusely from areoles at the top of the stems. Each trumpet-shaped, white bloom is about 8 inches long and 3 inches across. These enormous flowers open at night, usually fading during the morning of the following day. The normal flowering season for *T. spachianus* is summer.
See also CACTI.

PROPER CARE

Light Give these cacti direct sunlight all year long in order to ensure good spine color and prevent the stems from becoming unnaturally elongated. As with all columnar cacti grown indoors, the stems lean toward the source of light unless they are turned regularly (every three or four days) throughout the spring and summer period of active growth. Place them in outdoor sunshine during this period, if possible. They will benefit from the extra light and are less likely to grow one-sided.

Temperature Any normally warm room temperatures are suitable during the active growth period. During the winter rest period keep *T. spachianus* at a temperature below 50°F. This cactus can even withstand freezing temperatures under certain conditions (see "Watering," below).

Watering During the active growth period water moderately, enough to make the potting mixture moist throughout but allowing the top half-inch of the mixture to dry out before watering again. During the rest period give only enough to prevent the mixture from drying out completely. If, for any reason, indoor temperatures fall below about 35°F, do not water these plants at all. Let the potting mixture remain completely dry until the temperature rises. The plants will not be harmed as a result.

Feeding Apply a high-potassium, tomato-type liquid fertilizer to actively growing trichocereuses once every two weeks if they are potted in a peat-based mixture. If plants are in a soil-based mixture, feed them only once a month.

Potting and repotting Use either a standard soil-based or a peat-based potting mixture (see page 429). Because these cacti have vigorous root systems, a plant only 3 inches tall will probably need a 3-inch pot. Bigger specimens will need correspondingly larger pots, especially as the plants branch at the base. Repot every spring, using a folded newspaper to protect the plant (as well as the hands) while removing it from the pot. If the current pot is tightly packed with roots, move the plant into a pot one size larger. Otherwise, after gently shaking the potting mixture from the roots, return the plant to its old pot, which has been thoroughly cleaned and filled with fresh mixture.

Propagation If a trichocereus has grown large enough to form branches, cut off one of these at the base for propagation purposes. The best time to do this is in spring or summer. Allow the cut end to dry for three days before pressing it firmly into the surface of the standard potting mixture contained in a 3-inch pot. Then treat the newly potted branch as a mature specimen.

An obvious objection to cutting off a branch is that it can spoil the look of the parent plant. For this reason most growers prefer to raise these cacti from seed (see *CACTI*, page 119). Young trichocereus seedlings are attractive and grow well.

Special points With age, the stem of *T. spachianus* often becomes disfigured with corky markings, particularly around the base. (The branches, if any, are not affected.) This is natural but unsightly. It is advisable to cut across an affected unbranched stem about 6 inches from the base. Offsets will soon form around the edge of the cut surface. When these are 2–3 inches high detach them and treat as branches (see "Propagation," above) to make new, unmarked plants. This is best done in spring or summer. Use the top portion of the stem, provided it is not too badly marked, to produce a new plant by treating it in the same manner. Grow the parent plant on in the normal way.

Tulipa

LILIACEAE

Tulips
Tulipa hybrids

ALTHOUGH tulips are essentially outdoor plants, many kinds make delightful temporary house plants. The genus *Tulipa* includes about 100 true species of bulbous plant, but the showy hybrids are considered best for indoor use. The best of these have small leaves, short flower stalks, and large flowers. The bulbs of most kinds are 1½–2 inches in diameter, rounded or oval with a pointed end, and covered with a thin, chestnut brown skin, which is easily broken to reveal the cream-colored bulb beneath. An erect flower stalk topped by either a solitary, or several, cup-shaped blooms, rises from the neck of the bulb. Individual flowers may be single (with no more than six petals) or double (with several layers of petals). Flower color is most commonly pink, red, purple, yellow, orange, or white, but these colors are sometimes shaded with green or streaked or striped in any one of a number of combinations.

Tulip leaves are usually few (two to six), fleshy, roughly lance-shaped, 6–10 inches long, and 1½–2½ inches wide. They are produced just above the potting-mixture surface, either directly from the neck of the bulb or borne on the lower part of the flower stalk. Leaves can be almost any shade of green, often with a grayish cast.

The most suitable tulips for indoor use are those that flower in winter. They are commonly divided into two groups: early-flowering single tulips and early-flowering double tulips. Both types grow to a maximum height of about 14 inches and have flowers up to 5 inches across.

See also BULBS, CORMS, and TUBERS.

RECOMMENDED TULIPS

Early-flowering singles include the following forms: *T.* 'Bellona' (golden yellow); *T.* 'Brilliant Star' (scarlet); *T.* 'Couleur Cardinal' (orange-red); *T.* 'Diana' (white); *T.* 'Pink Beauty' (deep pink, marked with white); and *T.* 'Van der Neer' (dark purple).

Early-flowering doubles include the following forms: *T.* 'Electra' (carmine-pink, with petals bordered in paler pink); *T.* 'Madame Testout' (rose-pink); *T.* 'Maréchal Niel' (orange-tinted yellow); *T.* 'Peach Blossom' (rosy pink); *T.* 'Scarlet Cardinal' (scarlet) and *T.* 'Schoonoord' (white).

PROPER CARE

Plant tulip bulbs in early fall in order to enjoy the flowers indoors in mid- to late winter. Use either waterproof containers or pots or pans with drainage holes. Plant five or six bulbs together—not quite touching each other—with just the tips of the bulbs rising above the well-moistened potting mixture. Either a peat-based potting mixture or bulb fiber (see page 111) will do. If bulb fiber is used, moisten it thoroughly but squeeze out excess water before planting the bulbs.

Place planted bulbs in a dark position where the temperature will not rise above 50°F nor fall below freezing. Absence of light and warmth is essential for the development of a good root system before the development of top growth. Commercial growers "plunge" their containers in the ground outdoors under a thick layer of moistened peat moss. If this is not possible, enclose each container in a black plastic bag, and stand this on a shaded balcony or window ledge. Water the mixture as often as necessary to keep it moist, but not sodden. No feeding is necessary.

Keep the bulbs in cool darkness until 2–3 inches of leaf have emerged from the bulbs (probably in 8–10 weeks). Thereafter, uncover the containers and gradually expose the plants to medium light and to slightly higher temperatures. Water when necessary, as before, and keep the plants comparatively cool (below 60°, if possible) until flower stalks are at least 3–4 inches long and flower buds are clear of the foliage. As growth continues, more warmth becomes tolerable, but do not subject tulips to temperatures much higher than 60°. At 55°–60° the flowers will remain attractive for three or four weeks. Warmth will cause them to fade quickly.

Tulips cannot be grown a second time indoors. If the bulbs are planted outdoors, they will probably recover and flower in subsequent years.

Vallota

AMARYLLIDACEAE

Scarborough-lily
V. speciosa

VALLOTAS are bulbous flowering plants closely related to hippeastrums, which they resemble. The genus is composed of only one species, *V. speciosa* (also called *V. purpurea*; popularly known as the Scarborough-lily), which is an excellent plant for a sunny window. The leaves are dark green often tinged at the base with bronzy red, narrowly strap-shaped, and $\frac{1}{2}$–$\frac{3}{4}$ inch wide and up to 15 inches long. Flowers are trumpet-shaped,

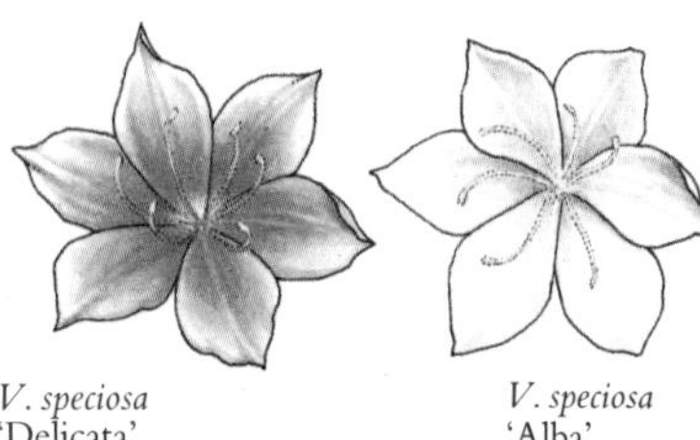

V. speciosa 'Delicata'   *V. speciosa* 'Alba'

bright scarlet, and 3–4 inches in diameter; they are produced in late summer in a cluster of from three to eight on a 2-foot-tall stem. The bulbs are brown-skinned, and of flowering size when about $1\frac{1}{2}$ inches in diameter. Forms with more delicate flower coloring—a white, *V.s.* 'Alba,' and a pale salmon pink, *V.s.* 'Delicata'—exist, but are relatively hard to obtain.
See also BULBS, CORMS, and TUBERS.

PROPER CARE

Light In order to flower, vallotas must have some direct sunshine, or very bright light.

Temperature Vallotas do well in normal room temperatures during the active growth period, but they should be rested in winter under cooler conditions (about 50°–55°F).

Watering Water newly potted vallotas sparingly—allowing the top two-thirds of the potting mixture to dry out between waterings. When they are well established (six to eight weeks after bulbs were planted), give them enough water to make the potting mixture just moist. During the winter rest period, water only enough to prevent the potting mixture from drying out completely.

Feeding From mid-spring to mid-summer feed established plants once every two weeks with standard liquid fertilizer; switch to a high-potash fertilizer (as used for tomatoes) during the late summer and through to the beginning of the rest period; then stop feedings altogether.

Potting and repotting Vallotas need a rich soil-based potting mixture (see page 429). The best time to pot up new, ready-to-flower bulbs is in spring or early summer. Plant one bulb to a 5-inch pot, half in and half out of the potting mixture. It is essential to pack the mixture firmly around the bulb. The roots should then be left undisturbed in the same pot for three or four years; during that time an annual spring topdressing (see page 428) of fresh mixture, incorporating a slow-acting fertilizer such as bonemeal, is all that is necessary.

Propagation Propagation is usually by division of overcrowded clumps in spring or early summer. The large bulb of the original plant will divide into several separate bulbs during the course of three or four years, and small, attached, side bulbs will also be produced; when the upper surface area of the pot is entirely filled with bulbs, detach the side bulbs carefully and divide the plant. Plant bulbs of flowering size—about as big as a mature shallot—in 5-inch pots, smaller ones in the 3-inch size, and move them on annually as they enlarge.

Vanda

ORCHIDACEAE

UNLIKE most other epiphytic orchids, vandas have a single stem rising from a tuft of roots and do not have pseudobulbs. Thick, fleshy aerial roots are often produced on the stem, and these may hang down outside the container in which indoor vandas are planted. Pale green leaves, which are generally strap-shaped, grow all along the stem, and flower stalks arise near its tip. Each stalk bears several fragrant flowers, which last for several weeks. Sepals and petals are usually of roughly the same shape and size, and the lip is often three-lobed. These plants have been widely hybridized, often with orchids of different genera.
See also ORCHIDS.

RECOMMENDED VANDAS

V. cristata has a stem up to 2 feet tall carrying nearly opposite, arching, strap-shaped, deeply channeled leaves 5–7 inches long and $\frac{1}{2}$–$\frac{3}{4}$ inch wide, with slightly toothed, blunt tips. Flower stalks 4–6 inches long appearing from leaf axils in spring and summer bear up to seven flowers about 2 inches across. The sepals and petals are yellowish green to creamy yellow. The short, oblong green-and-yellow lip has deep purple-red lines near the base.

V. sanderana has stems up to 2 feet tall carrying close-packed opposite pairs of strap-shaped, slightly arching leaves 12–15 inches long and 1 inch wide. Flower stalks 10–12 inches long bear up to 10 blooms each. The flower stems rise from leaf axils, mostly in late summer and fall. Each, flat, disklike flower is up to 5 inches across. The upper sepal and petals are rosy pink suffused with white, and the lower sepals are reddish yellow with darker markings. The very small, rounded, forward-jutting lip is reddish yellow.

V. teres has stems up to 7 feet high bearing nearly cylindrical, alternate leaves 4–6 inches long and $\frac{1}{2}$ inch thick. Flower stalks arise on the stem at points opposite the leaves, and each 7- to 10-inch-long stalk carries up to five flowers from late spring to early fall. Each bloom is 3–4 inches across. The broadly diamond-shaped, wavy-edged sepals and petals are pale pinkish purple suffused with white. The lip color is reddish yellow spotted and

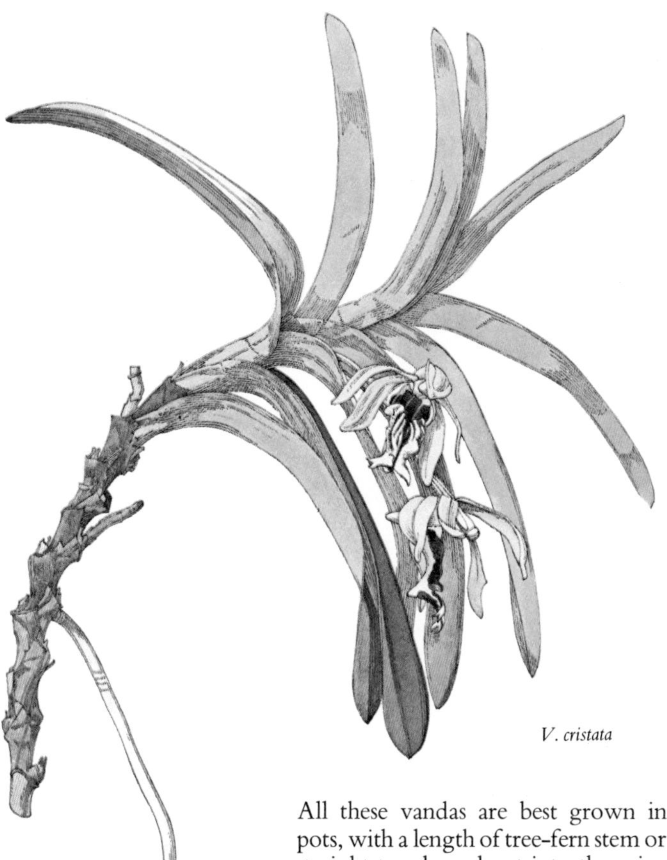

V. cristata

lined with red. There are also a large number of different-colored varieties.

PROPER CARE

Light Give vandas bright filtered light at all times. Supplement daylight with artificial illumination in winter, if possible (see page 446).

Temperature Normal room temperatures are ideal throughout the year. A night temperature about 15°F lower than the daytime level is desirable, however. For adequate humidity stand pots on trays of moist pebbles, and mist-spray plants daily.

Watering Water plentifully at all times, never allowing the potting mixture to dry out. Do not let pots stand in water, however.

Feeding Apply standard liquid fertilizer at half strength to these orchids with every other watering.

Potting and repotting Use any of the recommended mixtures for epiphytic orchids (see page 289). If the mixture includes fibrous material, use only big chunks of fiber. This is necessary for good drainage, as are plenty of clay-pot fragments and pieces of charcoal in the mixture. All these vandas are best grown in pots, with a length of tree-fern stem or straight tree branch set into the mixture to provide a support for the aerial roots. Place the plant in the middle of the container, and make sure that the base of the stem is not buried in the mixture. Move vandas into slightly larger pots every spring. When maximum pot size has been reached, cut up these plants for propagation.

Propagation The purpose of propagating vandas is mainly to reduce the size of an overlarge specimen. To do this, cut the stem at any desirable point above which there are plenty of aerial roots. Soak the cutting for two hours to make the aerial roots pliable before planting in a small pot of standard potting mixture. Place the cut base of the stem about 2 inches deep in the mixture, and try to bury some of the aerial roots as well. If any such root breaks, cut it cleanly above the break, and insert the cut end in the mixture. Support the cutting by staking it. During the first six weeks water only sparingly (permitting the mixture to dry out almost completely between waterings), and do not feed. Thereafter, treat the young plant as a mature vanda. The part of the old plant left in the original pot will usually branch and continue to grow at a reduced height.

Veltheimia

LILIACEAE

VELTHEIMIAS are all bulbous plants with attractive seasonal foliage and an interesting flower spike. The large, onionlike bulbs are normally planted in late summer, and the growth cycle begins in late fall. First each bulb sends up handsome foliage. This is followed by a flower spike of closely packed tubular florets that last for several weeks. In the late spring the bulb begins to go dormant, and the leaves turn yellow; they are shed in early summer. A few months later new growth begins again.

There is some confusion about naming the few species and hybrids of this genus. It is generally agreed, however, that two distinct types, as described below, are now in cultivation. *See also BULBS, CORMS, and TUBERS.*

RECOMMENDED VELTHEIMIAS

V. capensis has blue-green leaves up to 1 foot long and 2 inches wide, with strongly undulate edges. The stout flower stalk, also 1 foot long, is spotted with purple, and the flowers that are carried on its terminal spike are pale pink and pendent.

V. viridifolia has leaves up to 15 inches long and 4 inches wide, which are bright, glossy green, and less strongly undulate than those of *V. capensis.* The flower stalk may be as much as 2 feet long, and the blooms on the terminal spike are pinkish purple. It is also possible to obtain a rose-and-cream-flowered form sold as *V.v.* 'Rose-alba,' which has been developed in Holland.

Note: Veltheimias are sometimes sold as *V. glauca* and *V. deasii,* but these names are no longer valid.

PROPER CARE

Light Whether growing or dormant, veltheimias need at least three or four hours of direct sunlight every day. In their natural habitat (South Africa) these plants would get a thorough baking in the sun during the whole of the summer rest period.

Temperature Despite their need for sunlight, veltheimias do not like heat during the winter months of active growth and will not flourish if temperatures rise to even as much as 60°F at this time of year. Throughout the active growth period they should be

Veltheimia capensis

given a well-ventilated, sunny position at no more than about 55°. If this is impossible to achieve, the indoor gardener should not attempt to grow these plants.

Watering Water newly planted bulbs sparingly—only enough to make the entire potting mixture barely moist throughout—until some growth appears above the soil surface. Gradually increase the amount, but water only moderately at most, always letting the top half-inch of the mixture dry out between waterings. When the foliage begins to yellow, gradually reduce the amount. Once all leaves have died off, let the dormant bulb remain completely dry in its pot until new growth appears.

Feeding Apply a high-potash liquid fertilizer at half strength once a month from the time leaves are well developed until they start to yellow.

Potting and repotting Add one part of coarse sand or perlite to three parts of soil-based potting mixture (see page 429); and, for additional drainage, put plenty of clay-pot fragments in the bottom of the pot. Veltheimia bulbs are best planted in 5-inch pots, half in and half out of the potting mixture, in late summer or early fall. No repotting should be necessary for at least two or three years, although an annual late-summer topdressing (see page 428) with fresh mixture is beneficial. Repot veltheimias only when propagation becomes advisable (see "Propagation," below).

Propagation Once a veltheimia bulb reaches maturity, offsets begin to develop in quantity around its base, and in two or three years these are likely to crowd the pot. To propagate, use offsets with at least one pair of leaves. In late summer or early fall, detach them from the parent bulb and at the same time repot the parent in fresh potting mixture (either in its original 5-inch pot or another one). Plant each small new bulb in a 3-inch pot of the recommended potting mixture for mature veltheimias and keep it there until it is big enough to flower (after about three years). Then move it into a 5-inch pot.

Vriesea

BROMELIACEAE

THE genus *Vriesea* includes many house plants prized both for their handsome foliage and their showy flower spikes. These bromeliads have stiff, smooth-edged, sword-shaped leaves arranged in a loose rosette that is capable of holding water in the cup-like center. Like most bromeliads, vrieseas do not flower until they are several years old. Their strongly colored, usually erect, sword-shaped flower spikes, which can be produced at various times of the year depending on conditions, are very long-lasting—an effect largely derived from brilliant bracts rather than the short-lived flowers. In addition to the species named below, there are numerous hybrids well worth acquiring.

See also BROMELIADS.

RECOMMENDED VRIESEAS

V. fenestralis has about 20 shiny, arching leaves about 18 inches long and 2 inches wide, that are light green marked with pale green above and purple below. The 18-inch-tall flower stalk bears a terminal spike of up to 20 horizontal, shiny green bracts spotted with deep purple, and within these are $2\frac{1}{2}$-inch-long yellow to pale orange flowers. *V. fenestralis,* however, is grown primarily for its foliage.

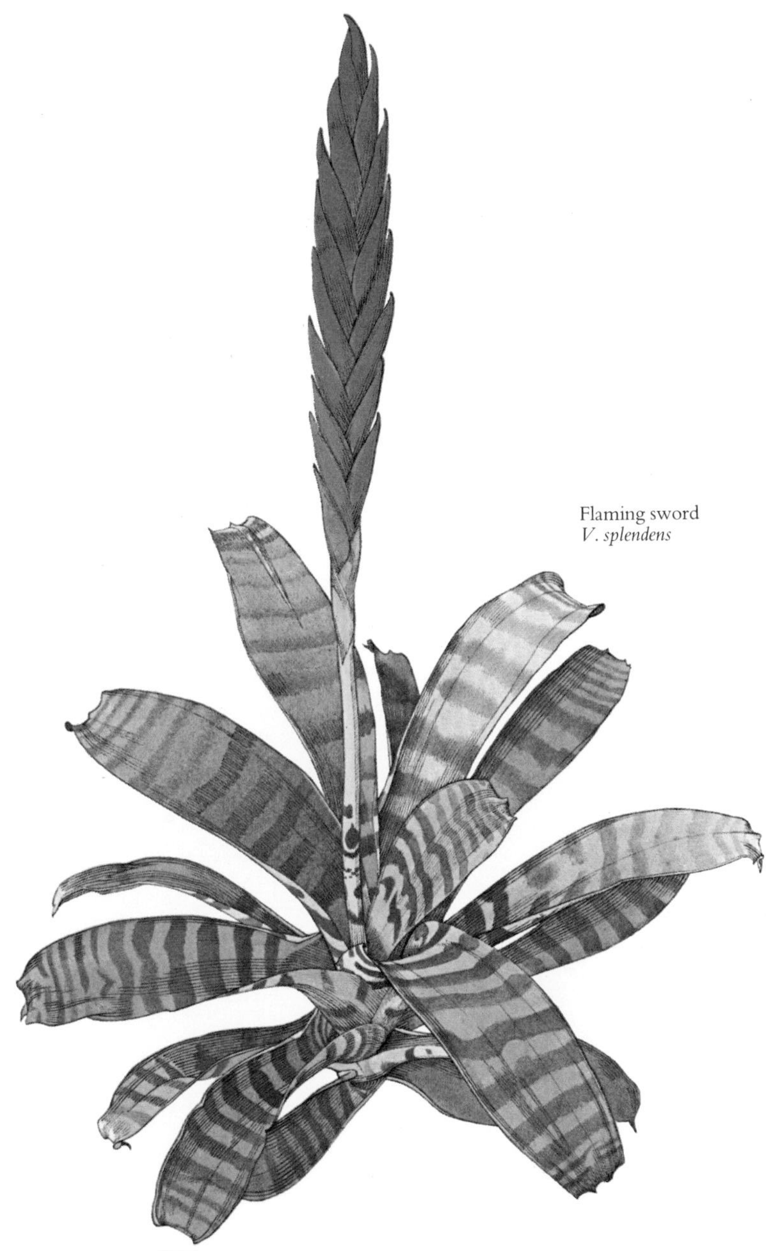

Flaming sword
V. splendens

V. hieroglyphica (often called the king of bromeliads) is also prized for its foliage. Leaves number 20 to 30, may be up to 2½ feet long and 3 inches wide, and are a shiny bright green with bands of irregular deep purple markings. Average spread of a mature plant is 3 feet. The 2-foot-tall flower stalk branches for the upper third of its length into numerous short, horizontal sections, each comprising inch-long pale green bracts that partly conceal tubular, yellow flowers.

V. psittacina has 15 to 20 soft leaves 8–10 inches long and 1 inch wide, which are pale green but may be colored violet-blue toward the rosette center. The 2-inch-wide inflorescence of green, yellow, and red on a 10-inch stalk comprises yellow flowers that are spotted green.

V. saundersii (previously called *V. botafogensis)* has 20 to 30 leaves, which are 8–12 inches long and 1½ inches wide, leathery, and dull gray-green thickly spotted on the underside with pinkish purple. Leaf tips are pointed and curve downward. There is a 12- to 15-inch flower stalk carrying yellow flowers backed with yellowish bracts 1-2 inches long.

V. splendens (flaming sword) has a loose rosette composed of about 20 leaves 15 inches long and 1½–2 inches wide, that are dark green with purple-black cross-banding. The flower spike up to 2 feet tall is capped by a foot-long, flattened blade of brilliant red bracts; and 1½- to 2-inch-long, yellow flowers emerge from this. There are many forms, some with darker foliage, some with larger or differently shaded flower spikes.

PROPER CARE

Light Vrieseas must have bright light, with three or four hours a day of direct sunlight, in order to flower. Do not subject them to the scorching midday sun, however.

Temperature Vrieseas need normal temperatures and high humidity; place pots on trays of moist pebbles.

Watering Water actively growing plants plentifully by filling the central cup of the rosette until water spills over into leaf axils and seeps through to the mixture. During the short-day months vrieseas may rest, when they should be watered just enough to make the mixture barely moist.

Feeding Give all actively growing plants half-strength standard liquid fertilizer once a month. Apply the fertilizer to both the potting mixture and central cup.

Potting and repotting Use the mixture recommended for bromeliads (see page 107). Repot vrieseas only when roots fill their pots—every two or three years—this is best done in spring. The largest pot size required is 5 inches. When repotting these plants, do not pack the mixture in too firmly; roots cannot penetrate heavy soil.

Propagation Around flowering time, most vrieseas will produce offsets either from leaf axils or around the base of rosettes. A basal offset should be from 3 to 6 inches long (depending on mature plant-size) before being detached with a sharp knife; retain roots if they have already been produced. Plant the offset in a 3-inch pot of moistened standard mixture, enclose it in a plastic bag, and keep it in a warm room in bright filtered light until roots are established (in about four to six weeks). Thereafter, treat the young plant as a mature vriesea. Offsets arising from leaf axils should not be detached but allowed to grow on in the normal way. They will take over from the parent plant (which, having flowered, slowly dies) over a period of about a year.

Vrieseas that do not produce offsets can be propagated from seed (see *BROMELIADS,* page 108).

Washingtonia

PALMAE

Desert fan palm
W. filifera

WASHINGTONIAS (Washington palms) are the popular fan palms used for street planting in California and other places where the climate permits. There are only two species; both grow in the wild in widely differing environments where they have adapted to a broad range of temperatures and other conditions. They are comparatively easy to grow as house plants. Both species have short, tapered, mahogany red trunks, and long, spiny leafstalks that carry large fan-shaped leaves cut into about twenty segments for up to half their spread. A distinctive feature of most of these palms is the fine fibers that hang from the edges of the leaf divisions.
See also PALMS.

RECOMMENDED WASHINGTONIAS

W. filifera, popularly called the desert fan or petticoat palm, has an open, uncluttered look. Its gray-green leaves have a span of 2 feet or more. The spiny leafstalks are 18 inches long, flat, and mostly green in color.

W. robusta, the thread palm, is taller, thinner, and faster-growing than *W. filifera*. Its leaves are bright green (except for a tawny patch where the leaf blade joins the leafstalk), and the leaf segments are much stiffer and much less deeply cut.

PROPER CARE

Light Washingtonias need bright light throughout the year, including, if possible, several hours of direct sunlight every day. Most growth is made during the summer months, and adequate light during this period helps produce large leaves of good color. If these palms get too little light, they may shed one or more lower leaves.

Temperature Though they prefer warm, or even hot, rooms, these plants can tolerate occasional temperatures as low as 50°F. Washingtonias can also tolerate rather dry air conditions, but they will produce larger leaves of a better color if they are stood on trays or saucers of pebbles kept constantly moist. These plants will do best if they are moved to a sheltered position outdoors from early summer to fall.

Watering During the active growth period water washingtonias plentifully as often as necessary to keep the potting mixture thoroughly moist, particularly if plants are kept close to a sunny window; but never allow the pot to stand in water. During the winter rest period water more moderately, enough to moisten the mixture throughout, but permitting the top half-inch of the mixture to dry out before watering again.
Feeding Apply standard liquid fertilizer every two weeks during the active growth period.
Potting and repotting Because a water-retentive potting mixture is essential for these plants, add one-third rotted leaf mold or peat moss to a standard soil-based mixture (see page 429). For good drainage put plenty of clay-pot fragments in the bottom of the pot. Repot these palms only when their roots are active—i.e., during the active growth period. They do not like to be overpotted so do not move them into pots one size larger until light-colored roots appear in quantity on the surface of the potting mixture.

This washingtonia needs repotting. The surface of the potting mixture is densely covered with brittle roots, which need careful treatment.

This should occur no more than once in two to three years. It is very important to plant washingtonias firmly, taking special care not to damage the main (thicker) roots, which are brittle; these plants are unusually sensitive to root damage.
Propagation Commercially, these washingtonias are normally raised from seed sown in considerable heat. Propagation is not practicable for the amateur indoor gardener.

Yucca

AGAVACEAE

Spanish bayonet
Y. aloifolia

THE genus *Yucca* includes about 40 species of stemless or erect, woody-stemmed plants with sword-shaped leaves arranged in a loose rosette. Yuccas are capable of growing to a considerable height (up to 40 feet) in the wild, but growth indoors is extremely slow and large specimens are relatively expensive to buy and difficult to find. The species most commonly used as house plants have short, brown, rough-textured, trunk-like stems topped with clusters of long, leathery leaves. Outdoor yuccas produce flower spikes up to 2 feet long from leaf-rosette centers. Each spike is composed of many white or violet-tinged blooms, that are bell- or saucer-shaped and up to 4 inches across. The flowers are not normally produced on indoor plants, however, unless they are grown in specially designed plant windows (see page 53).

RECOMMENDED YUCCAS

Y. aloifolia (Spanish bayonet, dagger plant) forms a single, normally unbranched trunk, which can grow 3–4 feet long and about 2 inches thick in a large pot or tub. The trunk terminates in tufts of rigid, sharp-pointed, dark, blue-green leaves up to 2 feet long and 2 inches wide. Leaf edges are minutely toothed; do not keep this plant in a position where the leaves are likely to get knocked.

There are a number of interesting forms of this species. *Y. a. draconis* is a much-branching plant with outward-arching leaves that are pliable instead of rigid. The leaves of most other forms are similar to those of the type species but differently colored. *Y.a.* 'Marginata,' for example, has dark green leaves bordered in yellow. The leaves of *Y.a.* 'Quadricolor' have green, white, yellow, and reddish lengthwise stripes. In *Y.a.* 'Tricolor' there are white and yellow stripes running along the middle of the green leaves. Newly produced leaves are tinged with red. *Y.a.* 'Variegata' has leaves with white lengthwise stripes.

Y. elephantipes (otherwise known as *Y. guatemalensis*; commonly called spineless yucca) produces a thickened stem (or trunk) 3–6 feet long and 1½–2 inches thick. The base of the stem is often greatly swollen. The somewhat thinner, much shorter branches at the top of the stem are topped with rosettes of downward-arching, non-rigid leaves. Each glossy, dark green leaf can grow 4 feet long and 3 inches wide. Leaf edges are roughly toothed, but leaf tips are soft. The general effect is of softness as compared with the hard rigidity of *Y. aloifolia*. One form, *Y.e.* 'Variegata,' has leaf edges that are banded with creamy white.

PROPER CARE

Light These yuccas need bright light, with at least three hours a day of direct sunlight, throughout the year. Very little growth will be made if these plants are given insufficient light (see "Temperature" below).
Temperature Normal room temperatures are suitable at all times. These yuccas can tolerate a wide range of temperatures, however, down to about 50°F. In places where plants are likely to get insufficient light during the short-day winter months, keep them as cool as possible (but not below 50°). Yuccas are tolerant of extremely dry air and will thrive in conditions unsuitable for most plants.
Watering During the active growth period (spring, summer, and fall) water plentifully as often as necessary to keep the potting mixture

thoroughly moist, but never allow containers to stand in water. During the winter rest period water yuccas sparingly, giving only enough to keep the mixture from drying out.

Feeding Apply standard liquid fertilizer every two weeks during the active growth period.

Potting and repotting Use a soil-based potting mixture (see page 429). Because of the weight of the rosettes of leaves at stem ends, some specimens may become top-heavy and easy to knock over. For this reason it is advisable to use clay pots rather than plastic. Move plants into containers one size larger in the spring, but only if they have filled the current container with roots (see page 426). After maximum convenient container size (probably a 12-inch pot or 15-inch tub) has been reached, topdress plants annually (see page 428) with fresh potting mixture.

Propagation Professional growers propagate these yuccas by cutting up and rooting sections of the thick stems, but this is a tedious process. The only practical way for amateur gardeners to propagate an indoor yucca is to use offsets, which are sometimes produced. With a sharp knife or razor blade, cut away an offset that carries at least four 6- to 9-inch-long leaves. This is best done in spring. Insert the offset in a 4- to 5-inch pot containing a moistened equal-parts combination of soil-based potting mixture and coarse sand or perlite. Stand the pot in bright filtered light, and keep the mixture barely moist until rooting occurs (in six to eight weeks). As renewed growth indicates that new roots have formed, begin to water moderately, enough at each watering to moisten the rooting mixture thoroughly, but allowing the top inch of the mixture to dry out before watering again. Start regular feedings (as recommended above) about four months after the beginning of the propagation process, and continue until the onset of the winter rest period. Move the young plant into a slightly larger pot of standard potting mixture the following spring, then treat it as a mature yucca.

Special points Indoor yuccas do best when they are kept out of doors during the warm summer months. If possible, stand plants outdoors from late spring to early fall. Be sure to choose a position that gets at least three to four hours a day of direct sunlight.

Zantedeschia

ARACEAE

Calla lily
Zantedeschia hybrid

THE small genus *Zantedeschia* (formerly, and still occasionally, termed *Richardia*) comprises stemless plants with large, usually arrow-shaped leaves and showy flowers often called calla lilies (though they are not true lilies). Zantedeschias have fleshy rhizomes that run just below the surface of the potting mixture, and from which fleshy feeding roots grow down into the mixture. The inflorescence is a typical arum flower with a central erect spadix surrounded by a showy spathe. It is carried on a long, stout stalk that rises among—sometimes above—the long leafstalks. In the wild these plants grow in swampy marshland, which tends to dry up during the summer months—a period of dormancy for the plants, when they too dry off and lose their foliage. This pattern must be followed with zantedeschias used as house plants; they can provide only a temporary display indoors during the early part of the year. Dormant rhizomes, however, once given suitable conditions, can be brought into new growth and can flower for many years.

RECOMMENDED ZANTEDESCHIAS

Z. aethiopica, the largest and best known of the so-called calla lilies (sometimes also called pig or arum lily), has deep green, arrow-shaped leaves up to 18 inches long and 10 inches wide, borne on leafstalks that may reach a length of 3 feet. Flower stalks can appear at any time from late winter to early spring; the inflorescence is a golden yellow spadix surrounded by a milky white spathe 5–10 inches long, which curves slightly outward near the edges. Particularly good as a house plant is *Z.a.* 'Childsiana,' which is more compact than the species type and also produces more flowers.

Z. albomaculata (spotted-calla) has dark green leaves marked with silvery white spots; the leaves are narrowly triangular—up to 18 inches long, but only 2–3 inches wide at the base, and are carried on stalks up to 3 feet long. The flowers are more trumpet-shaped than those of *Z. aethiopica*, with the 4- to 5-inch-long spathe forming a tube; its color varies from white to creamy yellow (or occasionally pink), with a purple stain at the inside base of the tube. The spadix is white.

Z. elliottiana (golden calla) has heavily white-spotted dark green leaves, which are broadly arrow-shaped, up to 11 inches long and 9 inches wide, with 2-foot-long stalks. The 6-inch-long showy spathe is bright yellow inside and greenish yellow outside, forming an open trumpet around the yellow spadix.

Z. rehmannii (pink calla) has narrow, medium green leaves often spotted with silvery white, that are tapered at each end; they grow up to 12 inches long and 2 inches wide, and have 12-inch stalks. The open-trumpet-shaped spathes are up to 5 inches long; they are usually pink but sometimes are red or purplish. They surround a creamy white spadix.

Many mixed hybrids have been derived from each of the four species that are described above. The flower shapes vary from narrow to open trumpets, and colors include a variety of shades of pink, cream, yellow, and bright red.

PROPER CARE

Light Provide bright light with some direct sunlight during the months when these plants have foliage. In the dormant period (usually from late spring to early fall) keep the dried-out plant in a sunny spot in the garden or on an outdoor terrace or balcony—an ideal position as long as there is no risk of frost or very wet weather (see "Watering," below).

Temperature When zantedeschias are starting into growth (usually from early fall onward), they should be kept cool—if possible, at a temperature of 50°–55°F—for about three months; thereafter, about 60° is best for *Z. aethiopica*, 65° for the other species and the hybrids, until flowering is under way. While they are flowering, keep the plants at normal room temperature; temperatures above 70° are likely to curtail flower life and to make the leaves wither prematurely. For rhizomes that are dormant, temperature is not a consideration.

Watering Water newly potted plants or old rhizomes starting into growth after the dormant period sparingly—just enough to moisten the potting mixture throughout at each watering and allowing the top two-thirds of the mixture to dry out before watering again. As growth develops, increase the quantity gradually until the zantedeschias are in full leaf. Thereafter, water plentifully as often as necessary to keep the potting mixture thoroughly moist; these are among the few plants that need constant moisture at their roots during the active growth period. When in full leaf, in fact, potted zantedeschias can stand in saucers of water. When the plant stops flowering, reduce the amount of water gradually, and stop watering altogether when the leaves become yellow and withered. Leave dried-out zantedeschias in their pots for the entire rest period, whether indoors or out. An occasional brief moistening from rain will not harm the dormant plants, but they must on no account be subjected to prolonged rainfall.

Feeding Once plants are in full leaf, apply standard liquid fertilizer every two weeks, and increase this to a weekly dose when flowers begin to appear, continuing until the end of the flowering season.

Potting and repotting Use a soil-based potting mixture (see page 429). A single flowering-size plant can be accommodated in a 6-inch pot but larger clumps need either larger pots or small tubs. In the fall, as plants start into growth, move them into pots one size larger, if necessary. When maximum convenient pot size has been reached, divide up plants for propagation (see below). Dry, newly purchased rhizomes can also be planted at this time, either singly in 6-inch pots or three together in an 8- or 9-inch pot. Place the rhizomes horizontally in pots about 2 inches below the surface of the potting mixture.

Propagation Divide rhizomes, or detach offsets that develop around the main rhizome for propagation. Either process is best done at the time of repotting in the fall. Pot single sections of a divided rhizome in 6-inch pots of slightly moistened potting mixture, and treat them as mature plants. Plant small offsets in 3- or 4-inch pots until they are big enough to move into bigger containers, but otherwise give them exactly the same conditions as the larger rhizomes.

It is also possible to increase zantedeschias from seed. This is the easiest way to get a stock of the mixed hybrids, since they are less readily available as rhizomes than the older forms. Raising these plants from seed, however, is a complicated, lengthy process best carried out in the carefully regulated conditions of a cool greenhouse. It is impracticable for most amateur growers.

Propagating a zantedeschia

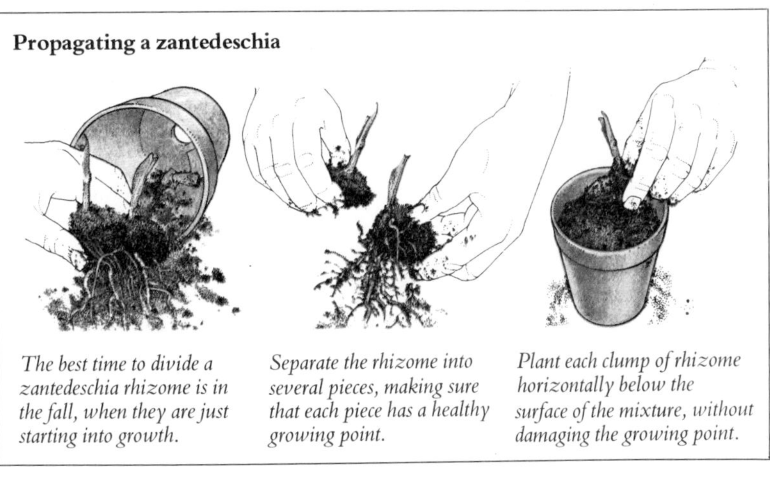

The best time to divide a zantedeschia rhizome is in the fall, when they are just starting into growth.

Separate the rhizome into several pieces, making sure that each piece has a healthy growing point.

Plant each clump of rhizome horizontally below the surface of the mixture, without damaging the growing point.

Zebrina
COMMELINACEAE

Wandering Jew
Z. pendula

THE only species of zebrina commonly grown as a house plant (often called wandering Jew, like its relations the tradescantias) is quick-growing and very decorative, particularly in hanging baskets, where its brilliant leaf coloring can be fully appreciated. These trailing plants have oval leaves roughly 2 inches long, with an iridescent upper surface and a rich purple underside. They produce clusters of small, three-petaled flowers in spring and summer. Zebrinas are suitable for mixed plantings in bowls or trained up fan-shaped trellises.

It is possible to train different-colored zebrinas up a fan-shaped trellis instead of growing them in the more usual hanging basket.

RECOMMENDED ZEBRINAS

Z. pendula (sometimes also known as *Cyanotis vittata*), the most popular species, is the parent of a number of varieties. Two glistening stripes of silvery green surrounding a medium green central portion run the length of the upper surface of its pointed-oval leaves. Its flowers are purple-pink.

***Z.p.* 'Discolor'** has thinner leaves, with slimmer silver stripes bordering a bronze-tinged center.

***Z.p.* 'Purpusii'** (also called *Tradescantia purpurea*) has larger leaves colored a very rich bronzy purple on the upper surface. Its flowers are purplish white.

***Z.p.* 'Quadricolor,'** with irregular pink, green, cream, and silver stripes on the leaves, is the most attractive form, but it is more difficult to grow.

PROPER CARE

Light Give these plants bright light at all times for close growth and brilliant leaf color. Plants can be grown at a short distance from a sunny window without too much loss of color, but growth will become straggly and colors will fade as this distance lengthens.

Temperature Zebrinas like warmth but they can tolerate temperatures down to 55°F. In cool conditions they grow very slowly.

Watering Water actively growing plants moderately, allowing the top inch of the potting mixture to dry out between waterings. When plants are resting, give them just enough water to make the mixture barely moist throughout, and allow the top half to dry out between waterings. Zebrinas that have been grown slightly on the dry side show the best color.

Feeding Give actively growing plants standard liquid fertilizer once every two weeks.

Potting and repotting Use a soil-based potting mixture (see page 429). Move zebrinas into pots one size larger whenever their roots fill the pot (see page 426). Plant several rooted cuttings together to create a bushy effect—as many as 12 to 15 in a single hanging basket.

Propagation Because older leaves of zebrinas dry up leaving bare stems, it is advisable to produce new plants quite frequently. Tip cuttings 3 inches long taken in spring or early summer will root easily in an equal-parts rooting mixture of peat moss and sand. Keep the cuttings in bright filtered light, giving them just enough water to make the mixture barely moist, and roots will develop in three or four weeks; plant four to six rooted cuttings together in a 3-inch pot of standard potting mixture, and treat them as mature zebrinas.

Alternatively, root tip cuttings in water. Place the cuttings in small—preferably opaque—glasses of water and keep them in bright filtered light. They will develop roots 1–2 inches long in two to three weeks and they can then be moved into the standard potting mixture and treated in the same way as mature plants.

Special points Pinch out growing points of lengthy shoots regularly to encourage the production of side branches. Remove all poorly colored stems in early spring.

Zebrinas rapidly become straggly and spindly if their growing points are not regularly pinched out.

Finder's guide

The following charts are designed to provide a quick reference to important features of plants described in the *A–Z Guide*, as well as to vital aspects of their cultivation needs. By examining these charts you can get a preliminary idea of which plants are most likely to fit into specific positions for decorative purposes, and whether or not a given plant is appropriate for the growing conditions available in any such position. Each entry relates to a particular genus. In cases, however, where certain species look very different from the rest or require a different kind of care, those species are treated separately from the genus to which they belong. Occasionally more than one species fits this secondary description. In such cases only one species is mentioned but it is followed by an asterisk (*). Consult the relevant genus entry in the *A–Z Guide* for more detailed information on the differences between these species. Such differences may only be subtle but they are certainly worth noting. (It should be emphasized that the material in the charts covers only the genera and species discussed in the *A–Z Guide* articles of this book.)

A few comments on details within the *Finder's guide*:

1. The word "foliage" is used here to cover not only leaves but also the stems of such leafless plants as cacti.
2. The guide to plant shape is based largely on the list of shapes that appears on pages 26-27. As explained on those pages, such a guide can indicate shape only roughly, since plants are so variable in form that precise classification is virtually impossible. Therefore, most creeping plants are listed below as "climbing and trailing," and "bushy" refers to the general look of a plant rather than to whether or not it literally fits the accepted definition of the word "bush". Descriptions of some plants (for instance, "globular" for many cacti) are self-explanatory.
3. Many plants change their appearance as they age. Some palms, for example, become tall and upright after a period of bushy, lower growth. Descriptive terms in these charts normally apply to plants of the size most frequently available in garden stores and nurseries.
4. Watering instructions and maximum and minimum recommended temperatures are usually given for both active growth and rest periods. Rest-period recommendations are omitted, however, for plants that grow actively throughout the year in normal room conditions.
5. As stated above, these charts are to help you make *preliminary* choices. Never make a final decision without consulting the *A–Z Guide* for qualifying details.

Key

These plants require no special attention and are easy to grow indoors.

These plants require some special conditions and are unlikely to thrive without them.

These plants require special conditions and will not thrive without them.

CHARACTERISTICS

	Foliage: Green	Foliage: Colored	Foliage: Variegated	Features: Flowers	Features: Fragrance	Features: Fruits or berries	Growth cycle: Evergreen	Growth cycle: Deciduous	Growth cycle: Temporary	Shape: Rosette	Shape: Bushy	Shape: Grassy	Shape: Upright	Shape: Treelike	Shape: Climbing and trailing
Abutilon			●	●			●				●				
A. megapotamicum	●			●			●				●				
*Acalypha hispida**	●			●			●				●				
*A. wilkesiana**		●					●				●				
A.w. 'Godseffiana'*			●				●				●				
*Achimenes**	●			●				●							●
A. grandiflora	●			●				●					●		
Acorus	●						●					●			
A. gramineus 'Variegatus'*			●				●					●			
Adiantum	●						●				●				
A. raddianum 'Fragrantissimum'	●				●		●				●				
Aechmea			●	●			●			●					
A. 'Foster's Favorite'*		●		●			●			●					
Aeonium	●			●			●			●					

PROPER CARE

	Watering: Rest period: Sparingly	Watering: Rest period: Moderately	Watering: Rest period: Plentifully	Watering: Active growth period: Sparingly	Watering: Active growth period: Moderately	Watering: Active growth period: Plentifully	Light: Medium	Light: Bright	Light: Bright filtered	Light: Direct	Temperature: Rest period: Min °F	Temperature: Rest period: Max °F	Temperature: Active growth: Min °F	Temperature: Active growth: Max °F	Humidity: Low	Humidity: High
Abutilon	●				●					●	50	75	60	75	●	
A. megapotamicum	●				●					●	50	75	60	75	●	
*Acalypha hispida**	●					●			●		60	75	65	80		●
*A. wilkesiana**	●					●			●		60	75	65	80		●
A.w. 'Godseffiana'*	●					●			●		60	75	65	80		●
*Achimenes**						●		●			40	55	60	80	●	
A. grandiflora						●		●			40	55	60	80	●	
Acorus	–	–	–			●			●		40	75	60	75		●
A. gramineus 'Variegatus'*	–	–	–			●			●		40	75	60	75		●
Adiantum		●			●			●			50	75	60	75		●
A. raddianum 'Fragrantissimum'		●			●			●			50	75	60	75		●
Aechmea	–	–	–		●					●	–	–	60	75		●
A. 'Foster's Favorite'*	–	–	–		●					●	–	–	60	75		●
Aeonium	●				●					●	50	55	65	75	●	

	CHARACTERISTICS Foliage			Features			Growth cycle			Shape						PROPER CARE Watering						Light				Temperature				Humidity	
	Green	Colored	Variegated	Flowers	Fragrance	Fruits or berries	Evergreen	Deciduous	Temporary	Rosette	Bushy	Grassy	Upright	Treelike	Climbing and trailing	Rest period Sparingly	Rest period Moderately	Rest period Plentifully	Active growth period Sparingly	Active growth period Moderately	Active growth period Plentifully	Medium	Bright	Bright filtered	Direct	Rest period Min °F	Rest period Max °F	Active growth period Min °F	Active growth period Max °F	Low	High
A. arboreum 'Atropurpureum'*		●		●			●			●						●				●					●	50	55	65	75	●	
Aeschynanthus	●			●			●								●	–	–	–			●		●			–	–	60	75		●
A. marmoratus			●	●			●								●	–	–	–			●		●			–	–	60	75		●
Agave	●						●			●						●					●				●	50	55	60	75		●
*A. victoriae-reginae**			●				●			●						●					●				●	50	55	60	75		●
Aglaonema			●				●				●					●				●		●				60	75	60	75		●
*A. pictum**			●				●							●		●				●		●				60	75	60	75		●
Aichryson	●			●					●		●					–	–	–		●			●			–	–	60	75	●	
A. domesticum 'Variegatum'			●				●				●					●				●			●			55	75	60	75	●	
Allamanda	●			●			●								●	●				●			●			60	75	60	80		●
Aloe	●			●			●			●						●					●				●	45	50	60	75	●	
*A. variegata**			●	●			●			●						●					●			●		45	50	60	75	●	
Ananas	●			●		●	●			●						–	–	–		●					●	–	–	65	80		●
A. comosus variegatus			●	●		●	●			●						–	–	–		●					●	–	–	65	80		●
Anthurium			●	●			●				●						●				●	●				55	70	65	70		●
*A. scherzeranum**	●			●			●				●						●				●	●				55	70	65	70		●
Aphelandra			●	●			●				●					●					●		●			55	65	65	80		●
Aporocactus	●			●			●								●	●					●				●	45	60	60	75	●	
Araucaria	●						●							●			●				●	●				45	75	45	75	●	
Ardisia	●			●		●	●							●		●					●		●			45	60	45	70		●
Asparagus	●						●								●	●					●		●			55	75	60	75	●	
A. densiflorus 'Myers'	●						●						●			●					●		●			55	75	60	75		●
Aspidistra	●						●				●						●			●		●				45	65	60	80		●
A. elatior 'Variegata'			●				●				●						●			●		●				45	65	60	80	●	
Asplenium	●						●				●					●					●	●				50	75	60	75	●	
A. nidus	●						●			●						●					●	●				60	75	65	75	●	
Astrophytum	●			●			●				Globular					●				●					●	45	50	60	75	●	
Aucuba			●				●				●					–	–	–			●		●			–	–	40	75		●
A. japonica	●						●				●					–	–	–			●		●			–	–	40	75		●
Begonia	Too varied to specify																														
Beloperone	●			●			●				●					–	–	–	●				●			–	–	65	75	●	
Bertolonia		●		●			●				Creeping					●					●	●				60	75	60	75		●
Billbergia			●	●			●			●						–	–	–		●			●			–	–	60	75	●	
B. horrida			●	●	●		●			●						–	–	–		●			●			–	–	60	75	●	
B.h. 'Tigrina'		●		●			●			●						–	–	–		●			●			–	–	60	75	●	
B. nutans			●	●			●			●						–	–	–		●			●			–	–	45	75	●	
Blechnum	●						●			●							●				●		●			50	60	65	75	●	●
Bougainvillea	●			●			●								●	●				●					●	50	60	60	75	●	
B. glabra 'Sanderana Variegata'*			●	●			●								●	●				●					●	50	60	60	75	●	
Brassaia	●						●						●			●					●		●			55	65	60	75		●
Brassia	●			●			●				●					●				●				●		50	75	50	75		●

	CHARACTERISTICS: Foliage: Green	Colored	Variegated	Features: Flowers	Fragrance	Fruits or berries	Growth cycle: Evergreen	Deciduous	Temporary	Shape: Rosette	Bushy	Grassy	Upright	Treelike	Climbing and trailing	PROPER CARE: Watering: Rest period: Sparingly	Moderately	Plentifully	Active growth period: Sparingly	Moderately	Plentifully	Light: Medium	Bright	Bright filtered	Direct	Temperature: Rest period: Min °F	Max °F	Active growth period: Min °F	Max °F	Humidity: Low	High
Browallia	●			●					●		●					–	–	–		●			●			–	–	55	65	●	
Brunfelsia	●			●	●		●				●					●				●			●			50	55	60	75		●
Bryophyllum	●			●			●						●			●				●			●			60	75	60	75	●	
Caladium		●						●			●					●				●			●			60	65	65	75		●
Calathea			●				●						●				●				●	●				60	70	60	70		●
Calceolaria	●			●					●		●					–	–	–			●		●			–	–	50	70		●
Callisia elegans			●				●								●	●					●		●			50	60	60	75	●	
C. fragrans	●						●								●	●					●		●			50	60	60	75	●	
Callistemon	●			●			●				●					●					●				●	45	50	60	75	●	
Camellia	●			●			●				●					●					●			●		45	60	45	65		●
Campanula	●			●			●				●					●					●		●			40	50	60	70		●
Capsicum	●					●			●		●					–	–	–			●		●			–	–	55	75		●
Carex			●				●					●				–	–	–		●				●		50	60	65	70		●
Caryota	●						●				●						●				●			●		55	70	60	75		●
Catharanthus	●			●					●		●					–	–	–			●		●			–	–	50	75	●	
Cattleya	●			●			●						●			●					●		●			55	60	60	75		●
Cephalocereus	●						●						●			●				●					●	45	65	60	75	●	
Cereus	●			●	●		●						●			●				●					●	50	55	60	75	●	
Ceropegia		●		●			●								●	●			●						●	60	75	60	75	●	
Chamaecereus	●			●			●					Clustering				●				●					●	35	45	60	75	●	
C. sylvestri 'Lutea'		●		●			●					Clustering				●				●					●	35	45	60	75	●	
Chamaedorea	●						●				●					●					●			●		55	75	65	75		●
Chamaerops	●						●				●					●					●				●	50	60	60	75	●	
Chlorophytum			●				●					●					●				●		●			45	70	60	75	●	
Chrysalidocarpus	●						●				●					●					●			●		55	75	60	75		●
Chrysanthemum frutescens	●			●					●		●					–	–	–			●				●	–	–	55	65		●
C. morifolium	●			●					●		●					–	–	–			●		●			–	–	55	65		●
Cineraria	●			●					●		●					–	–	–			●		●			–	–	45	65		●
Cissus	●						●								●	●				●			●			55	60	60	75	●	
C. discolor		●					●								●	●			●				●			65	75	65	80		●
Citrus	●			●		●	●							●		●				●					●	50	55	60	75		●
Cleistocactus	●			●			●						●			●				●					●	40	50	60	75	●	
Clerodendrum	●			●			●				●					●					●			●		50	55	60	75		●
C. thomsoniae 'Variegata'			●	●			●								●	●					●			●		50	55	60	75		●
Cleyera	●						●				●						●			●			●			50	55	60	75		●
C. japonica 'Tricolor'			●				●				●						●			●			●			50	55	60	75		●
Clivia	●			●			●			●						●					●		●			45	50	60	75	●	
Codiaeum			●				●						●			●					●		●			55	75	60	75		●
Coelogyne	●			●	●		●				●					●					●			●		45	60	60	75	●	
C. pandurata	●			●			●				●					–	–	–			●			●		–	–	60	80	●	
Coffea	●			●	●	●	●				●					●					●	●				55	75	60	75		●

	CHARACTERISTICS: Foliage			Features			Growth cycle			Shape						PROPER CARE: Watering						Light				Temperature				Humidity	
	Green	Colored	Variegated	Flowers	Fragrance	Fruits or berries	Evergreen	Deciduous	Temporary	Rosette	Bushy	Grassy	Upright	Treelike	Climbing and trailing	Rest period: Sparingly	Rest period: Moderately	Rest period: Plentifully	Active growth period: Sparingly	Active growth period: Moderately	Active growth period: Plentifully	Medium	Bright	Bright filtered	Direct	Rest period: Min °F	Rest period: Max °F	Active growth period: Min °F	Active growth period: Max °F	Low	High
Coleus		●							●		●					–	–	–			●				●	–	–	60	75		●
Columnea	●			●			●								●	–	–	–	●				●			–	–	65	85		●
C. 'Evlo'		●		●			●								●	●			●				●			55	65	65	85		●
*C. linearis**	●			●			●				●					–	–	–	●				●			–	–	65	85		●
Cordyline		●					●						●			●					●			●		60	75	60	75	●	
*C. australis**	●						●			●						●					●				●	50	60	50	75	●	
C.a. 'Doucetii'*			●				●			●						●					●				●	50	70	50	75	●	
Cotyledon	●			●			●						●			●				●					●	60	75	60	75	●	
*Crassula arborescens**	●						●							●		●					●		●			45	55	60	75	●	
C. argentea 'Variegata'*			●	●			●							●		●					●		●			45	55	60	75	●	
*C. falcata**	●			●			●				●					●					●		●			45	55	60	75	●	
*C. lactea**	●			●			●							●		●					●		●			45	55	60	75	●	
Crinum	●			●			●				●					●					●				●	50	55	60	75	●	
Crocus	●			●					●			●				–	–	–		●			●			–	–	45	60		●
Crossandra	●			●			●				●					●				●		●				65	75	65	80		●
Cryptanthus		●					●			●						–	–	–	●				●			–	–	60	75	●	
*C. bromelioides**			●				●			●						–	–	–	●				●			–	–	60	75		●
Ctenanthe			●				●				●					●				●				●		55	75	60	75		●
Cuphea	●			●			●				●					●				●			●			50	55	60	75	●	
Cyanotis	●						●								●	–	–	–		●			●			–	–	60	75		●
Cycas	●						●			●						●				●			●			55	75	60	75	●	
Cyclamen	●			●					●		●					–	–	–		●			●			–	–	55	65		●
Cymbidium	●			●			●						●			●				●			●			60	65	60	75		●
Cyperus	●			●			●					●					●				●		●			50	75	60	75		●
C. alternifolius 'Variegatus'			●	●			●					●					●				●				●	50	75	60	75		●
C. papyrus	●			●			●					●					●				●		●			60	65	60	75		●
Cyrtomium	●						●						●			●				●				●		50	75	60	75		●
Cytisus	●			●					●		●					–	–	–			●		●			–	–	45	60	●	
Davallia	●						●						●				●			●		●				55	75	60	75	●	
Dendrobium	●			●			●						●			●					●		●			50	65	60	70		●
Dichorisandra			●				●						●			●				●		●				60	70	65	80		●
Dieffenbachia			●				●						●			–	–	–		●				●		–	–	60	80		●
D. oerstedii	●						●						●			–	–	–		●				●		–	–	60	80		●
Dioscorea		●						●							●	●					●		●			55	60	60	75	●	
Dipladenia	●			●			●								●	●				●				●		50	55	60	80		●
Dizygotheca		●					●						●			●			●				●			60	75	65	80		●
Dolicothele	●			●		●	●					Globular				●				●					●	40	55	60	75	●	
Dracaena			●				●						●				●				●			●		65	75	65	75		●
*D. draco**	●						●						●				●				●			●		50	75	60	75		●
D. fragrans 'Lindenii'*			●				●				●						●				●			●		65	75	65	75		●
Dyckia	●			●			●			●						●				●					●	50	75	60	75	●	

	CHARACTERISTICS															PROPER CARE															
	Foliage			Features			Growth cycle			Shape						Watering						Light				Temperature				Humidity	
																Rest period			Active growth period							Rest period		Active growth period			
	Green	Colored	Variegated	Flowers	Fragrance	Fruits or berries	Evergreen	Deciduous	Temporary	Rosette	Bushy	Grassy	Upright	Treelike	Climbing and trailing	Sparingly	Moderately	Plentifully	Sparingly	Moderately	Plentifully	Medium	Bright	Bright filtered	Direct	Min °F	Max °F	Min °F	Max °F	Low	High
Echeveria	●			●			●			●						●			●						●	55	60	60	75	●	
*E. leucotricha**		●		●			●				●					●			●						●	55	60	60	75	●	
Echinocactus	●						●					Globular				●				●					●	40	50	60	75	●	
Echinocereus	●			●			●						●			●			●						●	32	50	60	75	●	
E. pentalophus	●			●			●								●	●					●				●	32	50	60	75	●	
Echinopsis	●			●			●						●			●					●				●	32	50	60	75	●	
Elettaria	●						●						●			●				●		●				60	75	60	75	●	
Epidendrum	●			●			●						●			●					●		●			55	70	55	70		●
Epiphyllum	●			●			●								●						●	●				60	75	65	80		●
Episcia			●	●			●					Creeping				–	–	–				●		●		–	–	65	75		●
E. 'Cygnet'	●			●			●					Creeping				–	–	–			●		●			–	–	65	75		●
E. dianthiflora			●	●			●								●						●		●			–	–	65	75		●
Erica	●			●					●		●					–	–	–			●		●			–	–	45	65		●
Eriobotrya	●						●							●		●					●		●			50	55	60	75	●	
Espostoa	●						●						●			●			●						●	55	60	60	75	●	
Eucalyptus	●						●							●		●				●					●	45	75	60	80	●	
Euonymus			●				●				●					●				●				●		50	55	55	65		●
*Euphorbia milii**	●			●			●						●				●			●					●	55	75	60	75	●	
*E. pseudocactus tirucalli**	●						●						●			●			●						●	50	60	60	75	●	
E. pulcherrima	●			●					●		●					–	–	–		●				●		–	–	60	75	●	
Exacum	●			●	●				●		●					–	–	–			●		●			–	–	60	75		●
Fatshedera	●						●						●			●				●		●				45	65	60	75		●
F. lizei 'Variegata'			●				●						●			●				●				●		50	65	60	75		●
Fatsia	●						●						●				●				●		●			45	55	55	65		●
F. japonica 'Variegata'*			●				●						●				●				●		●			45	55	55	65		●
Faucaria	●			●			●					Low growing				●					●				●	50	55	60	75	●	
Ferocactus	●						●					Globular				●				●					●	45	60	60	75	●	
Ficus	●						●						●			–	–	–	●					●		–	–	60	80	●	
*F. pumila**	●						●								●	–	–	–		●		●				–	–	50	75		●
F. rubiginosa 'Variegata'*			●				●						●			–	–	–	●				●			–	–	65	80	●	
Fittonia			●				●								●	●			●			●				55	65	65	70		●
Fortunella	●			●		●	●							●		●					●				●	50	60	60	75		●
Fuchsia hybrids	●			●			●				●					●					●		●			55	65	55	65		●
F. variegated forms			●	●			●	●			●					●					●		●			55	65	55	65		●
Gardenia	●			●		●	●				●					●				●			●			60	75	60	75		●
Gasteria			●				●						●			●				●		●				45	60	60	75	●	
Geogenanthus			●				●					Low growing				–	–	–		●				●		–	–	65	80		●
Gesneria	●			●			●			●						–	–	–			●		●			–	–	65	80		●
Gloxinia	●			●				●					●			–	–	–		●			●			45	60	65	85		●
Graptopetalum		●		●			●			●						●				●					●	45	55	55	75	●	
Grevillea	●						●						●			●				●		●				45	65	65	80		●

	CHARACTERISTICS: Foliage: Green	Foliage: Colored	Foliage: Variegated	Features: Flowers	Features: Fragrance	Features: Fruits or berries	Growth cycle: Evergreen	Growth cycle: Deciduous	Growth cycle: Temporary	Shape: Rosette	Shape: Bushy	Shape: Grassy	Shape: Upright	Shape: Treelike	Shape: Climbing and trailing	PROPER CARE: Watering: Rest period: Sparingly	Watering: Rest period: Moderately	Watering: Rest period: Plentifully	Watering: Active growth period: Sparingly	Watering: Active growth period: Moderately	Watering: Active growth period: Plentifully	Light: Medium	Light: Bright	Light: Bright filtered	Light: Direct	Temperature: Rest period: Min °F	Temperature: Rest period: Max °F	Temperature: Active growth: Min °F	Temperature: Active growth: Max °F	Humidity: Low	Humidity: High
Guzmania	●			●			●			●						–	–	–			●			●		–	–	65	80		●
*G. monostachia variegata**			●	●			●			●						–	–	–			●			●		–	–	65	80		●
Gymnocalycium	●			●			●					Globular				●					●		●			40	60	65	80	●	
G. mihanovichii 'Ruby Ball'		●		●			●					Globular				●					●		●			40	60	65	80		●
Gynura		●					●								●	●				●					●	55	65	60	75		●
Haemanthus	●			●			●						●			●				●			●			55	70	60	75	●	
*H. coccineus**	●			●				●					●			–	–	–		●			●			55	65	60	75	●	
Hamatocactus hamatacanthus	●			●			●					Globular				●				●					●	40	55	60	75	●	
H. setispinus	●			●		●	●					Globular				●				●					●	40	55	60	75	●	
Haworthia			●				●			●						●				●		●				40	65	60	75	●	
H. cuspidata	●						●			●						●				●		●				40	65	60	75	●	
Hedera	●						●								●	–	–	–		●			●			–	–	60	75		●
H. helix 'Glacier'*			●				●								●	–	–	–		●					●	–	–	60	75		●
Heliocereus	●			●			●								●		●				●		●			60	75	60	75	●	
Hemigraphis		●					●				●					●					●		●			60	75	60	75		●
Heptapleurum	●						●						●			–	–	–		●					●	–	–	60	75		●
Hibiscus	●			●			●				●					●				●			●			50	60	60	75	●	
H. rosa-sinensis 'Cooperi'			●	●			●				●					●				●			●			50	60	60	75	●	
Hippeastrum	●			●			●						●			●					●		●			50	65	60	65	●	
Howea	●						●				●					●					●			●		55	65	60	75	●	
Hoya			●	●	●		●								●	●				●			●			50	75	50	75	●	
H. carnosa	●			●			●								●	●				●			●			50	75	50	75	●	
Hyacinthus	●			●	●				●				●			–	–	–		●			●			–	–	45	70	●	
Hydrangea	●			●					●				●			–	–	–			●		●			–	–	45	75	●	
Hypoestes			●				●				●					●				●				●		58	75	60	75	●	
Impatiens	●			●			●				●					●					●		●			55	75	60	80		●
Iresine		●					●				●					●					●		●			60	75	60	75		●
I. herbstii 'Aurio-reticulata'			●				●				●					●					●		●			60	75	60	75		●
Ixora	●			●			●						●			●				●					●	60	75	60	80		●
Jacaranda	●						●						●			●				●			●			45	60	60	75	●	
Jacobinia	●			●			●						●			●					●		●			50	60	60	75		●
Jasminum	●			●	●		●								●		●				●		●			45	60	45	60	●	
J. mesnyi	●			●			●								●		●				●		●			45	60	45	60	●	
Kalanchoe			●				●						●			●			●						●	50	55	60	75	●	
K. blossfeldiana	●			●					●		●					–	–	–	●						●	–	–	60	75	●	
*K. pumila**	●			●			●				●					●			●						●	50	55	60	75	●	
Kleinea	●						●						●				●			●					●	60	70	65	70	●	
Kohleria	●			●			●						●			●				●			●			45	50	60	80		●
Laelia	●			●			●						●			●				●			●			48	65	48	65		●
Laeliocattleya	●			●	●		●						●			●				●				●		55	75	55	75		●
Lantana	●			●			●				●					●					●		●			45	55	60	75		●

	CHARACTERISTICS: Foliage: Green	Foliage: Colored	Foliage: Variegated	Features: Flowers	Features: Fragrance	Features: Fruits or berries	Growth cycle: Evergreen	Growth cycle: Deciduous	Growth cycle: Temporary	Shape: Rosette	Shape: Bushy	Shape: Grassy	Shape: Upright	Shape: Treelike	Shape: Climbing and trailing	PROPER CARE: Watering: Rest period: Sparingly	Watering: Rest period: Moderately	Watering: Rest period: Plentifully	Watering: Active growth period: Sparingly	Watering: Active growth period: Moderately	Watering: Active growth period: Plentifully	Light: Medium	Light: Bright	Light: Bright filtered	Light: Direct	Temperature: Rest period: Min °F	Temperature: Rest period: Max °F	Temperature: Active growth period: Min °F	Temperature: Active growth period: Max °F	Humidity: Low	Humidity: High
Liriope	●			●			●					●				●				●			●			50	55	60	85	●	
Lithops			●	●			●						Low growing			●			●						●	50	70	60	75	●	
Livistona	●						●				●					●				●				●		45	60	60	75	●	
Lobivia	●			●			●						Globular			●				●					●	45	55	60	75	●	
Lycaste	●			●	●		●						●			●				●		●				60	70	60	70		●
Mammillaria	●			●		●	●						Globular			●				●					●	40	55	60	75	●	
Manettia	●			●			●								●	●					●		●			50	60	60	75	●	
Maranta			●				●				●					●					●	●				55	70	65	70		●
Maxillaria	●			●			●						●			●				●				●		50	60	60	70		●
Medinilla	●			●			●				●					●				●			●			65	80	65	80		●
Microcoelum	●						●				●						●			●			●			60	80	60	80		●
Miltonia	●			●			●						●			–	–	–		●		●				–	–	62	75		●
Mimosa	●			●					●				●			–	–	–		●			●			–	–	60	75		●
Monstera	●						●						●			●			●					●		60	75	60	75		●
M. deliciosa 'Variegata'			●				●						●			●			●					●		60	75	60	75		●
Myrtus	●			●	●		●				●						●				●				●	45	60	55	75		●
M. communis 'Variegata'			●	●	●		●				●						●				●				●	45	60	55	75		●
Narcissus	●			●	●				●				●			–	–	–		●					●	–	–	40	60		●
Neoregelia			●	●			●			●						–	–	–		●			●			–	–	50	75		●
N. carolinae	●			●			●			●						–	–	–		●			●			–	–	50	75		●
Nephrolepis	●						●						●				●				●		●			50	55	55	75		●
Nerium	●			●			●						●			●				●					●	45	60	60	75	●	
N. odorum 'Variegata'			●	●	●		●						●			●				●					●	45	60	60	75	●	
Nertera	●			●		●	●								●		●			●			●			45	60	50	65		●
Nicodemia	●						●				●					●				●			●			50	75	60	75	●	
Nidularium			●	●			●			●						–	–	–		●				●		–	–	55	75		●
Notocactus	●			●			●						Globular			●				●					●	45	55	60	75	●	
*N. leninghausii**	●			●			●						●			●				●					●	45	55	60	75	●	
Odontoglossum	●			●	●		●						●			●				●				●		55	65	55	65		●
Oncidium	●			●			●						●			●			●						●	50	60	60	75		●
Ophiopogon	●			●		●	●					●				●				●			●			50	65	50	75	●	
O. jaburan 'Variegatus'*			●	●		●	●					●				●				●			●			50	65	50	75	●	
Oplismenus			●						●			●				●					●		●			55	70	60	75	●	
Opuntia	●						●						●			●				●					●	45	60	60	75	●	
Osmanthus	●						●				●					●				●			●			45	55	45	65	●	
O. heterophyllus 'Variegatus'*			●				●				●					●				●			●			45	55	45	65	●	
Pachyphytum		●		●			●			●						●				●					●	45	60	60	75	●	
Pachystachys	●			●			●						●			–	–	–		●				●		–	–	60	75	●	
Pandanus			●				●						●			●					●				●	55	70	60	75		●
Paphiopedilum	●			●			●						●			●				●		●				60	75	60	75		●
Parodia	●			●			●						Globular			●				●					●	45	60	60	75	●	

	CHARACTERISTICS															PROPER CARE															
	Foliage			Features			Growth cycle			Shape						Watering						Light				Temperature				Humidity	
	Green	Colored	Variegated	Flowers	Fragrance	Fruits or berries	Evergreen	Deciduous	Temporary	Rosette	Bushy	Grassy	Upright	Treelike	Climbing and trailing	Rest period: Sparingly	Rest period: Moderately	Rest period: Plentifully	Active growth period: Sparingly	Active growth period: Moderately	Active growth period: Plentifully	Medium	Bright	Bright filtered	Direct	Rest period: Min °F	Rest period: Max °F	Active growth period: Min °F	Active growth period: Max °F	Low	High
Passiflora	●			●			●								●	●					●		●			45	60	60	75	●	
Pedilanthus	●						●						●			●			●				●			55	70	60	80	●	
P. tithymaloides smallii 'Variegatus'			●				●						●			●			●				●			55	70	60	80	●	
Pelargonium domesticum hybrids	●			●			●				●					●				●			●			45	55	60	75	●	
P. hortorum hybrids			●	●			●				●					●				●			●			45	55	60	75	●	
P. peltatum hybrids	●			●			●								●	●				●			●			45	55	60	75	●	
*P. quercifolium**	●				●		●				●					●				●			●			45	55	60	75	●	
Pellaea rotundifolia	●						●				●					●					●	●				45	55	55	75		●
P. viridis	●						●						●			●					●	●				45	55	55	75		●
Pellionia			●	●			●								●	●					●			●		55	70	60	75	●	
Pentas	●			●			●				●					●				●			●			50	70	65	80	●	
Peperomia	●			●			●				●					●			●					●		55	70	60	75		●
P. scandens 'Variegata'			●				●								●	●			●				●			55	70	60	75		●
Pfeiffera	●			●		●	●								●		●				●		●			60	75	60	75	●	
Phalaenopsis			●	●			●						●			–	–	–		●				●		–	–	68	70		●
P. amabilis	●			●			●						●			–	–	–		●				●		–	–	68	70		●
Philodendron	●						●								●	●				●				●		55	75	55	75	●	
P. 'Burgundy'		●					●								●	●				●				●		55	75	55	75	●	
*P. selloum**	●						●			●						●				●				●		55	75	55	75	●	
Phoenix	●						●				●					●					●				●	45	60	60	75	●	
Phyllitis	●						●				●					●				●		●				50	55	55	75	●	
Pilea			●				●				●					–	–	–	●			●				–	–	55	75		●
*P. nummulariifolia**	●						●								●	–	–	–	●			●				–	–	55	75		●
Piper			●				●								●	–	–	–		●				●		–	–	60	75		●
Pisonia			●				●				●					●				●			●			50	75	50	75	●	
Pittosporum	●			●	●		●							●		●					●		●			45	60	60	75	●	
P. tobira 'Variegata'			●	●	●		●							●		●					●		●			45	60	60	75	●	
Platycerium	●						●								●	●					●		●			55	65	65	75		●
Plectranthus			●		●		●								●	●					●		●			50	65	60	75		●
P. australis	●				●		●				●					●					●		●			50	65	60	75		●
Pleomele	●						●						●			–	–	–		●			●			–	–	55	75		●
P. reflexa variegata			●				●						●			–	–	–		●			●			–	–	55	75		●
Plumbago	●			●			●				●					●					●				●	40	60	60	75	●	
Podocarpus	●						●							●		●				●				●		50	60	60	75	●	
Polypodium	●						●				●						●				●	●				45	55	55	75		●
P. aureum 'Mandaianum'		●					●				●						●				●	●				45	55	55	75		●
Polyscias	●						●				●					–	–	–		●			●			–	–	65	75		●
P. balfouriana 'Pennockii'*			●				●				●					–	–	–		●				●		–	–	65	75		●
Polystichum	●						●				●						●				●		●			55	60	60	75		●
Primula	●			●	●				●	●						–	–	–			●		●			–	–	45	65		●
*P. sinensis**	●			●			●			●						●					●		●			45	65	45	65		●

	CHARACTERISTICS															PROPER CARE															
	Foliage			Features			Growth cycle			Shape						Watering						Light				Temperature				Humidity	
																Rest period			Active growth period							Rest period		Active growth period			
	Green	Colored	Variegated	Flowers	Fragrance	Fruits or berries	Evergreen	Deciduous	Temporary	Rosette	Bushy	Grassy	Upright	Treelike	Climbing and trailing	Sparingly	Moderately	Plentifully	Sparingly	Moderately	Plentifully	Medium	Bright	Bright filtered	Direct	Min °F	Max °F	Min °F	Max °F	Low	High
Pseuderanthemum			●	●			●						●			–	–	–		●				●		–	–	60	75		●
Pteris	●						●				●						●				●		●			55	60	60	75		●
P. cretica 'Albo-lineata'*			●				●				●						●				●		●			55	60	60	75		●
Punica	●			●		●	●				●					●					●		●			50	60	60	75	●	
Rebutia	●			●			●			Globular						●				●			●			35	55	60	75	●	
Rhapis	●						●				●					●				●				●		45	60	60	75	●	
R. excelsa 'Zuikonishiki'			●				●				●					●				●				●		45	60	60	75	●	
Rhipsalidopsis	●			●			●				●					●					●	●				50	75	50	75		●
Rhipsalis	●			●			●								●		●				●	●				50	75	50	75		●
Rhododendron	●			●			●				●							●			●		●			45	65	45	65		●
Rhoeo	●			●			●			●						●					●		●			60	75	60	75		●
R. spathacea 'Variegata'			●	●			●			●						●					●		●			60	75	60	75		●
Rhoicissus			●				●								●	●					●		●			45	60	55	75	●	
Rochea	●			●			●						●			●				●					●	45	60	60	75	●	
Rohdea	●			●		●	●			●						●					●	●				45	55	55	70		●
R. japonica 'Marginata'			●	●		●	●			●						●					●	●				45	55	55	70		●
Rosa	●			●	●		●				●					●				●			●			35	50	50	75	●	
Ruellia			●	●			●								●	●				●				●		55	75	55	75		●
Saintpaulia	●			●			●			●							●			●				●		55	60	65	75		●
S. 'Bicentennial Trail'*	●			●			●								●		●			●				●		55	60	65	75		●
S. 'Midget Bon Bon'*			●	●			●			●							●			●				●		55	60	65	75		●
Sanchezia			●	●			●						●			●				●				●		55	75	55	75		●
Sansevieria			●				●						●			●				●					●	55	80	55	80	●	
S. trifasciata 'Hahnii'			●				●			●						●				●					●	55	80	55	80		●
Saxifraga			●	●			●			●						●					●		●			40	60	50	75	●	
Schizocentron	●			●			●								●	–	–	–		●				●		–	–	55	75		●
Schlumbergera	●			●			●								●		●				●	●				60	75	60	75	●	
Scilla			●	●			●						●			●				●			●			45	65	60	75	●	
*S. tubergeniana**	●			●					●				●			–	–	–			●			●		–	–	40	60		●
Scindapsus			●				●								●	●				●				●		50	65	60	75		●
Scirpus	●			●			●					●				●					●	●				45	55	55	75		●
Sedum	●			●			●				●					●				●					●	40	55	60	75	●	
S. morganianum	●						●								●	●				●					●	40	55	60	75	●	
S. rubrotinctum		●					●						●			●				●					●	40	55	60	75	●	
S. sieboldii 'Medio-variegatum'*			●	●			●								●	●				●					●	40	55	60	75	●	
Selaginella	●						●								●	–	–	–			●	●				–	–	60	75		●
S. martensii variegata			●				●				●					–	–	–			●	●				–	–	60	75		●
Senecio	●						●								●	●				●					●	45	55	60	75	●	
S. macroglossus 'Variegatum'			●				●								●	●				●					●	45	55	60	75	●	
Setcreasea		●		●			●								●	–	–	–		●			●			–	–	45	75	●	
Siderasis			●	●			●			●						–	–	–		●		●				–	–	65	80		●

	CHARACTERISTICS: Foliage: Green	Colored	Variegated	Features: Flowers	Fragrance	Fruits or berries	Growth cycle: Evergreen	Deciduous	Temporary	Shape: Rosette	Bushy	Grassy	Upright	Treelike	Climbing and trailing	PROPER CARE: Watering: Rest period: Sparingly	Rest period: Moderately	Rest period: Plentifully	Active growth period: Sparingly	Active growth period: Moderately	Active growth period: Plentifully	Light: Medium	Bright	Bright filtered	Direct	Temperature: Rest period: Min °F	Rest period: Max °F	Active growth period: Min °F	Active growth period: Max °F	Humidity: Low	High
Sinningia miniatures			●	●			●			●							●				●			●		60	75	65	80		●
S. rechsteineria group	●			●				●					●			●					●			●		40	60	65	80		●
S. velvet slipper gloxinias			●	●				●					●				●				●			●		40	60	65	80		●
Smithiantha	●			●					●				●			–	–	–		●		●				–	–	65	75		●
S. zebrina			●	●					●				●			–	–	–		●		●				–	–	65	75		●
Solanum	●			●		●	●				●					●					●				●	50	60	60	75		●
Sonerila			●	●			●				●					–	–	–		●				●		–	–	65	80		●
Sparmannia	●			●			●				●					●				●				●		50	70	55	75		●
Spathiphyllum	●			●	●		●							●		●				●		●				55	60	60	75		●
Stapelia	●			●		●	●						●			●				●					●	60	75	60	75	●	
Stenocarpus	●						●						●			●					●		●			50	75	50	75	●	
Stenotaphrum			●				●					●				●					●		●			55	75	55	75		●
Stephanotis	●			●	●		●								●	●					●		●			60	75	60	75		●
Strelitzia	●			●			●						●			●				●			●			50	60	60	75		●
Streptocarpus	●			●		●	●			●						●				●			●			45	55	55	80		●
S. saxorum	●			●		●	●								●	●				●				●		45	50	50	75	●	
Strobilanthes		●					●						●			●				●				●		55	75	55	75	●	
Stromanthe			●				●				●					–	–	–		●		●				–	–	60	75		●
Syngonium			●				●								●	●				●				●		55	75	60	75		●
S. auritum	●						●						●			●				●				●		55	75	60	75		●
Tetrastigma	●						●								●	●				●				●		55	75	60	75	●	
Thunbergia	●			●					●						●	–	–	–			●		●			–	–	50	75	●	
Tibouchina	●			●			●						●			●					●			●		45	55	60	75		●
Tillandsia			●	●			●			●						●			●					●		55	75	60	75		●
T. usneoides	●						●								●		●			●				●		55	60	60	75		●
Tolmiea	●						●				●					●				●			●			50	75	60	75		●
Trachycarpus	●						●				●					●				●			●			45	75	60	75	●	
Tradescantia	●			●			●								●	●					●		●			50	75	70	75	●	
T. albiflora 'Tricolor'*			●	●			●								●	●					●		●			50	75	70	75	●	
Trichocereus	●			●			●						●			●				●					●	35	50	60	75	●	
Tulipa	●			●					●				●			–	–	–		●		●				–	–	45	60	●	
Vallota	●			●			●						●			●				●					●	50	55	60	75	●	
Vanda	●			●			●						●			–	–	–			●			●		–	–	60	75		●
Veltheimia	●			●				●					●			●				●			●			45	60	45	60	●	
Vriesea			●	●			●			●						●					●		●			60	75	60	75		●
Washingtonia	●						●				●						●				●		●			50	75	60	80	●	
Yucca	●						●						●			●					●		●			50	75	60	75	●	
Y. aloifolia 'Variegata'*			●				●						●			●					●		●			70	75	60	75	●	
Zantedeschia			●	●				●					●								●		●			–	–	50	70	●	
Z. aethiopica	●			●				●					●								●		●			–	–	58	70	●	
Zebrina			●	●			●								●	●				●			●			55	75	60	80	●	

Caring for House Plants

Caring for house plants

All plants live and grow in basically the same way. Their essential needs are air, light, water, mineral food materials, and a suitable range of temperatures. Terrestrial plants also require a suitable medium for the roots to grow in. Most plants, even if epiphytic in the wild, adapt to a terrestrial environment indoors, and so they must have containers in which to put down roots.

Although they have the same *general* needs, however, plants differ enormously in the quality and quantity of those needs that they must have in order to grow successfully. Whether the air for a given species should be dry or humid, the light strong or weak, the water plentiful or sparse, the temperature high or low, the potting mixture acid or alkaline will depend on the original habitat of the species. The manner in which it grew in the wild will largely determine how it ought to be grown indoors.

An understanding of the growth processes common to all plants can be extremely helpful in trying to grow house plants. It should not be forgotten that an indoor domestic environment is basically unsuitable for them. For that reason it is vital to consider each plant's natural preferences when selecting specimens for a certain position. Although plants are remarkably adaptable, a plant that needs shade will not grow healthily in full sunlight, nor a tropical plant in an ice-cold room. A big house is likely to have plenty of suitable places. In a small apartment the possibilities are far more limited.

These comments may seem too obvious to bear repetition. Yet they cannot be repeated too often. The indoor gardener who fails to realize that plants have limitations is doomed to a long series of disappointments. Remember that the appearance of a plant in a nursery or garden shop often gives no clue as to how it will perform in the home. This is why each essential growth factor is discussed in every entry in the *A–Z Guide*. Treat your plants as recommended, and they and you will reap the rewards of proper care.

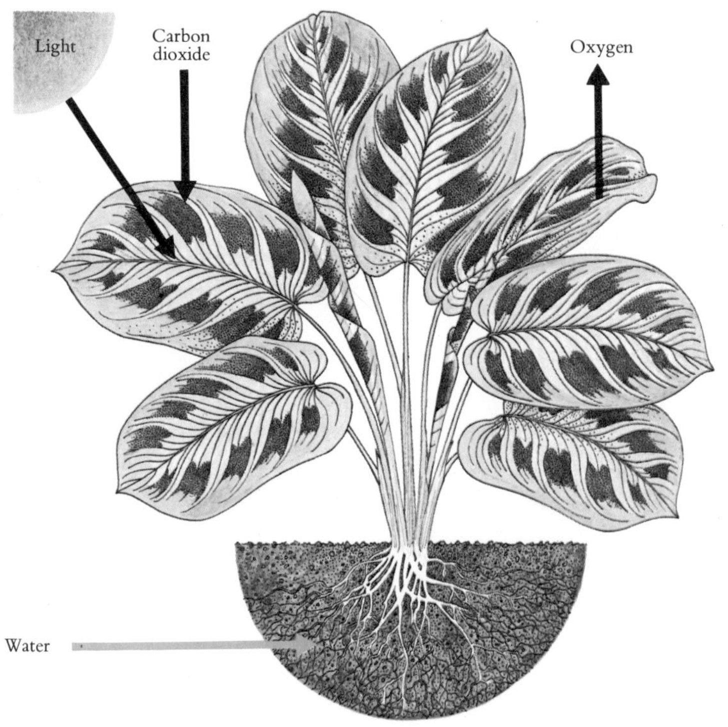

Photosynthesis
Light acts on green chlorophyll in stems and foliage to provide energy that the plant uses for making nourishing sugar. Essential for this process are carbon dioxide (from the air) and water (from the soil). Oxygen is a waste product.

Other plant processes

Plants breathe. Respiration, which involves taking in oxygen and emitting carbon dioxide, goes on constantly.

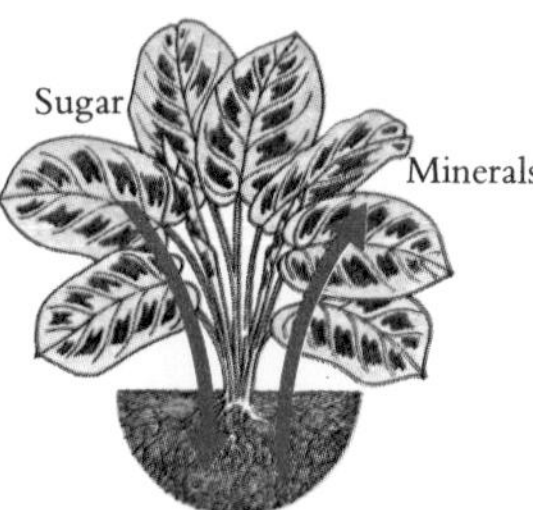

Water that roots absorb from soil contains minerals that are transformed into sugar by photosynthesis.

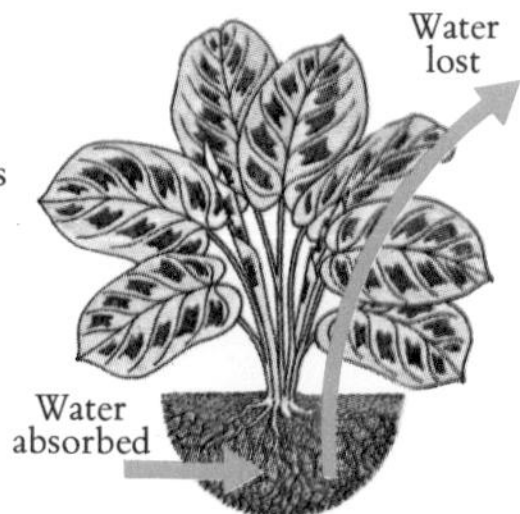

Some of the water is lost through pores (stomata) in leaves when these are open. This is transpiration.

HOW PLANTS LIVE

The key to all the activity in a plant that keeps it alive and growing is the process called *photosynthesis*. Photosynthesis, which provides the plant with the energy it needs in order to nourish itself, occurs as a result of the action of light upon the green pigment, chlorophyll, that is present in the leaves and stems of leafy plants. In leafless plants such as cacti, the chlorophyll resides in the green stem alone. Even leaves colored entirely by other pigments must contain green chlorophyll which is simply masked by the other color. Without chlorophyll there can be no photosynthesis.

The energy provided by photosynthesis converts simple elements into a range of essential food materials, which are all based on the production of sugar. Two elements necessary for manufacturing sugar are carbon dioxide and water. The plant takes carbon dioxide from the air, and water from the soil (or the potting mixture, for house plants) through its roots. Carbon dioxide and water, though vital, are not in themselves enough to create the nourishing sugar that the plant must manufacture for itself. Every plant also needs certain minerals that are—or should be—present in the soil. The roots absorb these minerals, which are carried up to the leaves.

The process of photosynthesis goes on continuously while light acts upon the chlorophyll in a plant. This means that the plant is constantly taking in carbon dioxide from the air, using it, and emitting oxygen as a waste product. At night, or whenever light is denied to a plant, the plant stops photosynthesizing. At all times, however, in addition to taking in carbon dioxide and emitting oxygen, the plant takes in oxygen and breathes out carbon dioxide. This process, known as *respiration,* is necessary for plant metabolism. The tradition of removing plants from sickrooms at night stems from the fact that plant life uses up some of the room's oxygen without replacing it as a waste product of photosynthesis like it does in the daytime.

Roots absorb water through fine root hairs at their ends. The roots never stop growing while the plant itself is in active growth. As the plant grows, it needs increasing amounts of moisture, and so the roots are continually reaching out, searching for more.

Water absorbed from the soil contains unprocessed minerals, which photosynthesis transforms into sugar. Parallel channels run through every part of the plant. One channel conducts unprocessed minerals from the roots to the leaves. The other channel takes processed food materials back through leaves, flowers, and stems to the roots.

Tiny pores *(stomata)* in the undersides of leaves are the openings through which the photosynthesizing plant takes in carbon dioxide and water vapor from the air and emits oxygen and moisture. Through those same stomata it respires, taking in oxygen and emitting carbon dioxide, when not photosynthesizing. The stomata open or close according to the external conditions. Because carbon dioxide exists in the atmosphere in only small quantities, the stomata have to be wide open throughout the hours while the leaves are absorbing light. As a result, the plant can lose a great deal of water through evaporation from the stomata. If the roots cannot absorb sufficient water from the soil to compensate, the plant quickly suffers from lack of moisture. This causes the loss of rigidity that we call wilting.

Loss of water through the stomata is called *transpiration*. And it is to minimize the effects of transpiration that gardeners are advised to keep atmospheric humidity high around many potted plants. If the air is already well charged with water vapor, loss of water through transpiration is greatly reduced, since a very humid atmosphere cannot absorb more water.

THE FLOWER

Any form of life must be able not only to stay healthy and grow but also to reproduce itself. Reproduction in most plants is the function of the flower. A few species have separate male and female flowers, but in the majority of species each flower bears the organs of both sexes. In essence these organs consist of the ovary-bearing pistil and the pollen-bearing stamen. When pollen produced at the tip of the stamen (the anther) is introduced into the ovary via the stigma, seed is created.

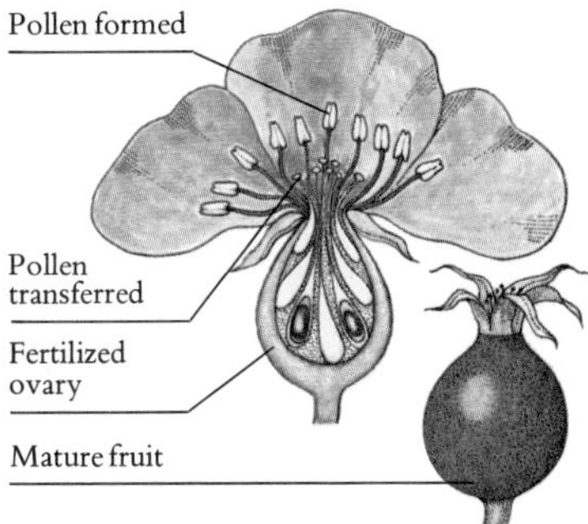

Pollen from the anther reaches the ovary of a flower via its stigma. The resultant fertilization will produce seed-bearing fruit if the flower is not destroyed.

Flowers are the product of maturity in a plant. Since many indoor plants cannot grow big enough to reach full maturity, such plants are grown primarily for their foliage and overall form. If flowers are produced, it is advisable to remove them when they begin to fade unless you are hoping to use the seed for propagation. Picking off the fading flowers prevents the channeling of food products into seed production and thus gives the plant more overall vigor.

With annuals acquired primarily for their flowers—the cinerarias, for example—picking off dead blooms is likely to stimulate the production of new ones, because the only purpose of an annual is fulfilled once it sets seed. If permitted to set seed, it will then put all its energy into ripening the seed. If flowers are removed before the reproductive function is completed, the plant will keep trying to reproduce itself by producing more flowers.

The growth cycle

The plant-growth cycle most familiar to everyone living in the Temperate Zone is that of deciduous trees. Everyone is accustomed to seeing a beech or maple tree put out leaves every spring and lose them every fall—an unchanging cycle controlled partly by the seasonal temperature changes and partly by variation in hours of daylight. Thus, it can be said that deciduous trees have extremely well-defined growth stages: an *active growth period* between spring and fall, followed by a winter *rest period*.

Deciduous trees are not alone in this respect. Their growth-and-rest cycle is an obvious one, but there are many other types of plant that grow and rest periodically even though they do not actually lose their foliage in the course of the rest period.

When such plants are cultivated indoors, they suffer if artificially deprived of their annual rest and many will eventually die if forced to grow out of season by being kept abnormally warm and well nourished.

Most house plants are evergreens—so they retain their leaves throughout the year. This should not blind indoor gardeners to the fact that the cold-climate evergreens do not actively grow during the winter. Such Temperate Zone plants as the ivies *(Hedera)* must have an annual rest period in order to thrive. They should be given no fertilizer and reduced amounts of water during the winter months. The temperature should also be kept relatively low at this time.

Only a few kinds of house plant are Temperate Zone plants, however. The growth-cycle problem is less straightforward with most potted plants, which are of tropical or subtropical origin. Some—for instance, the desert cacti and certain other succulent plants—have distinct growth and rest periods in the wild because of either seasonal temperature changes or seasonal rains. But many either continue to grow without pause in their native habitats or do not have specific seasons of active growth and rest. A great number of indoor plants come from tropical rain forests, where there is little change in growing conditions as the year progresses.

Growth cycles

Temperature, light, water and food all affect the natural growth pattern of plants. It is important to recognise the needs of different types of plant, as illustrated here.

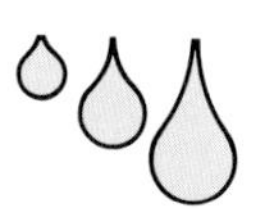

Watering
Size of blue symbol, left, represents watering needs: sparing, moderate or plentiful.

Feeding
Size of green symbol, left, represents feeding needs: small, moderate or great.

	Spring Daylength increases and temperatures begin to rise.	**Summer** Light and temperatures reach their maximum.	**Fall** Days shorten and temperatures drop.	**Winter** Minimal daylength and temperature.
Deciduous plants	 *As leaves begin to appear from bare stems, apply moderate amounts of water and fertilizer.*	*The fully active plant must be watered and fed moderately throughout the summer.*	 *When flowers are gone and leaves begin to die, reduce amounts of water, and stop feeding.*	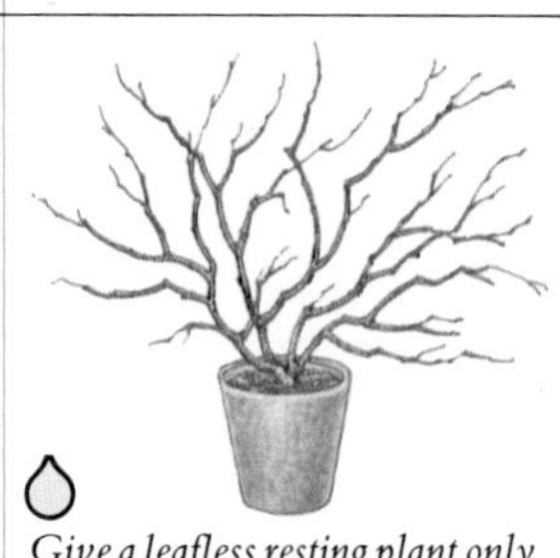 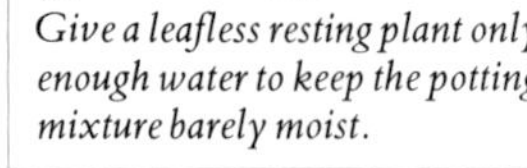 *Give a leafless resting plant only enough water to keep the potting mixture barely moist.*
Evergreens	*Evergreen plants begin to put forth new shoots in spring. Water and feed the plant moderately.*	*Moderate watering and regular feedings will keep the plant thriving throughout the summer.*	 *Because this evergreen must maintain its leaves, it should still be watered and fed moderately.*	 *During the short day winter months, give evergreens less water and do not feed.*
Plants that go dormant	 *During the active growth period when the plant is in flower, feed and water moderately.*	 *This tuberous plant should be neither watered nor fed during its summer dormancy.*	 *When leaves begin to sprout from the tuber, start to water sparingly, but do not feed.*	 *The winter growth period calls for moderate applications of water and fertilizer.*
Annual or temporary plants	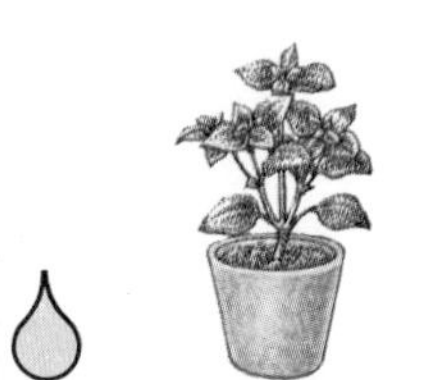 *Once a seedling is a few inches high it requires a moderate amount of water but no fertilizer.*	 *Water and feed the plant plentifully as long as it remains in full flower.*	 *In the fall, as the plant dies down, stop watering, and do not apply any more fertilizer.*	 *Seed sown at the end of winter should be watered sparingly until it germinates. Do not feed it.*

You might suppose that a plant without a well-defined growth cycle would present no problems in this respect to the grower who keeps all rooms comfortably warm in winter. This would be true if all other conditions remained unchanged, but unfortunately this is not so. There is one factor in indoor cultivation that does fluctuate in most Temperate Zone homes: the amount of daylight, measured in both length and strength. Because of this factor, plants that do not rest in the wild will often flourish in pots only if given regular rest periods. (Rest may not be necessary if plants are grown under artificial light. For a full discussion of artificial lighting, see page 446.)

FORCED REST

If you encourage a tropical plant to grow actively during periods of low winter light, it will eventually suffer even if other factors (such as warmth, watering, and feeding) are satisfactory. In particular, it will become spindly and pale, with consequent loss not only of beauty but of health. The reduction in the number of daylight hours thus becomes the major limiting factor preventing healthy growth in many kinds of house plant.

Instead of being encouraged to grow in winter, then, most indoor plants should be forced to rest. They adapt quickly to regular rest periods even if they are not naturally cyclical. The artificial winter rest slows down the plant's growth until conditions are again right for renewed growth. The usual way to achieve this effect with tropical or subtropical plants is to restrict watering and to stop applications of fertilizer. Such treatment is especially important with some cacti and other succulents that have pronounced rest periods during which watering must be greatly reduced.

The small number of house plants with leaves that drop off in winter must have an almost complete rest. In some cases they should be given only enough water during the rest period to prevent the potting mixture from becoming entirely dry. Very often, too, they need a drastically lowered temperature. Where this last requirement is specified in the *A–Z Guide* think twice before introducing such a plant into your collection. It is virtually impossible in many homes to provide a place for plants where the right light is combined with a low but above-freezing temperature throughout the winter rest period. These plants are not generally frost-proof, nor can they survive in darkness.

There are some plants, however, that become *dormant* while resting. Many bulbs, corms, and tubers, for example, have an annual period of dormancy, during which all above-the-surface growth dies back. A completely dormant bulb or tuber should generally be given no water at all, but should be stored dry throughout the dormant period, when it also needs no light. There are exceptions to this rule, especially among plants of the family *Gesneriaceae* (see *GESNERIADS*); the scaly rhizomes of these plants contain far less moisture than bulbs do, and so they might need to be given a little water while they are dormant to keep them from shriveling up. Always consult the *A–Z Guide* for advice on water requirements during the dormant period.

The end of the rest period is obviously signified by the production of new leaves and stems from buds. But there are a few plants that disconcertingly produce flowers during periods of evident rest. The succulent *Euphorbia milii* and some of the winter-flowering begonias are examples of this type of plant. If unexpected activity of some sort occurs in one of your plants during an apparent rest period, do not assume that it should therefore be fed or watered more generously. Consult the *A–Z Guide*.

ANNUALS

Annual plants such as cinerarias and exacums, which are grown for their floral display, are different from the plants discussed so far. The entire growth cycle of an annual is carried out within one twelve-month period (not necessarily a calendar year). Length of the active growth period varies considerably, depending on genus. During that period, regardless of its length, the seed germinates, the plant develops into maturity, flowers are formed, seed is produced, and the plant dies. It can be said that the rest period of an annual is the period during which it exists only as an inert seed. (Some plants, known as biennials, take two seasons to develop from seed and to flower, but none of the familiar indoor plants belongs in this category.) Indoor gardeners normally raise very few annuals from seed. Instead, these plants are usually bought in flower and discarded when the flowering period has ceased.

BRINGING PLANTS HOME

The growth cycle helps to determine the best time to introduce a new plant into the artificial environment of the home. Obviously, commercial growers are able to bring house plants to maturity under the best possible, most carefully controlled conditions of light, temperature, and humidity. In late spring and summer the difference between these excellent conditions and those in the average home will not be too great. For this reason a plant that is bought in spring or summer is unlikely to suffer from a drastic change of environment. Commercial growers produce plants all year long, however, and, by giving them constantly superior conditions, keep the plants in active growth when home gardeners would be letting them rest. It is between early fall and late spring that the differences between conditions in the greenhouse and in the home are at their greatest. To move a plant at this time is to run the highest risk of harmfully interfering with its natural growth cycle.

Moreover, the fall-to-spring transition from nursery to home is likely to cause shock to a plant in another way: During the course of the move it may suffer from sudden exposure to drafts and low temperatures. The most delicate species react badly to such changes. If a plant collapses after being brought into your home during the winter months, it could be because it has been chilled beyond recovery on its way from the nursery.

When buying plants in cold weather, make sure the supplier wraps them in several layers of paper secured with adhesive tape. If you have to move some of your plants in cold weather yourself, wrap them in the same way and protect them from the cold by packing them together in a cardboard box. For a long journey, place a hot-water bottle filled with hot (not boiling) water in the box. Similarly, if as often happens, you are given a plant during the winter holiday season, take especially good care of it. Give it the best possible conditions at home to help it become acclimatized to the new conditions.

Light

In their native habitats plants have adapted to vastly differing amounts of light. Plants that live at ground level in tropical rain forests, for example, flourish in the shade, whereas cacti in the open desert need and get full sunlight. The indoor gardener tries to give each house plant the kind of light it requires in order to remain healthy and grow well. It is obviously pointless to put a shade-loving fern at a sundrenched window, or a sun-loving pelargonium in a dark corner. In selecting a suitable position for a plant the first step is to determine its general light requirements. You must then assess the amount of light in various parts of the room.

The light level of direct sunlight remains fairly constant wherever the rays fall. Once a position is out of range of the direct rays, however, the situation changes greatly. The amount of light received through a window diminishes at a rapid rate as distance from the window increases. The human eye is a poor judge of the quantity of light at different points in a room. If you test a few guesses with a light meter, you will almost certainly find that you have overestimated the brightness. You will discover, for instance, that areas on either side of a window are not, as you might suppose, among the brighter spots.

Instruments for measuring the amount of light at a given point are available at many garden centers. You can also check light intensity with a photographic light meter, or a camera with a built-in light meter. Using a film speed setting of ASA 25, and a shutter speed of a quarter-second, the following f-stops indicate approximately the given light levels: f32 or f64 is direct sunlight, f16 is bright light and an f-stop reading of f8 is an indication of medium light. Take the readings from a white sheet of paper at the exact location of the plant.

The amount of light that enters an unobstructed window depends, of course, on which point of the compass it faces. In the northern hemisphere, windows facing south (or in the quadrant from southeast to southwest) receive several hours of direct sunlight on clear days, with the sun's rays moving around within the room. Windows facing east or west will have direct sunlight in the morning or evening only; and the western evening sun is usually stronger and hotter. North-facing windows get little effective direct sunlight. But the northern light, though generally weaker than that of other exposures, is also a great deal less variable.

Certain phrases used in the *A–Z Guide* for indicating different levels of lighting may be interpreted in the northern hemisphere as follows (with figures in brackets representing the approximate amount of light as registered by a meter):

Direct sunlight (100 percent) enters an unobstructed south-facing window throughout most of the day. For a few hours it enters windows facing east, southeast, southwest or west.

Bright filtered light (60–75 percent) is direct sunlight that is filtered through a translucent blind or curtain, or through a leafy tree outside the window. A thin gauze or muslin curtain will normally temper the sun's rays enough to prevent scorching of a delicate plant. For the very strong sunlight of lower latitudes, however, thicker curtains or a plastic venetian blind may be needed.

Bright light (20–25 percent) is found mainly in areas close to those reached by direct sunlight. It is the brightest light entering a sunny room that is not direct sunlight. It is much

Effects of direct sunlight

Wherever rays of direct sunlight fall in a room, the effect is almost constant. Brightness of light is then reduced as distance from the source increases (see below). Areas on either side of the window are much darker than expected (see right).

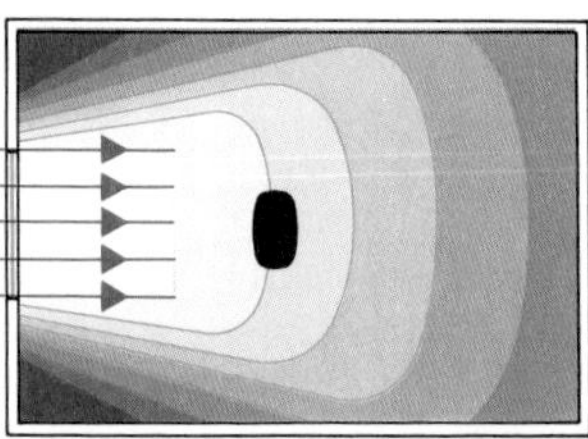

Effects of indirect light

Brightness of light in areas close to windows that do not receive direct sunlight is considerably less than those that do (see below). Also, light falls off more rapidly as distance from the window increases. Light at the sides is poor (see right).

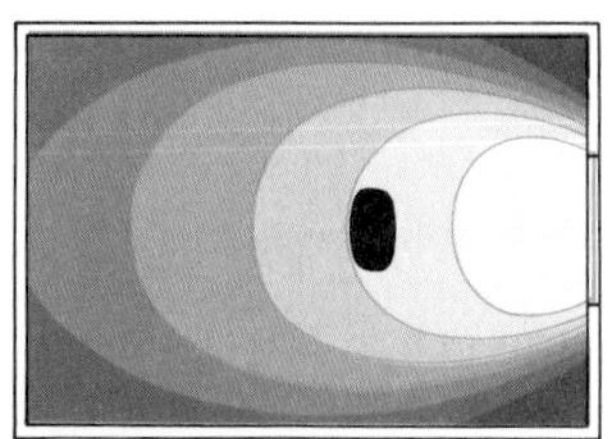

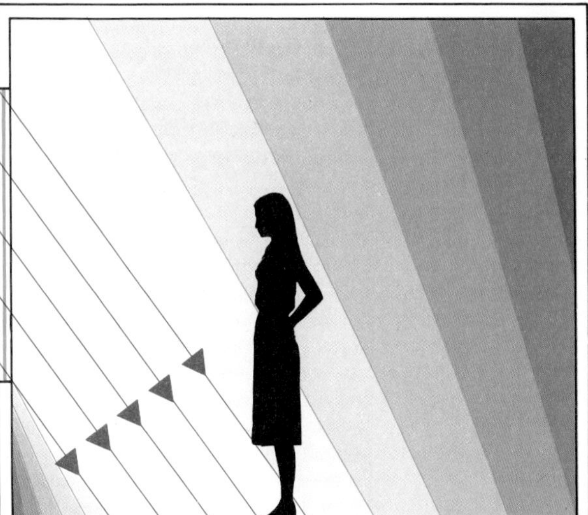

The sources of light

MEDIUM LIGHT
A constant level of daylight, normally without direct sunlight, enters a north-facing window.

MEDIUM LIGHT
The bright light through a west-facing window is reduced by the leafy shade of a nearby tree.

BRIGHT LIGHT
A west-facing window gets good light all day, with direct sunlight during the afternoon.

BRIGHT LIGHT
A west-facing window can get reflected sunlight if there is an appropriate surface nearby.

DIRECT SUNLIGHT
An unobstructed south-facing window gets the strongest light for most of the day.

BRIGHT FILTERED LIGHT
The direct sunlight normally entering a south-facing window is filtered through a translucent blind or curtain.

POOR LIGHT
The normally bright light entering an east-facing window is substantially reduced by the proximity of a blank wall.

POOR LIGHT
The intensity of light in a corner nowhere near a good source of light is extremely weak.

BRIGHT LIGHT
An east-facing window gets good light all day, with direct sunlight during the morning.

BRIGHT FILTERED LIGHT
The direct sunlight normally entering a south-facing window is filtered through the leaves of a nearby tree.

less strong than direct sunlight, as a light-meter reading will always show.

Medium light (9–10 percent) is the level of light found close to a north-facing window, where no sun enters, or at an east or west window where an outside obstruction such as a tree or building deflects the sun's rays. In such situations the level of light is further reduced by 1–2 percent for every three feet that a plant is moved deeper into the room. Medium light is also the light found in shaded areas within sunny rooms—for instance, along side walls—where the plant is well out of reach of direct sunlight, yet no more than 6–8 feet away from a sunny window.

Poor light (3–5 percent) exists in corners that do not face windows, in areas more than about 8 feet away from the source of light, or even directly in front of windows darkened by buildings or other obstructions.

The amount of light entering a given room depends upon such factors as the size and the number of windows, the seasons, and the surroundings. Light that comes through even the best of big-city windows is seldom entirely unobstructed, and trees in the suburbs or country can play a significant part in reducing light level. A tree outside a south-facing window can filter direct sunlight well enough to prevent damage to sensitive plants. However, a nearby building does not always keep out bright light. Light may be reflected into windows from white or glass-fronted buildings.

Rooms with white or pale walls are literally brighter than those decorated in darker, more light-absorbent colors. It is always wise, in fact, to place plants against a white background, where some of the available light will be reflected onto the back of the plants. There will be a noticeable contrast between their growth and that of

The extra light reflected from a white wall has evidently benefited the iresine on the left. A similar plant backed by a dark wall has grown only toward the window.

similar plants in a similar position backed by, say, a dark bookcase. The amount of light on the portion of a plant facing away from a window may be negligible. Even at best, right in a window, only half the plant is exposed to all the light.

It is generally true, however, that too little light may be less harmful to plants than too much. Very few house plants react well to full, unbroken summer sunlight, which is likely to scorch them and dry out the potting mixture. Even normally sun-loving specimens can be scorched at a closed window because the glass cuts off most of the ultraviolet rays, and the remaining light is unbalanced.

Recommended quantities of light for all plants are given in general terms in the *A–Z Guide*. The surest way to test whether a specific position is suitable for a plant in this respect is obviously by means of a light meter. Quantity is only part of the problem, though. The quality of light is equally important. Everyone is aware, for instance, that the summer sun is much stronger than the winter sun (it can be up to twice as hot) and that—in the northern hemisphere, at least—sunlight is always stronger in southern areas than in northern ones.

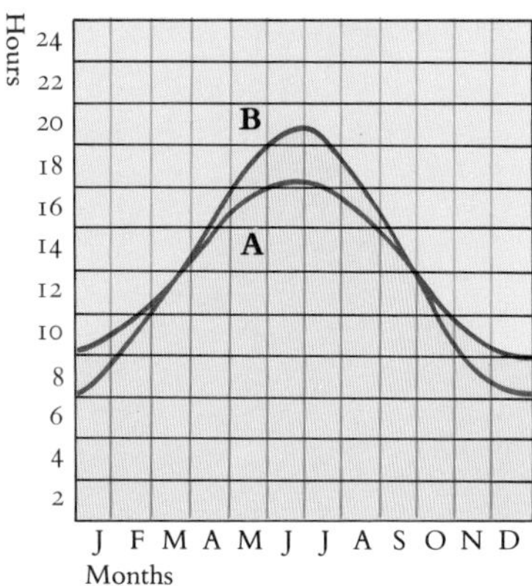

Plants farther north (B) receive more but less intense daylight in summer and less adequate light in winter than those farther south (A).

PLANT TOLERANCE

Most potted plants, apart from cacti and plants grown primarily for their flowers, neither require nor like high light intensities. However, granting all that has been said so far, do not forget that plants are amazingly tolerant. For instance, although cacti and flowering plants should have some sunlight every day, they rarely die if denied it for a while. Similarly, plants with variegated or purple leaves require bright light to retain their striking coloration, but they will not fade irrevocably if kept in medium light for a few weeks. The right kind of light is certainly important, especially for a plant that is growing actively, or that is about to flower. But a plant just maintaining itself in a rest period can survive for a long time in less light than it needs for active growth.

Plants that do best when grown in full or filtered sunlight can tolerate medium light for up to a month. And plants that should normally have bright light can be kept in medium-to-poor light for up to two months.

Shade-loving plants—aglaonemas, ferns, and fittonias, for example—are less tolerant of the wrong kind of light. Obviously, they cannot live in the dark. Furthermore, they should not be exposed to bright light, and they should *never* be subjected to direct sunlight, for it will rapidly scorch them. In fact, only plants specified as sun-lovers should be placed in strong sunlight.

On average, plants require 12–16 hours of light a day in order to maintain active growth. A plant getting fewer hours than this will grow slowly, or not at all. But there is a vast difference between a plant that is not actively growing because of inadequate light and a plant whose health is impaired. Most healthy plants *need* rest periods in order to remain healthy. Occasional periods of diminished light are no cause for worry if the plant is encouraged to rest by being given less water and no extra food during any such period. If active growth seems desirable, however, artificial light can promote plant growth by lengthening the hours of light in shorter days. (Techniques for the use of artificial light are discussed on pages 446-448.)

Because of their ability to tolerate deviations from the preferred norm, plants that "require" a certain type of light can be kept in relatively unsatisfactory light for quite a long time if this seems desirable for decorative purposes. However, they should be returned to the recommended light level for periods of recuperation—preferably for at least one week out of every seven or eight.

A plant can be shifted from bright to dimmer light without ill effects. Moving a plant from relatively poor to bright light, however, is sometimes harmful if done too abruptly. If a plant has been in a dim spot for several weeks and you want to move it to brighter light, shift it to conditions of maximum brightness gradually, over a period of 10–15 days. The same cautious approach applies to plants that are being moved outdoors in summer. Even cacti that have been in less than the brightest indoor light should be gradually acclimatized to the direct outdoor rays of the sun over a period of a week or two.

HOW PLANTS SEEK LIGHT

Whatever its requirements, almost every plant will turn its leaves toward a window so that the upper leaf surfaces can receive an evenly distributed supply of light. The only exceptions to this behavior are such stiff-leaved plants as sansevierias and rosette-forming kinds as the bromeliads.

If a plant is close to a window, the result of its leaf-turning will be that only the backs of the leaves will be visible from inside the room. If the plant itself is within the room, the light-seeking leaf surfaces may be seen to better advantage, but the plant may grow more on the side facing the light and become lopsided. A white background will help reduce this tendency.

It is possible to make a plant grow evenly all around by turning it regularly. However, if you choose to follow this rather tiresome procedure, do not turn a flowering plant that is already in bud. A flower bud suddenly exposed to a drastic change of light can react by dropping off.

The leaves of this fatshedera have become unattractively twisted toward the source of light. This result could have been avoided if the plant had been turned every few days.

Light is one vital factor in plant growth that the indoor gardener can control by intelligent planning. Begin by understanding fully the extent and limitations of the amounts of light provided by window and wall arrangements in areas where plants are to be positioned. Acquire plants that will not only look decorative but that will grow well in the light that can be provided for them. If this is done, there should be no problems. If a plant suffers from the effects of poor light, it will generally indicate its distress in a number of ways. For one thing, it will begin to lean toward the source of light. For another, the stems will become unnaturally thin and lanky, and the leaves will grow smaller, paler, and more widely spaced than they should be.

If such symptoms become apparent, bring the plant gradually into better light. It may be too late, however, to improve the condition of already over-elongated stems and sparse foliage. If the plant does not react fairly quickly to better light, it may be necessary to remove the affected portion and encourage the stems to sprout again from lower down.

Temperature and humidity

Temperature

Every plant grows best within a preferred range of temperatures. Most plants can also tolerate temperatures somewhat above and below the preferred levels, but they will die if exposed for very long to temperatures outside the tolerance range. The most satisfactory house plants, therefore, are those with a preferred temperature range of about 65°–75°F. This range is considered to be a reasonable year-round average for normally warm room temperatures in modern homes within the Temperate Zone.

In general, a nighttime temperature 5°–10° lower than the daytime level is advisable. Too great a difference between daytime and nighttime temperatures should be avoided. Fluctuations of more than about 20° in the course of 24 hours are bad for almost all house plants. They are better able to endure a lower temperature than the recommended level, as long as the low temperature remains fairly steady.

There are a number of species that do well *only* in relatively low temperatures. Many of the temporary flowering plants are of this type, and the life of the flowers of many other types is shortened by too much warmth. Moreover, a cool winter rest period is essential for a variety of evergreen species. For such plants the steady winter warmth of most modern rooms is unsuitable. It is sensible not to acquire plants of this sort unless the indoor gardener can reserve a room or two to be comparatively cool. The natural heat of summer does not present a similar problem. Summertime temperatures of 80° to 90° will not harm most indoor plants, even those that require cool winter temperatures, just as long as humidity is kept high at the same time (see "Humidity," below).

Whatever the general level of warmth in the home, there are certain danger spots for sensitive plants in virtually all rooms. When the weather is cold, a potted plant placed close to a window that is not protected by a storm window can be subjected to drafts or chills. If a plant is closed in between a window and a heavy curtain on a cold night, it becomes insulated from the indoor warmth, and serious chilling can occur. Ill-fitting doors and windows can create cold

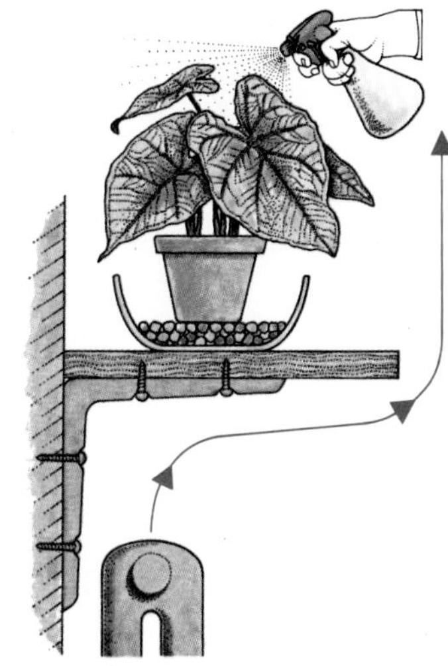

Heat-loving plants will thrive in hot air rising from a radiator but deflected by a shelf, if they are also given high humidity.

Temperature ranges

The ideal ranges for most plants listed in the *A-Z Guide*

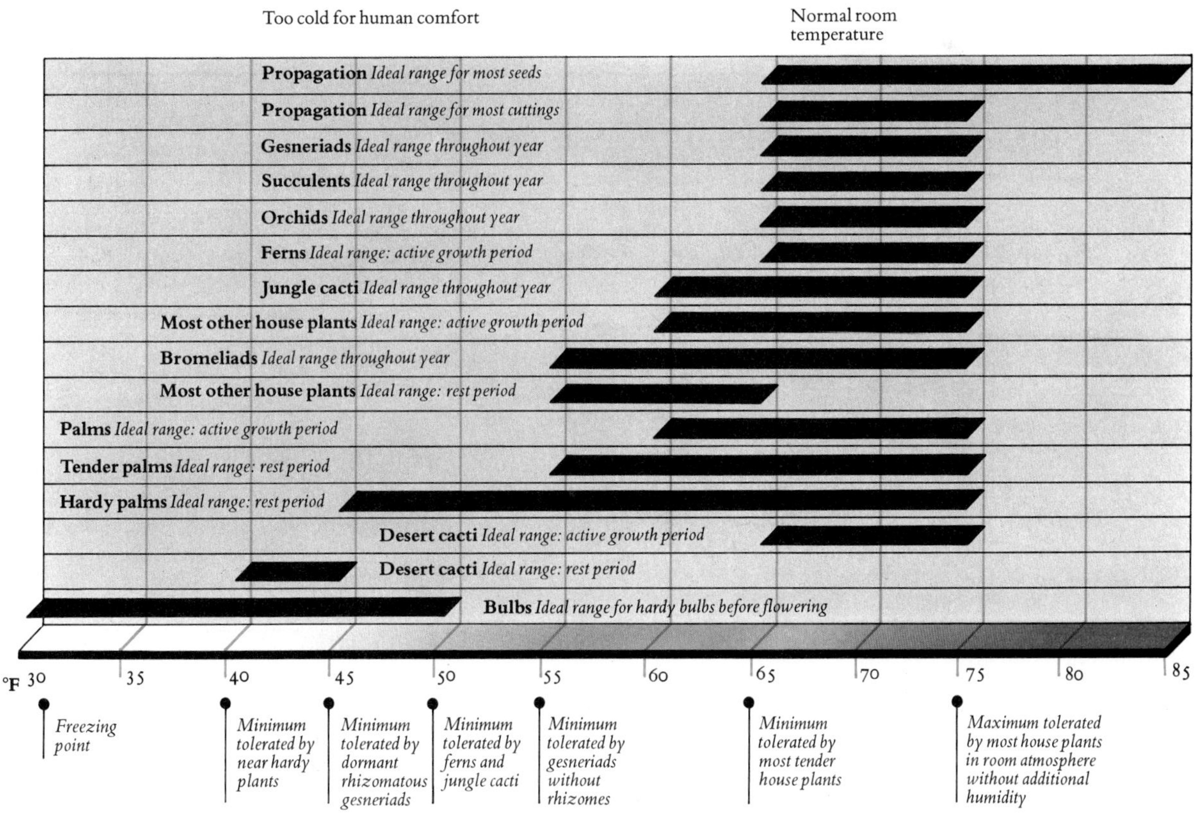

Too cold for human comfort

Normal room temperature

Propagation *Ideal range for most seeds*

Propagation *Ideal range for most cuttings*

Gesneriads *Ideal range throughout year*

Succulents *Ideal range throughout year*

Orchids *Ideal range throughout year*

Ferns *Ideal range: active growth period*

Jungle cacti *Ideal range throughout year*

Most other house plants *Ideal range: active growth period*

Bromeliads *Ideal range throughout year*

Most other house plants *Ideal range: rest period*

Palms *Ideal range: active growth period*

Tender palms *Ideal range: rest period*

Hardy palms *Ideal range: rest period*

Desert cacti *Ideal range: active growth period*

Desert cacti *Ideal range: rest period*

Bulbs *Ideal range for hardy bulbs before flowering*

°F 30 35 40 45 50 55 60 65 70 75 80 85

Freezing point (30)

Minimum tolerated by near hardy plants (40)

Minimum tolerated by dormant rhizomatous gesneriads (45)

Minimum tolerated by ferns and jungle cacti (50)

Minimum tolerated by gesneriads without rhizomes (55)

Minimum tolerated by most tender house plants (65)

Maximum tolerated by most house plants in room atmosphere without additional humidity (75)

Trouble spots

This diagram shows some typical problem areas where changes in temperature occur, with possibly damaging results to any nearby plants.

Heat rising from a refrigerator motor should not be ignored when positioning plants in the kitchen.

Plants placed between a window and a curtain can be trapped in cold air whenever the curtains are drawn.

Plants between facing doors are in danger of being subjected to cross-currents of air.

Strong direct sunlight is harmful to certain plants because of the drying and scorching effect.

Although stoves are an obvious source of extreme heat, some people carelessly place plants on nearby shelves.

The strong flow of cold air from an air-conditioning vent affects the area below it.

Even a well-fitting window conducts cold air through the glass, and sensitive plants can suffer as a result.

Heat rising from a radiator is potentially damaging if there is no deflector between the radiator and the plant.

drafts at any time. And plants near radiators or heating ducts can suffer from the effects of rising currents of hot, dry air, which can damage the foliage by scorching it.

It is occasionally wise to place a potted plant directly above a source of heat such as a radiator, where it can benefit from a combination of warm potting mixture around the roots and warm air around the leaves. A baffle or deflector between the radiator and the plant will minimize the risk of leaf scorch. Some extra local humidity should almost certainly be provided as well. A shelf a little wider than the spread of the plants concerned will deflect the hot air and provide space for a pebble tray. When advisable, such positioning is recommended in the *A–Z Guide*.

HOW TO MEASURE RANGE

The temperature at any moment is easily measured with a conventional thermometer. But experienced indoor gardeners recommend the use of a maximum/minimum type of thermometer with two linked columns of mercury. These move little metal indicators up or down, and the indicators stay in place at whatever extremes of temperature have been reached. Thus the maximum and minimum temperatures for a given period are automatically recorded.

When using a maximum/minimum thermometer you can not only check the accuracy of domestic thermostats but can find out how the temperature fluctuates during a day or week in various parts of a room. As a result of the thermometer's findings, you can judge with some accuracy whether or not a particular spot suits the temperature preferences of a particular plant.

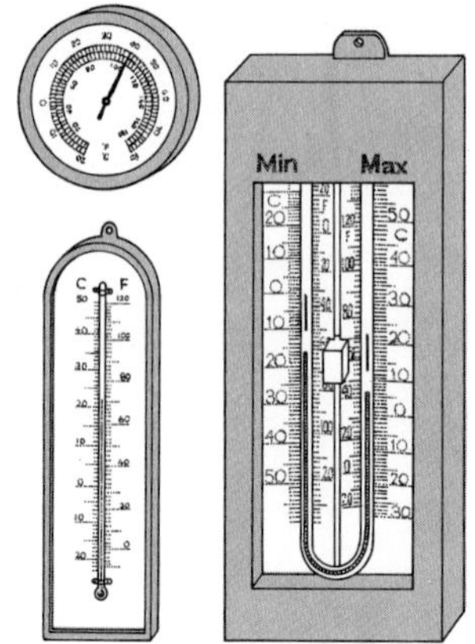

Both the thermometers on the left show temperatures in °C and °F, but the one on the right also records the maximum and minimum during a given period.

Humidity

It is not very difficult to specify and measure preferred or tolerable temperature ranges. A related factor vital to plant well-being, however, is humidity, which is less easy either to gauge or to provide. Humidity is the relative amount of water vapor contained in the air; it has nothing to do with the moistness of the potting mixture. All leaves have innumerable tiny stomata (pores) through which the plants take in vital gases from the atmosphere. As the stomata open to receive the gases, water in the leaves is lost through a process known as transpiration, with consequent water loss to the plant. If the air itself is sufficiently moist, however, it can accommodate less additional moisture, and so a plant's water loss through transpiration diminishes as external humidity increases. Thus, the lower the humidity, the greater the possibility that leaves will dry up and shrivel away, that buds will fall, and flowers wither prematurely.

The moisture in the air is measured on a scale of "relative humidity" ranging from 0 percent—air that is absolutely dry—to 100 percent—air that is saturated. The presence of fog, for

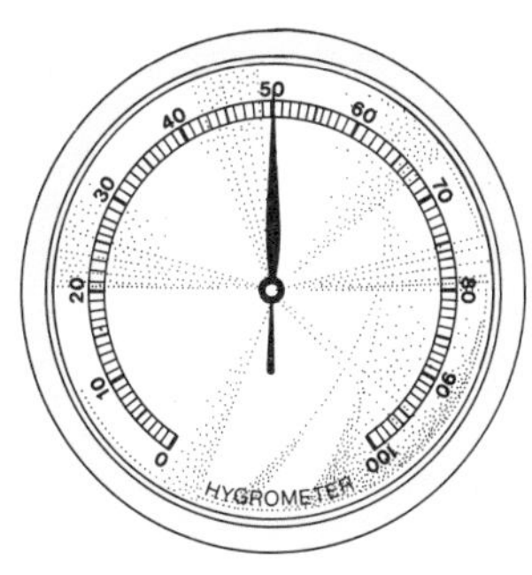

Hygrometers such as this one measure relative humidity on a percentage scale from 0 (dry air) to 100 (saturated air).

instance, can indicate a relative humidity of nearly 100 percent; there is so much vapor in the air that it can be seen. Mostly, though, humidity is invisible, and relative humidity can only be guessed at unless a hygrometer is used. These can be bought quite cheaply in most garden centers, and are among the indispensable tools of experienced indoor gardeners.

A relative humidity of at least 40 percent is an absolute requirement for most plants, including even cacti grown indoors. Many species that come from tropical rain forests need much more. A general level to aim at is about 60 percent. If an indoor plant is placed in air that is too dry, its leaves will soon begin to shrivel or show symptoms of scorching. Watch out for the drying up of leaf tips on plants with long, narrow leaves, such as chlorophytums and palms; this is a common indication of insufficient humidity around the plant.

The thinner and more papery-looking the leaf of a plant, the greater the likelihood that it needs extra-high humidity. Thick, leathery leaves are better able to withstand dry air. But increased humidity should be provided for all plants, virtually without exception, if they are placed directly above, or close to, a radiator or other source of heat.

HOW TO PROVIDE HUMIDITY

The amount of moisture that the air must contain to maintain a given level of humidity increases as the temperature rises. For example, the water content in the air must be roughly doubled to attain the same relative humidity at 70°F as there was at 50°.

Greenhouse gardeners usually add moisture to the air on hot days by splashing water on the floor—not a practical method in the home. There are several other ways to achieve a similar effect. For plants alone, it helps to spray a fine mist of water around them at least once a day preferably in the morning, soon after the heating system or sunshine begins to warm the room. The drawback to this procedure is that the effect is short-lived.

Probably the best and easiest solution to the problem is to provide a fairly constant level of water evaporation around the foliage by artificial means. There are several possible ways to do this. The most common method, frequently recommended in the *A–Z Guide*, is to stand the pot in a shallow, waterproof container (any sort of tray or dish) in which a 2- to 6-inch-deep layer of pebbles or gravel has been placed. Pour water over the pebbles, which should be no bigger than half an inch in diameter, but do not let the water level rise above that of the pebbles. The objective is to create vapor, *not* to provide extra water for absorption by the potting mixture. Add water at regular intervals to make sure the pebbles do not dry out. The pebble tray will have most effect if the width of the tray is the same as the spread of the plant. All the leaves will then benefit from the rising water vapor. If pebbles or gravel are difficult to find, stand the pot on a block of wood or a brick in a water-filled container, with the water not quite up to the level of the pot base.

For a plant growing in a hanging basket, suspend a dish of water, or one filled with pebbles kept permanently moist, about six inches beneath the basket. To do this, pierce a number of holes in the rim of a plastic dish,

The temperature/humidity ratio

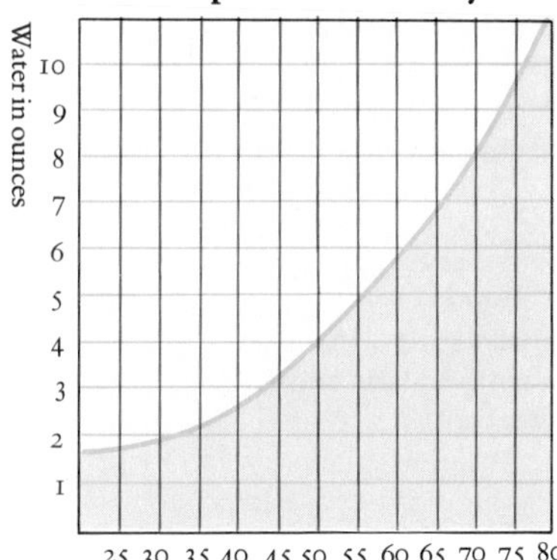

The higher the temperature, the greater the requirement for moisture in the air in order to maintain adequate humidity.

Alternative ways to provide humidity

The water in this saucer evaporates without moistening the mixture, because the pot is on a wooden block.

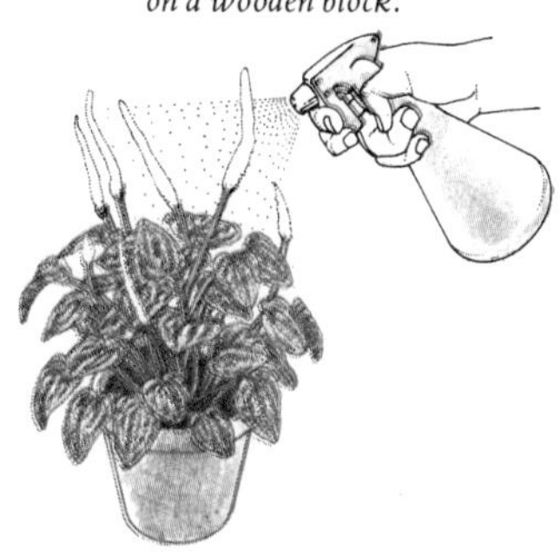

It is beneficial to regularly mist-spray the flowers and foliage of plants that require high humidity.

Another method is to stand a potted plant in a large container and fill the space between with constantly damp peat moss.

Grouping plants together on a tray of damp pebbles helps retain the humidity by trapping it between the leaves.

thread wire supports through the holes, and attach the dish to the basket. Some hanging baskets have built-in drip trays. These should never be filled with water to create humidity, however, because most plants must not be allowed to stand in water.

A water-filled dish suspended under a hanging basket can both provide humidity and act as a drip-tray.

Where groups of plants are concerned, stand all the pots together on a large tray of pebbles, or plunge them into moistened peat or sphagnum moss in a deeper container. They also benefit just from standing close together. The water vapor transpired by each plant tends to be trapped in the close-packed foliage instead of being dispersed, and this creates a slightly moister atmosphere all around the plants. Some people use humidifiers, which benefit human beings as well.

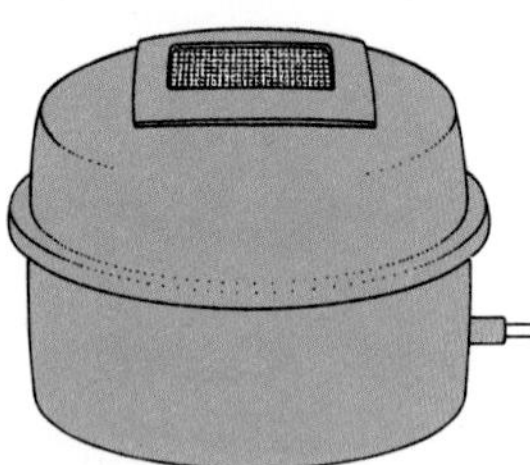

An electric humidifier vaporizes water over a period of several hours, thus creating constant high humidity.

With a limited number of very delicate plants, none of the simpler methods of providing localized vapor in an ordinary room may prove satisfactory. The only possible solution is to enclose them in a glass or plastic container, such as a terrarium or bottle garden (see pages 54 and 56). In such a well controlled atmosphere water evaporating from the potting mixture usually maintains high humidity.

Watering

How much water should you give a plant, and when? The amount that a plant requires depends primarily on the type of plant and its natural way of life. A desert-living cactus will use much less water than a marsh-dwelling rush. A caladium resting in winter needs only enough water to prevent the tuber from shriveling, while a Christmas-flowering begonia has to be watered moderately during the winter months.

The conditions under which an indoor plant is grown also affect its requirements. In hot, dry weather or well-heated rooms, an unusually large amount of water is lost through transpiration from the leaves and evaporation from the potting mixture. If hot sun shines directly onto a pot, the evaporation and drying out of the mixture is surprisingly rapid. In situations where temperatures are naturally cool, potted plants lose a great deal less water.

During the active growth period budding leaves and blossoms need their full ration of life-giving water. When resting, the plant can often survive with very little. Whether active or resting, the more roots it has, the more quickly it will use up water.

Two final considerations are the type of container and the medium in which the plant is being grown. For example, water will evaporate more rapidly from an unglazed clay pot than from a glazed, plastic, or plastic foam (Styrofoam) one. A plant in an unglazed pot, therefore, needs more water than an identical plant in one of the other types. Similarly, a potting mixture made porous by the addition of sand or perlite will lose water faster than will a standard soil- or peat-based mixture (see page 429). And the size of a plant relative to its pot makes a difference: The larger the plant, the quicker the mixture will dry out.

Because of these different but interacting factors, never water routinely by the calendar. The best way to determine when to water is to examine all plants every day or two to assess individual needs.

WHEN TO WATER

The most obvious indication that a plant requires water is drooping or wilting leaves. It is not the most useful indication, for it may come too late. Although thin leaves that have wilted can usually be revived quickly, thicker ones often cannot. In any case, repeated periods of wilting and resuscitation inhibit plant growth and flower production, and cause leaves to turn brown and fall off. Some plants—mainly succulents, orchids, and other tropical plants with stiff leaves—indicate lack of water by shrinking stems; but by the time this danger signal is apparent, severe damage may have been done. Wilting can even result from too much water rather than too little, because roots can be damaged or destroyed by waterlogging.

Therefore, it is unwise to try to judge the water content of the potting mixture from the appearance of the plant. Testing the potting mixture is really the only safe guide. Moisture meters, available in most garden-supply shops, are mechanical devices for measuring the moisture content of potting mixture on a precise scale. They are perhaps a bit elaborate for people with small collections of plants. But they are particularly useful for anyone who grows large plants in outsize pots or tubs, because the water content of these is difficult to determine in any other way.

Somewhat less sophisticated than moisture meters are small indicator sticks (sometimes called "plant probes"), which are also widely available from garden centers. When they are pushed into the potting mixture,

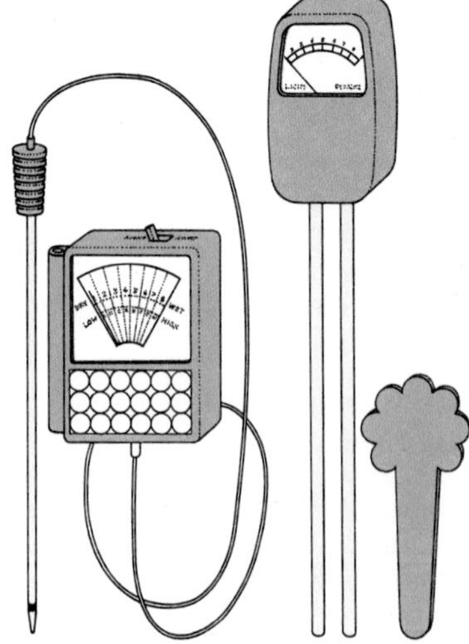

The instrument at left measures both light and moisture. The meter at center is used only for moisture. The simplest device (right) shows moisture content by color.

they indicate the extent of dryness or dampness by changing their color.

Without special instruments, there are various other ways to assess the condition of the potting mixture, but do not put too much trust in superficial evidence. A dry surface can hide a substantial amount of underlying moisture. If the mixture is shrinking away from the rim of the pot, the upper portion of the potting mixture is certainly dry, but the lower levels are not necessarily so. An extremely dry mixture is likely to shrink all the way down to the bottom of the pot. In this case, water with special care; if water is poured in, it can run out without moistening the potting mixture.

To test moistness within an inch or two of the surface of the mixture, probe with a finger. Use a pencil or thin wooden stake to go farther down. Where the mixture is moist, it will stick to the probe and discolor it slightly. If still in doubt, lift the pot up and test its weight in your hand. Dry potting mixture weighs much less than moist. It takes practice to feel the difference, but once familiar with this method of checking moisture content, you will find it quite helpful.

GIVING THE RIGHT AMOUNT

Watering instructions in the *A–Z Guide* almost always incorporate at least one of three basic guidelines to recommended quantity and frequency: to water a given plant *plentifully,* or *moderately,* or *sparingly.* These words are often further defined as they apply to specific cases. In general, however, here is what they mean:

Watering plentifully To water plentifully (or liberally) is to keep the potting mixture moist throughout all the time. Do not permit even the surface of the mixture to dry out. Give enough at each watering to let some water flow through the hole in the base of the pot. Except in rare cases (as indicated in the *A–Z Guide*), do not let the pot stand in excess water. Remember that even plants that require a lot of water will suffer if given too much.

Water is usually poured on to the top of the potting mixture but some growers prefer to water plants by filling the saucer in which the pot stands rather than letting water seep down to the roots (see page 422). If you want to water plants plentifully in this manner, continue filling the saucer

Giving the right quantity of water

The density of blue in the cutaway diagrams to the right of the illustrations indicates the amount of water the mixture should contain at each stage.

Watering plentifully

Refresh a plant that needs watering plentifully when the surface of the potting mixture begins to feel dry to the touch.

Flood the surface with water until the entire mixture is saturated and water flows through the drainage hole.

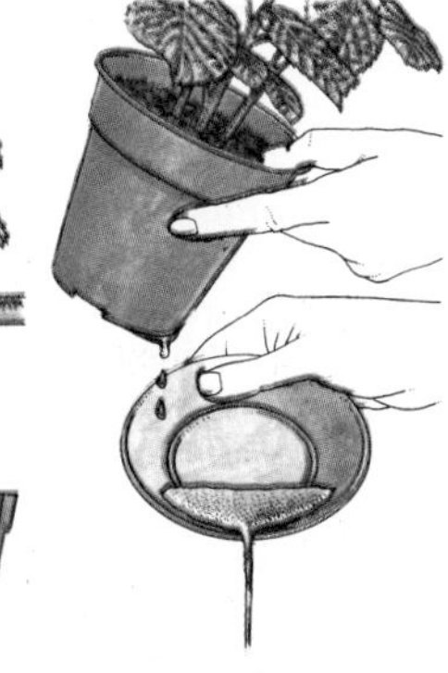

As soon as excess water has drained from the mixture, remove the plant and empty the saucer before replacing it.

Watering moderately

Refresh a plant that needs watering moderately when the top half inch of the mixture feels dry to your finger.

Pour water onto the surface until the entire mixture is thoroughly moistened but not saturated.

It is time to stop adding water when a few drops appear from the hole in the bottom of the pot.

Watering sparingly

Refresh a plant that needs watering sparingly when two-thirds of the mixture has dried out. Test with a stake.

Just cover the surface with water, so that it percolates down through the mixture, but does not appear in the saucer.

Test with the stake again—the entire mixture must be barely moist, so if there are still dry patches water a little more.

until the potting mixture can absorb no more and its surface feels thoroughly moist to the touch. Pour out any water that remains in the saucer for longer than half an hour.

Watering moderately To water moderately is to moisten the potting mixture right through, but to allow the top half-inch (sometimes a little more) of the mixture to dry out before watering again. When watering, stop in time to prevent more than a few drops from dripping through the drainage hole. If watering from the bottom up, put only a little at a time into the saucer—to a depth of about ¼ inch—and wait until all this has been absorbed before putting more in. As soon as the surface of the potting mixture feels barely moist, pour away any water that remains in the saucer.

Watering sparingly To water sparingly is to make the potting mixture barely moist throughout and to allow as much as two-thirds of the mixture to dry out before watering again. To barely moisten the mixture, give just enough to dampen the entire surface area, and then stop. Allow this to seep down through the mixture, then use a thin wooden stake to test the depth to which the water has penetrated. If the potting mixture still has dry areas, repeat the procedure. Never give so much water that it appears through the drainage hole in the bottom of the pot. If water is to be absorbed from below, put no more than a quarter-inch in the saucer at a time. Test the potting mixture for dry areas and add a little more water if necessary. When advised to water sparingly, remember that too little water is preferable to too much.

CONTAINERS WITHOUT DRAINAGE HOLES

In the rare case of a plant growing in a container without a drainage hole, water with extreme caution. Let only a little at a time flow in. Even when watering plentifully, do not continue beyond a point at which the mixture seems to have absorbed nearly all it can. If there *is* surplus water left in the container, the only way to get rid of it is to tip the container on its side and drain off the excess.

OVER- AND UNDERWATERING

It is never wise to water a plant little but often—in order, for example, to keep the potting-mixture surface wet. This can rapidly waterlog the mixture and waterlogged mixture is lacking in air—a condition that most plants cannot tolerate. It is much better to soak the mixture thoroughly after a slightly longer-than-necessary interval. When in doubt, do not water; wait a day or two, and then water thoroughly. Waterlogging is more likely to kill a plant than damage from wilting. Follow instructions for much-diminished quantities during the rest period with extreme care. Too much water at this time will rot the roots of certain plants and cause unseasonal, abnormal growth in many other plants.

If you are concerned that you are endangering a plant by giving it more or less water than it needs, look at the condition of the roots and potting mixture. Remove the plant from its pot as if for repotting (see page 427), and see whether the mixture is dry or over-wet. Finger the roots gently. If they are soft to the touch and come away easily, they are probably being rotted by overwatering.

HOW TO APPLY WATER

For indoor use, choose a lightweight watering can with a long, thin spout from which the stream of water can be aimed directly onto a surface concealed by foliage, or into separate pots grouped together. Just as effective, if available, is an indoor hose, with a narrow nozzle controlled by an on-off valve. The hose can be connected to a nearby faucet. By either method water can be directed straight into the pot, the center of a bromeliad rosette, or a saucer below.

An obvious advantage of watering from below is that it avoids the risk of wetting leaves; hairy leaves and those of rosette plants other than the bromeliads are particularly susceptible to decay or unsightly spotting from drops of water. Moreover, if absorbed from below, the moisture is sure to reach the lower levels of potting mixture. However, there is a risk of excess mineral salts collecting in the upper layer of the potting mixture. To avoid this, water occasionally from above and allow water to drain from the hole in the bottom of the pot. This helps to flush away the unwanted mineral salts. The other drawback when watering from below is that water can be left standing in the saucer through an oversight of the busy indoor gardener. It may therefore be advisable to adopt an alternative method such as a self-watering device.

A self-watering device is simply a reservoir placed below the potted plant. Sometimes the reservoir is built right into the plant container, and sometimes it forms the bottom section of a two-level apparatus, with the container in the upper level. In some models a wick in contact with the potting mixture draws water up from the tank by capillary action. In others the "wick" consists of potting mixture in a narrow vertical cavity within the plant container.

Three ways to apply water

The long nozzle on this watering can permits water to be directed straight onto the mixture without wetting the foliage.

If leaves permit little or no free entry to the surface, water the plant from below but do not let pots stand permanently in water.

Water on the foliage of bromeliads does no harm. Keep the cup of rosettes such as this one constantly topped up.

In an efficient self-watering arrangement the amount of water lost through transpiration controls the amount drawn up from the reservoir, and so there is no risk of overwatering. There is little risk, too, of a plant drying up, for the tank holds enough water for several days or even weeks, and there is usually a dependable water-level gauge. Because all these devices are costly, however, they are most often found in offices and public buildings rather than in many private homes. There are some less elaborate devices for allowing water to permeate the potting mixture slowly and steadily—for example, a flask-shaped earthenware "irrigator" that can be buried up to its rim in the pot, or a tank that stands mainly above the surface of the mixture and drips water into it. Such irrigators are cheaper than a true self-watering apparatus, but they lack the important element of plant-controlled timing.

WATER QUALITY

It is always best to use water that is lukewarm or at least at room temperature, because cold water can check growth and stray drops can spot the foliage. The water should also be as nearly as possible lime-free. If you are uncertain whether the water in your area is hard (containing a lot of lime) or soft (nearly lime-free), ask the local water company. Or make your own test for lime in the water by means of a pH-indicator strip obtainable from aquarium suppliers (for a definition of "pH" see page 430).

Not all plants react badly to hard water, but it affects the well-being of many; camellias, for instance, may become quite sickly as a result of it. The simplest solution, where possible, is to collect and use rainwater. It should not be used in big cities and industrial areas, where the rain is likely to be polluted by harmful chemicals. Distilled water is also safe to use.

One way to soften hard water and make it more suitable for lime-hating plants is to boil it. In the boiling process some of the lime is deposited in the pot. This method becomes tedious if the water is extremely hard and there are many plants to be serviced. Experienced growers recommend the purchase of a simple water filter or demineralizator, which will filter out impurities. The equipment, which is available at most hardware stores, is also effective against the strong chlorination that makes the water in some places harmful for plants. Do not use an ordinary domestic water softener (the kind that improves the lathering of soap), however. Any such softeners will damage your plants instead of helping them.

VACATION-TIME WATERING

Indoor gardeners who are going to be away from home for only a few days should not worry unduly about lack of water for their plants. A thorough watering just prior to departure is generally enough. As additional precautions, plants should be grouped in a cool room where there is no direct sunlight, and they should be either placed on trays or saucers of moist pebbles or plunged deep into large containers of moist peat moss.

For longer periods, try to improvise self-watering methods. For example, you can buy special wicks that conduct water by capillary action from a filled container to the tops of pots arranged at a lower level. Or there are large felt capillary mats on which plastic pots can be placed. In this latter system one end of the mat hangs down into a reservoir of water, and the entire mat remains constantly moist. The most convenient place to set up such a system is the drainer surface next to the kitchen sink. But further felt-mat systems can be accommodated in bathrooms and elsewhere.

A word of warning, however: The felt-mat system does not work efficiently with clay pots, which are too thick to permit the potting mixture to come into contact with the mat. If you want to use a capillary mat with a clay pot, insert a wick into the drainage hole of the pot to keep the potting mixture in contact with the wet mat.

A different method is to cover all plants with plastic bags immediately after the potting mixture has been thoroughly watered and allowed to drain; the bags will keep moisture in for two or three weeks. Support each bag on three or four thin stakes pushed into the edges of the mixture. Making sure that the plastic does not touch the foliage, tie the bag around the rim of the pot. Or, if you plan to be away for less than 10 days, simply let the bag hang loosely. Store bagged pots out of direct sunlight, in as cool a place as possible in summer or at a temperature of 60°–65°F in winter.

EMERGENCY TREATMENT

If, in spite of all precautions, you discover that the mixture in a pot has dried out, your best hope of saving the plant is to immerse the pot in a bucket or sink full of water. Leave the pot

Watering in vacation periods

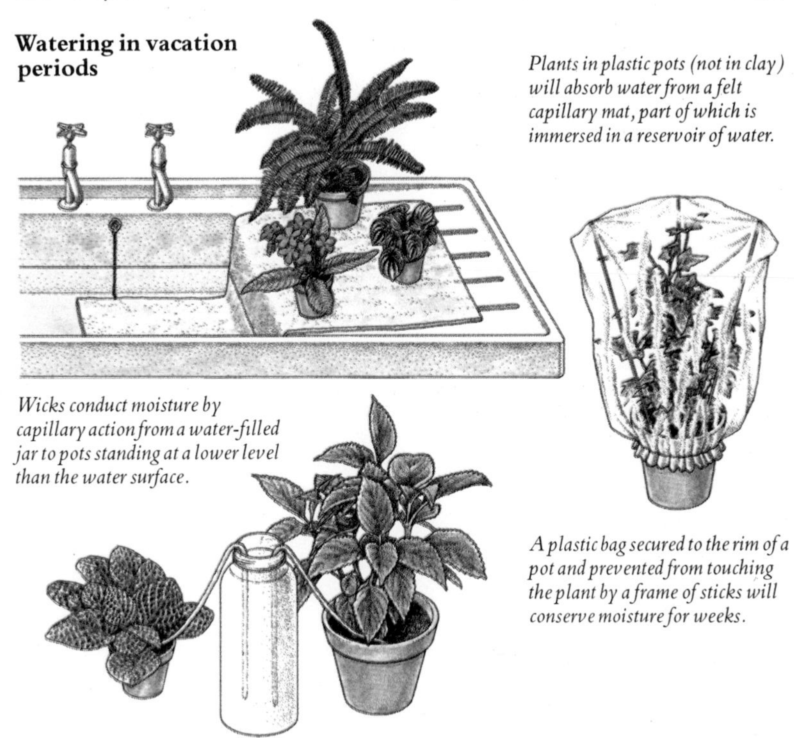

Plants in plastic pots (not in clay) will absorb water from a felt capillary mat, part of which is immersed in a reservoir of water.

Wicks conduct moisture by capillary action from a water-filled jar to pots standing at a lower level than the water surface.

A plastic bag secured to the rim of a pot and prevented from touching the plant by a frame of sticks will conserve moisture for weeks.

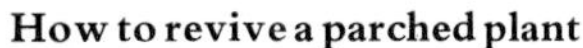

How to revive a parched plant

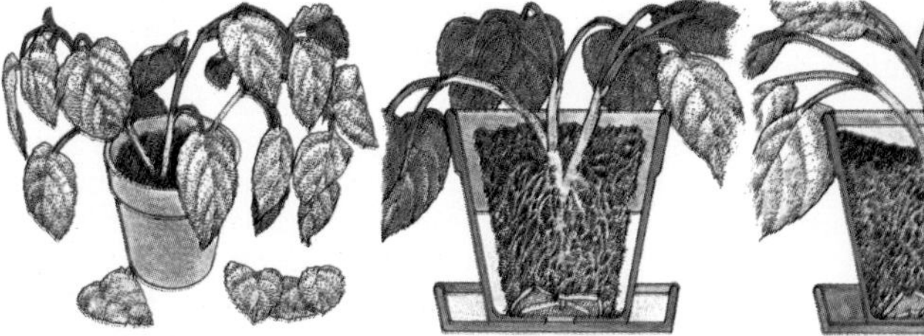

The leaves of this plant are wilting and falling, obviously because water is not getting through to them.

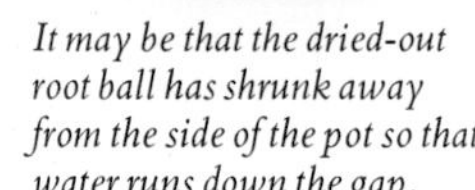

It may be that the dried-out root ball has shrunk away from the side of the pot so that water runs down the gap.

Or the potting mixture may have become compacted and insufficiently porous, so that water cannot penetrate.

To revive the plant begin by breaking up the surface of the mixture with a pointed tool, taking care not to harm roots.

Then immerse the pot in a bucket of water, until bubbles stop rising from the mixture. Meanwhile, spray leaves.

Let excess water drain away. If the problem recurs after a week, assume that the mixture is wrong, and repot the plant.

entirely immersed until bubbles stop rising up from the potting mixture. Excess water can then be permitted to drain away. While the pot is still under water, spray the foliage.

Most plants will profit from being given this type of deep-water treatment once or twice in the course of a summer even if they are not desperately in need of it. Total immersion moistens any persistently dry areas in the potting mixture.

One indication that a plant may be endangered, even though the foliage looks healthy, is a potting-mixture surface that does not absorb water easily. Be wary of a surface on which puddles collect and linger. They probably mean that the top layer of the mixture is so caked that water cannot seep down to the roots. Try breaking up the surface with a screwdriver or similar tool. If the trouble persists, the potting mixture is probably compacted all through. The only solution is to repot the plant in a more porous medium after freeing the roots from the old mixture.

QUICK-REFERENCE WATERING GUIDE

Water needed more often if:

The plant container is made of unglazed clay.
The plant is large but the pot it is in is small.
The plant has filled the pot with tightly packed roots.
The plant is in an active growth period.
The temperature is high.
The humidity is low.
The plant has large, thin leaves.

Water needed less often if:

The container is glazed clay or any type of plastic.
The plant is small and the pot large.
The plant has not filled the pot with roots.
The plant has just been repotted.
The plant is in a rest period.
The temperature is low.
The humidity is high.
The plant has succulent leaves or stems.

Feeding

Every plant needs various nutrients in order to grow satisfactorily. A newly bought plant should have a supply of the necessary nutrients already in the potting mixture, but these need to be replaced as they are gradually used up. That is why it becomes necessary to feed house plants.

Three chemical elements are essential for the balanced growth of all plants: nitrogen, phosphorus, and potassium. Nitrogen (in the form of nitrates) is vital for the growth of stems and leaves and for the production of energy-making chlorophyll. Phosphorus (supplied to plants as either phosphoric acid or phosphate) promotes healthy root production. Potassium (supplied as potash) is necessary for the production of flowers and fruit as well as general sturdiness. In addition to these three essentials, every plant needs much smaller quantities of a number of other minerals (known as trace elements).

The label of any fertilizer bottle or package always indicates the relative amounts of the three main nutrients, which are each abbreviated (by international agreement) as follows: N (nitrogen), P (phosphorus), and K (potassium). On some labels the relative amounts may simply be shown in a code consisting of three numbers —for instance, 6-10-6. Do not let the coding worry you. It is enough to know that the order is always the same—N-P-K. Thus, 6-10-6 will tell you that there are roughly the same amounts of nitrogen and potassium in this product, but that there is a greater amount of phosphorus.

FERTILIZER FORMULAS

A generally suitable fertilizer for house plants is one with evenly balanced proportions of the essential elements, and often with major trace elements as well. Any such product is known as a *standard* fertilizer. Various manufacturers produce somewhat different standard fertilizers. Every fertilizer recommended as generally suitable will undoubtedly serve its purpose. But the following distinctions are worth noting:

Fertilizers with a relatively high nitrogen content are especially good for leafy plants, and are useful for other types of plant, too, in the first half of the growing season when leaf production is at its peak. Formulas that include a notably large proportion of phosphorus make for slower growth, but they are good for building the root system; moreover, they are often recommended for plants just before and during the flowering period. After a plant flowers, it must build itself up toward the next flowering season, and fertilizers high in potash are good for specimens that have just finished flowering (especially permanent bulbs and flowering shrubs). High-potash fertilizers are sometimes called "tomato-type" fertilizers because they are normally given to tomatoes when the plants start to develop fruit.

Many manufacturers market fertilizers for specific purposes or groups of plants. There are preparations, for example, labeled as particularly suitable for leafy plants, flowering plants, etc. Among products worth keeping in mind for your collection are the so-called "acid reaction" (or simply "acid") fertilizers recommended for plants that do best in acid mixtures.

There are also specially formulated liquid fertilizers that are meant for spraying over foliage, which absorbs the chemical elements. Such *foliar feeding* is recommended in the *A–Z Guide* for certain plants. It has an immediate tonic effect on almost any plant that looks starved or in need of a boost. Foliar feeding is particularly useful for plants that absorb little food through their roots—many bromeliads and other epiphytes, for example. Never use foliar sprays near home furnishings, however. Take plants outside, or spray them in a bathtub.

HOW THEY ARE PACKAGED

Apart from the foliar sprays, standard and other fertilizers come in a variety of forms—such as liquids, powders. crystals, granules, and solids such as pills and "spikes." The most convenient to use are the liquids and soluble powders or crystals that are dissolved in water and applied when plants are being watered.

Always follow manufacturers' recommendations for dilution or mixing. An excessive amount of fertilizer can damage roots. It is always better to dilute the product in more than the prescribed quantity of water rather than less. Undiluted fertilizer used in a spray can damage the foliage.

Nonsoluble powder or granular fertilizers are sometimes included as an ingredient of homemade potting mixtures (see page 429). Otherwise, they are not generally used in feeding house plants. Pills and "spikes" are extremely easy to use because they are simply pushed into the mixture according to instructions on the package. Unfortunately, they tend to produce a concentration of food materials in one place, which can damage nearby roots. To overcome this, most solid fertilizers are constructed so that they release food materials slowly.

Some pill and granular products are specially designed to release their nutrients over a period of three to six months. These products, sometimes termed *slow-release* (or timed-release) fertilizers, can be of real value in repotting. A slow-release pill placed under the root ball or slow-release granules combined with fresh potting mixture will provide much-needed minerals for a long time to come.

WHEN TO FEED

Newly bought or repotted plants should not require immediate feeding. A plant in soil-based mixture may not need to be fed for three months, because the soil contains its own minerals apart from those in any added fertilizer. The fertilizer in soilless mixtures, however, is used up in six to eight weeks, and feedings should begin within two months for newly bought or repotted plants that are being grown in such mixtures. (See "Potting mixtures," page 429.)

Most plants should be fed only when in active growth. If fertilizer is applied to a plant during its rest period, it may well result in spindly growth and the production of abnormally small, pale, fragile leaves. Do not give fertilizer to a plant just because it seems sickly. Fertilizer provides food; it is not a medicine. Before feeding a plant that appears to be doing badly, consider whether the trouble can be due to overwatering, drafts, or wrong temperatures.

The feeding instructions in the *A–Z Guide* are not unalterable rules. Recommendations for individual plants, as well as for such special groups as the bromeliads, cacti, orchids, and palms, are based on the assumption that indoor gardeners want their plants to develop as rapidly as possible. If you prefer to let your plants grow more slowly reduce the frequency of feeding. As few as three or four applications of a standard fertilizer during the growing season will generally provide enough to keep a plant healthy as long as it is repotted or topdressed with fresh potting mixture at regular intervals.

Different ways to feed a plant

A liquid fertilizer that can be absorbed through the leaves often has a speedy tonic effect on unhealthy foliage.

For a long-term effect, use the blunt end of a pencil to push a slow-release nutritive pill deep into the mixture.

Spikes of fertilizer are easy to apply, but keep them as far as possible from roots, which can be damaged by a concentration of food.

Potting and repotting

A plant can stay in the same container without a change of potting mixture for quite a while if regularly fed. After a time, however, growth will slow down, and the plant will eventually become unhealthy because its roots take up more and more space while the amount of mixture steadily diminishes (literally turns to dust and disappears). That is why plants must be moved into larger pots of fresh mixture at fairly regular intervals—a procedure known as repotting, potting on, or moving on.

Annual plants grown from seed normally need several repottings between the first pot and the final flowering pot, all within a few months. Permanent house plants generally require repotting once a year until they attain a stable size. Thereafter, the intervals can be longer, or a plant can eventually remain in the same pot, with the annual addition of fresh potting mixture. This is known as topdressing (see page 428).

In the *A–Z Guide* repotting is recommended for most plants at stated intervals.

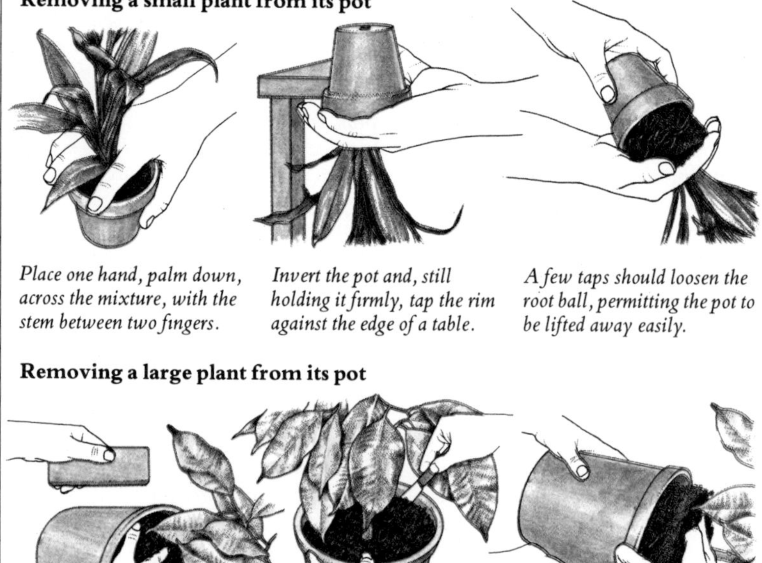

Removing a small plant from its pot

Place one hand, palm down, across the mixture, with the stem between two fingers.

Invert the pot and, still holding it firmly, tap the rim against the edge of a table.

A few taps should loosen the root ball, permitting the pot to be lifted away easily.

Removing a large plant from its pot

Lay the pot on its side, and turn it slowly, tapping the rim with a block of wood.

With the pot right way up again, run a knife blade around the inside of the rim.

A second pair of hands is a help when it comes to pulling the pot off the root ball.

HOW TO JUDGE THE NEED

To determine whether a plant needs repotting look at its roots. In some kinds—chlorophytums, for example—the fat, fleshy roots indicate that a bigger pot is required by pushing up through the surface of the potting mixture. The finer roots of most plants start to protrude from drainage holes in the pot. This is not a sure sign that repotting is necessary, however, because a few roots can often push through drainage holes even though the rest do not yet fill the pot. The only sure way to discover the state of the roots is to turn the plant out of its pot and examine them.

To remove a small or medium-size specimen from its pot, place one hand, palm downward, over the surface of the potting mixture, with the plant's strongest stem in between the fingers. In the case of small rosette plants, such as saintpaulias, place the fingers over the surface of the potting mixture but under the spreading foliage. Invert the pot, and tap its rim gently against the edge of a table, or tap the bottom of the pot with the palm of the other hand. After a few taps it should be easy to lift it off the root ball. If there is continuing resistance, slide a sharp knife all around between the root ball and the side of the pot.

This technique will not work for all plants, of course. For instance, easily damaged plants with brittle leafstalks or prickly ones such as cacti require very careful handling. Consult the appropriate entries in the *A–Z Guide* for further guidance.

In dealing with large plants, try laying the pot on its side and tapping the rim with a block of wood before running a knife blade around the inside of the rim. You may need an extra pair of hands to help pull the pot away from the root ball; and you may have to break the pot or, if it is plastic, cut it away with shears or tin snips. If there are many roots projecting from the drainage holes, break or cut through the pot to avoid damaging those roots in the turning-out process. This problem will not arise if repotting is done in good time.

When the pot has been removed, examine the roots for one of three signs that a move to a larger pot is advisable. If fresh root tips are showing all over the surface of the root ball, repot the plant. And if the roots are densely matted on the exterior of the root ball, or are forming a thick spiral at the base of the pot, a move is most probably overdue.

There are a few plants, however, that *should* be allowed to fill their pots with roots for long periods. Some fleshy-rooted plants such as clivias, for example, and certain bulbs and shrubs will flower more readily if pot-bound (the technical term for the condition). This special preference is pointed out, where applicable, in the *A–Z Guide*.

WHEN TO REPOT

The best time for repotting most plants is at the beginning of the growing season, whenever that occurs. Never move plants in a rest period. If a plant is not in active growth when potted on, its roots will not make their way quickly into the fresh potting mixture. As a result, the mixture can get waterlogged and unwholesome.

If a plant is ailing for any reason other than constricted roots (see *Plant Health*, page 452), do not repot it. A move at such a time risks inflicting an additional shock on the already weakened plant. So wait until its recovery seems assured.

HOW TO REPOT

The repotting operation is messy. If doing it indoors, work in large plastic trays, if possible, and protect nearby furniture with newspapers or sheets. Do as many plants as possible at one time, and gather them all together, along with fresh pots, drainage materials, and various suitable potting mixtures, before starting to work on the first specimen.

Give each plant a thorough watering an hour or so in advance; this will ease the task of removing the plant from its pot. Soak new unglazed pots in water for a few minutes (until air bubbles no longer rise); dry clay would absorb moisture too rapidly from the potting mixture. This is not necessary for glazed or plastic containers. Scrub all used containers with hot water and a germicidal soap or cleansing powder. Use a soft brush to remove lumps of mixture and old roots, as well as deposits of lime. Then rinse the pots in clean water and allow surface water to dry from them. If wet pots are used, the mixture tends to stick to them.

Select an appropriate new-size pot for every plant. Choose pots that are no larger than absolutely necessary because an excessive amount of new potting mixture can easily become waterlogged and "sour." When repotting from the 1½-inch size up to 4 inches, you will find an increase of ½ inch at a time just about right. With 5-inch and larger pots the availability of sizes will impose increases ranging from 1 to 1½ inches, with a final jump from a 12-inch to a 15-inch container.

To begin with, place drainage material in the bottom of the new pot. In a clay pot with a large drainage hole, a single clay-pot fragment big enough to cover the hole, placed concave side down, is adequate (unless extra drainage is recommended in the *A–Z Guide*). In plastic pots with numerous small holes, drainage material is rarely needed. If a pot is to stand in a saucer, however, cover the bottom with a shallow layer of pebbles or gravel. These must be big enough not to dribble through the drainage holes. In a clay pot the single clay-pot fragment at the bottom will serve as a floor for the pebbles. The pebbles give protection against waterlogging if water is inadvertently left in the saucer.

There should also be just enough fresh, slightly moist potting mixture in the new pot to provide a base for the root ball. The depth of this bottom layer of mixture should allow for room between the top of the root ball and the rim of the pot for watering. Leave ½ inch between root-ball surface and rim in any pot up to 5 inches in diameter; ¾ inch in a 5½- to 7½-inch pot; 1 inch in an 8- to 8½-inch pot; 1½ inches in a 9- to 12-inch pot; and 2 inches in 15-inch pots. Make sure the surface level of the root ball remains the same, and put no further mixture on top of it except to cover exposed roots.

The repotting process

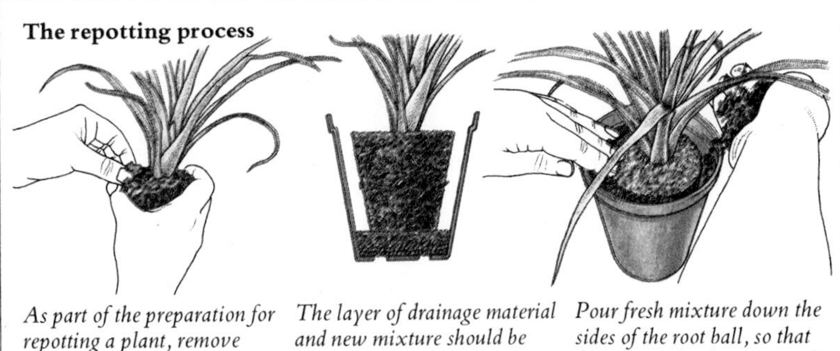

As part of the preparation for repotting a plant, remove moss from the surface of the old mixture. *The layer of drainage material and new mixture should be deep enough to keep the root ball at the correct level.* *Pour fresh mixture down the sides of the root ball, so that the plant is firmly supported in the new pot.*

The first step after turning the plant out of its present pot is to check the roots. If any are rotten or entirely dried up, cut or pull them carefully away. Look for such pests as root mealy bugs and grubs, and deal with these as suggested in *Plant Health* (page 455). Free the roots from any foreign matter—clay-pot fragments or pebbles—that may be clinging to them. Pinch off any moss growing on the upper surface of the root ball.

Next, seat the plant firmly on the bottom layer of fresh mixture, and pour more mixture around the root ball. Pack the mixture down gently with the fingers or a flat piece of wood. Except where otherwise specified in the *A–Z Guide*, the degree of firmness in packing depends mainly on the type of potting mixture. Soil-based mixtures should be packed down more firmly than other kinds. Do not overdo the pressure or the mixture will become impenetrable to water and you are liable to damage roots. To fill air pockets and to settle the mixture evenly, tap the pot on a hard surface several times as filling proceeds. Finally, water thoroughly around the edges of the pot.

With very big, bushy or prickly plants and with flat rosettes, the so-called "mold" method of repotting is perhaps easier than the traditional technique. To use the mold method, begin by removing the plant from its current pot. Cover the bottom of the new, larger container with a layer of fresh, slightly moistened potting mixture. Determine the depth of the layer by standing the old pot on top of it. The depth is right if the upper rim of the smaller pot reaches a point about half an inch below the rim of the big one; this will assure a suitable level of mixture when the new container is filled. Leaving the old pot in position within the new one, let fresh mixture trickle around the outer edges of the smaller pot. Moisten the mixture slightly and press it down with the fingers until it surrounds the contours of the old pot. When this pot has been removed there will be a firm mold in which to place the root ball, and you will have sidestepped the difficulty of trying to pour mixture into the pot past the branches or leaves of the plant.

To prepare a firm mold for the root ball, fill the space between the new pot and the present smaller one with fresh mixture, and remove the small pot.

It is often possible in the repotting process to correct the way in which the plant has been growing. For instance, if the stem is slanting, place the root ball at a slight tilt in the new pot. Be sure that the plant is firmly supported by the potting mixture.

TOPDRESSING

Although the biggest available pot size is 15 inches, there are larger containers for plants—round or square wooden tubs, for instance. The largest *convenient*-size container for a given indoor situation, however, may be only 8 or 10 inches. When the maximum convenient pot size has been reached, the easiest and most effective alternative to annual potting on is a procedure known as "topdressing."

To topdress a plant, scrape away the top inch or two of potting mixture with a small trowel or an old spoon. Remove as much of the mixture as possible without exposing major roots. Then refill the pot with fresh mixture up to the original level. Use the standard potting mixture and add either some slow-release fertilizer at the manufacturer's recommended rate (see *Feeding*, page 424) or one part of dry, rotted cow manure to every two of the mixture. The top layer of fresh, enriched mixture will provide extra food for the congested roots below. And it will also be more moisture-retentive than the mixture it replaces.

It must be understood that topdressing is only a partial solution to the problem of a plant that cannot be repotted. The plant's roots can become steadily more congested and unable to absorb water and food efficiently, and growth will gradually slow down. Even so, it is possible to keep large plants healthy for many years by topdressing them regularly at normal repotting time.

The topdressing process

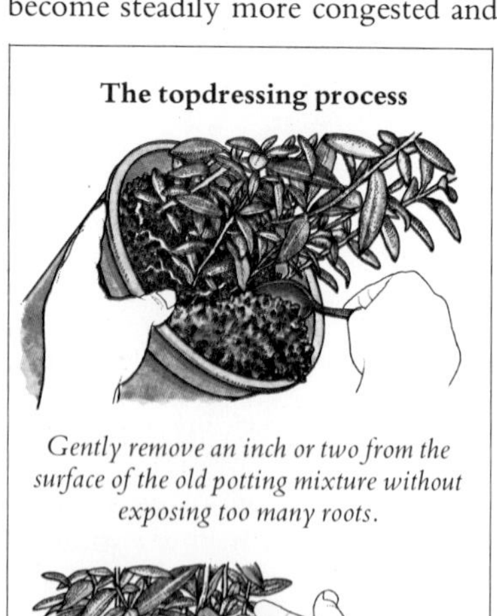

Gently remove an inch or two from the surface of the old potting mixture without exposing too many roots.

Use fresh mixture to refill the pot to its original level. Incorporate some fertilizer in the new mixture.

An alternative sometimes recommended is the actual cutting back of roots—root pruning. To prune a root ball, use a sharp knife to cut slices an inch or so thick from the sides and base. Then repot the plant in its old pot as if it were being moved on from a smaller one.

Sometimes the only feasible way to deal with pot-bound plants is to prune the roots by cutting inch-thick slices from the sides of the root ball.

However, root pruning is a drastic measure and can cause considerable shock to a plant. Give a root-pruned specimen the best possible growing conditions, to encourage it to produce new roots swiftly. Even under the best of conditions, however, it may not survive the shock. Unless root pruning seems essential—for instance, to save a beloved old plant that cannot be repotted but no longer responds to topdressing—it is probably best to propagate from the plant and then discard it afterward.

Pots and tubs

Pots are usually made of either unglazed clay or plastic. Each of these materials has advantages as well as one or two drawbacks.

Clay pots offer far more protection from waterlogging, because excess water is lost by evaporation through the sides. For the same reason, potting mixture needs to be watered more often in clay than in plastic. The surface of clay pots sometimes develops an unsightly crust, because clay readily absorbs mineral salts from the soil and water. (To remove the crust wash empty pots in bleach, and rinse them in diluted vinegar.) The chief advantage of a clay pot is its weight, which completely counterbalances the weight of a big plant.

Plastic pots are less likely to break than clay, although some are brittle and should not be picked up by the rim. They do not lose water through their sides, they are easier than clay to keep clean and are conveniently lightweight. But they are not heavy enough to counterbalance the weight of large plants. They are especially useful for self-watering with capillary felt mats (see page 423), which do not work with clay pots. Styrofoam pots have recently become popular, chiefly because, as an insulating material, styrofoam keeps the potting mixture relatively warm.

From the standpoint of appearance, plastic pots have the advantage of being available in different colors. Unglazed clay is on the whole functional, and many gardeners prefer its appearance. Glazed clay pots are also ornamental and they have the added advantage of not losing water through the sides.

POT SHAPE

Pots are normally round, but square pots are also available. Choice of shape is purely a matter of taste.

A typical pot is about as deep as it is wide. If clay, it will usually have only one large, central, bottom hole, but a very big clay pot may also have three side holes. Plastic pots generally have a number of small holes near the outer edge of the bottom.

Half-pots (sometimes called bulb pans or azalea pots), are much less deep than broad. These are useful for propagation purposes (see page 441). They also make suitable containers for mature plants with shallow roots, especially for such low-growing, spreading plants as fittonias. And they are often used for massed displays of thin-stemmed plants like setcreaseas, tradescantias, and zebrinas.

POT SIZE

Most types of pot are available in sizes ranging from a diameter of $1\frac{1}{2}$ inches to a diameter of 15 inches. It is usually possible to find all sizes at $\frac{1}{2}$-inch step-ups throughout the range from $1\frac{1}{2}$ to 9 inches. In pots larger than 9 inches the step-up is likely to be more.

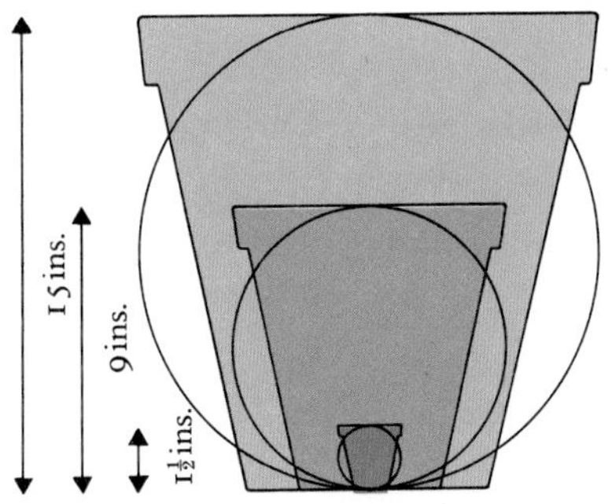

All pots, from the smallest at 1½ inches to the largest at 15 inches, are alike in that the depth equals the diameter at the rim.

Ordinary unglazed clay or plastic pots do not normally come in an 11-inch size, for instance, and you are unlikely to find anything between the 12- and 15-inch sizes.

Half-pots usually can be obtained in sizes from 3½ to 8 inches.

TUBS

Plants that have grown too big for ordinary pots are sometimes potted in wooden or plastic tubs. These are not made in regular sizes, and they are often simply containers adapted to indoor gardening needs. Plastic tubs made expressly for holding plants are stouter and less brittle than ordinary plastic pots, and they have large drainage holes. Wooden tubs that are made by cutting old barrels in half are likely to lack drainage holes. Use a drill with a minimum ½-inch bit to bore several drainage holes in the bottom of any such tub.

Potting mixtures

Garden centers carry a wide range of prepared potting mixtures. Those that contain soil are known as *soil-based* mixtures; those in which peat moss is substituted for soil are known as *peat-based* (or soilless) mixtures. The recommended type for each kind of house plant is indicated in the *A–Z Guide*, along with suggested modifications of the basic potting mixture wherever this is advisable. There are many slightly differing formulas for each of the two types. Some are designed for the individual requirements of particular plants (for instance, African violet mix) or situations (a terrarium mix).

Highly specialized plants such as orchids seldom thrive unless potted in precisely the right mixture. Most plants are adaptable, however, and do well as long as they get adequate amounts of fertilizer. Perhaps the major consideration for most plants is the acidity or alkalinity of the mixture. Most house plants like an acid mixture and react badly to an excess of alkaline. (For a discussion of acidity and alkalinity as they affect specific plants see page 430.)

It would be both simple and cheap to dig up some earth somewhere and put it in a pot if you were certain of getting what you wanted. Outdoor soil varies enormously in quality and texture, however, and is almost certain to contain all sorts of pests, disease organisms, and weed seeds. You are far more likely to have success with house plants if you use a ready-made potting mixture (in which the soil, if any, has been sterilized) or make up your own from a careful selection of the ingredients described below.

SOIL VS. PEAT MOSS

The chief advantage of a soilless, peat-based mixture is that it is clean, lightweight, and easy to handle. The composition of the peat moss used in ready-made mixtures is also standardized to a dependable degree. The chief disadvantage of peat-based mixture is that it lacks built-in nutrients. These are normally added to any supply of fresh peat-based mixture, but they are soon used up. Regular feeding is therefore essential for plants potted in soilless mixture.

Soil-based mixtures are less pleasant to handle and impossible to standardize, because the composition of soil is relatively unpredictable. The heaviness of such mixtures is an advantage when it comes to potting up large, top-heavy plants. The main advantage of soil, however, is that, even after it has been sterilized, it contains microorganisms that break down organic matter into essential minerals, thus eliminating the need for frequent artificial feeding.

DO-IT-YOURSELF MIXTURES

For people who prefer to make their own mixtures there are three basic recipes. All three combine the dual virtues of being able to hold water while at the same time providing good drainage. One or another of the recipes will be suitable for nearly every kind of house plant. Where modifications are advisable, instructions appear in the *A–Z Guide* (as do the different formulas recommended for a few special groups: bromeliads, cacti and other succulents, ferns, gesneriads, and orchids). A brief description of each kind of material used in formulating all types of potting mixture follows the three recipes.

Soil-based mixture:

1 part sterilized fibrous soil
1 part medium-grade peat moss, ground tree bark, or leaf mold
1 part coarse sand or fine perlite

Add 1 part dehydrated cow manure, if available. Otherwise, add a balanced granular or powdered fertilizer (according to instructions on the package).

Peat-based mixture:

1 part coarse peat moss
1 part medium-grade vermiculite
1 part coarse sand or medium-grade perlite

Add dolomite limestone powder at 2 tablespoonfuls to 2 quarts of mixture, and follow fertilizer instructions for soil-based mixture.

High-humus peat-based mixture:
This mixture is for plants such as ferns and other foliage types whose natural habitat is the loose organic litter on jungle floors.

3 parts coarse peat moss
3 parts leaf mold
2 parts coarse sand or medium-grade perlite

Add 1 cup of charcoal granules to 2 quarts of the mixture, and follow the same fertilizer instructions as for soil-based mixture.

ORGANIC INGREDIENTS

Leaf mold This is made of decayed leaves, rich in organic matter. Like soil, leaf mold has bacterial activity in it, and it therefore contains some nutrients. Beech and oak leaf molds are excellent; coniferous leaf molds are useful in cases where some rough texture is desirable.

Manure The only animal manure recommended for house plants is cow manure, generally available in dehydrated form. (It should not be used until it has dried out.) Nutrient-rich cow manure improves any mixture.

Peat moss Although composed of the remains of plants that have partly decayed under water in bogs or marshes, peat moss is almost entirely lacking in nutrient value. It holds water and fertilizer well and improves any unsatisfactory soil structure. In buying peat moss for house plants, choose the coarser, light brown type rather than the finely milled dark brown or black type.

Soil The main components of soil are sand, clay, and organic matter (the remains of plants and animals). There are also teeming masses of bacteria, fungi, and other microorganisms, as well as larger living creatures, in any quantity of soil. The best soil for house plants has the three main ingredients in roughly equal proportions, with the organic matter thoroughly decayed but still fibrous. Soils that are too sandy or that contain too much clay are unsatisfactory unless improved by the addition of peat moss (and, in the case of heavy clay, coarse sand, vermiculite, or perlite).

To destroy harmful living organisms, soil for potting mixtures must be sterilized. It can usually be bought already sterilized, but many indoor gardeners prefer to sterilize their own. This is not hard to do. Simply place a quantity of moist—not sodden—soil in a baking tin, cover it, and bake it for exactly one hour in a 180°F oven. Do not exceed that temperature. This will destroy weed seeds, soil pests, and disease organisms without simultaneously killing useful bacteria.

Soils vary by degrees between extremely acid and extremely alkaline (see *Acidity and alkalinity*). Alkaline soils (chalky soils, for instance) should not be used in potting mixtures.

Sphagnum moss This is a type of bog moss mainly used in mixtures for such plants as orchids, which need a very open, moisture-retaining material. Sphagnum moss has almost no nutrient value. A layer of it is often placed at the bottom of pots holding jungle-dwelling, and moisture-loving specimens. Milled sphagnum, in which the strands are reduced to small fragments, is ideal as the top layer of a seed-sowing mixture for very small seeds (see page 442).

Sphagnum peat moss This is peat moss derived from the decay of sphagnum moss. It is widely available and often used instead of ordinary peat moss.

Tree bark Various kinds of ground bark are used in the same way as peat moss. For routine potting mixtures the finely ground grades are best; the coarser grades are often used in mixtures for orchids and bromeliads.

INORGANIC INGREDIENTS

Charcoal By absorbing excess mineral salts and products of decay, charcoal helps keep potting mixtures "sweet." It is most often used, however, in situations where there is no drainage (for example, in bottle gardens or bowls of bulbs), where an excess of water might cause decay of the roots. Large pieces can also be placed at the bottom of pots, and smaller fragments can be mixed with the potting mixture to help maintain air space in the root area.

Dolomite limestone powder (also known as magnesium limestone). The carbonate in dolomite limestone reduces the acidity of a potting mixture, and so the powdered stone may be added for just this purpose. In addition, the magnesium content helps to counteract magnesium deficiency which can cause yellowing leaves in plants grown under acid conditions. It should be used, however, only in conjunction with pH tests (see *Acidity and alkalinity*). Using too much can make the mixture excessively alkaline and completely unsuitable for the house plant concerned.

Eggshells Crushed eggshells contain calcium carbonate, which is alkaline, and they are sometimes added to peat-based mixtures in order to reduce the acidity. Crushed eggshells also assist drainage.

Limestone chips These have much the same effect, and are used for the same purpose, as eggshells. They come in various sizes. The best size for opening up a potting mixture is in the region of a quarter-inch.

Perlite This is a sterile volcanic rock that has been ground fine, medium, or coarse. It helps give an open texture to the potting mixture, and it also absorbs water and minerals.

Sand Coarse sand is a valuable addition for opening up potting mixtures, in particular those that contain heavy soil. The most suitable sand is lime-free river sand. It must be coarse-grained and rough to the touch. Do not use seashore sand, which is likely to contain harmful salts, unless it is specified as "washed."

Vermiculite Mica expanded under heat forms flakes known as vermiculite, which can absorb and retain exceptionally large amounts of water and nutrients. Vermiculite is a useful material for rooting mixtures and is occasionally used in potting mixtures.

Acidity and alkalinity

Alkaline soils contain a quantity of lime, chalk, or related substances. Acid soils contain little or none of these. Most house plants prefer more or less acid conditions and will suffer if potted in an alkaline potting mixture. The typical symptom of an acid-loving plant subjected to too much alkalinity is yellowing of the leaves, technically known as chlorosis (see *Plant Health*, page 458).

The acidity or alkalinity of soil, water, or fertilizer is measured on what is termed the pH scale. The symbol pH stands for hydrogen ion concentration. The pH scale ranges from 0 to 14, with the number 7 standing for a neutral acid/alkaline balance; increasing acidity is indicated by pH numbers running *down* from 7 to 0, and increasing alkalinity is indicated by numbers running *up* from 7 to 14. Plants can live only in the range between pH 4 and pH 8.

The pH of soil varies according to its origin. If you intend to use ordinary garden soil in your potting mixture, be sure to test its pH first. This is important because certain types of plant (orchids and rhododendrons, for example) must have an acid mixture, while a few others (mainly succulents and pelargoniums) do well in a mildly alkaline mixture. Such common potting-mixture materials as peat moss, leaf mold, and tree bark are all acid in reaction. In spite of their acidity, however, some peat-based mixtures are unsuitable for plants that do best at the lower levels of the pH scale. This is because of the type of fertilizer added. So do not assume that the absence of soil or the presence of peat in a mixture guarantees its acidity. The pH level of most ready-made mixtures is stated on the package.

For a rough check of the acidity level of a substance, make a solution of the substance and dip litmus paper in it. The paper will turn red if the substance is primarily acid in reaction, blue if alkaline. More sensitive papers giving a range of colors to be read against a scale are also available, primarily at stores that sell supplies for small aquariums. For precise measurements of soils and potting mixtures, however, use one of the soil testing kits specifically for this purpose. Such kits are not expensive and can be bought in any garden center.

Pruning

In general, house plants need little pruning of the kind required for such outdoor plants as rose bushes and fruit trees. Still, house plants can sometimes become too big or unbalanced in growth. Pruning can either prevent or remedy such conditions. In addition, pruning stimulates new shoots to emerge from the dormant growth buds closest to the point of cut. (These are buds that produce leaf-carrying stems, not flower buds.) There are, basically, two ways to prune house plants: pinching and cutting back.

PINCHING

To "pinch" or "pinch out" part of a stem is to remove its small growing tip—a portion usually only $\frac{1}{4}$–$\frac{1}{2}$ inch long. The break is normally made just above a node, which is the point of growth at which a leaf or pair of leaves emerges. If nodes are close together, it may be necessary to remove the tip down to the second node.

To do this small-scale pruning—often known as "stopping" or "nipping," as well as "pinching"—pinch the growth between the thumb and a

To encourage branching, prune on a small scale by pinching out the growing tip of a stem just above a node.

finger or use scissors or a razor blade, particularly with slightly tough or woody growing tips.

Pinching is often advisable once newly rooted cuttings are growing well. With mature plants it is useful for producing dense, bushy growth on such fast-growing, soft-stemmed plants as beloperones, coleuses, and tradescantias, which tend to grow long, lanky stems. Whenever a growing tip is pinched out, one or two dormant growth buds lower down the stem are likely to start into growth. And the sideshoots thus produced can be pinched out later on to thicken the growth even further.

CUTTING BACK

Thicker and harder stems than those at the growing point are "cut back" with a sharp knife or, especially in woody plants, with a pair of pruning shears. Shears that work like scissors are preferable to the anvil type because they are less likely to crush the stem. Crushing can cause decay, and the rot can spread swiftly.

To cut a stem back very drastically make the cut directly above a growth bud. Any such cut will normally heal fast, whereas cuts midway between nodes cause unsightly dieback to the lower node, or even further decay. It is also important to make the cut straight across the stem, or else on a slope from a point above the growth bud down to a point opposite the bud; never cut down *toward* the bud, because you are likely to damage it.

TIMING

Begin to pinch out the growing tips on fast-growing plants as soon as the active growth period begins and continue the process throughout the growth period. This, as well as all other kinds of light pruning to reduce overcrowding of a shrub or climber, can be done whenever advisable.

Use pruning shears to prune an oversize or woody plant by cutting back to just above a node as far down the stem as desired.

Major pruning operations, involving drastic cutting back of main stems or sideshoots, are best done only at the beginning of the active growth season. At other times the dormant buds stimulated by pruning are less likely to grow effectively.

SPECIAL PRUNING NOTES

At the end of a season's growth, soft-stemmed bushy plants can have a number of over-long stems despite regular pinching. Cut back such stems almost to their base, leaving a framework of short growth from which new stems will eventually emerge. Do the same sort of drastic pruning on such flowering or fruiting plants as pelargoniums and solanums.

All shrubs will also benefit from the removal of crowded or crossing stems. If the center of a plant is congested, there is increased risk of mildew and other fungus disease attack. Cut away dead or unhealthy stems.

Cut back to the general level of other growths the long stems of woody shrubs—the citrus and the myrtus, for example—in order to keep the plants shapely. But prune most woody shrubs only to encourage new, compact growth. Plants like hibiscuses, oleanders and fuchsias will sprout if quite old growth is cut back. If their old stems have become leafless, pruning of this type will encourage new stems to grow from near the base of the plants.

When pruning a plant to reduce its height or spread, however, you may be frustrated just *because* pruning encourages new growth. If the top of a rubber plant is nearly touching the ceiling, you will achieve little by cutting back the top few inches; new sideshoots will soon be at ceiling height again. If a plant has become inconveniently tall and you want to retain it, cut it back by several feet. A few years will elapse before the problem again arises.

Some indoor climbers, such as bougainvilleas and passifloras, are rampant growers and may need considerable cutting back after only a single season. Prune both side growths and main stems, if it seems necessary. It is often wise to cut back all side growths flush with main stems, and to reduce mainstem lengths as well. If you want a climber to branch, encourage it to do so by cutting back several inches of the main stem. If you prefer it to have only one stem, cut away all weak side growths as soon as they appear.

SPECIAL CASES

If an all-green shoot appears on a variegated-leaved plant, cut it right out at the point of origin. Green shoots grow more strongly than variegated ones and will soon swamp the latter if allowed to persevere.

Always pinch or cut off faded flowers from a flowering plant (unless, of course, you want to collect seed). This not only keeps the plant looking attractive, but also prevents its energy from being wasted on seed formation.

Support and training

Non-climbing foliage plants seldom need support. The few that do are those with long, slender stems that droop if not held up—dizygothecas and fatshederas, for instance. Support is more often needed by plants with large flower heads on thin stems, such as cinerarias and calceolarias, or such brittle-stemmed plants as an impatiens when it becomes unwieldy.

The simplest method of supporting such specimens is to tie the stems to a thin stake or split piece of bamboo inserted in the center of the potting mixture. Use garden twine, raffia, macramé cord, plant rings, or wire-and-paper twisters, and attach the stems loosely to the stake. When using twine or cord, provide a buffer against bruises by making a figure-8 loop. If only a few stems need support, begin by tying a long piece of string to the stake, then proceed to loop it around each stem before again attaching it firmly to the stake.

For better support use two or even three stakes spaced equally around the edges of the pot. Be sure to push the stakes well down into the mixture, and pass the twine around them well below the level of the flower heads. For the sake of neatness tie the twine to one stake, loop it gently around the stems and other stakes, and attach the tail end back to the first stake again. Use square knots, and cut off the ends of the twine neatly.

The degree of tautness of the twine between stakes depends on the bushiness of the plant. Never tie stems in such a way as to bunch them together unnaturally or to jam flower heads up against one another.

CLIMBING PLANTS

When they are young, many climbing plants—ivies, for example—are quite bushy. But as they put forth long shoots they need some sort of support to climb up (unless, as is not always possible, they are allowed to trail). For a while, at least, most such climbers can be supported by means of the two- or three-stake system that has been described above.

The climbing growth can be spiraled around the different stakes in any one of several patterns.

Supporting unwieldy stems

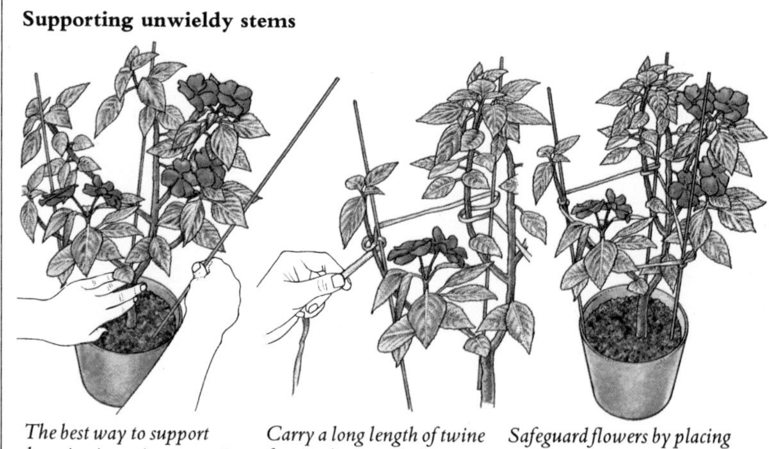

The best way to support drooping impatiens stems is to insert several thin stakes into the potting mixture.

Carry a long length of twine from stake to stake, looping it in figure-8s around all stems and stakes progressively.

Safeguard flowers by placing the twine well below flower level. Knot the twine to one of the stakes to secure the structure.

There are, however, more attractive methods of support. Wire frames, found in almost any garden shop, come in a variety of shapes: trellises, hoops, coils, globes, pyramids and obelisks. All of these are equipped with feet so that they can be pushed into the potting mixture at any appropriate place.

Bamboo and rattan are useful for forming your own shapes. Bamboo is strong but not very pliable and is therefore best used for straight shapes. Rattan can be steamed and bent into any sort of rounded form. For suggestions for ornamental supports from these materials, see opposite page.

In every case illustrated here, a number of different pieces of wood must be joined. The easiest way to do this to to tie the sticks together with wire or nylon thread or with wire-and-paper twisters. If done carefully, this may work well, but a single loose connection can result in the shifting—or even the collapse—of the whole structure. A more efficient method of securing the junctions is to drill a small hole in each stick at every point where it is to touch another stick; then simply pass wire through the holes, and twist it tight.

Various patterns can be woven around ordinary stakes. This cissus (left) is trained into an open rectangle; the philodendron (right) is decoratively twined across parallel supports.

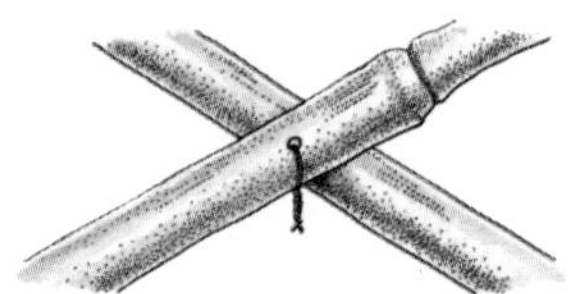

To join two stakes securely, drill a hole through them at the joining point, thread the hole with wire, and twist the wire until the joint is firm.

The size and strength of supports must be increased for large climbers in big containers. For example, a mature monstera in a 12- or 15-inch pot or tub will need long main supports of bamboo poles or else inch-square wood stakes.

EXTERNAL SUPPORTS

If a support designed to fit inside the pot becomes inadequate, it will become necessary to provide external support for the plant. This can mean making the plant a virtually permanent fixture in a given position, although there is a way to overcome the problem. Build a large trellis and fasten it to a small, movable wooden platform, instead of fastening it to the wall. Stand the pot on the platform, and its weight will help keep the trellis firmly upright.

Ornamental supports

These nine ornamental supports suggest only a few of the many possible support shapes for climbing plants. With ingenuity and strong wire or twine, the indoor gardener can combine tough bamboo and flexible rattan into any number of striking geometrical patterns.

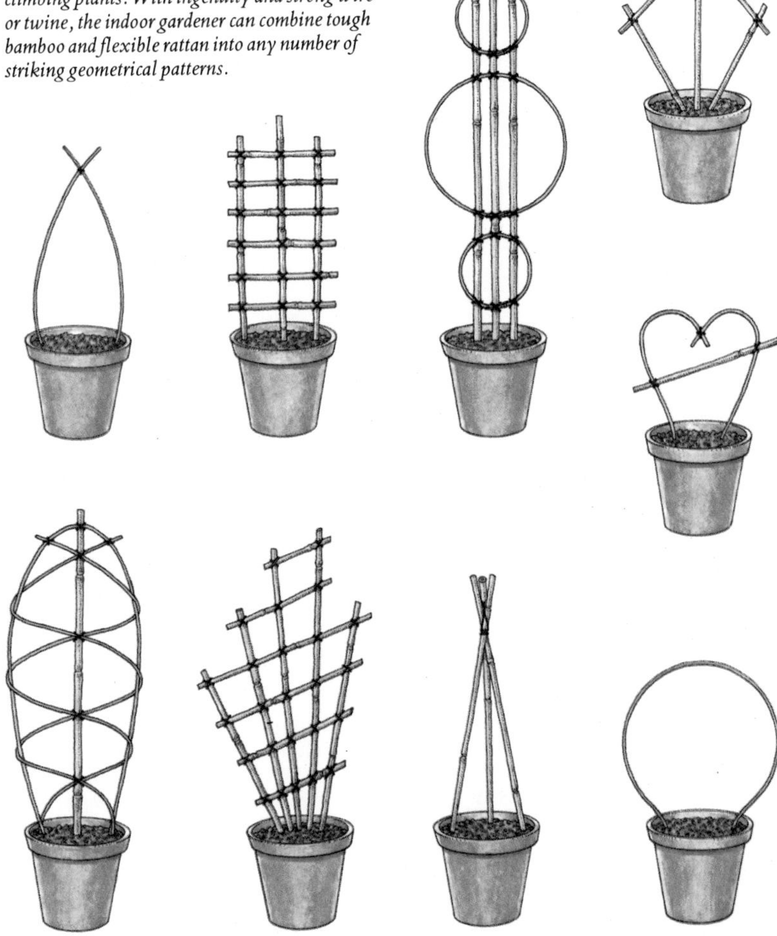

If the idea of a big, climbing plant in a fixed position does not disturb you, try growing one up a floor-to-ceiling wooden pole. The pole should be slightly shorter than full floor-to-ceiling height with flat squares of wood jammed in at top and bottom to keep the pole in position without damaging the ceiling or floor. Nails or screw eyes driven into the pole at regular intervals will provide convenient tying-up points.

Alternatively, a climbing plant can be trained right up a wall or around a window frame. This type of display requires one or more runs of wire or strong nylon cord strung between nails or screw eyes. Wire or cord stretched from floor to ceiling can also support the climbing growth of plants used as room dividers (see page 46). The bottom of the cord can be tied to hooks or eyes screwed into the floor or a wooden plant container, and the top tied to similar hooks or eyes in the ceiling. (The ceiling screw must either penetrate a wood joist or else must be adequately supported by some such device as an expanding toggle.)

If space permits, trellises can be fitted onto walls or around windows. Traditionally, trellises are wooden latticework, but modern ones are frequently made of metal or plastic strips or of nylon mesh, and they come in many different sizes. In order to protect walls, indoor trellises are usually affixed to wooden battens that are at least an inch thick.

TYING CLIMBERS

A climbing plant should be secured to its support in the same way as any other plant that requires staking (see above). Use loose figure-8 loops; if tied too tightly, a stem can become kinked or constricted, and this can kill the part above the knot. Do not wait too long before tying plant growth into place. It can rapidly become unmanageable, and difficult to bend. Even plants that grip the supports naturally are best encouraged with the aid of occasional ties.

The climbers that are perhaps least in need of human assistance indoors are those that twine (such as clerodendrums, dipladenias, and most hoyas) and those with particularly tenacious tendrils (cissuses and passifloras, for instance). Those that are most in need of tying up are the climbers that really ought to be called "scramblers": Such shrubs as bougainvilleas, jasminums, and plumbagos, which scramble up through the surrounding vegetation in their natural habitats. Unless they are systematically tied to their supports, these plants rapidly become a jumble of stems.

Some plants—notably the hederas, the climbing philodendrons, and the syngoniums—produce aerial roots, which grip supportive objects like tree trunks in the wild. Because these roots will not readily grip smooth or dry surfaces, this kind of plant also requires tying up. This becomes less necessary, however, if the plants are adequately supported by moss poles, as long as these are kept constantly moist (see page 44).

A few plants that are naturally trailers, not climbers, look attractive when trained up such supports as small trellises or wire hoops. Included in this group are the setcreaseas, tradescantias, and zebrinas.

Here a large jasmine climbing up a trellis stands on a movable base. To keep the growth under control most shoots should be tied to the support as soon as practicable.

Propagation

There are many reasons for propagating house plants. Even the most long-lived plant can outgrow its position or become in some respect less attractive, so that it only makes good sense to start again with a young specimen. The propagation process itself is so fascinating, though, that many amateur indoor growers spend time increasing certain house plants mainly for their own pleasure.

Two types of propagation are possible. The first, known as vegetative propagation, involves the use of some such part of a plant as an offset, stem, or leaf, or it may simply involve the division of a clump. Although this first method is in some cases a natural way for plants to propagate themselves, most vegetative methods have been devised, and are carried out, by man. Nature's main method of increasing plants is, of course, by means of the seeds that result from the sexual process of pollination.

Most house plants can be propagated by this second method. There is no other way, in fact, to increase annual plants grown for their short season of flowers. Even with permanent house plants, raising them from seed can be an engrossing and inexpensive source of pleasure and pride. But because it is often difficult to make seeds germinate, and because bringing a seedling to maturity can be an exceedingly slow process, the vegetative method is much more common among amateur growers of houseplants.

Summary of propagation methods

VEGETATIVE PROPAGATION

Plantlets A few species have a natural ability to increase their numbers by producing miniature replicas of themselves on leaves or stems, and indoor gardeners can use these little plants for propagation. In some

species the plantlets are produced complete with roots, and these will develop readily

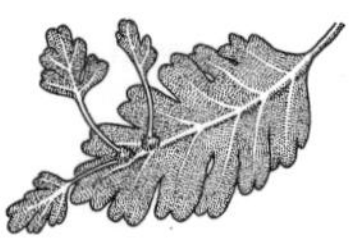

when potted up. More often, however, the plantlets are rootless. In such cases they need

more careful treatment in order to develop after separation from the parent.

Offsets The easiest way to propagate many species is from offsets, which are small replicas of the parent plant that spring directly from the main stem. If carefully cut away and potted up after reaching a certain size,

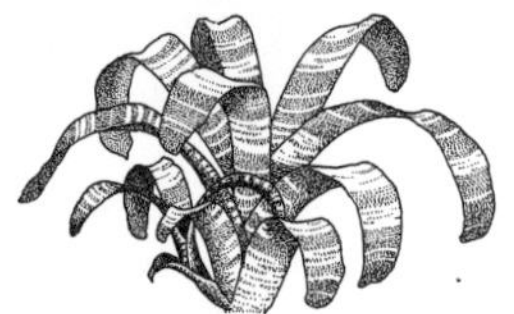

most offsets will rapidly grow into mature plants. This method of propagation is

especially appropriate for bromeliads, a number of cacti, and bulbous plants.

Division Plants that grow in clumps are generally propagated by being divided into two or more smaller clumps. It is often easy to pull a clump apart, but sometimes it is necessary to use a sharp knife to make the separation. For successful propagation each segment of a divided clump should carry a cluster of leaves

and should have well-formed roots. Some rosette-forming plants produce distinct clumps

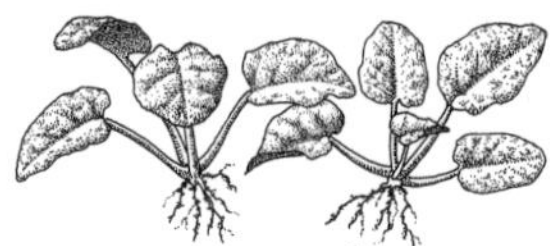

of new rosettes, which can be separated from one another by careful pulling.

Stem cuttings A common way to increase plants is by rooting pieces of stem, often taken at the tip. A tip cutting should ordinarily be trimmed a

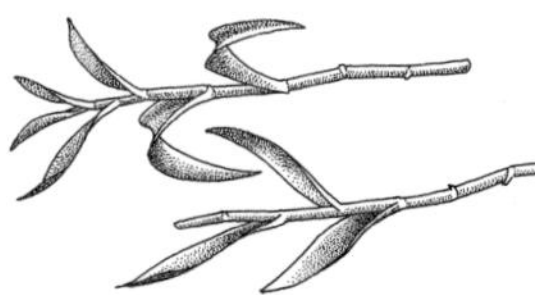

few inches below a growing point. In many woody plants the side growths are most

appropriate for propagation if the growth is pulled off along with a heel of older tissue from

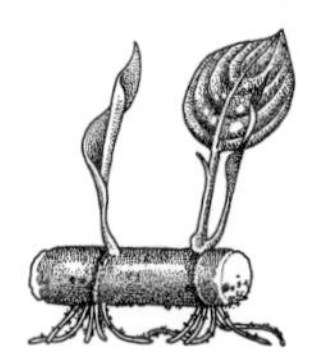

the main stem. Thick, old stems can often be cut into several short lengths, and pieces with two or more nodes can be rooted fairly easily.

Leaf cuttings It is possible to root leaves of some plants by inserting the leafstalk or base of the leaf into rooting mixture; new plants will develop from the roots. In a few cases the leaf can be cut into segments, each

of which will produce a young plant, often from a vein.

Layering In this method roots are encouraged to develop on stems still attached to the parent. The stem is pinned down

into contact with rooting mixture and severed from the parent after roots have formed.

Air layering For upright plants that do not root readily from cuttings, aboveground rooting can be encouraged by covering a carefully scraped

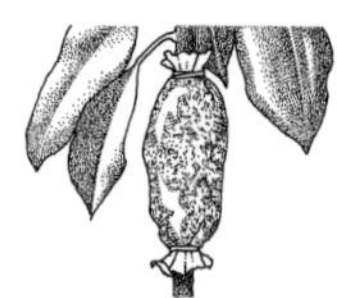

stem with damp sphagnum moss. The rooted top of the plant is cut away and potted up.

PROPAGATION FROM SEED

Large numbers of new plants can be raised from seed, and this is the only way to propagate annuals. A major drawback to raising perennial

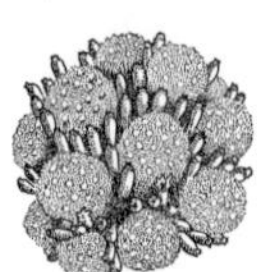

foliage plants from seed is that it can take years to bring most such plants to maturity.

Vegetative propagation

Plants may be propagated vegetatively by means of plantlets or offsets, by division of clumps, from stem or leaf cuttings, or by either of two special techniques known as layering and air layering. For some plants more than one of these methods may be feasible (as recommended where appropriate in the *A–Z Guide*).

PLANTLETS

A few house plants—for instance, some aspleniums, chlorophytums, and tolmieas—produce ready-made propagating material in the form of little replicas of themselves growing on mature leaves, at the ends of flower stems, or as miniature bulbs. In some cases these plantlets can be detached and planted individually; in others they need to be pinned down into rooting mixture while still attached to the parent (a method similar to layering, which is described below, page 439). Since so few plants produce plantlets, and since those that do are dealt with in different ways, full details are given for appropriate entries in the *A–Z Guide*.

OFFSETS

Offsets are side-growths that are identical in form to the parent plant. They may spring directly from the main stem, be produced (as in many succulents) at the end of short secondary stems, or be joined to the parent at the base, as in the case of bulbs. (Propagation of bulbs is discussed fully in *BULBS, CORMS, and TUBERS*. See *A–Z Guide*, page 111.) Sometimes the offsets have rootlets or roots already formed on them.

Offsets should not be used for propagation until they have grown to a reasonable size. Since "reasonable" size varies considerably, it is indicated where necessary in the entries for individual plants. When an offset is big enough, it may be severed from the parent. Use a sharp knife or razor blade, and cut as close as possible to the main stem. Push the base of the offset into a rooting mixture (see page 444) until it sits securely; if top-heavy, it may need to be held up by a couple of sticks. Make sure that the mixture is slightly moist, not sodden. Too much moisture can cause rotting.

Keep the offset warm; 65°–75°F will usually be satisfactory. And give it medium light, never direct sunlight, until adequate roots have formed. It is not always necessary to insert the offset in a propagating case or plastic bag (see page 443), but this may be done to speed rooting, if desired. As soon as adequate roots have formed, the new plant can be moved into the recommended potting mixture for mature plants of its species and treated in the same way as an adult specimen.

The chief producers of offsets (apart from bulbs) belong to three rather special groups. For additional points regarding propagation by offsets in these groups, see *BROMELIADS, CACTI* and *SUCCULENTS* which appear in the *A–Z Guide*.

Types of plantlet

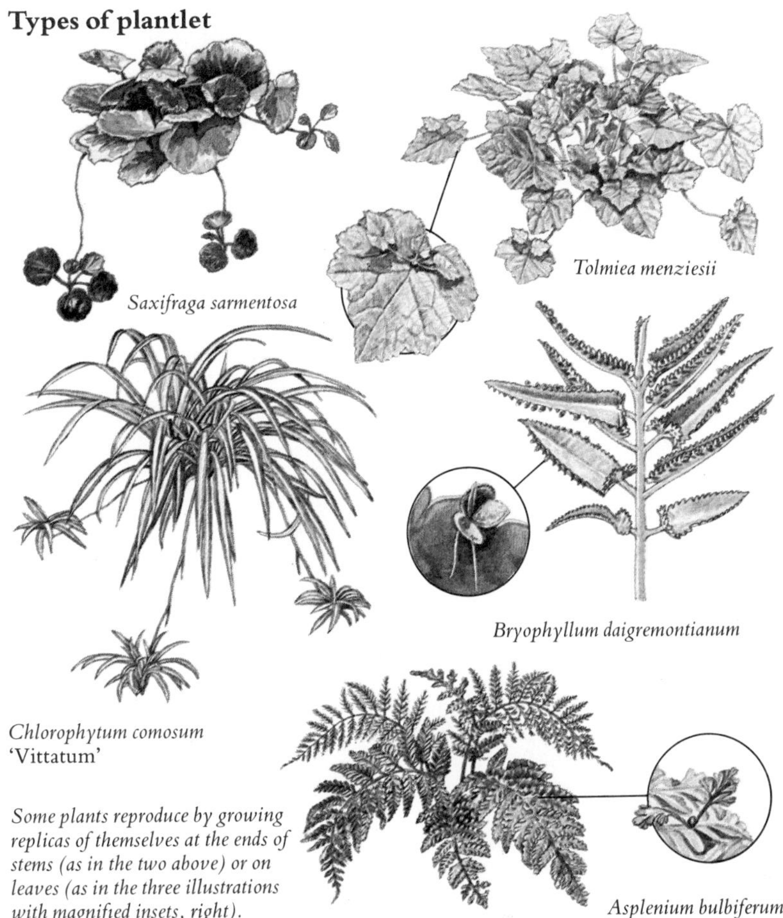

Some plants reproduce by growing replicas of themselves at the ends of stems (as in the two above) or on leaves (as in the three illustrations with magnified insets, right).

Taking a bromeliad offset

Separation of the leaves of this neoregelia discloses an offset for propagation.

After removing the plant from its pot, sever the offset as close as possible to the main stem.

Insert the detached offset into rooting mixture at the same depth as it was before.

DIVISION

The obvious way to increase plants that grow in clumps is to divide them into two or more smaller clumps. This is easy to do with plants that have erect, separate stems or rosettes. Take the plant out of its pot, find a point where separation seems possible, and gradually, pull the clump gently apart. It is sometimes necessary to shake or even to wash off much of the potting mixture, so that interlocked roots can be more readily disentangled. Try to avoid doing this, however, for it may well damage fine root hairs, making the divided clump harder to restore to normal growth.

It may be impossible to pull apart certain clumps by hand. For plants, such as ferns, that make tight clumps with dense root systems, or for those whose root sections form strong underground links (by means of rhizomes, for example), a knife may be required. Try to use the knife only to start with, however. If the division can be completed by pulling with the hands, the roots and stems are less likely to be damaged. Sometimes, though, the only way to divide a very large and tough old clump is by means of two hand forks. If there seems to be no alternative, insert the forks into the clump close together and back to back, and lever the sections apart. But remember that this clumsy method will probably injure at least some part of the plant.

Always plant a divided portion of a clump in a pot a little larger than the root-spread. If the root ball has lost much of its original potting mixture, take extra care not to hurt the naked roots during the repotting process.

Dividing a saintpaulia

The soft clumps of a saintpaulia with several rosettes make it suitable for pulling apart by hand.

One plant has now become two. Since both have roots they can be treated as mature as soon as they are potted.

Put only enough mixture in the pot to meet the lowest roots. Then hold the small clump in one hand at the proper level and trickle potting mixture between and around the roots with the other. To prevent air pockets, settle the mixture by tapping the pot gently on a hard surface before topping up as required. Soil-based potting mixtures should be pressed down firmly around the newly divided clump. Peat-based mixtures do not need to be packed tight in this manner.

Newly potted divisions seldom require any special after-treatment. If wilting does occur, place the plant in a propagating case or cover it with a plastic bag to improve the humidity (see page 443).

Do not try to divide either woody plants or palms, even if they form clumps by producing many stems. Such plants are unlikely to survive the treatment. On the other hand, division is the customary propagation method for orchids (see *ORCHIDS* for a discussion of their requirements).

Dividing a stromanthe

It generally needs a knife to slice right through the tough rhizome of a stromanthe.

Each clump should have some roots and leaves attached to a piece of the parent rhizome.

Leave the cutting in a small pot of rooting mixture until new roots have developed.

STEM CUTTINGS

The standard way to propagate a wide range of house plants is by rooting pieces of stem. Not all stemmed plants can be increased in this fashion. Although palms often have stems, for instance, their construction is such that the stems cannot be used for cuttings. But most soft-stemmed plants root readily from stem cuttings at any time of year, given suitable indoor conditions. Cuttings of woody plants are more difficult to root and often have to be taken at a specific season if successful rooting is to occur. Usually the best time to take stem cuttings is spring or early summer, at which time the parent plant is just beginning its annual growth period.

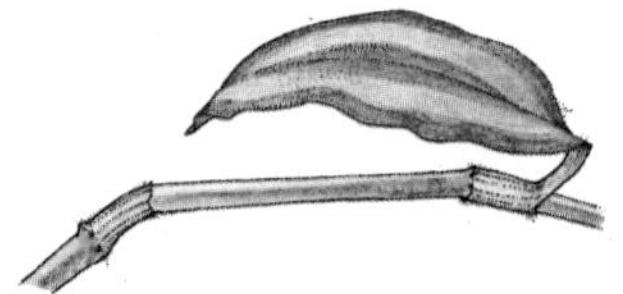

A node is the point where a leaf joins (or joined) the stem. The nodes on a tradescantia are easily visible.

The typical piece of stem used for propagation is a so-called "tip" cutting—one taken from the growing-tip end of the stem. The best length for such a cutting depends on the type of plant, but length is in part dictated by the desirability of cutting below a node. This is the point from which a leaf grows or grew. The node is frequently marked by a slightly raised ring of tissue, often along with a noticeable sheath that forms at the base of the leaf. On woody plants, where the ring and sheath may not be visible, the node can usually be identified by a thickening of the stem and the presence of a leaf scar and a bud if the leaf has fallen. A tip cutting should contain at least three nodes between the tip and the cut end. The best tip cuttings come from sturdy plants with stems whose nodes are relatively close together.

Taking a tip cutting from *Philodendron scandens*

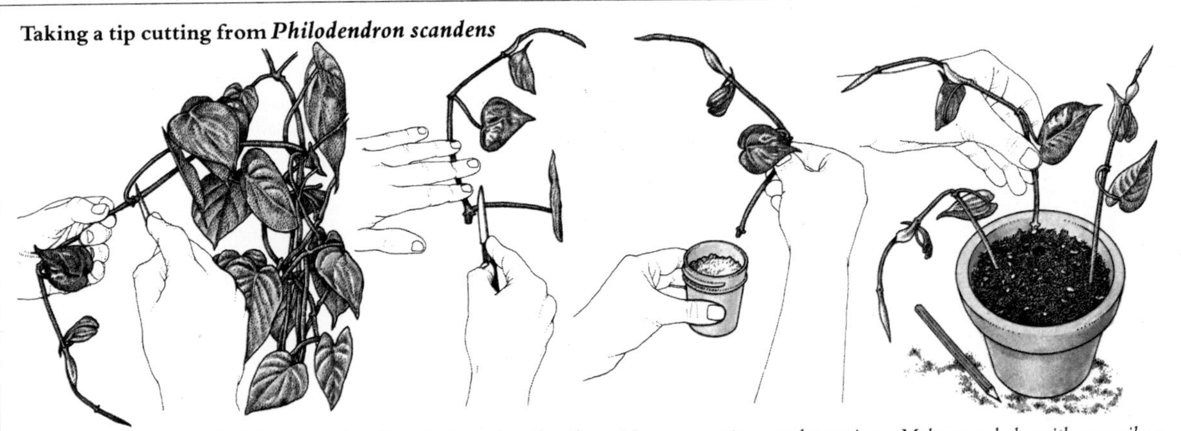

Make a clean cut at a point below a node, where you may find nodules which are rudimentary roots.

Cut off the leaf growing from the bottom node close to the stem. No leaf should touch the mixture.

Hormone rooting powder coating the severed end of the cutting will hasten the rooting process.

Make some holes with a pencil or stick to facilitate insertion, and plant several cuttings together.

Although the cut can be made with scissors or pruning shears, the cut end should be cleanly trimmed, with a sharp knife or razor blade, down to a horizontal line just below the bottom node. A clean cut is essential because torn or crushed plant tissue is likely to rot. If decay begins, it moves rapidly upward, and the only way to salvage a decaying stem is to trim it down to the next node.

For certain tough-stemmed plants a "heel" cutting is recommended. This consists of a sideshoot pulled off the main stem with a downward tug in such a way as to take with it a heel (a small piece of the skin of the main stem). Before inserting the heel in rooting mixture, be sure to trim off any ragged strands at the lower end and to remove rough edges from the torn-off portion.

For all cuttings use non-flowering shoots, if possible. Otherwise remove flowers or flower buds from the cutting. If a leaf is growing from the bottom node, remove it, too, for no leaf should be buried in the rooting medium. It is also wise to take off several lower leaves; this reduces the loss of moisture through transpiration. Removal of leaves is especially important if they are large. Trim away unwanted leaves with a razor blade, flush with the stem. This is better than pulling them off. An upward pull is not too harmful, but a downward pull can remove skin tissue from the stem.

Before inserting cuttings into containers of rooting mixture (see page 444), it is sometimes advisable to dip the cut ends into hormone rooting powder (see page 444) to stimulate root production. With or without the powder, it is best not to push the prepared cuttings directly into the rooting mixture unless it is extremely soft. To reduce risk of damage to the tissues make holes for easy insertion with some such implement as a pencil. Plant a single cutting in the center of a small pot, or else—usually more conveniently—plant three or more cuttings around the rim of a larger pot. When rooted cuttings are to be kept together to produce a bushy effect, as with tradescantias, insert several cuttings in the center as well as around the edges of the pot. After insertion, use your fingers to make the rooting mixture moderately firm, and top it up a little, if necessary.

It is normally helpful to keep cuttings covered while they are rooting. For a general discussion of the use of propagating cases and plastic bags see "Providing the right conditions," page 443. Humidity, temperature, and light requirements are broadly summarized in the same section. For specific instructions consult individual entries in the *A–Z Guide*.

Check potted cuttings occasionally to make sure they are not rotting at the base, and carefully remove decaying leaves, if any. Otherwise, do nothing further until new growth indicates that fairly sturdy roots have been formed. If in doubt, pull very gently on a cutting to determine whether roots are anchoring it down. As a last resort, cuttings may be tipped out of the container and examined. Once they are well rooted, most new plants can be moved into pots of standard potting mixture, with a little coarse sand or perlite added. They can then be treated as adults, though slight shading from strong light is desirable for another two or three weeks. (Where further special treatment is

Taking a sparmannia heel cutting

When giving the necessary downward tug to a sideshoot, be sure to hold the main stem firm.

The ragged ends of a heel torn away from the main stem must be carefully cut off to prevent rotting.

needed for very young plants, specific instructions will always appear under individual entries in the *A–Z Guide.*)

Many plant stems—among them, ivy (*Hedera*), aglaonema, impatiens, and all the tradescantias—root very readily in water. In fact, some cuttings that are difficult to root in a rooting mixture will eventually grow roots in a jar of water. Such roots are more brittle than those that are grown in rooting mixture. Do not let them grow more than about 2 inches long, or they may break when being transferred. In any case, moving a water-rooted cutting into a pot must be carried out with great care. Hold the cutting in position with one hand, and let the potting mixture, which should be fine-textured, trickle gently around the delicate roots from the other.

Rooting a stem cutting in water

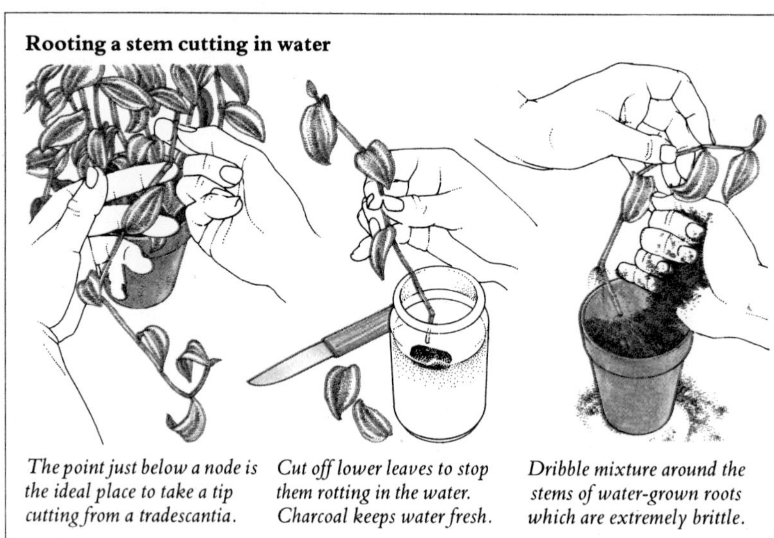

The point just below a node is the ideal place to take a tip cutting from a tradescantia. *Cut off lower leaves to stop them rotting in the water. Charcoal keeps water fresh.* *Dribble mixture around the stems of water-grown roots which are extremely brittle.*

Stem cuttings need not always be tip cuttings. Lower parts of stems will often root if the top of the piece is trimmed just above a node and the rest is prepared and treated as if it were a tip cutting. This fact is worth remembering when cutting back the stem from which a tip has been taken (and it is often necessary to remove such stems if the original plant is to regain its attractive shape). If the stem is a thick one—say, thicker than your thumb—quite short pieces may be used for propagation. Each piece need be only about 2 inches long, provided it includes one or two nodes; the position of the cuts in relation to the nodes is unimportant.

It is common practice to insert these short, thick cuttings into the rooting mixture horizontally, half-buried, with a node or leaf bud facing upward. In that way, the stem and leaf rosette that develop will be certain to grow upright. There is nothing wrong, however, with planting such cuttings vertically, as long as they are planted with the bottom end down, as on the original stem. Plants that can be propagated from woody stem cuttings include cordylines, dracaenas, and dieffenbachias. Gifts of the Polynesian ti plant, a variety of *Cordyline terminalis,* are often mailed to the recipient in the form of short cane pieces that are ready to plant.

Taking cuttings from thick-stemmed plants

An overgrown dracaena that has lost its lower leaves may no longer be attractive. This plant is an obvious candidate for propagation from thick stem cuttings.

Cut the stem into short pieces, each of which will take root as long as it contains at least one node.

Cuttings may be placed in rooting mixture either horizontally or the same way up as the original plant.

Whereas leaves develop from nodes exposed to the air, roots will sprout from buried nodes.

Cordyline terminalis *(good luck plant) is a popular example of a plant propagated by means of stem cuttings.*

LEAF CUTTINGS

A number of species will produce new plants from leaf cuttings. There is no dependable way to distinguish these plants from others, but most do have thick, fleshy leaves, which often grow in rosettes. Included among them are gloxinias, saintpaulias, peperomias, most rhizomatous, begonias, and many such fleshy-leaved succulents as crassulas and echeverias.

The basic way to handle a leaf cutting is to pull or cut from the parent plant a mature leaf with its leafstalk attached, and to insert the stalk for a small part of its length into a slightly moist rooting mixture. Because the weight of a leaf can overbalance its stalk if the aboveground portion of the stalk is too long, some leafstalks will need to be shortened before being planted. It is also wise to insert the stalk at a 45° angle. This will ensure sufficient underground support for the leaf without the need to bury an unreasonably long portion of its stalk. After a few weeks in ordinary room conditions, a young plantlet will form at the base. When the plantlet is about an inch across, the above-the-surface part of the parent leaf can be cut away and the plantlet left to grow in the pot. The parent leaf can be used again, but, unless the plant is particularly rare, it is better to start with a fresh leaf.

Long-stalked leaves of these species can be rooted in water. Begin by tying a piece of tinfoil or plastic firmly over the top of a glass jar partly filled with water, and punch a hole in this cover. Then drop a leafstalk into the water through the hole, letting the leaf rest on the cover. A few pieces of charcoal in the water will keep it fresh. Roots will soon form, and the long-stalked leaf will produce a new plant, ready for moving into standard mixture.

With some kinds of plant—one type of begonia, sansevierias, and streptocarpuses are examples—it is possible to make a number of plants from a single leaf by cutting the leaf itself into segments and rooting each segment separately. Because the procedure differs substantially for different species, it cannot be described in general terms. Where applicable, precise instructions for propagating a given plant from leaf sections are provided in the *A–Z Guide* entry for that plant.

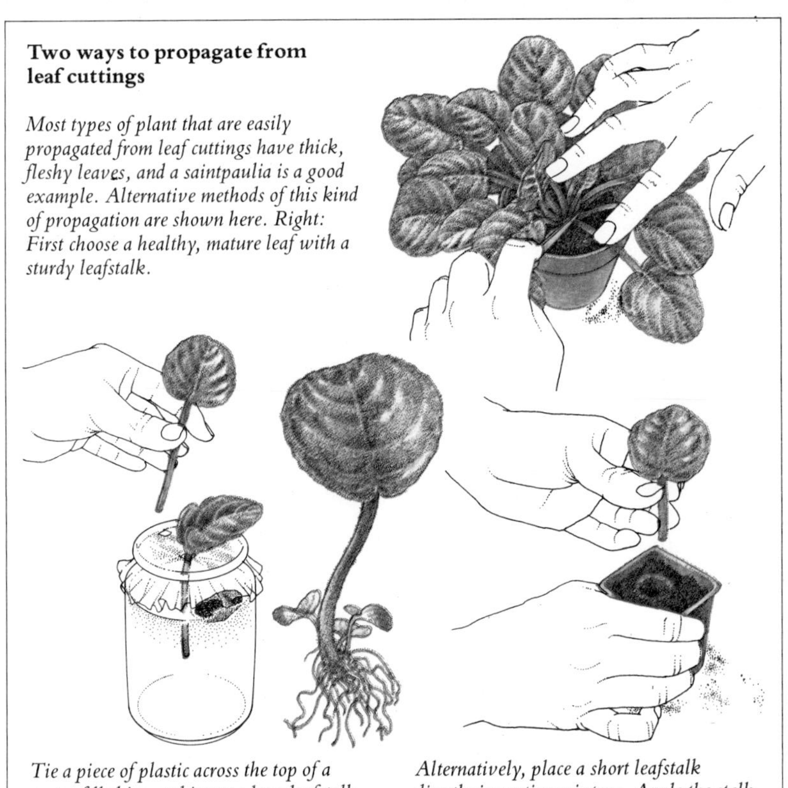

Two ways to propagate from leaf cuttings

Most types of plant that are easily propagated from leaf cuttings have thick, fleshy leaves, and a saintpaulia is a good example. Alternative methods of this kind of propagation are shown here. Right: First choose a healthy, mature leaf with a sturdy leafstalk.

Tie a piece of plastic across the top of a water-filled jar, and insert a long leafstalk through a hole punched in the plastic. Roots and small plantlets will form underwater.

Alternatively, place a short leafstalk directly in rooting mixture. Angle the stalk at 45° so that it will have underground support even though it is not buried deeply.

LAYERING

Layering is a procedure in which roots are encouraged to form on a trailing stem while it is still connected to the original plant. This is a useful propagation method for outdoor shrubs that resist rooting from cuttings. It is occasionally used indoors to speed up the rooting of such trailing or climbing house plants as ivies and philodendrons. The principle is simple: If the stem is forced into close contact with a rooting mixture, it will almost inevitably put down roots.

To layer a stem, pin it down into a pot of rooting mixture with a piece of wire in a U shape. Make sure that the section of stem under the wire is firmly in contact with the mixture or even buried. It may help if the stem is slightly bent, or a small cut is made in its underside, at or near the point where it is pinned down. This will stimulate rooting by checking the flow of sap. Soft-stemmed plants like ivies and philodendrons do not need much encouragement because they tend to form aerial roots at leaf nodes in any case.

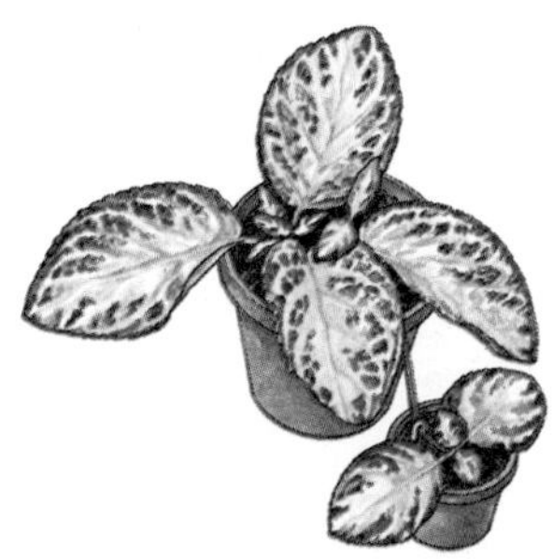

Here a stem of an episcia has been pinned down in a separate pot of rooting mixture, where it has taken root and will soon be capable of independent survival.

Several layers can be taken simultaneously from a healthy ivy. Merely surround the parent plant with small pots and pin a stem onto each one. When rooting has occurred (as indicated by renewed growth), cut the young plants free in such a way as not to spoil the shape of the parent.

Some creeping plants (fittonias and pellionias, for example) are virtually self-layering. That is, they will produce roots from their stems or from leaf clusters at the tips of stolons almost anywhere that these come in contact with damp potting mixture. Such rooted sections or plantlets can be cut off the parent plant and potted separately at any time.

Air layering *(Ficus benjamina)*

After scoring out two rings half an inch apart on the stem, peel off the bark between them.

Brush the stripped area of the stem with a thin dusting of hormone rooting powder.

Wrap the bottom of an oblong sheet of plastic tightly around the stem, tying it with thread.

Fill the cuplike piece of plastic with moistened sphagnum moss. Close the cup and secure it.

When roots appear through the moss, remove the plastic and cut the stem below the roots.

Place the new root ball in a pot, and work in potting mixture all around it.

AIR LAYERING

This method stimulates root formation in plants that are difficult to grow from cuttings and that have stiff, upright stems that cannot be layered by being brought down to soil level. If some such house plant as an aging rubber plant, codiaeum, or dracaena becomes unattractive as a result of losing its lower leaves, air layering can help to rejuvenate it. The aim of the procedure, as its name suggests, is to stimulate rooting at some point on the stem without lowering the stem to the surface of the potting mixture.

The first step is to wound the stem at a point below the lowest healthy leaf—preferably no more than 3 or 4 inches below it. One way to do this is to make an upward-slanting, inch-long cut with a very sharp, thin-bladed knife. The cut must not go beyond the center of the stem. Force open the cut just enough for the insertion of a small piece of matchstick or a grain of coarse sand. Cutting the stem in this way unfortunately weakens it, so that the top may break off if the plant is accidentally jostled. Many experienced growers prefer a less risky method: Using a sharp blade, scratch out two fine rings a half-inch apart in the bark or skin and peel off the area between the rings. This type of wound will leave the inside tissue of the plant undisturbed.

The next step is to dust the cut surface of the stem lightly with hormone rooting powder, and then to surround it with a double handful of moist sphagnum moss. There are two ways of keeping the moss in place. The more common method involves wrapping the narrow end of an oblong sheet of plastic around the stem. A plastic bag cut down the sides will do the job, as long as it is big enough for the ends to overlap. Tie the bag at the base with stout thread, or secure it with insulating tape. Then fill the bag with the moistened moss and secure the top of the bag around the stem to keep the moisture from escaping. In the alternative method, the moss is first secured to the stem with a few turns of stout thread. The plastic is then wrapped around the moss and secured at top and bottom with thread or insulating tape.

After a number of weeks, white roots should appear on the outside of the moss within the plastic covering. When the roots are visible, remove the plastic and sever the stem with a sharp knife, making a horizontal cut immediately below the ball of moss. Plant the new root ball in a pot large enough to allow about a half-inch of potting mixture to be worked all around the sides of the mossy root ball, and treat the plant as a mature specimen. If the new plant needs extra support until it develops more roots tie it temporarily to a stick that has been pushed into the potting mixture.

The original stem need not be discarded. It will almost always sprout again, usually near the top. When the new plant has been cut away, it is often wise to cut the old stem back to a point where new growth will make a more compact specimen. As long as the stem remains leafless, give the plant only enough water to make the potting mixture barely moist, allowing the top two-thirds of the mixture to dry out between waterings. After new growth appears, increase amounts of water, and begin to feed the plant.

If desired, the bare stem of a plant such as a dracaena that has been air layered can be cut into 2-inch lengths for use as stem cuttings.

If you cut back the leftover stem of an air layered plant, growth buds will soon begin to form new shoots.

Propagation from seeds

Seeds come in all sizes, from dustlike specks to berries, nuts, and stones an inch or more across. The smaller the seed, the harder it is to handle. But the general principles governing the raising of plants from seed are the same for all sizes.

CONTAINERS

The type and size of container in which to sow seeds depends on the kind and quantity of plants wanted. Because seed containers should be shallow, ordinary pots are not generally desirable, though half-pots can be used for small quantities of seed. For larger quantities it is best to use seed trays (often called flats). These are usually plastic and either 8 × 12 or 6 × 8 inches. They must have drainage holes. If a purchased flat has no holes, use a heated metal rod to make some in the plastic base. A convenient kind of seed tray is one that consists of a number of little pots joined together, or of rectangular depressions, in each of which a single seed can be sown. It is also possible to get various types of seed container in which the small pots themselves are made of compressed peat. Alternatively, you can obtain compressed peat pellets, which swell when moistened to become self-contained "pots".

Before filling the containers with a suitable rooting mixture (see page 444), line the bottom with a half-inch layer of small pebbles or fine bark for drainage. Most rooting mixtures are so porous that this is not essential, but if seeds are sown in relatively deep containers, a drainage layer has two advantages: It economizes on rooting mixture by taking up space, and it prevents the development of a harmfully soggy layer of mixture under the seedlings. The mixture throughout should be slightly moist, not sodden. The best way to get it right is to put dry mixture in a bowl or bucket and add a little water at a time, constantly stirring. There is too much moisture in the mixture if water can be wrung out when it is compressed in the hand.

If using a seed tray, be sure to put in enough mixture to fill the corners. Then, before sowing, use a slab of wood to press down the surface of the mixture so that it is slightly below the rim of the container.

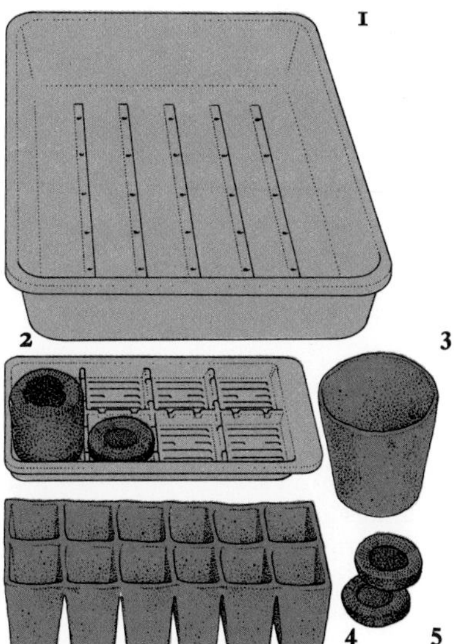

1 *Seed tray or flat.* **2** *Tray with eight divisions for peat pellets.* **3** *Large peat pot.* **4** *Small peat pots for individual seeds.* **5** *Peat pellets.*

SOWING THE SEEDS

In sowing, space seeds in such a way as to guard against overcrowding of the germinating seedlings. If small seedlings are crowded, they will become spindly, topple over, and rot at the base. To make furrows for sowing, press a ruler or pencil into the rooting mixture, leaving an inch between furrows for small seeds, more than an inch for bigger ones. Do not make deep furrows for very fine seed; the shallowest of markings will do.

The hardest seeds to sow are the dustlike ones of such plants as begonias and members of the gesneriad family. The hundreds of seeds contained in a single pinch can easily be blown away if sown in a draft or even breathed on, and it is also easy to sow them far too thickly, because they cannot be handled individually. The safest procedure is to begin by spilling the seeds into a shallow container, such as the lid of a small box. Then pick up a tiny pinch, and drop a trail of seeds across the rooting mixture by rubbing the finger and thumb together as the hand moves above the surface. Experts simply cut off a small corner of the seed package and, holding it by the diagonally opposite corner, tap it gently so that the seeds trickle out of the hole. Both methods take practice. It may help to experiment with some fine salt or dry sand.

Most seeds, fortunately, are big enough to distribute individually

Sowing fine seeds

Spread rooting mixture on top of fine gravel in the bottom of a flat. The layer of gravel prevents waterlogging and saves mixture.

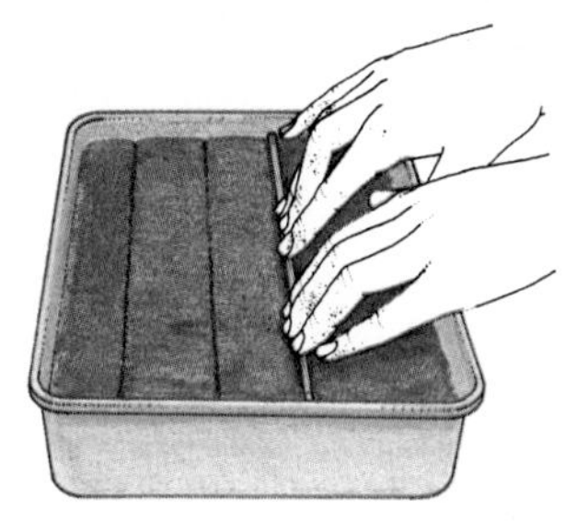

Because dustlike seeds sown at random can become overcrowded, mark out shallow furrows for sowing.

To avoid sowing too thickly, empty the seeds into a small container before sprinkling a fine pinch along each furrow.

Do not flood the mixture with water because it will bury or disperse the seeds. Instead moisten them with a fine mist-spray before covering the flat with a sheet of glass.

between finger and thumb, or tap out of a package in controlled quantities. Whatever their size, they should be well spaced along each furrow. Leave at least a quarter-inch between small seeds; sow medium-sized seeds a full inch apart; and space large seeds at twice the width of the seed. In fact, it is often better to sow the very big seeds singly in individual pots rather than in seed trays. Generous spacing gives seedlings room to develop without any overcrowding.

Most seeds bigger than a quarter-inch across will benefit from being soaked in warm (not boiling) water for 24 hours (or even longer with very large ones). Some seeds, too, have extremely hard coats and will not germinate unless the coat is nicked. To find out whether this is necessary for a given seed, consult the seed supplier. If it *is* necessary, nick the seed gently, taking great care not to damage the seed tissue inside. Make a very small cut in the coat by moving a sharp knife to and fro with a sawing motion until the skin is barely perforated.

Do not bury dustlike seeds in the rooting mixture. A light mist-spraying of the surface—*not* the heavy spray from a watering can—will settle such seeds adequately. On the other hand, cover small but visible seeds with a light dusting of fine mixture or milled sphagnum moss, and bury larger seeds at a depth of twice the width of the seed. Any such large, flat seeds as those of hippeastrums are best pressed in vertically and buried just below the surface. With the large, fully buried seeds, the rooting mixture should be watered lightly as soon as the seeds are sown, and the surface should then be firmly pressed flat with the help of a slab of wood.

Encouraging difficult seeds

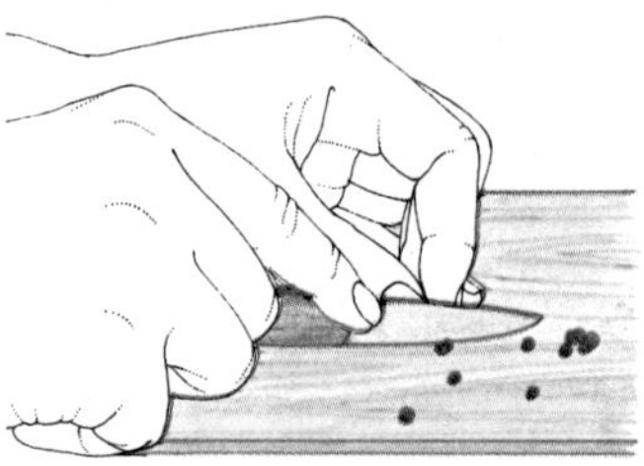

To facilitate germination of seeds with hard coats, nick each seed slightly, using a gentle sawing motion.

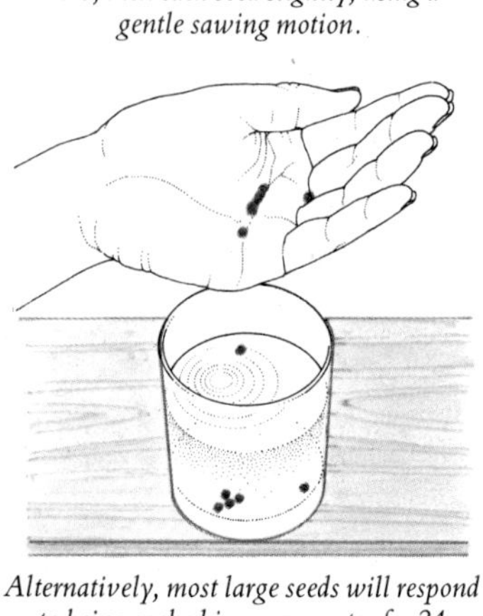

Alternatively, most large seeds will respond to being soaked in warm water for 24 hours before being sown.

PROPER CARE FOR SEEDLINGS

Seed containers must not be allowed to dry out, particularly in the case of dustlike and other small seeds planted at or barely below the surface of the rooting mixture. If left dry for even a few hours, tiny seedlings will shrivel and die. The best way to provide moisture for all but the largest seeds is not, as might be supposed, constant watering. Watering the mixture can disturb seeds or bury them too deeply, and there is an additional danger of rotting them by giving too much water. Instead, place the containers in a domed propagating case or similar plastic-topped device (see page 443). This ensures high humidity of the air above the mixture, and the moisture condensed in the propagator dome or plastic top keeps the mixture itself moist. Additional water is likely to be needed only for seeds that take more than two or three weeks to germinate. With such seeds, keep an eye on the container. If, after a few weeks, the mixture seems to be drying out, water it lightly with a fine spray.

Very large seeds well buried in relatively deep containers, need watering from the beginning. Instead of covering the container, water them often enough to prevent the rooting mixture from drying out.

In order to germinate, most house plant seeds need a minimum temperature of 65°F, but some need as much as 80° or even 85°. This is why most growers use heated propagating cases (see page 444). Temperature requirements are usually specified on seed packages. (They are also stated, where precise degrees of heat are important, in individual *A–Z Guide* entries.) Germination time is often unpredictable, except in general terms. Amateur indoor gardeners should not be too quickly discouraged if nothing seems to be happening. Large seeds in particular sometimes take more than two months to germinate.

Before germination light is not a vital consideration for most seeds. Very fine seed, however, does need bright light—but without direct sunlight, which would dry out the surface of the rooting mixture. Fluorescent lamps (see page 446) provide the right kind of light for such tiny seeds as those of the gesneriads. Fluorescent lighting is especially valuable after germination occurs, when bright all round light (without direct sunlight) becomes vital for all seedlings. Inadequate light will result in spindly growth, with consequent danger of toppling over and rotting; good light from only one side will produce a similar effect or, at least, will make for unbalanced growth. The ideal lighting situation is to keep seedlings 10–12 inches below fluorescent lights for 15 to 16 hours a day.

It is possible, of course, to give many kinds of seedling satisfactory light by placing them near a brightly lit window where they are nevertheless protected from the scorching direct rays of the sun. The seedlings most likely to react badly to inadequate light are those of fast-growing flowering annuals. Be especially careful to turn the trays or pots containing such seedlings daily. It is also helpful to put a piece of white cardboard or tinfoil behind the pots or trays—or on the darker side of the propagating case, if one is being used—in order to reflect the light.

After most of the seedlings have come up, reduce the temperature by 5°F or more, and gradually admit more outside air into the propagating case. Plastic domes often have ventilation controls, which should be opened up as the young plants grow. If there are no such controls, prop up the dome or plastic lid with a small piece of wood to allow a gap of ¼ inch at one side, and gradually enlarge the gap in the course of several days. Because seedlings are sensitive to dry air, they will not thrive in hot, dry room conditions. Under such conditions keep them in the plastic case, giving them plenty of ventilation, until they are big enough for transplanting. When they are finally placed in normal room conditions, maintain humidity levels as specified in the *A–Z Guide*.

Do not feed seedlings that are still lodged in rooting mixture if nutrients were added to the mixture before sowing (see page 445). Otherwise, give the new plants a quarter-strength solution of standard liquid fertilizer about every fourth watering. Never pour water on small seedlings directly from a can or spout. Use a mist-sprayer or fine-holed watering can; or else put the containers in a bowl of water, let the rooting mixture soak it up from below, and then allow the mixture to drain thoroughly.

POTTING UP SEEDLINGS

The first leaves to appear on seedlings (known as seed-leaves) do not resemble those of mature plants except in a few types of plant, such as the palms, hippeastrums, and members of the lily family. Always wait until a second or third pair of leaves has formed before considering transplanting. If the seeds were well spaced, there may be room enough in the original container to leave the seedlings for quite a while. In any case, consider how many adult plants you actually want. There are usually far too many seedlings, especially of flowering annuals. Thin them out at a very early stage by gently pulling out and discarding any unwanted seedlings and firming down those that are left. Leave only the healthiest-looking ones with plenty of space to grow; the space between seedlings should equal their height.

When it is time for transplanting, most house plants can be moved directly into individual pots of the appropriate potting mixture for mature plants of their species. With the fast-growing flowering annuals, however, it saves space to transplant a number of young seedlings into a larger tray of standard potting mixture until they are big enough to be planted in individual pots.

To move a seedling, lever it out of the mixture with a small, pointed tool. Always avoid handling the stem. Pick the young plant up by a leaf (ideally a seed-leaf). And replant the seedling in the same way that larger plants are repotted (see page 427), making sure that its lower leaves are not buried. After the new plant has been moved to an individual pot, it can be treated as an adult specimen.

For the propagation of ferns from spores, see the special article on ferns on page 208.

Thinning and transplanting

Do not hesitate to thin out seedlings drastically. Spaces between remaining ones should be equal to their height.

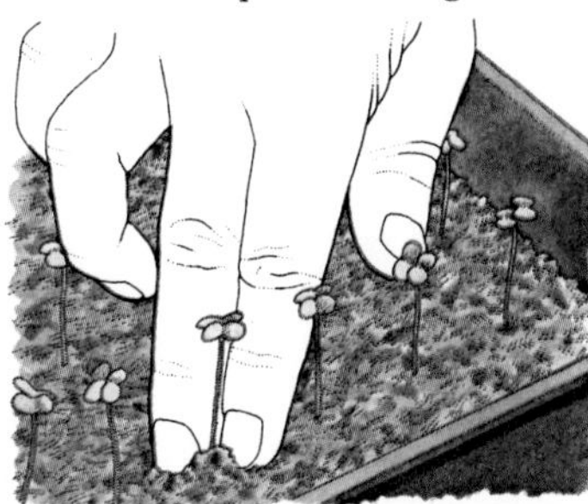

After thinning the seedlings, use your fingers to firm the potting mixture gently down.

When a seedling has developed at least two true leaves, ease it out of the mixture with an object such as a plant marker.

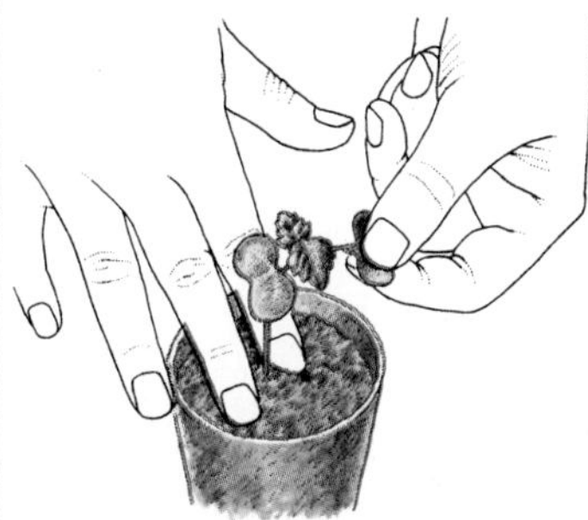

Move the seedling into a pot of the mixture for adult plants, taking care to hold the seedling only by a leaf.

Providing the right conditions

HUMIDITY

A humid atmosphere is essential for the satisfactory vegetative propagation of most plants (for humidity in seed-raising, see page 442). Humidity helps to prevent water loss from a cutting, which is unable to take up moisture readily because it has been deprived of its roots. Loss of moisture is greatest where leaves, or parts of leaves, are involved, because the leaves continue to transpire (i.e., to give off moisture) as long as they live. Leafless stem cuttings do not transpire, but if the rooting mixture in which they are planted dries out, they may wither. Humidity in the air is a better means than watering of maintaining the ideal degree of moisture in the rooting mixture. This is because even regular waterings can only be intermittent, with the result that there are inevitably wide fluctuations in the water content of the mixture.

Cuttings rooted in water do not normally suffer from dry air, of course. And humid air is not a requirement for the propagation of cacti, other succulents, and such fleshy-stemmed plants as pelargoniums. In fact, a humid atmosphere may cause the cuttings of these plants to rot. It is the most important factor, however, in the propagation of virtually all other types.

PROPAGATING CASES

The best way to maintain humidity for propagation indoors is by means of a plastic-topped propagating case. Such cases are available everywhere and can be bought quite cheaply. The simplest kind has a transparent lid, or dome, that fits over a plastic seed tray, and the propagator comes in various sizes. For potted cuttings there are deeper models in the form of miniature greenhouses. Somewhat less expensive (and much less efficient) than these plastic-topped cases are models consisting merely of a soft plastic cover fitting over metal hoops or a wire framework.

As a money-saving compromise, some indoor gardeners use ordinary plastic boxes designed for packing sandwiches or storing food. Those with transparent lids are excellent containers in which to start seeds. For individual cuttings planted in pots, the

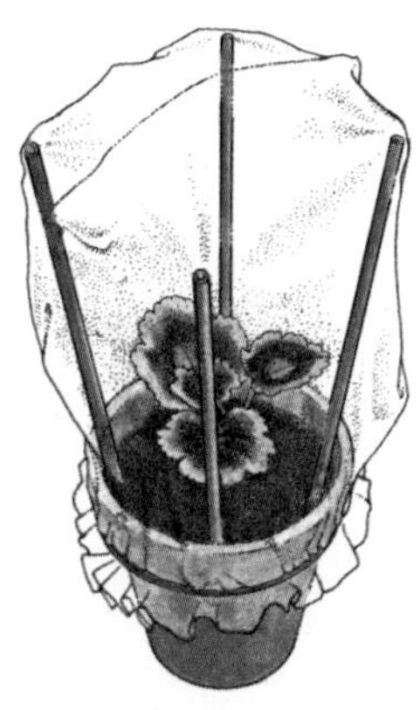

If you use a plastic bag to cover a potted cutting, you can keep the bag from touching the plant with a frame of four sticks.

simplest covering is a plastic bag. This must be big enough to fit over the pot and cutting without touching the plant material. To provide a frame for the bag, push three or four slim sticks into the potting mixture at the rim, or insert the ends of a wire hoop well down into the pot. Drape the bag over the frame, and close it around the top of the pot with a piece of string or a rubber band.

Alternatively, you can support the plastic by means of a wire hoop pressed well down into the potting mixture.

It is also possible to use any wide-necked glass jar of suitable size inverted over a cutting, with its rim supported on the rooting mixture. However, to prevent decay, all types of cover must be kept clear of the plant material being rooted.

Once rooting has occurred, high humidity becomes less essential. The newly rooted material of some plants can be exposed immediately to normal room conditions (taking due note of any humidity requirements specified in the *A–Z Guide*). In other cases—particularly with plants that need high humidity in an adult state—some acclimatization is necessary. With such plants, admit increasing quantities of outside air gradually, either by using the ventilation controls of plastic domes, opening sliding doors on large propagating cases, propping up the bottom of the dome or jar, rolling back plastic sheeting, or slitting one side of a plastic bag. After a few days of acclimatization most plants will be able to tolerate a relatively dry atmosphere.

One good way to protect a potted cutting is by means of an inverted glass jar with its rim resting on the rooting mixture.

TEMPERATURE

In order to germinate or root, almost any seed or piece of plant material needs a temperature of at least 65°F. It is usually possible to keep plant materials suitably warm in an inexpensive plastic-topped propagating case. But for plants that require a very high temperature—above 75°, say—a propagating case with a built-in heating element is essential.

HEATED PROPAGATING CASES

Heated propagating cases generally have their heating element either incorporated in the plastic base or in separate heating trays. Such cases are sometimes supplied with soil-warming cables. Small models may have a single heated tray, with a plastic lid or hood fitting over it. Larger cases may have several trays, each with its own lid. There are elaborate models that are, in effect, miniature greenhouses over 3 feet long and nearly 2 feet tall. Such propagators have sliding panels for access, and they can hold a large number of individual pots or seed trays, including quite big cuttings. They can even be used for seedlings after their initial transplanting but before their move into pots. Most electrically heated propagators and heating trays are equipped with thermostats. Thus the temperature can always be maintained at the desired level automatically.

LIGHT

Cuttings need bright light filtered through a translucent blind or curtain (see page 414) or medium light, such as the light at an unobstructed north-facing window. Given inadequate light, they will not only become lanky and weak but may never become satisfactory plants after rooting. They should never be subjected to direct sunlight. (For information on light in seed-raising, see page 442.)

HORMONE ROOTING POWDER

Hormone rooting powder is a synthesis of the growth-promoting hormones produced by plants. When applied to the cut end of a cutting, it stimulates root production. Because many soft-stemmed plants root swiftly without this treatment, the powder is most effectively used on cuttings of the woody-stemmed kinds. It does no harm, however, and may be used freely. Before planting a stem or leaf cutting, simply dip its base into the container of powder.

In buying hormone rooting powder, try to get a kind that contains a fungicide. This will help to prevent stem rot during the rooting period, when cuttings are particularly likely to decay at the base.

ROOTING MIXTURES

Standard potting mixtures are not suitable for germinating seeds or rooting cuttings. The texture of such mixtures is wrong, and they contain too much nutrient, which can scorch new roots. The right kind of rooting mixture for both cuttings and seeds is one that can hold moisture and yet prevent waterlogging (which is fatal to new roots) because its open texture allows for plenty of air spaces.

Rooting mixture must also be absolutely sterile, and no component of such a mixture should be used unless it has been sterilized. This lessens the risk of such diseases as the damping-off of seedlings or the various types of rot that attack cuttings at the base (see pages 456–459).

There are many prepackaged sowing or rooting mixtures for sale in garden centers. All are likely to be

Propagating cases

*Heated or unheated, propagating cases are available in a variety of shapes and sizes. The simple unheated model (**1**) is probably adequate for the needs of the average indoor gardener. It is basically a covered seed tray with adjustable air vents in the transparent lid. A similar seed-tray propagator has heated cables designed to run right through the potting mixture (**3**). More sophisticated propagators are designed to hold potted cuttings as well as seed trays. In its simplest form a propagator of this sort has a heating element incorporated in its base (**2**). Another type of case, which economizes by using flexible plastic as a cover, has its heating element in a sealed unit in the solid bottom, along with thermostatic control (**5**). The most elaborate propagator (**4**) is virtually a miniature greenhouse with sliding doors.*

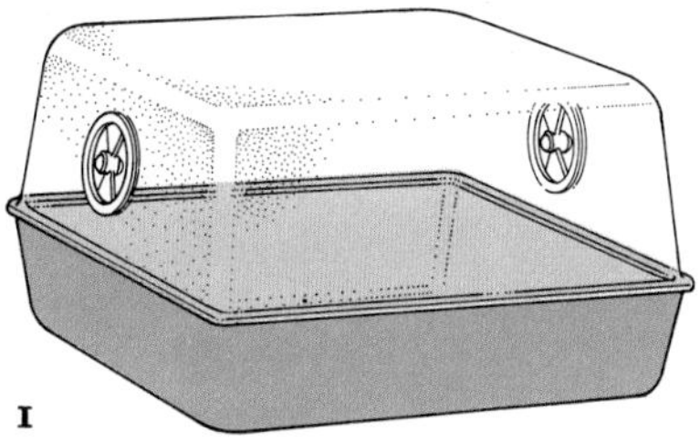

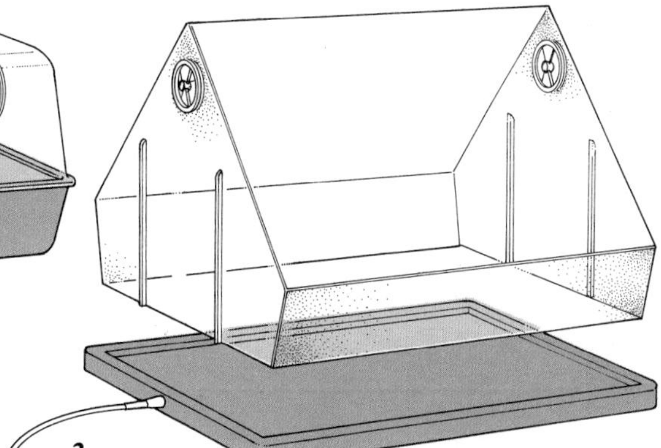

based on the same ingredients: perlite, vermiculite, coarse sand, peat moss, and sphagnum moss in differing combinations. What really matters, in fact, is whether the combination creates the necessary open-textured, moisture-holding mixture. Amateur gardeners can make their own by blending either equal parts of medium-grade perlite, medium-grade vermiculite, and milled (pulverized) sphagnum moss or equal parts of peat moss and perlite, vermiculite, or coarse sand (*not* fine builder's sand).

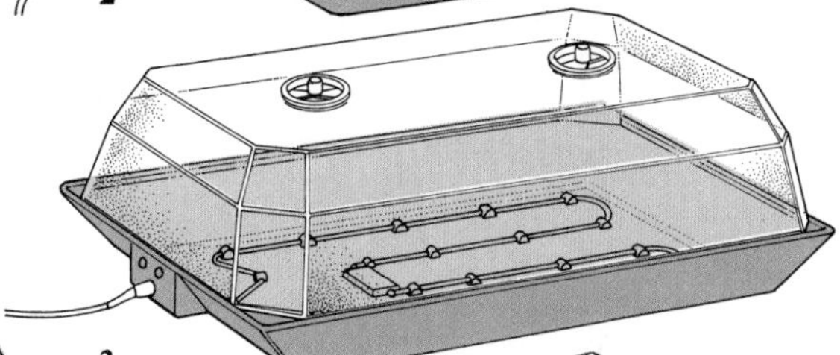

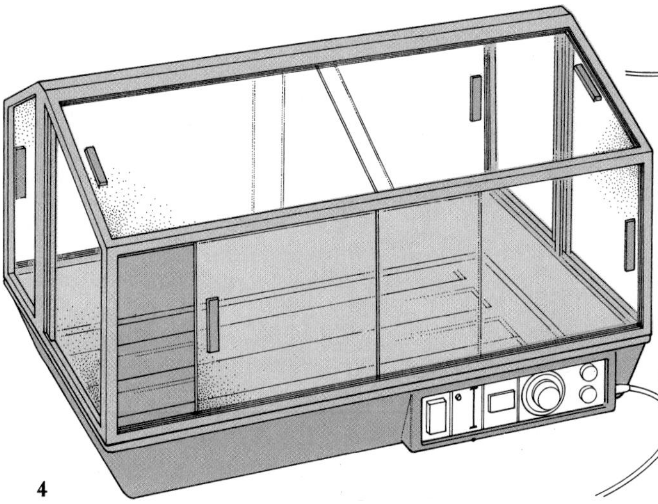

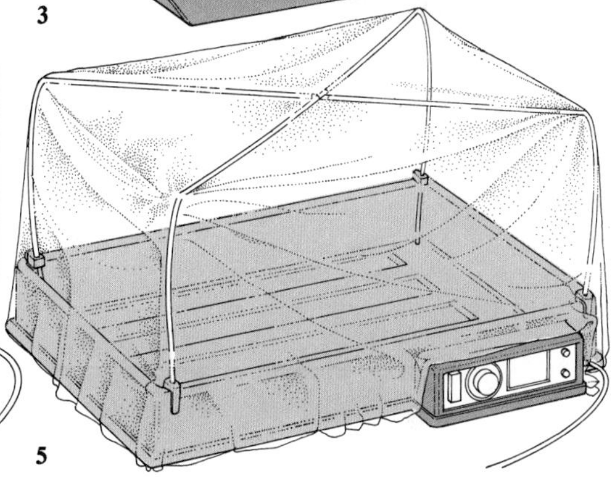

For very fine, dustlike seeds, spread a half-inch layer of milled sphagnum moss over the main mixture. If preferred, make this top layer by sifting some of the main mixture through an ordinary kitchen strainer. This coating of finely ground material upon which the minute seeds are sprinkled prevents them from falling into crevices so far down in the mixture that it becomes impossible for them to germinate successfully.

Cuttings require no extra food in the mixture, but seeds do. Before sowing, apply a solution of liquid plant food (about one-quarter normal strength) to the mixture. An alternative method of adding a little food is to change the blend of the rooting mixture for a given kind of seed. This can be done by adding a one-third portion of the potting mixture recommended for adult plants to a typical equal-parts mixture of, say, peat moss and perlite. This is particularly useful with larger seeds, which must often stay in the original containers for some time before being potted up. Another way to provide food for big seeds is to fill the bottom of the container with standard potting mixture, and cover this with a layer of non-nutritive rooting mixture in which to plant the seeds. As the seedling's roots develop, they will find this food supply just when they need it in order to keep the young plant alive and thriving.

Before sowing dustlike seed in rooting mixture, sift some mixture through a fine strainer. This finely ground top layer will stop the seeds from sinking too deeply.

Alternative growing methods

Artificial light

There are several reasons for growing indoor plants under artificial light. It can be used for supplementing daylight, or even for replacing daylight in poorly lit positions. It can also improve growth and health, especially in winter. And it can be used for decorative effect.

SOURCES OF LIGHT

There are three basic sources of artificial light: the incandescent filament bulb, the mercury-vapor lamp, and the fluorescent tube.

Incandescent Incandescent bulbs (such as domestic light bulbs) give out at least 70 percent of their energy as heat. Thus, if placed too near plants they can scorch the foliage and dry out the potting mixture. At a distance, however, the strength and the quality of such light are not enough to keep plants healthy. Incandescent bulbs are therefore useful for supplementing daylight, but not as the only source of light. Their chief value is decorative. For example, they can effectively "accent" the lighting of plants and plant groups. This may incidentally assist growth, but only slightly.

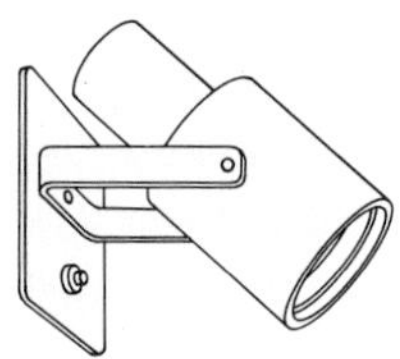

A spotlight like this one is capable of illuminating a plant effectively, but it has only limited value as an alternative to sunlight.

Incandescent floodlights are more effective than ordinary bulbs because the light that they produce is concentrated by means of internal reflectors. Floodlights are particularly useful for highlighting individual plants or small plant groups at night; and they do give a boost to growth, especially in winter (though again only along with—not instead of—adequate daylight). Most floodlight units are attractively styled, and they can be used to light large areas if several are arranged on a track system attached to the ceiling. One advantage of incandescent floodlights for decorative purposes is that the degree of brightness can be varied by means of a dimmer.

Mercury vapor The mercury-vapor floodlights are more powerful than the incandescent type, and they give out less heat. Their big drawback is that each such lamp is likely to have a wattage of at least 250, and therefore they are expensive to run. But indoor gardeners with large plant displays may find them worth the expense.

Fluorescent Undoubtedly fluorescent tubes provide the best kind of artificial light for house plants. They produce much more light per watt, and they waste less of their energy in heat, so that there is far less risk of scorched leaves or of over-rapid drying of potting mixture. They also come in a variety of shapes, "colors" and sizes. Lengths vary from 8 to 96 inches. And although the tubes are normally straight, they are also found as 8- or 10-inch circles. The circular tubes are usually used in round reflector fixtures, often with a stand.

This all-in-one fixture combines a covered circular fluorescent tube with a built-in pan for shallow-rooted plants.

Ready-made fixtures for conventionally shaped tubes accommodate from one to four tubes in parallel positions. Fixtures are available either in reflector housings hung on chains or as strip or batten arrangements without reflectors, designed to be fastened directly to an upper surface. Also available are fluorescent panels 12 inches square and 1½ inches deep. These are pleasing to the eye but, because they require special control devices, are not easy for do-it-yourself enthusiasts to install.

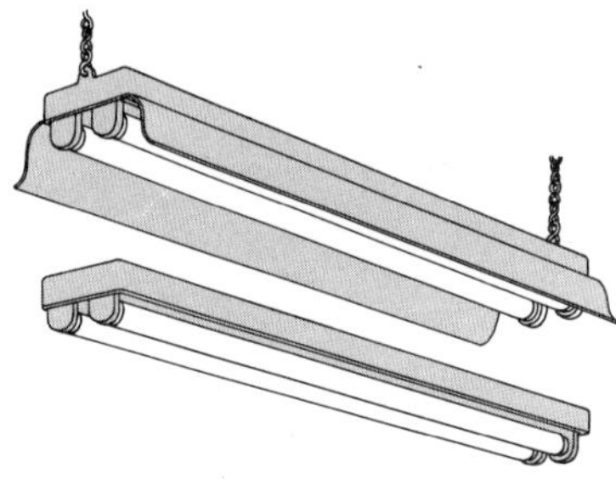

Long-tubed fluorescent-light fixtures can either hang above plants or be attached to an upper surface, such as a shelf. In the latter case no reflector is necessary.

QUALITY OF LIGHT

Of all the colors of the spectrum, two components—violet/blue and red—are the most important for plant growth. To be thoroughly effective, an artificial light must give out adequate amounts of these components. So-called "daylight" types of fluorescent tube are high in blue, but low in red; "warm white" and "natural white" tubes are high in red, but low in blue. In choosing a tube, therefore, look for one labeled as specifically made to assist plant growth. Such tubes produce blue and red light in quantities that closely match plant-growth requirements. This type of fluorescent light looks reddish—which heightens the visual impact of flower and foliage color.

Others—the so-called "wide spectrum" tubes—are especially good for plants that normally need extra amounts of sunlight, or that are just about to come into flower. It is a good idea to combine one plant-growth and one "wide-spectrum" tube over mixed plantings.

There are also tubes for special purposes. Some, for instance, are specifically recommended for raising plants from seeds and cuttings. If in doubt, consult your local electrical-appliances store or garden center.

LIGHT PLACEMENT

Incandescent lights The safe distance from plants is controlled by the amount of heat given off. A 15- to 25-watt incandescent bulb should be placed 12–15 inches from a plant; a 100-watt bulb, at least 24 inches away; and a 150-watt bulb, at a distance of 30–36 inches. Floodlights give off a little less heat. A 75-watt floodlight should be placed 18 inches away from a plant; a 150-watt floodlight 24 inches; and bulbs with higher wattages, 36 inches.

Mercury vapor With a minimum normal power of 250 watts, any such light should be placed at least 4–5 feet away from plants.

Fluorescent tubes Most of the tubes, including the plant-growth kind, give out 10 watts for every foot of their length. This wattage is mainly in the form of light, not heat, and so the heat produced by fluorescent tubes is not great enough to harm plants. The proper distance above plants at which to place tubes is governed by the intensity of light that plants need.

For foliage specimens the right distance lies somewhere between 12–24 inches, but most flowering plants need to be nearer the tubes (no more, say, than 6–12 inches away). For example, saintpaulias, which are often grown entirely under artificial light because it virtually assures continuous flowering, are best placed 9–12 inches under the tubes. The *precise* distance depends on plant size. (Measurements are based on the distance between tubes and the top of the foliage.)

Some flowering plants—certain bromeliads, cacti, orchids, and pelargoniums, for instance—require more than the average amount of illumination. For these the high-powered fluorescent tubes known as VHO (very high output) tubes should be used. VHO lights give nearly three times as much illumination (about 27 watts per foot) as the others, and they are placed 12–24 inches above any plants for which they are considered to be appropriate.

As the width of plants increases, more tubes in parallel arrangements are needed to provide the same intensity of light over the full extent of the foliage and flowers. Whereas a row of saintpaulias or similarly small plants can be grown under a single tube, a two-tube arrangement with a 6-inch gap is the minimum recommended for larger plants.

Experiment a bit before you decide upon the right placement of fluorescent fixtures for your plants. Watch the plants' behavior and adjust the lighting arrangements accordingly. If a plant is getting too much artificial light, it will indicate distress by fading colors, scorched foliage, or unnaturally stunted growth. If any of these symptoms occur, increase the distance between plant and light by 3 inches at a time, leaving the plants in the new position for a week before checking on their improvement or lack of it. On the other hand, elongated stems, small leaves, and lack of flowers at natural flowering time may indicate too little light. The remedy in this case is to bring the source of light closer to the ailing plant, again in 3-inch steps. Remember, however, that in moving a plant away from (or toward) a light source, the intensity of light reaching the plant is reduced (or increased) by much more than would appear. If a plant's distance from a light source is doubled, the amount of light falling on it is not halved, but quartered. Similarly, if its distance from the light is tripled, the intensity of light reaching the plant is reduced nine times. In moving plants toward a light source the converse is obviously true.

To keep the effective output of fluorescent tubes and reflectors as constant as possible, wipe them clear of dust every month or so. And, since tubes become progressively less efficient as they age, replace them as soon as the ends begin to darken. Ideally, they should be replaced at least once a year. In a fixture with two or more tubes, however, never put in more than one new tube at a time, because the shock of sharply increased light intensity can damage plants. To minimize this risk let three or four weeks elapse before following one replacement with another. One way to economize is to switch still-active older tubes to plants that have lower light requirements.

DURATION OF LIGHTING

As has already been mentioned, incandescent-bulb lighting is primarily decorative and has only a limited effect on plant growth. If you switch floodlights on for a period of several hours, growth will certainly be somewhat boosted. But ordinary floodlights cannot be used as a substitute for daylight, no matter how long they are permitted to shine.

Plants *can* thrive, on the other hand, on light entirely furnished by fluorescent tubes if the tubes are kept going for long periods. Most foliage plants do best when given 12–14 hours a day of fluorescent light. Flowering plants need 16–18 hours unless they are winter-flowering types (kalanchoes and poinsettias, for example). Such short-day flowering plants should have no more than 12–13 hours a day of artificial light. Most growers recommend using electric timer switches to make sure that the appropriate lighting programs are strictly adhered to.

USING LIGHTS INDOORS

Ordinary incandescent lights may be placed wherever they make a plant collection look its best, as long as they are not too close to the specimens. Fluorescent tubes, even when used merely to supplement daylight, are more truly functional. The simplest, most basic installation is either a hanging reflector or else a one- or two-tube batten attachment placed above a group of plants, according to what is most convenient for the grower. But there are many other possibilities.

The least complicated ready-made structure in which to grow artificially lighted plants consists of a reflector that holds one or two, two-foot-long fluorescent tubes. The reflector is supported on legs and can be placed over a tray of two or three average-size plants. Somewhat more elaborate is a similar fixture with a built-in tray. Even more complex are units incorporating a number of shelves for plants. Each shelf in a unit of this sort is equipped with an underlying tube that lights the shelf below, with an upper bracket for the topmost light. There are also "plant carts" designed on the same principle. These can be wheeled into different positions as required. The shelves on many such units can be adjusted to provide space for various plant sizes.

Although most commercially made structures look utilitarian, with metal shelves and reflectors and tubular or angular metal supports, it is possible to buy attractive furniture with built-in light units. Some indoor gardeners, however, prefer to design and construct their own arrangements. Any flat surface under a shelf can easily be converted into an illuminated plant-growing position. A row of fluorescently lighted plants at the rear of the working surface of a kitchen counter, for example, can be a refreshingly attractive backdrop.

Entirely dark areas such as cellars and attics can be converted into bright gardens by means of artificial lighting. Shelving of suitable widths and depths can be installed around the walls, with adequate banks of tubes fixed under the shelves. However, the builder should be sure to provide flexibility for a constantly changing plant collection and be generous enough with space between shelves so that tubes can be replaced without tearing the handiwork apart.

Ready-made units with artificial lighting

Left: This is simply a four-legged reflector equipped with short fluorescent tubes. More elaborate (and expensive) is the arrangement below, which has built-in tubes to light the three lower shelves. Each shelf of the movable "plant cart" at bottom left is lit by tubes attached to a bracket or the shelf above.

All electrical work should be carried out with special consideration for the high atmospheric humidity and flowing or dripping water everywhere. Each piece of equipment has to be grounded, and waterproof cable must be used throughout. All plants, finally, must be placed on waterproof trays, to minimize the risk of water dripping into electrical equipment. When constructing artificial-lighting units always leave the actual electrical work to a qualified electrician.

PLANT CARE

It may take a few weeks or even months for your plants to settle down under artificial lighting. Once they are established, they should grow well in comparison with daylight specimens. This will be especially true in winter, when natural light indoors is likely to be weak in both quality and quantity. Flowering plants are much more likely to bloom regularly under fluorescent tubes than in daylight.

Cultivation needs—temperature, watering, repotting, etc.—remain virtually unchanged for a plant grown under artificial lights. There are only one or two minor differences. For instance, in enclosed and possibly airless places such as attics or basements, some extra means of ventilation must be provided. It is also important to arrange for a temperature drop of a few degrees at night. Artificially lighted plants often need increased amounts of fertilizer because the roots require more minerals in order to sustain the extra growth of leaves and stems encouraged by constant light.

If left in position under fluorescent tubes, a plant is most likely to grow continuously. For many tropical plants—which is what most foliage house plants are—this does no harm. But plants that need a rest period (as indicated in the *A—Z Guide*) should be given one. The quality and quantity of artificial light should be temporarily reduced, along with prescribed modifications in temperature, watering, and feeding. Some growers recommend imposing a partial rest period on all artificially illuminated plants. To do this, simply reduce the time of illumination by three or four hours a day over an eight-week period. During this period stop feeding the plants, give them less water, and let the temperature drop a few degrees. An annual rest undoubtedly benefits most plants in a collection.

Hydroculture

Hydroculture (also called hydroponics) is a method of growing plants with their roots in water containing necessary plant foods. This nourishing liquid, technically known as "fertilizer solution," replaces the potting mixture—which is why hydroculture is often called "soilless" cultivation. The only solid materials required for plants being grown by this method are the containers and some substantial anchorage to keep the plants from toppling over.

The advantages of hydroculture for indoor gardeners, especially those in apartments, are that it saves time and space and is less messy than the orthodox method of growing house plants. There is no need to procure and store potting mixtures, and regular repotting and feeding requirements are much reduced. Watering and feeding become a matter of merely topping up the reservoir with plain water to which fertilizer has sometimes been added, and this makes vacation periods less of a problem. Many of the pests and diseases that can afflict plants growing in potting mixtures are avoided. As an added bonus, growth is often more vigorous in hydroculture than in conventional potting mixtures.

The idea of roots' being kept constantly in water may seem to conflict with warnings elsewhere in this volume about the dangers of overwatering. There is no conflict, however. Roots grown in water have a different structure from those grown in potting mixture. They do not suffer from waterlogging because their outer cells have expanded space for oxygen storage, whereas the cells of roots grown in non-liquid materials need to keep replenishing their store of oxygen from the potting mixture. Since root structure is so different, of course, it is generally risky to transfer a plant that has been living in one medium to the other. Virtually any plant can be successfully grown by hydroculture, but success is comparatively easy only with plants that originate from cuttings specifically raised for this method of cultivation. (For propagation from cuttings see "How to begin," below.)

Basic materials In the most elementary form of hydroculture, a plant grown from a cutting rooted in water sits in a specially shaped container, which provides support for the base of the plant while allowing its roots to hang down into water. The old-fashioned practice of growing hyacinth bulbs in glasses (see page 243) is a familiar example. It is theoretically possible to grow larger plants in this way, but the question of how to keep them upright without anchoring them down would soon arise. All modern hydroculture systems involve the use of an aggregate to provide necessary anchorage.

Every such aggregate consists of inert granular material made up of particles measuring approximately $\frac{1}{4}$–$\frac{5}{8}$ inch in diameter. This material can be grit, pea-gravel, gravel, crushed granite chips, lignite, perlite, vermiculite, or granules of expanded clay aggregate that are manufactured expressly for use in hydroculture. When bought in a garden center, these substances have normally been prepared and packaged for immediate, safe use. If you procure them from some other source, be sure the particles are within the recommended size range, and wash the aggregate thoroughly, sifting out any bits of dirt.

There are two main systems of hydroculture. The first is based on the use of a single watertight container. The second requires a specially designed double pot.

Single-container method Any type of unperforated pot may be used as long as it is watertight and is not made of unpainted metal (with which the chemicals in a fertilizer might react). Put in nearly enough aggregate to fill the pot, and pour over the aggregate a solution of standard liquid fertilizer at one quarter of the recommended strength (or use a fertilizer specially formulated for hydroculture and diluted as recommended). Let the liquid rise to a level where only the bottom quarter or third of the aggregate particles are submerged. The

Roots of plants grown hydroculturally in a single watertight pot are anchored in aggregate, some of which is submerged. Note the addition of a water gauge.

level of the liquid can be checked by means of a gauge. It is possible to buy pots with built-in gauges or you can buy a separate gauge in which a marker is moved up or down by the action of a small float that remains at water level.

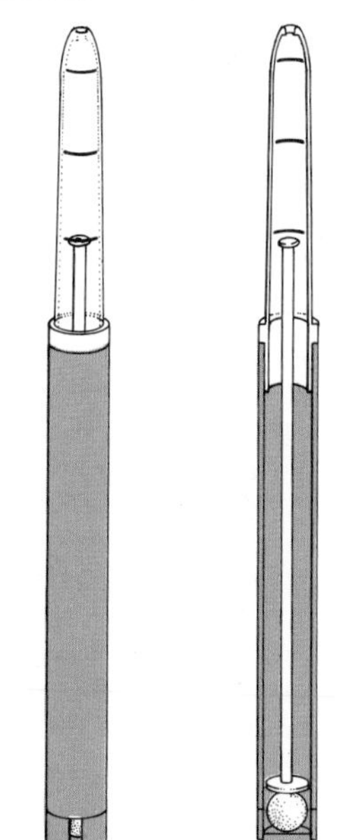

This typical gauge (cross-section at right) indicates fertilizer-solution depth with a marker moved by a float that drops with falling water level.

Keep the fertilizer solution topped up with room-temperature water so that it does not fall below the one-quarter or rise above the one-third level. It is important to keep the aggregate fairly free of excess fertilizer that may cling to the particles or to the roots of the plant growing in such a pot. For this reason it is advisable to pour out the fertilizer solution once a month and start afresh. Do it by upturning the pot, holding a hand over the surface of the aggregate to prevent it from spilling, and putting in new solution when the last of the old has dripped out. Even so, too much fertilizer is likely to build up in time, and this can result in unsatisfactory plant growth and discolored foliage. That is why the single-container system is most suitable for fast-growing plants—for instance, chlorophytums, hederas, plectranthuses, and zebrinas. Such plants can be renewed from cuttings at regular intervals and replanted in cleansed aggregate.

If a more permanent plant grown by this method of hydroculture shows signs of overfeeding, do not give it up for lost. Remove it from the container, and wash its roots thoroughly in fresh water. It should soon regain its health after being replanted in a container filled with clean aggregate.

Double-container method This system is more flexible than the other. The smaller of the two containers has holes in the bottom and is suspended at rim level within the larger one, which is watertight. The small container is filled with aggregate. The other holds fertilizer solution, the level of which must remain just above the base of the smaller container so that the liquid seeps into the aggregate by capillary action. A gauge to indicate the level of the solution is generally built into a ready-made double-container system. If there is no gauge, you can simply lift out the upper pot every so often to see whether the solution needs topping up.

In a double container, roots come into contact with solution seeping through holes in a small aggregate-filled pot, which can be lifted out of the big one.

At first the plant's roots do not extend beyond the aggregate in the small container, but they gradually grow down through the holes and into the liquid. The initial fertilizer solution can be topped up with room-temperature water whenever necessary. In general, however, it should be poured away and replaced with fresh solution after about four weeks.

To cleanse the aggregate, take out the inner pot every two or three months and let tap water run through the particles for a few minutes.

Using special ingredients The most recent form of hydroculture makes use of a special granular aggregate, in conjunction with a special kind of fertilizer. The clay granules are fired at a high temperature and have a hard skin around a honeycomblike center. These clay granules were originally designed for use as an aggregate in concrete mixes. Each granule is about ½ inch across, the best size for maintaining a satisfactory balance of air and liquid around plant roots. In addition to providing anchorage, these clay granules can absorb moisture when dry and release it as required.

This ability would be a drawback, however, with conventional fertilizers, which could not be washed out once they had been absorbed by the aggregate. As a result, an excess of chemical salts would eventually build up and damage plants anchored in the granules, if they were used along with ordinary fertilizer solutions. That is why special fertilizers are essential for use with this material.

The recommended fertilizer is unusual in that it provides a plant with a specific chemical nutriment only if and when the plant requires that particular chemical. Furthermore, any excess amount of a given chemical is taken up again by the particles of the fertilizer, thus shielding the plant from harmful overfeeding. And the particles also absorb any undesirable chemicals present in the water such as chlorine and fluorine.

The greatest value of hydroculture is that it takes care of a plant's feeding needs for many months at a time. Small plants can normally subsist on one dose of fertilizer for about a year, large ones for six months. Further amounts can be added to the water used for topping up. This water must be at room temperature; cold water can damage roots. The fact that the clay granules cannot be washed clean does not matter, of course, when the special fertilizers are used.

Repotting Plants grown in fertilizer solution can remain in the same fairly small container for a long time. Although individual roots are more fleshy than those of plants grown in potting mixture, the root systems of the products of hydroculture are much more compact. Annual repotting is therefore unnecessary. Repotting is usually done only when a plant begins to look awkwardly big for its small container, or when it becomes top-heavy. In the repotting process a plant being grown by the double-container method will need two somewhat larger containers instead of only one. This should present no problems, since the upper and lower pots are usually sold together as a complete package.

Begin the repotting operation for plants grown in both single- and double-container systems by putting an inch-deep layer of fresh aggregate in the pot that will hold the plant. Next, remove the plant carefully from its old pot and place it in the new one, holding the stem base on a level with its former depth. If the roots are extensive, spread them out evenly over the layer of aggregate. Then put additional clean aggregate around the roots until the plant is firmly held in place. The aggregate can be flush with the top of the container, if necessary. Try not to damage the roots; remove any fragments broken off during the operation, so as to avoid the risk of decay. Fertilizer solution should be provided, of course, as soon as the plant has been anchored down.

Plants can be bought already growing in containers designed for use with granular aggregate. In any such ready-made system there may be as many as three pots, since the plant itself is sometimes contained within a small granule-filled plastic pot, and the larger pot within which this plastic pot is enclosed sits in the still larger "reservoir." The roots of the plant protrude from slits or holes in the plastic pot through further openings in the larger pot and down into the liquid. The small plastic inner pot is to facilitate handling of the plant. If such a plant is to be repotted, do not tamper with the smallest of the three containers. Simply pour the aggregate around it within the new, larger pot.

Repotting in aggregate

Begin by covering the bottom of the container in which the plant is to be housed with an inch-deep layer of clean particles.

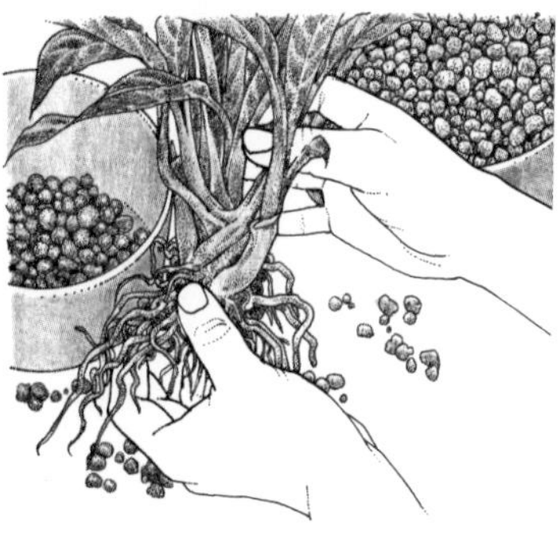

Gently remove the top layer of aggregate from the plant to be moved on. Gradually uncover all the roots, being careful not to damage them. Never pull the plant free.

Place the plant on top of the new layer of aggregate at the same depth as before, and spread the roots out. Add enough particles to hold them firmly in place.

Pour in just enough fertilizer solution to cover no more than the bottom third of the aggregate-filled pot.

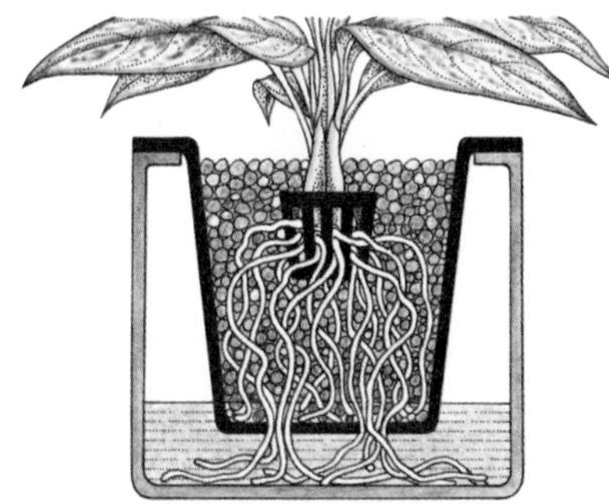

In this ready-made three-pot system, roots emerge through slits in a small pot whose only function is to ease plant handling. Leave this pot intact when repotting.

How to begin The easiest way to start growing plants hydroculturally is to acquire them already established in fertilizer solution. You may even find them in a plant shop growing in the tiny "nursery" containers just sitting in a large trough of fertilizer solution. This allows you to choose your own system. It is not difficult, however, to root cuttings from conventionally grown plants in such a way as to prepare them for hydroculture. Although most cuttings can be rooted in water alone, it is faster to root them with the support of one of the aggregates already discussed. For rooting purposes use small particles (no larger than ¼ inch in diameter). Spread the aggregate at least 2 inches deep in a watertight tray, and pour in enough quarter-strength fertilizer solution to keep the bottom inch of the aggregate continuously wet. Alternatively, if only a few cuttings are to be rooted, insert each cutting in an aggregate-filled 2-inch plastic pot, and stand the pots in a tray partly filled with the fertilizer solution. Capillary action will do the rest.

Cuttings of a given plant should be of the same size and should have the same amounts of light, warmth, and humidity as required for propagation in ordinary rooting mixtures. Except for the medium in which cuttings are inserted, the processes are identical. The only difference is that cuttings rooted in fertilizer solution will have hydroculture-type roots from the outset. Similarly, when the cuttings have made adequate roots and appear to be growing well, they are potted up for the chosen form of hydroculture in much the same way that they would be potted up in ordinary potting mixture (see page 437).

To start plants from seed, use vermiculite as the aggregate material. Put the vermiculite in half-pots or seed trays with drainage holes, and begin by moistening it with plain water

These cuttings are being rooted for hydroculture. Fertilizer solution in the tray moves upward into the aggregate by capillary action.

until it can absorb no more and the surplus emerges from the holes. Then sow the seeds exactly as they would be sown in potting mixture, and permit them to germinate normally (see page 441), keeping the vermiculite constantly moist but not sodden. After germination occurs, begin to apply a half-strength nutrient solution instead of plain water. Increase the strength gradually up to full strength during a period of about 10 days.

Move the seedlings into individual containers or another tray of aggregate when they are large enough to handle, as in normal seed propagation. This first move can be into further vermiculite or into one of the other aggregates with particles no bigger than ¼ inch in diameter. A small amount of vermiculite will cling to the roots of seedlings when they are lifted up for transplanting. Do not try to dislodge it, since the vermiculite will provide a reservoir of moisture and food in addition to protecting the fine roots from damage. When the seedlings are of fair size (which varies according to species), they can be moved into appropriate containers for permanent hydroculture.

As already pointed out, it is not generally advisable to transfer a plant previously grown in potting mixture to hydroculture. It can be done, however. The first step is to remove all traces of mixture from the roots of the plant. Wash the roots under slowly running water, if necessary. The plant can then be planted according to either of the systems described above.

This procedure is likely to result in considerable shock to the plant since most of its fine feeding roots will have been damaged. To minimize the effects of shock, keep the plant at a temperature of around 70°F, with fairly high humidity, for three to four weeks. Enclose the plant in a heated propagating case (see page 444) during this whole period.

When the plant seems to be growing normally, with no signs of limpness, you can assume it has recovered from the shock. But because the original roots die and decay as the new type are formed, the entire root system will need a thorough washing at the end of another six months. This is essential for removing decayed remnants of old roots. The aggregate must also be thoroughly rinsed. If rotting particles of old root are allowed to remain in contact with the new ones, the result will be unsatisfactory plant growth and, possibly, death.

Shifting a plant from mixture to hydroculture

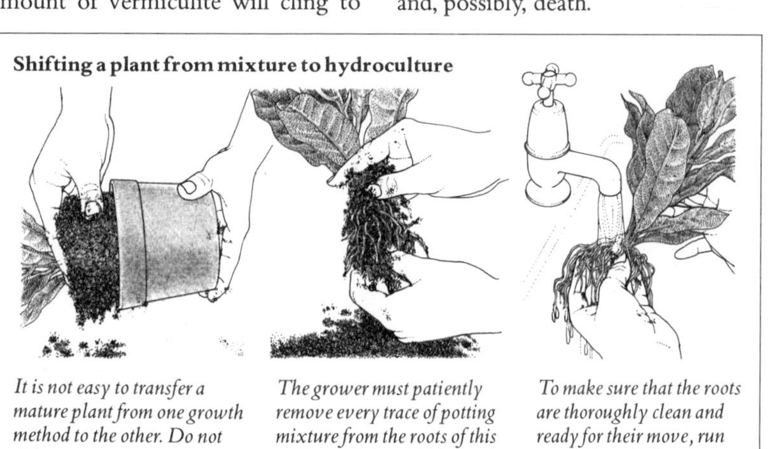

It is not easy to transfer a mature plant from one growth method to the other. Do not risk a rare specimen.

The grower must patiently remove every trace of potting mixture from the roots of this codiaeum before replanting it.

To make sure that the roots are thoroughly clean and ready for their move, run water through them.

Plant health

Keeping plants healthy

The best way to keep house plants healthy is to give them precisely the right growing conditions. Most troubles are due to improper care. If a plant seems not to be doing well, check its cultivation needs in the *A–Z Guide* to see whether you may have been inadvertently neglecting some of its requirements. Remember that there is usually a lag of some days or even weeks before symptoms of faulty care become apparent. It is therefore essential to think back carefully to possible causes of trouble.

Plant diseases must be differentiated from attack by pests. Most diseases result from poor cultivation, and the most common causes of disease are such factors as excessively dry or humid air, lack of air movement among crowded plants, and overwatering. It is generally easy to deal with such problems once they are spotted. Attack by the wide range of pests that do harm to house plants is harder to guard against. Some of these pests live indoors and cannot be excluded. Others enter through open windows or settle on plants that are temporarily placed outdoors. Still others can be brought into the home on newly acquired plants.

The first step to take in the constant battle against pests is to isolate newly acquired plants in a separate room for two or three weeks, during which they can be treated with a general purpose insecticide. If space does not permit isolation, new plants should at least be carefully examined, not only for small pests but for slugs and snails, which can wreak havoc if they spread. As for plants already in a general collection, they should be regularly examined for signs of infestation. The examinations should be linked with a cleaning routine that will help to ward off disease and discourage pests.

Cleaning It is essential to keep leaves free of dust and pollution deposits. This not only improves the appearance of the foliage but also prevents clogging of the pores through which plants breathe. The frequency with which plants need cleaning will obviously vary according to location. In an industrial area leaves quickly become dirty, oily, and discolored unless washed clean every week or two. In some rural or coastal places it can take months for dust to show. On the other hand, certain types of infestation from living organisms are more likely to occur in the country than in the city. Wherever you live, you should examine plants and clean leaves at least once a month.

Most comparatively small plants benefit from a light overhead spraying. The best place for spraying without wetting the furniture is outdoors; if this is not possible, use a large sink or bathtub. The spray should be rather fine and the water at room temperature, not cold. Sometimes the easiest way to clean the foliage of a little plant is to dip it bodily into water. Use slightly soapy water, if it seems advisable, but be sure to rinse the leaves in clear water. Avoid using detergents.

Plants too big to move, as well as those with large leaves, can have each leaf washed separately with a sponge or soft cloth. Again, if the kind of dirt warrants it, use soapy water followed by a clear-water rinse. When washing an individual leaf, support the leaf blade with one hand and pass the sponge or cloth lightly over the surface with the other. A gentle whisk of the underside of each leaf should be enough, since undersides usually need less attention than top surfaces. But because new leaves are soft, brittle, and easy to bruise, do not try to clean them in this way.

After washing a plant, do not let water remain on the leaves, in branch joints, or in the angles between stems and leafstalks. Lingering moisture can result in scorching or rotting.

Certain kinds of leaf—those that are hairy or scaly or have a waxy or powdery bloom—present special cleaning problems, which are not always easy to solve. Hairy leaves cannot be washed individually, for instance. Some can be sprayed lightly, as long as persistent drops of water are shaken off afterward. Probably the best way to clean hairy leaves, however, is with a soft brush. The type of brush often used for cleaning camera lenses is ideal for this purpose, especially if it is combined with a puffer for blowing dust away. But never use even the softest of brushes or cloths for scaly, waxy, or powdery leaves. An extremely gentle spraying, with some cautious shaking to dry off the moisture, is as much as these easily damaged surfaces can bear.

There is a belief in some quarters that wiping leaves with milk, beer, or vegetable oil will improve their appearance. It is not advisable, though, to use such substances; they may do more harm than good. This is also true of commercial leaf-shine products, whether applied with a cloth or by aerosol. These give an unnatural gloss to leaves, and some of them actually discolor foliage, especially if applied in low temperatures. If you use any such product, use it infrequently, and never risk clogging stomata by applying the product to the undersides of leaves.

In the course of examining and cleaning plants, always check the pots and potting mixture for signs of trouble. For instance, if the surface of the potting mixture has developed a white crust, this may indicate that the plant is being given excessively hard water or is being overfed. White deposits on the exterior of clay pots are a probable sign of the same sort of trouble. The green scum of algal growth or flat growths of liverwort on the mixture surface can indicate overwatering or poor drainage. And so on.

Interpreting symptoms The text and pictures on these and the following pages provide aids to prevention and cure of the common ailments that affect house plants. These guides to good health are designed to help you recognize and interpret symptoms of disease and types of infestation, and to do something about them where possible. In many cases a given symptom may be the result of a number of causes, including both inadequate care and attack by pests. If, for instance, leaves are yellowing for no apparent reason, the plant may be infested. But if close examination (which will sometimes require the use of a magnifying glass) rules out pests, the grower must consider whether any of a variety of cultivation needs is not being met. The following check list should help you pin down what may be wrong with your indoor plants.

CHECK LIST

Are you watering correctly?
Are you feeding the plant correctly?
Is the plant getting good light?
Is the temperature right?
Is the humidity right?
Is the pot size right?
Is the potting mixture right?

Disease

Diseases result from the invasion of plant cells by such microscopic organisms as fungi and bacteria. Apart from giving plants proper care, the best ways to stave off infection are to prevent water from settling on foliage and flowers and to space plants well apart from one another. Disease is contagious. Remove sickly-looking and dead leaves and flowers as soon as you spot them. Since bruised plant tissue is likely to become infected, watch such tissue carefully. If it begins to decay, cut it away with a clean, sharp blade, allow the wound to dry, and dust it with fungicidal powder. Infection can be kept from spreading by the use of chemicals and antibiotics. Use sterile potting mixtures to minimize the risk of diseased roots.

Blackleg

This ailment, also known as black rot or black stem rot, is a form of gray mold (see below). Stems of afflicted plants go black and rot at the base.

Prevention and cure Blackleg almost always follows overwatering or the use of rooting or potting mixture that is too water-retentive. Use porous, free-draining rooting mixtures for all cuttings. If only one cutting in a pot containing several is infected, throw away the diseased cutting and water the rooting mixture with streptomycin. Affected areas on stems will not recover, but sound parts of the stem above can be used for further cuttings. To reduce the risk of blackleg dip cut ends into hormone rooting powder containing fungicide.

Corm, root, or tuber rot

When the underground parts of a plant rot, the decayed areas usually become soft and slimy. Early indications of trouble may be leaf yellowing and wilting.

Prevention and cure This disease is much encouraged by overwatering and by water-retentive potting mixtures. Remove an afflicted plant from its pot, and discard it if the entire root system or storage organ is destroyed. If not, shake off the potting mixture, cut away damaged parts, and dust the rest (especially all cut surfaces) with a fungicide such as streptomycin, or sulfur. A precautionary measure is to drench the potting mixture of susceptible plants with terrazole.

Damping off

This term covers a group of diseases affecting seedlings. Stems of afflicted seedlings blacken or shrivel at or near rooting-mixture level and eventually topple over. There is no cure.

Prevention Damping off should not occur if sterile seed-sowing mixtures are used, but it is encouraged by excess moisture in the mixture, especially if the seedlings are crowded too close together. Sow seeds thinly, and thin out seedlings at the earliest feasible stage. Discard any that appear afflicted, and apply a fungicide to those that remain. As a precaution, rooting mixtures may be watered with fungicide before seeds are sown.

Gray mold

This fungus, which is also known as botrytis, covers affected leaves, stems, or flowers with a gray, fluffy mold. Any plant with soft leaves and stems is liable to attack. It is likely to occur only where the air is too humid.

Prevention and cure Gray mold is caused by mist-spraying too generously and permitting moisture to remain on the foliage. Cut away the affected parts, and throw the plant away, if necessary. To prevent further attacks, use a fungicide.

Leaf spot

Spots can be due to fungi or bacteria, or else to faulty growing conditions. Sometimes leaves develop brown or yellow blotches, and sometimes the blotches have a damp-looking center with yellow edges. Initially these diseased areas may be only about $\frac{1}{4}$ inch across, but they can spread and join together until the afflicted leaf dies.

Prevention and cure Leaf spotting often occurs when drops of water are permitted to remain on leaves. Watering with cold water can also result in spotting. Destroy affected leaves, and spray the plant with a fungicide. If spotting persists, try another type of fungicide or bactericide.

Damp spots sometimes develop into brownish, corky growths. This ailment, known as oedema or corky scab, is not caused by an organism. It is the result of overwatering and poor light conditions. Affected leaves will not recover, but new leaves will develop normally with reduction in watering and improvement in light conditions (as specified for each plant in the *A–Z Guide*).

Mildew

The leaves, stems, and (sometimes) flowers of plants suffering from this fungus disease—also called powdery mildew—become coated with a powdery growth of white mold. The mold can be distinguished from gray mold by color and by the absence of fluffy growths. Soft-leaved plants in general are prone to attack.

Prevention and cure Mildew is not a common disease of house plants. If mildew does occur, cut away affected parts. The rest of the plant should respond to spraying with a fungicide.

Sooty mold

This black mold does not directly attack leaves, but it is unsightly, interferes with photosynthesis, and blocks breathing pores.

Prevention and cure Sooty mold is a sure sign of attack by sap-sucking insects, which should be immediately treated (see "Pests," pages 454–456). Wash away the mold with a soft cloth dipped in soapy water, and then spray the leaves with clear water.

Stem and crown rot

Rot may attack any part of the stem of any plant. The area of decay usually becomes soft and slimy. Cacti may rot at the base. Plants forming crowns or rosettes are normally attacked at the center, so that the leaves are rotted away from their crown.

Prevention and cure Stem and crown rot always follows some sort of mistake in meeting a plant's cultivation needs (too much water or cold air, for example). Afflicted plants can rarely be saved except through cuttings of unaffected parts. If a stem begins to rot at some distance above the potting-mixture surface, cut it off just above the base, and dust the cut place with sulfur or streptomycin. The stem will probably sprout afresh.

Virus

Virus disease is caused by microscopic organisms or particles that change the basic composition of plant cells. The symptoms are usually yellow streaking or mottling of leaves, often with distortion of leaf shape, and stunting of the whole plant. There is no cure.

Prevention Be sure to destroy an infected plant immediately. Viruses are usually spread by aphids and other sap-sucking insects. This makes it all-important to combat these pests.

Pests

Most house-plant pests are tiny. The activity of those small insects or mites that suck plant juices results in a yellowing and distortion of the shape of leaves. Chewing insects bite off pieces of leaf edges, eat holes into the leaf, and attack stems and growing tips. The grubs of leaf-mining insects bore tunnels through leaves, eating plant tissues as they go. Meanwhile, other creatures, often in larval form, may be infesting underground parts, with consequent wilting of the plant.

As virtually any house plant can be attacked by pests, all specimens should be frequently inspected for symptoms of infestation and for the presence of the pests themselves. At the time of repotting, attention can be paid to roots as well as to junctions of stems and leaves and to fissures in the skin of woody stems.

On these and the following pages you will find important facts that every indoor gardener should know about pest control.

Ants

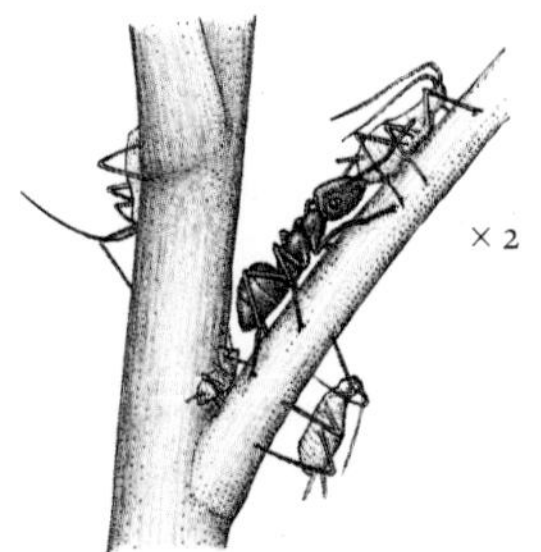

Ants can be indirectly harmful. They carry such sap-sucking pests as aphids to the soft upper parts of plants and feed on the "honeydew" excreted by the sap suckers. Thus ants spread pests from plant to plant. They also nest in pots, where their tunneling damages roots.
Control: In addition to using pesticides on plants, spread lindane dust or a borax-based antkiller wherever concentrations of ants appear.

Aphids

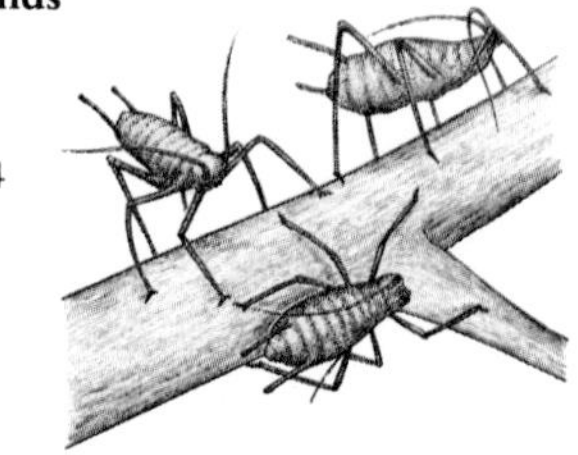

Aphids (or "plant lice") are sap-sucking insects about $\frac{1}{8}$ inch long and usually green, but may be black, brown, gray, or yellow. They multiply rapidly and molt often; white "skeletons" are visible evidence of infestation. Under attack, leaves, stems, and flowers become distorted, sticky, and very susceptible to sooty mold (see "Diseases," page 453). Aphids also carry incurable virus diseases. They attack all plants except those with hard, stiff tissues (like bromeliads).
Control: Remove and destroy badly distorted plant growths. Keep plants clean at all times, and use a pesticide regularly.

Bulb-scale mites

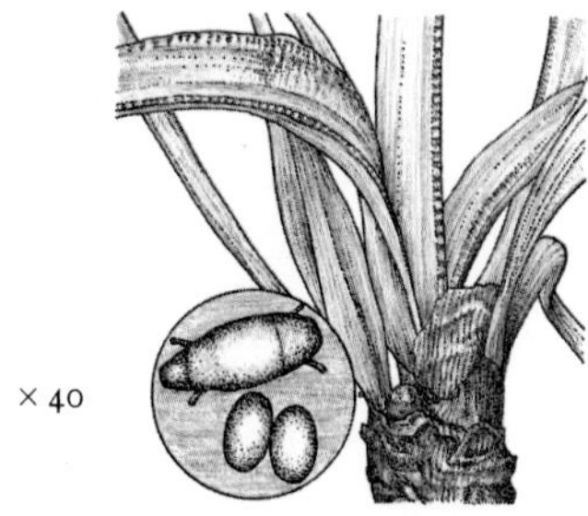

Bulb-scale mites are invisible sap suckers that attack bulbous plants. The only normally vulnerable house plants are hippeastrums. These pests cause red flecks and streaks on leaves and stems, especially near the bulb. In severe infestations leaf edges will become lightly notched and ridgy, and—though this rarely happens—flower buds can be distorted or destroyed.
Control: If reddish marks on emerging leaves and stems at the start of the growth period suggest the presence of mites, give a drenching spray of an appropriate pesticide, and repeat it weekly till new markings cease to appear.

Caterpillars

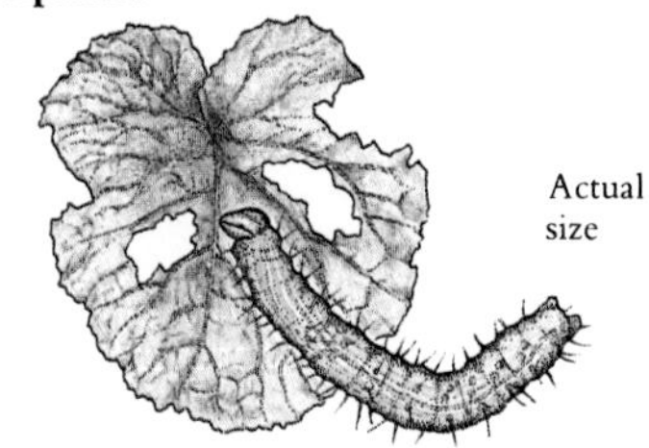

Caterpillars seldom infest indoor plants, but small ones may be introduced on newly acquired plants, and adult insects (moths and butterflies) sometimes fly in and lay eggs on established plants. Caterpillars chew leaves, making holes or notched edges. Some types (often called cutworms) attack stems near the base. Any soft-leaved plant is vulnerable.
Control: Pick off and destroy individual caterpillars. Apply an appropriate pesticide in cases of severe infestation.

Cyclamen mites

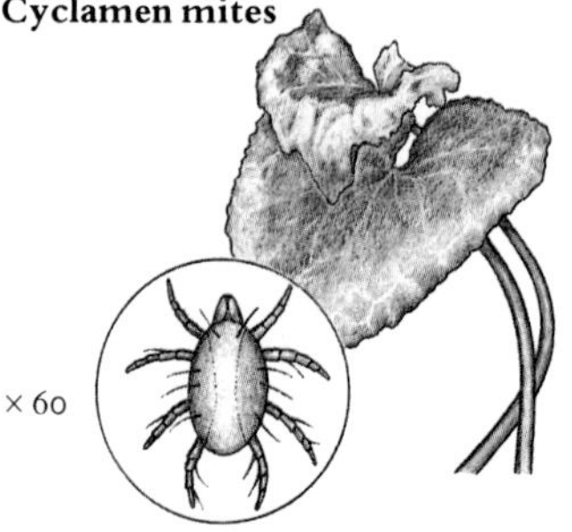

Cyclamen mites and the almost identical broad mites are minute sap suckers that lay eggs in such quantities that they look like a coating of dust. Leaves and flower stems become twisted, brittle, and (eventually) completely covered with small scabs. Flower buds may wither, and flowers lose color. These pests attack many kinds of plant in addition to cyclamens.
Control: Using a powerful magnifying glass, search suspicious-looking areas for concentrations of whitish eggs or mites. If necessary, spray with an appropriate pesticide, and spray again monthly until no sign of infestation remains.

Earwigs

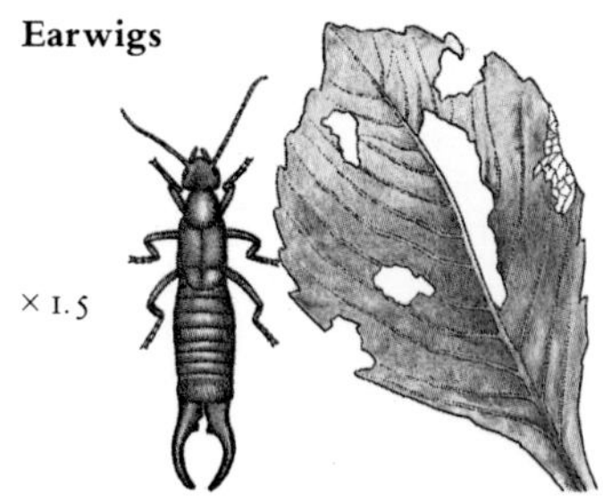

Earwigs are narrow, dark brown bugs up to 1 inch long, with a pair of pincers at the tail. They will chew up any aboveground part of almost any plant, can reduce leaves to skeletons, and can make flowers ragged.
Control: Pick off earwigs by hand, wearing gloves (the pincers do pinch). Otherwise use an appropriate pesticide. Domestic roach sprays kill these pests but must not be used on plants.

Fungus gnats

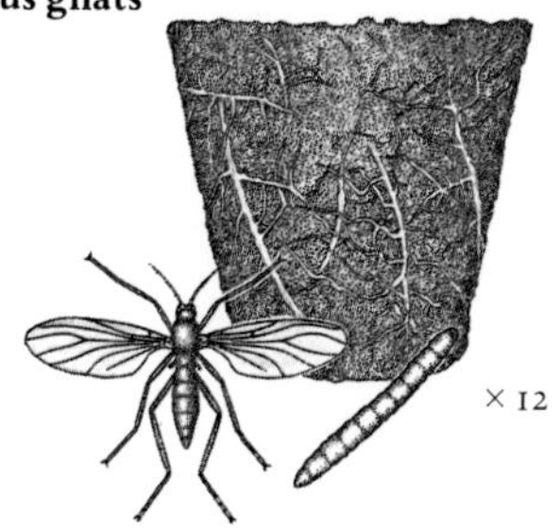

Fungus gnats (also called mushroom flies and sciarid flies) are tiny insects about $\frac{1}{16}$ inch long. They deposit their larvae, which are generally less than $\frac{1}{16}$ inch long and white with a blackish head, in potting mixture. Most such larvae feed harmlessly on decaying matter in the mixture or on naturally decaying roots, but one or two kinds are capable of seriously damaging roots, especially of seedlings.
Control: There should be no living larvae in sterilized potting mixture, but watch for them in peat and peat-based mixtures. Drench infested mixture with an appropriate pesticide, and spray adult gnats seen indoors with the same substance.

Leaf miners

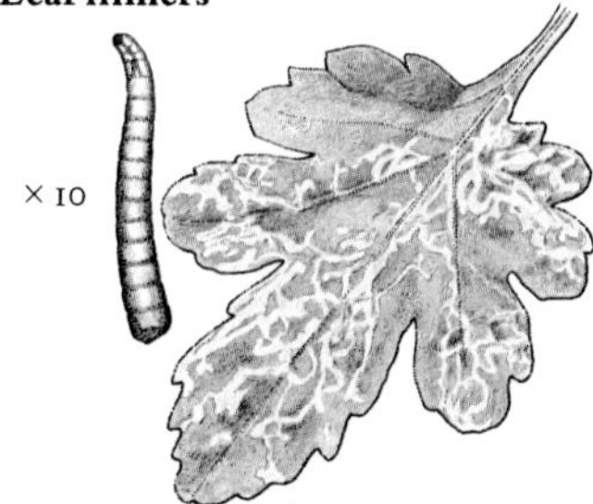

Leaf miners are sap-sucking grubs that tunnel through leaves between the surfaces, creating an irregular white pattern which is usually long and

narrow but can look simply blotchy. The grubs can often be seen if leaves are examined closely. The chief plants that become seriously affected are chrysanthemums and cinerarias, but others are sometimes attacked.
Control: Pick off affected leaves, and use an appropriate pesticide spray, or place granules of a systemic pesticide in the potting mixture.

Leaf rollers

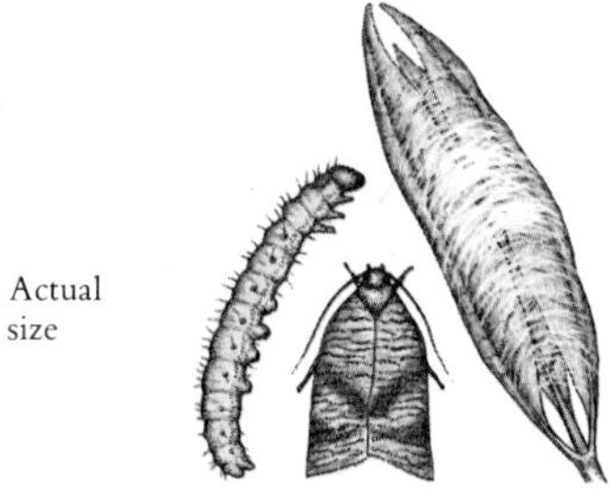

Leaf rollers are ½- to 1-inch-long, thin, green caterpillars (larvae of tortrix moths) that roll themselves up in leaves, occasionally emerging from this safe retreat to eat adjoining stems and foliage. They will attack almost any plant and can join adjacent leaves together with a sticky webbing if, for any reason, they cannot roll a single leaf around themselves.
Control: Pick off the leaf rollers and all damaged foliage. Spray with an anti-caterpillar pesticide if necessary. Get rid of intruding tortrix moths (nearly oblong in shape and ½ inch long with wings folded) by spraying them, too; failure to remove them before they lay eggs will result in the appearance of more leaf rollers.

Mealy bugs and root mealy bugs

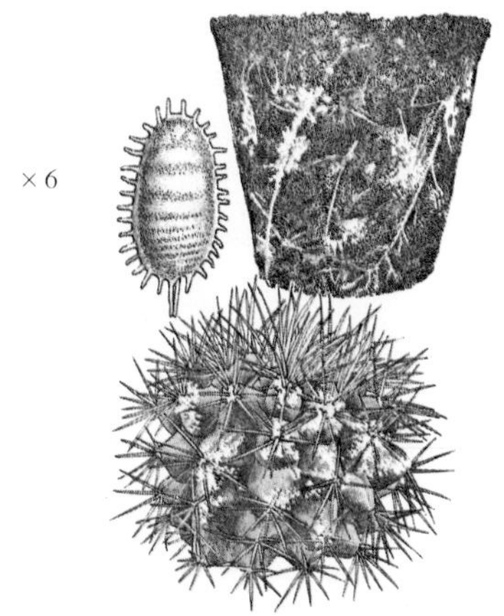

Mealy bugs are oval, ⅛ inch long, with filaments all around the body, which is pink overlaid by a whitish secretion. They tend to congregate on stems and leaves and in leaf axils. Individual bugs are often concealed in white, woolly "nests." They can attack almost any plant, causing leaves to yellow and wither rapidly, and they also excrete "honeydew," which attracts ants. Severe infestations can result in total loss of leaves.
Control: Remove visible bugs with a toothpick or a damp cloth, or swab them off foliage with a small, stiff paintbrush dipped in denatured alcohol or an insecticide solution. Then spray all top growth with an appropriate pesticide. Alternatively, place granules of a systemic pesticide in the potting mixture. During the next month examine plants weekly for traces of reinfestation.

Root mealy bugs infest roots, forming woolly, water-resistant "nests" like those of aboveground mealy bugs. By sucking the sap in roots these pests can cause stunting of top growth. Plants particularly prone to attack are cacti, other succulents, and saintpaulias.
Control: For small plants wash potting mixture from roots with tepid water, cut away worst infested parts, and soak the rest in an appropriate pesticide solution before repotting plants in clean pots of fresh mixture. For plants too large for this treatment drench the potting mixture with the pesticide every two weeks during a period of at least six weeks.

Nematodes

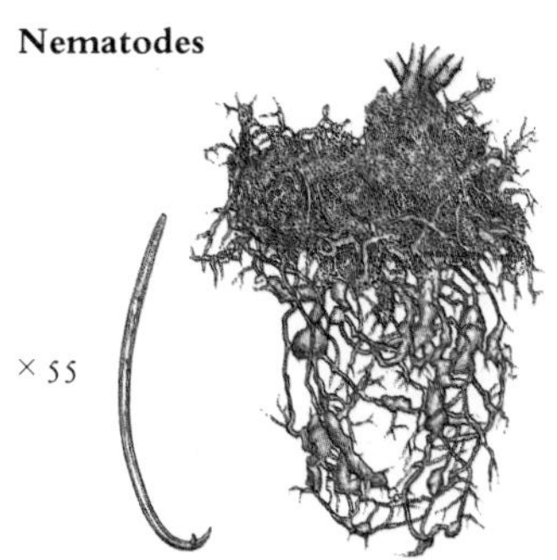

Nematodes (eelworms) are minute wormlike creatures that suck the sap of roots. The kind most likely to affect house plants—the root-knot nematodes—cause roots to swell, become unable to absorb water and food from the potting mixture, and eventually decay. Attacked plants look unhealthy and wilt for no apparent reason.
Control: Nematodes should not occur if sterilized potting mixtures are used. There is no way to combat these pests. Destroy infested plants, and dispose of potting mixture. Sterilize or discard pots. Avoid all contact between these materials and healthy plants. Do not take cuttings from lower parts of an infested plant before destroying it. Upper parts can be used.

Red spider mites

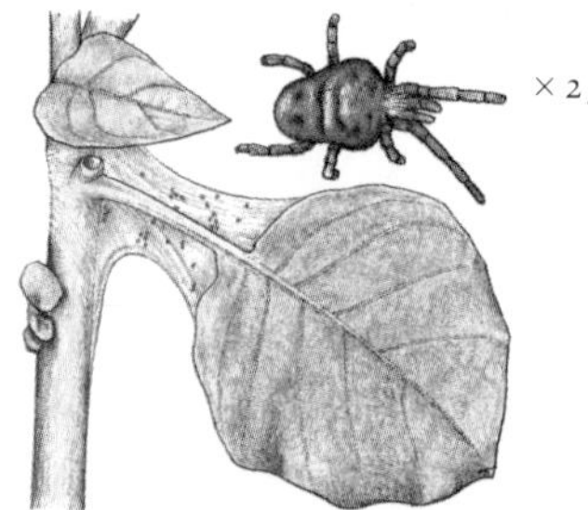

Red spider mites are minute red or pink sap suckers that make a silky webbing on the undersides of leaves. Mottled leaves gradually turning pale yellow, spotted with black dots (the mites' excreta), indicate infestation. Leaves curl up and fall, new growth may be stunted, and flower buds may be blackened. In severe attacks, infestation may spread from leaf to leaf until the whole plant is affected.
Control: These pests thrive in hot, dry air. Daily mist-spraying may help ward off attack. If an attack is suspected, confirm the presence of mites with a magnifying glass. Cut away badly infested leaves and adjoining stems, and spray plants with an appropriate pesticide. Repeat the treatment after 3 days, and again 10 days later. If mites persist, try a different pesticide.

Scale insects

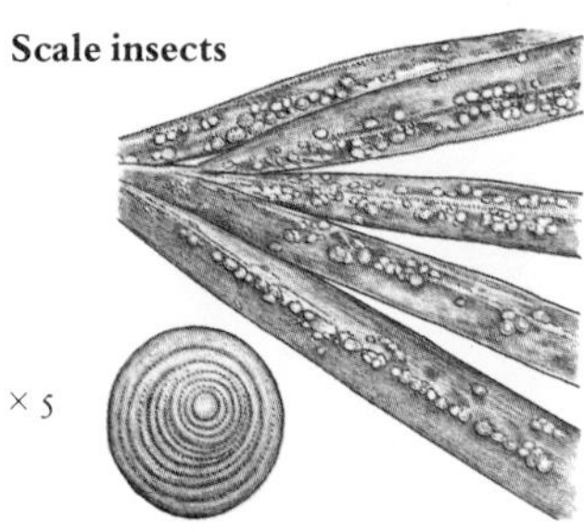

Scale insects are 1/16–⅛ inch long and mostly brown or yellowish (one type of fern scale is white). When mature, they are motionless, enclosed in a waxy cover (or scale). Thus protected, the insect sucks sap, causing the plant tissues to wither. Excreted "honeydew" attracts ants. Stickiness or resultant sooty mold (see "Diseases," page 453) is often the first sign of attack. All house plants are vulnerable to scale insects.
Control: Examine every crevice for scales, and wipe them off with a damp cloth or a fairly stiff brush dipped in soapy water or an appropriate pesticide solution. Then apply pesticide to the whole plant.

Springtails

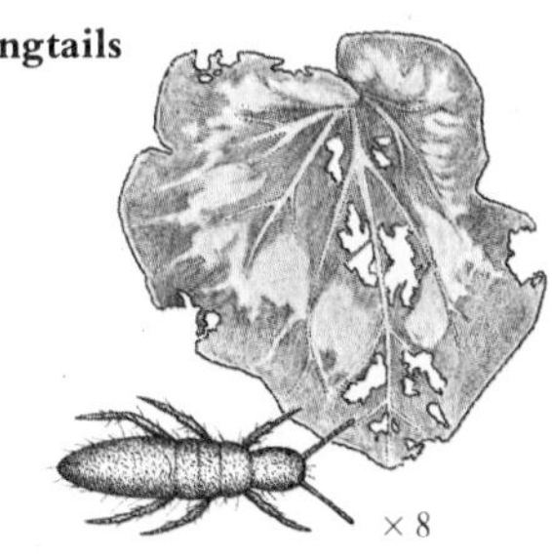

Springtails are wingless, jumping, white insects up to ⅜ inch long commonly found in unsterilized soil and peat. They usually do no harm, but some kinds gnaw the stems of young plants and feed on leaves that touch the potting mixture.
Control: To avoid possible trouble, always use sterile mixtures for seedlings. Otherwise, no action is generally advisable, though springtails will be destroyed if the potting mixture is drenched with an appropriate pesticide.

Symphilids

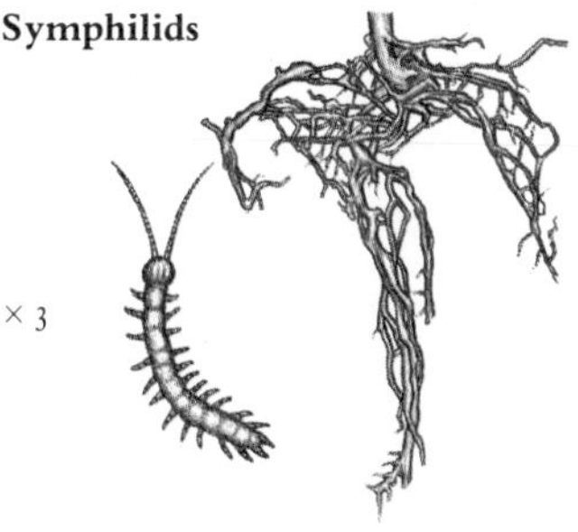

Symphilids look like tiny, cream-colored centipedes; but, unlike centipedes (harmless to plants), they destroy small roots and burrow into larger ones, where corky patches indicate areas that these pests have gnawed. Fortunately, they rarely occur in house plants.
Control: Symphilids cannot normally survive in sterilized potting mixtures. If infestation is suspected, test the mixture by stirring up a little in a container of water. The insects, if any, will rise to the surface. The mixture in the pot should then be drenched with an appropriate pesticide.

Thrips

× 7

Thrips (sometimes called thunderflies) are sap suckers about $\frac{1}{16}$ inch long, colored yellow, green, or black, with finely fringed wings that give them a fuzzy appearance. They seldom fly and are more likely to jump, like springtails. Thrips can attack any fairly soft foliage, causing mottling or streaking, and they also attack flowers, which then develop white spots. Drops of reddish fluid that these insects excrete turn black, speckling sickly leaves or flowers.
Control: After removing spoiled flowers and badly damaged leaves, spray plants with an appropriate pesticide.

Weevils

Actual size

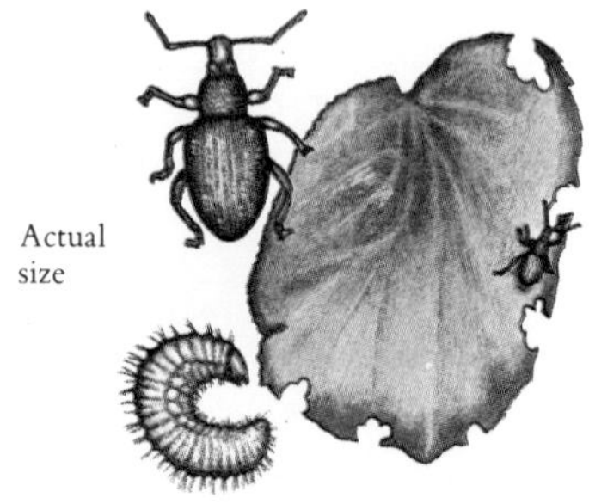

Weevils that damage house plants are 1-inch-long, leaf-chewing beetles. The most common ones are vine weevils. Their cream-colored, 1-inch-long grubs live in potting mixture, eat roots and storage organs, and can rapidly destroy the root system of a plant. Severely wilted top growth, especially if it occurs suddenly, is a likely sign of grub infestation. Grubs can be seen if the mixture is shaken out into a tray. Both grubs and adults attack a wide range of plants.
Control: Pick off and destroy adults. Plants with badly damaged roots or tubers cannot usually be saved. Immediately on sighting an adult weevil, drench the mixture with a suitable pesticide.

Whiteflies

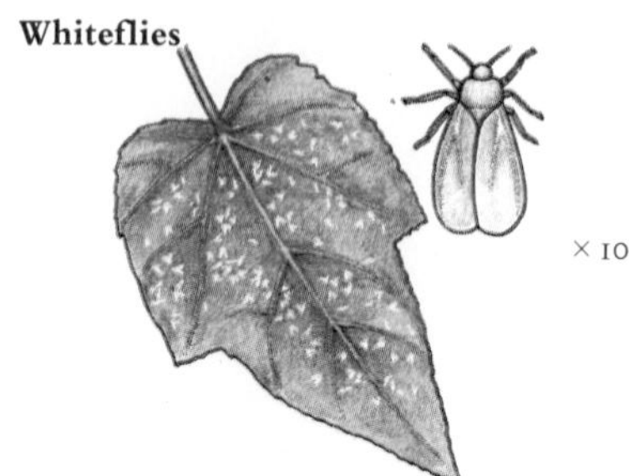

Whiteflies are wedge-shaped, white insects up to $\frac{1}{8}$ inch long. Winged adults deposit larvae in vast numbers on leaf undersides, where they suck sap and excrete sticky "honeydew." The larvae look like greenish or transparent scales.
Control: Whiteflies are difficult to get rid of. Spray repeatedly, trying different types of pesticide, until infestation appears to have ceased.

Diagnosing the problem

This chart is designed to help you recognize and interpret symptoms of plant ill health, whether due to pests, diseases, or inadequate care. Unfortunately, quite small deviations from the ideal growing conditions laid down in the *A–Z Guide* can cause markings, discolorations, or even decay. More generalized symptoms of ill health are usually caused by cultivation faults as diverse as giving too much or too little water, or an excess of fertilizer, providing too high or too low a temperature, or subjecting plants to drafts, hot, dry air, or to strong sunshine. The chart describes the symptoms from which a plant can suffer and the likely causes. Where the causes are cultural, the remedy lies in improving growing conditions while realizing that affected leaves and flowers are unlikely to recover. Where ill health is due to an attack by pests or to disease, it is important to diagnose the problem and to effect treatment as soon as possible. Once you have diagnosed the problem turn back to pages 452-455 for treatment instructions.

WHOLE PLANT

Collapse or wilting

The probable cause is either attack on the root system by pests or diseases (see "Roots," below) or faulty cultivation such as waterlogging, excessive dryness, or a severe, sudden chill.

Stunted growth

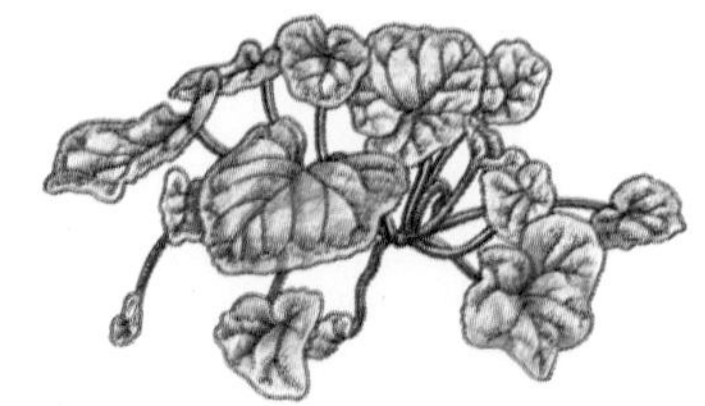

First, suspect attack by cyclamen mites or other sap-sucking pests, especially aphids, scale insects, or red spider mites. Otherwise, the cause may be an attack on the root system by pests or diseases (see "Roots," below). In perlargoniums, virus disease is a possibility.

TOP GROWTH

Fine web coating

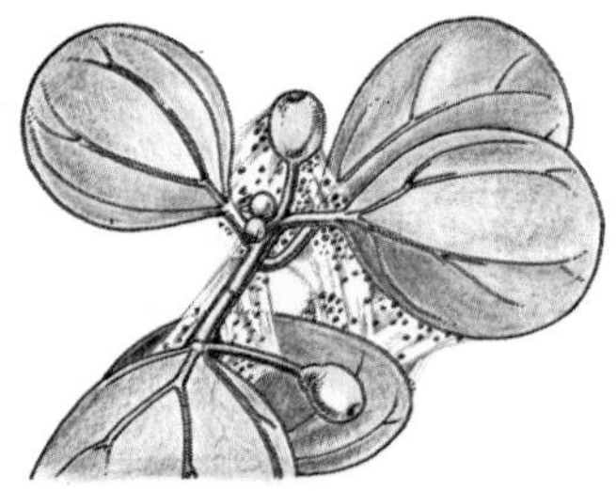

The web starts on leaf undersides and extends to clusters of leaves and shoots. It indicates attack by red spider mites.

Grayish mold

This indicates gray mold disease (botrytis).

Powdery white patches

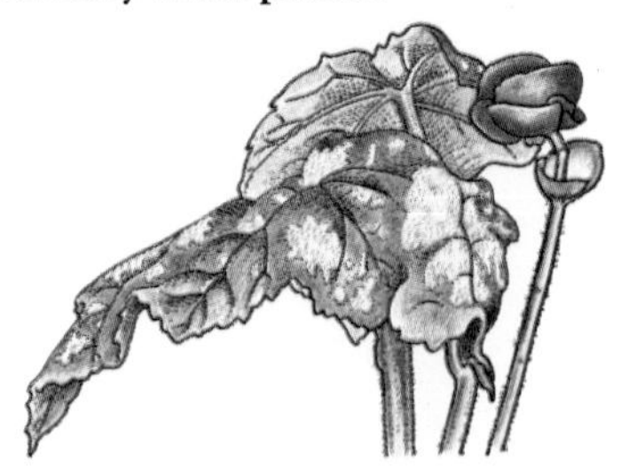

The cause of this is the fungus disease known as powdery mildew.

STEM OR CROWN

Black or brown decayed areas

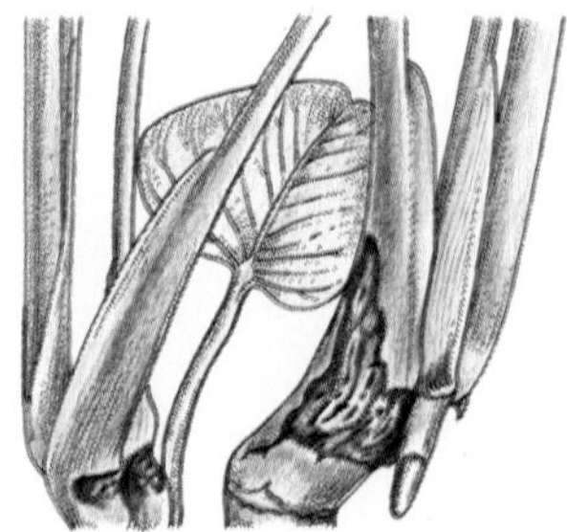

In mature plants the cause is probably stem and crown rot disease. If rotting is seen at the base of a cutting planted in rooting mixture, suspect blackleg disease. Rotting of seedling stems is due to damping off disease.

Disappearance of stem tips and irregular notching on stems

These plants are probably being attacked by caterpillars, earwigs, or weevils. Such irregular notching is caused by these pests literally chewing away the more succulent parts of a plant. They can do untold damage if not checked as soon as possible.

LEAVES

Black patches of mold

This is sooty mold, a fungus disease that is a side effect of infestation by such sap-sucking insects as red spider mites.

Blotches

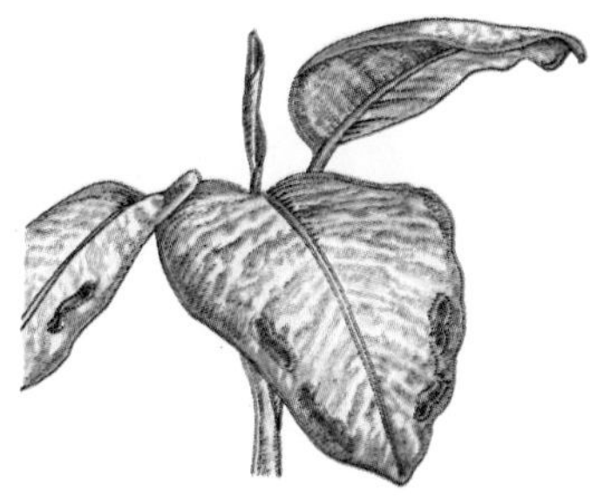

Large, irregular areas of discoloration—yellow, brown, or black—are usually a sign of unsatisfactory growing conditions. Consider all aspects of proper care.

Brown, withered tips

Plants with long, narrow leaves are most likely to suffer. Is the air or soil too dry? Are leaves being bruised by people brushing past the plant?

Corky growths

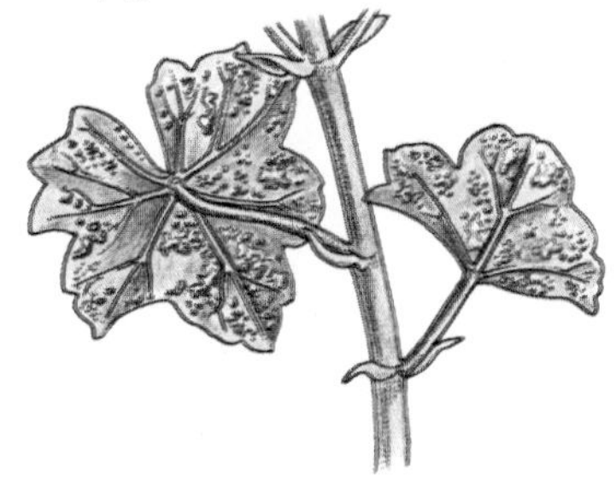

Damp spots on leaves can be the cause of these. The disease, known as oedema or corky scab, often results from overwatering of plants grown in poor light.

Distortion

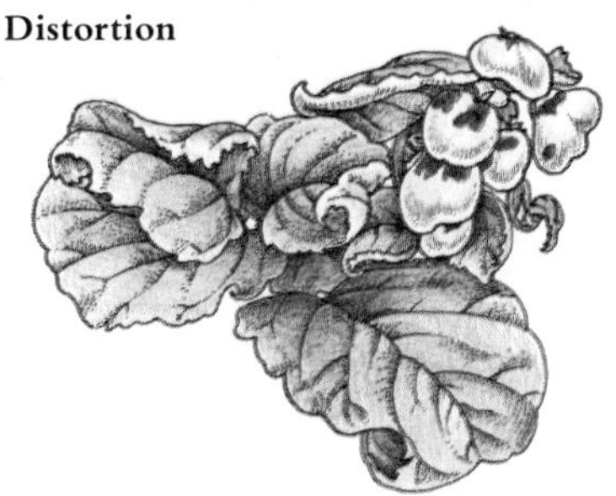

If leaves curl unnaturally or seem to be generally misshapen, suspect attack by sap-sucking pests such as aphids, cyclamen or red spider mites, or thrips. In pelargoniums, virus disease is a possible cause.

Falling leaves

If leaves suddenly start dropping off and the plant is not going into its dormant period, it has probably suffered severely from faulty cultivation. Consider all aspects of proper care.

Holes or notched edges

The cause is some type of chewing insect. Look for caterpillars, earwigs, or weevils.

Irregular white markings

These are the tracks of leaf-miner grubs.

Loss of variegation

This is not a disease. Variegated plants have a tendency to revert to the original type. Cut out all shoots bearing all green leaves. If leaves are losing color gradually, the cause is poor light.

Rolled-up leaves

If the edges are joined by a white web, look for a green caterpillar or brown pupa within the webbed leaf. It has been invaded by a leaf roller.

Spots

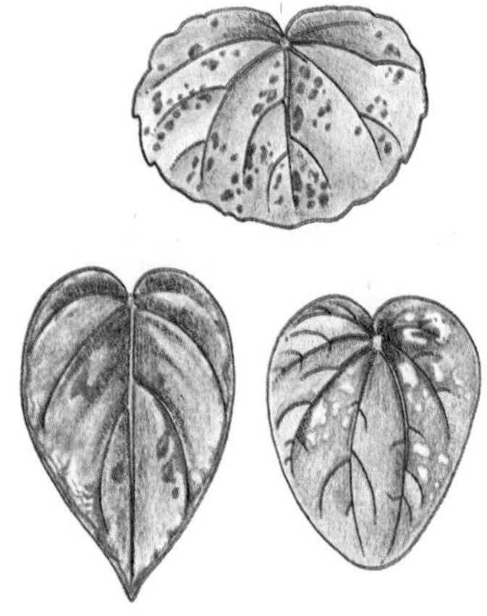

A wide range of spots and blotches varying from small and regular to large and irregular, and from moist and blistered to dry and depressed, can affect leaves. They are most likely to be caused by cultivation faults but can also be the result of bacterial or viral infection. Small, flat, roundish, brown spots, the most common problem, are usually caused by carelessness in watering and mist-spraying.

Stickiness

This is a secretion from sap-sucking insects—probably aphids, scale insects, or whiteflies. The accumulation of fluid can be so great that it drips from the tips of leaves.

Streakiness

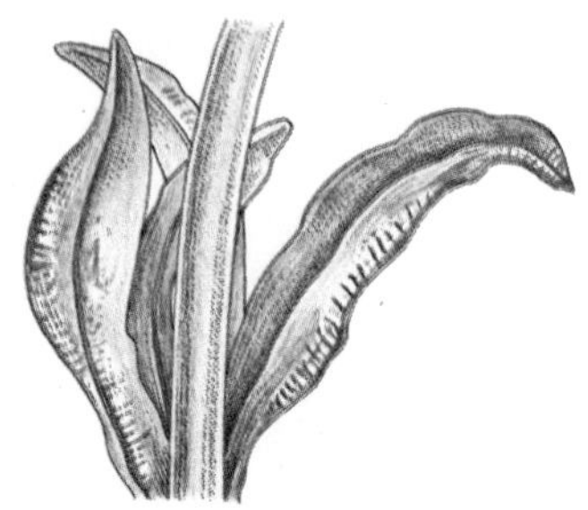

Undesirable pale or red streaks are probably caused by an infestation of bulb-scale mites in hippeastrums, or of thrips in any other plant. Long, narrow leaves of many bulbous plants may, at the same time, become twisted and malformed, and notched with rusty brown or red scars along their margins.

Yellow mottling

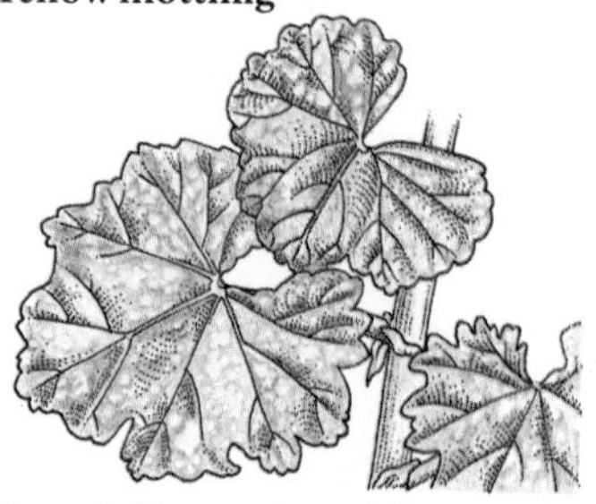

The probable cause is attack by sap suckers. In pelargoniums and peperomias this may be a sign of virus disease if leaves are also distorted.

Yellowing and withering

Is the plant being attacked by such sap-sucking pests as aphids, scale insects, red spider mites, or whiteflies? If not, growing conditions may be at fault. Consider all aspects of proper care.

Yellowing without withering

This is caused either by too strong light or by chlorosis—too much lime in the potting mixture or water. The latter can generally occur only in such acid-loving plants as camellias and gardenias. The easiest way to remedy chlorosis is to apply a sequestrine or chelate compound.

FLOWERS

Blackened buds

Is humidity too low? If not, suspect attack by cyclamen or red spider mites.

Distorted buds

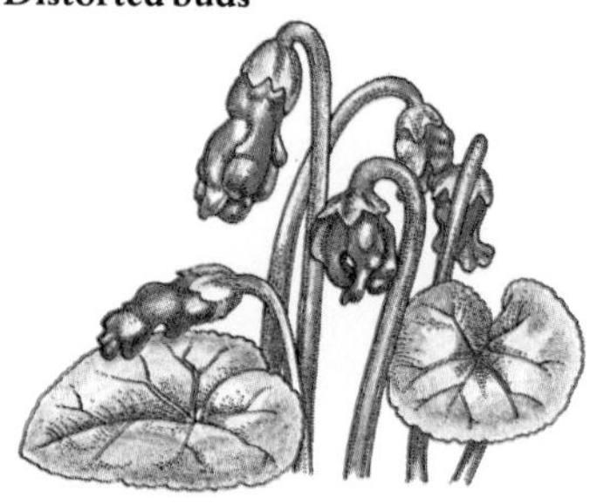

Suspect attack by thrips. This symptom can also be caused by a virus disease.

Premature dropping

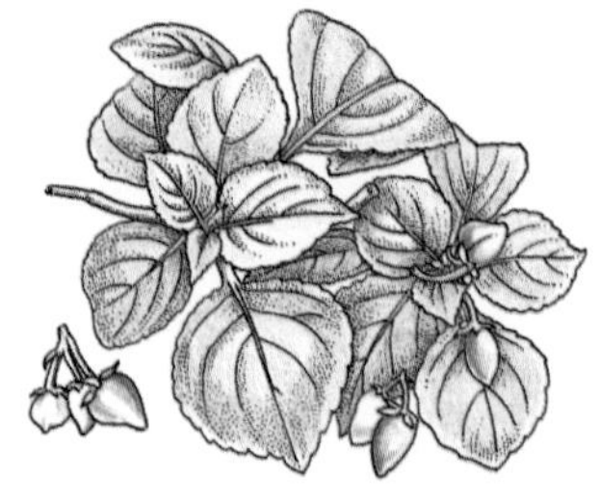

The cause is probably a succession of sudden, sharp changes in the growing conditions—for instance, irregular watering, big temperature drops or rises, or simply shifts in the location of the plant that cause it to be subjected to unfavorable lighting conditions or to drafts.

Streaking or speckling

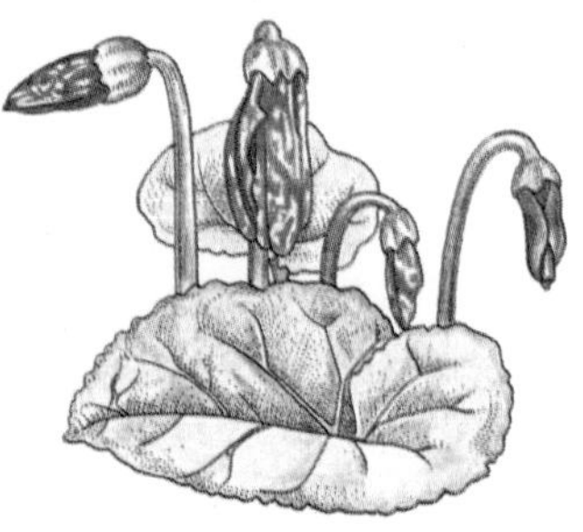

Suspect attack by cyclamen mites, thrips, or less likely, by virus disease.

ROOTS, BULBS, AND TUBERS

Abnormal swelling and bushiness

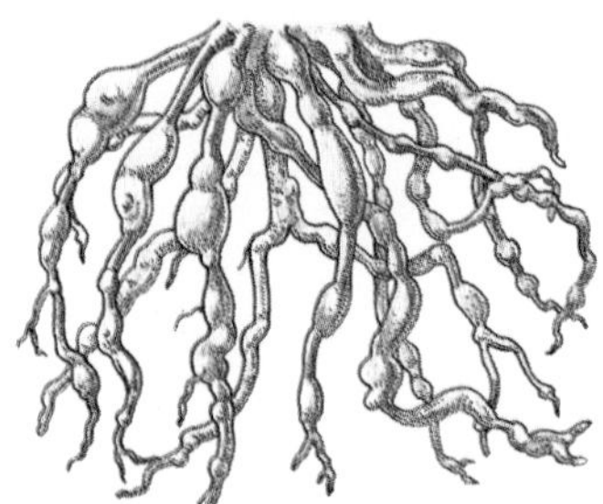

The most probable cause is attack by the pests known as root-knot nematodes.

Gnawed, corky patches

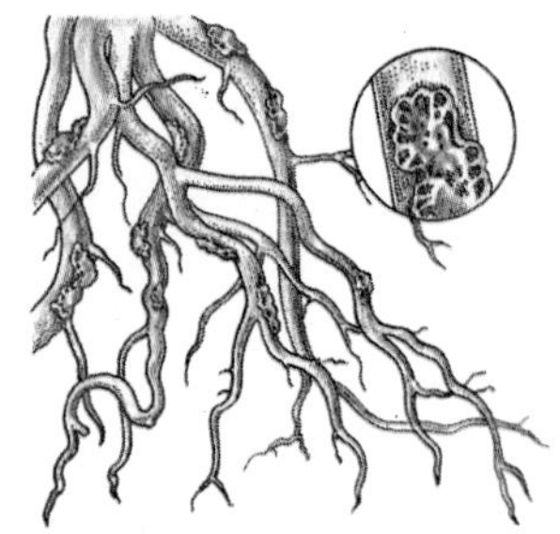

The cause is almost certainly due to an infestation of symphilids.

Reduction in quantity

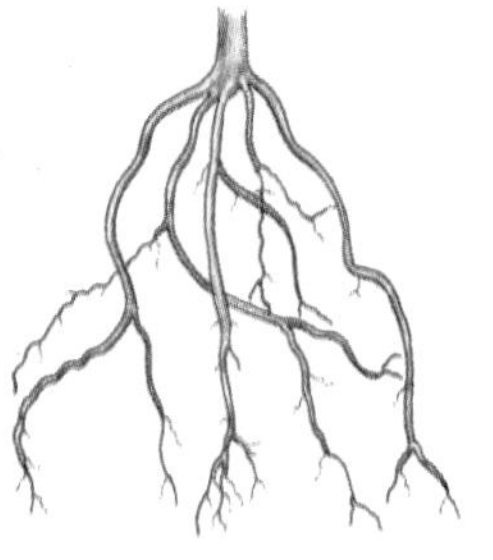

The roots are under severe attack by the larvae of fungus gnats or by nematodes, symphilids, or weevil grubs.

Rot

This may be a symptom of the disease known as corm, root, or tuber rot, or may be caused by any of a number of cultivation faults, the most likely of which are overwatering or blocked drainage holes in the pot or container.

White, woolly patches

These are a definite sign of infestation by root mealy bugs, which will be seen if the patches are closely examined.

Prevention and cure

Pesticides The earlier the presence of pests is noted, the easier they are to control. Most multiply very quickly and will spread from plant to plant. In the early stages it is sometimes possible to destroy visible pests—mealy bugs and weevils, for example—by picking them off plants, and to get rid of smaller creatures by removing all the infested parts of a plant. Often, though, simple methods of control are inadequate. Even if they seem to be successful, it is wise to apply a pesticide to the whole plant as a further preventive measure. Most pests can be killed by the application of a suitable pesticide (for specifics see page 461). And pesticides are generally available in different forms—liquids, powder, etc.—such as are discussed below under "Application methods."

Pesticides act against living creatures either by contact, when sprayed or dusted over them, or poisoning them after they have fed on plant tissue containing the poisonous substance. The latter poisons are of two types: Either they coat the external parts of the plant wherever applied, or they are absorbed by the plant and remain for a period within all its tissues, so that a pest feeding upon any part of the plant is destroyed. This second kind of pesticide, which is carried throughout the plant in its sap, is termed *systemic*, and systemic poisons are the best possible preventive measure, especially against such insidious pests as scale insects. They are less effective as a quick control, however, since it takes time for the poison to reach all parts of a plant. A contact pesticide applied as soon as infestation is observed does the job more swiftly, though probably less thoroughly. However, the two types of pesticide can sometimes be used in combination. This is effective against the widest possible range of pests.

In selecting pesticides for indoor use, remember that there are two important considerations other than effectiveness against pests: Those two considerations are plant health and human safety.

Certain pesticides are harmful to certain kinds of plant. Read the instructions on the package or bottle carefully; they should include lists not only of the pests that the product will kill but of the plants that it might harm. In particular, ferns, cacti, and other succulents can suffer from the use of certain chemicals. Be sure to follow instructions about quantities, too. Too much of a given product can damage the plant, and too little will be ineffective against the pest.

Furthermore, most pesticides are poisonous to human beings, when left on the skin. If used as directed, they should be safe enough, but careless handling is dangerous. Always follow safety instructions on the label to the letter, and always wash your hands after using these products. The only pesticides that are entirely harmless to human beings, even if swallowed, are pyrethrum and its derivative resmethrin. These are derived from plants and should therefore appeal to gardeners who prefer products of natural origin. Unfortunately, though, there are a number of pests that pyrethrum and resmethrin will not destroy. (Nicotine, usually in the form of nicotine sulfate, is also a commonly available natural pesticide, but this is poisonous to human beings.)

Some pesticides (such as rotenone) are deadly to fish. Cover ornamental fish tanks if such a pesticide is used on plants in the same room.

Disease control As has been emphasized, the best way to prevent disease is to grow plants under the best possible conditions. If disease occurs, the first thing to do is to remove and destroy affected parts of the plant. This is essential because diseases are so readily spread by microorganisms carried through the air.

The chemicals or antibiotics that can cure fungus and bacterial diseases are called fungicides and bactericides. As with pesticides, some of these are systemic and are therefore able to destroy microorganisms that attack any part of a plant.

Fungicides and bactericides are not generally harmful to either plants or human beings. But it is, as always, essential to obey safety instructions on the packaging.

Combined materials Products that combine a systemic pesticide and a systemic fungicide are now widely available. Because diseases are so much less likely than pests to attack house plants, it is seldom necessary to use such products indoors. It does no harm to use them, however. They can be a worthwhile insurance against possible attack.

Application methods Control materials are available in various forms. The most common form is a liquid to be diluted in water for use as a spray. It is always best to use pesticide sprays outdoors. If this is not possible, enclose the plant in a large plastic bag, tie the open end of the bag around the pot, and then spray the plant through a small hole made in the top of the bag. In any case spray with caution, directing the nozzle or spray valve only at the limited area being treated. Try to coat every part of the plant, however, paying special attention to young growths where sap-sucking pests are likely to congregate and to leaf undersides. It is often a good idea to place a large plant on its side in order to reach all sections of it. Diluted chemicals can also be used as a bath in which small plants can be dipped. When immersing the plant, spread one rubber-gloved hand over the potting mixture as you dip the upended plant into the solution, holding the base of the plant between two fingers.

Some pesticides are also available in aerosol form. These carry a warning about the minimum distance from which the spray should be directed at the plant. The foliage can be physically damaged by the force of the spray if such warnings are not taken seriously. Aerosol sprays are unlikely to harm furnishings, but in other respects they are as potentially dangerous as any other pesticide.

If it is necessary to soak the potting mixture with a pesticide in order to kill underground pests or to get systemic pesticide into the plant, do so by means of a watering can.

Many pest- and disease-control products are available as dusts. These are designed primarily for outdoor plants since they coat foliage until rain washes off the dust. Although they are not generally recommended for use on house plants, however, some fungicidal dusts can be usefully applied to cut or bruised surfaces.

Finally a few systemic pesticides are available in granule or tablet form. These can be placed on the surface of the potting mixture or pushed down into it, according to instructions. The pesticide is gradually released from the granule or tablet with each successive watering of the plant, and the poison is distributed throughout the plant. This method is convenient: it involves no mixing of solutions.

Pest and disease control chart

	chlorobenzilate	chlorothalonil	chlortetracycline	cycloheximide	diazinon	dichloran	dicofol	dinocap	disulfoton (systemic)
Ants									
Aphids					S G				S G
Black leg									
Bulb-scale mites	S						S		
Caterpillars									
Corm, root, or tuber rot									
Cyclamen mites	S						S		S G
Damping off (seedlings)				R					
Earwigs									
Fungus gnats									
Gray mold		S				S			
Leaf miners					S G				S G
Leaf-rolling caterpillars									
Leaf spot diseases			S						
Mealy bugs					S G				S G
Mealy bugs (root)									
Mildew		S		S		S		S	
Red spider mites	S				S G		S		S G
Scale insects					S G				S G
Sooty mold	S				S G		S		S G
Springtails					R G				
Stem and crown rot									
Symphilids					R G				
Thrips					S G		S G		
Weevils									
Whiteflies					S G				S G

*There is no cure for nematodes or virus disease

Key to application methods

D Dust plant
G Apply granules to mixture
R Soak mixture
S Spray plant

endosulfan	lindane	malathion	nicotine sulfate	pirimiphos-methyl	propoxur	pyrethrum	resmethrin	rotenone (derris)	streptomycin	sulfur	terrazole	tetradifon	thiophanate-methyl
		R		S	S	S	S						
S		S G	S	S	S	S	S						
									R				
S													
	S D G	S D G		S		S	S	S D					
									D	D	R		
S				S								S	
											R		
	S D	S G		S									
	S R G	S R G				S R	S R						
									S				S
	S G			S									
	S D G	S D G		S		S	S	S D					
									S				S
		S G	S	S									
		R G		R									
									S	S			
		S G		S	S								
		S G	S										
S		S G	S	S	S	S	S					S	
	R G	R G				R	R						
									D	D			
	R G	R G											
				S		S	S						
	S R D G	S R D G						S R D					
		S G		S	S	S	S						

Control products

Materials used for pest and disease control in plants are mostly complex organic compounds. Each compound has a technical name, which is the name that appears in the adjoining pest and disease control chart. Manufacturers, however, can apply trade names to their products regardless of the ingredients. Major ingredients and trade names of recommended compounds based upon them are listed below. All products should specify technical names of ingredients on their labels, but this information can be in very small print.

Technical name	*Trade names*
chlorobenzilate	Acaraban, Akar
chlorothalonil	Bravo, Daconil 2787
chlortetracycline	Acronize, Aureomycin
cyclohexamide	Acti-dione, Actispray
diazinon	Gardentox, Sarolex, Spectracide
dichloran (dicloran, DCNA)	Allisan, Botran
dicofol	Kelthane
dinocap	Arathane, Iscothane, Karathane, Mildex
disulfoton	Di-Syston
endosulfan	Cyclodan, Thifor, Thiodan
lindane (gamma-BHC)	Gammex, Gammexane
malathion	Cythion, Malathion
nicotine sulfate	Blackleaf 40
pirimiphos-methyl	Actellic
propoxur	Baygon
pyrethrum	Pratts Red Arrow Spray, Prentiss Pyrethrum Powder
resmethrin	Chryson, Synthrin
rotenone (derris)	sold as rotenone dust or spray
streptomycin	Agrimycin, Agri-Strep, Phytomycin
sulfur	sold as sulfur dust or spray
terrazole	Truban
tetradifon	Tedion
thiophanate-methyl	Cercobin-M, Topsin-M

Families of house plants

House plants belong to many different botanical families. In the following summary of the families of all plants included in this book, the genera involved are listed in italics. A knowledge of family relationships sometimes helps gardeners to understand cultivation needs.

Acanthaceae Mainly non-woody plants with simple, often attractively patterned leaves. Flowers often carried in long-lasting, colored bracts. Widespread, mostly in tropics. *Aphelandra, Beloperone, Crossandra, Fittonia, Hemigraphis, Hypoestes, Jacobinia, Pachystachys, Pseuderanthemum, Ruellia, Sanchezia, Strobilanthes, Thunbergia.*

Agavaceae Mostly woody plants with rosettes of narrow leaves on erect stems. Flowers usually small and numerous. From humid tropical and arid subtropical regions. *Agave, Cordyline, Dracaena, Pleomele, Sansevieria, Yucca.*

Aizoaceae Succulent, low-growing plants with daisylike flowers. From arid areas of southern Africa. *Faucaria, Lithops.*

Amaranthaceae Mostly non-woody plants with small flowers. Many have brightly colored leaves. Widely distributed. *Iresine.*

Amaryllidaceae Mostly bulbous plants with showy flowers and long leaves. Widely distributed in regions with long dry periods. *Clivia, Crinum, Haemanthus, Hippeastrum, Narcissus, Vallota.*

Apocynaceae Non-woody shrubby or climbing plants with simple leaves and showy flowers. Widespread, mostly in tropics. *Allamanda, Catharanthus, Dipladenia, Nerium.*

Araceae Non-woody and climbing plants, many very large, some epiphytic. Leaves variable. Flowers minute, in a spikelike spadix surrounded by a petallike spathe. From humid tropics. *Acorus, Aglaonema, Anthurium, Caladium, Dieffenbachia, Monstera, Philodendron, Scindapsus, Spathiphyllum, Syngonium, Zantedeschia.*

Araliaceae Shrubs and climbers, often with much-divided leaves. Flowers insignificant, in clusters. From temperate and tropical forests. *Brassaia, Dizygotheca, Fatshedera, Fatsia, Hedera, Heptapleurum, Polyscias.*

Araucariaceae Coniferous trees with small, spiky leaves. From temperate to subtropical regions. *Araucaria.*

Asclepiadaceae Shrubs, climbers, trailers and succulent non-woody plants. Flowers sometimes of curious appearance. Widespread in tropical regions. *Ceropegia, Hoya, Stapelia, Stephanotis.*

Balsaminaceae Non-woody or sub-shrubby plants, mostly with fleshy stems swollen at the nodes. Showy flowers, often with a spur. Worldwide distribution. *Impatiens.*

Begoniaceae Non-woody plants with lop-sided foliage or showy, variable flowers, or both. From humid tropics and subtropics. *Begonia.*

Bignoniaceae Trees and climbers with compound leaves and showy flowers. Widespread, mostly in tropics and subtropics. *Jacaranda.*

Bromeliaceae Mostly non-woody epiphytes with leaves in rosettes and long-lasting flower heads. Colored bracts often provide the main display. Native to tropical America. *Aechmea, Ananas, Billbergia, Cryptanthus, Dyckia, Guzmania, Neoregelia, Nidularium, Tillandsia, Vriesea.*

Cactaceae Succulent plants of varied form, mostly consisting of leafless stems that are treelike, columnar, globular, or creeping. Flowers are produced from areoles. Mainly from desert and jungle areas of the Western Hemisphere. Jungle cacti need humidity and are sometimes epiphytic. *Aporocactus, Astrophytum, Cephalocereus, Cereus, Chamaecereus, Cleistocactus, Dolicothele, Echinocactus, Echinocereus, Echinopsis, Epiphyllum, Espostoa, Ferocactus, Gymnocalycium, Hamatocactus, Heliocereus, Lobivia, Mammillaria, Notocactus, Opuntia, Parodia, Pfeiffera, Rebutia, Rhipsalidopsis, Rhipsalis, Schlumbergera, Trichocereus.*

Campanulaceae Non-woody plants with milky sap and bell- or saucer-shaped flowers, usually blue. Worldwide distribution. *Campanula.*

Celastraceae Trees and shrubs with simple leaves and insignificant flowers. Nearly worldwide distribution. *Euonymus.*

Commelinaceae Non-woody plants, often trailing, with fleshy, watery stems, simple leaves, and small flowers. Widespread, mostly in tropics. *Callisia, Cyanotis, Dichorisandra, Geogenanthus, Rhoeo, Setcreasea, Siderasis, Tradescantia, Zebrina.*

Compositae An enormous, very varied family, which includes some succulents and some plants with showy flowers. Worldwide distribution, mostly in temperate climates. *Chrysanthemum, Cineraria, Gynura, Kleinia, Senecio.*

Cornaceae Trees and shrubs with simple leaves and small flowers, sometimes with showy bracts. Mostly from temperate regions. *Aucuba.*

Crassulaceae Succulent perennials and shrubs. Leaves often in rosettes. Flowers small but can be brightly colored. House-plant genera often from drier parts of southern Africa and Central America. *Aeonium, Aichryson, Bryophyllum, Cotyledon, Crassula, Echeveria, Graptopetalum, Kalanchoe, Pachyphytum, Rochea, Sedum.*

Cycadaceae Slow-growing, palmlike, non-flowering plants with compound leaves in arching rosettes on woody trunks. Mainly found in the tropical regions. *Cycas.*

Cyperaceae Non-woody plants with grasslike leaves and tiny, greenish flowers, sometimes in heads of leaflike bracts. Widely distributed, especially in wet areas. *Carex, Cyperus, Scirpus.*

Dioscoreaceae Twining woody or non-woody climbers with heart-shaped leaves, tuberous roots, and small flowers. Widely distributed, mostly in tropics. *Dioscorea.*

Ericaceae Mostly evergreen, lime-hating shrubs and trees with simple leaves. Tubular or bell-shaped flowers are usually in clusters. Worldwide distribution, mainly in temperate climates. *Erica, Rhododendron.*

Euphorbiaceae Either non-woody plants, shrubs, or trees, sometimes succulent and cactuslike, often with poisonous milky sap (latex). Flowers insignificant but often surrounded by showy bracts. Widely distributed, frequently in tropics. *Acalypha, Codiaeum, Euphorbia, Pedilanthus.*

Gentianaceae Non-woody plants, mostly with simple leaves and showy flowers. Worldwide distribution. *Exacum.*

Geraniaceae Non-woody or sub-shrubby plants. Leaves often lobed and aromatic. Showy flowers. Worldwide distribution in temperate climates. *Pelargonium.*

Gesneriaceae Non-woody plants, often creeping or trailing, with simple leaves, often in rosettes, often colored and hairy. Some types have tubers or rhizomes. Flowers tubular and brightly colored. From humid tropical forests. *Achimenes, Aeschynanthus, Columnea, Episcia, Gesneria, Gloxinia, Kohleria, Saintpaulia, Sinningia, Smithiantha, Streptocarpus.*

Gramineae The grass family, with distinct stem nodes and sheaths. Flowers insignificant. Worldwide distribution. *Oplismenus, Stenotaphrum.*

Iridaceae Non-woody plants with bulbs, corms, or rhizomes. Leaves growing from the base. Flowers showy. Worldwide distribution. *Crocus.*

Labiatae Non-woody, sub-shrubby or shrubby plants. Leaves in symmetrical ranks. Stems usually square-sectioned. Flowers irregular. Widely distributed, but centered around the Mediterranean. *Coleus, Plectranthus.*

Leguminosae A huge family of shrubs, trees, climbers, and non-woody plants. Leaves usually compound. Flowers variable. Distributed throughout the world. *Cytisus, Mimosa.*

Liliaceae Non-woody plants. Can be bulbous, succulent, or short-trunked shrubs. Leaves usually arising at the base, or in rosettes. Flowers often showy. *Aloe, Asparagus, Aspidistra, Chlorophytum, Gasteria, Haworthia, Hyacinthus, Liriope, Ophiopogon, Rohdea, Scilla, Tulipa, Veltheimia.*

Loganiaceae Shrubs, trees and non-woody plants, usually with simple leaves and compound flowers. From warm-temperate to tropical regions. *Nicodemia.*

Lythraceae Shrubs, trees and non-woody plants with simple leaves. Flowers very variable. Worldwide distribution. *Cuphea.*

Malvaceae Shrubs, trees, and non-woody plants with lobed or compound leaves and often showy flowers in which the stamens are united into a long, projecting central tube. Distributed throughout the world. *Abutilon, Hibiscus.*

Marantaceae Family of clump-forming non-woody plants with simple, often colorful leaves. Flowers usually insignificant. Mostly from humid tropics. *Calathea, Ctenanthe, Maranta, Stromanthe.*

Melastomataceae Non-woody plants, shrubs, and trees with simple leaves. Flowers variable, usually showy. Widespread in tropics. *Bertolonia, Medinilla, Schizocentron, Sonerila, Tibouchina.*

Moraceae Trees, shrubs, climbers, and non-woody plants, mostly with simple leaves and tiny flowers. Widespread, mostly in tropics. *Ficus.*

Myrsinaceae Mostly trees and shrubs with leathery, simple leaves. Insignificant flowers are often followed by ornamental fruits. From tropical and subtropical regions. *Ardisia.*

Myrtaceae Trees and shrubs, usually with simple leaves, often aromatic. Small flowers are often crowded into variously shaped heads. Widely distributed. *Callistemon, Eucalyptus, Myrtus.*

Nyctaginaceae Trees, shrubs and non-woody plants. Flowers without petals, but often with colorful calyxes and bracts. Widespread in warm and tropical regions. *Bougainvillea, Pisonia.*

Oleaceae Trees, shrubs, and climbers. Leaves may be simple or compound. Flowers generally 4-lobed. Widely distributed. *Jasminum, Osmanthus.*

Onagraceae Variable shrubs, trees, and non-woody plants. Mostly from temperate climates in the Western Hemisphere. *Fuchsia.*

Orchidaceae Probably the largest plant family. Some epiphytic, some terrestrial, mostly rhizomatous. Flowers always have 6 segments. Widespread, mostly in tropics. *Brassia, Cattleya, Coelogyne, Cymbidium, Dendrobium, Epidendrum, Laelia, Laeliocattleya, Lycaste, Maxillaria, Miltonia, Odontoglossum, Oncidium, Paphiopedilum, Phalaenopsis, Vanda.*

Palmae Treelike or shrublike plants, either single-stemmed or clump-forming. Leaves mostly compound. From tropical and subtropical areas. *Caryota, Chamaedorea, Chamaerops, Chrysalidocarpus, Howea, Livistona, Microcoelum, Phoenix, Rhapis, Trachycarpus, Washingtonia.*

Pandanaceae Palmlike trees and shrubs with narrow leaves arranged in a spiral. Flowers insignificant. From Eastern Hemisphere tropics. *Pandanus.*

Passifloraceae Woody or non-woody climbers with simple leaves. Flowers often bright-colored, with a central crown of radiating filaments. Mostly from tropical America. *Passiflora.*

Piperaceae Mostly non-woody plants or shrubby climbers with simple leaves. Flowers minute. Widespread in tropics and subtropics. *Peperomia, Piper.*

Pittosporaceae Trees, shrubs, or woody climbers with simple leaves and small, often fragrant flowers. Widely distributed in warmer regions of the Eastern Hemisphere. *Pittosporum.*

Plumbaginaceae Shrubs or non-woody plants with simple leaves, often in rosettes. Flowers in clusters. Widespread, mostly from temperate or warm-temperate regions. *Plumbago.*

Podocarpaceae Coniferous trees and shrubs with flat, mostly narrow leaves. Widespread in temperate areas, mainly in the Southern Hemisphere. *Podocarpus.*

Polypodiaceae The main family of ferns. Flowerless, non-woody plants carrying reproductive spores on frond (leaf) undersides. Many are epiphytic, with creeping rhizomes. Leaves generally compound. Worldwide distribution. *Adiantum, Asplenium, Blechnum, Cyrtomium, Davallia, Nephrolepis, Pellaea, Phyllitis, Platycerium, Polypodium, Polystichum, Pteris.*

Primulaceae Non-woody plants, mostly with simple leaves. Flowers always 5-lobed. From cool-temperate climates. *Cyclamen, Primula.*

Proteaceae Trees and shrubs, usually with leathery leaves. Spectacular flowers, but not produced in house plants. Mainly from drier, warm-temperate regions of Southern Africa and Australia. *Grevillea, Stenocarpus.*

Punicaceae Shrubs or small trees with simple leaves. Flowers have persistent calyxes that surround fleshy fruits. From warm-temperate areas of Europe and Asia. *Punica.*

Rosaceae Shrubs, trees, and non-woody plants. Flowers often showy. From temperate areas of the Northern Hemisphere. *Eriobotrya, Rosa.*

Rubiaceae Non-woody plants, shrubs, and climbers with simple leaves. Flowers often in roundish heads. Widespread, mostly in tropics and subtropics. *Coffea, Gardenia, Ixora, Manettia, Nertera, Pentas.*

Rutaceae Shrubs and trees. Leaves may be simple or compound, often with aromatic sap. Flowers often followed by fleshy fruits. *Citrus, Fortunella.*

Saxifragaceae Mostly non-woody plants or shrubs. Leaves and flowers variable. Widespread, mostly from temperate climates. *Hydrangea, Saxifraga, Tolmiea.*

Scrophulariaceae Mostly shrubs or non-woody plants. Leaves and flowers variable. Worldwide distribution. *Calceolaria.*

Selaginellaceae Low-growing, flowerless plants allied to ferns. From moist shady areas, mainly in tropics and subtropics. *Selaginella.*

Solanaceae Shrubs, trees, climbers, and non-woody plants, funnel-shaped flowers often followed by showy berries. Mainly from Central and South America. *Browallia, Brunfelsia, Capsicum, Solanum.*

Strelitziaceae Mostly non-woody plants, but sometimes treelike. Leaves on long stalks. Flowers bizarre and showy. From tropics and subtropics. *Strelitzia.*

Theaceae Shrubs or trees with simple, usually leathery leaves and sometimes showy flowers. Worldwide distribution. *Camellia, Cleyera.*

Tiliaceae Mostly shrubs or trees with simple leaves and clusters of flowers. Worldwide distribution. *Sparmannia.*

Urticaceae Shrubs, trees, or non-woody plants with leaves that sometimes carry stinging hairs. Flowers insignificant. Worldwide distribution. *Pellionia, Pilea.*

Verbenaceae Shrubs, trees, or non-woody plants with stems often square-sectioned. Leaves simple. Flowers usually in clusters. Mostly from tropics and subtropics. *Clerodendrum, Lantana.*

Vitaceae Mostly woody climbers. Leaves usually divided into several lobes. Flowers insignificant. Mainly from tropics and subtropics. *Cissus, Rhoicissus, Tetrastigma.*

Zingiberaceae Non-woody, rhizomatous plants usually making clumps of stems with long, simple, leaves. Flowers are 3-lobed. Widespread in tropics. *Elettaria.*

Glossary

Acid Refers to a material (soil, potting mixture, water etc.) with a pH level below 7.0. Acidity is an indication of the absence of lime or other alkaline material. See also *neutral* and *pH*.

Active growth period The period within each 12-month season (not necessarily a calendar year) when a plant continues to put out new leaves, increases in size, and, generally, produces flowers. Compare *dormancy* and *rest period*.

Aerial roots Roots that arise in the air, from stems not necessarily in contact with a surface. Aerial roots are often capable of clinging to trees and other supports, and they can usually absorb moisture from the air.

Alkaline Refers to a material (soil, potting mixture, water etc.) which has a pH level above 7.0. Alkalinity can be an indication of the presence of lime. The opposite of *acid*. See also *neutral* and *pH*.

Alternate Refers to the placement of leaves on a stem. Alternate leaves are borne singly at different heights, more or less alternating from one side of the stem to the other. Compare *opposite*.

Annual A plant that grows from seed to flower and seed production and then dies within a single growing season. Compare *biennial* and *perennial*.

Anther The part of the flower that produces pollen (the male sex cells). Anthers are often carried on a long filament, and the combined organ is known as a stamen.

Areole An organ unique to the cactus family. A modified sideshoot, the areole is usually cushionlike and carries hairs and/or spines. From the areoles arise flowers and offsets; each areole flowers only once.

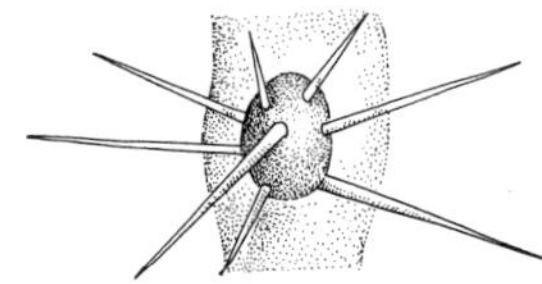

Axil The angle between the leaf or leafstalk and the stem that carries it. Any new growth or flower bud that arises from an axil is called axillary.

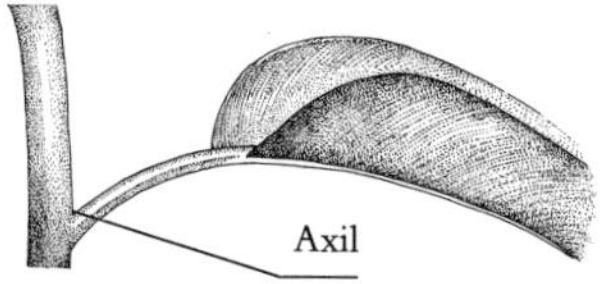

Biennial A plant that grows from seed to flower and seed production and then dies during two growing seasons. Compare *annual* and *perennial*.

Bigeneric Refers to a hybrid plant derived from the crossing of parents from two distinct genera. See also *intergeneric*.

Bipinnate Refers to leaves that are doubly pinnate—that is divided into segments each of which is itself divided into segments. See also *pinnate*.

Bloom An easily smudged powdery or waxy coating, generally whitish or bluish in color, on certain leaves and fruits. Alternatively, of course, a synonym for flower.

Bract A modified leaf, often part of a flower, which may be either leaflike or petallike and is sometimes highly colored and long-lasting.

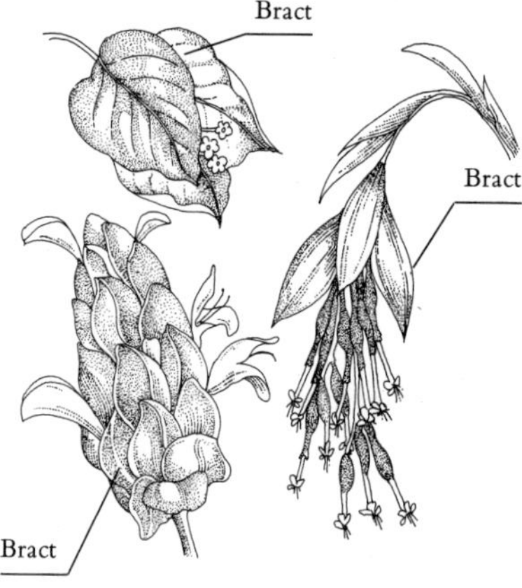

Bud A condensed shoot, often protected by overlapping scales. A growth bud contains embryo leaves. A flower bud contains embryo flowers or flower clusters.

Bulb A storage organ that usually grows underground and resembles a bud in that it contains the embryo leaves and sometimes flowers of the plant. Bulbs, which enable many plants to endure prolonged periods of total inactivity *(dormancy)*, often have a protective skinlike covering (the *tunic*).

Bulbil An immature, miniature bulb formed by certain bulbous plants either at the base of mature bulbs or on the stems. The word is sometimes applied loosely to miniature tubers, as in some begonias, or to leafy plantlets with smaller bases, as in certain ferns.

Calyx The outermost part of a flower, which can consist of separate sepals or be fused into a single organ. The calyx is normally tough and green and protects the corolla within. In some plants, however, it is brightly colored and resembles the corolla.

Channeled Hollowed like a gutter. Usually in reference to long, narrow leaves with upturned edges, but is also used to describe stems that are hollowed on one side to form a channel-like depression.

Chlorosis A condition in which leaves become unnaturally pallid, whitish, or yellow. The disease is usually due to lack of essential minerals.

Column An organ in which male and female parts of the flower are fused together. The column is a major identifying characteristic of orchids.

Compound Refers mainly to leaves that are divided into two or more segments, but can also refer to flowers or fruits composed of several similar parts. The opposite of *simple*.

Corm A solid underground storage organ formed from the thickened base of the stem, usually with a protective covering of papery scales (the *tunic)*.

Corolla The part of the flower that is usually its major decorative feature. It may consist of separate petals or be more or less fused into a single unit. The corolla tends to be colorful in contrast with the normally plain green calyx.

Cotyledon The first leaf or leaves to be carried by a seedling after germination. Cotyledons are often different in appearance from subsequent and adult leaves.

Cristate Crested, or cockscomb-shaped. Refers to abnormal-looking cockscomblike growth in one area of leaves, stems, or flowers. Varieties of house plants with cristate-leaved forms exist among the ferns, and cristate-stemmed forms are found among cacti and a few succulents.

Crown The area at the base or center of a herbaceous perennial from which top growth and roots emerge. The crown is the part of the plant where shoots and roots meet.

Cultivar Usually a variety that has originated in cultivation rather than in the wild. Cultivar plant names are generally in a modern language, not Latin, and are correctly enclosed within single quotation marks. See also *variety.*

Cutting A portion of stem, leaf, or root, or sometimes an entire leaf, removed from a plant and treated in such a way that it produces roots and eventually grows into a new plant.

Deciduous Refers to plants that lose their leaves annually at the end of the active growth period and produce new ones at the end of the rest period. The opposite of *evergreen.*

Dormancy A temporary state of total inactivity. The term *dormant* is broadly interpreted by many botanists. In its narrowest sense, however, a plant is considered to be not merely *resting* but *dormant* if its top growth has withered away (and sometimes, as with many bulbs, its roots as well). Compare *active growth period* and *rest period.*

Double Refers to a flower with at least two full layers of petals. Compare *single* and *semi-double.*

Drawn Applied to plants with stems that have become elongated and spindly, with small, often pallid leaves, generally because of inadequate light or, especially among young seedlings, serious over-crowding.

Epiphyte A plant that grows in the wild not rooted in soil but on the body of another plant or on rocks. An epiphyte clings to its support with aerial roots and gains its nourishment from the atmosphere or from the crevices in which it lodges. Epiphytes, among which bromeliads and orchids are prominent, are not parasitic.

Evergreen Refers to plants that retain their leaves throughout the year, even during the annual rest period, if any. The opposite of *deciduous.*

Eye A word with two different horticultural meanings. An eye is an undeveloped growth bud, as on a stem or tuber. And an eye is also the center of a flower, especially when the flower is circular and the color of the center contrasts with the rest.

Filament Any threadlike organ, but most commonly used in reference to the stalk of an anther-carrying stamen in a flower.

Floret A very small flower, especially one that is part of a large inflorescence composed of numerous such florets, as in the daisy family.

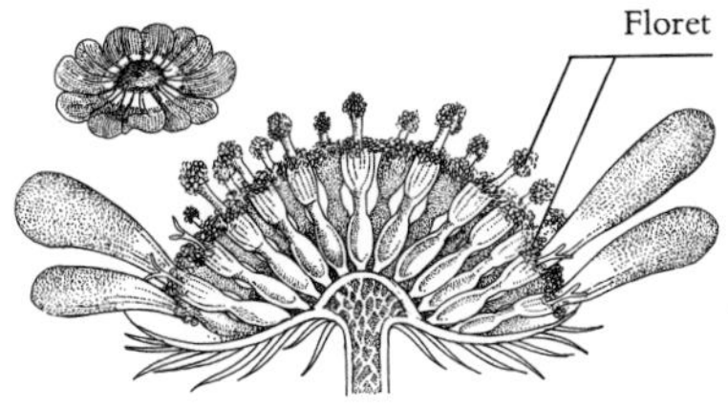

Flower The plant organ specialized for sexual reproduction, in which pollen from the male part (stamen) is transferred to the ovaries of the female part (pistil) so that fertilization occurs and seeds can be developed.

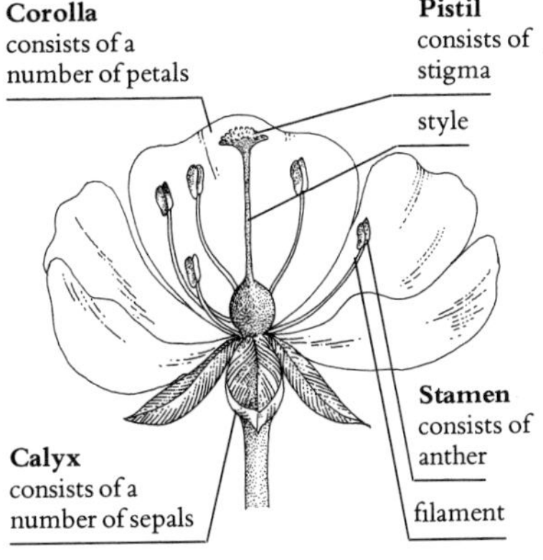

Forcing The process of bringing plants into growth and flower before their natural time by artificial means, most often gentle heat.

Frond Used mainly as an alternative term for fern leaves (whether simple or compound), but it is also frequently applied to the compound leaves of such plants as palms. See also *compound, pinnate, rachis.*

Glochid A tiny, barbed, bristly hair found in tufts in certain cacti (for instance, opuntias) in place of—or in addition to—woody spines. Like woody spines, glochids are borne by the areoles.

Growing point The extremity or tip of a stem, where extension growth is likely to occur.

Hardy Refers to plants that can survive in the open throughout the year at a given latitude, usually where there is an annual period of frost. The opposite of *tender.*

Heel A strip of bark and wood torn away from a main stem when a sideshoot is removed with a downward pull. Many plants root most readily from cuttings with a heel attached (called heel cuttings).

Herbaceous Refers to plants with soft, non-woody growth. Though the term is most often applied to those perennials that lose all their top growth and die down completely in winter, any type of plant that never makes woody stems may be characterized as herbaceous.

Hybrid A plant arising from the cross-fertilization of two dissimilar parents (which can be different varieties, subspecies, or species of a single genus, or even different forms of closely related genera). Crossing is not possible between plants of different families. Compare *cultivar, variety.* See also *bigeneric, intergeneric.*

Inflorescence A general term for the flowering part of a plant. Although it applies technically to any flower on any stem, the term is most commonly used in reference to a head, cluster, spike, or similar collection of small flowers grouped together on one main stem. See also *floret.*

Intergeneric Refers to a hybrid plant derived from the multiple crossing of parents belonging to more than two distinct genera. Hybrids with only two parents are sometimes called intergeneric, but they are more correctly categorized as *bigeneric.*

Keel A V-shaped ridge like the keel of a boat, formed on one side of a leaf or petal by a channel in the other surface.

Latex The milky sap produced by such plants as the euphorbias and some ficuses. Sometimes poisonous.

Leaf The organ in which the energy-producing process of photosynthesis is normally carried out by the unique green compound, chlorophyll. A few plants do not bear leaves (e.g. cacti).

Leaflet Any segment of a compound leaf. See also *pinna.*

Lip A lobe of the corolla that is distinct from the other segments and usually forms the lowest segment of a flower. The lip is a universal feature of orchids.

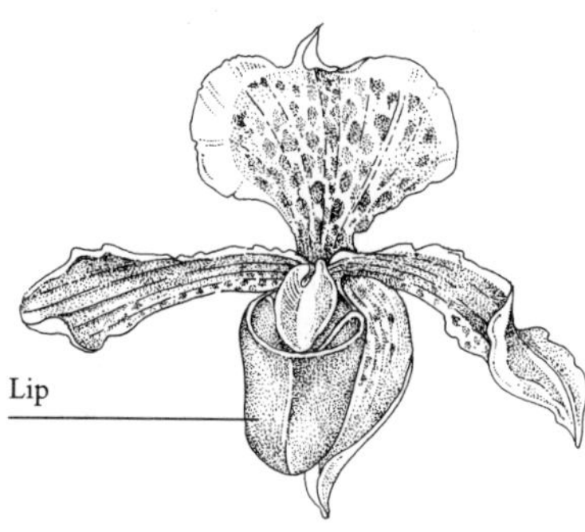

Lobe Any single projection (generally, though not always, rounded) of an organ such as a leaf or petal that is partly but not entirely divided into separate parts.

Margin The edge or boundary line of any plant organ; most often applied to the border area of a leaf.

Midrib The central rib of a leaf, which generally juts out from the leaf surface, runs its length, and divides it into equal halves. See also *rachis.*

Monopodial Refers to a stem that continues to grow indefinitely from a single growing point, very seldom branching; most often used of orchids. Compare *sympodial.*

Mouth Refers to the open end of the corolla of any bell-, trumpet-, or tube-shaped flower. Compare *throat.*

Neutral Refers to a material (soil, potting mixture, water, etc.) that is neither acid nor alkaline. On the pH scale neutral has a level of 7.0. See also *acid, alkaline,* and *pH.*

Node A point on a stem where leaves and sideshoots arise. Nodes are often called joints and are sometimes swollen. A node may have lost its leaf.

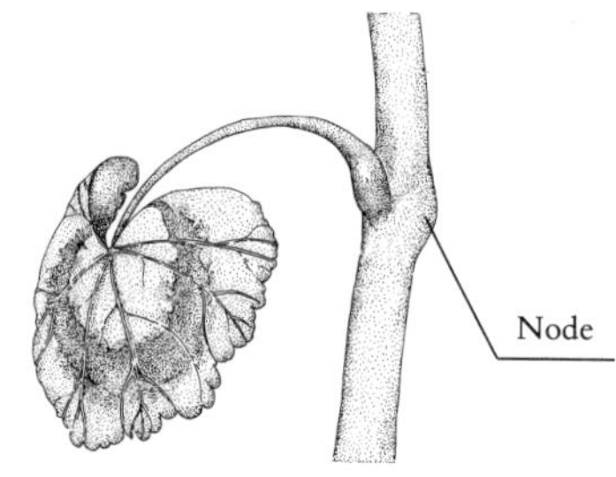

Offset A new plant produced naturally by an adult, usually at its base, as in bulbs, bromeliads, cacti, and some other succulents. Offsets are usually easily detached for propagation.

Offshoot A synonym for *offset.*

Opposite Refers to the placement of leaves on a stem: The leaves are borne in opposite pairs along the stem. Compare *alternate.*

Palmate This word does not refer to plants commonly known as palms. It means, literally, "hand-shaped" and is applied as a descriptive term to a leaf with three or more lobes or leaflets arising from a single point of attachment on the leafstalk.

Pendent Hanging, pendulous; usually applied to flowers.

Perennial A plant that lives for three seasons or more, usually indefinitely. Compare *annual* and *biennial.*

Perianth The outer parts of the flower, consisting of the calyx and corolla, which enclose the reproductive organs.

Petal In a flower, a separate segment of a divided corolla. Compare *sepal.*

Petiole The leafstalk.

pH Literally, the hydrogen ion concentration in soil, potting mixture, water, etc. The pH scale is used as a means of measuring the acidity or alkalinity of any of these substances. The scale extends from 0 to 14, with pure water (pH 7.0) as the standard. See also *acid, alkaline,* and *neutral.*

Pinching out The removal of the growing point of a stem, thus stimulating growth from buds lower down. Its effect is to encourage bushy growth and/or flower bud production. This operation, also known as *stopping,* is usually done with the finger and thumb but it can also be carried out with a sharp knife.

Pinna A single segment of a pinnate leaf or frond.

Pinnate Refers to a compound leaf with two or more leaflets (pinnae) carried on each side of the midrib (rachis) in more or less opposite pairs. In some compound leaves—those of ferns in particular—each pinna is itself divided into segments (pinnules), when the whole leaf is called bipinnate. In others the secondary segments are further divided, the leaf being tripinnate or quadripinnate.

Pinnule The smallest individual leaflet of a bi-, tri-, or quadripinnate leaf. See also *pinnate.*

Pistil The female organ of a flower. The pistil normally consists of an ovary (in which the seed develops), a stigma, and a style.

Pricking out (or off) The operation of transferring seedlings from the pots or boxes where the seeds were sown into other containers where the seedlings can be planted individually or spaced farther apart.

Pseudobulb Literally, a false bulb. In an epiphytic orchid the pseudobulb is a thick stem that rises from the rhizome at intervals and serves as a storage organ, not unlike an aboveground bulb, that often carries the leaves and flowers, if any.

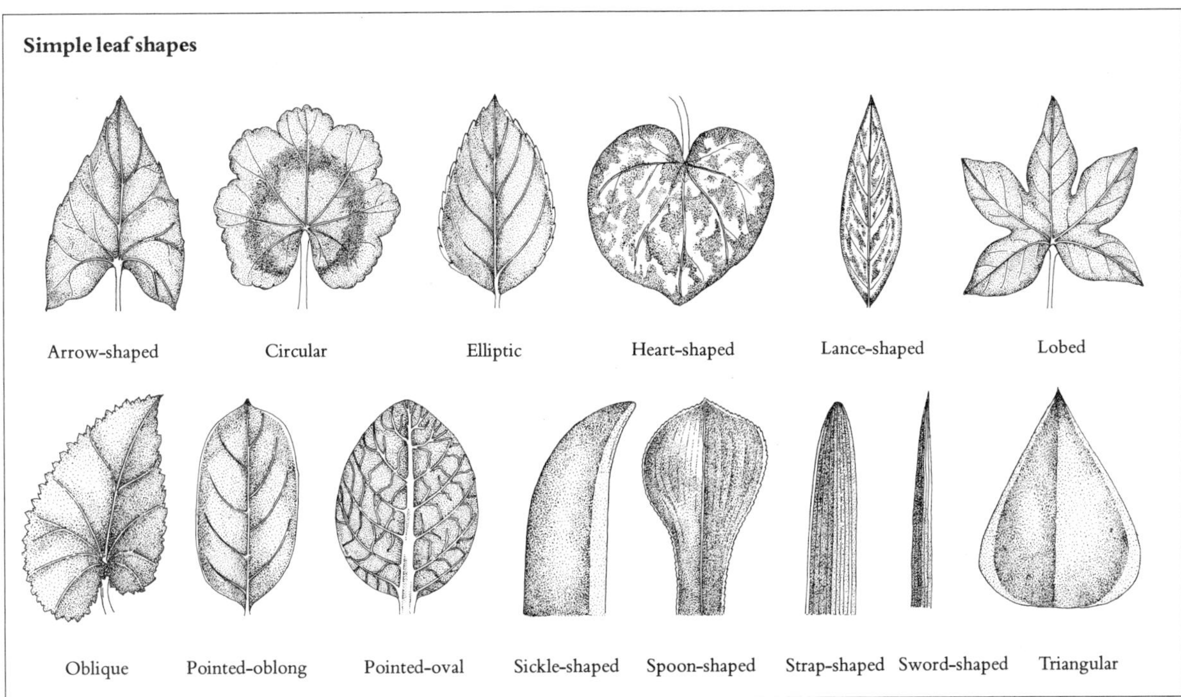
Simple leaf shapes
Arrow-shaped
Circular
Elliptic
Heart-shaped
Lance-shaped
Lobed
Oblique
Pointed-oblong
Pointed-oval
Sickle-shaped
Spoon-shaped
Strap-shaped
Sword-shaped
Triangular

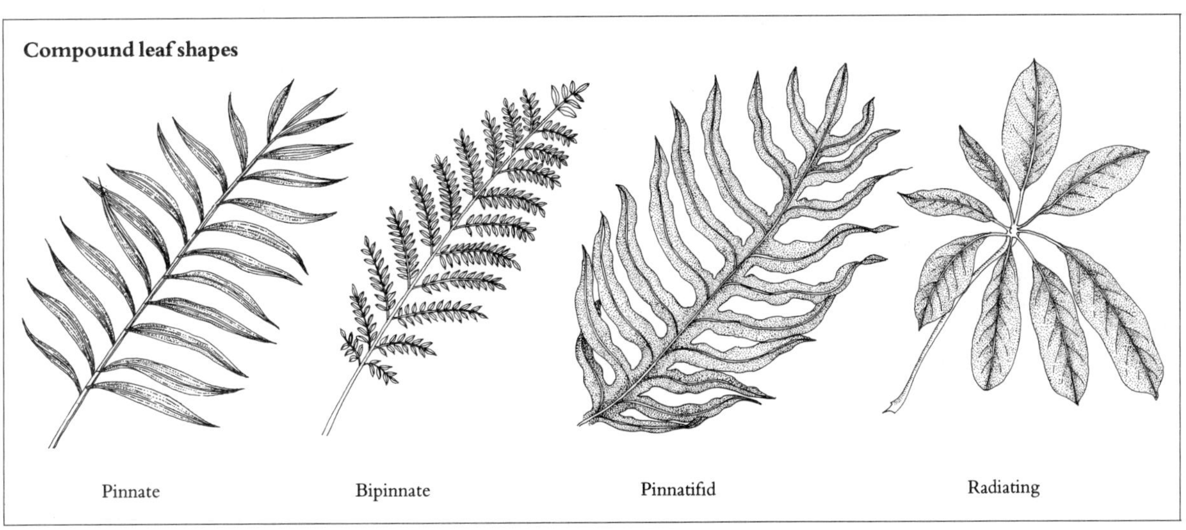
Compound leaf shapes
Pinnate
Bipinnate
Pinnatifid
Radiating

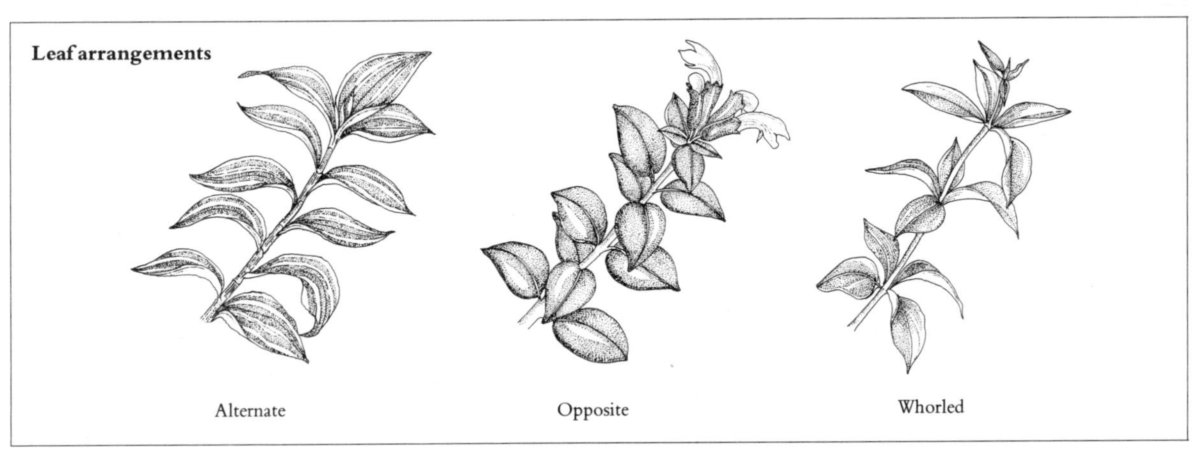
Leaf arrangements
Alternate
Opposite
Whorled

Rachis The midrib of a compound leaf. The rachis is an extension of the actual leafstalk.

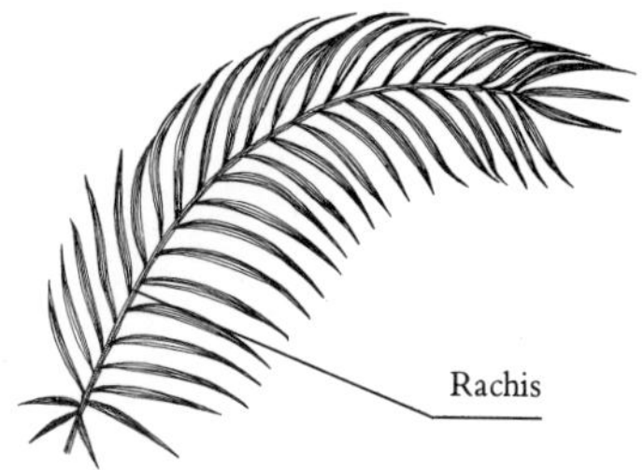

Rest period The period within each 12-month season (not necessarily a calendar year) when a plant is relatively inactive, retaining its foliage but producing little or no new growth. Compare *active growth period* and *dormancy.*

Rhizome A fleshy stem, usually (but not always) horizontal and underground, which lasts for more than one growing season and is often a storage organ. A rhizome normally produces subterranean feeding roots as well as top growth.

Rib Usually refers to prominent veins on a leaf, which typically project on the underside. But stems and fruits can also be ribbed. The ribs on cactus stems are frequently an especially prominent feature of the plant.

Root ball The mass of potting mixture and roots of a plant in a pot or some other container.

Rootstock The basal, root-carrying part of a plant on which another plant can be grafted. The term is also used to refer simply to the crown and root system as a unit; and it is sometimes loosely used as a synonym for underground *rhizome.*

Rosette An arrangement of leaves radiating from a crown or distinct center, either on individual stalks (as in saintpaulias) or in an overlapping spiral (as in many of the echeverias and bromeliads).

Runner An aboveground, more or less horizontal stem that produces buds at nodes, from which roots and new growth form. Compare *stolon.*

Scurf Minute scales or particles on the foliage that give it a dusty, or mealy, appearance.

Seedling A young plant soon after seed germination, still with a single, unbranched stem.

Sepal In a flower, a separate segment of a divided calyx. Compare *petal.*

Semi-double Refers to a flower with more than a single layer of petals, but with fewer than are found in a fully double flower.

Sessile Without a stalk; referring to leaves or flowers arising directly from a plant stem.

Sheath Any tubular structure protectively surrounding another plant organ—for example, the sheath that forms the basal part of a grass leaf.

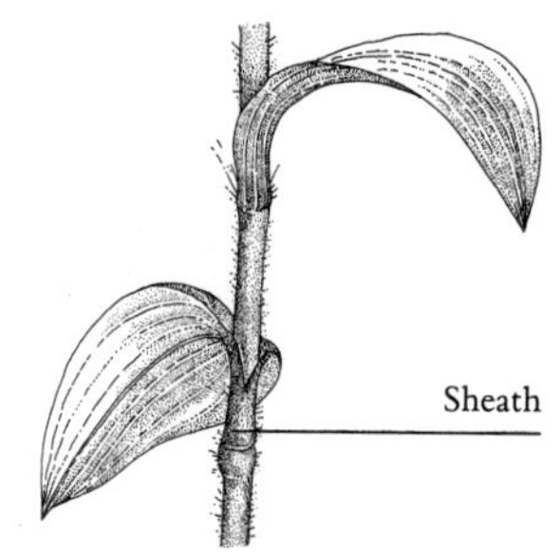

Shrub A plant that remains fairly small and produces permanent woody stems that normally branch from the base instead of having a single stem, or trunk. Compare *tree.*

Simple Refers to leaves that are not divided into separate segments. The opposite of *compound.*

Single Refers to a flower with only one layer of petals or corolla lobes. Compare *double* and *semi-double.*

Sinuate With wavy or scalloped margins in one plane (as differentiated from *undulate*); usually applied to leaves, but can also apply to petals and even sepals.

Spadix A special kind of flower spike, found chiefly in the family *Araceae,* in which the usually tiny flowers are embedded in the surface of a fleshy central axis. See also *spathe.*

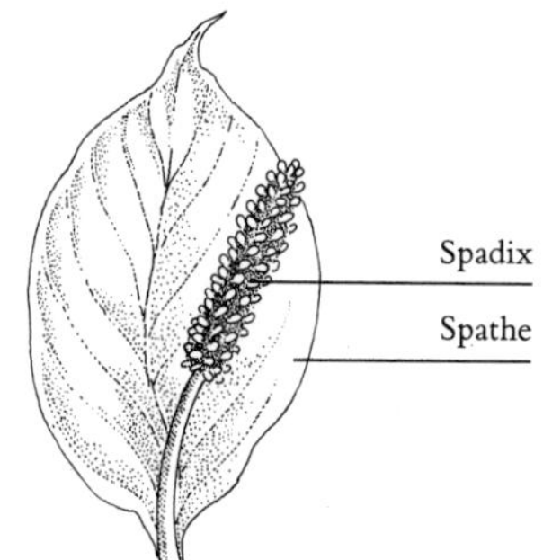

Spathe The large, sometimes brightly colored bract or modified leaf that usually surrounds or encloses the spadix in plants of the family *Araceae.*

Spore The tiny, single-celled reproductive body in such plants as ferns and mosses. The dustlike spores of ferns are usually carried in raised brown patches (spore cases or sori) on the undersides of fronds.

Spur In flowers, a spur is a hollow, usually conical or tubular projection from some part of the corolla, and it contains nectar to attract pollinating insects. The term is also used for a short side-branch that carries flower buds, as in hoyas.

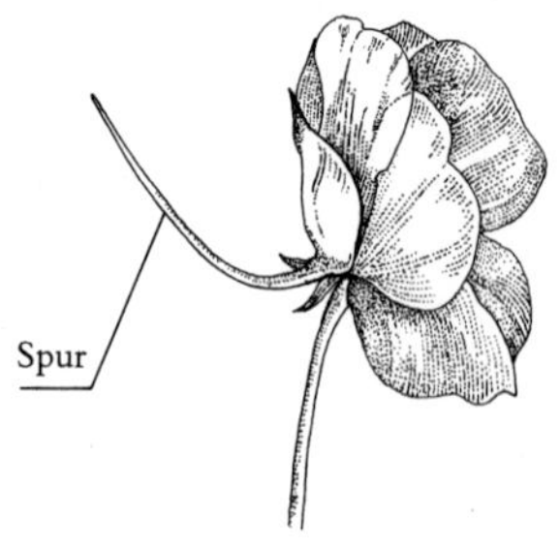

Stamen The male, pollen-bearing organ of a flower, usually consisting of two anthers on a slender filament.

Stigma The tip section of the pistil (female organ of the flower), which is receptive to pollen and generally becomes very sticky when the flower is ready for pollination.

Stipule A leaf- or scalelike growth, found at the base of the leafstalk in certain plants.

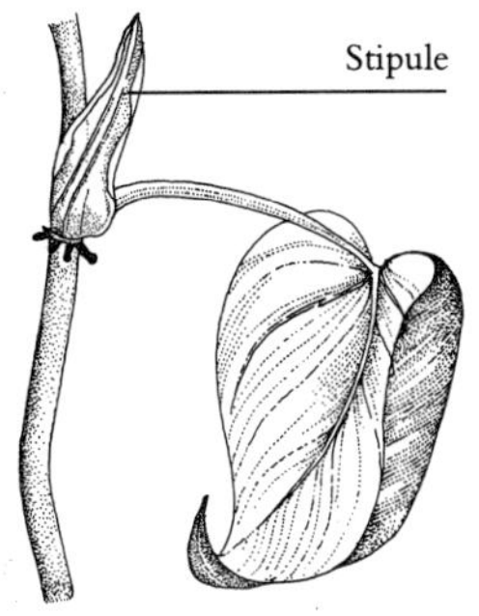

Stolon A shoot that creeps along the ground and roots and produces a new plantlet wherever it comes into close contact with the surface of the potting mixture or soil. Stolons differ from runners in that runners can root only at their nodes.

Stopping See *pinching out*.

Stomata (singular, stoma) The microscopic breathing pores of plants, most of which are found on the undersides of leaves.

Style The stalk that links the stigma with the ovary in the pistil of a flower. The style is variable in length and width and is entirely lacking in some types of flower.

Subshrub A perennial plant that is woody at the base but that produces soft, herbaceous growth on this framework.

Succulent Any plant, usually from relatively dry regions, that has fleshy stems and/or leaves that can function as water-storage organs.

Sucker A shoot that arises from the root or rootstock of a plant and develops leaves and roots of its own.

Sympodial Refers to stems or rhizomes in which successive growing points (pseudobulbs, for example) produce annual inflorescences, and further growth is carried on through branching; most often used of orchids. Compare *monopodial*.

Taproot Any strong root growing more or less vertically downward, especially if it is the only or main root of the plant.

Tender Refers to plants that are liable to injury from cold, especially in winter, at a given latitude. Most house plants are tender within the Temperate Zone. The opposite of *hardy*.

Tendril A threadlike organ of a climbing plant usually arising from a leaf axil, which twines around a support or attaches itself to a surface by means of terminal suckers. In some plants leafstalks act as tendrils.

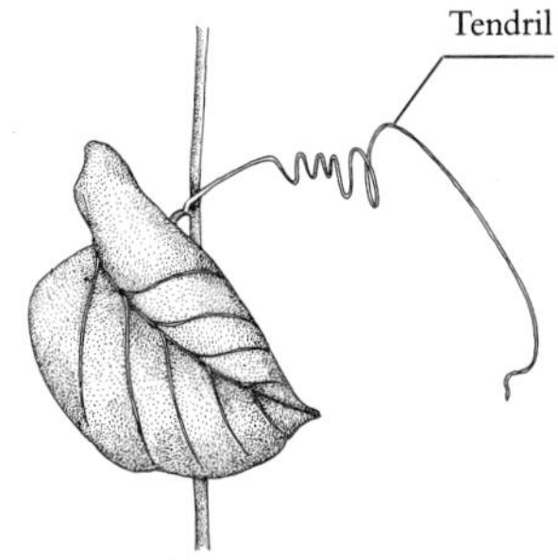

Terminal Refers to the uppermost, usually central bud, growth, or flower on a plant, or on a given stem of a plant.

Tessellated Checkered; applied to variegated petals and leaves which have a checkered or netted pattern in contrasting colors.

Throat Refers to the inner portion of the mouth of the corolla of a bell-, trumpet-, or tube-shaped flower when the inner portion is easily visible. See also *mouth*.

Topdress To apply a layer of fresh potting mixture to a potted plant, normally after removing an equal amount of old mixture. Topdressing is a generally acceptable alternative to repotting for a plant that has grown too large for moving on to a bigger pot or container.

Tree A woody plant with a single, distinct trunk between the ground and the first branches. Compare *shrub*.

Tuber A word used for fleshy storage organs of different kinds. The few tuberous house plants are stem tubers; in other words, a swollen stem stores food for the plant so that it can survive cold and/or drought. Stem tubers can grow above or below the surface of potting mixture and are sometimes found even on aerial stems. New shoots are produced from growth buds (eyes) on the tubers.

Tubercle A rounded, wartlike projection or swelling on a plant organ. Tubercles are especially abundant on the stems of many cacti; they are a characteristic feature of such plants.

Tunic The loose, membranous or fibrous outer skin of many types of bulb and corm.

Undulate With wavy up-and-down margins; usually applied to leaves, but can also apply to petals and sepals. Compare *sinuate*.

Variegated Refers to leaves (and sometimes flowers) that are either striped or spotted, or otherwise patterned in a color different from the normal green.

Variety A plant form that differs from the natural type species. The term *variety* as used by modern botanists refers only to variations that have originated in the wild, but the word is also frequently applied to variations arising in cultivation, which should technically be known as cultivars. Names of true varieties are usually in Latin and are not enclosed in quotation marks. See also *cultivar*.

Vein A strand of conducting tissue, primarily in a leaf. Large veins are called ribs, and the central vein (which is normally an extension of the leafstalk) is called the midrib or, in compound leaves, the rachis.

Viviparous Producing young plants (plantlets) asexually on the leaves or stems of the parent plant, sometimes from bulbils.

Whorl Three or more leaves or flowers that are produced in a radiating pattern—like the spokes of a wheel—at a single stem node.

Woody Refers to plant tissue that becomes lignified and hard, persisting throughout the plant's rest periods even if leaves die away. Thus, woody stems are more or less permanent. Compare *herbaceous*.

Index

A

B

G

H

I

J

K

L

M

N

Q

R

S

T

U

V

W

Y

Z

Credits and acknowledgments

Main illustrations by:

(*R* = right *L* = left)

Norman Barber *79L, 85, 88, 99, 156, 168, 178, 187, 188, 196, 237, 238L, 241, 247 (both), 252, 256, 257R, 259, 266, 270, 282 (both), 283, 291, 297, 306, 317, 324, 325, 330, 332, 339, 340R, 375, 383, 384*
Vicky Chesterman *79R, 86R, 90, 125, 126L, 129L, 136, 141, 149, 152R, 153, 157, 160R, 161, 167, 179R, 190, 203, 214, 219, 226 (both), 229, 230, 236, 248, 250, 263, 267, 269, 272, 273, 274, 275, 276, 279, 281, 298, 328, 340L, 342, 343, 347, 351, 356, 358, 368, 370R, 390*
Helen Cowcher *73, 84, 91, 98, 109R, 124, 129R, 132, 137, 140, 155, 163, 165, 183, 192, 200, 201, 216, 220, 221, 231, 234, 238R, 244, 257L, 265, 277, 299, 300, 301, 304, 322, 354, 359, 362, 364, 365, 367, 370R, 371, 374, 380, 385, 388, 389, 396*
Judy Dunkley *69, 103, 130, 164, 172, 175, 184, 194L, 227, 264, 319R, 323, 326R, 329, 335, 370L*
Victoria Gordon *179L, 195*
Richard Jacobs *110, 145, 146, 177, 193, 232, 245, 246, 268, 290, 310, 318, 361, 366, 369*
Sarah Kensington *228, 251*
Ken Lilly *100, 109L, 126R, 128, 131, 138, 148, 173, 194R, 202, 218, 249, 261, 271, 278, 292, 296, 305, 314, 316, 319L, 326L, 334, 386, 392, 398*
Donald Myall *66, 70, 75, 77, 86L, 87, 92 & 93, 127, 133, 135, 142, 147, 150, 159, 160L, 162, 166, 191, 197, 198, 209, 215, 239, 242, 253, 255, 258, 260, 309, 312, 341, 344 & 345, 348, 350, 352, 355, 360, 381, 391, 393*
Rodney Shackell *67, 68, 78, 89, 134, 139, 171, 176, 243, 284, 331 (both), 336, 387*
Harry Titcombe *71, 81, 83, 101, 102, 104, 123, 143, 152L, 169, 174, 180 & 181, 186, 254, 307, 321, 357, 372, 382, 394*
Elsie Wrigley *74, 189, 210 & 211, 233, 238, 373*

Other illustrations by:

Marion Appleton, David Ashby, David Baird, John Bishop, Leonora Box (Saxon Artists), Vana Haggarty, Nicholas Hall, Constance Marshall (Saxon Artists), Nigel Osborne, Jim Robins, Eric Thomas, Venner Studios.

Color reproduction by: Repro Singer Ltd.
Typesetting by: C. E. Dawkins (Typesetters) Ltd., Diagraphic Typesetters Ltd., Focus Photoset Ltd., S.P.S. Photosetting.

Special thanks to the following for their help:

Brighton Parks Dept.; Tom Deighton, Regents Park Parks Dept.; "The Exotic Collection"; Frederick Ford; Hollygate Nurseries; J. K. Hulme, University of Liverpool Botanic Gardens; Lancashire College of Agriculture; Le Petit Jardin; The Lock Shop, Camden Lock; Camilla Lomax; Maurice Mason; McBeans Orchids; Negs Photographic Services Ltd.; B. and W. Rittershausen, Burnham Orchid Nurseries; The Harry Smith Collection; Arthur Turner, RHS Garden, Wisley; Cambridge University Botanic Gardens.

Useful addresses:

In case you are unable to locate some plants, the following listing may be of help.

Most of the specialists' societies publish bulletins that include sources for plants and offer information about seed-exchange with other plant enthusiasts.

Be forewarned that the addresses of some organizations change from time to time but writing to these will put you on the track.

African Violet Society of America
Box 1326,
Knoxville, TN 37901
American Begonia Society
8302 Kittyhawk Avenue,
Los Angeles, CA 90045
American Bonsai Society
228 Rosemont Avenue,
Erie, PA 16505
American Fern Society
Biological Sciences Group,
University of Connecticut,
Storrs, CT 06268
American Fuchsia Society
Hall of Flowers,
Golden Gate Park,
San Francisco, CA 94122
American Gloxinia/Gesneriad Society
P.O. Box 174,
New Milford, CT 06776
American Hibiscus Society
P.O. Box 491F, Rt. 1,
Fort Myers, FL 33905
American Ivy Society
National Center for American Horticulture,
Mount Vernon, VA 22121
American Orchid Society
Botanical Museum of Harvard University,
Cambridge, Mass. 02138
American Plant Life Society
The American Amaryllis Society Group,
P.O. Box 150,
La Jolla, CA 92038
Bromeliad Society
P.O. Box 3279,
Santa Monica, CA 90403
Cactus and Succulent Society of America
P.O. Box 3010,
Santa Barbara, CA 93105
Cymbidium Society of America
1250 Orchid Drive,
Santa Barbara, CA 93111
Epiphyllum Society of America
P.O. Box 1395,
Monrovia, CA 91016
Gesneriad Society International
P.O. Box 549,
Knoxville, TN 37901
Herb Society of America
300 Massachusetts Avenue,
Boston, Mass. 02115
Holly Society of America
407 Fountain Green Road,
Bel Air, MD 21014
Indoor Light Garden Society of America
423 Powell Drive,
Bay Village, Ohio 44140
International Cactus and Succulent Society
P.O. Box 1452,
San Angelo, TX 76901
International Geranium Society
6501 Yosemite Drive,
Buena Park, CA 90620
Los Angeles International Fern Society
2423 Burritt Avenue,
Redondo Beach, CA 90278
National Fuchsia Society
c/o Bonita Doan, Dept. DH,
774 Forest Loop Drive,
Point Hueneme, CA 93041
Palm Society
1320 South Venetian Way,
Miami, FL 33139
Saintpaulia International
P.O. Box 549,
Knoxville, TN 37901
Terrarium Society
57 Wolfpit Avenue,
Norwalk, CT 06851

METRIC CONVERSION CHART

Under the Metric Conversion Act of 1975, the national policy is to work toward making the metric system dominant in all aspects of activity. In accordance with the act, the following conversion table is included.

Because it is easier to learn when the subject is immediately relevant, only the conversions for the measurements used in this book are listed in the table.

Capacity

US	liters
1 cup	0.2
1 quart	0.9
2 quarts	1.8

Height

ins	cm	ins	cm	ins	cm	ft	m	ft	m
$\frac{1}{10}$	0.2	$2\frac{1}{2}$	6.3	7	17.8	1	0.3	5	1.5
$\frac{1}{8}$	0.3	3	7.6	8	20.3	$1\frac{1}{2}$	0.4	$5\frac{1}{2}$	1.7
$\frac{1}{4}$	0.6	$3\frac{1}{2}$	8.9	9	22.9	2	0.6	6	1.8
$\frac{1}{2}$	1.3	4	10.2	10	25.4	$2\frac{1}{2}$	0.8	8	2.4
$\frac{3}{4}$	1.9	$4\frac{1}{2}$	11.4	12	30.5	3	0.9	10	3.0
1	2.5	5	12.7	15	38.1	$3\frac{1}{2}$	1.1		
$1\frac{1}{2}$	3.8	$5\frac{1}{2}$	14			4	1.2		
2	5.1	6	15.2			$4\frac{1}{2}$	1.4		

Temperature

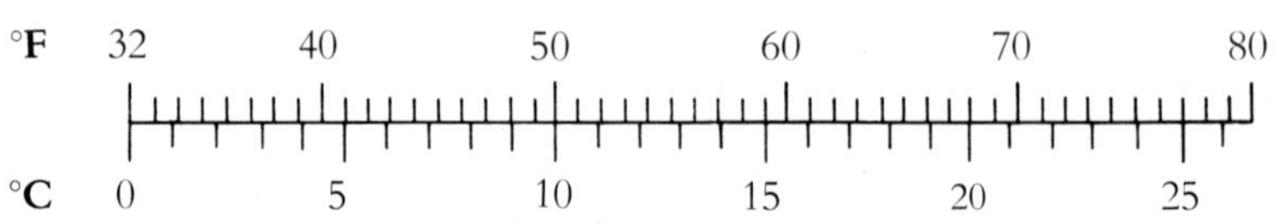